WAGGONER CRUISING GUIDE
2019

It is appropriate that this year's cover features one of the most popular cruising destinations in the Waggoner Cruising Guide, Prideaux Haven in Desolation Sound, British Columbia. While often crowded during the peak summer months, this beautiful July evening featured a stunning sunset and a peaceful evening on the hook with a stern-tie to the rocky shoreline. It just says "I want to be there. . ." Photo by Danielle Fellin Bernardo

p.472

Crossing Dixon Entrance

Dundas I.

DIXON ENTRANCE

Rose Point

p.462

Prince Rupert

Chatham Sound

p.444

BRITISH

COLUMBIA

Kitimat

Grenville

Channel

N

Finlayson Channel to Prince Rupert

Princess

Royal

Butedale

Channel

p.426

HECATE

Fiordland

Fitz Hugh Sound & Fisher Channel to Burke Channel, Dean Channel, Bella Coola

STRAIT

HAIDA GWAII (QUEEN CHARLOTTE ISLANDS)

Klemtu

Ocean Falls

Bella Coola

Milbanke Sound

New Bella Bella

FITZ HUGH SOUND

QUEEN

CHARLOTTE

Calvert I.

p.421

Rivers Inlet & Fish Egg Inlet

Dawsons Landing

SOUND

p.419

Smith Sound

Cape Caution p.411

p.478

KETCHIKAN

Ketchikan

Clarence Strait

p.417

Blunden Harbour to Slingsby Channel

QUEEN CHARLOTTE STRAIT

p.371 **Hardy Bay to Cape Scott**

Cape Scott

Port Hardy

p.358

North Vancouver Island

p.472

Crossing Dixon Entrance

Cape Fox

Cape Chacon

Dundas I.

p.373

Cape Scott to Quatsino Sound

Holberg Inlet

p.376

Quatsino Sound

Port McNeill

VANCOUVER

ISLAND

p.378

Quatsino Sound to Kyoquot Sound

Cape Cook

p.381

Kyoquot Sound

4

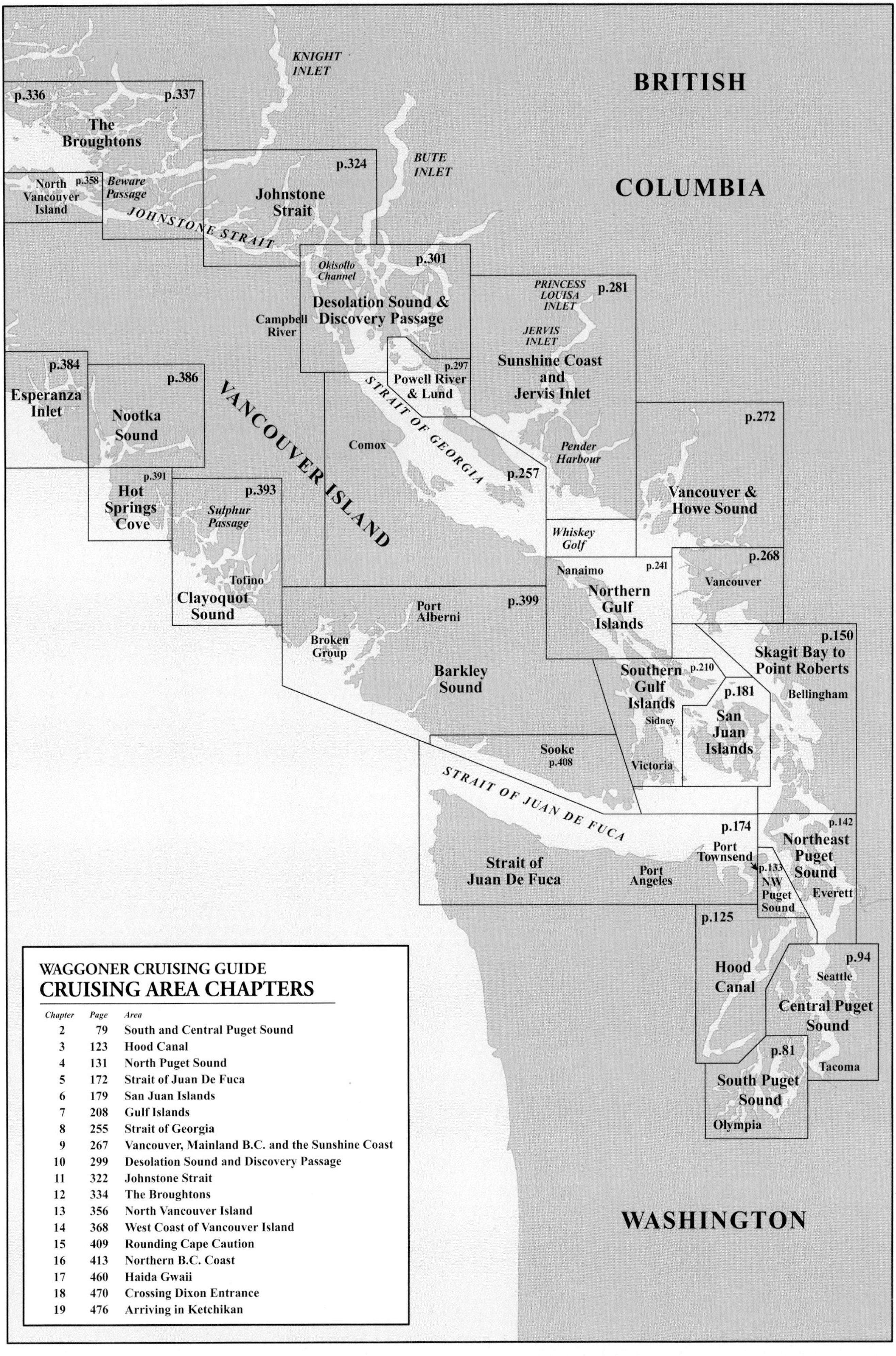

BRITISH

COLUMBIA

KNIGHT INLET

p.336 p.337
The Broughtons

North p.358 Beware Passage
Vancouver Island

JOHNSTONE STRAIT

BUTE INLET

p.324
Johnstone Strait

Okisollo Channel

p.301
Desolation Sound & Discovery Passage

Campbell River

PRINCESS LOUISA INLET
JERVIS INLET

p.281

p.297
Powell River & Lund

Sunshine Coast and Jervis Inlet

p.384
Esperanza Inlet

p.386
Nootka Sound

VANCOUVER ISLAND

STRAIT OF GEORGIA

Comox

Pender Harbour

p.272

p.257

Vancouver & Howe Sound

p.391
Hot Springs Cove

Sulphur Passage

p.393

Whiskey Golf

Nanaimo p.241

Vancouver

p.268

Tofino

Clayoquot Sound

Port Alberni

p.399

Northern Gulf Islands

p.150
Skagit Bay to Point Roberts

Broken Group

Barkley Sound

Southern Gulf Islands p.210

Bellingham

Sidney p.181
San Juan Islands

Victoria

Sooke p.408

STRAIT OF JUAN DE FUCA

p.174
Port Townsend

p.142
Northeast Puget Sound

p.133 NW Puget Sound

Everett

Strait of Juan De Fuca

Port Angeles

p.125

p.94
Seattle

Hood Canal

Central Puget Sound

p.81
South Puget Sound

Tacoma

Olympia

WASHINGTON

5

We want to hear from you!

Your comments, suggestions and corrections are invited. We appreciate hearing from anyone who finds errors in this publication.

We are interested in ideas about what you would like in future editions of the Waggoner Cruising Guide. There are a number of members of the Waggoner community who contribute to our website. Our readers are interested in your experiences and tips. We post cruising reports, pictures, video, updates about changes in specified areas, and tips that range from anchoring to restaurants to technical issues.

Contact us through our website www.WaggonerGuide.com, or by telephone, mail, or e-mail at WaggonerCruisingGuide@gmail.com.

CAUTION

This book was designed to provide experienced skippers with cruising information about the waters covered. While great effort has been taken to make the Waggoner Cruising Guide complete and accurate, it is possible that oversights, differences of interpretation, and factual errors will be found. Thus none of the information contained in the book is warranted to be accurate or appropriate for any specific need. Furthermore, variations in weather and sea conditions, a mariner's skills and experience, and the presence of luck (good or bad) can dictate a mariner's proper course of action.

The Waggoner Cruising Guide should be viewed as a reference only and not a substitute for official government charts, tide and current tables, coast pilots, sailing directions, and local notices to mariners. The Waggoner Cruising Guide assumes the user to be law-abiding and of good will. The suggestions offered are not all-inclusive, but are meant to help avoid unpleasantness or needless delay. Maps are not for navigation. Maps do not show all navigation marks, obstacles, hazards, and structures. Maps are for reference only.

The publisher, editors, and authors assume no liability for errors or omissions, or for any loss or damages incurred from using this publication.

WAGGONER CRUISING GUIDE

Founding Editor
Robert Hale

Editor/Publisher
Mark Bunzel

Managing Editors
Lorena Landon
Leonard Landon

Associate Publisher
Karla Locke

Art Director & Production
Sara White

Advertising Production
Melanie Haage, Karla Locke, Tony Locke, Sara White

Field Correspondents
Mary Campbell, Melissa Gervais, Deane & Arlene Hislop, Jim Norris & Anita Fraser, Brett & Sue Oemichen, Bob & Shino Posey, John Shepard

Correspondents/Contributors
Bruce & Margaret Evertz, Gil & Karen Flanagan, Gill Graham, Robert & Marilynn Hale, Jennifer & James Hamilton, Steve & Elsie Hulsizer, Tom Kincaid, John & Lorraine Littlewood, Kevin Monahan, Duart Snow, Rob & Jean Warner, Whale Wise

Office
Claudia Cole

Proofreading
Mary Campbell, Lara Dunning, Jim Norris, Brett Oemichen, Sue Peterson

Reference Maps
Melanie Haage, Leonard Landon

eBooks
Tony Locke

Photography
Danielle Fellin Bernardo, Mark Bunzel, Mary Campbell, Deane Hislop, Lorena Landon, Jim Niehaus, Jim Norris, Don Odegard, Brett & Sue Oemichen, Jim Redmond, Sara White

Government Data
BC Parks, BC Parks Forever Society, Canada Customs, US Customs, First Nations, National Weather Service, WA Dept. of Fish & Wildlife, WA Parks, WA Dept. of Ecology

Direct advertising inquiries to:
Waggoner Cruising Guide
Burrows Bay Associates
PO Box 726
Anacortes, WA 98221 USA
Phone (425) 780-5015
Fax (360) 299-0535
Email: WaggonerCruisingGuide@gmail.com
www.WaggonerGuide.com

Book Sales U.S.
Fine Edge Nautical Publishing
PO Box 726
Anacortes, WA 98221 USA
Phone (360) 299-8500
Fax (360) 299-0535
Email: orders@FineEdge.com
www.WaggonerGuideBooks.com

Book Sales Canada
Chyna Sea Ventures, Ltd.
Unit 4, 147 E. Fern Rd.
Qualicum Beach, BC, V9K 1T2
Phone: (250) 740-1184
Fax: (250) 740-1185
Toll Free: 866-627-8324
Email: orders@ChynaSea.com
www.ChynaSea.com

Like us on Facebook
Waggoner Cruising Guide
WaggonerGuide.com

Twitter
@TheWaggoner

25 Years . . .

It is interesting to look back over the last **25 years of boating** through the eyes of the Waggoner Cruising Guide. We take our responsibility to annually report all of the changes in our area seriously, all of the 400+ marinas, and the major anchorages that make this expansive area so special.

We cannot do it alone. Over the last 25 years we estimate nearly 150 people have contributed directly to the Waggoner Cruising Guide as editors, writers, correspondents, photographers, cartographers, artists, proofreaders, ad sales people, bookkeepers and even our printing crews at two separate plants in the Portland area. We also could not do this without the support of our 350+ advertisers over the years. It takes a village...

Many of our readers stop us on the dock and tell us how important the Waggoner Cruising Guide is to their time on the water. We are told that the Waggoner Guide is their "Bible for Northwest Cruising."

Our role at the Waggoner Cruising Guide has changed. We don't just publish a 500-page guidebook every year. We are in the nautical information business. Throughout the year we gather information for boaters with practical tips for enjoying our unique cruising area. We disseminate this information in our online newsletters, eBooks, email blasts, and of course, through the Waggoner Cruising Guide. With our seminars and flotillas, we share our expertise with several thousand through our Cruisers College, our Seattle Boat Show University programs and our Waggoner Seminars for cruising to Alaska and other destinations.

Going forward, watch for us to introduce innovative services that further embrace advances in technology and communications. We have a new group of boaters now exploring our cruising area who were practically born with a smartphone in their hands. While they may gather their information digitally, they, too, enjoy the beauty and natural wonders while exploring by boat.

While some of us love a good paper chart at the helm, we are using our sophisticated chartplotters with digital radar and satellite data communications to improve our safety and enjoyment on the water. Boating has changed in 25 years, but our goals of exploring this area are still the same.

We thank all of you, our readers, customers and contributors, for the last 25 years.

Mark Bunzel, Editor & Publisher

What's New in the 2019 Waggoner Cruising Guide?

At the end of each cruising season, we are always surprised by the large number of changes we find that are important to Northwest boaters. This season's longer than usual list of changes was driven by marinas upgrading and expanding capacity in response to more boaters that are cruising more often and for longer periods. Waggoner Field Correspondents were formally organized in 2018, ensuring better coverage of a wide area and have contributed greatly to the number of updates for the 2019 Waggoner edition. In this edition, you will find 20 new reference maps, including new stern-tie pins recently installed throughout many B.C. marine parks, and information about the new ROAM App for reporting your arrival into U.S. waters. Be sure to look for the information about Smartphone Apps, and the "Go-NoGo" weather checklists; new for 2019.

A Theme for 2019 Edition. Boaters love beautiful anchorages, charming villages and new-found friendships that enrich our cruising experience. Boating destinations become even more endearing when we know something about the area's history and colorful past. How many of us have anchored near the remnants of an old cabin or wharf and wondered who it was that once lived there? Or walked through a small village asking ourselves, "what prompted people to homestead in such a remote location?" "Nautical Tales through the Eyes of the Past," our theme for the 2019 Waggoner Cruising

Guide, will help shed light on some of these special places. Readers of the Waggoner Guide will find a synopsis of 17 non-fiction books that provide an intriguing background for many of our favorite boating destinations. There's a reason why the village of Sointula is a quiet community with a co-op grocery; a reason why the Golden Spruce on Haida Gwaii lives on; and a history that extends much deeper than we might first imagine at Ocean Falls. Most boaters are familiar with the story of the Nootka Sound Convention, but did you know that another story played out here when two Europeans were taken captive by Chief Maquinna? Or did you know that a 20th-Century prophet, called Brother XII, established his headquarters among the Gulf Islands, capturing the imagination of hundreds of people world-wide? You will find many other interesting stories from books that you will want to read before heading out on your next cruise, or take along for your quiet, at-anchor reading.

Lorena & Leonard Landon, Managing Editors

Mary Campbell came late to boating but has been making up for lost time. For the last 25 years, she has been sailing the Inside Passage, originally in her Colvin junk schooner and, for the last 10 years, in her Cascade 36. Retired, she spends each summer on the boat. Her travels have taken her through Southeast Alaska, across the Gulf of Alaska to Seward and the Katmai region; she has circumnavigated Vancouver Island and been captivated by the native villages of Haida Gwaii. She's also sailed in warmer climates, including the Sea of Cortez, the Pacific Coast of Mexico, Australia's north and east coasts, and parts of Indonesia. Still, her favorite cruising destinations are Prince William Sound and Haida Gwaii. Their pristine beauty and rugged coastlines present a last frontier of coastal cruising. Mary appreciates the challenge of cruising where the sight of another boat is a welcome surprise, and where the wildlife outnumbers the humans.

Melissa (Missy) Gervais has been boating for 20 years and is a member of the Royal Vancouver Yacht Club. She enjoys anchoring out in B.C.'s beautiful marine parks and taking photos of the many special, scenic destinations found in British Columbia. Her dog, Jonathan, is a companion aboard her 34-foot power boat, *As You Wish*. Melissa enjoys cruising the Gulf Islands and Sunshine Coast during vacation time from her active career with Pacific Yacht Systems. Melissa, who often goes by Missy, hosts a blog site which includes marine products, a photo gallery, and an events calendar geared to women boaters — missygoesboating.com. Melissa enjoyed cruising her favorite areas of the greater Gulf Islands region during the 2018 boating season.

Deane and Arlene Hislop call Anacortes their home. Between the two of them, they have over 75 years of Pacific Northwest boating experience, with the last 23 years cruising together. They enjoy visiting the many marinas and secluded coves that dot the inland waters of the Pacific Northwest. Deane and Arlene can be found cruising year-round between Olympia and northern Vancouver Island, spending more than 100 nights a year aboard their 381 Meridian, *Easy Goin'*. They enjoy meeting other boaters, exploring new locations, sampling local cuisine and collecting information, experiences and images for boating publications. Deane is a freelance writer and photographer specializing in recreational boating. His work has appeared in regional, national and international publications. Deane's images have also been featured in advertisements, websites and on magazine covers.

Anita Fraser and Jim Norris have been boating nearly their entire lives, having been engaged in commercial fishing, marine research, and more recently as active recreational boaters. They are Great Loop veterans, completing "The Loop" in 2008 on a 32-foot Grand Banks. Since 2010 they have cruised extensively between their home port of Port Townsend and Glacier Bay, Alaska on their 42-foot Krogen, Spirit Quest. Their northern trips have included the west side of Vancouver Island and Haida Gwaii. They have also cruised as far south as San Diego, spending a winter in Oxnard, California. Each year they explore their favorite destinations and personal secret places in Northern B.C. and Southeast Alaska.

Brett and Sue Oemichen reside in Port Ludlow and have been cruising the Pacific Northwest since 2010. They have traveled the Salish Sea from Olympia to the Northern BC Coast. Their first northwest boat was a Camano 31, and they are currently the proud owners of a 34-foot American Tug named *Joint Venture*. Their 2018 cruising season was spent in the San Juan and Gulf Islands, the Broughtons, and destinations north of Cape Caution. They are enthusiastic boaters who provide their perspective and insights into the process of discovery.

Bob and Shino Posey owned a PT 38 Trawler for many years in which they explored the Pacific Northwest and BC's lower mainland. Bob started boating with runabouts in the 60's. They currently own a 24-foot Sea Sport Explorer, based in Anacortes, which provides flexibility in planning a variety of cruising destinations. They spend most summers cruising the San Juan and Gulf Islands and enjoyed a recent trip to Chatterbox Falls in Princess Louisa Inlet. During the 2018 boating season, Bob and Shino trailered their boat to Prince Rupert BC and cruised the Inside Passage to Southeast Alaska where they rendezvoused with family members near the southern tip of Baranof Island.

John Shepard started sailing, racing, and instructing as a teenager in San Diego. As a Naval junior, John had free use of boats that provided recreational opportunities for servicemen, and he took full advantage sailing and racing in the waters of Southern California. John first started cruising the Pacific Northwest with a trailerable boat, exploring rivers, lakes and bays. Inspired by reading Jonathan Raban's book, *Passage to Juneau*, John purchased a Cal 35 Cruiser sloop, named *Hadley*. John undertook refurbishing s/v *Hadley*, making extensive repairs and refits. In 2017, with projects nearly complete, a fast-moving boat appeared out of the fog near Double Bluff on Whidbey Island and clipped his starboard stern. Thankfully the stern quarter and transom were mostly fiberglass repairs; a quick maneuver had helped avoid a more serious collision. Happily, *Hadley* was repaired over the winter and was ready in 2018 to once again weave through island passages in all sorts of weather and cross the straits that make up our water playground of the Pacific Northwest.

Lateral Buoys (R/G) No Light		Structures		Trail
Mid-Channel Buoys				Road
Lateral Lights (R/G)		Land		Boundary lines
Lateral Buoys (R/G) Lighted		Water		Railroad
Non-Lateral Lights (W/Y)		Shallow water		Curvilinear Route
Non-Lateral Buoys Lighted		Tidal area dries at chart datum (zero tide)	①	Key to Text
Non-Lateral Buoys No Light		Restricted Area - No entry or limited operation area		Anchorage
Mooring Buoy	Speed Limit Zone	Warning text		Lighthouse
Lateral Daymark Beacon Lighted		Special use area as described with each instance		Dock/float
Range Markers	+++	Rock awash at chart datum	✕	Stern-tie anchor pins
Beacon - shape and color as indicated	* * *	Rock which covers and uncovers	Even / Odd Slips	Even/Odd Slip Number Direction Indicator
	◎–◎	Linear Moorage		

ABOUT THE WAGGONER CRUISING GUIDE

Waggoner Guide (pronounced [wagənər] not [wagənir]) has been guiding boaters to the spectacular Northwest destinations since 1994. It provides the reader with information about marinas, anchorages, passages, and attractions from Olympia, Washington to Ketchikan, Alaska. It is referred to by boaters as *The bible for northwest cruising*. This all-inclusive guidebook is updated annually.

Waggoner Guide strives to be the most up-to-date cruising guidebook with the most accurate information. The writing style is intended to be as concise, factual, and informative as possible.

How the book is organized. The first section of the book, referred to as 'Front Matter,' contains valuable information that helps boaters plan and execute a successful trip. This Chapter 1, Front Matter has instructional material regarding customs, weather, anchoring, communications and other pertinent 'how-to' information

The body of the book is divided into chapters by geographic cruising area, starting in the south at Olympia Washington and progressing north to Ketchikan, Alaska. Keeping with the south to north organization, material within each chapter generally progresses northward. Each chapter begins with an overview of the area followed by detailed information for each marina along with passages and designated anchorages. Ports, harbors, and cities with multiple boating facilities also begin with an overview description to help the reader become familiar with the area

Reference maps for the chapter's coverage area are located at the beginning of the chapter with additional reference maps found throughout the chapter. A Legend of symbols used on Waggoner Guide reference maps can be found in this section. Area reference maps indicate destinations with numbers, which correspond to the numbered text for marinas and significant anchorages. Reference maps are not for navigation and do not show all navigation aids, beacons, marks, lights, and hazards. Maps are not to scale and are for reference purposes only. Boaters should carry up-to-date electronic charts and/or paper charts.

You will also find 'Local Knowledge' and 'Sidebars' within many of the chapters. Local Knowledge provides helpful tips and warnings regarding shoals, rocks, tides and current for specific locations, which may not be depicted on navigational charts. Short articles, called Sidebars, relate personal experiences that are informative and helpful to the reader. Sidebars also provide historical background for a number of destinations, enlightening the imagination and purpose of why we go there in the first place.

The Year's Theme. Some of the Sidebars in the Waggoner Guide focus on a chosen theme for the year. *Nautical Tales Through the Eyes of the Past* was chosen as this year's theme. How many of us have wondered what took place on an island, remote village, or abandoned farmstead? Knowing something about the history of the places we visit, brings a whole new appreciation and perspective for our many cherished boating destinations. This year's edition includes synopsis of 15 different non-fiction books, which provide an intriguing background for some of these favorite places.

How the Book is Made. The Waggoner Guide Team of Northwest boaters, cruise Northwest waters and the Inside Passage to Alaska each year, gathering updates for marinas, anchorages, and passages found in the Waggoner Guide. The Waggoner Team, along with experienced Field Correspondents and knowledgeable contributors, provide the many hundreds of updates included in each year's edition of the Waggoner Cruising Guide. While it is not possible to physically go to every anchorage or marina each year, every effort is made to get the latest information directly from marinas by phone or other means. Editorial work begins in September to incorporate these changes and updates, including new reference maps and photos. Editors, proof readers, and designers of maps, ads, and page layout spend untold hours preparing copy for final proofs, while meeting our print deadline. The much-anticipated announcement of the current edition of the Waggoner Guide is provided in our 'eNews.' Copies of the Waggoner Cruising Guide are made available at the Seattle Boat Show, where boaters enthusiastically purchase the new edition and begin making plans for their next adventure. Copies are also available at retailers throughout Washington, B.C., and Alaska and at the Anacortes Waggoner Book Store.

How to send us Comments and Feedback. The Waggoner Team invites your comments, suggestions and corrections. We appreciate hearing from our readers regarding ways we can improve our publication. Your ideas for future editions are always welcome along with your experiences and tips, which inform and help other boaters. Contact us through our website, www.WaggonerGuide.com, or by telephone (360) 299-8500; you can also find us on Facebook.

WaggonerGuide.com and eNews. At WaggonerGuide.com, we have a dedicated team of experienced boaters and travel experts who share a variety of articles each month about boating in Washington, British Columbia, and Southeast Alaska. Some of the topics include maintenance tips, cruising destinations, boat reviews, and on-the-water reporting. You'll also find boating seminar announcements, guidebook updates, access to free downloads, and our collection of boating and nautical-themed books in the Waggoner Store.

A great way to stay tuned into WaggonerGuide.com is to subscribe to Waggoner eNews. This newsletter is sent out twice a month and contains our latest boating related articles. It also gives you access to our eNews subscriber-only downloads. All of our content is geared toward you, our reader, who lives and breathes boating in the Pacific Northwest

To enroll in the Waggoner eNews visit WaggonerGuide.com. You'll find the subscribe button on the right column. Or, visit our Facebook page at https://www.facebook.com/WaggonerCruisingGuide and in the left-hand column, you'll find the Subscribe to eNews tab.

Advertisers. Advertising helps provide the best cruising information at the best price to you the cruising public; advertisements often provide more extensive information about the facility that is not part of the mission of the Waggoner Guide. Advertising helps us keep in touch with the marinas and service providers, who provide information about what is coming for the next cruising season. This symbiotic relationship helps the Waggoner Team stay in communication with the Marine Trade Industry and provide guidance regarding cruisers' needs. Combined ads, called Community Market Place, inform our readers of local events, farmers' markets, and other local points of interest.

eBooks. Waggoner Cruising Guide is available in a seven volume eBook series from Amazon. Volume 1 of the series is Chapter 1 of the guidebook, which includes how to go cruising topics. Volumes 2 through 7 cover the cruising area from Olympia, WA to Ketchikan, AK and are organized by common cruising areas. You can purchase Volume 1, along with one or more of the cruising area volumes where you plan to cruise. See WaggonerGuideBooks.com for more information.

IN THE BEGINNING

The Waggoner had its origins in 1993, when my wife Marilynn and I spent our summer vacation roaming the Canadian Gulf Islands on our Tolly 26, recording latitude/longitude coordinates for the upcoming Weatherly Waypoint Guide, vol. 2. This was when Loran was the hot new electronic navigation miracle, but required waypoint coordinates so it could tell how to get to where you wanted to go. Volume 1, covering Puget Sound and the San Juan Islands, was a success, and we saw a natural extension to other Northwest waters. We had never spent much time in the Gulf Islands, so we relied on existing guidebooks for cruising information. One in particular seemed to cover the anchorages, fuel docks and marinas, but its coverage was uneven.

In earlier times I had supported our family (modestly) as a freelance magazine writer, and spent two instructive years as editor of Nor'westing, then the leading Puget Sound area boating magazine. Tom Kincaid, a gem of a man, was the publisher. With this background, I fancied myself as something of a pro when it came to publishing, especially about local nautical subjects.

By the time we got home we had made a tentative decision to write and publish our own Northwest cruising guide, one that would address the shortcomings of others on the market. I confessed that I knew we could do better. It's not easy to create something from nothing. Every single element had to be

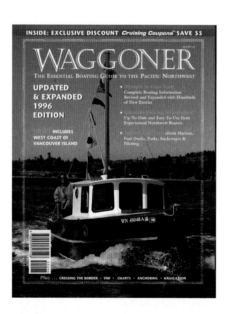

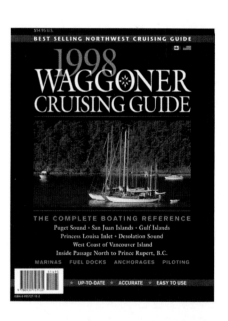

1994

The first Waggoner Guide, published in 1994 by Robert Hale & Co. Inc., included Puget Sound, San Juan Islands and the Gulf Islands, with 117 pages and sold for $9.95. The guidebook was first titled "The Pacific Northwest Waggoner" and included 18 advertisers. The price was raised the following year to $12.95, having expanded the coverage area to Desolation Sound and the Broughtons.

1996

The 1996 edition was expanded to include West Coast Vancouver Island and contained cruising discount coupons, "the green pages" and the "yellow pages" through 1997. The editorial text and photos for the Waggoner continued to be printed in black and white. The name of the guidebook changed in 1997 to its current name, the "Waggoner Cruising Guide."

1998

The 1998 edition saw the introduction of conversion tables added to other reference material like distance tables and VHF channels for U.S. and British Columbia waters, then identified as "the green pages." Included at the back of the book, was a list of fuel docks and their phone numbers. The page count had risen to 246 pages with a price change to $14.95.

decided and worked out, from what to include, how to include it, how to find and verify information—a blizzard of elements, all from square one. Finally, in early June 1994, the first edition went to the printer.

Thin though that first book was, it embodied several elements that have remained constant to today. First, the guiding philosophy, Serve the Reader. If the Waggoner was to succeed, it would be because people trusted the Waggoner, bought the Waggoner, and used the Waggoner. The notion of serving the reader has been proven valid. Today's Waggoners are the single most popular cruising guides in the Northwest.

Now, skip ahead 18 years to March 31, 2011. That was the date Mark Bunzel and I signed the papers that transferred the Waggoner Cruising Guide to Bunzel's ownership. When signatures were finished and hands were shaken, the time had come to say something I'd rehearsed for several weeks. I choked on the first try, gathered composure, and finally got it out: "Captain Bunzel, the helm is yours." My baby was moving to a new home.

[Robert Hale]

A HISTORY OF THE WAGGONER

About 1584 the Dutch pilot Lucas Janszoon Waghenaer published a volume of navigational principles, tables, charts, and sailing directions, which served as a guide for other such books for the next 200 years.

These *"Waggoners,"* as they came to be known, met with great success, and in 1588 an English translation of the original book was made. During the next 30 years, 24 editions of the book were published in Dutch, German, Latin, and English. Other authors followed the profitable example set by Waghenaer. Soon, American, British, and French navigators had Waggoners for most of the waters they sailed.

The success of these books and the resulting competition led to their eventual demise. In 1795 the British Hydrographic Department was established, and charts and sailing directions were issued.

We hope you find this new Waggoner to be as useful as the Waggoners of old. *Waggoner* is an ancient name with a proud history. Use and enjoy.

OUR MISSION

The Waggoner mission is to provide essential boating information for Northwest waters in an easy-to-use format. Through printed publications, digital media, and instructional materials, Waggoner endeavors to empower the boating public to discover the rewards of cruising these waters. We encourage all boaters to explore the beautiful waterways of the Pacific Northwest. Waggoner strives to be the go-to source of boating information for cruising the Northwest and Inside Passage.

SERVE THE READER

Although its coverage was limited initially, this book had one quality boaters seemed to recognize: it was written for them. The book contained factual, unbiased information about Pacific Northwest cruising and marine facilities, and it was easy to read and use.

The first Waggoner Cruising Guide laid the groundwork for each succeeding annual edition. Today, the guide has grown in size and coverage area (now Olympia, WA to Ketchikan, AK), with the addition of many timely articles, tips and stories. It's beginning philosophy of "serve the reader" has continued over the years and it shows on every page.

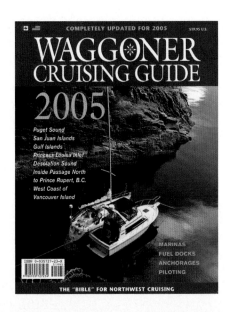

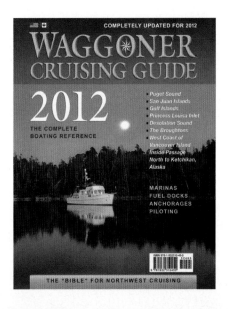

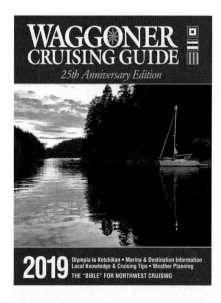

2005

2012

2019

Waggoner Cruising Guide was printed in color for the first time in 2005, and contained approximately 125 reference maps and many colorful photos and marine related ads. Many of the original advertisers continued their placement in the Waggoner Cruising Guide. At nearly 400 pages, the price of the Waggoner went to $19.95, and then to $21.95 in 2008.

Mark Bunzel purchased the Waggoner Cruising Guide in 2011 and continued to expand and improve its content, adding Dixon Entrance and Ketchikan in 2012. The VTS Radio section was expanded, and helpful "Local Knowledge" cruising tips were added to area chapters. Online Waggoner eNews was made available to over 10,000 boaters in the Pacific Northwest. Through the Fine Edge publishing business, flotillas and classes were made available in subsequent years.

In the fall of 2017, Mark brought in Lorena and Leonard Landon as managing editors. New marinas and anchorages were added, and major re-writes and updates were included in the 2018 and 2019 editions. Field Correspondents were formally organized and help cruise our waters for valuable updates. eBook Waggoner volumes were added in 2018. The 25th Anniversary Edition for 2019 now contains over 200 reference maps. The Front Section has been expanded to include the latest tools and techniques for boaters.

How to Cruise the Pacific Northwest

Inside Passage. The Inside Passage is one of the best cruising grounds in the world. The distance from Olympia, Washington to Ketchikan, Alaska is about 600 miles as the crow flies. On a boat, meandering through fjords and between islands, the distance multiplies. Most of these waters are protected; open water passages are relatively short, and anchorages are plentiful.

Wildlife is outstanding. Whales—orcas, humpbacks, grays, and more—are regularly spotted. Bald eagles are everywhere. Bears snatch salmon from seaside rivers or forage on the beach. Porpoises, seals, sea lions, sea otters, and myriad other life call the Inside Passage home.

Natural beauty overwhelms. The great volcanoes of the Cascade mountains are visible throughout Puget Sound and the San Juan Islands. Sandstone in the Gulf Islands, eroded by wind and water, forms fascinating patterns and shapes. Magnificent, glacier carved fjords run deep into British Columbia's interior. Waterfalls plunge thousands of feet from snow-covered peaks all the way to the waters' edge.

We have impressive cities, too. Seattle, Victoria, and Vancouver are easily visited by boat and have every amenity imaginable. Smaller cities like La Conner, Anacortes, Sidney, Cowichan Bay, Ladysmith—even Port McNeill, Port Hardy, Prince Rupert, and Ketchikan farther north—roll out the red carpet for visiting boats. They have restaurants, shops, and museums to explore or enjoy.

Small resorts and marinas, many family run, dot the coast. Some are as simple as local logs felled, milled, and lashed together to form a dock. Others have spas and high-end restaurants. Potluck dinners and happy hours are common at the smaller marinas.

You won't go hungry cruising this area. Bigger towns have grocery stores. Many marinas stock the essentials for their guests. Farmers markets, local bakers, artisan cheese makers, and craft wineries, breweries and now a few distilleries operate along the Inside Passage. Seafood, of course, is plentiful. Cruisers catch salmon, halibut, lingcod, prawns, and crab. They pick oysters and harvest sea asparagus.

The history is rich. Yaculta and Alert Bay have superb museums detailing the history of Native cultures. In Ketchikan, Totem Bight State Park has a remarkable collection of totems. Cruisers can follow in the footsteps of Capt. George Vancouver's 1790s expedition and the early expeditions of the Spanish explorers, during which many of the waterways and land masses in this area were named. Opportunities to enjoy the arts are readily available; in this book we describe the full range of museums at destinations along the way. Tacoma alone has six museums and a zoo, all within easy walking distance from the docks.

The variety of experiences, the majesty of the vistas, and the splendor of the wildlife and the variety of attractions in our towns and cities on the water keep us cruising.

"Gates" and Their Effect. The Pacific Northwest is a series of cruising areas separated by what we call "gates"— significant bodies of water that must be crossed. Although gates define our experience and abilities, they also serve as natural stopping points. Some cruisers stay in Puget Sound because the Strait of Juan de Fuca and San Juan Channel is a gate. Some stay in the Gulf Islands because the Strait of Georgia and Dodd Narrows crossing is a gate bringing concerns about the sea state conditions. Some go no farther than Desolation Sound because Johnstone Strait and the reversing tidal rapids north of Desolation Sound are gates. And some stay

south of Cape Caution because the ocean swells of Queen Charlotte Sound can be looked at as a gate. Gates exist all the way up the coast, all the way to Alaska.

Once beyond a gate and in a given cruising area, the waters are protected. Fortunately, summer weather usually is agreeable. With a study of the tide and current books, a close eye on the winds, an understanding of the weather, and a properly-equipped boat, the gates can be negotiated in safety, and often in comfort. The farther one decides to explore, the more time is needed. For the dedicated summertime Northwest cruiser, time is the principal element limiting cruising choices.

Chartering. The most popular charter boat waters run from the San Juan Islands to Desolation Sound, a distance of approximately 160 miles. These waters include the San Juan Islands, the Canadian Gulf Islands, the cities of Victoria and Vancouver, Howe Sound, Princess Louisa Inlet and the ever popular Desolation Sound. Most charters are for a week or two. It would take years of careful planning and repeat visits for a regular charter cruiser to see all there is to see in this area. For more information see *Chartering* in Chapter 1.

Trailering a Boat. Trailering is faster and more affordable than running a boat on its own bottom, and it avoids difficult passages across open water—the "gates" described earlier. Trailer boats can be towed to all the cruising grounds from Puget Sound to the far end of Vancouver Island. Even the sounds and inlets of the west coast of Vancouver Island

can be seen easily and safely. Some people trailer all the way up Vancouver Island, launch at Port Hardy, and—watching the weather carefully—cruise north past Cape Caution to Rivers Inlet and beyond.

Many boats are trailered from the B.C. Interior to launch at Bella Coola or Prince Rupert. It's a long drive, but the waters they get to are some of the finest in the world. From Prince Rupert, you can cruise north into Southeast Alaska, which is not accessible by road. Another option is to tow the boat and trailer onto the ferry. Although expensive, both the BC Ferries and the Alaska Marine Highway ferries allow trailered boats.

Anchoring vs. Marinas. Compared with the waters farther north, Puget Sound has relatively few good anchorages. Most Puget Sound cruising is from marina to marina, or hanging off state park buoys. The San Juan Islands and Canadian Gulf Islands have many marinas and many anchorages. Desolation Sound is mostly anchorages with a few marinas. State and provincial marine parks dot the waterways from Puget Sound to Desolation Sound, many but not all with mooring buoys. The Broughtons have a wide variety of marinas and many, many anchorages. The west coast of Vancouver Island and the waters north of Cape Caution have a few marinas but mostly anchorages. It is possible to cruise all the way to the top of Vancouver Island and stay only at the dock in a marina. For more information see *About Anchoring* in this chapter.

Moorage Reservations. Many marinas accept advance reservations for transient moorage. Reserving moorage in advance is always a good idea and highly recommended during the busy summer season. A telephone call is the most universally accepted means for making reservations. Increasingly, some marinas have web-based reservation systems and a few accept email requests. Some marinas don't require any credit card information, but others do. Ask about their policy for charging your credit card and about their cancelation policy in case weather or unexpected delays cause a change in plans. Some marinas charge for no-shows. Ask about your slip assignment; a few marinas assign a slip at the time of reservation, while others request you contact them by radio upon arrival.

It's best to contact the marina directly for slip reservations. There are a few third-party centralized marina slip reservation providers,

which began on the U.S. East Coast and have a very limited number of west coast marinas under contract. There are some websites that purport to have relationships with local marinas but do not. Check with the marina first before contacting any third-party web provider.

Have Flexible Expectations. Marina facilities run the range from elegant to, shall we say, rustic. Managements span the same range. A person who expects 5-star facilities and service at every stop will be disappointed. Especially in the remote areas, the docks and other facilities can be rather on the rough side. Service at the Native villages up the coast, for example, is provided on their terms, in their way, and that's different from the city approach most Waggoner readers are accustomed to. When we're out cruising we have found it helpful to relax and take things as they come. We appreciate the places that do things our way, but we get along with the places that don't.

The one area we have less patience with is cleanliness. We think public washrooms, showers and laundry areas should be clean and in good condition, always. If we could have one message for marina operators, it would be, *keep those areas sparkling.*

About the Boat. Northwest cruising is coastal cruising in generally protected waters, so blue-water ocean voyaging vessels are not required. But the waters can get rough. Whether power or sail, good Northwest cruising boats are strongly built and seaworthy. Lightweight pontoon boats or open ski boats that are so

popular on inland lakes are not well suited to these waters.

The weather can be cool and often wet. Northwest cruising powerboats tend to have large cabins and ample window area. Northwest cruising sailboats tend to have dodgers across the fronts of the cockpits or even full cockpit enclosures. Winds often are light and on the nose—"noserlies"—so sailboats should have good power.

Most Northwest cruising boats are equipped with cabin heat. It could be heat generated while the engine is running, a diesel heater or diesel furnace, or electric space heaters on the dock's shore power. Heat can add comfort when it is raining, on a cool night, or when cruising in the off-season.

GPS has become so affordable that no Northwest cruising boat should be without a GPS system. A chartplotter, whether a dedicated marine unit or computer software on a PC or pad/tablet device, makes it easy to always know your position. There is even chartplotter software that runs on your smartphone.

AIS (Automatic Identification System) is increasingly popular. AIS receivers display vessel name, course, speed, and closest point of approach for nearby boats equipped with an AIS transponder, which broadcasts the vessel's boat information, course, and speed. Large commercial craft, such as ferries, cruise ships, and freighters, all broadcast AIS signals.

Radar has grown better and prices are trending down. In the last two years new digital radar systems now require less power, are lighter and often plug right into a chartplotter. Most important the new digital radar units are very sensitive and provide a better resolution and presentation in color. Since fog and rain clouds can lower visibility to near-zero any time of the year, cruising boats in the Northwest often end up with radar. Autopilots take the uncertainty out of steering in fog and make long passages less tiring. They too are quickly added.

Dinghies and tenders and convenient dinghy launching/ recovery systems are important. When anchored or tied to a

mooring buoy, the dinghy will be used to travel to shore. Some cruisers use their dinghies extensively for exploring and fishing.

Substantial anchoring systems are important. See the *Anchoring* section of Chapter 1 for more information.

The minimum size for a cruising boat probably is in the 18- to 20-foot range, and that's pretty minimum. Most mom-and-pop cruising boats fall into the 25- to 50-foot size range, with the majority in the 32- to 50-foot range—large enough to be comfortable, small enough to be handled by two people.

Be Self-reliant. Don't venture out with the idea that if things go wrong, you can always call the Coast Guard. An important part of good seamanship is being able to handle whatever's thrown at you. Calling the Coast Guard is for true emergencies.

Best Months. The prime cruising months begin in April and end by October, with July-August the most popular. Boats are used year-round in Puget Sound. On winter weekends Puget Sound's popular ports are surprisingly busy. Cabin heat is a must in the winter. As mentioned above, cabin heat is almost a must the rest of the year.

North of Puget Sound, pleasure boating is best done between early May and late September. Really dependable summer weather (little rain, long days of glorious sunshine) normally doesn't arrive in the Northwest until July. September can be an outstanding cruising month. The crowds are gone and the weather can be perfect.

Use caution with winter cruising north of Puget Sound. (Be careful in Puget Sound, too.) Storms lash the British Columbia coast. A Northwest boat with a warm and dry pilothouse is the way to enjoy winter cruising. Some, with flexible schedules, cruise yearround. It takes a good understanding of the weather, and a warm, dry boat. There are many resources available to understand the weather and help keep you from an unexpected surprise. See the *Interpreting Northwest Weather* section for our approach to understanding the weather.

About GPS Chartplotters, Charts and other Publications. To keep this book informative and up-to-date, we have stuck our nose into many ports, bays, and coves along the coast. In the process we have become unyielding advocates of chartplotters, charts, and navigation publications. Properly used, charts not only keep a boat out of trouble, they allow one to enter areas you wouldn't want to try without the chart.

With advancements in electronic charting in recent years, more mariners are asking whether carrying paper charts is still worthwhile. For years, we would not leave the dock without a set of paper charts. Even with computer navigation and a complete selection of electronic charts, it seemed wise to have paper charts as a backup.

But times are changing. Tablets and smartphones, with built-in GPS receiver systems and robust batteries, provide excellent redundancy. Low cost, highly effective chartplotting software is available for most tablet platforms. Many of these "apps" make updating charts easy. If relying on a tablet or smartphone as a backup, consider carrying an extra battery pack. They're inexpensive and greatly extend battery life.

When using electronic charts, be aware that hazards can disappear at certain zoom levels. We always examine our route at several zoom levels to ensure that it is free of hazards.

Whatever form of charts you decide to carry, keep them updated. While rocks haven't changed location, navigation aids do change. Recently, for example, significant buoyage changes were made in Swinomish Channel. In British Columbia, some buoys were determined as unnecessary or redundant and were removed to meet budget goals. New charts reflect the change whether on paper or on new electronic updates. A five year old (or older) chartplotter may have very old charts and not reflect navigational updates.

Many cruising guides cover the Inside Passage and each offers a different point of view. We carry as many as we can fit, and keep several open at the helm. The U.S. Coast Pilot and Canadian Sailing Directions are good resources to have aboard, but they are focused on large commercial craft navigation.

Accurate tide and current tables are essential. Many electronic charting packages include tide and current data. However, we've found these are often inaccurate because they are based on old or estimated data. Note: Both U.S. and Canadian government tide tables are not corrected for Daylight Saving Time, so you'll have to make the corrections manually. Capt'n Jack's, covering Puget Sound, and Ports and Passes, covering Olympia to Prince Rupert and Southeast Alaska, are excellent and inexpensive, and times are corrected for Daylight Saving Time. Ports and Passes is updated each year with official government data. We have found some chartplotter tides and currents information to be off by as much as 45 minutes. Full disclosure: We are also the publishers of Ports and Passes.

U.S. Coast Guard Local Notices to Mariners, Canadian Notices to Shipping, and Canadian Notices to Mariners provide updated information on navaids and regulatory changes. U.S. and Canadian light lists are useful, too. The links to these sites are available in the "cruise planning" section of the Waggoner website.

We do not understand the mentality of the owner that will make a major investment in a boat and fuel, then hold back on charts and other navigation information. At the other extreme is the person who has very little invested, and won't buy navigation information because it costs too much compared to the value of the vessel. *Remember:* the rocks, tides and weather are indifferent to how much the boat cost. They treat all boats equally.

It Takes Teamwork. Like many boating couples, we work together as a team, checking and doublechecking routes, depths, and charted hazards along a chosen course. If we question or doubt our path, we come to a stop until the safest course can be verified before continuing on. This is not the time for wounded pride or "I told you so's," it's a matter of successfully accomplishing the task at hand, and the opportunity to learn and grow as a team. Everything looks different on the water, so it's easy to mistake land marks and aids to navigation. The more experienced you are as a team, the better off you will be when the going gets tuff, or when you are faced with a true emergency. Both partners should know how to use the radio, handle the helm, navigate, and manage sea conditions for a safe arrival into port. Docking and line-handling should be shared responsibilities, it's a good idea to schedule time for practice as well as a shake-down cruise for boat maintenance checks. The more comfortable you become with your own skills and know what your boat can handle, the more fun you will have. On a power vessel, it is imperative to conduct engine room checks, requiring a confident partner to take over the helm. Extended excursions or overnight passages for both power and sail, require taking turns at the helm so your partner can get some rest. The more you learn, the more opportunities you will have for new adventures further afield.

Use FRS Radios. Inexpensive, handy, no license required. Excellent for replacing shouts or if you get separated at the county fair or at Costco. If cruising with other boats, they keep needless chatter off VHF channels.

Don't Be Cheap. It's bad form to use a private marina's facilities and not pay for the privilege. Even if a direct charge is not made, usually something can be purchased. When we overnight at a marina, we pay the moorage, just as our readers do. We're glad the marina is there, and we want it to be there for the future. We are pleased to do our part.

WHAT TO BRING AND HOW TO EQUIP THE BOAT.

Carry Tools and Spares. Our tool box is in the main cabin, available for immediate access. It seems like we are in that box at least once a day, usually for something minor, but it has to be fixed. Carry all owner's manuals, extra engine oil, transmission fluid, hydraulic fluid, coolant, and distilled water (for the batteries), spare V-belts, ignition parts, impellers and filters. Carry a spare raw water pump. The list of tools and spares has no end. You can't prepare for everything, but you can prepare for likely problems.

Carry Charts, Tables & Guides. Carry charts for each area you will be cruising. Electronic charts are the most cost effective and cover the largest geographic area. Make sure you have multiple backups on separate independent devices. Don't forget tide and current tables. Local guidebooks have good information that add to the enjoyment of the trip.

Carry Self-amalgamating Tape. This is stretchy tape that sticks to itself but not to what it's wrapped around. Usually it is available in black or white. The black is stronger. We have used self-amalgamating tape to repair a leaking high pressure fuel line, and to repair a broken oven door handle. The stuff is magic. We wouldn't cruise without it.

Carry Shore Power Cords & Adapters. If your boat has 30 amp shore power, you will need adapters for 15 amp, 20 amp and 50 amp outlets. It hasn't happened often, but there have been times when the nearest power receptacle was more than 50 feet away. We carry a second 50-foot shore power cord.

First Aid. Nobody knows when an accident might occur (that's what makes it an accident). In many areas you will need to be self-reliant. It could be hours or even the next day before medical aid might be available at your location. Carry a comprehensive

medical kit and know how to use it. Carry spare medication for many of the common ailments. Call the Coast Guard if you do have a medical emergency. The U.S. Coast Guard has a medical professional on duty somewhere (it might be Kodiak, AK); they can be patched through for medical advice if needed. If you have guests onboard, ask if there are any medical issues or allergies. While your cruising may be recreational boating, the captain has responsibility for crew and guests.

Clothing. Except for some areas of Desolation Sound in the summer, most of the waters of the Northwest are cold. Even during warm weather you may welcome a sweater or jacket. Layering clothing works well. Rain gear is essential on sailboats.

On an enclosed powerboat, rain gear makes exploring shoreside attractions more pleasant when it is raining. Rubber boots are useful. Shoreside attire can be as nice as you want; most people do fine with comfortable sports clothes.

CRUISING TIPS & TECHNIQUES.

Shore Power Connection. Since not all docks have breakers to turn off individual outlets, we turn the boat's 110-volt switch to OFF before we hook up or unplug shore power. If the dock power has its own breaker, we turn it to OFF, too. When everything is hooked up, we turn the dock switch to ON, and then the boat switch.

Update Credit Cards. Credit and debit cards seem to be the preferred form of payment on both sides of the border. Even the remote areas have some means of accepting credit or debit cards. Some credit card companies have a very favorable exchange rate and withdrawing cash at ATMs may be cheaper than exchanging money beforehand. Before traveling out of

the country call your credit card companies to tell them where you will be and the dates of your trip. Otherwise they might (will) refuse a charge, usually at the most awkward moment. Getting it straightened out is exasperating.

Public Toilets. Take your own paper to public toilets. Especially outhouses at parks and campgrounds. We speak from experience.

Pets. Keep pets on leash, and clean up after them. Many people cruise with pets. Some marinas are more pet-friendly than others. Use the designated pet-walking areas. Don't let the dog lift his leg against the water faucet or power box. Carry plastic bags and clean up if the pet doesn't make it to the potty area.

Assisting Others. When helping arriving boats, follow the skipper's instructions. When we take a line we hold it loosely, awaiting instructions. Most skippers have a plan that will stop the boat and lay it alongside the dock. A bow line pulled tight at the wrong time can

ruin the plan: the bow swings toward the dock and the stern swings away. Obviously, if the landing plan has failed and the boat is being swept off, the dock crew goes into action. Even then it's a good idea to confirm with the skipper rather than acting on one's own.

Mooring Buoys. Pick up mooring buoys from the stern, not the bow. If the bow of the boat is very high off the water it may be impossible to loop a line through a mooring buoy ring. Carry a line aft to a low point of the hull (it may be the swim step), loop it through the ring on the buoy, then carry the line back to the bow. You may want to cleat or tie off one end of the line amidships to keep control of it throughout the process. Mooring buoys are often limited to small or medium sized boats. State and provincial park buoys are generally limited to boats under 45 feet; for specifics see the *State and Provincial Parks* section of Chapter 1 and the write-up for your planned destination.

Squeaky Fenders. De-squeak fenders with dishwashing soap. Joy, Ivory Liquid, whatever is handy seems to work. Slather it on. One application lasts for hours.

Use Scoot-Gard. This is the bumpy, rubbery material carried on big rolls at the marine store. It keeps things from sliding around. We use it for drawer and shelf liners. The microwave oven and the laptop computer with our charting and navigation program sits on it. Whenever we want something to stay where we put it but don't want to bolt or tie it into place, we use Scoot-Gard. It's inexpensive and it works.

Boat Cards. Consider making a boat card. One of the joys of cruising is the people you meet along the way. Boat cards are like business cards for your boat, and make it easy to stay in touch with people you meet.

Finger Food. Pack finger food for happy hour gatherings, potlucks, and entertaining on board. Impromptu gatherings are common.

FLOATPLANE TRAVEL ALONG THE INSIDE PASSAGE

For cruisers who need to travel home during a cruise, need parts shipped to them, or want to have guests join them in remote areas, floatplane travel can be a good option.

Floatplane flying provides a new perspective for boaters. If you can, sit in a window seat, or even the co-pilot seat up front. Take a small map, or this book, and pick out the islands as you fly by. The view is unforgettable—especially on a sunny day, the islands unfold dramatically. Currents are visible. Sometimes whales are spotted, and the pilot may even spend a few moments circling for a better view. On cloudy days you'll fly low—300 to 500 feet above the water.

Be prepared for a flight to have several stops along the route. If transiting from one country to the other, there will be a stop for customs clearance.

Many marinas offer boat watching service, perfect for when owners fly home. Some can even clean, fuel, and provision boats. For time-strapped cruisers, these services can be useful.

Floatplane operators are accommodating. We've seen floatplanes deliver parts and people to boats in remote anchorages.

The cost to use a floatplane service may initially appear high, but the time savings and convenience are huge. Consider that it's only a 3-hour flight from Port McNeill, near the north end of Vancouver Island, to Vancouver or Seattle.

THE BEAVER

For airplane buffs, a floatplane ride can be particularly thrilling. The venerable de Havilland DHC-2 Beaver is among the most widely used floatplanes in the northwest. De Havilland began producing the Beaver in 1948, and built nearly 1700 of them during a 19-year production run. Although the last Beaver was produced in 1967, operators and enthusiasts alike still appreciate its unparalleled combination of short field performance, durability, and versatility. Kenmore Air, Pacific Coastal, NW Seaplanes, Seair, Inland Air, and Tofino Air all operate Beavers. Pilots rave about flying them.

Equipped with a powerful engine (450 h.p. for piston Beavers) and a large wing optimized for short takeoff and landing distances, Beavers can reach places other planes can't. They can carry things other planes can't, too. De Havilland engineers designed the Beaver with doors wide enough to accommodate a 45-gallon drum and the ability to carry 2100 pounds of payload. Piston Beavers cruise at about 100 knots burning about 23 gallons of fuel per hour—enviable economy compared to many powerboats. Some operators have upgraded the original piston power plant to a newer turbine engine, increasing speed, payload capacity, and range.

The Beaver is so popular that well maintained examples have actually appreciated in value. When new, Beavers sold for about $50,000. Today, they can fetch more than $500,000.

KENMORE AIR
(866) 435-9524
Seattle (Lake Union or Kenmore)
to Sullivan Bay and Port McNeill

NW SEAPLANES
(425) 277-1590
Seattle (Renton) to Hakai Pass
and many points in between

FRIDAY HARBOR SEAPLANES
(425) 277-1590
Friday Harbor and San Juan Islands

PACIFIC COASTAL AIRLINES
(800) 663-2872
Victoria, Vancouver, Comox, Campbell
River, Powell River, Port Hardy,
Bella Bella, Masset

HARBOUR AIR VANCOUVER
(800) 665-0212
Victoria to Gulf Islands and
Sunshine Coast

SEAIR SEAPLANES
(800) 447-3247
or
(866) 692-6440
Vancouver to Gulf Islands
and Nanaimo

INLAND AIR
(888) 624-2577
Prince Rupert, North B.C.,
Haida Gwaii

TOFINO AIR
(866) 486-3249

WILDERNESS SEAPLANES
(800) 343-5963
B.C. Central Coast

U.S. AND CANADIAN CUSTOMS INFORMATION

U.S. / CANADA BORDER CROSSING

Customs must be cleared whenever the U.S.-Canada border is crossed in either direction. Generally, the process is quick and straightforward; but if the skipper isn't prepared with the proper information, it can be time consuming. It is extremely important to follow all the rules and be polite. While customs officers are trained in courtesy and usually are cordial, they have at their disposal regulations that can ruin your day. Take border crossing seriously, failure to follow the rules can have onerous consequences. Prepare ahead of time by inventorying items on board that need to be declared. Declare everything that must be reported, have a written list, don't trust your memory. Follow all the rules and report to customs as soon as possible after crossing the border. We know of an instance where a pleasure boater had their vessel seized by customs officials for failure to report their arrival in a timely manner. Their boat was finally returned, but only after paying a fine of $1,000. Another boater neglected to sign their new passport, which caused some significant delays and anxiety for family members. Be prepared and follow the rules so border crossings are non-events.

All vessels are required to clear with Customs when arriving in either the U.S. or Canada from a foreign port. Canadian and U.S. vessels do not need to clear out when leaving Canada. U.S. vessels do not need to clear out when leaving the U.S., except if the vessel is being exported. Canadian vessels with a U.S. Cruising License do not need to clear out when leaving U.S. waters. All non-U.S. flagged vessels (including Canadian) without a U.S. Cruising License are required to check-out when leaving U.S. waters.

Customs hours, rules, and requirements can and do change with short notice throughout the year. We urge readers to check the U.S. Customs and Border Protection (CBP) website www.cbp.gov and Canada Border Services Agency (CBSA) website www.cbsa-asfc.gc.ca for the latest. Check the Waggoner Guide website www.WaggonerGuide.com for border crossing updates.

Passports. If you don't have passports, we encourage you to get them. Lacking a passport, carry proof of citizenship such as an enhanced driver's license, enhanced identification, birth certificate, certificate of citizenship or naturalization, and photo ID. Standard (non-enhanced) drivers licenses are not proof of citizenship and are not accepted for border crossing. Citizens of some countries need visas as well. Carry birth certificates for all minors aboard — you may be asked for them.

Trusted Traveler Programs. Canada and U.S. have a number of Trusted Traveler Programs that expedite border crossings for boaters when all on board the vessel are enrolled in one of these programs. Nexus is a joint Canada and U.S. program that is recognized on both sides of the border and can expedite customs clearance going either direction. Most other programs are singular to one side of the border or the other.

Nexus. With Nexus, each person applies online and then contacted to set an appointment for an interview by both Canadian and U.S. customs agents at the Vancouver, B.C.; Blaine, WA or Seattle, WA CBP offices. The card is good for 5 years, and the cost is $50 U.S. or CDN per person. From start to finish, the entire process takes several months. If you cross the border by car along with your card, you'll have the additional benefit of using the Nexus lanes at the border. For general information or to begin the application process, U.S. citizens can go to www.cbp.gov, and Canadians go to www.cbsa-asfc.gc.ca.

Clearance Numbers. A clearance number will be issued to you when you have successfully completed reporting to the respective U.S. or Canadian customs agency. Keep a record of your clearance number, along with the date, time and location of clearance. You may be asked for this number later. Canada requires that foreign flagged vessels post their clearance number on a dockside viewable window while in Canadian waters. Keep a record of interactions with border officers. If you have received permissions or instructions from a customs officer via telephone, record the date and time of the conversation along with name or badge number.

Contact Customs or Coast Guard.
If unforeseen circumstances don't allow you to report to customs authorities as soon as possible after crossing the border, telephone customs authorities and report your circumstances. If you don't have cellular coverage, hail the Coast Guard on VHF and report your situation. This applies to crossing the border in either direction and with both Coast Guard agencies.

Don't Cross Border with Marijuana. Even though recreational marijuana may be legal in both British Columbia and the State of Washington, it is illegal to transport marijuana in any quantity across the Canada-U.S. border in either direction.

Be sure to have your passports ready when clearing customs.

22

CANADIAN CUSTOMS INFORMATION

CANADA BORDER SERVICES AGENCY (CBSA) Proof of citizenship and identification, such as Canadian or U.S. passport, U.S. Passport card, Trusted Traveler Program cards (Nexus and Sentri), State or Provincial issued enhanced driver's license, is required of all on board when entering Canada. If you are bringing a child other than your own into Canada, carry a notarized statement authorizing you to take the child into Canada and proof that the person signing the statement has custody of the child. The letter should include parents' or guardians' addresses and phone numbers. Canada Border Services Agency website has a sample letter.

Reporting to Canada Customs. All vessels arriving in Canada from a foreign country must clear Border Services immediately after the vessel comes to rest. The master, or the master's designated representative, must report to Border Services in-person or by telephone from a Border Services direct land line phone, or by calling (888) 226-7277. No one else may leave the vessel, and no baggage or merchandise may be removed from the vessel. You must report at a designated port of entry unless you have Nexus or Canpass. At some locations, Border Services officers will be present; at many other locations you will report by telephone. Even if you report by telephone, your boat may be subject to inspection. To avoid delays, have the following information ready when you report:

- Vessel name, length, and Coast Guard documentation number or state/province registration number

- Number of people on board

- Names, addresses, citizenship, birth dates and passport numbers of all passengers

- Purpose of the trip

- Number of pets on board – proof of vaccination needed

- Declare if you have cash over $10,000

- Length of absence from Canada (Canadian boats); Length and purpose of stay in Canada (U.S. boats)

- Quantity and type of alcoholic beverages

- Declare all goods being imported, including firearms

Once cleared, either by phone or by an officer, you will be given a clearance number. Post your clearance number in both side windows. Log this number with the date, time, and place of clearance. Vessels are subject to re-inspection while in Canadian waters, usually by RCMP officers when their patrol boat reaches a marina. The officers are well trained and polite, but be sure you don't have anything on board you shouldn't have.

Nexus. If all passengers aboard a boat have a Nexus permit, a vessel can clear Canada Border Services Agency by calling, toll-free, (866) 996-3987 at least 30 minutes and up to 4 hours before arriving at a designated CBSA or Nexus reporting station. The vessel must physically check in at a designated CBSA or Nexus reporting station. At the time of Nexus call-in, the Border Services officer will ask for the vessel's identification number, vessel's intended reporting station, estimated time of arrival (ETA), purpose of the trip, and length of stay. You must appear at the appointed reporting station before your declared ETA and wait at the station until the ETA. If no officer is present at the reporting station before the ETA, you may continue on your way, without further action. We usually take a photo, with date and time stamp, of ourselves and our boat at the reporting station – just in case. In the accompanying list of designated reporting stations, note that some are for Nexus/Canpass vessels only and can only be used by vessels where all on board have Nexus or Canpass.

Canpass-Private Boats. Canpass-Private Boats program was discontinued in 2018. New applications for the program are no longer being accepted. Those with valid and unexpired Canpass cards can continue to use them until the expiration date.

Firearms Restrictions. You may not bring switchblades, most handguns, automatic weapons, anti-personnel pepper spray or mace into Canada. Under certain circumstances, some long guns are allowed. Bear spray, if labeled as such, is permitted if declared. A Non-Resident Firearm Declaration Form is needed to bring firearms into Canada. Call the Canadian Firearms Centre at (800) 731-4000 for a copy of the form, or download

B.C. POINTS OF ENTRY

Designated B.C. Points of Entry for Pleasure Craft Reporting
All locations contact Canada Border Services Agency
Toll-free (888) 226-7277 (7 days a week, 24 hours a day)

Bedwell Harbour:	May 1 to Friday before Victoria Day 9:00 a.m. to 5:00 p.m. Friday before Victoria Day to Labour Day 8:00 a.m. to 8:00 p.m. Labour Day to Sept. 30 9:00 a.m. to 5:00 p.m. Oct. 1 to Apr. 30 (Canpass/Nexus only)
Cabbage Island:	(Canpass/Nexus only)
Campbell River:	Coast Marina; Discovery Harbour Marina
Galiano Island:	Montague Harbour Marina (Canpass/Nexus only)
Mayne Island:	Horton Bay (Canpass/Nexus only) Miners Bay (Canpass/Nexus only)
Nanaimo:	Nanaimo Port Authority Basin–E Dock Summer 8:00 a.m. to 5:00 p.m. Winter 8:00 a.m. to 4:30 p.m. Townsite Marina (Canpass/Nexus only)
North Pender Is.:	Port Browning Marina (Canpass/Nexus only)
Prince Rupert:	Lightering Dock Cow Bay Marina Fairview Govt. Dock Prince Rupert Rowing and Yacht Club Rushbrooke Government Dock
Saltspring Is.:	Ganges Harbour–Seaplane Dock First floating breakwater (Canpass/Nexus only) Royal Victoria YC Outst.(Canpass/Nexus only)
Sidney:	Canoe Cove Marina Port Sidney Marina Royal Victoria YC Outstation Tsehum Marina Van Isle Marina
Ucluelet:	52 Steps Dock June 1–Sept 30 only 8:00 a.m. to 10:00 p.m. Oct. 1–May 31 (Canpass/Nexus only)
Vancouver:	False Creek Fisherman's Wharf Steveston Harbour Authority (Canpass/Nexus) Royal Vancouver Yacht Club–Coal Harbour Harbour Green Dock
Victoria:	Oak Bay Marina Royal Victoria YC (Cadboro Bay) Raymur Point CBSA Dock
White Rock:	White Rock Government Dock Crescent Beach Marina

one from www.cfc-cafc.gc.ca. The cost is $25 CDN, and it is good for 60 days. All weapons and firearms must be declared to CBSA. See www.WaggonerGuide.com for links for more information and the application form.

Liquor & Tobacco Restrictions. Not more than 1.14 liters (38.5 oz.) of hard liquor, or 1.5 liters of wine, or a total of 1.14 liters of wine and liquor, or 24 12-ounce bottles of beer or ale per person of legal drinking age (19 years old in B.C.). Not more than 1 carton of cigarettes and 2 cans (200 grams) of tobacco and 50 cigars or cigarillos, and 200 tobacco sticks per person 19 or older without paying duty and taxes on the excess amount.

Food Restrictions. Food restrictions are subject to change without notice. Check the CBSA website at www.WaggonerGuide.com for updates. Canadian customs has an interactive website where you enter the food item you are planning to bring into Canada, and after selecting options regarding the items origin and planned use, you will get an Approved or Not Approved determination. See the CBSA website for a link to this Automated Import Reference System (AIRS) website. Other than restricted foods, you can carry quantities of food appropriate for your stay. Be aware of the following restrictions and limitations:

• No houseplants (including potted herbs)

• No apples, no pitted fruit (apricots, plums, peaches) Cherries are sometimes okay

• Potatoes from US are allowed – 1 bag per person of US #1 commercially packaged

• All firewood is prohibited

If in doubt, call (204) 983-3500 for inspection.

Duty-free Limits. Canadian residents returning to Canada may be eligible for a personal exemption on duty for goods brought into Canada. An exemption on goods up to $200 CDN is allowed for out-of-country stays of more than 24 hours. The exemption for stays of 48 hours or more is $800 CDN and may include alcohol and tobacco items. See the CBSA website for full details.

Declare All Items. If in doubt, declare it to CBSA. This is especially true for food items. If you are not sure, simply declare it and let the CBSA officer make the decision. It is always best to inform CBSA agents of items that you have on board. Failure to declare items can result in fines and penalties.

Pets. Owners of dogs and cats must bring a certificate issued by a licensed U.S. or Canadian veterinarian clearly identifying the pet and certifying that it has been vaccinated against rabies during the previous 36 months.

Currency. Cash or other monetary instruments in excess of $10,000 CDN per boat must be reported. For current rules and regulations, check out the Canada Border Services Agency website at www.cbsa-asfc.gc.ca.

U.S. Customs Information

U.S. CUSTOMS AND BORDER PROTECTION (CBP)

CBP requires approved identification, such as a U.S. or Canadian passport, U.S. Passport card, Trusted Traveler Program cards (Nexus and Sentri), I-68, State or Provincial issued enhanced driver's license, for entry to the U.S. We recommend that everyone aboard have a passport.

Reporting to U.S. Customs. You must report arrival and obtain clearance from U.S. CBP at a designated point of entry; OR by using the CBP ROAM smartphone App; OR if all on board are enrolled in Nexus, I-68, or Global Entry. Clearance may be conducted by calling (800) 562-5943. Whether in-person, by ROAM App, or by voice call, have the following information at-hand in order to avoid delays:

- Name, date of birth and citizenship of all persons on board (including passport number or citizenship identification)

- Name of the boat and vessel registration or documentation number

- Nexus BR Number

- Vessel homeport and current location

- CBP user fee decal number (if over 30 feet in length), or Cruising License Number for foreign flagged vessels (including Canadian)

- Canadian customs clearance number for U.S. flagged boats.

- Estimated length of stay in U.S. for Canadian vessels

- For U.S. vessels, date you departed U.S. and how long you were in Canada

Designated U.S. Ports of Entry. Arrivals requiring an in-person report may be made at any of the following Ports of Entry: Friday Harbor, Roche Harbor, Port Angeles, Point Roberts, and Anacortes. All other ports require appointments to be made in advance for in-person inspections (during regular business hours only). Don't assume that if you call for an appointment you will get one. To save time and avoid problems, clear U.S. Customs at one of the five designated Ports of Entry. If you arrive after normal business hours, call (800) 562-5943 for further instructions. Local customs office numbers are listed later in this section. I-68s are available at all locations listed.

CBP ROAM APP. ROAM is an official CBP smartphone App that can make your arrival reporting within U.S. waters a lot easier and may expedite your U.S. customs clearance requirements. New for 2019, boaters can check-in with CBP using the App as soon as they enter U.S. waters and have cell phone coverage. CBP officers access your boat and traveler information with the App and can open a video chat with you to obtain and verify information if needed. CBP will then either clear you for entry with a clearance number, or direct you to a designated U.S. Port of Entry for further processing. Those approved for entry do not need to report in-person at a Port of Entry. CBP ROAM is planned to be available for clearance 7/24. At press time, CBP was establishing support for off-hours processing. Check with CBP regarding hours of operation.

You don't need to be a member of a Trusted Traveler program to use ROAM; it can be used by U.S. and foreign travelers. The ROAM App can be used when entering at Washington and Alaska Ports of Entry for pleasure craft. The App supports iOS and Google Android phones and tablet mobile devices. The App works best with 4G or LTE service and is reported to also work with 3G service. Boaters needing a Cruising License, or that must pay duty, will need to report in-person to a Port of Entry. For more about the App and its use, see the www.cbp.gov website or www.WaggonerGuide.com.

Clearing by Telephone. Boaters with nothing to declare normally can clear U.S. Customs by telephone, if all on board have Nexus, I-68s or Global Entry. With Nexus, I-68 or Global Entry, you can call the Small Boat Reporting Office after entering U.S. waters, at (800) 562-5943 to report arrival and request clearance. When calling underway, call from an area with good reception. While you report, slow to idle speed to reduce background noise and remain in the good reception area. The Small Boat Reporting Office operates from 7:00 a.m. to 10:00 p.m. from May through September, and from 7:00 a.m. to 8:00 p.m. the balance of the year. If you enter the U.S. outside these hours, you must remain aboard your boat until you can clear.

Indications are that clearing by telephone with the Small Boat Reporting Office's 800 number will be replaced by ROAM App in the future.

I-68. The I-68 Permit is valid for 1 year from the date of issue. U.S. citizens, Lawful Permanent Residents, Canadian citizens and Landed Immigrants of Canada who are nationals of Visa Waiver Program countries are eligible to apply. The cost is $16 per person, $32 for families. Apply at CBP offices within the Puget Sound area. Bring proof of citizenship, such as a passport, certified copy of your birth certificate, and photo ID. Vessel information also helps. Each person applying must appear. Children under 14 can be listed on parents' I-68.

Small Vessel Reporting System (SVRS). The Small Vessel Reporting System program was replaced in 2018 with the CBP ROAM App. SVRS program is no longer available.

Entering Alaska. All vessels entering Southeast Alaska from a foreign country must clear U.S. Customs. Vessels my clear customs by reporting in-person in Ketchikan; OR with the CBP ROAM App; OR by telephone if all on board are enrolled in Nexus, I-68 or Global Entry. For detailed instructions on clearing U.S. Customs in Alaska, see *Chapter 19 – Arriving in Ketchikan.*

Processing Fee. Pleasure vessels 30 feet in length or more must pay an annual processing (user) fee of $28.24 to enter or re-enter the United States. U.S. vessels less than 30 feet are not subject to the fee, provided they have nothing to declare. Payment is required at or before the vessel's first arrival each calendar year. If you report by telephone, they charge your credit card. A non-transferable decal will be issued upon payment. Renewal notices for the next year's decal are mailed or emailed in the autumn. Vessels with a valid Cruising License do not have to pay this fee and do not require a decal. Order your sticker before you need to enter the U.S. Even if you have Nexus, I-68 or Global Entry preclearance, lack of a current-year sticker may direct you to a designated port of entry for inspection. User Fee stickers are not sold at CBP offices, but can be ordered online at https://dtops.cbp.dhs.gov, or by phone (317) 298-1245, or email decals@cbp.dhs.gov.

Cruising License. A Cruising License is available to Canadian and most foreign flagged vessels. A Cruising License saves time and money for foreign flagged vessels frequenting U.S. waters. Foreign vessels without a Cruising License must complete form CBP-1300 and pay a $19.00 Navigation Fee upon entering U.S. waters, with each movement within U.S. waters, and upon exiting U.S. waters. With a Cruising License form CBP-1300, the Navigation Fee is only required at the vessel's initial reporting and clearance with CBP. To get a Cruising License, foreign vessels upon entering U.S. waters must report to one of the designated CBP Ports of Entry where they submit form CBP-1300 and pay the $19.00 fee. CBP will inspect the vessel and process CBP-1300. A Cruising License can then be requested.

There is no charge for the Cruising License. Cruising Licenses expire after one year or upon surrendering to CBP when leaving the U.S. Vessels with a Cruising License do not need the $28.24 decal. Cruising Licenses cannot be extended and are available only when the vessel reports and clears-in at a CBP Port of Entry. Foreign flagged vessels made outside of the U.S. must wait 15 days after expiration of their Cruising License before requesting a new one. During this 15-day period, the vessel may enter and depart U.S. waters by submitting a CBP-1300 and paying $19.00 upon entry, exit, and movement. Vessels made in U.S. are exempt from this 15-day waiting period. Cruising Licenses do not affect customs reporting requirements. Vessels must report and clear in with CBP upon entry to U.S. waters by reporting in-person; OR by reporting arrival with the CBP ROAM App; OR by telephone with one of the trusted traveler programs like Nexus. You will need your Cruising License number when reporting in with CBP.

Food Restrictions. Food restrictions are subject to change without notice. See www.WaggonerGuide.com for updates and for a downloadable copy of CBP information regarding food products that may not be brought into the U.S. For specific food related questions, contact an Agricultural Specialist at (360) 332-8661 or (360) 988-2971. As a general guideline, any food you bring into the U.S. must be made or grown in Canada or the U.S., and labeled as such. Don't bring fresh tropical fruits or vegetables in, even if you bought them in the U.S. CBP recommends declaring all meat and produce when entering the U.S. If declared, prohibited goods will be seized but no fine will be levied. Subject to change without notice, use the following list to minimize problems:

- No sheep lamb or goat in any form, this includes pet food

- Meat (beef, pork, chicken, turkey) and meat products from Canada are allowed

- Keep pet food in original packaging

- No fresh citrus, regardless of where you bought it

- No fresh produce (vegetables or fruit) grown outside the U.S. and Canada

- Canned fruits and vegetables, however, are unrestricted regardless of origin; leave labels/stickers on cans

- No tomatoes

- No garlic, chives, green onions, leeks, and other green Allium vegetables from Canada

- No potatoes

- No cut flowers or potted plants (they are subject to so many restrictions that it's better to leave them in Canada and avoid the hassle)

- Seafood is okay

- Dairy products are okay

- Eggs are usually okay

- All firewood is prohibited; boaters with firewood may be required to return to Canada to dispose of it

Pets. Dogs and cats must be healthy, and dogs require current rabies certificates. Birds are subject to USDA Veterinarian inspection to enter or re-enter. It is usually not advisable to bring birds across the border.

Currency. Cash or other monetary instruments in excess of $10,000 U.S. per boat must be reported.

Duty-free Limits. U.S. residents outside of the U.S. less than 48 hours can import merchandise up to $200 in value per person without duty. If the stay is more than 48 hours, the limit is $800 per person. For ease and simplicity, try to restrict what you bring back home to products made or grown in Canada (sometimes even that isn't sufficient). For the latest customs information, go to the U.S. Customs and Border Protection website pages for pleasure boats at www.cbp.gov/travel/pleasure-boatsprivate-flyers/pleasure-boat-overview.

Declare All Items. If in doubt, declare the item to CBP. This is especially true for food products. If you are not sure, simply declare it and let the CBP officer make the decision. It is always best to inform CBP agents of items

that you have on board. Failure to declare items can result in fines and penalties.

Pilotage Exemption for Foreign Flagged (other than U.S. or Canadian) Vessels. Foreign flagged vessels (other than Canadian) in Washington waters are required by Washington State law to have an exemption in order to operate without a professional Pilot. To request an exemption, download and submit an application from the www.pilotagewa.gov website or call the Washington Board of Pilotage Commissioners at (206) 215-3904.

Aquatic Invasive Species (AIS) Prevention Permit. New for 2018, most boats operating in Washington State waters that do not have a WA State registration sticker need to purchase and carry an AIS Prevention Permit. Boats from neighboring states operating on shared waters are exempt along with dinghies. Permits can be purchased online or at any WA State Department of Fish and Wildlife license retailer. The permit is good for one year. For more details about this new permit see the AIS Prevention Permit sidebar in this chapter.

U.S. POINTS OF ENTRY
Anacortes (360) 293-2331
Office at Cap Sante Marina
8:00 a.m. to 8:00 p.m. Summer
8:00 a.m. to 5:00 p.m. Off-season
closed 1 ½ hours mid-afternoon)
Friday Harbor (360) 378-2080
Customs booth at the dock with phone
Office at Spring & First Streets
8:00 a.m. to 8:00 p.m. Summer
8:00 a.m. to 5:00 p.m. Off-season
Point Roberts (360) 945-5211
or (360) 945-2314
Customs Dock near Fuel Dock
8:00 a.m. to 8:00 p.m. Summer
8:00 a.m. to 5:00 p.m. Off-season
Port Angeles (360) 457-4311
Office Boat Haven
8:00 a.m. to 9:00 p.m. Summer
8:00 a.m. to 5:30 p.m. Off-season
Roche Harbor (360) 378-2080
Customs dock at Roche Harbor Marina
8:00 a.m. to 8:00 p.m. Summer
8:00 a.m. to 5:00 p.m. Off-season
Ketchikan (907) 225-2254
Call and wait for agent at assigned slip
6:00 a.m. to 6:00 p.m. Summer
Other Customs Offices
(by appointment only, call 24 hours ahead for availability and instructions):
Bellingham (360) 734-5463
Blaine (360) 332-6318
Everett (425) 259-0246
Port Townsend (360) 385-3777
Seattle (Boeing Field) (206) 553-0667
Tacoma/Olympia (253) 593-6338

Clearing customs at Roche Harbor on San Juan Island

131°	130°	129°	128°	127°	126°	125°	124°	123°	122°

U.S. CUSTOMS – NEW ROAM APP AVAILABLE IN WASHINGTON AND ALASKA

The new U.S. Customs and Border Protection (CBP) ROAM App can now be used when entering at state of Washington and Alaska Ports of Entry. The App can make your arrival reporting with U.S. Customs a lot easier. **R**eporting **O**ffsite **A**rrival – **M**obile, **ROAM** App, is an App that can now be used at Washington pleasure craft Port Of Entry locations including Anacortes, Point Roberts, Friday Harbor, Roche Harbor, and Port Angeles. In Alaska the App can be used at Ketchikan and Wrangell Ports of Entry. This official CBP App will support Apple iOS and Google Android phones and tablet mobile devices. Travelers entering the U.S. can check-in with the App, and CBP officers can initiate a video chat for information verification, or an interview if required. If approved for entry, boaters do not have to report in-person at a Port of Entry.

To use the ROAM App, input your biographic, vessel, and trip details into the App. Then submit your arrival for CBP Officer review by pressing the App's **Report Arrival** selection on your mobile device. A CBP Officer may initiate a video chat to further interview travelers. Once the CBP Officer reviews the information, you will receive a notification and email with your clearance status and next steps, if applicable. The App needs to have cellular data connection or Wifi service to report and process your arrival. The App works best with 4G or LTE cell service. However, boaters are successfully using it on 3G as well.

The ROAM App can be used by U.S. and foreign travelers to report arrival. You don't need to be part of a trusted traveler program to use ROAM. Reporting arrival in-person at one of the Port of Entry locations is still available. Travelers requiring a Cruising License, or that must pay duties, will need to report in-person to CBP at the nearest Port of Entry. Travelers with I-68 or Nexus may still report by calling the CBP Small Boat Reporting Office; however, this option may be replaced by ROAM at some future date.

To install and prepare the App, you will need an iOS or Android phone or tablet with camera. You will also need an email address. The App is free and available from the Apple App Store and the Google Play Store. To get started, download, install and prepare the App on your mobile device.

1. Download and install the App from the Apple App or Google Play store.
2. Setup a Login.gov account (if you don't already have one). Login.gov is a U.S. General Services Administration website and service, providing a single sign-in account to multiple participating government programs. If you are enrolled in Nexus you probably already have a Login.gov account. You can create an account from the ROAM App or at the Help menu selection at Login.gov website. You will need an email address.
3. Open the App and sign-in with your Login.gov account.
4. Add information about your mode of transportation – your boat (make, year, registration number, length). You can add and save information for more than one boat.
5. Add information about the travelers who will be on your boat when reporting in with ROAM. The App has a feature to populate the traveler information by scanning each person's travel document. Travel documents accepted include: Passport, Passport Card, Nexus, Enhanced U.S. Drivers License, Global Entry, Birth Certificate (kids 15 and under), Permanent Resident Card.
6. With the App, take a picture of each person's travel document.

That's it. You're now ready to use ROAM App to report your arrival into U.S. waters.

To use the ROAM App and report arrival:
- Report Arrival as soon as possible after entering U.S. waters. Report Arrival requests made outside of U.S. waters will be rejected.
- Ensure that you have a good cell signal and that you will be able to maintain cell coverage.
- Open and sign-in to the ROAM App.
- Press the **Report Arrival** selection, then select the mode of transportation (boat) and select travelers from saved profile information and designate one of the selected travelers as the vessel master. Answer all detail and declaration questions.
- Press the **Submit** selection
- You will receive a notification on the App and a message to the email address on your Login.gov account profile. The notification will provide you with a clearance, or instructions for further processing; which may include instructions to proceed to a Port of Entry location for in-person processing.

The ROAM App is currently available for download. For more about ROAM on the CBP website, see www.cbp.gov/travel/pleasure-boats-private-flyers/pleasure-boat-overview/roam.

[Leonard Landon]

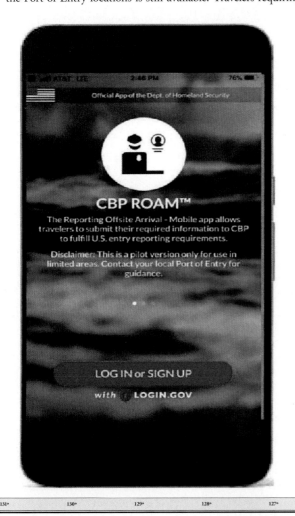

131°	130°	129°	128°	127°	126°	125°	124°	123°	122°

DIFFERENCES BETWEEN U.S. & CANADIAN CHARTS

Canada and the United States are two separate nations, and their charts, while similar in many ways, have important differences.

U.S. charts are in fathoms and feet; most Canadian charts are metric. *With all charts, read the chart title and margin information to see if the chart is metric, fathoms and feet, or feet.* Metric charts show soundings and heights in meters. A meter (spelled metre in Canada) equals 39.37 inches, or 3.28 feet. Two meters equals 6 feet 7 inches, or just over one fathom. The difference is significant. Don't confuse fathoms with meters.

Waters appear to be deeper on U.S. charts of Pacific Northwest waters. This difference is important wherever the water is shallow, and is the result of the two countries using different *chart datums*.

Depths on a chart are measured from the chart datum, also called the reference plane or **tidal datum**. On Canadian charts, the chart datum is either Lowest Normal Tides, or Lower Low Water, Large Tide. For that

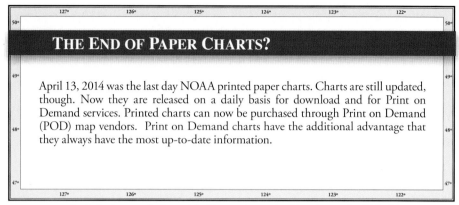

THE END OF PAPER CHARTS?

April 13, 2014 was the last day NOAA printed paper charts. Charts are still updated, though. Now they are released on a daily basis for download and for Print on Demand services. Printed charts can now be purchased through Print on Demand (POD) map vendors. Print on Demand charts have the additional advantage that they always have the most up-to-date information.

reason, you don't find many "minus tides" in Canadian tide tables.

On U.S. charts of Pacific Northwest waters, however, the chart datum is Mean Lower Low Water. Mean Lower Low Water is the mean, or average, level of the lower of the two low tides each day. Since the U.S. chart datum has half the lower waters above it and half below it, U.S. tide books show minus tides.

It's not a question of whether the tide drops lower in Canada or the U.S. It's a question of where the depth is measured from. U.S. charts start their measurements from a point higher than Canadian charts. The difference can be as much as 1.5 meters, or almost 5 feet.

Example: Assume that you are in the U.S., skippering a sailboat. The sailboat's keel draws 5 feet, and you want to anchor overnight in a bay with a charted depth of one fathom (6 feet). According to the tide table, low tide will be minus 1.5 feet at 0700. Knowing that your boat, with its 5 feet of draft, would be aground in 4.5 feet of water, you would look for a more suitable anchorage.

If this bay were in Canada, the chart would show a depth of perhaps just 1 meter (assuming a Lowest Normal Tide lower than the tide at 0700). The tide table would show a low tide at 0700 of perhaps .4 meters. You would add the 1 meter depth from the chart to the .4 meter low tide from the tide table, and get 1.4 meters of water at 0700. Since you draw more than 1.4 meters (55 inches), you would not anchor in the bay that night.

Important Exception: Both Canadian and U.S. charts show soundings in the other country's system when the charts cover both sides of the border. The U.S. chart would convert Canadian meters to U.S. fathoms, but would adopt the Canadian chart datum in Canadian waters. The Canadian metric chart would convert U.S. fathoms to meters, but would adopt the U.S. chart datum in U.S. waters. This is explained in the chart legends.

Clearances appear to be greater on U.S. charts. U.S. charts for Northwest waters measure clearances from Mean High Water. One-half the high waters are above the mean. Canadian charts measure clearances from Higher High Water, Large Tides. The same bridge, over the same waterway, would show less vertical clearance on a Canadian chart than on a U.S. chart. Metric Canadian charts show heights and depths in meters; Canadian charts in fathoms and feet show heights in feet and depths in fathoms. A Canadian metric chart might show a bridge clearance as "3," meaning 3 meters above Higher High Water, Large Tides. A U.S. chart would show a bridge clearance as "12" or more, meaning 12 feet or more above Mean High Water.

PUGET SOUND NO DISCHARGE ZONE

All of Puget Sound waters up to the Canadian border are a State of Washington designated No Discharge Zone (NDZ). It is illegal to discharge any (treated and untreated) black water sewage in this NDZ. In 2018, state law established the NDZ to improve area water quality and aid in the state's Shellfish Restoration initiative. Gray water is not included in the new regulations and there is no change for gray water discharges from onboard sinks and showers.

The Vessel Sewage NDZ includes all Washington marine waters east of New Dungeness Light, at the east end of the Strait of Juan de Fuca, plus Lake Washington, Lake Union, and the waters that connect them to Puget Sound.

Compliance means using an approved marine sanitation holding tank, securing the overboard thru-hull in the closed position and using pumpout facilities. If you have a Type I or Type II Treatment Marine Sanitation Device, you will need to secure it in a manner which prevents discharge of treated or untreated sewage by closing the seacock and removing the handle, or using a wire-tie.

Washington State boaters already practice good stewardship of state waters. The vast majority of vessels have holding tanks for use at pumpout facilities. State enforcement agents are first emphasizing outreach and education for this new law.

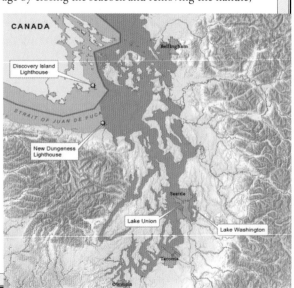

Canadian charts use more symbols to show buoys and tide rips. Canadian charts use symbols that approximate the shapes of buoys, with letters to indicate the buoy's characteristics. U.S. charts use a single diamond-shaped symbol for nearly all navigation buoys, with descriptive letters to indicate the buoy's characteristics.

For example, U.S. Chart 18421, Strait of Juan de Fuca to Strait of Georgia (1:80,000), shows the bell buoy marking Buckeye Shoal, north of Cypress Island, as:

U.S. Chart 18421

But on Canadian Chart 3462, Juan de Fuca Strait to Strait of Georgia (1:80,000), the buoy is shown as:

Canadian Chart 3462

Canadian charts may use arrows to show the location of the buoy or beacon. If other detail on the chart makes precise location

difficult, the Canadian chart will offset the symbol slightly, in the direction of the preferred navigable water. The offset is indicated by an arrow pointing to the actual location of the buoy or beacon. Sometimes the arrow is easy to overlook.

Chart No. 1 cracks the code. Nautical charts are filled with important navigation information. Unfortunately, so much of the information is in the form of symbols, abbreviations and undefined terms that it can be confusing. Each country has published a book that shows each symbol and defines each term used on its charts. The U.S. book is titled *Chart No. 1*; and the Canadian book is titled *Chart 1*. The Canadian book is available from Canadian Hydrographic chart agencies. The U.S. book is produced by several private publishers. Copies are available at marine supply outlets.

The Canadian Coast Guard publication *The Canadian Aids to Navigation System* explains the Canadian buoyage and light system, and is highly recommended. A PDF version is available on the Canadian Coast Guard website. The cost for the print version is $7.50 (Cdn) from Canadian Hydrographic chart agents, nautical bookstores and chandleries.

The introduction pages of both these books are filled with essential information. Don't overlook them.

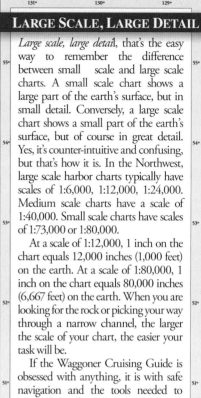

LARGE SCALE, LARGE DETAIL

Large scale, large detail, that's the easy way to remember the difference between small scale and large scale charts. A small scale chart shows a large part of the earth's surface, but in small detail. Conversely, a large scale chart shows a small part of the earth's surface, but of course in great detail. Yes, it's counter-intuitive and confusing, but that's how it is. In the Northwest, large scale harbor charts typically have scales of 1:6,000, 1:12,000, 1:24,000. Medium scale charts have a scale of 1:40,000. Small scale charts have scales of 1:73,000 or 1:80,000.

At a scale of 1:12,000, 1 inch on the chart equals 12,000 inches (1,000 feet) on the earth. At a scale of 1:80,000, 1 inch on the chart equals 80,000 inches (6,667 feet) on the earth. When you are looking for the rock or picking your way through a narrow channel, the larger the scale of your chart, the easier your task will be.

If the Waggoner Cruising Guide is obsessed with anything, it is with safe navigation and the tools needed to accomplish safe navigation. *Large scale, large detail*. It works.

ABOUT ANCHORING

Learning to stern-tie can provide additional mooring options.

One of the unique features of boating is the freedom of movement and independence to make any protected body of water home for a quick lunch stop or an overnight. Some people look forward to dropping anchor in an unfamiliar cove or bay. Many people do not share this enthusiasm. There are a few general principles that will help everyone anchor successfully. Cruising from dock to dock is fun, and no one can fault the conveniences. But a world of possibilities opens to those who have good anchoring gear and know how to use it.

Use good gear. Big, strong anchors work; small, cheap anchors don't. The most experienced cruisers seem to carry the biggest anchors. Well-equipped, wide-ranging boats carry all of the common designs: Bruce, CQR (plow), Danforth, Delta, Northhill, Rocna, Manson Supreme, and Ultra. Make sure your anchor is made of high quality steel. If it's wedged in a rock, you don't want it to bend. While Danforth style anchors are easiest to bend, within the limits of their design they can be made strong and expensive or weak and cheap. There are no strong, cheap Danforth style anchors. Read the sizing charts carefully, and size your anchor for storm conditions. Some sizing charts are written for 20-knot winds. Others are written for 30 knots. The Bruce chart is written for 42 knots and Rocna sizing is based upon 50 knots. When the wind comes on to blow hard at 3:00 a.m., you don't want a 20-knot anchor out there.

Pick your spot. Unless you're setting out a stern anchor or running a stern-tie ashore, plan on your boat swinging through an entire 360-degree circle. You don't want to bump up against a rock, a dock or another boat. Be sure to account for tidal changes. We've seen anchored boats aground at low tide because they didn't allow for drying flats or a sand bar in their swing circle. Other anchored boats will tend to swing as your boat swings, but not always. One night at Jones Island in the San Juans, swirling tidal currents had anchored boats swooping toward one another in a "dance of death."

Carry ample rode. For an anchor to bury and hold properly, you should pay out anchor rode at least five times the water depth. In 20 feet of water you would want 100 feet of rode out. In 60 feet of water you would want 300 feet out. Often, especially in crowded anchorages during high summer season, it will not be possible to anchor on 5:1 scope (five times the depth of the water). That is understood. In fact, the norm for most Northwest anchorages seems to be 3:1. But I've watched people put out 30 feet of rode in 20 feet of water, and wonder why the anchor wouldn't bite. For the deep waters of the Pacific Northwest, carry at least 300 feet of anchor rode, whether all-chain or combination chain and rope. Opinions vary about how much chain a combination rode should include, but no one would criticize you for having at least a foot of chain for every foot of boat length. Mark your rode well with something that is easily seen and clearly indicates the length. We have seen people with all chain that have no markers and therefore no way to know how much rode is out.

Rope or chain? For years we used a combination anchor rode—a length of chain backed up with 300 feet of top-quality nylon rope—and we anchored successfully. On a smaller boat with no anchor windlass, a combination rode is the way to go. When we moved to the 37-footer we found a new religion: all-chain. With all-chain, if we let out 100 feet of chain in 30 feet of water, 70 feet of chain will be lying on the bottom after the anchor is set. At a pound a foot, that's 70 pounds of chain that must be lifted off the bottom before we get to the anchor. During settled conditions we now get by with less scope, and our swinging circle is smaller. In storm conditions, of course, we're back to 5:1, or as close to 5:1 as we can manage.

Pay out all-chain rode as you move astern, not in a pile on top of the anchor. Use the clutch on your windlass to allow chain to pay out as you back-down. Initially, allow enough chain out to place the anchor on the bottom, then use movement astern to lay the chain along the bottom. Then secure the windlass clutch and begin to set the anchor.

Read the tide tables. If the overnight low tide isn't very low, a shallow anchorage can be just right. On the other hand, if the moon is either new or full (the two times during the month when the tidal range is the greatest) the shallow anchorage might go dry at low tide. You also want to know the maximum height of the tide during your stay. Set your scope for five times the water depth at high tide, or if you can't get five times, as much as you can get away with.

Set the anchor well. To get the best bury in the bottom, you want the angle between the anchor and the boat to be as flat as possible. After lowering the anchor, back well down before you set the hook. As you set, the rode should seem to stretch almost straight out from the bow. If the rode angles downward very much, you don't have enough scope out. When the anchor is set, you can shorten up to avoid swinging into other boats or onto a sandbar. You'll know, by the way, when the anchor is set. The anchor rode pulls straight and the boat stops. If you have any doubt as to whether the anchor is set, then it probably isn't. Weeds can foul an anchor, especially a Danforth style anchor, and many bottoms have weeds. Once the anchor is set, you don't have to pour on all 600 horsepower to prove your point. Anchors gain holding power through pulling and relaxing over time, a process called soaking. An anchor put down for lunch might be recovered with little effort. Left overnight it might feel as if it had headed for China.

Look at your chart. For happy anchoring you want a good holding bottom, appropriate depths, and protection. The nautical chart can help with all these needs. If the chart says Foul, don't anchor there. If the chart shows submerged pilings at the head of the bay, avoid the head of the bay. If the chart shows 200-foot depths right up to the shoreline, that's a bad spot. If it shows the bay open to the full sweep of the prevailing wind and seas, find another bay or you could be in for a rough night. I find the easiest anchorages to be in 20 to 50 feet of water, with a decided preference for the 20- to 30-foot depths. Approach slowly, take a turn around the entire area to check the depths, and decide where you want the boat to lie after the anchor is set. Then go out to a spot that will give you sufficient scope and lower the anchor. Back way down, set the hook, and shorten up to the desired location.

Anchor bridle snubber lines should be long enough and secured aft of the bow sprit.

Anchor in the right places. Don't anchor in cable crossing areas or near charted underwater pipeline areas. Increasingly, some communities and locales are discouraging anchoring in or near eelgrass. Anchoring gear, especially anchor chain, can be harmful to eelgrass. Eelgrass areas are not generally charted so check the Waggoner Cruising Guide or check for signage on spar buoys in the area marked, "no anchoring."

Use an anchor watch. There are a number of GPS based anchor watch systems that monitor your boats position and signal an alarm if the boat moves outside of a predetermined boundary circle. There are a number of Android and iOS smartphone Apps available with anchor watch features. Some chartplotters and chartplotter PC software have boundary circle features. For these anchor watch systems to work well, place the center of the boundary circle at the spot where you drop the anchor. This may mean taking the anchor watch system to the bow when you center the circle. After centering the boundary circle, set the radius of the circle equal to the scope, plus the distance from the bow roller to the place on the boat where the anchor watch

will rest while anchored, plus an appropriate GPS error factor, plus any significant tidal exchange that increases your swing. Anchor watch systems monitor the boats current location and sound an alarm if outside of the boundary circle. Some smartphone apps can also SMS text or email an alarm to another phone that goes ashore with you.

How to use a trip line. If there is any indication that your planned anchoring area is prone to fouling or snagging your anchor, use a trip line to help recover your anchor. Anchors prepared for trip lines have a small hole at the nose of the anchor, somewhere near the top and far forward. Before deploying the anchor, attach a length of line that is longer than the maximum tidal water depth at your intended anchoring location. To the other end of the line attach a small float or buoy. Later when you go to weigh anchor and it is snagged on something, use the trip line to help free the fouled anchor. The float or buoy also alerts other boaters of your anchor's location.

Bridles and Snubbers. Anchor bridles and snubbers are lengths of nylon line attached to a chain hook. When the hook is attached to a

deployed anchor chain and the nylon lines are attached to cleats on the boat, the bridle acts as a shock absorber to keep the anchor from breaking loose and to reduce chafe on the bow roller. As the wind and waves raise the boat, flex in the nylon lines absorb shock loads to avoid pulling the anchor free. Attached aft of the bow, bridles help reduce the boat's wind sailing and reduce yawing. To be effective the snubber lines need to be at least 30 feet long and should allow the chain attachment point, when deployed, to be below the waterline. Several pre-made bridles are available at marine suppliers or make your own.

Carry a stern-tie. In some anchoring locations, where swing room is limited, you will set the anchor offshore, back toward shore to set, and take the dinghy in with a line from a stern cleat to a securing point on shore such as a rock, tree, or stern-tie pin. Boats line Tod Inlet, near Butchart Gardens, and Prideaux Haven, in Desolation Sound, tied this way. In many small bays, with limited swing room, it's the only way you can anchor. Sometimes you'll find a little niche that will hold just your boat—if the stern is tied to shore. We carry 600 feet of inexpensive polypropylene rope for stern ties. Some popular anchorages necessitating stern-tie have metal pins embedded in rock with rings or a length of chain, through which you can pass your stern-tie line. After passing the end through the ring, bring the end back to the boat. That way, when you are ready to depart, you can release and recover the stern-tie line without leaving the boat. When there are no stern-tie anchor pins, find something secure on shore to anchor your stern-tie line. Carry a disposable short length of rope, about 5 feet long, that can be looped around something solid on shore like a rock outcropping. As a last resort loop your stern-tie around a dead tree. Many parks in BC and Washington frown on using live trees.

Up-slope anchoring. Up-slope anchoring is used when the only convenient anchoring depths are near to shore. Up-slope anchoring involves dropping the anchor on the upsloping sea bottom as it shallows. Once the anchor is set, back-down toward the nearby shore and stern-tie to shore. The stern-tie holds the boat in a position where it is always pulling the main anchor up the slope and keeps the anchor set.

Secure the anchor rode to the boat. We have all heard stories about boaters losing their all chain anchor, when they discover that the end, buried under hundreds of pounds of rode in the anchor locker, was not attached to the boat. Be sure the end of your anchor chain is attached to the boat – but not hard attached. The anchor should be attached to a length of nylon rope that is secured to the boat. Instead of leaving this nylon rope buried under a pile of chain in our anchor locker, we coil the line and keep it high and dry attached to the side of the anchor locker. In the event the anchor is stuck or if you need to get away from the anchor quickly, the rope can be cut. Secure a floating buoy to the end of the nylon rope so that you can retrieve the anchor and chain later.

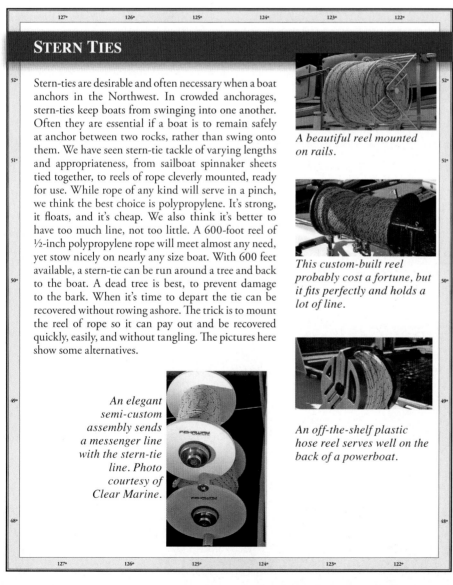

STERN TIES

Stern-ties are desirable and often necessary when a boat anchors in the Northwest. In crowded anchorages, stern-ties keep boats from swinging into one another. Often they are essential if a boat is to remain safely at anchor between two rocks, rather than swing onto them. We have seen stern-tie tackle of varying lengths and appropriateness, from sailboat spinnaker sheets tied together, to reels of rope cleverly mounted, ready for use. While rope of any kind will serve in a pinch, we think the best choice is polypropylene. It's strong, it floats, and it's cheap. We also think it's better to have too much line, not too little. A 600-foot reel of ½-inch polypropylene rope will meet almost any need, yet stow nicely on nearly any size boat. With 600 feet available, a stern-tie can be run around a tree and back to the boat. A dead tree is best, to prevent damage to the bark. When it's time to depart the tie can be recovered without rowing ashore. The trick is to mount the reel of rope so it can pay out and be recovered quickly, easily, and without tangling. The pictures here show some alternatives.

A beautiful reel mounted on rails.

This custom-built reel probably cost a fortune, but it fits perfectly and holds a lot of line.

An elegant semi-custom assembly sends a messenger line with the stern-tie line. Photo courtesy of Clear Marine.

An off-the-shelf plastic hose reel serves well on the back of a powerboat.

ELCI PROTECTED SHORE POWER

ELCI Breaker with Test/Reset on Eaton Pedestal

Shore Power Changes Are Coming.

Since 2011, efforts have been underway from both the building code side and from the boat building side to address safety issues due to stray electrical current in and around docks and marinas. The National Electrical Code Article 555 addresses electrical shock drownings caused by leakage of electrical current from A/C shore power facilities on docks and marinas. Concurrently, the American Boat & Yacht Council (ABYC) section E-11.11 has made changes to address A/C power leakage from boats into surrounding waters that endanger people.

As marinas upgrade their facilities, they will be required by building code to add Equipment Leakage Circuit Interrupter (ELCI) ground fault protection breakers to shore power receptacles. ELCI-protected breakers are designed to 'trip' and turn-off power if an imbalance is detected between the power (amperage) going to the boat and returning back to the shore power receptacle. In the past, marina shore power receptacle breakers only protected wiring and cables from over-amperage. The new ELCI-protected breakers will trip, turning off power, if the boat incorrectly leaks amperage or too much amperage is consumed.

Newly built boats and older boats upgraded to current ABYC standards include ground fault protection with an onboard ELCI (sometimes known as an RCD – Residual Current Detector). In the past, a boat's A/C breakers only protected wiring and cables from over-amperage problems. Onboard ELCI breakers now add electrical leakage protection to the boat.

How ELCI-Protected Power Might Affect You.

Your first visit to a marina with upgraded shore power may require some extra time and effort. Fortunately, this is a one-time process, so once you have successfully connected to ELCI-protected shore power you can rest assured that your boat is ready for the next one.

Before attempting your first-time connection to ELCI-protect power, make sure you know how to reset the ELCI feature on the shore power receptacle. There are a variety of different ELCI-protected breaker configurations and the ELCI reset isn't always easy to find make sure it's the ELCI reset as differentiated from the over-amperage reset.

Some breakers have a single "reset" position on the breaker toggle switch for resetting both the ELCI trip and the over-amperage trip. Others have two separate reset positions. Some ELCI-protected shore power installations have no ELCI reset at each power receptacle. Instead, they have one ELCI-protected breaker located at the power distribution panel providing power for a section of the marina. Any boat leaking excessive amperage within that section of the marina will trip the single ELCI-protected breaker, turning off power to all of the boats in that section of the marina, and marina staff will need to be notified to correct the problem.

First, try your usual connect and power-up sequence for shore power. If this works, great kick back and enjoy your now safer stay, knowing that your boat doesn't have A/C power leakage issues.

If the ELCI breaker trips as soon as you bring shore power to your panel, then try some alternate sequences of turning switches and flipping breakers on your boat's A/C power panel.

1. Turn off Shore power on your breaker panel.

2. Turn off all A/C panel breakers on your boat, including A/C breakers on the separate inverter panel, if equipped. Also, turn off all main A/C and Inverter breakers (double-pole breakers – the ones where two breaker switches are tied together).

3. Reset the dockside ELCI breaker and then turn the breaker to ON.

4. If the ELCI-protected breaker trips again, you likely have a boat wiring issue that will need to be addressed by a marine electrician. You will need to find shore power without ELCI-protection or go without shore power until the problem is fixed.

5. If the ELCI-breaker has not tripped, then retrn to your boat's breaker panel.

6 Switch the power source to Shore Power.

7. Try different sequences of turning main-double pole breakers on and individual circuit breakers on to discover what is causing the ELCI Breaker to trip. This may take some time as

you will need to restart the process by resetting the on-shore ELCI breaker with each attempt. Having someone on the dock resetting the ELCI breaker helps to facilitate this trial and error process.

What is causing the ELCI Breaker to Trip?
Reverse Y-splitters (adapters that combine two 30 amp receptacles into one 50 amp or two 50 amp into one 100 amp) are a known source of ELCI-protected breaker problems and unless specifically designed for ELCI-protected power, will likely not work.

Marine inverters appear to be a possible source of inadvertent ELCI breaker issues. Properly installed marine inverters may trip the ELCI breaker if other onboard A/C breakers are switched on before the inverter completes its process of synchronizing with shore power. Marine inverters correctly tie or connect the boat's neutral (white) A/C wire with the ground (green) wire when the inverter is creating A/C from DC battery power. When the inverter senses A/C shore power, it begins a process of synchronizing and switching to pass-thru mode.

Once the syncing and switching process is complete, the inverter breaks its neutral to ground connection and correctly leaves the boat's ground and neutral connected to shore power ground and neutral. If other main double-pole A/C breakers are ON during this syncing process, amperage on the neutral wire is conducted to the ground wire through the inverter's neutral to ground bonding and may trip the ELCI breaker.

Wait for about 30 seconds after supplying shore power to the inverter before turning other main and individual breakers on.

Marine battery chargers are another potential cause of ELCI breaker issues. Try turning off or lower the amperage setting to provide a temporary solution.

Self-testing galvanic isolators may also be a cause of ELCI breaker problems. Replace with a newer galvanic isolator.

A possible source of an unwanted, problematic, neutral-to-ground connection occurs when home-store (non-marine) appliances are installed on boats.

Inverter installation may be a source of incorrect neutral-to-ground connection when the neutral conductors are not separated into two busses; inverted and non-inverted. ABYC recommendations call for separating all neutral and ground wires for inverter loads from non-inverted. A neutral/ground connection should only be present at a source of power.

If you experience problems with these new ground fault systems, have a qualified electrician check your boat's wiring.

Do I Need an Isolation Transformer?
An isolation transformer is not required in order to use ELCI-protected power sources. If your boat is properly wired and powered up correctly, there is no requirement for an isolation transformer.

Isolation transformers all but eliminate the

possibility of tripping dock ELCI breakers. They also bring other benefits and are generally a good addition to the boat. Transformers are available in a variety of different voltages and amperages ranging in price from $1,000 to $4,000.

If an isolation transformer is installed within 10 feet of the boat's shore power inlet, an onboard ELCI breaker is not required in order to be ABYC compliant.

Why ELCI Breakers?

ELCI Breakers are safety devices to prevent Electric Shock Drownings. While more dangerous in fresh water, drownings happen in both fresh and saltwater when people become better electrical conductors of leakage A/C current than the surrounding water. Faulty dock or boat wiring is a common cause of dangerous electrical power in waters around docks and marinas. The danger only becomes known when someone enters the water and is immobilized by the electrical shock. These tragedies grow when rescuers enter the same dangerous waters in an attempt to help, and become victims as well.

ELCI Breakers detect amperage difference (imbalance) between the hot (black) wire and the neutral (white) wire and trip if there is a significant difference (leakage) between power going to the boat (hot wire) and that coming back (neutral wire) from the boat to shore power.

ELCI, RCD, GFCI, GFI Different or Same?

All of these devices perform the same function of detecting an amperage imbalance. The difference is in the level of imbalance, or leaking amperage (actually milliamps), that trips the breaker. In-home GFI and GFCI breakers trip at very low imbalance levels while ELCI breakers trip at much higher imbalance levels. RCD's trip at imbalance levels between GFI and ELCI.

Marinas with ELCI-protected Power.

ELCI-protected breakers first appeared at new or rebuilt marinas in Southeast Alaska; North Harbor in Petersburg, Thomas Basin in Ketchikan, and some docks at Bar Harbor South in Ketchikan.

In Washington State, Rosario Resort, Poulsbo Marina, Eagle Harbor Marina, and Eagle Harbor Waterfront Park dock, have upgraded all their docks to ELCI-protected power. Roche Harbor, Point Roberts Marina, Friday Harbor, and Skyline Marina in Anacortes, have upgraded some of their docks. Saltspring Marina, in Ganges Harbour, is one of the first in British Columbia with ELCI-protected power.

In the Waggoner Cruising Guide, marinas that have upgraded their shore power are identified with the label "ELCI-protected power."

Onboard Blue Sea Systems ELCI and Over-amperage breaker

It's Not the Marina's Shore Power.

If you are having problems with upgraded shore power, the first place to look is your boat. Ground fault monitoring and interrupt technology has been protecting us in our homes for many decades with GFCI outlets.

One way to prepare your boat is to install an ELCI or RCD breaker on your boat. This will not only help ensure that you won't have unexpected problems while cruising, but will also make for safer boating. If there are any electrical leakage issues on your boat, an ELCI will bring them to your attention and will do so at your schedule.

ELCI breakers cost about $500 or less and can be added to your existing panel or in a separate enclosure near your boat's shore power inlet.

[Leonard Landon]

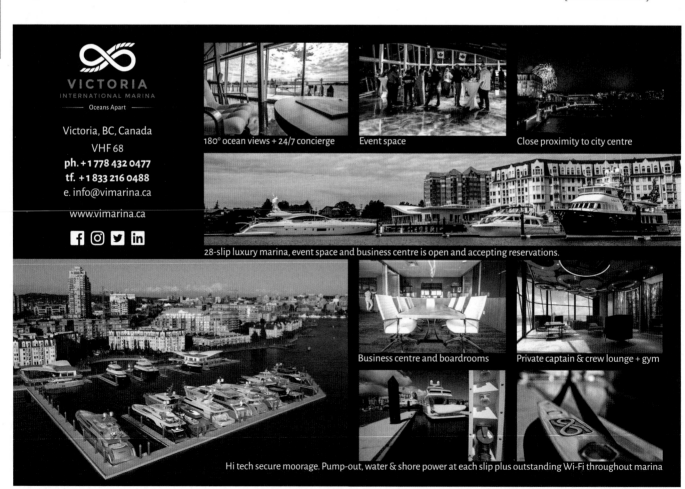

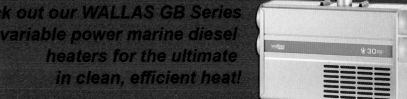

CHARTERING

Bareboat or crewed; sail or power; small and intimate or large and luxurious; one week or one month; on your own or with a group; chartering is an excellent way to not only cruise the Northwest waters and the Inside Passage, but it's a great way to try different styles of cruising. It's also an option for those who routinely cruise Puget Sound and San Juan Islands, but have always wanted to cruise farther north. You could charter a boat in Comox B.C. and cruise Desolation Sound or The Broughton Archipelago. Or charter a smaller, faster boat and use on-shore accommodations for overnighting. See the *Cruising Inn to Inn* section of this chapter for more information on this option.

Charter cruising is really all about flexibility. If you do not own a boat, you can rent one and cruise some of the most beautiful destinations in the world. Already have a boat, but need a larger boat with extra staterooms for family and friends? You can rent one. Or, do you want to try cruising with a different design before you consider purchasing. No experience is required. The charter company can provide an instructor-skipper to teach you how to handle a boat, or you can hire the captain to guide you to the most beautiful places. First mates, chefs and naturalists are available too. The surprising thing is that chartering a boat is relatively inexpensive compared to staying at luxury inns and hotels. Your destination can change every day without having to pack and unpack your luggage between destinations. The trips are memorable for all the wildlife experiences, secluded anchorages, and the choice of fine dining destinations – right on the water.

Flexibility includes the type of boats from which to choose, everything from sailboats and power trawlers, to large yachts. Take a look at the different companies' websites and the variety of boats they offer. Often the search starts with selecting power or sail. Then how many people will be on the boat. How many staterooms will you need? Do your guests mind sharing a head (bathroom), or do you need individual en-suite heads for all cabins? The age of the boat may vary the price. Next, how much do you want to spend versus how much room do you need or want? The range can go from about 26 feet up to 65-foot yachts.

Some charter operators offer a stay-the-night-before option so you can get an early start cruising on the first day of your charter. This option allows you to get onboard, load your personal items, equipment, and provisions. You can sleep aboard the boat but may not leave the dock until the morning of your planned charter. This option is usually charged at half the daily charter rate.

You might consider an organized flotilla where you can travel with a group of like-minded mariners guided by a professional that knows the area. Often activities are arranged every day and you meet some of the greatest people in the world.

At the end of your charter you will be expected to do some basic cleaning to return the boat in good order. Wash the dishes and put things away in the galley; re-fill the fuel and water tanks; empty holding tank(s); and hose down the exterior of the boat.

Some charter operators offer concierge services where they will provision the boat for you, set an itinerary and help with trip planning, and cleanup the boat afterwards.

You can plan and take your dream trip without the cost of owning a boat. Or, if you live and boat in a different area of the world, charter a boat and enjoy Pacific Northwest and Inside Passage cruising.

For a list of charter companies and further tips for charter cruising, see our website at WaggonerGuide.com.

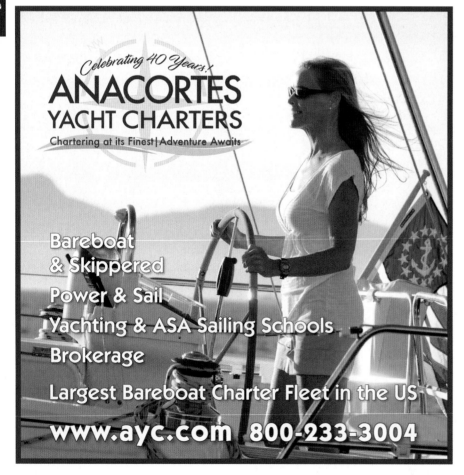

FLOTILLA CRUISING WITH NEW FRIENDS

There are many boaters who prefer cruising with other boats and crews as a group flotilla. For some, it is with a group of friends from a yacht club, a boat club, or with an organized commercial venture. They believe in safety in numbers, and often travel with one or more experienced crews to lead the group. Many use a flotilla trip as an opportunity to learn before they cruise on their own.

In the Northwest, there are several styles of flotilla cruises offered by different companies. They are all unique and have something different to offer. People who choose flotillas come in all ages, with varied boating experience. The common thread throughout is the opportunity for social interaction with other boaters, and the opportunity to gain a broader understanding of our Pacific Northwest waters.

Northwest Explorations in Bellingham, offers trips where customers charter a high-end yacht for multiple weeks with planned legs to Southeast Alaska, and planned legs for the return trip. Participants can purchase a chosen leg along the routes, depending on the amount of time you have to spend. Northwest Explorations supplies the boats, but you are captain and crew of your assigned vessel. Their fleet offers a variety of beautiful Grand Banks yachts and other brand yachts, including a

DeFever and a Fleming 55. They call their flotilla trips "Mother Goose" flotillas, where most of the boats follow along together. A mother ship leads with crew, a naturalist, and a mechanic to support 5-8 boats. Activities are planned along the way. This format is ideal for those who live and boat in another area of the country or the world, or if you have limited time to take your boat up to Southeast Alaska. Northwest Explorations also offers flotilla trips to Desolation Sound

The Waggoner Cruising Guide has a flotilla program for the passage from Anacortes to Ketchikan in Southeast Alaska, and an additional flotilla from Anacortes to Desolation Sound. Boaters use their own vessels in this program. The group usually consists of 6-8 boats that vary in size and speed. Some boats stay clustered during each day's leg, while others choose to meet up at the end of the day at the designated rendezvous location. The complete trip is organized and planned around an itinerary with activities and education along the way, including weather and seamanship. This program offers seminar courses, conducted in the months prior to departure, to develop the skills needed for a confident passage home. Trip leaders prepare daily briefings and guide all the participants on the trip to help insure

a safe, pleasant passage. Friendships are made on the flotilla trips that last a lifetime.

Jim Rard and Crew from Marine Servicenter offer a 12-week "Sail Alaska" program for power and sailboats. Participants learn while cruising to Alaska. Once in Southeast Alaska, Jim reveals his favorite destinations through organized special events and wildlife viewing. Imagine building and firing up a stone pizza oven and having homemade pizza cooked on hot rocks at a remote island in Southeast Alaska.

Slowboat, led by former Waggoner Guide Managing Editor, Sam Landsman, and experienced cruisers Laura Domela and Kevin Morris, Slowboat specializes in adventure cruising. Their flotilla program takes boaters to unique, out of the way destinations. They offer flotilla cruises to and from Southeast Alaska, destinations within Southeast Alaska, and the West Coast of Vancouver Island for beginner and experienced cruisers traveling with their own boats. They too work with the participants to share their knowledge for the unique situations presented in remote locations.

All flotilla cruisers say they come back from these trips with new skills, confidence, and many new friends from their time on the water.

37

MAINTAINING YOUR BOAT LIKE A PRO

The Waggoner Cruising Guide team takes boat maintenance very seriously. A breakdown can ruin your day, or even a week. For us and the boats in our flotilla trips, or when we are out researching for the Waggoner Guide, we cannot afford to breakdown. We certainly don't want a breakdown while underway in the remote areas of Northern B.C. or while crossing an open body of water like Dixon Entrance or rounding Cape Caution. You do not want to breakdown either. Time for summer cruising is a valuable commodity. The worst thing that can happen is when you have a breakdown and your family and friends are stuck waiting for repairs or parts. It is important to develop a maintenance program that is pro-active and preventative.

We have established a maintenance program that starts in the fall just after the cruising season ends. We begin by updating the list of our normal maintenance items such as taking an oil sample before changing the oil and filters. Coolant is inspected and changed. We inspect all systems to see what has broken or needs repair; we like to take care of this in the fall before the boat is laid up for the winter. Corrosives in used oil sitting over the winter can add to the wear on an engine.

It all starts with a checklist specifically tailored for our boat, identifying work to be done. After completing annual maintenance items, we start on upgrade items or refit. Scheduling work in the fall allows us to order needed parts that are often on sale during the winter months or available at boat show prices.

We also inspect our spares. When we purchase spares, the new spare is installed and the old part becomes the spare. This way we know the spare works and has all of the hardware it needs for installation. We carry a spare water pump – the old one stands by and ready to be installed. Parts stores are typically hard to find in our cruising areas. The old part probably has plenty of life in it for a temporary fix. We pack more spares for a single engine boat than we do for a twin-engine boat, where our second engine is our spare.

Look at spares as systems. For example, we do not believe in carrying a rebuild kit for the head. We do carry a complete, working pump assembly ready to be installed and carry spare duckbill valves. Rebuilding a pump for the head is not a pleasant task, nor would it go over well with the rest of the crew.

Our inspection checklist includes due dates for many items like hoses and belts. Dates are also set for various systems: the cooling system on the engine is sent out for flushing at a radiator shop every 5 years; the exhaust

BOAT SYSTEMS FOR INSPECTION AND SERVICE

- Engine Systems
- Control Systems
- Heat and Water Heater
- Electrical – Batteries, Inverters and Power Cables
- Fuel System – Filters and Tanks
- Water – Filters, Pumps and Tanks
- Heads and Waste systems
- Lighting – External and Internal
- Fire Suppression – All Extinguishers
- Emergency Kits, Flares and First Aid
- Electronics and Communications
- Charts and Cruising Guides
- Anchor Systems
- Galley and Refrigeration
- Dinghy
- Bedding and Soft Goods
- Accessories and Recreational Gear

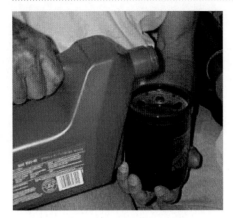

Prefill new filter with clean oil when changing engine oil.

system is removed and inspected annually. If you have a stainless steel or ceramic coated exhaust system, the interval can be much longer. For gensets and small diesel auxiliaries, the exhaust systems may be very hard to remove and inspect. It may be cheaper to just replace the exhaust system at a cost for parts of about $200. The transmission oil cooler is replaced every 5 years. Some transmission coolers can be sent to a radiator shop to flush, pressure test and service. Soft goods such as dripless seals, sail drive boots, hoses, belts etc. are inspected every year; after 10 years they are all replaced. We service the windlass

system with an inspection and lubrication annually. Every 5 years the windlass gets a major inspection, and every 10 years the windlass motor is sent out to a motor shop to be rebuilt. An anchor windlass is a single point of failure, keeping the windlass in great shape can save you from a real headache on the summer cruise.

Our maintenance checklist is divided among the boat's systems. The engine and propulsion systems are well understood, but we also breakdown our checklist into the other systems, such as the anchoring system, refrigeration, furnaces and heat, including the water heater. Electrical systems are checked – both 12V and 120/240V. Start and House Batteries are serviced and possibly replaced. We plan to replace batteries every 7-10 years for sealed batteries, and every 4-7 years for lead acid batteries, if they were properly maintained. And, remember when you replace battery banks, you need to replace all the batteries in the bank, even if just one is not performing to specifications. We even view the dinghy as a system and make sure the outboard is serviced and the fuel replaced annually. We check the dinghy's steering system, anchor system and the gear bag for first aid supplies and other safety items.

You do not have to do all the work, but often you do have to manage the work to make sure it gets done. If you elect not to

do some things on your checklist, have your shop update your checklist and ask them to sign off on the inspection and service items to ABYC standards.

Determine what items on your checklist you want to work on and those you would prefer a marine professional handle. For example, inspecting and remarking your anchor chain may be a day project you want to do.

A boat is a complex series of systems, all working in a corrosive environment. Your boat's systems are in standby through most of the year, ready for those good months when you go boating. It is best for boats to be used on a regular basis; you may want to use your boat more often and go boating once or twice every other month, but with our busy lives that may not be practical. The key is to have a process for good routine maintenance built into your boat ownership to maximize fun with family and friends for an enjoyable cruise.

For more information on the Checklist Approach, see Maintaining Your Boat Like a Pro at WaggonerGuideBooks.com. The checklist is in MS-Word format and you can modify it for your boat. Maintenance courses are offered at the Seattle Boat Show University and Cruisers College programs.

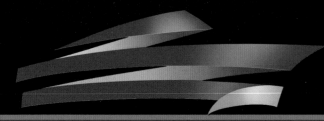

VHF Radio Procedures

The VHF radio is an important piece of safety equipment, and VHF 16 should be monitored when the boat is underway. While monitoring, you will hear weather and safety warnings, and be aware of what's happening around you. A boat close by, for example, may be having problems and call for help. By monitoring your radio, you can respond.

Station Licenses, U.S. Vessels. Until 1996, U.S. pleasure craft were required to have station licenses for their marine VHF radios. In 1996, however, the requirement was dropped for pleasure craft under 20 meters (65 feet), operating inside the U.S. only. All U.S. vessels operating in foreign waters, including Canada, still need a U.S. station license. With the 1999 dropping of station licenses in Canada (see below), it was hoped that pleasure craft exempted from station licenses in the U.S. no longer would need a station license to travel in Canadian waters. It now appears that it would require an act of Congress—literally!—to exempt U.S. pleasure craft from needing a station license for Canadian travel, and that's not likely. As a practical matter, Canadian authorities do not enforce U.S. radio license laws, and U.S. authorities are not going to follow a boat into Canada. In other words, there's no enforcement. We have our station license, however, and would not be without it, enforcement or no enforcement. We recommend that our readers do the same. Apply for your station license at the same time you register for your Maritime Mobile Service Identity (MMSI) number. You will need this number to use the Digital Selective Calling (DSC) and emergency calling features all VHF radios have. You can register online at www.fcc.gov, using the Universal Licensing System (ULS). The online process is cumbersome, but the processing time is short. The forms are also available from the FCC at (888) 225-5322 (Monday through Friday), if you apply by mail. If you call, choose menu option 2, Licensing. The woman who took our call was well-informed and helpful. A station license serves the entire vessel, regardless of the number of VHF radios the vessel has. The station license also covers the use of a tender's VHF radio (such as a handheld model) as long as the radio is used

in tender service, and as long as it is not used on land. It's all right for two or more radios from the same vessel with the same call sign to talk to each other via handheld VHF radio. U.S. pleasure craft longer than 20 meters, and all U.S. commercial vessels, are required to have an FCC station licenses.

Station Licenses, Canadian Vessels. Beginning in March 1999, station licenses no longer were issued to Canadian vessels so long as 1) the vessel is not operated in the sovereign waters of a country other than Canada or the U.S.; 2) the radio equipment on board the vessel is capable of operating only on frequencies that are allocated for maritime mobile communications or marine radio navigation. Canadian vessels not meeting those two requirements must have station licenses.

Operator's Permit, U.S. The U.S. does not require operator's permits for VHF radio use within the U.S. For foreign travel, however, a Restricted Radio Operator's permit is required. The U.S. individual permit is issued for life, and costs $60. If you are from the U.S. and take a boat to Canada, you will need a Restricted Radio Operator permit. Use Schedule E of FCC Form 605 to apply, and Form 159 to remit payment. If you are applying for both a station license and a

Restricted Radio Operator permit you will need a separate Form 159 for each application. The forms can be downloaded from www.fcc.gov, or you can apply electronically on the FCC website.

Operator's Permit, Canada. Canada requires each person operating a VHF radio to have a Restricted Operator's Certificate. For Canadian residents a test must be passed, but the certificate is free and issued for life. Training for the test and the issuing of certificates is handled by the Canadian Power and Sail Squadrons.

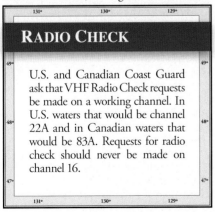

Radio Check

U.S. and Canadian Coast Guard ask that VHF Radio Check requests be made on a working channel. In U.S. waters that would be channel 22A and in Canadian waters that would be 83A. Requests for radio check should never be made on channel 16.

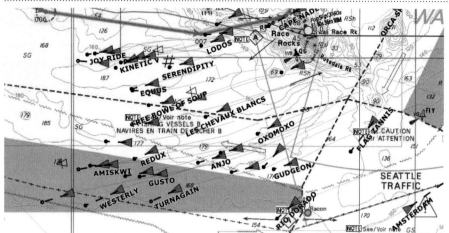

AIS display shows nearby vessels and potential conflicts. In this case it shows the fleet of sailboats at the start of the Swiftsure International Yacht Race.

SCOLDING ON THE RADIO

When a fellow boater does something that is dangerous or inconsiderate, proper VHF radio protocol does not allow the injured party to start yelling at "the boat that just went by" without identifying themselves – especially not on high power. If it's necessary to talk to the other boater – first switch to LOW POWER – then try to hail the boat by name and switch to a working channel.

Most people don't realize they're doing something wrong, so start by explaining the situation. Make sure it's a conversation and not a lecture. Explain the situation and listen to the response. A civil conversation is more likely to get results than an angry lecture. Make sure you are on a working channel and on low power.

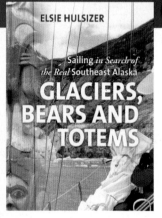
How to Use the VHF Radio. The easiest way to get a general sense of radio use is to monitor VHF 16, the hailing and distress channel; VHF 22A, the U.S. Coast Guard channel; VHF 83A, the Canadian Coast Guard channel, and the working channels. The VTS channels are good, too, because you'll be listening to professional mariners at work. VTS transmissions are brief and often informal, but you'll be listening to experienced people in action. On VHF 16 and the ship-to-ship working channels, you'll also hear inexperienced people. The difference will be obvious. To use the radio, call on the calling channel, VHF 16. When communication is established, switch to a working channel for your conversation. Except instances of distress, you may not have a conversation on VHF 16. VHF 09 may be used for conversations; but because it is an alternate calling channel in the U.S., the conversations should be brief.

The Low Power Switch. VHF radios can transmit at 25 watts, their highest power rating, or at 1 watt, the low power mode. Handheld VHF radios usually have a maximum power of 5 watts and low power of 1 watt. Whenever practical, use the low-power mode. Other vessels a few miles away can then use the same channel without interference from you. The difference between high power and low power affects transmission distance only. Reception ability is unaffected. Handheld radios should use low power whenever possible. The battery lasts longer. When making a securite call, such as transiting Dodd Narrows or Malibu Rapids, be sure to have your VHF radio set on low power (1 watt). A securite call is for traffic safety purposes only and is not a call for right-

SECURITÉ CALL INSTEAD OF BIG WAKE SCOLD

When a nearby boat is creating a large and potentially dangerous wake, instead of getting on the VHF radio and blindly scolding – do everyone a favor and issue a Securité call to alert other boats in the area. First switch to LOW POWER, then call: *"Securité, Securité, this is the 34-foot sailing vessel WINDY– caution for a potentially dangerous wake from a fast-moving large black-on-white power boat in Mosquito Pass."*

"Securité"
"Securité"
"Securité"

of-way. Vessels traveling with the current are the 'stand-on' and vessels traveling against the current flow are the 'give-way.'

When Not to Call on Channel 16. Large vessels in the VTS traffic lanes usually do not monitor VHF 16. They monitor the VTS channel for their area. In Puget Sound waters covered by Seattle VTS Traffic, large vessels also must monitor VHF 13, the bridge-to-bridge communications channel. Seattle Traffic covers all U.S. waters and the entire Strait of Juan de Fuca, including the Canadian side. If you are disabled in a traffic lane and a large vessel is bearing down on you, call the vessel on the appropriate VTS channel (see VTS Radio Channels chart in the What Recreational Boaters Need to Know About VTS section in this chapter). If you are still unsure about what to do, call the Coast Guard on VHF 16 and ask them to contact the vessel for you, or to provide you with the correct channel.

DSC & GMDSS. DSC stands for Digital Selective Calling, and is part of the Global Maritime Distress and Safety System (GMDSS). Basically, if you have a DSC radio with a valid MMSI (Maritime Mobile Service Identity) number in its memory and push the covered red button, the radio will send an automatic digital distress message on VHF 70. This message contains the MMSI number, which is linked to a database that includes your name, vessel information, emergency contacts, and other information. If the vessel's GPS is connected to the VHF, or the radio

is equipped with a GPS receiver, the radio also transmits GPS coordinates. For this to work, the radio must have the vessel's MMSI number stored in its memory. MMSI numbers are issued in the United States by the FCC or Boat U.S., and in Canada by Transport Canada and Industry Canada. Important for U.S. vessels traveling to Canada: Officially, MMSI numbers issued by Boat U.S. are only for use in the United States. However, a Boat U.S. MMSI number will work in Canada., but the database information may not be available to Canadian authorities. The distress signal and your location, if your radio is connected to a GPS signal, will be transmitted to authorities and other DSC equipped vessels to alert other boats. Brief your crew before heading out on a passage on how to summon help using the red DISTRESS button on your VHF radio. Consider preparing a check-list for emergencies for your crew that includes summoning help on the VHF radio and even the location of your safety equipment. For more information on this critical topic, see WaggonerGuide.com and search for the article on What to do when the Captain drops dead - or is incapacitated. While it is a catchy title, the article has many useful tips on how to prepare an emergency manual for use by your crew in case of an emergency.

Mayday Hoaxes. Each year, hoax Mayday calls cost the U.S. and Canadian Coast Guards millions of dollars ($2 million in Seattle alone) and in some cases put lives at risk. Sometimes the hoax is Junior playing with Grandpa's radio, sometimes it is the

result of things getting too festive, sometimes the caller has a mental problem. Now that direction-finding equipment can locate the sources of radio calls, arrests can be made and penalties assessed. Radios are not toys, and hoax Mayday calls are not jokes. Large fines and even jail terms are the penalties.

LOCAL KNOWLEDGE

To Reach the Coast Guard by Cell or Smartphone App

U.S. Coast Guard Rescue Center Seattle 911 or (206) 220-7001

U.S. Coast Guard Rescue Center Juneau (for all of southeast Alaska) 911 or (907) 463-2000

Canadian Coast Guard 911 or *16 or (250) 413-8933

Android and iOS smartphones can access and hail U.S. Coast Guard with their free official USCG App. The App has an emergency button as well as access to other helpful information.

Automatic Identification System (AIS). AIS is a VHF-based radio tracking system for commercial and recreational vessels. Vessels equipped with AIS transponders transmit their name, course, speed, MMSI number, vessel size, and destination. Vessels equipped with AIS receivers display information from surrounding vessels and warn of potential conflicts. Large commercial vessels are required to have Class-A transponders while recreational vessels optionally have Class-B transponders. In the past, the high cost limited AIS transponders to only larger recreational vessels and AIS receivers to some recreational boats. The cost to equip your boat with both transmit and receive continues to get more affordable all the time. In 2017 Standard Horizon came out with a VHF radio that includes both transponder and receiver built-in to a single box. Simply replace your VHF radio to show boats your information and receive their AIS information. AIS is particularly valuable in low visibility situations and when operating near large commercial traffic. Vessel name and MMSI AIS information makes it much easier to call a nearby vessel regarding potential conflicts. The price to equip your vessel with an AIS receiver is very affordable and well worth the expense.

New AIS applications show up each season. Small AIS man-overboard devices that attach to lifejackets are available; when activated, show a MOB alert on all AIS equipped vessels nearby. AIS system design provides for a number of different message types that include virtual navigation aids, observed weather information, and local harbor/port information.

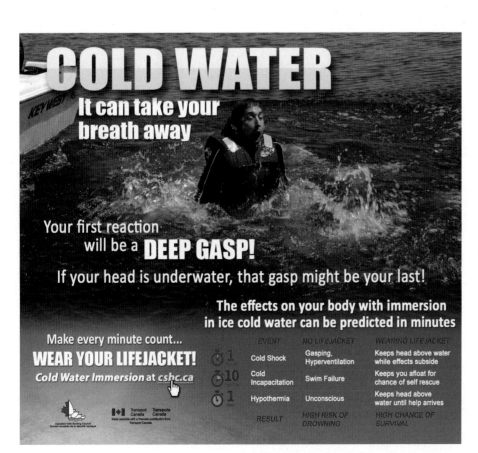

43

CELLULAR, INTERNET AND SATELLITE COMMUNICATIONS

Voice and data communications remain one of the priorities when cruising. Lately, with a multitude of smart and connected devices onboard, data communications have become a top priority for cruisers. Email, social media, weather information, financial transactions, marina slip reservations, and web browsing have all become essential elements of today's cruising. Cellular is the most cost effective solution for voice, messaging, and data communications in much of the Northwest cruising area. Satellite service provides the best geographic coverage, but at a higher cost. Wi-Fi internet service is available from a number of different free and for-fee providers. In more remote areas, service is not always available, or the service is slow and unreliable.

Cellular. In Washington waters, cruisers have a number of cellular providers to choose from, all with excellent voice, messaging, and data service. All of the Washington waters, except the western half of Strait of Juan de Fuca, have excellent cellular coverage. U.S. based cellular providers have a range of plans at reasonable rates. In 2017, reasonably priced plans were introduced with unlimited voice and data that include roaming in Canada. Today's cellular data speeds are good and service is very reliable. If you are on one of the newer rate plans, cellular is a cost effective way to handle your voice, messaging, and internet needs while cruising all of the Northwest waters. Be sure you have a voice, messaging, and data plan which includes roaming in Canada; if you don't, you may be shocked when you get the bill.

Three major cellular providers: Telus, Rogers, and Bell, operate in B.C. with voice, messaging, and data coverage. Voice, messaging, and data coverage is complete from the U.S. border on the south, to Campbell River/Desolation Sound on the north. There is no coverage in Jervis Inlet and spotty in mountainous areas. The west coast of Vancouver Island has coverage from Hot Springs south to Barkley Sound. There is coverage in Quatsino Sound in the north. From Campbell River/Desolation Sound to Port McNeill, cellular coverage is spotty. Johnstone Strait has the better coverage, with little if any coverage in the passages and inlets off of the Strait. Cellular towers high atop mountains near Port McNeill and Port Hardy provide coverage in much of Queen Charlotte Strait, and the edge of the Broughtons. Between Port Hardy and Prince Rupert, cell coverage is limited to the area around the towns of Bella Bella/Shearwater, Klemtu, Hartley Bay, Kitimat, and Bella Coola. The area around Prince Rupert has good cell coverage that continues north to the U.S. border in Dixon Entrance. Haida Gwaii has cell coverage in and around the city of Queen

Charlotte, Sandspit, and Masset. Cellular service keeps getting better every season with more and better coverage in remote areas. Coverage between Campbell River and Port McNeill keeps getting better each season.

Southeast Alaska coverage begins in Dixon entrance near Cape Fox but is spotty until you pass the entrance to Behm Canal on your way to Ketchikan. Four major U.S. cellular carriers provide voice, data, and messaging coverage in and around populated areas in Southeast Alaska.

Cellular Amplifiers. Cellular amplifiers are a good addition when cruising north of Campbell River and Desolation Sound. From Campbell River north, there are fewer cell towers and the distances between them are much greater. Cellular signals emitting

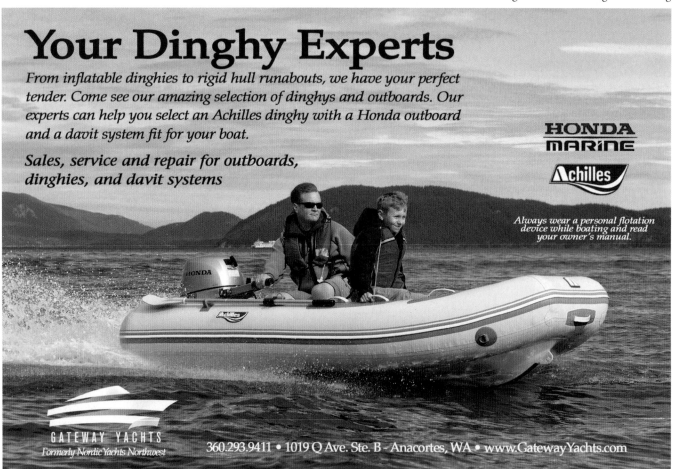

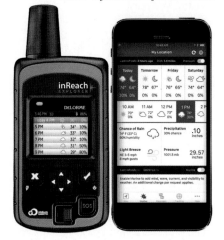

The InReach system now offers weather information from Ocens.

from the towers are powerful, but the return signals from your phone are relatively weak. A cell amplifier's main advantage is in boosting the signal from your phone so that the distant cell tower can "hear" your phone. The best amplifiers have an external antenna. Be sure and match the amplifier's frequencies to your phone, and the carriers for your planned cruising area.

Cruise ships have a predictable effect on cell service. In remote areas north of Campbell River and especially in southeast Alaska, cell phone service is noticeably degraded when a cruise ship or two are in the cell tower area. These remote systems, sized to limited cellular demand, are often swamped by the thousands of devices in the hands of cruise ship passengers.

Important: For emergency, distress, and rescue operations, cellular telephones are not substitutes for VHF radios. If you have a problem and need help, get on channel 16 and start calling. The Coast Guard and neighboring vessels will hear you and may be your closest and fastest aid.

Satellite Communications. Satellite today is more than just phones. Two satellite providers, Iridium and Globalstar, offer a number of equipment and service plans with voice, message, and data communication services. Satellite phones give you voice communication nearly everywhere. Prices of satellite phones have come down, but airtime is still more expensive than cellular. Satellite messaging and data services have recently become much easier to use with the introduction of Iridium Go and Globalstar Sat-Fi devices. These devices bring satellite communications to your smartphone, tablet, and PC. Both Iridium Go and Sat-Fi connect your smartphone, or any Wi-Fi enabled device, to the respective satellite system for voice, data, and messaging. The devices are easy to use and allow multiple devices to connect to the satellite service. Data speeds are slow to very slow, with bandwidth for simple email and light browsing. Some weather information services are available, designed for transmission over satellite service. Satellite phone rentals are available. See www.WaggonerGuide.com for more information about satellite phones.

Satellite Messengers. Satellite messengers like those from SPOT and Garmin offer an inexpensive way for cruisers to track and check in. Depending on the device and service plan selected, satellite messengers can send automated position reports, link to smartphones to send and receive text messages via satellite, or send a distress signal. Basic weather forecasts and marine weather forecasts are now available on Garmin's InReach device. Satellite messengers rely on private satellite constellations, not the internationally organized Cospas-Sarsat network that EPIRBs and PLBs use. SOS messages go through a private emergency center that passes on the message to government emergency services. Satellite messengers are not EPIRBs and should not take the place of an EPIRB, but they can provide low-cost communications far beyond cell phone service. Satellite messengers offer the coverage of satellite service at a lower cost.

WiFi Internet. Wi-Fi may be one of the most universal and inexpensive means of accessing the internet when cruising. However, availability, speed, and reliability are often problematic. Most marinas have Wi-Fi available for their guests. How the marina

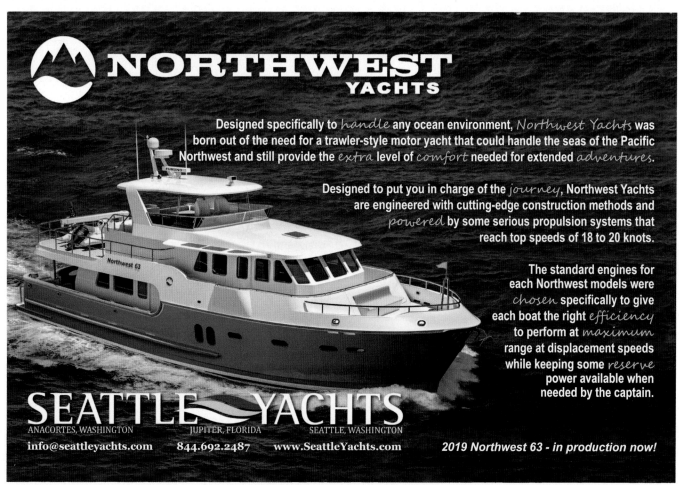

provides this Wi-Fi service varies from marina to marina. The larger, popular marinas have in-house installed commercial grade Wi-Fi systems that are accessible, and reliable with bandwidth for most internet needs. Other marinas have contracted with commercial Wi-Fi providers such as Shaw-Go and Beacon (formerly BBX) for commercial grade Wi-Fi service. A few marinas with commercial grade Wi-Fi systems offer high bandwidth, for a fee, as an alternative to their lower bandwidth free Wi-Fi. A number of marinas have in-house installed Wi-Fi, built from home-grade equipment connected to residential bandwidth internet service. In remote areas of B.C., where there are no landlines, marina Wi-Fi is via limited bandwidth Dish Satellite Internet providers. Satellite internet service is much slower and at a much higher cost than landline data service. Marina operators provide this service to guests at a high price; and it is metered. Every bit (pun intended) of data is a cost to the marina operator.

A decade ago, when a boat pulled into a marina moorage space, the boat might use one or possibly two Wi-Fi connection ports, and their usage consisted of simple emails and some limited bandwidth web browsing. But today, every person onboard has a smartphone that they want to connect to Wi-Fi, and they may have a tablet or PC. In addition, the boat has its own devices, including a chartplotter, wanting to connect. Young people onboard may have gaming devices as well. Then there's Fire TV that attemps to connect for streaming video or movies. Every piece of electronics today is Wi-Fi enabled. The demand for internet bandwidth has increased tenfold, putting an enormous strain on Wi-Fi systems.

Wi-Fi user expectations have changed dramatically; at home the average internet user has grown accustomed to large bandwidth internet connections with almost limitless amounts of data transfer. We all assume that any internet connection will be fast, available, and constant.

Marinas are challenged to keep up with this increasing demand. Remotely located marinas, where landline internet is not available, have an almost impossible task trying to meet demand with very limited bandwidth satellite internet connections.

How to be a Good Wi-Fi citizen. Adjust your expectations and your internet usage for Wi-Fi. Be prepared for internet access slower than you might be accustomed to; allow extra time for the online task and have an alternate plan. Most importantly, adjust your internet usage to minimize data transfer. Be especially aware of data upload, as upload speeds are the slowest on nearly every type of connection.

1. Turn off automatic updates. Not always as simple and straight-forward as it sounds.

2. On smartphones, tablets, and PC's, turn off automatic photo backup to cloud storage. Do you really need all 200 images uploaded to the cloud right now?

3. Smartphones – almost all of the Apps on our smartphones are searching for App updates. This constant 'pinging' to check for updates is largely unnecessary internet traffic when we are out boating. So go through your Apps one-by-one and turn off updates. Each App is different.

4. Don't even think of using Apps like Facetime, Netflix, Amazon Video, and gaming Apps.

5. Limit your use: email with no attachments; Facebook, scrolling slowly and no video viewing; voice only Skype, no video; and limit smartphone usage when Wi-Fi is the only signal available.

Wi-Fi Amplifiers. When your assigned slip is far out on the end of the most distant dock, the marina's free Wi-Fi may not help you much if you don't have an amplifier onboard. Relatively inexpensive, Wi-Fi amplifiers boost the often weak marina signal. Amplifiers allow you to reach otherwise unusable Wi-Fi signals from the surrounding area. These include Wi-Fi from providers like Shaw and Xfinity. Wi-Fi amplifiers connect to an onboard Wi-Fi router to bring the amplified signal throughout your boat. Wi-Fi amplifiers often allow boats at anchor to use nearby Wi-Fi.

SMARTPHONE APPS FOR CRUISERS

There are literally any number of Apps for just about every topic imaginable. Android and iOS Smartphone Apps can help with so many boating related activities. But it's important to keep in mind that onboard dedicated marine systems should remain the primary systems. Apps are often free and easy to download and install. Free Apps can contain advertising. Occasionally, an enhanced version of the free App can be purchased for a small price. Apps can be very cost effective additions to onboard equipment and serve as excellent backup and augmentation to dedicated equipment like chartplotters, VHF radio, depth sounder, and radar. Increasingly, smartphone Apps are the human-interface through WiFi to control and monitor equipment and devices on board; a good example is the Watchmate App listed below.

Apps are usually free and easy to download and install. Before becoming too dependent upon the App's information, learn where the App came from and where it gets its information. Tides and currents information is a great example. There are a number of Apps that display tides and currents for various Northwest locations. But where is the information coming from and how accurate is it?

Here are some of the more popular boater related Apps.

U.S. Coast Guard – This official App is configurable and saves your information as well as details of one or more of the boats you use. Once configured, you can use the App to: request Emergency Assistance; geo-locate the nearest NOAA weather buoys and view the latest conditions; file a float plan; report a hazard to navigation; report a problem with a navigation aid; report a marine life issue; consult navigation rules; request a vessel safety check; and report suspicious activity. Good information resource and an Emergency Assistance function that sends you Lat/Lon information to the Coast Guard.

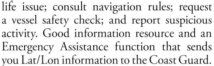

Marine Traffic - Provides up-to-date marine traffic information. It works well for monitoring ship traffic or monitoring friends. It can be used to monitor commercial vessel traffic, including ferries, if you don't have an onboard AIS.

Barometer - There are a number of good barometer Apps for both Android and iOS that use the device's sensors to measure and, more importantly, track barometric pressure. Much better than tapping the glass face on the brass encases, wall mounted mechanical barometer.

U.S. Customs CBP ROAM – This official Customs and Border Protection App supports Android and iOS devices. Travelers entering the U.S. can check-in with the App, and CBP officers can initiate a video chat for information verification, or an interview if required. If approved for entry, boaters do not have to report in-person at a Port of Entry. The App that can be used at State of Washington and State of Alaska pleasure craft Port Of Entry locations. Reporting Offsite Arrival

A TRIBUTE TO DON DOUGLASS AND REANNE HEMINGWAY-DOUGLASS

"No one has done more to open up the entire West Coast for the recreational boater than this pair. By visiting and recording information about every nook and cranny from San Diego to Glacier Bay, they answered the question every captain looking at a chart asks; I wonder what that cove is like? I have used every one of their books and have found their chartlets and diagrams spot on. Their guides relieve anxiety . . . they give us confidence . . . and inspire us to explore. I think the sheer volume of their work impresses me the most. They literally explored every inch of this coastline in a systematic way, and still had time to write down the details of what they found. Whew!"

[Jim Norris]

When cruising the waters of our vast coastal and northern regions, we always marvel at the energy, commitment, and effort that went into researching and producing the Exploring Series guidebooks. We at Waggoner Cruising Guide pay special tribute to Don Douglass and Reanne Hemingway-Douglass, who have unselfishly given so much of themselves to the enjoyment of the boating community. Can you imagine spending 35 years cruising the West Coast and Pacific Northwest waters, recording what each bay looks like, noting the best anchorage spots, and mapping each bay and cove? Don Douglass and Reanne Hemingway-Douglass did just that; not for their own benefit, but for the rest of us boaters who dare to believe that we, too, can venture beyond our comfort zone. Reanne, along with her husband Don, transited river bars, narrow passage ways, and endured violent seas; they persevered with strength and courage through it all, sharing their personal stories and collecting data for their guidebooks.

We were first introduced to the Douglasses through Reanne's book, *Cape Horn; One Man's Dream, One Woman's Nightmare*. We marveled at what they had accomplished. Their Exploring Series guidebooks empowered us to extend our own boating territory, cruising to Mexico and back, and cruising the isolated areas of the Gulf of Alaska. When the weather forecast started to talk about gale force winds, we knew we could go to their guidebooks for an accurate description of anchorage options; we knew they had been there and could trust their writeup.

Thank you Don and Reanne for showing us the extent of what our region has to offer, and for inspiring us to seek out our own adventures.

[Lorena Landon]

– Mobile, ROAM App, is configurable and saves your profile information.

iNAVX – This very feature rich iOS and Android App has many of the functions found on full function chartplotters, including everything from real-time navigation on a full suite of downloadable nautical charts, to an anchor watch feature. Interfaces with Vesper's AIS Wi-Fi gateway and supports AIS transponders/receivers. Positioning, GRIB weather, routing, charting and tracking all combine to make this app a powerful navigation tool.

Anchor Watch – Both the free and charge version of this anchoring App are feature rich. The App uses the iOS or Android device's GPS receiver to track the boat's position relative to the set anchor and sounds an alarm if the position exceeds a preset set distance from the anchor. There are other anchor watch Apps available, but this one has the added feature that will send an SMS message to another phone (on shore) in addition to sounding an alarm on the device left on the boat.

PredictWind – This Android and iOS App displays a wind speed and direction forecast for the selected area. Users can choose from four different forecast models. PredictWind provides accurate and time-specific information in an hour by hour format for a seven day period. Geographical coverage is provided for the entire west coast up to the Gulf of Alaska. You can zoom in on the forecast map to see micro area forecasts; which can be very helpful in route planning. With the App, it's easy to navigate between wind, swell, rain, cloud, air and sea temperature forecasts in table, map and graph views. Android, iOS and Web App.

SailFlow – Graphical indicator of current wind conditions and predicted wind. The App is location-sensitive and presents a concise list if nearby stations with current conditions and hour by hour predicted winds for 7 days. Options include detailed and basic displays. Forecasts include sky conditions. Select from a number of prediction models. Android and iOS compatible

Navionics – This Android, iOs and Web App is a valuable navigation tool. The App is free and the cost for charts

varies by geographic coverage area. The route planning feature allows the user to program settings for boat draft, speed, and fuel consumption; then choose either automatic routing from start to end points, or manually enter waypoints. The App calculates distance, time en route and total fuel required. Route planning is only one of many features and functions in this App. The use is intuitive and features are far too many to list here.

iSailor – A full-function Android and iOS App that is free but requires regional chart purchase. Locates position using Apple iOS Location or on phone GPS if available. Quick entry of waypoints. Vector maps. Route tracking. AIS provided through purchased internet access service.

VesselFinder – Map display of AIS information on vessels worldwide. With the pro version you can build your own fleet of vessels you follow. Current and historical data. Tracking information. Android and iOS compatible.

Wunderground – Android and iOS, this is the Weather Underground App, an extensive weather forecasts and conditions service. This is a good full info weather resource with data from a network of stations providing area forecasts, weather radar, satellite maps, and severe weather warnings. Local weather stations with camera images provide helpful information about localized conditions. Use the camera images from a station on the other side of the fog bound strait to discover if it's clear on the other side. Select from "Forecast on Demand" or "NWS" for forecast information source.

Windy – This Android, iOS, and Web App is one of the best wind, wave, and weather forecasting tools available today. Forecast wind and wave conditions are put into motion on a map display that can be zoomed out to see coming weather patterns and zoomed in to see localized conditions. Professional weather forecast model options including ECMWF, NAM 5km and GFS 22km; allow comparison of models to improve your weather data interpretation. Forecast information is in data and graphical display format with color and movement. 10 day forecasts show what's happening local, regional, and global. Forecast conditions for ground level up to 13.5 kilometers let you see not only what is happening but what is steering the weather to you.

WatchMate – This App is the display and controls for the Vesper AIS transponder receiver device. The App is only useful in conjunction with the Vesper. We list this here because the App, in conjunction with the Vesper unit, has some well-done AIS traffic alarms and an excellent anchor watch feature. Android and iOS compatible.

Alltrails – This App helps all of us boaters find those often times little known walking paths, hiking trails, and pedestrian ways that are so important to boaters looking for exercise and just getting around without a car. The App is free and has complete information about the trails. Android and iOS compatible.

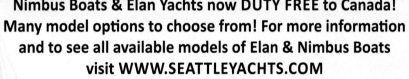

BOATING FROM INN TO INN

Boating from Inn to Inn

There is a new trend in boating where you can plan to use shore-side inns, hotels or cabins as extra staterooms. Many of them are designed for visiting boating guests and are very cool. You can boat with friends or family and give them the option of staying onshore. Handy if your boat does not have that second or third stateroom. This is also handy if you would like a night ashore and some of the options like yurts or bubble homes are very interesting. If you have a fast speedboat with a cuddy cabin, you can run up the Inside Passage to Alaska in two long days or less. There are lots of options.

When we started seeing this trend, we recognized the opportunity for guests aboard a boat to enjoy the day's cruise with the option to stay overnight onshore at an inn, cabin, or hotel room. There are even boats and houseboats in marinas that you can rent for the overnight stay. Some of these options can be booked through the marina or even on Airbnb. Grandparents can now join the fun of a day's cruise with the family and spend the night ashore in a comfortable bed with a normal sized bathroom facility. With a little creative planning and the Waggoner Cruising Guide in hand, you can create a cruising itinerary with stays in marinas that have nearby shore-side overnight stays. Accommodations range from luxury inns and hotel rooms to other boats in the marina, yurts, and even camp sites where the kids can stay in a tent.

Downsize your boat. We also see a trend where some cruising couples are downsizing their boat. They have owned a 45 foot to 60 foot displacement trawler, allowing them to cruise for weeks

Artisan Suites on Bowen Island sits atop the hill above Snug Cove, close to shops.

April Point Resort, Spa & Marina near Campbell River

Roche Harbor Resort on San Juan Island is a great family destination.

Camp in luxury at Backeddy Resort & Marina near Egmont, BC.

The cottage at Westbay Marine Village in Victoria

or months at a time. They have done the long trips and now want to downsize to reduce their boating costs, allowing them to experience other types of travel. Rather than letting go of the boating scene, they change their boating style and purchase a smaller vessel with basic overnight accommodations for two. They buy a faster boat and plan their trips to quickly dash to different places and stay ashore for most of the time during their trip. One owner who downsized from a 45-foot semi-displacement trawler to a new 28-foot Sea Sport with twin outboards, is planning a four-day passage from Anacortes to Ketchikan. He and his wife will be staying in cabins at Blind Channel and Echo Bay and then hotel rooms at Shearwater and Prince Rupert before arriving in Ketchikan. While their new 28-foot boat was not inexpensive, they save on moorage, insurance, and general maintenance with a smaller boat.

A growing family or bringing grandchildren along. If your cute young children are growing into gangly teenagers, and a new larger boat with cabins for all is not in your future, consider putting them off the boat ashore. There are many anchorages and marinas with camping areas and tent sites. It can be an adventure to arrive by boat and take the dingy to shore and set up camp. Some marina resorts have swimming pools, kayak rentals, and many recreational activities. Involve the kids in the planning. Let them research and make some of the choices on where to stay. This works for grandchildren too. The added benefit - with the kids ashore - you get your privacy back at the boat.

Seascape Waterfront Resort in Gowland Harbour near Campbell River

Hastings House has beautiful classic cottages overlooking Ganges Harbour on Salt Spring Island.

Denham Bay above Dent Rapids in Discovery Passage is a quiet, restful destination.

DEVELOPING AN ITINERARY TO DELIGHT THE ENTIRE CREW

Planning an itinerary for you and your crew generates enthusiasm for the trip and establishes team effort. For many, trip planning is part of the fun, starting months before the actual trip. You can dream about what your cruise will be like through the islands or Desolation Sound.

Involving the crew. You can start by involving the crew with pre-trip research, or you create the first draft as Captain. Look through the many cruising guides available (we stock most in the WaggonerGuide.com store). Also look through past issues of magazines that cover the Northwest like Pacific Yachting, Northwest Yachting Magazine, 48 North and SEA magazine to name a few. Start that short list of places you want to visit for the first time, re-visit, or see from a different point of view and share with guests who have previously never seen this beautiful area.

Everyone can prioritize activities and destinations based on their interests and work together to finalize the itinerary. Depending on how much time you have for the trip and knowing the distances involved, you can create an itinerary with reasonable expectations. Time should be factored in for provisioning, fuel stops, weather delays, and transiting any rapids along your route. Consider time for relaxing too. Those on a tight schedule might move to a different destination every day to see as much as possible. Others plan for a day or two, or plan short cruising legs to allow plenty of time to fully enjoy a destination.

A few questions to start. Asking a few basic questions will help you develop an itinerary. Many boaters have preconceived ideas about their anticipated cruise, or expect to see and do certain things they have in mind. A pre-planned itinerary, with some specifics, helps set the expectations for a pleasant and rewarding cruise. Consider:

How much time do you have, including the trip back? What speed do you expect to cruise at?

What do you want to see? This list could include wildlife, quaint villages, cannery ruins, museums, or simply relax at remote anchorages.

What activities do you want to do? Perhaps go fishing, swimming, or kayaking. Or you may prefer attending happy hours at the smaller marinas, or souvenir shopping when in town. Walking the beaches and hiking the trails found on many of the islands is always a favorite. You may have a crew that is split, where some will want to see the local museum, while others rummage through the shops in town. There are many locations that fit this criteria.

Are friends and family flying in to meet you? Options may include commercial airports, smaller community airports, or perhaps arriving by seaplane at more remote areas. You may want to factor in extra time for missed connections if you have guests arriving by plane.

Is this your first time cruising the Northwest? Are you planning a 1-week or 2-week bareboat charter? There are so many places to go and enjoy both near and far. Most people who are new to the area start by cruising among the San Juan Islands on a 1-week to 2-week itinerary, leaving from the charter bases in Anacortes or Bellingham. If you want to focus on the islands of British Columbia, there are bareboat charter companies in Sidney, Nanaimo and Vancouver. If you really just want to cruise Desolation Sound and the Broughton Islands area, there is a reputable charter company in Comox, BC where you can save a day or two by starting your cruise much closer to these areas.

Begin with the basics. With the basic information, we like to create an itinerary in a spreadsheet, or on a pad of paper. For those who like to work with spreadsheets, we have posted a few sample itineraries at www.WaggonerGuide.com/Itineraries. Start laying out a day on each line with a few notes.

There may be some special events such as the Saturday Market in Ganges, or the world-famous fireworks at Butchart Gardens. Your schedule may shift, so remain flexible. A 90-mile day of cruising may be too much, or a passage may miss slack at one of the tidal rapids.

At the Waggoner Guide, we like to start our itinerary with the "knowns" in place. For example, if we were planning a trip north to Desolation Sound, the Broughtons or Southeast Alaska and leaving from Anacortes, we know to plan for clearing Canadian Customs. We have three basic choices for clearance, heading north to Sidney, Bedwell Harbour, or Nanaimo. Nexus, i68 and Canpass holders will have many more options to clear Customs if the entire crew is registered in the programs.

Timing Dependencies. Typically we cross over to the Canadian Gulf Islands and work our way north through the protected waters of the islands. We then look at the times of slack water for Dodd Narrows, near Nanaimo. We record the time of morning and afternoon slack in our itinerary and then determine the approximate time and point of departure. It is a long day's cruise from Anacortes to Nanaimo at a cruise speed of 7-9 knots. If slack at Dodd Narrows is at noon, we probably will not be able to get there in time, especially if we need to allow nearly an hour to clear Canadian Customs in Bedwell Harbour. Instead we may elect to stay a day in the Gulf Islands and catch the morning slack at Dodd Narrows the following day, or plan for the evening slack and get to Nanaimo at around 7:00 p.m. This is where the different choices come into play. If you cannot get to Dodd Narrows in time, you can save an hour by planning to clear Canadian Customs in Nanaimo. This option would eliminate the stop at Bedwell Harbour (Poets Cove) and require an arrival at the Nanaimo Canadian Customs dock well before the closing time of 5:00 p.m. in the summers (4:30 p.m. in the off-season).

Why stop in Nanaimo? It is a good jumping off point for heading north to Campbell River or crossing over to the Sunshine Coast. The weather is typically better in the early morning when winds should be lighter. You can make the open water crossing before afternoon winds kick up. Nanaimo is also a good provisioning point. Markets and liquor stores near the marina allow you to stock up on food items that may have been restricted when clearing Canadian Customs.

There are other options you can build into the plan. When leaving from Seattle, you may need to allow a day to reach the Anacortes area or the San Juan Islands. Stopping in historic Roche Harbor or Friday Harbor may be a crew member's request. However, it may make more sense to save this stop for the return trip from Canada, since both locations are a U.S. Customs Port of Entry.

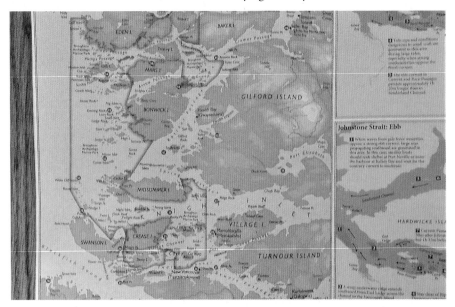

PROVISIONING YOUR BOAT FOR A WELL FED AND HAPPY CREW

Quality food on board is a big part of the cruising experience. Having that perfect meal surrounded by magnificent scenery is part of what makes our boating lifestyle so special. It is a fine balance between meals that are fun to prepare and keeping life and chores on board simple.

A few questions to start. How long is your cruise plan? Looking at an itinerary, roughly how many nights will you be dining on board versus eating at many of the very good restaurants along the way? Do you have anyone on your crew who has special food needs, is a vegetarian, needs gluten-free or likes milk in their coffee? Fat-free milk or whole milk? Does anyone on the crew have any allergies, or food items they like every day? You can see where this is going. If you are doing the cooking - how much work are you prepared to do? Pancakes in the morning or frozen waffles? It begs the question - do you have maple syrup on board? Or, do you like to sleep in and leave breakfast items out for crew and guests to help themselves. Are you headed to Canada, or from Canada into the U.S.? Will you need to purchase some items once you get into Canada due to border restrictions?

How much space do you have in your refrigerator or on-board freezer? Do you have a refrigerator or are you working from a cooler with ice. Your menu planning will change based on what foods you can store safely.

Headed up to the Broughtons? Be prepared to have your favorite dish to share for pot luck Happy Hours. Sometimes they are full meals and sometimes they are appetizer Happy Hours with finger foods. You will want to have a few recipes that are quick and easy to prepare. My favorite item is a supersize box with six packages of brownie mix. I make

it more indulgent with chocolate chips and cream cheese. It is quick, easy and I have never come back to the boat with anything left on the plate. I carry lots of cream cheese on the boat and can quickly mix in smoked salmon or a spice mix to make a quick dip for crackers or chips. Wine, beer, spirits for mixed drinks - don't forget the mixers. A warm day in the islands on Taco Tuesday begs for a margarita or a cold Corona. Stock what you need, being mindful of the limits imposed by Customs on either side of the border.

Make up your list. Indicate whether you should buy items in Canada or the U.S. depending on which direction you are headed across the border. Chocolate, candy, and liquor are generally more expensive in Canada due to the taxes imposed. The selection of wines at retail is better in the U.S. and maybe you should just pay the duty of 90% of the value

for a selection of good wines for your vacation cruise – that's right - almost double. Luckily many customs agents will average the value of your wine low when calculating the duty. Let them come up with a value. You can have a list of what is on board; but in reality, it is very hard to value liquor coming into the country. You will be surprised that an agent's estimate is probably lower than you might think.

Do not try to sneak extra alcohol into either country. We have seen too many bottles of very good liquor confiscated because the boater was not honest. Agents seem to be looking for liquor more than anything else. The irony is that laws go back to the thinking that one might be smuggling liquor into the country for profit, denying a country of duty and tax.

Don't forget the incidentals. A charcoal grill - needs charcoal and lighter fluid. Is your grill gas, do you need a supply of propane tanks? When cruising, you need to be self-sufficient. You do not have the ability to jump in the car and head to the store to purchase that missing ingredient or favorite food item. You could be a week or ten days between major grocery markets.

Pre-packaged Portions. One of our instructors and an excellent cook, Lynette Brower, likes to pre-prepare foods and place them into plastic bags for a complete meal. She keeps freezer bags filled with chicken or steaks broken down into portions for dinners. When she has guests; out come two bags. Often she will store the spices inside the bag along with the food item. By planning ahead with pre-packaged meals, time is saved and entertaining becomes more enjoyable.

Get rid of unnecessary packaging. Is your boat limited on storage space for food

or perishables? Consider removing food from boxes and bulky packaging. Mark the inner bag with a Sharpie. If it is a mix for preparation, cut the cooking directions from the box and tape it to the bag. Getting rid of the packaging before items are stored on your boat carries an additional benefit. Once north of Desolation Sound, getting rid of trash is a challenge and an expense. Many resorts charge by the bag or the pound to take your trash. Sometimes the trash needs to be stored for several days in a warm lazerette before it can be responsibly disposed. Getting rid of unnecessary packaging helps reduce trash.

Use plastic bins. A good system is to store dry food items in plastic bins sized to fit into the cabinets in the galley or other storage spaces. They can be segmented for how they are used. I have a bin for baking ingredients such as flour, sugar, baking soda and baking powder. The bin keeps the mess contained and supplies at-hand when doing a baking project. Bins keep canned goods from sliding around in rough seas and can be safely stowed.

Paper towels and paper plates are your friend. Unless you happen to be cruising on a mega-yacht, mealtime cleanup will be without a garbage disposal and dishwasher. Paper plates are a great option to reduce the dishwashing chore and reduce fresh water use (often a limited resource). You will likely be using more paper towels than at home. Paper towels make cleanup a breeze. It's best to wipe out greasy pots and pans rather than send oil and grease down the drain and into the sea water around your boat. Paper goods tend to be more expensive the farther north you go. Remember, everything has to be barged or flown in to the more remote locations.

Dining out. Options for dining-out disappear quickly the farther north you cruise. Beyond Desolation Sound restaurants are few and far between. Dining onboard is the rule, and it is important that you are prepared with the necessary items to make those tasty meals.

Don't overstock. In our experience, most people over stock their boats with food. It must be a comfort factor. There are plenty of places to purchase food items on the Inside Passage. Even the smallest marina markets try to support their guests with a means of purchasing food items and sometimes even fresh produce. We have not heard of anyone starving while out on a summer cruise. If anything, they come back refreshed and maybe even a pound or two content.

Keep it fun. Lastly, consider who is doing the cooking and cleaning up on your boat. It should not be the same person. This is a vacation in northwest paradise. Keep it light; keep it fun - and no galley slaves.

55

POTABLE WATER, CAN I DRINK IT?

"Is your water potable?" That's often one of the first questions boaters ask marinas when cruising Northern BC Coast, the Broughton Archipelago and sometimes even in the Gulf Islands. Boaters often find a 'boil water' notice or 'not-potable' sign at water spigots and hose-bibs on the docks. But what does this mean to boaters and why has this sign been posted?

What is not-potable water?
These notices indicate that the marina's private water system has not been certified by the Health Department as a public water system. Establishing a water system as a certified public water supply is an extensive and costly process, often not justifiable at remote, small marinas. Sometimes it requires a process for purification and exposure to UV light to kill certain bacteria. Sometimes the water is good and just needs to be tested regularly and sent in for certification. Water from private water systems may or may not be tested regularly but is used routinely, and may have been used for years with no ill effects. Remote resort locations like Pierre's Echo Bay Resort & Marina have been using the same well water for years with no ill effects. The hose bibs are marked non-potable and boil first; the water does have a slight brown tinge, but no one has reported problems with the water.

If other than owners are using or consuming water from a non-certified water system, the Government requires that a non-potable or boil notice be posted. The sign doesn't mean that the water is bad, but rather serves to inform guest users of the water source and allow the guest user to make a choice or further inquiries.

As boaters, what do we do with this information?
Depending on your comfort level, there are several options for non-potable water:

- Simply don't use the marina water, use only the water from your onboard tank.

- Do your own checking – ask locals if they regularly use the water for household needs. After your evaluation, you may choose to use the local source.

- Before your trip, you may wish to purchase a 3-stage water filter (the third stage needs to be a ceramic filter) and use this filter system to filter the marina water when filling your tank.

- If you have a watermaker onboard, you may wish to use your own established procedures for making water and filling or re-filling your onboard tank.

- Another option is to sanitize the marina water put in your tank with a chemical additive. You will need to research and purchase these additives before your trip.

- Lastly, installing filters and a UV light sanitizing system to your onboard water system will ensure you have safe water no matter where you fill your water tank.

What is the brown color in the water?
Additionally, boaters may have discovered that a few water sources on Northern BC Coast and in the Broughtons have a slight tannin or brown color to the water. While the water may be potable and not harmful, it certainly can be unappealing. Nature has its own filtration system that sometimes picks up coloring from cedar roots, resulting in the weak tea appearance to the water. This is an isolated issue, and nearly all of the marinas and water sources in the area have clear water.

In summary, small outlying marinas provide a surprising number of amenities for boaters, including acceptable sources of water. During their short business season, it's amazing what they can and do provide for the boating community. We encourage boaters to let them know how much we appreciate their facilities.

–The Waggoner Team

IT WILL NEVER HAPPEN TO ME...

We never plan to fall in and end up in the cold waters of the Northwest; but it happens, and in most cases, everything ends up OK. Every once in a while, we hear about an accidental drowning.

It's wise to be prepared, just in case. Have you thought about how you will get a person out of the water on your boat? You have only about 15 minutes or less until the situation becomes critical and life threatening. That's 15 minutes to spot and find the individual, bring the boat alongside, and pull them into the boat. You should have equipment available like a Lifesling Overboard Rescue System ready to deploy, or a block and tackle, or the use of a davit system. Next, you'll need to get them to a safe spot on the boat and a means of warming them up. You may be doing this in rough sea conditions singlehanded; or YOU may be the one in the water, hoping your crew knows the procedures and how to use the equipment on board. We recommend you practice the steps for a man overboard situation:

1. Instruct crew to keep eyes on the person overboard; arrest your forward motion.
2. Push the "Man Overboard" button on your Chartplotter or GPS.
3. Raise the RED safety cover on the Distress button on the VHF radio. Press the button for 3-4 seconds and make a Mayday Call on VHF 16 with the name of your vessel and that you have a Man Overboard situation with a person in the water. Give your lat/lon position.
4. Access the Man Overboard ring and line, or a Lifesling or other device, and deploy. Circle them to pull the float and line to them. Pull them to the side of the boat.
5. Deploy the swim ladder and assist climbing out of the water. They may not have the strength, and a line may have to be rigged to pull them out – most likely a davit system or block

and tackle rigged to a high position on the boat, or use the boom and winch on a sailboat.

6. Once on the boat, begin warming the victim with blankets. Communicate the situation on VHF 16 and determine if additional help is needed.

We make it a practice to wear life jackets while on deck and keep a VHF handheld with DSC in a pocket, and flares in another pocket. The crew wears the CrewWatcher system, where our location can be displayed on a smartphone. Most importantly, we have the Man Overboard procedure list in our Emergency binder at the helm.

See CruisersCollege.org for classes on Man Overboard situations

Mark Bunzel

FISHING AND SHELLFISH COLLECTING

How To Catch Dinner. If you love to eat salmon, halibut, rockfish, crab or prawns - you are boating in the right place. Washington, Alaska, and British Columbia all require licenses to harvest virtually any type of seafood. Washington and Alaska licenses can be purchased at sporting goods stores and other retail outlets, or online with a credit card. British Columbia licenses can be purchased at Independent Access Providers (check their website for a list), or online with a credit card. If you purchase online, consider how you will print the license; unless you have a printer on board, it may be best to do it at home ahead of time.

Investing in Gear. Crabbing is inexpensive and fun for even an inexperienced crew. Crabbing gear is relatively easy to purchase at a few hundred dollars, but the costs go up from there. Catching prawns can be more costly, especially if you purchase a pot puller to pull the weighted traps up from 250-350 feet deep. Many have outfitted their boats or dinghies to target salmon with all the best equipment, spending thousands of dollars for downriggers, trolling motors, special rods, reels, lures and a fishfinder. Some salmon fishing enthusiasts even tow a special boat set up to catch salmon. There is a lot of money invested, and we don't dare ask how much the investment totals compared to the cost of buying quality salmon at the market.

Charter Fishing. At the Waggoner Guide, we love to fish, or to put it more directly, we love to "catch" fish. Rather than investing a fortune "gearing up" to fish, we have gotten into the practice of hiring an expert with all the right equipment and going charter fishing for salmon or halibut once or twice a summer. Prices vary from reasonable to very expensive, ask before booking.

The experts know their local waters, where the fish are and how to fish. We nearly always fill our freezer with as much fish as we can handle and have a lot of fun. Your charter captain can conveniently issue fishing licenses for the charter, and has all the gear and fresh bait. Depending on the location, the charter captain also knows where to take the fish to be processed, flash frozen and stored in the freezer to be shipped home, where you can accept the shipment later.

Guests. We typically treat our guests to a fishing expedition in the Johnstone Strait areas, the Broughtons, Northern B.C. or in Southeast Alaska. A half-day charter will often do it; and with a good guide and good conditions, we limit out within the half-day charter and fill the freezer. We have also found it is best to ask the charter captain when to fish. Many start out the day early in the morning. We have also had excellent results when our charter captain suggested fishing on the evening change of tide.

Finding a Good Charter. Ask around at the marinas you will be visiting. They know the good local fishing guides. You may want to book a charter well in advance of your stay at a marina. When the bite is on, reservations with the best charter captains fill up quickly. The charter captains will often pick you up at your marina or even at your boat on the hook at an anchorage with a fast boat to quickly get you to the best fishing spots in the area. Most charter captains I have fished with take real pride in finding fish and helping you land them on the boat. They want you to catch fish, take them home, and tell your friends!

Catching Fish Without Fishing. There is another technique we have found to catch fish without even dropping a hook in the water. It all starts with being nice to people. Most fisherman catch more fish than they can use. We have seen some excellent techniques among pleasure boaters to catch fish with fresh baked bread, cookies and pies carried down a dock full of commercial fishing boats during the season, offering a trade. Many guys use the traditional technique of walking down the dock with a six pack of beer or a 20-dollar bill, which usually lands a catch. Keep in mind,

however, that some commercial operators are not allowed to sell fish to individuals unless the operator holds a special license.

Freeze the Bounty. Crab can be frozen and keeps well up to a year. Pack in freezer bags or vacuum bags with clean seawater or milk. When you are ready, defrost and squeeze the excess liquid out of the meat. Freezing in milk or seawater also works well for uncooked prawns. It keeps the meat from breaking down and getting freezer burn. While much of your catch may end up frozen for later, fresh fish, prawns and crab, consumed just an hour or two after coming out of the water is about as good as it gets.

Fishing Regulations. Fishing and shellfish collection have become much more complicated and onerous over the years. Laws not only require fishing licenses for specific species, at specific times, and for specific locations, but also set possession limits and storage requirements for fish and shellfish identification purposes. Field Correspondent Deane Hislop, and professional fisherman Gill Graham, share additional information below, regarding fishing in the waters of British Columbia.

SPORT FISHING IN B.C.

Know Before You Go. British Columbia Sport Fishing regulations cover 47 different management areas and vary from area to area, and from year to year, so it is important that anyone planning to wet a line, drop a pot, pick oysters or dig clams in British Columbia tidal water obtain the latest copy of the Department of Fisheries and Oceans (DFO) Canada, British Columbia Sports Fishing Guide from an authorized license dealer. Guides and licenses are also available online at www.pac.dfo-mpo.gc.ca. Beware, regulations can change during the season, so it is wise to monitor the website for any in-season revisions.

If you are going fishing or harvesting shellfish in tidal waters, you need a Tidal Waters Sports Fishing License. If you're going fishing in fresh waters for salmon or any other species, you're required to have a Non-Tidal Angling License issued by the Province of B.C.

Before going fishing, make sure you can answer these five questions:

1. Can I fish at this time, at this location?

2. Is the gear, and the manner in which I plan to use it, legal for catching fish, crab, shrimp or prawns?

3. What can I catch and keep, and in what amount?

4. Do I have the correct license (and supplementary salmon stamp if needed), and do I need to record my catch on the license?

5. How many fish, crab, shrimp, clams, oysters can I possess, and how am I allowed to clean, package and transport them to my residence?

Certain coastal areas are designated rockfish conservation areas (RCAs). Sport fishing is not allowed in RCAs. Gathering of invertebrates by hand picking or diving, or collecting crab, shrimp or prawn by trap, and smelt by gillnet may be allowed. Find out where B.C.'s RCAs are located at bcsportfishingguide.ca.

Reminders:

- Barbless hooks are required for all salmon and sea-run trout fishing. Treble barbless are acceptable in most areas.

- Know the size limit for the area fishing.

- In tidal waters, there's no limit to the number of fishing rods you can use.

- When filleting salmon, the tail must remain attached for the purpose of identification. The adipose fin or fin clip scar must also remain attached to determine if the fish is wild or hatchery.

- It's illegal to willfully hook a salmon. If you should foul hook a salmon, it must be released immediately.

- You must immediately record on your icense all adult chinook you keep.

- Harvesting of northern abalone, an endangered species in B.C., is prohibited.

For more information on sport fishing in B.C., including seasons, limits, gear requirements and restrictions, go to bcsportfishingguide.ca.

Deane Hislop

Posession Limits. The number of fish or shellfish of any species that you are allowed to keep as your daily limit and in possession is determined by the area in which you are fishing. Knowing the number of the area you are in is imperative to staying within your limits and therefore legal. The daily limits are what you are allowed to catch in one day, the in-possession limits are usually twice the daily limit. Once you have your possession limit you are done fishing, you must stop. The catch you eat, while still part of your daily limit, is not part of your possession limit. You may take or send your catch to your ordinary residence; once there, they are no longer part of your possession limit and you can fish again. However, the regulations are very clear on the explanation of your ordinary residence, and your boat is not included. The address on your driver's license is your ordinary residence.

Probably the most misunderstood, is the fact that if you are going to keep the crabs to take home, you cannot clean, cook and pick out the meat. The carapace, which is the shell on the top that you measure to determine his legality, has to be attached to the body. It is possible to lift it part way and clean out the innards, cook him, and then freeze him, however you cannot pick the meat from his shell. Technically, if you have frozen picked crab in your freezer, you committed an offence.

You can ship your catch to your ordinary residence, or someone else could take it home for you, however, there are certain criteria that have to be met to do this; check the regulations. Most importantly, remember the crabs have to have the carapace attached until they reach your residence. You cannot start catching more until your possession limit are in your ordinary residence.

Gill Graham

Rockfish Conservation Areas in B.C. Our coastal waters of British Columbia abound in wonderful delights from the sea. Rockfish species are one of these delicacies we can enjoy. Rockfish come in so many varieties, colours and shapes that a lot of people have no idea what they are catching. There are 37 varieties of Rockfish found on this coast. Yelloweye (red snapper) are rockfish. It is very important to know what species you are catching to stay within the regulations.

As man has learned over the ages, you just can't take and take and expect what you are taking to always be there. To protect our rockfish, Fisheries and Oceans Canada (DFO) designated protected areas for them in 2002. These areas are called rockfish Conservation Areas or RCAs. There are 16 RCA locations along our coast, and you should know where they are. Before you go fishing, go to bcsportfishguide.ca and locate the area in which you will be fishing and take note of the RCAs locations in that area. You might be surprised where some of these RCAs are located. Know before you go. Inside an RCA, you are not allowed to put a line in the water that is targeting any fin fish. You cannot troll for salmon in an RCA since rockfish will go after a lure; you cannot jig for Ling Cod since rockfish will go for your jig. You can handpick or dive for shellfish (invertebrates), you can fish for crab or prawns, you can catch smelt by gillnet, in the area. If your gear is attached to a fishing rod with a hook, jig, or lure, it cannot go in the water.

Many rockfish live to be over 100 years old, that 15-pound yelloweye you just brought up from 250 to 300 feet could be that old. Unlike salmon, rockfish don't survive well with catch and release. That is why there is no size limit for rockfish. If you catch a rockfish, DFO regulations state you have to keep that fish. If you are in an area that allows 1 rockfish per day, you have your one no matter how big he is or if you like him or not, he is yours.

Gill Graham

INTERPRETING NORTHWEST WEATHER

Weather is one of the biggest fears of many boat crews. There is a lot of information available, if you know how to understand it and make effective go, or no-go decisions.

Weather on the Internet, Cell Phone and VHF WX. At the Waggoner Guide, we have developed a means of using all of the weather information available to avoid getting into an uncomfortable situation. Many don't realize how you can use the internet to gather a good picture of the weather. No internet available? If you have cell phone coverage, you can call for weather and buoy reports. Out in a very remote area? If you have VHF WX coverage, you

can gather the right information you need over the radio; it just takes a little more effort. In remote areas of Haida Gwaii and Northern B.C., you can use satellite based systems such as Garmin InReach, Iridium Go, and Globalstar Sat-Fi to access weather information. There is a description of this system in the Cellular Internet and Satellite Communications section of this chapter.

Weather Overview. First, we start by using the internet to view weather information days before our intended departure. We use the NOAA Ocean Prediction Center, Pacific Region, Current Surface Analysis and then the 24, 48, and 96 hour forecasts to look

at the weather patterns as they develop and cross the Pacific Ocean. We look at the High and Low pressure systems and how they are forecast to move; typically from west to east. While this is offshore weather, it provides an indication of the weather systems that will pass over Puget Sound and the Inside Passage. Often in July and early August, a large high pressure system will sit offshore resulting in very good weather for an extended period of time. This is called the Pacific High and typically offers favorable conditions. Next, we look at the isobar lines over the coastal areas where we will be cruising. The isobar lines show the change in barometric pressure over a distance.

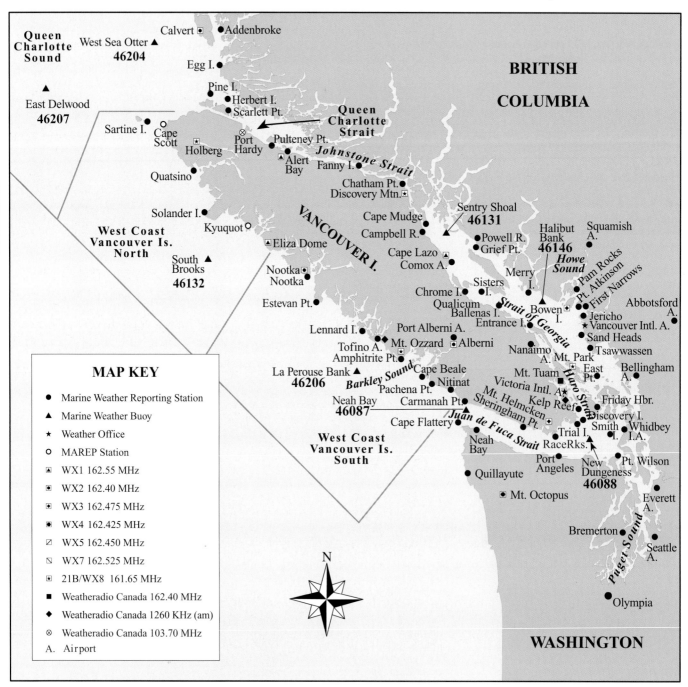

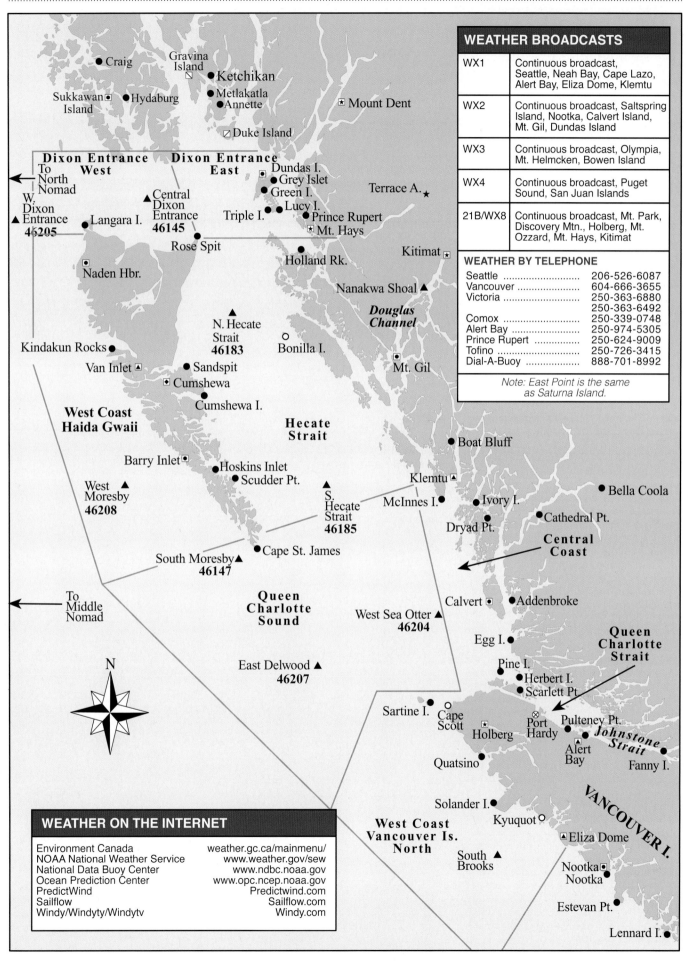

WEATHER BROADCASTS

WX1	Continuous broadcast, Seattle, Neah Bay, Cape Lazo, Alert Bay, Eliza Dome, Klemtu
WX2	Continuous broadcast, Saltspring Island, Nootka, Calvert Island, Mt. Gil, Dundas Island
WX3	Continuous broadcast, Olympia, Mt. Helmcken, Bowen Island
WX4	Continuous broadcast, Puget Sound, San Juan Islands
21B/WX8	Continuous broadcast, Mt. Park, Discovery Mtn., Holberg, Mt. Ozzard, Mt. Hays, Kitimat

WEATHER BY TELEPHONE

Seattle 206-526-6087
Vancouver 604-666-3655
Victoria 250-363-6880
                                       250-363-6492
Comox 250-339-0748
Alert Bay 250-974-5305
Prince Rupert 250-624-9009
Tofino 250-726-3415
Dial-A-Buoy 888-701-8992

Note: East Point is the same as Saturna Island.

Craig
Gravina Island
Ketchikan
Sukkawan Island
Hydaburg
Metlakatla
Annette
Mount Dent
Duke Island

Dixon Entrance West
To North Nomad
W. Dixon Entrance 46205

Dixon Entrance East
Dundas I.
Grey Islet
Green I.
Lucy I.
Terrace A. ★
Central Dixon Entrance 46145
Triple I.
Prince Rupert
Mt. Hays
Langara I.
Rose Spit
Holland Rk.
Kitimat
Naden Hbr.
Nanakwa Shoal

Douglas Channel

Kindakun Rocks
N. Hecate Strait 46183
Bonilla I.
Mt. Gil
Van Inlet
Sandspit
Cumshewa
Cumshewa I.

West Coast Haida Gwaii

Hecate Strait

Barry Inlet
Boat Bluff
Hoskins Inlet
Scudder Pt.
Klemtu
Bella Coola
West Moresby 46208
S. Hecate Strait 46185
McInnes I.
Ivory I.
Dryad Pt.
Cathedral Pt.
South Moresby 46147
Cape St. James
Central Coast

To Middle Nomad

Queen Charlotte Sound
Calvert
Addenbroke
West Sea Otter 46204
Egg I.
Queen Charlotte Strait
East Delwood 46207
Pine I.
Herbert I.
Scarlett Pt.
N
Sartine I.
Cape Scott
Port Hardy
Pulteney Pt.
Johnstone Strait
Holberg
Alert Bay
Fanny I.
Quatsino
VANCOUVER I.
Solander I.
West Coast Vancouver Is. North
Kyuquot
South Brooks
Eliza Dome
Nootka
Nootka
Estevan Pt.
Lennard I.

WEATHER ON THE INTERNET

Environment Canada   weather.gc.ca/mainmenu/
NOAA National Weather Service   www.weather.gov/sew
National Data Buoy Center   www.ndbc.noaa.gov
Ocean Prediction Center   www.opc.ncep.noaa.gov
PredictWind   Predictwind.com
Sailflow   Sailflow.com
Windy/Windyty/Windytv   Windy.com

61

Tighter isobar patterns show areas of wind and its counterclockwise direction around a low. We look for areas of big lazy (widely separated) isobars around a high indicating limited wind. Looking at the weather charts gives us a visual overview of the weather and which systems will be affecting our route over the next couple of days. Even if we do not have access to the internet while en route for a few days, we have the overview. To add to the overview, we look at one of the visual services on the internet at www.windy.com. This web site puts the weather prediction models into motion, where you can see the wind patterns circulating and how they flow across the Pacific. You can also see a visual of the offshore wind and sea conditions. Another popular weather App for mariners is PredictWind. It too presents a lot of visual information when an internet connection is available.

The Forecast. We then look at the NOAA Marine Forecasts for US waters, and when traveling north into British Columbia, we look at the Environment Canada Marine Pacific reports and forecasts. We compare the forecast in text format with the NOAA Surface Analysis charts. They should coincide. Even the 48-hour forecast should coincide with the forecast results. We take notes and start worksheets for the upcoming days.

Weather and Sea Conditions Worksheet. A two page worksheet to facilitate collecting and organizing weather and sea conditions information is available as a free download at the Waggoner Guide Store, free eBook section, Weather Checklist. This worksheet also includes a detailed description of the format and order of information presentation on VHF weather channels and telephone broadcasts. Recording the VHF WX forecasts with your smartphone allows you to replay relevant portions of the forecast.

Weather Reporting Stations. Using the maps in this section, we note and record the weather reporting stations along our route for the day on our worksheet. Next, we gather the weather reports for these stations from either the internet, by calling on a cell phone to the numbers shown on the weather maps, or by listening on the WX VHF. The list of weather reporting stations we need, keeps us focused on what stations we care to record when it is in a continuous audio format on either the phone or VHF WX. When we listen to the WX channels for our area, we listen for those places along our route. On the back of the weather sheet is the outline of the Continuous Marine Broadcasts for the U.S. and Canada. They are different. You can use this to determine where you are in the sequence of a WX broadcast. We write down the synopsis for the area. Next, we record the relevant station reports and then the lighthouse and buoy reports for our route with particular attention to the reported wind direction, speed and sea condition.

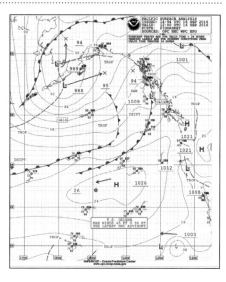

Current Surface Analysis Chart for September 16, 2016 shows High Pressure over the area from Seattle up through the Strait of Georgia. The big lazy isobar lines indicate light wind. Note how this lines up with both the U.S. and Canadian text forecasts on the next page.

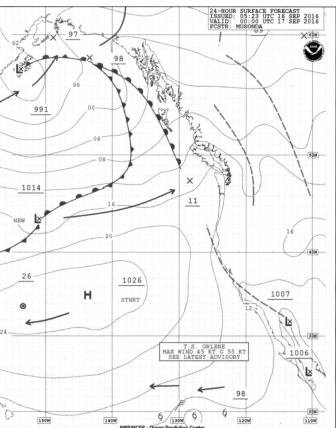

On the 24-Hour Surface Forecast we can see the low moving in from offshore and the isobars bunching up tighter. The text forecast shows the wind and waves picking up as the low comes ashore on Saturday through Saturday night. You can use this to make a go or no-go decision. From this you can see that it would be best to go north on Friday. If you cannot leave then you should most likely wait until Sunday.

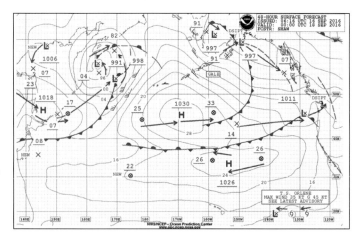

For the 48-Hour Surface Forecast you can see how another low is coming in for a forecast of 2 ft. seas. Tuesday's forecast returns to about 1 ft. seas.

*National Weather
Service Forecast
Synopsis for
Northern Waters*

```
National Weather Service Marine Forecast FZUS56 KSEW

FZUS56 KSEW 160957
CWFSEW

COASTAL WATERS FORECAST FOR WASHINGTON
NATIONAL WEATHER SERVICE SEATTLE WA
300 AM PDT FRI SEP 16 2016

INLAND WATERS OF WESTERN WASHINGTON AND THE NORTHERN AND CENTRAL
WASHINGTON COASTAL WATERS INCLUDING THE OLYMPIC COAST NATIONAL
MARINE SANCTUARY

PZZ100-161615-
300 AM PDT FRI SEP 16 2016

.SYNOPSIS FOR THE NORTHERN AND CENTRAL WASHINGTON COASTAL AND INLAND
WATERS...LIGHT ONSHORE FLOW CONTINUING TODAY. A COLD FRONT WILL
APPROACH THE WASHINGTON COASTAL WATERS FROM THE NW TONIGHT AND MOVE
THROUGH THE AREA DURING THE DAY SATURDAY FOR INCREASED ONSHORE FLOW.
A SURFACE TROUGH WILL MOVE ACROSS THE AREA ON SUNDAY. WEAK ONSHORE
FLOW WILL DEVELOP ON MONDAY AND CONTINUE INTO TUESDAY.


PZZ150-161615-
COASTAL WATERS FROM CAPE FLATTERY TO JAMES ISLAND OUT 10 NM-
300 AM PDT FRI SEP 16 2016

TODAY
N WIND TO 10 KT...BECOMING SW IN THE AFTERNOON. WIND WAVES
1 FT. W SWELL 3 FT AT 10 SECONDS.

TONIGHT
SW WIND 5 TO 15 KT...BECOMING S 10 TO 20 KT AFTER
MIDNIGHT. WIND WAVES 1 TO 3 FT. W SWELL 4 FT AT 9 SECONDS. RAIN
LIKELY IN THE EVENING...THEN RAIN AFTER MIDNIGHT.

SAT
S WIND 15 TO 25 KT...BECOMING SW 5 TO 15 KT IN THE
AFTERNOON. WIND WAVES 2 TO 4 FT. W SWELL 5 FT AT 8 SECONDS. RAIN
LIKELY IN THE MORNING...THEN A CHANCE OF RAIN IN THE AFTERNOON.
```

*Environment
Canada Forecast
for the Strait of
Georgia - South of
Nanaimo*

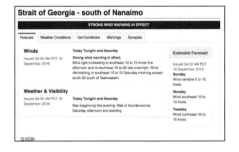

Check the Tides and Currents. Next, we look up in a Tide and Current Guide to determine whether we will be cruising with a Flood or an Ebb current, and the time of slack. This will be useful to understanding the sea state as the day continues over our route. We are looking to be aware or avoid wind opposing wave situations. This information is not included in a weather forecast and must be understood by the mariner using a tide and current guide or software to understand the sea state. Rather than just a go or no-go situation, we may see that it is best to delay a departure for a couple of hours to experience a different current situation. Lastly, we can see where we are in the lunar cycle by looking up the phase of the moon in the Tide and Current guide. A full moon or a new moon means tides and currents will be

at their strongest, and slack will be very short for tidal rapids. Once all this information is gathered, you have the information to develop a pretty good picture of the weather for your departure and route for the day. You will understand where the weather systems are and the resulting conditions for your route. You will know areas of wind; you can check to see if there will be wind opposing a current and determine your strategy. You can see if the forecast matches the conditions reported in a lighthouse or buoy report. If the forecast does not match, beware.

You and Your Boat's Tolerances. Next is comparing forecast conditions and observations with tolerances for your vessel and especially for your crew. You can minimize surprises while underway by gathering and evaluating as much information as possible from as many sources as possible. Gather the information described above and there should not be too many surprises while underway, though Mother Nature is known to shift plans. It's always a good idea to have Fail-safe Contingency plans or duck-in points if things change. For crossing the Strait of Georgia or Cape Caution, you can look to see if you have an opposing, beam-to, or following sea. This may change your go or no-go tolerances or the direction on your route.

Go-NoGo Checklists. Checklists to aid in evaluating conditions for a Go or NoGo decision are located in four chapters describing the passages: Strait of Juan de Fuca; Strait of Georgia; Cape Caution; and Dixon Entrance. These checklists summarize the more important conditions to consult before making that all important decision to proceed with the passage or wait for more favorable conditions. The lists include specifics for the area including weather forecasts, names and numbers for weather buoys, and names of lighthouse and weather station locations to consult when evaluating conditions. The checklists are intended to be summarized lists. Checklist items are grouped into these topic areas: Tides & Currents; Weather System Predictions; Weather & Seas Forecasts; Observations & Present Conditions; Go-NoGo Decision; Fail-Safe Contingency Plans. The heading line for each category includes a brief notation (Internet; Phone; Satellite; VHF) listing the sources for current information.

Underway – Monitor and Log Actual Conditions. At regular intervals along your planned route, make log entries noting the winds and sea conditions you encounter. Record how your boat handled the different seas. If your actual conditions are significantly different from forecast expected conditions, note this in your log and always be prepared to use your contingency plans. Sometimes the best option is to head to a safe port and wait for better conditions.

```
PZZ133-161615-
NORTHERN INLAND WATERS INCLUDING THE SAN JUAN ISLANDS-
300 AM PDT FRI SEP 16 2016

TODAY
LIGHT WIND...BECOMING S TO 10 KT IN THE AFTERNOON. WIND
WAVES 1 FT OR LESS.

TONIGHT
S WIND 5 TO 15 KT. WIND WAVES 2 FT OR LESS. A CHANCE OF
RAIN IN THE EVENING...THEN RAIN AFTER MIDNIGHT.

SAT
SE WIND 10 TO 20 KT...RISING TO 15 TO 25 KT IN THE
AFTERNOON. WIND WAVES 2 TO 4 FT. RAIN IN THE MORNING...THEN RAIN
LIKELY IN THE AFTERNOON.

SAT NIGHT
S WIND 5 TO 15 KT. WIND WAVES 2 FT OR LESS.

SUN
SW WIND TO 10 KT. WIND WAVES 1 FT OR LESS.

SUN NIGHT
SW WIND 5 TO 15 KT...BECOMING S AFTER MIDNIGHT. WIND
WAVES 2 FT OR LESS.

MON
SE WIND 5 TO 15 KT...BECOMING SW. WIND WAVES 2 FT OR LESS.

TUE
SW WIND TO 10 KT. WIND WAVES 1 FT OR LESS.
```

*National Weather Service Summary
Forecast for Northern Waters*

*The Halibut Bank - Buoy Report shows
actual conditions on Friday, September
16th with wave heights of 1 foot or less. A
DPD of 3 seconds gives you a warning of
a light chop.*

Reviewing these log entries over time will help develop your personal Go or No-Go thresholds for future planning.

Planned vs Actual. After arriving at your destination, review your log of actual conditions encountered along your route to help develop experience with the forecasting tools. This will help with future planning. For example, what a forecast of 15 to 20 knot winds felt like, and how your vessel handled in five to six foot seas with a Dominant Wave Period (interval) of 12-15 seconds, most likely a rolling swell.

For a better understanding of weather. Consider learning more and taking a weather course. The Waggoner Guide and our Seattle Boat Show University or Cruisers College programs offer a few different courses with weather experts, from 3-hour seminars to multi-day courses. Understanding the weather is a fascinating part of boating. The rewards when you get it right are substantial for you and your crew.

RUNNING IN THE FOG

Fog is an unavoidable reality of summer weather in the Northwest and on the British Columbia coast. On the Strait of Juan de Fuca, Vancouver Island's west coast, Johnstone Strait, Queen Charlotte Strait and Sound, and the Central Coast, you can pretty much depend on encountering fog almost daily from mid-July through September and sometimes much later in the season. So learning to navigate safely in "low viz" is critical.

The American Meteorological Society's *Glossary of Meteorology* defines fog as a collection of water droplets suspended in the atmosphere near the earth's surface that affects visibility. In temperate coastal areas like ours, fog results when warm air cools as it passes over cold water, which causes water vapor to condense and saturate the air. Fog may form in the evening, overnight or early-morning hours, then dissipate as the day warms. It may start sneaking over the trees into your anchorage near the end of cocktail hour – and you know you will wake up to pea soup.

When you do – and you will if you venture far from Puget Sound or the Strait of Georgia – here are some thoughts to help you prepare for your next "low-viz" passage.

Go or no-go? Should you set out in poor visibility in the first place? If you don't really have to go, don't. Running in fog is a stress-inducing business that can take the fun out of cruising, and it can be dangerous. The wisest course may be to wait for the fog to burn off, as it always does sooner or later.

In weighing a decision to run in fog, consider how well you know the waters you'll be navigating – a run through home water is a completely different challenge from transiting an area for the first time. Are the waters you'll navigate unobstructed – or encumbered with hazards that radar may not help you avoid? How much vessel traffic – big and small – might you encounter? High-traffic areas of Puget Sound, the Strait of Georgia and the Inside Passage are subject to vessel traffic management systems. Do you know how to listen for VTS operators' instructions to mariners around you and call them for guidance?

Make a Plan B. Where will you go if it becomes too risky to continue…or your nerves fail you? Is there a harbor en route that is clear enough to enter safely even if you can't see a thing?

And consider this: if you cruise long enough and seriously enough you will probably have to run in fog someday. If you can do it safely, why not try? It can be a tremendous learning opportunity and confidence-booster.

Slow down. This sounds obvious – but some boaters have trouble doing this under any conditions. Reducing your speed increases the amount of time you have to spot obstacles, hazards or vessels and take evasive action. If you hit something at reduced speed, it will do less damage and hopefully you will avoid catastrophic damage.

Trust your equipment. It goes without saying that you should have complete confidence in your navigation suite – plotter, sounder, radar, AIS and, yes, paper charts – you should know how to use them and know their limitations. We rely on sight to orient ourselves in space and find our way. Deprive us of visual cues and we veer off course or ramble in circles, still convinced we're on course. But magnetic compasses have helped mariners for centuries, so trust yours. Better yet, the electronic compass built into your vessel's autopilot is even more accurate and enables your pilot to steer a precise course for hours or days, freeing you to keep a closer watch.

Radar paints a clear picture of your surroundings, *as long you know how to read it*. It's a good habit to run with radar even in clear conditions so you can see how blips and images appear on screen in relation to vessels and objects around you while you can still see them. Add an AIS receiver/transceiver and you'll have a clear, precise reading of the course, speed and size of vessels you may not be able to see, especially the big, fast-moving ones.

However, it is the modern chartplotter running reliable electronic charts that brings safe passages in low visibility within reach of recreational mariners. Zoomed in to an appropriate level, a good plotter enables you to accurately pinpoint hazards you can't see and find safe water through them. (Remember: not all obstacles on all charts are depicted precisely, so a margin of error is prudent!). Set your radar range to the same scale as your plotter – or overlay it on the plotter if you can – so you can match charted features with radar for a clearer picture of your surroundings. Three-dimensional charts that show bathymetric data are better still. Use your plotter's predicted track feature to point your way past hazards.

Finally, use your VHF radio. Commercial vessels routinely broadcast their approach to points or channels which may bring them close to other traffic, so monitor Channel 16 and VTS channels. Follow their example and announce your intentions when you enter waters where you may meet other vessels; invite concerned craft to respond. If you spot a converging target on radar, call them to determine their intentions and discuss how to pass or cross safely.

Listen and look carefully. There is still a place for our own sharpened senses when we think we can't see diddly. In steamship days, skippers and pilots used to blow a whistle and listen for the time it took for echoes to return in order to determine their distance from shore. It makes sense to throttle back from time to time. Step on deck and listen for whatever you might hear: a horn, voices, a nearby outboard, birds calling, the lap of waves against the shoreline, the low thrum of really big engines…or nothing at all.

In restricted visibility, Collision Regulations require you to sound a single prolonged (four to six seconds) horn blast every two minutes if you are under way, and two prolonged blasts if you are stopped. Sound carries well over still water and in fog and sends a clear message to anyone around. Don't forget to use your nose, as well. Water smells different than land; the odor of guano may tip you off to a seabird colony on an isolated rock; a whiff of engine exhaust may warn you of vessels nearby.

Even when you're sure you can't see a thing, you often still can – if you look hard enough. Have your crew keep an intent bow watch for anything you may not see from the helm. Step outside and look around carefully yourself. The white hull of that lone sport fisher rolling in the chop may appear so faintly you aren't sure it's there. Or the superstructure of a container ship or ferry may float serenely through the top layer of the mist…and, hopefully, it won't be too close.

[Duart Snow]

BUOYS, BEACONS AND RANGES

Red, Right, Returning means leave **Red** navigation aids off your **Right** hand when you're **Returning** from seaward. If the navigation mark is not red, leave it off your left hand when you're returning from seaward.

This is the general rule in U.S. and Canadian waters, with three subtle refinements:

• Safe water mark. A buoy with red and white vertical stripes that marks an approach or mid-channel. Unobstructed water surrounds this mark. Both inbound and outbound, it is good practice to leave this buoy to port.

• Preferred channel mark. A buoy or a beacon with red and green horizontal bands. This aid marks a channel junction or an obstruction. While the aid can be passed on either side, the color of the top band indicates the preferred or main channel.

• Isolated danger mark. An aid—either a buoy or a beacon—with black and red horizontal bands that marks an isolated danger (an example would be the Blakely Island Shoal Isolated Danger Buoy DS, west of Blakely Island in the San Juan Islands). These marks have navigable water all around, but should not be approached closely without caution.

Nuns. All red buoys marking channels are shaped as cones, and are called nuns. Most nun buoys are painted solid red. If the nun buoy has a green horizontal band painted on it, the buoy marks the meeting of two channels, with the left channel being the preferred, or main, channel. (If you leave the buoy to starboard, you will be in the left channel.) If lighted, the light will be red.

Cans. All green buoys marking channels are called cans. They are shaped like, well, cans. Most can buoys are painted solid green. If the can buoy has a horizontal red band painted on it, the buoy marks the meeting of two channels, with the right channel the preferred, or main, channel. If lighted, the light will be green.

Beacons. Buoys float, and are held in place by heavy anchoring systems, but beacons are permanent navigation aids attached to the earth. Beacons can be located on land, installed on docks or breakwaters, or mounted on pilings. A lighthouse is a beacon. A beacon not on land will be placed in shallow water outside a channel. Do not pass a beacon close aboard. Give it considerable room.

An unlighted beacon is called a daybeacon. A lighted beacon is called a minor light. A minor light marking the right side of a channel will carry a red light (Red, Right, Returning). A minor light marking the left side of a

channel will carry a green light. If a minor light marks the meeting of two channels, it will be red if the left channel is preferred; green if the right channel is preferred.

Daymarks are the colored panels mounted on beacons. Red panels are triangle shaped; green panels are square. A triangle shaped red panel with a green horizontal stripe indicates the meeting of two channels, with the left channel the preferred, or main channel. A square panel painted green with a red horizontal stripe indicates the meeting of two channels, with the right channel the preferred channel.

Whenever a navigation aid is marked with a horizontal stripe of contrasting color, the color at the top of the aid indicates the preferred, or main channel.

Approaching a channel from seaward, buoys and beacons are numbered, beginning with the marks to seaward. Red buoys, daybeacons, and minor lights carry even numbers, such as 2, 4, 6, and so on. Green buoys, daybeacons, and minor lights carry odd numbers, such as 1, 3, 5, and so on. Depending on the channel, it might be appropriate to skip some numbers, so that buoy 6 is roughly opposite buoy 5, even if no buoy 4 exists.

Ranges. Ranges are used to help a boat stay in the middle of a narrow channel.

Ranges are rectangular panels stood vertically, each with a wide stripe running from top to bottom down the middle of the panel. Ranges are attached to the earth and arranged in pairs, one behind the other. The rear range board stands taller than the front range board. To use a range, steer until the rear range board appears to be on top of the front board. You can steer toward a range, looking ahead (leading range), or away from a range, sighting astern (back range).

Buoys and beacons are not selected and placed at random. They follow a plan, although to a newcomer the plan may at times seem obscure.

Despite the complexity of the buoyage and light system, you will find that as you understand it better your enjoyment afloat will increase. At some point you will want a thorough explanation of the entire system. For U.S. waters it will be found in the introduction to the Coast Guard Light List. For Canadian waters it will be found partly in the introduction to the Canadian Coast Guard List of Lights, Buoys and Fog Signals, and completely in the Canadian Coast Guard publication, The Canadian Aids to Navigation System. Latest editions of these publications should be aboard every boat. They are available at chart agencies and chandleries.

RED, RIGHT, RETURNING from the sea means the conical red nun buoy marks the right side of the channel. Vessels returning from the sea upstream will leave red navigation aids to starboard. Red aids are assigned even numbers, beginning with No. 2 at the seaward end of the channel.

Nun Buoy

A GREEN CAN buoy marks the left side of the channel. Vessels returning from the sea or upstream will leave green navigation aids to port. Green aids are assigned odd numbers, beginning with No. 1 at the seaward end of the channel. Buoys and beacons can be lighted or unlighted.

Can Buoy

A BEACON, such as this light at Webster Point in Lake Washington, is attached to the earth, and should be given a good offing. Port-hand beacons carry square green dayboards; starboard-hand beacons carry red triangular dayboards.

Lighted Beacon

CYLINDRICAL WHITE RESTRICTED OPERATIONS BUOYS, such as this one, mark speed zones, restricted anchoring areas, fish habitats and other important information.

Restricted Operation Buoy

BOARDINGS

"Welcome Aboard" – may not be the first thing that comes to mind when someone in uniform steps aboard your vessel. However, if we are prepared, it's more likely that we will be ready to welcome these agents of safety and law enforcement when we are out cruising. There are a number of different agencies and agents that may board recreational vessels.

U.S. Agencies. On the U.S. side of the border, the Coast Guard (USCG) routinely boards vessels to check for compliance with required devices and safety equipment. If underway and approached by a USCG patrol vessel for boarding, the officer may want you to slow down, but continue underway. They will come alongside and board while underway; however, you may choose to come to a stop. An officer will board and conduct a standard safety inspection. Their inspection includes checking for proper vessel documentation, personal floatation devices, and vessel safety equipment. The inspection takes about 15 to 30 minutes and includes a 'results form' with any deficiencies noted on the signed form. Any deficiencies noted on the form must be addressed and acknowledged by the Coast Guard. If there are no deficiencies, you will receive the same signed form noting the successful inspection. Keep this form on the vessel as it serves to waive any subsequent inspection boarding within the next 12 months.

State police, county Sheriff, city police, and port authorities have on-the-water patrol boats for safety, search and rescue, and law enforcement. Agents of these departments can and do board recreational vessels. Unlike

Retain the paperwork from a boarding, it will save you from future boardings for one year.

the U.S. Coast Guard's once-a-year limit on vessel boarding, there is no limit for these other law enforcement agencies.

Canada Agencies. On the Canadian side of the border, Canadian Coast Guard does not have maritime or law enforcement responsibilities and does not perform vessel inspections. Royal Canadian Mounted Police (RCMP) and city police have law enforcement responsibilities. RCMP does not routinely board vessels for marine safety inspections.

When cruising near the U.S. and Canada international border, you may be stopped and boarded by agents of the respective border patrol (U.S. Customs and Border Patrol, and Canadian Border Services Agency). They patrol the border crossings with their high-speed boats.

While fishing, crabbing, or prawning, agents from wildlife departments from Washington, Alaska, or British Columbia may board your vessel to check for compliance with seafood-collection rules and laws.

Preparation. While there are no guarantees, responsible cruisers can reduce their chances of boarding by keeping their boats clean, orderly, and in good condition; running the boat cautiously and competently, consistent with weather and sea conditions; doing nothing that would invite closer scrutiny. A current Coast Guard Auxiliary voluntary safety inspection sticker in the window might be a help. Consider doing your own inspection before the boating season to make sure you have all of your documentation, flares and approved life jackets or PFDs, placards and other items in order. For the complete list, you can search USCG Vessel Safety Checklist on the internet and find the same list used by the Coast Guard. Expect more checks by small boats. We watched armed USCG personnel in a mid-20-foot inflatable check the boats on moorings in Fossil Bay (Sucia Island) and board one of them.

Have all required boat documentation, licenses, and other paperwork ready in the event you are boarded. It is helpful to have a folder with the most current official documents. Keep a second folder for copies of original documents in the event you need to leave a copy with an official. Record each boarding event in your log, including the agent's name and authority. These agents help keep our cruising waters safe; thank them with a smile.

U.S. Coast Guard may want to board your vessel while remaining underway.

HOMELAND SECURITY

Here are some do's and don't's, drawn from material published by the U.S. Coast Guard and expanded upon by our own experiences.

Keep your distance from all military, cruise line or commercial shipping. For U.S. naval vessels, slow to minimum speed within 500 yards, and do not approach any U.S. naval vessel within 100 yards. Violation of the Naval Vessel Protection Zone is a felony offense. If you must pass within 100 yards of a U.S. naval vessel, you must contact the vessel or its Coast Guard escort vessel on VHF 16. The only exceptions to these requirements would be in a congested area, where there is no way to give this kind of room, or in a narrow channel, such as the mouth of the Snohomish River in Everett, which fronts on the Navy base there. In such cases, navigate slowly, predictably, and obey all instructions.

Observe and avoid all security zones. Also avoid commercial port operation areas, especially those that involve military, cruise line, or petroleum facilities. Observe and avoid other restricted areas near dams, power plants etc. Violators will face a quick, determined, and severe response. Translation: You risk being blown out of the water. The buoyed security zone protecting the Trident submarine base at Bangor, in Hood Canal,

is a good example. The restricted area is patrolled by four high-speed small craft, at least two of them with impressive guns mounted on the decks. Although we give the security zone a wide berth as we go by, it is obvious that we are being watched. When we increase our speed from 8.5 knots to 16 knots one of the patrol craft will turn abruptly and run on a parallel course at our speed until we pass the far boundary. We thought about taking photos of the base with at least one of the patrol boats in view, but decided it would be prudent to motor along as predictably and innocently as possible.

Don't stop or anchor beneath bridges or in the channel. If you do, you can expect to be boarded by law enforcement officials.
Be alert for anything that looks peculiar or out of the ordinary. Report suspicious activities to local authorities, the Coast Guard, or port or marina security. Do not approach or challenge those acting in a suspicious manner. Suspicious behavior includes:

- Suspicious persons conducting unusual activities near bridges, refineries, or around high security areas on or near the water
- Individuals establishing roadside stands near marinas or other waterfront facilities

- Persons photographing or making diagrams of things, such as the underside of a bridge, the area around nuclear powerplants, and waterfront facilities near what might be high-risk vessels
- Unknown or suspicious persons loitering for long periods of time in waterfront areas
- Suspicious persons renting or attempting to procure or "borrow" watercraft
- Suspicious vendors attempting to sell or deliver merchandise or drop off packages in waterfront areas

Always secure and lock your boat when not on board. Do not leave your boat accessible to others. Always take the keys with you. **When storing your boat, make sure it is secure and its engine is disabled**. If the boat is on a trailer, make the trailer as immovable as possible.

Be Prepared for a Vessel Boarding. Expect to see U.S. Coast Guard surveillance and vessel boardings. The physical size and geographic complexity of Northwest waters make these waters difficult to patrol and quite "porous" for vessels doing illegal things. More "assets," as the military calls them, are being deployed here.

STATE AND PROVINCIAL PARKS AND PUBLIC WHARVES

The waters from Puget Sound north into B.C. are dotted with more than 200 state, provincial, and national parks, and in B.C., more than 220 public wharves.

Washington Parks. At the state level, parks are administered by the Washington State Parks and Recreation Commission and by the Department of Natural Resources (DNR). Usually, DNR sites are on the primitive side. State parks, which tend to be more developed, charge for moorage at buoys and docks. For docks and floats, expect to pay $.70 per foot, $14 minimum. Mooring buoys are $15. The dock or buoy fee applies after 1:00 p.m., payable for even a stop-and-go visit, such as walking the dog. *Unless otherwise marked, buoys are for boats 45 feet and less; boats longer than 45 feet are not allowed.* Rafting is allowed for boats 36 feet and less. Each rafted boat must pay a moorage fee.

State parks charge moorage fees year-round. Annual moorage permits are available and valid from January 1 to December 31, $5 per foot, $60 minimum. Contact Washington State Parks Information, (360) 902-8844 (Monday through Friday), or infocent@parks.wa.gov. Or check their informative website at parks.state.wa.us/435/Boating.

Campsite fees are paid in addition to dock or mooring buoy fees. Self-register ashore for moorage or campsites.

Boat launch sites. State parks with boat launches charge fees of $7. The launch fee includes the daily parking fee. Annual launch permits cost $80 and are valid for a year from date of purchase. Contact Washington State Parks, (360) 902-8844, or from www.parks.wa.gov/boating/launch/.

Reservations. Moorage is unreserved. Leaving a dinghy or other personal property at a buoy or dock does not reserve moorage. Rafting is permitted, but not mandatory. Rafting is allowed on buoys, within specified limits. Reservations (for campsites only) in all state parks are accepted. Call toll-free (888) 226-7688.

Department of Natural Resources parks generally are primitive or have few facilities, and most do not charge fees.

Washington Boater Education Card. All operators of boats with motors of 15 horsepower or more born after January 1, 1955 are required to have their Washington State Boater Education Card. Washington State Parks administers this program. See their website at http://boat.wa.gov/ or call (360) 902-8555.

If you are boating in Canadian waters for longer than 44 days a Canadian Operator Card, or the equivalent issued by a state in the U.S. is required. The Washington Boater Education Card qualifies for cruising more than 44 days, as do U.S. Coast Guard licenses such as Captain's or Mate's license.

Public docks provide access to parks and islands.

Canadian Boater Pleasure Craft Operator Card (PCOC). Canada has a similar program for its boaters, requiring boater education and certification. In B.C., several firms offer classes and testing services to prove competency. A special program called "Rental Boating Safety Checklist" is for power-driven rental boats and bareboat charter boats. Consult your Canadian charter company for more information and requirements.

B.C. Parks, Including Gulf Islands National Park Reserve Parks. Most B.C. marine parks have floats or mooring buoys, and safe, all-weather anchorages. Marine parks are open year-round. Some have no on-shore facilities, others have day-use facilities, picnic areas, and developed campsites. Most parks have drinking water. Overnight moorage fees ($12 for a buoy; $2/meter for dock moorage) are charged at a number of the more developed parks. No rafting is permitted on mooring buoys. No charge for anchoring, even with a stern-tie to shore. Tent sites are extra. Contact B.C. Parks General Information at www.env.gov.bc.ca/bcparks. For more information on the Gulf Islands National Park Reserve, contact (866) 944-1744, or see their website at www.pc.gc.ca. On the homepage select "Find a National Park" and select "Gulf Islands National Park Reserve."

Public Wharves. In British Columbia, public wharves provide moorage for commercial vessels (primarily the fishing fleet) and pleasure craft. Especially in the off-season, public wharves are filled with fish boats, leaving little or no moorage for pleasure craft. Facilities vary, from a dock only, to fully-serviced marinas. Most of the public wharves now are operated by local harbor authorities or their equivalents. Locally-run public wharves charge market rates, and may reserve space for pleasure craft. Moorage fees vary. Public wharves are easily identified by their red-painted railings.

NO DISCHARGE IN PUGET SOUND
In 2018 Washington State designated all of Puget Sound waters up to the Canadian Border as a No Discharge Zone. It is illegal to discharge any (treated and untreated) black water in this zone. Compliance means using an approved sanitation device holding tank and having thru-hull valves secured with wire ties or zip ties. Gray water is not included in these regulations.

NO DISCHARGE ZONES IN B.C.
Discharge of black water is not allowed in the following areas. Approved holding tanks are required in these areas. Macerator treatment systems, even if approved in the U.S., do not qualify. "Gray water" is not included in the regulations. It's okay to take a shower and wash dishes.

– Pirates Cove (no gray)	– Tod Inlet	– Ladysmith Harbour
– Prideaux Haven	– Victoria Harbour	– Mansons Landing
– Roscoe Bay	– Carrington Bay	– Montague Harbour
– Smuggler Cove	– Cortes Bay	– Pilot Bay
– Squirrel Cove	– Gorge Harbour	

WHAT RECREATIONAL BOATERS NEED TO KNOW ABOUT VTS

Much of the information below is general in nature. It is intended to give recreational boaters a broad understanding of the Vessel Traffic Service (VTS) and how VTS can improve safety for all boats.

VTS is primarily for commercial vessels, although all power driven vessels 40 meters (131 feet) or longer, commercial or recreational, must be active participants. Active VTS participants are required to maintain radio watch on the assigned VTS channel for the waters they are in, and to call in at designated points with their location, course, speed, and estimated time of arrival (ETA) at the next call-in point. The VTS centers keep track of all active participant vessels and advise of any traffic that might interfere.

All power driven vessels between 20 meters (66 feet) and 40 meters (131 feet) must be passive participants, meaning they must keep a radio watch on the appropriate VTS radio channels.

Pleasure craft should monitor VTS. Although recreational vessels shorter than 20 meters are exempt from being active or passive participants in VTS, they must know how to keep out of the way of large, slow-maneuvering vessels. We keep our radio set on the VTS channel for the area we are cruising to hear where the large commercial vessels are operating.

Turn Point Special Operating Area. Turn Point is the northwest corner of the San Juan Islands' Stuart Island, where Haro Strait joins Boundary Pass. Turn Point is a blind corner. A recreational vessel could be completely unaware of a fast approaching ship on the other side. Monitor channel 11.

Separation Zones. The VTS lanes in Puget Sound, the Strait of Juan de Fuca, and the approaches to Haro Strait and Rosario Strait are divided into inbound and outbound lanes, with a separation zone between the two. The separation zones vary in width and are shown in magenta on the charts.

With the following precautions, pleasure craft are free to operate in the Puget Sound VTS lanes:

Pleasure craft, even vessels under sail, do not have right-of-way over VTS participant vessels and must not impede them in any way.

Wherever practical, pleasure craft should stay out of the VTS lanes, or at least minimize the length of time spent in the lanes. Large commercial vessels are required to remain in the VTS lanes unless cleared to do otherwise. It makes no sense to compete for that space.

If inbound in the VTS lanes, run in the inbound lane; if outbound, run in the outbound lane. Keep a lookout astern for overtaking vessels.

If crossing the VTS lane(s), try to cross at right angles to minimize the time spent in the traffic lanes. This is not always possible or practical, but it should be the objective.

Do not loiter or fish in the VTS separation zones.

Be aware of what is going on—ahead, astern, and to the sides. In the jargon this is called "situational awareness." Give large vessels lots of room. Make early and substantial course adjustments. Show them some side, meaning the side of your boat. (This is good practice whenever two vessels meet, regardless of size.)

If there's any doubt at all, cross behind a large vessel, not in front of it. A container ship traveling at only 11 knots needs more than a mile to come to a complete stop. Many container ships travel at 20 knots or more, which lengthens their stopping distance.

If you see a tug, look for a tow. Never, ever, pass between a tug and its tow. Leave ample room when crossing behind a tow.

Radio communication. While active VTS participants (large vessels and tugs with tows) are required to maintain radio watch on the appropriate VTS radio channel, such as VHF 14 in Puget Sound south of Bush Point, they are not required to monitor VHF 16, and many do not. Participants in Seattle Traffic waters also are required to monitor VHF 13, the U.S. bridge-to-bridge channel. Canada does not use VHF 13.

To contact a large vessel in Seattle Traffic

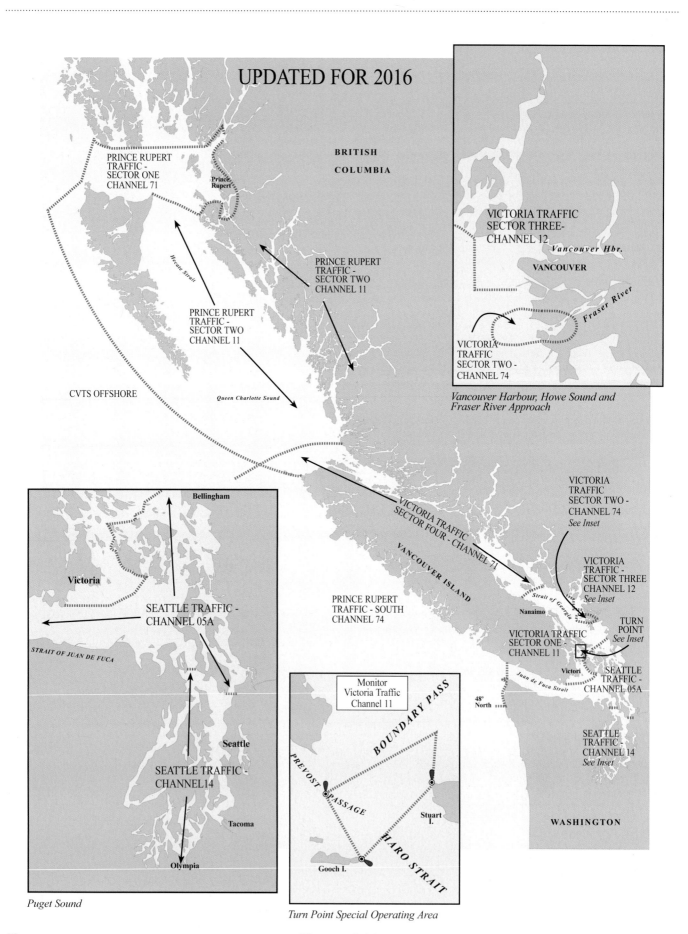

UPDATED FOR 2016

BRITISH COLUMBIA

PRINCE RUPERT TRAFFIC - SECTOR ONE CHANNEL 71

Prince Rupert

Hecate Strait

PRINCE RUPERT TRAFFIC - SECTOR TWO CHANNEL 11

PRINCE RUPERT TRAFFIC - SECTOR TWO CHANNEL 11

CVTS OFFSHORE

Queen Charlotte Sound

VICTORIA TRAFFIC SECTOR THREE- CHANNEL 12

Vancouver Hbr.

VANCOUVER

Fraser River

VICTORIA TRAFFIC SECTOR TWO - CHANNEL 74

Vancouver Harbour, Howe Sound and Fraser River Approach

VICTORIA TRAFFIC SECTOR FOUR - CHANNEL 71

VANCOUVER ISLAND

PRINCE RUPERT TRAFFIC - SOUTH CHANNEL 74

VICTORIA TRAFFIC SECTOR TWO - CHANNEL 74 *See Inset*

VICTORIA TRAFFIC - SECTOR THREE CHANNEL 12 *See Inset*

Strait of Georgia

Nanaimo

VICTORIA TRAFFIC SECTOR ONE - CHANNEL 11

TURN POINT *See Inset*

Victori

SEATTLE TRAFFIC - CHANNEL 05A

Juan de Fuca Strait

SEATTLE TRAFFIC - CHANNEL 14 *See Inset*

WASHINGTON

Bellingham

Victoria

SEATTLE TRAFFIC - CHANNEL 05A

STRAIT OF JUAN DE FUCA

Seattle

SEATTLE TRAFFIC - CHANNEL 14

Tacoma

Olympia

Puget Sound

Monitor Victoria Traffic Channel 11

BOUNDARY PASS

PREVOST PASSAGE

Stuart I.

48° North

HARO STRAIT

Gooch I.

Turn Point Special Operating Area

VTS RADIO CHANNELS

TRAFFIC AREA	AREA DESCRIPTION	VHF CHANNEL
Seattle Traffic	Puget Sound west of Whidbey Island and south of Bush Point.	14
Seattle Traffic	Strait of Juan de Fuca (including Canadian waters), and Puget Sound north of Bush Point on the west side of Whidbey Island, including the San Juan Islands and Rosario Strait. Also the entire east side of Whidbey Island.	05A
Prince Rupert Traffic – South	West Coast of Vancouver Island & approaches to the Strait of Juan de Fuca.	74
Victoria Traffic – Sector One	Southern Area, Race Rocks (Victoria) to Ballenas Island/ Merry Island. This includes Haro Strait, Boundary Pass, the Gulf Islands, and the southern part of the Strait of Georgia, except for Vancouver Harbour and the Fraser River.	11
Turn Point Special Operating Area	Haro Strait/Boundary Pass. See map and text.	11
Victoria Traffic – Sector Two	Fraser River, Sand Heads to Shoal Point, New Westminster.	74
Victoria Traffic – Sector Three	Vancouver Harbour and approaches.	12
Victora Traffic – Sector Four	Ballenas Island/Merry Island north to Cape Caution. This includes the northern part of the Strait of Georgia and Inside Passage waters north to Cape Caution.	71
Prince Rupert Traffic – Sector One	Prince Rupert Harbour & approaches, including the north end of Grenville Channel, Chatham Sound, and all of Dixon Entrance to Langara Island.	71
Prince Rupert Traffic – Sector Two	Remainder of Zone. Hecate Strait, Cape Caution north to Alaska on the west side of Haida Gwaii.	11

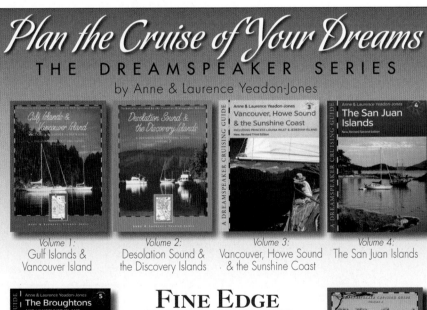

Volume 1:
Gulf Islands &
Vancouver Island

Volume 2:
Desolation Sound &
the Discovery Islands

Volume 3:
Vancouver, Howe Sound
& the Sunshine Coast

Volume 4:
The San Juan Islands

Volume 5:
The Broughtons

FINE EDGE
Nautical & Recreational Publishing

Available in the U.S. at nautical bookstores, and
WaggonerGuide.com or call 360-299-8500.

Available in Canada through HarbourPublishing.com
or call 800-667-2988 to order.
Also on Amazon

Volume 6:
The West Coast of
Vancouver Island

waters call on VHF 13. In Canada VTS waters call on the appropriate VTS channel, such as VHF 11 in southern Strait of Georgia waters.

We have made such calls a few times with excellent results. Twice in narrow channels, the large vessel voluntarily reduced speed to lower its wake. One time it was a cruise ship in northern B.C.; the other time it was a deadly-looking U.S. warship at the mouth of Admiralty Inlet.

Consolidation of Canadian Marine Communications and Traffic Services (MCTS) Centres.
The following stations consolidated in 2016 were:
• Vancouver Coast Guard Radio consolidated to Victoria Coast Guard Radio

• Comox Coast Guard Radio consolidated to Victoria Coast Guard Radio

• Tofino Coast Guard Radio consolidated to Prince Rupert Coast Guard Radio

Monitor VTS channels. This is called being a passive VTS participant. Many of the transmissions are extremely brief: a vessel calls in and is off the air almost before you realize it. But by monitoring you'll learn that a ferry is departing the dock, or that a large vessel is about to emerge from a channel just around the next point, or that a container ship is calling in from 5 miles behind you, traveling at 22 knots.

These are good things to know, even in clear weather. In thick weather, at night or in fog, the information is invaluable. We have even called the VTS center ourselves, such as prior to a fog-bound crossing of Puget Sound. We kept our transmission brief, and made sure we weren't a pest. Their response advised us of any potentially conflicting traffic and was always helpful, polite, and professional.

VESSEL TRAFFIC SERVICE
PHONE NUMBERS

Washington:
USCG Puget Sound Vessel Traffic Center (206) 217-6040

B.C.
Prince Rupert MCTS Centre (250) 627-3074 or (250) 627-3075

Victoria MCTS Centre (250) 363-6333

71

B.C. Marine Parks – a name you recognize and one that conjures up great memories and mental images. **B.C. Marine Parks Forever Society** – probably a name not as recognizable but one that should be. Through the work of the B.C. Marine Parks Forever Society, marine parks in BC have been expanded and made more accessible. Their financial support enables land acquisitions for new or expanded marine parks. Through their work and support, stern-tie pins, chains, and plates have been installed in many of the most popular parks. All this, thanks to financial donations from organizations, yacht clubs, and individual boaters like you.

Installations at Melanie Cove, Prideaux Haven, Smugglers Cove and Halkett Bay came about through the Forever Society working directly with B.C. Parks. As of December 31, 2017, the Society picked up 100 percent of the $45,000 project for stern-tie installations. In 2018, more than 100 new pins, chains, and ID plates were installed in 8 marine parks at an estimated cost of $70,000. The 2018 stern-tie project included installations at the following locations: Gulf Islands – Conover Cove and Princess Cove on Wallace Island; Howe Sound – Halkett Bay; Sunshine Coast – Copeland Islands and Smugglers Cove; Desolation Sound – Galley Bay, Grace Harbour, Laura Cove, Melanie Cove, Roscoe Bay, Tenedos Bay, and Walsh Cove.

A standard design for the pins and chains was selected based on a study provided by a qualified engineering firm paid for by the Society. Boaters using these installations will notice that the pins are anchored above the high-tide line to which a length of chain is attached long enough to reach the low-tide level. There is no ring attached to the chain. The chains have large links that allow stern-tie lines to pass through a link at any position along the chain. This design makes it easier for boaters to attach their stern line at all tide levels. As boaters, we all love marine parks, which are often full during the busy summer months. Additional stern-tie installations at these popular beautiful marine parks help insure that everyone gets a chance to experience these very special destinations.

If there are no stern-tie pins available, find a secure object on shore such as a large rock or downed log. Have a length of disposable line to form a loop around the object, then run your stern-tie line through the loop so that you can release your stern-tie line from the boat. If possible, try not to tie around live trees, which may scar or damage the tree.

Part of the Society's ongoing work is the acquisition of islands and island property for future marine parks. The Forever Society recently negotiated the purchase of a 6-acre island in the Harmony Islands group near the mouth of Jervis Inlet. The eastern side of the island, closest to the mainland, is completely protected and is an ideal location for moorage. Past acquisitions by the Forever Society include Octopus Island, Smugglers Cove, Jedediah Island, Pirates Cove, Wakes Cove, and Wallace Island among other locations; these islands continue to be favorite destinations on both sides of the international border.

The B.C. Marine Parks Forever Society was formed in 1990 to assist B.C. Parks in protecting recreational boating interests and to raise funds for the purchase of B.C. Marine Parks and other programs like the Stern-tie Program. The B.C. Parks Department approached the Council of BC Yacht Clubs in 1989 to set up a "charitable organization" for such a purpose. Members of the Society are volunteers and work hard to protect the interests of all boaters, from kayaks to sailboats and yachts.

We at Waggoner Cruising Guide encourage fellow boaters to support the Forever Society, which is committed to making improvements that enhance the boating experience. The Forever Society is a Canada non-profit organization. To learn more about the Society and their work, go to www.marineparksforever. ca. Financial contributions can be sent to **B.C. Marine Parks Forever Society**, 400 Newcastle Avenue, Nanaimo, B.C. V9S 4J1 Canada. Donations coming from the U.S., with a requested tax donation receipt, can be sent to American Friends of Canadian Land Trusts (www.afoclt.org), 702 Kentucky Street #663, Bellingham, WA 98225; you can request that your contribution be applied to the B.C. Marine Parks Forever Society Stern-tie Program. Contact Sandra Tassel at 360-515-7171 or info@afoclt.org for assistance concerning U.S. donations.
[Lorena Landon]

CONTACT PHONE NUMBERS & WEB ADDRESSES

U.S. COAST GUARD
U.S. Coast Guard Emergencies	**VHF CH 16 or call 911**
	(206) 217-6001 or (206) 220-7001
U.S. Coast Guard Emergency Juneau	**911 or (907)463-2000**
Cellular Phones Only	**911**
U.S. Coast Guard District Office: Seattle	(206) 220-7000
U.S. Coast Guard Smart phone App	

U.S. TOWING
Fremont Tugboat Co.	(206) 632-0151
Towboat U.S. all locations 24-hour dispatch	(800) 888-4869
Towboat U.S. Anacortes	(360) 675-7900
Towboat U.S. Everett	(425) 344-3056
Towboat U.S. San Juan	(360) 378-1111
(Friday Harbor & Roche Harbor)	
Towboat U.S. Lake Washington	(206) 793-7375
Towboat U.S. Oak Harbor	(360) 675-7900
Towboat U.S. Olympia	(360) 790-9008
Towboat U.S. Port Townsend	(360) 531-4837 or (360) 301-9764
Towboat U.S. Port Hadlock	(360) 301-9764
Towboat U.S. Seattle	(253) 312-2927
Towboat U.S. Tacoma	(253) 312-2927
Marine Services Whidbey (Deception Pass)	(360) 675-7900

U.S. WEATHER INFORMATION NUMBERS
Seattle	(206) 526-6087
Dial-A-Buoy	(888) 701-8992

U.S. CUSTOMS CLEARANCE NUMBERS
For customs entry call:	(800) 562-5943
The office numbers below are for weekdays only.	
Anacortes	(360) 293-2331
Friday Harbor/Roche Harbor	(360) 378-2080
Point Roberts	(360) 945-5211 or (360) 945-2314
Port Angeles	(360) 457-4311
Aberdeen	(360) 310-0109 or (360) 532-2030
Bellingham	(360) 734-5463
Blaine	(360) 332-8511
Everett	(425) 259-0246
Port Townsend	(360) 385-3777
Seattle	(206) 553-0770
Tacoma/Olympia	(253) 593-6338
Ketchikan	(907) 225-2254

WA PARKS INFORMATION NUMBERS
WA State Parks Launch & Moorage Permit Program	(360) 902-8500
San Juan County Parks	(360) 378-8420

CANADIAN COAST GUARD
Canadian Coast Guard Emergency Numbers	**VHF CH 16**
Cellphone	*16
Search and Rescue: Vancouver	VHF CH 16 or (800) 567-5111
Search and Rescue: Victoria	(250) 413-8933 or (800) 567-5111
Search and Rescue: Other areas	(800) 567-5111
Canadian Coast Guard District Office: Victoria	(250) 480-2600

B.C. TOWING
Vessel Assist Gulf Islands	(800) 413-8222
C-Tow	VHF CH. 07A or (888) 419-2869
Covers Victoria to the north end of Vancouver Island & the Tofino area	
Port McNeil	(250) 974-5305

CANADIAN WEATHER INFORMATION NUMBER
Vancouver	(604) 666-3655
Victoria	

CANADIAN BORDER SERVICES CLEARANCE NUMBER
All locations & CANPASS
contact Canada Border Services Agency toll-free: (888) 226-7277

CANADIAN PARKS INFORMATION NUMBERS
B. C. Parks General Information	(604) 582-5200
Gwaii Haanas National Park Reserve	(250) 559-8818
Gulf Islands National Park Reserve	(250) 654-4000 or (866) 944-1744

MARINE MAMMAL RESOURCES
San Juan County Marine Mammal Stranding Network is a collaborative program of the Whale Museum (Friday Harbor) and the National Marine Fisheries.
To Report a Stranding in San Juan County
Call 1-800-562-8832 or email hotline@whalemuseum.org
This hotline is a voicemail system that is checked frequently throughout the day. Leave your name and phone number.

NOAA Marine Mammal Disentanglement Network is a program for boaters to help entangled marine mammals in U.S. waters.
To report entangled whales call NOAA Fisheries hotline at (877) 767-9425.
NOAA 24/7 Hotline - To report injured or stranded whales, dolphins, porpoises, seals and sea lions, or to report incidents of marine mammal harassment:
Call NOAA's 24/7 hotline at (800) 853-1964.

BC Marine Mammal Response Network – handles marine mammal matters in B.C. waters; they ask that boaters report all injured, distressed and dead marine mammals and sea turtles.
Call their 24/7 hotline (800) 465-4336

FISHERIES & FISHERIES MANAGEMENT

Paralytic Shellfish Poisoning PSP shellfish closures can be expected without warning at any time during the season.

For PSP closures in Washington, phone (800) 562-5632. Washington State Dept. of Health Paralytic Shellfish Poisoning page: www.doh.wa.gov and search PSP. The website has a PSP fact sheet and links to PSP toxin closed areas of Puget Sound and San Juan Islands.

Washington State Dept. Fish and Wildlife information on fish and wildlife action plans: wdfw.wa.gov/conservation/cwcs/

Washington State Dept. Fish and Wildlife information fishing and shellfishing: wdfw.wa.gov/fishing/

U.S. Fish and Wildlife Service Fisheries and Habitat Conservation: www.fws.gov/fisheries/

For PSP closures in B.C., phone the Openings and Closures Toll Free Line: (866) 431-3474 or (604) 666-2828 in the Lower Mainland, or go to: www.pac.dfo-mpo.gc.ca/fm-gp/contamination/biotox/index-eng.htm

Fisheries Management Areas. Download map of Fisheries Management Areas to enable you to decipher closure areas at: www.pac.dfo-mpo.gc.ca

Rockfish Conservation Areas booklet contains chartlets of all conservation areas. Many people do not realize that RCA's prohibit ALL hook and line fishing, not just fishing for rockfish. To view or download a copy of the booklet, go to: www.pac.dfo-mpo.gc.ca

VHF CHANNELS FOR PLEASURE CRAFT

WASHINGTON WATERS

05A VESSEL TRAFFIC SERVICE SEATTLE—Northern Puget Sound and Strait of Juan de Fuca. Vessels not required to participate are highly encouraged to maintain a listening watch. Contact with VTS is encouraged if essential to navigational safety.

06 INTERSHIP SAFETY. Only for ship-to-ship use for safety communications. For Search and Rescue (SAR) liaison with Coast Guard vessels and aircraft.

09 INTERSHIP AND SHIP-SHORE ALL VESSELS and CALLING & REPLY FOR PLEASURE VESSELS (optional, U.S. only). Working channel.

13 Vessel BRIDGE to Vessel BRIDGE, large vessels. Low power only. May also be used to contact locks and bridges BUT use sound signals in the Seattle area to avoid dangerous interference to collision avoidance communications between large vessels. Call on Channel 13 or by phone at 206/386-4251 for nighttime bridge openings (after 2300) in the Lake Washington Ship Canal, Seattle.

14 VESSEL TRAFFIC SERVICE SEATTLE—Southern Puget Sound. Vessels not required to participate are highly encouraged to maintain a listening watch. Contact with VTS is encouraged if essential to navigational safety.

16 INTERNATIONAL DISTRESS AND CALLING. Calling channel. Used only for distress and urgent traffic, for safety calls and contacting other stations. Listen first to make sure no distress traffic is in progress; do not transmit if a SEELONCE MAYDAY is declared. Keep all communications to a minimum. Do not repeat a call to the same station more than once every two minutes. After three attempts, wait 15 minutes before calling the same station. Pleasure vessels may also use Channel 09 for calling.

22A COAST GUARD LIAISON. A government channel used for Safety and Liason communications with the Coast Guard. Also known as Channel 22 US. The U.S. Coast Guard does not normally monitor 22A so you must first establish communications on Channel 16.

66A PORT OPERATIONS. Marinas in Puget Sound are being encouraged to use this common frequency for arranging moorage.

67 INTERSHIP ONLY FOR ALL VESSELS (U.S. only, Puget Sound.) Working channel.

68 INTERSHIP and SHIP-SHORE FOR PLEASURE VESSELS ONLY. Working channel.

69 INTERSHIP and SHIP-SHORE FOR PLEASURE VESSELS ONLY. Working channel.

70 DIGITAL SELECTIVE CALLING ONLY (No Voice) FOR DISTRESS AND CALLING.

72 INTERSHIP ONLY FOR ALL VESSELS (U.S. only, Puget Sound.) Working channel.

78A INTERSHIP and SHIP-SHORE FOR PLEASURE VESSELS ONLY (Not available in Canada). Working channel. Marinas in Puget Sound are being encouraged to use this as a secondary working channel.

BRITISH COLUMBIA WATERS

05A VESSEL TRAFFIC SERVICE SEATTLE—Strait of Juan de Fuca west of Victoria.

06 INTERSHIP SAFETY. Only for ship-to-ship use for safety communications.

09 INTERSHIP AND SHIP-SHORE. All vessels. Working channel.

11 VESSEL TRAFFIC SERVICE VICTORIA—Strait of Juan de Fuca east of Victoria; Haro Strait; Boundary Passage; Gulf Islands; Southern Strait of Georgia.

VESSEL TRAFFIC SERVICE PRINCE RUPERT—North of Cape Caution.

12 VESSEL TRAFFIC SERVICE VANCOUVER—Vancouver and Howe Sound.

16 INTERNATIONAL DISTRESS AND CALLING. Calling channel. Used only for distress and urgent traffic, for safety calls and contacting other stations. Listen first to make sure no distress traffic is in progress. Do not transmit if a SEELONCE MAYDAY is declared. Keep all communications to a minimum. Do not repeat a call to the same station more than once every two minutes. After three attempts, wait 15 minutes before calling the same station.

66A PORT OPERATIONS. Most marinas in southern B.C. will use this channel.

67 INTERSHIP AND SHIP-SHORE. All vessels. Working channel.

68 INTERSHIP AND SHIP-SHORE. Pleasure vessels. Working channel.

69 INTERSHIP AND SHIP-SHORE. Pleasure vessels. Working channel.

70 DIGITAL SELECTIVE CALLING ONLY (No Voice) FOR DISTRESS AND CALLING.

71 VESSEL TRAFFIC SERVICE COMOX—Northern Strait of Georgia to Cape Caution.

VESSEL TRAFFIC SERVICE—Prince Rupert, Dixon Entrance and Chatham Sound.

72 INTERSHIP. All vessels. Working channel.

73 INTERSHIP AND SHIP-SHORE. All vessels. Working channel.

74 VESSEL TRAFFIC SERVICE VICTORIA—Victoria-Fraser River.

VESSEL TRAFFIC SERVICE TOFINO—West of Vancouver Island.

83A COAST GUARD LIAISON. Primary Canadian Coast Guard Safety and Communications Channel. Also known as Channel 83 U.S. mode.

To contact the Canadian Coast Guard, use Channel 16 to call the station nearest you: Victoria, Vancouver, Comox, Prince Rupert or Tofino.

Even though you may use alternate communication means such as cellular phone, MONITOR VHF 16. The safety of yourself, your family and your friends is enhanced by a watch on 16 by all vessels.

RADIO EMERGENCY SIGNALS

MAYDAY	Vessel threatened by grave and imminent danger and requests immediate assistance.
PAN PAN	Urgent message concerning safety of vessel or person on board or in sight.
SECURITÉ	Message concerning safety of navigation or meteorological warning.
SEELONCE MAYDAY	Mayday in progress, do not transmit normal communications.
SEELONCE FEENE	Resume normal communications.

CONVERSION TABLES

TEMPERATURE (FORMULAS)

FAHRENHEIT TO CELSIUS
To convert temperature from Fahrenheit to Celsius:

(F° - 32) × .555 = C°

Example: Convert 40° F to C:
(40 - 32) = 8; 8 × .555 = 4;
thus 40° F = 4° C

CELSIUS TO FAHRENHEIT
To convert temperature from Celsius to Fahrenheit:

(C° × 1.8) + 32 = F°

Example: Convert 4° C to F:
(4 × 1.8) = 7.2; 7.2 + 32 = 39.2 (round to 40); thus 4° C = 40° F

VOLUME

U.S. GALLONS TO LITERS
1 U.S gallon = 3.7854 liters

To convert U.S. gallons to liters, multiply U.S. gallons × 3.785.
Example: 40 U.S. gallons × 3.785 = 151 liters

To convert liters to U.S. gallons, divide by 3.785.
Example: 151 liters ÷ 3.785 = 39.89 U.S. gallons (round to 40)

IMPERIAL GALLONS TO LITERS
1 Imperial gallon = 4.546 liters

To convert Imperial gallons to liters, multiply Imperial gallons × 4.546.
Example: 40 Imperial gallons × 4.546 = 182 liters

To convert liters to Imperial gallons, divide by 4.546.
Example: 182 liters ÷ 4.546 = 40.035 (round to 40)

U.S. GALLONS TO IMPERIAL GALLONS
1 U.S. gallon = .833 Imperial gallons

To convert U.S. gallons to Imperial gallons, multiply U.S. gallons × .833.

Example: 40 U.S. gallons × .833 = 33.32 Imperial gallons

To convert Imperial gallons to U.S. gallons, multiply Imperial gallons × 1.20.

Example: 33 Imperial gallons × 1.20 = 39.6 U.S. gallons

LITERS AND QUARTS
1 liter = 1.0567 quarts, or 33.8 ounces
1 quart = .9467 liters, or 947 ml

SPEED

Convert knots to miles per hour: Knots × 1.15
Convert miles per hour to knots: MPH × .868

WEIGHT

1 kilogram (kg) = 2.2 pounds (lbs.)

1 pound = .4545 kilograms (454 grams)

1 U.S. gallon of fresh water weighs 8.333 lbs. or 3.787 kg

1 Imperial gallon of fresh water weighs 10 lbs. or 4.545 kg

1 liter of fresh water weighs 2.2 pounds or 1 kg

1 U. S. gallon of gasoline weighs 6.2 lbs. or 2.82 kg

1 Imperial gallon of gasoline weighs 7.44 lbs. or 3.38 kg

1 liter of gasoline weighs 1.64 lbs. or 0.744 kg

1 U.S. gallon of No. 2 diesel fuel weighs 6.7 pounds or 3.05 kg

1 Imperial gallon of No. 2 diesel fuel weighs 8.04 pounds or 3.66 kg

1 liter of No. 2 diesel fuel weighs 1.77 pounds or 0.8 kg

DISTANCE

1 inch = 2.54 centimeters

1 foot = .3048 meters

1 meter = 3.28 feet

1 fathom = 6 feet

1 fathom = 1.83 meters

1 cable = 120 fathoms

1 cable (British) = 0.1 nautical mile

1 statute mile = 5280 feet; 7.4 cables; 1.609 kilometers

1 nautical mile = 6076 feet; 8.5 cables; 1.852 kilometers

1 statute mile = 0.868 nautical mile

1 nautical mile = 1.15 statute mile

QUICK REFERENCE

32° Fahrenheit = 0° Celsius
0° Fahrenheit = -17.8° Celsius

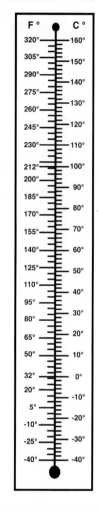

BAROMETRIC PRESSURE

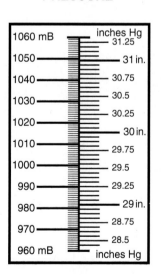

NORDHAVN

Oceans Apart from the Rest

After almost six million documented ocean miles, no production motor yacht or any other builders' motoryachts combined can come close to matching the incredible accomplishments of our Nordhavns. Consider the following facts;

- Over 150 Nordhavns have successfully crossed the Atlantic, Pacific and/or the Indian Ocean
- Ten Nordhavns have successfully circumnavigated the world
- Four Nordhavns have rounded Cape Horn – multiple times
- A Nordhavn 40 holds the world record for the fastest circumnavigation by a production power boat of any size
- A Nordhavn 68 has traveled further North than any private production motoryacht – to 81 degrees - 27 minutes north
- A Nordhavn 57 has transited the Northwest Passage from East to West
- South Georgia Island has been visited by only one production powerboat – a Nordhavn 63

- *RELIANCE*, a Nordhavn 76, has visited the continent of Antarctica
- The largest fleet of production power boats to cross the Atlantic in convoy – not once or twice but three times
- Dozens of north - south transits of the South China sea
- Dozens of east - west Mediterranean transits
- At least three Australian circumnavigations

If you dream of safe and comfortable worldwide Adventure Cruising without limitation, you will conclude, as have the world's most accomplished cruisers, there simply is no better choice than a Nordhavn.

Please visit Nordhavn.com for a detailed overview of why Nordhavn is "Oceans Apart from the Rest".

For information, visit nordhavn.com or contact us at info@nordhavn.com

Visit Nordhavn Yachts in Seattle at 2601 W. Marina Place, Suite S, or call 206-223-3624.

INDIAN RESERVE LANDS ON THE BC COAST

When navigating the BC Coast, boaters often see "IR" or the words "Indian Reserve" on charts. Many wonder what this designation means, as there may, or may not be, evidence of habitation.

Indian Reserve (IR) are tracts of land set aside under the Indian Act and treaty agreements for the exclusive use of an Indian band. Reserves are governed by one or more band Chiefs and Councils. A single band may control one or several reserves, while some reserves are shared between multiple bands. Band members possess the right to live on reserve lands, and band administrative and political structures are frequently located there. Reserve lands are not strictly "owned" by bands but are held in trust for bands by the Crown.

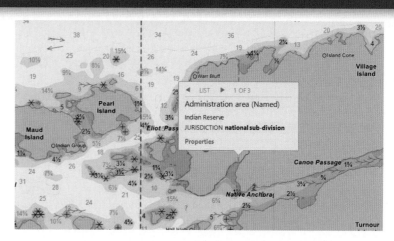

Of the 638,000 First Nations people who reported being Registered Indians, nearly half live on one of the 3,100 Indian Reserves in Canada. Many reserves, especially on BC waters, are small, remote, non-contiguous pieces of land that may or may not have year-round resident population. Some are used only seasonally by the band. In the Broughtons, Health Bay (Gilford Island) and New Vancouver (Harbledown Island) are examples of communities with small populations of band residents. In fact, both of these communities have docks that welcome visiting boaters. Others, such as Mamaliliculla (Village Island) and Karlukwees (Turnour Island) are settlements that are not currently inhabited but have historic buildings and structures from previous habitation. See separate entries in the Waggoner Guide for more information on these sites. Many others have no local names, buildings or other signs of habitation except, perhaps, a centuries-old midden. They may only be marked by signs indicating the named band territory.

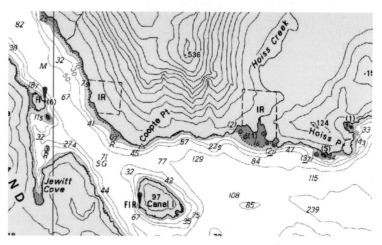

Regardless of whether First Nations people are present, all of these lands should be treated as private land and respected by visitors. Some Reserves, such as Mamaliliculla on Village island, require formal permission to visit and charge a fee to see the village. All of these reserve lands are protected by British Columbia's Heritage Conservation Act (http://www.bclaws.ca/civix/document/id/complete/statreg/96187_01), which prohibits damage to the sites or removal of material that constitutes part of the site. For personal safety and out of respect for First Nations property, visitors should not enter abandoned buildings.

Indian Reserves recognize and respect the 10,000-year inhabitation of the BC Coast by First Nations people. Each site is unique and some, like New Vancouver, offer tours to visitors. Check the Waggoner Guide for information about contacting Band offices for permission to visit. If you visit, please respect these places that are sacred to the people to whom they are entrusted. Take only photos and leave only footprints.

State of Washington

AIS Prevention Permit
Non-Resident Vessel

John Doe
5555 Washington Drive
Olympia, WA 98501
(360)-555-5555
JohnDoe555@gmail.com

Permit #: (Document Number)
Registration #: (Alphanumeric to 10 digits)
Registration State or Province:
Registration Country:

Valid: 01/01/2017 to 12/31/2018

Out-of-State Boaters Need A Washington State AIS Prevention Permit. Most out-of-state watercraft and floatplanes are now required to have an Aquatic Invasive Species (AIS) Prevention Permit when operating in Washington State waters. The $24 permit can be purchased online or at any WDFW license sales location throughout the state. Watercraft registered in the State of Washington automatically pay an annual fee as part of their registration and therefore do not need to separately purchase a permit.

Who Needs the AIS Prevention Permit? Operators of recreational vessels not registered in Washington, seaplane operators, and commercial transporters of watercraft are required to purchase and carry an AIS Prevention Permit. Permits can be purchased online or at any Fish and Wildlife license dealer. Online purchased permits are mailed and a temporary permit, good for 10 days, can be printed. Permits are valid for one year from date of activation.

The following are exempt from the required permit:

- Recreational vessels registered in Washington with a valid WA State registration sticker

- Small watercraft (Washington or out-of-state) that do not require state or country registration, such as canoes and kayaks

- Watercraft used solely as tenders to larger boats

- Vessels registered in Idaho or Oregon, when used in shared state waters

- U.S. and foreign documented commercial vessels

- Military, federal, tribal, state, and local government vessels used for government purposes

What's the Purpose of the Permits? AIS Prevention Permits were authorized in 2017. Fees from non-resident permits and resident vessel registrations help support the department's efforts to keep Washington's waters free of aquatic invasive species and manage infestations.

Invasive species such as zebra mussels and guagga mussels, European green crab and New Zealand mud snails (to name a few) are often spread by boats and trailers. Both marine saltwater and freshwater can harbor invasive species. WDFW's task of controlling invasive species in Washington waters is costly and permit and registration fees help fund the department's work.

What About Enforcement? This new permit has prompted a number of questions for boaters regarding enforcement of the permits and vessel inspections. WDFW's permit enforcement and inspection for invasive species is focused on boat trailers and boats transported overland.

- AIS Prevention Permits are for fundraising and do not automatically trigger vessel inspections

- Inspections of watercraft for aquatic invasive species are currently land-based, focused on trailered boats and boat trailers

- As of 2018, there were no on-water check/inspection stations for invasive species

Where to Get More Information. Aquatic Invasive Species is an important topic for all Northwest boaters. British Columbia, Washington, Oregon, and Idaho remain relatively free of invasive species. WDFW's efforts, along with those of similar agencies in neighboring states and provinces, are imperative to keep the region's waters free of invasive species. Increasing numbers and types of watercraft routinely on the move, make the containment job more difficult.

WDFW's website provides valuable information on this topic and a link to purchase the permit online. Please click through to learn more about their work and invasive species. Learn about some possible ways that both trailerable and non-trailerable vessels may unwittingly harbor and carry invasive species.

Aquatic Invasive Species Information https://wdfw.wa.gov/ais/ AIS Prevention Permit Information https://wdfw.wa.gov/licensing/ais_prevention/

[Leonard Landon]

South & Central Puget Sound

CHAPTER 2

SOUTH PUGET SOUND
Olympia • Case Inlet • Carr Inlet • Tacoma Narrows

CENTRAL PUGET SOUND
Gig Harbor • Tacoma • Vashon Island • Seattle
Bremerton • Poulsbo • Bainbridge Island

South Puget Sound begins at Olympia and ends at Tacoma Narrows. For scenic quality, relatively calm seas and solitude, South Puget Sound is an excellent region to explore. For some reason, Seattle boats that voyage hundreds of miles north often do not consider venturing just a few miles south. Yet South Sound is dotted with marine parks and served by enough marinas to meet most needs. We like South Sound and recommend it.

The waters are generally flatter in South Sound, good for cruising year-round. The channels are relatively narrow and have enough bends to minimize fetch and prevent most wind from creating large seas. Tide-rips, of course, still form where channels meet, and skippers must be aware of them.

Olympia is South Sound's only significant city. Getting away from civilization is easy, yet it is always close by. First-time visitors usually are surprised at the beauty of this area. Mt. Rainier, an inactive volcano 14,410 feet high, dominates many vistas. The islands and peninsulas tend to be either tree-covered or pastoral, with pockets of homes or commercial enterprise. Most marine parks have docks, buoys, and anchoring. The marinas are friendly and well-kept.

BUDD, ELD, TOTTEN INLETS

Budd Inlet. The mile-wide entrance to Budd Inlet is between Dofflemyer Point and Cooper Point. Approaching from the north,

simply round Dofflemyer Point, where a white-painted light blinks every 4 seconds, and head for the Capitol dome.

Anchorage in Budd Inlet is along both shores in 10 to 20 feet, mud bottom, with Butler Cove and Tykle Cove preferred. Private mooring buoys line the shores, so consider your swinging room when anchoring.

Launch Ramps: Swantown Marina has a 2-lane launch ramp. Another launch ramp is at the Thurston County park just south of Boston Harbor near Dofflemyer Point. Boston Harbor also has a launch ramp and parking for tow vehicles and trailers.

The City of Olympia's Priest Point Park, on the east side of Budd Inlet, has one of the finest sand beaches in southern Puget Sound.

Olympia. Olympia is one of the most charming stops in Puget Sound, the more so because so few boats from central and northern Puget Sound ever visit. Olympia is an undiscovered treat for many northern boaters.

Moorage in Olympia is at five marinas: NorthPoint Landing, Port Plaza Dock, Percival Landing, West Bay Marina, and Swantown Marina. Fuel is available at Boston Harbor Marina and Swantown Marina.

To get to the marinas, continue past Olympia Shoal, marked by lighted beacons on the shoal's east and west sides. From Olympia Shoal, pick up the 28-foot-deep dredged and buoyed channel leading to the harbor. A spoils bank from channel dredging is east of the channel. The spoils area is quite shoal and parts of it dry. Stay in the channel.

The channel branches at a piling intersection marker east of the privately-owned West Bay Marina. The dayboard on the marker is green on top, red on the bottom. The green top-color marks the main channel. If you leave the marker to port you'll proceed down the western leg past the Port of Olympia large ship docks, to Percival Landing, and to the Olympia Yacht Club at the head of the inlet. If you leave the marker to starboard, you'll take the eastern leg to the Port of Olympia's Swantown Marina and Boatworks. On both sides of each channel the water shoals rapidly to drying flats. The Olympia harbor has a no-wake rule.

West Bay Marina has a few guest slips and a restaurant, but no fuel dock. The Olympia Yacht Club has guest moorage for members of reciprocal clubs only. In the western channel, Percival Landing has guest moorage. In the eastern channel, the Port of Olympia's Swantown Marina has guest moorage.

A beautifully landscaped walkway surrounds the Percival Landing area. It's a popular place for strolling, with an excellent view of harbor activities. Good restaurants, a supermarket, a fish market, and wine shop are nearby. Some boaters find the number of people walking just above their boats disconcerting, although we have found nights to be quiet. Swantown Marina, in East Bay, does not have the crowds walking by the boats.

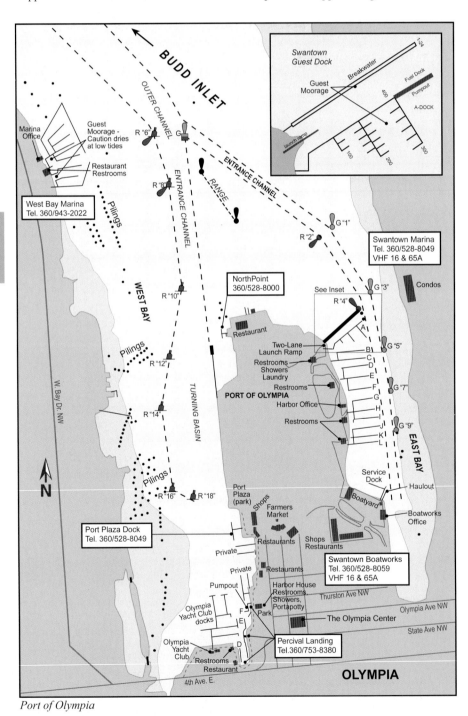

Port of Olympia

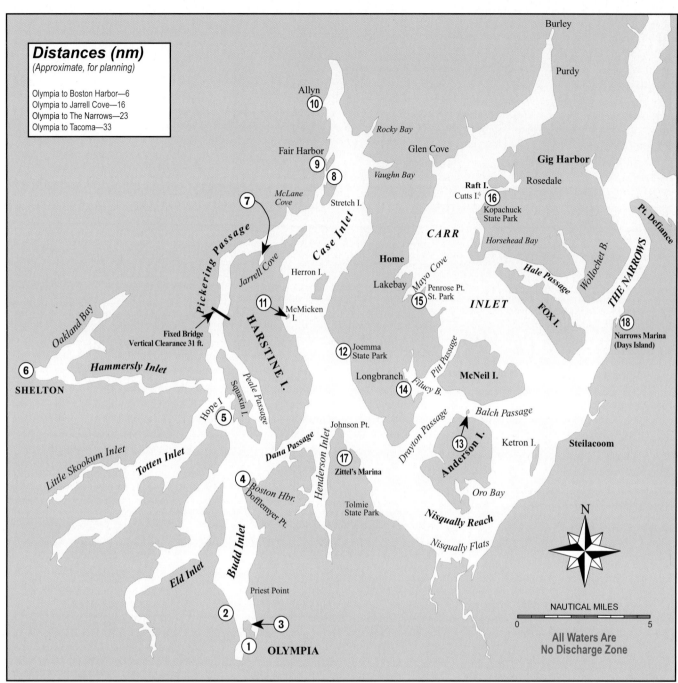

Distances (nm)
(Approximate, for planning)

Olympia to Boston Harbor—6
Olympia to Jarrell Cove—16
Olympia to The Narrows—23
Olympia to Tacoma—33

South Puget Sound

Deschutes Basin, the southernmost tip of Puget Sound, and Capitol Lake are blocked by a dam and crossed by city streets. They are used by small boats launched from the city park just across the road from Percival Landing and the yacht club.

Olympia is the state capital, and we urge a tour of the Capitol Campus and its buildings. Besides housing the largest chandelier ever made by Louis Comfort Tiffany, the Capitol dome, at 287 feet tall, is one of the tallest masonry domes in North America. The grounds are beautiful and the buildings are magnificent. Informative tours are conducted on the hour, 10:00 a.m. to 3:00 p.m. on weekdays, 11:00 a.m. to 3:00 p.m. on weekends. No charge for these tours. The free Dash shuttle bus runs regularly from the farmers market to the campus and back.

Downtown Olympia has its own charm. Parts of it got stuck in the '50s. If you've seen the film "Pleasantville," you'll recognize the storefronts. The State Theater's tall art deco sign is not a bit out of place in Olympia's downtown. The Eastside Club Tavern was the inspiration for Moe's Tavern on "The Simpsons" TV show. Some of the restaurants have employees who have been there 20 to 40 years, and they're open every day of the year so regular customers have somewhere to go, even at Christmas.

Take the self-guided Historical District Walking Tour to learn local history: www.olympiawa.gov/city-services/history-preservation/walking-tours-of-historic-Olympia.

About 20 antiques stores are located in the downtown area and out past Percival

Landing. Art galleries are springing up. If you need a jolt of caffeine, coffee roaster Batdorf & Bronson is just east of the farmers market. They have a tasting room, just like a winery, only with coffee. Samples are free, but we always buy at least a couple bags of coffee. We enjoy it.

Olympia Farmers Market. The Olympia Farmers market is located between Percival Landing and the Port of Olympia's Swantown Marina. The market is open Thursdays through Sundays from April through October. Hours are 10:00 a.m. to 3:00 p.m. The market is open weekends in November and December, and and Saturdays only January through March. Everything sold is grown or made locally, except for a few fruits that come from Yakima. Musicians perform on a covered stage, and take-out food is available

The marinas in Olympia are in the shadow of the Capitol building.

from several outlets. No pets allowed. The market's roof is topped by a weathervane in the shape of a traditional flying pig.

Olympia hosts several festivals each year. For additional information visit: www.downtownolympia.com or www. visitolympia.com.

Fuel. Olympia has a fuel dock at Swantown Marina with marine gas and diesel.

With all the services and shopping opportunities of a major city, combined with beauty and the friendliness of a small town, Olympia makes a truly pleasant destination for boaters exploring south Puget Sound.

 THINGS TO DO

1. Washington State Capitol. Take a short walk from the marinas for a free 60-minute tour of the architecturally magnificent legislative building.

2. Washington State Capital Museum. Good exhibits on the history of Washington State. Seven blocks from the Capitol.

3. Hands On Children's Museum. This children's museum has exhibits and an outdoor discovery center. A must-see for kids. Adjacent to Swantown Marina.

4. Olympia Farmers Market. One of the largest farmers markets in all of Puget Sound. It is open Thursday through Sunday, April to October, and limited days during the off-season. Located between Swantown Marina and Percival Landing.

5. Percival Landing Park. See classic boats, sculptures, and views of the Capitol on this landscaped walkway around the harbor.

6. Antique and specialty shops. More than 20 in the downtown area, a short walk from the waterfront.

7. Batdorf & Bronson Coffee Roasters. Taste the difference and learn the finer points of coffee.

① **Percival Landing.** 217 Thurston Ave., Olympia, WA 98501; (360) 753-8380; www.olympiawa.gov. Percival Landing has nice showers and restrooms. The park, with moorage, is adjacent to downtown Olympia near shopping, restaurants, and other facilities. Four hours day moorage, no charge. Guest moorage is along E float on the east side of the waterway. Water, 30 & 50 amp power are available on E float. Pumpout is on F float. D float, below the Olympia Oyster House restaurant on the west side, has limited space, no power or water. Register at The Olympia Center, east of E float. Group reservations available from October 1 to April 30.

The floats have access to toilets, showers, and portapotty dump. After-hours or weekends, self-register at the kiosk next to the parking lot. Cash or checks only at the kiosk, no credit cards. First-come, first-served. Maximum 7 days in a 30-day period. No manager is on site, so you may have to search for everything, including the registration kiosk. Good grocery shopping at Bayview Thriftway, west of the yacht club. The Harbor House meeting center was built as part of the Percival Landing renovation and is available for group gatherings up to 30 people. Call (360) 753-8380. There are also two outdoor pavilions.

Limited guest moorage during the Wooden

Boat Show in May, and Harbor Days in early September, which includes tugboat races.

① **Port Plaza Dock.** 701 Columbia St. NW, Olympia, WA 98501; (360) 528-8049; marina@portolympia.com; www. swantownmarina.com. Monitors VHF 65A. This is a modern, all-concrete set of floats on the east side of the waterway leading to Percival Landing and Olympia Yacht Club. The docks are intended for day use but are available for overnight. Location is convenient to dining and shopping, 4 hours no charge. No water, no power. Self-register at the kiosk at the head of the ramp. Reservations accepted for a $5 non-refundable fee.

The Port Plaza itself is a work of art. The sculpted concrete work suggests waves. It's completely flat but very effective. Bronze shells, golf balls, drafting tools— all sorts of things are set into the cement. The more you look. the more you see.

704 Columbia St. NW
(360) 357-9700

① **NorthPoint Landing.** 1675 Marine Drive NW, Olympia, WA 98501; (360) 528-8000; www.portolympia.com. Small dock operated by the Port of Olympia, at the north end of the waterway leading to Percival Landing and Olympia Yacht Club. Day use only. Max 4 hour stay. No power or water. 4 feet of depth at zero tide. Anthony's Hearthfire Grill is adjacent to the dock.

1675 Marine Drive NE
(360) 705-3473

② **West Bay Marina.** 2100 Westbay Drive NW, Olympia, WA 98502; (360) 943-2022; westbaymarina@hotmail.com; www. westbay-marina.com. On the west side of Budd Inlet. Guest moorage to 40 feet; call ahead for availability. Facilities include 30 amp power, restrooms, showers, coin-

The docks at Percival Landing Park

operated laundry, pumpout. Use caution, docks are in disrepair and may be unsafe. Tugboat Annie's restaurant and pub, a longtime favorite, is on site.

③ **Swantown Marina.** 1022 Marine Drive NE, Olympia, WA 98501; (360) 528-8049; marina@portolympia.com; www.swantown marina.com. Certified Clean Marina. Monitors VHF 65A. This is the Port of Olympia small boat moorage. Open all year, 50+ guest moorage slips for vessels to 100 feet. Fuel dock located on A Dock with diesel and ethanol-free gasoline. Nice restrooms, showers and laundry. Pumpout, portapotty dump, 30 & 50 amp power,

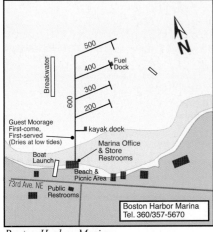

Boston Harbor Marina

garbage drop, waste oil dump, security patrols, well-tended grounds, free Wi-Fi, ice. Reservations accepted for $5. Dry boat storage, 2-lane launch ramp. Block and crushed ice at the Harbor Office. Groceries are a 15-minute walk away. The Olympia Farmers Market and downtown attractions are within walking distance.

The channel leading from the intersection beacon, with its green and red dayboard, can be confusing. If the weather is clear, you'll see a long, low 2-story condominium block on the eastern shore. Aim for those condominiums.

Guest moorage is on A-dock a short distance inside the entry next to the launch ramp. Register and pay moorage at the kiosk at the head of the ramp, or in the office at the head of I-Dock. Swantown Marina is parklike: clean, quiet, spacious and well-maintained.

Swantown Boatworks, (360) 528-8059, with 82-ton Travelift, is at the south end of the marina. Pettit Marine chandlery is located in the same building.

Burfoot County Park. 6927 Boston Harbor Rd. NE, Olympia, WA 98506. Located a half-mile south of Dofflemyer Point. This is a 60-acre county park, open all year, day use only. Restrooms, picnic tables, trails, and play area. Anchoring or beaching only. Buoys mark an artificial diving reef.

④ **Boston Harbor.** Boston Harbor is a halfmoon-shaped bay between Dofflemyer Point and Dover Point. Anchorage is limited but possible. Much of the bay is taken up by the Boston Harbor Marina.

④ **Boston Harbor Marina.** 312 - 73rd Ave. NE, Olympia, WA 98506; (360) 357-5670; www.bostonharbormarina.com. Phone ahead for slip assignment. Open all year with very limited guest moorage. Gas and diesel at the fuel dock. Guest moorage is located in front of the store on the west side of the 600 Dock and in unoccupied slips. Caution: the south end of the 600 Dock dries at low tide. The north docks, which were damaged in recent storms, will be under repair for the next few years. 20 amp power, picnic area, beach access, free Wi-Fi, restrooms, but no showers. The launch ramp dries on minus tide. The store has groceries, ice, beer on tap, wine, fresh seafood, some marine supplies, gifts, clothing, and books. Sandwiches, soups, and soft-serve ice cream at the store. Rental kayaks and SUPs available.

This is a real neighborhood place, a throwback to when small marinas up and down Puget Sound served surrounding communities. The quaint old store is built on pilings, and there's not a level floor to be found. The store and docks are gathering places for locals, and a cheery bunch they are. On Fridays, from Memorial Day to Labor Day, live music with beer tasting is held

83

The large deck adjacent to the Boston Harbor Store is popular.

on the pier. Breakfast is served on the pier Sunday mornings from 10:00 a.m. to 1:00 p.m., summer season only. If you relax and just let it happen, you'll think Boston Harbor is a delight.

No-wake zone: Several white warning buoys off the mouth of Boston Harbor mark a no-wake zone. Please slow down. Wakes from passing craft play havoc with the moored boats.

Eld Inlet. Eld Inlet is immediately west of Budd Inlet, and extends about 5 miles south from Cooper Point before it becomes aptly-named Mud Bay. Hold to a mid-channel course past Cooper Point, which has an extensive drying shoal northward from the point.

Eld Inlet has no marinas, but anchorage is good, mud bottom along both shores. Directly across the inlet is the waterfront activities center for The Evergreen State College. The center has a float and buildings to store canoes and other small craft used by students.

Frye Cove County Park. 4000 NW 61st Ave., Olympia, WA 98502. Just north of Flapjack Point in Eld Inlet. Open all year, day use only. Toilets, no other services. Anchoring or beaching only. Picnic shelters, barbecues, hiking trails.

⑤ **Hope Island Marine State Park.** (360) 426-9226. Junction of Totten Inlet and Pickering Passage. Boat access only. Trails crisscross the island leading through forest, meadows, and old orchards. Interpretive signs explain the island's history and ecology. Visitors rave about this park. A Park Aide lives on the island during the summer. The park has 3 mooring buoys on the west shore, 2 mooring buoys off the south shore and decent anchorage in 30 feet or less on the east side. Campsites, pit toilets, no fires, no pets. Pack out all garbage.

Totten Inlet. Enter Totten Inlet past Steamboat Island, connected to the the mainland by a causeway from Carlyon Beach. Homes and a private marina are on the island and mainland beach. The beach

is marked by a quick flashing light. All of Totten Inlet is less than 60 feet deep. The inlet shoals to drying mud flats toward its south end, called Oyster Bay.

The entrance to **Skookum Inlet** is on the west side of Totten Inlet, about 3 miles southwest of Steamboat Island. Skookum Inlet is called "Little Skookum" by locals, to differentiate it from nearby Hammersley Inlet, which they call "Big Skookum." Little Skookum is a pleasant exploration, but not navigable beyond Wildcat Harbor except by dinghy. Little Skookum is one of south Puget Sound's major oyster growing areas.

HAMMERSLEY INLET & SHELTON

Hammersley Inlet extends westward about 6 miles to Oakland Bay and the city of Shelton. Note the shoal area that blocks the entire south side of the entrance to Hammersley Inlet. Enter Hammersley Inlet on the north shore past Point Hungerford, marked by a beacon with a flashing red light. As Chart 18457 shows, depths range from 10 to 30 feet. Currents to 4 knots flood in and ebb out. The strongest currents occur around Cape Horn, a sharp, constricted bend just inside the entrance. Be mindful of tugs with tows. Moorage is at the Port of Shelton's Oakland Bay Marina, about a mile from Shelton.

Shelton. Shelton is the site of a major lumber mill, with rafted logs in storage in front of the town. Oakland Bay grows shallow north of Shelton, but is navigable at other than extreme low tide, and could offer anchorage on a mud bottom.

⑥ **Oakland Bay Marina** (Port of Shelton). 21 W. Sanderson Way, Shelton, WA 98584; (360) 426-1425; www.portofshelton.com. Open all year, 120 feet of guest moorage, 30 amp power. No fuel. The visitor dock is between the boat houses. Least depth 10 feet. Pumpout, portable toilet above the dock. Home to the friendly Shelton Yacht Club. Groceries, restaurants, and services are in town, about a mile away. The Port continues making improvements to the pier and uplands. Visitors welcome.

PEALE AND PICKERING PASSAGES AND CASE INLET

Pickering Passage extends northward from Totten Inlet past the west sides of Squaxin Island and Harstine Island. A fixed bridge connects Harstine Island to the mainland with a mean high-water vertical clearance of 31 feet. A ferry service once crossed Pickering Passage between 1922 and 1969. The passage was named by Charles Wilkes during his 1838-1842 expedition in honor of the crew's Naturalist, Charles Pickering.

Peale Passage runs along the east side of Squaxin Island. Shallow but passable depths.

Harstine Island is connected to the mainland at Graham Point by a bridge with a mean high water vertical clearance of 31 feet.

The small marina between Jarrell Cove and Dougall Point is private.

Jarrell Cove. Jarrell Cove is off Pickering Passage near the northwest corner of Harstine Island. Jarrell's Cove Marina and 43-acre Jarrell Cove State Marine Park occupy this pleasant, sheltered cove.

LOCAL KNOWLEDGE

SHALLOW AREA: A shallow spit at Jarrell Cove State Park extends from the point that protects the second park dock, the dock deeper in the cove. Boats sometimes cut the point too closely on low tides and go aground.

⑦ **Jarrell's Cove Marina.** 220 E. Wilson Rd., Shelton, WA 98584; (360) 426-8823. Open 7 days a week Memorial Day to Labor Day. The fuel dock has diesel and gasoline. In the winter, the store is closed and fuel is by appointment. Facilities include 3 RV sites, 30 amp power, restrooms, showers, laundry, pumpout, limited guest moorage. Get a slip assignment from the fuel dock before landing, even for a short stay. The store has groceries, beer, ice, some marine hardware, books, propane. The piña colada shaved ice sno-cones are popular with adults who might add a little something when they get back to the boat. Lots of other flavors available, too. Gary and Lorna Hink are the owners.

⑦ **Jarrell Cove Marine State Park.** 391 E. Wingert Road, Shelton, WA 98584; (360) 426-9226. Northwest end of Harstine Island. Open all year. This is a large, attractive park, with 650 feet of dock space on two docks, 14 mooring buoys (boats 45 feet and under). 30 amp power. Clean and well-maintained restrooms and showers, picnic shelters, RV sites and standard campsites. Except for the single buoy between the inner dock and shore, mooring buoys have minimum 10 feet of water at all tides. The inner end of the outer dock can rest on mud bottom on minus tides. The inner dock has 6 feet of water on zero tide. The outer end has sufficient depths for most drafts on all tides. Fishing, clamming, hiking, and bird watching. This park is a wonderful off-season destination.

McLane Cove. Across Pickering Passage from Jarrell Cove. Protected, quiet, lined with forest. Anchorage in 10 to 20 feet.

⑧ **Stretch Island** has good anchorage in the bay south of the bridge to the mainland. The bridge has a mean high water clearance of 14 feet. The channel under the bridge dries at low tide.

⑧ **Stretch Point Marine State Park.** On Stretch Island. Open all year, accessible only by boat. No power, water, restrooms or showers. Day use only, 5 overnight mooring buoys for boats 45 feet and under. Buoys are close to shore because of a steep dropoff. Swimming and diving, oysters and mussels, and a smooth sand beach. The park has no garbage drop and a "pack it in—pack it out" policy. The rustic shelters built behind the beach are on private land and not part of the park.

Reach Island. At the southern end of Reach Island is Fair Harbor, the location of Fair Harbor Marina. The bay has limited anchorage. The channel north of the marina, under a bridge with a mean high water clearance of 16 feet, dries on a minus tide.

⑨ **Fair Harbor Marina.** 5050 E. Grapeview Loop Rd., P.O. Box 160, Grapeview, WA 98546; (360) 426-4028; info@fairharbormarina.com; www.fairharbormarina.com. Open during the summer months with limited side-tie guest moorage on an 88-foot dock. Concrete launch ramp, water, 20 & 30 amp power, garbage, Wi-Fi, restrooms and showers. Picnic areas. Owners Susan and Vern Nelson have retired and the marina is currently for sale. Best to call ahead for moorage. The fuel dock and gift store are closed. Permanent moorage during the winters.

⑩ **Allyn Waterfront Park (Port of Allyn).** P.O. Box 1, Allyn, WA 98524; (360) 275-2430; portofallyn@aol.com; www.

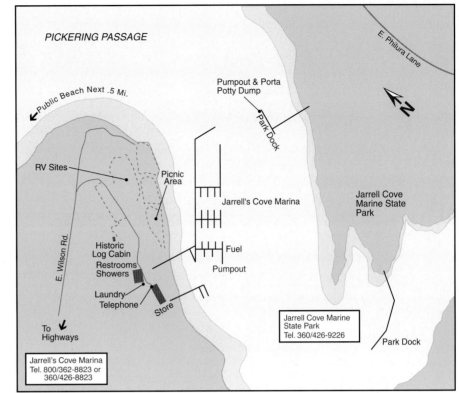

Jarrell's Cove

portofallyn.com. Open all year, launch ramp, 250 feet of moorage for boats to 45 feet on a "T" shaped float at the end of a public pier. Restrooms on site. Potable water at the docks; 30 & 50 amp power. The dock is exposed to winds. No fuel. Allyn is surrounded by shoal water, but can be approached by favoring the east side of the channel until opposite the wharf, then turning in. Depth at the mooring float is 5.25 feet at zero tide. Office hours are Monday through Friday, 11:00 a.m. to 4:30 p.m.

A waterfront park, 100-year-old church, grocery and liquor store, post office, restaurants, wine tasting room, kayak rentals, and the George Kenny School of Chainsaw Carving are a short walk ashore.

If you're experiencing a craving for a manly, heart-stopping burger and shake, visit Big Bubba's Burgers, an Allyn landmark, across the

road from Waterfront Park. Golfing available at nearby Lakeland Village Golf Course.

Rocky Bay. The best anchorage is behind a small sandspit extending from Windy Bluff. Enter with caution and round the little rocky islet off the end of the spit before circling in to anchor.

Vaughn Bay. Vaughn Bay can be entered at half tide or higher. Take a mid-channel course past the end of the spit, then turn to parallel the spit until safe anchoring depths are found near the head of the bay. Jet skis and water skiers sometimes roar around during the day, but they quit at sundown and leave the bay peaceful at night. A launch ramp is on the north shore of the bay.

Herron Island. Privately owned.

Jarrell's Cove Marina has great snow cones. It's a popular stop.

Joemma Beach State Park dock

⑪ **McMicken Island Marine State Park.** (360) 426-9226. On Case Inlet, off the east side of Harstine Island. Open all year, day use only, no overnight camping. Toilets, and 5 overnight mooring buoys for boats 45 feet and under. Mooring buoys, are on the north and south sides of 11½-acre McMicken Island. The buoys on the north side are a little close to shore on minus tides. Self register and pay mooring buoy fee on shore. Anchorage is on either side of the island, good holding bottom.

A trail on McMicken Island leads to a nice view of the beach and surrounding waters. A sign says to watch for poison oak. An artificial reef is north of the island. Fishing, good clamming and oyster gathering, swimming. McMicken Island is accessible only by boat except on low tides, when it and Harstine Island are connected by a drying spit. The spit comes up quickly, and you could find yourself aground if you try to pass between the two islands. The park has no garbage drop and a "Pack it in–Pack it out" policy.

Harstine Island State Park. This park is across the bay from McMicken Island. Open all year, day use only. No power, water, or toilets. At low tide you can cross to McMicken Island State Park. Anchoring only. Clamming, beachcombing.

⑫ **Joemma Beach State Park.** (360) 902-8844. Formerly Robert F. Kennedy Recreational Area, southeast Case Inlet, just north of Whiteman Cove. Cascadia Marine Trail campsite, 500 feet of dock space in place from mid-May through mid-October, 4 mooring buoys (boats 45 feet and under), boat launch, vault toilets. No power, no showers. The docks are good. Camping and picnic sites (including a covered shelter) on shore. Red Rock crabbing has occasionally been reported as excellent, right at the dock. The docks are exposed to southeast storms.

DRAYTON PASSAGE, PITT PASSAGE, BALCH PASSAGE

Taylor Bay. Taylor Bay, on Anderson Island, offers limited anchorage near the entrance, but is exposed to southerlies.

Oro Bay has a shallow, well-marked entrance with good anchorage inside. Oro Bay has a tranquil, rural feeling about it. Entering, the first dock you come to is a Tacoma Yacht Club outstation. Burwell's Landing is a Bremerton Yacht Club outstation. The Oro Bay Marina is home to Oro Bay Yacht Club, with some reciprocal moorage.

Two major parks, managed by the Anderson Island Park District, are the highlights of Oro Bay. Jacobs Point Park, the newer of the two, occupies most of the peninsula between inner and outer Oro Bay. Historically a pioneer farm, Jacobs Point Park provides 82 acres of trails, woodlands and beaches. Access is via a wooden staircase located north of the two red buoys. Andy's Park at the northeast corner of the bay provides 180 acres of wetlands, tidal estuary, and forest with a 2-mile nature trail loop. Access to Andy's Park is from Eckenstam Johnson Road, or through Jacobs Point Park.

Amsterdam Bay indents Anderson Island and is very shallow. Safe anchoring depths are right in the middle, when that spot is not already occupied by local residents' boats. The shores are rural and picturesque. If low tide isn't too low, it's a good place to spend the night. Observe a 5 mph or lower no-wake speed to prevent damage along the shoreline.

⑬ **Eagle Island Marine State Park.** (360) 426-9226. Ten-acre island on Balch Passage, off north side of Anderson Island. Open all year, day use only, 1 overnight mooring buoy on the east side, 2 overnight mooring buoys on the west side. Mooring buoys for boats 45 feet and under, self-register and pay mooring buoy fee on shore. No toilets, power, or water. Boat access only. Avoid the reef, marked by a buoy, off the west side of the island. Fishing and clamming. Watch for poison oak. No fires, no garbage drop and a "Pack it in–Pack it out" policy, no camping.

Eagle Island is a lovely spot. Except for the current which can roar through, this is an excellent South Sound layover location. Lots of seals, a fine view of Mt. Rainier, and good anchoring on the east side. The island is covered with dense forest, but well-maintained trails lead through the trees. Correspondents James and Jennifer

Hamilton call Eagle Island "a gem." Don't be oversold, but do expect a good place to spend some time.

Filucy Bay. Filucy Bay is a popular destination and a fine anchorage. Anchor inside the spit to the south of the entrance, or in the north section, farther in. The north section is wooded, quiet, and protected with good holding over a mud bottom. The view of Mt. Rainier from the entrance of Filucy Bay is stunning. Longbranch Improvement Club Marina welcomes visiting boaters. Homeowners around the bay shoot off impressive fireworks on the 4th of July, which can be seen from the Club Marina docks.

⑭ **Longbranch Improvement Club Marina.** 5213 Key Penninsula Hwy. S., Longbranch, WA 98351; (253)884-5137; (253) 307-1873 cell; licdockmaster@gmail.com; www.longbranchimprovementclub.org. Longbranch is a good South Sound stopover, and especially popular as a destination for boating club cruises. Open all year, but hours vary in winter. The marina has 540 feet of side-tie dock space for guest moorage, 30 amp power, ice, Wi-Fi, garbage drop, water, portable toilets. No showers. No charge for 4-hour day moorage. Advance notification for groups is requested. Group cruises stack the boats in tightly, and raft several deep. Check their website for the schedule of group cruises. The guest moorage bull rails are painted yellow. The docks have a large covered area with roll-down canvas sides, lights, tables, chairs, heaters, barbecues, book exchange. This marina has a warm, friendly atmosphere.

If you've anchored out, the dinghy dock is on the west side of the main dock, next to the ramp. Mechanic and divers are on call. Dances are held Memorial Day, July 4th, and Labor Day at the historic Longbranch Improvement Club Hall, located about a half-mile away. The dances are popular and usually sell out.

Pitt Passage is a winding, shallow passage between McNeil Island and the mainland. Because the passage is shoal, many skippers avoid it. Safe transit, however, can be made by following the navigation aids between tiny Pitt Island and McNeil Island. The waters

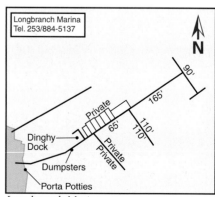
Longbranch Marina

west of Pitt Island are shoal.

Red, Right, Returning assumes you are returning from the north. This means that from the north, run an S-shaped course to leave the green can Wyckoff Shoal Buoys 1 and 3 to port, then turn east across the north side of Pitt Island to leave the red Daybeacon 4 to starboard. Continue between Pitt Island and McNeil Island, to leave the red nun Buoy 6 to starboard. Study the chart carefully before making your first run through Pitt Passage. Note how Wyckoff Shoal extends westward from McNeill Island almost across the mouth of the passage.

McNeil Island was a major state prison, which closed in 2011.

CARR INLET

Mayo Cove. Mayo Cove is pretty. The bay is shallow, however, and drying shoals are on either side. For exploring, take the dinghy part way up the inlet leading to Bay Lake.

Lakebay Marina & Resort. 15 Lorenz Road, Lakebay, WA 98349; (253) 884-3350; www.lakebaymarina.com. Open May through Labor Day. Located across Mayo Cove from Penrose Point Marine State Park. Beware that waters are shallow approaching the marina and park docks. Charts may not accurately depict water depths.

Lakebay Marina was built on a historic Mosquito Fleet landing. 30 guest slips, 30 amp power, water, restrooms, boat launch, a small store, and a large meeting/dining room. Free Wi-Fi. Pumpout planned for 2019. Ethanol-free gasoline at the fuel dock, no diesel. Campsites and cabins for rent. A tandem bicycle is available for overnight guests. Kayaks and stand-up paddleboards can be rented.

The Lakebay Cafe is on site and has good meals, bar, fishing tackle and clothing items. It is open 7 days a week in summer; closed Mondays and Tuesdays in winter. Breakfast Saturday and Sunday. A large dining room, with theater seats and old photos of the marina, is nice for groups.

Clam digging for overnight guests. The marina has a cocktail bar and regularly hosts beer tastings and live music in the summer. See their website for the schedule.

⑮ **Penrose Point Marine State Park.** (253) 884-2514. In Mayo Cove, west shore of Carr Inlet. Open for mooring and camping year-round. The 158-foot dock has 270 feet of side-tie space. The inner side of the dock grounds on lower tides. 8 mooring buoys for boats 45 feet and under. Self register and pay mooring fee on shore. Facilities include Cascadia Marine Trail campsite, picnic sites, restrooms, seasonal showers, pumpout, portapotty dump. No power. Standard campsites, 2.5 miles of hiking and biking trails, clamming, oyster picking, swimming, fishing. At low tide enter the cove with care.

Von Geldern Cove. Von Geldern Cove is a shallow bay exposed to northerly winds.

Anchorage is possible near the entrance. Most of the shoreline is residential. The town of Home, with a launch ramp, has some supplies. Take the dinghy under the bridge at the head of the bay and explore the creek until it's too shallow.

The town has an interesting past. Home was founded in the late 1800's by three men and their families, who wanted to establish a community based on an anarchist philosophy. Land was provided to those who became members of the community's Association and agreed to the anarchist ideals. The community later divided into factions and eventually dissolved in 1919.

Glen Cove is protected by a spit, but is very shallow and not recommended for overnight anchorage.

Rosedale. Rosedale is a small community tucked in behind Raft Island. Good anchorage. Enter the bay to the north of Raft Island, since a causeway connects the island to the mainland across the very shoal south side. The small and quaint Island View Market, with groceries and liquor, has a dinghy dock.

Cutts Island Marine State Park. (253) 265-3606. Open all year, day use only, 8 overnight mooring buoys for boats 45 feet and under. Self-register and pay mooring fee on shore. Accessible by boat only. No power, no water, no toilets, no camping or fires allowed. Easy row to Kopachuck Marine State Park. Cutts Island is connected to Raft Island by a drying shoal. Watch your depths if you try to cross between Cutts Island and Raft Island. We are told that in bygone days, Cutts Island was an Native American burial ground, and its local name is Dead Man's Island.

⑯ **Kopachuck Marine State Park.** (253) 265-3606. Three miles north of Fox Island, just north of Horsehead Bay. Open all year for day use and mooring. 2 overnight mooring buoys for boats 45 feet and under. Self-register and pay mooring fee on shore. Good bottom for anchoring, but unprotected. Underwater park with artificial reef for scuba diving. Kitchen shelters, picnic sites. Playground, trail, clamming, fishing. Swimming in shallow water off the beach area. The campgrounds are permanently closed due to hazardous trees.

Horsehead Bay. Horsehead Bay is an excellent anchorage, surrounded by fine homes. A launch ramp is near the harbor entrance. Good holding ground is a short distance inside the bay.

Hale Passage separates Fox Island from the Olympic Peninsula, and is crossed by a bridge with a mean high water clearance of 31 feet. A short distance east of the bridge, a green can buoy marks a drying, boulder-studded shoal. Pass to the north of the buoy. Currents run strongly through Hale Passage, with 1 to 2.5

knots common, flooding west and ebbing east. The ebb current is stronger than the flood.

Fox Island is connected to the mainland by a bridge with a mean high water clearance of 31 feet. Good anchorage can be found behind Tanglewood Island, which has a pavilion used by yacht clubs and other groups for special occasions. Residents of Fox Island are protective of their privacy, so it is a good idea to stay aboard unless invited ashore.

Wollochet Bay. Wollochet Bay winds a couple of miles into the mainland off Hale Passage. The shores of the bay are lined with homes, many with mooring buoys, but good anchorage can be found. The mouth of the bay is open to southerly winds. Inside, the waters are protected. Tacoma Yacht Club has an outstation near the head of the bay.

We've had good luck catching crab at the mouth of the bay.

A favorite pastime while visiting Wollochet Bay is launching the dinghy and exploring the saltwater marsh and estuary area at Wollochet Bay Estuary Park. The park, at the very head of the bay, has 854 linear feet of shoreline including the confluence of Artondale Creek.

Ketron Island. Privately owned.

HENDERSON INLET, NISQUALLY, STEILACOOM, TACOMA NARROWS

Henderson Inlet extends about 5 miles south from Itsami Ledge. The inlet has been the site of major logging operations over the years, and log rafts are still stored along the west side. Anchorage is good along approximately half of the inlet before it becomes too shallow near the entrance to Woodward Creek.

⑰ **Zittel's Marina Inc.** 9144 Gallea St. NE, Olympia, WA 98516; (360) 459-1950; www.zittelsmarina.com. Open all year, hours may vary in the winter. Ethanol-free gasoline and diesel at the fuel dock. Guest moorage in unoccupied slips and side-tie up to 65 feet when available (don't count on availability), 30 amp power, launch ramp, restrooms,

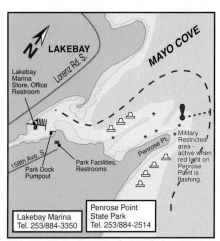

Penrose Point State Park & Lakebay Marina

pumpout, portapotty dump, showers. Haulout and repairs, limited marine supplies, boat rentals, groceries, bait and tackle. Owned and operated by Mike and Kathi Zittel.

Johnson Point is a popular salmon fishing area. Two launch ramps are at Johnson Point, but no facilities for visiting boaters.

Tolmie Marine State Park. (360) 753-1519. Eight miles northeast of Olympia. This 105-acre park is open all year for day use and overnight moorage, except closed for day use Mondays and Tuesdays in winter. Restrooms and showers. 5 mooring buoys for boats 45 feet and under are well offshore; beach and shallows extend out some distance. Self-register and pay mooring fee on shore. The underwater park for scuba diving includes sunken wooden barges. Hiking trails, picnic sites with barbecues, meeting room. Nice sandy beach. The park includes a small saltwater lagoon marsh area good for watching wildlife. No camping.

Nisqually Reach is the body of water south of Anderson Island, between the island and the mainland. The channel is marked by buoys along the extensive mudflats of the Nisqually River delta. The delta is a wildlife refuge, and is accessible by boat at half tide or better, by way of the Luhrs Beach launch ramp near Nisqually Head. Tom Kincaid has entered the river itself by dinghy, but from the water side the entrance is hard to spot.

Steilacoom. Picnic area on a small pebble beach, launch ramp, and fishing pier adjacent to the ferry landing. A year-round 60-foot day-use dock available for hourly moorage, limited to boats 23 feet and under, adjacent to the ferry landing. Steilacoom, incorporated in 1854, is the oldest incorporated town in Washington. A museum, restaurants, and other services are nearby. Steilacoom Marina, at Gordon Point, is abandoned and dilapidated.

Tacoma Narrows. All of the water in southern Puget Sound flows through Tacoma Narrows, with 4- to 6-knot currents common. Day Island Yacht Club, Narrows Marina, and Day Island Marina are on the east side of the south end of the Narrows. The Tacoma Narrows bridges, more than a mile long and 180 feet above the water, are two of the world's longest suspension bridges.

Back eddies form along the sides of the narrows, useful when transiting with an opposing current.

⑱ **Narrows Marina.** 9007 S. 19th St. Suite 100, Tacoma, WA 98466; (253) 564-3032; nmbt@narrowsmarina.com; www.narrowsmarina.com. Open all year except Christmas week, three days during Thanksgiving, and Easter Sunday. Ethanol-free gasoline and diesel at the fuel dock, restrooms, pumpout, transient moorage, long term parking, convenience store, tackle and

live bait. Full service repairs on-site with a 9-ton lift.

Painted boards along the docks indicate where you can tie up. Green indicates free moorage for visits less than three hours. Blue indicates reserved transient moorage; call ahead for a slip assignment. The fuel dock is inside the breakwater in the northeast corner of the marina. Currents can run strongly at the docks.

The Boathouse 19 restaurant and Narrows Brewing Company are on site. The top of the bar at Boathouse 19 is made from the old Day Island Bridge and the table tops are from Nalley Valley pickle barrels. Narrows Brewing Company has a tasting room where you can bring your own food and sample a variety of beers.

Narrows Marina is a 10 minute taxi ride from Chambers Bay Golf Course, the site of the 2015 U.S. Open.

Days Island. If your destination is the Day Island Yacht Club at the back of the lagoon, run down the west side, close to Days Island and its boathouses. At lower tides this will be obvious, because a big drying shoal blocks the middle. Time your passage for mid-tide or higher. Least depth at zero tide is said to be 4 feet.

Titlow Park. Tacoma Narrows Waterway. Located on the Tacoma side, about 1 mile south of the Tacoma Narrows Bridge. Open all year, park with tennis courts and 'Spray Ground' (splash park). Restaurants a short walk away. Titlow Park is a marine preserve with excellent diving.

CENTRAL PUGET SOUND

 LOCAL KNOWLEDGE

SPEED LIMIT: A no-wake speed of 5 mph or less is enforced within Gig Harbor and 200 feet outside the entrance.

⑲ **Gig Harbor.** www.gigharborguide.com. Gig Harbor is one of the most perfectly protected harbors in Puget Sound, and one of the most charming towns. The south shore is lined with moorages for the substantial commercial fish boat and pleasure boat fleets. The entrance to Gig Harbor is narrow, especially at low tide. Maintain a mid-channel course around the end of the spit.

Gig Harbor has overnight moorage, marine supplies, major repairs, and haulout. Anchorage is in 20 to 42 feet with good

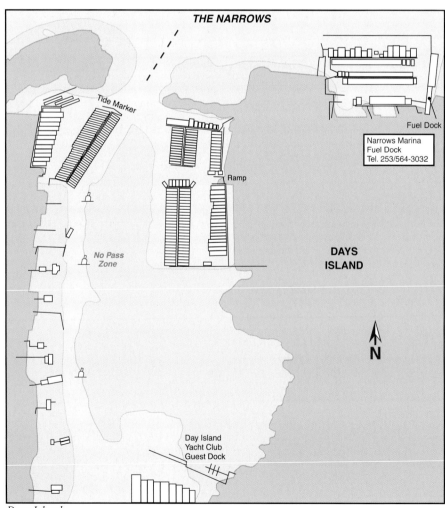

Days Island

holding, although the bay shoals close to both shores and toward the head. In some areas, weed on the bottom can foul anchors.

The City of Gig Harbor maintains Jerisich Park with its dinghy dock, long moorage float, 30 amp power, water and holding tank pumpout. The Gig Harbor Maritime Pier, 40-feet, next to Tides Tavern, has temporary moorage, restrooms and pumpout.

We enjoy walking Gig Harbor's village-like commercial streets. The harbor is lined with shops, galleries, specialty shops and antiquing are excellent, and the architecture turn-of-the-20th-century. At least two shops serve enormous ice cream cones and have chairs out front where you can enjoy your treat in the shade. Several good restaurants, from casual to elegant. On the casual side, Tides Tavern, a short distance inside the mouth of the bay, is a longtime favorite. If you are lucky, you'll find room to tie the boat at their private dock. Tides Tavern personnel can come to your boat to take your order and deliver your meal dockside, a nice option for families. Anthony's, near the head of the bay, also has a dock. More likely, you'll take the dinghy or approach by land. The JW Trolley at the Gig Harbor Marina & Boatyard is a local Gig Harbor favorite for informal dining. Open 8:30 a.m. to dusk.

Finholm's Market and Deli, The Harbor General Store, and The Waterfront Natural Market offer some groceries within easy walking distance of the waterfront. Several supermarkets are uptown, best reached by

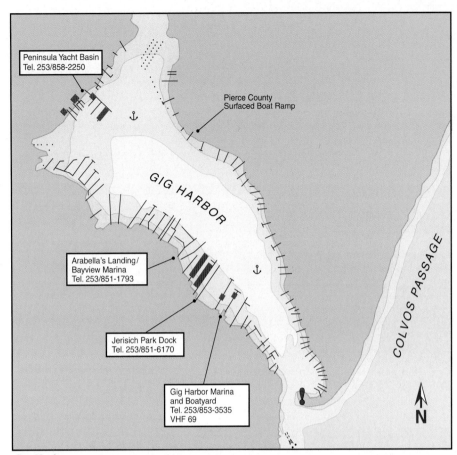

Gig Harbor

Marinas, anchorages, and restaurants abound in gorgeous Gig Harbor.

bus or taxi. In the summer months, a trolley-themed bus service runs seven days a week, frequently between the waterfront and uptown areas.

For a great view of Gig Harbor and Mt. Rainier, the local Lions Club built an observation area called the Finholm View Climb. The stairway is at the head of the bay, across the street from Anthony's Restaurant. Lee's SUP & Kayak rentals are located in front of Anthony's Restaurant.

For a romantic time with someone special, grab your favorite refreshment and take a gondola tour of the harbor (gigharborgondola.com). A small snack box of cheese, fruit and chocolates is provided.

The beautiful Gig Harbor History Museum (www.harborhistorymuseum.org) is superb. Located at the west end of Harborview Drive, the main road along the waterfront.

⑲ Gig Harbor Marina and Boatyard. 3117 Harborview Drive, Gig Harbor, WA 98335; (253) 858-3535; www.gigharbormarina.com. Monitors VHF 69. Open all year with guest moorage in unoccupied slips, 30 amp power, water, garbage drop, and free Wi-Fi. Restrooms with showers. Reservations accepted. Full service boatyard with haulout to 50 tons. "The Club" building and classroom space are available for rendezvous and other events.

⑲ Arabella's Landing. 3323 Harborview Drive, Gig Harbor, WA 98335; (253) 851-1793; info@arabellaslanding.com; www.arabellaslanding.com. Open all year, 225 feet of guest side-tie moorage for boats up to 175 feet, six 50-foot slips, and one 60-foot slip; 30 & 50 amp power, water, Wi-Fi, restrooms, showers, laundry, secured gate, pumpout. ADA accessible. Reservations recommended.

Stan and Judy Stearns developed this classy marina, located a short distance past the city dock, close to shopping, restaurants, services, and groceries. Excellent concrete docks, beautiful grounds, and brick walkways. They have a well-trained crew to help with landings, make dinner reservations, or assist in finding someone to repair your boat if necessary. The moorage fee includes power, water, and showers. Group gatherings may make use of the clubhouse with lounge, fireplace, and coffee service.

Enjoy Netshed No. 9 restaurant at the top of the docks for breakfast and lunch, and make reservations for a 5-star dinner at Brix 25. Ship to Shore Marine Supply, on site, has an excellent stock of marine supplies and kayaks which you may try-out in their infinity pool. Arabella's has two Airbnb suites for their guests that want to stay ashore. See GigHarborAirbnb for reservations for the "The Sail Loft" and "The Cove Suite."

Bayview Marina, just east of Arabella's Landing, is under the same ownership, with 250 feet of dock, 30 & 50 amp power and water on the dock.

⑲ Jerisich Dock. 3211 Harborview Drive,

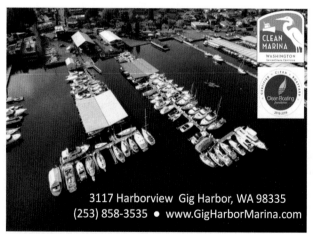

CRUISING THE SHOULDERS

Prime cruising season in the Pacific Northwest is in July and August, that's when you find the largest number of boats out cruising. In the past, boating activity didn't get started until well after Memorial Day and dropped-off after Labor Day. More recently, boating activity starts earlier in the season and continues well into fall. There are several factors stretching the boating season into the shoulder months of spring and fall.

The Pacific Northwest and the Inside Passage have been discovered. More out-of-area boaters are enjoying the protected waters, mild climate, and the unique boater friendly destinations this area has to offer. Western Washington and specifically the Seattle metro area have seen an influx of people in recent years that are eager to enjoy the area's great boating. Add to this a vibrant economy, providing people with time and money to get out on the water, and you get a significant increase in boating activity seen over the last three to five years.

Spring and fall shoulder cruising seasons have much to offer the boater that has the flexibility to take advantage of these opportunities. Before Memorial Day and after Labor Day, there are so few recreational boaters out there that VHF channel 16 is almost silent. We sometimes switch to VHF weather channels to ensure the radio is working. There are far fewer boats during a shoulder season, easing competition for moorage, anchorage, and access to services. Yes, there are some trade-offs; marina staffing levels may be reduced, and hours and days of operation may be curtailed. In early spring, you may find marina facilities and staff that may not be completely ready for your visit. So, when cruising in shoulder season, be adaptable and flexible. You may need to leave a message and wait for a callback to your inquiry for moorage. You may have to arrive a little earlier and depart later to accommodate off-season office hours.

The rewards for cruising in the shoulder season are many. Prices are often reduced and availability is greater. Often people have more time to share insider information about places to visit or things to do. You may find other cruisers more eager to visit and share boating stories. You will get more use out of your annual state parks pass. You will have your choice of prime spots in popular anchorages.

For marina operators in the Broughtons and elsewhere, the boating season is unfortunately too short. Marinas welcome a longer season and tend to open earlier and stay open later if demand calls for it. Cruising the shoulder season can bring new friendships and new opportunities, and in the process, help to convince marinas to extend their season. Give it a try, get out there early and come back later in the season.

Which areas are best for shoulder season cruising? South, Central, and North Puget Sound are some areas that start the earliest and run much later in the season. These areas are effectively year-round boating destinations. Next, the San Juan Islands, Gulf Islands, Vancouver B.C. destinations are good early and late season areas. Desolation Sound, north to and including the Broughtons, tend to be later in the shoulder season with facilities ready for full operation around Memorial Day, and curtailing operations by mid-September. Because of resort fishing activity, West Coast Vancouver Island around Barkley Sound and Tofino get started earlier than Desolation Sound.

September and October can often be a surprisingly good time of the year to cruise the Pacific Northwest waters from Olympia to Desolation Sound. Despite the occasional early fall storms that will have you sheltered for a few days, there can be some excellent fall cruising with settled weather, gorgeous sunsets, and empty anchorages.   *[Landons]*

Gig Harbor, WA; (253) 851-6170; www.cityofgigharbor.net. Open all year, 420 feet of first-come, first-served dock space, 30 amp power, seasonal water, free seasonal pumpout. Two mooring buoys for vessels 32 feet and under (no charge), but required to register. This is an attractive and well-used public dock and park, located just west of Tides Tavern on the downtown side of Gig Harbor. Maximum 3-night stay within a 10-day period. Pay overnight moorage fees at self-payment kiosk adjacent to the dock, credit and debit cards accepted. Dinghy dock is near shore on the west side. Restaurants, groceries, and a seasonal trolley café are all within walking distance. Check your tide table; close to shore you could touch at low tide.

The Welcome Plaza is located upland from the Jerisich Dock in Skansie Brothers Park. Restrooms, showers, and laundry facilities for visiting boaters are located at the plaza. The Splash Fountain is popular with children. A viewing deck, with tables and chairs, is located above the restrooms.

⑲ **Peninsula Yacht Basin.** 8913 N. Harborview Drive, Gig Harbor, WA 98332; (253) 858-2250; dockmaster@peninsulayachtbasin.com; peninsulayachtbasin.com. Open all year, no transient moorage, reciprocal privileges with Gig Harbor Yacht Club only. Maximum boat length 85 feet, 6-foot depth at zero tide, 20 & 30 amp power, restrooms, showers. Located on the north shore of Gig Harbor, next to Anthony's Shoreline Restaurant.

ANTHONY'S AT GIG HARBOR
8827 Harborview Dr. N.
(253) 853-6353

TACOMA AREA

Commencement Bay. The southern shoreline of Commencement Bay is mostly parks, interspersed with buildings, housing, restaurants, and other facilities. At least two

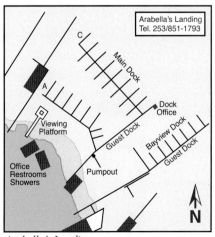

Arabella's Landing

RESTAURANTS, SHOPS & SERVICES

ANTHONY'S

Anthony's at Gig Harbor serves premium NW seafood and offers a spectacular view of the harbor and Mt. Rainier. Enjoy the view from our expansive deck. Downstairs in our Shoreline Room lounge is a lighter menu and a more casual dining experience.
253-853-6353 • 8827 Harborview Dr. N., Gig Harbor, WA 98335 www.anthonys.com

HARBOR HISTORY MUSEUM

Harbor History Museum creates opportunities to experience the heritage of the greater Gig Harbor communities by collecting, preserving, and sharing the rich history of the area. Artifacts, video kiosks, hands-on exhibits, computer interactives, and a small theater bring Peninsula history to life in our permanent galleries. In addition, the Museum provides 3-5 special exhibits throughout the year so there is always something new to see and experience for our members and visitors.
253.858.6722 ext. 5 • 4121 Harborview Drive, Gig Harbor, WA 98332 • www.harborhistorymuseum.org

HERITAGE DISTILLING CO.

Heritage Distilling Company (HDC) is a craft distillery with 2 tasting
room locations in Gig Harbor. HDC makes award winning vodkas,
gins, and whiskeys. Learn more at www.heritagedistilling.com.
**253.509.0008 • 3207 57th St Ct NW & 3118 Harborview Dr.,
Gig Harbor, WA 98335 • www.heritagedistilling.com**

GIG HARBOR COMMUNITY EVENTS

Monthly First Saturday FREE Art Walk at various downtown galleries www.gigharborwaterfront.org

April - Annual Gig Harbor Paddlers Cup www.gigharborpaddlerscup.com

May - Street Scramble - An urban scavenger hunt! www.gigharborguide.com

May - Gig Harbor Beer Festival www.gigharborbeerfestival.com

June - Maritime Gig Festival www.maritimegig.com

June - Aug 14 Summer Sounds at Skansie Every Tuesday - Enjoy an outdoor concert! www.gigharborguide.com

July - Gig Harbor Wings and Wheels Air Show and Car Show www.freedomfair.com

July - Chalk the Harbor www.gigharborwaterfront.org

July - Peninsula Art Leauge's ArtFest www.peninsulaartleague.com

July - Gig Harbor Wine & Food Festival www.gigharborwaterfront.org

September - Race for a Soldier Half Marathon and 5K www.raceforasoldier.org

October - Gig Harbor Film Festival www.gigharborfilmfestival.org

November - Annual Girls Night Out www.gigharborwaterfront.org

November - Donkey Creek Chum Festival www.harborwildwatch.org

November - Turkey Trot www.gigharborturkeytrot.com

December - Lighted Boat Parade gigharboryachtclub.wildapricot.org/

Visit GigHarborGuide.com for events and information

restaurants provide moorage for their patrons. Following this shoreline southeastward leads to the Thea Foss Waterway.

Tacoma's Commencement Bay is busy with commercial traffic. Most visiting boats choose to moor at one of several marinas in the Thea Foss Waterway. Museums, restaurants, and other attractions are a short walk from the docks.

Point Defiance. Point Defiance marks the northern end of Tacoma Narrows and is noted for swirling currents and excellent salmon fishing. The entire point is a major Tacoma park, complete with trails, a zoo, aquarium, gardens, sports facilities, and picnic areas.

20 Breakwater Marina. 5603 N. Waterfront Drive, Tacoma, WA 98407; (253) 752-6663 (office); (253) 752-6685 (service); www. breakwatermarina.com. Certified Clean Marina. Open all year, 15 & 30 amp power, restrooms, showers, laundry, portapotty dump, pumpout, propane, store. Guest moorage is in unoccupied slips for boats up to 45 feet, call ahead. Repairs available.

5910 N. Waterfront Drive
(253) 752-9700

20 Point Defiance Boathouse Marina. 5912 N. Waterfront Drive, Tacoma, WA 98407; (253) 591-5325; pointdefiancemarina.com. Certified Clean Marina and 5-Star EnviroStar rating. Open 7 days a week all year except Thanksgiving and Christmas. Guest moorage is on the dock between the ferry landing and the 8-lane boat launch, 72 hour maximum stay. Pay at the boat launch kiosk. Ethanol-free gasoline, restrooms, free pumpout, some 30 amp power, dry storage for small boats, boat rentals. Bait, tackle, snacks, souvenirs and gift items at Point Defiance Boathouse Tackle Shop. Public fishing pier. Anthony's Restaurant is at the east end of the marina. The marina is within walking distance of the Point Defiance Zoo & Aquarium and Point Defiance Park. Bus service to greater Tacoma.

Ruston. Point Defiance below the community of Ruston is the Tacoma terminus of the ferry to Vashon Island. The Point Defiance Boathouse Marina and Anthony's Harbor Lights restaurant are west of the ferry dock. A large launch ramp, operated by the Parks Department, is east of the ferry dock. Long-term tow vehicle and trailer storage is available a couple of blocks up the hill from the launch ramp.

The small town of Ruston was the site of a smelter. The site has recently been redeveloped, and a substantial footbridge now leads to the ferry terminal. A half-mile east of Point Defiance is the impressive Point Ruston development, consisting of classy condos and apartments, shops, cafes, and a theater.

A 'splash pad' overlooks the waterfront and pathway that connects Point Ruston to Point Defiance. Point Ruston is definitely worth a visit for the grand views, eateries, and park-like atmosphere.

Old Town Dock. Next to Jack Hyde Park (formerly Commencement Park). The docks are usable, but don't appear to get much traffic. Smaller boats only.

LOCAL KNOWLEDGE

STRONG CURRENTS: Currents, especially on large tides, can run stronger than expected in Thea Foss Waterway. Plan landings and departures accordingly.

Thea Foss Waterway. The Thea Foss Waterway (formerly City Waterway) has gone through a major renewal and revitalization.

Just inside the mouth of the waterway, the Foss Waterway Seaport is a fascinating stop. It is housed in the century-old Balfour warehouse, once part of a mile-long row of wheat warehouses. The 300-foot-long by 150-foot-wide building is itself a museum exhibit. Displays inside include a lab, a working boat building shop, Willits canoe exhibit, marine biology exhibit, and an extensive display detailing Puget Sound's maritime history. Some 1200 feet of public floats make boat access easy.

Up on Pacific Avenue, the Union Railroad Station has been restored and rebuilt as the Federal Courthouse, and decorated with Dale Chihuly glass sculpture. The must-see Washington State History Museum, which shares the courthouse's beautiful architecture, is next door.

The Washington State History Museum is excellent. Allow at least two hours to see it; three or four hours is better. The museum is enjoyable for both children and adults.

At the head of the waterway, the Museum of Glass fronts on the waterway, immediately east of the courthouse and the Washington State History Museum.

The Chihuly Bridge of Glass connects the courthouse and history museum complex with the Museum of Glass. You can spend several hours there. The hot shop furnaces roar, and the crew may create a bowl, a vase, or candlestick holders before your eyes. Exhibits in the galleries rotate. The works on display are impressive.

The Tacoma Art Museum features regularly rotating exhibits, and the building itself is a work of architectural art.

LeMay-America's Car Museum, across the road from the Tacoma Dome, draws large crowds. More than 350 cars, trucks and motorcycles are on display, dating from the beginning of motorized transport. Open 7 days a week, 10:00 a.m. to 5:00 p.m. Check website for weekly events. Highly recommended.

Downtown Tacoma is very different from other Puget Sound cities. Many of the old buildings are beautiful, and some are historic. One building has a plaque commemorating Russell G. O'Brien, who on October 18, 1893, originated the custom of standing during the playing of the Star Spangled Banner. We learn the most interesting things when we walk around.

Guest Moorage: Dock Street Marina, with guest moorage, is in front of the Museum of Glass. Guest moorage is also available at Foss Harbor Marina. Side-tie guest moorage is available at Foss Waterway Seaport.

No Anchoring Zone: All of the Thea Foss Waterway is a no anchoring zone.

Breweries: Area breweries include McMenamins Elks Lodge on 565 Broadway; Odd Otter Brewing at 716 Pacific; Pacific Brewing & Malting at 610 Pacific Ave.; and 7 Seas Brewing at 2101 Jefferson Ave.

Farmers Market: On Broadway between 9th and 11th Streets, a farmers market with 70 to 90 vendors. Thursdays, May through October from 10:00 a.m. to 3:00 p.m.

Light Rail: Light rail runs from the theater district at the north end of downtown Tacoma to a last stop, 2½ blocks from the Tacoma Dome and LeMay-America's Car Museum. At the museum district, the tracks are in the middle of Pacific Avenue, fronting the Washington State History Museum. The

93

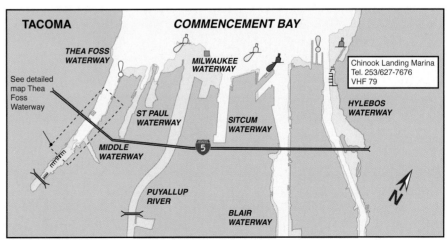

Commencement Bay

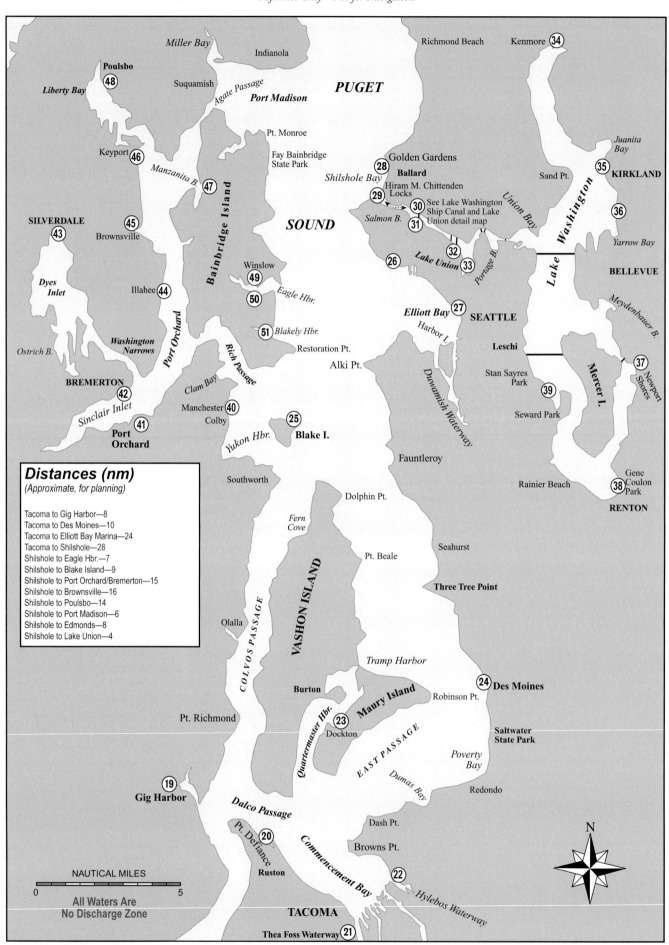

Distances (nm)
(Approximate, for planning)

Tacoma to Gig Harbor—8
Tacoma to Des Moines—10
Tacoma to Elliott Bay Marina—24
Tacoma to Shilshole—28
Shilshole to Eagle Hbr.—7
Shilshole to Blake Island—9
Shilshole to Port Orchard/Bremerton—15
Shilshole to Brownsville—16
Shilshole to Poulsbo—14
Shilshole to Port Madison—6
Shilshole to Edmonds—8
Shilshole to Lake Union—4

NAUTICAL MILES

0   5

**All Waters Are
No Discharge Zone**

Central Puget Sound

free trains are clean and safe. They run every 12 minutes from morning to evening.

With the accomplishments and ongoing efforts of the Port of Tacoma, city leaders and others, The Foss Waterway and downtown Tacoma is a first class urban boating destination.

THINGS TO DO

1. LeMay-America's Car Museum. This museum is housed in a dramatic building, just up from the waterfront. See over 350 cars, trucks and motorcycles on display in the world's largest auto museum.

2. Museum of Glass. With its iconic architecture near the waterfront and beautiful glasswork, this has become a key part of the Tacoma art scene.

Looking south in the Thea Foss Waterway, as seen from the 11th St. bridge

3. Tacoma Art Museum. Art in Tacoma continues with photography, paintings, and Chihuly glass.

4. Washington State History Museum. Learn about Washington's past.

5. Tacoma Glassblowing Studio. See how glass art is made.

6. Point Defiance Zoo & Aquarium. See an Asian Forest Sanctuary, elephants and tigers. The large aquarium has octopi, sharks, and a beluga whale.

7. Children's Museum of Tacoma. The museum serves young children and their parents through self-directed play.

8. Daffodil Festival. See the annual Daffodil street parade held in early April, followed by the parade of boats all decorated in daffodils, held mid-April.

㉑ **Foss Waterway Seaport.** 705 Dock St, Tacoma, WA 98402; (253) 272-2750; info@fosswaterwayseaport.org; www.fosswaterwayseaport.org. Located at the mouth of Foss Waterway. Visitor moorage

along 1200 feet of floating dock. From the middle gangway to the south end, 30 & 50 amp power and water are available. No power or water north of the middle gangway. No restrooms or garbage drop. Pumpout available April through September. Reservations only for groups. Payment is made at the Seaport office, or drop box after hours, 4 hour free stay. A dock for floatplanes is attached to the northwest end of the Seaport Facility; watch for floatplane activity.

㉑ **Foss Harbor Marina.** 821 Dock Street, Tacoma, WA 98402; (253) 272-4404; info@fossharbor.com; www.fossharbormarina.com. Certified Clean Marina. Monitors VHF 71. Open all year, ethanol-free gasoline and diesel at end of D dock. Visitor moorage to 95 feet in unoccupied slips. Restrooms, showers, laundry, water, fixed and slip-side pumpout, portapotty dump, 30 & 50 amp power, free Wi-Fi in lounge area, Wi-Fi on the docks for a fee, kayak and SUP rentals. The docks have recently been improved and are excellent. Store has expanded beer and wine selection, deli sandwiches, convenience groceries, bait, tackle, marine supplies. An indoor lounge and outdoor patio are available for customers. Convenient walk to downtown.

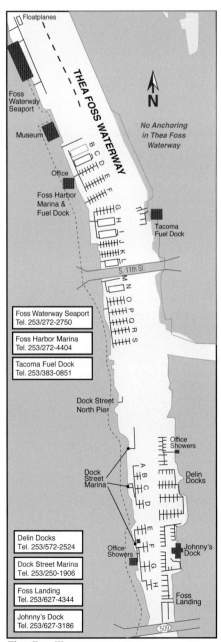

Thea Foss Waterway

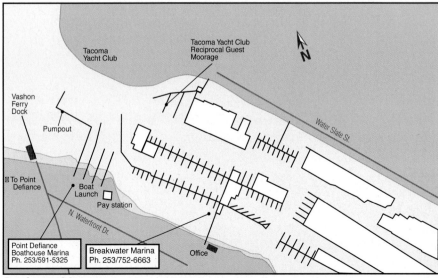

Breakwater Marina

TACOMA MUSEUM DISTRICT

Your Bridge to Culture

LeMay – America's Car Museum

Washington State History Museum

Museum of Glass

Foss Waterway Seaport

Tacoma Art Museum

Children's Museum of Tacoma

Six great museums. One low price.

www.TacomaMuseumDistrict.org

TACOMA REBORN

For years Tacoma was an industrial port and not friendly to recreational boaters. The city waterfront had been neglected, facilities were limited and there wasn't much to do. The city was famous more for its pulp mills than its historic buildings, museums, and restaurants.

In the late 1980s Tacoma's political leaders got serious about rejuvenating their city. The Simpson Paper Mill spent tens of millions of dollars on renovations, reducing emissions and sweetening the air. In 1990 the University of Washington established its Tacoma campus, which now has more than 4000 students just up the hill from the Thea Foss Waterway. Tacoma Link light rail was built to help the growing population get around the city.

Foss Waterway Seaport

Museum of Glass and waterfront walk

Much of Tacoma's redevelopment has been centered around the Thea Foss Waterway. In 1992 the former president of University of Puget Sound conceived of the idea for a glass museum. Working with Dale Chihuly, a Tacoma native, he proposed the glass museum be built in Tacoma. In 2002 the high-profile, 75,000 square foot Museum of Glass opened a few steps up from the Thea Foss Waterway. Exhibits show a variety of glass, from both Chihuly and other artists. The working hot-shop, visible to visitors, is a highlight.

Part of Tacoma's revitalization is the emergence of its museum district, conveniently located just upland from the Thea Foss Waterway. Above the Glass Museum is the outstanding Washington State History Museum, housed in a distinctive brick building. The Tacoma Art Museum is just north of the History Museum.

Seaport. The century-old Balfour Dock building was originally built for cargo arriving by rail and departing by sail. After a recent renovation, it now houses the Working Waterfront Maritime Museum. Inside you'll find notable classic boats and sailing vessels along with displays of boat building and restoration. The extensive guest dock along the waterfront offers four hours of free moorage, perfect when visiting the museum.

Looking south from the 11th Street bridge to the LeMay Museum

What would any progressive city be without a Children's Museum? The Children's Museum of Tacoma believes in the "Power of Play" and "Play to Learn", and play is the right of every child. The museum is new and bright, a fun place for kids. It moved to its current location on Pacific Avenue in 2012.

A single, discounted admission ticket to the Tacoma Art Museum, Museum of Glass, the LeMay America's Car Museum and the Washington State History Museum is available for $52.50, or $42 for students, active duty military, and seniors aged 65 and over. The pass is good for a seven day period while visiting Tacoma and includes a discount for the Foss Waterway Seaport. The Children's Museum of Tacoma is a "pay-as-you-will" museum.

Union Station

Tacoma has grown into one of the region's best urban destinations with an esplanade, restaurants and museums to explore, all within a short walk from marinas of the Thea Foss Waterway.

Tacoma Waterfront

Slightly further away is LeMay—America's Car Museum. Harold LeMay, now deceased, was a garbage pioneer. He started LeMay Inc. in 1942 and grew it into the 10th largest garbage hauler in the country. The wealth generated from his business endeavors allowed him to indulge his automotive hobby. Over time he and his wife collected more than 3,300 cars, trucks, and motorcycles—the largest private collection in the world. Today, more than 700 of his cars are on display in his namesake museum.

At the entrance to Thea Foss Waterway is Foss Waterway

㉑ Dock Street Marina. 1817 Dock St., Tacoma, WA 98402; (253) 250-1906; info@dockstreetmarina.com; www.dockstreetmarina.com. Call ahead by phone for slip assignment. Certified Clean Marina. Concrete docks, security gates, 30, 50 & 100 amp power, water, slip-side pumpout, garbage, recycling drop, laundry, restrooms, free showers, free cable TV, some wheelchair access, kayak rentals. Complimentary bicycles for marina guests. This is the marina in front of the Museum of Glass. It is made up of two sets of docks—G and H docks are the southern, guest moorage docks. The permanent moorage 17th St. docks are immediately north.

The office, showers, and laundry are above the guest moorage docks, 30 slips 36-60 feet, with 127-foot pier ends. Concierge service. Pet-friendly. Moorage in the north docks is by assignment in unoccupied slips only. A 320-foot dock is in the north moorage.

Special events such as the Daffodil Marine Parade completely fill the marina. See their website for the complete list of special events. Rendezvous sometimes fill the marina, too. Reservations recommended, even in the off season.

Dock Street Marina is first-class, with an easy walk to many Tacoma restaurants and museums. Don't be surprised to find a courtesy newspaper in the cockpit on Sundays, or a red rose on Valentine's Day.

The dramatic highway 509 bridge is just south of Dock Street Marina.

㉑ Dock Street North Pier. (253) 272-4352; This is the long concrete float north of Dock Street Marina. No power, water, or garbage, reservations 24-hours in advance. Watch your depths at zero tide or lower.

㉑ Delin Docks. 1616 East D St., Tacoma, WA 98421; (253) 572-2524; info@delindocksmarina.com; www.delindocksmarina.com. Certified Clean Marina. Open all year, 30 & 50 amp power, water, restrooms, free showers, laundry, pumpout, portapotty dump. These are nice docks with 30- to 60-foot slips, located immediately north of Johnny's Dock on the east side of Foss Waterway. They're primarily permanent moorage, although occasionally unoccupied slips might be used for guest moorage.

Note: Dock Street Marina and the Delin Docks are under the same management.

㉑ Johnny's Dock. 1900 East D St., Tacoma, WA 98421; (253) 627-3186; www.johnnysdock.com. Open all year with limited moorage to 55 feet, power, and water. Transient moorage primarily serves Johnny's Dock restaurant.

㉑ Tacoma Fuel Dock. 820 East D St., Tacoma, WA 98421; (253) 383-0851; (800) 868-3681, www.cbmsi.com. Fuel dock open all year except Thanksgiving, Christmas, and New Year's Day. Summer hours 8:00 a.m. to dusk, winter hours 8:00 a.m. to 4:30 p.m. Monitors VHF 69, summer only. Gasoline, diesel, ice, frozen herring, soft drinks, snacks. Located on the east side of Thea Foss Waterway; look for the large Tacoma Fuel Dock sign. The uplands house Commencement Bay Marine Services and the Tacoma Youth Marine Center, training young people in the skills needed for work on boats and along the waterfront. A portion of fuel sales supports the Sea Scouts and Tacoma Youth Marine Center.

Hylebos Waterway. The Hylebos Waterway follows the north shore of Commencement Bay and includes a number of moorages, boat builders, and boat service businesses. The shores are lined with heavy industry of many kinds, not all of it scenic. Still, an interesting exploration.

TACOMA MARKETPLACE

RESTAURANTS, SHOPS & SERVICES

ALFRED'S
We serve Breakfast, Lunch and Dinner all day, and we have a full service bar. Want a great breakfast, come see us. With its great food, generous cocktails, fun, old fashioned atmosphere and friendlier than average staff, Alfred's is a favorite with locals and visitors alike. Take the free link train to the Dome District.
253-627-5491 • 402 Puyallup Ave • One block west of the Dome at the corner of East D St and Puyallup

CHILDREN'S MUSEUM OF TACOMA
We encourage all ages to celebrate play with our playscapes and innovative design that celebrates imagination and encourages creativity. The museum has five main play areas – Woods, Water, Voyager, Invention and Becka's Studio. We are open Wednesday to Sunday from 10am to 5pm. Admission is by donation. Come play with us!
253-627-6031 • 1501 Pacific Ave. • www.playtacoma.org

DOCK STREET MARINA
Dock Street Marina is Tacoma's only dedicated guest moorage facility. Located in front of the Museum of Glass and just steps away from the Chihuly Bridge of Glass that leads to more museums, shops and restaurants. Reservations recommended. Please call.
253-250-1906 • www.dockstreetmarina.com.

FOSS WATERWAY SEAPORT
The Foss Waterway Seaport celebrates Tacoma's rich maritime heritage—past, present and future. Located on the waterfront in a century-old wheat warehouse built cargo arriving by " rail and departing by sail!" Features maritime heritage exhibits, land and boat based marine science, heritage boat shop and hands on activities for ages. Short term moorage, power & water. Home of Festival of Sail (tall ships) June 15 -18, 2017.
253-272-2750 ext 100 • 705 Dock Street • www.fosswaterwayseaport.org

LEMAY – AMERICA'S CAR MUSEUM
Celebrating America's love affair with the automobile. The four-level, 165,000 sq. ft. museum features rotating exhibits and 300 cars, trucks and motorcycles on display. Free Tacoma Link Light Rail from Union Station to the Dome District.
253-779-8490 • 2702 E. D Street • www.americascarmuseum.org

MUSEUM OF GLASS
The world famous Museum of Glass is located at the south end of the Foss Waterway with adjacent guest moorage. Featuring multiple exhibitions and art installations, hands-on art studio, diverse educational programs, and a fully functioning glass blowing Hot Shop, the museum offers a unique and entertaining experience for all. Hours are 10am to 5pm, Tuesday through Sunday.
253-284-4750 • 1801 Dock St. • www.MuseumofGlass.org

NORTHWEST YACHTNET BROKERAGE
Our brokers have the knowledge, contacts and yachting expertise to give you optimal service in any area that you require. NW Yachtnet Brokerage brokers complete the continuing education required to be "Certified Professional Yacht Brokers." Our highly skilled team will treat you with honesty and respect. We are here to make boating the enjoyable experience it is meant to be. We have offices in Tacoma, Seattle, and Olympia.
1-888-641-5901 • www.nwyachtnet.com
1717 Dock Street (next to the Museum of Glass)

ROCK THE DOCK
Always great food, friends and fun on the Thea Foss Waterway! Live music every weekend - never a cover charge. Dock side outdoor seating. Full menu on line, find us on Facebook or visit our website for a full calendar of events.
253-272-5004 • 535 Dock St. • www.RocktheDockPub.com

TACOMA ART MUSEUM
Tacoma Art Museum serves the diverse communities of the Northwest through its collection, exhibitions, and learning programs, emphasizing art and artists from the Northwest and broader western region. We are open Tuesday to Sunday from 10am to 5pm.
253-272-4258 • 1701 Pacific Avenue • www.tacomaartmuseum.org

WASHINGTON STATE HISTORICAL SOCIETY
Our museum is dedicated to collecting, preserving and vividly presenting Washington's rich and storied history. We invite you to explore our interactive exhibits and high-tech displays, listen to theatrical storytelling, discover dramatic artifacts and learn about Washington State's unique people and places.
253-272-9747 • 1911 Pacific Ave. • www.washingtonhistor.org

TACOMA COMMUNITY EVENTS

April	Daffodil Festival • Sailing Schooner Zodiac Easter Brunch Cruises www.fosswaterwayseaport • Tacoma City Marathon
May	Apple Blossom Festival
June	NW Pinball Show • Festival of Sail (tall ships) * Scottish Highland Games • www.tacomagames.org
July	Freedom Fair • Tacoma Pride Festival - 2nd week in July Tacoma Food Truck Fest • www.metroparkstacoma.org/food-truckfest
	Vintage Motorcycle Festival • www.americascarmuseum.org
August	Brew Five Three, Tacoma's Beer and Blues Festival www.broadwaycenter.org
Oct.	Tacoma Film Festival • www.TacomaFilmFestival.com
Nov.	Annual Holiday Tree lighting at the Broadway Center Day after Thanksgiving
Nov-Jan	Ice Skating Rink in Tacoma Polar Plaza

Dockton Park has extensive moorage.

Guest moorage is at Chinook Landing Marina, a short distance up the waterway.

㉒ **Chinook Landing Marina.** 3702 Marine View Drive Suite 100, Tacoma, WA 98422; (253) 627-7676. Monitors VHF 79. Certified Clean Marina. Open all year, guest moorage available. Snacks and ice cream at the office. This is an excellent facility, 30 & 50 amp power, restrooms, showers, laundry, free Wi-Fi, pumpout, portapotty dump, 24-hour security. Larger boats should call ahead for availability. No shops or restaurants nearby. The well-stocked J&G Marine Supply chandlery is located about a mile away.

Tyee Marina. 5618 Marine View Dr. Tacoma WA 98422; (253) 383-5321. Permanent moorage only.

Browns Point Park. Open all year, day use only. Picnic tables and a swimming beach. The lighthouse is the focal point, with free tours of the light keepers cottage on Saturdays 1:00 p.m. to 4:00 p.m., May to October. For more information call the Points Northwest Historical Society (253) 927-2536.

VASHON ISLAND, COLVOS PASSAGE, EAST PASSAGE, DES MOINES, BLAKE ISLAND

Colvos Passage. The current always flows north in Colvos Passage, so heading north on a flood tide is a good choice. Colvos Passage offers little to entice a boater to stop, although you can anchor off Olalla and dinghy to the little store for a snack.

Harper State Park. Located 1.5 miles west of the ferry landing at Southworth. Open all year, day use only. Anchoring only. The gravel launch ramp is usable at high tide only, but is the closest launch to Blake Island, 1 mile away.

Quartermaster Harbor. Quartermaster Harbor indents the south end of Vashon Island about 4 miles. It is protected on the east side by Maury Island, which connects to Vashon Island by a narrow spit of land. Dockton Park is a popular destination.

Anchorage is good throughout most of Quartermaster Harbor. Anchorage is no longer available off the village of Burton due to a field of private mooring buoys laid out by the State Department of Natural Resources (DNR). Anchorage is available farther to the east, or on the south side of Burton Peninsula.

The Quartermaster Yacht Club (members of reciprocal clubs welcomed) is at Burton, as is the Quartermaster Marina. The village of Burton has a well-stocked convenience store and several small shops. Taxi service is available on Vashon Island (Vashon Taxi (206) 434-1121).

Jensen Park, on Burton Peninsula, has a launch ramp, beach, picnic tables and barbecues. Vashon Watersports rents kayaks, canoes, and stand-up paddleboards at the park.

㉓ **Dockton Park.** 9500 SW Dock Road, Dockton, WA 98070; (206) 477-6150. Operated by King County Parks. Open all year, concrete launch ramp, 58 guest slips, rafting okay, restrooms, free showers, no power, no garbage pickup, no services within walking distance. Four days maximum stay. Dockton is a popular 23-acre park on the west side of Maury Island in Quartermaster Harbor. The park has play equipment, trails, fire pits, picnic shelters, picnic tables, barbecue areas. Call for group reservations.

About two blocks down 260th street, which runs eastward just above the dock, trailheads lead southward into 152-acre Dockton Forest, with one of the largest madrona forests in the area.

Anchoring Note: Holding can be fair to poor in the area north of the Dockton Park docks. If anchoring, be sure of your set.

Quartermaster Marina. 23824 Vashon Highway SW, Vashon, WA 98070; (206) 919-2318 (manager); (206) 463-3624 (office). Open all year, transient moorage in unoccupied slips. Call ahead for availability. Water, 30 & 50 amp power, restrooms, garbage drop, pumpout, Wi-Fi.

East Passage. Located between Vashon Island and the mainland. Large ships bound to or from Tacoma or Olympia use this route.

Tidal currents flood south and ebb north, and normally are a little stronger in East Passage than in Colvos Passage on the west side of Vashon Island.

Dash Point State Park. 5700 SW Dash Point Rd., Federal Way, WA 98023; (253) 661-4955. Open all year, 398 acres, restrooms, showers, no power. Sandy beach, swimming, and primitive, partial utility, and full utility campsites.

Redondo. A launch ramp, with 2 floats and a floating breakwater, is operated by the city of Des Moines. Fishing pier with coffee hut. Highline Community College operates the Marine Science and Technology Center (MaST), open to the public Saturdays 10:00 a.m. to 2:00 p.m. Anchor out and take the dinghy in.

Saltwater Marine State Park. 25205 8th Place South #1, Des Moines, WA 98198; (253) 661-4956. Two miles south of Des Moines. Open all year, overnight camping. Two day-use-only mooring buoys. Restrooms, showers, no power. Artificial reef for scuba diving, and outside shower for scuba rinse-off. Sandy swimming beach. Vault toilets, primitive campsites, picnic tables and shelters, kitchen shelter, children's play equipment. Seasonal concession stand.

Maury Island Marine Park. 5405 SE 244th Street, Dockton, WA. This is a 300-acre park at the site of what once was a sand and gravel operation, 1.5 miles south of Point Robinson. Trails lead through the park. The anchorage, with fair holding, is well protected in a northerly breeze. Popular with locals. On sunny days the winds are warmed as they cross Maury Island, making for good sunbathing. Operated by King County Parks.

Point Robinson. Point Robinson is surrounded by a 10-acre county park that can be approached by dinghy. The lighthouse is beautiful and the park has a nice beach, but no facilities for boaters.

Tramp Harbor, where Vashon Island joins Maury Island, has convenient anchoring depths, but only minimal protection from winds, particularly from the north. It is seldom used for overnight anchorage.

㉔ **Des Moines.** The City of Des Moines, between Tacoma and Seattle, is a good

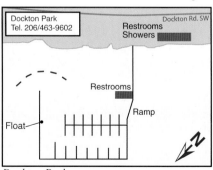

Dockton Park

Des Moines Marina is protected by a rock breakwater.

Inside the breakwater at Des Moines Marina. Fuel dock is on the right, guest moorage on the left.

destination for clubs and groups. The Des Moines Marina has full services available.

Des Moines Beach Park is within easy walking distance of the marina.

㉔ **City of Des Moines Marina**. 22307 Dock Ave. S., Des Moines, WA 98188; (206) 824-5700; marinainfo@desmoineswa.gov; www.desmoinesmarina.com. The marina does not monitor VHF. Certified Clean Marina. Open all year. Gasoline, diesel, propane, 30 amp power, free Wi-Fi. This 840-slip marina and public pier has 1500 feet of guest moorage, much of it side-tie, for boats to 100 feet. Maximum boat length in permanent slips is 62 feet. The parking lot is paid parking. Channel depth is 13 feet at zero tide. Stop at the fuel dock for directions to an empty berth. Free moorage for 4 hours. Restrooms, free showers, 2 free pumpouts. Reservations accepted for boats 32 feet and larger, or groups of 5 or more boats, 1 day in advance.

The marina can assist yacht clubs or rendezvous with planning and special needs, including free shuttle service upon request.

Des Moines Marina is the closest marina to Sea-Tac Airport. The marina can provide shuttle service to and from the airport.

The guest area has a 25×100-foot concrete activity float with shelter, and concrete moorage floats. An 80-foot-long ADA-compliant ramp available. The grounds are beautifully landscaped. Plans are underway to develop an attractive connection, with easy access, between the waterfront and downtown shops.

Services, including laundry, groceries, and several restaurants, are within walking distance of the marina. Shuttle service by request. The 670-foot public fishing pier runs east-west. To enter the marina, leave the fishing pier to port and turn to starboard at the north end of the breakwater. At low tide the entrance is tight, especially with opposing traffic. At the south end of the marina, Des Moines Yacht Club has guest moorage for visiting members of reciprocal clubs.

Farmers market on Saturdays, June through September. July 4th "Fireworks over Des Moines."

CSR Marine operates the repair yard, with a Travelift haulout to 25 tons.

ANTHONY'S
HOMEPORT RESTAURANT
421 South 227th St.
(206) 824-1947

Yukon Harbor offers good anchorage, well protected from the south but open to the northeast.

㉕ **Blake Island Marine State Park.** (360) 371-8330. Open all year, 475 acres with 1500 feet of dock space in the breakwater-protected marina. 24 mooring buoys for boats 36 feet and under ring the island. Pumpout, water, 30 amp power. No garbage drop and a "pack it in–pack it out" policy. Moorage is limited to 7 consecutive days. Buoys on the east side are exposed to wakes from passing ships. Self-register and pay mooring buoy fee on shore.

The marina is on the northeast shore of the island. To enter, follow the dredged channel marked by red and green beacons. Stay in the marked channel; the water is shoal on both sides of the beacons. Immediately inside the breakwater, one float is for the boat that brings guests to Tillicum on Blake Island, and another is for the State Parks boat. The rest of the floats are available on a first-come, first-serve basis. Expect to find them full during high season and on weekends year round.

Blake Island has primitive campsites, including a Cascadia Marine Trail campsite. An underwater reef is good for scuba diving. The park has picnic shelters, volleyball courts, nature trail, approximately 16 miles of hiking trails through dense forest, and 5 miles of

Traditional salmon bake dinner is a popular event at Tillicum Village.

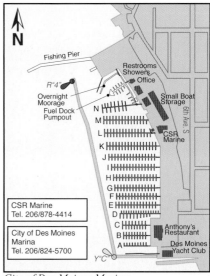

City of Des Moines Marina

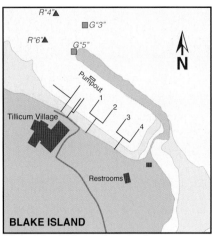

Blake Island Marine State Park

shoreline to explore. The Tillicum restaurant venue is a replica of an Indian longhouse. It is open only when tours are scheduled, and features dinner with fish cooked on stakes facing an open fire. Tours include dinner and a show with dancing and masks, and compares favorably with the show at Alert Bay. Call Argosy Tours (888) 623-1445; (206) 623-1445. Internet search, Argosy Cruises Tillicum Excursion. Individuals arriving by private boat should call ahead for dinner reservations.

Wildlife is abundant, including a high raccoon population not fearful of people. They roam the grounds and docks day or night looking for food. As in all state parks, there is a policy not to feed the animals. Park rangers recommend securing all garbage, pet food and ice chests; yes they can open an ice chest. Do not leave hatches open or you might find an unwelcomed surprise in your salon.

Blake Island is just a short hop from Elliott Bay Marina or Shilshole Bay Marina. The park is accessible only by boat and is one of the most popular stops on Puget Sound. A gem of a park.

SEATTLE

Elliott Bay, the center of Seattle's shipping industry, is a busy ocean port. Keep a sharp watch for ferries coming and going from Colman Dock, for tugs with tows, and for commercial vessels of all kinds. Large vessels are slow to maneuver, and should always be given a wide berth. When there's any doubt at all, cross behind commercial vessels, not in front of them.

Piers 89, 90, and 91 in Smith Cove are heavily used by commercial ships. The Port of Seattle's grain terminal occupies part of the shoreline north of the regular commercial piers. Myrtle Edwards Park, including a fishing pier, stretches about a mile along the Elliott Bay waterfront. The piers on the central waterfront, too small for modern maritime commerce, have been converted to other uses, including a hotel, shops, museums, an aquarium, and places to sit and watch the harbor activity.

At Pier 36, south of the Colman ferry dock, the U.S. Coast Guard has its Seattle headquarters, including the Coast Guard Museum and Vessel Traffic Service.

Downtown Seattle is served by two excellent marinas: Elliott Bay Marina on the north shore below Magnolia Bluff, and Port of Seattle's Bell Harbor Marina at Pier 66. These two marinas make downtown Seattle easy and safe to visit.

Seattle is often referred to as the "Boating Capital of America" and with little wonder. With abundant first-class visitor moorage, there is good reason to cruise to the Emerald City to find out what makes it so special.

THINGS TO DO

1. Pike Place Market. Unique shops with many specialty food items, even the first Starbucks. You can see cheese being made at Beechers. Watch out for flying salmon in the market. Don't miss the nearby Olympic Sculpture Park.

2. Seattle Aquarium. See a coral reef, giant Pacific octopus, pinecone fish, and potbellied seahorses. Located at Pier 59, a few blocks south of Bell Harbor Marina.

3. Seattle Art Museum (SAM). Locally curated exhibits and rotating exhibitions from the best art collections of the world.

4. Fremont Farmers Market. Year-round on Sundays in this funky neighborhood. You never know what you might find.

5. Burke-Gilman Trail. Rent a bike and see Seattle from Shilshole to Kenmore, mostly along the city's lakefront. Some detours on streets through Ballard.

6. Seattle Center. Tour the Space Needle, or MoPop, the museum of pop culture formerly known as EMP—the Experience Music Project, and the Chihuly Garden and Glass Museum.

7. Pacific Science Center at Seattle Center. Enjoy the IMAX Theater, the Planetarium or unique exhibits. Great for kids and adults.

8. Tillicum, Blake Island. Take your boat to Blake Island State Park and make a reservation for a tribal salmon buffet dinner and show. Experience the Coast Salish people through storytelling and dance.

9. Center for Wooden Boats. Walk around the antique restored boats on South Lake Union. With membership and checkout, you can even rent a classic sailboat or powerboat for a cruise on the lake.

10. Museum of History and Industry (MOHAI). Located in South Lake Union. Many exhibits on Seattle's heritage.

11. Kenmore Air Tour. What better way to learn the islands and waterways of this spectacular cruising area than from the air? Stay local or take an extended flight from Lake Union to the San Juan Islands and back.

12. Museum of Flight. A short taxi ride away is one of the nation's best flight museums. The Concorde, WWII aircraft, a Space Shuttle Simulator, a Boeing 707 and 787, and more.

13. Seattle Zoo. An outstanding zoo for the day or an afternoon, just a cab ride away.

14. Seattle Children's Museum. Over 22,000 sq. ft. of hands-on exhibits for kids, ages 10 months to 10 years, to explore, and daily educational programs.

15. Seattle Great Wheel. Take a ride on one of Seattle's newest attractions. Great views day or night. Located at Pier 57.

Enjoy an afternoon of sailing along the Seattle waterfront.

Ride the Great Wheel on the Seattle waterfront.

CHIEF SEATTLE AND THE TOWN THAT TOOK HIS NAME
- By David M. Buerge

Publisher: Sasquatch Books; ISBN: 978-1-63217-135-1

The town of Seattle and greater Puget Sound is seen in a whole new light after reading the historic accounts of an earlier world of inhabitants and their prominent chiefs, including Seattle's name sake, Chief Siatle or Sealth. Teacher and historian, David Buerge, provides an in-depth look at the relationships between Native tribes, European settlers, and the struggles of a changing world from 1792-1887, along with today's perceptions of the past. The book is not a casual read, made up of many historic threads weaved together, but does serve as an enlightening and thought-provoking account of Chief Siatle and his enduring message.

Author Buerge begins with the environment in which "the boy," Chief Seattle, grew up. The boy's father belonged to the Suquamish who lived on the Kitsap Peninsula and **Bainbridge Island**. His mother's tribe, the Duwamish, lived near **Elliott Bay** on the Duwamish River and connected tributaries. Several-thousand people lived in Suquamish and Duwamish winter villages around the late 1700's in which "the boy" was born in 1786. Native legends and myths of the time included the prophecy of a coming apocalypse. Indeed, a terrible sickness that arrived with the Europeans swept through the population, killing thousands; and eventually Natives were forced onto reservations.

Native tribes competed for wealth and warred against one another for power and prestige. When the Europeans arrived, including the Hudson Bay Company of the 1820's, competition for wealth among the tribes was spurred on. Puget Sound tribes mostly feared the Cowichan from the mouth of the Cowichan River on Vancouver Island. It is during this time that "the boy" became a warrior. His role in building Chief Kitsap's confederation and his likely participation in the raid against the Cowichan, earned him the title of war leader. The subsequent intermarriage between Cowichan and Puget Sound groups helped keep the peace and strengthen ties, which was the customary solution to settle tribal friction and share resources. Native women also married Company men, again to ease tensions and form important bonds.

On the heels of deadly epidemics, Natives were taking an interest in Christianity, and ministries arrived around the 1830's to teach and gain converts (Chief Seattle later became Catholic and was baptized around 1857). Still a warrior at the time, Chief Seattle led a raid on a Chemakum village at Hadlock, many Chemakum were killed, effectively wiping out the tribe. By 1849, Seattle now in his 60's, was rethinking his attitude toward the British as well as the Americans who had arrived on the scene. In 1850, Seattle met Robert Fay, a whaler captain and businessman whom Chief Seattle partnered with to form the Elliott Bay salmon-fishing venture. The Chief's ability to organize his people, attract Americans, and conduct business, illustrates his transformation from war leader to a community leader. In November of 1851, the Denny-Low party of settlers arrived at Alki followed by William Bell and Carson Boren, all welcomed by Seattle; and pioneer Doc David Maynard, who took over Fay's position, became a good friend of Seattle's.

Settlers were scattered among dense populations of Natives due to the Donation Land Claim Act that required settlers to live on their claims. The settlers were vulnerable to attack, and it was hoped that Seattle and his brother Curley would keep them safe. The Americans fenced off land for their crops and cattle, but the idea of land as a commodity to be bought and sold was unfamiliar to Native culture. Chief Seattle's vision was to create hybrid-racial communities to expand trade, share wealth, and live together in peace. While cultures clashed, the Americans recognized their continuing need for Seattle's support and unanimously named their settlement after him. Seattle hoped his people and the settlers would prosper together, and he worked to mitigate conflicts. In 1852, Henry Yesler arrived in **Seattle** and established a saw mill, which became the town's ticket to success. A year later, Congress established the Washington Territory. By now, Chief Seattle was approaching his 70's and older chiefs had passed away. Younger Natives questioned the intentions of the Americans and violence broke out once again among Native tribes; opinions also differed among whites. The liquor trade contributed to a growing problem among Natives, who were more susceptible to alcohol. Isaac Stevens, appointed Governor and territorial superintendent of Indian Affairs in 1853, declared that the guilty would be punished, while other Natives would benefit by receiving goods and schooling in exchange for giving or selling property.

As author David Buerge explains, "Seattle and other headmen had invited Americans into their country to live together and share in prosperity. But the treaty stipulated that upon ratification the people had one year to move away from growing centers of commerce to isolated reservations. As this sank in, anger grew." Resentment mounted among those like Chief Leschi, whose lands were coveted by settlers. Chief Leschi threatened war, and terrified settlers crowded into forts. Chief Seattle developed a plan that enabled his Duwamish kin to escape the conflict and arrive safely at **Port Madison**. Seattle Natives considered to be "friendlies" were housed by David Maynard and Henry Yesler. Chief Seattle learned of Leschi's plan to attack the city with a large force and sent word to his American friends. The city defended itself with gunfire from blockhouses and shell shot from the ship *Decatur*. Plans were laid to defeat Natives coming across the pass to join Leschi. Chief Leschi was eventually, caught, tried, and hung in 1858.

Native people still outnumbered American settlers, and Seattle's hybrid community remained vital through the 1860's. Despite the order to move to reservations, many native people remained, providing labor and trade to whites happy for their business. After ratification of the **Point Elliott Treaty**, Native people began moving to reservations; but during and after the States' Civil War, Congress was not eager to spend money on reservations, which exacerbated poor conditions. Many Natives remained at old village sites well into the 1880's. Chief Seattle spent his last days visiting friends, resolving disputes, and doing business with merchants, farmers, and government officials. In the spring of 1866, Chief Seattle grew weak and passed away on June 7th. Four hundred people, both Native and white, assembled for his memorial service.

Above all, Chief Seattle was known as an inspirational orator with an authoritative voice. Chief Seattle's 1854 speech later gained worldwide fame. Henry Smith, (of Seattle's Smith Cove), a Seattle pioneer and writer, was one of the first to document Chief Seattle's now famous speech. Other variations of the Chief's speech were interpreted by writers and professors who followed, but the message has predominantly remained the same, a combination of questioning despair, hope, and reconciliation.

㉖ **Elliott Bay Marina.** 2601 W. Marina Place, Seattle, WA 98199; (206) 285-4817; info@elliottbaymarina.net; www.elliottbaymarina.net. Monitors VHF 78A. Certified Clean Marina. This is a beautiful marina, immaculately maintained, open all year. The fuel dock has gasoline, diesel, free pumpout, and a store with convenience groceries. Contact the office for waste oil disposal. Transient moorage available in unoccupied slips, first-come, first-served. Reservations can be made for vessels 50 feet and longer. The marina has free cable TV, 30 & 50 amp power, up to 100 amp on outside moorage, restrooms, laundry, pumpout, free showers, free use of kayaks, SUPs and bikes, and excellent 24-hour security. Enter through either end of the breakwater.

The marina office is on the ground level of the main building, near Maggie Bluffs marina grill. Elegant dining at the Palisade restaurant is located upstairs. It's 5 minutes by cab or Uber to downtown Seattle. There is easy access to the Seattle public transportation system within walking distance.

The marina is headquarters for the Downtown Sailing Series; 10 informal races Thursday evenings during the summer, with barbecue and awards afterward.

Whole Foods Market and West Marine are about 1 mile away. A bike and walking path runs from the marina along scenic Myrtle Edwards waterfront park to the downtown waterfront. We took about an hour each way to walk between the marina and Pier 70. Seattle

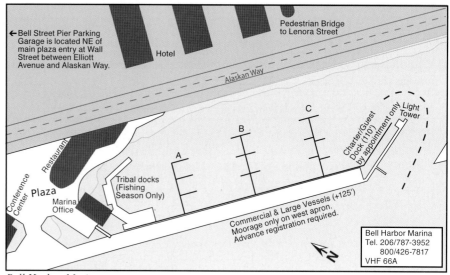

Bell Harbor Marina

Yacht Club has an outstation (no reciprocal moorage) at the marina. Views of downtown, Mt. Rainier, Olympic Mountains.

㉗ **Bell Harbor Marina.** Pier 66, 2203 Alaskan Way, Seattle, WA 98121; (206) 787-3952; bhm@portseattle.org; www.portseattle.org. Monitors VHF 66A. Certified Clean Marina. Open all year, 30, 50 & 100 amp power, water, restrooms, free showers, garbage/recycling drop, pumpout, 24-hour security. Entrance at 47°36.55'N/122°20.85'W—

look for the distinctive spire as a landmark. Moorage reservations can be made by telephone or email.

The Port of Seattle's Bell Harbor Marina, with 37 slips, is part of Seattle's Central Waterfront Development, and is an easy cruising destination. Depending on the mix, the docks will hold as many as 70 visitor boats, 30 feet to 70 feet. The waterfront, with the Seattle Aquarium, a variety of shops, and the Seattle Great Wheel, is just outside the marina. It's a safe, 2-block walk to the always interesting Pike Place Market.

Visitors can leave their boat at Bell Harbor and take in a game at Safeco Field for the Mariners or CenturyLink Field for the Seahawks or the Sounders. Three restaurants are just above the marina with many more restaurants and shops within walking distance.

Bell Harbor's facilities are top-notch, with excellent wheelchair access. The staff is professional and alert.

Because of rough water in Elliott Bay, the breakwater entry is narrow. Boats larger than 70 feet will find the entry and turning basin a little tight. The Port of Seattle provides approximately 1900 feet of outside pier apron devoted to large vessels including superyachts and cruise ships.

2201 Alaskan Way
(206) 448-6688

East Waterway. Both sides of East Waterway are lined with docks for commercial vessels, most of them loading or unloading containers. The waterway is navigable to Spokane Street, where a fixed bridge and foul ground block further navigation.

West Waterway. West Waterway and the connecting Duwamish River make a splendid sightseeing voyage. Use large-scale Chart 18450.

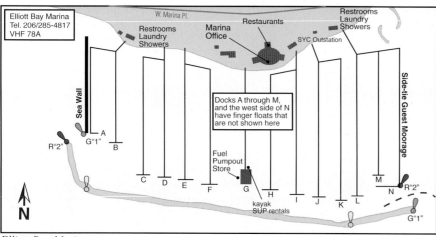

Elliott Bay Marina

Enter past busy Vigor Industrial shipyard (formerly Todd Shipyard) and the now-closed Lockheed Shipyard at the mouth, and motor along a fascinating variety of docks, ships, barges, small pleasure boats, mega-yachts, and abandoned hulks. Commercial buildings and the modest homes of South Park are on both sides.

You will go under the 1st Ave. S. Bridge, vertical clearance 39 feet, and past the former site of the Boeing Company's Plant 2, to the 16th Ave. S. Bridge (renamed the South Park Bridge). The 1st Ave. S. Bridge will open on signal, except during rush hour traffic. The famed Delta Marine facility, builder of commercial fish boats and megayachts, is a short distance beyond the 16th Ave. S. (South Park) Bridge.

Not far past Delta Marine, a low bridge blocks progress to all but small, open boats.

Don Armeni Park and Seacrest Park are located between Harbor Island and Duwamish Head. Don Armeni Park has a 4-lane launch ramp with floats. Seacrest Park has a fishing pier.

Harbor Island Marina. 1001 Klickitat Way S.W., Seattle, WA 98134; (206) 787-3006; him@portofseattle.org; www.portofseattle.org. This Port of Seattle marina is located on the south end of Harbor Island and caters to long term tenants. No transient moorage.

ELLIOTT BAY MARKETPLACE

RESTAURANTS, SHOPS & SERVICES

BOAT INSURANCE AGENCY
Boat Insurance is what we do at the Boat Insurance Agency, and we have been doing just that for over 30 years! Owned by Neal Booth and staffed by knowledgeable boaters and insurance folks, we are the first choice for thousands of boaters in the West. Representing all of the best markets, we do the shopping for you so you don't have to! Ask about our yacht club discounts, education and experience credits!
206-285-1350 • 2601 W Marina Pl. #B • www.boatinsurance.net

ELLIOTT BAY MARINA
With 360 degree views of downtown Seattle and the Olympic Mountains, Elliott Bay Marina offers a relaxing place to moor. Enjoy two restaurants, repair facilities, 24-hour security, fuel dock, convenience store, year round events, and friendly customer service from our marina staff.
206-285-4817 • 2601 West Marina Place • www.elliottbaymarina.net

MONKEY FIST MARINE
Keeping you on the water. Providing quality services from stem to stern; heating, bow and stern thrusters, electronics, plumbing, electrical, head systems, propulsion/engine, and generator.
206-285-2600 • 2601 West Marina Place Ste. K • www.monkeyfistmarine.com

PALISADE RESTAURANT
Palisade, where Seattle celebrates! Come up from the marina and join us for lunch, happy hour, dinner or weekend brunches with endless mimosas. Dining overlooks the marina with indoor and outdoor seating. Palisade is Seattle's landmark destination for elegant catering, inspiring views and memorable dining experiences. Let us be your onshore galley.
206-285-1000 • 2601 West Marina Place • www.palisaderestaurant.com

SHILSHOLE BAY

LOCAL KNOWLEDGE

Shallow Area: Do not stray south of the buoyed channel in Shilshole Bay. The water between the channel and Magnolia Bluff shoals rapidly.

Shilshole Bay indents the shoreline of Puget Sound north of West Point, and leads via a dredged channel to the Hiram M. Chittenden Locks (Ballard Locks) and the Lake Washington Ship Canal. Shilshole Bay Marina is north of the dredged channel, with entrances around the north and south ends of a long rock breakwater.

Lacking local knowledge, boats bound for the locks should follow the channel, marked by buoys, to the locks.

㉘ **Shilshole Bay Marina.** 7001 Seaview Ave. NW, Suite 100, Seattle, WA 98117; (206) 787-3006; (800) 426-7817; sbm@portseattle.org; www.portseattle.org. Certified Clean Marina. Monitors VHF 17. Open all year, office hours 8:00 a.m. to 4:30 p.m., Monday through Saturday. This is a large, busy, well-equipped marina, operated by the Port of Seattle. The marina has guest moorage for more than 100 boats to 250 feet, 30, 50, & 100 amp power, restrooms and showers (to be upgraded in 2019), laundry, free cable TV on the guest docks, pumpout, portapotty dump. Complimentary bikes and shuttle. The marina shuttle provides transportation for guests to Ballard shopping and dining. Waste oil disposal stations, recycling and garbage drop.

A complete boatyard (Seaview West) with 55-ton Travelift haulout is at the south end of the marina. The boatyard has repair-yard supplies and propane. A wide launch ramp is at the north end of the marina.

A coffee shop is onsite. Walking distance to restaurants, a fast-food stand, and a West Marine store. Golden Gardens Park, with beach and picnic areas, is a short walk north of the marina. Construction of a Duke's Chowder House is anticipated to start in 2019.

The large Central Plaza, in front of the office building and adjacent to the guest docks, is nice for gatherings. Contact the office for event planning.

㉘ **Shilshole Bay Fuel Dock.** 7029 Seaview Ave. NW, Seattle, WA 98117; (206) 783-7555. Open 7 days a week except Thanksgiving and Christmas. Ethanol-free gasoline, diesel, kerosene. At the end of H dock, the Port of Seattle operates a pumpout, bilge pumpout, and portapotty dump at the outer end of the dock. Convenience store carries ice, beverages, snacks, local guidebooks. Friendly people, clean and efficient operation.

LAKE WASHINGTON SHIP CANAL

The Lake Washington Ship Canal connects the Hiram Chittenden Locks with Lake Washington, a distance of approximately 5.5 miles. Except for a marked course in the middle of Lake Union, a 7-knot speed limit is enforced all the way to Webster Point, at the entrance to Lake Washington. Most boats travel about 6 knots. If no bridge openings are needed, allow about 30 minutes between Lake Union and the locks, and about an hour between Lake Washington and the locks. The Lake Washington Ship Canal has fuel docks, ship repair yards, boatyards, and moorages. Keep an alert lookout for vessels pulling out or turning. This can be an active area.

LOCAL KNOWLEDGE

Sound Signals: For all of the bridges, the sound signal to request an opening is 1 long blast and 1 short. The bridge tender will answer with 1 long and 1 short blast if the bridge can be opened or 5 short blasts if it cannot.

Ship Canal Bridge Information. From west to east, the Lake Washington Ship Canal is crossed by the Ballard Bridge, vertical clearance 46 feet at the center; Fremont Bridge, vertical clearance 31 feet at the center; University Bridge, vertical clearance 45 feet at the center; and the Montlake Bridge, vertical clearance 48 feet at the center.

Rush Hour Restricted Openings: The Ballard, Fremont and University Bridges do not open

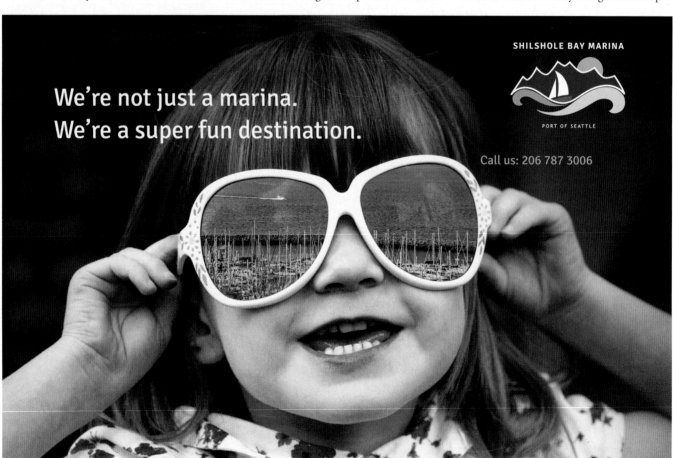

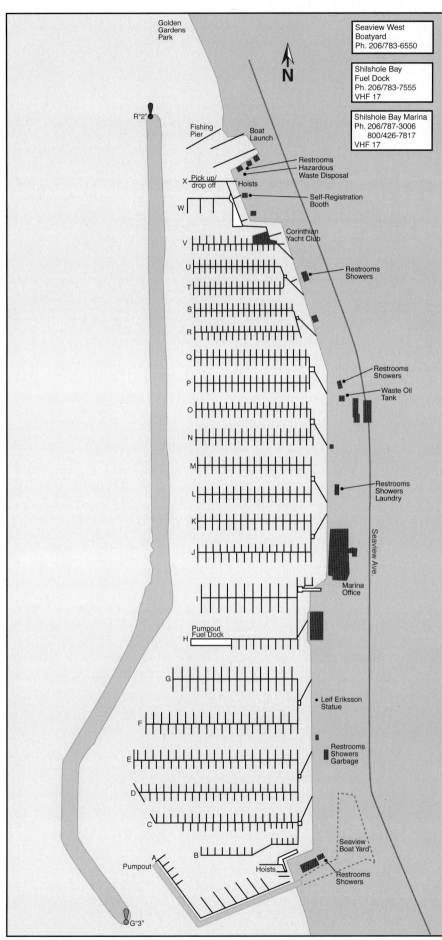

Golden Gardens Park

R"2"

Seaview West Boatyard
Ph. 206/783-6550

Shilshole Bay Fuel Dock
Ph. 206/783-7555
VHF 17

Shilshole Bay Marina
Ph. 206/787-3006
800/426-7817
VHF 17

N

Fishing Pier

Boat Launch

Restrooms
Hazardous Waste Disposal

X Pick up/drop off
Hoists

W

Self-Registration Booth

V

Corinthian Yacht Club

U

T

Restrooms
Showers

S

R

Q

P

Restrooms
Showers

Waste Oil Tank

O

N

M

L

Restrooms
Showers
Laundry

K

J

Seaview Ave.

Marina Office

I

Pumpout Fuel Dock

H

G

Leif Eriksson Statue

F

Restrooms
Showers
Garbage

E

D

C

Seaview Boat Yard

B

A

Pumpout

Hoists

Restrooms
Showers

G"3"

Shilshole Bay Marina

for recreational vessel traffic weekdays from 7:00 a.m. to 9:00 a.m. and 4:00 p.m. to 6:00 p.m., except holidays.

Nighttime Bridge Openings: The Ballard, Fremont and University Bridges are untended at night between 11:00 p.m. and 7:00 a.m. One crew, based at the Fremont Bridge, stands by to open bridges for vessel traffic. For openings call one hour ahead on VHF 13, or by telephone (206) 386-4251.

The Montlake Bridge is tended 24 hours a day, but between 11:00 p.m. and 7:00 a.m. vessels needing an opening must call ahead on VHF 13 or by telephone, (206) 720-3048.

㉚ **24th Avenue Landing.** At the foot of 24th Ave. NW on the north side of the Ship Canal, east of the locks. Open all year, day-use only up to 2 hours free of charge; no overnight stays. Dock has 300 feet of space, 40-foot maximum boat length. No power, water or showers. The Ballard business district is within walking distance.

㉚ **Ballard Oil Co.** 5300 26th Ave. NW, Seattle, WA 98107; (206) 783-0241; info@ ballard oil.com; www.ballardoil.com. Open Monday through Saturday. Just east of the locks, on the north side of the Ship Canal. Diesel only. Set up to handle larger pleasure craft and commercial vessels.

㉛ **Salmon Bay.** The Port of Seattle's Fishermen's Terminal is located on the south side of the Lake Washington Ship Canal at Salmon Bay, a half-mile east of the locks. Although Fishermen's Terminal caters primarily to the large Seattle-based fishing fleet, guest and permanent moorage is available for pleasure craft. A short term guest float is located along the inner bulkhead at the head of the west wall, often used by boaters while dining at Chinook's restaurant. Major repair facilities are nearby, as are stores offering a variety of marine services and supplies.

㉛ **Salmon Bay Marine Center.** 2284 W. Commodore Way #100, Seattle, WA 98199; (206) 450-9100; www.sbmc.com. On the south side of the Ship Canal, this facility has 18 slips to accommodate vessels from 60 to 240 feet. Most slips are sold or on long term lease. Short term moorage for large vessels may be available by reservation. Slips are 30 feet to 45 feet wide with a minimum depth of 12 feet. Power is single and 3-phase 240/480 and 208 volt–200 amp. A 50-cycle transformer is available. Black water connection at each slip with gray water pumpout. Free Wi-Fi, parking, and 4 electric utility cars for dock use. Marine repair companies and several large yacht brokerages are in the shoreside building.

㉛ **Salmon Bay Marina/Port of Seattle.** 2100 W. Commodore Way, Seattle, WA 98199; (206) 787-3395; salmonbay@portseattle. org; www.salmonbaymarina.com. Staff at Fishermen's Terminal respond to phone calls and email. Restrooms, showers, and laundry

107

HIRAM M. CHITTENDEN LOCKS

The dredged, well-marked channel leading to the Hiram Chittenden Locks passes under the Burlington Northern bascule bridge. *Caution: Although Chart 18447 shows vertical clearance of this bridge to be 43 feet from mean high water, Local Notice to Mariners reports that the actual clearance may be closer to 41 feet. Clearance gauges have been installed at the draw.* The bridge is kept open unless a train is due. The opening signal is one long and one short blast, the same signal as for the Ballard, Fremont, University, and Montlake Bridges. Remember, though, if a train is due you will be ignored.

Your wait at the locks, in either direction, can be as short as zero or as long as several hours depending on the flow of commercial traffic.

Approaching From Puget Sound: If you are approaching from Puget Sound, you'll starboard-side tie to the wall on the south side of the channel under the railroad bridge. If traffic is heavy, as it often is at the end of fair weather summer weekends, you may end up port-side tying to the wall west of the railroad bridge. Normally, only large commercial craft tie to that wall, but if the waiting area is crowded, you may be there too. The current always flows from the lake into the Sound. Approach carefully and be ready with extra fenders. Wait your turn and do not crowd ahead. Government vessels and commercial vessels have priority over pleasure craft, and will be directed into the locks ahead of pleasure craft.

Red and green lights on the large and small locks signal when you can enter. Red light means no; green light means yes. A loud hailer system also announces directions to the traffic waiting to transit.

Lock attendants do not respond to most radio calls from pleasure craft, but if you must communicate with them, call on VHF 13, using the 1-watt low-power mode. If you need help, they will answer. If you're calling to complain, forget it.

There are two locks: a large lock 825 feet long and 80 feet wide, and a small lock 150 feet long and 30 feet wide. On a busy summer weekend, the large lock can take a half-hour or more to fill with vessels. Lock attendants will direct entering vessels to one lock or the other by light signals and the loud hailer. Each vessel should have bow and stern mooring lines at least 50 feet long with a 12-inch eye in one end. Fenders should be set out on both sides of the boat. You may be placed against the lock wall or rafted to another boat.

The lock attendants are conscientious, experienced, and helpful. They make eye contact with the helmsman of each vessel as it enters, and signal their intentions clearly. They are polite, but they give direct orders. Do exactly what they tell you to do. They have seen everything and know how to deal with problems.

If directed into the large lock, larger vessels will be brought in first and tied along the walls. Smaller vessels will raft off. Large vessel or small, be sure you have 50-foot mooring lines, bow and stern, in case you are put along the wall. The lock attendants will throw messenger lines to you. Tie your mooring lines to the messenger lines and they will take them to bollards on top of the lock wall.

There is usually some current in the locks, flowing from the lakes toward the Sound. Enter slowly but with enough speed for steerage. Once your lines are made fast, prepare to assist boats that lie alongside you. When the lock is closed and the water begins to rise, the vessels along the wall must keep a half-turn on their cleats and continuously take in slack. When the water has stopped rising, make all lines fast until you are told to leave.

If directed into the small lock, you will lie alongside a floating wall equipped with yellow-painted "buttons." Loop your bow and stern lines around the buttons, bring the lines back, and make them fast to cleats. The floating walls rise or fall with the water level, so you don't need to tend your lines during the transit. Caution: It is always possible that a floating wall could jam in its tracks. Stand by to slack your lines quickly if that happens.

When directed to do so, loosen your lines and move out of the locks slowly but with good steerage.

Approaching From The Lake: If you are westbound from the lake to the Sound, you still need 50-foot mooring lines, bow and stern, in case you lie along the wall of the large lock. However, you will be able to hand your lines to the attendant instead of tying them to messenger lines. Boats along the large lock wall will slack their lines as the water drops.

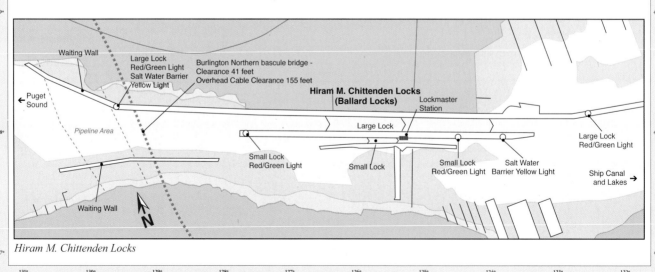

Hiram M. Chittenden Locks

facilities, 30 & 50 amp power. This marina was purchased by the Port of Seattle in June of 2018 and is for full time leased moorage only. Seattle Marine & Fishing Supply, a large chandlery, is across the street. Walking distance to restaurants and Fishermen's Terminal.

㉚ Covich-Williams Chevron. Dock Office, 5219 Shilshole Ave. NW, Seattle, WA 98107; (206) 784-0171; www.covichwilliams.com. On the north side of the Ship Canal, next to Salmon Bay Sand & Gravel. Open weekdays

8:00 a.m. to 5:00 p.m., Saturdays until noon; closed Sundays. Gasoline, diesel, kerosene. Carries filters, absorbent products, antifreeze, environmental products, fuel additives.

㉚ Ballard Mill Marina. 4733 Shilshole Ave. NW, Seattle, WA 98107; (206) 789-4777; ballardmillmarina@gmail.com; www.ballardmillmarina.com. Open all year, no guest moorage, 28 to 60 feet. Restrooms, pumpout, 20 & 30 amp power, showers. East of Covich-Williams Chevron fuel dock on the

north side of the Ship Canal. Free pumpout on the east dock. Stores, restaurants, marine supplies, haulout and repairs nearby.

㉛ Fishermen's Terminal/Port of Seattle. 3919 18th Ave. W., Seattle, WA 98119; (206) 787-3395; (800) 426-7817; ft@portseattle.org; www.portseattle.org. Monitors VHF 17, 24 hours a day, 30, 50 & 100 amp power, water, restrooms & showers, security cameras, free pumpout (sewage and bilge), recycling, waste oil dump. Major repair and supply facilities nearby. Restaurants, fish sales, shops, small grocery store, chandlery, postal service on site. The marina is on the south side of the Ship Canal, immediately west of the Ballard Bridge. Guest moorage welcomed, first-come, first-served, call for slip assignment. Make payment at building No. C15 located at 3919 - 18th Ave. West.

Dining: Chinook's at Salmon Bay is good for sit-down dining. A takeout seafood window is on the east side of the building. Tables and chairs are on the deck or in a covered area. An excellent fish market is in the front of the building. The Highliner Pub and the Bay Café also offer dining. The side-tie guest mooring float is in front of the restaurant building; complimentary 4-hour moorage.

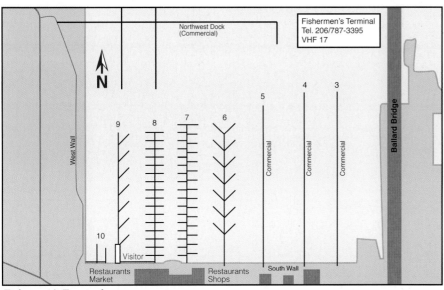

Fishermen's Terminal

1900 W. Nickerson St.
(206) 283-4665

Lake Union is lined with ship and boat moorages, houseboat moorages, and boating related businesses. It's the center of Seattle's boat sales industry. In the middle of the lake, a speed range marked by 4 buoys, is for sea trials. Other than the speed range, a 7-knot speed limit is enforced. A launch ramp is on the north shore, east of Gas Works Park. Gas Works Park is easily identifiable by the painted remnants of an industrial coal gas plant. Tyee Yacht Club and Puget Sound Yacht Club have moorages on Lake Union. The large Fisheries Supply marine store is located near Gas Works Park. Transient moorage is limited on Lake Union.

The south end of Lake Union is the home of Northwest Seaport. Next door is the Center for Wooden Boats and lovely Lake Union Park with the Museum of History and Industry (MOHAI). Kenmore Air's seaplane base is on the southwest shore, just across from the park. Flight operations are in the center of the lake. A vertical line of lighted buoys north of the MOHAI building marks the runway. Aircraft taking off and landing will trigger flashing lights to indicate air operation. Be aware of floatplanes.

A major ship repair yard, Lake Union Drydock, is on the eastern shore near the south end of the lake. Ivar's Salmon House, a popular waterfront restaurant, is at the north end of the lake under the I-5 freeway bridge, with temporary moorage for tenders and small boats while dining.

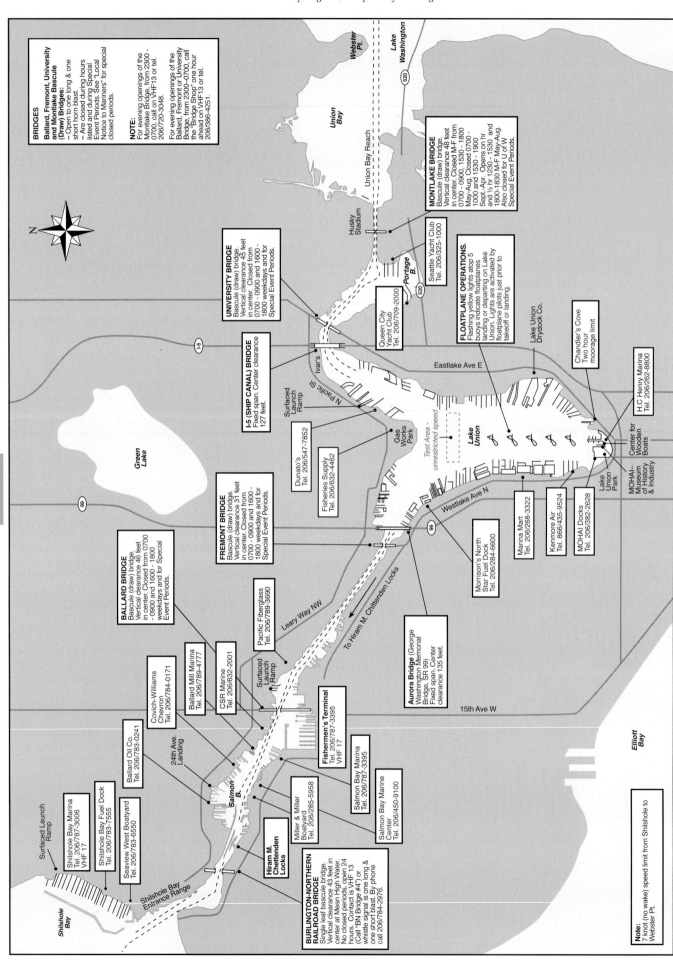

BRIDGES

Ballard, Fremont, University and Montlake Bascule (Draw) Bridges:
– Open to one long & one short horn blast.
– Are closed during hours listed and during Special Event Periods. See "Local Notice to Mariners" for special closed periods.

NOTE:
For evening openings of the Montlake Bridge, from 2300 - 0700, call on VHF 13 or tel. 206/720-3048.

For evening openings of the Ballard, Fremont or University Bridge, from 2300-0700, call the "Bridge Shop" one hour ahead on VHF13 or tel. 206/386-4251.

MONTLAKE BRIDGE
Bascule (draw) bridge. Vertical clearance 48 feet in center. Closed M-F from 0700 - 0900, 1530 - 1800 May-Aug. Closed 0700 - 1000 and 1530 - 1900 Sept.-Apr. Opens on hr and ½ hr 1230 - 1530 and 1800-1830 M-F May-Aug. Also closed for U of W Special Event Periods.

UNIVERSITY BRIDGE
Bascule (draw) bridge. Vertical clearance 45 feet in center. Closed from 0700 - 0900 and 1600 - 1800 weekdays and for Special Event Periods.

I-5 (SHIP CANAL) BRIDGE
Fixed span. Center clearance 127 feet.

FLOATPLANE OPERATIONS.
Flashing yellow lights atop 5 buoys indicate floatplanes landing or departing on Lake Union. Lights are activated by floatplane pilots just prior to takeoff or landing.

FREMONT BRIDGE
Bascule (draw) bridge. Vertical clearance 31 feet in center. Closed from 0700 - 0900 and 1600 - 1800 weekdays and for Special Event Periods.

BALLARD BRIDGE
Bascule (draw) bridge. Vertical clearance 46 feet in center. Closed from 0700 - 0900 and 1600 - 1800 weekdays and for Special Event Periods.

Aurora Bridge (George Washington Memorial Bridge, SR 99) Fixed span. Center clearance 135 feet.

Fishermen's Terminal
Tel. 206/787-3395
VHF 17

BURLINGTON-NORTHERN RAILROAD BRIDGE
Single leaf bascule bridge. Vertical clearance 43 feet in center at Mean High Water. No closed periods, open 24 hours. Contact is VHF 13 (Call "BN Bridge #4") or whistle signal is one long & one short blast. By phone call 206/784-2976.

Hiram M. Chittenden Locks

Shilshole Bay Marina Tel. 206/787-3006 VHF 17

Shilshole Bay Fuel Dock Tel. 206/783-7555

Seaview West Boatyard Tel. 206/783-6550

Ballard Oil Co. Tel. 206/783-0241

24th Ave. Landing

Covich-Williams Chevron Tel. 206/784-0171

Ballard Mill Marina Tel. 206/789-4777

CSR Marine Tel. 206/632-2001

Pacific Fiberglass Tel. 206/789-3690

Miller & Miller Boatyard Tel. 206/285-5958

Salmon Bay Marina Tel. 206/787-3395

Salmon Bay Marine Center Tel. 206/450-9100

Surfaced Launch Ramp

Dunato's Tel. 206/547-7852

Fisheries Supply Tel. 206/632-4462

Morrison's North Star Fuel Dock Tel. 206/284-6600

Marina Mart Tel. 206/268-3322

Kenmore Air Tel. 866/435-9524

MOHAI Docks Tel. 206/382-2628

Lake Union Drydock Co.

Chandler's Cove Two hour moorage limit

H.C Henry Marina Tel. 206/262-8800

Center for Wooden Boats

MOHAI– Museum of History & Industry

Lake Union Park

Queen City Yacht Club Tel. 206/709-2000

Seattle Yacht Club Tel. 206/325-1000

Surfaced Launch Ramp

Ivar's

Gas Works Park

Test Area - unrestricted speed

Eastlake Ave E

Westlake Ave N

Leary Way NW

To Hiram M. Chittenden Locks

15th Ave W

N Pacific St

Lake Union

Salmon B.

Green Lake

Shilshole Bay

Shilshole Bay Entrance Range

Elliott Bay

Union Bay

Union Bay Reach

Lake Washington

Webster Pt.

Husky Stadium

Portage B.

Note:
7 knot (no wake) speed limit from Shilshole to Webster Pt.

Lake Washington Ship Canal and Lake Union

Heading up in the small lock

㉜ **Morrison's North Star Marine.** 2732 Westlake Ave. N., Seattle, WA 98109; (206) 284-6600; www.morrisonsfueldock.com. Open all year, 7 days a week. Fuel dock with ethanol-free gasoline and diesel, no guest moorage. Restrooms, free pumpout, water. Handles oil changes; call for appointment. Limited marine hardware, local charts, groceries, beer, wine, ice. Friendly and well-run.

㉜ **Nautical Landing Marina.** 2500 Westlake Ave. N., Seattle, WA 98109; (206) 464-4614; info@nautical-landing.com; www.nautical-landing.com. Open all year for permanent and transient use with 1900 feet of moorage, 30, 50 & 100 amp power, security, Wi-Fi, garbage and recycling drop. This facility is popular with superyachts and has services to match.

㉝ **MOHAI Docks** Center for Wooden Boats. Docks located in front of the Museum of History and Industry, on the south end of Lake Union, are managed by the Center for Wooden Boats (206-382-2628). The North Wall has 160 feet of side-tie moorage and one 61-foot slip. Overnight stays at $1.30 per foot. Reservations are available by phone or email at knanen@cwb.org. The Parks Department may be taking on more responsiblility for moorage along the North Wall in the near future. 30 amp power no water. Two-week

maximum stay. The small concrete Art Float in front of the gazebo structure is for human-powered craft only. The West Wall has 140 feet of side-tie moorage on a first-come, first-serve basis, no charge. Day-use only from sunrise to sundown, no overnight moorage.

㉝ **Chandler's Cove.** 901 Fairview Ave. N., Seattle, WA 98109. An 85-foot guest float at the north end of the pier, two-hour day moorage limit, no overnight stays. Several restaurants are in the area. It's an easy walk to the Center for Wooden Boats and the Museum of History and Industry (MOHAI).

A time-line for re-development of South Lake Union by Vulcan Inc. is currently undetermined and plans remain in limbo.

㉝ **H.C. Henry Marina.** 809 Fairview Place N., Seattle, WA 98109. Located on the south end of Lake Union. Short-term public moorage on the south side of H dock, 2-hour limit while dining at area restaurants, no overnight stays.

㉝ **Marina Mart.** 1500 Westlake Ave. N., Seattle, WA 98109; (206) 268-3322; www.marinamart.com. Permanent moorage only, no guest moorage.

Portage Bay. East of the University Bridge, vertical clearance 42 feet at the center, Portage Bay is the home of Seattle Yacht Club and Queen City Yacht Club. The University of Washington has several facilities along the north shore. The University Bridge opens to 1 long blast and 1 short.

Montlake Cut. East of Portage Bay, the Montlake Cut connects to Union Bay and Lake Washington. The cut is narrow. When boat traffic is heavy, boat wakes can be turbulent as they bounce off the concrete side walls. Slow, steady speeds are called for. The Montlake Bridge, which crosses the cut, has a vertical clearance of 46 feet at the center. The bridge opens to 1 long blast and 1 short.

Union Bay. Union Bay is just east of the Montlake Cut and connects with Lake Washington. The dredged channel is well buoyed. The University of Washington's waterfront activities center is on the north shore, and the arboretum is on the south shore. Except for the dredged channel, the bay is shoal.

LAKE WASHINGTON

Lake Washington, 16 miles long, defines the eastern border of Seattle, and washes the edges of Kenmore, Bothell, Kirkland, Medina, Bellevue, Mercer Island and Renton. Summer weekends will be busy. Watercraft of all types crisscross the lake and party-raft in the bays. Opening Day of Boating Season celebration in early May of each year fills the waters from Lake Washington to Portage Bay, with hundreds of decorated boats parading through the Montlake Cut. Seafair celebration weekend borders on madness.

The Lake Washington shoreline is filled from the waterline to the tops of the ridges with waterfront homes and mansions. Cruising the shores while admiring the elegant to modest homes is a perfect day-long experience. There is a 7-knot speed limit within 100 yards of shore, docks, and bridges throughout Lake Washington. Kirkland, Bellevue, Leschi, Madison Park, Juanita Bay, and Renton are some nice boater friendly day stops for lunch or dinner. Limited overnight transient moorage is available at marinas and public docks in Kirkland, Kenmore, Newport, and Renton. Restrictions on overnight anchoring

on Lake Washington are enforced. Overnight anchoring is only allowed in Andrews Bay on the south end. At the north end of the lake, overnight anchoring is allowed in Juanita Bay; in Kenmore, off of Log Boom Park; and in fair weather, off St. Edwards Park.

Two floating bridges, I-90 and SR 520, cross Lake Washington and limit boater access to the south end of the lake with a maximum 70 feet of vertical clearance. Construction on the replacement SR 520 bridge floating span is complete. Work on the western connection to I-5 near Montlake continues. The replacement floating span does not have an opening section for boat traffic. Boat traffic passes under the fixed bridge at high-rises on either end along two navigation channels. Vertical clearance is 65 to 70 feet at the east high-rise and 42 to 49 feet at the west high-rise. Vertical clearances vary as the seasonal lake level is adjusted; higher water levels in spring and early summer, and lower levels in fall and winter. The I-90 floating bridge has a maximum vertical clearance of 34 feet at the west end and 37 feet at the east end. Least clearance at each end is 28 feet. The East Channel I-90 fixed bridge has a vertical clearance of 70 feet.

Sand Point. North from Webster Point, the first notable landmark is the former Naval Aviation base of Sand Point. Sand Point now includes Magnuson Park, which has a 2-lane launch ramp with floats. It is

The annual Seafair festivies draw thousands of people to Lake Washington for air shows, hydroplane races, and parties.

also the Northwest District headquarters for the National Oceanic and Atmospheric Administration (NOAA), which has a long piling pier along its north shore. Facilities west of NOAA are part of the park.

Kenmore. Kenmore offers two marinas: North Lake Marina, with permanent moorage slips, fuel dock, and repairs; and Harbour Village Marina with transient guest moorage. Kenmore is home to Kenmore Air, a major seaplane operation. Stay well clear of seaplane operating areas. Kenmore is at

the mouth of the Sammamish River. Shoal water abounds. Find the buoys and stay in the dredged channel. The river is navigable by small, low, shallow-draft boats all the way to Lake Sammamish.

㉞ **Harbour Village Marina.** 6115 NE 175th St., Kenmore, WA 98028; (425) 485-7557; harbormaster@harbourvillage.net. Open all year with 400 feet of side-tie moorage on the outside of the breakwater. Office hours vary. 30 & 50 amp power, restrooms, and showers. Reservations online at www.dockwa.com.

Caution for shallow water; follow the marked charted channel until abeam the marina.

㉞ **North Lake Marina.** 6201 NE 175th St., Kenmore, WA 98028; (425) 482-9465; susan@northlakemarina.com; www.northlakemarina.com. Open all year, closed weekends November through March. Ethanol-free gasoline at the fuel dock, no diesel. Permanent moorage only, no transient space. Parts, accessories, ice. Complete repairs available. Haulout to 20 tons.

Logboom Park. North shore of Lake Washington, Kenmore. Open all year, day use only moorage. Restrooms, no power, no showers. Trails, fishing pier, children's play equipment, picnic areas, and outdoor cooking facilities. The park is on the Burke-Gilman Trail, a walking and cycling trail that runs from Lake Union to the Sammamish River Trail. Note: Docks are in a state of disrepair and may be unsafe. Anchoring south of the park for up to 72 hours is allowed, watch for shallow water.

Saint Edward State Park. 14445 Juanita Drive NW, Kenmore, WA 98028; (425) 823-2992. Located on the northeast shore of Lake Washington, this 326-acre day-use park has trails and picnicking. Anchoring is possible off the park in fair weather for up to 72 hours. Beach landing only. A playground is located at the top of the bluff. A park pass can be purchased at the automated pay station. The historic brick building on the grounds served as a Catholic seminary in the 1930s, with hundreds of students in residence.

Juanita Bay. Anchorage for up to 72 hours is possible in Juanita Bay, which shoals gradually toward all shores. In nice summer weather, the bay is a crowded, popular, party-rafting destination. Off-season, the bay is quieter. The waterfront city park and estuary, at the head of the bay, provide paddling and beach-landing opportunities.

Kirkland. Kirkland is an outstanding cruising destination. The City of Kirkland's Marina Park visitor docks are well maintained, and connect directly with downtown. A good launch ramp is immediately north of the docks. If you enjoy tree-lined streets, superb dining, interesting boutiques and upscale galleries, you will not be disappointed. Kirkland is prosperous and it shows.

Next to Marina Park is the Kirkland Homeport Marina, which is primarily full-time, leased moorage; www.kirklandhomeportmarina.com.

A mile south of Marina Park is privately-owned Carillon Point Marina, with some guest moorage and access to restaurants and other businesses. Several restaurants in the area have their own docks for patrons.

㉟ **Marina Park.** 25 Lakeshore Plaza Drive, Kirkland, WA 98033; (425) 587-3300; www.kirklandwa.gov. Launch ramp adjacent. Open all year, 90 guest slips, restrooms, 30 amp power in some slips, Wi-Fi. No showers. This is a large and popular Lake Washington destination. Moorage is first-come, first-served and paid through electronic public pay stations located on the dock. Between 8:00 a.m. and 10:00 p.m. the first 3 hours free, ticket provided at pay station. Excellent access to downtown Kirkland. Nearby groceries, ice, and post office.

Use of the launch ramp can be purchased for a fee (each way) at the on-site pay station; a bollard in front of the ramp will lower upon payment. A key card for the season can be purchased from the city office at 123-Fifth Avenue. Use of the ramp is free from November 1st through March 31st. For additional information call (425) 587-3300.

Guest moorage can also be found along 150 feet of side-tie on the Second Avenue South Dock (Anthony's Restaurant), managed by the city. Check with Anthony's Restaurant for moorage while dining. The dock is located on the south side of a private marina. Make payment at the public pay station at the Marina Park.

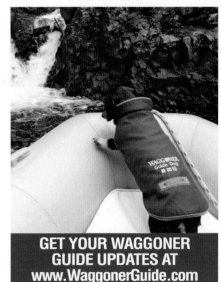
SHIP CANAL BRIDGE OPENINGS

BRIDGE	HEIGHT	CLOSED HOURS	
Burlington-Northern Railroad Bridge	43 feet MHW		
Ballard Bridge	46 feet at center	Weekdays 0700-0900, 1600-1800 and Special Events	1-hour notice 2300-0700
Fremont Bridge	31 feet at center	Weekdays 0700-0900, 1600-1800 and Special Events	1-hour notice 2300-0700
University Bridge	45 feet at center	Weekdays 0700-0900, 1600-1800 and Special Events	1-hour notice 2300-0700
Montlake Bridge	48 feet at center	May 1- Aug. 31: Weekdays 0700-0900, 1530-1800; Sept. 1-April 30: Weekdays 0700-1000, 1530-1900	May 1-Aug 31: 1230-1530 and 1800-1830 opens only on the hour and half hour
SR 520 *West End*	44 feet	SR 520 replacement bridge no longer has an opening span.	
SR 520 *East End*	65 feet 70 feet	on the shore side of the channel on the deep water side of the channel	

㊱ **Carillon Point Marina.** 4100 Carillon Point, Kirkland, WA 98033; (425) 822-1700; www.carillon-point.com. Certified Clean Marina. Open all year, guest moorage, 30 & 50 amp power, Wi-Fi, restrooms, showers, pumpout, portapotty dump. The public pier on the north end of the marina has 150 to 200 feet of side-tie, 2-hour tie-ups at no charge. The inside of the pier is for boats 32 feet and under and the outside of the pier is for larger vessels. Overnight moorage in unoccupied slips as available. This is a nice marina adjacent to a high-quality hotel with restaurants, spa, and shopping. Downtown Kirkland is 1.5 miles away by road.

㊱ **Yarrow Bay Marina.** 5207 Lake Washington Blvd. NE, Kirkland, WA 98033; (425) 822-6066; service@yarrowbaymarina.com; www.yarrowbaymarina.com. Open all year with ethanol-free gasoline and diesel, no guest moorage. Marine parts, restrooms, pumpout, haulout and repairs.

Cozy Cove and Fairweather Bay. Cozy Cove and Fairweather Bay are entirely residential, but anchorage is possible.

Meydenbauer Bay. Meydenbauer Bay is the home of Bellevue Marina and the Meydenbauer Bay Yacht Club, which has some moorage for reciprocal clubs. Meydenbeauer Beach Park underwent extensive renovation in 2017 and 2018. Downtown Bellevue, with outstanding shopping, is nearby. Anchorage

Montlake Bridge has a clearance of 46 feet. On sunny summer days boat traffic ranges from heavy to very heavy.

is possible in Meydenbauer Bay, although the water is deeper than most pleasure craft prefer. The marina off Beaux Arts Village, a short distance south of Meydenbauer Bay, is reserved for Beaux Arts residents.

Bellevue Marina. 99th Avenue NE, Bellevue, WA 98004; (425) 443-1090 Dock Master. Small boat visitor moorage between Pier 2 and Pier 3, day use only up to 4 hours between 8:00 a.m. and 9:00 p.m. daily.

Seasonal portable toilets. City park Rangers monitor the facilities.

Luther Burbank Park. 2040 84th Avenue SE, Mercer Island, WA 98040; www.mercergov.org. Open all year, day use only, dock space for 30 or more boats. Restrooms, no power, no showers. No anchoring. Park has picnic areas, swimming areas, trails, tennis courts, amphitheater.

East Channel Bridge. The I-90 fixed bridge over the East Channel on the east side of Mercer Island, has a vertical clearance of 65 feet.

㊲ **Newport Shores.** 3911 Lake Washington Blvd. SE, Bellevue, WA 98006; (425) 641-2090; www.seattleboat.com. Newport Shores has a large private marina (Seattle Boat-Newport), with an adjacent public launch ramp and fuel dock. Open all year, call or visit website for hours. Fuel dock with

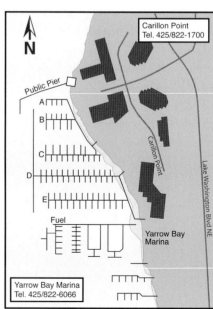

Carillon Point Marina, Kirkland

Gene Coulon park, with dockside eateries and day-use moorage

gasoline and diesel, located just south of the I-90 East Channel Bridge at Newport Yacht Basin; snacks, beverages, and ice. Complete repairs available. Marine supplies and parts, new and used boats, self-serve storage. Haulout to 35 tons.

㊳ Gene Coulon Memorial Beach Park. 1201 Lake Washington Blvd., Renton, WA 98055; (425) 430-6700; www.rentonwa. gov. Open all year, day use only. Slips for small boats and side-tie for larger vessels. Restrooms, showers, no power. Pay at the automated pay box. Showers in summer only, at the swim center. Ivar's and Kidd Valley restaurants in the park. Eight lanes for boat launching, very well organized, credit and debit cards only. No overnight parking in winter. This is a big, attractive, and much-used park with picnic shelters, playground equipment, tennis courts, horseshoe pits, volleyball courts, grassy areas and beaches. It has a fishing pier and a paved walkway along the water. Popular with everyone, especially families. Located on the southeast shore of Lake Washington, next to Boeing's Renton 737 complex.

Rainier Beach. Has a launch ramp and a private marina. It is the home of the Rainier Yacht Club. Limited guest moorage for visiting members of reciprocal clubs.

Andrews Bay. 5895 Lake Washington Blvd. S., Seattle, WA 98118; (206) 684-4396; www. seattle.gov. Andrews Bay is a popular anchoring spot, with room for many boats. Nestled in between Seward Park on Bailey Peninsula and the mainland, it is one of the few authorized pleasure boat anchorages in Lake Washington. Signs on the Seward Park shoreline mark the anchorage area, denoted by buoys marked with the letter "A". Put the hook down in 25 to 50 feet, excellent mud bottom, 72-hour maximum stay in a 7-day period. There is a 3 knot speed limit in Andrews Bay. A Seattle Parks swim area with bathhouse and lifeguards is at the head of the bay. A large grassy playfield is adjacent. Miles of trails lead through dense forest. Excellent stop, especially for families.

㊴ Lakewood Moorage. 4400 Lake Washington Blvd. S., Seattle, WA 98118; (206) 475-6559; www.seattle.gov. Open all year. No guest moorage. Permanent moorage only.

Stan Sayers Memorial Park. www.seattle. gov. Open all year. Temporary, day use moorage only, not enough depth for larger boats. Restrooms, no power, no showers. Launch ramp with boarding floats. Tie up to the floats. This is the pit area for hydroplanes during the annual Seafair races.

RICH PASSAGE, PORT ORCHARD, BREMERTON, SILVERDALE

LOCAL KNOWLEDGE

HEAVY TRAFFIC: Rich Passage is the ferry route between Seattle and Bremerton. Keep a sharp lookout ahead and astern and stay well clear of the ferries. Naval vessels also use Rich Passage to and from the Bremerton Naval Shipyard.

Rich Passage is winding but well-buoyed. From the west entrance, the city of Bremerton and the Naval Shipyard are clearly visible. For security reasons, stay well off the Naval facilities.

Currents run to 2 knots at the east entrance and 5.5 knots at the west entrance, flooding west and ebbing east.

Manchester State Park. 7767 E. Hilldale, Port Orchard, WA 98366; (360) 902-8844; www.parks.wa.gov. Open 7 days a week in the summer, 111 acres, day use and overnight camping. Open weekends and holidays in winter. Restrooms, showers, no power. Anchoring only; a bit rough because of boat traffic in Rich Passage. Park is in a shallow cove, good for wading in summer and scuba diving offshore. Picnic tables and shelters with fireplaces, campsites, nature and hiking trails. Old gun battery and emplacements are fun to explore.

㊵ Port of Manchester. P.O. Box 304, Manchester, WA 98353; (360) 871-0500; www.portofmanchester.com. Open all year, 400 feet of guest dock space, restroom, no overnight moorage. Dock can be dry on zero or minus tide. A launch ramp is adjacent to the dock. Overnight parking allowed. No power or other facilities at the dock. A restaurant and pub are a short walk away.

Fort Ward Park. 2241 Pleasant Beach, Bainbridge Island, WA 98110; (206) 842-2306; www.biparks.org. Open all year. Anchorage is exposed to wind and wakes from passing boat traffic. Toilets, launch ramp and hiking trails. Because of strong currents in Rich Passage, the underwater park is for expert scuba divers only. Bird watching from 2 bird blinds. Remains of

Manchester has an inviting sandy beach, day-use moorage, and spectacular views of Seattle.

historic fort emplacements to explore. No camping.

Port Orchard. The city of Port Orchard has long been a popular destination for Puget Sound boaters. It has a number of marinas that welcome visiting boats, including one, Port Orchard Marina, that is operated by the Port of Bremerton. Port Orchard Yacht Club, which welcomes visiting reciprocal yachts, is west of the Port Orchard Marina. Several other marinas have permanent moorage. Anchorage is in 50 to 60 feet, mud bottom. A passenger ferry runs between Port Orchard and Bremerton. Water Street boat launch has long term parking for tow vehicles and trailers.

Downtown Port Orchard has several antique and collectibles shops, and restaurants. Seasonal farmers market, 9:00 a.m. to 3:00 p.m. on Saturdays, mid-April through mid-October. The Port Orchard Public Market is open daily with a variety of local food and beverage vendors. Concerts by the Bay are held at Marina Waterfront Park June through September.

Besides a walkable waterfront featuring family friendly activities, playgrounds, parks and an array of excellent dining and shopping options, there are many events and festivals year round, www.exploreportorchard.com.

㊶ **Port Orchard Marina.** 707 Sidney Pkwy., Port Orchard, WA 98366; (360) 876-5535; kathyg@portofbremerton.org;

www.portofbremerton.org. Certified Clean Marina. Monitors VHF 66A. Enter the marina around the west end of the breakwater. The entrance is marked with navigation lights. Open 7 days a week all year, except for fall/winter holidays. Gasoline and diesel at the fuel dock, guest moorage in 50 slips (40-foot), and side-tie moorage along 1500 feet of inside breakwater with another 1500 feet available on the outside. The marina is well-managed and well-maintained, with clean restrooms and beautiful landscaping.

The marina has 30 amp power, water, restrooms, laundry, free showers, free pumpout, portapotty dump, and free Wi-Fi. An excellent children's play area is at the north end of the marina grounds. This is one of Puget Sound's popular destinations. Reservations accepted, 4 hours of day use free. It's one block to downtown Port Orchard. Repairs are nearby. Shuttle service by appointment.

Bremerton. The Bremerton waterfront was redeveloped several years ago and offers excellent facilities. The Bremerton Harborside Kitsap Conference Center, with a Starbucks, Anthony's Restaurant, and Cold Stone Creamery, overlooks the marina. The Hampton Suites Hotel is next door. Bremerton is doing its best to shed a dowdy image and make a name for itself.

Points of interest include the Naval Museum, the historic destroyer USS Turner Joy, and the attractive city boardwalk. Many boaters take

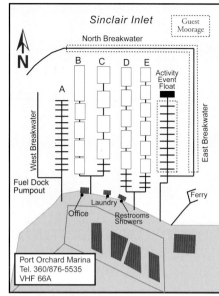

Port Orchard Marina

the passenger ferry for the 10- to 12-minute ride to Port Orchard, where the dining, the seasonal farmers market, antiques shopping, and boutiques are popular. Bremerton Marina is secured by a locked gate. Kitsap County buses in the adjacent transportation center can take you anywhere you wish to go, or take the ferry to downtown Seattle.

There is always something happening in Bremerton with its line-up of festivals and concerts. The Blackberry Festival is held Labor Day weekend, with booths ashore selling wonderful blackberry treats and more. We just happened to be there, and the festival was a hoot.

LOCAL KNOWLEDGE

STRONG CURRENTS: Tidal currents can make boat handling tricky in Bremerton Marina. It is best to time arrival and departure to coincide with slack water.

㊷ **Bremerton Marina.** 120 Washington Beach, Bremerton, WA 98367; (360) 373-1035; kathyg@portofbremerton.org. www.portofbremerton.org. Monitors VHF 66A. Certified Clean Marina. Located next to the ferry dock. Open all year, except for fall/winter holidays. Guest moorage in 80 to 100 slips and 990 feet inside of side-tie dock space, 30 & 50 amp power, water, garbage, restrooms, free showers, laundry, free Wi-Fi, 2 portapotty dumps. Shuttle service by appointment. No fuel is available. The nearest fuel dock is at Port Orchard.

This quality marina has excellent docks and a breakwater to protect against ferry wakes. Fountain Park, a short walk to the other side of the ferry dock, is lovely. The dramatic fin-like sculptures are fountains meant to resemble the superstructure (called the sail) of a modern submarine.

Washington Narrows connects Sinclair Inlet with Dyes Inlet. The narrows are crossed by two bridges with a minimum vertical clearance of 80 feet. Tidal currents, averaging over 2 knots, flood west and ebb east. Signs ask boaters to maintain minimum speed to reduce wake damage to the shore and to boats moored at the marina. A launch ramp with float and fishing pier is on the north side of the narrows about halfway along, part of the Lebo Street Recreation Area.

Bridgeview Marina. (360) 876-2522; Permanent moorage only, no transient space; pumpout is for moorage customers only.

Phinney Bay. Phinney Bay is the home of the Bremerton Yacht Club, with guest moorage for visiting reciprocal boats. Anchorage is good throughout the bay, which shoals toward each shore.

Ostrich Bay. Ostrich Bay offers good anchorage, mud bottom. The most popular anchorage is along the west side of the bay, facing dense forest. We have spent several pleasant nights at this spot. For some reason this entire area is overlooked. Even when the docks at Port Orchard and Bremerton are full on summer holiday weekends, Ostrich Bay has been almost empty.

Caution: Unexploded ordnance from years ago, when the Navy pier was used for loading munitions, has been found in the bay, especially in the vicinity of the pier.

Oyster Bay. A narrow but easily-run channel leads off Ostrich Bay into Oyster Bay, where perfectly protected anchorage is available toward the center of the bay. To enter, keep between the lines of mooring buoys and mooring floats on both sides of the channel. The channel shoals to about 6 feet at zero tide. Oyster Bay is surrounded by homes.

Dyes Inlet indents the Kitsap Peninsula northwest of Bremerton. Silverdale is on the north shore of Dyes Inlet and has a marina, waterfront park, boat ramp, and boardwalk. Dyes Inlet is connected to Sinclair Inlet via Port Washington Narrows.

㊸ **Silverdale Marina** (Port of Silverdale). P.O. Box 310, Silverdale, WA 98383; (360) 698-4918; portofsilverdale@wavecable.com; www.portofsilverdale.com. Open all year. Guest moorage along 1300 feet of wide, side-tie dock with a least depth of 10 feet at zero tide. No rafting. Moorage is on the honor system, but confirmed by security patrols that record the moored boats. Three-night maximum stay. Group reservations accepted online for a $75 fee. Restrooms, 30 amp

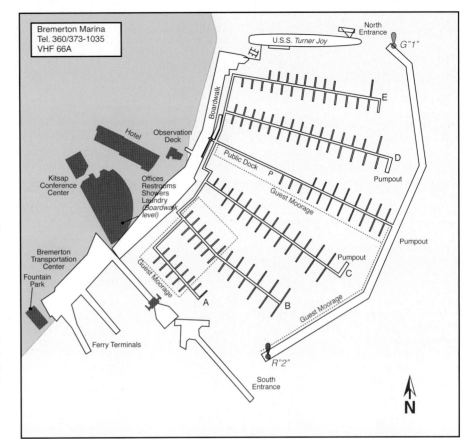

Bremerton Marina

power, seasonal potable water, pumpout, showers, 2-lane concrete launch ramp. No long-term parking. The pumpout operates 8:00 a.m. to 10:00 p.m., weekends, May to October.

The marina is adjacent to county-run Silverdale Waterfront Park. The park has picnic tables, restrooms, fire pits, children's play area, pavilion and a Veterans Memorial. Interesting shops and dining are in adjacent Old Town Silverdale. Complete shopping is at the Kitsap Mall about a mile away. The Trails shopping center is about 1.5-miles away. The nearby Clear Creek Trail & Interpretive Center is a good walk.

Whaling Days, a 3-day celebration the last weekend of July, draws big crowds, both from land and the water. Plan to anchor out. If you're on the dock, expect to be included in the carnival atmosphere. It's a big fair with live bands all weekend, activities for kids, outrigger canoe races, a fun run and more. See their website at www.whalingdays.com. Silverdale hosts the Kitsap Peninsula Water Trails Festival during the fourth weekend in June. Events include a 50K triathlon, kayak races, and waterfront activities.

BROWNSVILLE, POULSBO, NORTHERN PORT ORCHARD

Northern Port Orchard separates Bainbridge Island from the Kitsap Peninsula. Rich Passage and Sinclair Inlet are at the south end; Agate Passage is at the north. Brownsville and Poulsbo are the major marina destinations. The Agate Passage bridge has a vertical clearance of 75 feet. Currents in Agate Passage run to 6 knots on spring tides, flooding south and ebbing north.

LOCAL KNOWLEDGE

ROCK: A nasty rock, almost awash at zero tide, is inshore from the mooring buoys at Illahee Park, approximately between the

Bremerton harborside boardwalk leads to the USS Turner Joy.

buoy nearest the dock and shore. Thanks to Correspondents Al & Becca Szymanski, S/V Halona, for the report.

---

④④ **Illahee Marine State Park.** 3540 NE Bahia Vista Drive, Bremerton, WA 98310; (360) 478-6460. Located 3 miles northeast of Bremerton. Open all year, mooring and overnight camping. Guest moorage with 356 feet of side-tie dock space, 5 mooring buoys for boats 45 feet and under. Restrooms and showers, no power. The dock is protected by a floating concrete breakwater. Park has 3 kitchen shelters, picnic tables, campsites, horseshoe pits, ball field, hiking trails, and portable toilet. Popular for fishing and

sunbathing. Most services are in the upland area, reached by a steep trail.

④⑤ **Port of Brownsville.** 9790 Ogle Rd. NE, Bremerton, WA 98311; (360) 692-5498; jerry@portofbrownsville.org; www.portofbrownsville.org. Certified Clean Marina. Monitors VHF 16, switch to 66A. Open all year, 7 days a week. Fuel dock has ethanol-free gasoline, diesel, and propane. Guest moorage in 25 24-foot slips, 20 40-foot slips, and 550 feet of side-tie moorage along the breakwater, 30 & limited 50 amp power, free Wi-Fi, restrooms, showers, laundry, book exchange, free pumpout, portapotty dump, in-slip pumpout service (MV Ms le Pew). Paved 2-lane launch ramp with ample parking.

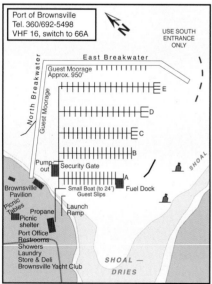

Port of Brownsville

The Port of Brownsville Marina is a popular venue for club events.

Up on the wharf, a covered picnic/gathering pavilion, with tables, is inviting. Additional picnic tables are on the docks and in Burke Bay Overlook Park above the wharf, with barbecue. This is a popular destination for club cruises. Group reservations invited.

A breakwater marks the entrance to the marina. The channel and area around the fuel dock has been dredged to 9 feet at minus tide and well marked with green buoys to port on entrance, so you don't have to hug the south side of the dock. The Deli has snacks, beer, and wine selection. They make take-out food and can cater a gathering. This is a pleasant, friendly marina.

Groceries are available a short walk (city block) up the road at the Daily Stop.

Brownsville Appreciation Day: Fourth Saturday of September. Folksy and fun, small community at its best. Classic boats and cars, treasure hunt, unicycles, hot dogs and hamburgers. All proceeds (not just profits) divided among the local elementary schools.

Savory Treat: A short walk up the road from the marina, Sweeney's Country Meats has mouth-watering specialty meats. We tried a marinade jerky and some of the bacon. All were delicious and well worth a visit.

㊻ **Port of Keyport Marina.** P.O. Box 195, Keyport, WA 98345; (541) 760-0176; www.portofkeyport.com. Concrete docks with five 50-foot slips for guest moorage, first-come, first-served. Water, 30 amp power. No restrooms. Six hours free, 3-day maximum stay. Be mindful of the current when approaching the dock. Boat launch ramp. Make payment at the Keyport Mercantile, located upland. There are several restaurants in the area, and the must-see Naval Undersea Museum (360-396-4148).

A pedestrian gate, open 10:00 a.m. to 4:00 p.m., is about a quarter of a mile straight up Washington Street from the dock. The gate leads onto the Naval Base and the Naval Undersea Museum. You can view a simulation of a nuclear fast attack submarine, torpedoes and torpedo tubes, a Confederate mine from the Civil War, and learn the history of naval diving. The museum is open daily. Admission is free.

Fletcher Bay. Fletcher Bay is shallow and not a good anchorage.

㊼ **Manzanita Bay.** Manzanita Bay is a good overnight sheltered anchorage for Seattle-area boats. The bay is all residential and has no public facilities, but the holding ground is excellent. Observe the 5-knot no-wake speed limit beginning halfway down the bay. Although the bay is lined with lovely homes, the surrounding hills give a feeling of seclusion.

At the north end of the bay, Manzanita Landing, a former Mosquito Fleet landing, provides access to the trail system of Manzanita Park. From the landing take Manzanita Road NE to NE Day Road West. Walk east to the park, which is on the left (north) side of the street.

Liberty Bay. The entrance to Liberty Bay is past the Keyport Naval torpedo research and testing facility and around Lemolo Point. The Navy requests boats travel at no-wake speed past its facility. A power cable with 90-foot clearance crosses overhead. A sign on the beacon off Lemolo Point asks boaters to slow down in all of Liberty Bay; buoys post the speed limit. Much of Liberty Bay is covered by Wi-Fi. Three major marinas are along the north shore of Liberty Bay: a private marina; the Poulsbo Yacht Club; and the Port of Poulsbo Marina.

The private marina has no guest moorage. At the Poulsbo Yacht Club, reciprocal moorage is along the northwest perimeter of the floating breakwater. Some reciprocal moorage is still available on the inside of the older breakwater.

㊽ **Poulsbo.** Poulsbo, on Liberty Bay, is one of the most popular destinations on Puget Sound, partly because it is close to the major population centers, and partly because it is such a delightful place to visit. Settled originally by Scandinavians, the downtown business district still loudly (to say the least) maintains its Norwegian heritage. Everything most visitors need is available either near the water or at the malls located on the highway about a mile away.

The waterfront portions of Poulsbo make for a lovely walk. Victorian homes and gardens have been restored and preserved to perfection.

Restaurants, bakeries and many shops that specialize in gifts, collectibles and home accessories are a few steps away in downtown

119

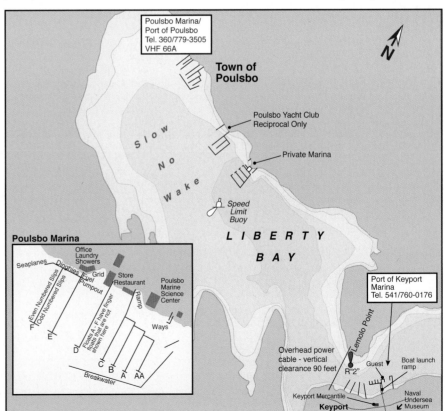

Poulsbo

Port of Keyport Marina. Transient moorage is to the left of the boathouse.

Poulsbo. Dining and shopping are popular. Sluys Poulsbo Bakery, Boehm's chocolates and Mora's Ice Creamery are favorites. Longship Marine is one of the few remaining second hand marine stores offering marine supplies and woodworking materials. The nearby Poulsbo Marine Science Center is fun for families. Don't miss the Maritime Museum on Front Street, showcasing the rich maritime history of Poulsbo and the Mosquito Fleet that transported supplies, mail and people to and from the islands. Special events include the Saturday Farmers Market, May - October; Viking Fest, 3rd weekend in May; Scandinavian Midsommer Fest, June; 3rd of July Celebration; Traditional Street Dance, August; Yule Fest, December and the Chip Hanauer Winter Rendezvous held the second weekend in February.

Looking for a great day trip or a weekend getaway? Look no further, Poulsbo has it all.

(48) Poulsbo Marina / Port of Poulsbo. 18809 Front St., P.O. Box 732, Poulsbo, WA 98370; (360) 779-9905; (360) 779-3505 ext. 1 (for reservations) office@portofpoulsbo. com; reservations@portofpoulsbo.com (for reservations); www.portofpoulsbo.com. Monitors VHF 66A. Open 7 days a week, all year, except Christmas Day and New Year's Day. Register by 4:00 p.m. to get the combination for the showers and restrooms. The fuel dock has ethanol-free gasoline and diesel. The marina has 130 guest slips, 10-foot depths at low tide, and 30 amp ELCI-protected power on all docks. Side-tie on the end of E dock. The Port utilizes permanent slips for transient moorage when available. Reservations accepted but may be limited during special events. Good restrooms and showers, laundry, pumpout, portapotty dump, launch ramp, free Wi-Fi. A meeting room and activity float are available. Groceries, fine restaurants and shops within walking distance.

If anchored out, dinghy tie-up is on the shore side of the dock closest to shore.

Agate Passage connects Port Orchard with Port Madison, and is crossed by a highway bridge with a vertical clearance of 75 feet.

Currents in the pass run as high as 6 knots at spring tides, flooding south and ebbing north. The channel through the pass is well marked, but in general, a mid-channel course will serve.

For some reason, many craft go through Agate Passage too fast, creating havoc for slower craft. Agate Passage isn't very long. Keep the speed down, look astern to judge your wake, and give fellow boats a break.

PORT MADISON AND BAINBRIDGE ISLAND

Miller Bay. Miller Bay indents the Northwest corner of Port Madison. It is very shallow and should be entered only at half tide or better, or with local knowledge. Like many bays on Puget Sound, Miller Bay has a drying shoal in the middle, so navigable water can be found only around the perimeter.

Mattson's Bay Marine. 20622 Miller Bay Rd. NE, Poulsbo, WA 98392; (360) 598-4900; mattsonsbaymarine@gmail.com. Open Tuesday through Saturday all year. Haulout to 30 feet, parts and complete repairs. Launch ramp, dry storage.

Suquamish. Suquamish is best known as the winter home of Chief Seattle and the former site of his longhouse, the Old Man House village. With its restaurants and other cultural attractions, it makes a good day trip from Seattle.

The Suquamish community dock and float, just north of Agate Pass, provides short-term moorage for visiting boats. The east side of the float is exposed to chop from boat traffic and weather in outer Port Madison. If the protected space on the west side is not available, boaters can anchor and take the dinghy to the float. Good anchorage is northeast of the float. A boat ramp is south of the float; it's not usable at low tide.

Today, the town of Suquamish is the center of the Suquamish Indian Reservation. A community center across the street from the dock is patterned after the Old Man House. The Suquamish Museum is up the hill.

Visible above the community center is an impressive veterans memorial, with carved figures honoring Chief Kitsap, Chief Seattle, and Suquamish veterans.

From the veterans memorial, follow signs to Chief Seattle's grave in the Suquamish Tribal Cemetery behind the white church of St. Peter's Catholic Mission. The original gravestone placed by Seattle pioneers is still there, along with more recent Native carvings and inscriptions of Chief Seattle's words.

From Chief Seattle's grave, continue walking uphill to the Suquamish Museum. The museum is open 10:00 a.m. to 5:00 p.m., daily.

Since 1911, the Suquamish Tribe has been celebrating Chief Seattle Days on the third weekend of August. Activities include a traditional salmon bake, canoe races, baseball, drumming and dancing, and a memorial service honoring Chief Seattle.

Sully's Bistro & Bar is within easy walking distance of the dock. Agate Pass Cafe and Scratch Kitchen have closed.

Indianola. Indianola is distinguished by the long pier that served passengers and freight during Mosquito Fleet days. A float is installed during the summer to give access

Who can resist stopping in for fresh bakery treats at Sluys Bakery?

Poulsbo fuel dock

to the town, max boat size 30 feet, max stay 30 minutes. The float grounds on low and minus tides. The Indianola Country Store, just a few blocks from the pier, has been in business since the 1920s. It has a good selection of grocery items, beer and wine, and a popular deli.

Inner Port Madison. The inner, residential bay extends for about 1.5 miles into the north end of Bainbridge Island. This is where Port Madison Yacht Club and a large Seattle Yacht Club outstation (no reciprocals) are located. Anchorage is good throughout, with a wide bight about 0.75 mile inside the entrance. Shore access is possible from a dinghy dock at Hidden Cove Park just west of the SYC outstation. Farther in, Hidden Cove is a lovely spot. For Seattle area boats, this is an often-overlooked area to have a picnic lunch or a quiet night at anchor. The shores are private but the setting is idyllic.

Fay Bainbridge Park. www.biparks.org. South of Point Monroe on Bainbridge Island. Open all year; exposed, anchoring only. Restrooms, showers. The park has 3 kitchen shelters, fireplaces, fire rings, a beach area, launch ramp, utility and primitive campsites, children's play equipment, horseshoe pits, fishing, clamming, and a concession stand in summer.

Murden Cove. Murden Cove has convenient anchoring depths, but little protection from winds. It's a long row to shore, partly over drying flats. The residential community of Rolling Bay is at the head of the bay.

LOCAL KNOWLEDGE

NO ANCHOR ZONE: The bottom around the south entrance to Eagle Harbor has been capped to prevent the spread of pollutants from a former creosote facility. Do not anchor in this area.

Eagle Harbor. Eagle Harbor is the location

of the Winslow neighborhood of the City of Bainbridge Island. The entire island is considered the City of Bainbridge, which includes several neighborhood areas. Winslow is the western terminus of a ferry from downtown Seattle.

The neighboorhood of Winslow has a guest dock and boat launch at Eagle Harbor Waterfront Park. Linear moorage and mooring buoys are located in the harbor. Anchorage in Eagle Harbor is available west of the Ferry Maintenance Yard, and at least 200 feet south of the marinas on the north shore. Anchorage for the first 2 days is without charge, a fee is charged for additional days, maximum 30-day stay. The nominal anchorage fee provides access to showers and garbage drop at the Park. Moorings in the harbor are part of the Eagle Harbor Waterfront Park facilities. A self-registration payment box for dock moorage, buoys, linear moorage and extended anchorage is located at Eagle Harbor Waterfront Park.

Several marinas in the area provide guest moorage if a permanent tenant is away. All but one marina, Eagle Harbor Marina on the south shore, are on the town side of the harbor. Queen City Yacht Club, Meydenbauer Bay

Yacht Club, and Seattle Yacht Club have outstations in Eagle Harbor. A pumpout station is located at Eagle Harbor Waterfront Park, and in-slip pumpouts are provided at Eagle Harbor Marina.

We enjoy walking the streets of town, which offer boutiques, art shops, and a variety of good restaurants. The grocery store, within walking distance, has everything. The beautiful Bainbridge Island Museum of Art has a cafe. The Alehouse on Winslow, located next to the museum, has a nice selection of beer and cider on tap; patrons may bring in outside food. The grounds and gardens at Bloedel Reserve, on the north end of the island, are worth a visit. Kitsap Transit, at the ferry terminal, provides service during weekdays and Saturdays.

Eagle Harbor is entered through a marked channel past foul ground that extends south from Wing Point. Nun Buoy 2 is at the end of this foul ground, and the Tyee Shoal Beacon is a short distance south of Buoy 2. The ferries round Tyee Shoal Beacon, but other craft can use Buoy 2 safely, following the rule of Red, Right, Returning. Follow the markers all the way in. Shoal water extends out to the channel on both sides. Observe the 5-knot speed limit from Buoy 5. The far west end of the inner harbor is an Aquatic Conservancy area where power boats are not allowed.

No Discharge Zone.

㊾ **Eagle Harbor Waterfront Park**. 280 Madison Ave. N., Bainbridge Island, WA 98110; (206) 786-7627; www.ci.bainbridge-isl.wa.us. Open all year. 500 feet of transient side-tie moorage at the dock. Water, 30 & 50 amp ELCI-protected power, and pumpout. 400 feet of linear moorage and 4 mooring buoys in the harbor. All moorage facilities are first-come, first-served. Washrooms, free showers, and garbage drop are located upland from the dock in the Waterfront Park. Rafting is encouraged. There is a nominal fee for stays up to 3 hours. Boat launch ramp is next to the dock. Public washrooms are open all hours. Showers are accessible with an entry

The cold water didn't deter these swimmers at Indianola.

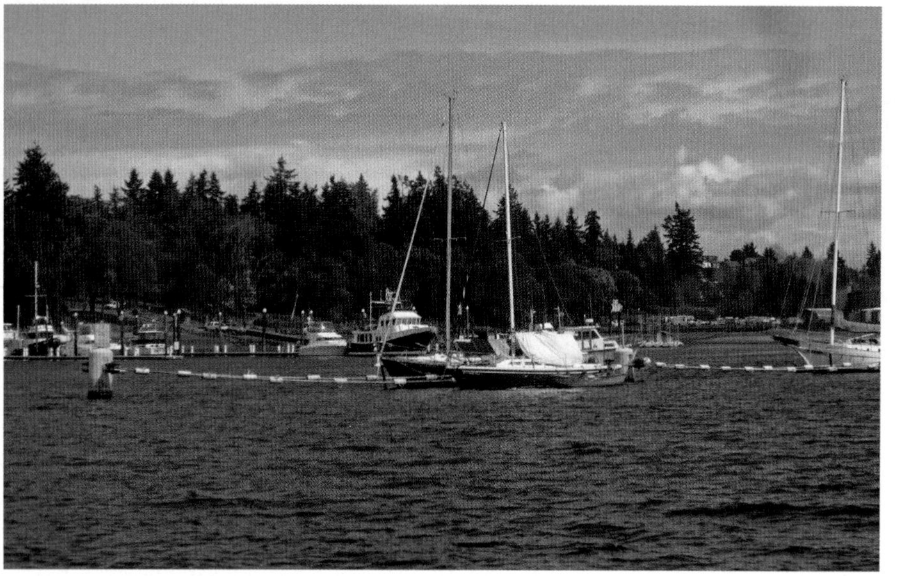

Linear moorage in Eagle Harbor

code available by calling the harbormaster. Payment for these City moorage facilities is made at the self-registration payment box located at the Park. Maximum 2-day stay in a seven-day period at the dock.

A short quarter-mile walk north from the Waterfront Park brings you to the center of town and the grocery store on Winslow Way. Half-mile long Winslow Way is lined on both sides with small shops, restaurants, pubs, and a bakery. One block north of Winslow Way on Ericksen Avenue is the Bainbridge Island Historical Museum.

Upgrades to the park dock facility were completed in 2018. The main dock was lengthened by 100 feet and a 200-foot end cap added. Bathroom facilities were also upgraded.

㊾ **Winslow Wharf Marina.** P.O. Box 10297, 141 Parfitt Way SW, Bainbridge Island, WA 98110; (206) 842-4202; dave@winslowwharfmarina.com; www. winslowwharfmarina. com. Monitors VHF 09. Open Tuesday through Saturday, 9:00 a.m. to 5:00 p.m. Guest moorage in unoccupied slips. Maximum boat length 50 feet, 30 & 50 amp power, clean remodeled restrooms, free showers. Wi-Fi, laundry, book exchange, pumpout, portapotty dump. Reservations required. Chandlery Marine, a well-stocked marine supply store, has a little bit of everything, (206) 842-7245. Seattle Yacht Club and Meydenbauer Bay Yacht Club have dock space reserved for their members. The spaces are clearly marked, and non-member boats may not use them.

㊾ **Harbour Marina.** 233 Parfitt Way SW, Bainbridge Island, WA 98110; (206) 550-5340; info@harbour-marina.com; www.harbour-marina.com. Open all year. Unoccupied slips used for guest boats, call ahead for availability. Facilities include 30 amp power, restrooms, free showers, laundry, pumpout. Located directly below Harbour Public House, an English-style pub with beer, wine, and food. No kids allowed in the pub. Moorage for visiting the pub and Pegasus Coffee House is clearly marked. Close to the Waterfront Trail and a short walk to downtown.

㊿ **Eagle Harbor Marina.** P.O. Box 11217, 5834 Ward Ave. NE, Bainbridge Island, WA 98110; (206) 842-4003; harbormaster@eagleharbormarina.com; www.eagleharbormarina.com. Open all year. Primarily permanent moorage with limited transient moorage, call ahead. Marina has 30, 50 & 100 amp ELCI-protected power. Restrooms, showers, laundry, pumpout, free Wi-Fi. Docks were recently replaced and upgraded, including monitored shore power, in-slip portable pumpout, year-round water, and security. This marina is on the south side of Eagle Harbor away from town; there are no restaurants or stores in the immediate area.

(51) **Blakely Harbor.** In the early days Blakely Harbor was the site of major lumber and shipbuilding activities. Now it is a quiet residential neighborhood. Some stub pilings remain from the old docks. The head of the bay, including the old mill pond and ruins of the concrete powerhouse, is now a park. Good anchorage in 35 to 50 feet can be found far enough into the bay to be well protected, yet still have a view of the Seattle skyline. Sunset on a clear evening is beautiful. Blakely Rock is 0.5 mile off; give it a good offing. Enter Blakely Harbour in the middle of the mouth of the bay. A drying reef extends from the north shore, and shoals are along the south side.

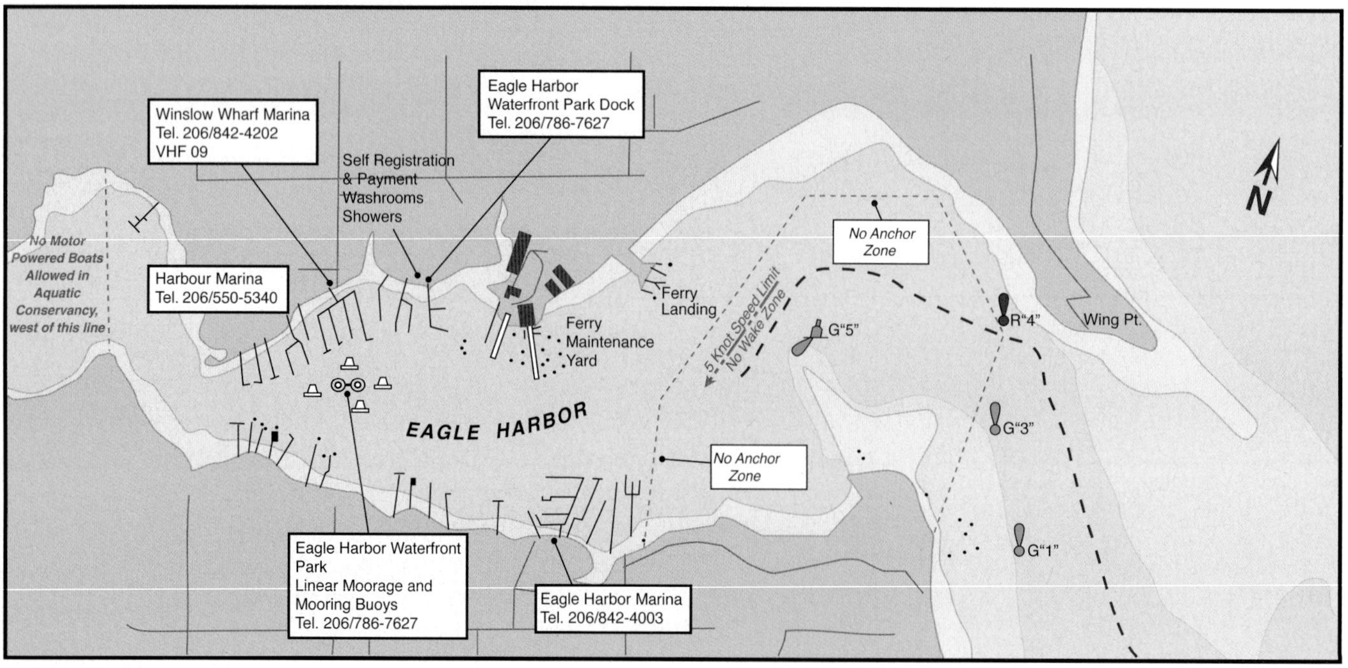

Eagle Harbor

Hood Canal

CHAPTER 3

HOOD CANAL
Dabob Bay • Pleasant Harbor • Alderbrook

See Area Map Page 125- Maps Not for Navigation

Hood Canal is a 65-mile-long glacier-carved fjord. Because the shorelines are fairly straight with few protected anchorages, Hood Canal is less used by pleasure craft than many other waterways. Most boaters don't realize that shrimping, oyster gathering, clamming and fishing can be outstanding. The shrimping season is short: usually 3 weeks in May, just 2 days each week. But on those days, the boats are thick. In clear weather the views of the Olympic Mountains from Hood Canal are outstanding. Other than shrimpers and knowing fishermen, however, Hood Canal is largely undiscovered.

Several rivers flow from the Olympic Mountains into Hood Canal, and each has formed a mudflat off its mouth. Although the shoal off the Dosewallips River, a couple of miles south of Pulali Point, is marked, the shoals off the Duckabush, Fulton Creek, Hama Hama, and Lilliwaup rivers are not marked, nor is the extensive shoal off the Skokomish River at the Great Bend. Care must be taken to avoid running aground.

Pleasant Harbor and the Alderbrook Inn Resort can take larger boats, but many of the other marinas and parks on Hood Canal are aimed at trailerable boats. This has disappointed some people with larger boats.

Hood Head. Anchorage can be found behind Hood Head on the western shore of Hood Canal, but the water shoals rapidly to drying flats near the head of the bay.

Shine Tidelands State Park. Stretches 1 mile north of the Hood Canal Bridge into Bywater Bay on the west shore of Hood Canal. Day use only, toilets, no power, water or showers. Anchoring only, well offshore. Launch ramp, crabbing and clamming, hiking trails.

Bywater Bay. Anchor in 6 to 12 feet, good holding on a soft bottom with room to swing. The spit provides wave protection from north winds. A shallow draft boat can easily enter the lagoon in the undeveloped Wolfe Property State Park at the northwest corner of the bay. [Hamilton]

Port Gamble. Port Gamble is a fine anchorage, protected from wave action by a sandspit at the entrance. Anchorage in 18 to 30 feet is possible everywhere. Many people prefer the area just inside the spit. At present, there is no guest dock or designated landing area. Port Gamble is charming and historic. The remnants of the sawmill are being removed, and the town has been restored. A museum, restaurants and small shops are on the tree-lined main street. Having established a sawmill, Port Gamble began as a company-owned town, founded in 1853. The mill was in operation until 1995. The Port Gamble Historic Museum (360) 297-8078 covers the history of the mill and town site. The museum is open daily, May through September, and on weekends only during the winter months.

Main street in historic Port Gamble

LOCAL KNOWLEDGE

DANGEROUS ROCKS: Sisters, two substantial rocks about 200 yards apart, lie 0.4 mile south of the Hood Canal bridge on the west side. The rocks dry at half tide. The southern rock is marked by a large lighted beacon, yet from time to time an unwary boat manages to go up on these rocks. For safety, if you have passed under the western end of the bridge, turn eastward at once and run parallel to the bridge to the middle before turning south into Hood Canal.

Hood Canal Floating Bridge. The east end of the Hood Canal Floating Bridge has 50 feet of vertical clearance. Clearance on the west end is 33 feet. The bridge can be opened for larger vessels, but it is not manned. To arrange an opening call (360) 779-3233, which connects to a State Department of Transportation office in Tacoma. They will take your name, telephone number, name of your vessel, date and time of desired opening, and whether you are inbound or outbound. They also will ask what width opening you need (300 feet or 600 feet). One hour's notice is needed to get a crew to the bridge and prepare it for opening. No bridge openings between 3:00 p.m. and 6:15 p.m. daily, from Memorial Day to Labor Day.

Salsbury Point County Park. Just off the northeast end of the Hood Canal Bridge. Day use only, restrooms, no power. Anchoring only, 2 launch ramps. Picnic tables, fireplaces, children's play area. Nature trail. Sandy beach for experienced divers only because of strong currents.

Kitsap Memorial Marine State Park. (360) 779-3205; Four miles south of Hood Canal Bridge. Open all year, day use and overnight camping, 2 mooring buoys for boats 45 feet and under. Self-register and pay mooring buoy fee on shore. Restrooms, showers, no power. Picnic sites, kitchen shelters, fireplaces. Standard campsites, swimming beach, playground, horseshoe pits, volleyball courts, baseball field. Buoys are exposed to tidal currents and wind.

Squamish Harbor. Squamish Harbor has convenient anchoring depths, but the harbor is quite open and has numerous rocks and reefs that must be avoided. It is seldom used for overnight anchorage.

Thorndyke Bay. Thorndyke Bay is too open to provide a snug anchorage.

LOCAL KNOWLEDGE

RESTRICTED AREAS: Boaters should take great care not to enter the Restricted Area in front of the Bangor Naval Station on the east side of Hood Canal, about 4 miles south from Vinland, which is patrolled constantly to keep passing vessels well away. The patrol craft are fitted with guns and are authorized to shoot. Best practice is to stay west of mid-channel when transiting this area. A second Naval Restricted Area is located off Point Whitney in Dabob Bay.

NAVAL OPERATING AREAS: Two adjoining Naval Operating areas cover a majority of Hood Canal, from South Point to Hazel Point. When transiting this area, boaters should monitor Channel 16. Look for Naval vessels flying a "Bravo" (red) flag during periods of Naval operations. A passage corridor outside the Operating Areas follows the west side of Hood Canal, hugging the eastern shoreline of Toandos Peninsula. Another Naval Operating & Exercise Area is in Dabob Bay, where flashing lights along the shoreline indicate the status of operations.

Naval Base Kitsap (Bangor). This is the location of Bangor Naval Station, homeport for a fleet of nuclear submarines. Several of

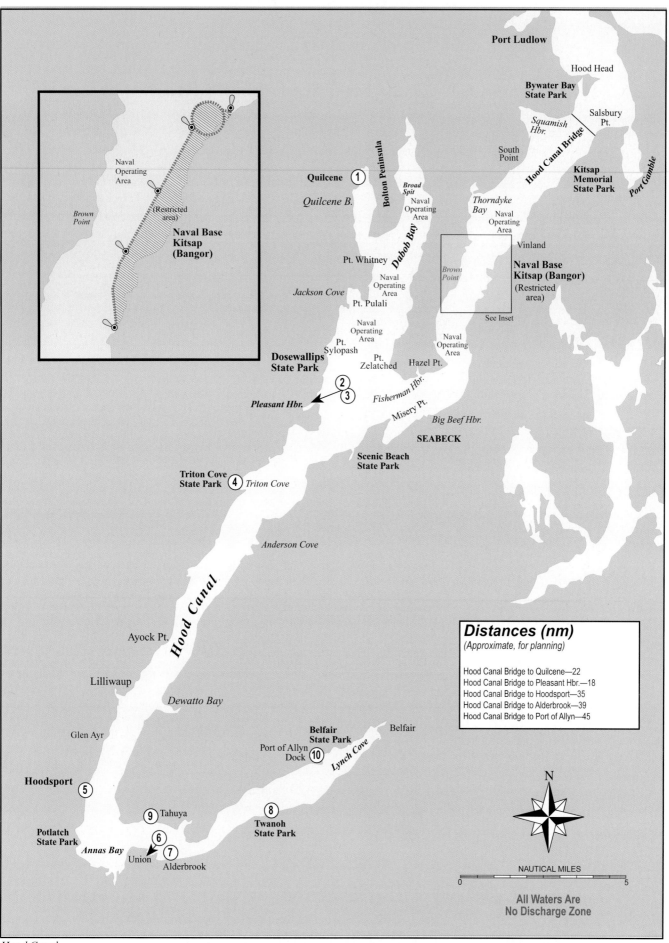

Distances (nm)
(Approximate, for planning)

Hood Canal Bridge to Quilcene—22
Hood Canal Bridge to Pleasant Hbr.—18
Hood Canal Bridge to Hoodsport—35
Hood Canal Bridge to Alderbrook—39
Hood Canal Bridge to Port of Allyn—45

Hood Canal

Stay well clear of Bangor Naval Station.

these awesome machines often are visible to passing craft. Stay outside of the marked restricted area.

Seabeck Bay. Anchorage is possible behind Misery Point, with good protection from the south and west. The Seabeck General Store can be accessed by dinghy. The Olympic View Marina is for permanent moorage only.

Scenic Beach State Park. South of Seabeck. Open for day use all year and overnight camping in summer only. Anchoring only. Standard and primitive campsites. Kitchen shelter, fireplaces, fire rings, horseshoe pits, volleyball areas. Scuba diving, swimming, hiking, shellfishing.

Fisherman Harbor. Fisherman Harbor can be entered only at high water, but once inside offers protected anchorage in 5 to 15 feet. Follow the natural channel into the bay, then turn south and follow the spit until anchoring depths are found. All the land around the bay is privately owned. Years ago, we tiptoed into Fisherman Harbor in a sailboat at something less than high tide. It was careful going, with a close watch from the bow and a bit of luck, but the boat got in without touching. Less foolish souls should wait for higher water. [Hale]

Dabob Bay. Most of Dabob Bay is a Naval Operating & Exercise Area with 5 warning lights. Flashing amber lights indicate Naval operations are in progress; boaters may enter the area on an amber light but should keep well clear of Navy vessels. Flashing red lights indicate the area has been closed to navigation. If the lights turn red while you are inside the Operations Area, shut down engines and depth sounder until operations have ended. The 5 warning lights are located

at Whitney Point, Pulali Point, and Sylopash Point on the west side of the bay; Zelatched Point on the east side of the bay; and at the north end of the bay on the southeast side of Bolton Peninsula. South of Pulali Point (western shore of Dabob Bay) is outside the Operating Area and includes Jackson Cove, where good anchorage can be found. Boaters should be aware of the Restricted Area just off Point Whitney, a charted no anchoring zone.

A State Department of Fish and Wildlife oyster research laboratory is at Whitney Point with a good launch ramp alongside. A breakwater-protected marina, Herb Beck Marina, is at the village of Quilcene.

Caution should be exercised when transiting Dabob Bay and Quilcene Bay to avoid the large number of shrimp pots during the season.

Broad Spit Park. On the east shore of Bolton Peninsula in Dabob Bay. Anchor on either side of the spit, depending on wind direction.

Easy beach access, trails ashore. Lagoon that fills at high tide. Field Correspondent Jim Norris reports "We anchored two nights just north of Broad Spit in Dabob Bay. The wind was SE 20-25 all day. Given the full fetch of Hood Canal for waves to develop, I feared a nasty swell would bend around the spit and make life uncomfortable. Not so. The spit offered good protection from the waves, but not the wind. We swung around on the anchor, but no other motion in the boat."

Quilcene Bay. Anchor in 12 feet, good holding in mud along the east shore opposite the marina, with protection from moderate southerly winds. On a 10-foot tide, a shallow draft vessel can travel at least a quarter mile up Donovan Creek through winding grasslands at the head of the bay. [Hamilton]

① **Herb Beck Marina.** 1731 Linger Longer Rd., Quilcene, WA 98376; (360) 765-3131; www.portofpt.com/marinas/. Managed by the Port of Port Townsend. Monitors VHF

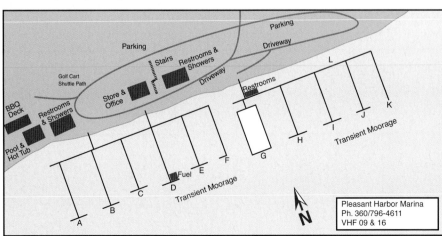

Pleasant Harbor Marina

TIME, TIDE & TIMBER OVER A CENTURY OF POPE & TALBOT
-By Edwin T. Coman, Jr. and Helen M. Gibbs

Publisher: Stanford University Press

Time, Tide, & Timber is about one of the most successful mill operations in our country's history. Building a mill at **Port Gamble** in the mid-1800's, Andrew Pope and William Talbot grew a company which lasted over 124 years. Woven into the story about the Puget Mill Company is the history and development of the West Coast. San Francisco and Seattle were just small settlements, and Washington was still part of the Oregon Territory.

A fifty-one-day journey around Cape Horn from Maine, necessitating passage on three different steam ships, brought Andrew Pope and Frederic Talbot to San Francisco in 1849. California was in the process of becoming a state, and the two men saw that lumber shipped by Pope's relatives in Boston could not arrive fast enough, cheap enough, or in great enough quantities to meet demand. Frederick Talbot returned to Maine to inform their brother, Captain William Talbot, who made the journey to **Puget Sound**. In December 1852, Pope, Talbot, and family members, Captain Keller and Charles Foster, signed an agreement to form the Puget Mill Company.

Captain William Talbot searched for an ideal location for a mill in Puget Sound; such a place needed to have good anchorage in a harbor close to viable road access, and dependable winds for sailing vessels; Port Gamble became the chosen site.

With the acquisition of more efficient equipment in 1854, the company became the largest operation on the Sound; 52 vessels arrived to load lumber and the mill operated around the clock. But the company was not without challenges – threats came from local Natives, a Depression hit in 1857, and the labor market was adversely affected during the 1858-1859 Fraser River Gold Rush. With good management, a good sales force, and a company store generating additional revenue, the mill at Port Gamble prospered. Shipments of lumber went to San Francisco, Victoria B.C., Japan, Hong Kong, Hawaii, Australia, and New Zealand. The risk of losing vessels and cargo at sea was always present, and losses occurred.

Controlling shipping costs was another challenge. Pope and Talbot turned to their East Coast relatives to purchase vessels in order to acquire their own fleet. The Civil War, which began in 1861, presented other obstacles. Later years saw the acquisition of timber lands, improved equipment and efforts to upgrade tugboat operations.

With the death of Andrew Pope in 1878 and William Talbot in 1881, carrying on the company legacy was left to a new generation of Popes and Talbots. During this decade, the railroads reached the Pacific Northwest. It was time to diversify once again. The Puget Mill Company adapted and entered the rail trade in 1919. As the U.S. prepared for WWI, northwest spruce lumber was needed for airplane construction, but the labor force was limited. The company then faced the Great Depression of the 1930's and WWII in the 1940's. Through it all, the company was made profitable through wise decisions and diversification. Naval housing projects and housing developments after WWII bolstered the business in addition to rehabilitation of timberlands and the establishment of tree farms.

The 1960's saw continued housing developments, including Port Ludlow, Everett, and the construction of the missile submarine base at Bangor, Washington in 1973. Keeping abreast of the times, the Company produced specialty products like veneers, particleboard, and plywood; and acquired other mills and timber lands in British Columbia. During the 1970's the U.S. entered a Recession and housing starts plummeted, still Pope & Talbot remained viable through conservative spending and aggressive positioning.

Generations of Popes and Talbots left rich accomplishments woven into the history of the Pacific Northwest. The book, *Time, Tide & Timber* is not only a look at the past, but serves as a study in good management practices, through good times and bad. This rare book is an interesting read.

THE MILL AT PORT GAMBLE, 1890
Reproduced from a photograph supplied by Dexter S. Kimball.

Pleasant Harbor Marina, a clean, attractive facility with guest moorage

66A. Open Wednesday through Sunday 8:00 a.m. - 4:30 p.m. in the summers; Tuesday, Friday, and Saturday 8:00 a.m. - 4:30 p.m. winters. Ethanol-free gasoline and diesel at the fuel dock. Limited guest moorage to 40 feet, 20 & 30 amp power, water, showers, restrooms, pumpout, garbage drop. Reservations accepted. This is a small, rustic marina.

Dosewallips State Park. (360) 796-4415; South of Brinnon. Park open all year for day use and overnight camping. Accessible by kayak or canoe. Restrooms, showers. Hiking trails, picnic areas, standard, utility, and primitive campsites.

Pleasant Harbor. Pleasant Harbor is a major stopping point on Hood Canal with a good destination resort marina and a state park dock. Enter through a narrow channel with least depth of 8.5 feet at zero tide. Inside, there's room to anchor, 18 to 42 feet, mud bottom. Pleasant Harbor Marina has excellent facilities for visiting boaters. Home Port Marina of Pleasant Harbor (formerly, Pleasant Harbor "Old" Marina) has no guest moorage.

Pleasant Harbor is full of boats in May, when the annual shrimping season is under way. For dates, go to www.wdfw.wa.gov.

② **Pleasant Harbor Marina.** 308913 Hwy 101, Brinnon, WA 98320; (360) 796-4611; (800) 547-3479; reservations@phmresort.com; www.pleasantharbormarina.com. Monitors VHF 09 & 16. Open all year. Closed Thanksgiving and Christmas. Ethanol-free gasoline, diesel and propane at the fuel dock. The marina has approximately 60 guest slips and unoccupied slips as available, 30 & 50 amp power. Side-tie moorage to 150 feet. Facilities include sparkling clean restrooms and free showers, laundry, free Wi-Fi, on-site security, and free pumpout at the fuel dock. A floating

washroom called "The Caboose" is moored at the north docks with a clean shower and two toilets.

The main building houses the marina office, restaurant, lounge, and store. The store has a selection of gifts, clothing, some groceries, beer and wine. At the fuel dock you'll find ice cream, ice, crab and shrimp bait, tackle, and marine hardware.

A shuttle van can take you to several local hikes that range in length from a 0.2 mile trail to a 130-foot-high waterfall, to a 3.5- mile loop of Dosewallips State Park.

This is a popular destination. Reservations strongly recommended, especially on weekends and holidays. Many of the permanent tenants spend considerable time at the marina, and life on the docks is quite friendly. Amenities include a barbecue and picnic area, swimming pool, hot tub, laser skeet range, and children's play area. Kayak, and SUP rentals. Live music May through September. Diane and Christy are the very capable managers.

③ **Pleasant Harbor Marine State Park.** (360) 796-4415. Open all year for day use and overnight mooring. No camping. Dock has 120 feet of space, 3-night maximum stay, first-come, first-serve. This is the first dock on the right as you enter Pleasant Harbor.

Triton Head. A state park launch ramp is at Triton Head, and anchorage is possible off this little bight.

④ **Triton Cove State Park.** (360) 796-4415; West side of Hood Canal, south of the Dosewallips River. Open all year, day use only. Vault toilet, no power, no showers. Concrete launch ramp, picnic area.

⑤ **Hoodsport.** Hoodsport is popular with scuba divers as a place to view the giant Pacific octopus. Local marine preserves such

as Octopus Hole and Sund Rock offer divers the chance to see octopus, wolf eels, rockfish, anemones and other marine life.

The town has a grocery store, hardware store, restaurants, an espresso shop, a beauty salon, and gift shops. The Washington Department of Fish and Wildlife operates a fish hatchery in town.

Glen Ayr Resort. 25381 N U.S. Hwy 101, Hoodsport, WA 98548; (360) 877-9522; office@garesort.com; www.glenayr.com. Open all year. Nice docks and friendly staff. Moorage for boats up to 35 feet, motel and townhouse guests have priority. Space for transient boaters, except during shrimp season. Restrooms, guest showers, laundry. No power at the docks. Attractive location and popular diving destination.

⑤ **Port of Hoodsport.** P.O. Box 429, Hoodsport, WA 98548; (360) 877-9350; portmail@hctc.com; www.portofhoodsport. us. Docks with 6 guest moorage slips for boats up to 16 feet, one outside 40-foot slip subject to wave action. No power, no water. Garbage drop. Self-register at head of dock. Grocery store is located across the highway from the dock; other Hoodsport businesses are within walking distance.

Sunrise Motel & Resort. 24520 Hwy 101, Hoodsport, WA 98548; (360) 877-5301; sunrise@hctc.com; myweb.hcc.net/sunrise. An older resort open all year, no power, laundry. Restrooms and showers in motel rooms. Maximum boat length 20 feet. Moorage for those staying ashore. Underwater park, scuba air station, barbecue, hot tub.

Potlatch Marine State Park. (360) 877-5361. South of Hoodsport. Open all year, day use and overnight camping and mooring. Restrooms, showers, no power. Five mooring buoys (boats 45 feet and under) are offshore in deep water, except the second buoy as you approach from the north. We are told this buoy swings into 5-foot depths at zero tide. Self-register and pay mooring buoy fee on shore. The park has a picnic area, an underwater park for scuba diving, hiking trails, campsites. Good wildlife-watching.

⑥ **Hood Canal Marina.** P.O. Box 305, 5101 E. Hwy 106, Union, WA 98592; (360) 898-2252; hoodcanalmarina@hctc.com; www.hood-canal-marina.com. Certified Clean Marina. Open all year. Fuel dock with ethanol-free gasoline and diesel, open daily 8:00 a.m. to 5:00 p.m., call ahead in off season; 30 amp power, free Wi-Fi, washrooms, and pumpout. Limited transient moorage, maximum 40-foot vessels. Call ahead for moorage. Moorages fill quickly in May during shrimp season. The Union launch ramp is adjacent and has off-site secured parking. The Union City Market, at Hood Canal Marina, offers food items, crafts, books and clothing.

PLEASANT HARBOR
—MARINA & RECREATION COMMUNITY—

CALL NOW
360-796-4611

More Than Just A Marina...

YEAR ROUND MOORAGE

- 312 Slip Protected Marina
- 30 & 50 Amp Power
- Non-Ethanol Gas & Diesel
- Vacuum Pump Out
- Heated Pool & Hot Tub
- Permanent / Guest Moorage
- Groceries / Gift Shop

LODGING

- 4 Suites
- Queen Size Beds
- En-Suite Bathrooms
- Outside Deck with BBQ
- Heated Pool & Hot Tub
- TV + WiFi
- Full Kitchen

GALLEY & PUB

- Delicious Food
- Local Beers On Tap
- Local Wine Selection
- Roof Top Patio
- Live Music
- 3 Big Screen TVs

ACTIVITIES & ADVENTURES

- Children's Play Area
- Kayak Racing
- Kayak & SUPs
- Laser Skeet Shooting
- Horsehoes
- Hiking
- Boating
- Lawn Games
- Shrimping/Crabbing

CLEAN MARINA
WASHINGTON
EnviroStars Certified

Play, Relax, Enjoy
www.pleasantharbormarina.com

ENVIROSTARS
CERTIFIED

Docks at Alderbrook Resort & Spa

⑦ **Alderbrook Resort & Spa.** 10 E. Alderbrook Drive, Union, WA 98592; (360) 898-2200; (360) 898-2252; cindy.sund@alderbrookresort.com; www.alderbrookresort.com. Monitors VHF 16, then switch to a working channel. Open all year, 1500 feet of guest moorage. Restrooms, showers, 30 & 50 amp power, water, swimming pool and whirlpool spa, free Wi-Fi. Pumpout available, check for availability in advance. Seaplane dock. Kayak, paddleboard, hydrobike and seacycle rentals. The classic schooner *Pleiades* and the trawler *Twanoh* are available for scheduled trips and charters.

If you're looking for a quality resort experience, you'll find it here. The rooms are beautifully appointed, the grounds are immaculate, and the dining room is superb. Moorage is free while dining. They have an indoor pool, with a spa adjacent. Hiking trails surround the property. Everything you're looking for in a weekend getaway is here, including golf. Best to call ahead for reservations and prices.

⑧ **Twanoh Marine State Park**. (360) 275-2222. Eight miles west of Belfair. Open all year, day use and overnight camping and mooring, except no camping in winter. Has 200 feet of overnight and day-use moorage dock, 6 mooring buoys for vessels 45 feet and under. Self-register and pay mooring fees on shore. Restrooms, showers, pumpout, portapotty dump, power, no water. Be aware that water depth at the dock is only 3 feet at zero tide. This is a large and popular park, with launch ramp, playground, picnic areas, kitchen shelters, fireplaces. Launch ramp; docks removed from November through April. Standard, utility and primitive campsites, tennis courts, hiking trails.

⑨ **Summertide Resort & Marina.** P.O. Box 450, 15781 NE Northshore Rd. Tahuya, WA 98588; (360) 275-9313; www.summertideresort.com. Guest moorage, 50-foot maximum boat length. Reservations required. Restrooms, showers, Wi-Fi, no power. Launch ramp, RV spaces with hookups. Boat moorage is for those staying in one of the resort's rental cottages. Store carries groceries, beer, wine, snacks, ice, bait, and tackle; boats may stop to visit the store.

Belfair State Park. (800) 452-5687. Three miles southwest of Belfair on the north shore of Hood Canal. Open all year for day use and overnight camping. Restrooms and showers. Anchor far offshore if at all. Drying mudflats restrict approach to small, shallow-draft boats only. Popular park, camping reservations required in summer.

⑩ **Port of Allyn North Shore Dock.** P.O. Box 1, Allyn, WA 98524; (360) 275-2430; www.portofallyn.com. Open March through October, with 240 feet of side-tie dock space. Water, 30 amp power, portable toilets, seasonal pumpout and portapotty dump, no showers. Overnight moorage for boats up to 45 feet with a 14-day limit. Self-registration payment box on-site. Launch ramp with credit, debit card payment.

Hood Canal with splendid views of the Olympic Mountains

North Puget Sound

CHAPTER 4

NORTHWEST PUGET SOUND
Kingston • Admiralty Inlet
Port Ludlow • Port Townsend

NORTHEAST PUGET SOUND
Edmonds • Everett • Langley
Saratoga Passage • Coupeville
Oak Harbor • La Conner • Deception Pass
Anacortes • Bellingham • Semiahmoo Bay
Blaine • Point Roberts

Kingston. Kingston, in Appletree Cove on the west side of Puget Sound, is the western terminus of the ferry run to Edmonds, and possibly the only city in Washington State where you can get an authentic French crepe at five o'clock in the morning while waiting for the ferry. A Port-owned marina, with a park, is located behind the breakwater. The park's meticulously maintained lawn and gardens are inviting. Kingston's tree shaded main street is lined with cafés with great food and colorful names, many with outdoor seating. Farther uptown is a grocery store and hardware store. On the north side of the ferry holding area a deck overlooks Puget Sound. A path leads to a Port-owned broad sandy beach filled with driftwood. It's a pleasant walk and great for families. On the the park grounds next to the marina a farmers market, quite popular, is open 9:00 a.m. to 2:00 p.m. Saturdays, May to mid-October. Concerts on the Cove, with a beer garden, are held Saturday evenings during July and August.

A pavilion on the park grounds, just up from the marina, is used for music concerts, gatherings, and weddings.

Anchoring is good south of the marina breakwater. Watch your depths. It gets shallow close to shore.

① **Port of Kingston.** P.O. Box 559, Kingston, WA 98346; (360) 297-3545; info@ portofkingston.org; www.portofkingston. org. Monitors VHF 65A but prefers telephone calls. Open year-round, 49 guest slips to

Port of Kingston marina. Fuel dock is in the foreground; visitor moorage parallels the breakwater.

50 feet, water and 30 amp power. At the outer end of the guest dock an 86-foot-long float, with water and 30 & 50 amp power, accommodates larger boats. The marina has restrooms, laundry, portapotty dump, free showers, free pumpout, in-berth pumpout on the guest dock, and free Wi-Fi. The fuel dock has ethanol-free gasoline, diesel and Delo lubricants. A dual-lane concrete launch ramp, with a float between the two lanes, is available. A kayak center is located on A Dock; key cards issued by the Port office are required for access. Parking (fee charged) for tow vehicles and trailers. Two electric courtesy cars are available through the Port office for local trips to shopping several blocks away. They are fun to drive and popular; 30-minute usage recommended.

Four mooring buoys for boats to 35 feet are outside the breakwater north of the ferry dock. They are exposed to winds and the wakes of passing boat traffic.

Moorage reservations are accepted with one day advance notice; call the Port office during business hours. Kingston is quite popular during the summer months, reservations are important. Reserved slips are marked and are not available, even for temporary use.

Enter the marina around the end of the rock breakwater. Leave two pilings that mark the edge of the dredged channel to port. Leave the red buoy marking the end of the breakwater to starboard. Guest moorage is in slips extending from the dock that runs

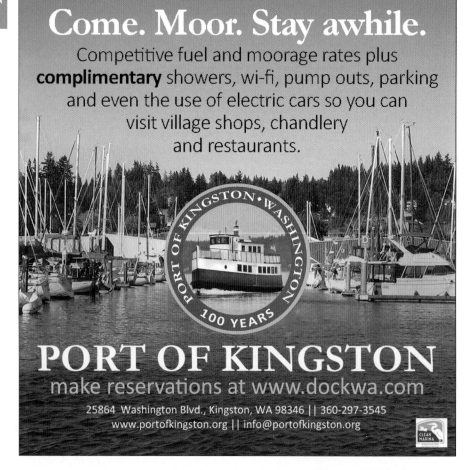
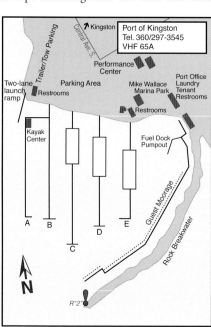

Kingston

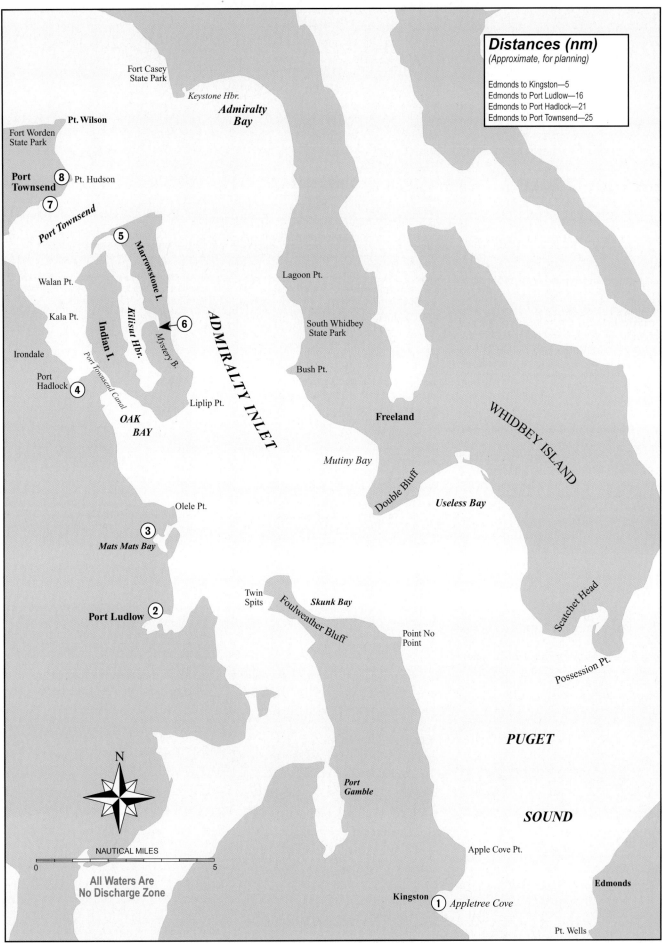

Fort Casey
State Park

Keystone Hbr.

*Admiralty
Bay*

Distances (nm)
(Approximate, for planning)

Edmonds to Kingston—5
Edmonds to Port Ludlow—16
Edmonds to Port Hadlock—21
Edmonds to Port Townsend—25

Pt. Wilson

Fort Worden
State Park

**Port
Townsend** ⑧ Pt. Hudson

⑦

Port Townsend

⑤

Marrowstone I.

Walan Pt.

Lagoon Pt.

Kala Pt.

Kilisut Hbr.

Indian I.

⑥

South Whidbey
State Park

Irondale

Port Townsend Canal

Mystery B.

ADMIRALTY INLET

Bush Pt.

Port
Hadlock ④

*OAK
BAY*

Liplip Pt.

Freeland

WHIDBEY ISLAND

Mutiny Bay

Olele Pt.

Double Bluff

③

Useless Bay

Mats Mats Bay

Scatchet Head

②

Port Ludlow

Twin
Spits

Foulweather Bluff

Skunk Bay

Point No
Point

Possession Pt.

PUGET

N

*Port
Gamble*

SOUND

NAUTICAL MILES

0 ____ 5

**All Waters Are
No Discharge Zone**

Apple Cove Pt.

Edmonds

Kingston ① *Appletree Cove*

Pt. Wells

Northwest Puget Sound

parallel to the breakwater, plus the side-tie float for larger boats at the outer end. The fuel float is at the shore end of the guest dock. Working from the shore end of the guest dock: the first five are 20-foot slips; then two 50-foot Kingston Cove Yacht Club reciprocal slips; then the 50-foot slips; then the 40-foot slips; and then the 30-foot slips. Moor in any unreserved guest dock slip and register at the Port office.

See the website for a schedule of music events. On the guest dock, two 22'x8' gazebos with picnic tables and power are popular with visiting boaters. First-come, first-served.

ADMIRALTY INLET

Admiralty Inlet begins at Point No Point in the south and ends at Point Wilson in the north. Admiralty Inlet is wide, deep, and straight, with no hazardous reefs or shoals. It makes up for this good design by often being the only patch of rough water for miles. Flood current or ebb, Admiralty Inlet waters swirl and lump up. If the wind is light, you'll see the swirls. If the wind is blowing, you'll be in the lump. Use the Bush Point current tables to predict the times of slack water, and the time and strength of maximum current.

If Admiralty Inlet is rough and you have to be there anyway, try to favor the eastern or western shores. The western shore is preferred. A suggested route is along Marrowstone Island, far enough off to avoid the rocks shown on the chart. Approach around Marrowstone Point inside the rough water just outside, and into Port Townsend Bay.

If you are northbound past Point No Point and you can see that Admiralty Inlet is rough (you can see it), head west across the south tip of Marrowstone Island, and go through Port Townsend Canal into Port Townsend Bay. Port Townsend Canal currents are based on the Deception Pass current tables.

Point No Point. Point No Point, on the west side of Puget Sound, is a popular salmon-fishing spot and a place where boats heading up-sound and down-sound tend to converge. Boat traffic can get heavy, especially when the salmon are running and the waters are literally covered with small sport fishing boats working along the tide-rip.

Watch out for this tide-rip. When a strong wind opposes a big tide, the waters off Point No Point can turn dangerous.

LOCAL KNOWLEDGE

NAVIGATION NOTE: Check your chart before entering the landlocked Port Ludlow inner harbor and be sure to pass between the two islets. Passing outside of either islet could put you aground.
SPEED LIMIT: A 5-mph "no wake" speed limit is in effect throughout Port Ludlow and applies to all vessels, including dinghies.

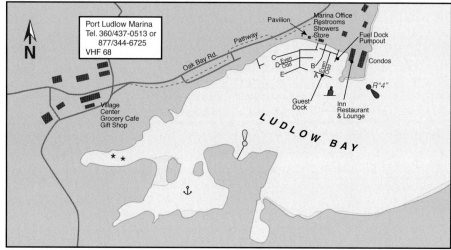
Port Ludlow

② **Port Ludlow.** Well-protected Port Ludlow indents the western shore of Puget Sound. It was once the site of a major Pope & Talbot sawmill, and now is a nice residential area, a destination resort and a marina. Anchorage is in the landlocked inner harbor, reached by passing between two little islands near the head of the bay. Deeper draft boats should watch the depth sounder closely when entering the inner harbor at low tide. The passage is shallower than the bays it connects. Good anchorage, mud bottom, is in about 15 feet. An 8-foot shoal area a short distance northeast of the entrance is noted on large scale Chart 18477. Anchorage can also be found south of the marina; note the charted cable area immediately west of the marina.

The inner harbor is a favorite destination in Puget Sound, protected from all winds. Upscale homes are set well back and often screened by trees, providing privacy and a lovely harbor charm. Meydenbauer Bay Yacht Club has an outstation on the peninsula that forms the inner harbor. A level, scenic one-mile pathway parallels Oak Bay Road, leading west from the marina to the Village Center which has a grocery, gift shop, pizza shop, and a café.

② **Port Ludlow Resort and Marina.** 1 Gull Drive, Port Ludlow, WA 98365;

(360) 437-0513; (877) 344-6725; marina@portludlowresort.com; www.portludlowresort.com. Monitors VHF 68. Certified Clean Marina. Open 7 days a week, all year. Ethanol-free gasoline and diesel at the fuel dock. Concrete docks, some of which are beginning to show their age. Guest moorage in 50 slips and along 460 feet of dock, plus unoccupied slips as available, 30 & 50 amp power, water, restrooms, Wi-Fi, gazebo with barbecue, pumpout, portapotty dump, free showers. Pavilion tent for groups. Kayak, SUPs, and skiff rentals. Reservations recommended.

A resort restaurant and lounge are within walking distance. Locals speak highly of the restaurant. Free shuttle for marina guests to the resort's 18-hole golf course. The marina store carries limited groceries, hot dogs, ice cream, beer, wine, ice, books, propane and limited marine hardware and supplies. Shops, medical services, and a post office are nearby. Marine mechanics from Port Townsend may be available. With its large grounds, pavilion tent, dining and golf, this is a popular destination for groups and rendezvous.

The marina often runs cruise-in specials that include moorage, golf, and restaurant credit. Check the marina website.

③ **Mats Mats Bay.** A course between Port Ludlow and Mats Mats Bay should avoid

Port Ludlow Resort and Marina

DOGS ONBOARD

There are really only two types of boaters—those who cruise with dogs, and those who don't. Those who don't think cruising with dogs is for the birds. The main reason we cruise with dogs lies at the heart of why we cruise in the first place. Cruising is about exploring, and on those routine shoreside jaunts, dog people come to know the terrain with an intimacy one wouldn't have thought possible. When our fellow-cruisers are

still abed, listening to the coffee perk while cold rain drums on the deck above them, we're ashore in full foul-weather gear, hiding under the dripping trees, while Buddy sniffs out the perfect spot to lift a leg. Led by The Nose, we hike to the ends of obscure trails—and beyond. We scramble over slippery rocks and dig up the coast's finest beaches. We come to know this extraordinary place in all its moods. Dogs initiate us into the world of wildlife, both living and dead. One night my wife Jan took our dachshund Rosie ashore for her evening visit. Suddenly, Spouse was leaping over rocks and crashing through bushes in hot pursuit of Hound, who was in hot pursuit of a rank-smelling wild goat. To Rosie, a city beast with a hunter's heart, the goat's scent trail must have seemed as wide as the I-5 freeway. Dead wildlife also has its attractions, especially if it's decaying and smelly. If you are a canine, getting in touch with your Inner Hunter means disguising your scent so your prey can't smell you coming. A beach walk is not complete without a roll on a dead crab, a seagull or fish carcass . . . or worse. On one occasion, for example, it was my turn to chase Rosie as she bounded over logs and disappeared around a bay. From afar I watched in horror as she sniffed the rotting remains of a seal, then looked at me for permission to roll. All I could do was yell "Nooooo!" at the top of my lungs. Rosie looked mighty put out but, incredibly, she left her prize untouched. Aboard the boat, settling down with Rosie in my lap gives me an ironclad excuse for not moving when my mate asks me to do something. In fact, it allows me to issue orders: "Could you pass up my sweater (my binoculars, my wine glass, my dinner . . .)?" It's not unknown for the crew of our little ship to have a debate about whose knee gets Rosie. These arguments are more frequent on chilly off-season cruises, when Rosie gives off the warmth of a modest cabin heater. What dogs really teach us is how to enjoy the simple things. When the trails have been walked, the beaches dug and the goats chased, it's time for us all to sit down together, to listen to the sounds or the silence, feel the tide turn, watch the birds fly and the sun set, and savor life on this coast in all its perfection. Yes, cruising with dogs is best.   *-Duart Snow*

Snake Rock, close to shore, and Colvos Rocks and Klas Rocks, farther offshore. Colvos Rocks are marked by flashing lights at the north and south ends, and Klas Rocks by a diamond shape dayboard with a flashing white light. Snake Rock is not marked.

Mats Mats Bay has a dogleg entrance with a least depth of 5 feet at zero tide. A lighted range shows the center of the narrow channel. A rock once almost blocked the entrance to the bay. It was blasted out years ago, and buoys now mark the channel. Pay attention to all buoys, and do not stray from the marked channel, especially at low water. Anchor in 18 feet in the middle or south part of the bay. The large number of boats on permanent moorings restrict anchoring options. Mats Mats Bay is well protected from almost any wind. A launch ramp is at the south end of the bay.

Oak Bay. Oak Bay, with convenient anchoring depths, is at the southern approach to Port Townsend Canal. Oak Bay County Park is on the west side of the channel, approximately one mile south of the entrance to the canal.

Oak Bay County Park. Northwest shore of Oak Bay. Open all year, restrooms, launch ramp, campsites, picnic tables, no power, no water. Anchoring or beaching only. Marked by a rock jetty. Swimming, scuba diving, clamming, crabbing.

Point Hudson Marina entry at the east end of Port Townsend

Port Townsend Canal. Port Townsend Canal (also known as Hadlock Canal) runs from Oak Bay to Port Townsend Bay through a relatively narrow dredged channel. The canal is well marked, easy to transit, and spanned by a bridge with 58-foot vertical clearance. Currents run to 3 knots. Port Townsend Canal is a secondary station under the Deception Pass reference station in the current tables.

Port Hadlock and Irondale. The towns of Irondale and Port Hadlock are west of the northern entrance to Port Townsend Canal. Limited transient moorage at Port Hadlock Marina and a day-use dock at Irondale.

Anchorage is good, sand bottom. Stay north of Skunk Island, due west from the marina.

④ **Port Hadlock Marina.** 173 Hadlock Bay Rd., Port Hadlock, WA 98339; (360) 385-6368; harbormaster@porthadlockmarina.com; www.porthadlockmarina.com. Permanent moorage marina with limited transient moorage in unoccupied slips, call for availability. 30 & 50 amp power, water, restrooms with showers. Laundry, garbage, pumpout and free Wi-Fi. Open all year.

Hadlock Public Dock. A Port of Port Townsend day-use dock, located at Irondale. 75 feet of side-tie guest moorage, with 4-hour

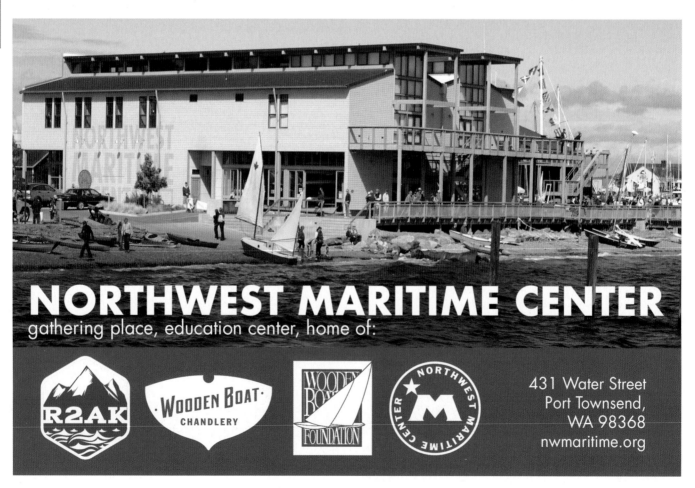

There are many fine eateries and shops in the Port Townsend Victorian buildings.

An incredibly wide variety of boats are seen in the harbor.

maxiumum stay at no charge. The much loved Ajax Cafe, located upland, reopened for business in October 2018; dinners served Thursday - Sunday with scheduled live entertainment. The adjacent **Northwest School of Wooden Boat Building** is worth a visit. Guided tours of the school are offered to the public on the first Friday of every month,

Port Hadlock Marina

starting at 3:00 p.m. The tour is approximately an hour and a half, covering boat building techniques and the school itself, which attracts students from around the world.

Fort Townsend Marine State Park. (360) 385-3595. Open summers only, 367 acres, 3 mooring buoys for boats 45 feet or less, restrooms, showers, no power. The park has campsites, swimming, playgrounds, hiking trails, picnic tables, fire rings, and kitchen shelters. Self-guided nature trail, clamming, fishing and scuba diving. Self-register and pay mooring buoy fee on shore.

Kilisut Harbor. Kilisut Harbor is entered through a channel between Walan Point and the spit protecting the harbor. When approaching the entrance, stay clear of the Navy restricted area off Walan Point. The channel is well marked though shallow, averaging about 11 feet. Currents can run strongly. The channel swings past Fort Flagler State Park on the north shore, then continues through Kilisut Harbor to Mystery Bay. Mystery Bay State Park, on the north shore, has a long dock and mooring buoys. At the head of Mystery Bay is the village of Nordland, and a great old general store with its small dock. Mystery Bay is a voluntary no anchoring zone to protect local shellfish.

⑤ **Fort Flagler Marine State Park**. (360) 385-1259. On Marrowstone Island. Open all year, 784 acres, day use, overnight mooring and camping. Has 256 feet of dock space with 6-foot depths at zero tide (docks removed in winter), 6 mooring buoys for boats 45 feet or less, launch ramp. The current can run strongly through this area; allow for it when mooring. Restrooms, showers, portapotty dump, no power. Self-register and pay mooring fee on shore. Easy trails lead to old fortifications along the north shore of Marrowstone Island. Underwater park for divers. Snack and grocery concession. Boat rentals, fishing supplies. Standard, utility, and primitive campsites. Campsite reservations are a good idea in summer, call (800) 452-5687.

⑥ **Mystery Bay Marine State Park.** (360) 385-1259. In Kilisut Harbor on Marrowstone Island. Open all year, 10 acres, 683 feet dock space with 4.5-foot depth at zero tide, 7 mooring buoys for boats 45 feet or less. Pumpout, portapotty dump, toilets, launch ramp, no power, no showers. This park is open for day use only, but overnight mooring is permitted at the dock. The dock runs parallel to shore. Call Fort Flagler office for more information (360) 388-1259. Self-register and pay mooring fee on shore. The charming Nordland General Store is at the shallow end of the bay with a dock in front. Dinghy landing only.

PORT TOWNSEND MARKETPLACE

RESTAURANTS & SHOPS

ELEVATED ICE CREAM & CANDY SHOP

We use the freshest local Ingredients in our flavorful ice creams, ices and sherbets, and handcraft our own chocolates and truffles. See our assortment of dark chocolate bars, candies and gifts. We're open late during boating season! Just two blocks west
of Point Hudson.

360-385-1156 • 627 Water St. • www.elevatedicecream.com

THE FOUNTAIN CAFE

Downtown Port Townsend is a casual and intimate cafe known for its excellent lunches and dinners enjoyed in a cozy setting one block from the hustle and bustle of Water Street. This popular eatery is located in the entertainment zone around Haller Fountain, a historic landmark famous for its statuesque, nude maiden and her attending sprites.

360-385-1364• 920 Washington St.
www.fountaincafept.com

MARINE THRIFT

Marine Thrift is a place where builders, sailors, DIYers, and the curious can find amazing deals on hardware, tools, and all kinds of other interesting boat gear. We keep good materials out of the landfill and in circulation while ensuring costs of boating stay accessible to many.

360-379-5807 • 315B Haines Place, Port Townsend
info@marinethrift.com • www.nwmaritime.org/marine-thrift

THE SWAN HOTEL AND COTTAGES

Located on the water front near the Point Hudson Marina, the NW Maritime Center and Historic Downtown. The Swan features suite,
studio, and hotel-style rooms, as well as deluxe cottages. Within walking distance of most of Port Townsend's restaurants, shops & attractions.

360-385-1718 • 222 Monroe at Water Street
frontdesk@theswanhotel.com • www.theswanhotel.com

THE WINE SELLER

The Small Town Wine Shop With a Big City Selection, since 1982. Amazing selection of fine wines, champagne, beer & ale, ciders, gourmet foods, cheese, coffee chocolate & cigars. Surprisingly competitive prices! Generous mixed-whole and 1/2 case discounts. Knowledgeable friendly wine specialists!! OPEN 7 DAYS a WEEK. Marina delivery available!

360-385-7673 • 1010 Water St. • www.PTwineSeller.com

THE WOODEN BOAT CHANDLERY

Everything for wooden boats and the people who love them. For boat owners, we have bronze hardware, copper nails, rope, oakum, varnishes and more. For boat lovers, we have NOAA charts, cruising guides, galley ware, maritime books, nautical gifts and toys, and affordable apparel and more.

360-379-2629 • 431 Water Street • Yellow Building at NW Maritime Center • woodenboatchandlery.com

PORT TOWNSEND COMMUNITY EVENTS

Strange Brew festival	January
Shipwrights' Regatta	February
WBF Maritime Swap Meet	April
Port Townsend Rhododendron Festival	May
Classic Mariner Regatta	June
Steampunk Festival	June
Raker's Car Show	June
Centrum's Jazz Festival	July
Centrum's Acoustic Blues Festival	July
Wooden Boat Festival	September
Crafts By the Dock Fair	September
PT Film Festival	September
Kinetic Skulpture Weekend	October
Holiday Craft Fair	November
Festival of Lights	December

Port Townsend. Port Townsend has two Port-owned marinas, Point Hudson Marina and the Port of Port Townsend's Boat Haven. Boat Haven is closer to a supermarket, but Point Hudson is closer to downtown.

Port Townsend is a major boatbuilding and repair center with craftsmen skilled in every nautical discipline. It is the home of the annual Wooden Boat Festival at Point Hudson Marina, held the weekend after Labor Day. Next to the Point Hudson Marina is the Northwest Maritime Center and the Wooden Boat Chandlery. Northwest Maritime Center often has boat building projects underway, visitors welcome. Wooden Boat Chandlery carries an array of nautical items. A Maritime Thrift Store for used gear is located in Boat Haven, 315 B Haines Place.

Port Townsend is a favorite destination. The commercial district is lined with imposing stone and brick buildings from before 1900. At that time, residents hoped Port Townsend would become the western terminus of the transcontinental railroad and the principal city on Puget Sound. Victorian homes, many of them beautifully restored and cared for, are on the hill above the business district. Port Townsend's upper business district is at the top of a long flight of stairs from the lower district on Water Street. The town of Port Townsend is a haven for writers, craftspeople and artists of all kinds. Tourists overwhelm the town during the summer, but that shouldn't keep anybody away.

Whether you're a woodenboat fan, history buff or antique collector, Port Townsend has a little bit of everything. Even with limited time to spare, the town's distinctive charm and spectacular views of Admiralty Inlet are enough to make the trip worth it.

⑦ **Port of Port Townsend Boat Haven.** P.O. Box 1180, 2601 Washington Street, Port Townsend, WA 98368; (360) 385-2355; (800) 228-2803; info@portofpt.com; www.portofpt.com. Monitors VHF 66A. Open all year. Guest moorage along 900 feet of side-tie linear dock and unoccupied slips as available, 30 & 50 amp power, restrooms, showers, laundry, pumpout, portapotty dump, for-fee Wi-Fi, launch ramp. Garbage receptacles are locked. Make sure you get the code before carrying a load of garbage up the docks.

Point Hudson Marina

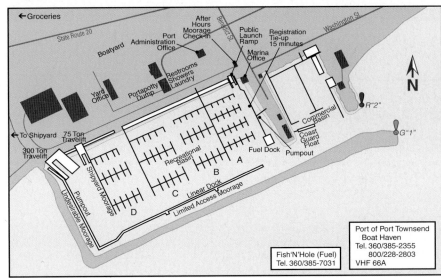

Port Townsend Boat Haven

The Wooden Boat Festival in Port Townsend

Port Townsend Boat Haven Marina & Boat Yard

The West Coast's premier location for marine services.
A full-service yard with 300 & 75 ton lifts, that also welcomes DIY work.
Over 100 vendors for services and supplies.
Fuel dock, laundry, showers, provisions, chandleries.

360-385-2355
PortofPT.com
info@portofpt.com

Ethanol-free gasoline and diesel fuel at the fuel dock (The Fishin' Hole).

The marina is west of the ferry dock, and entered between a rock breakwater and a piling wavebreak. The first basin on the right has the Coast Guard float and slips for commercial vessels. The next basin is the recreational basin with combination fuel dock and registration dock, moorage slips, linear dock, launch ramps, and haulout facilities. Fuel/registration dock is on the right, after passing the Coast Guard float.

Call ahead or check-in at the marina office for guest moorage availability and slip or side-tie assignment, which may be in the recreational basin or commercial basin.

Vessels over 50 feet should call a day in advance. Spaces may be available through the marina for reciprocal yacht club members with Port Townsend Yacht Club. After hours, empty slips are marked on a map board at the top of the launch ramp and fuel dock. Temporary tie-up is just past the fuel dock, towards the launch ramps, for use only while checking for an empty slip, 15-minute limit.

Customs clearance by appointment only during standard business hours 8:00 a.m. to 4:00 p.m.; call (360) 385-3777. There is only one CBP agent stationed in Port Townsend in an office at Point Hudson. Please plan accordingly.

A hardware store and a large Safeway supermarket are across the highway. The local co-op market is a few blocks closer to town. The Chamber of Commerce Visitor Information Center is just beyond Safeway. Key City Fish, an excellent fish market, is in the repair yard area. Several good restaurants are nearby. More restaurants and a brew pub are in the Boat Haven. The main part of the town, with more restaurants and shops, is a 5-7 block walk.

A 300-ton Travelift and a smaller Travelift are available for haulout. Major boatbuilding and repair facilities and a chandlery (Admiral Ship Supply) are at the Boat Haven, and a West Marine store is nearby.

⑦ **The Fishin' Hole.** (360) 385-7031. Ethanol-free gasoline and diesel fuel, open all year. Located inside the Boat Haven breakwater. Floating store carries soda, snacks, ice, bait, tackle.

⑧ **Point Hudson Marina** & RV Park. P.O. Box 1180, Port Townsend, WA 98368; (360) 385-2828; (800) 228-2803; pthudson@portofpt.com; www.portofpt.com. Monitors VHF 09. Open all year, moorage slips to 70 feet. Side-tie dock space accommodates larger boats. Water, 30 & 50 amp power, restrooms, showers, pumpout, laundry, for-fee Wi-Fi. Reservations recommended. Temporary tie-up is available for up to 4 hours, call ahead for space assignment. Ice, event facility, RV park and restaurants are on the property or nearby. The marina is within easy walking distance to town.

Enter the marina between two piling breakwaters that force the channel into a distinct bend, directly into the prevailing northwesterly summer winds. The limitation on the size of boats is mainly due to the turns required to enter the breakwater. Breakwater repairs that were planned for 2018 have been postponed indefinitely. The marina office is in a white building on the north side.

The Sea Marine haulout and boatyard facility is at the north end of the basin. There's no grocery store nearby, so Sea Marine has ice, propane, and beer. Three restaurants are in the historic white buildings on the north side of the harbor. Other marine businesses around the harbor include Hasse & Co. sailmakers, Brian Toss Rigging, and the Wooden Boat Chandlery located in the NW Maritime Center on the south side of the harbor entrance. The coffee shop at the Wooden Boat Chandlery has free Wi-Fi.

Customs clearance by appointment only during standard business hours 8:00 a.m. to 4:00 p.m.; call (360) 385-3777. There is only one CBP agent stationed in Port Townsend in an office at Point Hudson. Please plan accordingly.

Fort Worden Marine State Park. (360) 344-4400. North of Port Townsend. Open all year, 120 feet of dock space, 5 mooring buoys. Restrooms, showers and no power. The dock is protected by a wharf. Use the dock or a buoy—this is not a good anchorage, although

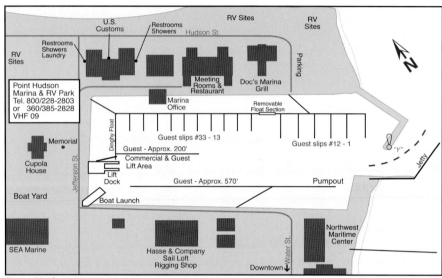

Point Hudson Marina

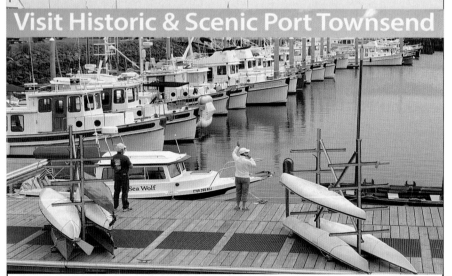

Point Hudson Marina is near the Northwest Maritime Center, a must see.

a friend found good sand bottom in about 18 feet. He also reported that the wakes from passing ship traffic rolled him out of his bunk all night, and he won't overnight there again. Others say they've had no trouble at all. Underwater park for scuba diving. Boat launch with two ramps. Tennis courts, picnic areas, snack bar concession near moorage area. Hiking trails, swimming, fishing. Utility and primitive campsites. Campsite reservations taken year-round. Call (800) 452-5687. Self-register and pay mooring fees on shore.

Upland, the old officers' quarters can be rented overnight. Fort buildings house the Marine Science Center and the Centrum Foundation, which conduct workshops and seminars on the arts each summer.

LOCAL KNOWLEDGE

TIDE-RIP: The tide rip at Point Wilson can be dangerous to cruising boats. The bigger the ebb, the greater the chance for a tide-rip. A small ebb can produce no rip at all, particularly if the wind is light. Use the Bush Point current tables to predict the time of slack water and strength of maximum current. Those who think that a fast boat makes current tables unnecessary are wrong, and Point Wilson will prove them so.

Point Wilson. Point Wilson is the corner where Admiralty Inlet turns into the Strait of Juan de Fuca. On an ebb, a nasty tide-rip can build immediately north of Point Wilson, and stretch well across the mouth of Admiralty Inlet. If it's a big ebb and opposed by strong westerly winds, the seas in this area are not merely nasty, they are dangerous. They are high, steep and close together. They break. They are not long rollers; they are pyramid-shaped, and have no consistent pattern except for being ugly.

Since boats bound for the San Juan Islands or out the Strait of Juan de Fuca often schedule their passages to take advantage of the ebb, skippers must be aware of what can happen at Point Wilson, especially if a westerly is blowing. In such conditions, the

wise approach is to favor the Whidbey Island side. The even wiser choice is to wait until slack water or the beginning of the flood. Better yet, wait for the wind to drop and then go at slack water.

For information on crossing the Strait of Juan de Fuca, see Chapter 5, Strait of Juan de Fuca.

WEST WHIDBEY ISLAND

South Whidbey State Park. On Admiralty Inlet on the Whidbey Island side, just south of Lagoon Point. Open all year, day use only. Campground closed October 15 to March 15. Restrooms, showers, no power. Anchoring in calm conditions or beaching only. Picnic sites, hiking trail, underwater park for scuba diving.

Fort Casey State Park. (360) 678-4519. Admiralty Head, adjacent to Keystone Harbor on Admiralty Inlet. Open all year, day-use and overnight camping, restrooms, no power, no showers. Has a 2-lane launch ramp with boarding floats. Not a good anchorage; beachable boats are best. Underwater park with artificial reef for scuba divers. Picnic areas, standard and primitive campsites. Lighthouse and interpretive center. Historic displays and remains of the old fort to explore. Guided tours during summer.

Fort Ebey State Park. (360) 678-4636. Open all year for day use and overnight camping. The park has restrooms and showers. Anchoring only, or small boats can be beached. Standard campsites, picnic sites. Interesting bunkers and gun batteries are in the old fort.

Joseph Whidbey State Park. (360) 678-4636. Northwest shore of Whidbey Island on Admiralty Inlet. Open April through September, day use only. Toilets. Anchor or beach only. One mile of sandy beach on Puget Sound. Picnic sites.

NORTHEAST PUGET SOUND

⑨ Edmonds. Edmonds, a prosperous community with a small-town feel to it, is about 8 miles north of Shilshole Bay on the east side of Puget Sound. Edmonds has a major rock breakwater-protected marina (the Port of Edmonds Marina) with excellent facilities for visiting boats. At the marina and in the town

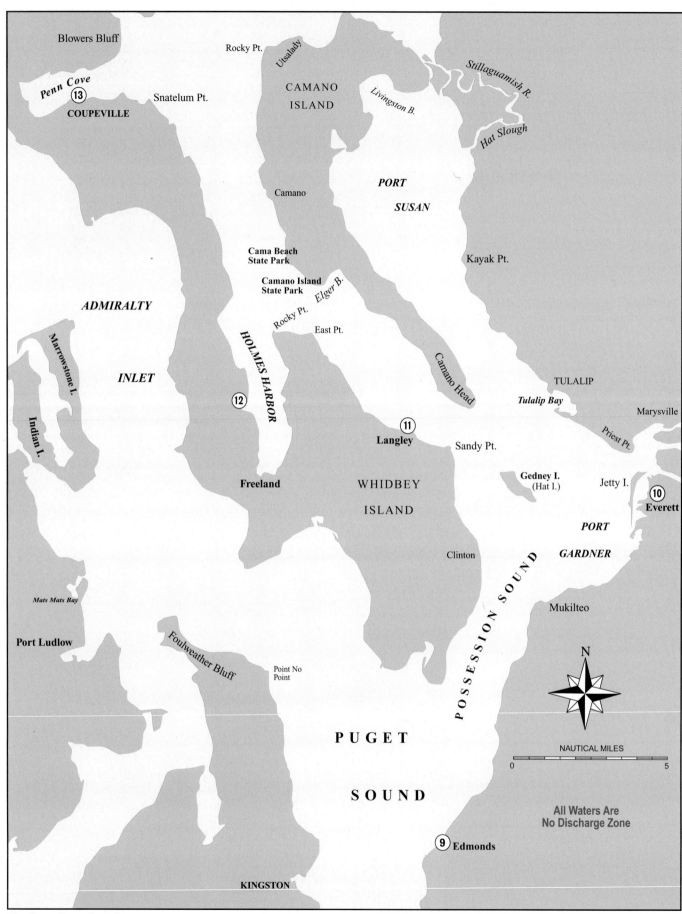

Blowers Bluff

Rocky Pt.

Utsalady

Stillaguamish R.

Penn Cove
⑬
COUPEVILLE

Snatelum Pt.

**CAMANO
ISLAND**

Livingston B.

Hat Slough

PORT

SUSAN

Camano

Kayak Pt.

ADMIRALTY

Cama Beach
State Park

Camano Island
State Park

Elger B.

Rocky Pt.

East Pt.

INLET

Marrowstone I.

HOLMES HARBOR

Camano Head

TULALIP

⑫

Tulalip Bay

Marysville

Indian I.

⑪

Langley

Sandy Pt.

Priest Pt.

Freeland

**WHIDBEY
ISLAND**

Gedney I.
(Hat I.)

Jetty I.

⑩
Everett

PORT

Clinton

GARDNER

Mats Mats Bay

Mukilteo

Port Ludlow

Foulweather Bluff

Point No
Point

POSSESSION SOUND

N

P U G E T

NAUTICAL MILES

0   5

S O U N D

**All Waters Are
No Discharge Zone**

⑨ **Edmonds**

KINGSTON

Northeast Puget Sound

a short distance away you'll find a number of very good restaurants, antiques stores, a lively art scene, an historic 252-seat movie theater, art museum, performance theaters, and interesting shops and galleries. Edmonds "walks" well. This is an ideal destination for a weekend getaway, year-round.

THINGS TO DO

1. Edmonds Waterfront Festival (June)

2. Marina Concert Series: Wednesday evenings and Sunday afternoons (June - mid-September).

3. Taste of Edmonds (Around the second week of August.)

4. Edmonds Public Art Walking Tour: 12 of 15 art pieces are in the city's central core.

5. Edmonds Historic Site Walking Tour: This self guided tour takes you past 29 sites in a one-square-mile section of the city's historic center.

6. Scratch Distillery: Learn about the distilling process for handcrafted vodkas and gin in a relaxed contemporary atmosphere. Tour & Tasting on Saturdays and Sundays.

7. Cascadia Art Museum The museum showcases American regional art from the mid-19th to the mid-20th century.

8. Edmonds Center for the Arts has theatre productions, comedy, film series, and live music.

9. Edmonds Segway Tours: Learn about Edmond's history or take a sunset tour. Book online or call (206) 947-5439.

⑨ Port of Edmonds. 336 Admiral Way, Edmonds, WA 98020; (425) 775-4588; info@portofedmonds.org; www.portofedmonds.org. Monitors VHF 69. Certified Clean Marina and Certified Clean Boatyard. Open 7 days a week all year. The fuel dock has ethanol-free gasoline & diesel. The marina

The Port of Edmonds building with restaurant and showers

has 500 feet of guest side-tie dock space, plus unoccupied slips when available. They can accommodate boats to 100 feet. The docks are served by 30 & 50 amp power, free Wi-Fi, restrooms, showers, two pumpouts, a covered outdoor weather center, and public plaza. Used oil drop.

Enter through the middle of the breakwater. Guest moorage and the fuel dock are immediately to the south. The marina has a large do-it-yourself work yard, a 10,000-pound public sling launch and a 50-ton Travelift. Close to two popular public beaches and a public fishing pier. An artificial reef for scuba diving (the first such site in the state) is next to the ferry dock just north of the marina. Fishing charters are available. It's a short walk to several restaurants. Groceries and shops are in town, about 9 blocks away. On Saturdays a market is set up near the downtown business district. The marina provides courtesy van service to downtown Edmonds. The marina personnel are friendly and helpful.

456 Admiral Way
(425) 771-4400

456 Admiral Way
(425) 771-4400

Possession Sound is on the southeast side of Whidbey Island between Possession Point and Mukilteo.

Mukilteo. (425) 263-8180. Mukilteo Lighthouse Park has a 4-lane launch ramp with floats in summer. It is exposed to ferry wakes and waves generated by winds on

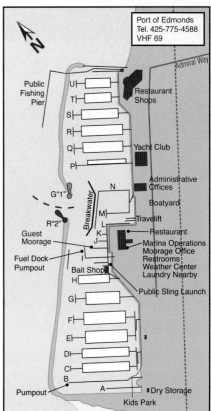
Port of Edmonds

Possession Sound and Port Gardner. A launch fee is charged. Call for more information. Tucked behind the ferry wall and pilings next to Ivar's Restaurant are 3 seasonal, 24-foot Port of Everett floats for access to restaurants and other businesses ashore; caution is advised, floats shift forward and back between pilings. The Mukilteo Lighthouse is open for visitors April through September.

Gedney Island. (425) 327-2607. Gedney Island, known locally as Hat Island, is privately owned. The marina on the north shore is for Gedney Island property owners and their guests, and members from reciprocal yacht clubs.

Tulalip Bay. Anchorage is possible, but Tulalip Bay is very shallow, with a reef guarding the entrance and drying shoals inside. Several private floats and mooring buoys owned by members of the Tulalip Indian Tribe often occupy the bay.

LOCAL KNOWLEDGE

STRONG CURRENTS: Currents in the Snohomish River can be quite strong, particularly on an ebb tide. Allow for the current as you maneuver.

Night Lights: At night, lights ashore in Everett's Navy facilities make the entrance channel buoys very difficult to see and identify. A vessel approaching at night should be extremely cautious.

⑩ **Everett.** The Port of Everett Marina is home to a fishing fleet as well as private pleasure craft. Entry is about a mile upstream from the marked mouth of the Snohomish River. Information about moorage can be obtained from the fuel dock just inside the piling breakwater.

When you are in the river and approaching the marina entrance, watch for debris in the water and pay close attention to your navigation. Several aids to navigation, including one buoy marking a sunken ship, can be confusing. Although the channel can be entered between Lighted Buoy 3 and Light 5 off the south end of Jetty Island, the water between them is somewhat shoal. For complete safety we recommend entering by leaving Lighted Buoy 3 to port. The channel leads past the U.S. Navy homeport facilities.

The marina is a long hike from the central business district, but bus and taxi service are available.

Everett offers numerous activities of interest. The Everett Marina hosts a farmers market in Boxcar Park at the disabled-access dock, Sundays, 11:00 a.m. to 4:00 p.m. May through October. The Port of Everett hosts a summertime waterfront concert series at Port Gardner Landing June through August, from 6:30 p.m. to 8:30 p.m. on Thursday and Saturday. The Xfinity Arena at Everett (www.xfinityarenaeverett.com) brings big-name entertainment. For professional sports with an intimate feeling, take in a minor league baseball game and cheer on the Aquasox. The July 4 fireworks show is Puget Sound's largest outside Seattle, and right in the laps of the Everett moorage.

Across the river from the marina is a Port-owned float at Jetty Island, which has what is probably the largest pure sand beach on Puget Sound. The Langus Waterfront Park, with a good launching facility, is on the north shore of the main river channel, a short distance up the river from the Port of Everett Marina.

Farther up the Snohomish River, Dagmar's Landing is a large dry-land storage facility with a huge fork lift truck and a long float. A detailed chart or local knowledge are required before continuing beyond Dagmar's.

THINGS TO DO

1. Boeing Aircraft Factory. Take a 90-minute tour of the world's largest aircraft plant. Children must be at least 4 feet tall. A cab ride away.

2. Flying Heritage Collection. A remarkable collection of one-of-a-kind military aircraft from the past 75 years. Located at Paine Field, adjacent to the Boeing factory.

3. Tulalip Casino Resort. Adult gaming and

~ Plan Your Best Day Everett ~

Visit the Port of Everett Marina to see and experience the waterfront transformation. Offering state of the art boating amenities, waterfront access to dining, retail and relaxation, Everett is the perfect place to stopover or make your home Port.

Visit **portofeverett.com/marina**
Call **425.259.6001**

1205 CRAFTSMAN WAY, EVERETT, WA 98201

RESTAURANTS, SHOPS & SERVICES

Calendar of Events

ALL SUMMER LONG:
Waterfront Farmer's Market
Music at the Marina
Jetty Island Days
Harbor Tours

APRIL
Everett Half Marathon

APRIL
Milltown Sailing Swap Meet

MAY
Opening Day of Boating

JUNE
Marina Cleanup Day

JULY
Fourth of July Celebration
Sail-In Cinema

AUGUST
Fresh Paint Festival of Artist at Work
Sail-In Cinema

SEPTEMBER
Mukilteo Lighthouse Festival
Wheels on the Waterfront Car Show

DECEMBER
Holiday on the Bay

Port of Everett
www.portofeverett.com/events
or 800-729-7678

Photos courtesy of Port of Everett

ANTHONY'S HOMEPORT EVERETT

Located on Port Gardner Bay, the restaurant offers fresh northwest seafood with majestic views of Puget Sound islands and the Olympic Mountains. Lunch served Monday-Saturday, Sunday brunch and dinner served daily. Located at Everett Marina Village. Visitor moorage along the dock in front of the restaurant.
425-252-3333 • 1726 West Marine View Drive, Everett Marina Village
www.anthonys.com

ANTHONY'S WOODFIRE GRILL

Featuring specialties from its custom-built rotisserie, applewood-burning oven and applewood grill. Serving signature fresh northwest seafood selections, as well as northwest beef selections at lunch and dinner daily. Located at Everett Marina Village. Visitor moorage along the dock in front of Anthony's HomePort.
425-258-4000 • 1722 West Marine View Drive, Everett Marina Village
www.anthonys.com

BAYSIDE MARINE AND DRYSTACK

Offering consignment brokerage, used boat sales, parts and service for most major brands of pleasure boats and inside boat drystack. Keep your boat inside with secure rack storage with private dock and launching.
425-252-3088 • 1111 Craftsman Way •
www.baysidemarine.com

SCUTTLEBUTT BREWING COMPANY

Brewing handcrafted beer from the Northwest's finest ingredients since 1995. Come visit our family friendly brewery and pub. Offering a variety of handcrafted ales and root beer and a full menu, we have something for everyone. Just steps from the dock, on the water at the north end of the Everett Marina.
425-257-9316 • 1205 Craftsman Way •
www.scuttlebuttbrewing.com

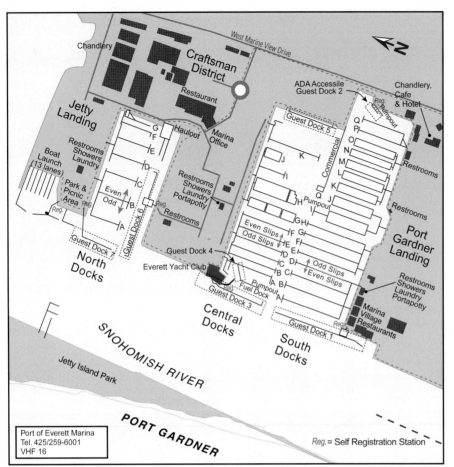

Port of Everett Marina

Port of Everett Marina
Tel. 425/259-6001
VHF 16

Reg. = Self Registration Station

good restaurants. The Tulalip Amphitheatre often has live music.

4. Seattle Premium Outlet Stores. Features over 130 designer names; outlet stores next to the Tulalip Casino.

5. Imagine Children's Museum. Hands-on activities for kids and many special events. About 1.5 miles from the marina.

6. Port Gardner Bay Winery. A boutique winery with relaxed tastings. They also offer classes in winemaking. About 1.5 miles from the marina.

7. Everett Farmers Market. Every Sunday at Boxcar Park, just up from the marina.

8. Port Gardner Landing. Summer Concerts.

9. Legion Memorial Golf Course. Close to the marina.

⑩ **Port of Everett Marina.** 1205 Craftsman Way, Suite 105, Everett, WA 98201; (425) 259-6001; marina@portofeverett.com; www.portofeverett.com. Monitors VHF 16. Certified Clean Marina. Open all year, gasoline and diesel at fuel dock. Over 5000 feet of guest moorage with depths 10 to 16 feet, unoccupied slips used when available.

Moorage is first-come, first-served, and self-pay stations are on the docks. If staying less than six hours before 10 p.m., guest moorage is free. Water, 20, 30 & 50 amp power, restrooms, showers, laundry, multiple free pumpout stations, free portapotty dump, for-fee Wi-Fi.

Handicapped-accessible guest moorage available. Watch for strong currents when landing at the guest dock. The Port's Craftsman District has a Travelift haulout to 75 tons with yard storage, a boatyard for repairs and maintenance. The Travelift is at the east end of the moorage. The Jetty Landing launch, a 13-lane launch ramp (largest in the state), is just north of marina.

The Port of Everett's North Marina offers a first-class 42-slip guest moorage facility. The concrete docks are wide, stable and heavily built. Power is 30 & 50 amp, with 100 amp at the end moorages. A pumpout line is built into the main docks with attachments at each slip. The basin has its own restrooms, showers, and laundry. The Port of Everett is a large, complete marina, with shops, full repairs, services nearby, and and two chandleries. An attractive marina village with a hotel, shops, a West Marine store and good restaurants is adjacent to the south mooring basin. The wheelchair-accessible float is next to the street in the east end of the south basin. The Waterfront Center Building on the north side of the marina has an inside coffee area, a brew-pub restaurant and a distillery. Harbor

Marine, a complete marine supply store and chandlery, is on 10th Street between the north docks and the Jetty Landing launch ramps. They have added a snack bar and cafe with daily specials.

The Port of Everett is undergoing substantial development of the uplands to include a hotel, apartments, and splash park. Upgrades and replacement of docks are also taking place. New docks are planned to be in place for 2019, and additional upgrades to be completed in 2020.

Everett Marine Park. On the Snohomish River, north of the Port of Everett Marina. Open all year, 700 feet of overnight guest moorage, restrooms, pumpout, portapotty dump. Pay station on shore. No power, no showers. The park has a 13-lane launch ramp with boarding floats. An attendant is on duty summer and fall.

Jetty Island. (425) 257-8304; www.everettwa.org. Jetty Island is a lovely low sand island across the river from the Everett Marina and Everett Marine Park. Jetty Island is open all year. Two large docks provide space for a number of boats. Boats can overnight at the dock. Jetty Island has toilets but no showers, no power, and no water for boats. The toilets are closed in winter. Pay station on shore.

River currents can make landing at the docks challenging. Before approaching the dock, be sure your boat is well fendered, dock lines ready, and contingency plans agreed upon.

Jetty Island is a wildlife preserve with great birdwatching. The Parks Department offers nature programs during the summer, and runs boats from the launch ramp to the island, no charge, July 4 through Labor Day.

Snohomish River Delta. The Snohomish River Delta has three main mouths—Steamboat Slough, Ebey Slough, and the main river—each of which is navigable for all or part of its length. Cautious boaters can cruise the delta.

Contributing Editor Tom Kincaid has cruised all of this area, some of it several times, in a 30-foot sailboat, a 36-foot powerboat, and an outboard-powered dinghy. The waters are subject to tidal action. Drying flats are off the river mouths. Enter only during the hours of highest tides. The Snohomish River

The Port of Everett Marina is excellent, with attractions nearby.

Delta is a fascinating place with wildlife, calm anchorages, and quiet.

Langus Waterfront Park. North shore of the Snohomish River. The park is open all year and has restrooms, but no guest moorage, power or showers. This is a City of Everett park with a 2-lane concrete launch ramp and boarding floats. A wide concrete float is for fishing and launching rowing shells.

Port Susan. Port Susan is surrounded by Camano Island to the west and the mainland to the east. A swampy waterway connects the northern end of Port Susan with Skagit Bay. Kayak Point in Port Susan is a Snohomish County Park. North of Kayak Point, Port Susan shoals to drying flats, through which meander the two mouths of the Stillaguamish River. At high tide it is possible to cross over these flats and enter South Pass to Stanwood, although the bridge just beyond Stanwood is very low.

Kayak Point County Park. 15610 Marine Drive, Stanwood, WA 98292; (360) 652-7992. Open all year, restrooms but no showers. Anchorage only close to shore. The anchorage is exposed to southerly winds. Launch ramp with boarding floats. Fishing pier, no overnight moorage at the pier.

Saratoga Passage. Saratoga Passage separates Camano Island from Whidbey Island. The waters are better protected and often smoother than Admiralty Inlet, and the current is less. Boats running between Seattle and the San Juan Islands often choose this inside route via Deception Pass or La Conner when the wind and seas are getting up in Admiralty Inlet.

This is not to say the waters are always smooth. One year, Bob and Marilynn Hale ran into uncomfortable seas while southbound in Saratoga Passage during a 25-knot southerly storm, and were forced to run back to Oak Harbor for shelter.

Saratoga Passage is relatively free of dangers, but it does have two tricks: Rocky Point(s) and Holmes Harbor. A study of the chart shows two Rocky Points in Saratoga Passage. One is on Whidbey Island at the entrance to Holmes Harbor; the other is at the north end of Camano Island.

Southbound boats may be tempted to go straight into Holmes Harbor instead of turning southeast past the Whidbey Island Rocky Point. If you're not watching your chart, the appeal is quite strong. Follow the Camano Island shoreline.

Cama Beach State Park. (360) 387-1550. Twelve miles southwest of Stanwood. Open all year, anchoring only. Restrooms, showers, small store, 15 miles of hiking and biking trails, 24 cabins, 7 deluxe cabins and 2 bungalows. The Center for Wooden Boats runs the boathouse and boat rental operation, first-come, first-served. Many classic rowboats and sailboats are available for hourly or daily rentals. The workshops on shore may have a boat building project or two underway. See the CWB website (www.cwb.org) for information on classes offered at Cama Beach and available boat rentals. Advance contact is recommended for hours and days of operation (360) 387-9361 or cama@cwb.org.

Elger Bay. Elger Bay is a good anchorage, mud bottom, with surprisingly good protection from northerly winds. Watch your depths close to the head of the bay.

Camano Island State Park. (360) 387-3031. Fourteen miles southwest of Stanwood. Open all year for day use and overnight camping, first-come, first-served. Restrooms, showers, no power. Anchoring only. Launch ramp. Underwater park for scuba diving. Cabins, standard and primitive campsites.

⑪ **Langley.** The Langley Boat Harbor serves the delightful village of Langley. If the boat harbor is crowded, as it usually is during the summer, anchorage is good south and east of the harbor, unless strong northerly winds

Jetty Island Wildlife Preserve is a short dinghy ride form Everett Marina.

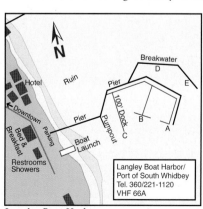

Langley Boat Harbor

Glass art at the Langley fire station

The historic village of Coupville offers shops, cafes, and a museum.

make the area uncomfortable. Langley Boat Harbor has a long history of being creative about getting another boat tied up. Their motto is, "We'll try to fit you in." Be sure you have fenders set on both sides.

The town of Langley itself has streets lined with historic buildings that house interesting shops, excellent galleries, fine restaurants, a whale museum, a craft brewery, and a vintage 250-seat movie theater. Langley is a good walking town. You'll find beautiful views of Saratoga Passage from the bluff above the marina. A couple blocks from the cozy commercial district is where the farms begin.

⑪ **Port of South Whidbey/Langley**. P.O. Box 872, Freeland, WA 98249; (360) 221-1120; harbormaster@portofsouthwhidbey.com; www.portofsouthwhidbey.com; Monitors VHF 66A. Guest moorage year-round. Approximately 1,100 feet of moorage. Docks D and E are located behind the outer breakwater; docks A, B, and C are behind the wall of the inner harbor. Depths shallow to approximately 8 feet at zero tide south of the breakwater. Check your depth.

Reservations accepted online 48 hours in advance, highly recommended during the peak season. Restrooms, showers, 20, 30, 50 & 100 amp power, launch ramp (higher tides only), pumpout barge, free Wi-Fi. Friendly service staff tries to help every boat dock. Nearby groceries, unique shops, boutiques, bakery, and laundromat are up the hill in town. Free shuttle to town in season. Crabbing for everyone at the upper wharf, and by reservation only off D and E docks at the marina.

Holmes Harbor. Holmes Harbor indents the eastern shore of Whidbey Island for about 5 miles in a southerly direction. It is deep and relatively unprotected from strong northerlies. The harbor has a good launch ramp at the head and anchorage along either shore. Honeymoon Bay is a good anchorage. Holmes Harbor is subject to williwaws, the unusually strong gusts of wind that spill across the lower portion of Whidbey Island.

⑫ **Honeymoon Bay.** Honeymoon Bay is a favored anchorage on the west shore of Holmes Harbor. Private mooring buoys take up most of the good spots; but with a little diligence, satisfactory anchoring depths with adequate swinging room can be found. Honeymoon Bay is exposed to northerly winds.

Penn Cove. Penn Cove is about 10 miles north of Holmes Harbor. The cove extends nearly 4 miles west from Long Point, with the town of Coupeville on the southern shore. Anchorage is good along both shores and toward the head of the bay, but be aware that strong winds from the Strait of Juan de Fuca can blow across the low neck of Whidbey Island at the head of the cove. This is where the famous Penn Cove mussels come from. Watch for mussel-growing pens.

⑬ **Coupeville**. The town of Coupeville is served by the Coupeville Wharf, a 415-foot-long causeway on pilings extending over the beach to deep water. Coupeville is quaint, old, and friendly, with a variety of shops, galleries, and restaurants. A display of tribal canoes is 200 feet from the head of the wharf.

⑬ **Coupeville Wharf.** P.O. Box 128, Green Bank, WA 98253; (360) 678-6379. Open all year, 450-plus feet of dock space, first-come, first-served, free moorage before 5:00 p.m. Watch depths at low and minus tides. Gasoline and diesel at the fuel dock. There is also room to anchor in front of town. Pumpout, restrooms and showers are on the wharf, no power or water on the float. Free Wi-Fi is available on the float and throughout town. A gift shop, a coffee shop, and a restaurant are at the outer end of the wharf. The town's shops and restaurants are within easy walking distance. Island Transit, with stops nearby, offers free bus service to key points on Whidbey Island.

Captain Coupe Park. 602 NE Ninth St., Coupeville, WA 98239-0577; (360) 678-4461. Open all year with restrooms and nearby portapotty dump, no power, no showers. Anchoring only. A launch ramp with a float is installed in the summer. The park is one-quarter mile by water from Coupeville wharf. It's better to anchor closer to the wharf. Mud flats surround the launch area at low tide.

Langley Boat Harbor with floating breakwater moorage and inner harbor docks

NORTHEAST PUGET SOUND

⑭ **Oak Harbor**. Oak Harbor is a shallow and well protected port with a major, city-owned marina. The entrance channel is marked by red and green buoys and beacons, beginning with Buoy 2, offshore about 1 mile south of Maylor Point. From Buoy 2 the entry channel runs northward into Oak Harbor, and makes a 90-degree turn to the east for the final mile that leads to the marina.

Do not pass between Buoy 2 and Maylor Point. The water there is shoal and littered with large boulders that have been known to tear stern drive units out of boats.

The only moorage is at the spacious Oak Harbor Marina. The marina has complete facilities and park grounds ashore for dog-walking, games, or strolling. It's a bit of a walk to town, and the nearest grocery store is 1½ miles away. Free bus service runs Monday through Saturday, or you can call a cab.

Anchorage can be found just outside the marina close to the entry channel. The bottom is soft; be sure your anchor is well set. A small float for dinghies is in front of the business district, about a 1-mile walk from the marina. The float dries at low tide.

Events: Holland Happening is the last weekend of April; the town's celebration of their Dutch heritage. Whidbey Island Race week is mid-July.

Festivals: Oak Harbor Music Festival is Labor Day weekend; free admission.

Taxi: (360) 682-6920 or (360) 279-9330.

LOCAL KNOWLEDGE

ENTRANCE CHANNEL: Shoals line

Sailboats lined up during Whidbey Island Race Week

each side of the channel all the way into Oak Harbor. At low tide especially, you will go aground if you stray.

⑭ **Oak Harbor Marina**. 865 SE Barrington Dr., Oak Harbor, WA 98277; (360) 279-4575; csublet@ohmarina.org; www.ohmarina.org. Monitors VHF 16, switch to 68. Open all year (closed Sundays & holidays, October through March) with at least 26 slips for guest moorage. The fuel dock has mid-grade ethanol-free gasoline, diesel and propane. The marina has 20 & 30 amp power, restrooms, showers, laundry, pumpout, porta-potty dump, and free Wi-Fi. The guest moorage dock has picnic tables along the breakwater. In the adjacent park, there are Bocce ball and Petanque courts. One set of restrooms and showers is on the lower level of the administration building at the head of the docks. Additional restrooms, showers, and laundry are in buildings a short distance away. A floating restroom facility is on the guest moorage F-dock. Military and retired military (with DoD I.D.) can walk onto the Navy base area and use the Navy Exchange for shopping and provisioning. The Exchange is in one of the large buildings that formerly was a hangar. A seasonal convenience store is open in the summer. A 100-foot-wide concrete launch ramp, built in 1942 to launch PBY Catalina patrol seaplanes, is at the south end of the marina. Extended parking for trailers and tow vehicles. Mariners Haven has repairs and a chandlery. Free bus service to town. Whidbey Island Race Week is held mid-July. Reservations recommended for the Oak Harbor Music Festival on Labor Day weekend. Hydroplane races are held mid-August.

Oak Harbor Marina is protected by a floating concrete breakwater. Guest moorage is in slips on the inside of this breakwater and along the long float leading to shore. A dredged channel, 100 feet wide with a least depth of 12 feet at zero tide, leads along the west face of the breakwater and around the end, to side-tie moorage on the float that leads to shore. Water outside the channel is shoal. Entering Oak Harbor, keep red buoys and beacons close to starboard (see Local Knowledge Entrance Channel). If you plan to moor along the north side of the marina, the safest approach is to head directly for the entrance light at the south end of the breakwater. When you reach the breakwater, turn to port and proceed along the outside (west side) of the breakwater to the north moorage. The Oak Harbor Marina is well maintained, easygoing, and friendly.

Crescent Harbor. Just east of Oak Harbor. The Navy facility along the western shore near the head of the bay has large old hangars that once housed PBY Catalina flying boat patrol aircraft. Crescent Harbor is exposed to southerly winds, but in northerlies or westerlies it's a good anchorage.

Rocky Point. Tidal currents meet off Rocky Point. North of the point they flood south out of Deception Pass and Swinomish Channel. South of the point they flood north out of Saratoga Passage.

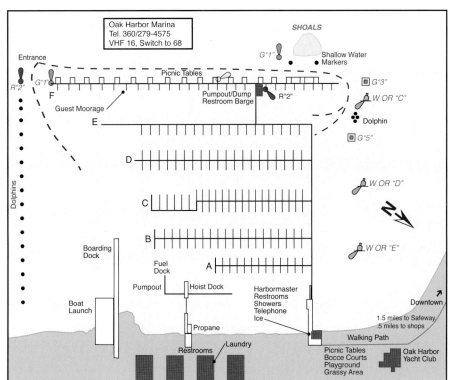

Oak Harbor Marina

Reference Only – Not for Navigation

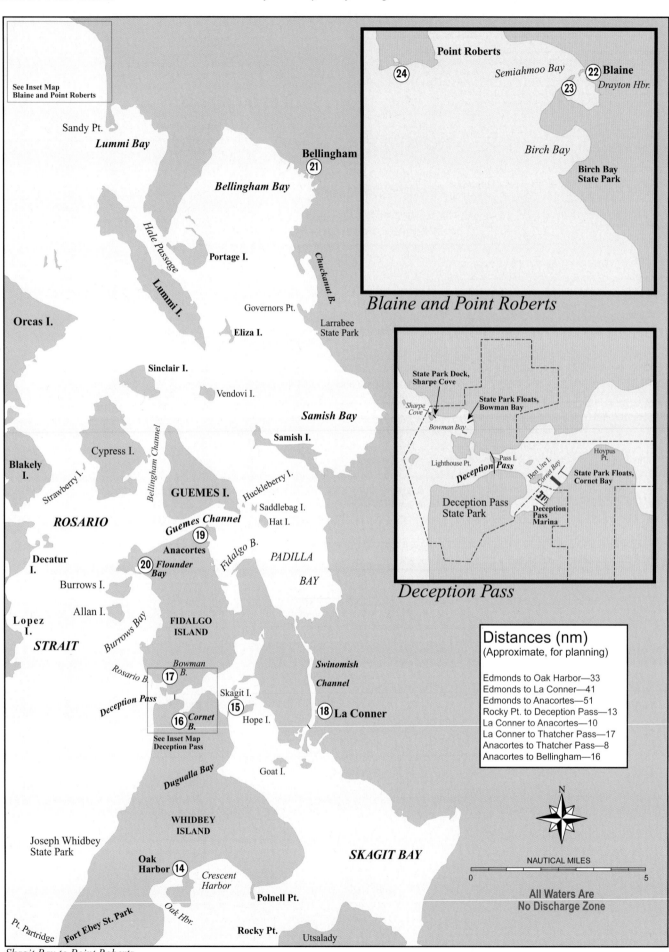

See Inset Map
Blaine and Point Roberts

Sandy Pt.

Lummi Bay

Hale Passage

Lummi I.

Portage I.

Orcas I.

Bellingham Bay

Bellingham
㉑

Governors Pt.

Chuckanut B.

Eliza I.

Larrabee
State Park

Sinclair I.

Vendovi I.

Samish Bay

Samish I.

Cypress I.

Bellingham Channel

GUEMES I.

Huckleberry I.

Saddlebag I.

Hat I.

Blakely
I.

Strawberry I.

Guemes Channel

ROSARIO

⑲

Anacortes

Fidalgo B.

PADILLA

Decatur
I.

⑳ *Flounder
Bay*

BAY

Burrows I.

Allan I.

Lopez
I.

FIDALGO
ISLAND

Burrows Bay

STRAIT

Rosario B.

*Bowman
B.*

⑰

*Swinomish
Channel*

Deception Pass

Skagit I.

⑮

⑯ *Cornet
B.*

Hope I.

⑱ **La Conner**

See Inset Map
Deception Pass

Dugualla Bay

Goat I.

**WHIDBEY
ISLAND**

Joseph Whidbey
State Park

SKAGIT BAY

Oak
Harbor
⑭

*Crescent
Harbor*

Pt. Partridge

Fort Ebey St. Park

Oak Hbr.

Polnell Pt.

Rocky Pt.

Utsalady

Blaine and Point Roberts

Point Roberts

㉔

Semiahmoo Bay

㉒ **Blaine**

㉓

Drayton Hbr.

Birch Bay

**Birch Bay
State Park**

Deception Pass

**State Park Dock,
Sharpe Cove**

*Sharpe
Cove*

**State Park Floats,
Bowman Bay**

Bowman Bay

Hoypus
Pt.

Lighthouse Pt.

Pass I.

Deception Pass

Ben Ure I.

Cornet Bay

**State Park Floats,
Cornet Bay**

**Deception Pass
State Park**

Deception
Pass
Marina

Distances (nm)
(Approximate, for planning)

Edmonds to Oak Harbor—33
Edmonds to La Conner—41
Edmonds to Anacortes—51
Rocky Pt. to Deception Pass—13
La Conner to Anacortes—10
La Conner to Thatcher Pass—17
Anacortes to Thatcher Pass—8
Anacortes to Bellingham—16

N

NAUTICAL MILES

0   5

**All Waters Are
No Discharge Zone**

Skagit Bay to Point Roberts

150

SWINOMISH CHANNEL

In October, 2013, the U.S. Coast Guard changed the buoyage in Swinomish Channel. The "change point," noting "return from the sea (Red Right Returning)" was moved to the center of La Conner. It previously was about 2 miles north of La Conner. Old charts do not reflect this change. Buoy R22 has been changed to G35; G23 to R34; R26 to G31; and G25 to R32.

Swinomish Channel current predications and slack water timing are dependent upon tidal high and low water level differences and river outflow. Therefore, time of slack water and current flow can only be estimated. According to Ports and Passes, slack water occurs at La Conner Landing 2.0 to 3.5 hours after high or low tide; current flows north from 2.0 to 3.5 hours before and after high tide; current flows south from 2.0 to 3.5 hours before and after low tide. General rule of thumb is to use Seattle tides and add 30 minutes (adjust for daylight saving). Tides and helpful information for transiting the Swinomish Channel are found in Ports and Passes in the La Conner section.

The southern entrance to Swinomish Channel is just north of Goat Island. Do not turn into the channel until the range markers in Dugualla Bay, to the west, are in line. The channel is well marked but narrow, particularly if you meet a tug with a tow of logs. Check the range markers as you go. Rock piles lie immediately outside of the dredged channel. Tidal currents flow across the channel and can sweep a boat off course. Occasionally a deadhead log will imbed itself in the shallow bottom. At Hole in the Wall the channel bends sharply around a high rock outcropping. Swirling currents in this area call for close attention.

From Hole in the Wall to the railroad swing bridge to the north, the channel is a no wake zone. Be particularly mindful of your wake when passing through the town of La Conner.

Red, Right, Returning: The buoyage system for Swinomish Channel south of the town of La Conner assumes "return" is from the south. North of La Conner and in Padilla Bay, the dredged channel assumes "return" is from the north. Red navigation aids in Padilla Bay are on the west side.

Rainbow Bridge (now painted orange), located just south of La Conner, has an overhead clearance of 75 feet.

Swinomish Channel is dredged every four to six years, but it silts up between dredgings. Maintenance dredging of the channel was completed in November 2018. Keep in mind that the silting occurs at the same locations each time, so at low tide the wary boater can avoid them. Here are the troublesome shoaling areas:

1. West of Goat Island, the very entrance to Swinomish Channel is shoal. Especially on a low tide, swing wide and don't cut any of the entry buoys close. The channel leading past Goat Island is quite shoal. On very low tides deep draft vessels such as sailboats should wait for more water.

2. South of town at Shelter Bay, a shoal extends from the west side of the channel, approximately from the southernmost house north to the entrance channel of the Shelter Bay development. Favor the center of the channel.

3. About midway along the main La Conner waterfront, a shoal extends from the west side of the channel, approximately between the middle of the restaurants on the La Conner side and a tall pole with antennas on the west side. Favor the east side of the channel.

4. Just south of the highway bridges and the railroad swing bridge, at the location marked "Pipeline Area," sand accumulates on top of the pipeline to create another shoal.

5. The most troublesome shoal is opposite Buoy 29, north of the railroad swing bridge and the highway bridges. This shoal stretches across the entire channel.

Shelter Bay, with its private moorage, indents the western shore of Swinomish Channel just north of Hole in the Wall.

Then comes lovely Rainbow Bridge (now orange), vertical clearance 75 feet in the center. North of Rainbow Bridge the town of La Conner stretches along the eastern shore of the channel. Three city public floats, La Conner Marina, and several privately-owned floats serve restaurants and other businesses along the town waterfront. Across from La Conner the Swinomish Indian Reservation occupies most of the west side of the channel.

Just north of La Conner is a point where the flood and ebb currents meet, ebbing south past La Conner and north toward Anacortes. The channel is marked by buoys and a range, but follows a generally northerly direction until

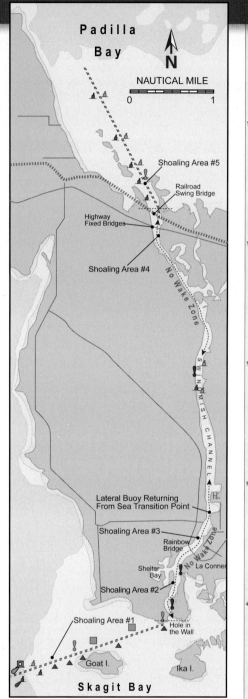

Swinomish Channel

it passes under a swinging railroad bridge and fixed highway bridges to enter Padilla Bay. The highway bridges have a vertical clearance of 75 feet. The railroad bridge is very low. Hundred-car-long crude oil trains headed to the local refinery can close the bridge for 20 minutes or more, holding up boat traffic. If you are there at the wrong time, consider dropping the anchor until the train has passed. Currents can be strong. Overhead power and telephone cables cross at several charted locations, with a minimum vertical clearance of 72 feet.

See Area Map Page 150 - Maps Not for Navigation

Skagit Bay. Skagit Bay extends from Polnell Point and Rocky Point to Deception Pass. The bay becomes increasingly shoal toward the east due to Skagit River outflow. The navigable channel parallels the Whidbey Island shore, and is well marked by buoys. Use caution in this channel; buoys can be dragged out of position by tugs with tows. The village of Utsalady, with a launch ramp, is on the Camano Island side of the channel. Anchorage there is not protected from northerly winds and waves, but Correspondents James & Jennifer Hamilton report anchoring through a southeast gale without difficulty.

(15) **Skagit Island, Hope Island, Similk Bay**. Hope Island is a state marine park with 4 mooring buoys on the north side and good anchorage, particularly along the south shore. Check the depths before using the buoys. No power, water, restrooms or showers. Trails lead around and through the island. Skagit Island, just to the north, has 2 mooring buoys along its north side. Self-register and pay mooring buoy fees on shore. Similk Bay is shoal but navigable in shallow draft boats. Anchorage is possible almost anywhere.

Kiket Island/Kukutali Preserve. Located just east of Skagit Island. Kiket Island is part of the Deception Pass State Park and jointly managed with the Swinomish Tribal Community reservation. The Island is open to the public for day-use only from dawn to dusk. Although technically an island, Kiket is connected to Fidalgo Island by a thin tombolo. Kiket Island can only be accessed by non-motorized boats. Access to Flagstaff Point on the west end of Kiket Island is restricted. Trails, a viewing platform, and pit toilets can be found on Kiket Island.

(16) **Cornet Bay.** Cornet Bay, tucked in behind Ben Ure Island, indents the north shore of Whidbey Island just east of Deception Pass. A dredged channel marked by pilings leads to Deception Pass Marina and a state park, both of which offer visitor moorage, and serve as a place to hole up while waiting for the tidal change. The passage west of Ben Ure Island should not be attempted except at high tide,

Note the currents in this view of Deception Pass looking west.

and then only by shallow draft boats. The channel to a county dock at the south end of the bay is very shallow and should only be attempted with local knowledge. Vessel Assist towing and emergency rescue office nearby.

(16) **Deception Pass Marina**. 200 West Cornet Bay Road, Oak Harbor, WA 98277; (360) 675-5411. Open all year. The marina has some slips reserved for visiting boats and uses unoccupied slips as available. The docks have 30 amp power, but only limited room for larger boats up to 65 feet. Ethanol-free gasoline, diesel, and propane at the fuel dock. The store carries convenience groceries, bait, tackle, charts, books, beer and wine. Restrooms, no showers (showers are available at the state park next door). Call ahead for availability of guest moorage. Nearby laundry and haulout.

(16) **Deception Pass Marine State Park**, Cornet Bay area. Open all year for day use and overnight moorage; first-come, first-served. Payment boxes on the floats and at a kiosk on shore. The park has 600 feet of side-tie dock space, restrooms, showers and pumpout, but no power. Two additional 100-foot floats are anchored offshore and not connected to land. A 5-lane launch ramp has boarding floats. Hiking trails and picnic areas nearby. Groceries, laundromat and services are at Deception Pass Marina. Park has campsites, but not near this area. On Ben Ure Island, a

single cabin is available for rent. Reservations online or call (888) 226-7688.

LOCAL KNOWLEDGE

STRONG CURRENTS: Currents run to 8 knots in Deception Pass with strong eddies and overfalls. Dangerous waves can form when a big ebb current meets strong westerly winds. It is best to time an approach to enter the pass at or near slack water. Try to travel single-file.

Deception Pass. Deception Pass narrows to 200 yards at Pass, Island, one of the anchors for the spectacular 144-foot-high bridge that connects Whidbey Island and Fidalgo Island.

Tidal current predictions are shown under Deception Pass in the tide and current books. An even narrower pass, Canoe Pass, lies north of Pass Island. Kayaks use Canoe Pass, but lacking local knowledge we wouldn't run our boat through it.

From the west, the preferred route to Deception Pass is just to the south of Lighthouse Point and north of Deception Island.

North of Lighthouse Point, **Bowman Bay**, also known as Reservation Bay, is part of Deception Pass State Park.

(17) **Deception Pass Marine State Park, Bowman Bay** (Reservation Bay). Open all year for day use and overnight camping and mooring. Restrooms with showers, no power. Bowman Bay has a gravel 1-lane launch ramp. Standard campsites are on the north shore. The park has picnic sites and outdoor kitchens. An underwater park for diving is near the mouth of Bowman Bay, near Rosario Head. When entering take care to avoid Coffin Rocks and Gull Rocks, which cover at high tide. Safe entry can be made by staying fairly close to the Reservation Head side of the entrance.

A mooring float, approximately 100 feet long and not connected to shore, is located behind Reservation Head. On the east side of the bay the 40-foot-long float on the park dock is for dinghies.

Anchorage is also possible in the bay north of Rosario Head, but it is exposed to wave action from Rosario Strait.

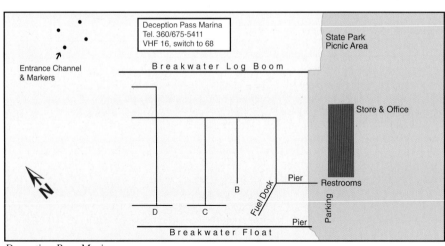

Deception Pass Marina

Deception Pass Marine State Park, Sharpe Cove. Open all year for day use and overnight camping and mooring. The park has 160 feet of dock space, no power. Restrooms, showers, portapotty dump, picnic sites, kitchen. Campsites are east of Sharpe Cove. The onshore facility is the Walla Walla University Rosario Beach Marine Laboratory.

Shelter Bay Marina. 1000 Shoshone Drive, La Conner, WA 98257; (360) 466-3805; www.shelterbay.net; kemerson@shelterbay.net. Shelter Bay Marina is on the west side of Swinomish Channel just south of La Conner. Primarily permanent moorage, but some transient space is available. Water, 30 & 50 amp power, pumpout, restrooms, showers, no laundry.

⑱ **La Conner.** The Port of Skagit's La Conner Marina, with two large moorage basins, is a short distance north of downtown La Conner. Both moorage basins have guest moorage and full facilities for visitors. Fuel is available adjacent to the marina at La Conner Landing, and propane is available at Boater's Discount marine supply store between the two basins.

The town of La Conner has three public floats for guest moorage for boats up to 45

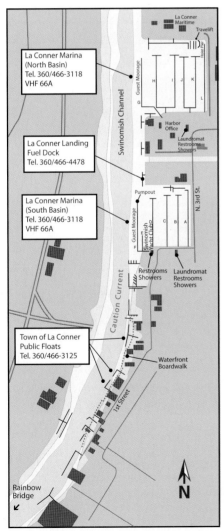

La Conner

Several small public docks line the waterfront at La Conner.

feet, with stays of 24 hours, located along the quarter-mile long waterfront boardwalk.

Current in Swinomish Channel can be strong and difficult to predict. Allow for current before landing anywhere along the channel.

The town of La Conner is thoroughly charming. It has excellent restaurants, galleries, museums, wine tasting rooms, and shops. During the summer, hordes of visitors arrive by car and tour bus. Even when crowded, the town is enjoyable. Free outdoor concert, parade, food vendors and fireworks on the 4th of July. On summer Sundays in Gilkey Square, live music from mid-June to August.

⑱ **La Conner Marina.** P.O. Box 1120, 613 N. 2nd St., La Conner, WA 98257; (360) 466-3118; www.portofskagit.com/la-conner-marina. Monitors VHF 66A. Open all year with 30 & 50 amp power, free Wi-Fi, restrooms, showers, laundry, pumpout. Reservations accepted for G dock only. Haulout to 82 tons. Complete repairs available through La Conner Maritime.

All shopping and services are within walking distance. A monorail launch can handle boats to 14,000 lbs. Trailers must be roller style, no bunks. A paved and lighted storage yard is available for trailers and tow vehicles.

This marina, owned by the Port of Skagit, is where most visiting boats tie up. F dock at the south basin has 1200 lineal feet of side-tie guest moorage. G dock at the north basin has another 1200 feet of side-tie moorage. E dock, near shore in the south basin, has 450 feet of guest moorage for the Swinomish Yacht Club. Reservations accepted. Unoccupied slips are used when available. If the moorage appears full, call anyway. They try to fit everybody in.

⑱ **La Conner Landing Fuel Dock.** P.O. Box 1020, La Conner, WA 98257; (360) 466-4478. Open all year. Summer hours from 8:00 a.m. to 6:00 p.m. daily. Hours and days vary during the fall and winter, call ahead. Fuel dock with ethanol-free gasoline and diesel, pumpout. The store has tackle, bait,

ice, marine items, and snacks.

Caution: Strong current flows past the dock. Look for the directional sign on the fuel shed labeled 'CURRENT' with an arrow indicating which way the current is running.

⑱ **Town of La Conner Public Floats.** (360) 466-3125. The town of La Conner has three floats with first-come, first-serve moorage for vessels 45 feet and under for stays up to 24 hours. The three separate floats are along the waterfront boardwalk that parallels the Swinomish Channel. The street-end floats are located at Benton, Calhoun and Washington Streets. Larger vessels may be accommodated at Benton float with prior approval by calling ahead. Self-registration and cash payment at payment drop boxes located at each of the floats. Call for stays longer than 24 hours. No water, no power; public restrooms are available in town and near the La Conner Marina.

Caution: Strong current flows past the floats, check the current before approaching.

Padilla Bay. The well-marked channel through Padilla Bay is about 3 miles long between drying flats. Don't take any shortcuts until north of Beacon 2, which marks the edge of Guemes Channel. Deeper draft boats, such as sailboats, should hold to a mid-channel course, especially at low tide. To the west of the channel are long docks serving ocean-going tankers calling at the two major oil refineries in Anacortes. Often tankers, barges, or tug boats lie at anchor in the bay awaiting room at the docks.

Red, Right, Returning: In Padilla Bay, Red, Right, Returning assumes "return" is from the north. Red navigation aids are on the west side of the channel from Padilla Bay to La Conner. South of La Conner, red navigation aids are on the east side of Swinomish Channel. Approaching La Conner from north or south, remember Red, Right, Returning.

Saddlebag Island Marine State Park. Open all year for day use and overnight anchoring and camping. Boat access only. Anchorage is good off the north or south shore. Water

LA CONNER MARKETPLACE
RESTAURANTS, SHOPS & SERVICES

Calendar of Events

JANUARY
Skagit Valley Winter
Birds Festival

FEBRUARY
Annual Smelt Derby

MARCH
Annual La Conner
Daffodil Festival

APRIL
Skagit Valley Tulip Festival

MAY
Opening Day Boating
Season Parade

JUNE
MoNA Auction

JULY
Hometown 4th of July
Celebration

AUGUST
Annual Classic
Boat & Car Show

OCTOBER
Festival of Family Farms
Annual Brew on the Slough –
La Conner's Beer Fest

NOVEMBER
Arts Alive!

DECEMBER
Community Tree Lighting
Lighted Boat Parade

Dates may change, check website
www.loveliaconner.com

*Boardwalk photo courtesy of
La Conner Chamber of Commerce
Town photo courtesy of Aimee Beckwith*

LA CONNER CHAMBER

A beautiful village on the banks of the Swinomish Channel. Shop, Dine, Art and Wine! Come experience the LaConner love. Located just 60 miles north of Seattle in the heart of Skagit Valley

**360-466-4778 • 413 Morris Street,
La Conner, WA • www.LoveLaConner.com**

LA CONNER CHANNEL LODGE & COUNTRY INN

Enjoy Deluxe Accommodations! The Channel Lodge features water views and private balconies. The Country Inn on Second Street is charming with spacious rooms. Enjoy continental breakfast, free parking, and Wi-Fi at both locations!

**1-888-466-4113 • 360-466-1500
205 N. First St. & 107 S. Second St.,
La Conner, WA
www.LaConnerLodging.com**

LA CONNER LANDING FUEL DOCK

The friendliest and most convenient fuel dock around! Fuel up and pump out at the same time. Quality marine diesel and ethanol free gas. Located on the Swinomish channel just north of town. Ice, bait, food and marine supplies. Hours vary by season.

**360-466-4478 • 541 North 3rd Street,
La Conner, WA**

LA CONNER BREWING COMPANY

Unique Northwest-style family-friendly brewpub featuring wood-fired pizzas, burgers and other fresh local pub fare served with our small-batch, hand-crafted beers. Wines and hard ciders available too. Enjoy by the fireplace or on the garden terrace.

**360-466-1415 • 117 S. First Street,
La Conner, WA
www.LaConnerBrewery.com**

LA CONNER MARITIME

Servicing, building and equipping boats for nearly 40 years, we take pride in our reputation as a friendly, professional boat yard that can handle every customer need from pressure washing the hull to rebuilding the engine.

**360-466-3629 • 920 W. Pearle Jensen Way
La Conner, WA
www.LaConnerMaritime.com**

LA CONNER MARINA
Your Premier Destination on the Swinomish Channel

Port of Skagit

Our full-service marina is walking distance from great dining and shopping in historic downtown La Conner, WA. Courtesy shuttle for guests! The Swinomish Channel is your safe and comfortable route to the San Juan Islands.

360-466-3118 • VHF 66A • www.portofskagit.com/la-conner-marina

155

YOUR FULL-SERVICE REPAIR AND REFIT YARD
IN DESTINATION LA CONNER

▸ Haul outs to 110 tons
▸ 30,000+ SF heated, indoor work space
▸ Providing solutions for safe and reliable boating for over 30 years

LA CONNER MARITIME SERVICE

service@laconnermaritime.com

- Long & Short Term Storage
- Gas & Diesel Repair & Repowers
- Paint, Fiberglass & Wood Repair
- Bow & Stern Thrusters
- Full System Service
- Wood Boat Specialist
- Heating Systems
- Sanitation Systems
- Electrical

ABYC MEMBER

NORTHERN LIGHTS VOLVO PENTA NAIAD DYNAMICS ALEXSEAL

See the Hide-A-Davit in action on our website!!

Hull Paint & Repair

Hydraulics & Systems Engineering & Installation

920 W. Pearle Jensen Way ▪ La Conner, WA 98257 (360) 466-3629 ▪ www.laconnermaritime.com

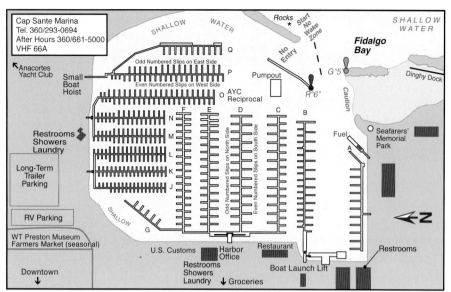

Cap Sante Marina

depths are inconveniently deep on the west side, and inconveniently shallow on the east. Vault toilets, primitive campsites. Cascadia Marine Trail campsite. One-mile hiking trail. "Hot spot" for crabbing.

Huckleberry Island. North end of Padilla Bay, owned by the Samish Indian Nation. Open all year, day use only. No services. Undeveloped 10-acre island with anchoring or beaching only. No fires or camping. Pack out all garbage. Attractive to kayakers and scuba divers. Gravel beach on the southwest side of the island.

⑲ **Anacortes.** www.anacortes.org. Anacortes is a major boating center, with fishing and pleasure craft facilities in Fidalgo Bay and along Guemes Channel. The city's marine businesses can provide for a boater's every need, including food, fuel, and repairs. With seven haulout yards, Anacortes has the marine trades for any repair. For pumpout service, call PumpMeOut at (425) 903-3137.

U.S. Customs: Anacortes is a U.S. Customs port of entry with an office in the Cap Sante Marina harbormaster's building. There is no U.S. Customs dock. Call the marina office for a slip assignment and proceed to the slip. Then call the Anacortes Customs Office at (360) 293-2331 for instructions. Between 1:00 p.m. and 3:00 p.m. during the summer agents are apt to be 4 miles away at the Washington State Ferry terminal, clearing arrivals on the international ferry from Sidney, B.C. You'll have to wait aboard for the agents to return. Otherwise, they will ask the captain to walk up to the Customs Office, Suite F, to the right of the harbormaster's office for clearance.

Fidalgo Bay is shallow. If you stray from the dredged and marked channels during low water, you could find yourself aground.

Four marinas are located on the Fidalgo Bay side of town. Three additional marinas are located on the west end of Fidalgo Island. From north to south on Fidalgo Bay, the first is Cap Sante Marina, owned by the Port of

Anacortes, with guest moorage, fuel, water, electricity, pumpout and haulout facilities. Enter between the arms of a piling breakwater due west of Cap Sante.

The second, behind a prominent breakwater, is Anacortes Marina, where Marine Servicenter has fuel, pumpout, 55 ton Travelift haulout, and repairs. Open seven days a week from 8:00 a.m. to 4:30 p.m. and 8:00 a.m. to 8:00 p.m. from Memorial Day weekend to Labor Day weekend. Permanent moorage only. Anacortes Yacht Charters and many bareboat charter boats are based in this marina. Follow the dredged channel to the marina entrance on the south side. The north entrance in the breakwater is for exiting boats only.

Next is the 360-foot-long dock and haulout ramp for Pacific Marine Center (360) 299-8820. Large vessels can be hauled out with their 200-ton Travelift and blocked in their extensive yard complex for maintenance and repairs. They also have multiple KMI Sea-lift machines for haulout on their ramp for vessels up to 65 feet. Limited moorage is available on their docks, typically reserved for repair or dry storage customers.

The fourth is Fidalgo Marina, where Cap Sante Marine has a 50 ton Travelift and the haulout ramp for North Harbor Diesel. The marina is protected by a piling breakwater, and is entered through the dredged channel marked by pilings extending from deeper water near Cap Sante.

Moving east to west, Dakota Creek Industries is a large shipyard on Guemes Channel with Syncrolift ship lift and drydock for vessels to 400 feet.

Next to the Guemes Ferry is Anchor Cove, a private marina with no transient moorage.

Lovric's Sea-Craft is on Guemes Channel, with two marine ways for haulout, and a small dry dock.

Skyline Marina is in Flounder Bay on the west side of Fidalgo Island, 3 miles from downtown Anacortes. It has some transient moorage and a DIY yard with 55 ton Travelift haulout and a stationary lift accommodating

16,000 pounds.

Farmers Market: Saturdays 9:00 a.m. to 2:00 p.m. next to the Depot Arts & Community Center; seasonal.

Events: Wine Festival, early April; Anacortes Waterfront Festival, early June at Cap Sante Marina; Shipwreck Day, July; Anacortes Arts Festival, early August; Oyster Run, late September; Bier on the Pier, early October. www.anacortes.org; info@anacortes.org; (360) 293-7911.

THINGS TO DO

1. Charming downtown. Visit the shops, galleries, antique stores, and restaurants along Commercial Avenue.

2. W. T. Preston, an old snag boat, is part of the Anacortes History Museum. Located across from the north end of Cap Sante Marina.

3. Live music. On Fridays and some Saturdays in July and August, the Port of Anacortes hosts free concerts at Seafarers' Memorial Park.

4. Skagit Cycle. Rent a bike and ride the Tommy Thompson Trail, or just around town. Catch the Tommy Thompson Trail from R Avenue at Cap Sante Marina.

5. Cap Sante Park. Walk to the top and view Mt. Baker and the marina from this scenic vantage point. Sunsets from here are particularly beautiful. A steep switchback trail leads from the gazebo on the point at Cap Sante.

6. Seabear Smokehouse. Learn the difference in taste between smoked pink, king and sockeye salmon at their processing plant and factory store at 30th Street and T Ave.

7. Crabbing. Fidalgo Bay often has great crabbing.

⑲ **Cap Sante Marina/Port of Anacortes.** 100 Commercial Ave., 1019 Q Ave., Anacortes, WA 98221; (360) 293-0694; (360) 661-5000; marina@portofanacortes.com; www.portofanacortes.com. Monitors VHF 66A. Formerly Cap Sante Boat Haven. Open all year with moorage to 120 feet. Call or radio ahead for slip assignment. There is a $5 fee for reservations. No fee for same-day reservations. The 18×120-foot fuel dock, with ethanol-free gasoline, and diesel is to port inside the breakwater. A high-volume fuel delivery hose is available. Propane at boat launch. The marina has 20 & 30 amp power with some 50 & 100 amp power available, ELCI protected shore power on docks A & B. 5 pumpout carts (free), 2 portapotty dumps, restrooms, showers, and laundry. Guest boaters are given an access code to the laundry. A pumpout float is located just inside the harbor entrance. Used oil dump near the office. Free Wi-Fi throughout the marina. Loaner wheelchair available. Complimentary bicycles with baskets are available for marina guests. A monorail launch can handle boats to 25,000 pounds. A small hoist and dry storage yard for hand launching small boats is in the North Basin on P-Q dock. Call (360) 293-0694. Most of the transient area marina floats have been replaced by wide, stable concrete floats, with wide slips and wheelchair accessible ramps to shore. The floats are first-class in every way.

Follow the dredged and marked channel, and enter between the arms of a piling breakwater due west of Cap Sante. The area to port just inside the breakwater, towards Seafarers' Memorial Park, is shoal and should not be attempted. The harbormaster's office and U.S. Customs office are just north of C & D floats.

This is a clean and popular stop, located in the heart of downtown Anacortes. Complete facilities, including many good restaurants, large Safeway and Marketplace grocery stores, well-stocked Ace Hardware and Sebo's hardware stores, and two marine stores (West Marine, Marine Supply & Hardware) are within walking distance. An esplanade leads from the marina to the Seafarers' Memorial Park and building, and around the marina to Rotary Park. A dock for dinghies is behind a small breakwater at Seafarers' Memorial Park. The lawn and beach areas are used as a kayak launch.

The Anacortes Farmers Market is open Saturdays from 9:00 a.m. to 2:00 p.m. May to October.

Cap Sante Marina is one of the top three most popular marina (rated by marina moorage nights) in the state. It is considered the homeport of the San Juan Islands and is often used as a supply and provisioning jumping-off point for cruises into the islands and further north.

ANTHONY'S
CAP SANTE MARINA
1207 Q Avenue
(360) 588-0333

THE CABANA
1207 Q Avenue
(360) 588-0333

⑲ **Anacortes Marina.** 2415 T Avenue, Anacortes, WA 98221; (360) 293-4543. Primarily private moorage. Marine Servicenter, with fuel dock, haulout, and repairs, is located there. Enter through the dredged channel to the south opening in

157

Cap Sante Marine

Haul-outs to 50 Tons
Custom Davit Installation
Nordic Tug Specialists
Dinghy & Outboard Service
Mechanical & Electrical Service
Propeller & Running Gear Repair
Thruster & Stabilizer Installation
Fiberglass & Paint Services

Everything in Boating Since 1979
360.293.3145 • 2915 W Avenue Anacortes • www.CapSante.com

ANACORTES MARKETPLACE

RESTAURANTS, SHOPS & SERVICES

CALENDAR OF EVENTS

JANUARY
First Friday Gallery Art
Walk

FEBRUARY
First Friday Gallery Art
Walk

MARCH
First Friday Gallery Art
Walk
Anacortes Salmon Derby

APRIL
First Friday Gallery Art
Walk
Spring Wine Festival
Island Chicks Antique
& Vintage Show, Port
Warehouse
Skagit Valley Tulip
Festival
Anacortes Annual Quilt
Walk

MAY
First Friday Gallery Art
Walk
Anacortes Boat & Yacht
Show

JUNE
Kids Fishing Derby
Chamber Gallery Art
Walk
Anacortes Waterfront
Festival, Cap Sante Marina

Dates may change, check website
www.anacortes.org
360-293-7911

ACE HARDWARE
Ace Hardware of Anacortes is your locally owned and operated hardware store, specializing in marine hardware, stainless fasteners, electrical, Craftsman Tools, fishing licenses, tackle, bait, rain gear and all your hardware needs.
360-293-3535 • 1720 Q Avenue,
Anacortes, WA 98221 • 360-378-4622
www.AceAnacortes.com

Mary LaFleur

ALT INSURANCE GROUP
An all lines broker with a specialty niche in yacht insurance, Mary LaFleur has over 30 years in the insurance industry, represents over 30 insurance carriers, and is a life-long boater. "Most times we can save our boaters enough on their auto, home, commercial and RV insurance to put fuel in their tanks." Customer Service is second to none.
253-222-7519 • 360-899-4653
819 Commercial Avenue, Ste D,
mary@altinsurancegroup.com
www.altinsurancegroup.com

ANACORTES MARINE INSURANCE
One of only a few Insurance agencies in Washington State, and the only one in Skagit County/Anacortes, offering direct access to the top Yacht Insurance markets in the world. Featuring CHUBB, REDSHIELD and PANTAENIUS, as well as PREMIER, SAFECO, and TRAVELERS, our experienced staff can find the best coverage/best pricing to fit your needs. Additional access to brokers allows us to handle all types of Marine-related Business Pursuits.
360-588-8112 • 1116 12th St
www.AnacortesMarine-Ins.com

ANACORTES RIGGING & YACHT SERVICES
Pleasure marine, industrial, and architectural wire and rope rigging services. Standing rigging, running rigging, mooring, tow lines, lifting bridles, davit service. Large selection of rope in stock and fast turn around. Consultation, inspection, refits.
360-293-2030 • www.AnacortesRigging.com

ANTHONY'S
Anthony's at Cap Sante Marina - Lunch and dinner daily in a scenic waterfront setting, overlooking the marina with two view decks. Serving fresh northwest seafood from our own seafood company. Adjacent is The Cabana by Anthony's, a casual seafood restaurant with a classic "to-go fish & chips" bar. Both restaurants are steps from the marina.
360-588-0333 • 1207 Q Avenue •
www.anthonys.com

ANTHONY'S THE CABANA
The Cabana is located adjacent to Anthony's at Cap Sante Marina. The Cabana offers casual family-friendly dining as well as a classic fish & chip "to-go" bar for quick service dining. The Cabana has two full-size Bocce Ball courts available for guests while dining.
360-588-0333 • 1207 Q Avenue • www.anthonys.com/restaurants/detail/anthonys-cabana

THE BROWN LANTERN ALE HOUSE
Serving the locals & visitors to Historic Anacortes since 1933, just steps from the waterfront in the heart of oldtown. Featuring outstanding burgers, creative pub fare, 15 beers on draft, and over 50 different whiskies alone! See why we are voted the "Best Tavern in Anacortes" year after year. Now family friendly.
360-293-2544 • 412 Commercial Ave.
www.brownlantern.com

CAP SANTE MARINE
Over 30 years of experience with professional service and factory-trained and authorized service technicians. We offer full mechanical services, electrical installation and repair, Fiberglas, gelcoat, and paint in our heated shop. Fully-stocked parts department and haulout up to 50 tons on our Travelift.
360-293-3145 • 2915 W Avenue •
www.capsante.com

INSIDE PASSAGE YACHT SALES
Boating is not about a boat, it is about a lifestyle. Our passion is not simply boats, it is matching perfect boats to individual buyers and that is what makes us different. Here at Inside Passage Yacht Sales we proudly represent brands such as Lindell, Parker, and Sargo in the Pacific Northwest. In addition we carry a large inventory of new and used saltwater and sports fishing, center consoles, cruisers, and pilot house boats.
(360) 468-4997 • 409 30th Street
www.insidepassageyachtsales.com

Statue Photo Courtesy of Anacortes Chamber of Commerce, Steve Berentson, photographer

ANACORTES MARKETPLACE

RESTAURANTS, SHOPS & SERVICES

CALENDER OF EVENTS

JULY
First Friday Gallery
ArtWalk
4th of July Parade
Shipwreck Day
Anacortes

AUGUST
First Friday Gallery
ArtWalk
Anacortes Arts Festival
Fidalgo Bay Day

SEPTEMBER
First Friday Gallery
ArtWalk
Oyster Run Motorcycle
Rally

OCTOBER
First Friday Gallery
ArtWalk
Bier on the Pier
Anacortes Fall Boat
Show
Trick or Treat Downtown

NOVEMBER
First Friday Gallery
ArtWalk
Fall Vintage Market

DECEMBER
Tree Lighting,
Holiday Parade
Holiday ArtWalk
Lighted Boat Parade

Dates may change, check website
www.anacortes.org
360-293-7911

NORTH HARBOR DIESEL & YACHT SERVICE
North Harbor Diesel and Yacht Service has been in Anacortes since 1985. Come see us for boat storage, engine services, hull and bottom repairs, maintenance and modernizing. Open year round Monday–Friday, we are the region's premier boat yard.
360-293-5551 • 720 30th Street
www.northharbordiesel.com

ROCKFISH GRILL & ANACORTES BREWERY
The Rockfish Grill serves Northwest food including seafood and wood fired pizza made with fresh local ingredients. They proudly pour Anacortes Brewery beers made right next door. Live music weekly. Full bar. Family friendly.
360-588-1720 • 320 Commercial Avenue •
www.anacortesrockfish.com

SALISH MARINE LLC
Marine maintaince and repair. Working Anacortes and Laconner.
360-707-1257 • 16840A Bennett Rd, Burlington, WA 98273
www.facebook.com/Salishmarine

SEATTLE YACHTS
Serving the Pacific Northwest for over 33 years, Seattle Yachts is the premiere dealership for trawlers, cruising sailboats and motoryachts, both new and brokerage. Now with 2 offices to serve you; one at Shilshole Marina in Seattle and the other at the Anacortes Marina.
844-692-2487 Ext 2
Anacortes Marina
2415 T Ave, Suite 112
www.SeattleYachts.com

MARINE SERVICES GROUP is the management company that owns and operates North Island Boat, Anacortes Marine Electronics, 3C Canvas, and Jensen's Shipyard. Our divisions work together to create and efficient "one stop shop" environment to repair and maintain every system within your vessel. With multiple locations and mobile capabilities, we can provide the same level of superior service from Everett to Bellingham and throughout the San Juan Islands.
Headquarters: 1910 Skyline Way • Anacortes, WA 98221 • 360.293.2565
www.marineservicesgroup.com

ANACORTES MARINE ELECTRONICS
At Anacortes Marine Electronics our NMEA and MEI certified technicians can troubleshoot, install, and network any component on your vessel. We specialize in designing and configuring custom navigation and communication packages that meet your individual needs and help you take full advantage of your boating season.
A Division of Marine Services Group
1910 Skyline Way Anacortes, WA 98221
360.293.2565
www.anacortesmarine.com

NORTH ISLAND BOAT
North Island Boat is a full-service boat yard open year-round. Our team of ABYC certified technicians are trained to service all brands and are equipped to handle any of your mechanical, gas, diesel, hydraulic, electrical, or shipwright needs. With mobile capabilities, we can provide service from Everett to Bellingham.
A Division of Marine Services Group
1910 Skyline Way Anacortes, WA 98221 • 360.293.2565
www.northislandboat.com

3C CANVAS
Our fabrication shop is dedicated to sewing, cutting, and bending your marine canvas and upholstery visions into reality. Using top of the line material to create custom fit designs, our canvas makers provide quality dodgers, biminis, enclosures, and covers for any vessel.
A Division of Marine Services Group
1910 Skyline Way Anacortes, WA 98221 • 360.293.2565
www.3ccanvas.com

Great experiences come in small islands

Relax and enjoy a weekend (or more!) on Fidalgo Island. With mild temperatures, lush forest lands to explore, and water that surrounds, staying here is a great way to spend your time away from home. Visit by car, ferry, plane or boat. Experience amazing restaurants, boutique shopping in historic downtown, nature viewing, multiple festivals across the year, live music, and so much more.

From Anchors to Zincs you can cover all of your boating needs in Anacortes! We have first class marinas and over 50 marine trades companies and professionals that are dedicated to providing quality parts and services. Let us help you buy, insure, store, moor, maintain, repair, and enjoy your boat, right here on beautiful Fidalgo island.

the pilings. Exit the marina through the north opening in the breakwater. Marine Servicenter's fuel dock, pumpout and a 55 ton Travelift are straight ahead when you enter the marina.

⑲ **Marine Servicenter.** 2417 T Avenue, Anacortes, WA 98221; (360) 293-8200; service@marinesc.com; www.marinesc.com. Open all year. Fuel dock with ethanol-free gasoline, diesel, propane, pumpout, portapotty dump, lubricants, engine oil. Complete repair facilities with yard and haulout to 55 tons.

⑲ **Fidalgo Marina.** 3101 V Place, Anacortes, WA 98221; (360) 299-0873. No transient overnight moorage, but a number of marine businesses are located there. Enter through

the opening at the end of the dredged channel on the north side. First, to starboard, is the dock with a 50-ton Travelift for Cap Sante Marine, a full-service boatyard for repairs and refits (360) 293-3145.

Next are the staging docks with temporary moorage for the marine repair businesses. The city dock has marked temporary hourly moorage but no overnight. The ramp at the end of the small basin is for the 45-ton capacity KMI Sea-Lifts for North Harbor Diesel's repair yard and dry storage yards, and Banana Belt Boats brokerage storage yard.

Guemes Channel. On an ebb tide, waters in Guemes Channel can be very rough, especially west of the mouth of Bellingham Channel.

Watch for the Guemes ferry, a small car and

passenger ferry that makes frequent crossings between Anacortes and Guemes Island.

Next to the ferry dock is Anchor Cove Marina, a private condo marina with covered and open slips.

Farther west is Lovric's Sea-Craft (360) 840-3271, a commercial shipyard and moorage with large marine ways for haulout.

Ship Harbor was once the primary harbor for Anacortes and offers some protection and reasonable anchorage. Watch for ferry traffic from the busy Washington State Ferries terminal in Ship Harbor. *Cross behind the ferries, not in front.*

Guemes Island. Guemes Island has no facilities specifically for boaters, although anchorage can be found along the north shore. Anchorage also can be found on the eastern shore in a tiny notch called Boat Harbor. A ferry connects Guemes Island to Anacortes.

Washington Park. www.cityofanacortes.org. West shore of Fidalgo Island on Guemes Channel. Open all year for day use and overnight camping. Restrooms, portapotty dump, showers. Anchoring or beaching only. Two-lane launch ramp, parking area, picnic tables, picnic shelters, fireplaces, campsites. Playground equipment. The loop road is 2.2 miles in length and is good for walking or jogging. The park has forested areas and viewpoints along the beaches overlooking Rosario Strait to Burrows Bay.

Flounder Bay. Flounder Bay has been dredged to provide moorage for the Skyline real estate development. Skyline Marina and several charter companies are inside the spit. Also a small chandlery, Travelift, and other facilities, including a large dry storage

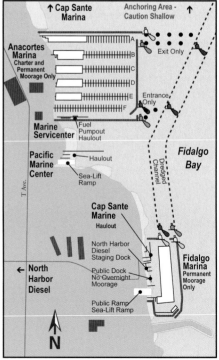

Anacortes

Cap Sante Marina

A year-round all weather marina, Cap Sante Marina in Anacortes is one of the boating capitals of the Northwest. Centrally located between Victoria, BC and Seattle, Cap Sante offers the ultimate location for guests planning to explore the region. Within walking distance to downtown, you can enjoy our many local restaurants, shops, festivities and amenities.

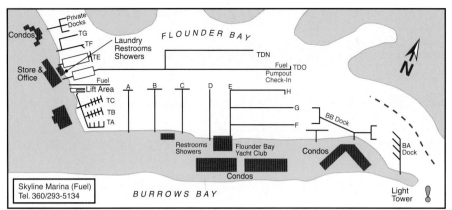

Skyline Marina

building. Entry is from Burrows Bay along a dredged channel marked by lighted pilings.

⑳ **Skyline Marina**. 2011 Skyline Way, Anacortes, WA 98221; (360) 293-5134; info@skylinemarinecenter.com; www. skylinemarinecenter.com. Open all year, guest moorage, 30 amp power (ELCI-protected power on some docks), laundry, showers. Fuel dock with ethanol-free gasoline, diesel and pumpout. A seaplane float is at the fuel dock. Propane and a coffee bar at the marina office.

Complete boat repairs and services are available. The yard has space for DIY repairs. A convenience store with grocery items is a block away. Other marine services nearby. Secure inside and outside storage for boats, vehicles, and trailers. Water taxi to the San Juan Islands. The marina is 4 miles from downtown Anacortes.

In 2017, the inner area around TA-TC docks was dredged and new docks installed. A 16,000 pound stationary lift was added and the nearby 55 ton Travelift area was rebuilt. A building housing a kayak tour operator, a marine brokerage, bareboat charter and other marine related businesses are located upland. The nearby North Island Boat Company (360-293-2565) accepts used oil.

Burrows Island State Park. Open all year, no facilities. Undeveloped 330-acre state park. Anchor in Alice Bight on the northeast shore, or beach. No camping or fires. Pack out all garbage. Do not disturb wildlife or surroundings. Most of the shoreline is steep cliffs. The Burrows Island Lighthouse is on the west tip of the island.

Allan Island. Allan Island is privately owned, but anchorage can be had in the little bight on the east shore.

Cypress Island. A park ranger told us he considers Cypress Island to be the "crown jewel" of the San Juans, we agree. This island, now largely in public ownership, is beautiful, and is an excellent place to stretch the legs. Access is hindered by a shortage of good anchorages, so you won't be bothered by large crowds. Several trails lead off from Pelican Beach at the northeast corner of the island. They can provide leisurely walks or vigorous hikes, with beautiful views.

About a half-mile south of Pelican Beach, just past a small headland, two little coves are quite pretty and have room for one or two boats each.

Pelican Beach Recreation Site. Dept. of Natural Resources (DNR) park on the northeast side of Cypress Island. Open all year for day use and overnight camping and mooring. The park has 6 mooring buoys, a gravel beach, 5 campsites, compost toilets, picnic shelter, fire pit, information board. Many kinds of wildlife and birds can be observed. Public DNR beaches extend from the park around the north end of Cypress Island for 1.5 miles until just south of Foss Cove, and south of the park for 0.5 mile to Bridge Rock. The moorage is unprotected to the north. If anchored or moored to a buoy and the northerly wind comes in, you'll not want to stay. Current runs through the moorage, and is subject to wakes from passing traffic.

Eagle Harbor. East side of Cypress Island. Eagle Harbor is shallow, especially at low tide, but has 15 mooring buoys. Use care in approaching all but the outermost of these buoys. The bay's shallow spots are truly shallow. The innermost 4 buoys display red tags cautioning the user to verify depths at lower tide levels. Convenient beach access to the island's trails. No fires, no camping. If you have sufficient depth, Eagle Harbor is quite protected. Views of Mount Baker are breathtaking.

Cypress Head. East side of Cypress Island. Open all year for day use and overnight camping and mooring. The park has 4 mooring buoys and 5 campsites, picnic sites, compost toilets, no other facilities. Three miles of public tidelands extend from the moorage/recreation area. Many types of birds and wildlife, good fishing. Tide-rips at the south end of the island cause high wave action.

Deepwater Bay. East side of Cypress Island. Deepwater Bay has several fish farm net pens. In 2017, strong currents collapsed one of the pens, releasing 300,000 Atlantic Salsmon.

Skyline Marina in Fidalgo Bay is one of the closest marinas to the San Juan Islands.

Strawberry Island State Park. West of **Cypress Island** in Rosario Strait. Open all year. Anchoring or beaching only, anchorage in settled weather only. Strong currents and submerged rocks make landing difficult; skiffs or kayaks are best for landing. Park has three Cascadia Marine Trail campsites, vault toilet.

Vendovi Island. San Juan Preservation Trust, www.sjpt.org. Day use only, open April 15 through October 15, 10:00 a.m. to 6:00 p.m Thursday through Monday. No anchoring. A 70-foot dock behind a rock breakwater is on the north shore. All visitors must sign in and review visitor guidelines at the head of the dock upon arrival. A public restroom is in the building at the top of the hill.

Sinclair and Eliza Islands. A piling breakwater protects a loading and unloading dock on the south shore of Sinclair Island, but there are no facilities specifically for pleasure boaters. Eliza Island is privately owned, with a private dock and float on the north side. Anchorage is possible several places around the island.

Larrabee State Park. (360) 676-2093. Seven miles south of Bellingham on Samish Bay. Open all year for day use and overnight camping. The park has restrooms and showers. This was Washington's first official state park, dedicated in 1923. It covers 2000 acres and is heavily used. Facilities include a launch ramp, kitchen shelters, picnic tables, standard, utility, and primitive campsites. Fishing, clamming, crabbing, scuba diving. Trails provide access to two freshwater lakes within the park. A 5.5-mile walking/bicycling trail connects with Bellingham.

Chuckanut Bay. Chuckanut Bay is a good anchorage with protection from prevailing winds in the north or south arms. Enter close to Governors Point to avoid extensive rocky shoals that partially block the entrance. The land around the bay is privately owned. Correspondents James and Jennifer Hamilton anchored in Pleasant Bay, just inside Governors Point, during a southeast gale. "The winds howled up to 49 knots, but the water was reasonably calm. Good holding over mud." [Hamilton]

㉑ **Fairhaven Moorage.** (360) 714-8891; www.boatingcenter.org. Nine mooring buoys, a side-tie linear mooring system, and two boat launch ramps at Fairhaven are managed by the Community Boating Center. Moorage and boat launch May through October, 38-foot maximum. Launch ramps are tide-dependent and best suited to smaller boats. Pay moorage at the CBC office or pay box. Walk up to shops and restaurants in Fairhaven's lovely Victorian buildings. Just south of the business district you'll find a beautiful old park with mature plantings and great expanses of lawn. The Seaview Boatyard Dock (360) 676-8282 is located east of the Bellingham Cruise Terminal and transient linear moorage. The boatyard dock is used for staging in preparation for Travelift haulout.

㉑ **Bellingham.** Bellingham is the largest city between Everett and the Canadian border, and has complete facilities for commercial and pleasure craft. Moorage, fuel, marine supplies, and repairs are available at the Port of Bellingham's Squalicum Harbor. Bellingham Yacht Club and Squalicum Yacht Club are nearby. BYC has moorage for members of reciprocal yacht clubs.

Charming Hotel Bellwether is near the mouth of the Squalicum Harbor south basin, adjacent to the Marina Restaurant and shops. The port runs a courtesy shuttle to downtown grocery stores, and the historic Fairhaven area shops and restaurants.

Mooring buoys and a linear moorage system are at Fairhaven, in the south part of Bellingham Bay. Fairhaven is a delightful stop with turn-of-the-20th-century Victorian buildings, boutiques, a large bookstore and other interesting shops. Fairhaven is also the southern terminus of the Alaska Marine Highway Ferry System. As with Squalicum Harbor, you can take a bus or taxi to downtown Bellingham. Many shops, restaurants and a supermarket are within walking distance in this historic area. The Bellingham International Airport is convenient for arriving or departing guests.

Bellingham's scenic surroundings and its proximity to the San Juan Islands alone would be enough to draw many boaters. Bellingham is a college town with incredible shopping opportunities including provisioning for the galley. Squalicum Harbor has comfortable moorage and is a convenient base for cruising.

165

The day-use dock at Vendovi Island provides access to hiking trails and beautiful scenic vistas.

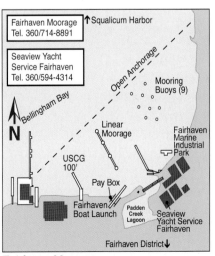

Fairhaven Moorage

THINGS TO DO

1. Spark Museum of Electrical Invention. Over 1,000 radios and many other electrical devices on display.

2. Bellingham Railway Museum. Model and actual trains, including a simulator.

3. Whatcom Museum. Art, photography, and a family interactive gallery. Downtown.

4. Historic Fairhaven. Good shopping and restaurants surrounded by period buildings. Peruse Village Books.

5. Bellingham Farmers Market. Held in Depot Square, a glass and steel building modeled after a railroad station, with beams and arches salvaged from a local highway bridge. Wonderful local vendors every Saturday from 10:00 a.m. to 3:00 p.m. One of the largest markets in the state.

6. Boundary Bay Brewery & Bistro. Across from the farmers market. Great beer garden and good food.

7. Mount Baker Theatre. Enjoy a performance in this magnificently restored art deco theater built in 1927.

8. Mindport. Not quite a science museum.

Bookstores, cafes, and pubs make up the charming village of Fairhaven.

Exhibit themes are exploration, observation, creativity, play, and of course, fun.

9. The Big Rock Garden. More than 37 sculptures in this 2.5-acre park. Local and internationally acclaimed artists represented. Near Lake Whatcom, a cab ride away.

LOCAL KNOWLEDGE

SHALLOW AREA: A shoal habitat enhancement bench (4-foot depth at zero tide) is along the breakwater protecting the western basin of Squalicum Harbor. The bench extends approximately 200 feet out from the breakwater and runs approximately 400 feet along the breakwater. White cylindrical can buoys mark the outer corners. From its outer edge, the bench slopes another 100 feet into Bellingham Bay until it meets the sea floor. Give the buoys a good offing when running along the face of the breakwater.

㉑ **Squalicum Harbor/Port of Bellingham.** 722 Coho Way, Bellingham, WA 98225; (360) 676-2542; squalicum@portofbellingham.

BELLINGHAM MARKETPLACE

RESTAURANTS, SHOPS & SERVICES

ANTHONY'S AT SQUALICUM HARBOR

Located in Bellwether on the Bay, offering spectacular views of the San Juan Islands. Serving fresh Northwest seafood from our own seafood company along with seasonal local produce - lunch, Monday through Saturday; Sunday brunch; and dinner served daily. Visitor moorage nearby on side-tie docks.
360-527-3473 • 360-647-5588 • 25 Bellwether Way, Bellingham
www.anthonys.com

ANTHONY'S HEARTHFIRE GRILL

On Squalicum Harbor in Bellwether on the Bay, offering guests spectacular views of the San Juan Islands. Serving premier northwest beef and fresh northwest seafood, this high-energy restaurant specializes in hearthfire cooking. Lunch and dinner served daily. Visitor moorage nearby on side-tie docks.
360-527-3473 • 7 Bellwether Way, Bellingham
www.anthonys.com

BELLHAVEN YACHT SALES AND CHARTERS

The premier choice for sail or power boat charters, certified sailing and power instruction, and yacht sales. Boats of varied specifications are available to suit your cruising style and preferences. Your exclusive dealer for Bali catamarans.
877.310.9471 • 700 Coho Way, Bellingham, WA 98225
www.bellhaven.net • bellhaven@bellhaven.net

LFS MARINE & OUTDOOR

Located within easy walking distance of Squalicum Harbor docks. Boaters will appreciate the wide selection of fishing gear and crab pots, boat equipment and supplies, safety supplies, outdoor clothing, boots, and rain gear, plus Pacific Northwest gifts, nautical books, and cards.
Open Weekdays 8 to 5, Saturdays 9 to 5.
800-426-8860 • 360-734-3336 • 851 Coho Way
Bellingham, WA 98225 • www.LFSmarineoutdoor.com

NW EXPLORATIONS

NW Explorations is a premier brokerage, charter and marine services company offering first class customer service in all areas. Whether you want to charter, buy/sell a vessel, or care for your existing boat, NW Explorations can help meet your needs.
360-676-1248 • 2623 South Harbor Loop Dr., Bellingham, WA 98225 • www.nwexplorations.com

SAN JUAN SAILING

A family run business for over 30 years, we strive to provide our guests with sail and power instruction, charters (sailboats, trawlers, motoryachts, sail and power catamarans), and brokerage services in a manner that consistently exceeds their expectations.
360-671-4300 • Gate 3, Squalicum Harbor, Bellingham
www.sanjuansailing.com

TRI-COUNTY DIESEL MARINE

We're factory trained and authorized for servicing the top brands covering maintenance, repair, and repower of marine propulsion and power generation. With over 100 years of combined experience, no job is too big or too small for our friendly team of professionals.
360.733.8880 • 2696 Roeder Ave. , Bellingham, WA 98225
care@tricountydieselmarine.com
www.tricountydieselmarine.com

Harbor Events

May — Ski-to-Sea -

July — Haggen Family 4th of July - Fireworks & fair

April - Christmas — Farmers Market - Saturdays

September — Sea Feast

Contact the Port of Bellingham
www.portofbellingham.com • 360-676-2500

Maintenance tips

Basic engine service: Oil change, fuel filter change, refrigeration re-charge and diagnosis, battery maintenance, stuffing box adjustment, prop cleaning, and new zincs installed.

Inspect and service the tender: check for leaks in the inflatable, have the outboard serviced, ensure that all davit and hoist systems onboard are functioning.

Electronics: Ensure that all local charts are loaded onto nav-gear, and or charts are procured. Keep an updated version of the Waggoner Guide in the chart table.

Inspect and service all charging gear: High output alternator, regulator, inverter, and genset service.

com; www.portofbellingham.com. Certified Clean Marina. Monitors VHF 16, switch to 68. Open all year, guest moorage along 1000 feet of dock in two basins. Unoccupied slips are used when available, please call ahead. The marina has 20, 30 & 50 amp power (mostly 30 amp), restrooms, showers, laundry, pumpout, portapotty dump, and fee-based Ecco Wi-Fi. Three-day maximum stay in any 7-day period for visiting boats with longer stays subject to approval. The docks in both basins are gated for security. Restaurants and a snack bar nearby. Also chandleries and repair shops.

Seaview Boatyard runs the shipyard adjacent to the westernmost moorage basin. The yard has a 150-ton Travelift and a 35-ton Travelift.

Squalicum Harbor is divided into two moorage basins, each with its own entrance and guest moorage. The westernmost has restrooms located about halfway out the main pier, and onshore at the top of the dock ramp. Portable pumpout carts are kept at the restroom station.

In the eastern basin, guest moorage is just inside the breakwater entrance. Hotel Bellwether, with its dock, is located on the east side near the entrance. The hotel is part of a larger Port of Bellingham Bellwether development with park grounds, restaurants, boutiques, and a coffee shop. Seasonally, you can buy fresh fish right off the boat. A marine life tank (great for kids) also is near the streetside parking lot. A 3-lane launch ramp, with extended-term parking for tow vehicles and trailers, is just east of the east basin.

Harbor Marine Fuel. (360) 734-1710. Open all year. Fuel dock with diesel and gasoline (containing ethanol). Store carries motor oils. Located in northern Squalicum Harbor, behind the breakwater.

25 Bellwether Way
(360) 647-5588

7 Bellwether Way
(360) 527-3473

㉑ **Hotel Bellwether**. 1 Bellwether Way, Bellingham, WA 98225; (360) 392-3178; reservations@hotelbellwether.com; www.hotelbellwether.com. Open all year, side-tie moorage along 220-foot concrete float, 30, 50 & 100 amp power. Larger boats tie outside, smaller boats tie inside. This is a classy small hotel, done to 5-star standards. Outstanding dining. Located just inside the mouth of the Squalicum Harbor east basin. Reservations required. Dog friendly.

Hilton Harbor Marina. 1000 Hilton Ave., Bellingham, WA 98225; (360) 733-1110; info@hiltonharbor.com. Fuel dock with gasoline only. Located at the south entrance to Squalicum Harbor at the foot of Hilton Avenue. Two 3 ton hoists., repairs. Oil disposal available.

Lummi Island. Lummi Island is high (1480 feet) and has no facilities specifically for visiting boaters. Anchorage is good in several places, including Inati Bay and along both shores of Hale Passage. A ferry connects Lummi Island to the mainland. Restaurants and other businesses are near this dock. The Lummi Nation's people haul their boats, including reef net boats, on the beach south of the ferry dock.

Inati Bay. Inati Bay is on the east side of Lummi Island, approximately 2 miles north of Carter Point. It is the best anchorage on Lummi Island, protected from all but northeasterly winds (rare in the summer) with good holding. Members-only allowed at the Bellingham Yacht Club outstation property (change from earlier years, when all were welcome ashore).

When entering Inati Bay, leave the white cautionary buoy well to starboard to avoid the rock that extends northward from the buoy. Stay close to the point of land on the south side of the entrance.

Lummi Island Recreation Site. Southeast shore of Lummi Island. Open all year, toilets, campsites.

Sandy Point. Sandy Point is a private real-estate development consisting of several canals with homes on them. No public facilities. Long docks serving a refinery and an aluminum plant extend from shore north of Sandy Point.

Birch Bay. Birch Bay at the southeastern end of Strait of Georgia is a large bay with excellent anchoring depths over a flat mud bottom. However, the bay is so large that it affords little protection from wind and waves. Open to the northwest, west, and southwest, Birch Bay is best used in calm conditions. Popular in the summer, you will find almost as many small craft as crab pot buoys. Large sections of the head of the bay are drying tidal areas. The cluster of buildings on the east shore marks the town of Birch Bay and the group of masts on the north shore marks the private Birch Bay Marina with no services for transient boaters.

LOCAL KNOWLEDGE

Shoal Entry: The approach to Blaine through Semiahmoo Bay is shoal at all stages but high tide. Pay close attention to the buoys along the drying bank on the south side of the bay, and turn into the entrance channel before getting too close to the eastern shore.

㉒ **Blaine.** Blaine has two moorages in Drayton Harbor. One is owned by the Port of Bellingham; the other, Semiahmoo, is privately owned and has both permanent and transient moorage at this nice resort.

The Port of Bellingham's Blaine Marina is on the east (port) side as you enter. Entry to that marina is through an opening in the piling breakwater. Once through the breakwater follow the signs to the guest moorage in the middle of the harbor.

The Semiahmoo Marina is on the west side of the entrance channel and has fuel. Both marinas have water, power, and other facilities

ashore. The Port's marina gives access to the town of Blaine and a number of boating-related businesses and a good selection of restaurants. Semiahmoo Marina has access to two world-class golf courses. In the summer, Friday through Sunday, the classic foot ferry, *Plover,* operates between the two marinas or you can dinghy between the two.

With all that Blaine has to offer, no lack of things to do and fantastic sunsets, it makes a nice cruising destination.

Drayton Harbor is a sensitive shellfish harvesting area.

No Discharge Zone. Gray water okay.

Bellingham offers extensive moorage options, marine services, and waterfront parks.

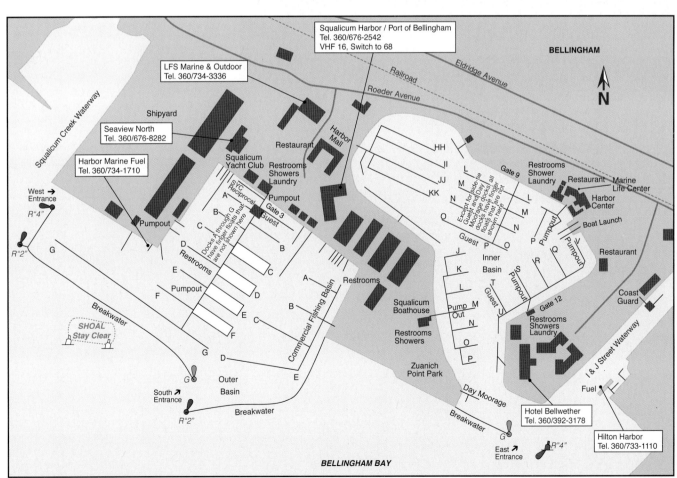

Port of Bellingham, Squalicum Harbor

㉒ **Blaine Harbor/Port of Bellingham**. P.O. Box 1245, 235 Marine Drive, Blaine, WA 98230; (360) 647-6176; blaineharbor@portofbellingham.com; www. portofbellingham.com. Monitors VHF 16, switch to 68. Certified Clean Marina. Side-tie guest moorage along 800 feet of wide dock, unoccupied slips up to 120' used when available. Services include 30 & 50 amp power, water, restrooms, showers, laundry, pumpout carts, portapotty dump, and fee-based Ecco Wi-Fi. Repairs, haulout, supplies available. Waste oil disposal. Two blocks to town. Concrete launch ramp with parking. Restaurants nearby. Courtesy shuttle to grocery store in town.

The side-tie guest (visitor) dock is served by a wide fairway for easy maneuvering. The shoreside facilities are built to a turn of the 20th century theme. The marina office is in the Boating Center building. A 65-person public meeting room, with kitchen, is also in this building at Gate 2. An attractive park with a children's playground and beach access is across the road on the north side of the spit. Walking distance to the Peace Arch at the border.

㉓ **Semiahmoo Marina.** 9540 Semiahmoo Parkway, Blaine, WA 98230; (360) 371-0440; moorageoffice@semiahmoomarina.com; www.semiahmoomarina.com. Monitors VHF 68. Open all year. Ethanol-free gasoline and diesel at the Semiahmoo Marina fuel dock, which offers a fuel discount for guests; propane, free pumpout. Guest moorage in unoccupied slips when available. One 50-foot slip is reserved for reciprocal yacht clubs. Call for availability for all guest moorage, reservations accepted. Services include 30 & 50 amp power, restrooms, free showers, laundry, pumpout, portapotty dump, Wi-Fi. Marina store with gifts, clothing, beer, wine, and marine items. Marina Cafe serves breakfast and lunch.

The Semiahmoo Resort has a hotel, spa with pool, restaurants and kayak, SUP, and bicycle rentals. It is a full resort with all the amenities. If you have bicycles on board or have rented a bike, you can ride the 1.2-mile scenic pathway to the Alaska Packers Association Cannery & Fishing Museum, located at 9261 Semiahmoo Parkway. Museum displays, housed in an original cannery building, include machinery and historic photos. Open weekends 1:00 p.m. to 5:00 p.m., Memorial Day through September.

The par 72 Semiahmoo course is outstanding. Day passes available for marina guests. Telephone (360) 371-7015.

㉔ **Point Roberts.** Point Roberts is a low spit of land extending south from Canada into U.S. waters. Although physically separated from the U.S., Point Roberts is U.S. territory and part of the state of Washington. The Point Roberts Marina is on the south shore. Enter via a dredged channel skirted by drying flats. The channel was last dredged in the fall of 2017. Four ocean-front parks, one located at each corner of 4.9 square mile Point Roberts, can be reached by bicycle. Bicycle rentals are available through Peddle Pushers Bike Rentals (360-990-0193).

㉔ **Point Roberts Marina Resort**. 713 Simundson Drive, Point Roberts, WA 98281; (360) 945-2255; prmarina@pointrobertsmarina. com; www.pointrobertsmarina.com. Monitors VHF 66A. Open all year. Fuel dock with mid-grade gasoline, diesel, propane, ice, beer & wine, fishing licenses, tackle, convenience items. The fuel dock is open daily during the summer season until 5:00 p.m., Sunday through Thursday; and until 8:00 p.m. on Friday and Saturday. Transient

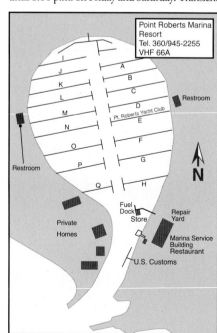

Point Roberts Marina

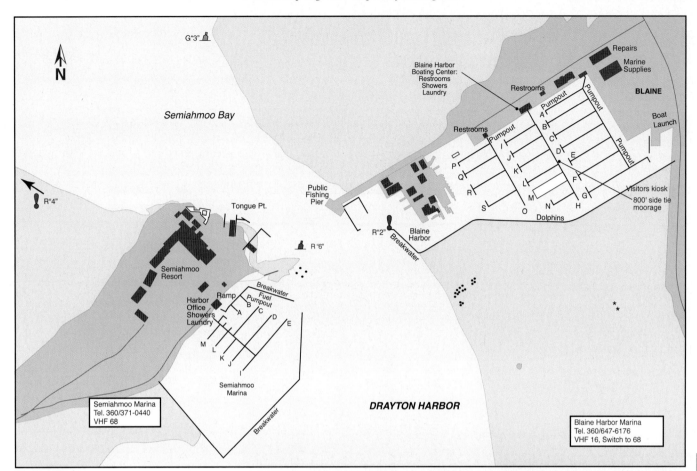

Drayton Harbor

moorage in unoccupied slips. Phone ahead for slip assignment, reservations required. Services include 30 & 50 amp power, (ELCI-protected power on some docks) free Wi-Fi, restrooms, showers, laundry, garbage drop, free pumpout. Used oil drop. The remodeled Compass Rose Bar & Grill at the marina is delightful, reservations recommended for large groups; (360) 945-7673. Other restaurants, golf and groceries are nearby. Haulout to 35 tons. Westwind Marine Services, with repairs and a chandlery, is in the main building and has seasonal hours.

Point Roberts is a U.S. Customs port of entry. The first dock to starboard has a direct-dial telephone to customs. Agents typically drive over from the Point Roberts border office. Summer hours 8:00 a.m. to 8:00 p.m., winter hours 8:00 a.m. to 5:00 p.m. Consider calling ahead at (360) 945-5211.

Lighthouse Marine County Park. (360) 945-4911; lthouse@pointroberts.net; www. whatcomcounty.us. Open for day use and overnight camping in summer, day use only in winter. On the southwest corner of Point Roberts. Anchor north of the park and row in, or moor at Point Roberts Marina and walk or ride a bike over. Facilities include boat launch ramp with seasonal staging float, campsites, picnic shelters, fire pits, barbecues, restrooms, showers, sand and gravel beach. Also a whale exhibit, playground, boardwalk, and picnic shelters. Whales can sometimes be seen from the park. A small public airstrip is along the eastern perimeter of the park.

Strait of Juan De Fuca

CHAPTER 5

CROSSING THE STRAIT OF JUAN DE FUCA

Sequim • Port Angeles • Clallam Bay • Neah Bay

The Strait of Juan de Fuca is about 100 miles long and 12 miles wide. Depending on the weather, it can be flat calm or extremely rough. The typical summertime pattern calls for calm mornings with a westerly sea breeze rising by mid-day, increasing to 30 knots or more late in the afternoon. If this sea breeze opposes an outflowing ebb current, the seas will be unusually high, steep, and close together. Often, however, the "typical" weather pattern does not prevail, and the wind blows around the clock. Or, it can be calm, even on a warm summer afternoon. Weather reports must be monitored. If wind is present or predicted, we stay off the strait.

CROSSING THE STRAIT OF JUAN DE FUCA

The Strait of Juan de Fuca has a well-earned reputation for being rough at times. It's true that a boat crossing the strait can take a beating that its crew will not want to repeat, but often the crossing can be almost flat. If conditions truly are foul, alternate routes exist. The secret to an easy crossing lies in picking your times and not being foolhardy. Routes suggested below are approximate and for reference only. They assume good conditions and the absence of current. Since current is always present, appropriate course adjustments will be needed.

Summer weather pattern. During the high summer cruising season, the "typical" weather pattern calls for near-calm conditions in the early morning when the air over the entire region is cool. As the summer sun heats the land, air over the land rises and colder ocean air funnels down the Strait of Juan de Fuca to replace the rising land air. This is called a sea breeze, and it usually develops in the late morning or early afternoon. By late afternoon the sea breeze can be quite strong, creating short, high seas, especially on an ebb. After sundown, as air in the interior cools, the sea breeze dies away.

Given this pattern, early morning crossings are preferred. Carefully monitor the official weather reports and forecast. If the morning report says the wind already is blowing 15 to 20 knots, and more wind is expected, don't cross. Wait until the wind subsides or take an alternate route.

Fog can develop unexpectedly. Sometimes it is only a thin mist, other times it can be pea-soup thick. Normally when the wind moves in, the fog blows out.

LOCAL KNOWLEDGE

DANGEROUS TIDE RIPS. Ebbing tidal currents can set up dangerous tide-rips at Point Wilson, and at the south end of Rosario Strait, at Cattle Pass, and off Discovery Island. Do not underestimate the viciousness of these tide-rips. Whenever possible, plan your passage to transit these danger spots near the turn of the tide or on a flood.

Point Wilson to San Juan Channel. The most direct route from Point Wilson to Friday Harbor is via San Juan Channel. A direct course between the two intersects Smith Island. Shoals, covered with dense kelp, extend westward from Smith Island for nearly 2 miles. Partridge Bank, between Point Wilson and Smith Island, should be avoided. Heavy kelp is an obstacle, and if the wind is up, seas are worse in the shallow water over the bank.

At Point Wilson you'll set a course of approximately 301° magnetic until you're abeam the Smith Island light, where you'll turn to a course of 330° magnetic to fetch Cattle Pass. (From Cattle Pass to Point Wilson reverse the process: run 150° magnetic until the Smith Island light bears abeam to port, then turn to 121° magnetic to fetch Point Wilson.)

When using this route, it's best to time your arrival at Cattle Pass for shortly after the current turns to flood. The current can run hard through Cattle Pass, so it's best not to fight it. Use the San Juan Channel current predictions.

If you do it right, you'll carry the last of a dying ebb out Admiralty Inlet, past Point Wilson, and well across the strait.

Just before reaching Cattle Pass, the current will turn to flood, flushing you nicely through the pass and into San Juan Channel. Since you can have 2 to 4 knots of current in Admiralty Inlet, and a couple knots of current in the strait, riding the ebb can save considerable time, even in a fast boat. The less time you're exposed, the less time you have to meet trouble.

To Rosario Strait or Deception Pass. From the mouth of Admiralty Inlet, plot a course that leaves Point Partridge bell buoy off Whidbey Island to starboard. If you're bound for Rosario Strait, stay out of the traffic lanes as much as possible. As noted above, the mouth of Rosario Strait can be filled with dangerous tide-rips on an ebb tide. Be prepared to favor the eastern shore.

To Haro Strait (Roche Harbor). Leaving Point Wilson, run a course of approximately 301° magnetic until the Smith Island light is abeam to starboard. Then turn to approximately 305° magnetic to run toward Lime Kiln Point on the west side of San Juan Island. Once near Lime Kiln Point, follow the San Juan Island shoreline north.

If you're returning south from Roche Harbor, follow the San Juan Island coastline until you're a little south of Lime Kiln Point, then turn to approximately 125° magnetic until the Smith Island light is abeam to port. At Smith Island turn to 121° magnetic to fetch Point Wilson.

Both the flood and ebb currents run strongly along the west side of San Juan Island. Even in a fast boat it is best to make this passage with favorable current. The Canadian Hydrographic Service book, *Current Atlas: Juan de Fuca Strait to Georgia Strait* illustrates these current flows in convincing diagram form. *Waggoner Tables,* published annually, provide the time schedule for the Current Atlas.

To Victoria. From Point Wilson, a course of approximately 275° magnetic takes you 30 miles to Victoria. Returning from Victoria, a course of about 095° magnetic should raise Point Wilson in time to make late-run corrections for the effects of current. In slow boats, the trip between Victoria and Point Wilson usually can be made on a single favorable tide. In all boats, utilizing favorable current can save significant time.

Even the best plan can go awry. While over the years we have made many easy

The entrance to John Wayne Marina is unusual and requires close attention.

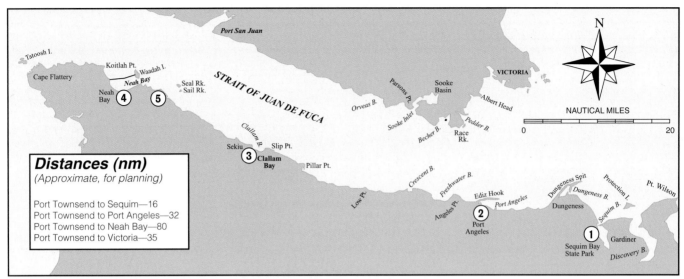

Strait of Juan de Fuca

crossings of the strait (only a few have been "memorable"), it's important to understand that conditions can change with little warning. When you're several miles offshore and the wind decides to kick up, you can't pull over until things improve.

The Strait of Juan de Fuca is not to be feared, but it should be respected. Be sure your boat is seaworthy, well-equipped, and in excellent condition. Carry plenty of fuel. Check the typically easterly flowing offshore weather systems. Let the weather and tide and current tables set your plans. Don't be afraid to wait, but be confident enough to seize opportunities as they arise.

Discovery Bay. Discovery Bay is west of Point Wilson. It is somewhat protected from the Strait of Juan de Fuca by Protection Island, a wildlife refuge. Discovery Bay is open and unobstructed, but it is seldom used by pleasure craft as an overnight anchorage. Gardiner, halfway down the bay, has a launch ramp.

Sequim Bay. Sequim Bay is a beautiful, quiet anchorage with a public marina and a state park with floats. The bay is protected by Travis Spit, extending from the eastern shore. To enter, steer for the middle of this spit, then turn sharply west and run parallel to the spit.

Actor John Wayne, who visited Sequim Bay often aboard his yacht *Wild Goose,* donated 22 waterfront acres to the Port of Port Angeles on condition that the Port build a marina on the site.

 LOCAL KNOWLEDGE

SHOAL AREA: Sequim Bay has a large shoal in the middle with passage around the eastern and western sides. The marked channel, which leads to John Wayne Marina, is on the west side. This route is best when approaching Sequim Bay State Park.

① **John Wayne Marina.** 2577 W. Sequim Bay Road, Sequim, WA 98382; (360) 417-3440; rona@portofpa.com; www.portofpa.com. Open all year, gasoline and diesel at the fuel dock, guest moorage in 22 slips and 200 feet of dock. Services include 30 amp power, restrooms, showers, free Wi-Fi, laundry, pumpout, portapotty dump, and launch ramps. The Dockside Grill restaurant is ashore. Picnic area and beach access are nearby. Check in at the first float inside the breakwater. John Wayne Marina is operated

by the Port of Port Angeles. For those desiring onshore accommodations, the John Wayne Waterfront Resort (360-681-3853) has cabins and camp sites a short walk away.

① **Sequim Bay Marine State Park**. (360) 683-4235; Sequim Bay Marine State Park occupies 92 acres along the western shore of Sequim Bay. Open all year, day use and overnight mooring and camping, 424 feet of dock space and 5 buoys (for boats 45 feet and under). Facilities include restrooms,

STRAIT OF JUAN DE FUCA GO-NOGO CHECKLIST

Tides & Currents - See Ports & Passes; Canadian Tides & Current Tables Vol. 5
- ☐ Phase of the moon – Spring or Neap Tide
- ☐ Flood or Ebb - Ebbing tidal currents can set up dangerous tide-rips at: Point Wilson, Cattle Pass, and South end of Rosario Strait

Weather System Predictions – via Internet or satellite
- ☐ Check NOAA Ocean Prediction Center forecasts for any approaching significant weather systems
- ☐ Check Windy.com, Predictwind.com, SiriusXM Marine, or Sailflow.com
- ☐ See Environment Canada and NWS NOAA forecasts for the Synopsis for East Entrance Juan de Fuca Strait, and Haro Strait

Weather & Seas Forecasts – via Internet, phone, or VHF
- ☐ See NWS NOAA Zone Area Forecasts for East Entrance Strait of Juan de Fuca, Northern Inland Waters Including San Juan Islands, and Admiralty Inlet; note wind speed and direction, wave height and interval, and trends
- ☐ See Environment Canada Forecast for Juan de Fuca Strait – East Entrance; Check for warnings, note wind speed, direction and trends

Observations & Present Conditions – via Internet, phone, or VHF
- ☐ Check Buoy Report for New Dungeness (46088); note wind and sea conditions
- ☐ Check Lighthouse and Station Observation Reports from Smith Island, Race Rocks, Port Townsend, Trial Island, and Entrance Island; note wind and sea conditions

Go-NoGo Decision
- √ Check wind direction in relation to direction of travel.
- √ Are you prepared to clear U.S. or Canada Customs?
- √ Is there a wind against wave or current situation?
- √ Are the more protected, but longer, alternate routes a better option?

Fail-Safe Contingency Plans
- √ Duck-in locations along the route: Dungeness Spit, and Oak Bay on Vancouver Is.

See *Chapter 1 Interpreting Northwest Weather* section for telephone numbers, website addresses, VHF channels, and buoy numbers.

showers, portapotty dump, picnic sites, campsites, kitchen shelters, and launch ramp. No power. The mooring buoys are in deep water. Pay nightly mooring buoy fee on shore. The water around the dock and mooring float is shallower. Watch your depths at low tide. Boarding floats at the launch ramp are removed in the winter.

Dungeness Spit. Beautiful Dungeness Spit, 5.5 miles long, is the world's longest natural sand spit. The spit provides protection from westerly weather, and convenient anchoring depths along its inner edge before an attached cross-spit forces the channel south. Shallow draft boats can continue into the inner harbor, where there is a launch ramp and protected anchorage. Dungeness Spit is a wildlife refuge and open to hikers but has no public facilities.

② **Port Angeles**. Port Angeles is a substantial small city on a bay protected by Ediz Hook. The Port Angeles City Pier, with visitor moorage, is near the south end of the business district. Guest moorage with full services is available at the breakwater-protected Port of Port Angeles Boat Haven marina at the southwest corner of the bay.

Port Angeles is a U.S. Customs port of entry. The *Coho* car and passenger ferry runs from Port Angeles to Victoria (www.cohoferry.com). It is possible to moor the boat in Port Angeles, take the *Coho* ferry as a walk-on passenger in the morning, tour Victoria, B.C. for the day, and return to Port Angeles in the late afternoon.

The outer end of Ediz Hook is a Coast Guard station. Just west of the Coast Guard station is the Port Angeles Pilot Station, where Puget Sound Pilot tenders shuttle pilots to ships bound to or from Puget Sound ports.

Port Angeles has a number of attractions.

The walkable town has many shops and restaurants to explore. The Feiro Marine Life Center, on the city pier, focuses on the marine life in the Strait of Juan de Fuca. Open daily, 10:00 a.m. to 5:00 p.m. in summers and 12:00 p.m. to 5:00 p.m. in winters. In late June, free summer concerts begin on the pier, Wednesdays 6:00 p.m. to 8:00 p.m. The Juan de Fuca Festival with music, workshops and crafts is on Memorial Day weekend. For general tourist information see the North Olympic Peninsula Visitor & Convention Bureau website: www.olympicpeninsula.org.

Farmers market: Saturdays year-round, from 10:00 a.m. to 2:00 p.m at the corner of Front Street and Lincoln Street.

Olympic Discovery Trail: The Olympic Discovery Trail for walking and bicycling, runs from Port Angeles to the town of Blyn. Eventually this trail will extend all the way from Port Townsend to La Push. Bike rentals are available in Port Angeles.

② **Port Angeles Boat Haven**. 832 Boat Haven Drive, Port Angeles, WA 98362; (360) 457-4505; pamarina@olypen.com; www.portofpa.com. Open all year, ethanol-free gasoline and diesel at the fuel dock, and high-volume fuel delivery for larger vessels. The marina has concrete docks, side-tie guest moorage, and a guest arrival float. Maximum boat length 164 feet. Services include 30, 50, and 100 amp power, restrooms, Wi-Fi, showers, waste oil disposal, pumpout. Security system with locking gates. Call ahead for after-hours arrival. Online reservations available through Dockwa.com. Excellent 2-lane launch ramp with ample room for tow vehicles and trailers. Customs clearance is available from a dedicated phone on the water side of the harbor office, (360) 457-4311. Haulout on a 70-ton Travelift. Groceries,

doctor, post office, and laundry are nearby. The Castaway Restaurant, located on the northwest end of the moorage basin, is a full service restaurant and night club frequently featuring live music.

② **Port Angeles City Pier**. Foot of North Lincoln St., Port Angeles, WA 98382; (360) 417-4550; www.cityofpa.us. Six new floats, one of which is ADA accessible, were installed at Port Angeles City Pier in 2018. Transient overnight side-tie moorage available for boats up to 80 feet. No power, no water; first-come, first-served. A self-registration pay station is located near the docks. Maximum 10-day stay.

Crescent Bay. Crescent Bay is a possible anchorage if conditions on the Strait of Juan de Fuca become untenable. A little protection can be found close to the western shore, but swells can still work into the bay and make for an uneasy stay.

Pillar Point. Pillar Point has a fishing resort with launch ramp and float but is not available for transient moorage. In a westerly the area close to and east of the point is a notorious windless spot–a "hole" in sailboaters' language. A Waggoner reader wrote to tell us anchorage is good along the eastern shore.

CLALLAM BAY AND SEKIU

Clallam Bay. Clallam Bay, with Sekiu on its western shore, is somewhat protected from westerlies and has convenient anchoring depths along the shore. A serious reef, marked by a buoy at its outer end well offshore, extends from the eastern point. Leave the buoy to port when entering the bay. Three marinas offer transient moorage.

175

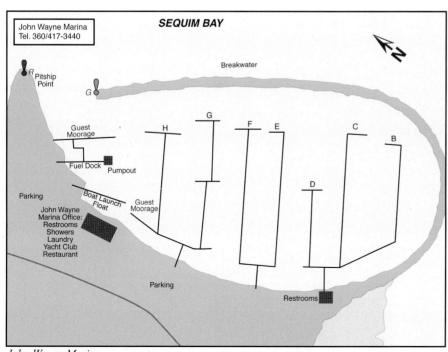

John Wayne Marina

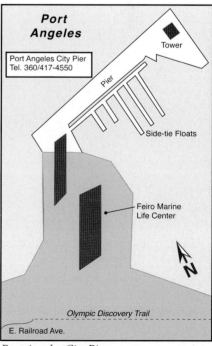

Port Angeles City Pier

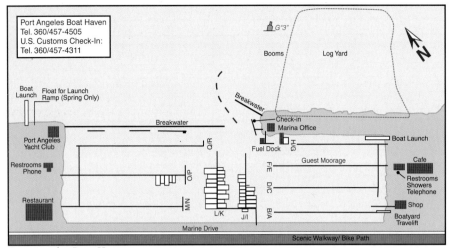

Port Angeles Boat Haven

③ **Van Riper's Resort.** P.O. Box 246, 280 Front Street, Sekiu, WA 98381; (360) 963-2334; www.vanripersresort.com. Open summers, closed winters. Guest moorage on five docks with 450 feet each. Facilities include restrooms, showers, free Wi-Fi, campground, concrete launch ramp. No power. Boat and motor rentals, charter service, ice, groceries, charts, and books. Nearby post office, restaurant and bar, and marine supplies.

③ **Olson's Resort.** P.O. Box 216, 444 Front St., Sekiu, WA 98381; (360) 963-2311. Open March through September. Gasoline and diesel at the fuel dock. Guest moorage in 300 slips behind a breakwater, 35-foot maximum boat length. No power. Services include restrooms, showers, laundry, 3-lane concrete launch ramp, and Wi-Fi near the office. Motel units available. Busy during salmon season. After 80 years of family ownership, the Olson family sold the resort in late 2014. The Mason family now owns and operates the resort.

③ **Curley's Resort.** P.O. Box 265, Sekiu, WA 98381; (360) 963-2281; (800) 542-9680; www.curleysresort.com. Open May through September, guest moorage while staying in one of the cabins. 750 feet of dock space, 30-foot maximum boat length. This is a private resort with moorage, motel rooms, and cabins for rent. Pets must remain on the boat.

NEAH BAY

The Makah Tribe town of Neah Bay is popular with sport fishermen, who trailer their boats in during the summer. It's also a good place to wait for a favorable weather window to round Cape Flattery and head down the Pacific Coast. Most boats bound to or from Barkley Sound, however, choose to stay along the Vancouver Island side of the Strait of Juan de Fuca. For cruising boats that do stop, moorage is at the Makah Marina docks, managed by Big Salmon Resort.

A long breakwater connects the mainland and Waadah Island, blocking ocean waves from getting in. Anchorage is good, sand bottom, throughout the bay. A second breakwater protects the Makah Marina. The Coast Guard station at the entrance to the bay serves the west end of the Strait of Juan de Fuca and the northern Pacific Ocean coast.

Neah Bay is not a U.S. Customs port of entry, although entrants with Nexus cards may be able to phone in for clearance. Those without Nexus must clear at a designated port of entry. Port Angeles is the nearest location.

The Makah Cultural & Research Center Museum features artifacts from the Ozette archaeological dig site. The museum is world-

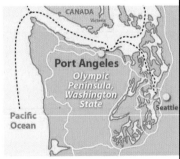

class—a must see. The Ozette dig unearthed a village site buried by a mudslide 500 years ago, before European contact. It is a time capsule of coastal Native life. The tools, clothing, furniture, weapons, and fishing implements are exquisitely preserved and displayed.

Neah Bay's general store is well-stocked, except for spirits. Neah Bay is dry.

④ **Makah Marina**. P.O. Box 137, Neah Bay, WA 98357; (360) 645-3015. www.makah.com/activities/marina Open all year, guest moorage, 30 & 50 amp power, free Wi-Fi, potable water, restrooms, showers, laundry nearby, pumpout station, portapotty dump, 2-lane launch ramp with extended parking available for tow vehicles and trailers. Summertime visitor moorage is managed by Big Salmon Resort, see listing below. Shopping (on the rough and ready side) and lodging are nearby. The extraordinary Makah Museum is an easy walk.

The marina is spacious and well-built. The concrete docks are stable, and each mooring slip is served by sturdy mooring cleats. The slips and the fairways between docks are wide. On shore, the administration building

Totems at Makah Cultural Center

has restrooms and showers. Summertime moorage can be crowded with commercial boats and their gear, however, so don't expect a resort environment.

④ **Big Salmon Resort**. P.O. Box 140, 1251 Bay View Ave., Neah Bay, WA 98357;

(360) 645-2374; (866) 787-1900; www.bigsalmonresort.net. Open April 1 to September 15. Gasoline and diesel at fuel dock. Pumpout. Haulout to 30 tons and 2-lane concrete launch ramp with long-term parking. Guest moorage at Makah Marina. A small store carries tackle, some groceries, local charts. Motels are nearby.

If the fuel dock is closed for the season, fuel is available at the Makah Mini Mart's commercial dock just beyond the commercial fish offloading pier.

⑤ **Snow Creek Resort**. P.O. Box 248, Mile Marker 691, Hwy 112, Neah Bay, WA 98357; (360) 645-2284; snowcreek@gmail.com. Open from April 15 to October 1. Guest moorage for up to 40 boats plus 25 buoys. Maximum boat size 26 feet. Restrooms, showers, campsites and RV parking, cabins, limited groceries, diving air, haulout, beach launch, and hoist launch.

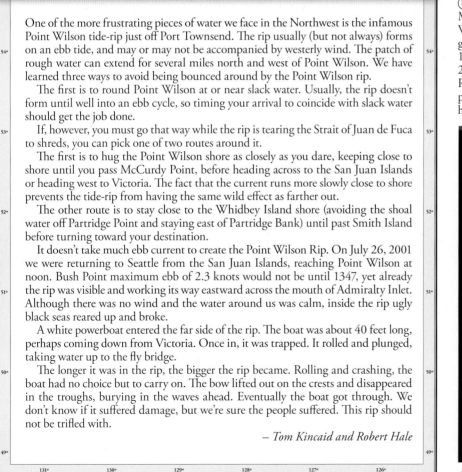

THE POINT WILSON RIP

One of the more frustrating pieces of water we face in the Northwest is the infamous Point Wilson tide-rip just off Port Townsend. The rip usually (but not always) forms on an ebb tide, and may or may not be accompanied by westerly wind. The patch of rough water can extend for several miles north and west of Point Wilson. We have learned three ways to avoid being bounced around by the Point Wilson rip.

The first is to round Point Wilson at or near slack water. Usually, the rip doesn't form until well into an ebb cycle, so timing your arrival to coincide with slack water should get the job done.

If, however, you must go that way while the rip is tearing the Strait of Juan de Fuca to shreds, you can pick one of two routes around it.

The first is to hug the Point Wilson shore as closely as you dare, keeping close to shore until you pass McCurdy Point, before heading across to the San Juan Islands or heading west to Victoria. The fact that the current runs more slowly close to shore prevents the tide-rip from having the same wild effect as farther out.

The other route is to stay close to the Whidbey Island shore (avoiding the shoal water off Partridge Point and staying east of Partridge Bank) until past Smith Island before turning toward your destination.

It doesn't take much ebb current to create the Point Wilson Rip. On July 26, 2001 we were returning to Seattle from the San Juan Islands, reaching Point Wilson at noon. Bush Point maximum ebb of 2.3 knots would not be until 1347, yet already the rip was visible and working its way eastward across the mouth of Admiralty Inlet. Although there was no wind and the water around us was calm, inside the rip ugly black seas reared up and broke.

A white powerboat entered the far side of the rip. The boat was about 40 feet long, perhaps coming down from Victoria. Once in, it was trapped. It rolled and plunged, taking water up to the fly bridge.

The longer it was in the rip, the bigger the rip became. Rolling and crashing, the boat had no choice but to carry on. The bow lifted out on the crests and disappeared in the troughs, burying in the waves ahead. Eventually the boat got through. We don't know if it suffered damage, but we're sure the people suffered. This rip should not be trifled with.

– Tom Kincaid and Robert Hale

A tribal mask in the Makah Museum at Neah Bay

OZETTE – EXCAVATING A MAKAH WHALING VILLAGE
- By Ruth Kirk

Publisher: University of Washington Press; ISBN: 9780295994628

If you have marveled at the 300-500-year-old artifacts at the Makah Museum in **Neah Bay**, you won't want to miss reading Ruth Kirk's book in which she describes these discoveries and the excavation methods used to uncover Native houses and their contents at Ozette, buried in a mudflow around 1700.

Makah Natives were forced to leave their year-round whaling village at **Ozette** and settle 16 miles north in Neah Bay so that their children could attend school, a requirement by the Federal Government, begun in the 1920's. In 1966, storm waves were beginning to undercut and expose artifacts at Ozette; the Makah tribe contacted archaeologist Richard Daughtery, a PhD faculty member at Washington State University. Daughtery had conducted extensive midden surveys in 1947 along the West Coast and was a logical choice to call upon for assistance. The wet sea banks fit the ancient Makah oral tradition of a mudflow that swept into the village one night, knocking down houses and burying them.

After Daughtery's visit in 1966, efforts to excavate the site at Ozette began almost immediately; 30 archaeology students were recruited from around the U.S and Canada; high school and college-age Makah students were also given the opportunity to work at the site. Students unearthed 72 artifacts in a single day. By the end of July 1966, more than 2,000 items had been found, and by late August the count was more than 4,000. Unearthed artifacts included hats, baskets, wood carvings, tools and other household items. Radiocarbon dating indicated that an earlier village was 1,600 years old. Trench walls were mapped and recorded, and monolith sections were lifted out to study time periods. When a buried house was discovered, it became clear that it would take many years to excavate the entire site. The mudflow or "wet site" capped by clay, had preserved the houses and their contents.

Excavation of the site was interrupted for three years while additional funds for the project were being sought. The additional challenge of the "wet site" required new and different techniques. So as not to destroy the houses and artifacts by conventional digging, hydraulic excavation was required. The mudflow deposit was so deep that the hydraulic excavation was on a scale never before attempted by archaeologists; a partial solution was to use fire hoses to pump water from the ocean. Structural elements of the first house discovered were carefully unearthed and studied along with household furnishings and personal possessions. By spring 1971, almost 5,000 artifacts had been recovered; by summer's end of 1972, 13,000 artifacts and pieces of artifacts had been flown to the laboratory and storage facility at **Neah Bay**. By 1976, the number of artifacts had grown to 40,000 and awareness of the Ozette project had spread worldwide. Bowls, looms, benches, woven mats, seal clubs, and harpoon pouches were among the many items discovered. A second house revealed infant cradles, children's toys, and a copper pendent. A third house revealed a three-quarter ton support post and a lovely feast dish. Five other homes were subsequently located and mapped.

The excavation of the Ozette site is as fascinating as the artifacts themselves. Author Ruth Kirk, who had lived on the **Olympic Peninsula** and became the wife of archaeologist Richard Daughtery, documents the excavation in her book and describes the extraordinary artifacts found, and their cultural significance. Her long-awaited book was published in 2015 and is an easy read for the lay person.

San Juan Islands

CHAPTER 6

SAN JUAN ISLAND
Friday Harbor • Roche Harbor • Garrison Bay

LOPEZ ISLAND
Fisherman Bay • Spencer Spit • Watmough Bay

ORCAS ISLAND
Eastsound • Deer Harbor • Rosario Resort

Blakely Island • Sucia Island • Jones Island
Shaw Island • Stuart Island • James Island

See Area Map Page 181 - Maps Not for Navigation

The world-famous **San Juan Islands** are the dream destination for thousands of boaters each year. The scenery is stunning, the fishing is good, the anchorages are plentiful, and the amenities—marine resorts, settlements, villages and towns—are many and varied. The islands contain large flocks of bald eagles. Sailing in the company of porpoises and whales is almost commonplace.

The San Juans have a feel about them that is different from most other coastal cruising areas. In the San Juans we don't just head down the coast to another bay, or out to a little clutch of islets for the night. Instead, we are cruising among the peaks of a majestic sunken mountain range, and each island peak is different from the others. We've truly left the bustle of civilization behind and found a corner of paradise.

The San Juans have so much to see and do that a first-time visitor can be overwhelmed. We have a short list of stops that we recommend. They are not the only places to experience, but nothing like them exists anywhere else. Our short list is as follows: Rosario Resort, Roche Harbor, English Camp (Garrison Bay), Stuart Island (Prevost Harbor and Reid Harbor), Sucia Island, Friday Harbor. You will make many other stops as well. But these six are highly recommended, especially for the first-time visitor, or when you have guests.

Rosario Resort is a mansion and estate built in the early 1900s by Robert Moran, a turn-of-the-20th-century pioneer ship builder. The facilities include a luxury resort hotel and marina. Roche Harbor is another century-old monument, this one built around limestone quarrying. It's now a deluxe resort and a not to be missed experience. English Camp is at Garrison Bay, a short distance from Roche Harbor. This is where the British garrison was stationed during the historic 1859–1872 Pig War. The blockhouse, formal gardens, and several buildings remain. They are now a National Historical Park, with an interpretive center. You can anchor in the bay and visit by dinghy.

Stuart Island is a gem. In both Prevost Harbor and Reid Harbor you can anchor, tie to a mooring buoy, or moor on the coveted, but space-limited, State Park docks. Whichever you do, you will be surrounded by beauty. A hike along a well-marked, up-and-down trail leads to the dirt road that runs out to Turn Point Lighthouse. Along the way are the Stuart Island one-room school, library, and museum.

Sucia Island, with its weather- and water-sculpted sandstone, its fossils and fascinating shoreline, is the definitive anchorage of the San Juans. The problem will be choosing which of Sucia Island's five bays to stay in.

Friday Harbor is a lovely little town where you can browse the shops, or enjoy one of the many restaurants or pubs. Friday Harbor is the commercial hub of the San Juans, with more services than any other destination.

No, we've not mentioned the charming village of Eastsound on Orcas Island, or

The San Juan Islands are understandably popular. The scenery is impressive.

Lopez Village on Lopez Island, or the Shaw General Store at the Shaw Island ferry landing, or Spencer Spit, or a dozen other delightful places to see, although we certainly describe them in detail later in the chapter. This is the problem with the San Juans. There are so many choices.

Although summertime tourism is a major industry in the San Juan Islands, the settlements have retained a small village atmosphere. Minutes out of town, you will be on winding roads in pastoral farm country. Island people are easygoing and friendly, and many of them are highly accomplished. Movie stars and industrialist families have estates there. The late author Ernest Gann lived on San Juan Island. One famous author's book bio says simply that he lives on an island. What it doesn't say is that the island is in the San Juans.

Drinking water is in short supply in the San Juan Islands. In almost every case you'll find no water for boat washing. Go to the San Juans with full water tanks, and conserve while you are there.

Personal Watercraft Restriction: Because some people were hot-dogging on their PWCs and harassing whales and other wildlife, San Juan County has banned PWC use in the San Juan Islands.

San Juan Islands National Wildlife Refuge: The San Juan Islands National Wildlife Refuge consists of 83 islands, islets, rocks and reefs. Boaters must remain 200 yards offshore from any refuge property.

Getting to the San Juan Islands. If you are approaching from the east, you'll enter the San Juans through one of four passes: Lopez Pass, Thatcher Pass, Peavine Pass, or Obstruction Pass.

At times the waters outside these passes can be turbulent, dangerously so, the result of tidal current and wind opposing each other. Be sure you have a complete tide and current book, and are able to read it. You can't go wrong with the official government publications, but our preferred tide book is

Ports and Passes, available at marine supply stores or www.WaggonerGuide.com. Ports and Passes uses a tabular format, covering the area from Olympia to the Alaska border and is corrected for Daylight Saving Time.

① **James Island Marine State Park.** (360) 376-2073; Open all year for day use, overnight mooring, and camping. James Island is a favorite spot, with trails to hike and wildlife to view. Visiting boats can use both sides of the 128-foot-long float located on the west side of the island. The float was extended and the pilings upgraded in 2018. Toilets, no power or water. Strong currents and a rocky bottom make anchoring difficult in the west cove, use the float.

The east cove is exposed to wakes from passing traffic in Rosario Strait, but has 4 mooring buoys for boats 45 feet or less. Self-register and pay nightly mooring buoy fee on shore. The park has a picnic shelter and 13 primitive campsites. A Cascadia Marine Trail campsite is at Pocket Cove (high bank gravel beach). Excellent hiking, picnicking, scuba diving. Pack out all garbage. If at the dock, raccoons will go aboard unattended boats if

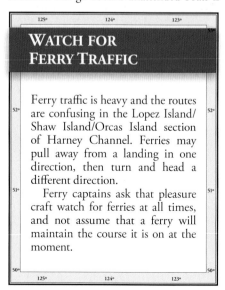

WATCH FOR FERRY TRAFFIC

Ferry traffic is heavy and the routes are confusing in the Lopez Island/ Shaw Island/Orcas Island section of Harney Channel. Ferries may pull away from a landing in one direction, then turn and head a different direction.

Ferry captains ask that pleasure craft watch for ferries at all times, and not assume that a ferry will maintain the course it is on at the moment.

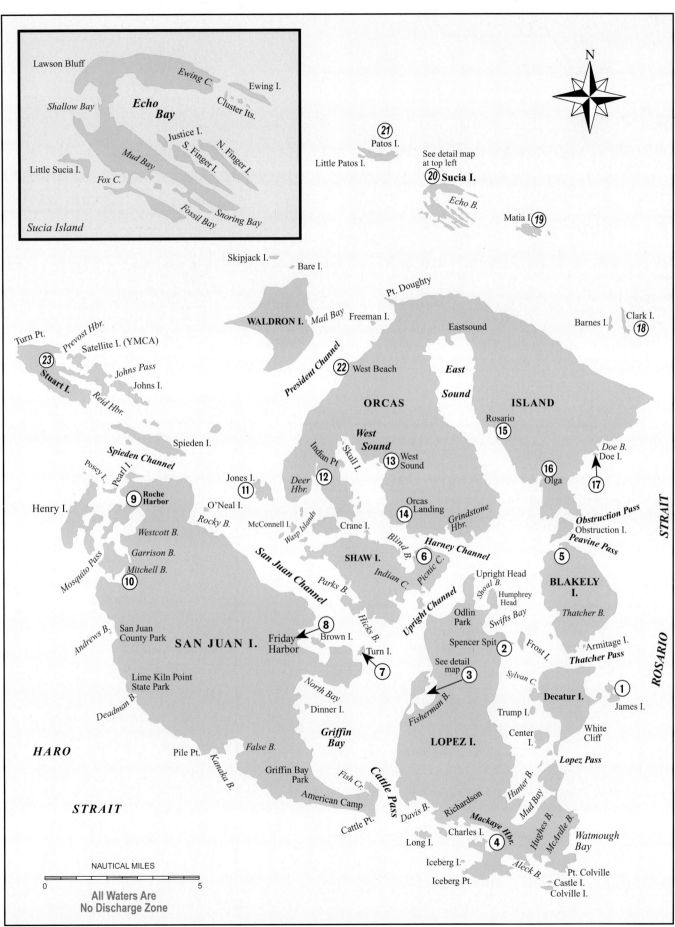

Lawson Bluff

Ewing C.

Ewing I.

Echo
Bay

Cluster Its.

Shallow Bay

Justice I.

N. Finger I.

S. Finger I.

Little Sucia I.

Mud Bay

Fox C.

Snoring Bay

Fossil Bay

Sucia Island

N

㉑ Patos I.

Little Patos I.

See detail map
at top left

⑳ **Sucia I.**

Echo B.

Matia I ⑲

Skipjack I.

Bare I.

Barnes I.

Clark I.

⑱

Pt. Doughty

WALDRON I.

Mail Bay

Freeman I.

Eastsound

Turn Pt.

Prevost Hbr.

Satellite I. (YMCA)

East
Sound

Johns Pass

President Channel

㉒ West Beach

ORCAS

ISLAND

㉓

Stuart I.

Johns I.

Reid Hbr.

Rosario

⑮

West
Sound

Spieden I.

Doe B.
Doe I.

Spieden Channel

Indian Pt

Skull I.

⑬ West
Sound

Posey I.

Pearl I.

Jones I.

Deer
Hbr.

⑫

⑯

Olga

⑨ **Roche**
Harbor

⑪

O'Neal I.

Orcas
Landing

⑭

Grindstone
Hbr.

⑰

Henry I.

Rocky B.

McConnell I.

Wasp Islands

Crane I.

Obstruction Pass

Obstruction I.

Westcott B.

Blind B.

Harney Channel

Peavine Pass

Garrison B.

Mosquito Pass

Mitchell B.

SHAW I.

⑥

Picnic C.

⑤

BLAKELY
I.

⑩

Indian C.

Upright Head

San Juan Channel

Parks B.

Upright Channel

Shoal B.

Humphrey
Head

Thatcher B.

Hicks B.

Odlin
Park

Swifts Bay

Andrews B.

San Juan
County Park

SAN JUAN I.

⑧

Brown I.

Spencer Spit

Frost I.

Armitage I.

Friday
Harbor

Turn I.

②

Thatcher Pass

⑦

See detail
map

③

Sylvan C.

Decatur I.

①

Lime Kiln Point
State Park

North Bay

Dinner I.

Fisherman B.

Trump I.

James I.

Deadman B.

LOPEZ I.

Center
I.

White
Cliff

HARO

Pile Pt.

False B.

Griffin
Bay

Lopez Pass

Kanaka B.

Griffin Bay
Park

Fish Cr.

Cattle Pass

American Camp

Davis B.

Richardson

Hunter B.

Mud Bay

Hughes B.

McArdle B.

STRAIT

Cattle Pt.

Charles I.

Mackaye Hbr.

④

Watmough
Bay

Long I.

Aleck B.

Pt. Colville

Iceberg I.

Castle I.

Iceberg Pt.

Colville I.

ROSARIO

STRAIT

NAUTICAL MILES

0　　　　　　　　5

All Waters Are
No Discharge Zone

181

San Juan Islands

Sylvan Cove is a lovely anchorage, but the land ashore is all private.

Visitors enjoying the view from the end of Spencer Spit

food or garbage is left in the open. Best to stow food well and close the boat tight.

LOCAL KNOWLEDGE

TIDE-RIP: When the current is ebbing and the wind is blowing from the south, be particularly mindful of the tide-rips that form at the eastern entrance to Thatcher Pass.

Thatcher Pass. Thatcher Pass runs between Blakely Island and Decatur Island, and is one of the main entrances into the San Juan Islands. Currents can run strongly.

Washington State Ferries use Thatcher Pass, so keep a sharp lookout.

Decatur Island. Decatur Island is east of Lopez Island and south of Blakely Island. Decatur Island has three vacation communities and about 50 full-time residents. No public services.

Sylvan Cove. Sylvan Cove, at the northwest corner of Decatur Island, has good holding bottom in convenient depths. The bay is truly beautiful, with New England-style buildings ashore. All the land is private, as are the mooring buoys, the dock, and float that serve homeowners on the island.

Brigantine Bay. The area between Trump Island and Decatur Island is pretty, and has anchorage in 24 to 42 feet. The dock and all the land ashore are private. Center Island has good anchorage which can be found by simply cruising around Center Island into Reads Bay until you find an area out of the prevailing wind.

Unnamed Island #3 (Reads Bay Island). This island, an undeveloped Bureau of Land Management property, is in the little bay at the south tip of Decatur Island, and joins Decatur Island at low tide. Open all year, day use only. Anchor out. No fires or overnight camping. Pack out all garbage. Do not disturb wildlife or alter the surroundings. This was one of Tom Kincaid's favorite anchorages. When the Kincaid children were small, they used the concrete structure on the island as a fort.

Lopez Pass. Lopez Pass connects Rosario Strait to Lopez Sound. Currents can flow strongly through Lopez Pass and the area calls for careful navigation.

Lopez Island. Lopez Island offers a variety of anchorages and moorages. On the northern end, sandy Spencer Spit is a favorite. Fisherman Bay, on the west side, has the village of Lopez, with marinas, a museum, a grocery store, and restaurants.

The southern end of Lopez Island is indented by several bays, and guarded by rocks and reefs. The geography is rugged and windblown, the result of the prevailing westerly winds from the Strait of Juan de Fuca. It's an interesting shore to explore when the wind is down.

Lopez Sound. Lopez Sound is the large body of water between Decatur Island and Lopez Island. This broad area has easy anchoring depths with few hazards. A selection of anchoring locations in Lopez Sound affords wind protection from a variety of directions. Among them are Hunter Bay and Mud Bay. Although Lopez Sound is surrounded by private homes and docks, it's very picturesque and feels special. A variety of scenery captures

CAUTION IN ROSARIO STRAIT

Lopez Pass, Thatcher Pass, Peavine Pass and Obstruction Pass all connect with Rosario Strait. Especially on an ebb, when current in Thatcher Pass and Lopez Pass flows east into Rosario Strait, expect rougher water off their mouths. If a big southflowing ebb in Rosario Strait is opposed by a fresh southerly wind, expect severe turbulence. The tide-rips and heavy seas can persist completely across the strait.

We have seen some vicious rips at the south end of Rosario Strait. Walt Woodward *(How to Cruise to Alaska without Rocking the Boat Too Much)* recalls that a rip outside Lopez Pass was the worst he had ever encountered.

The waters between Guemes Channel and Thatcher Pass can be rough or even dangerous in these conditions (southflowing ebb in Rosario Strait opposed by fresh southerly wind). Guemes Channel enters Rosario Strait from the east, and Thatcher Pass enters from the west. Bellingham Channel angles in from the northeast. The conflict of the four currents, combined with the opposing wind, creates confused, high and steep beam seas as you cross. It seems that all experienced local yachting families (ourselves included) have their own horror stories of crossings in such conditions.

We have learned to treat Rosario Strait with great respect. Thus, one year when a 20-knot southerly was blowing, we left the San Juans for Seattle via Peavine Pass, at the north end of Blakely Island. As we suspected, Rosario Strait was rough, especially to the south. We angled northward and eastward across the top of Cypress Island, and looked down Bellingham Channel. It too was a mass of whitecaps.

So we continued eastward, and found calm water on the east side of Guemes Island. Our route plan back to Seattle then went past La Conner and south through Saratoga Passage. It was longer and slower than a fast run across the Strait of Juan de Fuca and down Admiralty Inlet, but it was unruffled.

– Robert Hale

Hunter Bay is a popular, scenic anchorage on the southwest corner of Lopez Sound.

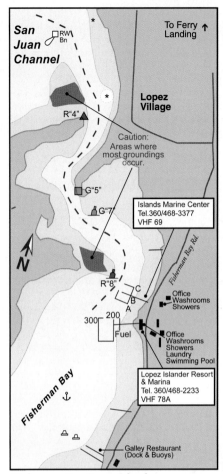

Fisherman Bay, Lopez Island

the mind's eye, everything from wind swept slopes and rocky beaches, to tree-covered hillsides and open pastures. Crabbing and clamming are popular local past-times.

Mud Bay. South end of Lopez Sound. This large bay has ample room for anchoring with good holding in 12 - 14 feet over a mud bottom. Watch your depths, charted shallow areas in the bay. Good protection except in strong northeast and southeast winds. Buoys in the bay are private. Tiny Mud Bay County Park (360) 378-8420, located along the southeast side of the bay, is open all year for daytime use. No shore side signage at the park. The park beach is a popular departure point for kayakers. Clamming on the mud flats is reported to be good.

Hunter Bay. Southwest corner of Lopez Sound. Hunter Bay is a good place to anchor, consistent depths of 15 feet over a mud bottom. The bay is surrounded by forest and protected from all but northeast winds. Located on the southeast side of the bay, just south of Crab Island, is a public launch ramp and public pier with a 45-foot float for day use, no overnight moorage.

② **Spencer Spit Marine State Park.** 521 A. Bakerview Road, Lopez Island, WA 98261; (360) 468-2251; www.parks.wa.gov. On the northeastern shore of Lopez Island. Open all year, day use and overnight mooring and

camping. The park has 12 mooring buoys; self-register and pay nightly mooring buoy fee on shore. The buoys, for boats 45 feet and under, typically fill up quickly during the summer, but anchoring is good. Restrooms are located upland, no showers. Restrooms are closed from the end of October to March. Water is available at the bottom of the trail to the uplands.

Spencer Spit is a popular park. A saltwater lagoon, fed from the north side, is in the middle of the spit. If you are on the north side, you must walk around the tip of the spit and back down the south side to get to the upland areas of the park. The park has standard and primitive campsites. To reserve a campsite call (888) 226-7688. Rabbits abound, and interpretive signs aid exploration. Spencer Spit is a Cascadia Marine Trail campsite. Although the pass between Spencer Spit and Frost Island is narrow, it is deep and safe.

Swifts Bay. Swifts Bay, behind Flower Island and Leo Reef, is shallow, but a usable anchorage in settled weather. Anchor on a sand bottom in 10 to 20 feet.

Shoal Bay. Shoal Bay indents the northern tip of Lopez Island between Humphrey Head and Upright Head offering good, fairly protected anchorage. We think the best spot is behind the breakwater and off the private marina along the east shore. Numerous crab pot floats must be avoided in picking an anchorage.

LOCAL KNOWLEDGE

SHOAL ENTRY: The entrance to Fisherman Bay should not be attempted by deep draft boats at less than half tide.

③ **Fisherman Bay.** Fisherman Bay extends southward about 1.5 miles into the western shore of Lopez Island. The entrance is winding and shallow. About 200 yards off the entrance, a non-lateral sector light marks the center of the entrance channel; you can pass

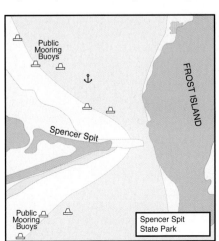

Spencer Spit State Park

Large Mud Bay, on the south end of Lopez Sound, has ample room for many boats at anchor; mooring buoys in the bay are private.

on either side, but stay close to remain in the deepest water. Caution: watch for the charted rock awash approaching red Daybeacon 4. Leave this beacon to starboard, then follow the well-marked channel into the bay. Cutting any of the corners risks grounding.

The northernmost marina in Fisherman Bay belongs to Islands Marine Center. The docks next door belong to the Lopez Islander Resort. About one-half mile south of the Lopez Islander, the Galley Restaurant, (360) 468-2874, has two mooring buoys and a 180-foot dock with slips for boats to 38 feet; moorage can be arranged while dining at the restaurant.

Anchorage in Fisherman Bay is shallow, with a mud bottom. When entering or departing, resist the urge to cut inside any navigation marks. Departing, it's tempting to cut inside red nun Buoy 8, and there you are, aground. Remember: Red, Right, Returning, also means Red, *Left, Departing.*

Lopez Village is a little less than a mile away. You'll find excellent dining, a well-stocked grocery store, galleries, all the usual services, and the famous Holly B's Bakery.

The Lopez Historical Museum is open noon to 4:00 p.m., Wednesday to Sunday, May through September, with exhibits inside and on the field outside. A farmers market takes up an entire field at the village, 10:00 a.m. to 2:00 p.m. on Saturdays, May through September.

Keep one hand free to wave to passing vehicles as you walk or cycle the roads. It's the custom on Lopez Island. Everybody waves.

184

Islands Marine Center in Fisherman Bay offers moorage and full-service repairs.

Note: Floatplanes typically use the northwest side of the bay for landing. This is also where local boat repair centers conduct on-water testing. Consider anchoring in other areas of the bay.

③ **Islands Marine Center.** 2793 Fisherman Bay Rd., Lopez, WA 98261; (360) 468-3377; imc@rockisland.com; www.islandsmarinecenter.com. Monitors VHF 69. Open all year, Monday through Saturday. Guest moorage along 1000 feet of dock space, 30 amp power, Wi-Fi, ATM, restrooms, showers, garbage, recycling, pumpout. Call ahead.

This is a well-run, full-service marina, with haulout to 25 tons, launch ramp, repairs, fishing supplies, and a fully stocked chandlery. One view guest room available for overnight lodging. Good depth at all docks. The marina offers a free 2-hour tie-up for boaters going to the nearby Lopez Village for shopping.

③ **Lopez Islander Resort & Marina**. P.O. Box 459, 2864 Fisherman Bay Rd., Lopez, WA 98261; (360) 468-2233; (800) 736-3434; desk@lopezfun.com; www.lopezfun.com. Monitors VHF 78A. Open all year, gasoline & diesel at the fuel dock. Guest moorage in 64 slips plus 600-foot dock. Reservations recommended on busy weekends. Services include 30 & 50 amp power, restrooms and showers, laundry, swimming pool (heated June through September), year-round Jacuzzi, free Wi-Fi in the lodge. The seasonal dock store has ice, beer, wine, and bait, along with basics like milk, eggs, cheese, and snacks. Nearby bicycle and kayak rentals.

Rental kayaks are available on the beach at the Lopez Islander Resort.

The resort has a good restaurant with an outdoor deck and sports lounge, a workout facility, a spa, massage, camping, and water-view lodging by reservation. Live music in the Tiki Bar most weekends June through September. The docks are solid, and the management is attentive. Shuttle service available for a fee.

Odlin Park. 350 Court St. #8, Friday Harbor, WA 98250; (360) 378-8420; parks@ sanjuanco.com. sanjuanco.com/495/Lopez-Island. West side of Lopez Island. Located between Flat Point and Upright Head. Open all year. Good bottom for anchoring, but exposed to northwest winds. Five mooring buoys are available, a nightly use fee is payable at the park office, located up the road past the baseball field. Small float for boats 30 feet and under with a 2-hour limit, or take your small craft ashore. Campsites, restrooms, beach area and sea wall, baseball diamond, picnic sites, cooking shelter, fire pits.

Upright Channel Park. Northwest side of Lopez Island 1/4 mile east of Flat Point. Day use only. Restrooms, 4 picnic sites.

④ **Mackaye Harbor.** Mackaye Harbor and Barlow Bay at the south end of Lopez Island are a good overnight anchorage for boats planning an early morning crossing of the Strait of Juan de Fuca. Swells from a westerly wind can make their way into the harbor.

A county dock/boat launch is located at the northeast end of Mackaye Harbor. The Southend General Store & Restaurant (360) 468-2315 is located a half mile away. The restaurant is open for lunch and dinner noon to 8:00 p.m., Wednesday through Saturday. The well-stocked grocery includes a collection of local foods, art and jewelry. Docks and mooring buoys in Barlow Bay are private. Dinghy or kayak ashore at Mackaye Harbor.

Dangerous Wreck: A sunken boat is on the east side of the entry to Barlow Bay, approximately at the 2 fathoms, 5 feet sounding on Chart 18429. The wreck is visible at low tide. Mackaye Harbor is the site of a fish boat marina, and during the summer months a large fish boat fleet can be found in the harbor.

Iceberg Island. An undeveloped state park in outer Mackaye Harbor. Open all year, day use only. Anchor out. No facilities, no fires, no overnight camping. Pack out all garbage. Do not disturb wildlife or alter the surroundings.

Aleck Bay. Aleck Bay is not particularly scenic, but it is big and easy to get into. Anchor close to the head of the bay in 30 to 36 feet.

Hughes Bay. Hughes Bay is exposed, but Tom Kincaid has anchored overnight as far into the bay as he could get and still have swinging room.

McArdle Bay. McArdle Bay provides good anchorage in 24 to 30 feet, but is completely exposed to southerly winds coming off the Strait of Juan de Fuca. Lovely homes are on the hills above the bay. Just outside, the chart shows a rock in the passage between Blind Island and Lopez Island. The rock is actually a reef.

Castle Island. Castle Island is part of the San Juan Islands National Wildlife Refuge. Boats must stay 200 yards from shore to protect wildlife; no shore access.

Watmough Bay. A beautiful high sheer rock wall is on the north side of Watmough Bay. The chart shows the bottom as rocky, but we have found excellent holding in blue mud in 12 to 18 feet about halfway in. Three public mooring buoys are for boats 45 feet and under. They are free to use for up to 72 hours. The bay looks sheltered from southerly weather, but we've found waves work their way into the bay.

A pretty trail leads back through the woods from the head of the bay. A short but steep trail leads to the top of Chadwick Hill. The head of the bay and the trails are part of a San Juan County Land Bank preserve, made possible by donations from private citizens.

LOCAL KNOWLEDGE

TIDE-RIP: Nasty tide-rips can form off the

185

eastern entrance to Peavine and Obstruction Passes when the wind is blowing from the south and the tide is ebbing.

Obstruction Pass and Peavine Pass. Obstruction Pass runs between Obstruction Island and Orcas Island. Peavine Pass runs between Obstruction Island and Blakely Island. Both passes connect the inner San Juan Islands to Rosario Strait. Currents run to 6.5 knots, and can make these passes challenging. Peavine Pass is preferred, but be alert for occasional ferry traffic. The ferries usually use Thatcher Pass. Peavine Pass is their storm route, although sometimes it is used in fair weather as well.

Blakely Island. Blakely Island is east of Lopez Island and Shaw Island. Both Blakely Island and tiny Armitage Island off the southeast corner of Blakely Island are privately owned, with no shore access. Anchorage is possible in Thatcher Bay, and, with care, behind Armitage Island. The Blakely Island Store & Marina, at the north end of Blakely Island, has guest moorage. Blakely Island is private, including the roads. Please confine your stays to the marina property.

⑤ **Blakely Island Store & Marina.** #1 Marina Dr., Blakely Island, WA 98222; (360) 375-6121; info@blakelyisland.com. Monitors VHF 66A. Moorage in 12 guest slips and in permanent slips as available. Phone or email reservations a must. Fuel dock has gasoline and diesel, with a kiosk for self-serve credit card purchases from 6 a.m. to 8 p.m. during the summer months. Facilities include excellent concrete docks, 30 amp power, Wi-Fi, water, restrooms, showers, laundry and covered picnic area.

The store is open from June until mid-September. The store cafe serves dinner on Fridays until mid-August, and breakfast and deli lunch daily. Fresh donuts, made on site, are available in the morning. Beer on tap. They also carry a good selection of books and some gift items.

The channel leading to the boat basin is shallow, and may restrict deep draft vessels at the bottom of a very low tide. Other than those conditions, you should have plenty of water. If in doubt, call the marina office for guidance.

Shaw Island. The marina is adjacent to the Shaw Island ferry terminal. Resident boats occupy most of the dock space. Maximum length for short term guest moorage is 25 feet, call ahead at the Shaw General Store. It's better to anchor in Blind Bay and take the dinghy over. Tie up in a place that doesn't block a permanent boat. Wakes make their way into the moorage, either from the ferries or from boat traffic in the channel. Consider this when tying up to the dock.

Safety Note: Do not under any circumstances run the dinghy under the bow of a ferry tied up at the landing.

Stop at Blakely Island for a fresh donut and fuel. Fuel self-pay station is at the top of the ramp.

 LOCAL KNOWLEDGE

Dangerous Rocks: Charted rocks obstruct the waters west of Blind Island. While it's possible to get through safely, our advice is do not pass west of Blind Island.

Blind Bay/Blind Island Marine State Park. Blind Bay, on the north side of Shaw Island, has good anchorage throughout the center portion. Blind Island is a minimally developed state park and Cascadia Marine Trail campsite, with 4 mooring buoys on its south side for boats 45 feet and under. Self-register and pay nightly mooring buoy fee on shore at Blind Island. Toilets are on the island.

Pack out all garbage.

East of Blind Island a white daymark, installed and maintained by Bellingham Yacht Club since the 1950s, marks a rock that lies between Blind Island and the Shaw Island shore. Enter Blind Bay midway between that mark and Blind Island. The water shoals abruptly as you enter, but there's no danger unless you are close to the island. Several rocks are just under the surface on the west side of Blind Island. Transit should not be attempted on the west side without local knowledge.

⑥ **Shaw General Store.** P.O. Box 455, Shaw Island, WA 98286; (360) 468-2288; www.shawgeneralstore.com. Open 7 days a week in summer, closed in winter. Very

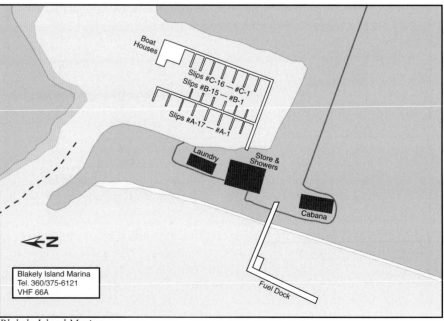

Blakely Island Marina

limited short-term, day-use guest moorage, maximum 25 feet, call ahead. Groceries, beer and wine, ice, gift items, soup, sandwiches, ice cream cones in summer, local organic produce, and coffee roasted in-house. The back area of the store is a coffee shop. Restrooms adjacent to the ferry dock.

You'll enjoy anchoring in Blind Bay and taking the dinghy over to meet Steve and Terri Mason, who have owned the store for 15 years.The store was built in 1924. It's as charming as can be, with its straight-grain wood floors, old shelving and displays, and posters and signs from days gone by. The store is a local hangout for Shaw Island residents.

Parks Bay. An excellent anchorage in a southern blow; Parks Bay is a fine anchorage, but you can't go ashore. Except for three privately-owned parcels at the north end and a single parcel at the south end, the land surrounding Parks Bay is owned by the University of Washington as a biological preserve, and is off limits to visitors. Stub

pilings are at the closed end, but there is plenty of anchoring room, mud bottom, throughout the bay. Parks Bay Island, at the mouth of the bay, is no longer a state park.

Hicks Bay. Hicks Bay has good anchorage, although it is exposed to southerlies. When entering, take care to avoid a reef extending from the southern shore.

Indian Cove. Indian Cove, a popular anchorage area has a big open feeling. Exposed to the south but well protected to the north. Watch for drying rocks between Canoe Island and Shaw Island, and a shoal 200 yards west of the southern point of Canoe Island. The Shaw Island County Park, with launch ramp, has an excellent beach. Anchor in 15 to 40 feet with good holding.

Picnic Cove. Picnic Cove is immediately east of Indian Cove. It's a pretty little nook with room for a couple boats. A mid-channel entrance is best, to avoid reefs on each side of

the cove. The head of the cove shoals to drying flats. Anchor in 20 to 25 feet. The mooring buoys in the cove are private.

SAN JUAN ISLAND

San Juan Island is the second largest of the San Juan Islands, and has the largest population. Friday Harbor, the only incorporated town, is the seat of county government.

Cattle Pass. Cattle Pass is the local name for the narrow channel between the south end of San Juan Island and Lopez Island. It is the only southern entrance to the San Juan Islands, and connects with San Juan Channel. Whale Rocks lie just south of Cattle Pass. It's easy to get close to them if you're not careful. When we enter Cattle Pass from the south, we try to favor gong Buoy 3, marking Salmon Bank, to port, and make a course for the middle of the entrance. This avoids Whale Rocks.

Shaw General Store next to the Shaw Island ferry landing serves ice cream, sandwiches and more.

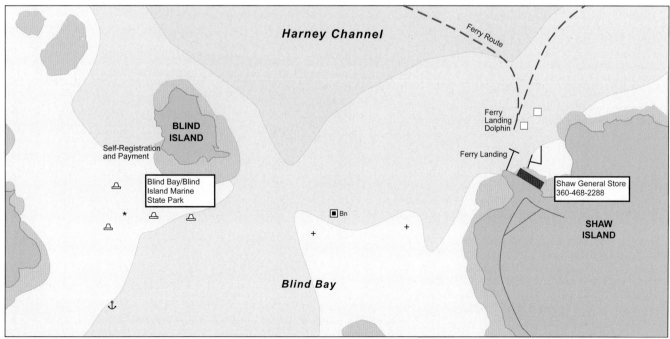

Blind Island and Shaw Island

BE WHALE WISE

Know the Law. Observing marine life, including whales breaching, feeding or on the hunt, is always a thrill to see. The diversity and complexity of marine life in our coastal waters is truly extraordinary. It's one of the reasons boaters come to the waters of Washington State, British Columbia, and Alaska. Unfortunately, increased vessel traffic and noise threatens the whale population along with other factors like pollutants and lack of prey.

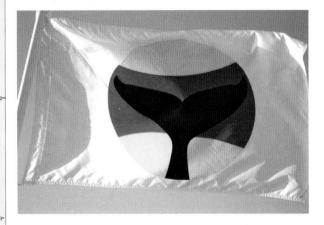

Research has shown that underwater noise and sudden loud spikes of noise cause harm to whales, including Killer Whales (Orcas), an endangered species in the dolphin family. Killer Whales are constantly on the move, traveling 70 to 100 miles per day in search of food. Boats that get too close to a whale, can prevent the whale from having a successful catch of prey. Killer Whales, like other marine mammals, are protected by law.

It is important that boaters understand the laws governing the operation of vessels near whales. Laws in both Canada and the U.S. regulate approach distances and viewing distances for whale watching as well as approach speeds. These regulations are strictly enforced by various officials or agencies of Washington State and the Province of British Columbia. Don't be tempted to speed towards a whale, or get too close, you can be cited and fined; fines can be very expensive.

If whales surface unexpectedly within 100 to 200 yards, slowly move away perpendicular to the whales' direction of travel. If they're within 100 yards, shut down until the whales are a safe distance away. Be aware that you can still be cited, even if the incident was not intentional. Positioning the boat directly ahead of a whale, including shutting down, is not permitted under law. U.S. law requires vessels give 400 yards of clearance in front of whales. Traveling behind whales should also be avoided.

Judging Distance. Keep in mind that 100 yards is 300 feet, so binoculars are your friend. Judging distance at sea can be challenging. It may be helpful to think in terms of boat lengths. For a distance of 100 yards, a 50-foot boat would need to stay six-boat lengths away, and a 30-foot boat would need to stay ten boat lengths away. For those used to visualizing distance in miles, one-quarter statute mile is 440 yards, and a half statute mile is 880 yards. Radar, especially digital radar, may be a useful tool for accurately measuring distance from an object.

U.S./Canada Regulations:

100 yards/meters No approach zone for all marine mammals; (Humpback Whales only, AK)
200 yards/meters No approach zone for Killer Whales, CN; (Southern Resident Orcas only, U.S.)
400 yards/meters Keep-clear in front of whales, U.S.
400 yards/meters No wake, slow zone; recommended 7 knots or less
800 yards/meters Slow approach zone

Enforcement. Law enforcement personnel may board your vessel if you are in violation of whale watching regulations. In the U.S. that may be NOAA, Washington Department of Fish and Wildlife (WDFW), or the County Sheriff's Department. Canadian Fishery officers and BC Conservation officers provide enforcement in Canada.

Whale Warning Flag. While being good stewards of whale watching regulations, boaters can also help protect our whales by flying a 'Whale Warning Flag' when sighting whales. San Juan County is running a new pilot project through the 2019 boating season. If you see this flag, slow to 7 knots or less, be prepared to adjust your course, and follow the whale watching regulations. If you would like one of these flags, contact Frances Robertson, Marine Program Coordinator for San Juan County, at francesr@sanjuanco.com. Don't forget to lower the flag once you or the whales have left the area.

Voluntary No-Go Zone. Boaters should be aware of the voluntary no-go zone, which runs from Cattle Point to Mitchel Bay along the southwest coast of San Jun Island. The area offers a sanctuary from underwater noise for sensitive marine species, including Southern Resident Orcas. The area extends one-quarter mile offshore and a half-mile offshore around Lime Kiln Lighthouse.

For more information, go to sjcmrc.org.

Graphic Courtesy of Chyna Sea Ventures

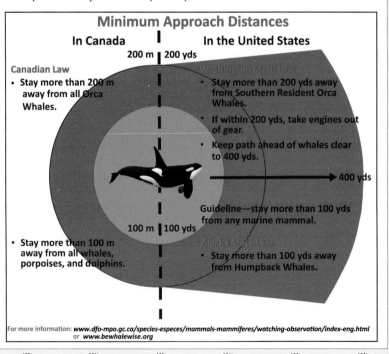

Minimum Approach Distances

In Canada | **In the United States**

200 m | 200 yds

Canadian Law
• Stay more than 200 m away from all Orca Whales.

Washington State Law
• Stay more than 200 yds away from Southern Resident Orca Whales.
• If within 200 yds, take engines out of gear.
• Keep path ahead of whales clear to 400 yds.

→ 400 yds

100 m | 100 yds

• Stay more than 100 m away from all whales, porpoises, and dolphins.

Guideline—stay more than 100 yds from any marine mammal.

Alaska State Law
• Stay more than 100 yds away from Humpback Whales.

For more information: www.dfo-mpo.gc.ca/species-especes/mammals-mammiferes/watching-observation/index-eng.html or www.bewhalewise.org

Anchoring at Turn Island can be tricky due to strong currents. Several mooring buoys provide an alternative.

After we clear Cattle Pass northbound, we've felt a definite tendency to favor the Lopez Island shore. Maybe it's just us. In any case, this course leads dangerously close to *Shark Reef,* about one-half mile north of Cattle Pass. We recommend sagging west a little toward Griffin Bay until past Shark Reef.

Tidal currents can run strongly through Cattle Pass, and the waters can be turbulent with rips and eddies. Watch out for a big ebb current flowing out of San Juan Channel against a fresh westerly wind in the Strait of Juan de Fuca. We've seen this ebb current as much as a mile outside Cattle Pass. Against a fresh westerly it will create high, steep seas, the kind you definitely want to avoid. Current predictions are shown under San Juan Channel in the tide & current books. In Cattle Pass, it's possible to run behind Goose Island and avoid foul current, but local knowledge is called for.

Fish Creek. Fish Creek is a tiny indentation near the southern tip of San Juan Island, lined with the docks and mooring buoys of the homes along its shores. Fish Creek has no public facilities, and swinging room is very restricted between the homeowners' floats.

Griffin Bay. You can anchor in several places in Griffin Bay. A stretch of beach inshore from Halftide Rocks is Griffin Bay Park, a public campground. American Camp, maintained by the U.S. Park Service as an historical monument to the 1859-72 Pig War, is a short walk from the campground. The Pig War resulted in setting the boundary between the U.S. and Canada in Haro Strait, keeping the San Juan Islands in the U.S.

Griffin Bay Park. Next to American Camp. Open all year. Toilets, no other facilities. Four campsites and a picnic area. Two inland campsites are exclusively for boaters arriving by human- or wind-powered watercraft. Vessels with motors are not allowed to moor at the park overnight. Watch for shallow water and pilings.

Unnamed Island #119. Griffin Bay, south of Dinner Island. This island is part of the San Juan Islands National Wildlife Refuge. Boats must stay 200 yards from shore; no shore access.

⑦ **Turn Island State Park.** (360) 376-2073; In San Juan Channel, at the southeast entrance to Friday Harbor. Turn Island is open all year for day use and overnight mooring. Boat access only; *land only on the west or southwest beach.* Pets are not permitted on shore. Outhouse and campsites. No fires. Pack out all garbage. Hiking, fishing, crabbing.

Turn Island is a beautiful park, completely wooded, with many trails. It's a popular stop for kayaks and beachable boats. Along the south side of the island the trees (madrona, cedar, hemlock, cypress) are bent and twisted, with much evidence of blowdown. The wind must howl though here in the winter.

Approximately three mooring buoys, for boats 45 feet and under, are placed along the west side, at the mouth of the pass separating Turn Island from San Juan Island. Currents can be quite strong in this pass, but these buoys are located safely out of the current. If you anchor to seaward of them, you will be in the current. We recommend the buoys. Self-register and pay nightly mooring buoy fee on shore.

Correspondents James and Jennifer Hamilton have anchored off the southwest tip of Turn Island in about 10 feet of depth at zero tide. Although the current ran noticeably, the anchor held perfectly. Other boats, anchored farther out and closer to the eastern mouth of the pass, appeared to have less current.

Turn Island is part of the San Juan Islands National Wildlife Refuge. Do not disturb animals in their natural habitat.

⑧ **Friday Harbor.** www.fridayharbor. org. Friday Harbor is the government and commercial center of the San Juan Islands. It is a U.S. Customs port of entry, and the terminal for ferries from Anacortes that also serve Sidney, B.C. The town swells with tourists during the summer months and has many boutiques, shops, galleries, restaurants and pubs to serve them. King's Market, a well stocked grocery store, is on the main street (Spring Street) two blocks up from the waterfront. They will drive you back to the marina with a sizable purchase.

189

Friday Harbor

Port of Friday Harbor
Tel. 360/378-2688
VHF 66A

Port of Friday Harbor
Fuel Pier
Tel. 360/378-3114

Breakwater A
Slip Assignment Station (Summer)
Customs Kiosk
Breakwater B
Guest (Side-Tie)
H
G
Guest
Guest
F
E
C
Seaplane Terminal
Breakwater C
M
Breakwaters C & D have Guest Moorage for vessels over 45 ft.
K
M
Breakwater D
Guest Moorage
J
Guest Check-In (summer)
Pumpout
Crane
Spring Street Landing Terminal & Restrooms
W
Restrooms
Fuel
Garbage
Ferry Dock
Dinghies
Guest Check-in
Showers
Port Office
Fairweather Park
Laundry
Restrooms
Front St.
Shuttle Bus
Yacht Club
U.S. Customs on First St.
Spring St.
San Juan Island

Friday Harbor

190

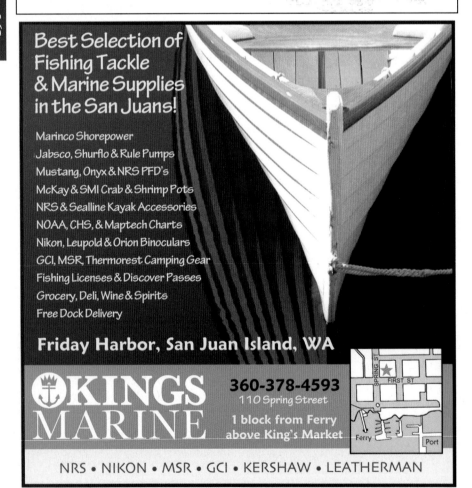
Puget Sound Express (360-385-5288) has daily passenger only ferry service between Port Townsend and Friday Harbor; operates early May to late September. Kenmore Air flies in from Lake Union and Boeing Field in Seattle, with a shuttle to Sea-Tac Airport. Friday Harbor Seaplanes flies in from their location on south Lake Washington in Renton. Check their websites for seasonal schedules.

Moor at the Port of Friday Harbor marina or anchor out. Anchorage is good in the cove north of the marina, and behind Brown (Friday) Island. Do not anchor in the cable-pipeline area between San Juan Island and Brown Island. Our friend John Mifflin cautions that the water close to Brown Island contains several sunken wrecks, "requiring diver assistance when raising anchor."

Enter Friday Harbor around either end of Brown Island. An unlighted daybeacon marks the end of a drying reef off the southwest corner of Brown Island. Brown Island is privately owned, and has its own dock and floats.

Take care to avoid interfering with the ferries and the large number of float planes taking off and landing in the harbor. The fuel dock is located between the Port marina and the ferry dock. The floats just south of the ferry dock are owned by the condominium apartments ashore. Jensen's Marina, in the southeast end of the harbor, can handle repairs. Jensen's is owned by the Port of Friday Harbor and managed by Marine Services Group; 35-ton Travelift. No transient moorage. The Port marina office can provide a list of repair people. Kings Marine carries marine supplies, fishing gear and apparel.

The Downriggers Restaurant is in a new building on the same site after a devastating fire destroyed the earlier historic building. Other businesses in the building include San Juan Excursions, San Juan Safaris, and the Rip Tide Cafe.

Bus Transportation: San Juan Transit, next to the ferry landing, has scheduled service and tours all around San Juan Island; www.sanjuantransit.com; (360) 378-8887.

Taxi: Classic Cab, (360) 378-7519; Bob's Taxi, (360) 378-6777; Friday Harbor Taxi, (360) 298-4434; Rhodes Trips Taxi & Tours, (360) 298-6975; San Juan Taxi, (360) 378-8294.

Mopeds: Susie's Mopeds (800) 532-0087 (cars, mopeds, ScootCoupes).

Bicycles: Island Bicycles Transportation (360) 378-4941.

Trolley: Friday Harbor Jolly Trolley Transportation (360) 298-8873. Offers guided rides to island attractions with hop on/hop off all-day passes.

Summer Concerts: Live music Sundays at 2:00 p.m. and Fridays 5:00 p.m. to 7:00 p.m. July and August in the small park next to the marina.

Farmers Market: San Juan Farmers Market, Saturdays 10:00 a.m. to 1:00 p.m. mid-April through mid-October in the Brickhouse Plaza, 150 Nichols St., about 5 minutes from the marina.

Spring Street in Friday Harbor is lined with shops and restaurants. Photo by Michael Bertrand.

THINGS TO DO

1. The Whale Museum. In Friday Harbor. Learn about orca whales that frequent the San Juan Islands.

2. Lime Kiln Point State Park. Watch for whales that often cruise by this park.

3. Tastings. San Juan Vineyards has a tasting room near Friday Harbor. San Juan Island Distillery, with a variety of apple-based spirits, has a tasting room within walking distance of Roche Harbor.

4. Westcott Bay Sculpture Park. More than 100 superb sculptures in iron, bronze, stone and wood displayed in a 20-acre park near Roche Harbor.

5. Pelindaba Lavender Farms. Walk through fields of purple lavender and shop for all things lavender.

6. Saturday Farmers Market. Fresh vegetables, flowers, plants, honey and more at the Brickworks in Friday Harbor.

7. English Camp. See the gardens, hike the trails, learn the history. In Garrison Bay near Roche Harbor.

8. Roche Harbor Mausoleum. Walk from Roche Harbor resort to this beautiful setting steeped in mythology.

9. Blackberries. In late summer they are everywhere, big, tasty, and free.

10. Krystal Acres Alpaca Farm. See alpacas and learn what they can be used for.

11. Susie's Mopeds. Rent mopeds or electric bicycles. Rental office in Friday Harbor 360-378-5244.

12. The "Retirement of the Colors" ceremony at Roche Harbor at sunset is unforgettable.

13. Friday Harbor Seafood. Fresh shrimp, oysters, crab, or fish for sale on the main dock.

14. Shuttle Bus Tour. Regular schedule in the summer. Ride the bus, getting on and off at locations such as the lavender farm, Lime Kiln Point, and English Camp.

⑧ **Port of Friday Harbor.** P.O. Box 889, 204 Front Street, Friday Harbor, WA 98250; (360) 378-2688; tamih@portfridayharbor.org; www.portfridayharbor.org. Monitors VHF 66A. Certified Clean Marina. Open all year, gasoline and diesel at the fuel dock. Side-tie guest moorage along 1500 feet of dock, plus moorage on the guest dock and in unoccupied slips. Reservations accepted. Only 30% of the transient space is available for reservations; 70% is first-come, first-served. If reservations are full, space may be available on the day you arrive.

The slips handle boats to 44 feet. Longer boats (to 200 feet) side-tie along the breakwaters (see marina diagram). Breakwater A has no power or water. Marina services include 120-volt 30 & 50 amp power, 240-volt 50 amp power, and some 240-volt 100 amp power. Guest docks G and H were upgraded in 2018, including new ELCI-protected shore power pedestals. Free excellent Wi-Fi, restrooms and showers, excellent laundry, garbage and recycling drop. Used oil drop behind the office, key required. The Pumpty Dumpty pumpout service is available seasonally to come to your boat for a small charge, or you can use the self-serve pumpout carts. A stationary pumpout is located on a float between C and M docks. At low tides, deep draft vessels should not venture shoreward of the pumpout. An ADA-compliant ramp connects the wharf above with the floats and slips below. A floating restroom is on the long float leading to guest moorage, dock G. A covered activity barge is available for groups or rendezvous. Ten or more vessels earn a group moorage discount. Individual boats staying four nights get a fifth night free from September 15 to June 15. Check the Port's website for seasonal specials and events.

If you do not have reservations, call on VHF 66A for a moorage assignment, but wait until you are within sight of the marina before calling. In the summer, a slip assignment station is staffed at the end of Breakwater A. A dinghy float and day moorage are available. Nearby haulout and repairs.

191

This is one of the busiest marinas in the Northwest, and the pressure on staff and facilities is enormous. To their credit, they maintain the docks, showers and restrooms quite well. Because they are so busy, when you depart it is courteous to call the marina on VHF 66A to let them know your slip is available.

Customs: U.S. Customs clearance is on Breakwater B. Tie up in the designated customs area and check in at the direct-phone kiosk on the dock. During the summer months the kiosk may be manned by a CBP agent. Occasionally customs officials will have you walk to the U.S. Customs office. The office has moved to the corner of Spring Street and First Street, about 3 blocks from the marina.

⑧ **Port of Friday Harbor Fuel Pier.** 10 Front Street, Port of Friday Harbor, Friday Harbor, WA 98250; (360) 378-3114; www.portfridayharbor.org. Between the Port of Friday Harbor marina and the ferry dock. Open 7 days a week, all year. Ethanol-free gasoline, diesel, oil, lubricants, propane, and ice.

Rocky Bay. Rocky Bay, close inshore from O'Neal Island, is a good anchorage and fairly well protected. Take care to avoid a drying shoal and a covered rock.

Lonesome Cove Resort. (360) 378-4477; located along the north shore of San Juan Island on Spieden Channel. Guest moorage

for those staying in one of the on-shore accommodations. Five adorable cabins, Boat House, and Eagles Nest apartment; beautiful grounds and lovely views of Spieden Channel and Spieden Island. Maximum boat length 28 feet.

⑨ **Roche Harbor.** Roche Harbor, (pronounced Rohsh Harbor) on the northwest corner of San Juan Island, is popular, attractive, and has a number of interesting anchorages and moorages. From the north (Spieden Channel), enter Roche Harbor on the west side of Pearl Island. The passage east of Pearl Island is shallow, and is in line with dangerous rocks outside. From the south (Haro Strait), entry is through Mosquito Pass.

Roche Harbor is one of the busiest U.S. Customs ports of entry in the country for recreational boats. During the prime summer season, the floating customs office and the harbormaster's office are located on G-dock. The customs landing area on G-dock is noted with signs on the pilings. Moor between the signs only when clearing customs. On busy days, boats tend to create an informal line on the water, waiting for room on the customs dock. Be patient. It can be a challenge to maintain a place in line among boats at anchor, especially when a good breeze kicks up. Note that the seaplane dock is near the customs dock, and arriving seaplanes will need to cut through the line of boats. One summer we watched as one of the area's large wooden sailing

schooners pulled up to the dock to clear customs. The space was much too small to lie alongside. The captain commanded her crew of high school students to drop the anchor at the right time, as she turned stern-to the dock. With an audience watching, she backed down and tied off, stern-to. She placed a 133-foot vessel into less than 20 feet of dock space, impressive.

Note: During fall, winter, and spring, the customs and harbor offices are floated inshore to the main float, just west of the fuel dock. Approach as though you are going to the fuel dock. The customs dock is to starboard, marked with signs, just below the ramp. Once tied to the dock, all crew must stay on the boat until cleared. The U.S. Customs agents are particular about procedures here.

Many boats anchor in Roche Harbor, but we've heard of anchors dragging in strong winds. Check your set and use ample scope. Anchorage is also possible in Open Bay on Henry Island, although it is exposed to southerly winds.

Bus Transportation: San Juan Transit has scheduled service to Friday Harbor and all around San Juan Island. The pick-up area is on the road across from the Roche Harbor Market. Call (360) 378-8887; www.sanjuantransit.com.

⑨ **Roche Harbor Marina**. P.O. Box 4001, Roche Harbor, WA 98250; (800) 586-3590; (360) 378-2155; marina@rocheharbor.com;

www.rocheharbor.com. Monitors VHF 78A. Open all year, up to 250 guest slips, including moorage for boats to 150 feet. Call ahead for reservations. They work to fit everyone in, even on busy holidays. Last-minute holiday moorage may mean Med-tying stern-to on the cross docks. The dock crew provides plenty of help. Ethanol-free gasoline and diesel at the fuel dock, open 9:00 a.m. to 6:00 p.m. Services include 30, 50, and some 100 amp power (ELCI-protected power on some docks), restrooms, showers, laundry, portapotty dump, propane, and free Wi-Fi (best reception is in the hotel lobby). Pumpout is at the north end of the fuel dock, or call for the "Phecal Freak," for a courtesy pumpout at your slip. Their motto: "We take crap from anyone." Tips are appreciated. The moorage fee includes water, power, pumpout, trash disposal, and use of the pool and resort facilities. Excellent management. When we visited at the end of a busy day at the end of summer, we found all the facilities, including the showers, to be clean and in good condition.

This is one of the most popular spots in the islands, and in our opinion is a must-see destination. The historic Hotel de Haro, the heated swimming pool, formal gardens, tennis courts, Afterglow Spa, well-stocked grocery store, gift shops, and excellent restaurant and lounge are something apart from the usual tourist fare. An informal café also is available. Try the Roche Harbor donuts

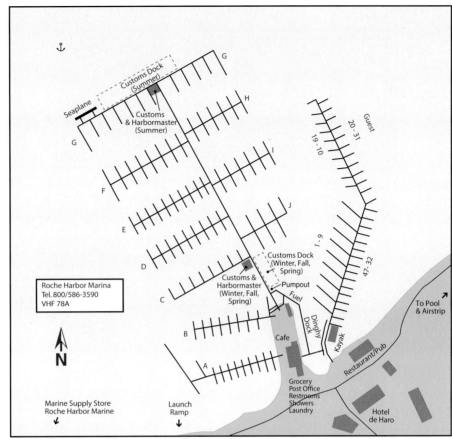

Roche Harbor Marina

ROCHE HARBOR

EST. 1886 | SAN JUAN ISLANDS, WASHINGTON

Dining | Lodging | Marina | Air Strip
Grocery & Shopping | Pool & Tennis
Formal Gardens | Weddings | Spa | Hiking
Kayaking & Whale Watching

800-586-3590 Marina | 800-451-8910 Lodging
www.rocheharbor.com

at the café, made fresh each morning.

Be sure to take a walk up to the Afterglow Vista Mausoleum. You've never seen anything like it. Another good walk is up the small mountain behind the resort, past the limestone quarries, to a lookout. The trail is easy and well-maintained, and the view is excellent. The entire loop took us approximately a half-hour. If we had stopped to smell the flowers it would have taken an hour. The hotel lobby has complimentary walking tour maps. For $1.00 they also have a pamphlet detailing the remarkable history of Roche Harbor. See the guest registry on display, and the pictures on the wall showing the history of Roche Harbor.

The Westcott Bay Sculpture Park is on the edge of the Roche Harbor property, across the road from the airstrip. The park is a display of outdoor sculpture—approximately 100 pieces—set in a large grassy field and along several trails through the woods. This description completely understates how impressive the display is. We spent an hour in the park and should have spent three more hours. It's magnificent. The pieces are first-rate and the setting works.

Major development continues on the hillside up from the hotel. Great effort has been made to design the new construction in keeping with the classic century-old style of the existing buildings. Many of the units are available for overnight or longer stays.

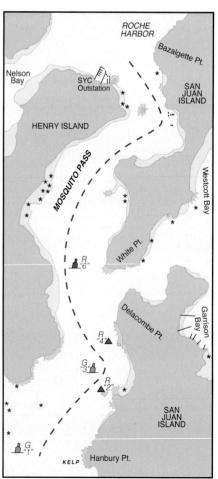

Mosquito Pass Route

SAN JUAN ISLAND MARKETPLACE

RESTAURANTS, SHOPS & SERVICES

ACE HARDWARE
Ace Hardware is your locally owned and operated hardware store, specializing in marine hardware, stainless fasteners, electrical, tools, fishing licenses, tackle, bait, rain gear and all your hardware needs.
360-378-4622 • 340 Argyle Ave, Friday Harbor, WA
www.AceAnacortes.com

THE GOURMET'S GALLEY
Since 1969 a favorite source of rare ingredients for the adventurous cook. Proper teas, teapots, and kettles. Quality tools for the serious chef. Whimsical gifts with food and marine themes. Monday-Saturday 10 - 5:30.
360-378-2251 • 21 Spring Street

ALBERT JENSEN & SON'S SHIPYARD
Brings full services back to the original site that started it all. Since 1910 Jensen's has been providing superior mechanical, electrical, plumbing, finishing, and shipwright services to San Juan Island. Our boat yard, Travelift, and certified technicians operate year-round to keep you cruising. A Division of Marine Services Group
1293 Turn Point Road • Friday Harbor
360.378.4343 • www.jesnsenshipyard.com

KING'S MARINE CENTER
Best selection for your outdoor adventure gear. Everything from fishing gear, kayak accessories, marine supplies and camping gear to sportswear, shoes & boots, sunglasses, books and more.
360-378-4593 • 110 Spring St. W • Above King's Market • www.kings-market.com

LAVENDERA MASSAGE
Rest, renew, revitalize with a smoothing massage: Therapeutic, relaxation, combo, hot stone, couples, prenatal massage. Prices: 60 min $95, 75 min $120, 90 min $135. *Clothed massage and chair massage $1 per minute.* Body wrap, body exfoliation, foot therapy, and energy work also available. Call or email to book, go to our website for more info.
360-378-3637 • 285 Spring Street, Friday Harbor
www.lavenderamassage.com

SAN JUAN ISLANDS MUSEUM OF ART
The museum is committed to promoting the arts of the Pacific Northwest and Southwest British Columbia. We offer rotating exhibitions through our three galleries, with approximately 8-10 exhibitions per year, as well as a lecture series titled Art as a Voice.
360-370-5050 • 540 Spring St. • www.sjima.org

SUSIE'S MOPEDS
Explore San Juan Island at your leisure with an electric bike, moped, Scoot Coupe, or car. Let our professional and friendly staff help plan your island adventure which includes plenty of spectacular scenic stops. Hourly and daily rates. An island tradition since 1986. Reservations suggested.
360-378-5244 • At the Ferry Landing
www.susiesmopeds.com

THE WHALE MUSEUM
Be Whale Wise! Founded in 1979, The *Whale Museum* in Friday Harbor is a natural history museum and is an easy walk from the docks. Our mission is to promote stewardship of whales and the Salish Sea ecosystem through education and research programs. Come learn about the endangered Southern Resident Orcas and other marine mammals. Browse the gift shop for that perfect Friday Harbor Whale Museum gift or souvenir. Our Orca Adoption Program is a great way to support us and makes a very unique gift.
360-378-4710 ext. 30 • 62 1st Street N., Friday Harbor
www.whalemuseum.org

SAN JUAN ISLAND COMMUNITY EVENTS

May
Opening Day Boat Parade, Friday Harbor
Memorial Day Parade & Ceremony, Friday Harbor

June
San Juan Island Artists' Studio Tour
Three Lakes Triathlon & San Juan Island Marathon, Half Marathon & 10K Day
Orca Sing Annual Concert

July
July 4th Parade, Pig War Picnic, Friday Harbor
Rock the Dock dance, Fireworks, Port of Friday Harbor
Roche Harbor Old Fashioned Fourth - Games and Fireworks
San Juan Island Lavender Festival & Summer Arts Fair
San Juan Island National Historical Park Encampment
Summer Concert Series "Music in the Park" Port of Friday Harbor (July-Labor Day)
Music on the Lawn, July - August at the San Juan Historical Museum grounds

July – August
Shakespeare under the Stars

August
Shaw Island Classic Sail Boat Race,
Jazz at the Labs
San Juan County Fair
Concours d'Elegance of the San Juan Islands

September
Friday Harbor Fly-In & Open House
San Juan Vineyards Harvest Festival
Savor the San Juans

October
Savor the San Juans
Friday Harbor Fall Farm Parade

November
Friday Harbor Film Festival
Artisans' Holiday Marketplace

December
Island Lights Festival – Friday Harbor
Lighted Boat Parade & Santa's Arrival – Friday Harbor
San Juan Historical Museum – Old Fashioned Christmas Celebration

www.visitsanjuans.com

A view of the gardens, blockhouse, and dinghy dock at English Camp National Historical Park.

Contact Roche Harbor Lodging at www. rocheharbor.com. The Afterglow Spa offers massage and other treatments for the crew. Advance reservations recommended.

Located just under a mile west of the Resort at 12 Anderson Lane, is San Juan Distillery (360-472-1532). Open for tastings on Saturdays from 1:00 p.m. to 4:00 p.m. Their specialties include gins, liqueurs, flavored brandies and small batch ciders.

A lovely bell concert rings out from the church at 9:00 a.m., noon, and late afternoon. At sundown each evening during the summer season the marina conducts a formal retirement of the colors. The Roche Harbor flag is lowered, followed by the British flag to "God Save the Queen," and the Canadian flag to "O Canada." Then the cannon fires— BOOM!—and the U.S. flag is lowered to "Taps."

Dinghy Docks: Dinghy docks are at the bottom of the ramp to the main wharf, or to port just past the fuel dock.

Bus transportation: San Juan Transit has scheduled service all around San Juan Island, with regular stops at Roche Harbor. Guests can take the shuttle from the ferry landing in Friday Harbor to Roche Harbor; www. sanjuantransit.com; (360) 378-8887.

Mopeds: Susie's Mopeds is near the airstrip; www.susiesmopeds.com; (360) 378-6262.

Posey Island Marine State Park. www. parks.wa.gov. North of Roche Harbor. Day use and overnight mooring and camping. Pit toilet, no other facilities. Cascadia Marine Trail campsite (primitive). The island is less than 1 acre in size. Water surrounding the island is shallow. Motorized vessels are not permitted; anchor out and row in. Great sunset views on the west side.

Mosquito Pass. Mosquito Pass connects Roche Harbor to Haro Strait, and provides access to Westcott Bay and Garrison Bay. The flood current sets north in Mosquito Pass and the ebb sets south, out of Roche Harbor. Currents can be strong at times. The channel is narrow but well-marked. Navigate carefully. See Mosquito Pass Route map.

Westcott Bay. Westcott Bay is a large bay with good anchorage for many boats. Depths are consistently shallow throughout but adequate. Westcott is a quiet, scenic anchorage alternative to the often crowded Garrison Bay. Nearby English Camp National Historic Park, Westcott Bay Shellfish Co. (open to the public for sales), and Roche Harbor are all a dinghy ride away. Hiking trails connect English Camp Park with Westcott Bay Shellfish Co. The public beach near Bell Point reportedly has excellent clamming.

Westcott Bay Shellfish Co. (360-378-2489). Located on the southeast shore of Westcott Bay, open daily in the summer months 11:00 a.m. to 5:00 p.m. from Memorial Day weekend through Labor Day. Retail shellfish sales. As time permits, staff will show you how to shuck your oysters. Local bakery bread, cheeses, and charcuterie are available for purchase from their deli to enjoy with your hand-shucked shellfish along with beer, wine, sodas or water. Picnic tables overlooking the bay complete this unique experience. Anchor in the bay; boaters are welcome to tie dinghies (bow-tie only) to the Shellfish Company's working docks to go ashore and make purchases. Barbequed oysters are available on select days. During the 1970's, Westcott Bay oysters were known in oyster bars around the world. This family-run aquaculture farm continues the legacy of providing quality oysters as well as clams and mussels.

Garrison Bay. Garrison Bay, the site of English Camp, is a popular and excellent anchorage, with room for a large number of boats.

English Camp National Historical Park. P.O. Box 429, 4668 Cattle Point Road, Friday Harbor, WA 98250; (360) 387-2240 ext. 2244; www.nps.gov. Open all year; Visitor Center open seasonally. Anchor in the bay and dinghy to the park dock. British troops were garrisoned here during the 1859-72 Pig

Westcott Bay Shellfish Dinghy Dock

Westcott Bay Shellfish Co. 360-378-2489

Westcott Bay

N

Bell Point

English Camp National Historic Park 360-387-2240 x2244

Historic Buildings

Visitor Center

Restrooms

Dinghy Dock

Blockhouse

Garrison Bay

Formal Gardens

SAN JUAN ISLAND

Guss Island

Garrison Bay and English Camp

196

War, and the U.S. Park Service has restored the buildings and grounds as a historical site. You can tour the grounds, some of the buildings, and the cemetery, where several people from that era are buried. Rangers are on duty to provide information, and a film tells the history. It's a good stop for families with children. Restrooms, no other facilities. A steep trail leads to the top of 650-foot-high Young Hill, for a marvelous view.

Mitchell Bay. A shoal extends from the south shore almost to the middle of the entry. A rock is at the outer end of the shoal. Leave this rock to starboard when entering. Large scale Chart 18433 shows the entrance clearly.

⑩ **Snug Harbor Resort.** 1997 Mitchell Bay Road, Friday Harbor, WA 98250; (360) 378-4762; sneakaway@snugresort.com; www. snugresort.com. Monitors VHF 66A. Snug Harbor is open all year and welcomes visitors. Maximum boat length 60 feet. Depth at zero tide is 9 feet. Services include 30 amp power, Wi-Fi, restrooms, showers, garbage drop, recycling, barbecues, fire pits. Reservations recommended. The on-site convenience store has ice and limited groceries, gifts, propane, fishing and boating supplies. Mitchell Bay Coffee has free Wi-Fi, espresso, fresh pastries, waffles and soup. Canoes and kayaks available for guest use free of charge. Beautiful cabin accommodations.

Lime Kiln Point. Lime Kiln Point is a favorite place to watch for orcas, the so-called "killer whales," that often cruise within a few yards of shore. Anchorage offshore from this park would be very difficult and is not recommended. A small interpretive center with information about orca whales is in the park. Best visited by taking the San Juan Transit shuttle bus from Roche Harbor or Friday Harbor.

San Juan County Park. 4289 West Side Road N., Friday Harbor, WA 98250; (360) 378-2992; www.sanjuanco.com. Open all year. Facilities include launch ramp and restrooms. No power, no showers. A popular park for kayak campers who can pull up on the beach.

Henry Island. A Seattle Yacht Club outstation (no reciprocals) is in Nelson Bay. Nelson Bay is shallow, so use your depth sounder and tide table before anchoring. The rest of the island is private.

Unnamed Island #40. On the southwest side of San Juan Island, approximately 1 mile northwest of Pile Point. Open all year, day use only, no facilities. Anchor out at this undeveloped DNR (Dept. of Natural Resources) property. No fires or overnight camping. Pack out all garbage. Do not disturb wildlife or alter the surroundings.

Unnamed Island #38. On the southwest side of San Juan Island, near the center of Kanaka Bay. Open all year, day use only, no facilities. Anchor out at this undeveloped DNR property. No fires or overnight camping. Pack

out garbage. Do not disturb wildlife or alter the surroundings.

 LOCAL KNOWLEDGE

DANGEROUS REEFS: TowBoatU.S. reports the Wasp Islands are the number-one area for groundings in the San Juan Islands.

Wasp Islands. The Wasp Islands on the east side of San Juan Channel are a rock and reefstrewn area requiring careful navigation. The underwater hazards are charted but not all of them are marked, and the unwary can come to grief. Wasp Passage, however, is free of hazards, and the skipper who stays in the channel will have no problems.

All the major Wasp Islands are privately owned except Yellow Island, which is owned by The Nature Conservancy.

Yellow Island. (206) 343-4344; www. nature.org. Open all year, 10:00 a.m. to 4:00 p.m. Yellow Island is owned by The Nature Conservancy and administered as a wildlife preserve. No pets. Land dinghies on the southeast beach, below the wooden Dodd cabin.

Northwest McConnell Rock. Northwest of McConnell Island. Part of the San Juan Islands National Wildlife Refuge. Boats must stay 200 yards from shore; no shore access.

⑪ **Jones Island Marine State Park.** (360) 376-2073; Open all year, day use and overnight mooring and camping. The bay at the north end of Jones Island is an excellent anchorage, but is exposed to northerlies. Boats anchoring near the beach run stern-ties ashore, leaving swinging room for boats anchored in the middle. Currents can swirl through the bay, so leave ample room when you anchor.

Normally, 4 mooring buoys, for boats 45 feet and under, are in the bay. A seasonal 160-foot-long mooring float connects to a wharf that leads to shore. Self-register and pay mooring buoy fee at the head of the dock. Composting toilet facilities are ashore. A well provides drinking water, but may run dry in late summer. Use the water sparingly.

A few mooring buoys are in the small bay on the south side of the island. Self-register and pay mooring buoy fee on shore. No dock for shore access, kayak or dinghy ashore. In the middle of this bay, watch for a rock that lies awash at zero tide. The rock is shown on the charts, but the symbol is easy to overlook. Choose your anchorage based on which side of the island provides the best protection from the wind. We've had a pleasant night in the south anchorage when the wind was blowing from the north, while cruisers anchored in the north bay reported a difficult night.

The south bay is a Cascadia Marine Trail site, with 24 campsites and several camp shelters; toilet facilities at the campsite. Look for the fruit trees of a long-ago orchard, deer

Lime Kiln Point lighthouse. Orca whales are often spotted offshore.

often go there. South bay is a popular kayak destination, with excellent views.

This is a wonderful park, popular for families with children. An easy trail connects the north and south moorages, with a 1.2-mile south loop trail branching off through forest and along rock headlands over the water. If you look carefully along this trail, you'll see low patches of prickly pear cactus growing along the way. At the north moorage especially, you probably will meet tame deer. If you dine at a picnic table they may try to join you. During the summer, mooring buoys and float space can be hard to get.

Caution: Raccoons will go aboard unattended boats at the dock if food is left in the open. Stow food well, and close the boat tightly.

Orcas Island. Orcas Island is the largest island in the San Juans, deeply indented by Deer Harbor, West Sound and East Sound. Various locations around the island offer services ranging from float plane flights, to groceries, to luxurious spa experiences, to boat repairs. The island hosts several festivals and has a seasonal Saturday farmers market in Eastsound. See www. orcasislandchamber.com/orcas-island-events for more information.

Getting Around: Car rental delivery service is available through "Orcas Island Shuttle" (360-376-RIDE), offering a variety of interesting vehicles. We spotted a 2-seater Miata with the company logo; cars can be delivered anywhere on the Island. For taxi service, call (360) 376-TAXI. San Juan Transit has shuttle bus service around the island on Fridays, Saturdays, and Sundays.

⑫ **Deer Harbor.** Deer Harbor is a quiet, protected bay on the west end of Orcas Island that is home to two marinas. Deer Harbor Marina is the first marina entering the bay from the south with transient moorage, guest services, and outstations for several yacht clubs. At the north end of the bay is Cayou Quay Marina with permanent moorage only and no transient services. The entire bay north of Fawn Island has good anchorage. A charted Cable Area surrounds Fawn Island and extends westward to the shore of Orcas Island.

⑫ **Deer Harbor Marina.** P.O. Box 344, 5164 Deer Harbor Road, Deer Harbor, WA 98243; (360) 376-3037; mbroman@deerharbormarina.

com; www.deerharbormarina.com. Monitors VHF 78A. Certified Clean Marina. Open all year. Facilities include ethanol-free gasoline and diesel at the fuel dock, guest moorage for vessels up to 120 feet, 30 & some 50 amp power, free Wi-Fi, restrooms and showers, pumpout, laundry, and floating dock with BBQ for parties and rendezvous. Air service by Kenmore Air.

The docks are excellent, and the restrooms and showers are clean and spacious. A small store at the outer end of the wharf carries groceries, beer, wine, espresso, Lopez Island Ice Cream cones, and has an ATM. A small cafe in the store serves breakfast, lunch, and snacks. Fresh donuts made before your eyes on Saturdays and Sundays. A gift store on the dock has books and items for kids. Kayaks for rent from an operator on site. Whale watching, boat charters, and fishing charters available. 12-passenger loaner van is available (weekdays only during summer), inquire at the office. We took the van to Turtleback Mountain for a hike with an impressive view of the area. We have also used it to pick up crew arriving by ferry at Orcas Landing.

A beautiful sand beach next to the wharf will entertain the little ones. At the north end of the beach, a small but lovely park has been built. The Resort at Deer Harbor is across the road. Marina guests have access to the resort's swimming pool. The Deer Harbor Inn Restaurant, a ten-minute walk north, is excellent. If you don't want to walk, you can ride the restaurant's courtesy "limousine." The entire area has an easy and relaxed "vacation" feeling. Even the quaint post office fits right in. During the busy months it's best to call ahead for mooring reservations. The marina purchased the restaurant building across the street from the marina. The Island Pie, with indoor and outdoor dining on the deck, serves pizza, beer, cider and wine.

Cell Phones: Cell phone service is spotty at the marina. A free courtesy phone is available in the laundry room.

LOCAL KNOWLEDGE

SPEED LIMIT: A 7-knot zone marked by white cylindrical buoys extends from just west of Pole Pass eastward almost to Bell Island.

Pole Pass. Boats transiting between Harney Channel and Deer Harbor usually go through Pole Pass, a narrow notch separating Crane Island from Orcas Island. Rocks obstruct the edges and approaches, and currents can run swiftly through the pass. A mid-channel course is safe. For most skippers, good sense dictates slow speeds. Unfortunately, not all skippers have seen it that way, and wakes have damaged docks along the shoreline. So now

speeds are limited by county law to 7 knots maximum. Sometimes the sheriff is there, ticketing speeders.

⑬ **West Sound.** West Sound is the middle inlet of Orcas Island, where the Wareham family's West Sound Marina offers limited overnight moorage and complete service facilities. Next to the marina is the Orcas Island Yacht Club, with reciprocal moorage for visiting members. A day-use-only public dock is west of the Orcas Island Yacht Club dock. At press time, the Westsound Inn and Cafe located upland from the public dock was for sale. It is not known if the Inn and Cafe will be open for the 2019 season.

Good anchorage is available at the head

Deer Harbor Marina

Deer Harbor Marina is a popular destination for families.

Looking east toward Orcas Landing from Wasp Passage. Watch for ferry traffic, current, and charted rocks.

of the bay (stay well clear of Harbor Rock, marked by a daybeacon). Anchorage is also good off the village of West Sound, and behind Double Island.

⑬ West Sound Marina. P.O. Box 119, 525 Deer Harbor Road, Orcas Island, WA 98280; (360) 376-2314; info@westsoundmarina. com; www.westsoundmarina.net. Monitors VHF 16, switch to 09. Open all year, except closed Sundays in the winter. Facilities include ethanol-free gasoline and diesel at the fuel dock, propane, 400 feet of guest moorage, reservations 24 hours in advance, 30 amp power, restrooms, shower, pumpout. Recycling and used oil drop. Haulout to 30 tons with full service and repairs, including an enclosed area for major work. The chandlery has most boating supplies. When approaching, stay well off Picnic Island. A rock ledge extends into West Sound from the island. Once at the marina, stay close to the docks. The water shoals toward Picnic Island.

Victim Island. West side of West Sound. Open all year, day use only, no facilities. Anchor out at this undeveloped BLM property. No fires or overnight camping. Pack out all garbage. Do not disturb wildlife or alter the surroundings.

Unnamed Island #80 (Massacre Bay Rocks). West of Indian Point in West Sound. Open all year, day use only, no facilities. Anchor out at this undeveloped Bureau of Land Management (BLM) property. No fires or overnight camping. Pack out all garbage. Do not disturb wildlife or alter the surroundings.

Skull Island. North end of Massacre Bay. Open all year, day use only, no facilities. Anchor out at this undeveloped BLM property. No fires or overnight camping. Pack out all garbage. Do not disturb wildlife or alter the surroundings.

Unnamed Island #81 (Trinka Rock). South of West Sound Marina, north of Picnic Island. Open all year, day use only, no facilities.

Anchor out at this undeveloped BLM property. No fires or overnight camping. Pack out all garbage. Do not disturb wildlife or alter the surroundings.

⑭ Orcas Landing. Orcas Landing has a float next to the ferry dock, but stays are limited to 30 minutes. The grocery store at the head of the ferry dock is well stocked, and has a good selection of wine and cheese. Other shops in the village, aimed at serving the summer ferry lineup, are good. Great sandwiches and ice cream cones, too. Be well-fendered and securely tied to the dock at Orcas Landing. Passing boat and ferry traffic in Harney Channel throw a lot of wake towards the dock.

Grindstone Harbor. Grindstone Harbor is a small, shallow anchorage, with two major rocks in its entrance. One of these rocks became famous a number of years ago when the Washington State ferry *Elwha* ran aground on it while doing a bit of unauthorized sightseeing. Favor the east shore all the way in. Private mooring buoys take up much of the inner part of the bay, but there's room to anchor if you need to.

Guthrie Bay. Guthrie Bay indents Orcas Island between Grindstone Harbor and East Sound. It's a pleasant little spot with private mooring buoys around the perimeter and homes on the hillsides. Anchor in 24 to 42 feet.

East Sound. East Sound, the largest of Orcas Island's indentations, extends about 6 miles north from Foster Point. The shores on both sides are steep, and offer few anchorage possibilities. Rosario Resort is on the east side, a short distance up the sound past the village of Olga. The village of Eastsound is at the head. Fresh winds sometimes blow in East Sound, while outside the air is calm. Anchorage is also possible in Fishing Bay on the west Shore.

Eastsound. The village of Eastsound, at the head of East Sound, is the largest settlement on Orcas Island. A 40-foot seasonal county dock is on the eastern shore, small boats or dinghies only. A 10-minute walk leads to town. Eastsound has several very good restaurants, a large grocery store, an excellent museum, many interesting shops, and on Saturdays during the summer, a busy farmers market.

The pool at Deer Harbor is available for marina guests.

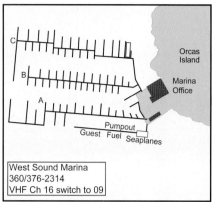

West Sound Marina
360/376-2314
VHF Ch 16 switch to 09

West Sound Marina

County Dock at Orcas Landing, a convenient stop for grocery and gift shopping. East end of the dock is reserved for a whale watch boat.

Anchoring Note: A sign on the county dock announces that the bottom inshore, from a line between the dock and the small islet off the town, is sensitive eelgrass habitat. It requests that you anchor to seaward of that line. Anchorage is possible in Fishing Bay on the west shore.

Fishing Bay & Judd Bay. West of Eastsound village and at the head of East Sound are Fishing Bay and adjacent, Judd Bay. Anchorage can be found in 20 to 45 feet of water. The bays are protected from all but southeasterly winds. The anchorage is semi-private with one or two cabins and homes along the shore. Judd Cove Preserve is accessible at the head of Judd Bay on a pebble beach. A restored stone lime kiln from the late

1800's marks the correct public beach access area; private lands are to the north and south.

(15) **Rosario Resort & Spa.** 1400 Rosario Rd., Eastsound, WA 98245; (360) 376-2222; (800) 562-8820; harbormaster@rosarioresort.com; www.rosarioresort.com. Monitors VHF 78A. Certified Clean Marina. Open all year, diesel and ethanol-free unleaded gasoline at the fuel dock (fuel dock by appointment October through April), 45-50 slips with unlimited water for filling tanks and boat washing, 30 & 50 amp ELCI-protected power, 8 mooring buoys, garbage drop with recycling, restrooms, showers, café, convenience store, swimming pools, excellent Wi-Fi, seaplane service to Seattle via Kenmore Air and NW Seaplanes. Reservations for moorage are

strongly recommended. Buoys are for boats 50 feet and under, first-come, first-served. There's room to anchor, though the sound is exposed to southerlies. The outdoor swimming pool, nearest the docks, welcomes families as does the spa-pool inside the resort's Mansion; the Mansion's outdoor pool below the hotel is for adults only. Two hours of day-use moorage is free if space is available. For those wanting to explore Eastsound or the island, car rental delivery service is available through "Orcas Island Rental Car" (360-376-RIDE). "San Juan Transit" runs to Eastsound, Deer Harbor, Rosario and other locations on Orcas Island in the summer months on Fridays, Saturdays, and Sundays.

A 200-foot breakwater dock accommodates larger vessels up to 180 feet. The outer end of

200

A collection of historic log cabins make up the Orcas Island museum in Eastsound.

Rosario Resort's new dock configuration accommodates more boats and improves access.

the breakwater is for seaplanes only. New docks in a U-shape configuration allow easy access into the marina through a center fairway. Moorage includes power, water, restrooms and showers. A pumpout cart is located on the dock. Boats on buoys pay a buoy fee and boats anchored out pay a landing fee of $25 for use of the marina pool, shower and restrooms; spa facilities are extra. The Cascade Bay Grill and Store at the head of the dock is open from Memorial Day through mid-September and has snacks, sodas, beer and wine, gift items, and limited groceries. The Grill serves great burgers, fish & chips, and casual fare, inside or out. Live entertainment two nights a week, check their website.

The centerpiece of the resort is the magnificent Moran Mansion, listed on the National Register of Historic Places. The mansion houses a restaurant, lounge and the spa. The mansion itself is also a fascinating museum (open 8:00 a.m. to 9:00 p.m. daily), a chronicle of Robert Moran's history as a shipbuilder, the mayor of Seattle, then as the builder of Rosario. Christopher Peacock, longtime resident artist and musician and now resort manager, presents a slide presentation on the history of the resort, with musical accompaniment performed on the giant room-sized Wurlitzer pipe organ. The concert begins at 4:00 p.m. Tuesdays to Saturdays mid-June through mid-September,

and Saturdays only through the winter. It's wonderful. Don't miss it. Moran State Park is about a 30-minute walk.

Figurehead: The beautiful figurehead above the marina is a replica from the wreck of the *America*, a wooden clipper ship converted to barge use. The ship went aground near False Bay on San Juan Island in 1914 while under tow from Seattle to Vancouver. During periods of small tides and slack water, the wreck's bones are still a dive site at False Bay (from *Northwest Dive News*).

⑯ **Olga.** Olga, a tiny pastoral village, is near the entrance to East Sound, on the east shore. Olga has a dock and 105-foot-long mooring float, but no power, restrooms, or showers. The float is removed in winter. A box for overnight moorage payment is at the bottom of the ramp. Three-day overnight limit. Day-use stay up to two hours. Limited anchorage offshore exposed to southeasterly winds. Numerous private mooring buoys and charted cable area limit the possible anchoring opportunities.

A sign above the dock lists local stores and locations. Up the road you will find the Artworks co-operative, the James Hardman Gallery, and the Catkin Café housed in the reconstructed Strawberry Barreling Plant building.

Twin Rocks. West of Olga. Open all year, day use only, no facilities. Anchor out at this undeveloped state park property. No fires or overnight camping. Pack out all garbage. Do not disturb wildlife or alter the surroundings.

Lieber Haven Resort. P.O. Box 127, Olga, WA 98279; (360) 376-2472; www.lieberhavenresort.com. In the middle of Obstruction Pass. Overnight moorage on the resort docks for cottage guests only. Two rental cottages along a nice sandy, light gravel shoreline. Store carries some groceries, beer and wine, and some marine supplies.

Obstruction Pass State Park. www.parks.wa.gov. Southeast tip of Orcas Island. Open all year, moorage at 3 buoys for boats 45 feet and under. Self-register and pay moorage

The Moran Mansion is a distinctive landmark when approaching Rosario Resort.

The public dock and pier at the charming village of Olga on Orcas Island

buoy fee on shore. Toilets, no power or showers. Good anchoring on a gravel bottom. Campsites with fireplaces, picnic tables, hiking trails.

⑰ **Doe Island Marine State Park.** (360) 376-2073; On the southeast side of Orcas Island. Normally, open all year for day use and camping. This is a beautiful tiny island with a rocky shoreline dotted with tidepools. A trail leads around the island, through dense forest and lush undergrowth. Toilets, but no power, water, or showers. Pack out all garbage. Adjacent buoys are privately owned. Currents run strongly between Doe Island and Orcas Island. The 30-foot mooring float was damaged in a storm in 2010. As of 2018, the dock has not been replaced. The park is still open to small boats and kayaks.

⑰ **Doe Bay Resort and Retreat.** 107 Doe Bay Road, Olga, WA 98279; (360) 376-2291; office@doebay.com; www.doebay.com. Doe Bay is an interesting off-the-beaten-path destination, with 2 guest buoys (call for reservations) and anchorage space for 3 to 6 boats. Dinghy ashore to the rocky beach to

visit the café or use the creekside clothing-optional soaking tubs and cedar sauna. Buoy mooring fees include use of the soaking tubs and sauna for two; anchor guests can use the cafe, soaking tubs and sauna for $15 per person.

The café has an intriguing menu and is open for breakfast, lunch and dinner, with indoor and outdoor seating. A store has convenience groceries and items from local artisans. The resort has cabins, geodesic domes, yurts, a beautifully crafted treehouse, and campsites for rent. Doe Bay Fest, a popular music festival, is held in August.

Smuggler's Villa Resort. P.O. Box 79, Eastsound, WA 98245; (360) 376-2297; smuggler@rockisland.com; www.smuggler.com. No transient moorage. Smuggler's Village has condos for rent, a swimming pool and hot tubs. Reservations required. Good base for trailer boaters who can rent a condo for overnights and explore the northern San Juans during the day.

⑱ **Barnes and Clark Islands.** These two beautiful islands lie parallel to each other in

Rosario Strait, between Orcas Island and Lummi Island. Barnes Island is privately owned, but Clark Island is a state park, with mooring buoys installed during the summer. Camping and picnicking sites are ashore, and trails meander along the island.

⑱ **Clark Island Marine State Park.** (360) 376-2073; Open all year, day use and overnight mooring and camping. Clark Island is exposed to Rosario Strait and the Strait of Georgia, and is best in settled weather. Mooring buoys are deployed between Clark Island and Barnes Island, and in the bay on the east side. The park has 9 mooring buoys for vessels 45 feet and under: 6 on the east side and 3 on the west side. Self-register and pay mooring buoy fee on shore. Toilets, picnic sites, fire rings, and primitive campsites. No power, no water. Pack out all garbage.

Note: A nasty rock is in the entrance to the bay.

Visitor Report: Correspondents Bruce and Margaret Evertz spent a night on a buoy on

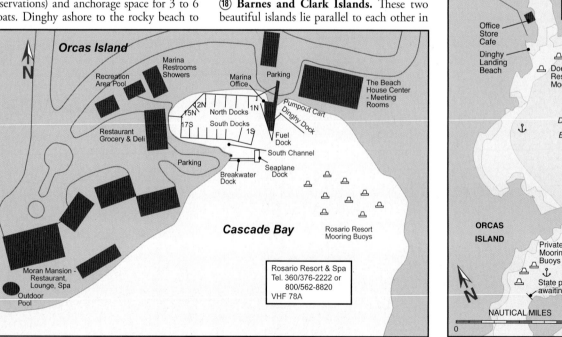

Rosario Resort

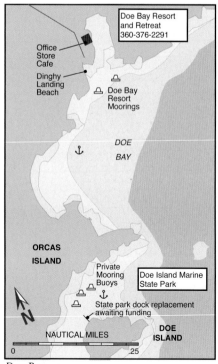

Doe Bay

Though small, Matia Island has a cove for anchorage and a public dock.

Exploring the caves on Sucia Island.

the east side of Clark Island and ". . .woke up three times in the middle of the night hanging onto the mattress as we rolled in the wake of something big. Next time we'll try one of the buoys on the west side."

⑲ **Matia Island.** (360) 376-2073; Open all year, day use and overnight mooring. Matia Island is part of the San Juan Islands National Wildlife Refuge. All access is restricted except the loop trail and the designated 5-acre moorage and picnicking area at Rolfe Cove. The rest of the island is off-limits to protect wildlife. Pets are not allowed on shore.

The favored Matia Island anchorage is in **Rolfe Cove**, which opens from the west. Strong currents can run through Rolfe Cove and the bottom is rocky. Be sure the anchor is well set and swinging room is adequate. Facilities include a 64-foot-long moorage float, 2 buoys (limit 45 feet), 6 campsites, toilet. No power, water or showers. The mooring float is removed in winter. Self-register and pay mooring buoy fee at the head of the dock.

Those confident in their anchoring ability might try the little 1-boat notch between

Rolfe Cove and Eagle Point, although you can't go inland from there. A stern-anchor will be required to keep the boat positioned. High cliffs surround this cove. It's very secluded and serene.

Anchorage is good in the bay indenting the southeast corner of the island. The remains of an old homestead are located at the head of that bay.

There is some disagreement about the pronunciation of Matia. Bruce Calhoun's book, *Cruising the San Juan Islands*, says it's pronounced "Mah-TEE-ah." We've been told, however, that a number of genuine old hands have always pronounced it "Mah-CIA," as in "inertia" or "militia." However the name is pronounced, Matia Island is a popular destination, beautiful and interesting.

LOCAL KNOWLEDGE

DANGEROUS REEFS: A reef extends westward from Little Sucia Island nearly to the shoal water near West Bank. Sucia Island is surrounded by such hazards. We strongly

recommend that vessels in these waters carry and use Chart 18431.

⑳ **Sucia Island.** Open all year, day use and overnight mooring and camping. For information call (360) 902-8844; for campsite reservations call toll-free (888) 226-7688. Facilities include dock space, linear tie mooring systems, numerous mooring buoys, and toilets. Water, but no power, no showers. This probably is the most heavily used marine park in the system. As many as 500 boats can visit on one weekend in the high summer season.

Like Matia and Patos Islands, Sucia Island is made of sandstone carved by water and wind into dramatic shapes. Many fossils can be found in Sucia Island's sandstone. It is illegal to disturb or remove fossils.

The park has 55 primitive campsites and 2 group campsites, which can be reserved. Camping is permitted in designated areas only. A day use/picnic area, with picnic shelters, is on the neck of land separating Echo Bay and Shallow Bay, and can be reserved. The park has several miles of hiking trails and

203

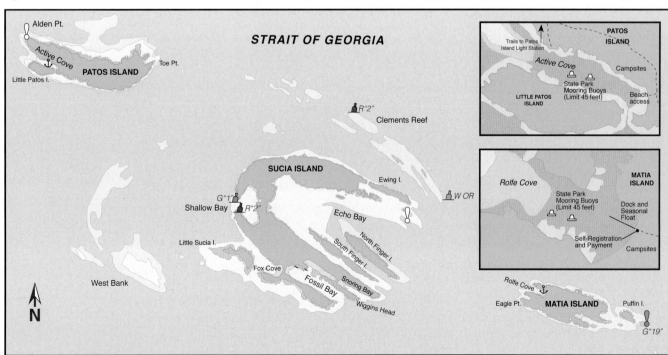

Sucia, Patos, and Matia Islands

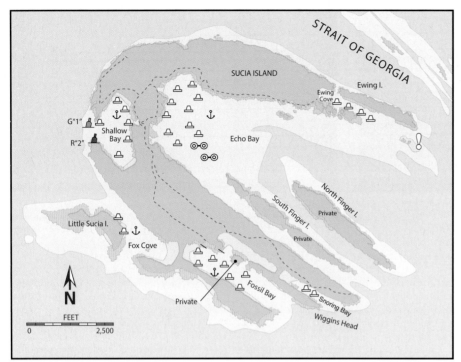

Sucia Island Marine State Park

service roads. Fresh water is available at Fossil Bay and near Shallow Bay April through September. The most developed facilities are at Fossil Bay.

Sucia Island has several fingers that separate small bays. Facilities are as follows: Fox Cove: 4 mooring buoys; Fossil Bay: 2 docks, 13 mooring buoys; Snoring Bay: 2 mooring buoys; Echo Bay: 14 mooring buoys, 2 linear moorings; Ewing Cove: 4 mooring buoys; Shallow Bay: 8 mooring buoys. All mooring buoys are limited to boats 45 feet or less. Rafting allowed at the docks based on the size of boats. All docks and moorings are Washington State Parks facilities, self-register and pay a fee at the designated on-shore stations. The mooring buoy count can change based on winter weather and repairs.

Shallow Bay. Shallow Bay is an excellent, popular anchorage. Lots of room except on minus tides. Mooring buoys take most of the obvious good spots, so if they are taken you'll be looking at the south side of Shallow Bay. Check the tides before anchoring, and be sure you'll have enough water under the keel at low tide. Easy entry as long as you pass between the two buoys marking the entrance. The best place to beach the dinghy is on the narrow neck of land separating Shallow Bay from Echo Bay. Sunsets in Shallow Bay are beautiful.

Fox Cove. Enter Fox Cove from either side. Waters off the southern entry can be turbulent. At the west entry foul ground extends west farther than you expect. Tie to mooring buoys or anchor behind Little Sucia Island. A pretty spot with sandstone cliffs.

Fossil Bay. Fossil Bay is easy to enter, nicely protected, and beautiful. Anchor out, tie to

one of the mooring buoys, or moor at the docks. In winter one of the docks is moved to a more protected area of the park. At the head of the outermost dock a plaque commemorates the yacht clubs that were members of the Interclub Boating Association of Washington, when Interclub worked to collect funds from ordinary citizens, then bought the island and gave it to the state as a state park. One of the points of land overlooking Fossil Bay is named for Ev Henry, the first president of Interclub, who conceived the idea and carried out the project.

Depths in Fossil Bay at zero tide are 6 feet at the outer end of the innermost dock, and they shoal rapidly toward the head of the bay. The park ranger told us depths are only 5 feet at zero tide near the outer dock. Be careful on low tides. A substantial day use shelter,

excellent for group functions, has been built at the head of the dock. Call (360) 376-2073 for reservations.

Snoring Bay. Snoring Bay is easy to enter and has 2 mooring buoys. A good spot. As we understand the story, a park ranger was caught sleeping on duty in this bay, hence the name.

Echo Bay. Echo Bay is the largest of Sucia's bays. Although it is the most exposed, it is the most popular. Mooring buoys line the western shore, and 2 linear mooring systems are just outside the buoys. Picnic facilities are on the narrow neck of land separating Echo Bay from Shallow Bay.

The fine gravel beach at the head of Echo Bay is fairly steep, making dinghy landing much more convenient. We were able to step ashore without getting our feet wet.

The two long islands in Echo Bay (North Finger and South Finger Island) are privately owned. The south half of Justice Island (the small island off South Finger Island) is park-owned but closed to the public as a nature preserve.

Caution: A reader reported that he grounded his Cal 39 sailboat, which draws 6 feet 8 inches, on an uncharted rock in Echo Bay. The grounding occurred in the area marked 1 fathom, 5 feet extending from the small islet northwest of South Finger Islet, as shown on large scale Chart 18431. He sounded the area carefully after the grounding, and found the depths to be somewhat less than charted. The keel of his boat confirmed the soundings. On low tides especially, give the tip of this islet a good offing.

Despite occasional stories of anchor dragging in Echo Bay, we have found the bottom to be heavy, sticky clay, with excellent holding.

No-anchor Zone: A no-anchor zone is marked by buoys near the head of Echo Bay. They want to protect eelgrass from boat anchors and dragging chain rode. Mooring

Active Cove on Patos Island is one of the most scenic anchorages in the San Juan Islands.

TURN POINT SPECIAL OPERATING AREA

The Turn Point Special Operating Area was created in 2001 to manage the high volume of commercial ship and recreational boat traffic around Turn Point. Ships longer than 100 meters (328 feet) must call in to Victoria Traffic on VHF channel 11 prior to entering the area and report their intended navigation movements and any other information necessary to comply with standards of care.

Recreational vessels should monitor VHF channel 11 in this vicinity so they can be aware of any ships. If ships are in the Special Operating Area, stay well clear until they are past. In a crossing situation, *cross behind the large ship*, not in front of it.

Turn Point is a blind corner. A recreational vessel could be completely unaware of a fast approaching ship on the other side. Monitor VHF channel 11. We had a near-miss in fog a few years ago. It was scary.

Also see "What Recreational Boaters Need to Know about VTS" in Cruising Information section in the front of the Waggoner.

— *Robert Hale*

buoys in the bay use eco-friendly anchors that do not disturb eelgrass.

Ewing Cove. In our opinion, cozy little Ewing Cove, tucked in behind Ewing Island on the north side of Echo Bay, is the most charming of Sucia Island's bays. The cove has 4 mooring buoys and a lovely beach at the western end. We have reports of a rock in Ewing Cove's southern entrance, from Echo Bay. The rock is east of a white can that marks a fish haven, shown on large scale Chart 18431. We're told the rock is black and hard to see, and feeds on propellers at low tide. Be extra cautious. Reader Bruce Farwell sent lat/lon coordinates of 48°45.794'N/122°52.924'W. We've found the narrow pass at the northwest end of Ewing Cove to be deep and easily run as long as you pay attention. Danger Reef lies just outside.

㉑ **Patos Island.** (360) 376-2073; Open all year, day use and overnight mooring and camping. Facilities include 2 mooring buoys (limit 45 feet) in Active Cove, toilets, primitive campsites. Self-register and pay mooring buoy fee on shore. The remains of the dock that served the lighthouse on Alden Point are still there, but barely recognizable. A one-mile trail leads from the beach at the head of Active Cove to the lighthouse. Pack out all garbage. The island is a breeding area for birds.

㉑ **Active Cove.** The only possible Patos Island anchorage is in Active Cove, on the west tip of the island. The cove, with its sculpted sandstone walls, is one of the most scenic spots in the San Juans. Considerable current activity is outside the entrances. Inside the cove the currents are reduced, but it's tight. Use the mooring buoys when possible. If the mooring buoys are taken, anchoring gets interesting. A stern-tie to shore probably will be called for.

Freeman Island. On President Channel. Open all year, day use only, no facilities. Anchor out at this undeveloped state park property. No fires or overnight camping. Pack out all garbage.

㉒ **West Beach Resort.** 190 Waterfront Way, Eastsound, WA 98245; (360) 376-2240; (877) 937-8224; vacation@westbeachresort.com; www.westbeachresort.com. Open all year, ethanol-free premium gasoline at the fuel dock, 10 mooring buoys in the summer and 3 in the winter, restrooms, showers. A new pumpout station was installed in 2018; the service is free and accomodates boats up to 60 feet. You can pick up a free pumpout kit, provided by Washington Sea Grant (WSG), at the marina office. Floats in deeper water accommodate larger boats. Larger powerboats and keel sailboats tie to mooring buoys. Most of the docks are removed from mid-September to late May, limited moorage in the winter. The fuel dock is open year round. The store has a little bit of everything, including groceries, ice, beer, wine, espresso, ice cream, and free Wi-Fi. Limited dock space in the off-season.

West Beach is a popular fishing resort with cabins, tent cabins, RV, camping, children's activities, food service, private launch ramp (free for guests, a fee is charged for non-guests) and parking. Be careful if you anchor out. The eelgrass bottom does not offer good holding in many places and you can drag.

Waldron Island. Waldron Island has no public facilities. In settled weather, anchorage is good in Cowlitz Bay and North Bay. Mail Bay, on the east shore, is rocky but usable. The mail boat from Bellingham used to arrive here, leaving the mail in a barrel hung over the water.

㉓ **Stuart Island.** The center portion of Stuart Island, including Reid Harbor and Prevost Harbor, is a state park with campsites, potable water, and clean, spacious composting toilets. A trail and dirt road from Reid Harbor and Prevost Harbor lead out to the automated Turn Point lighthouse. The distance is about 3 miles, each way. It's an excellent walk, although the trail to the road goes over a mountain, and will have you puffing. The view down into Reid Harbor is excellent, however.

Once you get to the road, it's 0.7 mi. to the school house (1 room, K-8), library and museum, which in our opinion are on the must-see list. The school house is modern, but the library and museum buildings go back to earlier days. The museum is filled with information about island life, which, despite being close to big cities, is pretty primitive. There is no public electric power, for example. Every resident is responsible for his or her own electricity, and a few choose to do without. Ditto water and telephone, although cell phones have filled that void. Handmade postcards are for sale in the library on the honor system.

One island family, Ezra and Loie Benson and their children, have created a small business called Boundary Pass Traders. They operate the Treasure Chest, near the schoolhouse, and a second Treasure Chest along the road at Prevost Harbor. T-shirts and coloring books, with local scenes, are for sale. Strictly the honor system. Select the items you like and mail a check for your purchases, or you can pay online.

Prevost Harbor. Open all year, day use and overnight mooring and camping. Facilities include 256 feet of dock space, 7 mooring buoys (limit 45 feet), a linear mooring system, 18 primitive campsites, toilets. Self-register and pay dock moorage, mooring buoy, and linear mooring fee at the head of the state park dock. The favored entrance to Prevost Harbor is around the west end of Satellite Island. A county dock on the northwest end of Prevost Harbor, suitable for dinghies, shortens the walk to the Island school and Turn Point lighthouse. No overnight stays at the county dock.

Caution: Two reefs in the Prevost Harbor entrance cover at high tide. One is off the Stuart Island shore and dries at 6 feet. The other is off Satellite Island and dries at 4 feet. The reefs are clearly charted, but when they cover, the route to the dock looks to be wide open. If you're entering at higher tide when the reefs are covered, don't wrap tightly to port around the tip of Satellite Island. That's where one of the reefs is lying in wait. Proceed a short distance straight into the harbor (but not too far; that's where the other reef is located), then turn to port.

Except for the reefs noted above, anchoring is good throughout Prevost Harbor. After dinner we took a slow dinghy ride around the shoreline. A grass airstrip is at the east end of the harbor, beyond the docks. As we putt-putted along we found the houses, rock forms, and beaches fascinating.

The passage to the east of Satellite Island is foul. It has been reported that, with care, these waters are passable at half tide or better, or by shallow draft boats; use caution. Shoreside facilities are shared with Reid Harbor, on the narrow but steep neck of land that separates them.

Satellite Island East Cove. "The little cove on the eastern shore of Satellite Island has good holding in mud in about 40 feet. Wonderful view across Boundary Pass. Inside, Prevost Harbor was packed with boats; we were alone." [Hamilton]

Reid Harbor. Open all year, day use and overnight mooring and camping. The entrance is straightforward. A 192-foot mooring dock is on the north shore. 13 mooring buoys (for boats 45 feet and under) dot the bay, and mooring floats (not connected to land) and a linear mooring system are within easy dinghy distance of the landing dock. Self-register and pay mooring fees at the head of the dock. Toilets, pumpout, and portapotty dump are located on a float along the north shore. Reid Harbor is long and narrow, and protected by high hills. The bottom is excellent for anchoring, and the harbor holds a great number of boats. It's a popular destination. The setting is beautiful. Shoreside facilities are shared with Prevost Harbor, on the narrow but steep neck of land separating them. The county dirt road leading to the Turn Point

One of the small, intimate marinas among the San Juan Islands; West Beach Resort has mooring buoys and seasonal dock moorage.

Lighthouse, with its museum (and the school house, museum and library along the way), begins at the head of Reid Harbor. No dock at the head of the bay, but if tides are favorable you could beach your dinghy there without having to carry it back through the mud.

Gossip Island. "Reid Harbor had too many boats for our taste. Preferring a view anyway, we dropped anchor just outside, in the cove formed by Gossip Island and the unnamed island immediately northwest of Gossip Island. It was very private, with two white sand beaches nearby. Good holding ground for the anchor. Southerly swells rocked us a couple times, but no worse than in the east cove of James Island. We had an excellent view through the islets to the Olympic Mountains, and of large ship traffic away off in Haro Strait." [Hamilton]

Johns Pass. Johns Pass separates Stuart Island and Johns Island, and is used regularly. At the south end of the pass foul ground, marked by kelp, extends about half of a mile southeast from Stuart Island. Boats heading southeast through Johns Pass should head for Gull Reef, then turn when well clear of the kelp. Anchorage is possible in Johns Pass and along the south side of Johns Island.

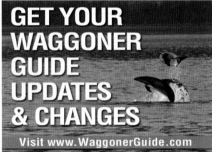

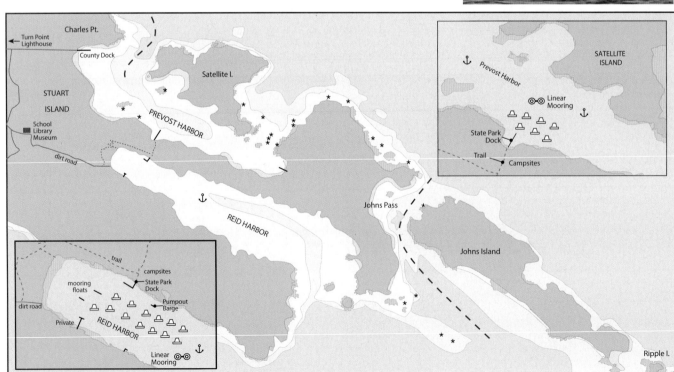

Stuart Island Marine State Park

THE PIG WAR, STANDOFF AT GRIFFIN BAY
- By Mike Vouri

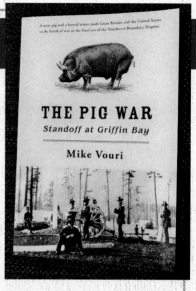

Publisher: Discover Your Northwest; ISBN: 978-0-914019-62-6

One of the most interesting border disputes in history played out on **San Juan Island**. Mike Vouri, Chief of Interpretation and Historian for San Juan Island National Park, writes the fascinating account of how the conflict over the San Juan Islands was finally resolved.

In June 1846, the Treaty of Oregon established the boundary between British and American possessions at the 49th parallel extending from the Rocky Mountains "to the middle of the channel which separates the continent from Vancouver's island," then south through the channel to the Strait of Juan de Fuca and west to the Pacific Ocean. The "channel," however, was actually two channels, Haro Strait and Rosario Strait. The San Juan Islands lay between the two channels, leaving them in a state of limbo; both sides claimed that the group of islands belonged to them, creating a conflict that nearly led to war.

Mike Vouri begins the story with a concise, chronological view of the earlier maritime explorers and their claims to Pacific Northwest lands, including Robert Gray's discovery of the Columbia River in 1792. Both British and American fur traders established posts in the Oregon Territory – American John Jacob Astor at Astoria, near the mouth of the Columbia; and the British Hudson Bay Company at Fort Vancouver (Vancouver, Washington), under John McLoughlin. From 1841 to 1845, the American population in the Oregon Country skyrocketed. A compassionate man at heart, McLoughlin helped many of the American settlers, which ultimately led to the fort's undoing.

The formation of the Washington Territory in 1853 meant that more Americans would come north of the Columbia River to settle in the Puget Sound basin. Author Mike Vouri expounds on how James Douglas, Governor of the Crown Colonies of B.C., established British presence in the San Juan's with a plantation on the south end of San Juan Island. In December 1853, Hawaiian herdsmen, led by Chief Agent Charles J. Griffin, brought nearly 1,400 sheep in addition to other farm animals, including several Berkshire boars. U.S. Customs Inspector, Isaac Neff Ebey, threatened seizure of the British property on **San Juan Island** in order to collect duties; but the British saw the tax collector as a common offender – thus began the first standoff on the Island. Ebey and Douglass wrote to their respective governments. The U.S. temporarily backed off; but Governor Stevens of Washington Territory soon moved his Army garrison from Fort Steilacoom to **Port Townsend** near San Juan Island. In 1855, U.S. troops landed on San Juan Island in pursuit of northern Natives; U.S. Revenue vessels as well as Whatcom County continued to attempt collecting taxes on the Hudson Bay Company's "Belle Vue Sheep Farm." The story continues with the account of how Sheriff Barnes, with an armed party, captured and removed a group of rams from the Island, one of many interesting stories in Vouri's book.

Between June and December of 1857, Captain James Prevost, British Boundary Commissioner, and U.S. Boundary Commissioner, Archibald Campbell, met six times but could not agree on a water boundary. In 1858, the U.S. felt it should establish a military naval station at **Griffin Bay** on the shores of San Juan Island to overlook inner waters equally with Great Britain, who had a station at Esquimalt Harbour near Victoria. American settlers who had arrived on the Island were viewed as squatters by the British; and likewise, the HBC was viewed by the territorial government in Olympia as an alien squatter.

An American settler by the name of Lyman Cutlar had homesteaded on 160-acres of land under U.S. pre-emption laws, and made several complaints to Charles Griffin about the Company pig (a Berkshire boar), that was rooting up potatoes in his garden. One day in 1859, Cutlar shot "the pig;" he confessed the shooting and offered remuneration, but the damage had been done and accusations and threats flew between the two men and their respective countries. Americans on San Juan Island decided to provide support for Lyman Cutlar, and held a flag-raising party. Raw emotions continued the controversy of island ownership between the two countries, resulting in the arrival of ships with naval guns and the establishment of military camps on the Island — the American Camp on the south end of the Island with "gun platforms," and the English camp in **Garrison Bay** on the north end. In his book, author Mike Vouri expounds on the military maneuvers and political maneuvers that took place in 1859. The situation nearly came to blows between British Captain Hornby of the HMS Tribune, and the Ninth Infantry American commander Captain George Pickett (a Virginian who later fought for the Confederate Army during the Civil War). Fortunately, calmer heads prevailed and fighting was averted. Like most events in history, the facts are more complicated than they first appear; author Mike Vouri does an excellent job of painting the big picture.

Military Generals came and went from both sides of the conflict for purposes of posturing and saving grace. The commander of each respective camp on the Island kept the peace and actually became friends. Captain George Bazelgette of English Camp, and Captain Pickett of the American Camp, spent most of their time sorting out Indian and civilian matters involving drunkenness, theft, and prostitution; the two Captains cooperated with one another in these matters, and even took trips together to Victoria. Likewise, soldiers from both camps enjoyed comradery through joint athletic contests and social events. A tone of mutual cooperation had been set; no one believed that a joint military occupation would have lasted 12 years.

By December 1860, the British were willing to seek arbitration to settle the water boundary issue, which proved to be an interesting series of events which Vouri outlines in his book. At last, in May of 1871, the Treaty of Washington was signed by the British and Americans. Kaiser Wilhelm of the newly constituted German Empire had served as arbiter, along with his three-man commission who deliberated for more than a year. It was determined that Haro Strait had to be the "southerly channel" dividing Vancouver Island from the mainland. The judgement was endorsed by the emperor, and the ruling was issued on October 21, 1872.

San Juan Island remains a beautiful and beloved Island to this day, visited by all who know her. Boaters of the Pacific Northwest won't want to miss reading the extraordinary account of "The Pig War" as written by Mike Vouri.

207

Gulf Islands

CHAPTER 7

GULF ISLANDS
*Victoria • Sidney • Butchart Gardens • Chemainus
Wallace Island • Pirates Cove • Nanaimo*

SALTSPRING ISLAND
Ganges • Vesuvius • Fulford Harbour

NORTH & SOUTH PENDER ISLAND
Bedwell Harbour • Port Browning • Otter Bay

GALIANO ISLAND
Sturdies Bay • Montague Harbour

Victoria Harbour Authority's Causeway Floats are right in front of the Empress Hotel.

For convenience, the Gulf Islands section of this book includes the southern tip and the east side of Vancouver Island as far up-island as Nanaimo.

The Gulf Islands are British Columbia's version of the Washington's San Juan Islands. The San Juan Islands are the peaks of a sunken mountain range. The Gulf Islands, for the most part, are a different geology, made of sandstone that has been folded and uplifted until it sticks out of the sea. Together, the San Juan Islands and Gulf Islands create a superb cruising area.

Like the San Juan Islands, the Gulf Islands are in the lee of mountains. They receive much summertime sun and little summertime rainfall. Water is in short supply. Boat washing is something that just isn't done, at least in the islands themselves.

The Gulf Islands are blessed with dozens of anchorages, from one-boat notches to open bays that hold many boats. Marine parks provide anchorage, mooring and docking possibilities, and facilities ashore. Private marinas run the spectrum from rustic to deluxe, many with excellent dining on-site or nearby.

The largest town in the Gulf Islands proper is Ganges on Saltspring Island. If your definition of the islands expands (as ours does) to include southern and eastern Vancouver Island, then Victoria, Sidney, Ladysmith and Nanaimo are larger than Ganges.

The best provisioning stops are Victoria, Sidney, Ganges, Ladysmith, Chemainus, and Nanaimo. Fuel is available throughout the islands.

Navigation is straightforward, but pay attention. It's easy to get confused, and the waters are dotted with rocks and reefs. You want to know where you are at all times. Unfortunately for those who rely solely on paper charts, no single chart sheet covers all the waters, so you will be working among the 1:40,000 scale Charts 3440, 3441, 3442 and 3443, plus several large-scale charts and plans charts. Plans charts are a collection of large-scale charts all on one sheet. The Canadian Hydrographic Chartbook 3313 is an excellent chartbook for the Gulf Islands. This chartbook is not inexpensive, but it has everything.

Customs – Entering Canada. Vessels entering Canada are required to clear Canadian Customs at their first stop in Canada. Most boats will clear customs at Bedwell Harbour on South Pender Island, Victoria (includes Victoria Inner Harbour, Oak Bay and Cadboro Bay), Sidney, or Nanaimo. Bedwell Harbour is just 4 miles north of Stuart Island in the San Juan Islands, but its station is open only from May 1 through September 30. See *Chapter 1 U.S. and Canadian Customs Information* for a more detailed explanation on the process of clearing Canadian Customs.

Gulf Islands National Park Reserve. The Gulf Islands National Park Reserve came into

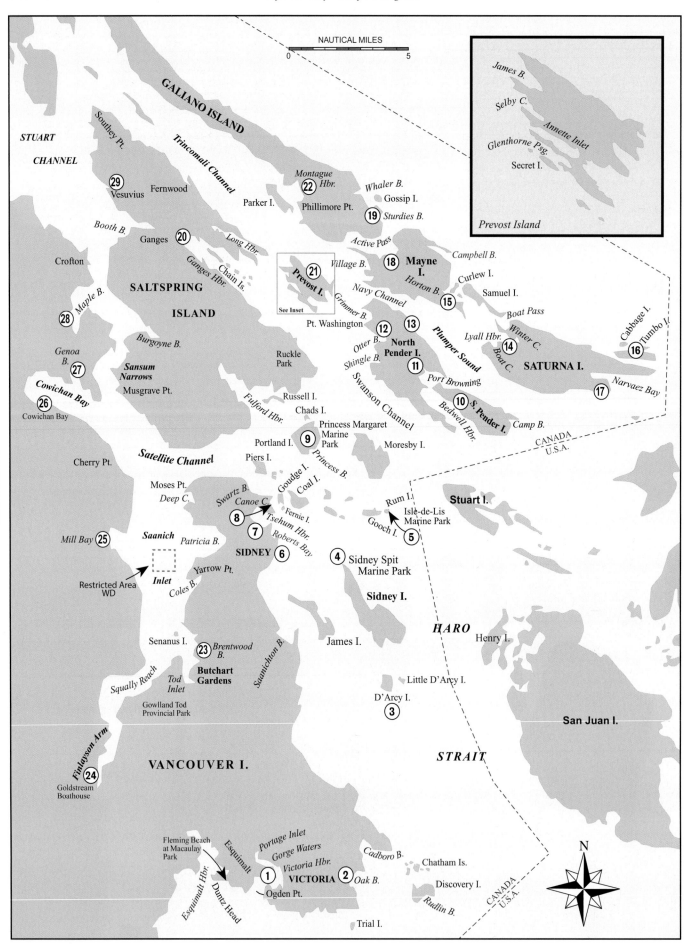

NAUTICAL MILES
0   5

James B.
Selby C.
Annette Inlet
Glenthorne Psg.
Secret I.
Prevost Island

STUART
CHANNEL

GALIANO ISLAND

Southey Pt.
㉙ *Fernwood*
Vesuvius

Trincomali Channel

Montague Hbr. ㉒

Whaler B.
Gossip I.
㉙ *Phillimore Pt.*
Sturdies B. ⑲

Booth B.
Ganges ⑳
Crofton

Long Hbr.
Chain Is.

Active Pass

Village B.
⑱ **Mayne I.**

Campbell B.
Curlew I.
Samuel I.

Maple B.
㉘
Ganges Hbr.
SALTSPRING ISLAND

Prevost I.
㉑
See Inset

Navy Channel
Horton B.
⑮
Boat Pass
Winter C.
Cabbage I.
Tumbo I.

Grimmer B.
⑫ ⑬
Lyall Hbr. ⑭
Plumper Sound
Boat C.
SATURNA I.
⑯

Burgoyne B.
Genoa B.
㉗
Sansum Narrows
Musgrave Pt.

Pt. Washington

Otter B.
Shingle B.
North Pender I.
⑪
Port Browning
Narvaez Bay
⑰

Ruckle Park

Cowichan Bay
㉖
Cowichan Bay

Fulford Hbr.
Russell I.
Chads I.

Swanson Channel
Bedwell Hbr.
⑩ **S. Pender I.**
Camp B.

CANADA
U.S.A.

Cherry Pt.

Satellite Channel
Portland I.
⑨
Princess Margaret Marine Park
Princess B.
Moresby I.

Moses Pt.
Deep C.
Piers I.

Swartz B.
Canoe C.
⑧
Goudge I.
Coal I.
Fernie I.

Rum I.
Stuart I.
Isle-de-Lis Marine Park
Gooch I.
⑤

Mill Bay ㉕
Saanich
Patricia B.
⑦ *Tsehum Hbr.*
Roberts Bay
④ *Sidney Spit Marine Park*

Restricted Area WD
Inlet
SIDNEY ⑥
Yarrow Pt.
Coles B.

Sidney I.

HARO

Senanus I.
㉓ *Brentwood B.*
Butchart Gardens
Saanichton B.

James I.
Henry I.

Squally Reach
Tod Inlet
Gowlland Tod Provincial Park

Little D'Arcy I.
D'Arcy I.
③

San Juan I.

Finlayson Arm
㉔
Goldstream Boathouse

VANCOUVER I.

STRAIT

N

Fleming Beach at Macaulay Park
Esquimalt
Portage Inlet
Gorge Waters
Victoria Hbr.
①
VICTORIA ②
Cadboro B.
Chatham Is.
Oak B.
Discovery I.
Esquimalt Hbr.
Duntz Head
Ogden Pt.
Rudlin B.
CANADA
U.S.A.

Trial I.

210

Southern Gulf Islands

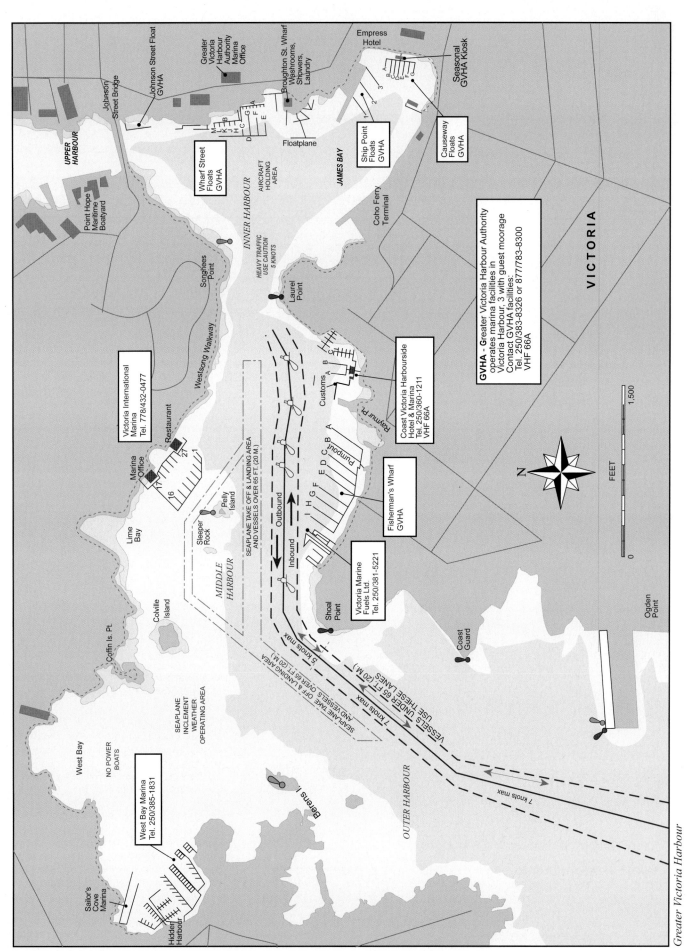

Greater Victoria Harbour

211

Enjoy the views along the Westsong/Songhees mile-long pathway, where you can get on and off at various foot ferry landings.

being in 2004. Many former provincial parks, and most of the uninhabited islands and islets south of Active Pass, were transferred to the new national park, plus a number of other properties that were purchased. Land continues to be purchased and added to the Reserve. Park lands have green and white location signs, or small yellow boundary signs bearing the stylized beaver symbol of Parks Canada. Dogs must be on leash. Camping is in designated areas only. Nominal usage fees are charged, often collected through honor boxes on shore.

For more information see www.pc.gc.ca/gulf; gulf.islands@pc.gc.ca; (250) 654-4000; (866) 944-1744. For emergencies or to report problems on park lands, call toll-free (877) 852-3100.

iOS and Android App: The Parks Canada Explora app, available free for iOS and Android, provides geo-tagged maps, photos, information, and quizzes about sites throughout the Gulf Islands National Park Reserve.

VICTORIA AREA

Esquimalt Harbour. Esquimalt Harbour is a wonderful but often overlooked anchorage, with excellent holding in thick mud southeast of Cole Island, with room to swing. Protection is reasonable, even with big winds blowing in the Strait of Juan de Fuca. With this bottom you're not going anywhere, anyway, but you might be rocking and rolling at times due to swell or wind waves. The Canadian Navy guards the entrance with a high speed inflatable and will advise you to keep 100 meters away from their ships and property. Anchor north of a line between the south end of Richards Island and the north end of Smart Island.

The British Navy once used Cole Island for munitions storage. The large brick buildings from the late 1800s on the island are still intact and make interesting exploration. Cole Island is a National Historic Site where visitors are welcome. A dinghy dock is located on the southwest side of Cole Island and boardwalk pathways connect all the buildings. For a map of the buildings on the island, go to www.coleisland.ca.

Security Zone: All vessels entering or departing Esquimalt Harbour are requested to contact QHM Operations on VHF channel 10 or by telephone (250) 363-2160. Give your vessel name, make, and direction of travel at Fisgard Lighthouse and Duntze Head. Fisgard Lighthouse was the first lighthouse on Canada's west coast (1860) and is still in operation.

You can anchor the dinghy off the beach at the lighthouse to tour Fisgard Light and the historic Fort Rodd Hill military site. Payment to enter the grounds should be made at the entrance gate to Fort Rodd Hill located above the lighthouse. The grounds are open from June through October. Gun emplacements, magazines, defensive walls and military houses from the late 1800's can be seen at Fort Rodd Hill; Fisgard Lighthouse contains archival photos and historical information about the lighthouse.

Fleming Beach at Macaulay Park. West of Victoria Harbour, in Esquimalt. Open all year. Facilities include launch ramp (fee charged) and washrooms. This is a charming little cove, protected by a rock breakwater, overlooked by most boating people. It is the home of Esquimalt Anglers' Association, a private sportfishing and fish enhancement group. The boarding floats at the launch ramp have room for temporary moorage while shopping nearby, or you can anchor out. Walkways and picnic areas have been built. Fleming Beach is adjacent to old coastal gun emplacements, which make for good exploring.

LOCAL KNOWLEDGE

Victoria Mandatory Traffic Lanes: All vessels 65 feet LOA and less must enter and depart Victoria's Inner Harbour between Shoal Point and Laurel Point along the south shore, as shown in the accompanying harbor map. Inbound vessels favor the docks; outbound vessels a little farther out. The traffic lanes are marked by buoys (keep the buoys to port when entering and exiting). The more open water in the middle of the harbor is used by the large number of float planes that land and take off constantly. Because of the volume of boat and float plane traffic, no sailing is allowed inside the breakwater. Sailboats under power must have sails lowered.

① Victoria. Victoria is the provincial capital of British Columbia, and the largest city on Vancouver Island. Vancouver Island is served by ferries from Port Angeles, WA to Victoria; from Tsawwassen to Sidney and Victoria through Swartz Bay; and from Vancouver (Horseshoe Bay) to Nanaimo. The fast-running Victoria Clipper passenger ferry connects Victoria and Seattle. Scheduled float planes also connect with Vancouver and Seattle, and other destinations.

Victoria is beautiful. The Empress Hotel, for which the word "majestic" could have been created, dominates the Inner Harbour. The Empress is flanked on the south by the B.C. provincial parliament buildings, themselves the embodiment of dignity, thoughtful deliberation, and orderly progress—the buildings, that is. Between the Empress and the parliament buildings stands the Royal British Columbia Museum, a must-see, especially for families. A giant ice-age mammoth dominates the entry, and the rest of the museum delights with a re-creation of Capt. Vancouver's ship, a Victorian town exhibit, a west coast seashore, a First Nations Big House and much, much more. Highly recommended.

The Maritime Museum of British Columbia (250) 385-4222 is located downtown in Nootka Court at 634 Humboldt Street, across from the Empress Hotel. This excellent museum is open 10:00 a.m. to 4:00 p.m. Tuesday through Saturday.

The Visitor Information Centre is on top of the causeway at the head of the Inner Harbour, across from the Empress Hotel. It's easy to find. The entire Victoria Inner Harbour is covered by Wi-Fi.

Inside Ogden Point, marinas and public wharves begin with Fisherman's Wharf and progress inward to the well-marked customs dock at Raymur Point. East of the customs dock is the Coast Victoria Harbourside Hotel & Marina. Next, in James Bay, comes the Causeway Floats, in front of the Empress Hotel. These docks are popular and fill first. Northward from the Causeway Floats comes Ship Point Floats. Continuing north are the Wharf Street Floats, and Johnson Street Float. On the north shore of the Middle Harbour is the Victoria International Marina. With the exception of Harbourside Hotel & Marina and Victoria International Marina, all moorage facilities are managed by the Greater Victoria Harbour Authority. Details regarding these facilities are described below.

For an interesting side trip, take the dinghy through Gorge Waters to Portage Inlet. You'll travel through the industrial part of the city, then through park and residential areas. It's about a 3-mile trip; currents are a factor if you intend to row.

Customs: The customs dock is located at Raymur Point, just east of Fisherman's Wharf in front of the Harbourside Hotel & Marina. When arriving, check in using the dedicated phone at the customs dock.

Greater Victoria Harbour Authority: The Greater Victoria Harbour Authority

Victoria's promenade is alive with people, street entertainers, and food venders.

operates 6 facilities, 3 of which have transient moorage: Causeway Floats, Ship Point Floats (large vessels), and Wharf Street Floats. Laundry, showers, and washrooms for all three transient facilities are located on the Broughton Street Wharf—look for the gray building with a red roof. The Harbour Authority has a "meet and greet" program for visiting boats. When you enter the Inner Harbour, call on VHF 66A and they will direct you to available guest moorage.

Reservations: The Coast Victoria Harbourside Hotel & Marina, adjacent to the Fisherman's Wharf, accepts reservations. The Greater Victoria Harbour Authority accepts reservations for any size vessel. The Harbour Authority recommends that vessels greater than 60 feet LOA call ahead so space can be found: (250) 383-8326; (877) 783-8300; reservations@gvha.ca.

Symphony Splash: On the first weekend in August enjoy symphony music from a barge in the Inner Harbour, punctuated with cannons and fireworks. Over 40,000 people line the Inner Harbour for the evening event.

No Discharge Zone. Discharging raw sewage is prohibited in Victoria Inner Harbour, defined as beginning at the Ogden Point breakwater. This applies to "black water" only. "Gray water," such as from dishwashing or showers, is okay (if biodegradable).

Pumpout: A for fee pumpout station is located on the B Dock of Fisherman's Wharf. Tokens to operate the pump are available at Victoria Marine Fuels and the Harbour Authority seasonal kiosk at the Causeway Floats.

THINGS TO DO

1. Royal British Columbia Museum. An extraordinary museum covering the human and natural history of British Columbia is just above James Bay in Victoria.

2. B.C. Maritime Museum. Displays

on B.C. marine history, the voyages of Captain George Vancouver, and other rotating exhibits.

3. Afternoon tea at the Empress Hotel. A special treat, high tea offers pastries and piano music in an elegant setting.

4. Victoria Inner Harbour. Watch street musicians, mimes, and artists. The waterfront comes alive in the summer. Great boat watching, too.

Greater Victoria Harbour Authority - GVHA. The Victoria Harbour Authority operates marina facilities in the Victoria harbour area, three of which have short and long-term transient moorage.

① Fisherman's Wharf - GVHA. Fisherman's Wharf is reserved primarily for commercial and monthly moorage. No transient space.

① Causeway Floats - GVHA. (250) 383-8326 ext. 235 or 225; (877) 783-8300 ext. 235 or 265; reservations@gvha.ca; www.gvha.ca. Monitors VHF 66A. Open all year with 2000+ feet of side-tie dock space for vessels up to 60 feet, 30 amp power, potable water, free Wi-Fi, garbage and recycling drop. Limited transient moorage October 1 through May 15. Docks are gated all hours throught the year. The check-in kiosk, located beside the ramp to shore, is open June 15 through September 15.

These are the picturesque and popular docks directly in front of the Empress Hotel. Downtown Victoria beckons with fabulous restaurants, shopping, hotels, museums, and sightseeing. Public washrooms (no showers) are located under the Visitors Centre building. Private, clean Harbour Authority operated showers, laundry, and washrooms are at the Broughton Street Wharf.

① Ship Point Floats - GVHA. (250) 383-8326 ext. 235 or 225; (877) 783-8300 ext.

235 or 225; reservations@gvha.ca; www. gvha.ca. Monitors VHF 66A. Open all year for larger vessels to 280 feet, slips and side-tie, gated all-hours. Reservations highly recommended. Potable water, 30, 50, 100 amp single phase/208 & 3-phase/480 power, free Wi-Fi, garbage, recycling drop. Public washrooms (no showers) are located under the Visitors Centre building. Private and clean Harbour Authority-operated showers, laundry and washrooms are at the Broughton Street Wharf.

① **Broughton Street Wharf - GVHA.** Showers, washrooms, and laundry facilities, serving Harbour Authority

The foot ferry will carry you between waterfront promenades that encircle the harbour.

transient moorage guests, are located on the Broughton Street Wharf (site of the old customs dock). No transient moorage at the Broughton Street Wharf.

① **Wharf Street Floats - GVHA.** (250) 383-8326 ext. 235 or 225; (877) 783-8300 ext. 235 or 225; reservations@gvha.ca; www. gvha.ca. Monitors VHF 66A. Open all year for vessels to 375 feet, more than 1000 feet of side-tie visitor dock space. Limited guest moorage October 1 to end of May. Potable water, 30, 50 & 100 amp power (single phase/208), free Wi-Fi. Power availability varies depending on location. Washrooms, showers, laundry, garbage & recycling drop

are located on the adjacent Broughton Street Wharf. Conveniently located downtown, just not quite as picturesque as the Causeway Floats in front of the Empress Hotel.

① **Johnson Street Float- GVHA.** This marina facility is for monthly moorage only, primarily used by fish boats and commercial vessels.

① **Victoria Marine Fuels Ltd.** (250) 381-5221; www.marinefuels.com. Fuel dock with gasoline and diesel, located at Erie Street Fisherman's Wharf at 1 Dallas Rd. Open all year, but with shorter winter hours, closed Christmas Day and New Year's Day. Store stocks snacks, food items, charts. This is the only fuel dock in the Inner Harbour.

① **Coast Victoria Harbourside Hotel & Marina.** 146 Kingston Street, Victoria, V8V 1V4; (250) 360-1211; coastvictoria@ coasthotels.com; www.coasthotels.com. Guest moorage May through September, limited availability October through April; 30 & 50 amp power, potable water on the docks, washrooms and showers. Marina guests have full access to the dining room and lounge, indoor/outdoor pool, Jacuzzi, sauna, and fitness facilities. Reservations accepted. Within walking distance of downtown.

① **Victoria International Marina.** 1 Cooperage Place, Victoria, BC V9A 7J9; (778)

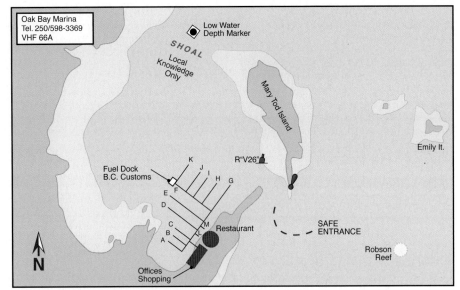

Oak Bay Marina

432-0477; info@vimarina.ca; www.vimarina. ca. On the north shore of Victoria Harbour, northeast of Pelly Island, two symmetrical one-story buildings sit on either side of this 28-slip marina designed to accommodate boats 65 to 175 feet in length. Seven slips are leased for 40 years; seven slips are available for one-year renewable leases; seven slips for monthly leases with a 3-month minimum stay; and seven slips are reserved for transient moorage with a 3-day minimum stay. This is a world-class marina with first-class marina services and crew quarters. The marina is designed and built with luxury yachts in mind. Due to Victoria Harbour traffic restrictions imposed by Transport Canada, this marina is for yachts 65 feet and over. Future plans for the marina include a restaurant that will be open to the public. The beautiful Westsong/ Songhees Walkway meanders along the shore offering outstanding views. Three water-taxi landings are located along the Walkway with departures to Victoria's downtown waterfront.

① **Westbay Marina.** (250) 385-1831; www. westbay.bc.ca; located in Victoria Harbour, west side; permanent moorage with transient slips occasionally available.

② **Oak Bay.** Oak Bay is on the east side of the south tip of Vancouver Island, west of the Chatham Islands. The channels between the various rocks and reefs are well marked. This is the route taken by many tugs with tows, and commercial fish boats of all sizes. The Oak Bay Marina and a separate small repair yard are located behind the breakwater.

② **Oak Bay Marina**. 1327 Beach Drive, Victoria, BC V8S 2N4; (250) 598-3369; (800) 663-7090 ext. 247; obm@obmg.com; www.oakbaymarina.com. Open all year with gasoline and diesel at the fuel dock. Customs clearance telephone at the fuel dock. Guest moorage for boats to 80 feet, 15 & 30 amp power, washrooms, showers, laundry. Call ahead for availability.

The marina has excellent docks and a good licensed waterfront restaurant. Outdoor seating on the deck overlooking the marina. The restaurant offers a coffee house for quick casual dining, and a gift shop with local products and sundry items. A small chandlery carries essential boating supplies. Repairs are at the Gartside Marine boatyard in a neighboring building, no haulout. The Oak Bay Beach Hotel is nearby for elegant dining. Complete shopping at quaint Oak Bay Village a short distance away. Regular bus service to downtown Victoria.

Discovery Island Marine Park. Open all year. An undeveloped park suitable for beachable boats only. The island was once the home of Capt. E.G. Beaumont, who donated the land as a park. The northern part of Discovery Island, adjacent Chatham Island, and some of the smaller islands nearby are Indian Reserve lands: no landing.

Cadboro Bay. Cadboro Bay is entirely residential except for the Royal Victoria Yacht Club, which has a breakwater-protected marina on the western shore. Moorage at Royal Victoria Yacht Club is for members of reciprocal clubs only. Customs clearance is available.

Anchorage in Cadboro Bay is excellent, mud and sand bottom. A 100-foot long concrete replica of Cadborosaurus, the elusive sea monster of Cadboro Bay, is prominent in the playground above the broad sandy beach at Cadboro-Gyro Park.

③ **D'Arcy Island (Gulf Islands National Park Reserve).** Open all year. This is an undeveloped island with no facilities other than some primitive campsites and a toilet. Dogs must be on leash. The island is surrounded by intimidating rocks, reefs, and shoals. Even if you study the chart carefully, kelp-covered rocks will pop up and surprise you. Approach with great caution. As far as we are concerned, there are no "good" anchorages at D'Arcy Island, only acceptable spots in the right weather. The cove on the east side of the island has depths of 10 to 25 feet with fair holding and some protection from, west and northwest winds. The single Parks staff mooring buoy is in this cove. This cove is closest to the island's campsites and pit toilets. If conditions allow, the cove on the west side of the island, south of the light, will work. Two coves on the northwest end look okay, but we didn't put the anchor down to confirm.

D'Arcy Island was B.C.'s first leper colony; from 1891 until 1925 it housed Chinese lepers. The colony was closed in 1925 and the island reverted to provincial jurisdiction. Ruins from the colony located just south of the west side light remain. A rustic shore side trail runs from the east cove campsites around the south end of the island to the west side light. A well-marked trail cuts across the island from just south of the campsites to the colony ruins. Plans for the island as a federal penitentiary were never realized. D'Arcy Island remained undeveloped, and was established as a marine park in 1961. *A Measure of Value*, by Chris Yorath, provides a good history of D'Arcy Island. To the east, Little D'Arcy Island is private property.

④ **Sidney Spit (Gulf Islands National Park Reserve).** The park, open all summer, occupies about one-third of Sidney Island, and all of the mile-long Sidney Spit with its white sand and shell beach extending northwest from the island. The island is closed to

215

visitors from November through February to facilitate traditional hunting by First Nations to control the fallow deer population. Anchor or tie to one of 12 mooring buoys, or moor on the seasonal dock. Anchoring depths are shallow and the area has considerable eel grass. Self-registration and payment box located at the dock. Buoys are limited to vessels of 50 feet or less in winds up to 30 knots; 40 feet for winds up to 37 knots; no mooring in large waves. In the summers, a passenger ferry runs between Sidney Spit dock and Sidney Beacon Ave dock.

Picnic and camping areas are ashore. Dogs must be on leash. An easily walked 2-km loop trail winds around the park through a dense forest of cedar, hemlock, fir, big-leaf maple and vine maple. A herd of fallow deer is reported to be on the island. A large saltwater lagoon is habitat for many animal and plant species and is off limits; markers show its borders. The remains of a brick-making factory are near the lagoon, where a beach is covered with broken red bricks.

⑤ **Isle-de-Lis at Rum Island (Gulf Islands National Park Reserve).** Open all year, anchoring only, campsites and a pit toilet. This is a small, undeveloped, and very pretty park with a walking trail and beaches. Dogs must be on leash. Rum Island is located at the east end of Gooch Island (private), where Prevost Passage meets Haro Strait. Anchorage is on either side of the gravel spit connecting Rum Island and Gooch Island. The northern anchorage is preferred. Rum Island is said to have come by its name honestly during Prohibition. In 1995 the warship HMCS *Mackenzie* was sunk in approximately 100 feet just north of Gooch Island to create an artificial reef for divers. It is marked with 2 cautionary/information buoys.

Saanichton Bay. Just off Cordova Channel between James Island and the east shore of Saanich Peninsula is Saanichton Bay. This large bay is open to the north but protected from south and west winds. Good anchoring in 15 to 30 feet with room to swing. Along the shore to the southeast is Cordova Spit Park with nice sand and gravel beaches. Most boat traffic transits Sidney Channel farther to the

east so there is minimal boat wake. A large barge is normally moored in the bay but is not a factor for anchoring.

Roberts Bay. Good anchorage, centrally located about a mile from both Sidney and Tsehum Harbour. Anchor in the center of the bay where the large shallow bay gives separation from the homes lining the shore. Good holding on a flat mud bottom, but exposed to north and northeast winds. Large wakes from boats entering and exiting Tsehum Harbour occasionally find their way into the anchorage but the bay becomes settled in the evening.

THINGS TO DO

1. Butchart Gardens in Brentwood Bay. A 55- acre display of flowers and gardens. Fireworks on Saturdays in the summer. Take the bus from Victoria or visit the area by boat.

2. Shaw Ocean Discovery Centre in Sidney. Learn more about the ecosystem of the B.C. coastal waters.

3. Bookstores. Downtown Sidney has numerous bookstores, everything from books for kids to collectors. Even a haunted bookstore. See why Sidney is called Booktown.

4. Lochside Regional Trail along the waterfront. Rent bikes for this flat and easy-to-ride trail from Victoria to Sidney.

⑥ **Sidney.** For boats crossing from Roche Harbor or the northern San Juan Islands, Sidney is a natural first stop to clear customs, stroll around, and restock with fresh produce, meat, spirits, and more. Downtown Sidney and nearby Tsehum Harbour have much to attract boaters, including excellent bakeries just up Beacon Avenue (Sidney's main street). The town also has art galleries, interesting shops, liquor stores, several bookstores, several museums, and three supermarkets. Summer concerts are held on the lawn at the base of Beacon Street. A paved walkway stretches 2.5 km along the Sidney waterfront between Port Sidney Marina and south beyond the Washington State Ferries terminal. It is part of the 29 km multi-use Lochside Regional Trail stretching from Swartz Bay to Victoria.

The Sidney Historical Museum occupies the lower floor of the old Post Office Building, up at the corner of 4th and Beacon. The museum has an excellent exhibit of early history in Sidney, admission by donation. Highly recommended, especially for families. Located at the nearby Sidney airport is the BC Aviation Museum, a short cab ride away.

The Shaw Ocean Discovery Centre in the Sidney Pier building has outstanding exhibits of marine life from local waters.

For an entirely different feeling from downtown Sidney, try Tsehum Harbour, a short distance north of downtown. The pace in Tsehum Harbour is much slower, and many of the moored boats are funkier. This is where the fishing fleet moors, and where the boat yards are. Van Isle Marina is the major marina.

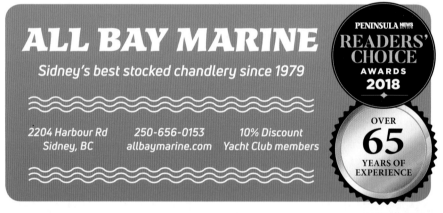

Sidney invites a stroll along the waterfront promenade.

Rum Island has a feeling of seclusion, with views across Haro Strait to nearby Turn Point.

217

Something about Tsehum Harbour attracts good restaurants, too. Tsehum Harbour's only disadvantage is the long walk to major shopping. Regular bus service runs into Sidney, or you could take a taxi or rent a car. Thrifty Foods charges $5 per order for delivery.

Market: The Sidney Street Market takes over the lower part of Beacon Avenue Thursday evenings May through September, 5:30 p.m. to 8:30 p.m.

Customs: Sidney is the western terminus of the Washington State Ferries that run from Anacortes and Friday Harbor, and is a Canada Customs port of entry. Customs can be cleared by telephone at Port Sidney Marina, Van Isle Marina or Canoe Cove Marina.

Wi-Fi: Free Wi-Fi throughout town. Select Sidney WiFi network and accept terms to connect.

⑥ **Port Sidney Marina**. 9835 Seaport Place, P.O. Box 2338, Sidney, BC V8L 4X3; (250) 655-3711; admin@portsidney.com; www. portsidney.com. Monitors VHF 66A. Open all year. Facilities include 30, 50 & 100 amp power, water, excellent washrooms, showers, laundry, Shaw Go Wi-Fi on the docks and free Wi-Fi in the comfortable marina lounge. This is a popular marina, modern and well-maintained, adjacent to downtown Sidney. Reservations recommended. A for-fee pumpout, located between D and E docks, accommodates boats up to 40 feet. The marina is part of the Mill Bay Marine Group, a company that owns several marinas throughout B.C.

Call on VHF 66A low power before entering and exiting the breakwater. When approaching from the north, pass between the two buoys just outside the breakwater entrance. The easternmost of these buoys marks a reef. Do not try to enter between the

north end of the breakwater and shore. If you are directed to the shore side of the long, main pier, do not stray outside the marked channel. The bottom has been dredged alongside the shoreside dock, but shoal water lies just a few feet inshore.

Customs: The customs check-in dock is on the end of G dock. Customs can be cleared by using the direct-line telephone on the dock. During summer months customs officers may be stationed there for inspections after calling in. Space at the dock is limited to one or two boats and once inside the breakwater maneuvering room is limited. The marina office has a video camera pointed at the dock and they can advise over the VHF if boats are waiting to clear customs.

⑥ **Sidney Beacon Ave. Public Wharf.** Sidney Beacon Avenue Public Wharf is used only for the summertime ferry to Sidney Spit Marine Park and does not have public dock space. A snack bar, café and a fresh fish market are at the end of the pier.

⑦ **Tsehum Harbour.** Tsehum Harbour (Tsehum is pronounced "See-um"), a shallow but navigable inlet about 1.5 miles north of downtown Sidney, contains a number of public, private, and yacht club moorages as well as chandleries. Enter favoring the Armstrong Point (south) side to avoid a marked rock. This is the working waterfront of Sidney, with several excellent boatyards. Van Isle Marina, the first marina on the south

Port Sidney Marina

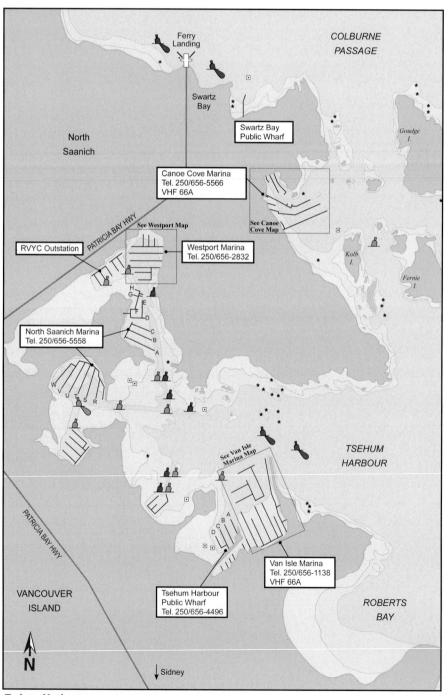

Tsehum Harbour

side, has a customs check-in telephone, fuel, and guest moorage. Westport Marina has guest moorage, and many services including haulout and free showers. Other moorages in Tsehum Harbour are North Saanich Marina, Capitol City and Sidney North Saanich yacht clubs, a Royal Victoria Yacht Club outstation, and private marinas. The main fuel dock is in Van Isle Marina. Fuel is also available at North Saanich Marina.

Speed limit: A speed limit of 4 knots is in force in Tsehum Harbour. Watch your wake.

Repairs: Haulout and complete repairs are available.

LOCAL KNOWLEDGE

ROCKS: Stay close to the end of the dock when rounding the west end of the fuel and customs dock at Van Isle Marina. A substantial drying rock lies a short distance off, and each year a few boats manage to find it. The rock is marked by a beacon, but the rock extends toward the dock from the beacon.

⑦ **Van Isle Marina.** 2320 Harbour Road, Sidney, V8L 2P6; (250) 656-1138; info@vanislemarina.com; www.vanislemarina.com. Monitors VHF 66A. Open 7 days a week, all year. Gasoline and diesel at fuel dock, customs clearance with dedicated phone in the small shed at the end of the fuel dock, Shaw Go Wi-Fi, 15, 30, 50 & 100 amp power, excellent washrooms, showers and laundry, pumpout, launch ramp for marina guests, oil pumpout. Internet is provided free through an installation by Shaw Go. Passwords available from the office. A business center with computer connections, copy machine, fax machine, and conference room is available for marina guests.

A side-tie dock, 451 feet long and 15 feet wide, runs parallel to the breakwater on the

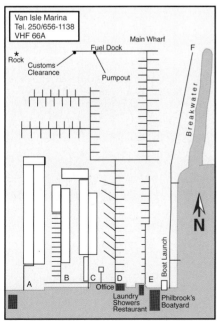
Van Isle Marina

east side of the marina. It is set up for yachts up to 200' and more, with 100 amp power, telephone, cable, and internet connections. Large boat or small, it's best to call ahead for guest moorage availability.

Van Isle is a large and busy marina, about a mile from downtown. Full repair services, haulout to 45 tons, and dry storage are available. The Thrifty Foods in Sidney will deliver groceries to the marina. The Sea Glass Waterfront Grill is at the head of the dock, call (778) 351-3663 for reservations. The famous Latch Country Inn Restaurant is a short walk away. The marina offers bicycles at no charge to ride into Sidney or on the popular Lochside Trail, nearby.

Since 1955 Van Isle Marina has been owned and managed by three generations of the Dickinson family. The family's long-term commitment to doing things right is evident. The staff is excellent, and the facilities are top-notch.

⑦ **Tsehum Harbour Public Wharf.** (250) 655-4496. Open all year, 1043 feet of dock space, 20 & 30 amp power, washrooms, shower, Wi-Fi available at the office. This is a commercial fish boat harbor that accepts very limited transient moorage. Call in advance for availability. Fresh fish for sale.

⑦ **Westport Marina.** 2075 Tryon Road, Sidney, BC V8L 3X9; (250) 656-2832; westport@thunderbirdmarine.com; www.

CANOE COVE MARKETPLACE

RESTAURANTS, SHOPS & SERVICES

ALL THINGS MARINE THRIFT STORE

The Maritime Museum of BC has opened the marine focused thrift store which will take in donated surplus marine equipment to be sold by volunteers of the Museum. This is a great way to reuse and recycle the many extra pieces of marine equipment that most boaters gather and see them go to a good use. The MMBC will be accepting donations of saleable marine equipment and tools at their location at Canoe Cove Marina on Fridays and Saturdays.

Open Fridays and Saturdays • 250-385-4222 ext. 102
www.mmbc.bc.ca

BLACKLINE MARINE INC.

Blackline delivers industry leading service in yacht rigging, composite repair, AwlGrip paint refinishing, custom metal fabrication, and seasonal maintenance. Canoe Cove Marina has been our home for 37 years and we are proud to be an active member of this service community.

Service & Haul Outs: 250-656-6616
www.blacklinemarine.com

CANOE COVE MARINA & BOATYARD

Canoe Cove Marina has been a preferred "one-stop" full service marina for over 75 years. Commitment to customer service, ongoing upgrading of technical skills, and regular expansion of facilities, has been the hallmark of the Marina's success.

250-656-5566 • 2300 Canoe Cove Rd.
www.canoecovemarina.com

NW EXPLORATIONS

NW Explorations is a premier charter, marine service and brokerage company offering first-class customer service in all areas. Whether you want to charter a yacht or need service for your existing boat, NW Explorations can help meet your needs.
236-237-6939 • Bldg. 6 • www.nwexplorations.com

RAVEN MARINE

Providing professional yacht services to the Pacific Northwest for over 20 years. Our accredited technical teams are experienced with installations, maintenance, and repairs. Our professional brokers will provide the advice and expertise you need to make an informed decision.
250-655-3934 • info@ravenmarine.ca

VECTOR YACHT SERVICES

Vector Yacht Services is the premier marine repair, service, and repower center for Vancouver Island. With over 30 years of service, our factory trained service technicians are experienced in all aspects of boat systems. We pride ourselves on providing quality workmanship and exceeding customer expectations.
Chandlery & Service 250-656-5515 • www.vectoryacht.com

thunderbirdmarine.com. Open all year. 15, 20, 30 & 50 amp power, washrooms, free showers, Wi-Fi. Guest moorage in unoccupied slips, call ahead for availability. Haulout to 55 tons. Well stocked chandlery, charts, limited groceries.

⑦ **North Saanich Marina.** P.O. Box 2001, 1949 Marina Way, North Saanich, BC V8L 3S3; (250) 656-5558; nsm@obmg.com; www.northsaanichmarina.com. Open all year. Gasoline and diesel at fuel dock, not always attended. Wi-Fi. Washrooms at main office. Permanent and visitor moorage usually available for vessels to 70 feet, 15, 30 & 50 amp power. Recent dock refurbishments, large dog walking area, and a short taxi ride to the nearby town of Sidney. Rental bikes available to ride the paved trails to Sidney and Victoria. Store carries sundries, fishing tackle, boat cleaning supplies, ice. Call ahead for moorage availability. The marina is part of Oak Bay Marine Group, a company that owns several marinas and fishing resorts throughout B.C.

⑧ **Canoe Bay.** Canoe Bay, commonly called Canoe Cove, is tucked in behind a group of islands, only some of which have navigable passages between them. The clearest passage is **John Passage**, along the west side of Coal Island. From John Passage turn west into **Iroquois Passage**, and follow Iroquois Passage between Fernie Island and Goudge Island into Canoe Bay. From the south, Page Passage, west of Fernie Island, leads to Canoe Bay, and many boats use **Page Passage**. Canoe Bay has moorage with all amenities.

Caution: Page Passage should be run only with local knowledge or close study of large-scale Chart 3479. Tidal currents can run strongly, especially on spring tides.

⑧ **Canoe Cove Marina & Boatyard.** 2300 Canoe Cove Road, North Saanich, BC V8L 3X9; (250) 656-5566; (250) 656-5515; www.canoecovemarina.com. Monitors VHF 66A. Open all year, gasoline, diesel, propane at fuel dock, 30 & 50 amp power, washrooms, showers, laundry, 24-hour customs clearance at fuel dock, free Wi-Fi. This is a 450-berth marina with permanent and visitor moorage. Best to call ahead.

Navigate carefully on approach. A number

Princess Bay, a popular anchorage on Portland Island National Park Reserve.

of islands and rocks surround the entrance to Canoe Cove. They are well marked on the charts and easily avoided as long as you pay attention.

Canoe Cove Joe's Cafe is in the center of the marina, and the excellent Stonehouse Restaurant is nearby. A short trail leads to the Swartz Bay ferry terminal for arriving or departing guests from Tsawwassen, on the B.C. mainland. A harbor taxi shuttle connects the marina with Sidney. Pacifica Paddle Sports (250) 665-7411 at Canoe Cove offers kayak, canoe, and paddleboard rentals along with lessons and tours.

Canoe Cove's major thrust is its environmentally friendly full repair facility. They recently added an 83-ton Travelift, and they have extensive covered work areas and a well-stocked chandlery now run by Vector Marine. The staff and management are friendly and competent. Together with Vector Marine, Blackline Marine, Raven Marine, Sea Power Marine Centre, Jespersen Boat Builders, Reyse Marine, and Lightship Marine Mobile, they can do anything.

Customs: The customs clearance dock is located on the fuel dock pier.

Swartz Bay Public Wharf. Open all year, adjacent to the ferry terminal, with 85 feet

of dock space. No facilities. Watch for heavy ferry traffic near Swartz Bay.

Piers Island Public Wharf. Open all year with 200 feet of dock space, no facilities.

⑨ **Portland Island (Gulf Islands National Park Reserve).** Formerly Princess Margaret Provincial Marine Park. Open all year, picnic and campsites, toilets, no other facilities. Dogs must be on leash and cleaned up after. In honor of her last visit to Victoria, Portland Island was donated to Her Royal Highness Princess Margaret, who later deeded the island to British Columbia. The park is now part of the Gulf Islands National Park Reserve.

Portland Island is wooded and hilly. Hiking trails follow the coastline. Easy-walking service roads and trails crisscross the center of the island. It would be easy to spend an entire day exploring. Reader Tyson Nevil says the coastline trail is easier to follow when walking in a counter-clockwise direction.

Anchor in Royal Cove (behind Chads Island) on the north side of the island, or in Princess Bay, behind Tortoise Island on the south side. The Royal Cove anchorage is exposed to the wakes of passing BC ferries, and Princess Bay also receives wakes. At Royal Cove you can have a quiet night if you can get

221

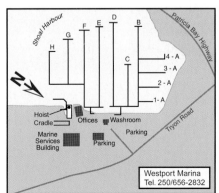

Westport Marina

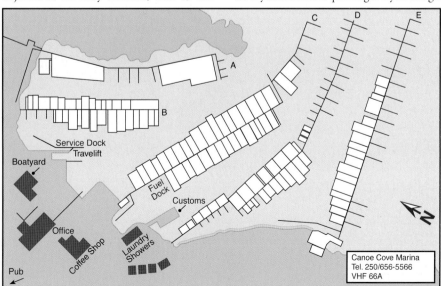

Canoe Cove Marina

well inside. Three red marked stern-tie rings are along the northeast shore in Royal Cove.

There's room for a couple of boats behind Brackman Island, off the southwest corner of Portland Island. Watch your depths at low tide. Brackman Island is a protected wildlife and bird sanctuary. No access is allowed above the high tide line and no pets are allowed.

Princess Bay is roomier and far more popular, but somewhat exposed to southerly winds. In summer it's usually fine. With its shallow depths, not much anchor rode need be paid out, and the boats squeeze in pretty tightly. Watch your depths as you approach the head of Princess Bay. The bottom shoals rapidly, farther from shore than you might expect. Dinghy docks in Royal Cove and Princess Bay provide shore access.

The host float in Princess Bay is staffed by yacht club volunteers during the summer. They answer questions and give out information.

The *G.B. Church*, a sunken freighter off the southwest shore of the island, is an artificial reef for divers. The freighter lies in 100 feet and is marked with bow and stern buoys.

PLUMPER SOUND AREA

Bedwell Harbour. Bedwell Harbour has a luxury marina resort, Poets Cove, with docks that give complete access to the facilities ashore. North of the resort, anchorage is good (except in a southeasterly) off the Beaumont/ Mount Norman portion of Gulf Islands National Park Reserve. Anchorage also is good, if tight, in Peter Cove, on the west side of the harbor.

Slow Coast Coffee and Medicine Beach Liquor store are located a short walk from Medicine Beach, at the north end of Bedwell Harbour. No dock, but easy anchoring just offshore, and a sandy beach for the dinghy.

Customs clearance: The Canada Border Services Agency (Canada Customs) dock is adjacent to Poets Cove Marina and well marked. Open from May 1 to September 30. Except for landing, only the skipper can leave the boat until customs is cleared. The procedure is for the captain to go up the ramp to the direct-line telephones along the wall of the customs office. Have all of the vessel's paperwork and crew's passport information ready. Call in for clearance. In most cases the agent on the telephone will give you a clearance number, but you may be asked to stand by for agents to inspect your vessel. Canpass or Nexus permits only from October 1 through April 30. See the U.S. and Canadian Customs

Information section for more information on clearing Canadian Customs.

Peter Cove. Peter Cove is at the southern tip of North Pender Island. It is a well protected little anchorage, but permanently moored boats make anchoring a bit tight. A significant reef guards the mouth of the cove. Enter and depart north of the reef.

⑩ **Poets Cove Marina.** 9801 Spalding Road, RR #3, South Pender Island, BC V0N 2M3; (250) 629-2100; (250) 629-2111 marina; marina@poetscove.com; www.poetscove. com. Open all year, gasoline, diesel, and ice at the fuel dock. Guest moorage to 100 feet in 95 slips and side-tie, 30 amp power. If slips are filled, a floating dock is available at a reduced rate. Liquor store, cafe, pub with dining, heated pool, hot tub, spa, Eucalyptus Steam Cave, fitness center, and free Wi-Fi. Day passes for the pool are available for guests who anchor out. Coin-operated laundry machines are located adjacent to the pool.

The casual Moorings Cafe is located in the building adjacent to the pool and serves sandwiches, espresso, and baked goods. The cafe also sells liquor and convenience items. Syrens Bistro and Lounge, open April

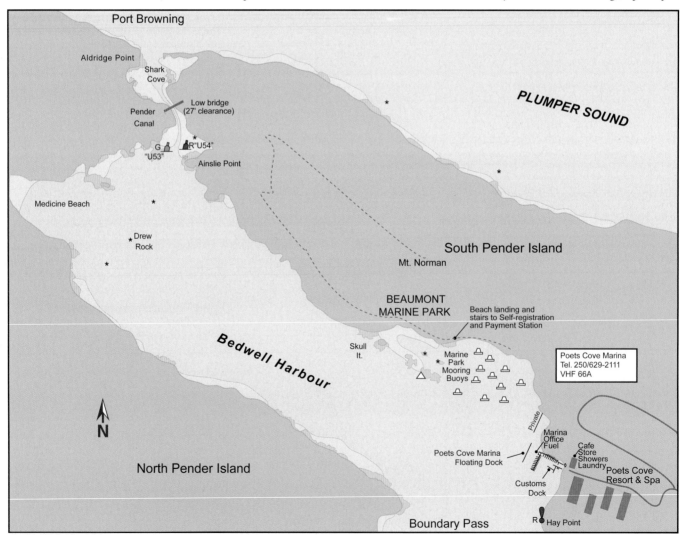

Bedwell Harbour

The large swimming pool at Port Browning is a hit with the kids.

through October, serves lunch and dinner noon to 9:00 p.m. and has seating indoors or out on the patio. Aurora, a fine dining venue, serves breakfast and dinner, open seasonally.

Poets Cove has plenty of activities. Book an aerial whale watching excursion, rent a bike or kayak and explore the island, play a round of golf, or try out the disc golf course. Kids Camp programs are available through Dog Mermaid Eco Excursions (250) 222-0015. Shuttle service is available for a charge.

Beaumont/Mount Norman Park (Gulf Islands National Park Reserve). In Bedwell Harbour, west side of South Pender Island, in Bedwell Harbour. Open all year. Facilities include 15 mooring buoys (pay buoy fees at honor box top of staircase above the beach northwest of the buoys, no charge before 3:00 p.m.). Mooring buoys accommodate boats up to 50 feet, or 40 feet depending upon wind conditions. Signage for size limits are posted on the buoys. Toilets, no showers or fresh water. Walk-in campsites, picnicking, excellent walking and hiking trails. Hike to the top of Mount Norman, elevation 800 feet, for a memorable view. Dogs must be on leash.

Enter from Swanson Channel from the south, or from Plumper Sound and Port Browning through Pender Canal (27-foot clearance).

Pender Canal. Pender Canal is a man-made dogleg channel between North Pender Island and South Pender Island, connecting Bedwell Harbour and Port Browning. The canal is crossed by a bridge with 27 feet of vertical clearance. Pender Canal is narrow, shallow, and often has a swift current running through it. Because of its dogleg shape, vessels approaching from opposite directions cannot see each other until they are in the narrowest section.

Before entering, signal your intentions on VHF 16, low power: *Securite, Securite, this is the 34-foot motor vessel* Happy Days, *northbound from Bedwell Harbour to Port Browning. Any concerned traffic please advise, channel one-six.*

⑪ **Port Browning.** Port Browning has a resort (Port Browning Marina) with moorage and other facilities. Anchorage is good throughout the harbor. The Driftwood Centre shopping area is about a half-mile walk from the marina or you can call the Pender Island Cab at (250) 629-2222. The center has a beautiful Tru-Value Foods, a bank, gift shop, book store, bakery, liquor store, and pharmacy. The gas station now has marine supplies. The award winning Sea Star Vineyards is nearby.

⑪ **Port Browning Marina.** P.O. Box 126, North Pender Island, BC V0N 2M0; (250) 629-3493; contact@portbrowning.ca; www. portbrowning.ca. Monitors VHF 66A. Canpass/Nexus-only reporting station. Open all year, 3000 feet of guest moorage, 15 & 30 amp power, free Wi-Fi, ATM, excellent

223

washrooms, laundry, launch ramp, seasonal swimming pool, beer & wine sales. Kayak and SUP rentals.

Port Browning Marina offers two dining venues: the licensed family Port Browning Pub, with large picture windows facing east, overlooks the bay; and the adults-only bar named Bridgeman's Bistro, with a separate entrance, occupies the back portion of the restaurant building. Bridgeman's Bistro is open for dinner on Friday, Saturday and Sunday; open for breakfast on Saturdays and Sundays only. A glass-enclosed side-patio provides partial views of the marina and kayaking activities. Similar menu selections are available at both dining venues. Port Browning Marina is a local's favorite.

The Mill Bay Marine Group recently purchased the property with plans to install new docks in the future.

Browning Harbour Public Wharf. Open all year, 89 feet of dock space, no facilities. Commercial fish boats have priority.

Shingle Bay (Gulf Islands National Park Reserve). This is a recent addition to the Gulf Islands National Park Reserve. Open all year, picnic tables, campsites, composting toilets. Dogs must be on leash and cleaned up after. See the remnants of the Shingle Bay fish reduction plant that operated intermittently between 1927 and 1959. It served as an important part of the local economy, employing 15 to 20 men at a time, mainly Pender Island residents.

Because the bay shoals rapidly, you must anchor well out, in line with the old reduction plant. Favor the north side, as a reef extends on the south. Anchorage is exposed to the southwest. The community park at the head of the bay is a welcome place to walk dogs, picnic, and access the island. A jungle gym is popular with children.

⑫ **Otter Bay Marina.** 2311 McKinnon Rd., North Pender Island, BC V0N 2M1; (250) 629-3579; info@otterbaymarina.ca; www.otterbaymarina.ca. Monitors VHF 66A. Online reservations highly recommended during the peak season. Moorage open all

Otter Bay Marina is a great place to relax and enjoy the views.

year, full services May 15 to September 30. Washrooms, showers, laundry, 15 & 30 amp power, 50 amp power on "A" dock, launch ramp, gazebo, children's play area, two heated pools, free Wi-Fi. Four buoys belonging to the marina are used for transient moorage when vacated by the permanent tenant. Scooters, kayaks and SUP rentals. A fee-based daily shuttle to Driftwood Center.

The upper pool is for families and is open mid-May through Labour Day. When both pools are operating, the lower pool is for adults. The small convenience store carries baked goods, prepared foods, frozen meat and ice. Daily breakfast specials are offered at the espresso bar; milkshakes, smoothies and lunch items in the afternoon. A daily or weekly day camp is offered for children through Dog Mermaid Eco Excursions (250) 222-0015.

This popular marina is on the west side of North Pender Island, facing Swanson Channel. Look for the tall flagpoles on the observation deck, just past the ferry landing. The marina was taken over by new owners in the fall of 2017, followed by upgrades to the lower pool and washrooms. Seating, with cozy fire pits, is located along the walkways among the colorful flower beds. Weekend meal events starting in June; see their website for the schedule.

An enclosed activity center, with a stone fireplace and rental barbecues, is a nice venue

for group events and rendezvous, even in the off-season.

For a short excursion, take the dinghy across the bay to Roe Island Park, a lovely spot to stretch the legs.

Caution: A green spar buoy is off the corner of the marina docks. Red, Right, Returning means you leave this buoy to port as you enter. Do not pass between the buoy and the dock. A rock 2 feet below the surface at zero tide lurks between the buoy and the dock.

The 9-hole Pender Island Golf Course is about a 15-minute walk from the marina. No tee times needed. The marina can give you a ride up the hill to the course for a small fee. Zuppa's Restaurant (250-629-3124) is at the golf course.

Roesland/Roe Lake (Gulf Islands National Park Reserve). Located on North Pender Island, deep in Otter Bay. Field Correspondent Deane Hislop reports: "We set the anchor, good holding, and took the dinghy to the park's dinghy dock. We discovered a former 1908 farmhouse that now serves as the Pender Island Museum, offering a glimpse into the island's past. This is also the location of Parks Canada's field office. We took the short walk to the end of Roe Islet to take in an amazing view of Swanson Channel, Saltspring Island, and Vancouver Island. Then it was back along the islet and up Shingle Bay road to the Roe Lake trail head and through the forest to beautiful Roe Lake, making for a full day of hiking and exploring."

Port Washington Public Wharf. On North Pender Island. Open all year, 147 feet of dock space on two floats. The northwest float is for transient boats, the portion marked in yellow is a 15-minute load/unload area; eastern float appears to be assigned, permanent moorage. Floats are subject to boat wakes from Swanson Channel. No facilities ashore. Watch for a rock off the southeast dock. One float is designated for aircraft.

⑬ **Hope Bay Public Wharf.** (250) 813-3321 Wharfinger. East side of North Pender Island, facing Navy Channel. Open all year, 300 feet of dock space, 2 day-use mooring buoys

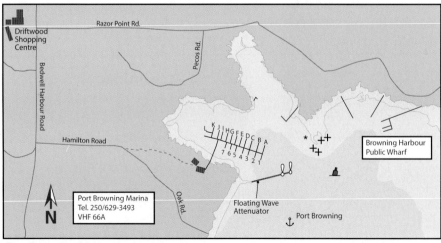

Port Browning Marina

Hope Bay Public Wharf

marked "Hope Bay Store." If the dock is full (it often is), tie to the mooring buoys and dinghy in. Wakes from passing ferries make rafting undesirable, and depths on the inside of the dock are shallow at low tide. Peter, at the upland Goldsmith & Clock shop, is the wharfinger.

This historic landing has attractive buildings on the pier which house a number of small businesses, including a chocolate shop, the Pender Island Veterinary Clinic (250) 629-9909, the Dockside Realty and a second-hand shop with antiques. Philly's Diner closed in 2018 and it remains to be seen if another restaurant will take its place.

Breezy Bay – Sea Star Vineyards. (250) 629-6960; www.seastarvineyards.ca. (Formerly the Saturna Winery.) At press time, new owners of the vineyards have not re-opened the winery or bistro. We were informed that the dock is closed for repairs, and boaters are requested not to dock or walk the grounds in 2019. The owners are working towards re-opening the vineyard grounds and a bistro in 2020.

Irish Bay. Irish Bay, on the west side of Samuel Island, is a good anchorage with scenic rock walls, but the island is privately owned. If you venture above the foreshore, the caretaker will shoo you off.

Winter Cove. A Gulf Islands National Park Reserve. Winter Cove, between Samuel Island and Saturna Island, has an attractive park on the Saturna Island side, and shallow anchorage. We think the best anchorages are behind Winter Point, north of the cable line, or just off the National Park Reserve lands. The charts show shallow water in the middle of the cove, but you can patrol around—carefully—with the depth sounder and find anchoring sites away from the preferred spots. The mooring buoys in the southwest corner of the cove are private. A public dinghy dock is on the eastern shore. It has been reported that a sunken boat lies in the middle of Winter Cove.

Minx Reef partially blocks the Plumper Sound approach to Winter Cove. Entering, we have found the best way to avoid the reef is to point the bow at the northern shore of Irish Bay, and run well past Winter Point before turning south into the cove.

The annual Canada Day (July 1) Saturna Island Lamb Barbecue at Winter Cove is a big event. The cove is packed with boats; islanders shuttle visitors ashore and back. For more information go to www.saturnalambbbarbeque.com.

The annual Saturna Lions Club Dog & Dogs Show is in early September. Prizes for best dog and owner look-alike, best puppy, best tail-wagger, and more. Bribes encouraged. Correspondents Bruce and Margaret Evertz happened upon the show and say it's wonderful. Bring your dog. For information see www.saturnalionsclub.net.

Boat Pass. Boat Pass connects Winter Cove with the Strait of Georgia. Currents in Boat Pass can run to 7 knots past several nasty rocks and reefs. Take this pass only at or near high water slack, preferably after seeing it at low water so you know where the rocks are.

⑭ **Lyall Harbour.** www.saturnatourism.com Lyall Harbour, on Saturna Island, is a

OTTER BAY
MARINA
PENDER ISLAND, BC

Otter Bay Marina is located 5 miles from the US border on the west side of North Pender Island, just east of the Ferry Terminal in the heart of the Gulf Islands.

Our management is dedicated to provide you with the best service

- 2 Heated Swimming Pools
- Boat & Kayak Launch
- 15, 30 & 50 Amp Power
- Potable Water & WiFi on the docks
- Kids' Playground
- Local Art & Gifts
- Store with Groceries, Clothing & Marine Supplies
- Bistro Style Restaurant serving Lattes, Espresso & Cappuccino
- Covered Gazebo with Propane & Charcoal BBQs
- Strong Cell Phone Signal & Payphone Service
- Excellent Showers & Laundry Facilities
- Dog Friendly Facility
- Nearby 9 Hole Golf Course—Shuttle Service

www.otterbaymarina.ca **Call (250) 629-3579 or VHF 66A**

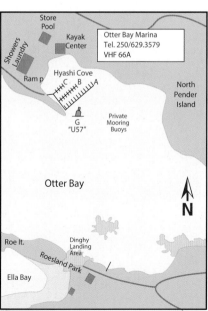
Otter Bay Marina

SWIMMING POOLS OF THE INSIDE PASSAGE

Swimming pools are a welcome treat at a marina. Over the years we've had many readers request a list of boat-accessible swimming pools in the Northwest. As it turns out, there are many choices, from Hood Canal to Gorge Harbour, and most of the pools are heated. You just need to know how to find them.

ALDERBROOK RESORT & SPA
The indoor heated pool is in a greenhouse adjacent to Hood Canal, with a beautiful view of the area.

PLEASANT HARBOR MARINA
The heated outdoor pool and hot tub are tucked among the trees above the marina. Open seasonally.

Pleasant Harbor Marina

ROSARIO RESORT & SPA
Three pools are located around the property. The family pool is adjacent to the marina. The adults-only pool is in front of the resort on a sun deck. A lap pool is tucked into the spa in the basement of the historic mansion.

LOPEZ ISLANDER RESORT & MARINA
Pool and hot tub are located across the street from the marina and main lodge building.

DEER HARBOR MARINA
The seasonal outdoor pool is up the hill and overlooks the marina.

Deer Harbor Marina

ROCHE HARBOR MARINA
The large heated pool is on the hill overlooking the marina. A dinghy dock provides access, or walk around from the main docks.

Roche Harbor Marina

SEMIAHMOO MARINA
The spa and pool are part of the Semiahmoo Health Club at the resort, and are available for a fee.

POETS COVE MARINA
The pool and hot tub overlooks the marina. Laundry is just a few steps away, so you can catch up with the wash while lounging at the pool.

Poets Cove Marina

PORT BROWNING MARINA
The pool is on the sloping hillside next to the pub. Kids love this pool.

OTTER BAY MARINA
The adults-only pool is just up the way, next to the main building and snack bar. The family pool is up the hill.

Otter Bay Marina

BRENTWOOD BAY RESORT & MARINA
The pool and hot tub are just outside the main building, overlooking the marina. The focus is on serenity and relaxation for adults.

GANGES
The new community center has a pool and shower facility for visitors. Ask the marina for directions.

OCEANFRONT SUITES AT COWICHAN BAY
Oceanfront Suites has moorage and an indoor pool. Guests of other marinas can use the pool for a fee.

BEACH GARDENS RESORT & MARINA
You can enjoy the indoor pool year round.

GORGE HARBOUR MARINA RESORT
The pool and hot tub look over the marina and the harbor.

Gorge Harbour Marina Resort

large, well protected anchorage, with a ferry landing and store near the entrance. Nearby **Boot Cove** is a beautiful spot with anchorage in 12 to 18 feet, but it is crowded with resident boats on mooring buoys, and can be subject to williwaws blowing over a low swale on Saturna Island.

Tom Kincaid anchored there one afternoon, and before night his anchor line was stretched tight by 40-knot winds that were still blowing the next morning. "I dinghied to the nearest beach that afternoon and walked to the store for a loaf of bread," he reports. "I asked the proprietor if he'd heard when the wind was supposed to die down. 'Oh, you must be in Boot Cove,' he said. 'It always blows in Boot Cove.' So we weighed anchor, set sail, flew out the entrance and coasted to a stop, windless, just outside."

Lyall Harbour is off the beaten path for the Gulf Islands. It is quiet and gradually being discovered. Your choice, anchor in the bay or tie at the dock. Nothing fancy. This is not Ganges. The Saturna Point Store is the center of activity in Lyall Harbour and just up the road from the Public Wharf. The Lighthouse Pub is downstairs in the same building and has very good food with fish and chips being their signature item, though some say their lamb burger is to die for. Lamb carries a special reverence on Saturna Island. Dine inside or out on the deck. The beer is cold and the drink menu is imaginative and available by the drink or by the pitcher. You get the idea. The people are very nice. They say hello. They like your business. The Pub is family friendly.

Need a "wake-me-up" in the morning? Hike a mile up the hill from the marina. Then treat yourself to darn good organic coffee and sweet and savory baked goods, or breakfast items at Wild Thyme (250-539-5589), open Thursday-Sunday. You can't miss it on the left. It is the pleasant green double-decker bus. If it is raining, sit on the upper deck of the bus and join the locals. You might need to get up to date on your Canadian politics - Saturna's point of view. Or enjoy the sun outside in a patio area. Visitors and locals rave about their food. Open for breakfast and lunch. Free Wi-Fi. After a hearty breakfast, it is downhill

back to the boat. You can rent bicycles at Saturna Cycle (250-857-4102) upland from the wharf. For an interesting island ride, visit the Saturna General Store & Freight (250-539-2936) beyond Wild Thyme, a 2.5km ride. Kayaks are for rent from the Saturna Paddle Shack (250-539-5553) located on the dock. An Outdoor Market is open seasonally on Saturdays in the store parking lot from 10:00 a.m. to 1:00 p.m.

⑭ **Lyall Harbour Public Wharf.** (250) 539-0195 wharfinger. Next to the ferry dock. Open all year, 200 feet of dock space. No power, water, washrooms or showers. Commercial fishing vessels have priority. Gasoline and diesel at the fuel dock. Pay for fuel at the Saturna Point Store, just above the dock. Moorage is collected at the honor box at the top of the dock. Note, there are day rates and overnight rates. Floatplanes arrive three times per day from the Vancouver airport for your guests. Laundry and showers are located at the campground ¼ mile up the road from the wharf. Wild Thyme Coffee House is up the road a bit in a cute converted double-decker bus named Lucy. Stay overnight and treat yourself and your crew to an evening at the Lighthouse Pub.

⑭ **Saturna Point Store & Fuel.** 100 E. Point Rd., P.O. Box 80, Saturna Island, BC V0N 2Y0; (250) 539-5726. saturnapointstore.com Open daily in summers. Gasoline and diesel at fuel dock, washrooms, convenience store with snack items, ice, ice cream, fishing gear. ATM and the Prism Art Gallery. The Saturna Lighthouse Pub downstairs (250-539-5725) offers sit-down dining inside or out. The pub is fully licensed for family dining.

Georgeson Passage. Georgeson Passage, between Mayne Island and Samuel Island, is short and pretty. Currents, based on Active Pass, are about half as strong as those in Active Pass, both flooding and ebbing. Still, they run vigorously. See the Georgeson Passage secondary station under Active Pass in the Tide & Current Tables Vol. 5, and Ports and Passes. If entering from the Strait of Georgia through the narrow pass between Campbell

Point and Georgeson Island, be aware that a drying reef extends from Campbell Point into the pass. Favor the Georgeson Island side. Watch for rapids.

⑮ **Horton Bay.** The public wharf is a Canpass/Nexus-only customs reporting station, and has room for a dozen 30-foot boats, plus rafting. Entering the area between Mayne and Samuel Islands requires some care but is completely navigable.

From the Gulf Islands side, the best route is through Georgeson Passage, east of Lizard Island. Be careful of a kelp-covered rock in less than 6 feet, fairly close to Mayne Island. If entering west of Lizard Island, the rock is in the middle of your path into Horton Bay. A reef extends from Curlew Island into Robson Passage, which separates Curlew Island from Mayne Island. Use Plans Chart 3477 (larger scale, much recommended) or 3442. A study of Chart 3477 shows a mid-channel course is called for. The bay is filled with crab pots and private mooring buoys in the best part of the bay. We have received reports of current running through the bay.

⑯ **Reef Harbour (Gulf Islands National Park Reserve).** Reef Harbour, along with nearby Cabbage Island and Tumbo Island constitute a marine park. The park is open all year, 10 mooring buoys, pit toilets, no water, no showers. Dogs must be on leash. Caution, some buoys are close together, watch swinging space. No rafting on the buoys. Maximum vessel size: 50 ft for winds 30 knots or less; and 40 ft for winds of 37 knots or less. This is a pretty anchorage between Cabbage Island and Tumbo Island, out on the edge of the Strait of Georgia. Caution for rocks and reefs on the approaches. From west northwest, approach between two long reefs. Approaching from south, cross the reef on the Tumbo Channel side, between two patches of kelp, a short distance from the north tip of Tumbo Island. This should show 30 feet under the keel all the way across. Chart 3441 shows good depths at that location. Field Correspondent Jim Norris noted a gentle swell in the anchorage in settled weather but notes that it might be a lumpy anchorage in northwest winds at high tide when the protective reefs around Cabbage Island are submerged.

Cabbage Island has picnic sites, campsites, and a wonderful sandy beach. Crabbing is reportedly good. Cabbage Island is interesting to explore. It isn't very big, so you can walk around the entire island in a reasonable time. Though tiny, the island is hardly dull. The beaches are different on every side, ranging from white sand, to sandstone reefs, to an aggregate of small rocks embedded in sandstone, to fine gravel. Inland, you'll find forests of Arbutus, (madrone), Garry Oak and Western Red Cedar.

Tumbo Island, privately owned until recently, is now part of the Gulf Islands National Park Reserve. Trails lead through the island where you will find remnants of the island's commercial past in the forests and

Anchorage off Lyall Harbour Wharf; pub, store, and more upland

Moorage at Fulford Public Wharf

fields. Coal mining was attempted in the early 1900s, but the shafts flooded and the effort was abandoned. In the 1920s and 1930s foxes were raised on the island. The original fox farm homestead, on the flatter northeast end of the island, can still be seen. Field Correspondent Jim Norris reports good access to the trailhead just opposite mooring buoys 3 and 4, where you will find an information kiosk, map, and a rope to help climb up the smooth rock face. The landowner who sold Tumbo Island to the reserve has a life tenancy for the house and a small area surrounding the house located on the northeast end of the island. If someone is in residence there, please respect their privacy.

⑰ Narvaez Bay (Gulf Islands National Park Reserve). Picnic tables and toilet, camping in 7 sites, ideal for kayakers. Dogs must be on leash. Beautiful Narvaez Bay indents the rock cliffs on the south shore of Saturna Island, and is open to southeasterly winds and the wakes of passing ship traffic in Boundary Pass. Parts of the bay's shoreline were added to the Gulf Islands National Park Reserve, including the small peninsula parallel to the western shore, a short distance in.

You can anchor in the little bight behind this peninsula and have shelter from wind and waves, although a reader wrote that in a northerly, they experienced williwaw winds of 20+ knots from the head of the bay. The wind in the Strait of Georgia was only 12 knots. The holding ground is not very good. It appears to be loose mud, the kind that washes off easily. It felt like a thin layer on top of rock—fine for a picnic in settled weather, but chancy for overnight.

The neck of land separating the peninsula

from the rest of Saturna Island holds the ruins of an ambitious homestead. We didn't find any buildings, although fruit trees and the remnants of fences are there. A dirt service road runs the length of the peninsula and leads up the hill to a main Saturna Island road.

ACTIVE PASS AREA

Active Pass. Active Pass separates Mayne Island and Galiano Island, and has long been one of the most popular fishing areas in the Gulf Islands. It also is the route taken by commercial traffic, including BC Ferries that run between Tsawwassen and Swartz Bay. Currents in Active Pass run to 7 knots on a spring tide. They flood eastward toward the Strait of Georgia. See the Tide and Current Tables Vol. 5, or Ports and Passes. Unless your boat is quite fast, slack water passage is recommended. If you are in the current, you can minimize turbulence by favoring Miners Bay.

Dinner Bay. Dinner Bay, between Crane Point and Dinner Point, looks to be a good anchorage, but is exposed to ferry wakes and northwest winds.

Village Bay. Village Bay is wide and deep, with convenient anchoring depths near the head. The bay is open to northwest winds and waves, but well protected from everything else. Village Bay has a ferry terminal.

⑱ Miners Bay. A public wharf is in the bay on the south side of Active Pass, and is subject to swirling tidal currents and the wakes from passing ferries. A float is on each side of the wharf, best suited for smaller boats. Convenient anchoring depths are close to shore—most of the bay is quite deep.

A bakery, inn, pub, and two grocery stores are up the hill from the wharf. A small museum on Fernhill Road covers the history of this area with indoor and outdoor exhibits. Across from the museum, on Saturday mornings, from 10:00 a.m. - 1:00 p.m., the Mayne Island Farmers Market, has local produce, handicrafts, baked goods, and art work. Beginning in the 1800s, this was a popular stop for miners on their way to the gold mines. The Springwater Lodge (250-

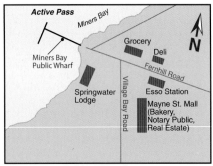

Miners Bay Public Wharf

539-5521), built in 1892, overlooks the bay. It remains the oldest continuously operated hotel in British Columbia.

Customs: Miners Bay wharf is a Canpass/Nexus-only customs reporting station.

⑱ Active Pass Auto & Marine. (250) 539-5411; www.activepassautoandmarine.com. Open all year. Propane, stove alcohol, tackle, bait, ice, snacks, ice cream, marine supplies, haulout, 24-hour towing and moped and bicycle rentals. Located at the service station 200 yards from the dock.

⑲ Sturdies Bay. Sturdies Bay, on Galiano Island toward the eastern end of Active Pass, is a landing for ferries coming to and from Tsawwassen and continuing on to the other Gulf Islands. A public float is alongside the ferry dock. The community of Sturdies Bay, just up the road, has a grocery store and shops. Galiano Oceanfront Inn & Spa is south of the ferry landing with its own dock.

Sturdies Bay is a convenient stop to exchange crew arriving from or departing to the mainland on the BC Ferries. They can disembark the ferry, walk across to the provincial dock, and board the boat.

⑲ Galiano Oceanfront Inn & Spa. 134 Madrona Drive, Galiano Island, BC V0N 1P0; (250) 539-3388; info@galianoinn.com; www.galianoinn.com. Located in Sturdies Bay, north of the ferry landing. Open all year but dock in place May to October only, call for exact dates. Wi-Fi, but no power or water on the dock. The dock is subject to wakes from passing ferries in Active Pass. Set fenders accordingly. Reasonable dock rates; free if using spa, restaurant, or inn. Suites were renovated in late 2018.

This is a high-quality inn and spa, with casual fine dining, natural spa, and gardens. Pizza from a wood-fired oven is served for lunch and early dinner from a pizza terrace overlooking the bay (seasonal). Village shops are a block away with more choices for dining, shopping and liquor store. Smart cars are available for rental (inquire in advance). If you're in Montague Harbour and want to dine at Atrevida Restaurant at the Inn, or have spa treatments, call for pick-up and reservations, (250) 539-3388.

The Kunamokst Mural from the 2010 Olympic games is displayed in the lobby of the Inn. The mural is made from individual tiles, each independently illustrated by a different artist. Collectively they form an image of an orca whale and calf. It's quite striking.

Whaler Bay. Whaler Bay is on the east side of Galiano Island, just north of Active Pass. It is full of rocks and shoal water. Enter carefully through a rock-strewn passage from the south, or through a more open passage around the north end of Gossip Island. Whaler Bay has a public wharf. Good protection is near the wharf, but there's very little swinging room.

A moonlit night over Ganges Harbour

Whaler Bay Public Wharf. (250) 539-2264. Open all year, 350 feet of dock space, no facilities. Commercial fish boats have priority.

MAYNE ISLAND, CAMPBELL BAY TO HORTON BAY

Campbell Bay. Campbell Bay, on the northeast side of Mayne Island, is entered between Edith Point and Campbell Point. It is open to southeasterly winds, but has anchoring depths near the head, mud bottom.

Bennett Bay (Gulf Islands National Park Reserve). Bennett Bay, south of Campbell Point, has good anchorage but is exposed to southeast winds. Curlew Island and Samuel Island are privately owned.

Note: Campbell Point, a portion of the waters of Bennett Bay, Georgeson Island, and the Belle Chain Islets including Anniversary Island, are part of Gulf Islands National Park Reserve. To protect sensitive ecosystems, access to Georgeson Island and the islets is prohibited.

SALTSPRING ISLAND, FULFORD HARBOUR TO LONG HARBOUR

Russell Island (Gulf Islands National Park Reserve). Russell Island is just outside Fulford Harbour. Anchor on the northwest side of the island, fair holding, with views of mountains above Fulford Harbour. A trail leads through open meadows and a forest of Douglas fir, arbutus (madrona) and Garry oak. The original house dates back more than a century. A caretaker lives on the island. A boater we trust reports, "Russell Island is wonderful!"

Fulford Harbour. Fulford Harbour is wide and open. A public dock for locals only is located on the north side of the ferry terminal. On the south side of the ferry terminal is a public float with transient moorage that is exposed to wind and ferry wash. No services at the float. The charming village of Fulford has a restaurant, a good grocery store at the Salt Spring Mercantile, and an assortment of art galleries and stores specializing in crafts and country clothing. Everything feels very "island."

By all means take a 15-minute walk down the road to St. Paul's Catholic church (called the Stone Church), built in 1880. The graveyard, with island history chiseled into its headstones, is adjacent. On one visit we found the church's door unlocked, and stepped inside. It was lovely. "This is where God lives," we thought.

Bus Transportation: Regular bus service on Saltspring Island connects Fulford Village, Ganges, Long Harbour, Vesuvius and Fernwood. For schedule see www.busonline.ca; (250) 537-6758.

Fulford Outer Harbour - Harbour Authority of Salt Spring Island. (250) 537-5711 Open all year. www.saltspringharbours.com A public wharf and float is located immediately south of the BC Ferries terminal, managed by the Harbour Authority of Salt Spring Island. The 54-foot public float provides moorage on both sides. Overnight moorage permitted. No water, no power. Payment envelopes, moorage rates, and a self-pay box are located on the wharf. Locals tend to use this float primarily for loading and unloading purposes.

Fulford Inner Harbour - Harbour Authority of Salt Spring Island. Located just north of the BC Ferries terminal is a public dock filled with local boats; no space for transient boats.

Isabella Island (Gulf Islands National Park Reserve). A smallish anchorage is available behind Isabella Island, a short distance west of the mouth of Fulford Harbour. Although exposed to the west, it's a cozy little spot for one or two boats. Anchor in 24 feet.

Ruckle Park. Beaver Point on Saltspring Island. Open all year, day use and overnight camping. No mooring facilities, exposed anchorage on each side of Ruckle Point. Probably the best of these anchorages is in the first cove south of Ruckle Point. Swinging room is limited, and the cove is exposed to ferry wakes and southeast winds. The anchorage is pretty, though, and in settled weather could be a good day stop. This is an extensive park, with miles of shoreline and rocky headlands. Walk-in campsites. Great views of the southern Gulf Islands.

DANGEROUS ROCKS & REEFS: Enter Ganges Harbour, leaving all the Chain Islands to starboard; *do NOT* cut through any of the islands. No short cuts. There are rocks and reefs throughout. The entry channel itself can be a 'minefield' with crab pot floats, many in dark colors; considerable boat traffic, and a charted, busy floatplane operations area.

There are two similarly named dangers in Ganges Harbour. *Money Maker Reef* is northwest of Third Sister Island near the entrance to the Harbour; *Money Makers Rock* is 2 miles to the northwest and is one of at least two dangerous rocks in a shallow area between and southeast of Saltspring Marina and Ganges Marina.

The dangerous shallow area, between Saltspring and Ganges marinas, has two charted rocks; one lies off the end of Ganges Marina C dock and the other lies off the southeast end of Saltspring Marina. The rock off Ganges Marina's C dock is locally known as Zachary Rock, however, Canadian charts show its name as Money Makers Rock. The rock south of Saltspring Marina is known locally as Money Makers Rock and is not named on Canadian charts. In 2018, locally known Money Makers Rock was in open water off the end of Saltspring Marina and marked with two small buoys. Saltspring Marina's expansion, planned for 2019, may cover part or all of the northerly charted rock with a floating breakwater. The exact location and water depth of both these charted rocks and the surrounding shallow area remain uncertain. Use extreme caution when approaching Ganges Marina's north docks and Saltspring Marina. The water depth at zero tide could be as shallow as 4 feet 3 inches.

㉀ Ganges. Ganges, at the head of Ganges Harbour, is a favorite destination. This bustling seaside village has marinas, good anchorage, shops, banks with ATM's, galleries, restaurants, and two large supermarkets with marina delivery. There is a dedicated centrally located dinghy dock. Thrifty Foods is the closest to the marinas. Above the store, entered from the street side, is "The Local," a liquor store associated with Thrifty Foods that also delivers to the marinas. Country Grocer (Liquor Agency in the store), at 374 Lower Ganges Road, has a "boaters van" with pick-up, drop-off services at any Ganges marina. Mouat's, a huge old hardware and household goods general store with a separate gift shop and apparel section, is a longstanding favorite. They also have fishing and marine supplies.

The sprawling Salt Spring Island Saturday Market, also called the Farmers Market, is held in Centennial Park at Grace Point on Saturdays 9:00 a.m. to 4:00 p.m., April through October. A Tuesday farmers market, no crafts, is held in the same location, 2:00 p.m. to 6:00 p.m. from June to the end of October. Although boats and tourists are

RESTAURANTS, SHOPS & SERVICES

BLACK SHEEP BOOKS

Get lost in a good bookstore. Explore two floors packed with volumes of enduring value, including familiar favorites, contemporary fiction, guides, and non-fiction titles covering everything from outer space to inner peace. Authorized dealer for CHS marine charts.
250-538-0025 • 3101-115 Fulford Ganges Rd. In Grace Point Square
www.blacksheepbooks.ca

LI READ SEA TO SKY PREMIER PROPERTIES

You love boating among the Gulf Islands. See Li Read to find your new dream home port. Visit Li for what is for sale, an island map and market conditions. Office located across the street from Ganges Marina, Salt Spring Island. Welcome!
250-537-7647 • #4 - 105 Rainbow Road
LiRead33@Gmail.com
www.LiRead.com

MOBY'S PUB

Moby's Pub offers a comfortable atmosphere. The friendly staff, great food, legendary live entertainment, waterfront patio, and excellent location make Moby's the best place on Salt Spring Island to meet people.
250-537-5559 • 124 A Upper Ganges Rd.
mobyspub@gmail.com
www.mobyspub.ca

SALT SPRING INN

Come and Experience one of Salt Spring's finest restaurants. A wide variety of different dishes from all over the world. From seafood to pasta, the Salt Spring Inn has it all in a beautiful newly renovated building, which includes seven guest rooms in one of the most wonderful locations in British Columbia.
250-537-9339 • 132 Lower Ganges Rd.
www.saltspringinn.com

EAGLE EYE MARINE

Eagle Eye Marine Services is the largest commercial assistance company in the southern gulf islands. We are the southern gulf islands' marine towing and salvage team. We pride ourselves on our professionalism and on being the right fit for any job.
250-883-SUNK (7865) • www.eagleeyemarine.ca

Salt Spring Island Community Calendar

Famous Saturday Market: April to October
Tuesday's Farmers Market: June to October
All Summer Long: Music under the Stars, ArtCraft, Salt Spring Studio Tours, ArtSpring Summer Performances, Live Music at Oystercatcher, Moby's Pub and Salt Spring Vineyards – and more!
January: Salt Spring Polar Bear Swim
February: February Festival • Family Day Concert • Seedy Saturday • Indoor Market
March: Documentary Film Festival • Salt Spring Home & Garden Show
April: Salt Spring Blooms in April • Easter Art Festival • Blossom Festival
May: Round Salt Spring Sailing Race • Ruckle Farm Day
June: Tour des Iles Festival Taste of Salt Spring • Solstice on Salt Spring
July: Canada Day Festivities • Classic Car Show • Lavender Festival
August: Firefly Lantern Festival • Movies in the Park
September: Pride Festival • Fall Fair Weekend • Working Boat Festival
October: Harvest Food and Drink Festival • Apple Festival • Sip & Savour Salt Spring • Harvest Grape Stomp • Halloween in Ganges Village
November: Remembrance Day Parade & Ceremonies • Christmas Light Up Events
December: Christmas on Salt Spring • WinterCraft at Mahon Hall
Christmas Craft Fairs • WinterCraft at Mahon Hall • Beaver Point Hall Fulford Hall ArtSpring Christmas Concerts • Annual Glowtini Contest
Community Christmas Dinner • New Year's Eve Celebrations
Plus… Special Events during most Canadian Holiday Long-weekends!

Saltspring Marina at the head of Ganges Harbour

The popular Salt Spring Island Fair, held in mid-September, is within easy walking distance from town.

important to summer trade, Ganges is not just a summer resort village. It's a bustling center of year-round local commerce.

Boats can anchor out in the bay. All buoys in the harbour are private. Moorage is available at Saltspring Marina, Ganges Marina, or the town's Kanaka Wharf. Larger vessels might side-tie along the 240-foot-long floating breakwater that extends into the bay from the Coast Guard dock. An airplane float, pumpout station, and some power and water are on the breakwater. A ramp leads to shore. Because of the breakwater's high freeboard, it is best suited to larger boats. If the wind blows (especially a southeasterly), expect some movement.

The Saltspring Island Sailing Club's docks, to port as you approach Grace Point, have some space for reciprocal clubs. It's about a 1-mile walk to town. The Centennial Wharf public dock behind Grace Islet is permanent moorage only with some transient "hot berths" available if you call the Harbour Authority office. Off Mouat's store, the Kanaka Wharf is within close proximity to shopping; Kanaka dock moorage frequently opens up during the day as boats come and go.

More than 40 artists' studios are in Ganges and scattered around Saltspring Island. In addition to painters and sculptors, they include artisan cheese makers, bakers, wineries, and now a microbrewery. Rental cars and vans are available at Saltspring Marina. A local map identifies stops and hours.

Artspring: Locally supported arts and theater, an easy walk from the village. See www.artspring.ca.

Bird Sanctuary: While you can anchor a short distance south of the Sailing Club's docks, Walter Bay and the spit that creates it are a sanctuary for black oystercatchers. Please leave the sanctuary area alone.

Swimming Pool: The Rainbow Road Indoor Public Pool is an easy walk away. Call (250) 537-1402 for hours.

Bus Transportation: Regular bus service on Saltspring Island connects Fulford Harbour, Ganges, Long Harbour, Vesuvius and Fernwood. For schedule see www.busonline.ca; (250) 538-4282.

Shuttle: A free shuttle goes to upper Ganges shopping center, call (250) 538-2398.

Taxi: Silver Shadow Taxi (250) 537-3030; Amber Cab Co. (250) 537-3277

Car Rental: Salt Spring Car Rentals (250) 537-3122

THINGS TO DO

1. Studio Tour. Map available at the Visitor Centre. Rent a car, van, or moped at the Saltspring Marina and visit some of the 40 artist studios. Most are open every weekend.

2. Salt Spring Island Cheese Company. See the many steps needed to make artisan cheese. Then taste 20 different cheeses.

3. Wine Tasting. Two wineries are on Saltspring Island and they regularly have tastings. Wine and farm tours available at TourSaltSpring.com.

4. Salt Spring Island Saturday Market. The largest farmers market in the islands.

5. Hastings House. Reserve for an elegant dinner or a bistro lunch. Walk the grounds of this manor style resort. A special experience.

6. Barb's Buns. Delicious coffee and fresh baked goods. Bring some back to the boat. Their breakfasts and lunches are also very good.

7. Embe Bakery. A "old style" full service bakery serving up freshly baked breads, pastries, dessert pies, meat pies, and other baked goods.

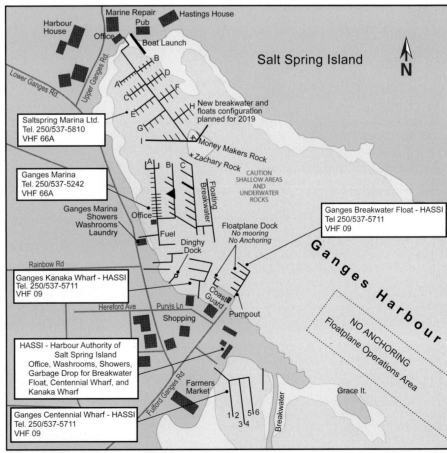

Ganges Harbour

131°	130°	129°	128°	127°	126°	125°	124°	123°	122°

GANGES & SALT SPRING ISLAND – FOODIE HEAVEN!

Salt Spring Island has been a foodie heaven since the late 1800s. Back then, fresh produce grown on the island was delivered to Hope Bay, where it was loaded on the ferry and shuttled to Vancouver.

Today, Salt Spring Island is home to brewers and vintners, farmers, cheesemakers, artisan bakers, and restaurateurs. If you love delicious food, Salt Spring Island is a fantastic destination.

FARMERS MARKET

Ganges hosts the best farmers market in the Gulf Islands. Each Saturday from March through October, the "Market in the Park" at Centennial Park is open for business. More than 100 vendors sell their wares, ranging from fresh produce to seafood to pastries and crafts. The variety is outstanding and everything is made locally.

Another, smaller, market is held Tuesday afternoons at the same location.

Both markets are perfect places for provisioning. We've found fresh seafood, unusual mushrooms, heirloom tomatoes, ripe melons, berries, a variety of sprouts, and more. Four artisan bakeries—ranging from Rendezvous French Patisserie (superb desserts) to the Salt Spring Island Bread Company and the Bread Lady—attend the market. Fair warning: it's best to go early, since many items sell out by closing time.

WINE AND BEER

Salt Spring has two wineries: Garry Oaks Estate Winery, and Salt Spring Vineyards. Each has a tasting room.

Both Garry Oaks and Salt Spring Vineyards require car transportation. Each winery hosts a variety of tasting events throughout the summer, some including food pairings or live music. Check their websites for a schedule of events.

The Sip and Savour festival in September celebrates Salt Spring Island's food and wine.

If beer is your preference, stop by one of B.C.'s smallest breweries: Salt Spring Island Ales, outside of Ganges. You can enjoy beer on tap, or pick up a bottle or growler for later. The beer is organic and made with locally grown ingredients—even the hops are from Salt Spring Island.

RESTAURANTS

Hastings House is one of the finest restaurants we've ever dined at. They've hosted movie stars and sports stars, royalty and heads of state. Almost everything, including bread and crackers, is prepared fresh in their kitchen. They grow many of their ingredients on site, and the garden is open to patrons. We recommend wandering through, either before or after your meal. It's not uncommon to see the chef gathering herbs, fruits, or vegetables.

You can choose a Bistro Dinner, or a Fine Dining menu. An optional cocktail hour in the Manor House precedes dinner. Recommended.

STILL HUNGRY?

If you're willing to travel beyond walking distance from Ganges, another world opens up. Salt Spring Auto Rentals (250 537-3122), located at Saltspring Marina, provides maps highlighting more than 40 destinations on Salt Spring Island. Many of these places are artisan food businesses, ranging from cheese makers to beekeepers.

One of our favorites is Salt Spring Island Cheese Company, near Fulford Harbour. A tour includes petting the goats and sampling some of their 20+ cheeses in a tasting room overlooking the production area. Afterword, customers can relax at outdoor tables and enjoy goat milk gelato.

Salt Spring Island's wide variety of food producers and restaurants, and their consistently high quality, make it the ideal destination for foodie boaters.

– Mark Bunzel

131°	130°	129°	128°	127°					

㉑ **Harbour Authority of Salt Spring Island.** 127 Fulford Ganges Road, Salt Spring Island, BC V8K 2T9; (250) 537-5711. Monitors VHF 09. www.saltspringharbours.com.

The Harbour Authority of Salt Spring Island manages eight marina facilities on Salt Spring Island: Ganges Centennial Wharf; Ganges Breakwater Float (which also includes the Wharfhead where the Coast Guard building is located); Ganges Kanaka Wharf; Vesuvius Bay; Fulford Inner Harbour; Fulford Outer Harbour; Burgoyne Bay; and Musgrave Landing. The Harbour Authority office and wharfinger are located at Ganges Centennial Wharf.

㉑ **Ganges Centennial Wharf - Harbour Authority of Salt Spring Island.** (250) 537-5711. Monitors VHF 09. www.saltspringharbours.com. This is the Grace Point facility. Mostly commercial and permanent moorage, but sometimes transient space is available, call the Harbour Authority Office.

㉑ **Ganges Breakwater Float - Harbour Authority of Salt Spring Island**. (250) 537-5711. Monitors VHF 09. www.saltspringharbours.com. This is the dock below the Coast Guard station. Moorage on the outside of the long floating breakwater or in several slips on the inside. Be sure to avoid the marked seaplane and Coast Guard areas. Limited 30 amp power and water. Pumpout

The Hastings House gardens are outstanding.

at the dock. Washroom, shower and garbage drop at the Harbour Authority office at Centennial Wharf. Two hours free moorage before 4:00 p.m.

Wharfingers collect moorage daily, or pay in the drop box at the head of the docks or at the Harbour Authority office.

㉑ **Ganges Kanaka Wharf - Harbour Authority of Salt Spring Island.** (250) 537-5711. Monitors VHF 09. www.saltspringharbours.com. These docks are immediately north of the floating breakwater, with 1400 feet of visitor moorage, water, 30 amp power. Good free Wi-Fi on the docks

or from nearby cafés. Washroom, shower and garbage drop at the Harbour Authority office at Centennial Wharf, about a block away. Free moorage for 2 hours. Boats come and go all day and moorage opens up after crews complete their shopping.

Wharfingers collect check or cash for moorage daily, or pay in the drop box at the head of the docks, or at the Harbour Authority office.

LOCAL KNOWLEDGE

EXPLORING ISLANDS: You can explore

Third Sister Island by dinghy or kayak to see the beautiful midden shell beach and creative outhouse made of driftwood.

⑳ **Ganges Marina**. 161 Lower Ganges Road, Salt Spring Island, BC V8K 2L6; (250) 537-5242; gangesmarina@gmail.com; www. gangesmarina.com. Monitors VHF 66A. Moorage for vessels up to 120 feet. Open all year, gasoline, diesel and limited lubricants at fuel dock, ample guest moorage. Reservations recommended in summer. Facilities include 30 & 50 amp power, washrooms, showers, laundry, free Wi-Fi, garbage drop. On-site marine mechanic. Groceries, restaurants, propane, and other services nearby.

A floating breakwater, 500 feet long and 24 feet wide, can handle vessels to 400 feet.

⑳ **Saltspring Marina.** 124 Upper Ganges Rd., Salt Spring Island, BC V8K 2S2; (250) 537- 5810; (800) 334-6629; info@saltspringmarina. com; www. saltspringmarina.com. Monitors VHF 66A. At press time, work was underway to replace all the docks with new and expanded floats, scheduled to be completed May 2019. The new floats will have guest moorage for a variety of boat sizes in a configuration that includes a floating breakwater covering Money Makers Rock. New electrical service will be ELCI-protected, one of the first in BC. 30 & 50 amp power, washrooms, showers, laundry, water, ice, recycling,

garbage drop, and mobile pump-out station. Shaw Go Wi-Fi and concrete launch ramp. No long term parking. At certain times of the year, when in short supply, water use at the docks may be restricted.

Adjacent Moby's Pub (take-out & off-sales) has a terrific menu, music and dancing. Check their website. Rendezvous French Bakery has fresh baked goods. Harbours End has full-service repairs with haulout to 40 feet (250-537-4202). Car, van, scooter, and bicycle rentals (250-537-3122).

Long Harbour. Long Harbour lies parallel to Ganges Harbour, but is much narrower. The BC ferry from Tsawwassen lands there. Good anchorage is beyond the ferry dock, taking care not to anchor over a charted cable crossing. Royal Vancouver Yacht Club has an outstation in Long Harbour.

PREVOST ISLAND

㉑ **Prevost Island.** Prevost Island is a favorite of many. Annette Inlet and Glenthorne Passage, on the northwest end, are particularly attractive. The bays indenting from the southeast also look inviting, but with a southeaster always possible and with ferry traffic flying by in Swanson Channel, they might get a little lumpy.

Acland Islands. The passage between the Acland Islands and Prevost Island is a pleasant anchorage, with dramatic sheer rock walls on

the Prevost Island side. Anchor in 25 to 35 feet with enough room to swing, or stern-tie to Acland Island.

Glenthorne Passage. Glenthorne Passage is the westernmost of the northern bays on Prevost Island. Well protected anchorage in 15 to 30 feet, good holding. Even though cabins line Secret Island, the surroundings are agreeable and the anchorage is popular. In summer months the sun sets in the narrow passage between Glenthorne Point and Secret Island.

Annette Inlet. Annette Inlet is a little wider than Glenthorne Passage, with few houses and a good sandy beach at the head. As you approach, note the charted rock that dries at 0.9 meter, off the mouth of the inlet. A rock at the point is marked by a small, private beacon. Approach from the Glenthorne Passage side and wrap around the point, leaving the beacon to starboard. The head of the bay shoals to drying flats. Anchor in 8 feet (zero tide) anywhere, gray mud bottom. Southeast winds can blow across the low swale separating Annette Inlet from Ellen Bay on the other side of Prevost Island, but there isn't enough fetch to build waves.

Selby Cove & James Bay. A house and dock are on the right side as you enter Selby Cove. Anchor in 18 feet and be sure of your set. We found poor holding in one spot. James Bay is the most northeast bay, open to

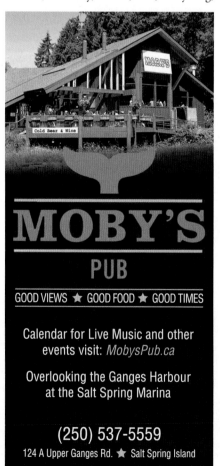

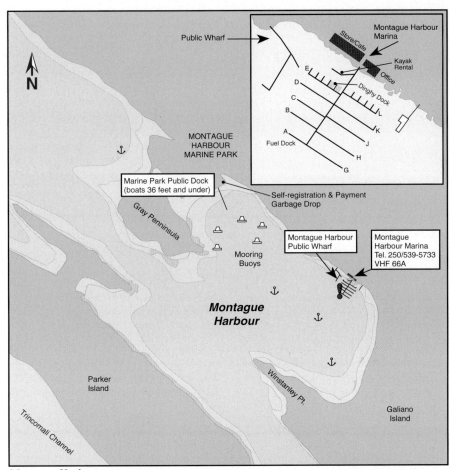

Montague Harbour

northwesterlies. It is a little deep for anchoring until close to the head. The lands surrounding James Bay and a portion of the north shore of Selby Cove are part of Gulf Islands National Park Reserve, as are the lands surrounding Richardson Bay and the Portlock Point light station at the southeast corner of Prevost Island. Ferries do not serve Prevost Island, thus it is less populated than the larger islands.

MONTAGUE HARBOUR

㉒ **Montague Harbour.** Montague Harbour is a popular stopping spot in the central Gulf Islands. It is well protected and has an outstanding marine park. Depending on wind direction, you can find good anchorages around the bay.

Entry is unobstructed, either from the southeast, past Phillimore Point, or from the northwest, between Parker Island and Gray Peninsula.

Caution: A shoal extends southeast from the tip of Gray Peninsula into Montague Harbour. We've seen a boat thoroughly grounded on that shoal, awaiting a rising tide. Continue well into the harbor before turning east to anchor or pick up a mooring.

Montague Harbour will hold a huge number of boats. We have anchored there during high season surrounded by more than 100 boats, yet no one was crowded. Anchor in about 40 feet over a mud bottom. The marina has a fuel dock, store, gift shop, scooter and kayak rentals, and restaurant. For-fee Wi-Fi is available throughout the harbor; cell phone reception is poor.

No Discharge Zone, Gray Water okay.

Customs: Montague Harbour is a Canpass/Nexus-only call-in customs clearance location.

Dining: Everybody enjoys the Hummingbird Inn Pub. A visit to Hummingbird Pub begins with a memorable ride on the Hummingbird Pub bus. Catch the bus on the road above the marina, about 300 yards to the right of the intersection. The bus also stops at the front gate of the marine park. Check the Hummingbird Pub website or signs at the marina and park entrance for the scheduled times for bus pick-up. The Hummingbird Pub serves food and is family friendly.

The Pilgrimme Restaurant (250-539-5392) operates in the former location of the French restaurant La Berengerie. It gets great reviews from visiting boaters. Reservations recommended. Walking distance from Montague Harbour Marina.

㉒ **Montague Harbour Marine Park.** Montague Harbour Marine Park, at the north end of Montague Harbour, is beautiful, exceptionally well-maintained and very popular. The park is open all year. It has excellent white sand beaches on the south side and astonishing rock beaches on the north and west sides. If you walk along the beach on the north side, opposite the head of the lagoon, you'll find a midden beach with numerous shells. There's no hint of the midden on the

235

trail above, but it's obvious from the beach. A tiny, secluded beach is on Gray Peninsula, facing Parker Island. The park has walk-in campsites, a picnic area and toilets. A dock with a 300-foot-long float is for dinghies and boats up to 11 meters (36 feet). Designated dinghy area is on the shore end of the float. There are approximately 39 mooring buoys off the dock. No boat size limitation is marked on the buoys but as a practical matter, be careful not to endanger other boats or damage buoy equipment. An honor box for paying moorage is at the top of the stairs. The Park Ranger will also accept VISA and MasterCard and will visit your boat in late afternoon/early evening to collect your payment. The park has anchorage for many boats on both sides of Gray Peninsula depending on wind direction. Garbage disposal for a fee is available, located up the stairs from the dock.

㉒ **Montague Harbour Marina.** 3451 Montague Rd, Galiano Island, BC V0N 1P0; (250) 539-5733; montagueharbourmarina@gmail.com; www.montagueharbour.com. Monitors VHF 66A. Open May 1 to September 30. Guest side-tie moorage, 15 & 30 amp power, no water at the docks, free Wi-Fi, and washrooms. Reservations strongly recommended during the high season. Garbage and recycle drop-off with overnight moorage. Dog friendly. Licensed restaurant, groceries, marine supplies, and gift shop. Diesel and ethanol-free gasoline at the fuel dock. Fuel is available during the off-season on Saturdays from 10:00 a.m. to 2:00 p.m. or by arrangement. Moped, kayak, and motor boat rentals.

The store carries an expanded variety of goods, including smoked fish, meats, and local produce, fishing tackle, a good selection of books, souvenirs, and hand-dipped ice cream cones. Cappuccino bar service available. The licensed Crane & Robin is open for breakfast, lunch and dinner. Check their happy hour specials. Dinghy dock available for any boaters on anchor or mooring buoys who want to enjoy the marina's shopping and dining. Check in with store if you plan to leave the property. Limited Wi-Fi for anchored boats is available for a fee.

㉒ **Montague Harbour Public Wharf.** Open all year, 160 feet of dock space, no facilities. 2-hour complimentary tie-up for dingies and boats. Fee for additional stays, pay at self-registration payment box at head of the ramp. Video monitoring and the wharfinger enforce the 2-hour free limit. Surveillance ensures that everyone has an opportunity to use the dock. Wharfinger always greets you with a smile.

Walker Hook. Walker Hook, on the west side of Trincomali Channel, has a beautiful beach on its eastern shore, where it connects with Saltspring Island. Anchor in 24 feet. An approach between Atkins Reef and Saltspring Island takes the worry out of identifying just where the various rocks are.

Dinghies on one side of Butchart Gardens dock, the other side is reserved for floatplanes.

Fernwood Public Wharf. Located on the Trincomali Channel side of Saltspring Island north of Walker Hook, opposite Victoria Shoal and just south of Wallace Island. Open all year, 44 feet of dock space, no facilities. Correspondents Fred and Judy Triggs visited and say they'd stop again. They enjoyed the locals who came down to visit, and concluded, "A pleasant and unexpected surprise was the Fernwood Road Café, located at the head of the pier, 50 meters up the road. Well stocked, good bakery items, sandwiches and pizza – excellent food." We visited, and agree.

SAANICH INLET

Saanich Inlet extends south into Vancouver Island for about 12 miles. The northern part of the inlet is fairly civilized, especially along the Saanich Peninsula shore to Brentwood Bay, where Butchart Gardens is located. For a beautiful and often-overlooked trip, continue south through Squally Reach and Finlayson Arm. Boat traffic usually is minimal.

Holding Tank Pumpout Service: J.R. Pump Out, a mobile pumpout boat, serves the Brentwood Bay/Butchart Gardens area of Saanich Inlet. Because of a sill at the mouth of the inlet, Saanich Inlet does not exchange its water well and is growing increasingly lifeless along the bottom. Saanich Inlet is not a good place to pump overboard. J.R. Pump Out at (844) 507-3451 or VHF 88 (seasonally). During the summer season the pumpout boat goes out every evening. In winter, every two weeks.

Restricted Area: In Saanich Inlet, Area Whiskey Delta (WD) is restricted when the government is conducting certain operations. Before entering, listen to the continuous marine broadcast or call the Coast Guard on VHF 83 to ensure the area is not restricted before entering.

Deep Cove. Wain Rock, with good water on both sides, lies about 0.2 mile off Moses Point. The remains of a public wharf are in the south part of the cove. Deep Cove Marina is adjacent to this pier and is for permanent moorage; transient moorage available only when there is space available which is rare, call (250) 733-2991 Ext 300.

Boaters can anchor in front of The Chalet restaurant on the north end of Deep Cove and land the dinghy on their private beach, while enjoying lunch or dinner. Call ahead for reservations (250) 656-3541, open Wednesday-Sunday. This is a unique venue overlooking Deep Cove and Saanich Inlet. The home was built as a teahouse for the B.C. Electric Rail Line in 1913 and has been a restaurant ever since. After coming ashore, leave your boots behind and slip on your nice shoes; this is a fine dining venue with prices to match. Remains of several pilings in front of The Chalet help locate the restaurant; see www.deepcovechalet.com for more details.

Patricia Bay. Patricia Bay, locally called Pat Bay, is open, but all the facilities are reserved for the Canadian Government's Institute of Ocean Sciences. It is here that the Canadian Hydrographic Service develops and maintains charts and related publications for western Canada and the Arctic.

Coles Bay. Coles Bay is east of Yarrow Point. It is good for temporary anchorage but open to southerly winds. If approaching from the north, the Canadian Small Craft Guide recommends that you give Dyer Rocks, off Yarrow Point, a 0.5-mile berth to avoid shoals extending south from the rocks.

LOCAL KNOWLEDGE

DANGEROUS ROCKS: A reef, marked by red nun buoy U22, is a short distance off the Brentwood Bay ferry dock. Approach Brentwood Bay Resort & Marina from the north, leaving buoy U22 to starboard. Dangerous rocks lie on the other side of the buoy, and west and south of the resort's docks. Locals report that these rocks are hit frequently.

㉓ **Brentwood Bay.** Although Brentwood Bay can be entered on either side of Senanus Island, prawn trap floats often clog the water between the north end of the island and Henderson Point. Best to leave Senanus Island to port. The Mill Bay ferry departs a short distance south of Sluggett Point. The Seahorses

Elegant Brentwood Bay Resort near Butchart Gardens

Cafe, with a dinghy dock, is north of the ferry dock. Nearby Blue's Bayou Café to the south has Cajun/Creole style food. Open for lunch and dinner, reservations recommended (250) 544-1194. The Brentwood Bay Public Dock, next to the Cafe, is suitable for dinghies and small watercraft.

Pumpout is available monthly on the second Saturday throughout Brentwood Bay for free (donations appreciated) through J. R. Pumpout, (844) 507-3451 or VHF 88. This program is funded by Butchart Gardens. Butchart Gardens is one of the main attractions around Brentwood and is well worth a visit. Another popular attraction is the Victoria Butterfly Gardens (877) 722-0272 located about two miles from Brentwood Bay.

The village up at the highway has some shopping. Moorage is at Brentwood Bay Resort & Marina and limited moorage at Portside Marina and Angler's Anchorage Marina.

㉓ **Portside Marina.** 789 Saunders Ln., Brentwood Bay, BC V8M 1C5; (250) 652-2211; info@portsidemarina.net; portsidemarina.net. Open all year with limited guest moorage for boats up to 50 feet, reservations accepted. 30 amp power, water, washrooms, showers, and laundry. The marina is located in Brentwood Bay north of the BC Ferries terminal and next to the Seahorses Café. New owners took over the marina in 2017 and have been steadily making improvements. Transient moorage space was expanded in 2018. A small marine ways and boatyard that specializes in wooden boat building and repair is adjacent to the marina. Pacifica Paddle Sports (250-665-7411) is located at the marina and has rental kayaks, canoes, and SUPs.

㉓ **Brentwood Bay Resort & Marina.** 849 Verdier Ave., Brentwood Bay, BC V8W 1C5; (250) 652-3151; (888) 544-2079; marina@brentwoodbayresort.com; www.brentwoodbayresort.com. Monitors VHF 66A. The reservation-only marina has 22 slips of guest moorage and side-tie moorage for vessels to 125 feet, 15, 30 & 50 amp power, water, washrooms, laundry, garbage, recycling, showers, adult pool with drinks and pub food service, sushi and sake, cold beer

& wine off-sales in the pub, free Wi-Fi. Live music and beer samplers on Sundays.

This is a highly rated resort and spa, with excellent views of Saanich Inlet, beautiful landscaping. A shuttle boat runs to Butchart Gardens for a fee (make reservations at the marina office), or it's a short dinghy ride away. Kayak and SUP rentals, bicycle rentals, and Paddle Sports eco-adventure tours available.

㉓ **Angler's Anchorage Marina.** (250) 652-3531; info@anglersanchorage.com; www.anglersanchoragemarina.com. Some transient moorage available in slips to 50 feet, call ahead, 30 & 50 amp power, washrooms, showers, laundry, garbage drop, pumpout. Reservations are accepted and recommended. Call or see their website for reservations. A new patio and ramp were added in 2017 to create a welcoming entrance to the refurbished marina office.

㉓**Butchart Gardens**. 800 Benvenuto Avenue, Brentwood Bay, BC V8M 1J8; (250) 652-5256; (866) 652-4422; www.butchartgardens.com. Locally named **Butchart Cove** just outside the mouth of Tod Inlet is the back door to the celebrated and astonishing Butchart Gardens. The Gardens are a must-see attraction. They are lighted at night, creating an entirely different effect from the day. On Saturday evenings during the summer a fireworks display is held on a large field in the gardens. Many people arrive early and have a picnic dinner while waiting for darkness. A little known secret is — The Dining Room restaurant will prepare a special picnic basket to enjoy on the grounds — see their website for the menu. Bring blankets and cushions. Even for jaded viewers, it's worth the trip. The most interesting fireworks are done at ground level, accompanied by music — you have to be at the field for the full experience.

The Gardens' dinghy dock is in tiny Butchart Cove with 4 free mooring buoys for boats 40 feet and under (a fifth mooring ball for vessels 18 feet and under) that are first-come, first-served, maximum 24 hour stay. Eyes for stern-ties are set into the rock wall. Most visitors put the anchor down in adjacent Tod Inlet and go by dinghy to the dinghy dock. Dinghy dock is closed from December 1 to January 6.

Tod Inlet. *No Discharge Zone, Gray water okay.* Tod Inlet reaches back behind Butchart Gardens into Gowlland Tod Provincial Park, and has ample anchoring room. Anchor in water deeper than 20 feet to protect eelgrass. Green can Buoy U21 marks a rock. Leave the bouy to port when entering. The inlet is narrow when seen from Brentwood Bay, but opens somewhat after a bend. In the narrow sections you should plan to run a stern-tie to shore. Boats in the more open sections around the bend often can swing without a stern-tie. On Saturday nights the inlet is crowded with boats that come to see the fireworks display at the Gardens.

The dinghy dock on the southeastern shore of the inlet is provided by the Marine Conservation Society and BC Parks, look for the green Marine Ecology float building. A trail to the south leads to the main entrance of Butchart Gardens, about a 10 minute walk. Stay left at the 'Y' in the trail. It's also a short dinghy ride to Butchart Cove where you can tie to the shore side of the dinghy dock and pay admission to the gardens at the backdoor entrance. The dinghy dock in Tod Inlet serves as an access point for the Gowlland Tod Provincial Park with hiking trails connecting through the Gowlland Range. During the summer months, volunteers set up a float in Tod Inlet to provide information

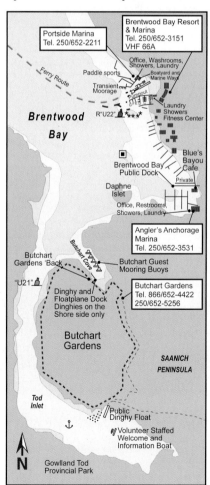

Brentwood Bay and Tod Inlet

and answer questions. The float is staffed by members of the Capital City Yacht Club on behalf of BC Parks.

Finlayson Arm. Goldstream Boathouse is located at the head of Finlayson Arm, at the edge of drying flats off the mouth of the Goldstream River. The shoal water seems to be extending farther north, so come in close to the docks. If the approach is made from mid-channel, an unsuspecting skipper could run aground. Unique homes dot the hillsides and shoreline along Finlayson Arm. Look for the cute 'crooked little house' on a small point just before the power lines on the western shore at 48°31.14'N/123°32.5'W.

㉔ **Goldstream Boathouse.** 3540 Trans-Canada Hwy, Victoria, BC V9B 6H6; (250) 478-4407; admin@ goldstreamboathousemarina.com; www. goldstreamboathousemarina.com. Open all year, gasoline and diesel at fuel dock. Minimal guest moorage available, but even during the summer season they usually have room, call ahead. Complete repair facility and haulout by trailer up to 50 feet, small convenience store, 2-lane concrete launch ramp, 15, 30 & 50 amp power, washrooms, no showers. Future plans include rebuilding upland structures.

㉕ **Mill Bay.** Mill Bay is a good anchorage. The west shore provides a lee from the usual summer west or northwest winds. The bay is, however, open to southeast winds. Just north of the Mill Bay Marina is a spar buoy zone marking a no-anchoring area. A charted pipeline extends from the northwest corner of the bay.

㉕ **Mill Bay Marina.** 740 Handy Road, Mill Bay, BC V0R 2P1; (250) 743-4303; contact@ millbaymarina.ca; www.millbaymarina.ca. Monitors VHF 66A. 700 feet of transient moorage to accommodate boats to 200 feet, 30 & 50 amp power, water, gasoline, diesel, pumpout, laundry, showers, free Wi-Fi. Reservations recommended in season. Wide roomy slips and side-tie moorage on concrete docks. State-of-the-art marina with great views of Mt. Baker.

Picnic tables and propane barbeques for guest use are on the docks. The Bridgemans Bistro restaurant, open for lunch and dinner, and brunch on weekends is a hit. Soft drinks, ice cream. Live music on Sundays. Blue Dog Kayaking (250) 710-7693 located at Mill Bay Marina offers kayak and SUP rentals, instruction, and expeditions.

The Mill Bay Shopping Centre is a short walk up the hill. The center has a supermarket, drug store, liquor store, hardware store, bank and gift stores. Several restaurants and the Visitor Centre are also located there.

A public launch ramp is on the north side of the marina. Spar buoys north of the marina and boat launch, located in front of the Brentwood College School (a college prep boarding school), mark a no-anchoring area. The no-anchoring area protects an ocean loop geo-exchange system used for heating and cooling the school's buildings.

㉕ **Mill Bay Community Wharf.** Open all year, 50 feet of dock space, no facilities. Three hour maximum stay, no overnight moorage.

㉖ **Cowichan Bay.** www.cowichanbay. com. The waterfront village of Cowichan Bay is located near the southwest corner of Cowichan Bay. Docks at Fishermen's Wharf are behind a floating breakwater. The floating breakwater dock is not connected to land. A dinghy is needed for shore access. Two privately owned marinas are west of the public wharf and offer transient moorage. Mooring buoys for vessels up to 55 feet are available for transient boaters from Classic Marine. At the other end of town, Hecate Park has a launch ramp with ample trailer storage. In settled weather anchorage is possible but not advised. We are told crabbing and prawning are good. The annual Cowichan Bay Regatta is held the first weekend in August, a popular event drawing many participants. The village is full of life. It has numerous shops and businesses, including liquor stores and good restaurants, not one of them part of a major chain. Interesting little shops are tucked away everywhere. The True Grain Bakery is superb as is Hilary's Cheese Shop. Udder Guys Ice Cream has some of the best ice cream on the

coast. The Cowichan Bay Maritime Centre, built on a wharf extending from shore, has many interesting displays.

The Ocean Front Suites has a pub and restaurant. A grass tennis court, just like Wimbledon, is 3 miles west of town at 2290 Cowichan Bay Rd (250) 746-7282. For brewery tours of the area, see CheersCowichan.com (250) 710-7391.

Water Shuttle: The water taxi service between Genoa Bay Marina and Cowichan Bay is no longer operating.

㉖ **Cowichan Bay Fishermen's Wharf Association.** P.O. Box 52, Cowichan Bay, BC V0R 1N0; (250) 746-5911; cbfwa@shaw.ca. Monitors VHF 66A. Open all year, 900 feet of dock space for vessels to 100 feet, 30 amp power, free Wi-Fi, clean washrooms, laundry, showers, free pumpout, garbage and recycling drop, waste oil disposal. Short-term shopping stops are encouraged until 2:00 p.m.; check-in at the harbor office. Fish sales available on the dock, Saturdays, June through the first week in September, 4:00 p.m. to 6:00 p.m. off the fish boat *Charisma*.

㉖ **Oceanfront Suites at Cowichan Bay.** 1681 Cowichan Bay Rd., Cowichan Bay, BC V0R 1N0; (250) 715-1000; info@ oceanfrontcowichanbay.com; www. oceanfrontcowichanbay.com. Full service resort hotel. Overnight stays at the dock for hotel guests; hourly stays for restaurant and pub patrons; dock suitable for shallow draft boats only. No power on the docks. The Oceanview restaurant overlooking the bay is open seasonally. Located immediately south of the Fishermen's Wharf dock. Watch your depths on very low tides.

㉖ **Classic Marine Transient Moorage.** 1725 Cowichan Bay Rd, Cowichan Bay, BC V0R 1N0; (250) 746-1093; info@ classicmarine.ca; www.classicmarine. ca. Monitors VHF 66A. In 2018, Classic Marine Store added five (5) mooring buoys in Cowichan Bay for transient boats up to 55 feet. In 2019 there will be ten (10) buoys available for a nightly fee. The large orange

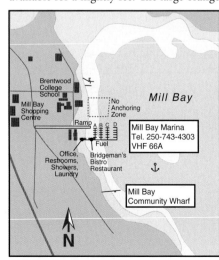

Mill Bay Marina

and white buoys are marked as "Classic Marine" and are numbered; number "1" is for boats up to 55 feet, the others are for boats up to 38 feet. Buoys are located north and west of the Fishermen's Wharf breakwater. Contact Classic Marine Store for assignment and to arrange for payment (credit card or cash). If arriving after store hours, call to hear a recorded message with payment instructions. A short-term dinghy dock is located below the store, or tie your dinghy at the Fishermen's Wharf.

Classic Marine Store is a well-stocked marine chandlery with marine parts, supplies, gifts, and fishing gear. Don't miss the Galley Café located in the store, with delectable bites, homemade clam chowder, and the all-day breakfast menu. Classic Marine also offers small boat rentals.

㉖ **Pier 65 (Dungeness Marina).** 1759 Cowichan Bay Rd., Box 51, Cowichan Bay, BC V0R 1N0; (250) 748-6789; info@dungenessmarina.com; www.dungenessmarina.com. Office hours 8:00 a.m. to 2:00 p.m. Tuesday through Saturday. 200 feet of transient moorage, maximum boat length 85 feet; 30 amp power in one box with 4 receptacles; water at the dock. First-come, first-served but may call ahead for available space.

㉖ **Bluenose Marina.** 1765 Cowichan Bay Rd., P.O. Box 40, Cowichan Bay, BC V0R 1N0; (250) 748-2222; deven@thebluenosemarina.

com; www.thebluenosemarina.com. Open all year. Guest moorage available on a 100 foot dock, reservations accepted. 15 & 30 amp power, washrooms, showers, laundry. Nearby launch ramp, public playground, and kayak shop. The Cow Cafe & Cookhouse serves seafood and steaks. The Vine Restaurant and Creperie, and Udder Guys Ice Cream shop are nearby.

㉗ **Genoa Bay.** Genoa Bay indents the north shore of Cowichan Bay. Anchorage can be found off the marina docks. The Genoa Bay Marina has transient moorage.

Water Shuttle: The water taxi between Genoa Bay and Cowichan Bay ceased operation in 2018.

㉗ **Genoa Bay Marina.** 5000 Genoa Bay Rd., Duncan, BC V9L 5Y8; (250) 746-7621; (800) 572-6481; info@genoabaymarina.com; www.genoabaymarina.com. Monitors VHF 66A mid-May through end of October. Open all year, guest moorage in 30 slips and along 1200 feet of dock space, call ahead. C Dock was widened in 2018, with plans to retrofit other docks in the near future. Excellent washrooms, showers and laundry, 15, 30 & 50 amp power, limited water. Launch ramp, covered picnic shelter, Wi-Fi. This is a popular summer stop. The Genoa Bay Gallery has lovely paintings, prints, and sculpture. The Genoa Bay Café is busy, reservations recommended. The "breakfast cabana" on the dock offers coffee, fresh baked goods, and other breakfast items daily, from the third

weekend in June through Labor Day.

The unusually good store carries convenience items, souvenirs, books, cruising guides, and snacks. Good crabbing in the bay.

Musgrave Landing - Harbour Authority of Salt Spring Island. (250) 537-5711 saltspringharbours.com/musgrave-landing/ Musgrave Landing is on the southwest corner of Salt Spring Island, at the mouth of Sansum Narrows. It is managed by the Harbour Authority of Salt Spring Island. Musgrave Landing is a popular stopover, although it has only a small public float for visitor moorage, no facilities, and very restricted anchorage nearby. Upland you'll find good hiking along miles of logging roads. On a pleasant roadside walk we picked a bouquet of thistle, foxglove, dandelion, fern, salal, nicotiana and pearly everlasting for the galley table. A housing development, with private dock, is on Musgrave Point.

SANSUM NARROWS TO DUCK BAY

Sansum Narrows. Sansum Narrows connects Satellite Channel to the south with Stuart Channel to the north, and leads between high hills on Saltspring Island and Vancouver Island. The wind funnels down the axis of the narrows, turning at the bends. It also funnels down the valleys leading to the channel, so wind directions can be erratic. Currents seldom exceed 3 knots; usually they are less.

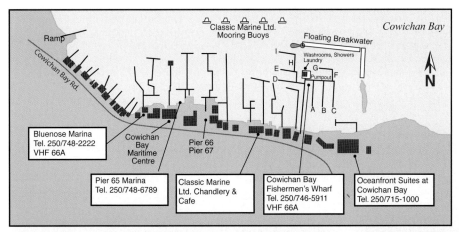
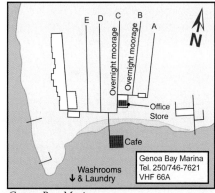

Genoa Bay Marina

Genoa Bay Marina

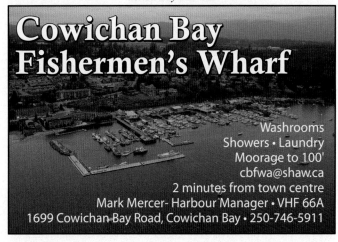

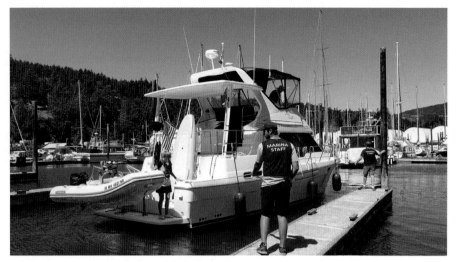

The friendly staff at Maple Bay are ready to assist.

Burgoyne Bay - Harbour Authority of Salt Spring Island. saltspringharbours.com/burgoyne-bay/; Burgoyne Bay has ample anchorage in 18 to 30 feet at its inner end, but is subject to williwaws that blow across a low swale on Saltspring Island. Most of the bay is too deep for convenient anchoring. A 65-foot public float for visitor moorage is at the head of the bay, next to the anchorage, no facilities. One side of the float is available for transient moorage stays up to 48 hours. The other side is reserved for local use.

㉘ **Maple Bay.** Maple Bay is a major pleasure boat center, with public moorages and all necessary facilities and services. Birds Eye Cove, off the southwest corner of Maple Bay, is home to the Maple Bay Yacht Club, with reciprocal moorage, and the Maple Bay Marina and Birds Eye Cove Marina. Anchoring is good in Birds Eye Cove, but avoid anchoring on the east side of the cove, opposite the marina docks. Markers designate the no anchoring navigation channel.

Birds Eye Cove Farm, located a half-mile south of Maple Bay, is a favorite local attraction. The Farm raises beef, pork and chickens as well as farm-fresh produce. Visitors can purchase vegetables, eggs, pies and meat dishes from the "Gypsy Wagon" open daily from 9:00 a.m. to 5:00 p.m. Food items are created on their spit grill and wood-fired pizza oven. "Pizza Nights" are held from 4:00 p.m. to 8:00 p.m. on Mondays in May, and from June until Labor Day on Mondays and Wednesdays. It's a treat to join the social events among 300 acres of beautiful rolling fields. Gatherings are held in the large hand-cut timber frame barn and there are two timber frame cabins to rent. For more information go to www.birdseyecovefarm.com or call (250) 748-6379.   One of the best farmer's markets on Vancouver Island is held in downtown Duncan on Saturdays at the Market Square, look for the Clock Tower. The market is open year-round, spring/summer hours 9:00 a.m. to 2:00 p.m. Taxi service is available through Duncan Taxi (250) 746-4444 or make reservations for the shuttle service from Maple Bay Marina.

㉘ **Maple Bay Marina.** 6145 Genoa Bay Rd., Duncan, BC V9L 5T7; (250) 746-8482; (866) 746-8482; info@maplebaymarina.com; www.maplebaymarina.com.   Monitors VHF 66A. Open all year. Gasoline, diesel, lubricants, propane and pumpout service at the fuel dock. High-flow fuel pumps available. Mostly 15 & 30 amp power, some 50 amp, garbage, washrooms, showers, laundry, water, waste oil disposal, Shaw Go Wi-Fi, and free Wi-Fi. A lovely picnic shelter provides space for yacht club group functions. Mariners Market & Espresso Bar has coffee, hot breakfast items, muffins, sandwiches, convenience groceries and local art and crafts. The marina office is in the Mariners Market store. A chandlery has marine supplies and charts. Call ahead for slip assignment. Reservations recommended.

A 55-ton Travelift provides haulout for repairs. It is run by Lindstrom Marine, who has the small marine supply store at the marina.

The washrooms are spacious and clean, with good showers. The Shipyard Restaurant & Pub has good food, with daily specials and live music on Friday evenings. The pub offers off-sale beer and wine. Shuttle service is available to downtown Duncan twice a day on weekdays and on Saturdays for a fee. There is charter shuttle service to two different local golf courses. Ask for a schedule at the marina office. Hiking trails and map are available for Mount Tzouhalem.

The marina offers float home and kayak rentals. Check the website for special events, including live music on Sundays, July through August.

Harbour Air has scheduled float plane service to Vancouver Harbour. Saltspring Air has scheduled service to Vancouver Airport and Vancouver Harbour.

㉘ **Birds Eye Cove Marina.** 6271 Genoa Bay Rd., Duncan, BC V9L 5Y8; (250) 746-5686; info@birdseyecoveduncan.ca. Limited guest moorage with 15 & 30 amp power, washrooms. No showers. The fuel dock at Birds Eye Cove Marina is no longer operating.

㉘ **Maple Bay Public Wharf.** Open all year. Located in Maple Bay, not in Birds Eye Cove, which extends from the south side of Maple Bay. Moorage along 300 feet of dock space, water to the bottom of the ramp but not out to the dock, no power. Self-register at kiosk. A nice beach is nearby. An underwater park is about 200 feet off the end of the dock. The wharf is managed by the Chemainus Harbour Authority and checked daily.

Crofton Public Wharf. Open all year, 1000 feet of dock space, 20 & 30 amp power, washrooms, showers, laundry, garbage drop. Breakwater protected. The docks are usually full with local boats. Crofton is the pulp and paper mill town on the west side of Stuart Channel. The public dock is next to the terminal for the ferry to Vesuvius on Saltspring Island. Walking distance to all services including groceries, restaurants, fishing supplies and licenses. Playground two blocks away. Nearby outdoor swimming pool, tennis courts, hiking trails.

㉙ **Vesuvius.** Located on the northwest side of Saltspring Island, the village of Vesuvius is the terminus for the ferry to Crofton on Vancouver Island. Vesuvius has a public wharf, coffee shop with tasty lunch items, and a restaurant all within easy walking distance. The Seaside restaurant has its own private dock suitable for dinghies and small craft. Vesuvius Bay has anchorage that is open to the northwest with limited protection to the south and southeast. The bay is regularly rocked with wakes from the arriving ferry. More protected anchorage can be found nearby in Duck Bay.

㉙ **Vesuvius - Harbour Authority of Salt Spring Island.** (250) 537-5711 saltspringharbours.com/vesuvius-bay.   The public wharf at Vesuvius, located behind the ferry landing, has side-tie visitor moorage

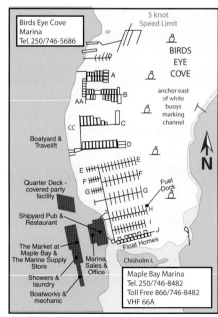

Birds Eye Cove and Maple Bay Marina

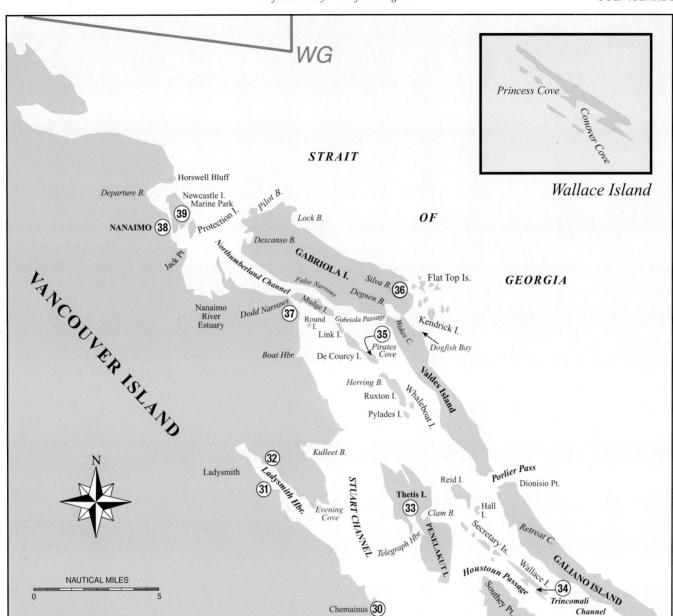

Northern Gulf Islands

on a 40 foot float; no power, no water. Self-registration, moorage rates and payment box are located at the wharfhead; first 2 hours stay at no charge 8:00 a.m. to 4:00 p.m. This is a popular well-used location.

Duck Bay. Just north of Vesuvius Bay, Duck Bay has good anchorage with steep, wooded cliffs rising on its east side. The bay is well-protected, except from northwest winds. A number of private docks, mooring buoys and homes surround the bay.

NORTHERN GULF ISLANDS

Stuart Channel. Stuart Channel runs from Sansum Narrows to Dodd Narrows. It is bordered on the west side by Vancouver Island, and on the east side by Saltspring, Kuper, Thetis and De Courcy Islands. Stuart Channel tends to be littered with drift because of extensive log towing to Crofton, Chemainus and Ladysmith. Keep a sharp watch ahead.

㉚ **Chemainus**. Chemainus is on the Vancouver Island side of Stuart Channel. It has a good public wharf and floats. Chemainus Bay, south of the Municipal Dock, is filled with commercial log boom operations and commercial maritime activities. The bay is not suitable for anchoring.

Chemainus is filled with boutiques, galleries, antique shops, and interesting-looking restaurants. More than 30 of the town's buildings have large, well-done murals, most of them depicting Chemainus' distant past as a Native seasonal campground and its more recent history as a mining, logging, and mill town. The mural project is now focused on celebrating Canadian artist Emily Carr's work. The first mural is a remarkable three-dimensional piece on the west side of the Chemainus Theatre Festival building. This is the initial step in a planned million-dollar outdoor gallery of Carr's art, both paintings and sculpture.

Chemainus has grown so popular that

a large parking area has been built for tour buses, and in they roll, filled with visitors from around the world. Horse-drawn tours are available. Two 49th Parallel grocery stores are located on Oak Street. The original historic general store is immediately above the municipal dock, and the new fully-stocked store is about half a mile up the road at 3055 Oak Street; call (250) 246-3551 for dock-side deliveries, a fee is charged. Also on Oak Street is the Chemainus Bakery with a good selection of fresh baked goods.

A ferry crosses between Chemainus and Thetis Island, about a 10-minute walk from either Thetis Island Marina or Telegraph Harbour Marina. This is a good way to visit Chemainus. If you take in an evening show in Chemainus, be sure you can get to the ferry before the last departure. Chemainus Water Taxi is another option (250) 246-7866 or (250) 246-9559.

Live Theater: The Chemainus Theatre Festival mounts live matinee and evening

Enjoy the wonderful cafes and large outdoor murals in Chemainus.

performances year-round (closed Mondays). Highly recommended. Call for tickets in advance: (250) 246-9820 or (800) 565-7738.

③⓪ Chemainus Municipal Wharf. P.O. Box 193, Chemainus, BC V0R 1K0; (250) 715-8186; (250) 246- 4655; harmen.chemainus. munimarina@ gmail.com. Monitors VHF 66A. Day and overnight moorage, 30 & 50 amp power, water, washrooms, showers, garbage drop, pumpout and Wi-Fi. Make

moorage reservations directly with the marina by phone or email; they have no relationship with third-party booking services. A nice laundromat is 1½ blocks away at 9870 Cross Street. This marina, with slips and side-tie, is next to the ferry terminal. Reservations recommended. Every two hours from morning to night, the ferry arrives and rolls things around a little. It's not bad, but first-time visitors should be aware of the wake.

Visitor boats will tie along 175 feet on the

outside of the main dock or moor in slips on the inside of the main dock. Because Chemainus is a popular day stop, landing fees have been instituted—$6 under 40 feet; $12 over 40 feet. They found that the docks were full during the day then empty at night, and they need moorage income to maintain the facility. The irrepressible Harmen Bootsma is the manager.

Mooring Buoys: Eight mooring buoys are available off the park at the entrance to the bay. One boat per buoy, 45-foot maximum length. Cost is $10 per night if you pay at the Chemainus Municipal Dock office; $20 if they have to come out to collect. Private mooring buoys are also in the bay; look for the buoys labeled 'public.'

③⓪ Jones Marine Services Ltd. Box 29, Chemainus, BC V0R 1K0; (250) 246-1100. Diesel and mid-grade gasoline. Fuel service is closed until further notice. A fire in March of 2018 caused considerable damage, and the building has been torn down. Fuel service will be restored once permits are in-hand and a new building for fuel services has been constructed. Fuel service is anticipated to be available for the 2020 boating season.

Evening Cove. Evening Cove, at the mouth of Ladysmith Harbour, is a possible anchorage. Correspondent Bruce Evertz reports: "We

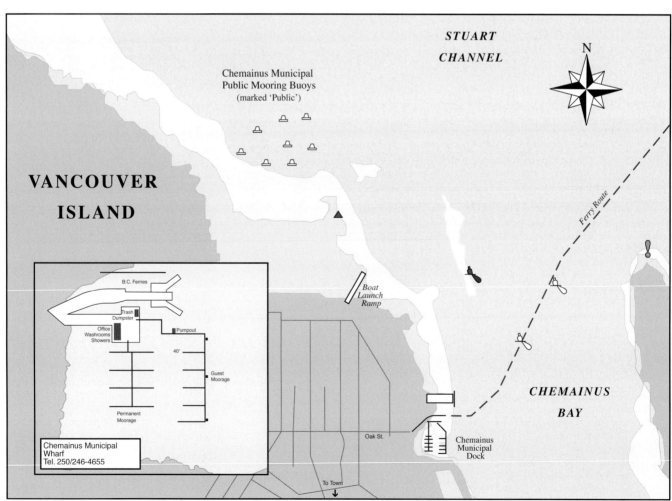

Chemainus

found good protection from northwest winds, but did have a few wakes from passing boats. There are several houses around the bay so it's not a good spot to take Fido ashore."

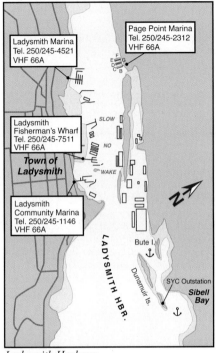
Ladysmith Harbour

㉛ **Ladysmith Harbour.** Ladysmith is on Vancouver Island, approximately 6 miles north of Chemainus. Ladysmith is an active sawmill town. Logs are stored on the north side of the harbor and in front of the mill on the south side.

Ladysmith itself is about one-half mile from Ladysmith Community Marina and Fisherman's Wharf, up the hill and across the highway. It's a bit of a hike, but worthwhile. Before reaching the highway, the big blue building is the Ladysmith Waterfront Arts Centre, with interesting galleries and the Ladysmith Maritime Society's office and historical collection of outboard motors. The building used to be a railroad equipment repair facility. The tracks are still there. A train occasionally rumbles by.

The main street of Ladysmith looks as if time passed it by. Movie scenes have been filmed here. A large and friendly 49th Parallel Grocery is several blocks west from the main downtown area, and will deliver to the docks. A private liquor store is next door to the grocery.

The Old Town Bakery at 510 First Avenue (main street through town) is "to die for," with the widest variety of fresh-baked cinnamon buns we've ever seen. We had an excellent and reasonably priced deli lunch there, too. Buoma Meats, at 412 First Avenue, is an old-fashioned butcher shop, all weights in pounds and ounces. The Beantime Cafe serves fresh roasted coffee. A broad selection

of restaurants are in town. Several restaurants will deliver to the marinas.

Ladysmith Community Marina, run by the Ladysmith Maritime Society, behind Slag Point on the south side of the harbor, is the first major set of docks. Ladysmith Fisherman's Wharf is adjacent, followed by Ladysmith Marina, farther into the harbor. Page Point Marina, on the north shore, sometimes has transient moorage available. Ladysmith Yacht Club, located at Ladysmith Marina has reciprocal moorage. Near the mouth of Ladysmith Harbour the long float in Sibell Bay, on the north side of the Dunsmuir Islands, is a Seattle Yacht Club outstation, member boats only, no reciprocal moorage.

The best anchoring is either in Sibell Bay or just west of Sibell Bay, inside the westernmost of the Dunsmuir Islands. Because of shoal water between Sibell Bay and the latter anchorage, it's a good idea to loop around the west end of the Dunsmuir Islands. Anchorage can also be found at the head of Ladysmith Harbour, off of Page Point Marina.

Repairs: Saltair Marine Services offers marine repairs and haulout to 40 feet, (250) 714-6206 Sealegs Kayaking Adventures, located upland from Ladysmith Community Marina, offers equipment sales, tours and lessons. The office, located at 200 Transfer Beach Blvd., is a short hike up the hill, phone (250) 245-4096. Concerts are held in the park at Transfer Beach.

No-Discharge Zone. Gray water okay.

Ladysmith Community Marina is a great place to relax and meet other boaters.

㉛ Ladysmith Community Marina. P.O. Box 1030, Ladysmith, BC V9G 1A7; (250) 245-1146; info@lmsmarina.ca; www. lmsmarina.ca. Monitors VHF 66A. Best to phone or email for availability. Open all year, 800 feet of guest moorage with 30 amp power, water, cube ice, pumpout, free Wi-Fi. Garbage and recycling (donations are appreciated). Reservations recommended and can be made online. The impressive Ladysmith Maritime Society Welcome Centre, on a float at the docks, has a fireside lounge, washrooms, showers, laundry, and the seasonal Oyster Bay Cafe, which is open from mid-May to Sept. from 8:00 a.m. to 3:00 p.m daily. Adjacent to the Oyster Bay Cafe is the Sea Life Center with interpretive displays and an underwater portal to view the marine life. It is a hit with the kids. The dinghy dock is on the cross dock by the Welcome Centre.

These are the first set of docks on the southwest side as you enter Ladysmith Harbour. The docks are very good and the historical displays, including restored museum boats and equipment, are fascinating. The Harbour Heritage Centre and an art gallery are up the hill in the large blue building. The town of Ladysmith is a short walk farther up the hill. Bus service runs to nearby shopping and a mall located outside the town center. Pick up for the bus is at the 49th Parallel grocery store in town.

The community is justifiably proud of this facility and its large meeting spaces. A large covered 40 X 20 foot picnic area with tables and grills, located on the docks, can accommodate up to 100 people. At the end of the day it is not unusual for a group to gather round, some grilling their dinners and some visiting others. Dine on the Dock programs are often held on Fridays during the summer and frequently sell out. Music on the Dock events are held every Thursday. Check the website for more information. The Ladysmith Maritime Society Community Marina really is a community marina, run by a small staff and over 250 volunteers. As guests, we could feel their enthusiasm.

㉛ Ladysmith Fisherman's Wharf. P.O. Box 130, Ladysmith, BC V9G 1A1; (250) 245-7511 or (250) 618-4720 after hours; office hours 10:00 a.m. to 1:00 p.m. Monday through Saturday. lfwa@telus.net; www. ladysmithfishermanswharf. com. Open all year, 1200 feet of dock space, 30 amp power, garbage drop, washrooms, showers, laundry services, waste oil disposal, trailer parking. Marine repairs, tidal grid and launch ramp. Limited transient moorage. Commercial fish boats have priority during the winter months. Stairs lead up the hill toward the town of Ladysmith, about one-half mile away.

㉛ Ladysmith Marina. 901 Gladden Rd., Ladysmith, BC V9G 1K4; (250) 245-4521; ladysmithmarina@obmg.com; www. ladysmithmarina. com. Monitors VHF 66A. Open all year, washrooms, showers, and a public laundry. 30 & 50 amp power. Picnic area. This marina has permanent moorage, but guest moorage is often available in unoccupied slips, call ahead for availability; reservations accepted. Dock A on the east side of the marina is occupied by the Ladysmith Yacht Club, with reciprocal moorage. The marina is part of Oak Bay Marine Group, a company that owns several marinas.

㉜ Page Point Marina Inc. 4760 Brenton-Page Rd., Ladysmith, BC V9G 1L7; (250) 245-2312; (877) 860-6866; moorage@pagepointmarina.com; www. pagepointmarina.com. Monitors VHF 66A. Open all year. Permanent and guest moorage to 66 feet, 30 amp power, water, free Wi-Fi, garbage drop, compost & recycling. Free shuttle service to the airport. Pet-friendly. Reservations recommended. The dinghy dock is next to the ramp at the head of G dock.

A cozy inn is available for short or long-term accommodations and private functions.

Tent Island. Tent Island is off the south tip of Penelakut Island (formerly Kuper Island), at the junction of Houstoun Passage and Stuart Channel. The small bay on the west side of Tent Island is a popular anchorage in settled weather.

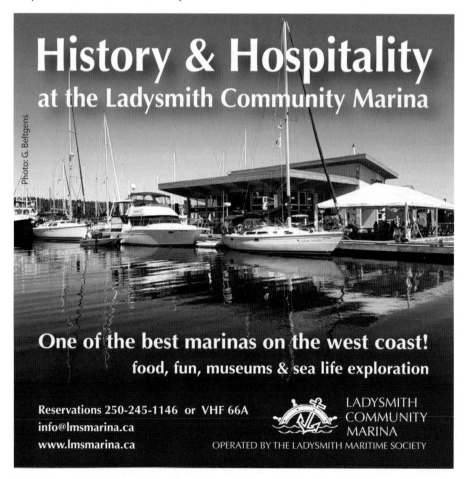

Preedy Harbour. Preedy Harbour indents the southwest corner of Thetis Island, due west of Telegraph Harbour. The ferry from Chemainus calls there. From the south, enter between Hudson Island and three long, thin reefs, marked with red (starboard hand) lights and day beacons. From Stuart Channel enter between Hudson Island and Dayman Island. Reefs, marked by green buoys on the Dayman Island side and a light on the Hudson Island side, extend from both these islands. Because the Hudson Island light is positioned upland from the toe of its reef, favor the Dayman Island buoys.

Entry from the north is clear as long as you stay mid-channel. For all three entries, check the chart carefully so you know where the reefs are, and how to avoid them.

A day-use-only community dock is in the northwest corner of Preedy Harbour, near the ferry landing. Anchorage is good in this area, keeping in mind the ferry comings and goings.

③③ **Telegraph Harbour.** Telegraph Harbour is one of the Gulf Islands' most popular stops. It is located across Stuart Channel from Chemainus, between Thetis Island and Penelakut Island (formerly Kuper Island). Two marinas are in Telegraph Harbour: Thetis Island Marina and Telegraph Harbour Marina. Both marinas are walking distance to an inter-island ferry to Chemainus. While you're at Telegraph Harbour, you may enjoy walking the roads of Thetis Island. You'll find a number of interesting stops, including the Pot of Gold Coffee Roasting Co.

White Restricted Operations buoys mark the edges of the anchoring area. Note the shoal areas on the starboard side of the channel and across from the Thetis Island Resort. Depths are shallower than charted.

Penelakut Island (formerly Kuper Island) is an Indian Reserve.

Farmers Market: A farmers market is held 10:00 a.m. to 2:00 p.m. on Saturdays, May through early September at Howling Wolf Farm at the corner of Marine Dr. and Pilkey Point Road.

LOCAL KNOWLEDGE

ENTRANCE CHANNEL: Channel markers indicate the channel between Thetis Island Marina and Telegraph Harbour Marina. Keep the marks to starboard when entering. On very low tides hug the breakwater outside the Thetis Island Marina fuel dock as you enter Telegraph Harbour. The channel has about 9 feet of depth at zero tide.

③③ **Thetis Island Resort.** 46 Harbour Rd., Thetis Island, BC ; (250) 246-1443; marina@ thetisisland.com; www.thetisisland.com. Monitors VHF 66A; (250) 246-3464 (pub, year round). To port, this is the first marina as you enter Telegraph Harbour. Open all year, gasoline and diesel at the fuel dock, propane on shore, over 3000 feet of side-tie dock space, 15 & 30 amp power, washrooms, showers, laundry, ATM. New docks were added in 2017. Additional improvements were made in 2018, including a new patio area, a refurbished deck for the pub, and renewed finishes on the outside of the main building. New owner, Wayne Proctor, is planning for continued improvements. The marina has three rental suites, and they're quite nice. This is a full-service marina with a liquor store, convenience groceries, snacks, ice, and post office. Wi-Fi on the docks; get the password at the pub or the fuel dock. A cell phone booster covers the pub and deck areas. It's a 10- to 15-minute walk to the BC Ferries to Chemainus.

The fully-licensed pub has inside and outside dining and separate areas for families. The pub has good food and an excellent selection of beers, porters, stouts, and single-malt scotches.

The Resort has its own water desalination system, no water at the docks however. A covered picnic and barbecue area with seating is available for groups. There is a Saturday Market from 10 a.m. to 2 p.m.

245

Stern-tied in lovely Princess Cove on Wallace Island

㉝ **Telegraph Harbour Marina.** Box 7-10, Thetis Island, BC V0R 2Y0; (250) 246-9511; (800) 246-6011; sunny@telegraphharbour. com; www.telegraphharbour.com. Monitors VHF 66A. This is the marina at the back of the bay. Although close to drying flats, the docks have at least 6 to 8 feet on all tides. Open 7 days a week, mid-June through mid-September, and weekends only from Easter through mid-June. In winter no facilities are available except moorage and electricity. Gasoline, diesel, and oil at the fuel dock. Moorage along 3000 feet of dock, 15 & 30 amp power, washrooms, showers, laundry, Wi-Fi, garbage drop, recycling, limited water.

The store carries convenience groceries including a variety of specialty meats, deli items to go, marine guides, books and gifts, and fresh-baked pies. The marina has pre-ordered homemade pizzas and fresh baguettes to go, and is the exclusive outlet

for Thetis Island's Pot of Gold coffee. They have an old fashioned soda fountain where you can still get guilt-filled hard ice cream and milk shakes.

The marina is clean and well-maintained. Staff helps arriving boats land. They have a playground for kids, a dog run, a large covered area for group functions, and a picnic area with tables and barbecues. It's a 10 to 15 minute walk to the BC Ferries to Chemainus. Boaters are permitted to use the community trail system, accessible from the marina. The Domaine Jasmin Winery (250) 246-9494 is a recent addition on the island located several miles north. Arrangements for group transportation to the winery are possible through the Telegraph Harbour Marina with a return trip provided by winery personnel.

Rendezvous: Many rendezvous are held here in spring or early fall, best to call ahead for reservations on weekends and during the peak season. A few rendezvous fill the marina, but most do not. Moorage space is usually available.

The Cut. The Cut is a straight and uncomplicated drying pass connecting Telegraph Harbour with Clam Bay. Red, Right, Returning assumes you are returning from Clam Bay. Cruising boats should only try The Cut at or near high water, with local knowledge. Signs at each end purport to show the depth, but they read approximately 3 feet too deep. We took the dinghy through at the bottom of a 4.3-foot tide, sounding the shallow spots with a leadline. Although the two signs said 6 feet of water was in the channel, we found only 2 to 2.5 feet in the shallow spots near the Telegraph Harbour entrance and at a couple of narrow places on the Clam Bay side.

North Cove. North Cove indents the north end of Thetis Island and is a good anchorage, although it is open to northwesterly winds. A substantial rock breakwater protects a private float and boathouse at Fraser Point, the entrance to North Cove. Camp docks are in the southwest corner of the cove. Anchor in 24 to 36 feet (zero tide) along the south shore. High tide covers fingers of rock that extend from the south shore, but the rock reappears

when the tide drops. Don't get too close. Stay clear of the rocks in the middle of the entry. The charts show them as ++, for dangerous rocks 6 feet or less beneath the surface.

Cufra Inlet. Cufra Inlet, about a mile long, extends into Thetis Island from the southeast corner of North Cove. Most of the inlet dries, but is good for dinghy exploring at higher water.

Clam Bay. Clam Bay is a large, relatively open bay with good anchoring in convenient depths. Reader Jerry Williams, who lived there, says his favorite spot is the little bight on the north shore, between Leech Island and Thetis Island. The mouth of the Clam Bay is partly blocked by Centre Reef. Rocket Shoal is in the middle of the bay. Lacking familiarity, the safest entry is south of Centre Reef, between Buoy U42 and Penelakut Spit, which extends from Penelakut Island (formerly Kuper Island). The charts show everything. Large scale Plans Chart 3477 is especially useful. Clam Bay is at one end of The Cut, the drying channel that separates Thetis Island from Penelakut Island.

Southey Bay. At the north tip of Saltspring Island, tucked in beside Southey Point, is a little notch that Tom Kincaid used as an anchorage in past years. An increasing number of private mooring buoys have restricted swinging room, but it's still a possible anchorage.

Secretary Islands. The Secretary Islands have several nice little anchorages, with the emphasis on *little*. One of the easiest is in the notch on the Trincomali Channel side between the two Secretary Islands.

Mowgli Island. Mowgli Island, off the northwest tip of the Secretary Islands, has good anchorage in a cozy bay between it and the first Secretary island. Swinging room is limited. We suggest a stern-tie across the gravel beach to driftwood ashore. The island is surrounded by reefs. They are easily seen at low tide, but be cautious at high tide.

㉞ **Wallace Island Marine Park.** www.env. gov.bc.ca/bcparks/explore/parkpgs/wallace/ Open all year. Wallace Island, a marine park purchased with the help of the local boating community, is a low and beautiful tree-covered island in Trincomali Channel. Enter from Houstoun Passage. You'll find sheltered anchorage and a dock at Conover Cove, anchorage for many boats in locally-named Princess Cove, and room for a couple of boats just inside Panther Point. The park has toilets, campsites and picnic areas, and trails crisscrossing the entire island. It's a fine place to walk through the forest and stretch the legs. Raccoons roam the area—especially at night, lock up all food items aboard and pack out refuse. Old cabins set in an orchard near Conover Cove are locked shut, awaiting funds for restoration. One cabin is festooned

Telegraph Harbour Marina
Ph. 250/246-9511
VHF 66A

THE CUT
Shallow

G H I J K L
B · Fuel
E C A
F D

N

Seaplane
Dock

Floating
Breakwater

Fuel

Thetis Island Marina
Ph. 250/246-3464
VHF 66A

Telegraph Harbour

Stern-ties are the rule at popular Pirates Cove Marine Park.

with carved name boards from visiting yachts. Please respect the two private properties on the island.

③④ Conover Cove. A reef directly offshore from the entrance to Conover Cove on Wallace Island can be avoided by going around either end. Especially from the southeast, give the reef ample room. When you leave, remember the reef is there. We are told that each year boats depart at high tide and drive up on the rocks. A dock for boats 36 feet and under provides access to the island, a nominal fee is charged. An honor-system pay-box is located at the head of the ramp. Conover Cove is fairly shoal at the dock and shoals even more toward both ends of the bay. You can anchor and stern-tie to pins, with chain, set in the rocks on shore. Be sure to check your depths. The entrance to Conover Cove is shallow at low tide.

③④ Princess Cove. Princess Cove is just northwest of Conover Cove, and has room for quite a few boats to anchor. 18 long chains, with large links for stern lines, are attached to existing pins set in the rock along the shoreline. If anchoring in the cove, set the anchor carefully in 18 to 24 feet (deeper toward the mouth of the cove), and maintain an anchor watch if the wind comes up. A dinghy dock is on the west side of the cove for convenient access to hiking.

③④ Panther Point. Panther Point is the southeast tip of Wallace Island. There's room for one or perhaps two boats in 30 to 36 feet just inside the mouth of the cove. If you anchor any farther inside, a rock on the north side will restrict your swing. The anchorage is exposed to southeast winds but protected from other winds.

Retreat Cove. Retreat Cove, a small notch protected by off-lying Retreat Island, indents Galiano Island across Trincomali Channel from the south tip of Wallace Island. The approach around the north side of Retreat Island is shallow and foul with rocks and reefs. Enter only from the south. The head of Retreat Cove shelves sharply. Anchor in 18 to 24 feet, but plan your swing to avoid the shelf. An 80-foot-long public dock, no facilities, is

on the southern shore of the cove. Local boats take much of the space on the dock.

North Galiano. North Galiano is on the west side of Galiano Island. It lies to the northeast of Hall Island and has anchorage and a small public dock, no facilities.

Dionisio Point Park. Open all year, day use and overnight camping, toilets, no power, no showers. Anchor only. The park overlooks Porlier Pass. It has sandy beaches, rocky headlands and forested uplands.

Porlier Pass. Porlier Pass separates Galiano Island and Valdes Island. Several times a year, currents on large tides reach 9 knots. Current predictions are shown in the Tide and Current Tables Vol. 5, and Ports and Passes. The current floods north into the Strait of Georgia, and ebbs south into the Gulf Islands. The best time to transit is at slack water. A study of the chart shows it is safest to transit Porlier Pass on the south sides of Black Rock and Virago Rock, staying toward the Galiano Island side of the pass.

From the Strait of Georgia, begin your approach near Lighted Bell Buoy U41. South of the buoy, pick up the range on Race Point and Virago Point. Follow that range into Porlier Pass to clear the rocks extending from the northeast tip of Galiano Island. Once clear of the rocks, you can turn to follow a mid-channel course between Virago Rock and Galiano Island. Charts 3442 and 3443 show the range and the rocks to be avoided on both sides, but the larger scale Chart 3473 really helps understanding. Chartbook 3313 also shows the pass in excellent detail.

De Courcy Group. The De Courcy Group has several interesting small anchorages. **Whaleboat Island,** just off the southeast shore of Ruxton Island, is a relatively undeveloped provincial park. The preferred anchorage is south of the island, taking care to avoid a drying rock. The north end of **Ruxton Island** has **Herring Bay**, one of the more attractive small anchorages in the northern Gulf Islands, and frequently used when the anchorage at **Pirates Cove** on De Courcy Island is full (which it often is in the summer). Herring Bay has a white

sand beach to enjoy. The De Courcy Group is named after Michael de Courcy, captain of the H.M.S. Pylades, who charted these waters from 1859 to 1861.

Whaleboat Island Marine Park. Just south of Ruxton Island. No facilities. Whaleboat Island is undeveloped, but provides an extremely limited alternate anchorage to Pirates Cove Marine Park. The preferred anchorage is south of the island, taking care to avoid a drying rock.

Pylades Island. Reader Jerry Williams, who grew up on Pylades Island, tells us the little hole just north of the dot islet off the northeast corner of Pylades Island is "magical." Most of the land is private, please do not take dogs ashore. A drying shoal is between Pylades Island and the dot islet, so approach from the north. In Whaleboat Passage, between Pylades Island and Ruxton Island, note the drying rock a short distance off Pylades Island.

Herring Bay. Herring Bay indents the northwest end of Ruxton Island, off Ruxton Passage. The bay is bordered by weather-carved sandstone walls and has a beautiful sand beach on the southeast side. Good anchoring in 24 feet, much to explore.

A charted rock ledge that dries at 1 foot is in the west entrance to Herring Bay at 49°05.08'N/123°43.01'W. We use the north entrance exclusively.

LOCAL KNOWLEDGE

DANGEROUS REEFS: The entrance to Pirates Cove is guarded by a reef that extends parallel to the shoreline to a point a little beyond a concrete beacon. When entering, you must leave this beacon to port. A range, consisting of a white-painted arrow on the ground and a white × on a tree above, shows where to make your approach. Align the × on the tree above the arrow on the ground and proceed slowly until just past the concrete beacon to port. Turn sharply to port and leave the red Spar Buoy U38 to starboard. The entry is shallow. At lower tides deep-draft boats should be especially cautious.

③⑤ Pirates Cove Marine Park. Pirates Cove is open all year, campsites, pit toilets, hand pump water (boil before use) on the south beach, no other facilities. It's a lovely little harbor, protected from seas but not all winds, with room for many boats (on a short scope). 24 stern-tie chains are set into the sandstone cliffs that encircle the bay; the boat's stern-tie line is run through a large link in the chain. Do not use trees for stern tie. Two dinghy docks are for shore access, one on the northeast and the other on the southwest side of the cove. Dinghies may go ashore at the south end beach. The small marina on the right as you enter is private.

Most of the land is a marvelous provincial park. The cove is surrounded by a forest of Douglas fir, Garry oak and arbutus (madrona). Well-maintained trails lead through the forest and along the rock shoreline with its sculpted sandstone formations and tide pools. Be sure to stay on designated trails to avoid brushing against poison oak, a rash-causing plant species protected by the Provincial Marine Park. Pirates Cove has only a fair holding bottom of sticky mud. If the wind comes up during the night, you can expect a fire drill as boats drag anchor. It's best to stern-tie. When departure time arrives, be prepared to spend extra time cleaning the anchor as it comes aboard.

No Discharge Zone, No Gray Water Discharge.

On Ruxton Passage, the little notch at the south end of De Courcy Island is also part of the park, and you can anchor there. The beach is good for dinghy or kayak landing, and campsites are ashore. Additional anchorage is available at Whaleboat Island Marine Park, nearby. Another "Pirates Cove overflow" notch is just north of Pirates Cove off Link Island.

Boat Harbour. 2275 Kendall Road, Nanaimo, BC V9X 1W8; (250) 802-9963; marina.boatharbour@gmail.com; www.boatharbourmarina.ca; VHF 66A. Located across Stuart Channel from De Courcy Island, Boat Harbour is home to **Boat Harbour Marina**. Open June-September, 9:00 a.m. to 6:00 p.m.; till 5:00 p.m. on weekends. Long-term moorage with some transient space. Two-day minimum stay on weekends.

Silva Bay offers several moorage options.

30 & 50 amp power, water, garbage drop, Wi-Fi. All new docks installed in 2018. The marina offers customized tours for groups of 8 or more. You can opt for hikes through the private upland trails, with a picnic at the lake, or you might choose cooking classes, catered parties or pig roasts.

The anchorage area in Boat Harbour is within a private 'water lot' and is a no discharge zone. Anchorage allowed only with a permit by calling or texting (250) 802-9963 for application. The no-anchoring zone is marked with a line of spar buoys and posted signage. All of **Kenary Cove** dries on low tide.

GABRIOLA PASSAGE TO NANAIMO

Gabriola Passage. Gabriola Passage (Gabriola is pronounced "GAY-briola") is the northernmost entrance to the Gulf Islands from the Strait of Georgia. From Bowen Island on the east side of the strait, it is 14 miles to Gabriola Passage, the shortest crossing between the lower mainland and the islands.

Tidal currents on spring tides can run to 8 knots in Gabriola Passage, both flood and ebb. Typical maximum currents are around 4 knots. Transiting is best at slack. The current sets east on the flood and west on the ebb. Times of slack and maximum currents are given in the Tide & Current Tables, Vol. 5 and Ports and Passes.

Degnen Bay. Degnen Bay, on Gabriola Passage at the south end of Gabriola Island, is a good anchorage but a little crowded with boats on moorings. Entering Degnen Bay, favor the east side, close to Josef Point, to avoid rocks in the middle. A petroglyph of a killer whale is on a slab of rock near the head of the bay. Correspondents John and Lorraine Littlewood report additional petroglyphs on the United Church grounds. A public dock provides access to Gabriola Island. All other docks are private.

Degnen Bay Public Wharf. Has 190 feet of dock space, power, garbage drop, but no other facilities. Commercial fish boats have priority.

Wakes Cove. Wakes Cove, on Gabriola Passage at the north end of Valdes Island, has a beautiful provincial marine park occupying almost the entire north end of Valdes Island. The park has trails and historical interpretation information. It is served by a small dock, approximately 40 feet, for RCMP and BC Parks personnel. The park is accessible by dinghy and kayak. Anchorage is a little iffy.

Dogfish Bay. Kendrick Island, on the northeast side of Valdes Island, creates a narrow and shallow bay known locally as Dogfish Bay. Dogfish Bay is well protected and the holding ground is good. West Vancouver Yacht Club has an outstation on Kendrick Island, members only, no reciprocal moorage.

Drumbeg Provincial Park. South end of Gabriola Island, overlooking Gabriola Passage. Open all year, day use only. Toilets, no other facilities. Has shelving sandstone rocks and a small sandy beach.

Flat Top Islands. The Flat Top Islands are appropriately named, and from the north or east they're a little hard to tell apart. If approaching from the Strait of Georgia, pass north of Thrasher Rock Light. The light marks the northern end of Gabriola Reefs. All the Flat Top Islands are privately owned.

LOCAL KNOWLEDGE

DANGEROUS ROCK: When entering Silva Bay between Vance Island and Tugboat Island, leave the beacon marking Shipyard Rock to port. Do not turn at once for the Silva Bay floats or other facilities. Shipyard Rock is larger than it appears on the charts. Continue instead until about halfway to Law Point before making your turn. Give the rock plenty of room.

㉟ **Silva Bay**. Silva Bay is a popular destination in the Flat Top Islands area, well protected, with good holding bottom. From the north, enter through Commodore Passage between Gaviola Island and Vance Island; from the south enter through Commodore Passage between Acorn Island and Tugboat Island. From Commodore Passage, enter Silva Bay

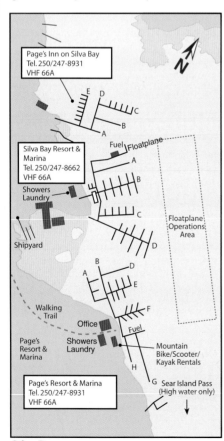

Page's Inn on Silva Bay
Tel. 250/247-8931
VHF 66A

E D
C
B
A

Fuel Floatplane

Silva Bay Resort & Marina
Tel. 250/247-8662
VHF 66A

A
B

Showers Laundry

C

Floatplane Operations Area

D

Shipyard

B D
A E

Walking Trail

Office

Page's Resort & Marina

Showers Laundry

F

Fuel

H

Mountain Bike/Scooter/ Kayak Rentals

G Sear Island Pass (High water only)

Page's Resort & Marina
Tel. 250/247-8931
VHF 66A

Silva Bay

You can purchase gifts, books, and ready-made dinners at Page's Resort.

between Tugboat Island and Vance Island, leaving Shipyard Rock to port; notorious Shipyard Rock lies along the south side of this passage. Entering Silva Bay from the south through Sear Island Passage between Gabriola Island and Sear Island is possible only on high water tides.

Silva Bay Shipyard, with marine railway and 12-ton Travelift, is next to Silva Bay Resort & Marina.

Anchoring: Anchoring is tight. Much of the bay is filled with private mooring buoys; a designated float plane departure and landing area is located along the front of the docks, where anchoring is not allowed.

㊱ **Silva Bay Resort & Marina**. 3383 South Road, Gabriola Island, BC V0R 1X7; (250) 247-8662 ext. 8; info@silvabay.com; www.silvabay.com. Monitors VHF 66A. Open all year with guest moorage, 30 amp & limited 100 amp power, water on the fuel dock, garbage drop, washrooms, showers and laundry. Reservations recommended. Diesel and mid-grade gasoline at the fuel dock. Daily floatplane flights to Vancouver.

The Silva Bay Bar & Grill was destroyed by fire in October 2017. Dan Chen and family, new owners of the marina property, have plans to construct a new pub to be completed some time during the 2019 season.

㊱ **Page's Resort & Marina.** 3350 Coast Road, Gabriola Island, BC V0R 1X7; (250) 247-8931; info@pagesresort.com; www.pagesresortgroup.com. Monitors VHF 66A. Open all year. Visitor moorage accommodates vessels to 40 feet; two slips accommodate vessels up to 60 feet; one slip can accommodate a 75-foot vessel. Mid-grade marine gasoline and diesel at the fuel dock. 30 amp power, washrooms, showers, laundry, garbage, recycling, bicycle and scooter rentals, ice, free Wi-Fi. Cottages and tent sites for rent. The grounds are well maintained.

Cab service and a community shuttle bus service can take you to Gabriola Island's shopping center, or you can rent bicycles or motor scooters at Page's.

For those interested in books, Page's is an attractive stop. The office feels more like a peaceful bookstore (which it is) with an extensive range of titles, especially books about local subjects and by local authors. The refurbished shop carries essential groceries, sundry items, bait, marine charts, and cruising guides. The shop's freezer is stocked with ready-made dinners that can be prepared back at the boat or on the barbeque.

This marina resort is friendly and well managed. Gloria Hatfield is the owner.

㊱ **Page's Inn on Silva Bay.** 3415 South Rd., Gabriola Island, BC V0R 1X7, (250) 247-9351; info@silvabayinn.ca; www.pagesresortgroup.com. This lovely Inn, formerly the Boatel, was

Every day at noon the cannon is fired from the historic Bastion above the moorage area.

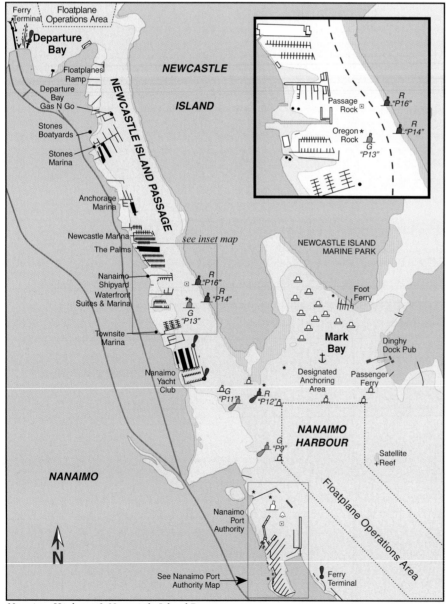

Nanaimo Harbour & Newcastle Island Passage

recently purchased by Page's Resort & Marina. Meeting space is available on the top floor. Located west of Page's Marina, the docks at Page's Inn offer transient moorage for boaters staying ashore in one of the suites. A farmers' market, selling produce, food, and Gabriolan art, is held on the grounds on Sundays during the summer season.

Silva Bay Shipyard. 3445 South Road, Gabriola Island, BC V0R 1X7; (250) 247-9800; info@silvabayshipyard.com; www.silvabayshipyard.com. A do-it-yourself boatyard with a 12-ton travelift and 80-ton railway. Ships chandlery, mechanical & electrical repairs, stern drive mechanics, and wooden boat repair.

False Narrows. False Narrows is east of Dodd Narrows, and is an alternate connection between the Gulf Islands and Northumberland Channel. If you choose to make this passage, you will be traveling between reefs in a shallow channel that is best used at half tide or better. Local knowledge says if you strictly follow the two ranges shown on the chart you'll be okay. Go slowly to keep your wake down. Maximum currents in False Narrows are about half of those in Dodd Narrows.

㊲ **Dodd Narrows.** Currents in Dodd Narrows run to 9 knots as water swirls through the narrow deep passage between cliffs. The narrows are best taken at slack water. For the hour or so before the predicted turn, boats collect at each end waiting for the right time. These boats include commercial craft, even tugboats with log tows or large barges, so the period around slack water can get pretty interesting. Generally, the boats on the upstream side go first, catching the last of the dying fair current. When they are through, boats on the other end go through, picking up the beginnings of the new (for them) fair current. It all works well as long as no one gets impatient. Vessels will be transiting in both directions during and around slack periods. Check for traffic by viewing AIS targets on both sides of the narrows and listen on VHF 16 for Securité calls from traffic that might pose a safety concern for other vessels. Tugboats with log tows and large commercial vessels will typically announce their intentions on VHF 16. In recent years, VHF 16 has been flooded with Securité calls from boats that may not need to announce themselves, so if your boat does not pose a safety concern for others, there is no need to make a Securité call. If you do make a call, be sure to use 1-watt low power. Don't be in a hurry, and don't try to pass a slower boat. Dodd Narrows is short. Travel single-file and leave room between your boat and the boat ahead and share the channel with opposing direction traffic.

Northumberland Channel. Northumberland Channel is the passage from the Gulf Islands to Nanaimo. It begins at False Narrows and runs northwest between Gabriola Island and Vancouver Island. Northumberland Channel exits in the Gulf of Georgia, or, at Jack Point, makes the turn to Nanaimo. Because of considerable log boom towing in the area, watch for floating debris. If you are not yet ready for civilization, you might lay over at Pilot Bay, on the north end of Gabriola Island.

Pilot Bay. Pilot Bay is on the north end of Gabriola Island. It's a good anchorage in a southeasterly, but is open to northwesterlies. *No discharge zone, gray water okay.*

Gabriola Sands Park. North end of Gabriola Island. Open all year, day use only. Toilets, but no other facilities. This park fronts on Taylor Bay and Pilot Bay. It has a sandy swimming area and a playfield. Good for kids.

Sandwell Park. Northeast side of Gabriola Island. Open all year, day use only, toilets but no other facilities. This is a small seafront park with a sandy beach and forested uplands.

㊳ **Nanaimo.** As you pass Jack Point the city of Nanaimo opens up. Head for the prominent high rise condominium building, easily seen from Jack Point. The harbor is wide and sheltered from the Strait of Georgia by Protection Island and Newcastle Island.

The Nanaimo Port Authority public marina is at the south end of the business district near Nanaimo's famous Bastion (blockhouse), with access to downtown Nanaimo. The Bastion was built in 1853 by the Hudson's Bay Company, and is Nanaimo's oldest man-made landmark still standing. A Thrifty Foods supermarket, London Drug, Pacific Place, ATM, B.C. liquor store, Starbucks and several fast-food and sandwich shops are in the shopping mall near the Port Authority marina. The Nanaimo Museum is in the Conference Centre, one block from the public marina.

The Canada Customs dock is marked at the head of E dock on the north side of the public docks, just behind the fuel dock area. Other moorages, including the Nanaimo Yacht Club, are in Newcastle Island Passage, the channel leading behind Newcastle Island to Departure Bay. The Nanaimo Yacht Club has guest moorage for visiting members of reciprocal clubs. Waterfront Suites & Marina has transient moorage and Stones Marina occasionally has room for transient boaters.

Satellite Reef caution: Buoy *PS* is west of Satellite Reef, approximately where boats entering from Northumberland Channel would plan to turn to anchor at Newcastle Island or continue through Newcastle Island Passage. Satellite Reef dries at zero tide and should be considered hazardous at all times. Stay west of Buoy *PS*.

Repair and haul-out facilities capable of handling any needed job are located along Newcastle Island Passage, known locally as Newcastle Channel.

Nanaimo is a natural point of departure for boats headed across the Strait of Georgia

or north to Campbell River or Desolation Sound and beyond. It is the second largest city (behind Victoria) on Vancouver Island. Shops of all kinds line the narrow, winding streets of old town Nanaimo. We've prowled through several impressive bookstores—new and used—in downtown.

Nanaimo offers excellent dining, from casual to elegant. Several restaurants are on the water in the marina. A winding promenade takes walkers along the waterfront for 4 km (2.5 miles), from the marina to the B.C. Ferry Terminal in Departure Bay.

An 1853 cannon, intended in its day to protect the Bastion but used instead to welcome ships into the harbour, is fired at noon each day at the Bastion beginning in May. It's a ceremony complete with a piper in full regalia and a booming explosion with a cloud of white smoke. Beginning in June the Brigadoon Dance Academy's highland dancers perform from 11:15 a.m. to 11:45 a.m. Get there early and bring your camera.

Nanaimo is home to the Annual 'World Championship Bathtub Race' held during the third weekend in July. The event is preceded by a parade of bathtub race participants, games, food, and concerts. See www.bathtubbing.com.

Floatplane Activity: Beware of floatplane arrivals and departures when motoring in the charted air operation area. A flashing white light, located on the Eco Barge pumpout dock, indicates air operation.

Chandlery: Harbour Chandler, south of the boat basin, is an excellent chandlery. At the north end is Stones Boatyard Marine Store.

Farmers Market: Just north of the Bastion, a farmers market, often with entertainment, is open 10:00 a.m. to 2:00 p.m. Fridays, May to mid-October.

Taxi: AC Taxi, (250) 753-1231

THINGS TO DO

1. Nanaimo Bastion. Located above the marina, the Bastion is the oldest standing building in Nanaimo. You can explore it, or watch the cannon ceremony at noon.

2. Newcastle Island. Hike to the sandstone quarry or rent a kayak, SUP, or bike. A foot ferry provides regular access to Newcastle Island from the Nanaimo waterfront or take your dinghy. A children's playground was recently added. Walking tours and a traditional tribal salmon bake are available on the island by reservation. See www.newcastleisland.ca for reservations information

3. Fresh seafood on the dock. Fishermen return to the Port Authority marina and sell their catch. You can prepare a fresh seafood dinner on your boat. Or, stop by Trollers for fish and chips.

4. Nanaimo Museum. Just up from the marina at 100 Museum Way. Learn the history of Nanaimo from its First Nations roots to the discovery of coal in the area.

5. Petroglyph Provincial Park. A taxi ride from the docks. See carvings of animals and sea creatures immortalized in the sandstone hundreds and thousands of years ago.

6. Dinghy Dock Pub. On Protection Island. Take your dinghy or the ferry ($9). Great sun deck, good food, and of course cold beer.

7. Walk or bike the multi-use Harbourfront Walkway trail along the downtown waterfront, and on north along the Newcastle Channel.

251

Boutiques, gift shops, and good restaurants are plentiful in Nanaimo.

③⑧ **Nanaimo Port Authority.** 100 Port Drive, P.O. Box 131, Nanaimo, -BC V9R 5K4; (250) 755-1216; (250) 754-5053; marina@npa.ca; www.npa.ca. During July and August call (250) 755-1216. Monitors VHF 67 (not 66A). Open year-round. Three hours of moorage complimentary, but call on VHF 67 for slip assignment. Fewer spaces have been reserved for transient moorage than in the past. Reservations recommended. Reservations must be made 48 hours in advance. Rafting is permitted. Dock assistants are available during the summer months to help you tie up. Numerous commercial fish boats are in the basin during the winter months, but pleasure craft moorage is available. Water at selected docks in the winter. Customs clearance available at the customs dock, just behind the fuel dock.

A floating breakwater dock is in the center of the harbour entrance, and the Eco Barge pumpout and portapotty dump is tied to the shore side of this dock. No charge for the Eco Barge. Arriving and departing vessels must pass south of the floating breakwater dock. The northern entrance is reserved for aircraft.

No Discharge Zone, Gray water okay.

The Port Authority harbour is actually two marina facilities: **Inner Boat Basin** and **W.E. Mills Landing & Marina** (formerly and locally known as Cameron Island Marina). We have used both and are happy either place.

Inner Boat Basin is mostly permanent moorage with some transient space. Facilities include extensive dock space, 20 & 30 amp power on all floats, some 50 & 100 amp power, water, free Wi-Fi, and waste oil disposal. Washrooms, showers with heated tile floors, and laundry are next to the wharfinger office.

③⑧ **W.E. Mills Landing & Marina.** Larger vessels and ships will tie on the outside of the breakwater pier, smaller boats on the inside. Facilities include 20, 30, & 50 amp power and water. Free Wi-Fi. Washrooms, showers, and laundry are located in the Inner Boat Basin near the wharfinger office, a short dinghy ride but a long walk. Wakes from boats headed for the fuel dock or the Inner Boat Basin rock boats at W.E. Mills Landing & Marina. The docks have a security gate that is open 7:00 a.m. to 11:00 p.m. Between 11:00 p.m. and 7:00 a.m., you'll have to use the combination supplied by the dock help or call security to let you in. Watch the current when landing at W.E. Mills Landing & Marina. Usually there's no problem, but be aware.

Seasonally, fresh fish is sometimes sold at the Nanaimo Fisherman's Market dock at the entrance to the Inner Boat Basin. The dock is 250 feet long, 15 feet wide, and wheelchair accessible. With its flags and specially designed gazebos, you can't miss it. Fish & chips, Mexican food, and other delights are available at floating restaurants. Theaters, a waterfront promenade, and tennis courts are nearby. The seaplane terminal is north of the Inner Boat Basin.. All of the Nanaimo commercial district is within a five-minute walk.

No Designated Dinghy Dock. If coming by dinghy, call the marina office on VHF 67 for tie-up instructions.

③⑧ **Petro-Canada Coastal Mountain Fuels.** 10 Wharf St., Nanaimo, BC V9R IP2; (250) 754-7828. Open all year, gasoline and diesel at the fuel dock. Lubricants, accessories, ice, snacks. At the end of "E" dock. May to mid-September, 7:00 a.m. to 7:00 p.m.; October to May, 8:00 a.m. to 5:00 p.m.

③⑧ **Waterfront Suites & Marina.** 1000 Stewart Ave., Nanaimo, BC V9S 4C9; (250) 753-7111; moorage@waterfrontnanaimo.com; www.waterfrontnanaimo.com. Open all year, moorage to 100 feet, 30 & 50 amp power, washrooms, showers, laundry, Wi-Fi available in the hotel lobby, 24-hour service and security. Reservations encouraged. The docks are modular and staff can configure a dock for odd sized boats. Often has space for transient boats when the other marinas are full.

③⑧ **Stones Marina.** 1690 Stewart Ave., Nanaimo BC V9S 4E1; Marina (250) 753-4232; www.stonesmarina.com. Open all year, 30 & 50 amp power, washrooms, showers, laundry, cable & internet. Limited transient overnight moorage by reservation only. The

Hike the network of trails on Newcastle Island.

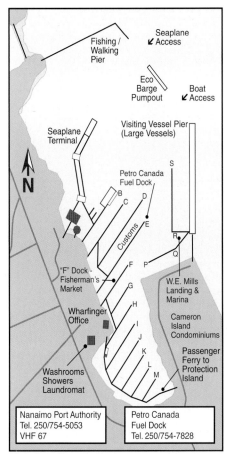

Nanaimo Port Authority

marina office is located in the white building up the driveway and along the main road. The marina complex has a pub and restaurant, liquor store, marine supplies store, boatyard, yacht charters, and day-use guest moorage dock. The 140 foot float in front of the pub restaurant has side-tie space for vessels visiting the Stones Marina complex. **Stones Boatyard & Marine Store** www.nanaimoboatyard. ca (250-716-9065) are located in the Stones Marina complex. The do-it-yourself or yacht services boatyard with 83-ton Travelift is available for scheduled and emergency repairs. Stones Boatyard & Marine Store is under separate ownership.

Caution: Waters are shallow around the day-use guest dock and Travelift; check your depth.

㊳ **Departure Bay Gas N Go.** 1840 Stewart Ave., Nanaimo, BC V9F 4E6; (250) 591-0810. Open all year. Fuel dock with gas and diesel at north end of Newcastle Channel. Small store carries snacks, tackle, some lubricants.

㊴ **Newcastle Island Marine Park.** www. env.gov.bc.ca/bcparks/explore/parkpgs/ newcastle/ Open all year, moorage with 1500 feet of dock space, excellent washrooms and showers, no power. Anchoring is prohibited in Mark Bay; 43 mooring balls are available for vessels 40 feet and under (some are limited to 30 feet). A nightly mooring fee is paid onshore at the head of the dock. Extensive anchorage

is still available just beyond Mark Bay and the docks. Several small bays, beaches, and playing fields. Many hiking trails. Walk-in campsites and picnic areas. Seasonal kayak, canoe, SUP and bicycle rentals. In summer a passenger ferry connects the island with Nanaimo.

The 1931 pavilion houses a dance floor, snack bar, visitor center, and excellent interpretive displays on the natural and human history of the area.

This is an extraordinary park. The pulpstone quarry astonishes. The bays and beaches intrigue. Before European settlement, Newcastle Island was a summer campsite for First Nations people. Since European settlement, it has supported a shipyard and been mined for coal. In the early 1870s it was quarried for sandstone that built the San Francisco Mint. Between 1923 and 1932 its sandstone was quarried for pulpstones, giant cylinders that ground wood into pulp for making paper. Before WWII, Japanese fishermen ran herring salteries here. Through it all, Newcastle Island has been a popular holiday spot.

You might see rare albino raccoons, and dozens of bunny rabbits. If moored at the dock, raccoons will try to board vessels searching for food. Secure your boat well, and don't leave any food or garbage out. Arrive early enough to get literature from the visitor center. Try to spend the night. The lights of Nanaimo are beautiful. The Dinghy Dock pub is a short dinghy ride away.

BROTHER XII, THE STRANGE ODYSSEY OF A 20TH-CENTURY PROPHET
- By John Oliphant

Publisher: Twelfth House Press; ISBN: 9780978097202

Nanaimo on Vancouver Island, along with **Valdez and De Courcy Islands** are familiar names, known to boaters who cruise the Gulf Islands of British Columbia; but how many of us are aware of the tale of a religious cult that was active on these islands during the 1920's. The story has mostly gone untold, until recently. Little was known about Edward Arthur Wilson, other than as a lingering legend. Author John Oliphant heard of the tale while cruising the Gulf Islands; intrigued, he wanted to learn more. Locating and interviewing surviving disciples and finding rare documents, author John Oliphant wrote the fascinating story of Brother XII (Edward A. Wilson).

Edward Arthur Wilson, later known as Brother XII, was a charismatic individual who evoked curiosity, awe, and inspiration, which enabled him to attract followers to his mystical cult. Most of his followers were from wealthy backgrounds who donated thousands of dollars to "The Work." A bizarre mixture of spiritualism, Greek mythology, astrology, black magic, and Christianity, membership became widespread, including members in Europe, the U.S., and Canada.

Edward Wilson claimed that he was the Messenger of an ancient mystical Brotherhood known as the Great White Lodge. A former sea captain, he had traveled extensively and had a knowledge of world religions. Edward, Brother XII, believed that he and his followers were destined to start a more evolved race of humanity and make ready for an impending Armageddon. He established the Aquarian Foundation for the teaching and saving of humanity; members would be the spiritual aristocracy, like knights of the Grail.

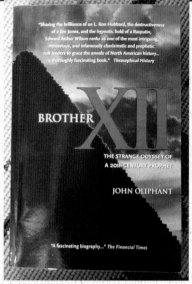

As a Center of Refuge for his disciples, he established a settlement in British Columbia in the farming district of Cedar, nine miles south of **Nanaimo**, which he called Cedar-by-the-Sea. The property included views of tiny Round Island, Dodd Narrows, and Gabriola Island. After the appointment of his Governors, the purchase of property, and the 1927 incorporation of the Aquarian Foundation in May, he began constructing buildings. Carpenters framed up houses and a Center Building was built with lumber from Chemainus. A power plant was installed, wells dug, and a water tower built. The property was fenced, including ten-foot-high gates at the entrance.

The following year, he purchased 400 acres in nearby **Valdes Island** and built a cabin at the top of a ridge on the east side of the Island. The new settlement on Valdes, called the Mandieh Settlement, was to be for select disciples, who were asked to surrender their personal possessions because their needs for food, clothing, and shelter would be provided. Brother XII planned to build several cabins, a freight shed, wharf, blacksmith shop, and a small schoolhouse. He had already completed a comfortable five-room log cabin for himself and an assembly hall.

Several months later, Brother XII traveled in his tugboat, the *Khuenaten*, from Valdes across Pylades Channel to the De Courcy group of islands. Onboard was one of his wealthy donors, Mary Connally. He wanted to show her a deserted farm located in the center of **De Courcy Island** which he believed could provide the colony with all the food it required. He told Mary that he would like this "idyllic sanctuary" to be the new headquarters of the colony. Apparently, Mary was seduced by the beauty of the islands and by Brother XII's vision. After returning to Nanaimo, Mary purchased De Courcy Island and Ruxton Island, putting the title in the name of Brother XII's secretary-treasurer. The story of Brother XII's political aspirations is equally fascinating. Wilson (Brother XII) began efforts to create a third party, the P.P.L. (Protestant Protective League) in the United States, and convinced Senator Tom Heflin to run as a presidential candidate for the party during the 1928 presidential election.

As time went on, Brother XII had become a different person, his temperament and behavior had become harsh. Residents of his cult settlements were made to work unreasonably long hours under horrible conditions. Some followers carried on longer than would be expected under the belief that their strength and loyalty were being tested. Around the same time, several lawsuits arose in which Brother XII was accused of the misappropriation of funds, and he in-turn brought suits against his original Governors. Ironically, Brother XII believed that personality should not be a part of the Brotherhood, but it was the conflict of personality that brought about many troubles.

In addition to his questionable finances, Wilson's views of marriage raised concerns with government authorities. Was Edward Wilson a sincere believer, or was he a talented charlatan? The author of the book provides in-depth detail of Edward Wilson's early life, religious philosophy and practices, and court case transcripts so that you can make your own assessment. Why did his personality change and take on a cruel nature? Had he become bitter, or was he suffering from a disease which affected his mental capacities? In a fit of rage, Brother XII destroyed many of the buildings at his settlements and died a mysterious death in 1934 in England after returning to his childhood homeland.

The story is a fascinating account of mystery and intrigue and is of interest when exploring the areas of Nanaimo, Valdes and De Courcy Islands.

The colony's school as it looks today. At one time, the building was used as a dormitory for the female members of the commune. Brother XII is believed to have concealed his gold in an underground vault in the basement. (Photo by Cecil Clark)

Treasure hole where Brother XII hid perhaps half a million dollars in gold and banknotes. Clericalism himself Harry Oliver, attempted to find the concealed gold and came away empty vaults. (Photo by Cecil Clark)

Strait of Georgia

CHAPTER 8

CROSSING THE STRAIT OF GEORGIA

STRAIT OF GEORGIA
Schooner Cove • French Creek • Denman Island •
Hornby Island • Comox Oyster River •
False Bay • Squitty Bay

Crossing the Strait of Georgia. The Strait of Georgia is not to be trifled with. It's a big body of water, 110 miles long and 15 to 20 miles wide. Pleasure craft cross the strait all the time, but locals know better than to go out when the wind is blowing. They are especially careful when wind blows against strong currents.

When conditions are right, the strait need not be intimidating. The "typical" summertime fair weather wind pattern calls for calm mornings followed by a rising northwesterly sea breeze by early afternoon. By mid-afternoon the sea breeze can be 20 to 25 knots. In the evening the wind dies down. We have crossed early in the morning and in the evening and had no problems.

Frequently though, the typical pattern doesn't hold. If a weak frontal system passes over the area, the higher pressure behind the front will produce northwesterlies of 20 to 25 knots, sometimes reaching gale force. These winds can blow around the clock for three days or even longer, effectively closing the strait to small craft.

Summer afternoon southwesterly winds known as Qualicums can blow across the strait between Qualicum Beach and False Bay at the northern tip of Lasqueti Island. Qualicum winds resulting from the passage of a cold front can reach 40 knots but are short-lived.

When wind opposes current in Sabine Channel, between Lasqueti Island and Texada Island, 8-foot seas can result. Malaspina Strait can be rough, especially when wind is against

The Strait of Georgia on a calm day

current. Currents from Howe Sound and Burrard Inlet meet off Point Atkinson, and create rough seas. Wind makes them worse.

When the wind is up it produces a difficult 4- to 5-foot chop—sometimes higher—in the middle of the strait away from land influences. These aren't long, lazy ocean swells. Strait of Georgia seas are steep and close together. In southeasterly winds, the largest seas are found near Chrome Island and Cape Mudge, both locations with significant fetch. When the wind blows from the northwest, the largest waves are found in Sabine Channel and near Sand Heads. A well-handled boat might run with these seas,

but taken on the bow or beam they are no fun at all.

Sometimes, the afternoon winds never materialize and the strait can be crossed all day. It's best to avoid being forced into crossing at a specific time or on a specific day. Wait for calm conditions and know that they don't always appear in the morning and evening. When the conditions are right, go. Be cautious yet decisive.

Even in calm conditions, you may find tide-rips off many of the points, and wherever passes or channels join the strait. When the current flows out of a pass or inlet into the strait, confusion results. Add wind, and big confusion results. While the ebb current flows from inlets into the strait, note that the flood current flows out of the Gulf Islands into the strait. At the eastern mouths of Active Pass, Porlier Pass, and Gabriola Pass, look for rough seas on the flood, especially when the wind is blowing.

We list these cautions not to frighten the reader but to inform. Weather patterns do exist and the bad spots are known. The skipper who monitors the VHF continuous marine broadcast will gather a sense of what is happening, where it is happening, and why it is happening. Go and no-go decisions get easier.

Here are a few tips for a safe and comfortable crossing:

- Monitor the buoy reports for Halibut Bank (Buoy 46146, off Gibsons) and Sentry Shoal (Buoy 46131, between Comox and Campbell River and below Mitlenatch Island). These reports provide frequent updates on sea state and wind conditions. They can be found online on Environment Canada's website, on the continuous marine broadcast, or by calling Dial-A-Buoy at (888) 701-8992.

- Monitor lightstation reports. Lightstations are at Chrome Island, Merry Island and Entrance Island. The lightkeepers provide information on visibility, wind speed and direction, and sea state, updated every three hours and broadcast on the VHF WX channels. You can also call directly on VHF 82.

CROSSING STRAIT OF GEORGIA GO-NOGO CHECKLIST

Tides & Currents - See Ports & Passes; Canadian Tides & Current Tables Vol. 5
- ☐ Time your crossing to be near mid-Strait at slack
- ☐ Flood or ebb; avoid wind against current conditions
- ☐ Ebbing currents flow out of inlets into the Strait, except in Gulf Islands
- ☐ Flooding currents from both north and south directions meet at Mitlenach Island

Weather System Predictions – via Internet or satellite
- ☐ Check NOAA Ocean Prediction Center forecasts for any approaching significant weather systems
- ☐ Check Windy.com, Predictwind.com, SiriusXM Marine, or Sailflow.com
- ☐ See Environment Canada forecast for the Synopsis report for Strait of Georgia North of Nanaimo and Strait of Georgia South of Nanaimo

Weather & Seas Forecasts – via Internet, phone, or VHF
- ☐ See Environment Canada Forecasts for Strait of Georgia North of Nanaimo and South of Nanaimo; check for warnings and note forecast wind speed and direction

Observations & Present Conditions – via Internet, phone, or VHF
- ☐ Check Buoy Reports for Halibut Bank (46146) and Sentry Shoal (46131); note wind speed and direction
- ☐ Check Lighthouse and Station Reports from Chrome Island, Merry Island, and Entrance Island; note wind speed and direction
- ☐ Check the status of Restricted Area Whisky Golf north of Nanaimo

Go-NoGo Decision
- √ Check wind and wave direction in relation to direction of travel. Straight line crossing is the shortest distance, but may not be the most comfortable.
- √ Will the typical summer weather pattern with afternoon winds affect conditions?
- √ Is Restricted Area Whisky Golf active?

Fail-Safe Contingency Plans
- √ Duck-in locations along the route: lees may lie off Texada Island and Lasqueti Island

See *Chapter 1 Interpreting Northwest Weather* section for telephone numbers, website addresses, VHF channels, and buoy numbers.

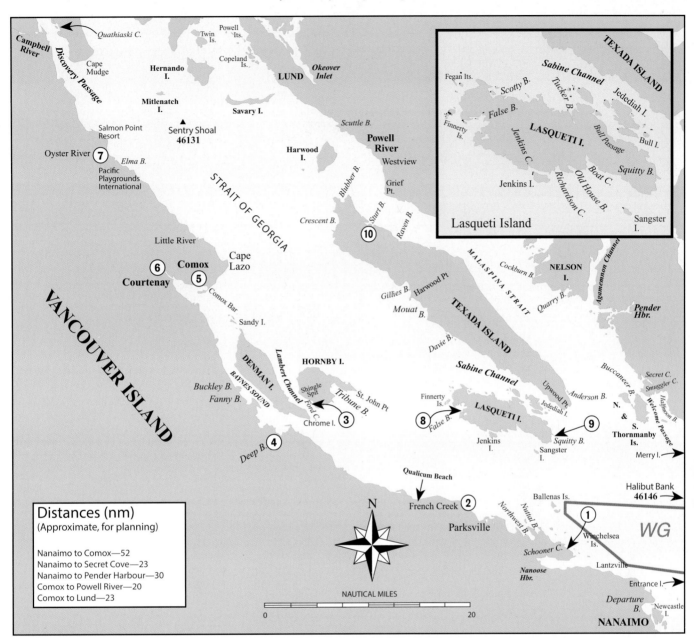

Strait of Georgia

- Based on the wind direction and sea state, choose the best angle and direction for your crossing. The most direct course may not be the most comfortable. Don't be afraid to change your destination if the weather isn't cooperating.

- The north-flowing flood current from Strait of Juan de Fuca meets the south-flowing flood from Discovery Passage near Mitlenatch Island. When traveling the length of the strait, time your departure to take advantage of currents flowing in the same direction as the wind. When crossing, especially in the south, try to time your departure to hit slack in the middle of the strait. Both strategies will minimize the effect of wind against current.

- The area between Qualicum Beach and Lasqueti Island can be subject to southwesterly winds coming through the Alberni "notch" in the Vancouver Island mountains. Check Chrome Island for local southwesterly winds. Old salts also recommend checking winds at Cape Beale, on the west coast of Vancouver Island. If a strong southwesterly wind is blowing there, often it will flow right over Vancouver Island through the Alberni "notch," affecting the waters off Qualicum Beach.

- Take advantage of lees along the way. For example, you may choose to go up one side or the other of 27-mile Texada Island to stay in the lee of a southwesterly or northeasterly wind. Always be prepared to turn around and go back if things do not look right.

Whiskey Golf. Boats headed north from Nanaimo often must navigate through or around the restricted area "WG" (Whiskey Golf) when it is "live." Whiskey Golf is a deepwater range operated by the Canadian and U.S. Navies, and is used to test torpedoes (always unarmed) and various ships' systems. The area consists of a network of underwater sensing devices joined by cables to a control site on Winchelsea Island. Torpedoes are fired from range vessels or aircraft along a predetermined course, and are tracked from the Winchelsea control center. After the run, the torpedoes are recovered either by helicopter or range vessels. Unauthorized craft are not permitted in the area while the range is in operation.

Typically, the range is active Mondays through Fridays, sometimes Saturdays, 7:00 a.m. to 5:30 p.m. Winchelsea Range Control monitors VHF channel 10 during operations. Notice of operation is included as part of the Canadian continuous marine broadcast on the weather channels. The Coast Guard

TUGBOAT LIFE- *By Captain Gerald Bell*

ISBN 978-1492825029 Publisher: CreateSpace Independent Publishing Platform

While cruising the Pacific Northwest waters, it's quite common to see tugs towing barges, and we often take their challenging job for granted. Tugboat captains make their transits look easy, but it's anything but; the risks and challenges are enormous. Author Gerald Bell in his book, *Tugboat Life,* shares his 50 years of experience as a "tugboater." He towed everything from canned salmon and beer to gravel, sand, crude oil, and scrap metal.

Gerald grew up on a farm in Skagit Valley near La Conner, Washington and started working for Dunlap Towing in 1959. He worked his way up from deckhand to mate, and then eventually as captain. As mate, he took his turn at the helm, which provided valuable experience. His book is filled with fascinating accounts of how tugboats evolved over the years and his personal experiences at sea. The book is filled with stories of near-death experiences and other mishaps that keep you on the edge of your seat, like the time he fell off a barge that ended up running over him. He tells of the time when towing a log boom across the Strait of Georgia and a storm came up, resulting in the loss of 300 logs; nearly half their tow. The logs were retrieved and they had to rebuild their tow.

Gerald spent ten years towing log booms before switching to towing barges filled with sand and gravel. Tugboats were getting larger and offered more crew comforts, but the challenges remained. One time, current pushed the barge sideways over a navigation buoy, which became tangled in the towline and dragged the buoy up a channel. In 1969, he was promoted to captain. One night, Gerald's mate awoke him, reporting that the barge full of crushed rock had rolled over. The barge had hit a tide rip and took a sharp turn, which caused the barge to lean; the rock slid to one side dumping nine-hundred tons of gravel into the sea. The tow bridle fell off the upside-down barge —read the book to learn the rest of the story.

Opportunities continued to present themselves for Gerald; and in July 1970, he became an employee of Puget Sound Freight Lines. In his book, Gerald explains how a tug is brought alongside a barge in order to maneuver the barge into place. Since the captain can only see one side of the barge, the mate gives rudder and throttle commands over the radio. Risks and challenges also continued. Gerald's runs to and from Canada became pretty much routine; but routine can be interrupted by shear fright. The culprit was usually bad

weather — wind, steep waves, tides and current — Gerald's stories make the gravity of these situations quite clear. In the 1980s, Gerald captained twin screw tugs and made trips from Port Alberni and Gold River, hauling large rolls of newspaper print. One night, he awakened to the words, "get up! we're on fire!" The wheelhouse was filled with a thick haze of smoke and the barge was still moving towards their tug. He tells of another instance when they were hauling scrap metal; a row of crushed cars peeled off the barge and went overboard in the deep waters of the Strait of Georgia – a new habitat for the fish.

Improvements for procedures and tug maintenance, and new laws and regulations for the industry are also covered in his book. The Seattle Vessel Traffic System (VTS) was established in 1972, and the Canadian Traffic System was established in 1979. Later, GPS came along and Automatic Identification System (AIS) was added. Gerald turned 70 years old in 2010 and decided it was time to retire. He had been working since 1959. He saw the towboat industry grow from the use of small wooden, single screw tugs to the very powerful twin screw steel hull tugs of today. He saw the many changes in electronics and navigation systems, and closer scrutiny by the Coast Guard. Gerald shares his stories through all of these changes and his personal stories of the ongoing challenges of towing barges at sea. *Tugboat Life*, by Captain Gerald Bell, is a book you'll find hard to put down.

Tribune Bay, with its sandy beach, is a busy spot in summer.

(VHF channel 83A) also knows if the range is active. If unsure, contact Winchelsea Range Control or the Canadian Coast Guard.

The Whiskey Golf restricted area is on the direct course across the Strait of Georgia from Nanaimo to Secret Cove, Smugglers Cove, Pender Harbour, and other destinations along the Sunshine Coast. We once saw an oblivious skipper cross right through the active range. Winchelsea Control made multiple calls to the offending vessel with no response. A patrol helicopter quickly flew over, hovered just in front of the offending vessel, and redirected it to safe water. Such encounters are best avoided.

The Canadian Navy established a safe transit route along the edges of the restricted area when the range is in use. After clearing Nanaimo Harbour or Departure Bay (being careful to avoid Hudson Rocks and Five Finger Island), head directly for the Winchelsea Islands. Pass east of Winchelsea Islands within 1000 yards. Turn to pass east of the Ballenas Islands within 1000 yards. Once well past the Ballenas Islands, steer a course for your destination on the mainland side of the strait, or northwest along the Vancouver Island side.

Nanoose Harbour. Anchorage is good just inside the sandy spit on the south side of the entrance. The docks and mooring buoys along the north shore are the base for Royal Canadian Navy and U.S. Navy vessels engaged in activity on the Winchelsea (Whiskey Golf) torpedo range.

Schooner Cove. Schooner Cove is north of Nanoose Harbour. The cove is well-protected with a breakwater on the northwest entrance. The Fairwinds Marina fills most of the cove
.

① **Fairwinds Marina.** 33521 Dolphin Dr., Nanoose Bay, BC V9P 9J7; (250) 468-5364; marina@fairwinds.ca; www. fairwinds.ca. Monitors VHF 66A. Fairwinds Marina, located at Schooner Cove, is open all year with gasoline and diesel at the fuel dock. Guest moorage for vessels up to 80 feet, 15, 30 & 50 amp power, washrooms, showers, and pumpout. Dock repairs were made in 2018, and renovation of the main upland building is on-going, with plans to include a restaurant and pub on the second floor; marina office facilities on the first floor. Facilities are anticipated to be available for the 2019 boating season. Easily accessed off of Ballenas Channel and Strait of Georgia, the marina has picturesque views of the Strait of Georgia and coastal mountains. Reservations recommended. Watch for a rock marked by a red buoy just inside the breakwater. Keep the buoy well to starboard when entering. The outstanding Fairwinds Golf club is part of the resort. A courtesy shuttle takes you there. The courtesy shuttle also goes to the Wellness Center, consisting of fitness facilities, an indoor pool, and tennis courts.

Schooner Reef. Schooner Reef is a short distance northward off the mouth of Schooner Cove and has caught a number of boats unaware. The light marking the reef is on the southernmost of its rocks. More rocks lie up-island from the light.

Nuttal Bay. Nuttal Bay is protected from southeasterly winds but exposed to northwesterlies. To enter Nuttal Bay, leave Dorcas Rock Buoy *P27* to port. Do not pass between Dorcas Rock Buoy *P27* and the land south of it. Buoy *P27* lies a good deal farther out than one might expect. If you are traveling up- or down-island, locate that buoy and pass to seaward of it.

Northwest Bay. Northwest Bay is home to a private moorage only marina with no services for transient boaters, and an active log dump and booming operation. The bay is protected from southerly winds but open to the north and northwesterly winds and seas. Suitable anchorage depths can be found at the head of the bay and in a bight along the west shore.

Mistaken Island. Privately owned and posted with "No Trespassing" signs.

Parksville. Parksville has a nice beach, but shoal water extends out some distance. Except for the marina at French Creek at the north end of Parksville, no facilities are available for boaters.

259

Fairwinds Marina

Strait of Georgia

Vancouver Island

N

Buoy marks rock.
Leave to starboard
when entering

Visitor moorage
available on
B, C and D docks

Schooner Cove

B

C

D

E

F

G

Pumpout

I

H

Odd Numbered Slips

Even Numbered Slips

A

Activity Dock

Fish Cleaning
Station

Fuel
Dock

Marina Office
Washrooms
Showers

Boat Launch

Dumpsters

Fairwinds Marina
Tel. 250/468-5364
VHF 66A

See Area Map Page 257 - Maps Not for Navigation

② **French Creek Harbour Authority.** 1055 Lee Rd., Parksville, BC V9P 2E1; (250) 248-5051; hafc@frenchcreekharbour. ca. Monitors VHF 66A. Open all year with gasoline & diesel. Commercial vessels have priority for moorage, but room may be available for pleasure craft. No reservations; rafting is required. Washrooms and shower, 20 & 30 amp power. A key from the office is required for waste oil and garbage disposal. Office hours are 8:00 a.m. to 5:30 p.m. Restaurant, pub, marine supplies, nearby launch ramp and haulout. A fish market in the large white processing building sells fresh seafood. Groceries are at the mall, a 15-minute walk away.

French Creek is the only breakwater-protected harbor in the 25-mile stretch between Northwest Bay and Deep Bay. The breakwater has recently been extended. French Creek is the western terminus of the passenger ferry to Lasqueti Island.

Hornby Island. Hornby Island has anchorages in Tribune Bay, Ford Cove, and south of Shingle Spit (where a small ferry runs to Denman Island). Tribune Bay and Shingle Spit are exposed to southeast winds.

A seasonal dock for dinghies and shallow draft water craft is located next to the ferry terminal. The dock is for guests dining at the Thatch Pub and Restaurant located above the dock. The fully licensed Pub and Restaurant has live entertainment, (250) 335-0136; thatchpub.com.

The annual Hornby Festival, held in early August, is a well-organized event drawing professional, award-winning musicians from around the country, see hornbyfestival.com.

Tribune Bay. Tribune Bay is a wonderful place to visit and justifiably popular. Anchor offshore in 18 to 30 feet and dinghy to a splendid sand beach. Visit Tribune Bay

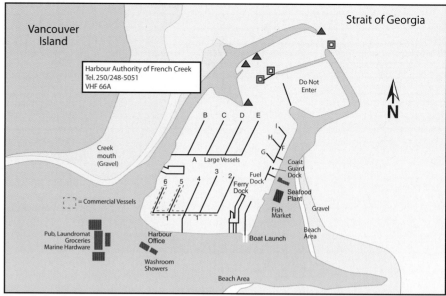
French Creek Boat Harbour

Provincial Park. Take the 3-mile hike to Helliwell Provincial Park, on St. John Point.

Caution: Tribune Bay has excellent protection from northwesterlies, but in a southeasterly the bay can get very rough. For a more private nook, try the little cove near St. John Point. Anchor in 20 to 30 feet.

③ **Ford Cove.** Upgraded harbor with greater capacity at the Harbour Authority public dock. A green spar buoy marks the southern end of Maude Reef. You'll see a rock breakwater and a floating breakwater. To enter, leave the rock breakwater to starboard. No fresh water on the dock. Good anchorage on rocky bottom.

A well-stocked grocery (250) 335-2169 is upland from the docks and sells fresh take-out pizza year-round. A seasonal fish & chips hut is adjacent. The store and eatery along with cottages, campsites, and RV parking make up a small resort called Ford's Cove Marina & Store.

There are numerous trails in the area. A well-traveled 1.5 mile trail leads northwest along the shore to Shingle Spit and the popular Thatch Pub.

③ **Ford Cove Harbour Authority.** 10800A Central Rd., Ford Cove, Hornby Island, BC V0R 1Z0; (250) 335-0003; VHF 66A; fordcoveharbour@gmail.com; www. fordcoveharbour.com. Open all year, guest moorage along 3000 feet of dock space and inside of the floating breakwater, 20 & 30 amp power, toilets, garbage drop, no water, no showers. Wi-Fi planned for the near future. Reservations accepted or call ahead for availability. Rafting allowed up to 20 feet deep. No rafting on the breakwater. Loading dock located near the ramp. Kayak and boat rentals.

Baynes Sound. Chart 3527 shows navigation aids not shown on Chart 3513. These aids are buoys marking extensive

shoals off Gartley Point, Union Point, Denman Point and Base Flat (Buckley Bay); 2 buoys near Repulse Point; and 2 buoys marking the shoal off Mapleguard Point. Baynes Sound, a 12-mile-long refuge, is protected from the Strait of Georgia by Denman Island. A ferry to Denman Island crosses from Buckley Bay. Comox is at the north end of Baynes Sound and Deep Bay is at the south end. The northern entry to Baynes Sound is across the Comox Bar, marked by buoys and a lighted range on the Vancouver Island shore. The southern entry is past Chrome Island.

LOCAL KNOWLEDGE

NAVIGATION NOTE: A considerable shoal extends into the mouth of Baynes Sound outside Deep Bay. The shoal, and shoaling along the shoreline of Denman Island, opposite, are marked by buoys shown on Chart 3527, but not on Chart 3513.

The dinghy dock at lively Thatch Pub is seasonal and dries on low tides.

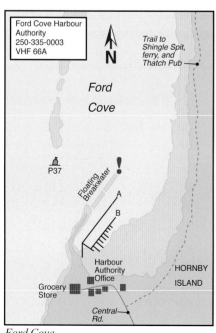
Ford Cove

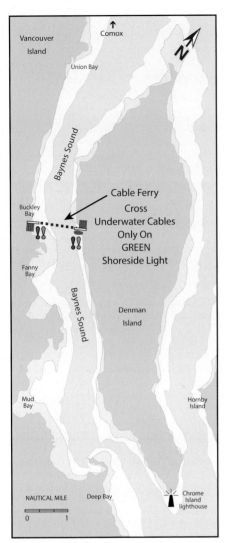

Denman Cable Ferry

LOCAL KNOWLEDGE

CABLE FERRY: The *Baynes Sound Connector* cable ferry runs between Buckley Bay and Denman Island. Red and green lights are at each terminal. When the green lights are illuminated, vessels may cross the ferry lane. When red lights are illuminated, the ferry is in transit and vessels may not cross the ferry lane.

Denman Island. www.denmanisland. com. A public dock and 60-foot float are alongside the landing for the cable ferry that runs to Buckley Bay on Vancouver Island. Six hours of moorage is free, 2-day maximum stay. No power or water; 5 mooring buoys. Self-registration and payment box at the top of the ramp. Denman Village is a one-third mile walk up a steep hill. The Denman General Store with groceries, a post office, and liquor store is in Denman Village. A small museum, community center, bistro, and a craft shop are also in the Village.

The north end of Denman Island stretches out into a long spit, dotted with small islands and rocks. One of these islands, Sandy Island, is a provincial park. Off the south end of Denman Island is Chrome Island lighthouse, a dramatic landmark.

Sandy Island Marine Provincial Park. This park includes the Seal Islets, and is accessible only by boat. Anchor in Henry Bay, south of Longbeak Point. Picnic areas, swimming, fishing, hiking trails, and wilderness campsites. Sandy Island is a popular overnight stop for kayakers. At low tide it is possible to walk along the sandy spit all the way to its end—halfway to Comox.

LOCAL KNOWLEDGE

NAVIGATION TIP: If you follow the buoyed channel over the Comox Bar in a fresh southeasterly you will have 4- to 5-foot seas on your beam. In these conditions it's better to ignore buoys *P54* and *P52* and instead work your way south until you can turn to fetch the inner Buoy *P50* while running with the seas. The chart indicates ample depths. Large scale Chart 3527 shows Buoy *P50*, but small scale Chart 3513 does not.

Comox Bar. The Comox Bar nearly joins Denman Island and Cape Lazo, with a shallow channel (least depth 15 feet) across the bar. A lighted range—white, with red vertical stripes—is on the Vancouver Island shore. The range's lights are visible in cloudy weather and at night, but in sunlight they are hard to see. Lighted red Bell Buoy *P54* marks the Strait of Georgia end of this channel. Red Buoys *P52* and *P50* show the course across the bar.

Boaters need to check the red/green light at each of the Denman-Buckley cable ferry terminals before crossing the ferry route in Baynes Sound.

④ **Deep Bay.** Anchorage is good in Deep Bay, though in deeper water than most boaters like. Derelict boats, which occupied a portion of the best space, have recently been removed. The Ship & Shore Cafe, which once sold convenience supplies, is now a full restaurant under new ownership. The restaurant is located near the head of the public wharf. Washroom and laundry facilities nearby.

④ **Deep Bay Harbour Authority.** 164 Burne Rd., Bowser, BC V0R 1G0; (250) 757-9331; deepbay-mgr@shawcable.com; www.dbha.ca. The government wharf and floats are open all year with moorage along 1130 feet of dock. Garbage drop, 20 & 30 amp power, free Wi-Fi, free pumpout, waste oil disposal, tidal grid, and guest dock. Washrooms and showers were upgraded in 2018. The pumpout is located at the loading zone on the main pier. Space is very limited and rafting is required, call ahead to see what is available.

Fanny Bay. Fanny Bay is primarily a camping area, with a small public float.

The Denman-Buckley ferry runs on three underwater cables across Baynes Sound.

See Area Map Page 257 - Maps Not for Navigation

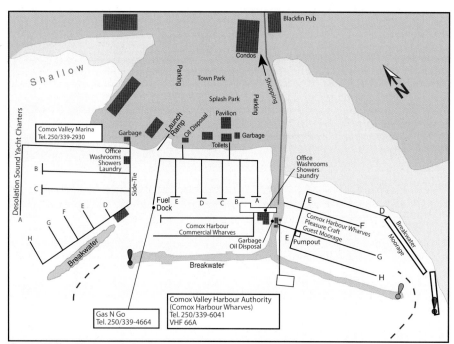

Comox Valley Harbour Authority

⑤ **Comox.** If you plan to go to Comox, we urge that you have Chart 3527 (1:40,000), with its 1:15,000 inset of Comox Harbour and the Courtenay River up to the Lewis Bridge. Chart 3527 shows the various ranges and other navigation aids in excellent detail, and could save you from much uncertainty.

Marine services at Comox include Desolation Sound Yacht Charters (250) 339-4919 offering cleaning, maintenance, hull inspection, and bright work (after-hours calls accepted); and Wills Marine Supply (250) 941-7373 offering electrical, mechanical, diving and repair services.

Comox is a busy little city, population 13,600, with breakwater-protected marina docks. HMCS Quadra, a Canada Sea Cadet camp, is on Goose Spit, across the bay from Comox.

The Comox Valley is a popular retirement area. Albertans from the oil patch can take daily flights to the Comox airport and enjoy golf and skiing within an hour of one another on Vancouver Island.

From Baynes Sound the entrance to Comox is well marked, but be careful of drying flats off Gartley Point and in the inner half of the bay. The breakwater in front of the town will be clearly visible. As the harbor map shows, the breakwater shelters four sets of docks: the Comox Bay Marina; the Gas N Go fuel dock and marina; the municipal marina; and one set of Comox Harbour Authority public docks used entirely by commercial fishing boats. A launch ramp and two tidal grids are behind the breakwater. The other set of Harbour Authority public docks, where pleasure craft are welcomed, is around the east end of the breakwater.

Showers and laundry are in the Harbour Authority's building at the head of its docks. A beautiful pavilion with meeting space overlooks the Comox Harbour Commercial Wharves and serves as a nice venue for club rendezvous.

A Splash Park located behind the pavilion is a hit with the kids. The seasonal food truck has been relocated near the pavilion.

Comox has good shopping and a number of restaurants within walking distance of the marina. The downtown area includes a supermarket and chandlery. Regular bus service runs from the Comox Mall to the town of Courtenay with more shops, restaurants and a museum. You can also go by dinghy up the slough to Courtenay. See the Courtenay section for more information.

When you're in Comox, take the short walk to the Filberg Heritage Lodge & Park. It's a 9-acre estate built in the 1930s by logging baron R. J. Filberg, furnished and maintained in its original splendor. The heavy wood construction, fabulous gardens, and interesting outbuildings (root cellar, chicken coop, dairy barn, potting shed, and so forth) are must-see attractions. Weddings and art shows are held there. The seasonal Pavilion Kitchen, located on the grounds, is open Thursday through Sunday. English Tea is held at the lodge in the spring and fall.

Float planes: A float plane landing and takeoff zone is southwest of the marina breakwaters, with regularly scheduled flights. It does not affect anchoring behind Goose Spit or the approach to the marinas.

Festival: The Filberg Festival, an arts, crafts, food, and entertainment celebration, draws 20,000 to 25,000 visitors each year. It's held at Filberg Park, east of the public floats in Comox Harbour. Dates coincide with Comox Nautical Days and B.C. Day long weekend in early August. The park will be closed the week prior to the festival and the week following. Special events also can result in closures. Call first to confirm they are open (250) 941-0727. www.filbergfestival.com.

⑤ **Comox Valley Marina.** 1805 Beaufort, Box 20019, Comox, BC V9M 1R9; (250) 339-2930; manager@comoxvalleymarina.

Fisherman's Wharf in Comox Harbour has guest moorage for an overnight stop on your way to Desolation Sound.

com; www.comoxvalleymarina.com. Side-tie moorage at a guest dock and in unoccupied slips. Water, 15, 30 & 50 amp power, shower, washroom, free Wi-Fi, 24-hour access to laundry, garbage, and nearby floatplane service. The amenities building and marina office are on the float at the base of the ramp.

⑤ **Gas N Go Marine Ltd.** 11 Port Augusta St., Comox, BC V9M 7Z8; (250) 339-4664; (888) 575-4664; gasngomarine@gmail.com; www.gasngomarine.com. Monitors VHF 66A. Open all year. Fuel dock with

gasoline & diesel. Transient moorage when slips are available (call ahead), 15 & 30 amp power, washrooms, small store, Wi-Fi. As you approach, look for the Gas N Go sign.

⑤ **Comox Municipal Marina.** 1809 Beaufort Ave., Comox, BC V9M 1R9; (250) 339-3141. Permanent moorage only.

⑤ **Comox Valley Harbour Authority.** 121 Port Augusta St., Comox, BC V9M 3N8; (250) 339-6041; info@comoxharbour.com; www.comoxharbour.com. Monitors VHF

66A. Located at east end of the Comox breakwater. Guest moorage available on 2100 feet of docks, 20, 30 & 50 amp power. Holding tank pumpout, garbage drop, cardboard recycling, waste oil disposal, free Wi-Fi (get the password at the office). Clean washrooms, showers, laundry, and an air-conditioned lounge with a bucket of biscuits for visiting boat dogs.

This is a working waterfront facility, only two blocks from downtown Comox. In the summer, harbor staff move the fishing boats to one float and set aside the other docks for overnight pleasure craft. Fresh seafood is available "off the boat," usually in the evening. The Harbour Authority staff works hard to make visiting pleasure boaters feel welcome and comfortable.

⑤ **Comox Harbour.** Anchorage can be found in Comox Harbour; with northerly winds, anchor south of the marina breakwater, taking care to avoid channel entrances on either end of the breakwater; in southerly winds, the favored anchorage is tucked into the cove north of Goose Spit. Mud bottom. The harbour is not as well protected as charts might suggest and can get uncomfortable in southerly winds.

⑥ **Courtenay.** For a pleasant diversion, take the dinghy a short distance up the Courtenay River to the town of Courtenay. A dredged channel, marked by ranges, leads through the delta to the river mouth. The river is an interesting break from the saltwater experience out on the strait.

Just before you reach Lewis Bridge (vertical clearance 10 feet) Courtenay Slough leads off to the right. Inside, an extensive Comox Valley Harbour Authority float parallels the shore, and a city float is at the head. Enter the slough at high tide only. The mouth is blocked by a weir that dries at 8 feet; without the weir the slough would empty completely at low tide.

The slough's Harbour Authority dock is gated and locked. Pick up a re-entry key at the Harbour Authority office in Comox. An imposing restaurant dominates the view at the head of the slough. Excellent shopping and several restaurants are within easy walking distance.

Museum: We highly recommend a visit to the Courtenay & District Museum, a 4-block walk from the slough. There, hung from the ceiling, is the 40-foot-long skeletal reconstruction of an 80-million-year-old elasmosaur, excavated from the banks of the nearby Puntledge River. This is the most dramatic exhibit in an outstanding paleontological display. Other things you will see are dinosaur footprints, an extinct marine reptile that resembles a 15-foot-long alligator, and an ancient fish they call a "sabre-toothed salmon." We toured the museum and were impressed. Families with inquisitive children will be rewarded. There's much more than we can cover here. The museum is in the old brick post office building at 4th St. and Cliffe Avenue. From

Comox you can get to the museum by bus or cab, or take the dinghy to Courtenay. Call for information: (250) 334-0686.

Cape Lazo. Cape Lazo is marked by a high cliff. *Be sure to stay to seaward of Buoys PJ and PB.* The buoys are well offshore, but shoals studded with boulders reach almost all the way out to them.

Somewhere just north of Cape Lazo is the point at which the tidal currents change direction and begin flooding south from the north end of Vancouver Island, rather than north from Victoria.

Little River. Little River, 3 miles up-island from Cape Lazo, is the western terminus for the ferry to Westview/Powell River. Marginal moorage for a few small craft can be found behind the ferry dock.

Oyster River. A channel, dredged annually and marked by pilings, leads to the protected Pacific Playgrounds Marina next to the mouth of the Oyster River.

⑦ **Pacific Playgrounds Resort & Marina.** (250) 337-5600; info@PacificPlaygrounds. com; www.Pacific Playgrounds.com; open year-round, secure marina with transient and permanent moorage up to 40 feet, a few 46-foot spaces; 15 amp power, water at the docks, restrooms, showers; reservations accepted. Payment made at the upland office open 9:00 a.m.-8:00 p.m. summer months. Payment can also be made at the dockside "fishing shack" summer hours 6:00 a.m.-8:00 p.m.; hours vary off-season. Located 16 miles south of Campbell River (49° 52' N / 125° 7' W), Pacific Playgrounds is accessed through a channel alongside, and south of Oyster River. This is a challenging entrance, check the tide tables; marina personnel advise that a minimum tide of 7 feet is needed for a boat with a 4.5 foot draft; the depth is shallowest at the outermost channel marker; access is not advised during high winds and swells

Oyster River Plaza is a short walk from the marina, with shops, cafes, a supermarket, and other services. A beautiful trail from the marina leads to a one-lane timber truss bridge over Oyster River, where you will find the Fishermen's Lodge Pub.

⑦ **Salmon Point Resort.** (250) 923-6605; sales@salmonpoint.com; www.salmonpoint. com. Gas, propane, launch ramp, store, laundry, pool, jacuzzi and kids' activity areas. Located 15 miles south of Campbell River on the western shore of Discovery Passage, this marina, built behind a riprap breakwater, has room for powerboats up to 32 feet. The entrance is very shallow and dries at low tide. "Stay-aboards" (overnighting on boat) not permitted. The resort is an RV park primarily serving recreational fishermen, with 1 to 2 bedroom cottages, rental RVs, and a licensed restaurant and pub on site.

LASQUETI ISLAND

Lasqueti Island is often overlooked by pleasure craft as they hurry across the strait between Nanaimo and the Sunshine Coast, or run along the Vancouver Island shore between Nanaimo and Campbell River. The island has a number of good anchorages. A convenience store is at the village of False Bay, located upland from the ferry landing on the left. The shores of Lasqueti Island are indented by a number of bays that invite anchorage. Along the south shore are Boat Cove, Old House Bay, Richardson Cove and Jenkins Cove, all of which are somewhat open to southerlies, but offer good protection from northerlies or in settled weather. This part of the Lasqueti shoreline is rugged and beautiful. Squitty Bay is at the southeast end of Lasqueti Island—tiny, but with a public float. Several little dogholes for anchoring can be found in Bull Passage. Little Bull Passage, between Jedediah Island and Bull Island, has a number of good anchorages in both ends, and is passable for most boats.

Other anchorages are Boho Bay, Tucker Bay and Scottie Bay. Spring Bay is only partially protected from the north by a group of small islands offshore.

⑧ **False Bay.** False Bay is the primary settlement on Lasqueti Island with a public float offering limited dock space and a float plane tie-up. A passenger-only ferry runs between False Bay and French Creek on Vancouver Island. Island residents transport not only themselves by ferry but also bring a large quantity of supplies, everything from food and clothing to appliances. It's quite a scene when the ferry arrives at False Bay. An open-air market is held at the arts center, a quarter mile up the road from the ferry landing, from mid-June to September.

Buoys adjacent to the ferry landing are private and fill most of the anchoring area near the public float. The preferred anchorage is the north shore of the bay, an easy dinghy ride to the public float. On warm summer afternoons strong winds, called Qualicums, can blow through False Bay; waves break at the dock, making tie-up difficult. If you must tie in these conditions, make sure you have robust dock lines and fenders. Kevin Monahan, a long-time resident of Lasqueti Island, reports that southwest gale force winds at Cape Beale often serve as a presage of Qualicum winds arriving at False Bay.

⑨ **Squitty Bay.** Squitty Bay is a tiny, narrow and shallow notch at the southeast corner of Lasqueti Island. It would be harrowing to enter Squitty Bay in a roaring southeasterly, but at other times entry should be easy. Rocks border the north side of the entrance; favor the south side. The unnamed point on the south side of Squitty Bay is an ecological reserve, noted for prickly pear cacti and Rocky Mountain juniper. The public dock, 150 feet long, may be largely occupied by local boats. Rafting is permitted. Ashore, the trees in this area are bent and broken, obviously by strong winds. Tall trees are rare. A walk along the road is fascinating.

Bull Passage. Bull Passage and the islands that lie off the south end of Jedediah Island are rugged and scenic.

Little Bull Passage. Between high rock cliffs, Little Bull Passage is narrow and beautiful. Watch for the charted rock on the Jedediah Island side. It hides at high tide. Our notes say, "The east end of Little Bull Passage is absolutely fabulous. So much variety and strength in the rock walls and islands. Worth a side trip just to see the sights."

Jedediah Island. Jedediah Island is a marine park. Although good anchorages are scarce and tight, Jedediah Island is increasingly popular. One of the best anchorages is in the little notch, called Deep Bay, opposite the south end of Paul Island, where chains have been installed around this small bay to facilitate stern-ties. It is impractical that all

Enjoy great views of Vancouver Island, while picnicking at False Bay on Lasqueti Island.

Jedediah Island is a small island that can easily be explored by dinghy or by foot.

these stern-ties could be used at the same time in this tiny, v-shaped bay, except for the smallest of boats. The large number of stern-ties are provided to allow different options for boaters. Long Bay just south of Deep Bay is usable, too. Long Bay goes dry a short distance inside the mouth. Codfish Bay on the southeast side of Jedediah Island has room for two or three boats to stern-tie. If nothing looks good at Jedediah Island itself, Boho Bay at Lasqueti Island, about 1 mile away, is an alternative.

One interesting spot is the narrow and protected steep-sided notch at the southeast end of Jedediah Island. Although its sheer walls might discourage much on-shore exploration, it is possible to scramble from the head of the notch up the bluffs on the north side. You will be rewarded not only with access to the rest of the island but also an excellent view toward Texada Island. [*Hamilton*]

For easy access to the island, take the dinghy ashore at Deep Bay and hike the short, well-marked trail across the island. A map of the island is posted at the head of the trail from both Deep Bay and Long Bay. A trail also leads from Codfish Bay. A visit to the old homestead on the east side of Jedediah Island is an exciting adventure and should not be missed. The homestead is frozen in time and left undisturbed. Please respect the property and leave things as found for others to enjoy. The island was owned by several families over the years. The Foote Family first purchased the island in 1890. Alan and Mary Palmer, the last owners, didn't want this island paradise to be developed so sold Jedediah Island to the Provincial Government in 1994 to be used as a Marine Park. A plaque on the island commemorates their generous forethought. You can learn more about the history of Jedediah Island

in the book - *Jedediah Days, One Woman's Island Paradise*, by Mary Palmer.

TEXADA ISLAND

Texada (pronounced "Tex-AY-da") Island has three main anchorages: Anderson Bay on Malaspina Strait at the south end; Blubber Bay at the northern tip; and Sturt Bay, a couple miles south along the Malaspina Strait (eastern) side. Although it has a ferry landing and public float, **Blubber Bay** is dominated by an enormous quarry and is not inviting, but anchorage is possible if needed.

Anderson Bay. Anderson Bay is at the south end of Texada Island on Malaspina Strait. It is a beautiful spot, lined with sheer rock walls. Anchor in 24 feet near the head.

The safest approach is from the southeast. In our opinion, the pass between Texada Island and the unnamed 20-meter island is not as open as the charts suggest. We explored this pass at the bottom of a 1.6-foot low tide and found rock shelves extending from the Texada Island side well into the pass. Be especially careful of the reef that extends from the southwest point of Texada Island. The reef dries at low tide, but at higher stages of tide it could be a nasty surprise.

⑩ **Sturt Bay.** Locally called Marble Bay, on Malaspina Strait near the north end of Texada Island; it has the best anchorage and moorage on Texada Island. Anchorage is in the bay, but beware of forest and mining equipment said to be lying on the bottom.

Hiking trails are close to the docks. An RV campground just up the hill from the garage has laundry facilities, coin-operated showers, and Wi-Fi. The full service grocery store has liquor, good meats and produce. A farmers

market is held Sundays at Gillies Bay Ballpark. Correspondents Al and Becca Symanski tell us the Texada Island Museum, housed in a wing of the local school, is a "must see."

Caution: Sturt Bay is a welcome haven if a northwesterly is kicking up Malaspina Strait, but not suitable in a fresh southeasterly. Blubber Bay provides better anchorage in a southeasterly.

Texada Boat Club. The Texada Boat Club has extensive floats, visitors welcomed. The floats have water and 15 amp power. Bob and Maggie Timms are the harbormasters, (604) 414-5897.

Van Anda (Vananda). A 98-foot public dock is located in Van Anda Cove. Guest moorage at the dock can be lumpy in northwesterlies. Nearby Sturt Bay is preferred.

Harwood Point Regional Park. Gillies Bay, Texada Island. Anchor out only and dinghy in to a 40-acre park. Grass fields, picnic tables, campsites, pit toilets.

JEDEDIAH DAYS ONE WOMAN'S ISLAND PARADISE
- By Mary Palmer

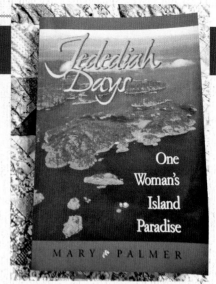

Publisher: Harbour Publishing; ISBN: 978-1-55017-452-6

Boaters who have visited **Jedediah Island** can't help but be captured by its beauty and intrigue — the small cozy coves, the forested trails, open meadows, and the old homestead and orchard that still seem to speak to us. It's easy to imagine an earlier time when homesteaders were busy with farm and household chores and children roamed the island at play. Jedediah becomes even more endearing after reading Mary Palmer's book, Jedediah Days One Woman's Island Paradise.

After WWII, couples were searching for new beginnings and new meaning in life. Mary Palmer and her husband, Ed, set sail among the islands of Puget Sound and British Columbia in search of an idyllic setting. Their search ended when they saw an ad in a Seattle newspaper that a 640-acre island in the Strait of Georgia was for sale. They left Kenmore, Washington in 1949 on a float plane to visit Jedediah Island and meet Mr. Shaw, the current owner. They looked over the barn and house, both of which were in need of repair; walked the trails; inspected the field and orchard; and gazed at the view from the house overlooking **Home Bay**. They also met Jimmy and Jenny, who lived in a float house on the island. Jenny, now an older woman, had been a previous owner of the island.

Author Mary Palmer, who had grown up among the mountains of the Olympic Peninsula and logging camps, fell in love with Jedediah; but Ed, a city fellow, expressed some reservations. Nevertheless, they purchased the property with the intent of using it as a summer retreat and then moving to the island permanently after retirement.

When school finished for the year, their sons Evan and Roger, were eager to spend a summer on Jedediah. Supplies were packed and they departed Seattle aboard their boat, the *PBY*; but shortly into the journey, the motor "sputtered, groaned, and died." They got a tow into Everett, where Ed stayed to make repairs while Mary and the boys continued north. Mary, along with her sons, found a ride on the *Cardena*, which carried freight, cannery workers, loggers, miners, and tourists to many ports along the coast. Arriving in Pender Harbour, the next challenge was to find a ride to Jedediah Island. "In the summer of 1949, **Pender Harbour** was a hive of activity." After several failed attempts, she eventually found a ride on a fish boat, which was headed in the right direction.

Ed arrived several weeks later and began helping with the summer chores which included gathering wood for the stove and fireplace, planting and tending the garden, and canning fruit. Swimming, fishing, and hiking were other activities. After a hike to the summit of Gibraltar, they added their names on a list enclosed in a glass jar at the base of a cairn. Beautiful views of neighboring **Lasqueti and Bull Islands**, where they often visited friends, could be seen from the summit. Feral goats also provided company for the family. It is believed that Spanish explorers, who plied the waters along the coast in the 1700's, kept goats aboard their ships for meat and milk; put off on islands to graze, some of these goats never made it back onboard. Their descendants still live on Jedediah.

While enjoying island life, Ed's nursery and landscape business in **Seattle** needed attention; Ed returned to Seattle to get things in order. After Ed's return, he suggested putting their Seattle home and business up for sale so they could live year-round on Jedediah. Unfortunately, the new owner of Ed's and Mary's landscape business was unable to make a go of it; they had to take back the business and start over again. Mary and the boys returned to Jedediah for the summers with never a dull moment, keeping busy with chores, reading, teasing wool, and carving miniature animals. They enjoyed frequent visits from boaters, neighbors, and island friends. Opportunities to ride on tugboats, float planes, and meeting many interesting people were unique experiences for the boys. Unfortunately, Mary and Ed had lived somewhat separate lives, which eventually led to an amicable divorce. Ed kept the business and Mary kept Jedediah.

Mary later met Albert Palmer, who worked for the Fisheries Research Institute and had served on merchant marine ships during WWII. Their shared love of the outdoors and the sea brought them closer together, and they married in 1959. With the shared goal of living on Jedediah Island, they worked to earn enough money to live there for most of their remaining lives. Once again, Mary packed up her belongings, having chartered a small tugboat from Nanaimo to **Jedediah Island**. After ten years of running a nursery business, Al and Mary were ready to live year-round on Jedediah, beginning in 1971. Al cut shakes from cedar blocks to replace the roof of the house and work shed. Farm animals and equipment were purchased, including a hay bailer, tractor, binder, and seeder which were delivered by barge along with sheep and cattle. A new kitchen was added to the house and new bathroom fixtures installed. Al enjoyed spinning wool as an evening hobby while Mary knitted sweaters, caps, and socks. By now, Mary had grandchildren who came to Jedediah and experienced many of the same activities she and her sons had enjoyed.

Rather than being island recluses, both Mary and Al were outgoing individuals and had many friends; they hosted annual summer picnics at their homestead which were attended by islanders, boaters, and family members. Baseball games were organized and Al provided hay rides for the children around the property. Al and Mary even hosted a school group from Kent Meridian High School, who enjoyed hands-on experiences on Jedediah Island – shearing sheep, milking a temperamental milk cow, chopping logs, making butter from fresh cream, and riding Will, their horse. **Seattle school teachers** knew Mary through her articles published in the Seattle Times and for her talks on island life and gardening.

At the end of twenty years, Al and Mary found their spirit willing, but their energy was winding down at 70 years of age. Without farm status, land taxes on Jedediah would become astronomical; it was time to make a change. But Al and Mary wanted "to preserve Jedediah in its pristine condition in perpetuity, without sacrificing its land, native plants, timber, beaches and other unique features." Through fundraising and a long legal process, Jedediah Island was designated a **marine provincial park** for all to enjoy. The original house, and the barn with its tractor now silent, still remain. Trails are maintained and visitors will often find feral sheep among the orchard trees.

Mary Palmer's writing style is so colorful and descriptive, that the reader comes to know and love each owner and family who came and went on Jedediah Island and can't help but feel their presence when visiting this special place. *Jedediah Days One Woman's Island Paradise* is one of those books that's hard to put down.

Vancouver, Mainland B.C. & The Sunshine Coast

CHAPTER 9

WHITE ROCK TO VANCOUVER
Boundary Bay • Fraser River • Steveston

VANCOUVER AND HOWE SOUND
False Creek • Vancouver Harbour • Indian Arm
Horseshoe Bay • Gibsons

GOWER POINT TO SECHELT INLET
Buccaneer Bay • Smuggler Cove • Secret Cove
Pender Harbour • Egmont • Sechelt Rapids • Sechelt

JERVIS INLET
Blind Bay • Ballet Bay • Hotham Sound • Jervis Inlet
Princess Louisa Inlet

MALASPINA STRAIT TO SARAH POINT
Grief Point • Westview • Lund • Copeland Islands

Reference Only – Not for Navigation

WHITE ROCK TO VANCOUVER

The coastline between Boundary Bay and Vancouver is an uninteresting river delta and the waters are often rough. Fraser River sediment, locally known as Sand Heads, has created shoal depths for some distance offshore. The prevailing winds tend to blow against the river current in the shallow water, and steep seas build quickly. Stay well off in deeper water, but even there, a 20-knot wind can make for a rough ride.

We listened to the VHF one day when a storm front blew through, and we sympathized with a terrified woman aboard a chartered 45-foot powerboat caught in steep seas near Roberts Bank. She kept repeating their lat/lon coordinates from the GPS and begging for help. The boat wasn't taking on water and no one was injured, but conditions were awful and they were scared. There was nothing another boat could do.

A few weeks earlier we spoke with a couple who had gone up that shore to Vancouver and had a very rough ride, the kind of ride they never wanted to repeat—period. We have run that coast in calm conditions and had no problems. If you decide to go that way, be sure conditions are favorable. [*Hale*]

Most pleasure craft choose to go north through the Gulf Islands, then pick a patch of good weather to cross the Strait of Georgia to Vancouver or Howe Sound. The shortest distance across the strait, from Gabriola Pass to Howe Sound, is 14 miles. Even slow boats can make the crossing in two or three hours; faster boats can cross in an hour or less. Listen for the weather report for the Halibut Bank buoy, or call Dial-a-Buoy at (888) 701-8992 and enter 46146 for the wind and wave conditions in the Strait of Georgia, off Sechelt.

Boundary Bay. The U.S./Canada border runs through Boundary Bay. Delta, B.C. is located on the northwest shore. Point Roberts, Washington, is to the southwest. White Rock and the Semiahmoo First Nation's reserve are on the southeast shore. The southeastern section of Boundary Bay, straddling the U.S./Canada border is known as Semiahmoo Bay. The northern tip of Boundary Bay is known as Mud Bay.

① **White Rock.** White Rock, in Canada, is almost due north of Blaine, in Boundary Bay. A long pier, with floats at the outer end, crosses tide flats. The waterfront village has interesting restaurants, shops, and galleries.

① **City of White Rock Pier.** (604) 626-5330. White Rock is a Canada Customs port of entry; call (888) 226-7277. The south side of the eastern float has about 50 feet of space reserved for transient moorage, 2 hours maximum stay, no power or water.

② **Crescent Beach.** North of White Rock, the Nicomekl River empties into Boundary Bay, creating a channel that leads to the village of Crescent Beach and the Crescent

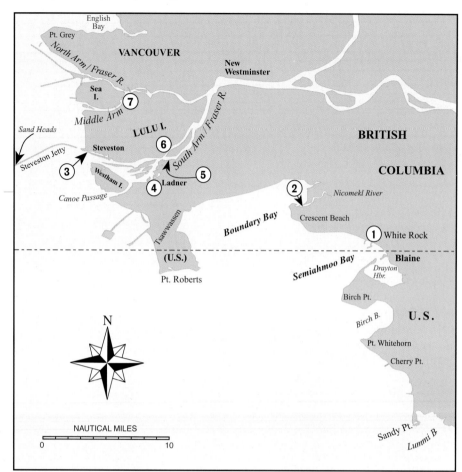

White Rock to Vancouver

Beach Marina. The channel is marked by port and starboard daymarks. The marina is located just beyond the Burlington Northern Railway swing bridge that crosses the river to Blackie Spit. Depending on tide, bridge clearance ranges from 9 to 20 feet. The bridge is manned 7 days a week, from 6:30 a.m. until 10:30 p.m., and will open to 3 horn blasts. Call the bridge at (604) 538-3233 or call the Crescent Beach Marina at (604) 538-9666, and they will contact the bridge tender.

② **Crescent Beach Marina Ltd.** 12555 Crescent Road, Surrey, BC V4A 2V4; (604) 538-9666; info@crescentbeachmarina.com; www.crescentbeachmarina.com. Open all year, gasoline & diesel at the fuel dock. Guest moorage for boats to 60 feet; call first. Haulout on hydraulic trailers to 30 tons, 15, 20 & 30 amp power, washrooms, ice, repairs, chandlery, launch ramp, showers, laundry, pumpout, dry storage. Used oil drop.

Canoe Passage. Canoe Passage is the southernmost mouth of the Fraser River. The seaward entrance is marked by a government buoy, but private dolphins mark its winding path through Roberts Bank. Although mainly used by commercial boats with local knowledge, Canoe Passage can be used by small craft, especially at half tide or better on a rising tide. The swing bridge connecting Westham Island with the mainland is manned 24 hours a day, and opens to 3

whistle blasts. Contact the bridge tender on VHF 74 or by telephone at (604) 946-2121. In 1997 the Canadian Hydrographic Service published large scale Chart 3492 (1:20,000) showing Canoe Passage, but we are skeptical. Locals who use the passage re-mark the channel yearly, after major runoff has moved the sand bars.

South Arm Fraser River. Sand Heads marks the mouth of the South Arm (also called the **Main Arm**) of the Fraser River. The South Arm is the Fraser's major entry, and is protected on its north side by the Steveston Jetty. Currents in the Fraser River can run to 5 knots, depending on the volume of water in the river, which in turn depends on rain and snow melt upstream. Large flood tides will at times slow or reverse the current.

Caution: An on-shore wind meeting an ebb current, combined with heavy outflow from the river, will create dangerously steep and high seas in the river mouth. Friends who keep their boats on the river tell of their entire boat being airborne in these conditions.

The lower part of the Fraser River is delta country, low and flat. The marshlands are havens for wildlife, and you'll see many eagles. The river itself contains much drift. The river is used heavily by fish boats, tugs towing barges or log booms, Coast Guard boats, work boats of all description, and freighters. Water-oriented industrial companies are located along the shores.

Steveston transient moorage across from the whale watch tour boats

Relatively few cruising boats go up the Fraser River, in part because the entire coast between Point Grey and Point Roberts is uninteresting to view, and hostile in any kind of wind. Most of the marinas on the Fraser River exist primarily for permanent moorage tenants, with few facilities for visitors.

③ **Steveston.** The first stop on the Fraser River is Steveston, a long, slender harbor on the north side of Cannery Channel, protected by a sand island (Steveston Island). Although Steveston is primarily a fishing town with moorage and other services for commercial fishermen, it has become a lively tourist destination as well. Transient moorage is available at the Steveston Wharf and at Imperial Landing located a third of a mile east of the wharf. Steveston has a fuel dock. Antique shops, bookstores, plenty of dining and all the other facilities of a small city are ashore. The streets of Steveston are quaint; the local movie industry sometimes films scenes there. Steveston has much to offer above and

beyond its attractive shops and cafes. The excellent Gulf of Georgia Cannery Museum on the west end of the Public Wharf is a must see, as is the Britannia Shipyards National Historic Site on the east end of the village, reached by a beautiful promenade along the shoreline. Hikers and bicyclists make use of the extensive trail system that leads to the North Arm of the Fraser River and to the City of Richmond. For a short hike, walk the trail west of town to Garry Point Park with beach access and great views over the South Arm and the Gulf Islands.

③ **Steveston Harbour Authority Wharf.** 12740 Trites Rd., Richmond, BC V7E 3R8; (604) 272-5539; www.stevestonharbour. com. Open all year, 30 amp power, water, washrooms, and showers. No Wi-Fi. Side-tie transient moorage is available by reservation only on the east side of the unlabeled float, east of the fish sales float (the eastern most Wharf float.) Additional side-tie transient moorage is available on the shore side of

A-dock on a first-come, first-serve basis. All transient guests must register and make payment by phone; the Harbour Authority office is located more than a mile away, at their Paramount Basin site. A key to the showers is provided upon request. Showers and public washrooms are located next to the Gulf of Georgia Cannery Museum.

③ **Steveston Chevron.** (604) 277-4712. Fuel dock with ethanol-free gasoline, diesel, washrooms. Limited marine supplies, lubricants, snacks.

③ **City of Richmond Imperial Landing.** Located a third of a mile east of the Steveston Harbour Authority docks; britannia@ richmond.ca; www.richmond.ca/parks. A Richmond City Parks Department facility (604) 244-1208. Transient side-tie moorage on this substantial 600-foot concrete dock; 30 amp power, no water, no washrooms, or showers. First three hours are free. Rates for stays over three hours are posted at the automated pay-station at the head of the ramp. Maximum stay is three consecutive days. This dock offers a more secluded moorage option when visiting the community of Steveston. Charted depths are deeper off the west end of this dock than around the Steveston Harbour docks.
Caution: Hazardous submerged piles are reported near the inside (shore side) of the east half of the dock.

④ **Ladner.** Ladner is a pretty town. Leave the main branch of the Fraser River and take Sea Reach to Ladner Harbour, fronted by float homes. Moorage for fish boats is on the port side, and pleasure craft are welcome when the fleet is out. Strongly favor the south shore as you enter Ladner Harbour, skirting the docks

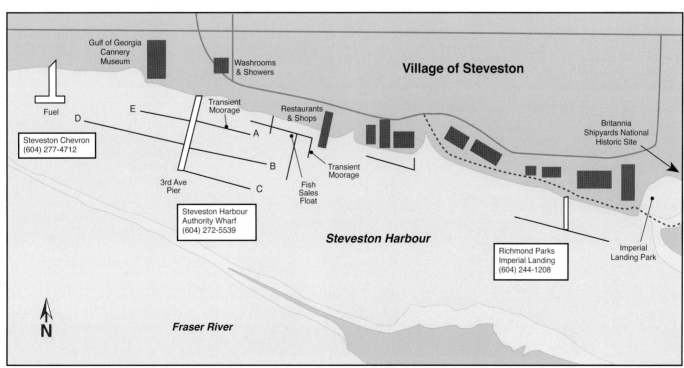

Steveston Harbour

of marinas and businesses located along River Road. A drying mud bank, studded with deadheads, extends a considerable distance from the north side of the harbor.

④ **Ladner Yacht Club.** (604) 946-4056; www.ladneryachtclub.ca. Reciprocal boats only if space is available. Water, restrooms, 30 amp power, secured marina.

Deas Slough. A little farther up the river from Ladner, Deas Slough is home to Captain's Cove, located behind Deas Island. A low bridge (Hwy. 99) blocks passage any farther up Deas Slough, except for small boats with no masts.

⑤ **Captain's Cove Marina.** 6100 Ferry Rd., Ladner, BC V4K 3M9; (604) 946-1244; info@captainscovemarina.ca; www. captainscovemarina.ca. Open all year, guest moorage available for boats from 24 to 60 feet, best to call ahead. The fuel dock has gasoline and diesel. Washrooms, showers, laundry, water, 30 & 50 amp power, waste oil disposal, pumpout, Wi-Fi. The facility is large and well cared for. Haulout to 60 tons, and a yard for repairs.

Golf: Cove Links, a pretty (and pretty challenging, we're told) 9-hole par 29 golf course next to Captain's Cove Marina, is part of a development that includes homes and condos.

⑥ **Shelter Island Marina Inc.** 6911 Graybar Rd., Richmond, BC V6W 1H3; (604) 270-6272; www.shelterislandmarina.com. Open all year, some guest moorage, call ahead. Washrooms, showers, laundry, water, 15, 30, & 50 amp power, several Travelifts for boats up to 220 tons, chandlery with hardware section in the marina office and a full-service chandlery across the parking lot. Restaurant and pub with free Wi-Fi, beer and wine store, and a full liquor store two blocks away.

Shelter Island Marina is behind Don Island at the south entrance to Annacis Channel. It is a busy facility with a number of boat repair companies.

New Westminster. New Westminster is located at the confluence of the North and South Arms of the Fraser River, and is heavily industrialized along the waterfront.

Tom Kincaid has run the river past New Westminster to the Pitt River, where he spent the night at the Pitt Meadows Marina. A few friends have continued to the Harrison River, running up the Harrison River to Harrison Lake and Harrison Hot Springs. All recommend having a fast boat and a knowledgeable pilot aboard before attempting to run either of these rivers. The Fraser River beyond Richmond is poorly marked, and sand bars are constantly changing. The river is navigable as far as Hope during high water stages, but mariners should rely on local knowledge before attempting this run.

North Arm Fraser River. The North Arm of the Fraser River is lined with boatbuilding and repair yards and other businesses that serve the marine community. A jetty runs through Sturgeon Bank along the south side of the North Arm, parallel to the Point Grey shoreline. A dredged basin, known locally as "Coward's Cove" or the "Chicken Hole," is on the north side of the channel, just before the North Arm enters the Strait of Georgia. The basin gives good protection to skippers while they assess conditions out on the strait.

⑦ **Richmond Chevron.** 7891 Grauer Rd., Richmond, BC V7B 1N4; (604) 278-2181. Beneath Arthur Laing Bridge. Open all year, gasoline, diesel, lubricants and waste oil disposal.

Middle Arm Fraser River. The Middle Arm of the Fraser River runs along the south side of Sea Island, which is almost entirely taken up by Vancouver International Airport. The west entrance is blocked by Sturgeon Bank with no marked channels. We have seen a small, fast cruiser enter the Middle Arm, but the tide was high and perhaps the skipper had local knowledge (or maybe was just lucky). Prudence dictates entry from the North Arm only. The Delta River Inn Marina and

Vancouver Marina are on the Middle Arm near a low swing bridge connecting the city of Richmond with the airport.

⑦ **Pier 73 Marina & Yacht Club.** 3500 Cessna Drive, Richmond, BC V7B 1C7; (604) 970-4882; info@pier73marina. com; pier73marina.com. Located 8 miles up the North Arm of the Fraser River in Moray Channel at the Pacific Gateway Hotel Vancouver Airport. Open all year, limited guest moorage, call ahead. This fully refurbished marina has slips from 30 to 80 feet, 30 & 50 amp power, water. The hotel has several restaurants, a bar, and a pool. They run a bus to the airport.

⑦ **Vancouver Marina.** #200-8211 River Road, Richmond, BC V6X 1X8; (604) 278-9787; mooring@vancouvermarina.com; www. vancouvermarina.com. Monitors VHF 66A. Open all year, call ahead for guest moorage. Gasoline & diesel at the fuel dock, 15, 20 & 30 amp power, garbage, pumpout, recycling and waste oil disposal, washrooms, no showers. They carry marine supplies, snacks, bait, and ice. Restaurant, mechanic and parts department, haulout to 30 feet, 24-hour security. Located in the heart of Richmond on the Middle Arm of the Fraser River.

⑦ **Skyline Marina.** 8031 River Road, Richmond, BC V6X 1X8; (604) 273-3977; www.skylinemarina.ca. Open all year, no transient moorage. The marina has a boatyard and 30 ton Travelift.

VANCOUVER

Vancouver is the largest city in British Columbia, and the major deepwater port on the west coast of Canada, handling cargo from across Canada and around the world. The city is clean, safe, and thoroughly cosmopolitan. Its architecture is exciting. Vancouver's parks, museums, hotels, and dining are wonderful.

If you are approaching Vancouver from the south, you could go up the North Arm of the Fraser River to a number of marinas in the Richmond area, and take a bus into the city. If you are approaching from the north, you could tie up at Horseshoe Bay on the north shore of West Vancouver, or at Snug Cove on the south side of Bowen Island. A private foot ferry runs between Snug Cove and Granville Island during the summer months. Or take the BC Ferries from Snug Cove to Horseshoe Bay, then board a bus for the trip into Vancouver—or as far south as White Rock if that's where you wanted to go. The Vancouver transit system is excellent and affordable.

For moorage in Vancouver proper, choose either the Vancouver Harbour area or the False Creek area. Each has advantages, and each is good. Once you're settled, Vancouver's bus system allows you to get around the entire area with minimum delay. A Costco store is located near the northeast end of False Creek at 605 Expo Blvd. (604) 622-5050.

Anchoring restriction: A permit, at no

Negotiating around the ships at anchor in English Bay on the way to False Creek

cost, is required for all vessels anchoring in False Creek (see False Creek area description for details).

Point Grey. Point Grey marks the southern entrance to Burrard Inlet. When approaching from the south, cutting too close to Point Grey risks grounding on Spanish Bank. Leave the buoys to starboard when entering.

Spanish Bank. Spanish Bank is an extensive drying bank off the north shore of Point Grey. The outer edge of the bank is marked with buoys. Royal Vancouver Yacht Club has its main clubhouse and sailboat moorage about 3 miles from Point Grey along the south shore of English Bay. A launch ramp is close to the former Kitsilano Coast Guard station near the entrance to False Creek.

FALSE CREEK

False Creek is an ideal centrally located bay with a number of marina moorage options, well-protected anchorage and a full service boatyard with Travelift. A well-monitored anchoring permit system helps to keep anchoring space available and prevents permanent anchorage abuses. Anchoring permits (free) are required for day anchoring longer than 8 hours and overnight anchoring. Permits can be picked up at Heather Civic Marina or online at http://vancouver.ca/ streets-transportation/anchoring.aspx. Boats without permits are subject to ticketing and fines up to $500.

False Creek Yacht Club, on the north shore of False Creek, usually has guest slips available. Quayside Marina, also on the north shore, has excellent facilities with guest slip and side-tie moorage. Foot ferries stop at Quayside. On the south shore, the Fishermen's Wharf marina, managed by the False Creek Harbour Authority, has transient moorage and good facilities. It is a short walk from the marina to the Granville Island Market, shops, and restaurants. False Creek is covered by Wi-Fi.

Blue Pacific Charters, on the west side of Granville Island near the Granville Market, sometimes has moorage available in unoccupied slips, reservations required. To reach these docks turn just before the Bridge Restaurant, on the south side when you enter False Creek, and work your way towards the docks. On the east side of Granville Island the Pelican Bay Marina, next to the Granville Island Hotel, has some guest moorage.

Granville Island is an active and vibrant place, full of people. You'll find a busy food market (similar in many ways to Seattle's Pike Place Market), many restaurants, galleries, shops, and a variety of marine supplies, both on the island and a short walk away. Docks face the waterway, and are posted for 3-hour maximum stay.

Two harbor foot ferry franchises serve False Creek, it's a great way to tour the harbour. These foot ferries no longer stop to pick up passengers from boats anchored in the bay.

First Narrows under Lions Gate Bridge

Fuel: Fuel is available at the False Creek Fuels.

Pumpouts: Pumpouts are located at Burrard Bridge Civic Marina, False Creek Harbour Authority Fishermen's Wharf, Heather Civic Marina (under the large "Monk's" sign), and Quayside Marina. The City of Vancouver and the Vancouver Park Board started a free mobile pump-out service pilot project in 2017, which is currently on-going. To schedule the service, contact Skookum Yacht Services at (778) 683-7867 or email at pumpout@ skookumyachtservices.com.

No Discharge Zone. Gray Water Okay.

THINGS TO DO

1. Granville Market. On Granville Island, a delight to the senses with flowers, spices, teas, fruit and other food markets, restaurants and crafts.

2. Foot Ferries. Crisscross the water from False Creek. Travel to different attractions or stay aboard to tour the entire harbor area. Some ferries allow bicycles.

3. Vancouver Maritime Museum. Learn more about B.C. maritime history from Vancouver to the Arctic. See tugboats, fireboats and even pirates. Easily reached by foot ferry.

4. Stanley Park. Several bike rental shops are on Denman Street, near Coal Harbour. Rent a bike and ride the trail along the seawall. Or, take a walk around the park. While in Stanley Park, learn more about B.C.'s First Nations people in Klahowya Village.

5. Vancouver Aquarium. Located in Stanley Park. Excellent. Don't miss the white Beluga whales.

6. Spirit Catcher Miniature Train. Take a ride and see the story of Sasquatch.

7. Science World. The distinctive domed glass building on False Creek with imaginative exhibits and hands-on experiments for young and old.

8. Bloedel Floral Conservatory. In Queen Elizabeth Park. Tropical plants; colorful birds flying about.

9. Museum of Anthropology. On the University of British Columbia campus. Study of First Nations people and other B.C. cultures.

10. Deeley Motorcycle Exhibition. Over 250 motorcycles on exhibit, spanning 115 years and 59 different manufacturers.

11. Yaletown or Gastown. Key shopping areas with many shops and boutiques.

Vancouver Maritime Museum. 1905 Ogden Avenue in Vanier Park, Vancouver, BC V6J 1A3; (604) 257-8300; www. vancouvermaritimemuseum.com. Vancouver Maritime Museum is on the south shore of English Bay at the entrance to False Creek. The museum's docks are for display boats only. The vessel St. Roch, which explored the Northwest Passage, is on display in its own building. The False Creek Ferry stops at the museum docks.

⑧ **Vancouver Boating Welcome Centre.** 1661 Granville St., Vancouver, BC V6Z 1N3; (604) 648-2628; welcome@fcyc.com. Hours 9:00 a.m to 5:00 p.m. Located in a boat at False Creek Yacht Club. The Welcome Center is a good resource to help with boating related matters. Anchor permits for False Creek are no longer available through the Welcome Centre. The Yacht Club is phasing out of their participation in the Welcome Centre over the next two years.

⑧ **False Creek Yacht Club**. 1661 Granville St., Vancouver, BC V6Z 1N3; (604) 648-2628 dockmaster; (604) 682-3292

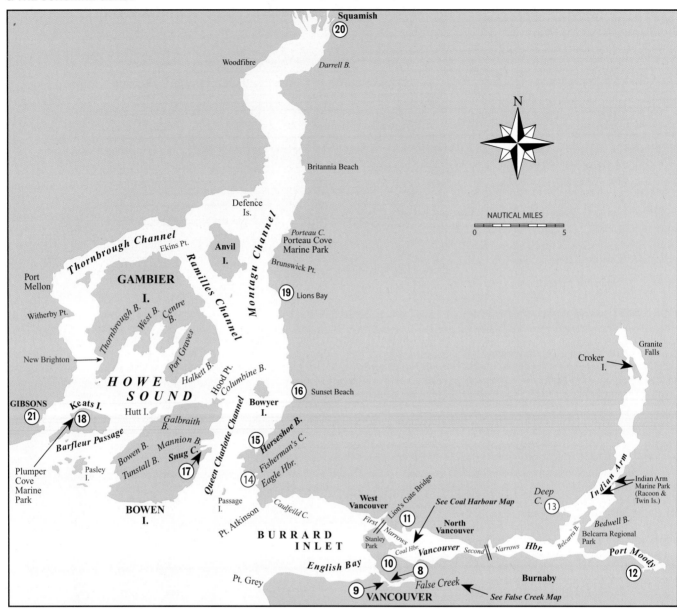

Vancouver and Howe Sound

administration & event scheduling; www.fcyc.com; welcome@fcyc.com. Washrooms, showers, laundry, pumpout, free Wi-Fi, 30 amp power, and lounge. Open all year on the north side of False Creek, directly under the Granville Street Bridge. Reciprocal and public guest moorage in unoccupied slips. Limited moorage for boats over 50 feet. Call the dockmaster upon arrival. A passenger foot ferry runs regularly to Granville Island.

⑧ Quayside Marina. 1088 Marinaside Crescent, Vancouver, BC V6Z 3C4; (604) 681-9115; (604) 209-6456; qsmarina@ranchogroup.com; www.ranchovan.com/marina. Monitors VHF 66A. Open all year for vessels to 125 feet, 30, 50 & 100 amp power, water on the docks, washrooms, showers, laundry, pay telephone, pumpout, garbage and recycling, ice, security. Wheelchair accessible. Online Reservations are available on their website. Slip sales and long-term lease information also found on their website.

The Quayside (pronounced "Keyside")

Marina is on the north shore of False Creek, in the middle of Vancouver's cosmopolitan Yaletown district. Most of the slips are for permanent moorage, but guest moorage is available on a 500-foot-long float extending from shore, or in vacant slips. Colorful Aquabus foot ferry boats come and go from their spot near the head of that float as do the small passenger False Creek Ferries. Moorage reservations are essential during high season and requested year-round. Although it's a bit of a walk from the guest dock to the office, check in promptly after you arrive. For provisioning, visit the Urban Fare Market, a block away, at 1688 Salt Street. Costco, located at 605 Expo Blvd., is a short walk or taxi ride away.

⑧ Pacific Boulevard Marina. Box 26, 750 Pacific Blvd., Vancouver, BC V6B 5E7; (604) 683-7035; info@pacblvdmarina.com; www.pacblvdmarina.com. Permanent moorage marina with transient space when available for vessels up to 40 feet; 30 amp power, water,

security gates. Located at the northeast end of False Creek. Reservations requested no more than one week in advance. Transient space is most likely available during March and April.

⑨ Burrard Civic Marina. 1655 Whyte Ave., Vancouver, BC V6J 1A9; (604) 733-5833 (604) 505-5833 cell; burrard.marina@vancouver.ca. The first marina in False Creek, with over 420 berths. Open 7 days a week all year. Operated by the City of Vancouver. Permanent moorage with some space for transient boats in vacant slips to 36 feet (occasionally up to 45 feet). Call for availability. Water, 15 amp power, washrooms, showers, pumpout, waste oil disposal, security gate with key-card, free Wi-Fi. The marina is convenient to the Vancouver Maritime Museum, walking and bike paths, and the False Creek foot ferries.

⑨ False Creek Fuels. 1655 Whyte Avenue, Vancouver, BC V6J 1A9; (604) 638-0209; fillup@falsecreekfuels.com;

www.falsecreekfuels.com. Monitors 66A. Just west of the Burrard Street Bridge, the fuel float carries gas, diesel, oil, lubricants. Open 7 days a week. Accommodates vessels to 165 feet. The store has drinks, snacks, ice cream, sandwiches (seasonal), and a coffee bar. It also has ice, bait, tackle, marine supplies, guidebooks.

⑨ **False Creek Harbour Authority Fishermen's Wharf**. Fishermen's Wharf. 1505 W. 1st Ave., Vancouver, BC V6J 1E8; (604) 733-3625; info@falsecreek.com; www. falsecreek.com. Monitors VHF 66A. This is a 5-Anchor Clean Marina rated facility. Open 24 hours a day year-round. Located on the south shore of False Creek, west of Granville Island. Contact the Harbour Authority office for docking instructions prior to arrival. 20 & 30 amp power on all docks; 50 & 100 amp power on some. Contact the Harbour office for access to locked power connection boxes. Water, washrooms, showers, laundry, ice, pumpout, recycling, waste oil disposal, free Wi-Fi, and 24-hour security. Ramps between shore and the floats are wide, long and compliant with Canadian Disability Policy Alliance. A fish sales dock is just east of

Fish Sales and Customs Dock at Fishermen's Wharf in False Creek

the Harbour Authority office, where you may purchase fresh seafood directly from the fish boats. The upland Go Fish Seafood Shack's fish & chips are not to be missed, take-out or enjoy at the outdoor bar and picnic tables. Expect long lines around noon time.

The Vancouver Maritime Museum in Vanier Park is a short walk away. The popular Shakespeare Festival, under the tents in Vanier Park, is held early June through mid-September. Granville Island, with its excellent market, shops, cafes and theaters is within easy walking distance from Fishermen's Wharf .

Customs Clearance. A courtesy customs clearance area is located in the yellow painted bull-rail area on the 'T' end of F-dock. There is no dedicated phone, you will need to use your cell phone.

⑨ **Blue Pacific Yacht Charters.** 1519 Foreshore Walk, Vancouver, BC V6H 3X3; (604) 682-2161; info@bluepacificcharters.ca; www.bluepacificcharters.ca. Open all year, moorage in unoccupied slips as available, 30 & 50 amp power, washrooms, and showers. Located on the west side of Granville Island.

⑨ **Granville Island Boat Yard**. (604) 685-6924; www.granvilleislandboatyard.com. A

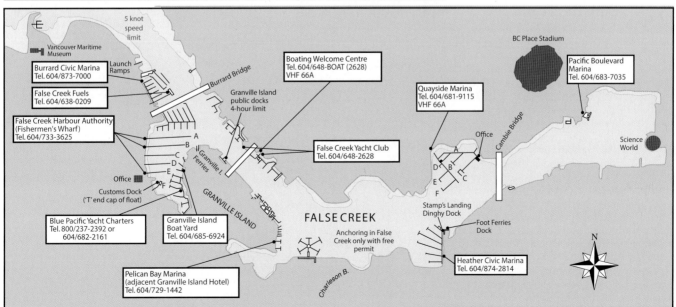
False Creek, Vancouver

Coal Harbour Marina is in the middle of downtown Vancouver and the most centrally located.

full service boatyard with 55 ton Travelift is located on the west side of Granville Island. The boatyard has repair service trades people available and welcomes do-it-yourself.

⑨ **Pelican Bay Marina**. 1708 W. 6th Ave., Vancouver, BC V6J 5E8; (604) 729-1442; pelicanbaymarina@mail.com. Open all year, adjacent to the Granville Island Hotel on the east end of Granville Island. Moorage in unoccupied slips when available, call ahead. Water, 15, 30 & 50 amp power, washroom, ice.

⑨ **Heather Civic Marina**. 600 Stamps Landing, Vancouver, BC V5Z 3Z1; (604) 874-2814; heather.marina@vancouver.ca; www.vancouver.ca/streets-transportation/heather-civic-marina.aspx. Open all year with guest moorage to 42 feet in unoccupied slips, call for availability. Washrooms, showers, pumpout, 15, 30 & 50 amp power. Restaurants and pub nearby. A passenger foot ferry runs to both sides of False Creek. The Heather Civic Marina office issues anchoring permits for False Creek.

LOCAL KNOWLEDGE

STRONG CURRENTS: Currents run strongly in both First and Second Narrows. Use caution, especially because of the heavy traffic that frequents the area.

Vancouver Harbour (South). Vancouver Harbour is entered under the Lions Gate Bridge through First Narrows, in the northeast corner of Burrard Inlet. Because of heavy commercial traffic, strong currents and narrow channels, sailing craft must be under power from westward of First Narrows until well into Vancouver Harbour. No sailing is permitted through Second Narrows, either. In First Narrows, a strong ebb current meeting a fresh onshore breeze can create high, steep seas. Current predictions are shown in the Tide and Current Tables Vol. 5, and Ports and Passes. Monitor VHF 12 for Vessel Traffic Services (VTS) information.

Watch for drifting logs, float plane traffic, and Vancouver Rowing Club rowers in Vancouver Harbour. Approaching Coal Harbour, leave Burnaby Shoal and the

Chevron fuel barge to starboard. Observe a 5-knot speed limit.

Once into Vancouver Harbour, your best bet for moorage is along the southern shoreline in the Coal Harbour area. Vancouver Rowing Club, located adjacent to Stanley Park, has moorage for members of reciprocal yacht clubs. Stanley Park is nearby.

Bayshore West Marina, next to the Harbour Ferries docks, offers some guest moorage.

Coal Harbour Marina, just east of the Bayshore Hotel, makes a visit to Vancouver a real pleasure. It is first class in every way, and is an excellent base for a few days in town.

These marinas are close to downtown Vancouver, a pleasant walk or short cab ride away. Wright Mariner Supply, occupying a floating structure in the Coal Harbour Marina, sells a complete range of marine supplies, clothing, charts, and books.

Robson Street's shops, galleries and wide range of restaurants are just a few blocks away.

Anchoring restriction: Pleasure craft may not anchor in Vancouver Harbour between First Narrows and Second Narrows.

Customs dock: (888) 226-7277 The customs dock is a Parks Board dock called "Harbour Green," east of Coal Harbour Marina. Day moorage up to 3 hours, no overnight.

⑩ **Coal Harbour Chevron**. (604) 681-7725. Fuel barge in Coal Harbour open 7 days a week 7:00 a.m. to 11:00 p.m., gasoline & diesel, washrooms, showers. They do oil changes and have waste oil disposal.

⑩ **Coal Harbour Marina**. 1525 Coal Harbour Quay, Vancouver, BC V6G 3E7; (604) 681-2628; guestservices@coalharbourmarina.com; www.coalharbourmarina.com. Monitors VHF 66A. Open all year, guest moorage for boats to 330 feet, reservations recommended. Facilities include 30, 50 & 100 amp single/3-phase power, Wi-Fi, pumpout, washrooms, showers, laundry. This is a first-class marina with wide concrete docks, 24-hour staff, security gates, a restaurant, marine supply store, and easy access to downtown Vancouver. Reservations in season highly recommended.

⑩ **Bayshore West Marina**. 450 Denman St., Vancouver, BC V6G 3J1; (604) 689-5331; info@bayshorewestmarina.com; www.bayshorewestmarina.com. Open all year, mostly permanent moorage with limited guest moorage to 80 feet; 30, 50 & 100 amp

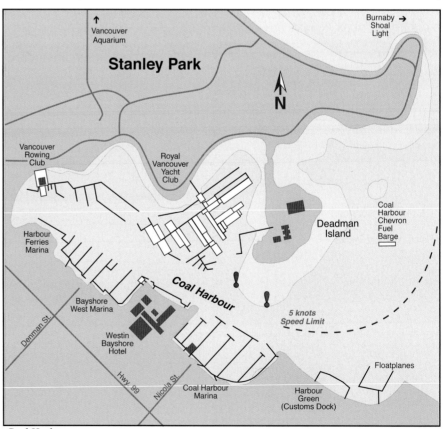

Coal Harbour

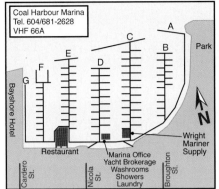
Coal Harbour Marina

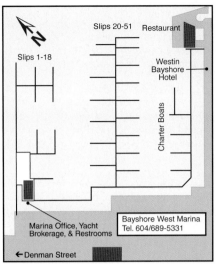
Bayshore West Marina

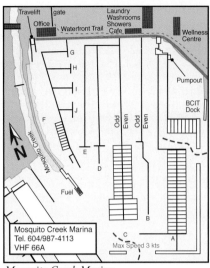
Mosquito Creek Marina

power, garbage, recycling Wi-Fi, washrooms, and pumpout. Located in Coal Harbour between Stanley Park and the Westin Bayshore Resort. Restaurants and shopping within easy walking distance. Guided fishing excursions available. The slips and fairways are wide for easy maneuvering.

Vancouver Harbour (North). With the exception of the re-developed Lonsdale area, the north shore of Vancouver Harbour is mostly heavy commercial. Transient moorage is available at Mosquito Creek Marina and at the City of North Vancouver's St. Roch dock. Both are near the Lonsdale area which has a selection of restaurants and pubs, grocery, and shopping. SeaBus foot ferry service at Lonsdale

Quay in North Vancouver runs to downtown Vancouver. The crossing takes 12 minutes and connects with other transportation options in downtown Vancouver. For more information see the Vancouver transit planning website: www.translink.ca.

A number of good marine repair shops are in Mosquito Creek Marina and at Lynnwood Marina, just west of Second Narrows.

Saturday Summer Concerts: July through August at Shipbuilders' Square at the foot

of Lonsdale. Shipyards Night Market: May through September from 5 to 10 p.m. on Fridays. Live music, fresh food and locally made products.

Caution: The SeaBus north terminus is just west of Lonsdale Quay with frequent arrivals and departures of two foot-passenger catamaran SeaBus ferries.

St. Roch Dock. (604) 982-3910; www.cnv. org. 80 feet of floating dock for short-term and

overnight moorage. Located east of Lonsdale Quay with its "Q" on top of the tower, just below the historic yellow crane and next to the re-developed 700x50 feet Burrard Dry Dock. This pleasure craft float is conveniently located but exposed to Vancouver Harbour on the south. No charge for the first 3 hours of stay. Thereafter, call the City of North Vancouver (604) 982-3910 to make payment.

The City of North Vancouver has two other docks nearby. The Goldsworthy Pier float has 36 feet of day-use only space with stays limited to 3 hours at no charge. The Burrard Dry Dock is for large vessels and requires prior arrangement scheduling and a signed agreement.

⑪ **Mosquito Creek Marina.** 415 West Esplanade, North Vancouver, BC V7M 1A6; (604) 987-4113; mcmb_dockmaster@ squamish.net; www.mosquitocreekmarina. com. Open all year with guest moorage in unoccupied slips, reservations recommended. 15, 30 & 50 amp power (100 amp on Dock A), washrooms and laundry, Wi-Fi, 50-ton Travelift, water, pumpout, marine repairs, security gates, 24-hour security. Fuel dock with mid-grade gasoline, high-speed diesel, ice, bait and fishing supplies. On-site cafe located in a double-wide trailer near the office.

The marina is operated by the Squamish Nation. A mixture of open moorage and covered moorage with a variety of slip sizes. Know your assigned slip and study the Mosquito Creek Marina dock diagram before entering the marina as dock and slip signage is lacking. Replacement of finger piers and decking is on-going. Future plans include removal of F-dock allowing a wider entrance to the marina.

A foot path connects the marina with Lonsdale Quay shopping, with restaurants and a farmers market. Several boat repair companies with complete services are on-site. It's a 10-minute walk to the SeaBus foot ferries to downtown Vancouver.

⑪ **Lynnwood Marina.** 1681 Columbia St., North Vancouver, BC V7J 1A5; (604) 985-

1533; info@lynnwoodmarina.com; www. lynnwoodmarina.com. Moorage for repair customers only. The marina has 15 & 30 amp power, complete repairs, and haulout to 60 tons. Shopping is about a 10-minute walk away.

BURNABY, PORT MOODY, INDIAN ARM

Second Narrows. To proceed eastward from Vancouver Harbour to Burnaby and Port Moody, you first must go through Second Narrows. On spring tides, flood currents can reach 6.5 knots and ebb currents 5.5 knots. The narrows are not to be treated lightly. Wind and current opposing each other can create standing waves and difficult seas. The best advice is to go through near times of slack, although on small tides the current should present few problems for boats with adequate power. Current predictions are shown as a secondary station in the Tide and Current Tables Vol. 5, and Ports and Passes. Due to extensive heavy displacement commercial traffic, monitor Vessel Traffic Service on VHF channel 12. Sailing is not permitted in Second Narrows.

Cates Park. Cates Park is at Roche Point, near the entrance to Indian Arm. The park has a paved launch ramp, beach, trails, playground, changing room, and picnic shelter. Temporary anchorage only.

Burnaby. The park at Burnaby is the site of an old sawmill. The park has no public float, but anchorage is good just east of the fishing pier.

Port Moody. Port Moody ends in drying flats, but a dredged channel on the south shore leads through the flats to Rocky Point Park. The park has a launch ramp, swimming pool and picnic areas, and is the location of the Port Moody Museum. A large designated anchorage area is located at the head of the bay with protection from all except northwesterly winds. This is an industrial area with commercial traffic.

⑫ **Reed Point Marina.** 850 Barnet Highway, Bldg. #1, Port Moody, BC V6H 1V6; (604) 937-1600; office@reedpoint.com; www. reedpoint.com. Open all year, mid-grade gasoline and diesel. Washrooms, showers, pumpout, haulout to 55 tons, chandlery, sundries, restaurant, marine supplies and service. Permanent moorage only.

INDIAN ARM

Indian Arm extends 11 miles into Coast Range mountains soaring to 5000 feet. Indian Arm is largely unpopulated beyond Deep Cove, because Deep Cove is the end of the road from North Vancouver. The waters in Indian Arm generally are calm, but can be ruffled by local downdraft winds off the mountains. Indian Arm is a little secret that Vancouver boaters cherish. It feels remote, yet it is close to the city.

Indian Arm Marine Park. In 1996 the Indian Arm Marine Park was expanded from the Twin Islands and Racoon Island to include most of the fjord. Croker Island and Granite Falls are part of the park.

Belcarra. Belcarra Regional Park is located on the east shore of Indian Arm, near the entrance. The public float is for loading and unloading only. Anchorage is good. The park has 2 lakes, 4 miles of shoreline, and complete facilities. It's a popular stop.

Strathcona. The small Strathcona municipal float is at the mouth of Indian Arm across from Belcarra, behind White Rock and the Grey Rocks Islands. The float dries at low tide.

⑬ **Deep Cove.** Deep Cove is a city of about 5,000 people. The public float provides access to shopping in the town of Deep Cove for vessels up to 36 feet, no overnight moorage. The commercial village, adjacent to the public float, is upscale. Deep Cove is the location of the Deep Cove Yacht Club. Deep Cove Northshore Marina has moorage, fuel, and other amenities. Speed limit in Deep Cove is 5 knots.

⑬ **Deep Cove Public Wharf.** The dock is 145 feet long, and is within walking distance of grocery stores, restaurants, live theater, and other facilities. Day use only, for boats up to 36 feet, no overnight moorage.

⑬ **Deep Cove North Shore Marina.** 2890 Panorama Drive, North Vancouver, BC V7G 1V6; (604) 929-1251; info@deepcovemarina. com; www.deepcovemarina.com. Open all year, gasoline and diesel at the fuel dock, limited guest moorage in unoccupied slips and side-tie. Call ahead. Facilities include washrooms, showers, laundry, and convenience store. Deep Cove Village with restaurants and shopping is located a mile to the west.

Bedwell Bay. Bedwell Bay has the best anchorage in Indian Arm. The bay is

Remote and scenic Deep Cove is a surprisingly short distance from metro-Vancouver.

sheltered from southerly winds. The anchorage can be crowded during peak season. Speed limit 5 knots.

Twin Islands and Racoon Island. The larger of the Twin Islands has a dinghy float on its east side, and picnic and sanitary facilities ashore. Anchorage offshore is quite deep (between 80 and 150 feet). Twin Islands and Racoon Island are used by kayakers and canoeists who pull their craft ashore.

Granite Falls. Granite Falls, the largest of the falls entering Indian Arm, tumbles off a cliff along the east bank. A small day dock makes access easy and serves campsites ashore. Anchorage is fair just offshore. The climb up the cliff is good exercise for cramped muscles. Because of the questionable anchoring bottom, overnight anchoring is not recommended if outflow winds are expected.

Wigwam Inn. The Wigwam Inn, at the head of Indian Arm, was a luxury resort whose rich history goes back to 1906. Today it is a Royal Vancouver Yacht Club outstation. RVYC members only. Burrard Yacht Club and Deep Cove Yacht Club have outstations nearby—members only, no reciprocals.

POINT ATKINSON TO HORSESHOE BAY

Caulfeild Cove. Caulfeild Cove is a tiny bight, protected from nearly all winds and seas, tucked into the shoreline just east of Point Atkinson. A 52-foot public float lies along the east side of the cove with 6 feet of depth alongside.

Point Atkinson. Point Atkinson is the north entrance to Burrard Inlet.

LOCAL KNOWLEDGE

TIDE-RIPS: The waters just off Point Atkinson can be very rough, especially on a large ebb flowing against a fresh onshore wind. Often, a course well to seaward is called for, and even that can be heavy going. Point Atkinson is well known to Vancouver boaters, who give this area great respect.

Eagle Harbour. Eagle Harbour is the home of the Eagle Harbour Yacht Club. No guest moorage.

Fishermans Cove. Fishermans Cove, the home of West Vancouver Yacht Club, is filled with Thunderbird Marina. West Vancouver Yacht Club has some guest moorage for members of reciprocal clubs.

Important: Enter on the northwest side of the 39-meter island and Eagle Island, leaving the flashing red light to starboard. A "false entrance" between the 39-meter island and Eagle Island could put you in real trouble.

The passage from Eagle Harbour east of Eagle Island is shown clearly on Plans Chart 3534 but not on smaller scale Chart 3481.

The daymark in the northern mouth of the passage east of Eagle Island has been changed from port hand to starboard hand. This daymark relates to craft approaching from the north side of Eagle Island. Those craft should leave that daymark to starboard, to stay between the daymark and the docks on the north side of Fishermans Cove. Vessels northbound from Eagle Harbour should leave the daymark to port.

⑭ **Thunderbird Marina.** 5776 Marine Drive, West Vancouver, BC V7W 2S2; (604) 921-7484; thunderbird@thunderbirdmarine. com; www.thunderbirdmarine.com. Permanent moorage only. Haulout to 25 tons for boats to 50 feet. Do-it-yourself or use trades people boatyard. Thunderbird Marine Supplies carries marine supplies and hardware.

HOWE SOUND

Howe Sound is a 23-mile long, deep-water inlet off the Strait of Georgia, with Squamish at its head. About 12 miles from Vancouver, Howe Sound is the "backyard" for Vancouver area boaters. Stunning Coast Range mountains surround Howe Sound.

Most boaters visit the communities and anchorages in the southern portion of Howe Sound. The town of Gibsons, on the west shore, is served by ferry from Horseshoe Bay, and offers two marinas and a fuel dock. Good restaurants, fun gift shops, a grocery and farmers market are available in Gibsons.

The village of Snug Cove on Bowen Island is another delightful destination with boutiques, pubs and cafes, two grocery stores and hiking opportunities. Bowen Island is served by ferry at Snug Cove. Smaller marinas dot the eastern shore of Howe Sound, frequented by runabouts and sport fish boats. The south end of Gambier Island has several anchorages, including Port Graves, with room for a large number of boats. Two yacht club outstations are on the north side of Gambier Island. Keats Island, near Gibsons, offers anchorage and moorage at Plumber Cove Marine Park, with upland park areas. On the eastern shore of Howe Sound, Porteau Cove has a lovely beach and detached 60-foot Park float and one mooring buoy.

Continuing north, the population becomes sparse in a wilderness setting with few anchorages. The water turns emerald green north of Anvil Island with stunning views of the Coast Range mountains. Glimpse views of the Sea-to-Sky highway, carved into the granite outcroppings, gives testament to this wilderness environment. "**Mariners Rest**," an islet off Mariners Rest Point, is a Provincially designated burial site for ashes at sea, look for the silver cross and anchor on the islet. Ashes are not buried on the islet, but rather at sea nearby, going ashore is not permitted.

In the distant northwest shore of Howe Sound are several large pulp and paper operations. Log booming areas fill the waters in front of these operations. Watch for considerable drift that may be present in Howe

Sound. The town of Squamish is at the head of Howe Sound. Squamish is a vibrant town that has attracted young families, and brings in tourists seeking hiking opportunities and special attractions like the Sea to Sky Gondola near town, and Whistler Blackcomb, a world-class ski resort, located farther north. Moorage is available at the Squamish Port Authority docks and at the adjacent Squamish Yacht Club docks, where guests are welcome from just about any yacht club. Squamish has excellent pubs and cafes; groceries, hardware and other necessities.

⑮ **Horseshoe Bay.** Horseshoe Bay is the eastern terminus of ferries serving the Gulf Islands, Sunshine Coast, and Vancouver Island. Sewell's Marina, a large breakwater-protected public marina, is located to the west of the ferry docks. Boaters transiting this area are urged to use caution because of the steady procession of large ferry boats.

⑮ **Sewell's Marina Ltd.** 6409 Bay St., West Vancouver, BC V7W 3H5; (604) 921-3474; info@sewellsmarina.com; www.sewellsmarina. com. Open all year, gasoline and diesel fuel, ice, limited 15 & 30 amp power, concrete launch ramp, frozen bait. Limited guest moorage, mostly for boats 45 feet and under, call ahead. Fishing charters. Restaurants, groceries, and a post office nearby.

⑮ **Horseshoe Bay Public Wharf.** (604) 925-7129. Guest float, approximately 100 feet, on the south side of the wharf for short-term tie-up, maximum 4 hour stay. A float on the east end of the wharf is a 10-minute pick-up, drop-off area.

⑯ **Sunset Marina Ltd.** 34 Sunset Beach, West Vancouver, BC V7W 2T7; (604) 921-7476; sunsetmarina@shawlink.ca; www. sunsetmarinaltd.com. Open from March 1 to October 15. Gasoline, guest moorage to 24 feet, haulouts to 25 feet (power boats only), repairs, launch ramp with long term parking, washrooms. They carry marine supplies, tackle, and bait.

Bowen Island. Bowen Island is served by ferry from Horseshoe Bay. Snug Cove has a public wharf and two marinas. It's a wonderful destination with shops, a number of good restaurants, and a 600-acre park. A co-op store up the hill from the harbor has provisions. On the northeast corner of Bowen Island, Columbine Bay and Smugglers Cove offer good anchorage. Galbraith Bay has a public float. Anchorage is in Bowen Bay and Tunstall Bay.

⑰ **Snug Cove**. Snug Cove on Bowen Island is a favorite stop. It has a public dock and two marinas, and is served by ferry from Horseshoe Bay. From there you can take a bus to downtown Vancouver. Or take the seasonal foot ferry that runs directly to Granville Island.

The commercial village at Bowen Island has several boutiques, restaurants, grocery store, bakery/coffee house, pharmacy, wine store and liquor agency, and a couple of pubs. Bowen Island residents are artistic, interesting, and eclectic, and the local shopping reflects the character of the population.

Pubs: Visit Bowen Island Pub located in an impressive building up the hill; new for 2019 is the Copper Spirit Distillery with a selection of locally crafted vodka, gin and whisky.

Dock Dance: The annual Dock Dance, a benefit dance for the local volunteer firefighters, is held in early August. Participants take over the dock at Snug Cove for a party that literally rocks the dock with music and dancing.

Golf: The 9-hole par 35 Bowen Island Golf Club is challenging and beautiful, with greens that are devilishly hard to read. Call (604) 947-4653. Union Steamship Co. provides transportation for its guests.

Ferry Noise: Ferry propellers make underwater noise that can sometimes be heard throughout Snug Cove. If you hear what you think is an onboard pump cycling ON whenever a ferry is at the dock, realize that it may actually be noise transmitted from the ferry's props to your hull.

⑰ **Bowen Island Marina.** 375 Cardena Dr., RR 1 A-1, Bowen Island, BC V0N 1G0; (604) 947-9710; www.bowen-island.com. Moorage for boats on an annual basis. No overnight transient moorage. Located on the starboard side when entering Snug Cove. Shops with ice cream, pies, pastries, gifts and kayak rentals.

⑰ **Snug Cove Public Wharf.** (604) 328-5499. This wide concrete dock, with 350 feet of space, is next to the ferry landing in Snug Cove and exposed to ferry wash. No water or electricity. First-come, first-served in areas that are not reserved for load/unload and water taxis. Some areas are reserved for monthly moorage from mid-September to mid-June. Self-registration and payment at the top of the ramp on the pier.

⑰ **Union Steamship Co. Marina**. P.O. Box 250, Bowen Island, BC V0N 1G0; (604) 947-0707; marina@ussc.ca; www. unionsteamshipmarina.com. Monitors VHF 66A. Open all year, ample guest moorage, pumpout, 30 & 50 amp power, a boaters lounge with washrooms and showers, laundry, free Wi-Fi. The washroom and shower building, one of the finest on the coast, also includes a comfortable lounge with big screen TV and a computer station, all near the showers and laundry.

This is an excellent place to stop. Rondy Dike, an architect by training, and his wife Dorothy have restored the Union Steamship Co. landing into a wonderful destination resort. Their daughter, Oydis Dike Nickle, now manages the resort and marina. The staff is attentive and standing by to help. A lovely boardwalk leads from the marina, connecting several shops, cafes, and Doc Morgan's Pub & Restaurant. Easy walking trails are found through the adjacent 600-acre park. It seems that everyone who stays at Union Steamship has a good report. Reservations recommended.

The marina has 8 cottages available on the hillside.

Mount Gardner Park Public Dock. Galbraith Bay, northwest side of Bowen Island. Has 110 feet of space.

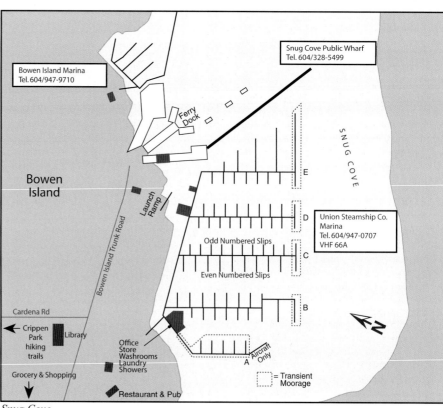

Snug Cove

Gambier Island. Gambier Island has three significant inlets, all opening from the south: West Bay, Centre Bay, and Port Graves. A smaller inlet, Halkett Bay, is at the southeast corner of the island. Thornbrough Bay, on the west side of the island, has a public dock. We are told that boats often tie to log booms on the western (Port Mellon) side of the island. In the summertime the water around Gambier Island warms to swimming temperatures. We know, we tried it.

Gambier Harbour Public Wharf has 100 feet of dock space.

Burrard Yacht Club and Thunderbird Yacht Club have outstations at Eakins Point at the north end of Gambier Island. Members only, no reciprocals.

West Bay. Favor the west shore when entering West Bay to avoid the reef extending from the eastern shore. West Bay once was a major log booming site and the bottom is apt to be foul with old cable and equipment.

Anchorage in West Bay is in at least two places. The first is on the north side of the reef, close to the reef. The second is in the bight at the northeast corner of the bay. Easy anchoring depths are close to shore in this bight, but because of real estate development, you probably shouldn't run a stern-tie to shore.

Centre Bay. Most of Centre Bay is deep, but the little bight on the west side, just inside the entrance, has 18- to 24-foot anchoring depths, and is delightful. Royal Vancouver and West Vancouver yacht clubs have outstations in Centre Bay. The docks belonging to the Centre Bay Yacht Station are at the head of the bay.

Port Graves. Port Graves is definitely the most scenic of Gambier Island's inlets and has good anchoring depths at the head. Because of real estate development in West Bay and Centre Bay, Port Graves is the best anchoring spot on the island. A small float at the public wharf, located at the head of the bay, is used for dinghy tie-up. The marked yellow side-tie is reserved for a water taxi. The adjacent floats belong to a Christian camp and are private. The wharf is under the auspices of the Sunshine Coast Regional District (604) 885-6802. A 2.5-mile trail near the head of the wharf leads to Lost Lake.

Halkett Bay. Halkett Bay at the southeast corner of Gambier Island has one mooring buoy, labeled B.C, Parks, and has room for 4 to 5 boats to anchor; beware that chop can be somewhat active in southerly winds. In 2018, 5 stern-tie pins, with chain, were installed along the western shoreline within the park boundary by BC Parks and the BC Parks Forever Society. Approach along the east shoreline as rocks lie on the west side of the bay. A dinghy dock provides access to Halkett Bay Marine Park with pit toilets, primitive campsites, and trails.

Plumper Cove Marine Park has an excellent dock, but no power or water. The yellow buoy pictured here marks a rock.

Halkett Bay Fircom Dock. A Sunshine Coast Regional District dock (604) 885-6800. Fircom dock is located on the southeast side of Gambier Island, along the west shore south of Halkett Bay. The 52-foot float is available on a first-come, first-serve basis for 24 hours at no charge. No water, no power. The Fircom Market, located upland, sells fresh produce on Friday evenings and Saturday mornings, seasonally.

Brigade Bay. Brigade Bay is on the eastern shore of Gambier Island. Anne Vipond, reporting in Pacific Yachting, suggests that because of deep water fairly close to shore, a stern anchor be set toward the beach and the main anchor set offshore.

Thornbrough Bay. The New Brighton Public Wharf in Thornbrough Bay has 390 feet of dock space.

⑱ **Plumper Cove Marine Park.** Plumper Cove Marine Park is in a cove formed by Keats Island and two small nearby islands. The park has 400 feet of dock space and several mooring buoys. Field Correspondent Jim Norris reports wave action at the dock. The bay has anchorage for quite a few boats. A rock, marked by a yellow buoy, lies a dozen yards off the dock.

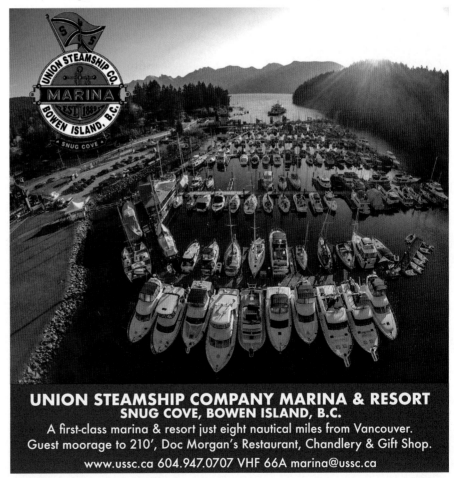

Porteau Cove. Porteau Cove is on the east shore of Howe Sound in Montagu Channel at latitude 49°33'N. The park is open all year; toilets, launch ramp, walk-in campsites, hiking trails and a picnic area. Tiny Porteau Cove itself has a 60-foot mooring float, not connected to land, and 1 mooring buoy. Two shallow-water buoys near the float mark shallow areas and are not mooring buoys. Sunken ships and man-made reefs provide excellent scuba diving. White caution buoys mark the yellow-buoyed diving area. Watch your depths; some of the cove dries at low tide. Anchoring within the park is prohibited.

⑲ **Lions Bay Marine Ltd.** 60 Lions Bay Ave., P.O. Box 262, Lions Bay, BC V0N 2E0; (604) 921-7510; www.lionsbaymarina.com. Open all year, except closed December 15 to January 15. In winter, closed on Tuesday and Wednesday. Gasoline, diesel and propane available. In summer they have transient moorage for boats up to 32 feet on 400 feet of dock space. Haulout to 30 feet (powerboats only) with repairs on site. Groceries and a post office are nearby.

⑳ **Squamish.** www.squamish.ca. The town of Squamish, pop. 20,000, is nestled against the Coast Range mountains at the north end of Howe Sound, between Vancouver and Whistler. Since the 2010 Winter Olympics at nearby Whistler, Squamish has become a vibrant town with young families and outdoor enthusiasts. A bus transit service (604-892-3567) runs to Whistler and the Sea to Sky Gondola, or you can rent a car. The Sea to Sky Gondola is about 2.5 miles from the docks and the views from the top are outstanding. At the top, a suspension bridge leads over a canyon to a trail with scenic overviews. There are many hiking and rock climbing opportunities near and around the gondola base station. The Squamish shopping district is about one-quarter mile from the docks where you will find excellent pubs and restaurants. There are

two grocery stores within a half-mile walk of the docks. A Saturday Market is held in a parking lot at the north end of Junction Park, April through October.

Summertime inflow winds usually begin between 11:00 a.m. and noon. By 2:00 p.m., the wind can make landing tricky. Best to go to Squamish in the early morning. The Harbour Authority docks are your best bet for moorage or the adjacent yacht club for reciprocal moorage from any yacht club. The Blue Heron Marina (604-898-3733) and Sea To Sky Marina (604-892-9282) are private permanent moorage marinas located farther up the channel beyond the Harbour Authority and yacht club. On a recent visit, we saw a sailboat anchored in the channel just north of the yacht club docks.

Transit Mamquam Blind Channel between the head of Howe Sound and the Squamish marinas with caution on a mid or high tide. The channel has a lighted range. On entry, follow the range, favoring the starboard side until abeam Stawamus River, then favor the port (west) side of the channel through the charted quarter mile shallow area. Stay close to the piling painted green/white/green at the charted shallowest area. The channel in front of the public dock and yacht club is marked with private red and green spar buoys

⑳ **Harbour Authority of Squamish Boat Harbour.** P.O. Box 97, Squamish, BC V8B 0A1; (604) 892-3725 or (604) 815-9658 Harbourmaster. VHF 69. Open all year. Located near downtown Squamish next to the Squamish Yacht Club. 80 feet of summer transient moorage; maximum boat length 55 feet. Pumpout, 15 and 30 amp power, washrooms, showers, garbage, boat launch. First-come, first-served; call ahead to check availability. Plans are in the works to add floats in the near future. Expect a relaxed, informal experience. They don't get many visitor boats.

⑳ **Squamish Yacht Club.** 37778 Logger's Lane, P.O. Box 1681, Squamish, BC V8B 0B2; (604) 815-9533, yacht club port captain; reciprocals are available for just about any yacht club, must display yacht club burgee. Guest moorage on docks D17-19 (the yellow zone) on a first-come, first-serve basis; call ahead to check available space. Maximum boat length 45 feet. 15, 20 and 30 amp power, water, restrooms, showers and garbage. Guest key assigned. Docks are within walking distance to downtown.

Shoal Channel (The Gap). The Gap is a sandy shoal with a least depth of approximately 5 feet at zero tide, between Keats Island and Steep Bluff, at the mouth of Howe Sound. Although waves off the Strait of Georgia tend to break on this shoal, if you know your draft and the state of the tide you can approach Gibsons from the strait via The Gap and have no problems—unless it's rough, and then you should go around Keats Island. Stay mid-channel. Boulders line the edges of the passage. The distance to Thrasher Rock,

outside Gabriola Pass in the Gulf Islands, is approximately 16 miles. Use Chart 3463 for the crossing, changing to Chart 3526 as you approach Popham Island. This approach, with Howe Sound islands backed up by the Coast Range mountains, is magnificent.

Correspondent Pat Shera says you can cross Shoal Channel at anything but low tides using a natural range. Keep the FlG (flashing green) light located east of the Gibsons Harbour entrance just barely visible in line with the base of Steep Bluff in the foreground. This transit takes you across the shoals with a minimum depth of 7 feet at zero tide. Travel along the 20- to 30-foot depth contour from either side until this natural range lines up, then stay on the range until you reach 20- to 30-foot depths on the other side. Not recommended when a strong southerly is blowing.

㉑ **Gibsons.** Gibsons is a charming seaside village, a good place to take the day off and stretch your legs. The lower Gibsons downtown area is filled with shops, restaurants, and pubs ranging from elegant to funky. The Sunshine Coast Museum & Archives is excellent. Hours are 10:30 a.m. to 4:30 p.m., Tuesday through Saturday.

The nearest supermarket is SuperValu in upper Gibsons. You'll need a ride. Be sure to see Fong's Market & Gifts in lower Gibsons, one of the more unexpected places on the coast. They have many of the essential grocery items, a good selection of Asian foods and a broad array of bowls, tea pots and other imported items. The Gibsons Market is just up from the Gibsons Marina. Some may remember the Market from earlier visits. In 2016 they expanded (rebuilt) the Gibsons market to be a two-story building with more local produce, meats, cheese and local crafts; an aquarium is located upstairs. They re-used the cupola from the old building by lifting it up to the top of the new building by crane.

As you enter the marina complex at Gibsons, you will see The Gibsons Landing Harbour Authority public dock to the north. Gibsons Marina and Fuel Dock are ahead and to the south. There are several private docks and a private marina behind the breakwater at Gibsons. A shoal extends from the shore between the public dock and the fuel dock. Approach each moorage directly from seaward.

Some boats anchor outside the breakwater and to the east of the pier, in front of the townsite. This is unprotected and suitable only in settled weather.

Sea Cavalcade: The Sea Cavalcade festival, featuring food, dancing, fireworks and other events, is held each July. See www.seacavalcade.ca.

㉑ **Gibsons Landing Harbour Authority.** P.O. Box 527, Gibsons, BC V0N 1V0; (604) 886-8017; glha@telus.net; www.gibsonsha.org. Monitors VHF 66A. Open all year, guest moorage, 15, 30, 50 and 100 amp power but mostly 15 amp with 20 amp receptacles, 3-ton crane, washrooms and showers, laundry, pumpout, garbage dumpster. Docks inside

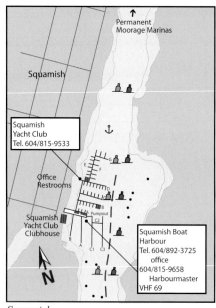

Squamish

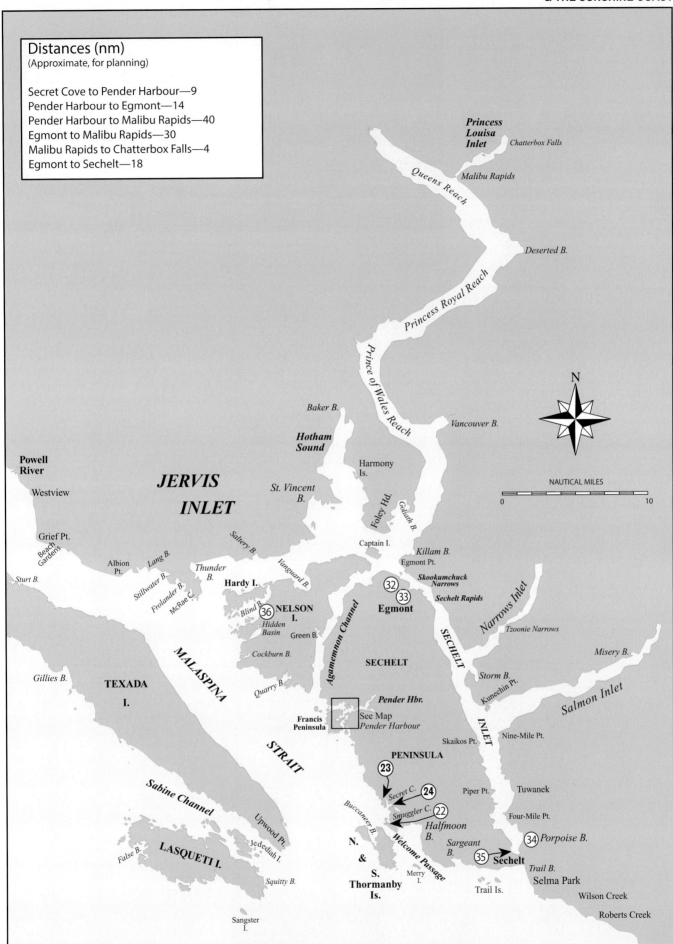

Distances (nm)
(Approximate, for planning)

Secret Cove to Pender Harbour—9
Pender Harbour to Egmont—14
Pender Harbour to Malibu Rapids—40
Egmont to Malibu Rapids—30
Malibu Rapids to Chatterbox Falls—4
Egmont to Sechelt—18

Sunshine Coast and Jervis Inlet

the breakwater are first-come, first-served; call ahead to check on available space. The public wharf has been upgraded with beautiful offices, improved shoreside amenities, and surveillance television security. Much of the moorage space is taken by permanent tenants, but they work to fit visitors in. Reservations accepted for vessels over 45 feet, which are assigned to the concrete float outside the harbour breakwater, located on the northeast side of the pier. No water on the float. Plans are in the works to add water and an additional concrete float for large vessel moorage in the near future. A year-round 80-foot long float for short-term stays up to 4 hours is on the shore side of the wharf outside the breakwater protected harbour, adjacent to the large vessel reserved moorage. Register and pay at the Harbour Authority Office.

㉑ **Gibsons Marina and Fuel Dock**. P.O. Box 1520, Gibsons, BC V0N 1V0; (604) 886-8686 (marina), (604) 886-9011 (fuel dock). Monitors VHF 66A. Open all year except Christmas Day. Reservations accepted. 15 and some 30 amp power, free Wi-Fi, washrooms, showers, well-stocked chandlery, laundry, pumpout, garbage, recycling, concrete launch ramp. The fuel dock has gasoline and diesel. The store on the fuel dock has lubricants, snacks, and ice cream.

GOWER POINT TO SECHELT INLET

From Howe Sound to Pender Harbour the coast is largely a barren run. The exceptions

Gibsons Harbour Authority docks provide easy access to shopping and great cafes.

are Buccaneer Bay, Secret Cove, Smuggler Cove, and to a lesser extent, Halfmoon Bay. When the weather gets up, the going can be wet and slow; but with a weather eye, the passages can be easy.

Trail Bay. A rock breakwater protects a small moorage at **Selma Park** on the south shore of Trail Bay. We once waited out a nasty southeasterly, riding on the hook in this hideout.

LOCAL KNOWLEDGE

STRONG CURRENTS: Currents run to 3 knots at the north end of Welcome Passage and 2 knots off Merry Island at the south end.

When wind and current oppose each other, the waters can be rough and uncomfortable. Watch for drift.

Welcome Passage. Welcome Passage separates South Thormanby Island from Sechelt Peninsula and is used by boats of all types bound up or down the Sunshine Coast. The passage west of Merry Island is deep and easily navigated.

Halfmoon Bay. Sunshine Coast Regional District facility (604) 885-2261. A public pier, with a 75-foot float, is at the head of Halfmoon Bay. It is very shallow on the land end of the mooring float. Side-tie available on the outside of the float. Onshore, you can walk about a half block through a residential neighborhood to an area with a store (a longtime landmark) and a cafe with fresh bakery goods. Henry Hightower, a resident of Halfmoon Bay, provided us with the following insider's view of the facilities and anchorage possibilities. He writes:

"The store at the Halfmoon Bay government wharf is well stocked, and has the best bacon and free-range eggs, as well as fresh and packaged meat, fruit, vegetables and staples, fishing gear, beer, wine and liquor, convenience store stuff, and a gift shop." After visiting, we agree.

If a strong wind is blowing or forecast, there will almost certainly be at least one tug with a log boom waiting for favorable weather, positioned across the open south side of Priestland Cove between the shore and the charted rocks. There is quite a bit of room to anchor behind its shelter.

Priestland Cove is southeast of the government dock.

㉒ **Smuggler Cove.** Smuggler Cove has a narrow entrance through the rocks, but opens to a beautiful anchorage that is protected from most weather. We have received reports that the cove is not protected from northwesterlies. Before entering, first-timers should have in hand Sheet 3 from Sunshine Coast Strip Chart 3311 or Plans Chart 3535. Both charts show Smuggler Cove clearly, but Chart 3311's scale of 1:6000 is even clearer than Chart

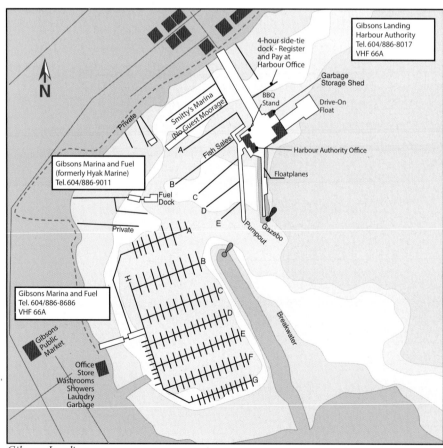

Gibsons Landing

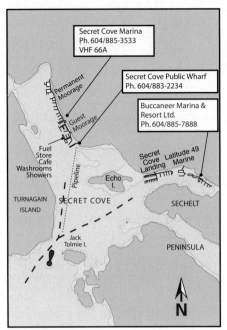

Secret Cove

3535's 1:10,000 scale. As both charts show, the channel is very close to the Isle Capri side of the entrance in order to avoid rocky shoals extending from the south shore. Inside is Smuggler Cove Marine Park, which has no facilities for boaters or campers, but does have trails through the park's 400 acres of woodlands. A favorite activity is paddling a kayak or dinghy among the little islets and coves. Reduce swinging room by taking one of many stern-ties (38), with lengths of chain, set in the rock ashore. New stern-ties were added in 2018 and old-stern-tie installations upgraded in 2018 by BC Parks and the BC Parks Forever Society.

No Discharge Zone. Gray water okay.

Buccaneer Bay. Buccaneer Bay is between North Thormanby and South Thormanby Islands, and has a beautiful white sand beach at the south end and west side.

Be careful to enter Buccaneer Bay by leaving the Tattenham Ledge Light Buoy Q51 to port. The buoy is well north of South Thormanby Island, but it marks the end of Tattenham Ledge and should be respected.

Once in Buccaneer Bay, anchor in 30 to 40 feet behind the Surrey Islands or in 20 to 30 feet in Water Bay. The Surrey Islands anchorage is particularly cozy and attractive.

A private moorage is in Water Bay. During the day small boat traffic to and from the dock will rock you some, but it dies down at night. The dock is posted for loading/unloading.

Watching your depths, you can also snug up to the shoaling waters off Gill Beach at the south end of the bay. In a southeasterly, you'll get some wind but no seas. There's no protection from a northwesterly, however. One year, we anchored in calm conditions only to have a northwesterly come in around midnight and ruin our night's sleep. It was pretty bouncy.

Secret Cove. Secret Cove has three branches, each with excellent weather protection and easy anchoring depths. Unfortunately, the Secret Cove bottom is notorious for anchor dragging in strong winds, so be sure you are well set if you do anchor.

Enter Secret Cove north of a light on a small rock in the middle of the entrance. Inside are the three arms. The southern arm has a very narrow entrance but adequate depths inside. This arm is lined with private docks that restrict swinging room in the middle. You can find room, however, off the Royal Vancouver Yacht Club outstation docks about halfway in. Correspondents James and Jennifer Hamilton have anchored there and report the holding ground is excellent. The center arm has Buccaneer Marina. The north arm is occupied almost entirely by Secret Cove Marina, but there is still plenty of room for anchoring, using stern-ties to shore if needed; a few chains and ropes are found along the west shore. A public float is adjacent to Secret Cove Marina.

㉓ **Secret Cove Public Wharf.** Managed by the Harbour Authority of Pender Harbour (604) 883-2234. Dock has 144 feet of moorage with 20 amp power, no water. Self-registration, payment box located on the wharf. Primarily used by local commercial fish boats and the Thormanby water taxi.

㉓ **Secret Cove Marina.** 511 Secret Cove Road, Sechelt, BC V0N 3A0; (604) 885-3533; info@secretcovemarina.com; www.secretcovemarina.com. Monitors VHF 66A. Reservations requested. Open April 1 through

John Henry's
MARINA & RESORT

YOUR FULL-SERVICE STOP IN PENDER HARBOUR!

For Your Boating Needs:

- Guest moorage for vessels up to 150ft. 20, 30 & 50 AMP power. Reservations strongly recommended
- Fuel dock - ethanol-free mid-grade gas & diesel. Fuel discount offered to overnight guests
- Well-provisioned General Store - food, liquor & gifts
- Showers & laundry facilities
- Marine supplies - charts & guides, basic parts, engine oils, fishing tackle & bait
- Provisioning service available - easy, convenient, tailored. Call ahead to order

For Your Adventure Needs:

- Bike, kayak, paddle board, & power boat rentals
- Guide books & information on local adventures & attractions

> *"We returned, after a great stay last year, to dock staff with the same helpful and attentive attitude as before. We'll be back!" (2018)*
>
> *"Amazing location, great food and friendly staff! Best crab cakes and burgers ever!" (2018)*
>
> *"Excellent service, amazing views great food and beer!" (2017)*

The Café:

- Open from May to September
- Indoor & outdoor seating with ocean view
- Great food and friendly staff

The General Store:

- Open daily year round
- Groceries, produce, dairy, ice (cubes & blocks)
- Specialty foods
- Fully-stocked liquor store
- Personal care & household products
- Eclectic gift selection
- John Henry's famous ice cream & candy bar
- Propane
- ATM
- Post office next door

Accommodation:

- 4 cozy oceanfront cottages
- 2 luxury 4-bed ocean view vacation rental homes
- 4 oceanfront RV sites
- 2 oceanfront campsites

Tel: (604) 883-2336 | 49° 37' 51.627" N / 124° 1' 56.273" W | VHF 66A | info@johnhenrysresortmarina.com
johnhenrysresortmarina.com

Canadian Thanksgiving. This is a full service marina in the north arm of Secret Cove, with gasoline and diesel fuel, guest moorage, 15 & 30 amp power, washrooms, clean showers, liquor agency, restaurant, store with groceries, gift items, clothing, block and cube ice, boating and fishing supplies, Wi-Fi. Fishing charters, kayak and paddleboard rentals. This marina resort is well managed and continues to receive excellent reviews.

The "Upper Deck," a five-star restaurant was closed in 2018 due to health issues. At the time of printing, reports from marina staff indicated that Chef Jennifer D'Amour would be back for the 2019 season. Dress code for dinner.

㉔ **Buccaneer Marina & Resort Ltd.** 5535 Sans Souci Rd., Halfmoon Bay, BC V0N 1Y2; (604) 885-7888; buccaneermarina@ telus.net; www.buccaneermarina.com. Open all year, gasoline and diesel fuel, limited guest moorage with 15 amp power, chandlery, engine and outboard repairs (weekdays), propane, haulout to 40 feet, paved launch ramp with long term parking. Fishing tackle and one of the few places with live herring bait. Water taxi to Thormanby Islands. Located in the center arm of Secret Cove. Owned and operated by the Mercer family since 1968.

Bargain Bay. Although its entry is actually off the Strait of Georgia, Bargain Bay is properly a part of the complex of bays that make up Pender Harbour. Enter between Edgecomb Island to the east and Francis Peninsula to the west. The entry is easy and open until you are part way inside, where a drying reef and an underwater rock extend from the west shore to the middle of the channel. Another underwater rock lies off the east shore. Pass between the two rocks and proceed into the bay.

Bargain Narrows, called Canoe Pass, is a drying channel spanned by a bridge with 4 meters (13.12 feet) vertical clearance. The pass runs between Bargain Bay and Gerrans Bay inside Pender Harbour.

PENDER HARBOUR

Pender Harbour is a natural stopover for boats heading north or south in the Strait of Georgia. For northbound boats, it's just the right distance for a day's run from Nanaimo, Silva Bay, or Howe Sound. For boats southbound from Desolation Sound, it's a good place to prepare for the long, exposed legs across the Strait of Georgia or down the Sunshine Coast. Boats bound to or from Princess Louisa Inlet often use Pender Harbour both going and coming.

Pender Harbour has good marinas, good anchorages, good eating, and good shopping. It has fuel and a haulout and repair facility. Diving services available through Wet Dock Divers (604-740-5969). The harbor is nestled against steep mountains; the scenery is beautiful. It's a good place for walking and hiking. If you carry trail bikes, the Madeira Park Public Wharf has a map of the nearby Suncoaster Trail, built and maintained by volunteers.

Pender Harbour is not a single large bay. It is a complex of coves, each with its own personality. Duncan Cove has a marina resort along the north shore. Gerrans Bay has marinas and anchorage. Hospital Bay and Garden Bay have marinas, fuel, shopping and dining. The best anchorages are in Garden Bay and Gerrans Bay, and in the bay between Garden Peninsula and Madeira Park. John Henry's Resort & Marina is the only place for fuel in Pender Harbour. Madeira Park, in the southeast corner of Pender Harbour, has moorage, haulout and repairs. A shopping center is a short walk from the Madeira Park dock.

Pender Harbour has several drying and underwater rocks throughout, but most of them are marked. With Chart 3535 (or good electronic charts) and a little care, you should have no problems.

Pender Harbour Music Festivals: The Pender Harbour Music Society sponsors a concert series throughout most of the year;

check their website for dates and tickets at www.penderharbourmusic.ca or call (604) 989-3995.

Transportation: There's no bus or taxi service. Use your dinghy, or try the **Slo-Cat Harbour Ferry**, based in Madeira Park, (604-741-3796) or VHF 66A, for excursions or shopping trips.

Irvines Landing Marina & Pub. Closed.

㉕ **Pender Harbour Resort and Marina.** 4686 Sinclair Bay Road, Garden Bay, BC V0N 1S1; (877) 883-2424; (604) 551-2742 (phone or text); info@phrm.ca; www.phrm. ca. Open all year with moorage to 50 feet. New docks, with a new configuration, were installed in 2018. Transient moorage is in unoccupied slips. Reservations accepted through "Swift Harbour" online booking. No VHF monitoring; call the marina a day ahead for slip assignment. Water, 15 & 30 amp power, Wi-Fi, showers, laundry, launch ramp, garbage and recycling drop. Marina guests have access to all resort amenities, including heated seasonal swimming pool, fire pit, gazebo, and sports field. Cottages, motel rooms, yurts, campsite, small boats, stand-up paddleboards, and kayaks are available to rent. There is a small store in the office with snacks, essentials, bait and gifts.

Hospital Bay. Hospital Bay is on the west side of Garden Peninsula, facing the mouth of Pender Harbour. The harbor is home to the former Fisherman's Resort and Marina (now part of John Henry's), John Henry's store and fuel dock. Hospital Bay Public Wharf is next door. Hospital Bay is also the site of the St. Mary's Columbia Coast Mission Hospital building, built in 1929.

A narrow isthmus divides Hospital Bay from Garden Bay with a walkway between the two. Dan's Grill, an old-fashioned diner (previously LaVerne's) is located here. Dan's, which opened in July 2018, carries on the tradition of tasty burgers, milkshakes, fish n' chips, and offers breakfast all day.

㉖ **Fisherman's Resort & Marina.** Fisherman's Resort and Marina was purchased in 2015 and is now part of John Henry's. See the listing below.

㉖ **John Henry's Resort & Marina.** P.O. Box 40, 4907 Pool Lane, Garden Bay, BC V0N 1S0; Moorage: (604) 883-2336 Store: (604) 883-2253; info@johnhenrysresortmarina. com; www.johnhenrysresortmarina.com. Monitors VHF 66A. Call for reservations. John Henry's and Fisherman's Resort are now operated as a single entity. Open all year with 2300 feet of moorage, water, 20, 30 & 50 amp power, washrooms, showers, laundry, Wi-Fi, garbage, recycling, ice, launch ramp. Gasoline, diesel, 50:1 pre-mix, and propane at the fuel dock. Moorage guests receive a fuel discount. Kayak, SUPs, powerboat, cottage, and RV site rentals available. Kenmore Air and Harbour Air provide float plane service

Pender Harbour has ample anchorage and many marinas with transient moorage.

Hospital Bay Public Wharf in Pender Harbour has transient moorage on two docks.

from Seattle and Vancouver.

This is a quiet, well-cared-for marina and resort with beautiful lawns and flower gardens. The well-stocked store above the fuel dock has fresh produce, meats, sandwiches, charts, cruising guides, books, liquor agency, post office, and an ATM. The store also carries tackle, bait, ice, gift items and hand-scooped ice cream. The store at the fuel dock carries snack items, fishing tackle, and boat supplies.

The nice restaurant, with indoor and outdoor seating, is very good and the portions are substantial.

Hospital Bay Public Wharf. P.O. Box 118, Madeira Park, BC V0N 2H0; Harbour Authority of Pender Harbour; (604) 883-2234; penderauthority@telus.net. Across from the fuel dock in Hospital Bay, 400 feet of first-come, first-served side-tie transient moorage on the south side of the middle float and both sides of the southern-most float. 20 & 30 amp power, water, garbage drop for fee, at the top of the dock. Portapotties are in the pocket park 200 feet up the road. Close to John Henry's and the pub in Garden Bay.

Garden Bay. Garden Bay is at the northeast corner of Pender Harbour. The Garden Bay Hotel hasn't been a hotel for a long time, so don't look for rooms to rent.

Seattle Yacht Club, Burrard Yacht Club and Royal Vancouver Yacht Club have outstations in Garden Bay—members only, no reciprocals. Many boats anchor out in Garden Bay and dinghy either to the marinas, John Henry's, or to Madeira Park. The Garden Bay holding ground is good and protection is excellent in most weather.

Garden Bay Provincial Park has about 50 feet of frontage on the north shore. The park has a dinghy dock, toilets, and a network of excellent walking trails, but no other facilities for boaters. Garden Bay Lake, a popular swimming destination, is within walking distance of the Provincial Park.

㉗ **Garden Bay Hotel Marina & Pub.** P.O. Box 90, Garden Bay, BC V0N 1S0; (604) 883-2674; gbhm@dccnet.com; www.gardenbaypub.com. Call ahead for space. Open all year, 1200 feet of side-tie moorage,

15 & 30 amp power, washrooms, showers on shore across from the pub entrance, Wi-Fi. This is a good-sized marina with a pub, including an outdoor seating area. The pub is open 7 days a week all year.

On a beautiful day, the deck overlooking Garden Bay is quite pleasant. A road leads from the pub to Hospital Bay and John Henry's store. A separate walking trail leads along the shore to the Royal Van outstation, and connects with the road to John Henry's.

Gunboat Bay. Gunboat Bay, surrounded by high, steep mountains, is entered through a narrow channel with a least depth of 4 feet. An underwater rock lies just to the north of the centerline of the entry channel. Currents in the entry channel are quite strong except at slack water. Although the bay is open and good for anchorage before it peters out into drying flats, few boats anchor there because Garden Bay is so much easier.

㉘ **Sunshine Coast Resort & Marina.** P.O. Box 213, Madeira Park, BC V0N 2H0; (604) 883-9177; (888) 883-9177; vacation@sunshinecoast-resort.com; www.sunshinecoast-resort.com. Monitors VHF 66A. Open all year with moorage for boats to 100 feet, call for reservations, 15 & 30 amp power, water, washrooms, showers, free Wi-Fi, hot tub on the deck, laundry, bait, small boat and kayak rentals, and a hillside lodge with 16 truly outstanding rooms.

The entire property is tidy and well-maintained. Manager Ralph Linnmann is committed to providing attentive customer service.

A steep mountainside rises above the docks. The laundry, showers, and road to town are a considerable climb up the hill, although the office and additional showers are in the lodge about halfway up. The marina is in the small bay to the right as you approach Gunboat Bay, about a half-mile north of Madeira Park shopping. You can walk to Madeira Park down the hill (and back up to return) or take the dinghy (we'd take the dinghy). Free transportation to the challenging Pender Harbour Golf Club.

㉙ **Madiera Park.** If you want to provision, Madeira Park is where you'll do it. The Harbour Authority Public Wharf is close to two grocery stores (the well-stocked IGA, and the Oak Tree Market with excellent meats and cheeses). The IGA is open 7 days a week 8:30 a.m. to 7:00 p.m., and 8:30 a.m. to 8:00 p.m. in July and August; delivery to the wharf by request. A drugstore, liquor store, bank with ATM, book store, and veterinarian are close by. No laundromat. Madeira Park has a full-service medical clinic. The Grasshopper Pub has been rebuilt and has temporary moorage at their dock while dining or shopping at their liquor store.

㉙ **Madeira Park Public Wharf.** P.O. Box 118, Madeira Park, BC V0N 2H0; (604) 883-2234; Harbour Authority of Pender Harbour; penderauthority@telus.net. Monitors VHF 66A. Open all year, 600 feet of first-come, first-served transient moorage space located on both sides of B-dock. 15, 20, 30 and 50 amp power, water, washrooms, showers, garbage drop for fee, recycling, pumpout, floatplane dock, free Wi-Fi. The dinghy dock (south side of A-dock) faces shore, adjacent to the launch ramp. No dinghy check-in is needed and no charge for daytime dinghy tie-up. Marine repair, chandlery, and mechanics nearby.

Madeira Park Public Wharf is a destination in its own right. A small park with a gazebo and benches overlooking the marina is ideal for relaxation or a picnic. Two well-stocked

grocery stores and a liquor store within walking distance make this a great place to provision. Stores allow customers to use their shopping carts to haul items to the Wharf, where the carts may be left. This well-managed facility is a popular destination.

㉙ **Madeira Marina.** P.O. Box 189, Madeira Park, BC V0N 2H0; (604) 883-2266; madeiramarine@telus.net. Open all year. Marine railway with haulout to 40 tons, complete marine repairs, parts, indoor painting facility for boats up to 30 feet, and chandlery. Prompt, competent repair service.

Pender Harbour Hotel & Grasshopper Pub. 12671 Sunshine Coast Hwy, Madeira Park, BC V0N 2H0; (604) 883-9013; penderharbourhotel.com. Located in Madeira Park high above Welbourn Cove. The Hotel's private dock has space for temporary moorage while visiting the Grasshopper Pub

or shopping at their liquor store. Call for moorage and courtesy pickup at the dock; it's a short but steep walk up the driveway to the Hotel and Pub. Good food and drink with outstanding views.

Gerrans Bay. Gerrans Bay is one of the larger bays in Pender Harbour with suitable anchoring depths. It is quieter and less traveled than other areas of Pender Harbour. The bay is dotted with rocks that are charted and or marked. It is mostly residential, with some of the homes obviously in the commercial fishing business. Two marinas, Coho Marina and Painted Boat Resort & Marina, and the Whisky Slough Public Wharf, have moorage for transient boaters. A private marina with no transient moorage is located on the west shore near the southwest head of the bay. Anchoring can be found in the southwest head of the bay or in the northeastern half of the bay over a mud bottom with good holding.

㉚ **Coho Marina and RV Resort.** 12907 Shark Lane, Madeira Park, BC V0N 2H0; (604) 883-2238; (604) 396- 3353 cell; info@ cohomarina.com; www. cohomarina.com. Open all year with guest moorage for boats to 40 feet in unoccupied slips, reservations accepted. Located on the east side of Gerrans Bay, the marina approach is through marked and charted rocks and reefs. 15 & 30 amp power, water, restrooms, and showers; 5-minute walk to Madeira Park shopping center with grocery and liquor. The docks were re-configured in 2018, making this a 100-slip marina.

㉚ **Painted Boat Resort Spa & Marina**. P.O. Box 153, 12849 Lagoon Rd., Madeira Park, BC V0N 2H0; (604) 883-2456; (866) 902-3955; reservations@paintedboat.com; www. paintedboat.com. Open all year with guest moorage to 70 feet, moorage reservations needed. The approach from east Gerrans Bay winds through rocks and reefs. We suggest

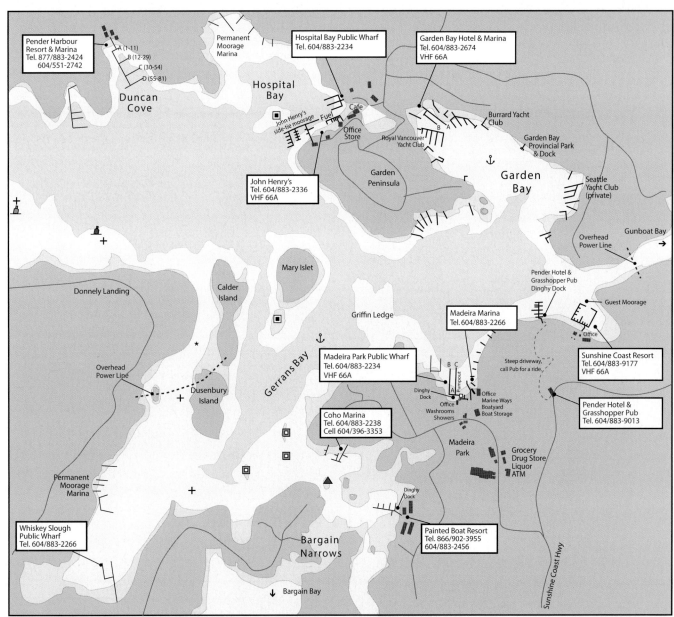

Pender Harbour

entering carefully with a bow watch. The docks have 15, 30 & 50 amp power and water, no washrooms, no showers, no laundry. This is a first-class resort. The upscale but relaxed Lagoon Restaurant at Painted Boat is open seasonally for dinner, with 58-feet of short term moorage and 92-feet of dinghy tie-up (near shore) for restaurant patrons. Restaurant reservations required. It is elegant with a great view. The full-service spa is available for an additional charge; swimming pool is for lodge guests only.

③ **Whiskey Slough Public Wharf**. P.O. Box 118, Madeira Park, BC V0N 2H0; (604) 883-2234; penderauthority@telus. net. Limited first-come, first-served side-tie transient moorage is available on two floats, with the best chance to find open space on the eastern most float. 20 & 30 amp power, limited access to potable water, no facilities or services. Mostly commercial fish boats here.

Agamemnon Channel. Agamemnon Channel runs northeast between Nelson Island and the mainland, and is the shortest route for those heading for Princess Louisa Inlet, Egmont, or Sechelt Inlet. The only reasonable anchorage is at Green Bay. A private marina is in Agamemnon Bay.

Green Bay. Green Bay is a well-protected small bay on the northwest side of Agamemnon Channel. Prime anchorage is at 30 feet in the cove on the west side of Green Bay in front of the lake shown on the chart. A stream with a waterfall runs from the lake to the cove. A drying reef nearly closes the pass to the back cove to the north of the prime anchoring area. Holding is fair on a hard mud bottom. Use caution approaching and within Green Bay as it is not well charted. Sailing Directions warns of rocks on the east side of the entry to Green Bay which are not shown on the chart. A large uncharted rock/pinnacle with 6 feet of water at zero tide is located mid-channel off a cabin with a small float, on the northeast side of Green Bay, east of the prime anchoring area. We entered favoring the west side of Green Bay. Several cabins, some with private docks, cling to the shore. The gentle sound of the waterfall makes for a restful anchorage.

SECHELT INLET

Egmont. Egmont, on the Sechelt Peninsula, is near the entrance to Skookumchuck Narrows and Sechelt Rapids. Sechelt Inlet lies beyond the rapids. Backeddy Resort & Marina and Bathgate General Store & Marina both have fuel. Backeddy Resort & Marina fronts on Skookumchuck Narrows; Bathgate is closer to the rapids, behind a well-marked reef in Secret Bay. The public dock is adjacent. Beautiful West Coast Wilderness Lodge, with fine dining, is immediately south and up the hill from Backeddy Resort & Marina. It's an easy walk between the two, and the view from the dining room and deck at West Coast Wilderness Lodge is a knockout. One of our correspondents reports that their dinner was as good as the view—world class, they said. We agree.

The Egmont Heritage Centre is a short walk up the main road from the marinas.

LOCAL KNOWLEDGE

STRONG CURRENTS: Strong currents can whip through Backeddy Marina. Watch the current as you approach the dock, although dockhands are usually available to assist. Sechelt Rapids currents in the Tide and Current guides will give you an idea of the current direction and force.

DANGEROUS ROCKS: The red triangle day beacon off Backeddy Marina's south docks means Red, Right, Returning for the channel outside. Approaching the docks, leave the beacon to port or you will run up on a rock shelf that extends from shore.

③② **Backeddy Resort & Marina.** 16660 Backeddy Rd., Egmont, BC V0N 1N0; (604) 883-2298; (800) 626-0599; info@backeddy. ca; www.backeddy.ca. Monitors VHF 66A. Open all year with guest moorage and services, reservations recommended. Gasoline and diesel fuel, 400 feet of moorage for vessels up

Sechelt (Skookumchuck) Rapids running at a 12 knot flood, less than full boil at almost 16 knots

to 120 feet. 15 & 30 amp power, washrooms, showers, laundry, garbage drop with fee, Wi-Fi, water at the fuel dock. Cabins, 5 geodesic domes for luxury camping, concrete launch ramp. Float plane access for Kenmore Air and West Coast Air. Small convenience store on site with ice. Backeddy Pub open for lunch and dinner, hours vary between October and April, call ahead.

The marina is opposite the Sutton Islets. This is a well-run marina, its rustic exterior hides the well-appointed pub and accommodations. Kayak and bicycle rentals available at the marina. Tours for Princess Louisa Inlet leave from the Backeddy dock. Water taxi service available. The Backeddy fuel dock is the first and last on the way to and from Princess Louisa Inlet.

㉜ **West Coast Wilderness Lodge**. 6649 Maple Road, Egmont, BC V0N 1N0; (604) 883-3667; lodge@wcwl.com; www.wcwl.com. This beautiful luxury lodge is located within easy walking distance from Backeddy Marina and offers a fine dining venue for boaters and lodge guests. Open for breakfast and dinner during the shoulder seasons; breakfast, lunch, and dinner during the summer. Reservations highly recommended during peak season, July and August. The float below the lodge is for seaplanes; however, dingies may tie-up while dining at the lodge, contact on VHF 68A. A steep trail leads from the dock to the lodge. Adventure tours can be booked through the Egmont Adventure Centre located below the Lodge (778-280-8619). Moorage can be found near the Lodge at Backeddy Marina or at Egmont Public Wharf.

㉝ **Bathgate General Store, Resort & Marina.** 6781 Bathgate Rd., Egmont, BC V0N 1N0; (604) 883-2222; info@bathgate.com; www.bathgate.com. Contact on VHF 16. Open all year, gasoline and diesel at the fuel dock, limited guest moorage, 15, 20 & 30 amp power, showers, washrooms, laundry. Reservations recommended. Shallow depths at the fuel dock restrict access. The store has fresh produce and a good selection of groceries, propane, marine supplies, liquor agency, bait and tackle, block and cube ice. It's the only well-stocked store for miles. Deluxe wheelchair-accessible waterfront motel unit available. Short and long term parking.

The reef in Secret Bay can confuse a first-time visitor, especially one who isn't that familiar with navigation aids. Remember: Red, Right, Returning. When entering, leave the red daymark well to starboard and you'll have no problems. If you still aren't sure, just remember to go around the ends, not between the two beacons.

㉝ **Egmont Public Wharf.** Managed by the Egmont Harbour Authority, 604-883-9652 or 604-883-9463, two public floats and one private float are accessed from the public wharf. The small float northwest of the wharf is private with no public access. The two large floats south of the wharf are public with permanent moorage on the southerly of these two floats and 150 feet of transient moorage for up to 48 hours on the northerly side of the north float. Self-registration and payment is at the head of the ramp. 20 & 30 amp shore power.

Sechelt Inlet. Beautiful Sechelt Inlet, with few anchorages and limited facilities for pleasure craft, is often passed by—especially with Princess Louisa Inlet at the end of nearby Jervis Inlet. Sechelt Rapids also serve as a gate to keep out all but the determined.

To explore Sechelt Inlet and its arms, use Chart 3512 (1:80:000) or Chartbook 3312. The inlet is shown at 1:40,000 in Chartbook 3312. Sechelt Inlet extends about 15 miles south of Sechelt Rapids. It ends at Porpoise Bay, the back door to the village of Sechelt, where there is a public float and easy anchorage. Two arms, Salmon Inlet and Narrows Inlet, run from the eastern side of Sechelt Inlet into the heart of the Earle Mountain Range. A number of provincial park sites are in Sechelt Inlet, most of them best suited to small boats that can be pulled up on the beach.

Inflow winds can blow from south to north in Sechelt Inlet and up Salmon Inlet and Narrows Inlet. Even when the northern part of Sechelt Inlet is near calm, the southern part can be increasingly windy. In Salmon Inlet and Narrows Inlet, the inflow winds will grow stronger as the inlets deepen and narrow. Outflow winds can develop at night, but in the summer they often don't unless a strong southeasterly is blowing out on the strait.

The tidal range does not exceed 10 feet in Sechelt Inlet, and the times of high and low tide are 2 to 3 hours after Point Atkinson. Two secondary ports, Porpoise Bay and Storm Bay, are shown in Tide & Current Tables, Vol. 5. Current predictions for Tzoonie Narrows, in Narrows Inlet, are shown under Secondary Stations in Tide & Current Tables, Vol. 5 and Ports and Passes. Depths at the head of the

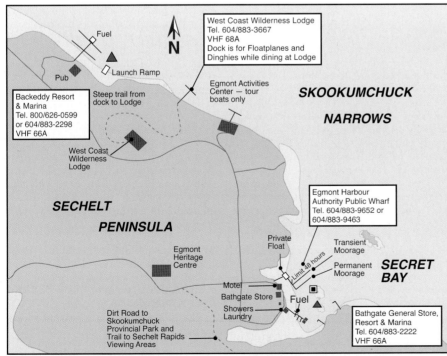

Egmont (Backeddy, Bathgate, Egmont Marinas & Wilderness Lodge)

Inlet are shallow enough for easy anchoring over a mud bottom. Usually there are other boats at anchor and a number of private buoys, but it's a large area with ample space.

For a complete description of Sechelt Inlet cruising, including excellent hiking trails, see our sister publication, *Cruising the Secret Coast,* by Jennifer and James Hamilton.

LOCAL KNOWLEDGE

DANGEROUS CURRENTS AND INCORRECT TIDE DATA: We've had reports that some current tables contained in electronic navigation programs don't agree with the printed tables for Sechelt Rapids. Use the Canadian Hydrographic Service or Ports and Passes tables.

Sechelt Rapids. On large tidal exchanges, Sechelt Rapids can run 16.5 knots, the world record holder. Sechelt Rapids, also known as the Skookumchuck Rapids (Sechelt is pronounced "SEE-shelt"; skookum means "big" or "strong," and chuck means "body of water"), provide the only water access to Sechelt Inlet.

Times of turn and maximum current are shown in the Tide and Current Tables, Vol. 5 and in Ports and Passes. Sechelt Rapids can be extremely dangerous except at or near slack water. At full flow the rapids are boiling cauldrons with 8-foot overfalls and 12- to 16-knot currents. Even an hour before slack, when many other rapids may have calmed down, the Sechelt Rapids can be menacing. Traverse the rapids only at slack water. Be aware of where you are time-wise in the lunar cycle. When close or on a full moon or a new moon, the period of slack water is short. When the rapids are running at full strength this area is deadly.

Lacking prior experience, do not go through without accurate charts for Sechelt Rapids and Secret Bay. Sailing Directions says the best route through the rapids is west of Boom Islet (choked with kelp, but safe) and west of the Sechelt Islets light.

We, however, have run a dogleg course without discomfort through the middle of the channel, between the Sechelt Islets and the unnamed islet directly north of the Sechelt Islets. This area is where dangerous whirlpools can develop on ebbs, so be careful. Give Roland Point a wide berth, especially on a flood.

Either direction, Sechelt Rapids are just fine at slack, and if you time it well (easily done) you'll slide through with no problems at all. But when the rapids are running, their roar can be heard for miles. Lives have been lost there.

Before making your own entrance it can be instructive to walk to the rapids from the public dock in Egmont to watch the channel in full boil.

Sechelt Rapids Viewing. On flood current watch standing waves and kayakers surfing

The view from the West Coast Wilderness Lodge. Backeddy Marina can be seen below.

the waves from Rowland Point Viewing Area; on ebb current watch whirlpools from the North Viewing Area. Viewing times are 30 minutes of max current. The 4km long trail is an easy walk from Bathgate, with minimal elevation gain; walking time is about 1 hour each way.

㉞ **Poise Cove Marina.** 5991 Sechelt Inlet Rd., Sechelt, BC V0N 3A3; (604) 885-2895. Open all year with limited guest moorage for boats to 25 feet, limited 15 amp power, concrete launch ramp for boats 25 feet or less. No long term parking. Located on the east side of Sechelt Inlet near Porpoise Bay Marine Park.

㉞ **Choquer & Sons Ltd.** 5977 Sechelt Inlet Rd., Sechelt, BC V0N 3A0; (604) 885-9244; choquerandsons@telus.net. Good docks with guest moorage for boats to 75 feet, deep enough for sailboats, 15 & 30 amp power, bathroom, showers. Launch ramp and trailer lift. Full marine repair. Their primary business is a machine and metal fabrication shop upland.

㉟ **Lighthouse Pub & Marina.** 5764 Wharf Rd., Sechelt, BC VON 3A0; (604) 885-9494; info@lighthousepub.ca; www.lighthousepub.ca. Located at the south end of Sechelt Inlet with easy access to Sechelt village. Docks with slips from 16 to 40 feet plus side-tie moorage, 30 amp power, showers, laundry, washrooms. Call ahead for moorage, make payment at the pub. The long and often empty dock extending from the pub is reserved for Harbour Air floatplanes. The dock to the east, marked 'Day Use' is used for transient side-tie. Dinghies may tie-up on the fuel dock, near shore, when dining at the pub or visiting in town. For taxi service call (604-885-3666). Gasoline and diesel at the fuel dock. Lighthouse Marine Store (778-458-3625) carries marine hardware, charts, fishing supplies, snacks, ice. Look for the lighthouse on top of the pub. We've heard the food at the pub is excellent. Three 2-bedroom "Bed & Boat" cottages are available for rent, reservations at bedandboatcottages.com.

㉟ **Royal Reach Marina & Hotel.** 5758 Wharf Rd., Sechelt, BC V0N 3A0; (604) 885-

7844. Open all year, moorage to 30 feet is for hotel guests only, limited 15 amp power, must call ahead. Located at the head of Sechelt Inlet. Watch your depths at low water.

㉟ **Porpoise Bay Government Wharf.** 5770 Wharf Street, Sechelt, BC V0N 3A0; (604) 740-7528. Next to the Lighthouse Pub & Marina. This dock usually is completely taken by local boats, but space does become available from time to time. Call Les, the Wharfinger, regarding available space. Docks accommodate boats up to 30 feet; 20 & 30 amp power, water, pumpout, and grid. Self-registration and payment box at the head of A-dock. Dinghies may tie-up in available space at the dock.

Narrows Inlet. Narrows Inlet is mostly 150 to 180 feet deep except at the head, where the Tzoonie River makes a delta. Tzoonie Narrows, about a third of the way along, is a spectacular cleft in the high mountains that surround the inlet. Tidal currents run to a maximum of 4 knots through Tzoonie Narrows, but the passage is free of hazards. All but the slowest or lowest-powered boats could run them at any time. Arguably the best anchorage in this area is in Storm Bay at the mouth of Narrows Inlet. Storm Bay is very pretty with a dramatic rock wall on its eastern shore. Anchor behind the little islets at the entrance or near the head of the bay.

Tzoonie Narrows Park. This park takes in both sides of the narrows and is good for swimming, fishing, diving, and picnicking. Walk-in campsites. The 1-meter islet shown on the chart is a long, narrow reef with large extensions under the surface. You can anchor inside the reef, or in the deep bight on the other side of Narrows Inlet.

Salmon Inlet. Salmon Inlet is very deep, although anchorage is good in Misery Bay, where the water is warm enough for swimming. A drying shoal almost blocks the passage across the inlet at Sechelt Creek. The shoal can be passed safely by staying close to the north shore.

MALASPINA STRAIT TO JERVIS INLET

Quarry Bay. Quarry Bay faces the Strait of Georgia and is too deep and exposed to be a destination of first choice. If you must anchor there, you could work your way in among the rocks in the southeast corner of the bay. It would be a good idea to run a stern-tie to keep from swinging onto a rock. At the north end of Quarry Bay a little cove, surrounded by homes, is well protected and has good anchoring depths. It would be a good hideout. Chart 3512 (1:80,000) and Chartbook 3312 (1:40,000) show a stream connecting this cove with Quarry Lake. Three rocks in this cove are shown in Chartbook 3312.

Cape Cockburn. An unmarked drying rock is a short distance off Cape Cockburn. Give the cape a good offing.

Cockburn Bay. Cockburn Bay is completely plugged by drying rocks and is accessible only by small craft at or near high water.

Hidden Basin. Hidden Basin is blocked by drying shoals and rocks, and currents run strongly through the restricted entrance. Chartbook 3312 (1:40,000) shows Hidden Basin better than Chart 3512 (1:80,000). Entrance to Hidden Basin should be made—carefully—at high water slack. Secure anchorage is available once inside.

㊱ Blind Bay. Blind Bay once had a number of good anchorages, especially along the Hardy Island side. Most of them now are taken with private homes and their docks, so the choices are fewer. One good spot on the south side is popular Ballet Bay. On the north side, Hardy Island Marine Park (formerly Musket Island Marine Park) has anchoring. Nearly all anchorages require a stern-tie. Use your chart and depth sounder, watch for rocks, and go slowly.

㊱ Ballet Bay. Ballet Bay, on Nelson Island, is a popular, well-protected anchorage in Blind Bay.

Ballet Bay can be entered from the north, but many rocks obstruct the path and close

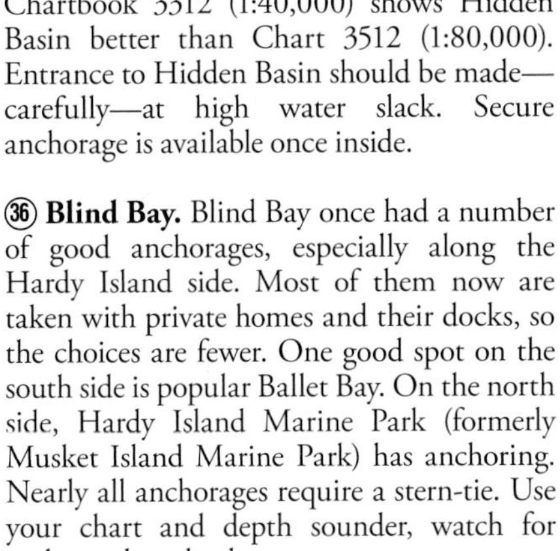

Blind Bay

At anchor in Hardy Island Marine Park

attention is called for. The easier entry is from the west, between Nelson Island and Clio Island. If you do enter from the west, the rock shown at the point before you turn into Ballet Bay truly is there, and farther offshore than you might expect. Give it a wide berth. Many rocks in the area around Ballet Bay are marked with sticks or small floats, but don't count on all of the rocks being marked. Not all the rocks are charted. Go slowly and pay attention.

The center of Ballet Bay is good-holding mud, but the bottom grows rockier toward shore ("a boat-eating rockpile" —*Evertz*). A trail reportedly connects Ballet Bay and Hidden Basin, although all Evertz found were "No Trespassing" signs.

Hardy Island Marine Park. Formerly Musket Island Marine Park. Located behind Fox Island, near the western entrance to Blind Bay. The upland area of the park is on Hardy Island. A beautiful spot. Anchor behind the tiny islet, or in the bay that opens up to the north of the islet. In most cases you'll stern-tie to shore. The bottom can be rocky, so be sure you have a satisfactory set. You also can anchor in the narrow, vertically sided, almost landlocked cove indenting Hardy Island immediately northwest of the park itself. Rock has been quarried on the peninsula high above the cove. It's quite dramatic. The area is poorly charted and some of the depths are deeper than charts show.

Telescope Passage. Telescope Passage connects Blind Bay with Jervis Inlet, but is partly blocked by underwater rocks that extend from the 70-meter island at the north entrance. Strongly favor the Nelson Island side until past the 70-meter island. Then, trend toward the middle of the passage to avoid charted and uncharted rocks along the Nelson Island side. When approaching Telescope Passage from Jervis Inlet, you might be confused (we were) by the presence of a tiny islet almost 100 feet high just outside the entrance. Check the chart closely; the islet is shown as the smallest oval imaginable with (26), for 26 meters high, directly beside it.

JERVIS INLET

Jervis Inlet extends 46 miles into Coast Range mountains and is the route to fabled Princess Louisa Inlet. Jervis Inlet is 1 to 1.5 miles wide and often more than 600 feet deep. Steep-to shores, with mountains rising directly above, make for few good anchorages. Currents in Jervis Inlet are light, and are often affected by winds. Watch for drift. Heading up-inlet, Backeddy Resort & Marina and Bathgate Marina in Egmont are the last fuel stops.

Once beyond Foley Head and Egmont Point, you'll find only indifferent anchorages at Vancouver Bay, Deserted Bay, and Killam Bay. The 30 miles of Princess Royal Reach, Prince of Wales Reach, and Queen's Reach do not have useable anchorages. Unlike the other deep fjords that penetrate from the sea, however, Jervis Inlet has a spectacular prize at the end: Princess Louisa Inlet.

Pictograph: Correspondent Pat Shera reports a good pictograph of what appear to be a group of salmon and other figures on the north side of Princess Royal Reach, midway between Osgood Creek and Patrick Point.

McRae Cove. Indenting the south end of the peninsula to the east of McRae Islet where Jervis Inlet joins Malaspina Strait, this small cove can be a day or overnight stop. The bay has consistent depths that are shallow for deep draft vessels. Watch for charted rocks at the entry and drying area at the head of the cove. The cove is scenic with windows to Malaspina Strait. A couple of homes occupy the north shore. This is a well-protected cove that is larger than it appears on the charts and has room for two or three boats.

Thunder Bay. Thunder Bay, immediately inside the north entrance to Jervis Inlet, has anchorage in the protected cove on the south shore, and in the open cove at the northwest corner. Correspondent Capt. Fred Triggs reports that in the southern cove, the rock drying at 2.1 meters appears to be farther offshore than charted. The cove looks a little small on the chart, but Capt. Triggs says it has room for several boats and good holding.

The shores are lined with vacation cabins. Mooring floats restrict anchoring room. Rocks extend from the point as you approach. Give the point a good offing. At low tide the charted rock looks like a small haystack. If you stay off the west shore you'll be fine.

Saltery Bay. Saltery Bay has a public float, picnic sites and a seasonal take-out eatery. It is the ferry landing for road travel along the Sunshine Coast. The Saltery Bay Provincial Park, with beach access, is about half a mile to the west. A log booming operation, with signs warning boaters of cables, fills most of the possible anchoring area in the bay, and what remains has several private mooring buoys. An underwater cable area is to the west of the ferry landing.

Saltery Bay Harbour. (604) 487-0196. Public floats are located adjacent and east of the ferry landing. Visitor moorage is available along 650 feet of space on three floats on a first-come, first-serve basis. The western most float is 240 feet long with stays limited to 48 hours on the outer western portion of the float. No power, no water. Most of the space is taken by local boats. Space for smaller boats can usually be found. Commercial vessels have priority.

Saltery Bay Provincial Park. Open all year, anchor only or moor at the public dock, a 1-km walk from the park entrance. Picnic facilities and a dive rinse station are located above the small sandy beach. Most of the shoreline is rock, however, and very impressive. In Mermaid Cove, scuba divers can look for the underwater statue of the mermaid. The dive reef is marked by white buoys. A launch ramp is a short distance west of Mermaid Cove.

St. Vincent Bay. Much oyster culture activity. Sykes Island and Junction Island may have anchorage.

Hotham Sound. Hotham Sound is a beautiful, 6-mile-long body of water, surrounded by high, rugged mountains. The sound is sheltered from most strong winds, and in the summertime the water is warm enough for swimming. Friel Lake Falls tumble 1400 feet down a sheer mountainside near the Harmony Islands. Unfortunately, good anchorages in Hotham Sound are few.

Wolferstan (*Cruising Guide to British Columbia Vol. 3*, Sunshine Coast, now out of print) devotes an entire chapter, with superb aerial photos, to Hotham Sound; but for the most part, even his advice comes down to finding little niches along the shoreline. Suitable anchorage is found in Baker Bay at the head of Hotham Sound.

Harmony Islands Marine Park. The Harmony Islands in Hotham Sound are lovely. Four islands comprise the Harmony Islands Group. Two of the islands, the southern-most and the northeastern-most, are part of the Marine Park. The middle

Running against a couple knots of current at Malibu Rapids

island is private property and is not part of the park. The northwestern-most island was acquired by BC Parks (with substantial help from BC Parks Forever Society) in 2018, and is expected to be officially dedicated as part of the park in the spring of 2019.

The best anchorage is in locally-named Kipling Cove, a nook surrounded by both of the northern islands and the middle island. The bottom is rocky, so be sure you have the right ground tackle and it's well set. You'll run a stern-tie to shore. The middle island is privately owned and posted with "Private Island, No Stern Ties, No Fires, No Kayakers" signs. The signs mean what they say, and private property must be respected. The two northern islands that make up Kipling Cove are owned by BC Parks, with no restriction on going ashore or stern-tying. The southern-most of the Harmony Islands (separate from Kipling Cove) is also part of the marine park.

Because anchoring inside Kipling Cove can be tight, some boats choose to put the hook down in the channel on the east side of the islands. Close to the islands the depths are fine, but the channel itself is around 100 feet deep. As long as you are set up for deeper anchorages, you should be okay. Rings for stern ties are along the high tide line.

We have been told that williwaws can blow down from the mountains and make anchoring interesting. And we have heard that flies can be aggressive. Our visits have been in late June. On one overnight, we were troubled by only a few flies in the evening—but they were definitely determined.

Dark Cove. Dark Cove is a little notch between Foley Head and Goliath Bay, and was recommended to us by an experienced sailboater we met at Princess Louisa Inlet. We motored through Dark Cove the next day but didn't stop. At 90 feet deep, Dark Cove isn't ideal for anchoring, although protection behind Sydney Island is excellent.

Malibu Rapids. Malibu Rapids mark the entrance to Princess Louisa Inlet. The rapids are narrow and dogleg-shaped, and boats at one end cannot see boats at the other end. It is courteous—and wise—to warn other vessels via VHF radio that you are about to enter the rapids, and the direction you are traveling. Most boats use channel 16 because it is the one VHF channel everyone is supposed to monitor. The transmission can be brief: *"Securité, Securité. This is the 34-foot motor vessel Happy Days, inbound to Princess Louisa Inlet. Any concerned traffic please respond on channel one-six."*

A VHF securite call is a notice of safety to boaters. When making a securite call at Malibu Rapids, it is for safety reasons and not for any right-of-way statement. Rules of the road for vessels operating in current flow are determined by current flow direction. Vessels traveling with the current are the 'stand-on' and vessels traveling against the current flow are the 'give-way.' The path through Malibu Rapids is 'S' shaped. While it might be tempting to 'cross over' the opposing traffic path to get a look at the rapids, this may create a conflict with boats coming in the opposite direction.

Currents in Malibu Rapids run to 9 knots and create large overfalls. Run this passage at slack water. High water slack occurs about 25 minutes after high water at Point Atkinson, and low water slack about 35 minutes after low water at Point Atkinson. High water slack is preferred because it widens the available channel somewhat. High slack or low, before entering or leaving Malibu Rapids, local knowledge says to wait until the surf created by the overfall subsides entirely.

Important: Use the Volume 5 Canadian Hydrographic Service or Ports and Passes tide tables for Point Atkinson tides.

Princess Louisa Inlet. Princess Louisa Inlet, 4 miles long, is the "holy grail" for cruising people from all over the world. Entered through Malibu Rapids, the inlet is surrounded by 3000-foot-high mountains that plunge almost vertically into 600-foot depths below. Entering Princess Louisa Inlet is like entering a great cathedral. The author Earle Stanley Gardner wrote that no one

292

Princess Louisa Inlet on a high-speed tour boat

could see Princess Louisa Inlet and remain an atheist. It is one of the most awesome destinations on the coast. What words can describe this place? All the superlatives have been used up on lesser subjects.

Please observe a no-wake speed limit. Larger wakes bounce off the sides of the inlet.

Malibu Club, a Young Life Christian summer camp for teenagers, is at the entrance to the inlet, just inside Malibu Rapids. The kids and staff are welcoming and polite. Tours are possible. It's probably best to visit by dinghy after your boat is settled at Macdonald Island or the park dock at Chatterbox Falls.

As you clear Malibu Rapids and motor up Princess Louisa Inlet, you will be treated to waterfalls streaming down the mountainsides. About halfway along, 5 mooring buoys are behind Macdonald Island.

Princess Louisa Park is at the head of the inlet, surrounded by a bowl of high sheer cliffs that astonish even repeat visitors. The 650-foot-long park dock will hold a large number of boats. The dock is available at no charge; maximum boat length is 55 feet and stays are limited to 72 hours. Snug up close to the boat in front to leave room for others. The float at the end of dock is for floatplanes.

If the dock is full, you will need to make use of one of the five mooring buoys at Macdonald Island. Anchorage is possible at Macdonald Island but may not be practical due to depths and lack of swinging space. Two dinghy docks are provided on the mainland shore opposite Macdonald Island for visitors to access a 1.5 km loop trail.

Since most people don't stay longer than a day or two, there's good turnover. A boat at anchor or on a mooring buoy need only wait for the twice-daily departure of boats from the dock running for slack at Malibu Rapids. Space then can be found before the next fleet

arrives from the rapids. Water (not potable) is available all the way out the dock (May 1 - Oct 30) but no power. Up-inlet thermal winds can develop on warm afternoons. Be aware if you're out in the dinghy.

The park is beautifully developed and maintained. Use the shoreside toilets. Limit generator use to 9:00 a.m. to 11:00 a.m. in the morning and 6:00 p.m. to 8:00 p.m. in the evening. Quiet hours are 11:00 p.m. to 7:00 a.m. The water is warm enough for swimming, even by adults who usually don't go in anymore.

No discharge zone. Gray water okay.

There's a covered fire pit for group get-togethers. For those who wish, a short walk to the pools near the base of Chatterbox Falls will yield a bracing bath/shower followed by a power rinse.

A delightful waterfall-fed pool is hidden in the forest on the north side of the inlet. From the dock you can see a large boulder that marks the spot. Land the dinghy on the small beach just beyond the boulder and walk a few steps to the pool. A bather we met yelped when he jumped in, but a moment later said the water was fine.

No hook-and-line fishing. Princess Louisa Inlet is a rockfish conservation area.

Trapper's Cabin is about a 2-hour very demanding hike from the dock area. The cabin is now completely collapsed. The trail is steep, and often muddy and slippery. We're not kidding about the hike being demanding, serious injuries have occurred.

With a fast boat, Princess Louisa Inlet could be seen in one day. Zoom up for the morning slack at Malibu Rapids, see the sights for a few hours, and zoom out on the afternoon slack. That, however, would be seeing Princess Louisa Inlet but not experiencing it. Something good happens to

people when they're at Princess Louisa Inlet. We suggest at least three days for the trip: one day up 46-mile-long Jervis Inlet; the next day at the park; and the third day back down Jervis Inlet on the morning slack.

Princess Louisa Society. The Princess Louisa Society was formed to buy and preserve the area around Chatterbox Falls for perpetuity. The Society gave the property to B.C. Parks, but maintains an active role in the care of the facilities. Fundraising continues to maintain and develop the facilities at docks and in the area. Annual memberships are $40 U.S or Cdn.; life memberships are $200 U.S. or Cdn. The Society website is www.princesslouisa.bc.ca.

MALASPINA STRAIT TO SARAH POINT

Malaspina Strait, 36 miles long, separates Texada Island from the mainland. Although the strait looks protected from the open water of the Strait of Georgia, storms can create high seas. Especially on an ebb tide, confused seas often build up off the mouth of Jervis Inlet and extend almost to Texada Island. Grief Point, at the north end of Malaspina Strait, is another bad spot in a southeasterly. Other than the mouth of Jervis Inlet, however, Malaspina Strait poses no threat in settled weather.

McRae Cove faces Malaspina Strait, just west of Scotch Fir Point at the mouth of Jervis Inlet. The cove is well protected but shallow. The charts show a straightforward entry between the 27- and 29-meter islands, then along a 36-meter island. Anchoring is in the vicinity of the 36-meter island in 6 feet at zero tide. Don't go much farther in—the bottom shoals quickly.

Westview basin at Powell River

Willingdon Beach in Powell River

㊲ **Beach Gardens Resort & Marina**. 7074 Westminster St., Powell River, BC V8A 1C5; (604) 485-6267; (800) 663-7070; beachgardens@shaw.ca; www.beachgardens.com. Monitors VHF 66A July & August. Reservations accepted. Open all year, moorage, 15 & 30 amp power, water, free Wi-Fi, washrooms, showers, coin laundry, fitness center, indoor pool, ice, well-stocked beer and wine sales store. Gasoline, diesel and lube oil at the fuel dock, seasonal only. This is a breakwater-protected marina with good docks, just south of Grief Point. Deluxe waterfront rooms are available. Kayak and paddle board rentals available.

Beach Gardens Resort features a new building overlooking the marina and fronting the older buildings of the resort. The laundry, beer and wine store, and the excellent Seasider Bistro, (604) 485-0996, are on the bottom level with beautiful views of Malaspina Strait. Check www.theseasider.ca for hours of operation. A market with a coffee bar is within walking distance of the marina. Free shuttle service from the marina to Powell River Town Centre Mall is available in July and August. The city bus stop is a short walk away.

Grief Point. Grief Point marks the northern end of Malaspina Strait on the mainland side. The seas around Grief Point get particularly rough when the wind blows.

㊳ **Westview/Powell River.** There are two main moorage areas at Powell River's Westview area: the North Harbour for permanent moorage located north of the ferry landing with its own entrance; and the working harbour and transient guest moorage facility with an entrance located south of the ferry landing. The guest moorage facility consists of two basins referred to as Westview and South Harbour; these two basins are accessed through the shared south entrance and the floats are used by working vessels and transient pleasure craft. Fuel, water and power are available at the Westview and South Harbour basins; nearby stores have marine supplies. Grocery stores and a major shopping center are a taxi or a free seasonal shuttle from the marina.

The section adjacent to the ferry loading area between the two main moorage areas, north and south, has been redeveloped and now houses the harbor office, new washrooms, showers, and laundry. Access to excellent restaurants, the Willingdon Beach Trail, and the historic "Townsite" district makes Powell River a destination worth visiting.

An excellent stock of marine and fishing supplies is available at nearby Marine Traders chandlery. Shops and a range of restaurants are on the main commercial streets, a short walk away. The Chopping Block, an old-fashioned butcher shop, is at the north end of Marine Avenue. Their meats, seafood, homemade smoked sausage, and cheese are delicious. The Town Centre Mall, with Save-On Foods, Safeway, Shoppers Drug Mart, Walmart, liquor store and other shops, is located some distance away, up a steep hill on Courtenay Street (they call it Cardiac Hill). It's a hike. Another shopping center has a QF grocery store that will deliver to the marina.

The original Powell River townsite is a couple of miles up the road from Westview. Visitors can walk or bicycle along the shoreline through a beautiful forested trail starting at Willingdon Beach on the north end of downtown Powell River. Numerous pieces of historic logging equipment are on display along the Willingdon Beach Trail, serving as a fascinating outdoor museum complete with interpretive signage. For energetic hikers, you can access the old "Townsite" district above the Mill off the end of the trail. Take a taxi for the return trip to Powell River. "Townsite" is the original settlement of Powell River and is a designated National Historic District. Four hundred of the original buildings from the early 1900s remain. Many have been refurbished and are still in use. A row of large

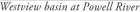

Beach Gardens Resort & Marina

oak trees and grand homes from the era stand proudly overlooking the mill and Malaspina Strait. Several cafes are found in "Townsite" and a brewery offering craft beer samplers.

In Powell River, history buffs may want to visit the small history museum adjacent to Willingdon Beach. The Blackberry Festival is in early August. Check the town's website (www.discoverpowellriver.com) for a schedule of activities.

㊳ Westview Harbour. 6790 Wharf Street, Powell River, BC V8A 1T9; (604) 485-5244; jkinahan@powellriver.ca. Monitors VHF 66A. Open all year, potable water, 30 & 50 amp power, washrooms, large showers, laundry, garbage drop, recycling, waste oil disposal, free Wi-Fi. Pumpout by appointment. Leave the daymark inside the harbor entry to port when entering. Guest moorage is available at both Westview Harbour and South Harbour basins, which share the same south entrance. Westview Fuels is the demarcation between the two moorage areas. First-come, first-served; call ahead for available space.

Westview Harbour floats 5 and 6 are the primary guest moorage floats; effort is made to accommodate most transient boats in Westview, rafting may be required or stern-tie to the main dock. South Harbour (floats 7-11) can accommodate vessels up to 150 feet (20-foot draft at zero tide). A short trail connects the South Harbour basin and the Westview Harbour basin.

Washrooms, showers, and garbage drop are available at both Westview and South Harbour; the newest facilities are located at Westview with the older more basic facilities

at South Harbour.

Two-hour complimentary moorage, call ahead. Free scheduled shuttle to the mall picks up outside the harbor office four times per day during the ten-week season. Schedule is posted at the marina office.

㊳ Westview Fuels. P.O. Box 171, Powell River, BC V8A 4Z6; (604) 485-2867. Monitors VHF 66A. Gasoline, diesel, lubricants, washrooms, and ice. Located between Westview Harbour and South Harbour. Joe and Debbie Hooper are the owners and they're great.

Dinner Rock. Dinner Rock, exposed at all tides, is approximately 0.2 mile off the mainland shore, slightly southeast of Savary Island. In 1998 a 1000-lb. cross was erected on the rock. It is a memorial to the five people who died there in October 1947, when the vessel *Gulf Stream*, proceeding in darkness with rain falling, struck the rock and sank.

Savary Island. Savary Island is a 4-mile-long sandy island that lies approximately east and west, and is served by water taxi from Lund. The island is a favorite destination for Vancouverites. The small public dock on the north shore is for loading and unloading only. Anchorage is good, sand bottom, within easy dinghy distance of shore. Savary Island has no real protected harbor, but the beaches are some of the best in B.C.

In summer months, Riggers a licensed pub-style restaurant, and a small general store are open. From the public dock turn right and follow the road for about one-half mile. Bicycles can be rented nearby. A number of years ago Bob Hale anchored off the north shore for the night and "got away with it." By contrast, Tom Kincaid once anchored overnight in the same area, but by morning the wind had come in from the north and he was on a lee shore. We visited Savary Island recently and anchored in 50-70 feet just off the dock and mooring field. We took the dinghy to shore and explored the island. The gently sloping beach makes landing and mooring the dinghy a challenge. Visiting by water taxi from Lund might be a better idea if you plan to spend the day there.

Nearby **Hernando Island** is surrounded by rocky shallows, and is seldom visited by cruising boats. Renowned authors Lin and Larry Pardey, however, report excellent anchorage with protection from southeast winds in Stag Bay, northwest of the pier. Anchor in 18 to 24 feet on a firm sand bottom.

Mitlenatch Island. Roughly west of Hernando Island, Mitlenatch Island appears to be an uninviting rock out in the middle of the Strait of Georgia. It is in fact a thriving and ruggedly beautiful wildlife refuge, with a small, protected anchorage on its east side. Park volunteers spend a week in turn each year on the island doing trail maintenance and guiding tours. Visitors are asked to stay on the trails to avoid disturbing birds. Those who visit will be rewarded, as this note from Correspondents John and Lorraine Littlewood suggests:

"If you can get there on a calm clear day in September, you'll see an incredible variety of wildlife, from Goshawks to huge sea lions. An additional benefit is water so clear that we could actually watch our Bruce anchor deploy. It hit the bottom in about 20 feet, flipped over, bit, and buried itself. This was on only 2:1 scope, although we later paid out to our normal 3:1."

We thank reader Sharl Heller for increasing our awareness of Mitlenatch Island.

㊴ Lund. Lund is the north end of the Pacific Coastal Highway, the road that leads all the way to the tip of South America. Lund is a busy place in the summer, a jumping-off point for Desolation Sound with fuel, provisions, and pumpout.

The historic Lund Hotel, with restaurant and pub, is at the head of the fuel dock. The small but well-stocked store, in the same building as the hotel, has a good deli, fresh (often local) vegetables, ice cream, frozen meats, liquor agency with good wine and beer selection, pet supplies, prawn bait, frozen herring, camping and picnic supplies, and more.

Lund is the mainland's closest launch site to Desolation Sound. Long-term auto, trailer and tow vehicle parking available. Lund Auto & Outboard is a few blocks away. Nancy's Bakery is in the modern, larger building overlooking the public docks. Nancy's pastries, pizzas, and other specialties are famous. Nancy's also has good Wi-Fi. Upstairs

Westview Harbour

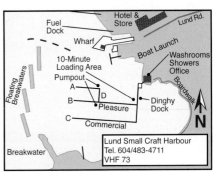

Lund Small Craft Harbour

Nancy's Bakery above the harbour at Lund

from Nancy's is Pollen Sweaters, specializing in locally made sweaters, and Terracentric Adventures, a kayak tour operator.

The town assumed operation of the public docks following divestiture by the federal government several years ago. With commercial fishing in decline, the docks and shoreside facilities were upgraded to make them more inviting to visiting pleasure craft. Rafting may be required. When the docks are full, you can moor along the inside of the breakwater and dinghy to the dinghy dock. There's a good launch ramp, and modern public washrooms with excellent showers.

Over on the north side of the bay a public float, with no access to shore, is in the middle of Finn Cove.

Fuel: The busy Lund Hotel fuel dock has gasoline and diesel.

Garbage: During the season a truck at the top of the boat launch will take your garbage for a fee. Recycling is available behind the hotel.

Haulout: Jack's Boatyard in Finn Cove has a repair yard, haulout to 50 tons and boat storage.

About Finn Cove: Sailing Directions and the charts call it Finn Cove, but the locals

call it Finn Bay. The road that leads from the village to the cove is named Finn Bay Road. The Waggoner will call it Finn Cove, however, to be consistent with the charts. No anchoring in Finn Cove.

㊴ **Lund Small Craft Harbour.** P.O. Box 78, Lund, BC V0N 2G0; (604) 483-4711 or (604) 414-0474; lundharbour-wharfinger@ twincomm.ca; www.lundharbourbc. wordpress.com. Monitors VHF 73. Open all year, more than 1700 feet of breakwater-protected dock space, 20, 30 & some 50 amp power. The harbor has one of the only pumpout stations in the area. Garbage drop, $3 to $6 per bag, is above the fuel dock; off-season, use the garbage drop at the general store. No oil disposal. Excellent washrooms and showers. Wide concrete launch ramp with 4 lanes, good for most launchings down to about 5 feet above zero tide, some say 3 feet.

Enter north of the floating breakwaters. The northern dock located inside the breakwater is reserved for pleasure craft, rafting required. Don't give up if the docks appear full. Office hours are 8:00 a.m. to 11:00 a.m. and 3:00 p.m. to 5:00 p.m. October to May, 8:00 a.m. to 5:00 p.m. June and September, 8:00 a.m. to 8:00 p.m. July 1 to Labour Day. Moorage is free for the first hour, 1 to 3 hours are charged at the half-day rate. Radio ahead for a slip assignment when near the entrance, even for short stays.

The floating concrete breakwater noted

above (no power or water) protects the inner docks. You can tie inside of these floats and dinghy to the marked dinghy dock area below the ramp. Overnight moorage is charged on the breakwater.

The area near the launch ramps had a green buoy to mark a shallow spot for years. It has been removed. Local knowledge says to be aware of a high spot there, about 4 feet at its shallowest.

㊴ **Lund Hotel.** 1436 Highway 101, Lund, BC V0N 2G0; (604) 414-0474; (877) 569-3999; info@lundhotel.com; www.lundhotel.com. Open year-round; An 80-foot dock provides limited overnight moorage on a first-come, first-serve basis. Free moorage for hotel guests. Free Wi-Fi. The laundry facility is clean, with good machines. The store and deli are well stocked. The fuel dock has gasoline, diesel, and lubricants.

The historic hotel, which dates back to 1905, has been restored and remodeled with a pub and separate dining area. The hotel has 31 rooms, all renovated in 2018, ranging from budget-sensitive to four "boutique superior oceanfront" rooms overlooking the water. Rooms feature unique hand-painted murals. The hotel, pub, general store, and fuel dock are under the ownership of the Tla'amin Nation. Tug Guhm Gallery & Studio, well known for lifelike seal heads carved from a single block of stone, is in the lower part of the hotel.

㊴ **Lund Water Taxi.** (604) 483-9749. Scheduled service to Savary Island. Can deliver parts or people to Desolation Sound and surrounding areas.

㊴ **End Of The Road Parking.** P.O. Box 94, 1440 Lund Rd., Lund BC V0N 2G0; (604) 483-3667. Daily and long-term vehicle and trailer parking in secure lots off-site.

㊴ **Lund Automotive & Outboard Ltd.** 1520 Lund Hwy, Lund, BC V0N 2G0; (604) 483-4612. Long-term tow vehicle and trailer parking in secure lots. Call ahead for reservations. Mechanics are on staff for mechanical and electrical repairs and they are an authorized service facility for several engine brands. Haulout to 30 feet.

㊴ **Jack's Boatyard (Finn Cove).** 9907 Finn Bay Road, P.O. Box 198, Lund, BC V0N 2G0; (604) 483-3566; info@jacksboatyard.ca; www.jacksboatyard.ca. Haulout to 50 tons, storage available. Can haul sailboats. Washrooms, showers, laundry, supply store, garbage and recycling drop, Wi-Fi in the boatyard well above the water. Owner Jack Elsworth blasted the boat storage yard out of solid rock and welded up the darndest haulout machine imaginable. Think Travelift, then make it completely different. You have to see it to understand.

In 2013, they added the structure to support a 50-ton Travelift, and a lower yard was cleared to allow for blocking four or more medium to large boats. The old lift is used to haul boats to 30 tons up the hill to the expansive upper yard. Since Quarterdeck Boatyard in Port Hardy closed in 2014, Jack's lifts and the lift in Campbell River are the only lifts until Shearwater, some 200 miles north.

Copeland Islands. The Copeland Islands (locally known as the Ragged Islands) are a provincial park. Anchorage is possible in several nooks and coves among the islands, although some of the coves are exposed to wakes from boats transiting Thulin Passage. Because of remnants of booming cable on the bottom, a buoyed trip line to the anchor crown is a good idea. Check your swing when you anchor. 19 stern-tie pins, with chains, were installed by BC Parks and the BC Marine Parks Forever Society in 2018,

making it easier for boaters to visit the Copeland Islands. Please watch your wake in Thulin Passage. There are environmentally sensitive areas in the Copeland Islands.

Sharpe's Landing. A private marina with no facilities for transient boaters is in a small bay on the north end and east side of Thulin Passage. Please watch your wake as you go by.

㊵ **Bliss Landing Estates.** (604) 414-9417; (604) 483-8098; bliss@twincomm.ca. Located in Turner Bay, north of Lund. Open May through October. First-come, first-served guest moorage for boats under 60 feet. The docks belong to the development. Transient moorage is in unoccupied slips or side-tie at the south side of the southerly docks. Washrooms, showers, laundry, 30 & 50 amp power, water, free Wi-Fi. Docks are exposed to westerly winds; moor bow-out. It's about a 15-minute dinghy ride to Lund.

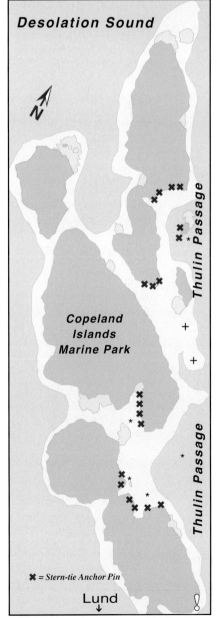

Copeland Islands Stern-tie Anchor Pins

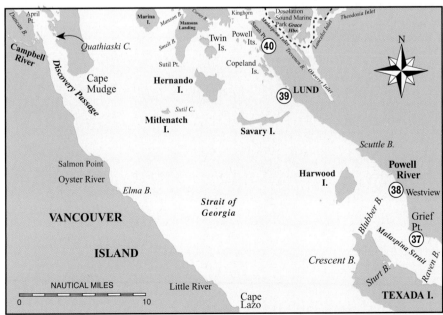

Powell River & Lund

THROUGH THE RAPIDS THE HISTORY OF PRINCESS LOUISA INLET - *By Charles William Hitz*

Publisher: Sitka Publishing; ISBN: 0-9720255-0-2

Chatterbox Falls in Princess Louisa Inlet is one of those special destinations on the must-see list. Some boaters come to the Inlet on an annual basis, passing through Malibu Rapids, snapping photos of the Young Life Christian camp, known previously as the Malibu Club of the rich and famous. Prior to the Malibu Club of the 1940's, early settlers staked land claims in the Inlet, built their cabins, and lived off the land. Author Charles W. Hitz details the fascinating history of the Inlet, including its geology, early maritime explorers, lives of former settlers, and the creation of the Malibu Club and eventual transformation into the Malibu Young Life Camp.

After the initial survey conducted by Captain Richards and the crew of the HMS Plumper in 1860, settlers later followed. Charles R. Johnstone was the first recorded settler, filing a pre-emption claim in 1910 near today's MacDonald Island. Sadly, one of his eight children, Ivan, died of the flu epidemic of 1918 and is buried at the entrance to Princess Louisa Inlet. The family adopted the natives' way of living and traveled by dugout canoe. Another settler, Steve Casper, was of German descent and settled in the Inlet around the early 1930's. A German firm had set up business in Sechelt, where many Germans decided to stay; the area became a haven for German refugees during WWI.

James F. MacDonald (Mac) was a friend to Casper, as well as with many Pacific Northwest boaters. Mac finished high school on Bainbridge Island in 1908, and then traveled the world. After serving in the Army, acquiring the rank of Captain, Mac cruised with his uncle's yacht to Princess Louisa Inlet. In 1927, Mac made a claim for crown grant property at the head of the Inlet; and in 1928, started building his cabin near the falls, which he named Chatterbox Falls. Mac had the comforts of hot water and electricity thanks to a generator creating electricity via a hydro water wheel. Mac's cabin was completed in 1930, but was later destroyed by fire in 1941. He then lived on a float, called the Seaholm, near the falls where he spent the summer months. Mac strongly felt that Princess Louisa Inlet should be protected from further commercial development; and upon hearing the plans to build the Malibu Club, he enlisted the help of Pacific Northwest boaters to create the Princess Louisa International Society, a non-profit organization dedicated to protecting the Inlet for all to enjoy. In October of 1953, Mac deeded his property to the Society. The Society was also to maintain the moorage floats around the falls. Seeking further assistance from the Province of British Columbia, Mac's land was transferred to the Government's Ministry of Parks in 1964 with the stipulation that the area be a public recreation area. The Society and Parks were able to obtain the land known as the 'Foreshore,' the flat land in front of Hamilton Island, near where the Johnstone's had first settled. The island was later renamed MacDonald Island.

The creation of the Malibu Club began when Tom Hamilton and his family were on vacation cruising in British Columbia on their yacht, the *Malibu*. They were moored at Campbell River next to Bill Boeing's yacht, the *Taconite*. Bill Boeing suggested they cruise to Princess Louisa Inlet, a must see before returning home. Taking the advice, Hamilton visited the Inlet, and his wife fell in love with its beauty. In 1940, Hamilton purchased the island from Mac, naming the island, Hamilton Island. In June of 1941, Tom Hamilton purchased land surrounding the Inlet in the Sechelt Forest Reserve from the Canadian Government, which made up nearly the entire Inlet with the exception of MacDonald's property

at Chatterbox Falls. Hamilton envisioned an exclusive resort for the Inlet and began construction on the finger of rock at the entrance to Princess Louisa. He built lodges, cabins, a boathouse, library, and dining hall. Artists were hired to add aesthetics such as native carvings and totem poles. Brochures and advertisements were sent to boating magazines and other publications, attracting the rich and famous, including movie stars and musicians.

Born in Seattle, Tom Hamilton had made his money in the aviation industry. In 1911, he began the construction of several unique seaplane designs. Then in 1914, as the Boeing Company was starting up, Tom Hamilton moved his operation to Vancouver BC to build trainers in preparation of WWI. The U.S. military also took an interest in Tom, bringing him to Milwaukee, Wisconsin to construct propellers and sea plane pontoons, eventually starting his own company. In 1927, he produced one of the first all-metal aircraft, called the Hamilton Metalplane H-18, christened the *Maiden Milwaukee*. Tom had always been a boating enthusiast, having grown up in Seattle on the shores of Lake Washington. It was in 1940 that he turned his attention to Princess Louisa Inlet.

The saddest chapter for the Malibu Club came when Hamilton abandoned the resort in 1950. Pots and pans remained in the kitchen, the tables were still set, and supplies were untouched. To learn why the resort was abandoned, and how Jim Rayburn, founder of the Young Life organization came to purchase and refurbish the property, don't miss reading Charles Hitz book, *Through the Rapids, The History of Princess Louisa Inlet*. Readers will also enjoy learning about the classic yachts and special aircraft that visited the Inlet over the years.

The Crowded Inner Harbor of Malibu (1948)

◄ 123 ►

Desolation Sound & Discovery Passage

CHAPTER 10

DESOLATION SOUND
Prideaux Haven • Homfray Lodge
Pendrell Sound • Refuge Cove • Teakerne Arm
Toba Inlet

CORTES ISLAND
Squirrel Cove • Cortes Bay • Von Donop Inlet
Gorge Harbour

QUADRA ISLAND
Rebecca Spit • Heriot Bay • Octopus Islands
Okisollo Channel

DISCOVERY PASSAGE
Campbell River • April Point • Brown Bay
Small Inlet

Captain George Vancouver had it all wrong when he explored and wrote about this area during his cruise in 1792. He named it Desolation Sound, saying, "there was not a single prospect that was pleasing to the eye." Granted, his crew did have a challenging time with weather, fleas, and even shellfish poisoning. In reality, Desolation Sound, located today literally just beyond the end of the road, is a place of extraordinary beauty. It's one of the Northwest's most dreamed-about and sought-after cruising destinations.

Officially, Desolation Sound is the body of water north of Sarah Point and Mary Point, and south of West Redonda Island. When most people think of cruising these waters they consider Desolation Sound to include the entire area north of Cape Mudge and Sarah Point, and south of Yuculta Rapids and Chatham Point, including Discovery Passage (Campbell River).

For those departing from the Seattle or Vancouver areas, the trip to or from Desolation Sound might take as long as a week, depending on boat speed, weather, and stops along the way.

Desolation Sound is not a huge area. Even slow boats can go from one end to another in a day. But Desolation Sound offers a wilderness setting, generally easy waters, many bays and coves to explore and anchor in, and marinas where fuel and supplies are available. On the west side of these cruising grounds, Campbell River on Vancouver Island is a vibrant small city. Campbell River has complete supplies and even a boatyard for haulout and repairs. Lund, on the B.C. mainland, is at the eastern entry to Desolation Sound. Lund is a quaint, small village that has several services vacationing boaters are apt to need, including a nearby boatyard and lift. Lund also is the northern terminus of Highway 99, a road that extends to Tierra del Fuego on the tip of South America. Small marinas scattered throughout Desolation Sound offer fuel, water, and limited supplies.

Since it is close to the point where the tidal currents meet on the inside of Vancouver Island, the water in Desolation Sound is not regularly exchanged with cold ocean water. During the summer, water temperatures of 70° to 80°F are not unusual in some of the bays, making for comfortable swimming.

Okeover Harbour Authority docks

Navigation is straightforward, with few hazards in the major channels. Closer to shore it's a different story, but the rocks and reefs are charted.

The most popular time to cruise Desolation Sound is from mid-July through the end of August, when the prospects for sunny, warm weather are best. It's also when the anchorages and facilities are most crowded. June weather can be cool and rainy, but crowds are not a problem. It's then that the waterfalls are most awesome and the resorts and businesses, while open and stocked, are the least harried.

If your calendar permits, the very best time to cruise Desolation Sound might be early- to mid-September. By then the high-season crowds have departed, yet summer usually hangs on for a last and glorious finale. Stock in the stores may be thin and the young summertime help has headed back to school, but the low slanting sunlight paints the hills and mountains with new drama, and the first colors of autumn make each day a fresh experience. Watch the weather closely. Leave before the fall storm pattern begins, although usually that's not before October.

Navigation Note: Tide information for locations in Desolation Sound is shown in Ports and Passes and Canadian Tide and Current Tables, Vol. 5 (they are shown as secondary ports based on Point Atkinson Tides). Currents for Beazley Passage, Hole in the Wall, and Discovery Passage are shown in Vol. 6 and Ports and Passes as are corrections for Upper Rapids and Lower Rapids in Okisollo Channel. Owen Bay tides and Okisollo Channel secondary port tide corrections also are in Vol. 6 and Ports and Passes.

Sarah Point. For boats running north through Thulin Passage, Sarah Point, at the tip of the Malaspina Peninsula, is the dramatic entrance to Desolation Sound. The high hills of the Malaspina Peninsula hide the Coast Range mountains. But on a clear day, once Sarah Point is cleared, the mountains come into magnificent view.

MALASPINA INLET

Malaspina Inlet, Okeover Inlet, Lancelot Inlet and Theodosia Inlet all are entered between Zephine Head and Myrmidon Point. On a spring flood tide you will most likely find current at the mouth of Malaspina Inlet, all the way to Grace Harbour. Much of Gifford Peninsula, to the east of Malaspina Inlet, is Desolation Sound Marine Park. Several good anchorages are in this area. You'll also find rocks and reefs, most of them covered in kelp in summer and easily identified. They'll keep you alert, though.

Aquaculture occupies several otherwise inviting anchorages, but there are still plenty of choices in this area. Many of the aquaculture sites indicated on charts are no longer active, but debris left behind can foul ground tackle.

Malaspina Inlet is popular with kayakers. Be mindful of your wake.

① **Grace Harbour.** Grace Harbour is a popular anchorage. The inner bay is surrounded by forest and almost completely landlocked, with anchorage for quite a few boats. Many of the anchorages are along the shore, so be prepared to run a stern-tie. In 2018 BC Parks and the BC Parks Forever Society added 10 stern-tie pins, with chains, for a total of 16 stern-ties in the harbour. A fire pit is in a little park-like area at the north end. A rock, shown on the charts, is in the middle of this innermost bay. The anchor just skids across the rock before finding holding ground on the other side. On a crowded summer weekend, the empty spot in the middle is there for a reason.

Cochrane Bay. Located on the west side of Malaspina Inlet, Cochrane Bay along with the two small islands in front of the bay, are within the Desolation Sound Marine Park. The only safe entrance into the bay is from the south. Field Correspondent Deane Hislop

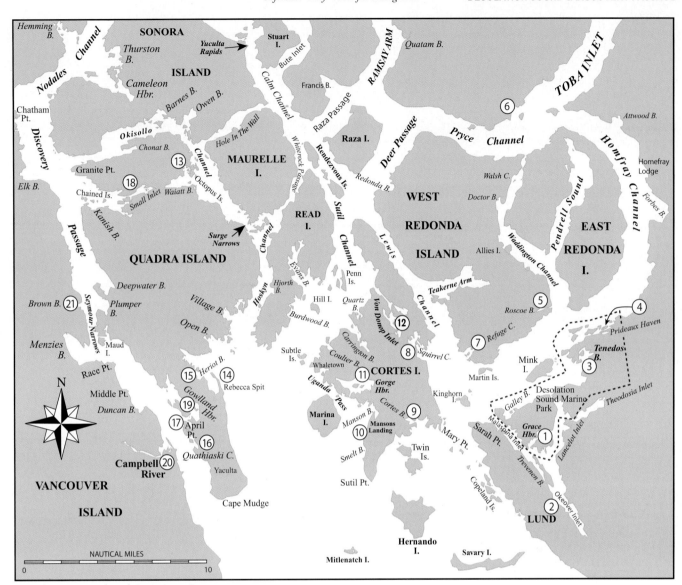

Desolation Sound and Discovery Passage

reports that there appears to be an entrance on the north side, but it's not safe due to uncharted rocks that lie below the surface. Set the hook in 35 feet of water over a sand and gravel bottom. A short trail on the western shore of the bay leads to the Sunshine Coast Trail system.

Trevenen Bay. The head of Trevenen Bay looks like a good anchorage on the chart, but the bay is largely taken by aquaculture.

Penrose Bay. Anchorage at the head of the bay. The Okeover Harbour Authority docks are on the west shore to the south.

② **Okeover Harbour Authority.** Okeover Inlet borders the Desolation Sound Marine Park area. The Okeover Harbour Authority docks are located on the western shore of Okeover Inlet a short distance south of Penrose Bay with road access to Lund. Oysters and other seafoods are grown in several places along beautiful Okeover Inlet.

The docks at Okeover are managed by the Okeover Harbour Authority (604) 483-

3258, contact via VHF 66A. Docks located behind the L-shaped breakwater are for local working boats. The large outer breakwater (440 feet each side) provides plenty of space for transient moorage, no power, no water; the seaward side of the breakwater is exposed to northerly winds. Moorage is on a first-come, first-serve basis; payment made to wharfinger or fill out the self-registration envelope and deposit at the office door-drop. Office located on the wharf is open 12:30 p.m.-6:30 p.m. daily during the summer months, hours vary during the off-season. Launch ramp on-site.

The Laughing Oyster Restaurant (604) 483-9775 is located above the docks. It is an excellent restaurant with outstanding cuisine, lovely surroundings and a stunning view. Reservations recommended. It's one of those gems not to be missed.

Lancelot Inlet. Isabel Bay in Lancelot Inlet is popular. The best anchorage is behind Madge Islands, with a beautiful view and room for one or two boats among the large rock formations. Good anchorage is also in Thors Cove. The bay is deep, except in nooks or close to shore.

Correspondent Pat Shera, from Victoria, wrote to tell us that in Isabel Bay he fouled his anchor on a section of bulldozer track at the head of the anchorage, just west of the north tip of Madge Island. If you have Chartbook 3312, it's where the 4.2-meter sounding is shown. He says another section of track was high and dry on a nearby rock.

Theodosia Inlet. Theodosia Inlet has a narrow, shallow, and kelp-choked entrance, but is navigable by most boats at all stages of the tide. Once inside, the bay opens up. Logging activity takes away from the remote feeling of the bay. Boomed logs can occupy much of the shoreline. Anchorage is in a number of gunkholes along the shoreline.

MINK ISLAND AREA

Galley Bay. Galley Bay is just east of Zephine Head. It is a good anchorage, particularly in the eastern end. In 2018, 9 stern-tie pins, with chain, were installed in the area by BC Parks and the BC Parks Forever Society.

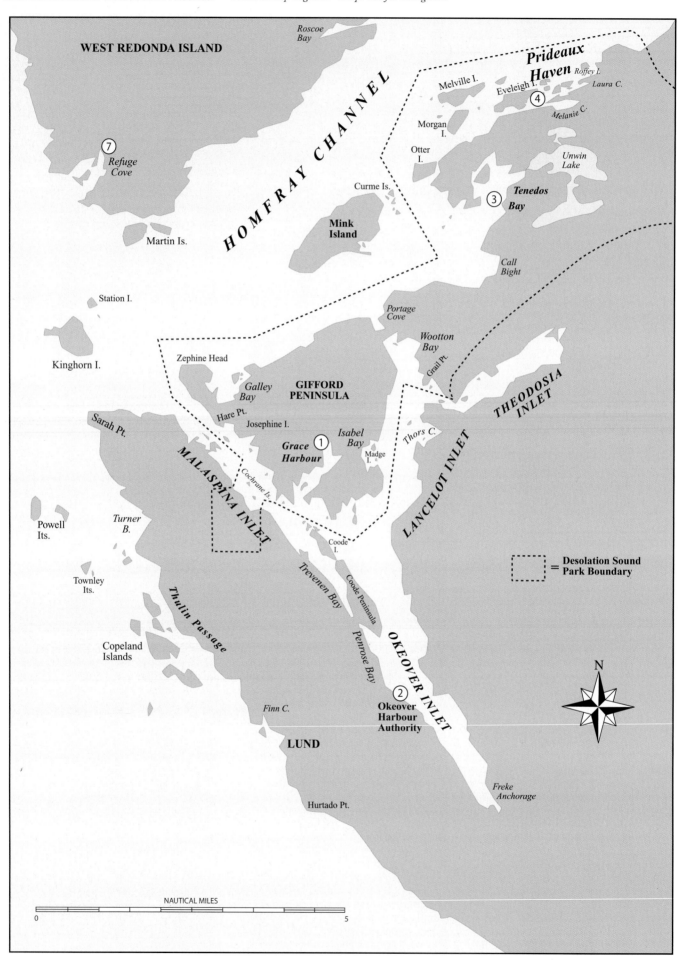

WEST REDONDA ISLAND

Roscoe Bay

Prideaux Haven

Melville I.

Eveleigh I. ④ Roffey I.

Laura C.

Morgan I.

Melanie C.

Otter I.

Unwin Lake

⑦ *Refuge Cove*

Curme Is.

③ *Tenedos Bay*

H O M F R A Y   C H A N N E L

Mink Island

Call Bight

Martin Is.

Station I.

Portage Cove

Wootton Bay

Grail Pt.

Kinghorn I.

Zephine Head

Galley Bay

GIFFORD PENINSULA

T H E O D O S I A   I N L E T

Hare Pt.

Josephine I.

Isabel Bay

Thors C.

Sarah Pt.

Grace Harbour ①

Madge I.

L A N C E L O T   I N L E T

M A L A S P I N A   I N L E T

Cochrane Is.

Turner B.

Powell Its.

Coode I.

= **Desolation Sound Park Boundary**

Townley Its.

Trevenen Bay

Coode Peninsula

Penrose Bay

Thulin Passage

O K E O V E R   I N L E T

N

Copeland Islands

Finn C.

② **Okeover Harbour Authority**

LUND

Freke Anchorage

Hurtado Pt.

NAUTICAL MILES

0   5

302

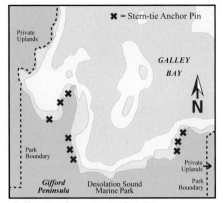

Galley Bay Stern-tie Anchor Pins

Exploring the rocky shores of Prideaux Haven

Mink Island. Mink Island is private property, but you'll find excellent anchorage in the bay that indents the southeast shore, particularly if you work in behind the little island in the center of the bay. You'll probably run a stern-tie to shore.

Curme Islands. Wolferstan describes navigation in the Curme Islands, east of Mink Island, as "challenging." Bailey and Cummings, in their *Gunkholing* book (now out of print), described the Curme Islands as extremely tight with shallow waterways, but with anchoring possibilities if the boat uses 4-way ties to hold position. For most people, dinghies and kayaks are probably the way to go.

③ **Tenedos Bay.** Tenedos Bay (also called Deep Bay) is a favorite, for a couple of reasons. First, it's a good, protected anchorage, with a landlocked basin behind the island off the northwest shore. This island is joined with

the mainland by a drying shoal, shown on the charts. Second, it's just a short dinghy ride to the mouth of the stream that runs from Unwin Lake, a popular freshwater swimming hole. A path beside the stream leads to the lake. Several of the stream's pools, screened by vegetation, make good bathing places.

In addition to the landlocked basin noted above, you'll find anchorages in coves along the shore of Tenedos Bay. 14 stern-tie pins, with chain, are located around the bay; installed by BC Parks and the BC Parks Forever Society. The center of Tenedos Bay is too deep (300 to 600 feet) for anchoring.

Caution: As you enter Tenedos Bay, a nasty rock lies submerged off the south side of Bold Head. Especially if you are headed to or from Refuge Cove, Mink Island, or around Bold Head to Prideaux Haven, this rock is right on your probable course. The rock lies farther offshore than you might expect. Give it an extra wide berth, just to be sure. Remember to study your charts before proceeding in these

waters. A number of rocks are shown. All are easy to avoid if you are aware of them.

Otter Island. A very narrow but navigable channel runs between Otter Island and the mainland. Ample space for a few boats to anchor on the north side, using stern-ties to shore.

PRIDEAUX HAVEN AREA

The coves that make up the area generally known as Prideaux Haven are the most popular spots in Desolation Sound, with several requiring stern-ties to increase the number of boats accommodated. The area is described in great detail by M. Wylie Blanchet in her classic book, *The Curve of Time.*

At the head of Melanie Cove you can find the remains of Mike's place, and in Laura Cove traces of old Phil Lavine's cabin site are visible (both from *The Curve of Time*). The evidence, however, is getting pretty faint.

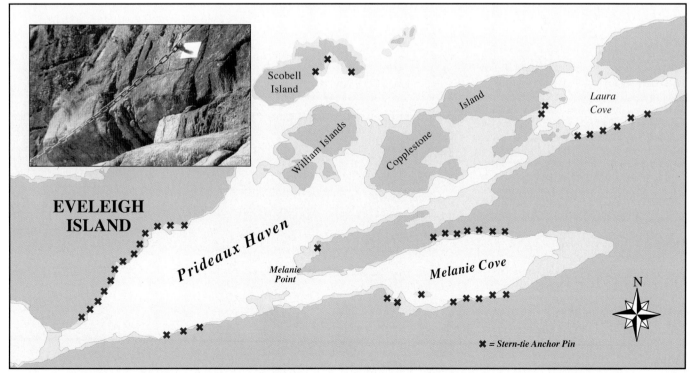

Prideaux Haven Stern-tie Anchor Pins

The entire clutch of islands and shallow waterways invites exploration by dinghy or kayak. The narrow pass between Scobell Island and the William Islands, for instance, is beautiful. During high season, the only thing missing is solitude. You'll have lots of company. There is some cell phone reception in the area, including Prideaux Haven.

No Discharge Zone. Gray water okay.

Eveleigh Island. Anchorage is in Eveleigh Anchorage, the western cove behind Eveleigh Island. A drying reef connects Eveleigh Island with the mainland. Entry to the other Prideaux Haven anchorages is around the east end of Eveleigh Island. A reef almost, but not quite, closes this entrance. Use Chart 3555 (recommended) or Chartbook 3312. Smaller scale Chart 3538 (1:40,000) shows the entry but with too little detail to inspire confidence. After rounding Lucy Point, strongly favor the Eveleigh Island side of the passage to clear the reef.

④ **Prideaux Haven.** Boaters will find numerous stern-tie installations throughout the Prideaux Haven area including: along the southeast shore of Eveleigh Island; along the southeast shore of Scobell Island; on the north and south shores of Melanie Cove; and on the south and west shores of Laura Cove.

No Discharge Zone. Gray water okay.

④ **Melanie Cove.** Melanie Cove is perfectly protected, with ample room along both shores for boats to anchor and stern-tie. 7 stern-ties were installed along the north shore in 2017 and 8 stern-ties installed along the south shore in 2018 as part of the BC Parks and BC Parks Forever Society stern-tie project. A few boats can anchor in the middle without a stern-tie. An overgrown apple orchard and the site of Mike's cabin, warmly described in *The Curve of Time*, are at the head of the cove. A small creek on the south shore, near the head, has a flowing hose. The water is untreated, and not recommended for human consumption.

Correspondent Gil Flanagan tells us a trail runs between Melanie Cove and Unwin Lake, with a new section that bypasses an earlier hand-over-hand section. He says the first half-mile is easy, and has a nice view at the end.

④ **Laura Cove.** Laura Cove has a fairly narrow entrance, with a least depth of approximately 10 feet at zero tide. Rocks extend from both sides. Enter cautiously. Once you're inside, the bay is beautiful. A few cherry trees and English Ivy mark Old Phil, the Frenchman's cabin site mentioned in *The Curve of Time,* at the head of this bay. Anchorage is to the east of Copplestone Point. The west end of the cove is a maze of rocks and reefs. In 2018, 6 stern-tie pins were installed along the south shore and 2 stern-tie pins on the northwest end of the cove by BC Parks and the BC Parks Forever Society.

Roffey Island. If you can't find a place at Prideaux Haven, Melanie Cove, or Laura

Cove, try the little bay behind Roffey Island. Room for one or more boats away from the crowd.

Homfray Channel. Homfray Channel curves from the south end of West Redonda Island and around East Redonda Island, until it merges with Toba Inlet. The only bays of consequence are Forbes Bay and Atwood Bay. The center of Atwood Bay is too deep for convenient anchoring, though we've successfully anchored in the nook indenting the north shore. Bob Stephenson, the former owner of Desolation Sound Yacht Charters, says Forbes Bay can be good for anchoring.

In Bill Wolferstan's book, *Desolation Sound and the Discovery Islands*, he tells of two Native pictographs on the west shore of Homfray Channel—one of a single fish, the other unidentified. Actually, there are several pictographs located about 10 feet above the high water line located across the channel from Lloyd Point.

Homfray Lodge. (604) 566-8026 or (844) 504-1391; info@homfraylodge.com; www.homfraylodge.com; VHF 66A. Office hours 9:00 a.m. to 5:00 p.m. Monday-Friday. Located just north of Forbes Bay. Beautiful and remote location with 250 feet of moorage and two mooring buoys. Moorage is for guests who have booked overnight stays at the lodge or in one of the cabins. Potable water, showers; Wi-Fi at the lodge. No power or food service. Guests can sit on the covered porch and enjoy a beautiful view up the channel. Fishing and sightseeing charters can be arranged. Reservations recommended during the high season.

WADDINGTON CHANNEL

⑤ **Roscoe Bay/Roscoe Bay Marine Park**. Roscoe Bay, on West Redonda Island where Waddington Channel meets Homfray Channel, is an excellent, protected, and popular anchorage. The bay is divided into an inner cove and an outer cove, separated by a drying shoal easily crossed by shallow draft

boats at half tide or better. If in doubt, go in on a rising tide. At high tide most sailboats can get in. 12 stern-tie pins, with chains, were added in 2018 by BC Parks and the BC Parks Forever Society for a total of 22 stern-ties in Roscoe Bay.

The inner cove is pretty, and except for the other boats enjoying the bay with you, it's a good example of what cruising in these waters is all about. Dinghy ashore and take the short hike up to the knob dividing the two bays.

At the head of the inner cove an old logging road with a short stream beside it connects with Black Lake. During summer months, the water in Black Lake is warm and excellent for swimming or bathing. Trout fishing is reportedly good. If you carry your dinghy up the road, you can launch it along the lake's shoreline.

On the west side of Roscoe Bay a large red float (a "scotsman") hangs in a tree marking the beginning of a trail to the top of a 2200-foot-high mountain. A rock cairn has been built at the summit, and on the cairn is a bottle with pencil and paper inside. Write your name on the paper and add it to the collection. The hike is demanding and a round trip takes several hours, so use your judgment.

No Discharge Zone. Gray water okay.

LOCAL KNOWLEDGE

SPEED LIMIT: Seed oyster growers in Pendrell Sound ask for a 4-knot speed limit in the vicinity of their operations to prevent damage.

Pendrell Sound. With summer water temperatures dependably in excess of 68°F, Pendrell Sound has been called the "warmest saltwater north of Mexico." Major oyster culture operations are in the sound, providing seed oysters to growers all along the coast.

Strings of cultch material (often empty oyster shells) are suspended from floats in the bay until the oyster spat adheres to them, at which point they are shipped.

Roscoe Bay is a scenic and popular anchorage. A lake is a short walk from the head of the bay, seen in this photo.

The favored anchorage is at the head of Pendrell Sound, probably stern-tied to trees ashore. Wear good shoes and sturdy gloves when you're clambering around on the rocks.

Another anchorage is on the western shore, about three-quarters of the way up the sound, tucked in behind a small islet at the outfall from a saltwater lagoon. "We tried this anchorage in deteriorating weather a few years ago, but found the best spots close to the islet taken. With nightfall approaching and conditions worsening, we got creative. The charts show the shore on the north edge of this cove as reefs, but we found a nice opening, perhaps 50 feet wide, between two fingers of reef. We were able to set the anchor in front of the opening and back in. A long stern-tie was run to rocks on shore. It took several changes in the stern-tie termination point to align the boat just right, but once done, the anchorage was snug and safe for the night—a windy night filled with rain, thunder and lightning." [*Hale*]

Elworthy Island. A delightful cozy anchorage lies behind Elworthy Island, a mile north of Church Point, roughly across Waddington Channel from the entrance to Pendrell Sound. The aquaculture noted on charts no longer is present. The island is called Alfred Island by Wolferstan, but in 1992 it was renamed Elworthy Island for seaman Richard Elworthy, who died serving freedom in 1942. A handsome plaque is set into rock on the northeast corner of the island. Enter

the anchorage from either end, but watch for a drying rock near the north entrance. The south entrance shallows to about 12 feet. The island's shoreline is covered with oysters.

Allies Island. Allies Island is connected to West Redonda Island by a drying reef. The north cove is pretty well choked with aquaculture; anchorage is possible in the south cove. The south cove offers a secluded anchorage for 1 to 3 boats and is exposed to the southeast. The rocks around the cove are full of oysters.

Doctor Bay. Doctor Bay is mostly filled with aquaculture. Correspondent Fred Triggs reports good anchorage in 35-40 feet north of the aquaculture operation. We've also heard reports that the aquaculture operation allows pleasure boats to tie up to some floats; check with an employee for instructions.

Walsh Cove Marine Park. Walsh Cove Marine Park is a beautiful little spot with room for several boats to stern-tie along the rocky shore. 15 stern-tie pins, with chain, were installed in 2018 by BC Parks and the BC Parks Forever Society. See Walsh Cove reference map for locations. Enter Walsh Cove from the south. At the north end of the cove, a rock-strewn reef connects Gorges Island to West Redonda Island. The middle of the cove is deep. The cove is well protected from down-channel winds but open to up-channel winds from the south. Two sets of Native pictographs are at Butler Point.

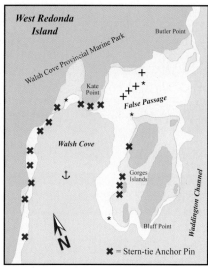

Walsh Cove Stern-tie Anchor Pins

⑥ **Toba Wilderness Marina.** (250) 830-2269; inquiries@tobawilderness.com; www.tobawilderness.com. Contact VHF 66A ahead of time for tie-up instructions upon approach. Reservations highly recommended during July and August. This is a quiet marina, located behind Double Island at the mouth of Toba Inlet. The views up Toba Inlet are breathtaking. The marina has 1400 feet of moorage, on concrete floats, for vessels up to 200 feet; cash payment. No requirement for rafting. Enjoy the attractive Welcome House located upland for afternoon and evening get-

Refuge Cove Store has food, supplies, and a selection of marine hardware.

togethers. 5 km of hiking trails, Wi-Fi, free ice, washroom, showers, and garbage drop-off (1 bag only per day with overnight moorage). Abundant clean clear water is available on the dock, with 30 and 50 amp power. Scheduled float plane service available through Kenmore Air, NW Seaplanes, and Corilair. Secure long-term moorage and boat watch available. Please do not go into the water while hiking to the base of the falls, as this is the source of the marina's drinking water. This marina is not setup for day visits or tours. Overnight guests only please. Anchoring in the bay adjacent to the dock is not recommended.

Toba Inlet. Toba Inlet extends 20 miles into the 8,000-foot-high Coast Range mountains until it ends in drying flats at the mouth of the Toba River. The water is very deep right up to the rock wall shores. Look for two Native pictographs in Toba Inlet: one along the west shore 1 mile south of Brem Bay and another on the north shore 3.6 miles east of Brem Bay. Magnificent waterfalls crash into the sea, especially early in the season when the snowpack is rapidly melting. Toba Inlet reminds us of the inlets north of Cape Caution. Limited anchorage is possible at the head of the inlet, and in Brem Bay off the mouth of the Brem River. We observed a boat stern-tied in a small bight off the north shore near a river inlet at approximately 50°26'N/124°32'W.

Correspondent Gil Flanagan reported that he has anchored, stern-tied, on the northeast side of Brem Bay, at the mouth of a cove created by a rock breakwater not shown on the chart. The views were beautiful.

Toba Inlet's most dramatic waterfalls are on the south side of the inlet, about 3 miles past Snout Point, which is located opposite Brem Bay.

LEWIS CHANNEL

Lewis Channel runs between West Redonda Island and Cortes Island.

⑦ **Refuge Cove**. Refuge Cove, with a public marina, fuel dock, shops and well-stocked store, is a good resupply stop in the heart of Desolation Sound. The busiest times are between 11:00 a.m. and 3:00 p.m. For easiest moorage and fuel dock use, early morning and late afternoon are recommended. Several homes, joined by boardwalks, surround the cove. Ample moorage is available. A floating dock, just off the fuel dock, is for overflow moorage, with no power or water. Dogs should be on a leash. A pet path is beside the used-book stand. Anchorage is possible toward the head of the bay.

Traffic can be heavy during high season. Approach slowly, and wait your turn for dock space or fuel. Turnover is rapid; you shouldn't have to wait long.   Refuge Cove is a scheduled stop for float plane service.

Garbage Barge: Around mid-June, an enterprising chap named Dave Cartwright moors a barge near the mouth of Refuge Cove. For a reasonable fee charged by the pound, he accepts bagged garbage and responsibly takes it away. If you have accumulated garbage from several days in Desolation Sound, this is one of the few places to dispose of it.

⑦ **Refuge Cove General Store.** General Delivery, Refuge Cove, BC V0P 1P0; (250) 935-6659; refcov@twincomm.ca; www.refugecove.com. Guest moorage along 2000 feet of side-tie dock space. No reservations; first-come, first-served. The fuel dock has gasoline, diesel, and propane. Washrooms, showers and laundry are up by the store. Free purified water, 15 amp power available during store hours, fee-based Wi-Fi.

The store carries groceries, fresh produce, deli items including cheeses and meats, hand-dipped ice cream, a complete liquor agency with interesting wine selections, some marine supplies and fishing gear, charts, cube and block ice, a good selection of books and magazines. It is also a post office. If Judith Williams' delightful book, *Dynamite Stories*, is in stock, pick up a copy. The stories are a blast, literally. The store has limited operating hours in the fall.

Most businesses, including the art gallery and gift shop, are open June through August. The cafe has fresh bakery items; open for breakfast, lunch and dinner. Licensed for wine and beer with Happy Hour specials.

Teakerne Arm. Teakerne Arm is a deep inlet extending from Lewis Channel into West

306

Redonda Island. Anchorage is just inside the entrance in Talbot Cove, or in front of the waterfall from Cassel Lake at the head of the north arm, or in the south arm. Both arms are deep, except very close to shore.

The area near the waterfall is a provincial park, with a dinghy float connected to shore by an aluminum ramp. Anchorage is in 90 to 150 feet. A cable in fair but serviceable condition hangs down the rock wall west of the waterfall for stern-ties. Several rings are set in the rock just above the high tide line and on either side of the dinghy dock. The waterfall is stunning, about 2½ stories high. Taking the short, vigorous hike from the dinghy float to Cassel Lake for a swim is a popular pastime. The water warms in the summer.

Talbot Cove. Talbot Cove is near the entrance to Teakerne Arm, on the south shore. The cove is marked with large yellow propane floats for a commercial operation. Anchor with a stern-tie in the southeast corner.

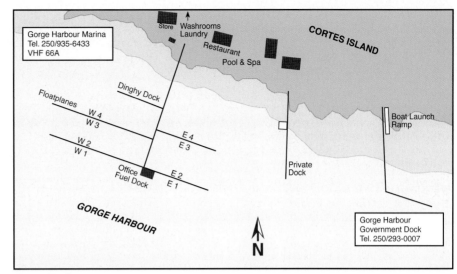

Gorge Harbour

CORTES ISLAND

Recommended book: Destination Cortez Island, by June Cameron, describes the early days on Cortes Island. In our opinion this book joins *The Curve of Time* as entertaining background reading about the B.C. coast. After reading *Destination Cortez Island* you will have an entirely different outlook about your explorations of Cortes Bay, Squirrel Cove, Von Donop Inlet, Whaletown, Gorge Harbour, Mansons Landing, and the entire Desolation Sound area.

Published in Canada by Heritage House and in the U.S. by Fine Edge Nautical Publishing.

⑧ **Squirrel Cove.** Squirrel Cove is made up of an outer bay and an inner bay. The outer bay provides access to the public wharf and the Squirrel Cove Trading Co. general store dock. The inner bay, consisting of two anchorage areas, has better protection and during the summer is often full of anchored boats. A saltwater lagoon is at the head of the inner bay. A connecting rapids runs into the lagoon at high tide and out of the lagoon at low tide. Be sure to plan an exit strategy if you enter the lagoon by dinghy.

The Flying Squirrel take-out stand and

The Cove Restaurant are located upland. A farmers market is held Sundays from 11:00 a.m. to 3:00 p.m.

At one time the inner bay was used for log booming. The late June Cameron wrote an article in Pacific Yachting telling of a tangle of sunken logs on the bottom. Our side-scan sounder showed the bay filled with logs scattered like matchsticks.

A trail leads from the northwest corner of Squirrel Cove to Von Donop Inlet.

The large building on the west shore is a Native Cultural Centre and offices.

No Discharge Zone. Gray water okay.

⑧ **Squirrel Cove Public Dock.** (Harbour Authority of Cortes Island), Box 329, Manson's Landing, B.C., V0P 1K0; (250) 293-0007; www.cortesharbours.ca; hacimgr@gmail.com. Open all year with 200 feet of floating dock that is often filled with local boats. First-come, first-served; commercial vessels have priority. There's always room for the dinghy. Rafting is encouraged. 15, 20, & 30 amp power. Self-registration and payment at the honor box located at the head of the ramp or pay with credit card, or Paypal at the Harbour Authority website. Garbage drop for a fee (cash).

The dock is close to the Squirrel Cove Trading Co. store and The Cove Restaurant.

A full-time diver is nearby for maintenance and recovery, phone number posted at the dock.

At very low tides the ramps from the wharf to the floats are quite steep. Local boats often take much of the dock space, although by being patient we've found room. A public mooring ball is available in front of the store.

⑧ **Squirrel Cove Trading Co. Ltd.** P.O. Box 1, Squirrel Cove, BC V0P 1T0; (250) 935-6327; squirrelcovetrading@yahoo.ca; www.squirrelcove.com. Open all year. Washrooms, showers and laundry are in a separate building just west of the store. Potable water at the dock. Gasoline, diesel, propane and kerosene available upland. Gas and diesel available at the dock via hoses from the upland pumps. The dock is 6 feet below the local tide chart and only accessible at high tides, plan accordingly. Plans are in the works to extend the guest fuel dock in the near future. Picnic tables available.

This is a good provisioning stop, with fresh produce, meat and fish, groceries, ice, books, marine hardware, post office, pay phone, Wi-Fi, liquor, and ATM. The expanded hardware section downstairs has just about anything a person might need.

A crafts shop and gallery is next to the store, stocked with island-made (or designed)

Squirrel Cove Store is under new management. The gift shop, on the right, carries locally-made items.

goods and clothing. Artists take turns staffing the shop. A Sunday market, with crafts, local produce, baked goods and musicians, runs from 11:00 a.m. to 3:00 p.m., summers only.

The Cove Restaurant reopened in 2018, and The Flying Squirrel take-out is now located within the restaurant.

⑨ **Cortes Bay.** Cortes Bay is well protected, but in some places the soft mud bottom doesn't hold well. Use Chart 3538 when approaching. Several charted rocks and reefs near the entrance have claimed the inattentive. These include Central Rock, north of Twin Islands, several rocks around Three Islets, and a rock off the headland midway between Mary Point and the entrance to Cortes Bay. To be safe, we always pass south of Three Islets.

Pay close attention to the beacon in the middle of the narrow entry to Cortes Bay. This beacon, with its red triangle dayboard, marks the south end of a nasty reef. Leave the beacon to starboard (Red, Right, Returning) as you enter. If you doubt the existence of this reef, one look at low tide will convince you. A small public wharf is at the head of Cortes Bay. It is usually full during the summer. Rafting is required.

Seattle Yacht Club has an outstation on the south shore of Cortes Bay, at the location of a former marina. Royal Vancouver Yacht Club has an outstation on the north shore. No reciprocals at either outstation.

Local knowledge says good holding ground is east of the Royal Van outstation, off the mouth of a small drying cove. During a 30- to 40-knot southeasterly blow, we saw several boats anchored successfully off the SYC outstation as well.

No Discharge Zone. Gray water okay.

Twin Islands. Twin Islands, located off the southeast side of Cortes Island, are really a single island divided by a drying spit. Anchorage is possible close to the drying spit on either side.

Sutil Point. Sutil Point is the south end of Cortes Island. A long, drying spit dotted with boulders extends south from the point, almost to buoy *Q20*. Give this buoy plenty of sea room.

A fresh southeast wind, especially if it is

blowing against an ebb current (see Point Atkinson tides), will set up high steep seas south of Sutil Point and east past Mitlenatch Island. Sutil Point can be dangerous in a southeasterly.

Smelt Bay Provincial Park. One mile north of Sutil Point on the west side of the peninsula. Good temporary anchorage is close to shore. The park has 23 campsites, picnic tables, and a white sand beach.

⑩ **Mansons Landing.** Mansons Landing on Manson Bay, located on the south side of Cortes Island has good anchorage, a public dock, a marine park, a lagoon, and a community village one mile from the public dock. The east shore of Manson Bay, the uplands and the lagoon to the east, are all part of the Mansons Landing Marine Park. The public dock also on the east shore provides access to the park and the road to the village. Anchorage is good north of the public dock. The entire area is exposed to the south.

The one mile walk to the village is uphill on a very lightly traveled road. The village has a well stocked co-op grocery store with a wide selection of organic foods and a café with Wi-Fi. The post office, community center, and take-out restaurant with outdoor seating, and a small store are across from the co-op. A small museum and visitor information center, housed in the historic Mansons Landing store building, are beyond the community center on the road to the west. A farmers market is held Fridays from 12:00 p.m. to 3:00 p.m at Mansons Hall Community Center (250-935-0015). Don't miss the homemade pies and rootbeer floats at the community center cafe.

No Discharge Zone. Gray water okay.

⑩ **Mansons Landing Marine Park.** Open all year, 117 acres. The park has no dock of its own, but can be reached from the Mansons Landing public dock, or you can anchor out. Hague Lake, with warm water and swimming beaches safe for small children, is a 10-minute walk from the public dock. The lagoon reportedly has clams and oysters.

⑩ **Mansons Landing Public Dock.** (Harbour Authority of Cortes Island), Box 329, Manson's Landing, B.C., V0P 1K0; (250) 293-0007; www.cortesharbours.ca; hacimgr@gmail.com. Open all year with a 240 foot float that is often filled with local boats. First-come, first-served; commercial vessels have priority. 20 & 30 amp power. First hour is free; up to 4 hours are at half-rate; thereafter, full-rate; rates apply to dinghies. Self-registration and payment in the honor box at the head of the ramp, or pay by credit card on their website. Garbage drop for a fee (cash). North end of the float is reserved for floatplane and load/unload.

⑪ **Gorge Harbour** is a large bay with many good spots to put the hook down. The entry is through a narrow cleft in the rock cliff. Orange-colored Native pictographs, including

a stick figure man, a man on what appears to be a turtle or fish, and several vertical lines, are on the rock wall to port as you enter. You have to look closely to identify them. Current runs through the entrance, but boats go through at any time. Inside you'll find good, protected anchorage. Several aquaculture operations are in the harbour. A field of private buoys is to port. The Gorge Harbour Marina Resort, on the northwest shore, has many amenities, including a restaurant. If the marina is full, anchor in the protected bay in 55 to 60 feet.

No Discharge Zone. Gray water okay.

⑪ **Gorge Harbour Marina Resort.** P.O. Box 89, Whaletown, BC V0P 1Z0; (250) 935-6433 ext. 4; moorage@gorgeharbour.com; www.gorgeharbour.com. Monitors VHF 66A. Open all year, gasoline and diesel at the fuel dock, guest moorage along 1800 feet of dock. Reservations are recommended May 15 to September 15; held-back moorage space is released daily at 4:00 p.m., first-come, first-served. Facilities include 30 & 50 amp power, water, swimming pool, hot tub, barbecue areas, washrooms, showers, laundry, Wi-Fi, pay phones. A well-stocked convenience store has fresh vegetables, meats, dairy products, liquor, ice, propane, DVD movie rentals. Four lodge rooms and a poolside cottage for rent. Garbage disposal is available for marina guests for a fee, no charge for recycling. Complete recycling instructions available. Dock staff will pick up garbage by your boat twice a day for a fee. The resort has an RV park, 2 trailer rentals, campground, lodge accommodations, and float plane service. Boats, kayaks, stand-up paddleboards, and cars for rent.

The resort features a pool and hot tub surrounded by attractive landscaping. A patio with a fireplace and barbecue area are available for guest use. Both overlook the harbor. Live music is often performed in the evening on the patio. There is an elaborate children's play area. Many boaters consider Gorge Harbour Marina & Resort to be on the list of special destinations. The Gorge Harbour Marina farmer's market is open from 10 a.m. to 1:00 p.m. on Saturdays during summer. Anchored guests are welcome to use the resort facilities; passes for use of the pool are available at the store for a fee.

The Floathouse Restaurant always gets excellent reviews. The atmosphere is cozy and conducive to multi-table conversations. Open from May through September, with reduced hours in winter. During peak season the restaurant offers breakfast, lunch, tapas (3:00p.m. to 5:00p.m.), dinner and a Sunday brunch. Espresso and pastries at the bar all day long. Year after year, they have a great chef. The restaurant has two areas, one part is covered with a bar and cocktail area; the other part is open with seating overlooking the harbor. Restaurant reservations recommended in the high season, outdoor seating can be requested.

⑪ **Gorge Harbour Public Dock.** (Harbour Authority of Cortes Island), Box

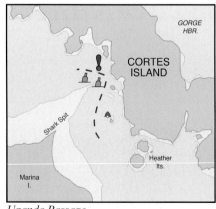

Uganda Passage

Whiterock Passage is narrow, with leading and following range markers to guide you through safely.

329, Manson's Landing, B.C., V0P 1K0; (250) 293-0007; www.cortesharbours. ca; hacimgr@gmail.com. Located a short distance east of the Gorge Harbour Marina. Open all year with a 100 foot float that is often filled with local boats. First-come, first-served; commercial vessels have priority. Self-registration and payment honor box at the head of the ramp, or pay by credit card on their website. Garbage drop for a fee (cash). Boat launch ramp located adjacent to the dock.

Uganda Passage. Uganda Passage separates Cortes Island from Marina Island. The pass is narrow and winding, but well marked and easy to navigate as long as you pay attention. Red, Right, Returning assumes you are returning from the south. See the Uganda Passage map showing the route through the passage. Shark Spit is long and low, with a superb sand beach. Swimming is good. Anchorage is south of the pass, on either the Cortes Island side or the Marina Island side.

Whaletown. Whaletown is the terminus of the ferry between Cortes Island and Quadra Island. The ferry dock is on the north side of the bay, and a 200-foot public float is on the south side. Watch for several marked and unmarked rocks, normally covered by kelp. The public float is mostly taken up by local boats. First hour free; stays up to 4 hours at half rate; stays over 4 hours at full day rate. Self-registration and payment box located on the wharf at the head of the ramp.

Subtle Islands. The two Subtle Islands are separated by a drying shoal. Good anchorage is off this shoal on the east side, particularly in settled weather. The little bay on the north side is very deep except at the head. It has a lovely (and exposed) view to the north. The islands are privately owned and marked with "stay off" and "keep away" signs.

Coulter Bay. Coulter Bay is pretty, but as the chart indicates, much of the bay is too shallow for anchoring. Most of the good spots are taken by local boats. You could anchor in the tiny nook behind Coulter Island, beside a little unnamed islet to the west. Some cabins are nearby, but they are screened from view.

Carrington Bay. Carrington Bay is pretty, and well protected except from the north. The bottom is rocky so be sure your anchor is properly set before turning in for the night. Carrington Lagoon, at the head of the bay, is interesting to explore. Drag the dinghy across the logs that choke the entrance to the lagoon. The late June Cameron, in *Destination Cortez*, says the lagoon entrance was blasted out of rock, with amazingly smooth sides—a tribute to the skills of the man who did the blasting. A good anchorage is to the right, near the entrance to the lagoon, with a stern-tie ashore. We've seen other boats anchored in the little bight a short distance to the left of the lagoon entrance and behind the tiny island just off the eastern shore of the bay.

No Discharge Zone. Gray water okay.

Quartz Bay. Quartz Bay is unusually pretty, with good holding bottom. The eastern cove of the bay has several homes and two private docks along the shoreline. You can anchor with swinging room in 30 to 42 feet near the head, but you're in their front yards. The western cove has some aquaculture, one cabin on the shore, and anchoring depths near the south and west shores. You may have to run a stern-tie to shore. It is exposed to north winds, but it's a nice spot.

LOCAL KNOWLEDGE

DANGEROUS ROCK: About halfway into Von Donop Inlet, a rock lies in the narrowest part of the channel. Look for two prominent rock outcroppings covered with lichen, moss and grass on the left side of the channel. The rock is opposite the second, or inner, of these outcroppings. Hug the right side and keep that rock to port, even if tree branches try to brush the starboard side of the boat or rigging.

⑫ **Von Donop Inlet.** Von Donop Inlet, on the northwest tip of Cortes Island, is a 3 mile long landlocked inlet entirely within the Hathayim Provincial Marine Park. The inlet is entered through a 2-mile long channel with a narrow neck mid-way along the channel. Caution at the neck for rocks in the middle of the channel; hug the south side of the channel. Best entry and exit is at high-water

slack. Once inside, several coves provide protected anchorage. The largest of these coves takes up the entire head of the inlet and has room for many boats. The bottom in this area is sticky mud. It is ideal for holding, but requires extra cleaning time when departing. The lagoon at the northeast end of the inlet can be explored by dinghy at high-water slack. The outlet of this lagoon has reversing tidal overfalls. All of the uplands are park lands. Several maintained trails lead from the head of the Inlet to the lagoon, lakes, Squirrel Cove, and a longer trail leads to the road to Squirrel Cove Store and Gorge Harbour. The trailhead is on the southeast shore at the head of the inlet.

⑫ **Háthayim Provincial Marine Park** (Von Donop). This 3155-acre park includes Von Donop Inlet, Robertson Lake and Wiley Lake.

Read Island. The east side of Read Island is indented from the south by **Evans Bay**, where several little notches are worth exploring as anchorages. Most have drying flats at their heads. **Bird Cove** is probably the best protected, although Tom Kincaid has spent a quiet night behind the little islets in the bay just to the north of Bird Cove. A small public float is near the entrance to Evans Bay.

Hill Island. Hill Island is privately owned. According to Sailing Directions, a private lodge with a floating breakwater is in Totem Bay. The island is not open to the public.

Burdwood Bay. Burdwood Bay has several possible anchorages, particularly on the lee side of the little islands that extend from the south side of the bay, and in a notch in the north end. Burdwood Bay is not particularly pretty, but could be a hideout in a storm.

Hoskyn Channel. Hoskyn Channel runs between Read Island and Quadra Island and connects at the north with Whiterock Passage and Surge Narrows.

Bold Island Anchorage. Bold Island is just north of Village Bay on the west side of Hoskyn Channel. Enter through Crescent Channel. Anchorage is in the basin at the northwest corner of Bold Island, approximately between the two drying reefs. Two oyster farms are in the area with one along the northwest shore of Bold Island. The bay opens to the south with views across Read Island. The anchorage might be exposed to southerlies.

Hjorth Bay. Hjorth Bay, on Hoskyn Channel along the west side of Read Island, is a good anchorage except in a strong southerly. Anchor in 50 to 60 feet, probably with a stern-tie to shore. A small cabin is on shore behind the island.

Whiterock Passage. Whiterock Passage is narrow, and the dredged channel is bounded on both sides by drying shoals studded with

309

angry boulders. Least depth at zero tide is 5 feet. Maximum currents are 2 knots. Running Whiterock Passage at half tide is a good idea—it exposes the shoals on both sides but provides a little extra depth. The uninitiated tend to avoid Whiterock Passage, but it's easy to run if you pay attention and know how. Here's how:

Carefully study Plans Chart 3537 or Chartbook 3312, both of which detail Whiterock Passage at a scale of 1:10,000. As the charts show, two ranges are on the Read Island side of the passage. Going either direction, one will be a leading range as you enter, and the other a back range as you depart. Approaching, find the leading range and stay exactly on it. Proceed slowly and watch astern as the back range comes into view. When the back range lines up, turn the appropriate direction and let the back range keep you on course as you complete your transit.

Remember that the course lines on the charts are true, not magnetic. You must subtract the magnetic variation from the true heading to get the magnetic course. Before entering, make sure you have a clear view astern from the helm to view the back range markers.

Rendezvous Islands. The Rendezvous Islands have a number of homes along their shores. Anchorage may be possible in a bight between the southern and middle islands, but a private float and dolphins restrict the room available.

CALM CHANNEL

Calm Channel connects Lewis Channel and Sutil Channel to the south, and with Bute Inlet and the Yuculta Rapids to the north. It is appropriately named, often being wind-free when areas nearby are breezy.

Frances Bay. A logging road and logging dump area are located on the westerly side at the head of the bay, indicating past logging operations. In 2017, no logging operations were observed and boats were seen anchored at the head of the bay in the eastern portion. It has been reported that the bottom is rocky throughout the rest of the bay and an anchor fouling cable is near the log dump.

Church House. Church House is an abandoned Indian Reserve opposite the

entrance to Hole in the Wall on Calm Channel, and near the mouth of Bute Inlet. The white-painted church, an often-photographed landmark, has collapsed in a heap.

Redonda Bay. Redonda Bay has the ruins of an old wharf left over from logging days, but otherwise is not a good anchorage. The wharf is no longer usable and the ramp leading from the float to the wharf is gone. Several rocks in the bay are charted.

Bute Inlet. Bute Inlet, approximately 35 miles long, is very deep. Except in small areas near the mouths of rivers and at the head of the inlet, it is not good for anchorage. Usually, the bottom drops away steeply, making a stern-tie to shore necessary. Anchorages should be chosen with an eye to strong inflow winds during the afternoon, followed by calm, then by icy outflow winds in the morning. Correspondents Gil and Karen Flanagan explain:

"The glaciers around Bute Inlet were melting and there are a lot of them. The water was milky by Stuart Island, and got darker and darker the farther up we went, turning from light green to gray to brownish. We saw considerable drift, including complete trees with roots sticking 8 feet or so into the air. At times we had to slow to idle, shift to neutral and coast through bands of drift. Jack Mold, the caretaker at Southgate Camp, said what we experienced was normal. Waddington Harbour, at the head of Bute Inlet, has a lot of good anchoring spots in 10 to 50 foot depths. We anchored as close to the northeast shore as we could get, and still were at least 100 yards from the beach (don't bother trying to stern-tie). There is no protection from wind, but we had no wind. We didn't see much driftwood on the beach, either. We doubt if inflow winds blow hard or long, probably because even on hot days the massive ice fields in the mountains above preclude high land temperatures.

Because of the ice fields, we had an overnight low in the upper 40s on September 1. It was 10 to 20 degrees lower than temperatures we had been experiencing in Desolation Sound. The morning air was cold enough that we needed heavy coats, even in the sun.

Mountains 6,000 to 7,000 feet high rise directly from the head of the inlet. They have snowfields, and are spectacular.

The milky water, drifting logs, huge harbor and high mountains create an environment that felt wild and different from anywhere we have been on the coast. We spent only 19 hours in Waddington Harbour, which wasn't long enough to take the dinghy up either river. We did see a grizzly bear on the beach near our anchorage. We definitely will go back." [*Flanagan*]

Reader Richard McBride sent a note about a tiny anchorage he calls "The Nook," just outside Orford Bay:

"It is a small crack in the mountain wall about 100 feet wide at the opening and about 150 feet deep, with a little waterfall at the head. This is a terrific spot for a couple of small boats to tuck in. Lat/lon 50°34.368'N/124°52.439'W."

OKISOLLO CHANNEL/ SURGE NARROWS

Owen Bay tides and Okisollo Channel Secondary Port tide corrections are contained in Canadian Tide and Current Tables Vol. 6, and Ports and Passes. Okisollo Channel runs along the east and north sides of Quadra Island, from Surge Narrows to Discovery Passage.

Surge Narrows & Beazley Passage. Surge Narrows and Beazley Passage should be run at or near slack water. Spring floods set eastward to 12 knots and ebbs set westward to 10 knots. Current predictions are shown under Beazley Passage in the Canadian Tide and Current Tables Vol. 6, and Ports and Passes.

Although Beazley Passage, between Peck Island and Sturt Island, has the strongest currents in the Surge Narrows area, it is the preferred route between Hoskyn Channel and Okisollo Channel. Especially on an ebb current in Beazley Passage, watch for Tusko Rock, which dries at 5 feet, on the east side of the pass at the north end. Stay well clear of Tusko Rock.

According to Sailing Directions, the duration of slack at Surge Narrows varies between 5 and 11 minutes. The passage north of the Settler's Group is useable following the deeper channel, avoiding the charted rocks and shoals.

⑬ **Octopus Islands Marine Park.** This is a beautiful, popular anchorage and exploration area, wonderfully protected. The park includes all of Waiatt Bay, the uplands south of Waiatt Bay, and all but the two large islands in the Octopus Islands group. The two islands charted on Chart 3539 as 50 meter and 71 meter islands are private and not part of the park. Octopus Islands Marine Park was expanded and Chart 3539 shows its present boundaries. Much of the upland areas to the north of Waiatt Bay are not part of the park and are private property.

You can enter Waiatt Bay from Okisollo Channel with care for the rocks, but the usual entry is by a narrow channel from the north.

Quiet anchorage in Octopus Islands Marine Park, northwest of the northerly narrow entrance channel

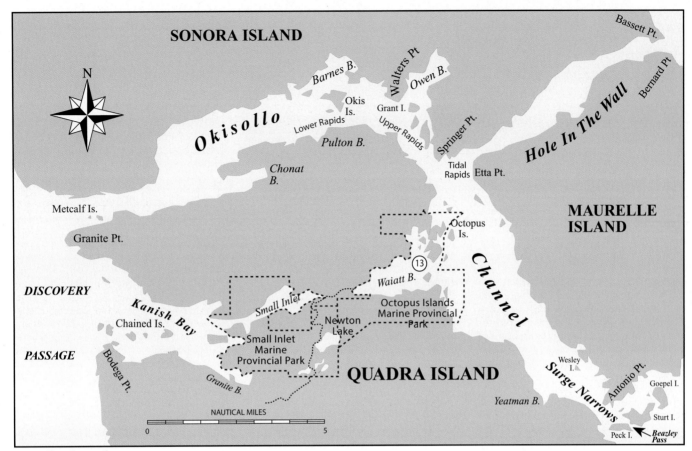

Okisollo Channel

Anchor in Waiatt Bay or any of several coves in the Octopus Islands group and run a stern-tie to shore. At the end of the narrow channel as you enter from the north, a rock, clearly shown on Plans Chart 3537, obstructs part of the entry to the first cove on the right. This rock is easily seen as a white smear under the water.

Waiatt Bay. Waiatt Bay is broad and protected, with convenient anchoring depths throughout. The entire bay is part of the Octopus Islands Marine Park. The bay's entrance is choked with islets and rocks, and Sailing Directions (written for large vessels) warns against entering. With the aid of large scale Plans Chart 3537, however, a small boat can pick its way in along the south shore, or in the middle of the islets, or along the north shore. The chart shows the possibilities. You

Middle entrance to Waiatt Bay in Octopus Islands Marine Park

might anchor in a notch along the shore, or at the head of the bay.

A half-mile easy trail connects the head of Waiatt Bay with Small Inlet. About half way between Waiatt Bay and Small Inlet, a sign points the way to Newton Lake with a less traveled trail branching to the northwest. Follow the Newton Lake sign direction, which also takes you to Small Inlet. A trail sign at the head of the cove in Small Inlet marks the end of the trail between Waiatt Bay and Small Inlet. From here, the trail to Newton Lake follows the south shore of Small Inlet cove before becoming difficult and steep. It is one mile from the trail head at Small Inlet cove to Newton Lake. Don't confuse a small pond, a short distance before Newton Lake, for the real thing. The crystal clear waters of Newton Lake invite a fresh water swim. From

Newton Lake a two-mile trail continues to Granite Bay Road and Granite Bay.

Hole in the Wall. Hole in the Wall connects Okisollo Channel with Calm Channel to the east. Boats accumulate on each side of the rapids at the western entrance to Hole in the Wall, waiting for slack water. In general, boats on the upstream side will catch the last of the fair current when the rapids calm down, leaving room for the boats on the other side to pick up the new fair current in the opposite direction. Slacks occur 50 to 55 minutes before Seymour Narrows, and last about 4 minutes (Seymour Narrows currents are shown in Canadian Tide and Current Tables Vol. 6, and Ports and Passes). The flood current sets northeast. Maximum currents run to 12 knots on the flood and 10 knots on the ebb.

LOCAL KNOWLEDGE

DANGEROUS CURRENTS: Upper Rapids and Lower Rapids in Okisollo Channel can be dangerous and should be run at or near slack. Slacks occur 50 to 55 minutes before slack at Seymour Narrows.

Upper Rapids. These are the first rapids in Okisollo Channel north of Hole in the Wall, and they are dangerous unless run at or near slack water. Slack occurs 55 minutes

Anchorage can be found on the Drew Harbour side of Rebecca Spit Provincial Marine Park, with dinghy access to the long beaches.

before Seymour Narrows (Seymour Narrows currents are shown in Canadian Tide and Current Tables Vol. 6, and Ports and Passes). At full rush on a spring tide, the rapids running at 9 knots are frightening to watch. A wall of white water stretches nearly across the channel almost until slack. When it's time to go through, steer a little east of mid-channel to avoid Bentley Rock. Chart 3537 makes the course clear.

Barnes Bay and several small indents in this part of Okisollo Channel could be good anchorages, except for the large amount of log booming and aquaculture. Owen Bay is the preferred anchorage.

LOCAL KNOWLEDGE

STRONG CURRENTS: Currents run strong through the islands that separate Owen Bay from Upper Rapids. If you explore these islands, exercise caution to avoid getting sucked into the rapids.

Owen Bay. Owen Bay is large and pretty. Our recommended anchorage is in the second little notch on the west side of the bay. This notch is quite protected, and has room for about 5 boats if the spots are well chosen and stern-ties are used. Enter Owen Bay through a narrow channel between Walters Point and Grant Island. A reef, marked by kelp, extends from Walters Point nearly halfway across this channel. It will inspire you to hug the Grant Island side. Correspondent Pat Shera adds that there is good holding and shelter near the small public float on the east side of the bay. Shera also says that the northeastern head of Owen Bay has "acres of good holding on a flat bottom." That area, however, is subject to being hit by strong (and cold) outflow winds from Bute Inlet. He was "kissed by the Bute" one sleepless night and knows what he's talking about.

Lower Rapids. Lower Rapids turns at virtually the same time as Upper Rapids—55 minutes before Seymour Narrows (Seymour Narrows currents are shown in Canadian Tide and Current Tables Vol. 6, and Ports and Passes). Currents run to 9 knots on spring

tides, and you must steer a course to avoid Gypsy Shoal, which lies nearly in the middle. Transit at slack water only.

We recommend avoiding Lower Rapids altogether by going through Barnes Bay, north of the Okis Islands. At times other than slack you will still see considerable current, but you will avoid the hazards of Lower Rapids.

Barnes Bay. Barnes Bay and several small indents in this part of Okisollo Channel could be good anchorages, except for the fair amount of aquaculture. Anchorage may be possible to the west in **Chonat Bay** and in the notch behind **Metcalf Island.**

QUADRA ISLAND, SOUTH

⑭ **Drew Harbour/Rebecca Spit Marine Park.** Drew Harbour is large, and in the right winds the open harbor can be lumpy. The preferred anchorage is in the bight immediately inside the north tip of Rebecca Spit. A drying shoal defines the south side of this bight. The shoal extends a considerable distance from shore, and it could fool you at high tide.

If the preferred bight is full, anchor south of the drying shoal in 24 to 36 feet, although it isn't as protected. Rebecca Spit Marine Park is popular. The Drew Harbour side of the spit has a lovely sand beach. Trails with picnic

tables run the length of the spit. The exposed Sutil Channel side has a beach of remarkable small round boulders.

Bill Wolferstan's cruising guide to Desolation Sound contains an excellent section describing silvered tree snags on the spit, the result of subsidence during a 1946 earthquake. Wolferstan also describes the mounded fortifications, thought to be defenses built 200 to 400 years ago by the local Salish tribe against attacks from the Native Kwakiutl.

⑮ **Heriot Bay.** Heriot Bay has a public wharf, a supermarket, the Heriot Bay Inn & Marina, and the Taku Resort. During the summer high season the public dock usually is full with boats rafted several deep. Anchorage area north of the public wharf is filled with private mooring balls. Transient anchorage is found further east in 50 to 60 feet of water. The Heriot Bay Inn & Marina is between the ferry dock and the public dock. Just south of Heriot Bay, in Drew Harbour proper, Taku Resort has excellent docks and facilities. Heriot Bay Tru-Value Foods, a short walk from the Heriot Bay or Taku resorts, is the best-stocked grocery store in Desolation Sound, with complete groceries, including fresh vegetables and meats, a post office, gift shop, and liquor store; Java Bay Cafe is located in the same building. Free grocery delivery to the docks from Tru-Value Grocery (250) 285-2436. Bicycles can be rented from a shop on the road above Taku Resort. The Quadra Island Golf Course is a short ride away.

⑮ **Heriot Bay Public Wharf.** (250) 285-3622; www.qiha.ca. Open all year, 670 feet of dock space, power, water, portable toilets, Wi-Fi, garbage drop, launch ramp. The docks have recently been rebuilt. Watch for ferry wash on the outer face. Heriot Bay Inn and shopping nearby. The dock is managed by the Quadra Island Harbour Authority.

⑮ **Heriot Bay Inn & Marina.** P.O. Box 100, Heriot Bay, BC V0P 1H0; (250) 285-3322; (888) 605-4545; info@heriotbayinn.com;

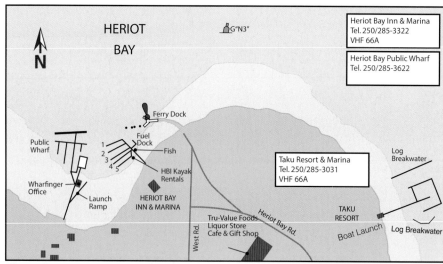

Heriot Bay

The Heriot Bay Inn & Marina has a pub, restaurant, and gift shop.

www.heriotbayinn.com. Monitors VHF 66A. Open all year, gasoline, diesel, propane, ice and fishing tackle. Guest moorage available on 1800 feet of side-tie dock, mostly 15 amp power with some 30 amp, washrooms, showers, laundry, limited Wi-Fi. Reservations recommended June through September. Fairways between the finger floats are narrow, larger vessels should 'starboard-tie' on the outside of Float 1. The outer docks and fuel dock are subject to wakes from passing ferries.

The hotel is delightful. This 1913 historic hotel has ten rooms, three cabins, and a suite. The restaurant has outdoor seating overlooking the bay, and the pub has live music on many nights. The gift store off the lobby has local guidebooks, local artisan jewelry, crafts, and souvenirs. The office can provide contact information for local tours and fishing guides. Heriot Bay Tru-Value Foods is a short walk up the hill. Bicycle and kayak rentals nearby.

In 2008 a group of 20 Quadra Island residents ("old hippies," one of them said) bought the property and set about making improvements. Among them they had all the needed skills: carpentry, electrical, painting, administrative, whatever else was required. In recent years the Heriot Bay Inn's public areas have been upgraded with lovely flower beds and walkways. The goal of this working community is to maintain the property with the spirit of welcoming the traveling public.

(15) **Taku Resort & Marina.** P.O. Box 1, Heriot Bay, BC V0P 1H0; (250) 285-3031; info@takuresort.com; www.takuresort.com. Monitors VHF 66A. Open all year. The docks have 30 & 50 amp power, potable water and Wi-Fi. Washrooms, coin showers, laundry and a 14-room resort are ashore, as are RV sites, tennis, volleyball, badminton and horseshoes. The docks are exposed to southeast winds across the bay, but the inside moorage is protected. The views and proximity to Rebecca Spit Marine Park make this a popular marina. A shopping center and Tru-Value Foods grocery store is a short walk away. A kayak tour operator is on site and a bicycle rental store is just up the road. The resort offers kayak, paddleboard rentals, and cooking classes. The facilities and service are high quality. Lynden McMartin is the manager.

DISCOVERY PASSAGE

Discovery Passage is approximately 20 miles long, and separates Quadra Island and Sonora Island from Vancouver Island. It is the main route for commercial traffic north and south along the east side of Vancouver Island. Cape Mudge is the south entrance to Discovery Passage. At the north end, Discovery Passage connects with Johnstone Strait at Chatham Point. An enormous amount of water flows through Discovery Passage, flooding south and ebbing north. Tide-rips are frequent.

Cape Mudge. The area around Cape Mudge and Wilby Shoals is a famous hot spot for salmon fishing and often full of small fishing craft during the summer months. Several resorts in the area cater to sport fishermen. Guides are available for hire in Campbell River.

On a flood tide, a backeddy often sets up at Cape Mudge running north along the western edge of Wilby Shoals all the way to the Cape Mudge Lighthouse.

LOCAL KNOWLEDGE

TIDE-RIPS: A strong southeasterly wind blowing against a large, south-flowing flood tide can set up high and dangerous seas. Lives have been lost off Cape Mudge in such conditions. Cape Mudge, at the south end of Quadra Island, has been a graveyard for vessels of all sizes, particularly in the winter months. If a southeaster is blowing, Sailing Directions recommends entering at or after high water slack. Good advice.

Yaculta. The First Nations settlement of Yaculta, located on Quadra Island, is the site of the Nuyumbalees Cultural Centre, with its splendid collection of potlatch regalia and historical artifacts and photos. Open 7 days a week, May to September. The Centre is a 3-block walk south from the public dock. We urge a visit. **Cape Mudge Boatworks** (250) 285-2155 is located here. They have a large marine ways and often work on recreational boats.

Yaculta Public Dock. Located at 50°01.4'N on the east side of Discovery Passage, next to the Cape Mudge Boatworks marine ways. Public dock with 220 feet of float; 30 amp power and water. No charge. Not recommended for overnight stays, exposed to winds and boat wakes, use at your own risk. Near the Yaculta village and the Nuyumbalees Cultural Centre. Moorage space on the more protected inside of the floats is normally occupied by local boats.

(16) **Quathiaski Cove.** Quathiaski Cove (known locally as Q-Cove) is the Quadra Island landing for the ferry to Campbell River. A public dock is next to the ferry landing and may be rolly from ferry wakes and passing vessels. A seasonal snack stand is in the ferry parking lot; a pub and restaurant are a short walk away. A shopping center with a good grocery store, a tasty informal café, pizza restaurant, bank with an ATM, and a variety of stores to peruse are a few blocks up the hill from the ferry landing. The grocery store will deliver to the dock. The Visitor Centre is next to the bank. A farmers market adjacent to the Visitor Centre is open Saturday mornings during the summer months.

Because of ferry traffic, the best anchorage is farther north in the cove behind Grouse Island. Fingers of current from Discovery Passage work into Quathiaski Cove at some stages of the tide, so be sure the anchor is well set.

See Area Map Page 301 - Maps Not for Navigation

⑯ **Quathiaski Cove Public Wharf.** (250) 285-3622; www.qiha.ca. Adjacent to the ferry landing. The dock has 20, 30 & 50 amp power, water, Wi-Fi, pay telephone, and launch ramp. Above the dock are washrooms and shower facilities, with a number to call for the keycode after hours. The dock has considerable mooring space, but we often find it crowded with local and commercial fish boats. Commercial fish boats have priority. South side of the south float is for seine fishing vessels. Managed by the Quadra Island Harbour Authority.

⑰ **April Point Resort, Spa & Marina**. P.O. Box 381 Quathiaski Cove, BC V0P 1N0; (250) 285-2222 x264; marina@northcoasthotelresort.com; www.aprilpoint.com. Monitors VHF 66A. Resort and spa open mid-May to October, moorage open all year. The resort lodge and spa are located at April Point and the marina is located in the cove a half mile southeast. The marina has moorage for vessels up to 200 feet, Wi-Fi, water, garbage, and 30, 50, & 100 amp power. Laundry, showers, and a picnic area are available at the resort lodge along with kayak and bike rentals. The resort lodge is a 10-minute walk from the marina or an easy commute by dinghy. In 2017 the G/H dock at the marina was replaced for an additional 600 feet of moorage.

Approaching, you will see a red spar buoy at the entrance to the bay. The buoy marks a shoal, keep the buoy to starboard as you enter (Red, Right, Returning). The proper channel will appear narrow, especially at low tide. You will be strongly tempted to leave the buoy to port, which might put you aground. The docks in front of the lodge are for resort boats and dinghies only; however, boats under 25 feet may be allowed to tie-up while dining at the lodge.

April Point Resort & Spa is a deluxe destination vacation resort. Notable stars from previous generations, like Bob Hope and John Wayne, vacationed here. It has everything for the most demanding guest, including excellent rooms, a beautiful spa, fishing guides, renowned dining, and scheduled air service by Kenmore Air. The marina and resort are owned by North Coast Hotel Resort Ltd, which operates a number of high-quality resorts. Painter's Lodge, north of Campbell River on the west side of Discovery Passage, is a North Coast Hotel resort and is accessible by the resort water taxi from April Point. April Point moorage guests have full access to the amenities at Painter's Lodge, including dining, swimming pool, hot tub and tennis courts.

Limited anchorage can be found in the cove near the marina. A rock-strewn passage, suitable for kayaks and dinghies only, leads between the cove and adjacent Gowlland Harbour.

⑱ **Steep Island Lodge.** P.O. Box 699, Campbell River, BC V9W 6J3; (250) 830-8179; info@steepisland.com; www.steepisland.com. Open May 15 to September

April Point marina with ample side-tie moorage is a short walk to the Resort Lodge and Spa (inset).

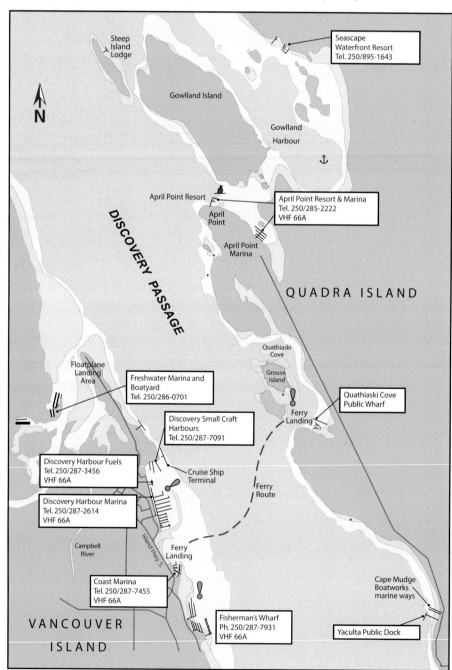

Campbell River

www.WaggonerGuide.com

30. Guest moorage for those staying in lodge accommodations. Water at the dock, no power. This is a beautiful resort with private cabins. It is on the east side of Steep Island, off the northwest corner of Gowlland Island. Fishing and kayak charters available. Float plane service. Jacuzzi. Dinner is all-inclusive and by reservation only.

Gowlland Harbour. Gowlland Harbour is a large, protected bay behind Gowlland Island, with considerable log booming activity along the shoreline. Before entering, study the chart so you can avoid Entrance Rock, north of Gowlland Island.

You'll find good anchoring depths at the north end of the bay, but it's much prettier at the south end, especially behind Stag Island. Although homes and docks are on the shores, we didn't feel closed-in-upon. Good anchoring is also behind Wren Islet, Crow Islet, and the Mouse Islets, all of them a little to the north of Stag Island. These islets, which are protected as provincial park preserves, make good picnic spots.

⑲ **Seascape Waterfront Resort.** P.O. Box 566, Quadra Island, BC V0P 1N0; (250) 895-1643; theseascaperesort@gmail.com; www.seascapewaterfrontresortandmarina.com. Located north of Stag Island in Gowland Harbour; 50°04.9'N 125°13.4'W Open all year, 1000 feet of guest moorage, 15 & 30 amp power, washrooms, showers, laundry, and kayak rentals. Docks and cabins were refurbished in 2018. The large upland octagon building serves as a venue for rendezvous and special events; the interior has beautiful wood finishes and sculptures, a nautical-themed bar, large stone fireplace and comfortable furnishings; wonderful views of the harbour. New owners of the resort continue to make plans for additional improvements.

CAMPBELL RIVER

Campbell River calls itself the "Salmon Capital of the World," and is working to become an important tourist destination. While dozens of guideboats take sportfishermen to prime fishing areas in Discovery Passage and off Cape Mudge, lunker-size salmon are still caught from marina breakwaters and the public fishing pier.

Campbell River has complete shopping, dining, and marine facilities, all close to the waterfront. Fisherman's Wharf and the Coast Marina are close to Tyee Plaza with drugstore, liquor store, excellent laundromat, and more. Discovery Harbour Marina is part of the extensive Discovery Harbour Centre with grocery and big-box general merchandise stores, liquor store, fast food, restaurants, and pubs. Buses leave hourly from a shelter at the mall, providing a convenient way to visit other areas of town.

An attractive promenade runs the length of the shoreline from Fisherman's Wharf marina to the ferry dock. The promenade is scheduled to be extended to the Discovery Harbour Marina; for now follow the sidewalk along the highway. At the north end of Discovery Harbour Marina, a Native-owned cruise ship terminal has been built.

As you approach Campbell River from the south you will find four marinas, with transient moorage, each protected by a breakwater. The southernmost marina is Fisherman's Wharf (formerly the Government Dock, now Campbell River Harbour Authority).

Coast Marina is the second breakwater protected marina, offering guest moorage as you progress northward. The BC ferry run between Quathiaski Cove on Quadra Island and Campbell River lands adjacent to Coast Marina. Coast Marina is closest to downtown Campbell River.

The third marina is Discovery Harbour Marina with considerable moorage, including slips and side-tie. The 52-acre Discovery Harbour Centre adjoins the marina for convenient shopping, including Ocean Pacific Marine Supply, a well-stocked chandlery. Adjacent to the shopping center is a repair yard with 110-ton Travelift haulout.

The fourth marina (north side of Discovery Harbour) named Discovery Harbour Authority Small Craft Harbours is located behind the same breakwater that protects Discover Harbour Marina. This fourth marina is located on the north side of Discovery Harbour Fuels sales dock and provides transient moorage and a boat ramp. All four marinas monitor VHF 66A. Located one half-mile up the Campbell River is

Freshwater Marina and Boatyard, offering permanent moorage, repair services and a 50 ton Travelift.

Marine Parts & Supplies: Well-stocked Ocean Pacific (250-286-1011) has overnight delivery from major suppliers in Vancouver for just about anything.

Museums: The Campbell River Museum & Archives, at 470 Island Hwy, is in the "don't miss" category. The care and imagination of the exhibits remind us of the Royal British Columbia Museum in Victoria, only smaller, and without the giant ice age mammoth.

The Maritime Heritage Centre, a short walk south from Fisherman's Wharf, features a number of fishing and maritime exhibits.

The Discovery Passage Aquarium is just above the docks at Fisherman's Wharf. It is small, but the exhibits are well done. Younger crew will enjoy it.

Farmers market: Sundays, May through September, 10:00 a.m. to 2:30 p.m. in the fishing pier parking lot at the Fisherman's Wharf docks. Fresh farm produce, baked goods, fresh fish, all the things you'd expect.

㉔ **Fisherman's Wharf (Campbell River Harbour Authority).** 705 Island Highway, Campbell River, BC V9W 2C2; (250) 287-7931; fishermans@telus.net; www.fishermanswharfcampbellriver.com. Monitors VHF 66A. Open all year, water on docks, 20, 30, limited 50 & one 100 amp power, pumpout, ample dock space, washrooms, showers, tidal grid, Wi-Fi, garbage, recycling. Reservations accepted. All but one of the docks are side-tie only, rafting permitted. Docks A, B, and C are in the North Basin and docks 1-6 are in the South Basin. Docks A,B,1,2 and the west side of 3 are reserved. Transient space is located on dock 5, the east side of 3, and the east side of C. The pumpout is on dock C in the north basin in the area marked "Loading Zone."

This was almost entirely a commercial fish boat moorage basin until the harbor authority took over operation. Several improvements have been made to attract pleasure craft. All the docks have been recently re-decked, and a new building completed with washrooms, showers, and the harbor office. The well known Dick's Fish and Chips moved from the Coast Marina to a new storefront across from the Wharf. Crabby Bob's on finger 6 on the south wharf has fresh and frozen seafood on the dock. Other boats sell fresh fish on the floats between fingers 2 & 3. Call the office for a heads-up on what's available. Office hours are 8:00 a.m. to 5:00 p.m., 7 days a week. If the office is closed, take an empty space and register in the morning.

㉔ **Coast Marina.** 1003 Island Highway, Campbell River, BC V9W 2C4; (250) 287-7455; coastmarina@gmail.com; www.coastmarina.ca. Monitors VHF 66A. The

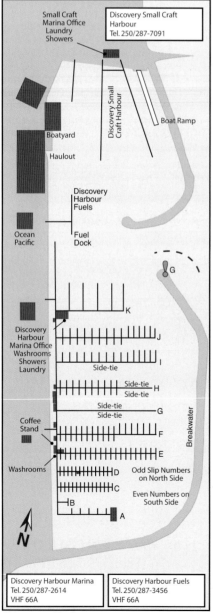

Discovery Harbour

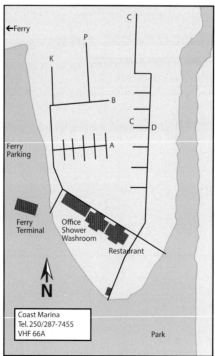

Coast Marina

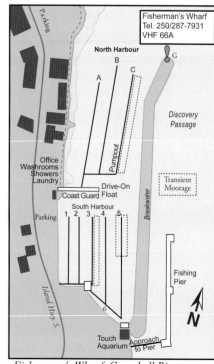

Fisherman's Wharf, Campbell River

SEYMOUR NARROWS

Seymour Narrows is a wide pass, clear of hazards, and offers a direct route north past the important provisioning town of Campbell River. It is the easiest connection from the Strait of Georgia to Johnstone Strait or Cordero Channel.

Most commercial vessels stay clear of Seymour Narrows except at slack. A ship or barge-towing tug cannot afford to go sideways for even a few seconds. Small fishboats and recreational vessels, however, often transit Seymour Narrows within an hour of the turn, especially if going with the current. We always take Seymour Narrows going with the current and we've rarely had an anxious moment.

Smaller tides, where maximum current is predicted at six knots or less, can be taken at any time for most boats (again, going with the current). Larger tides should be taken within a half-hour of the turn. If it's a strong current cycle, in the 14- to 16-knot range, arrive at the pass within 15 minutes of slack water and the current will be manageable. The strongest current doesn't extend very far in either direction, so the transit past whirlpools lasts only a few minutes.

Hydrographers say the strongest currents at the Narrows are in the vicinity of Ripple Rock (slightly west of mid-channel, directly beneath the hydro lines strung between Vancouver Island and Maud Island). On a flood, the strongest turbulence will be along the west wall and in the area south of Ripple Rock. On an ebb, the turbulence and the set starts between Maud Island and Ripple Rock. The ebb current sets northwest to the west wall.

Northbound vessels: On small tides, northbound vessels should arrive off the Maud Island light an hour before the end of the ebb, or an hour prior to high water slack, before the ebb begins. Once into the narrows, steer toward the tongue of the current stream (east of mid-channel) to avoid the whirlpools and eddies north of Maud Island up to North

Note how the current is pushing the barge to one side in Seymour Narrows.

Bluff. On big tides, low-powered vessels will find it prudent to be at the Maud Island light at high water slack, or just a few minutes into the north flowing ebb.

If the slack is at low water, arrive at the pass before the end of the ebb. Slack on large tides is not very long, five to ten minutes at most. You'll want to be past Brown Bay before the southflowing flood gets underway. It can be brutal in a slow-moving boat. You may find a back eddy along the eastern shore. On a large flood, Seymour Narrows can reach 16 knots, no place to be in any kind of boat.

Southbound vessels: Southbound boats should be opposite Brown Bay within an hour of the beginning or end of a neap (small) flood. On a large spring flood, it would be wise to be opposite Brown Bay within a half-hour of its end or beginning. Keep well off the sheer rock wall on the west shore of the narrows. Current turbulence can set a vessel onto that wall. The worst turbulence is usually south of Ripple Rock, especially if wind is against current. Stay on your side of the channel (i.e. to starboard) to be clear of any tugs or large ships headed the other way. The good news about Seymour Narrows is that there are no obstructions and just one strong, main stream.

– Bill Kelly
Anne Vipond and Bill Kelly are the authors of
Best Anchorages of the Inside Passage.

317

Coast Discovery Marina is a personable, friendly marina, with Dockside Fish & Chips.

Coast Marina is located behind the middle of Campbell River's three breakwaters, and has facilities for boats to 180 feet in length. Open all year, guest moorage, 30, 50 & 100 amp power, washrooms, showers, excellent laundry across the street in the plaza, garbage, recycling, water, and free Wi-Fi. Water taxi, whale watching, charter fishing, and adventure tours.

The marina has wide concrete docks with power and water to each slip. Docks C and D were extended in 2018. The marina is just steps away from Foreshore Park and downtown Tyee Plaza shopping. Dockside Fish & Chips is a fully licensed restaurant with indoor and outdoor seating right on the docks. An art gallery is located next door.

⑳ Discovery Harbour Marina. Suite 392-1434 Ironwood St., Campbell River, BC V9W 5T5; (250) 287-2614; info@ discoveryharbourmarina.com; www. discoveryharbourmarina.com. Monitors VHF 66A. Open all year, with a mixture of slips and side-tie. Washrooms, showers, laundry, garbage drop, ample guest moorage, 20, 30, 50 & 100 amp single/3- phase power, Wi-Fi. In-slip pumpout service. The G, H, I and J floats have side-tie moorage that can handle mega-yachts, additional side-tie on docks C and D. Finger piers have recently been added to docks A and C for 30, 40 and 50-foot slips. Customs clearance available. This is the largest of Campbell River's four breakwater-protected marinas. The marina

has excellent docks, landing assistance and friendly people.

The marina office, with showers, washrooms, and laundry, is in a two-story floating facility at the foot of the north ramp on K dock. Floating washrooms are also near E dock to save the long walk to the main washrooms. The docks can be busy with whale and bear tour operators. Water taxi located on the main dock.

The extensive Discovery Harbour Centre shopping plaza is adjacent to the marina, with everything you would expect to find in a major center.

⑳ Discovery Harbour Fuels. Box 512, Campbell River, BC V9W 5C1; (250) 287-3456; dhfs@telus.net; www. discoveryharbourfuel.com. Monitors VHF 66A. Located straight ahead as you enter the Discovery Harbour breakwater. Fuel dock open all year; gasoline, diesel, propane-exchange, self-service oil change system, and sani-pump station. Fresh water fill, water is excellent. A full line of cruising guides, maps, extensive charts, fishing gear, marine parts, ice, kerosene and convenience supplies.

⑳ Discovery Harbour Authority Small Craft Harbours. (250) 287-7091. Monitors VHF 66A. This marina was formerly for commercial boats only but is now open to recreational vessels; the marina is managed by the Discovery Harbour Authority. Open all year with 4000 feet of dock space located north of the fuel sales just inside the Discovery Harbour breakwater. Transient moorage with mandatory rafting; permanent slips for commercial vessels; launch ramp on site. 30 & 50 amp power and two 100-amp stations; no reservations, may call ahead for availability. Washrooms, showers, laundry, garbage drop with recycling and waste oil disposal; no Wi-Fi. Payment made at wharfinger office on site open 8 a.m.-4 p.m. daily; after hours use envelope payment drop at office door. Marina has a night watchman and camera surveillance.

Freshwater Marina and Boatyard. 2705 N Island Hwy, Campbell River, BC V9W 2H4; (250) 286-0701 Marina; (250) 203-2635 Boatyard; jwtimber@uniserve.com Marina; darcybain@gmail.com Boatyard; www.freshwatermarina.ca. Open all year Monday – Friday. Freshwater Marina is located about half a mile up the Campbell River from Discovery Passage; the Marina and Boatyard are accessible on a 6 foot tide or better for small craft and higher tides for larger vessels. River pilots are available, contact Freshwater Marina. Permanent moorage is available for vessels up to 65 feet, dryland storage for smaller craft. Tide dependent launch ramp. No transient moorage. Freshwater Boatyard has a 50 ton Travelift and do-it-yourself boatyard that also welcomes trades contractors.

DESTINATION CORTEZ ISLAND – A SAILOR'S LIFE ALONG THE BC COAST- By June Cameron

Publisher: Heritage House/Fine Edge; ISBN: 0-938665-60-X

June Cameron, along with her brother George and their parents George Sr. and Marjorie Griffin, lived aboard their 36-foot wooden boat for 19 years during the summers, traveling from Vancouver B.C. to Cortez Island to visit grandparents and cousins. Their explorations of the Sunshine Coast and Desolation Sound seem common place today, but it was a noble undertaking in the 1930's and early 40's before GPS, chart-plotters, depth sounders, guidebooks, and reliable weather information. Boats were prone to breakdowns and required constant maintenance, and non-perishable food stuffs weren't readily available.

Our Loggers Arrive

June's accounts include homesteading the islands of Desolation Sound during the 1920's, when her father's parents settled on Cortez Island. Stories of memorable people and happy times as well as unfortunate events serve as a colorful road to the past. The author provides insights into what it was like to survive on the islands and the challenges that early settlers faced on land and at sea.

The inconveniences, considered hardships today, are part of June's memorable experiences — bathing in salt water; hauling buckets of water back to the boat to do laundry; and boiling fish to store in jars. Some of the more pleasant activities included attending dances at Gorge Harbour, visiting the library at Whaletown, and shopping at Refuge Cove. The reader soon finds himself/herself immersed in a bygone age that is both fascinating and informative. You can purchase your copy of *Destination Cortez Island, A sailor's life along the BC Coast* at www.WaggonerGuide.com or through other retail outlets.

Destination Cortez

A common wartime scene on Cortez was the gathering of locals near the Manson's Landing post office (in background) when the Union Steamship approached with its cargo of groceries, mail, and freight. Walter Beasley is on the left, next to Nellie Jeffery. Her daughters Judy and Joan are in front, and her father-in-law is in the background on the left. Others in the scene include Postmaster Patterson, far right, and Ernie Bartholomew next to him. (Nellie Jeffery photo)

Upon finding her old family album, June's memories of her early childhood aboard the *Loumar* came flooding back. She decided it was time to share with others her stories and experiences filled with tidbits of history. Her writing style is captivating, sprinkled with humor and provides a fascinating insight into the early days of pleasure boating. Familiar place names take on a whole new meaning after reading her book — Granville Island was once an industrial area; the large imposing building in Pender Harbour once served as St Mary's Hospital, and a logging camp once stood above the falls in Teakerne Arm. Descriptions of other recognizable destinations include the old trading post at Manson's Landing; the company town at Powell River; and the machine shop at Squirrel Cove.

Seymour Narrows. Currents in Seymour Narrows run to 16 knots on the flood and 14 knots on the ebb, flooding south and ebbing north.

Northbound, you can wait for slack either in Menzies Bay on the Vancouver Island side, or in the good-size unnamed bay behind Maud Island on the Quadra Island side. South of Maud Island the flood forms a backeddy along Quadra Island, easily sweeping northbound boats toward Maud Island. Southbound, Plumper Bay is a good waiting spot on the east side, as is Brown Bay on the west side. Brown Bay has a floating breakwater, and a marina with a fuel dock and restaurant.

Both **Deepwater Bay** and **Plumper Bay** are too exposed and deep to be attractive as anchorages. **Menzies Bay** may have good anchorage, being careful to go around either end of a drying shoal which almost blocks the entrance. This area is used as a booming ground for the pulp mill in Campbell River.

Seymour Narrows is the principal route for northbound and southbound commercial traffic, including cruise ships. Give large vessels ample room to maneuver. Before going through, we urge you to read the Sailing Directions section on Seymour Narrows. Especially on a flood, Sailing Directions counsels against the west side because of rough water. Monitor the passage times of commercial traffic on VHF 71, the area Vessel Traffic Services (VTS) frequency.

The warship HMCS *Columbia* was sunk off Maud Island to create an artificial reef.

㉑ **Brown's Bay Marina & RV Park.** 15021 Brown's Bay Road, Campbell River, BC V9H 1N9; (250) 286-3135; marina@brownsbayresort.com; www.brownsbayresort.com. Monitors VHF 12 & 66A. Open all year, gasoline and diesel, side-tie moorage to 100 feet along 2000 feet of dock, 50 slips for boats to 24 feet, 15, 30 & 50 amp power, free Wi-Fi, washrooms, showers, laundry, ice, cable television, phone, garbage drop, marine & RV store, boat launch. Four rental cabins and tent cabins for camping available.

This marina is on Vancouver Island, at the north end of Seymour Narrows. Enter around the north end of the breakwater. Strong currents can sweep through the marina; be sure to take the current into account when maneuvering, and tie your boat to the dock securely.

The store has a variety of snack items, clothing, and fishing gear. The seasonal floating restaurant offers all-you-can-eat crab feed specials on Thursdays and Fridays, a signature event, along with their annual Luau. Call or check their website for the schedule.

Kanish Bay. Kanish Bay has several good anchorages. You could sneak behind the **Chained Islands**, and with some thought and planning find a number of delightful spots, especially in settled weather. A charted large aquaculture, or at least the buoyed anchor points for same, lies mid-channel

between 61-meter island and the entrance to Granite Bay. The small bay between Granite Bay and Small Inlet offers protection from westerlies. An aquaculture operation is in the mouth of this bay.

Correspondents James & Jennifer Hamilton anchored in the cove behind Bodega Point, just south of the 2-meter rock. "Really beautiful. Birds calling. Good holding in sticky mud."

Granite Bay. Granite Bay is well protected with a good bottom and room for several boats to anchor. The shore to the north is part of Small Inlet Marine Park and the shore on the south has a few houses. The Strathcona Regional District (250-830-6700) public dock has a 230 foot float with side-tie space that is mostly occupied by local boats. Self-registration and payment box at the head of the dock. Two 15 amp shore power receptacles located at the base of the ramp offer power during limited hours. No other services at the dock. A launch ramp (limited to boats 20 feet or less) and trailer parking are located at the park.

Small Inlet. A narrow but easily-run channel with a least depth of 8 feet leads from the northeast corner of Kanish Bay to Small Inlet. This inlet, surrounded by steep, wooded mountains, is beautiful, although we can confirm that a strong westerly from Johnstone Strait can get in and test your anchoring. Once through the kelp-filled entrance channel, a number of good anchorages can be found along the north shore. A couple of boats can fit behind a little knob of land near the southeast corner. The chart shows 3 rocks in this anchorage—actually, it's a reef with 3 high points. You also can anchor in the cove at the head of Small Inlet, behind two small islands.

A half-mile easy trail connects the cove

at the head of Small Inlet with Waiatt Bay. The trail head is at the head of the cove in Small Inlet with a trail sign pointing east to Waiatt Bay. To the west, a trail to Newton Lake follows the south shore of Small Inlet cove with two dinghy landing sites, one at the rock outcropping across from the two islands forming the cove, and the other at a rocky shore midway between the previous rock outcropping and the head of the cove. The trail to Newton Lake is a one-mile steep and sometimes difficult forest trail. Don't confuse a small pond, a short distance before Newton Lake, for the real thing. The crystal clear waters of Newton Lake invite a fresh water swim. From Newton Lake a two-mile trail continues to Granite Bay Road and Granite Bay

Small Inlet Marine Park. Located on the west side of Quadra Island bordering Octopus Islands Marine Park on the east, Small Inlet Marine Park has good anchoring opportunities in Small Inlet itself and in nearby Granite Bay and Kanish Bay. The marine park includes upland areas and trails. See *Okisollo Channel* map in this chapter.

Granite Point. If you are traveling between Discovery Passage and Okisollo Channel, you can safely steer inside Min Rock, north of Granite Point, and run close to Granite Point itself. You will be treated to the sight of some extraordinary rock formations on Granite Point.

Rock Bay Marine Park (Otter Cove). Otter Cove is just inside Chatham Point. It's a useful little anchorage, with convenient depths and protection from seas rolling down Johnstone Strait. If you need a place to hide until the wind or seas subside, it's a good spot.

The Strathcona Regional Public Dock is tucked in the south end of Granite Bay, a locals favorite.

Johnstone Strait

CHAPTER 11

JOHNSTONE STRAIT
*Yuculta Rapids • Stuart Island • Cordero Channel • Nodales Channel
Blind Channel • Greene Point Rapids • Whirlpool Rapids
Sunderland Channel • Johnstone Strait • Port Neville*

The southern tip of Stuart Island marks the northern boundary of Desolation Sound. North of Desolation Sound, you'll find colder water, harsher weather, fewer services, and a greater number of rocks, reefs and tidal rapids. You should have good ground tackle and know how to use it.

Fewer boats venture north of Desolation Sound. A greater percentage of those boats are 32 feet in length and larger. Many stay out for four to eight weeks or more, and the larger boats provide more comfortable accommodations. On average the occupants are older, too. The farther north you go, the more remote conditions become, all the way to Alaska.

It is possible to do a quick two- to three-week trip from Seattle to this area, although it might require long days on the water to get there. The reward is experiencing beautiful cruising grounds few others will see.

Garbage Drops. While occasionally you will find a lack of garbage drops in Desolation Sound and south, garbage becomes a much greater problem farther north. Garbage must be hauled from marinas and settlements to authorized dumps, usually on Vancouver Island. Since marinas must pay for hauling and disposal, most charge a fee for garbage, if they accept it at all. Those that do will sometimes take recyclables at no charge. Use as little glass as possible, wash and flatten cans, and pack paper out.

Fresh Water. Fresh water can be a problem even in Desolation Sound, and northward the supplies are fewer. Many marinas prohibited boat washing. Some marinas limited the amount of water for filling tanks. Check with marina staff before washing the boat or filling the tanks.

Some stops, such as Lagoon Cove or Blind Channel, have sweet spring water from deep wells. In some places, the potable water has a brown cast from cedar bark tannin. We don't know of anybody who has had a bad experience from it. We use an RV filter on the hose when filling the tank and a filtration system to a special tap in the galley for clean good tasting water. Others purchase large jugs of water for cooking and drinking.

Prices. The season is short and the costs are high. Everything must be brought in by water taxi, barge, or air. Don't be upset when prices are higher than at home. Remember, too, that during the season the marina personnel's workday starts early and ends late, and calls for a smile at all times.

Provisions. Going north there are major shopping centers and large grocery stores in Campbell River, Port McNeill and Port Hardy. There are small stores with many items and the essentials in Telegraph Harbour, Pierre's Echo Bay, Sullivan Bay, Sointula, and Alert Bay. You will not starve, though you may not always find those special ingredients for a unique recipe, like Old Bay for a prawn boil.

Chatham Point marks the Southern end of Johnstone Strait.

Everything must be brought in by boat and occasionally floatplane. Prices are higher and some resorts are now reserving perishables and other products for their marina guests only.

Recommended books. Peter Vassilopoulos's cruising guide, *Broughton Islands Cruising Guide,* is excellent. The book covers the waters from Yuculta Rapids to Port Hardy, and is packed with maps, history, and hundreds of aerial color photos.

A second book, *Local Knowledge: The Skipper's Reference, Tacoma to Ketchikan* by Kevin Monahan, is a compilation of useful navigation and trip-planning information, including mileage and conversion tables. It has a comprehensive section on tidal rapids, recommended strategies, and how to calculate timing for transit. We use the mileage charts regularly. Monahan's excellent Johnstone Strait diagrams are included in this chapter.

Exploring the South Coast of British Columbia, by Don Douglass and Réanne Hemingway-Douglass, is another excellent book covering this area.

THE INSIDE ROUTE TO THE BROUGHTONS

Most cruisers heading north choose the sheltered inside route through Cordero Channel, Chancellor Channel, Wellbore Channel and Sunderland Channel rather than face a long, possibly rough passage in Johnstone Strait against the prevailing northwest winds. Often the Johnstone Strait route is taken on the way home with the winds from astern and ideally on a flood tide. The inside route runs from the north end of Calm Channel (the south tip of Stuart Island), through five sets of rapids: Yuculta Rapids, Gillard Passage, Dent Rapids, Greene Point Rapids and Whirlpool Rapids. The route includes an open stretch of approximately 13 miles in Johnstone Strait (which cannot be avoided) between Sunderland Channel and Havannah Channel, after which the currents of Chatham Channel must be negotiated. Careful planning is paramount. You need to

know the times of slack water at each rapids, and you need to know how long it will take to get to each rapids.

Up-to-date charts and a copy of the Canadian Tide and Current Tables Vol. 6 or Ports and Passes are critical for safe navigation. Using the corrections shown in the Reference and Secondary Current Stations in the front part of the Tide and Current Tables (back of Ports and Passes), you must be comfortable calculating the times of slack water at the various rapids. For anchoring or transiting shallow channels, use the corrections in the Reference and Secondary Ports pages to calculate times and heights of tides.

The calculations can be daunting at first, but an evening spent reading the excellent instructions will clear matters considerably. For clarifications, don't be shy about asking a few old salts on the docks. They (we) love to help.

Since the waters north of Desolation Sound flood southward from the top of Vancouver Island and ebb northward, the northbound boat (if it wishes to clear a number of rapids in one run) has a timing problem. Assuming a start with Yuculta Rapids, all the rapids to the north will already have turned before slack water occurs at the Yucultas. It is best to approach Yuculta Rapids before the southbound flood turns to the northbound ebb, and utilize two backeddies (described below) to help your way against the flood for the two or so miles to Gillard Passage and Dent Rapids. Done correctly, you'll go through Dent Rapids against the last of the flood current, and let the new ebb current flush you out Cordero Channel.

The ebb will already have been running 13 miles away at Greene Point Rapids, which turned earlier. Depending on your boat's speed, the ebb could be at full force when you arrive. Rather than go through in these conditions, many choose to overnight at Blind Channel Resort. Shoal Bay and the Cordero Islands are other good places to wait for Greene Point Rapids to turn to slack.

The next day you can depart before high water slack and push through Greene Point

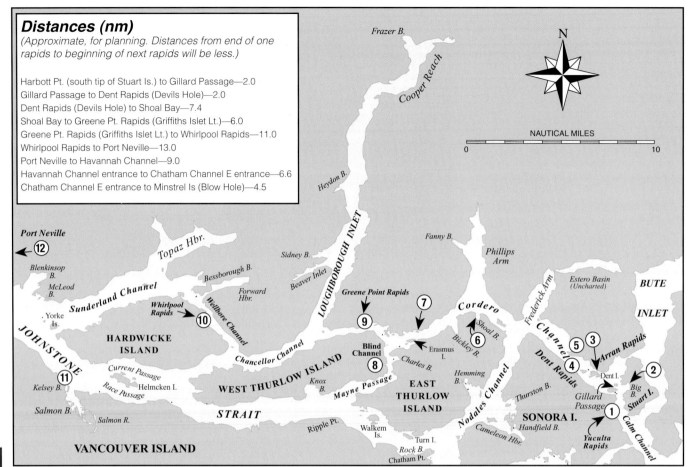

Distances (nm)
(Approximate, for planning. Distances from end of one rapids to beginning of next rapids will be less.)

Harbott Pt. (south tip of Stuart Is.) to Gillard Passage—2.0
Gillard Passage to Dent Rapids (Devils Hole)—2.0
Dent Rapids (Devils Hole) to Shoal Bay—7.4
Shoal Bay to Greene Pt. Rapids (Griffiths Islet Lt.)—6.0
Greene Pt. Rapids (Griffiths Islet Lt.) to Whirlpool Rapids—11.0
Whirlpool Rapids to Port Neville—13.0
Port Neville to Havannah Channel—9.0
Havannah Channel entrance to Chatham Channel E entrance—6.6
Chatham Channel E entrance to Minstrel Is (Blow Hole)—4.5

Johnstone Strait

Rapids in the dying flood current. Then you'll hurry to Wellbore Channel, to take Whirlpool Rapids early in the favorable ebb current. If this is done early in the morning, it is possible the wind will not have started building for the stretch in Johnstone Strait. With luck it can be a pleasant run down Sunderland Channel and into Johnstone Strait for the 13-mile run to Havannah Channel. How well this works depends on the speed of your boat, the time of day, the conditions, and the flexibility of your schedule.

Southbound the options are greater. Take your first rapids against the last of the dying ebb, and let the new flood current flush you south. Each rapids in succession turns at a later time. Given the right conditions even a slow boat can take all the rapids on one tide, with only a few hours' wait if the boat arrives at any given rapids when they are running too hard to risk transit.

Note: Canadian Tide and Current Tables *do not adjust* for Daylight Saving Time. Ports and Passes tide and current times are adjusted for Daylight Saving Time.

Caution: A tight schedule is not justification for taking a chance with bad conditions. The dangers are real.

① **Yuculta Rapids.** The Yuculta (pronounced "YEW-cla-ta") Rapids separate Stuart Island and Sonora Island. Taken at slack they are benign, but at full force on a spring tide, especially against an opposing wind, they

can be extremely dangerous. Northbound, Sailing Directions recommends that slow and low-powered boats arrive at the rapids an hour before high water slack, and use a backeddy along the Stuart Island shore until off Kellsey Point. Then cross to the Sonora Island shore to use a prevailing northerly current. This should position the boat to go through Gillard Passage and Dent Rapids satisfactorily. If you are late and unsure about transiting Dent Rapids, wait in Big Bay for the next slack.

② **Big Bay (Stuart Island).** For decades, Big Bay on Stuart Island has been a major fishing resort center. The public floats are behind a plank and piling breakwater at the head of Big Bay. The former Big Bay Marina is now a private fishing resort with no services for cruising boats. The Stuart Island Community dock has moorage and a store. Big Bay has seen an increase in development of exclusive, high-end fishing resorts and lodges over the past few years. Many boats criss-cross the bay during the summer and peak fishing seasons.

② **Stuart Island Community Dock.** P.O. Box 5-6, Stuart Island, BC V0P 1V0; (250) 202-3625; postmaster@stuartisland.info; www.stuartislandca.info. Monitors VHF 66A. Moorage, water, liquor, laundry, post office, store, ice, fishing guides, good cell phone coverage, free Wi-Fi. No power, no fuel. Staff is on call 24 hours a day in season.

The docks were rebuilt and expanded to

accommodate boats to 100+ feet. The store carries convenience items, liquor, locally made goods. Store hours are 8:00 a.m. to 5:00 p.m. seven days a week in season. A large deck with a covered picnic area connects to the store.

A well-marked road and trail lead to Eagle Lake, where a skiff is kept. It's a good walk, through beautiful forest.

Shoal: An important shoal lies a short distance off the dock. Approach from the south.

Gillard Passage. Currents run to 13 knots on the flood and 10 knots on the ebb. Transit near slack water. Times of slack are shown in Canadian Tide and Current Tables Vol. 6 and Ports and Passes. Pass south of Jimmy Judd Island. Big Bay is a good place to wait if the current is too strong.

If you're lucky, you might find the trees on and near Jimmy Judd Island filled with eagles that swoop down to the swirling waters to feed on hake, whose air bladders have brought them to the surface. It's a real sight.

③ **Fisherman's Landing & Lodge.** P.O. Box 5-3, Stuart Island, BC V0P 1V0; (250) 202-0187; fishermanslanding@hotmail.com. Monitors VHF 66A (previously known as Morgans Landing). All new concrete docks were installed by the new owners in 2018. 350 feet of guest moorage, with 30, 50 and 100 amp power. Some 200 amp power. Wi-Fi, water, washrooms, showers, laundry and ice. Reservations recommended. The 50-

RUNNING THE RAPIDS

The cautious advice—the first rule of thumb—for transiting tidal current rapids is to wait for slack water and go through then. This rule of thumb is fine but imperfect. There you sit, watching other boats go through before slack and after slack.

A second rule of thumb is a corollary of the first. It says that boats should arrive at a rapids an hour before predicted slack, so they're ready to go through as soon as the rapids grow quiet. Like most rules of thumb, this one doesn't always work either. Sometimes it appears as if the rapids would be safe much longer than an hour before or after. Sometimes one look tells you it's smarter to wait. With a little study, however, it's possible to predict when the window of opportunity will be wider or narrower.

Before going further, two definitions:

Slack water. Slack water is the time when rapids cease flowing one direction but haven't begun flowing the opposite direction. Another word for slack is turn, meaning the time when the water's flow turns from one direction to the other.

Window, or window of opportunity. For purposes of this article, window means a time when most boats can transit a rapids safely, without too much excitement.

This article gelled with me in Malibu Rapids at the mouth of Princess Louisa Inlet. It has its origins in the successful running of the Pacific Northwest's tidal current rapids over a span of nearly four decades.

Understand that my wife and I are the original cautious and conservative boaters when it comes to rapids. Several years ago we hiked from Big Bay, on B.C.'s Stuart Island, to Arran Rapids, one of the most deadly rapids on the coast. We arrived in what must have been the middle of a large tide exchange, with its frightening whitewater overfalls, upwellings and whirlpools that no sensible boat could be expected to survive. White water is full of air, and less buoyant than green water. Boats float lower, with less freeboard. Rudders lose effectiveness and propellers lose their bite. We got the message: Rapids are not to be trifled with.

With experience, we have developed a loose sense of when a rapids could be run at times other than slack. Until our transits of Malibu Rapids, however, this sense was not refined to any kind of structure.

For what it's worth, here's our thinking. But first,

Caution: Every rapids has its own personality and characteristics. What follows is general in nature, and may not apply to any given rapids. It is a way of looking at things, an approach to the problem. It is not a guarantee.

The determining factors are 1) high water slack vs. low water slack; 2) neap tides vs. spring tides; 3) the size of the exchange on each side of slack.

High water slack vs. low water slack. We entered Princess Louisa Inlet through Malibu Rapids without drama nearly two hours before high water slack. When we departed two days later we found definite swirls, overfalls and whirlpools only 20 minutes before low water slack. The two transits were entirely different.

Our entry to Princess Louisa Inlet was at high water, when the narrow, shallow channel was full. Our departure was at low water, when the channel was much less full and much narrower. The less water in the channel, the faster the current must run.

General Rule: The window of opportunity is wider at high water slack. The narrower and shallower the channel, the more this is true.

Neap tides vs. spring tides. Neap tides are small tides that occur around the times of half moon. Neaps often show only a small dip from one high water to the next. The widest windows of opportunity occur on that small dip.

Spring tides occur around the times of full moon or no moon. Low tides can be very low and high tides very high. On springs even the dip between two high tides can be significant. The

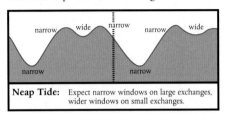

Neap Tide: Expect narrow windows on large exchanges, wider windows on small exchanges.

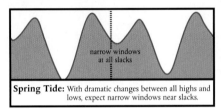

Spring Tide: With dramatic changes between all highs and lows, expect narrow windows near slacks.

windows of opportunity are narrower on spring tides than on neap tides.

Since it takes only a week to go from neap tide to spring tide (and another week to go from spring tide to neap tide), the experience from just a few days earlier has no bearing on the day you're going through. Each day, each transit, must be evaluated on its own.

Size of the exchange. Imagine this exercise. Using a garden hose, fill a five-gallon container in a minute. Then fill a one-gallon container in a minute. You had to turn the flow of water way down for the one-gallon can. Our neap tide entry through Malibu Rapids was near the top of a fairly small rise from lower low water to high water. The smaller the rise or fall, the less the current.

Conclusions

1. The window is narrowest at lower low water slack. The tide has dropped a long way and will be rising a long way. The farther the tide has dropped and the farther it is to rise, the narrower the window. Also, the shallower and narrower the rapids, the narrower the window at lower low water. At lower low water, plan to go through fairly close to slack.

2. The window at high water slack is wider on neap tides than on spring tides. The window is widest in the "dip" between the two high waters on neap tides.

3. At high water slack, the window is narrower on the rise from lower low water. The window is wider between the next two high waters.

Disclaimer. Skippers are responsible for the welfare and safety of their vessels and passengers. The purpose of this article is to provide tools for evaluating situations. It is not the purpose of this article to tell a skipper when to transit a rapids. When in doubt, the safest course is to transit at slack water, regardless of what other boats are doing.

– Robert Hale

See Area Map Page 324 - Maps Not for Navigation

MONAHAN'S LOCAL KNOWLEDGE

LOCAL EFFECTS – EBB

West of Port Neville, the ebb begins along the mainland shore and takes almost two hours to completely cover the strait from one side to the other.

Turn to flood occurs in Sunderland Channel 1h 40m before Johnstone Strait Central and 1h 20m before Camp Point.

To avoid heavy weather in Johnstone Strait (especially when wind opposes currents) Sunderland, Wellbore and Cordero Channels offer calmer conditions.

Current Passage turns to ebb 50m after Johnstone Strait Central, but 1h 15m before Camp Point.

Turn to ebb at Vansittart Point occurs up to 30m before Current Passage, almost two hours before Camp Point.

Freshet conditions in mainland rivers may encourage a premature turn to ebb in the vicinity of Mayne Passage.

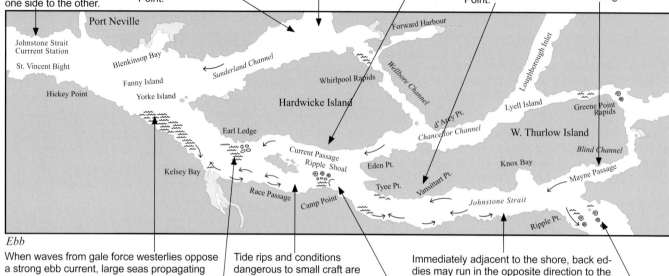

Ebb

When waves from gale force westerlies oppose a strong ebb current, large seas propagating southward are generated in this area. In this case, smaller boats should seek shelter at Port Neville or enter the harbour at Kelsey Bay and wait for the contrary current to moderate.

Tide rips and conditions dangerous to small craft are generated in this area during large tides, especially when strong westerlies oppose the ebb current.

A steep underwater ridge extends southward from Earl Ledge across the channel to the Vancouver Island shore. Deep tidal currents meet this steep topography and are deflected to the surface, causing extreme turbulence west of Helmcken Island during large tides.

Immediately adjacent to the shore, back eddies may run in the opposite direction to the main flow. However, at headlands between back eddies, the ebb current is strong right up to the shore.

Stay clear of Ripple Shoal. Dangerous whirlpools form to the west of the shoal during the ebb.

Tide rips and turbulent conditions are generated in this area during large tides, especially when strong westerly winds oppose the ebb current.

LOCAL EFFECTS – FLOOD

Near Port Neville, the mainland and Vancouver Island shores turn to flood up to one hour before the center of the channel.

In Current Passage, turbulence is weaker near the north shore.

To avoid heavy weather in Johnstone Strait (especially when wind opposes currents) Sunderland, Wellbore and Cordero Channels offer calmer conditions.

Stay clear of Ripple Shoal. Dangerous whirlpools form to the east of the shoal during the flood.

First ebb current in eastern Johnstone Strait begins between Mayne Passage and Vansittart Point, up to two hours before turn to ebb at Camp Point.

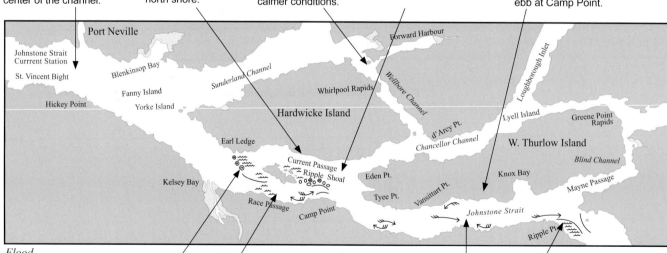

Flood

Tide rips and conditions dangerous to small craft are generated in this area during large tides, especially when strong southeasterlies oppose the flood current.

The ebb current in Current and Race Passages persists approximately 1h 20m longer than in Sunderland Channel.

Immediately adjacent to the shore, back eddies may run in the opposite direction to the main flow. However, at headlands between back eddies, the flood current is strong right up to the shore.

Tide rips and turbulent conditions are generated in this area during large tides, especially when strong southeasterlies oppose the flood current.

foot float on the west end is for float planes. Happy Hours are held on weekends. The dining room is expected to be open for 2019. Plans were underway in 2018 to provide additional moorage floats for the 2019 season, along with a fuel dock. Facilities include accommodations, eco tours and guided fishing charters, and meals by reservation. This is an upscale fishing lodge located at the mouth of the little bay that separates Dent Island from the mainland. Floatplane and water taxi service available.

③ **Dent Island Lodge.** P.O. Box 8, Stuart Island, BC V0P 1V0; (250) 203-2553; info@ dentisland.com; www.dentisland.com. Monitors VHF 66A. Open late May to mid-September, guest moorage for boats to 200 feet on wide, stable concrete docks, 30 & 50 amp power at every dock pedestal, plus single-phase 100 amp power upon request. Potable water on the docks, Wi-Fi, good cell phone service, fishing guides, restaurants, gift shop, sauna, showers, exercise room, hot tub.

The service at Dent Island Lodge is first class, with moorage and dinner prices to match. The main lodge was removed in 2017 for the construction of a new bigger and better lodge that opened in late June of 2018. The new lodge takes advantage of the gorgeous views. The enlarged dining room and other spaces flow out to the rapids of Canoe Passage.

The professional staff treats you like a special guest in a small, quiet, private retreat.

The Reversing rapids in Canoe Pass beside Dent Island Lodge are fascinating to watch.

At the end of the day after the guide boats have returned from fishing, an elegant appetizer table is set out. The dinner menu in the main dining room is limited but very well done. Less formal, the Rapids Outdoor Grill is a small-plate-style dining area with a view of Canoe Pass rapids. Tables surround the kitchen and the chef personally prepares each dish directly in front of you. Both dining options are popular; reservations recommended.

A hiking trail, rough in places, is a good place to work off some of the calories.

The lodge is at the back of a little bay separating Dent Island from the mainland, next to Canoe Pass rapids, where 10- to 12-knot whitewater tidal currents churn. A spacious deck overlooks the pass. Another

deck, screened by forest, holds a hot tub.

The lodge has a fast jet boat for eco-explorations and thrilling rides in the rapids. They offer tours to the head of Bute Inlet, including runs up the rivers in the inlet. Resort manager Justin Farr is an experienced fishing guide in these waters, and he knows every swirl, overfall and calm spot. The boat turns in its own length and dances through rough waters. The tour will make you respect the waters around Dent and Arran Rapids. Salmon charters can be arranged by the resort.

Schedule arrivals and departures to coincide with slack water in Gillard Passage, and approach from the southeast. Chart 3543 shows the lodge location, including the dock. Watch for a shoal area 0.9 meter deep at zero tide on the east side of the entry. Stay

327

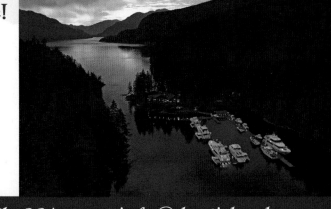

Small plate dinners at the Rapids Outdoor Grill at Dent Island Lodge are a special treat for the crew.

mid-channel. It is best to make reservations, even in the less-busy weeks of the season. Reservations are just about essential during high season.

④ **Dent Rapids**. Currents run to 9 knots on floods and 8 knots on ebbs. Time corrections are shown under Reference and Secondary Current Stations in Tide and Current Tables Vol. 6 and Ports and Passes. Per Sailing Directions, "In Devils Hole, violent eddies and whirlpools form between 2 hours after turn to flood and 1 hour before turn to ebb." People who have looked into Devils Hole vow never to run that risk again. Favor the Sonora Island shore of Dent Rapids.

Tugboat Passage, between Dent Island and Little Dent Island, avoids the potential problems of Devils Hole, and the current is less. Use the large-scale inset on Chart 3543, and favor the Little Dent Island side.

Arran Rapids. Arran Rapids separate the north side of Stuart Island and the mainland, and connect Bute Inlet with Cordero Channel. Current predictions for Arran Rapids are shown in Canadian Tide and Current Tables Vol. 6, and Ports and Passes. Arran Rapids are unobstructed, but tidal streams run to 13+ knots. These rapids have a long history of killing the unknowing or foolhardy. Run Arran Rapids at slack water only, if at all. We have hiked from Big Bay to Arran Rapids

and watched the water during a spring tide. The enormous upwellings, whirlpools, and overfalls were frightening.

⑤ **Denham Bay.** (250) 703-6978 (Peter); (250) 218-8538 (Sarah); denhamdocks@gmail.com; www.denhambay.com. Monitors VHF 66A. Denham Bay is located in a lovely setting with park-like grounds offering several well-appointed vacation cabins. Be sure to stay clear of Secord Rock located approximately 400 yards offshore lying northwest of Horn Point; there is currently no buoy marking this rock. Open May 15 to October 15, water, Wi-Fi, no power.

Owners Peter Geneau and Sarah Askwith are friendly and welcoming. Peter has worked in salmon enhancement and as a fishing guide in the area. Sarah worked as a high-end pastry chef for some of the local resorts.

A dock was added in June of 2017, increasing moorage space to approximately 500 feet. Reservations are taken for group events, priority is given to boats making use of the cabins. Denham Bay primarily caters to smaller boats but can accommodate boats up to 95 feet as space allows, call ahead for availability. A beautiful outdoor kitchen area with granite countertops is available for cabin guests, and boaters moored at the marina can make use of a separate shore-side kitchen area and the wood-fired pizza oven. The grounds are a delight, with lovely walkways and a

shore-side boardwalk. Hiking trails in the area. Salmon charters can be arranged with prior notification.

Frederick Arm. Frederick Arm is deep, with almost no good places to anchor. You can anchor in several nooks along the eastern shoreline, or near the head, where the bottom shoals rapidly.

Estero Basin. If the crowds are getting to you, uncharted Estero Basin, at the head of Frederick Arm, is where you can avoid them. The narrow passage into the basin, called "The Gut," is passable only at high water slack (very high water slack, we now are told), and slack doesn't last long. A dinghy with outboard motor is a good way to go, and you may have to drag it part of the way. We have not been in Estero Basin, but Wolferstan has. He writes convincingly about the strong currents in The Gut and the eerie stillness of the 5-mile-long basin with its uncharted rocks. Friends tell us that Estero Basin is absolutely beautiful, usually deserted, with small islands, sheer cliffs, and water that grows fresher the farther you go. "Bring your lunch and shampoo," we're advised.

Waggoner reader Patrick Freeny reported that he had just enough water for his inflatable dinghy on a 13-foot tide. On a 10-foot tide the dinghy had to be dragged in. Dinghies or skiffs only, no larger boats.

NODALES CHANNEL

Thurston Bay Marine Park. Thurston Bay Marine Park is large enough to hold many boats without feeling too crowded. We've had good overnight anchorages in Handfield Bay, and in 36 feet behind Block Island.

The landlocked inlet behind Wilson Point, on the south side of Thurston Bay, is best entered at half tide or higher. Wolferstan calls this inlet Anchorage Lagoon. At the entrance, least depth at zero tide is 2 feet or less. We tiptoed in near the bottom of a 2.9-foot low tide with the depth sounder showing 6 feet (our boat drew 3 feet). Inside we found four boats at anchor in a pretty setting, with 9 to 10 feet of depth. This is a good place to know your vessel's draft and the tidal range during your stay.

Be bear aware when ashore.

LOCAL KNOWLEDGE

Dangerous Rocks: Note that in the entrance to Cameleon Harbour, Douglas Rock, which dries at 1.5 meters, is detached from Bruce Point. Give Bruce Point ample room.

Handfield Bay. Enter via Young or Burgess Passages, located to port as you enter Cameleon Harbour. Chart 3543 (1:40,000) makes it clear that you should enter Handfield Bay leaving Tully Island to port. Once inside you'll find excellent protection, good anchoring depths, and shore access. The rock

Denham Bay docks just above Dent Rapids overlooking Cordero Channel

north of Tully Island is usually easy to spot at half tide. Handfield Bay is a favorite stop for many cruisers.

Cameleon Harbour. Cameleon Harbour is a big, open bay with ample protected anchorage, depending on where you need the shelter.

Hemming Bay. Enter leaving the Lee Islands well to starboard to avoid Menace Rock in the middle of the bay. Most of Hemming Bay is deep, but you can find anchoring depths near the head. Field Correspondent Deane Hislop reports a large booming operation on the north shore with signage warning of cables across the bottom; anchorage is possible at the southwest side of the bay, but the beauty of the bay is spoiled by the logging operation.

⑥ **Shoal Bay.** Shoal Bay has a public float with good anchorage off the outboard end. The water shallows dramatically at the head of the bay. Shoal Bay is protected from most winds blowing down Cordero Channel, but is open to wakes from passing boats. It has a beautiful view up Phillips Arm. It's a good place to wait for slack water at the rapids north or south. Rafting is mandatory; set out fenders on both sides. The docks fill quickly during the summer, so arrive early or be prepared to anchor out. No power or water at the docks. Mark MacDonald is the wharfinger, and moorage fees are collected at the Shoal Bay Pub, just up from the head of the wharf.

⑥ **Shoal Bay Pub.** General Delivery, Blind Channel, BC V0P 1B0; (250) 287-6818; shoalbay@mac.com; www.shoalbay.ca. Open May 1 to October 1, cash payments. Free Wi-Fi at the pub, washrooms, showers and laundry. Guest cabins through Airbnb. The pub has cold beer and other beverages, indoor seating, and a deck with breathtaking views up Phillips Arm.

A large vegetable patch, adorned with sculpture, is available for garden-deprived cruisers who like to get their hands dirty. All tools are provided. Pay by donation for what you pick. Mark's wife Cynthia is a talented potter, and her locally thrown and fired pottery is available for sale. Her work adorns the property.

For exercise, take the sometimes challenging hike up the mountain to the abandoned gold mine. Be bear aware.

The Shoal Bay International Blues Festival is held in early August, check their website for dates. What started out as a bunch of friendly folks jamming now has a stage with a schedule of acts. The dock and anchorage fill quickly, so arrive early. The music goes on into the wee hours and echoes across the bay.

Phillips Arm. Phillips Arm is deep, with little protection along the shores. Fanny Bay looks good on the chart, but has log booming activity. A northwest wind can blow through a saddle in the mountains at the head of **Fanny Bay.** On an earlier visit we found a stiff breeze in the bay; in Phillips Arm the air was calm. Large logging operations are located near the head of the inlet. A friend, much experienced, tells us not to anchor in the area of Dyer Point. The bottom there is foul with a tangle of sunken logs. *[Hale]*

Bickley Bay. Bickley Bay on Cordero Channel has anchoring depths toward the head of the bay. Favor the east shore to avoid a shoal area. Friends who have cruised in the area extensively warn of poor holding ground and won't go in anymore. Phil Richter at Blind Channel Resort also warns of poor holding. Caution advised.

⑦ **Cordero Lodge.** Cordero Lodge, General Delivery, Blind Channel, BC V0P 1B0;

currently no phone number; corderolodge@gmail.com; www.corderolodge.com. The Lodge and restaurant closed in 2017 due to the death of the previous owner and subsequent vandalism. New owners are making plans to return the facility to operation. At press time it was not known what services would be available in 2019. Boaters may tie-up at their own risk.

Please, please slow down. Passing boat traffic in Cordero Channel can put out damaging wakes that roll into boats moored at Cordero Lodge. As you approach the lodge location, throttle back to no-wake speed and hold that speed until you're past.

Crawford Anchorage. Crawford Anchorage, between Erasmus Island and East Thurlow Island, is chancy at best, with a rocky and poor holding bottom. Friends report they have anchored in Crawford Anchorage successfully, using a Bruce anchor and a stern-tie to Erasmus Island. We tried anchoring with indifferent results. Enter Crawford Anchorage from the west—rocks lie in the eastern entrance. Rocks also lie southeast of Mink Island.

Mayne Passage (Blind Channel). Mayne Passage connects Cordero Channel with Johnstone Strait. From Johnstone Strait, the entrance can be hard to spot, hence the local name "Blind Channel." The current in Mayne Passage reaches 5 knots at springs, flooding north and ebbing south. Chart 3543 (1:40,000) shows rips in the northern part of Mayne Passage, and Sailing Directions warns of whirlpools and overfalls. Passages near slack are recommended. Blind Channel Resort, on the west shore of Mayne Passage, is popular. On the east side of Mayne Passage, Charles Bay is a good anchorage.

Charles Bay. On the east side of Mayne Passage, Charles Bay has convenient

329

The view of Phillips Arm and Shoal Bay public floats from the Shoal Bay Pub

Blind Channel Resort's tidal turbine power generator is anchored just north of the resort.

anchoring depths around Eclipse Islet in the center of the bay. Just east of Eclipse Islet, however, the bay shoals to drying flats.

LOCAL KNOWLEDGE

STRONG CURRENTS: Current runs across the face of the floats at Blind Channel Resort and landing can be a little tricky. At the fingers themselves, the current runs from north to south about 90 percent of the time, regardless of the current in the middle of the channel. A short distance off the fingers, however, the current usually runs from south to north. You can verify the current direction at the docks by observing which way the fingers press against the pilings at the outer ends. Call on the VHF for docking instructions. One of the staff always comes down to help with landings. They know what to do.

⑧ **Blind Channel Resort.** Blind Channel, BC V0P 1B0; (888) 329-0475; info@blindchannel.com; www.blindchannel.com. Monitors VHF 66A. Open all year, gasoline, diesel, propane. Ample moorage on 2000 feet of dock, 15, 30 & some 50 amp power, washrooms, showers, laundry, UV-treated spring water, free Wi-Fi. Garbage drop for fee, no charge for glass and cans. Float planes stop here. This is a complete, well-run, and popular marina and resort, with water taxi, adventure tours, accommodations, well-stocked store, fresh-baked goods during the high season, post office, liquor agency, gift items. The nice gazebo overlooking the marina is a welcome addition in rainy weather. Several events are held throughout the summer months, check their website for the season's schedule.

The resort is surrounded by hiking trails, developed and maintained by Interfor. One trail leads to an 900-year-old cedar, 16 feet in diameter. It's a good hike and a splendid old tree. Recommended.

The fully-licensed Cedar Post Restaurant (open June-Labour Day) is excellent, akin to something that might be found in Whistler or Vancouver. The servers are well-dressed and the menu is varied. Breakfast and dinner are offered daily during the peak season. The Grill Shack on the seaside patio is open for lunch in July and August.

This is a real family enterprise, now spanning four generations. Edgar and the late Annemarie Richter bought Blind Channel in the early 1970s. Edgar designed and built all the buildings, and Annemarie's distinctive and lovely artwork decorates the dock and the restaurant. What they built, with long hours and hard labor, is a long way from what they bought 40 years ago.

Their son Phil Richter is general manager. Phil and Jennifer's sons Eliot and William grew up working on the docks and in the dining room. Eliot is now a partner in the business and lives on-site. You will most likely see Eliot's children running around the property, learning and having fun.

LOCAL KNOWLEDGE

Tidal Current Turbine Generator: July 2017, Blind Channel Resort added a tidal current turbine generator anchored in Mayne Passage less than 1/4 mile north of the resort and 400 feet from the West Thurlow Island shore. Most of the turbine generator is below the water's surface with part of the frame floating above. The turbine supplies electrical power to the resort.

⑨ **Greene Point Rapids.** Currents in Greene Point Rapids can run to 7 knots on spring tides. On small tides currents are much less. Sailing Directions warns of "considerable overfalls, whirlpools and eddies," and recommends transiting near slack. Slack water occurs about 1 hour and 30 minutes before slack water at Seymour Narrows. Current corrections are shown under Seymour Narrows in the Secondary Stations section in Tide and Current Tables Vol. 6, and in Ports and Passes. When eastbound on flood tides, low-powered boats, and boats with tows, are cautioned against being set against Erasmus Island.

Loughborough Inlet. Loughborough (pronounced "Loch-brough") Inlet, off Chancellor Channel, is deep, with steep-to sides and few good anchorages. The best anchorage used to be in Beaver Inlet, a short distance from the mouth on the western shore. Beaver Inlet is now a log booming ground with significant commercial activity, making it ill-suited to pleasure boats. Edith Cove in Beaver Inlet is occupied by a float home and log raft, so it's not an anchorage.

Sidney Bay. Sidney Bay indents the western shore of Loughborough Inlet, where resident homesteaders Dane Campbell and Helen Piddington operate a rustic 120-foot float for visiting boats, located on the south side of the bay 50°30.88'N/125°36.06'W. Payment can be made at the float shed, or across the bay at their home on the north shore. A picnic table and book exchange are in the float shed. Dane most likely will be ready to receive your painter line and provide good conversation. Field Correspondent Deane Hislop writes, "It's well protected from the wind and a beautiful location. We've stayed many times." Dane is a soft spoken commercial fisherman that we have found quite interesting to talk to. In 1975 he and his wife moved to Sidney Bay, where they raised their two children. Helen's book, *The Inlet*, describes life and their experiences in Loughborough Inlet." Her other book, *The Rumble Seat*, describes growing up in the 1930's near Victoria BC. The Landons report that Helen's health is failing; boaters may wish to visit this pioneer out-station, one of the last remaining from a bygone era, before it too passes with time.

WELLBORE CHANNEL

⑩ **Whirlpool Rapids.** Whirlpool Rapids on **Wellbore Channel** has currents to 7 knots. The time of turn is based on Seymour Narrows, and corrections are shown under Secondary Current Stations in the Tide and Current Tables Vol. 6, and Ports and Passes. The flood sets southeast and the ebb sets northwest. When the current is running, expect strong whirlpools, upwellings and back eddies on the downstream side. The turbulence occurs south of Carterer Point on the flood, and north of Carterer Point on the ebb. It is best to transit within a half-hour of slack, although on small tides boats seem to go through anytime. At low tide you might see bears on the beach near the south entrance to Wellbore Channel.

Forward Harbour. The entrance to Forward Harbour is narrow but unobstructed. Most of the harbor is 60 to 90 feet deep. Douglas Bay is a pretty anchorage, sheltered from Johnstone Strait westerlies that turn and blow through Sunderland Channel. The bottom of Douglas Bay drops off quickly, and you may find yourself anchored in 60 feet of water instead of 30 feet—a good reason to carry at least 300 feet of anchor rode. We've had a report that a southeast wind can make for a rough time for boats anchored along the northern shore. Field Correspondent Jim Norris reports cell reception outside and east of Douglas Bay, along the north shore.

A trail leads from Douglas Bay to a white sand beach at Bessborough Bay. In the past, the trail was well marked and easy to walk, but we received a report that winter blowdown has made the trail much more challenging.

If Forward Harbour is too full, good anchorage can be found in the little bay on Hardwicke Island, directly across from the mouth of Forward Harbour.

Bessborough Bay. Although you can find anchoring depths in the southeast corner, the entire bay is open to strong westerlies blowing up Sunderland Channel.

Topaze Harbour. Big and pretty enough, but little shelter for small boats.

Sunderland Channel. Sunderland Channel connects Wellbore Channel with Johnstone Strait. If the westerly is blowing and whitecaps are in Sunderland Channel, it will likely be worse in Johnstone Strait. Many boats wait out these conditions in Forward Harbour.

All of the channels northwest of Yuculta Rapids—Nodales Channel, Mayne Passage, Chancellor Channel, and Sunderland Channel—lead to Johnstone Strait. Each provides some protection and a chance to observe conditions on Johnstone Strait before venturing out. A strong westerly wind opposed by an ebb current can make Johnstone Strait difficult.

JOHNSTONE STRAIT

Johnstone Strait is a seductive and difficult body of water. The strait begins at Chatham Point in the east, and stretches 54 miles along the northeast side of Vancouver Island to Blinkhorn Peninsula. It is the shortest route up- or down-island. Especially on the Vancouver Island side, Johnstone Strait is bounded by steep, high and beautiful mountains. On a clear day the scenery is awesome.

That is the seductive part. The difficult part is what the wind and current in Johnstone Strait do to each other. The flood current flows eastward, down-island, toward Discovery Passage and Campbell River. The ebb current flows westward, up-island, toward Queen Charlotte Strait and the North Pacific Ocean. A residual ebb surface current exists in Johnstone Strait, increasing the west-flowing ebb current's strength and duration. In the summer, the prevailing wind in Johnstone Strait is a westerly, often a gale-force westerly, funneled by the mountains. The result is a classic wind-against-current heaping up of the seas.

Conditions are worst where the meeting of currents creates tide-rips, even in calm conditions. This stretch begins at Ripple Shoal, east of Kelsey Bay. It extends westward past Kelsey Bay, through Race Passage and Current Passage, and across the mouth of Sunderland Channel. Especially on an ebb, when the westerly is blowing you don't want to be there—period. Leave the heroics to others. Johnstone Strait can take all the pleasure out of a pleasure boat.

Monahan's Local Knowledge diagrams, earlier in this chapter, illustrate Johnstone Strait's trouble spots.

Despite the potential problems, we have run the length of Johnstone Strait, both directions, many times, and often had an excellent ride. But we listened to the weather and went when conditions were calm or near-calm. If the wind had come up, we were prepared to run for cover in a bay or seek out a friendly point to hide behind until conditions improved. We always keep a bail-out point in mind. Conditions can change quickly.

Watch for drift in Johnstone Strait. There's considerable current activity, and many shear lines where scrap wood, tree limbs, logs, and even entire floating trees accumulate.

Turn Island. Turn Island is off the southern tip of East Thurlow Island, at the intersection of Johnstone Strait and Discovery Passage. Anchor behind Turn Island, about where the 5.8-meter sounding is shown on the chart across from Turn Bay, with good holding and room to swing. The anchorage has nice views to Johnstone Strait and the mountains on Vancouver Island. *[Hamilton]* Charts show a log dump north of this anchorage. Reader Kelly Calvert reports snagging a logging cable when they anchored in small Turn Bay behind Turn Island.

Knox Bay. Knox Bay is located on the north side of Johnstone Strait, near the mouth of Mayne Passage. Knox Bay would be a poor choice for an anchorage, but a good hideout to escape a strong westerly in the strait. The northwest corner of the bay is best protected. Unfortunately, it is deep and occasionally has log booming.

Fanny Island. When the Environment Canada weather station was moved from Helmcken Island to Fanny Island a few years ago, Johnstone Strait weather reports improved dramatically (Helmcken Island could report 8 knots of wind when it was blowing 30). We're told, however, that while Fanny Island reports of northwest winds are fairly accurate, south and east winds can be reported less than what's actually going on.

Helmcken Island. Helmcken Island has protected anchorage on its north side in Billygoat Bay. Currents in this part of the strait run at 5 knots. When opposed by wind from the opposite direction large, dangerous seas can build rapidly. Billygoat Bay is a good place to hide out. Anchor in approximately 30 feet, although Correspondents James and Jennifer Hamilton found only poor holding over rock. Instead, they recommend the cove northwest of Billygoat Bay. They go up to the head of the cove, where they have found calm water, with an "awesome" view eastward. The cove is unnamed in Sailing Directions or on the chart. The Hamiltons call it Helmcken Cove.

⑪ **Kelsey Bay.** (250) 282-3623. Kelsey Bay, on the north side of Vancouver Island, has

a breakwater southeast of the harbor, made of old ship hulks—the Union Steamship *Cardena* and three WWII frigates: *HMCS Runnymede, HMCS Lasalle,* and *HMCS Longueil.* Enter leaving the light green breakwater to starboard and the old ships to port. Watch for current entering the breakwater. Transient moorage is on A, B, and C docks, maximum length 60 feet. Water, 20 and 30 amp power, garbage drop, recycling, oil disposal. Most of the moorage is occupied by commercial fish boats. Rafting may be required. Moorage is paid at the honor box at the top of the ramp, an attendant is on site during the summer months. We found the docks to be clean and well maintained The Straits View Cafe, located behind the breakwater, welcomes boaters at their 100-ft dock while enjoying breakfast, lunch, or dinner; the cafe is closed on Tuesdays. Overnight stays are permitted on the Cafe dock, moorage charged, 20-amp power, reservations accepted, call (250) 282-0118.

A small gift shop that doubles as a tourist office is located on the wharf at the north end of the marina. The small village of Sayward is approximately one mile south, some services but the grocery store is no longer open.

Yorke Island. Located in the middle of Johnstone Strait, west of Hardwicke Island, Yorke Island is the site of several gun emplacements which were installed in 1937. These ruins from WWII were originally intended to block enemy backdoor approach to the Strait of Georgia and the cities of Vancouver and Victoria. Well maintained trails by BC Parks lead from the south cove on the island to various gun and battery sites. The main gun emplacement is at the highest point on the island with great views of the Strait and is visible from passing boats. Yorke Island is a haunting place to visit and worth the stop in the right conditions. Maps of the island and more historical information can be found at www. wikipedia.org/wiki/Yorke_Island_(Canada). Temporary anchorage can be found in 30 to 45 feet of water, east of the unnamed cove on

the south side of the island. The cove is often covered with kelp and the bottom is rocky with poor holding. Wind and current are a consideration. Leaving the boat unattended is not recommended. Charted rocks lie south of the cove.

Blenkinsop Bay. Blenkinsop Bay has reasonably protected anchorage along the north shore of Johnstone Strait, but swells from westerly winds work into the bay. The chart shows tide-rips off Blenkinsop Bay. The chart isn't kidding. McLeod Bay and an unnamed bay inside Tuna Point are possible temporary anchorages.

⑫ **Port Neville.** Port Neville is an 8-mile-long inlet, a popular hideout for the fishing fleet, and an excellent spot to duck into if the weather in Johnstone Strait deteriorates. The inlet is a good anchorage. A government dock and float are a short distance inside, along the eastern shore. Boomed logs are stored in several places toward the inner end of the inlet. No public facilities or services are in the vicinity. The current can run swiftly past the government float, so plan your approach carefully. Remember, there's no shame in making several attempts before you get your landing right.

For years Olaf "Oly" Hansen, at the government dock post office, could be reached by radio for a report on conditions on Johnstone Strait. Oly died in January, 1997 at age 87, another legend gone from the coast. Oly's widow Lilly lived on in the family house for a few years, but finally had to move down-island. In 2003, shortly after her 90th birthday, she too left us. Their daughter Lorna (Hansen) Chesluk raised her daughter Erica in the house at the head of the wharf. Lorna was the postmaster, and she happily looked out on the strait and gave a report if you called on the radio.

The post office was closed in 2010, and Lorna moved to Campbell River to be closer to family. The Hansen family had lived at Port Neville since 1891. Until it closed, the Port Neville post office was the longest

continuously-operating post office in the province. Yet another page of coastal history is turned. A caretaker now looks after the property. The wonderful old store building is at the head of the wharf. Occasionally tour and whale watching groups stop by to see the old post office, still frozen in time.

If you go ashore, keep pets on a leash. Wild animals (grizzly bears and black bears) and protective mother deer are in the area.

On the west side of Robbers Nob, near the tip, several petroglyphs can be seen below the high tide line. The property above the high tide line is private.

Anchoring: Correspondents Elsi and Steve Hulsizer report after trying several anchoring locations in Port Neville, their preferred spot is across the inlet from the public dock where the water is protected from northwest winds by hills. Correspondents James and Jennifer Hamilton recommend anchoring in Baresides Bay, directly south of the MSh symbol on Charts 3545 and 3564 where you will be in 15 feet of water at zero tide, about 200 feet from shore. Excellent holding. Not the most protected but out of the worst of westerly winds.

LOCAL KNOWLEDGE

RESTRICTED AREA: Robson Bight, on the Vancouver Island side near the north end of Johnstone Strait, is an Ecological Reserve, a gathering place for Orcas. Unauthorized vessels (meaning yours and ours) are not allowed. Stay outside of the Reserve's boundary lines noted on the charts.

Robson Bight. The Robson Bight Ecological Reserve is a restricted area that runs 0.5 mile offshore and for 5 miles off Robson Bight. It is part of a reserve for Orca whales. The Reserve is not centered on the Bight and extends more to the east. The Reserve is shown on most charts but may be hard to see. If you stray into the restricted area, wardens will intercept your boat and instruct you to leave immediately.

Views of Johnstone Strait from Yorke Island's WWII gun emplacements   *The view from the Straits Bay Cafe at Kelsey Bay*

THE INLET: MEMOIRS OF A MODERN PIONEER - *By Helen Piddington*

Publisher: Penguin Group; ISBN: 978-0-14-200459-3

Helen Piddington was living in France during the 1960's, studying Lithography when she received photos of Haida totems in the mail from a friend. As Helen gazed at the photos pinned to her wall, she felt as if these faces were calling her home, and she soon returned to Vancouver, B.C. Helen visited the old Haida sites in 1968 with a friend and enjoyed sketching scenes found along the shores. Two years later she returned to Haida Gwaii, obtaining passage on a sailboat as a cook for Captain Dane. He and Helen became good friends and spent the summers sailing the Pacific Northwest; they married around 1970 and have been together ever since. Dane continued his photography and Helen continued selling her art work, purchased by buyers the world over.

After their sailing adventures and the arrival of their first child, they looked for land in a remote area with a cabin. Preferring a life style of self-sufficiency, they found such a place in **Sidney Cove** on **Loughborough Inlet**. After their arrival in Loughborough in 1975, it was evident that the Inlet had been a busy place in the 1930's and 40's — scattered ruins consisted of old homesteads, abandoned logging camps with railroad beds, a fenced graveyard, and terraced hillside gardens. The largest logging camp was at Heydon Bay, five miles up the Inlet from Sidney Cove, once sporting several homes, bunkhouses, a post office, store, and a school for children. Realizing those days had passed into history, Helen set about capturing what had been lost to time, through her writings, describing the people and activities that had come before. She also tells of their own experiences over the years, an excellent insight into remote coastal living.

Helen's colorful writing style, full of imagery like her sketches, helps us connect with the past while bringing us into the present. Past stories that played out in Loughborough and the surrounding waters, and those that played out for Dane and Helen, are both exciting and thought provoking. Throughout the book, Helen weaves in their own stories of survival, not unlike those of the past. "Time seems to be connected with threads of history, caught in recurring patterns." She talks about how they lived off the land, establishing a garden and fruit trees, raising chickens, and owning a herd of boars for a time. While many dream of the "simple life," Helen explains that living in a remote setting is neither simple nor easy. Machinery needs to be maintained and repaired; and they must grow their food for the whole year – staples that can be stored in the ground and foods that can be frozen, canned, pickled, dried, or jammed. They even made wine from grapes grown on the property. Dane engaged in fisheries and prawning, selling his catch to resorts and restaurants

The House from the Studio
charcoal/pastel

in Campbell River and to special customers as far away as Japan. When fishing and prawning tapered off, they established an oyster farm. Logging helped supplement their income through the Crown Woodlot Program. Unlike most logging, woodlots are ongoing operations run by resident loggers, but the same regulations, planning, and procedures must be followed. Protecting their animals and food crops from birds, deer, coyotes, and bear was an ongoing challenge. Helen tells of several close calls with bears and coyote that had helped themselves to chicken, fruit, and vegetables.

As Helen explains, once bear discover a food source, it becomes encoded; "try Sidney Bay when hungry; the apples are sour but the grapes are delicious; there are vegetables too, and chickens; it's all up for grabs." Helen also talks about the tough winter weather: wind storms that pull or snap lines holding rafts and storage sheds; heavy rain that threatens roof maintenance; and snowfall that makes transportation difficult.

She also tells of the social life during their earlier years living in the Inlet. While visits may be less frequent than in the city, Helen shares some of the social opportunities they enjoyed: pleasure boaters often stopped to tie-up at their guest float; people living in the Inlet came over to visit, or to help with building projects; and Helen hosted special gatherings at their place, including monthly film festival events. She explains that each inlet is a world unto itself with social connections made through common needs and necessities. Outings for Dane and Helen consisted of going to the Kupers' floating restaurant at **Cordero Lodge**; or going to the post office, store, and restaurant at **Blind Channel** on West Thurlow Island. Transportation is a time-consuming affair in remote locations. To sell his fish, Dane had to travel thirty miles by sea to **Kelsey Bay**, unload the boat, then load their parked van, then drive fifty miles over the mountains to Campbell River. While in town, he would take care of business and fill the van with groceries, animal feed, and other supplies to bring home.

What about their children, Arabella and Adam? Helen homeschooled their children until high school, at which time they left to attend boarding school in the 1980's and 90's; they returned home each summer, helping their parents with the busy chores at hand. Although not an official teacher, Helen had gained some teaching skills through her printmaking courses she taught in her studio; life drawing classes for students of architecture at University BC; and in a geology lab at Victoria College. Back in the mid-1950's, Helen taught thirty-five Inuit children at Fort Chimo, now Kuujjuuaq, located in Quebec, Canada.

"Life is not at all as it was when we came here. We are the only ones who get mail at Blind Channel now. There is no centre in Loughborough, no urge for the all-embracing parties . . . no monthly get-togethers like the Loughborough Film Society at our place – occasions that brought inlet people together." Dane and Helen now find themselves alone, the last remaining homesteaders in Loughborough Inlet. The colorful characters that once lived there have either moved on to other things or have since passed away. Helen weaves the tales of those who lived in the Inlet before she and Dane arrived in 1973, and those who lived there during the time they raised their family; tales of adventure and endurance. "Time fascinates me, how it shrinks and stretches our position in it. Time is so tenuous and difficult to grasp, we must run to keep up with it. Yet only when you sit absolutely still on the ground is it possible to feel the earth's pulse and be in its centre."

Dane and Helen still live in their cabin in Sidney Cove off Loughborough Inlet. Helen's health is now failing with the onslaught of dementia, but her stories have been written and are now woven through the fabric of time. If you have always wondered what it would be like to live in a remote area of the Pacific Northwest waters, don't miss reading Helen's book, *The Inlet, Memoir of a Modern Pioneer.*

The Broughtons

CHAPTER 12

THE BROUGHTONS
Port Harvey • Lagoon Cove
Kwatsi Bay • Echo Bay
Sullivan Bay • Jennis Bay

"The Broughtons" is an all-encompassing term for the inlets, islands and waterways on the mainland side of Queen Charlotte Strait, north of Johnstone Strait. This area includes the islands adjoining Blackfish Sound and Fife Sound. It also includes Knight Inlet, Kingcome Inlet, Tribune Channel, Drury Inlet, and Mackenzie Sound. For convenience we include Havannah Channel and Chatham Channel. Locals call this area the Mainland, to distinguish it from the Vancouver Island side from Sayward (Kelsey Bay) to the top of Vancouver Island, which they call North Island.

The Broughtons, or the Mainland, is one large, complex cruising ground. It offers anchorages from raw and wind-swept Fife Sound and Blackfish Sound, to the gentler waters of Simoom Sound, Greenway Sound and Drury Inlet. Small, family-owned resorts—no two of them alike—are spread throughout the Broughtons. Most cruisers anchor out some of the time and enjoy the social side of marina life the rest of the time. During the course of a cruising holiday, most cruisers either stop at or overnight at all the marinas: Port Harvey, Lagoon Cove, Kwatsi Bay, Pierre's at Echo Bay, Sullivan Bay, and Jennis Bay.

Resupply and repairs are on the North Island side, at Port McNeill, Alert Bay, Sointula, and Port Hardy. North Island is described in a separate chapter.

The rich history of the Broughtons begins with Native habitation dating back thousands of years. On Mound Island, 14 depressions in the earth are evidence of Native Big Houses and Long Houses, each of which held extended families. We're told that trading beads, the colorful glass beads exchanged for valuable pelts by early traders, can sometimes be found on beaches throughout the Broughtons.

The Broughtons were homesteaded in the late 1800s and early 1900s. Families were raised on rude farms. The men rowed across Queen Charlotte Strait to Alert Bay, or rowed—*rowed*—200 miles south to Vancouver or Victoria to conduct business and bring back supplies.

In most cases, the forest has erased all traces of the homesteaders' now-abandoned efforts. One notable exception is remarkable "Monks' Wall," at the north end of Beware Passage. There, hidden in the trees, are the remains of rock walls from William and Mary Anne Galley's wilderness trading post that was active from the late 1800s until after the First World War.

The Broughtons are a destination. Take your time and don't hurry through. See Billy Proctor's museum in Proctor Bay. Marvel at Lacy Falls on Tribune Channel. Anchor out in the coves and lagoons. Visit the marinas and meet the families who run them.

Ask questions, read the history, and take time to explore. If you spend your entire cruise in the Broughtons, you might—you just might—scratch the surface.

Marinas: Marinas in the Broughtons are different from marinas elsewhere on the

Beautiful Lacy Falls in Tribune Channel near Watson Cove and Kwatsi Bay

coast. They're small and often family run; each marina has its own character and charm. Some cruisers develop friendships with the owners, and come back year after year to catch up. Owners of these wilderness marinas make do with what they have in regards to power and water. Power is normally an additional charge and can be more expensive than elsewhere due to their remote locations.

Wi-Fi: Internet in the Broughtons is provided by satellite, and bandwidth is limited. Marina owners request that visitors refrain from downloading videos, sending large email attachments, using Skype, or engaging in other high bandwidth activities.

Potluck Hour: Many of the marinas in the Broughtons have a potluck hors d'oeuvre—or even a potluck dinner—gathering around 5:00 p.m. Bring your own beverages, leaded or unleaded and your own plate with utensils. It's an ideal time to meet other boaters and exchange information. Kids usually are more than welcome, although if they're the only ones they might get bored with grownups' chit-chat. You'll want to carry a stock of suitable fixings for your hors d'oeuvre or potluck contribution. The fixings don't have

to be fancy. If you're down to Doritos and salsa, they'll be hoovered into mouths in short order. If you enjoy preparing something special, this is a good time to show your stuff.

Good Books: Tide Rips and Back Eddies; and Full Moon, Flood Tide. Both by Bill Proctor, edited and illustrated by Yvonne Maximchuk. Published by Harbour Publishing. These books are highly recommended reading before or during a cruise to the Broughtons. If you are hungry for a little more, consider Yvonne's recently released book, *Drawn to Sea*, for more insights on life and the people of this area.

HAVANNAH CHANNEL

Havannah Channel leads northward toward Knight Inlet and other channels to the north and west.

① **Port Harvey.** Port Harvey is large, and although it is open to westerlies from Johnstone Strait, it is an excellent anchorage. If you're planning an early morning run on Johnstone Strait, it's a good place to overnight. You'll find anchorage in several notches along

Small intimate marinas are found among the Broughtons Islands.

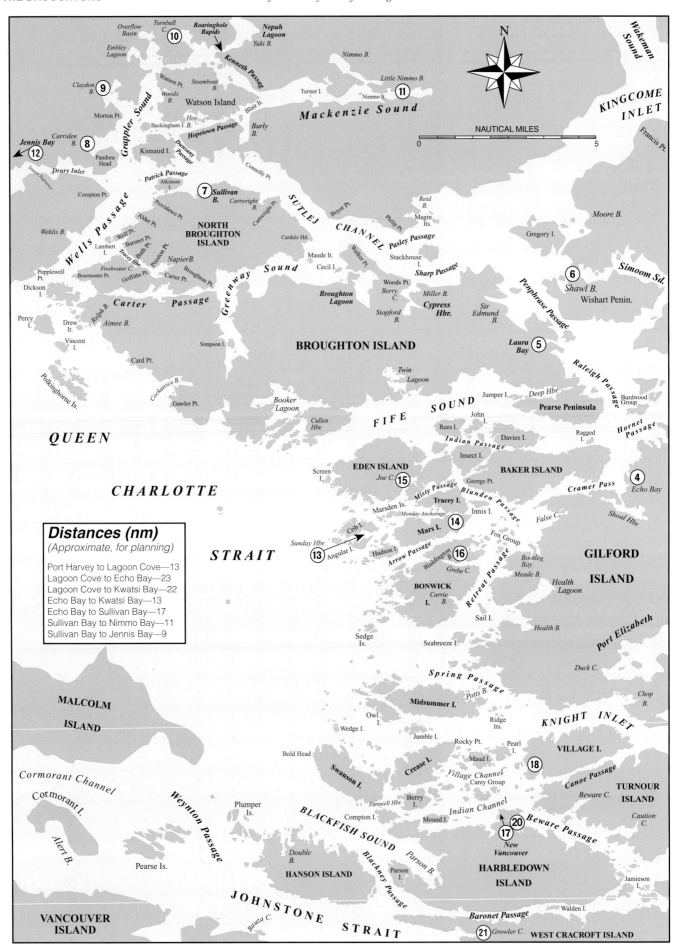

The Broughtons - West

Distances (nm)
(Approximate, for planning)

Port Harvey to Lagoon Cove—13
Lagoon Cove to Echo Bay—23
Lagoon Cove to Kwatsi Bay—22
Echo Bay to Kwatsi Bay—13
Echo Bay to Sullivan Bay—17
Sullivan Bay to Nimmo Bay—11
Sullivan Bay to Jennis Bay—9

336

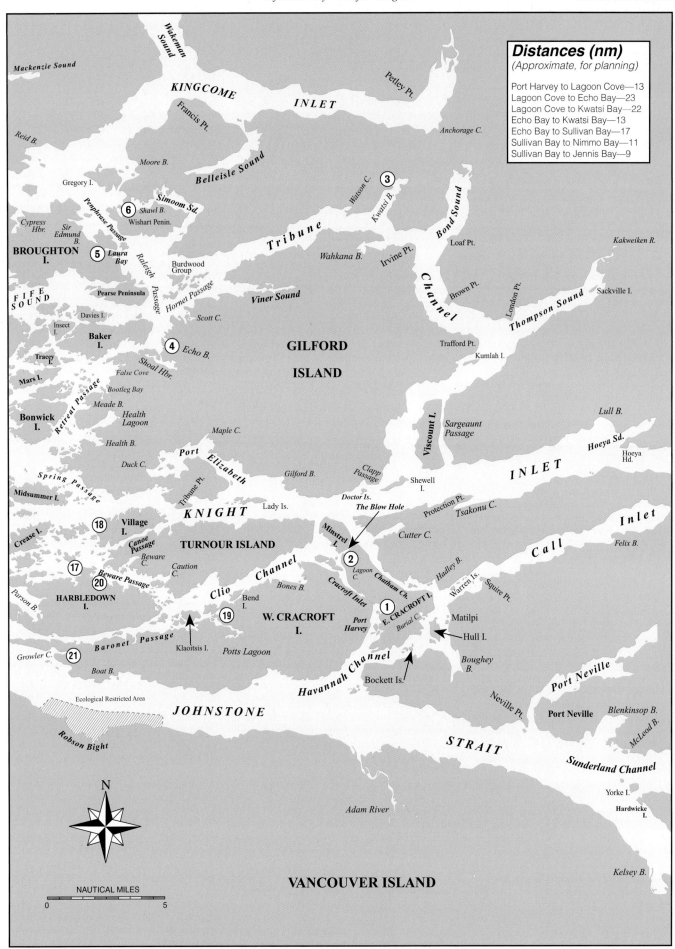

Distances (nm)
(Approximate, for planning)

Port Harvey to Lagoon Cove—13
Lagoon Cove to Echo Bay—23
Lagoon Cove to Kwatsi Bay—22
Echo Bay to Kwatsi Bay—13
Echo Bay to Sullivan Bay—17
Sullivan Bay to Nimmo Bay—11
Sullivan Bay to Jennis Bay—9

337

The Broughtons - East

The docks at Port Harvey

the east side before you reach the head of the bay, and ample anchorage at the head.

A big logging operation is on the west side of Port Harvey. A permanent house with private mooring floats is on the shore. The wind blows through Cracroft Inlet, and a gentle, low surge can come in if the wind is blowing on Johnstone Strait.

Caution: Do not attempt the narrow channel that leads between Port Harvey and Cracroft Inlet that dries and is studded with boulders.

Port Harvey Marine Resort is located at the head of Port Harvey. They charge a fee for landing the dinghy.

① **Port Harvey Marine Resort.** St. 108, 1434 Ironwood St., Campbell River, BC V9W 5T5; (250) 902-9003; portharveymarine@ gmail.com; www.portharvey.blogspot.com. Monitors VHF 66A. Guests welcomed with ample 1000 feet of side-tie moorage on good docks, with 15 & 30 amp power, water, and Wi-Fi. The power generator is turned off between 10:00 a.m. and 2:00 p.m. daily. Easy access to shore for walking the dog or walking the trail through the forest. Day pass available for guest moorage from owner, Gail Cambridge. The beach in front of the Cambridge house has clams and geoducks for those willing to do a little digging.

George Cambridge, who had the vision and created this special marina, passed away unexpectedly in July 2018. George was industrious and hard-working, he will be missed. At press time, it was not known if Port Harvey would be open to receive transient boaters for the 2019 boating season as George's wife Gail, and family, determine the next steps for the marina. The docks may be open for moorage at your own risk. There may be no power or water, and the store and restaurant may not be open. We recommend you call the number above for a recorded announcement on the status of the marina, or check WaggonerGuide.com for updates.

The marina isn't visible until you get all the way to the head of Port Harvey beyond Range Island. You will see the industrial operation on the shore first. Port Harvey Marina is just across the bay.

Bockett Islets. Tom Kincaid has anchored for a few hours among the Bockett Islets awaiting favorable current in Chatham Channel.

Boughey Bay. Anchorage is toward the south end of Boughey (pronounced "boogie") Bay. John Chappell (*Cruising Beyond Desolation Sound*) says easterly winds can spring up suddenly in the bay.

Matilpi. Matilpi (pronounced MAT-il-pi) is a former Indian village site. It is beautiful, with a white shell beach backed by dense forest. Anchor behind the northern of the two islands, or between the islands. Protection is excellent.

Burial Cove. Burial Cove is pretty, though open to most winds. It is well-protected from seas and has good holding in 25 feet. A few houses are on shore. We've anchored there twice.

Call Inlet. Call Inlet is approximately 10 miles long, and runs through beautiful, steep-sided mountains. You can find anchoring depths in the **Warren Islands**, near the mouth of the inlet. They are a pretty spot to wait for the current to change in Chatham Channel. A stern-tie to shore is a good idea for overnight anchorage. Field Correspondent Deane Hislop writes, "we spent two wonderful nights anchored in the protection of the islands with a depth of 35 feet over a good holding bottom; views of the islands and Call Inlet are outstanding."

Chatham Channel. Chatham Channel is easier to run than it appears from the chart. The southern section is the narrowest, with the least room in the channel, and requires the greatest attention. The current floods east and ebbs west. Near slack water is the most pleasant time to transit this southern section.

Slacks are based on Seymour Narrows predictions. Correction factors for the times of slack water are found under Secondary Stations in the Tide and Current Tables, Vol. 6, and Ports and Passes. Chart 3545 (1:40,000) shows the area, including the range locations. Chart 3564 (1:20,000), with its

1:10,000 insert of the southern section, really helps understanding. We highly recommend Chart 3564.

If you are running compass courses through the southern section, remember that the headings shown on the chart are true, and must be corrected to magnetic. We have found that in some lighting conditions, or if the trees are not trimmed, the ranges are hard to locate from the far ends of the lower channel. Going either direction, a sharp-eyed crew should sight astern at the back range until it grows difficult to see. By then the leading range should be visible. Maximum currents in the southern section run to 5 knots on a spring tide, with no significant swirls or overfalls. In our experience, the current usually is much less than shown (but not always; twice, we have found considerable current). Chatham Channel can be taken at times other than slack water, but you should know what you are doing, and in the southern section *keep your boat lined up on the range*. Keep your eyes open. We encountered a bear swimming across Chatham Channel one morning.

Cutter Cove. Cutter Cove, located across from Minstrel Island Resort (now closed) at the north end of Chatham Channel, is very pretty and a good anchorage. A fresh west or northwest wind can enter the cove. No swells, but aggressive little whitecaps. The bottom looks flat, as if it's pure mud. "At least one noisy old rock is down there, though, because the anchor chain dragged across it all night long." *[Hale]* Anchor in 24 feet (zero tide).

Minstrel Island Resort. The sad story of this once great stop continues. The buildings appear abandoned and vegetation is growing on the docks as they slowly decay, due to lack of maintenance. You may see several boats moored there.

LOCAL KNOWLEDGE

CAUTION: When entering Lagoon Cove from Blow Hole, give the Islet and shoal across the channel from Perley Island a wide berth as the shoal extends further west than chart 3564 indicates. Look for a private orange and/ or green round plastic float which should pass to your port side entering Lagoon Cove.

The Blow Hole. The Blow Hole is a short, shallow, easily-navigated channel between Minstrel Island and East Cracroft Island. The channel gets its name from strong westerly winds that sometimes blow through. Near the west end a reef, shown clearly on Chart 3564, extends from East Cracroft Island on the south side of the channel. Brave the kelp and favor the north side of the channel and you'll have no problems.

② **Lagoon Cove.** Lagoon Cove has good anchorage along the shorelines, although the middle of the bay is a little deep for most boats. Lagoon Cove Marina is on the east

Lagoon Cove docks and office with Clio Channel in the distance

Popular Happy Hour at Lagoon Cove is held at the historic workshop.

side of the bay. Locals recommend against anchoring on the west side of the bay, which they say is foul with logging cable. We got a note from a reader who said at least one cable can be found on the east side as well.

② **Lagoon Cove Marina.** c/o Minstrel Island P.O., Minstrel Island, BC V0P 1L0; (778) 819-6962; info@lagooncovemarina. com; www.lagooncovemarina.com. Monitors VHF 66A. Open all year. Reservations accepted; a portion of the docks are held open for drop-ins. Lagoon Cove has gasoline, diesel, propane; 15, 30, & 2×30 amp power, water, washroom & showers, gift shop. Wi-Fi has been extended to the docks with repeaters. A cell phone booster is located in the book exchange. Kenmore Air, Corair, and NW Seaplanes service to Seattle.

A do-it-yourself burn barrel is available for burnable garbage (no fair just dropping a bag of garbage in, for someone else to deal with). The fuel dock office carries fishing tackle, prawn and crab traps, ice, charts

and a few essentials. Pick up a jar of their Lagoon Cove prawn sauce or Lagoon Cove coffee. A separate store with the grand name "Edgewater Emporium" carries Lagoon Cove branded clothing.

The entire property has a whimsical quality about it. The workshop is a "historic" workshop full of old tools. A totem pole is made from pieces of outboard motors and all sorts of other junk. Two "exercise stations," one of them a pile of wood with an axe, the other a brightly painted lawnmower, invite the eager. Several hiking trails are maintained. A pet path is available for the four-legged crew. Be bear aware.

Lagoon Cove Marina is one of the most popular stops on the coast and fills during the summer months. Reservations accepted. Happy hour appetizer potlucks for marina guests are held almost every day in the "historic" workshop. Guests bring treats from their boats. Happy hour often morphs into a casual potluck dinner. Weather permitting, a marshmallow roast might be organized at

sunset. Ping-Pong under the fruit trees is also a popular passtime.

Everybody, by the way, goes to the happy hour and marshmallow roasts. "This is summer camp for adults," an enthusiastic lady told us.

Current owners, Jim and Lou Ryan, purchased the property in 2016 and began their first season in 2017 with lots of energy, making improvements to the marina while maintaining the beloved character and charm of Lagoon Cove. Their daughter Kelley and son-in-law Dan round out the family team. The Ryans are committed to "enhancing but not changing" this popular destination, as evidenced by dock repairs in 2018 along with other upgrades.

Knight Inlet. Knight Inlet (locally called Knight's Inlet) extends from its mouth at Midsummer Island to its head, at the mouth of the Klinaklini River. The inlet is about 70 miles long and 2 miles wide, the longest of the fjords indenting the B.C. coast. Along

339

THE SURPRISE ON KNIGHT INLET

More times than not, we have been cruising the calm protected waters of Chatham Channel when headed north, or down Tribune Inlet when headed south, and broken out into Knight Inlet to find 4-6 foot seas and 20+ knots of wind. What happened? When you look at the charts you can see what is happening. Winds typically come from the west or northwest during the popular summer cruising months. From Queen Charlotte Sound and Blackfish Sound there is 16 miles of fetch for wind-driven waves to build. This is enough to set up challenging wave conditions. If your timing adds an ebb current, you can see how you can go from fairly calm conditions to a 2-mile crossing of Knight Inlet that is very uncomfortable, especially when headed south. Consider timing your crossing of Knight Inlet early in the morning before winds pick up and on a flood tide.

most of its length, the shores rise steeply to 6,000-foot-high mountains. Anchorage is iffy at best, so for many, the inlet's upper reaches are explored mainly by fast boats able to make the round trip in a single day. Boats with limited fuel capacity should top off at Lagoon Cove before making the trip. Extensive logging activity has put considerable debris in the water. Watch carefully.

The section above Glendale Cove is reported to be more dramatic than Jervis or Bute inlets. Reader John Tyler reports, "Even with the distances involved, it's well worth the time to cruise up there."

In Knight Inlet, **Tsakonu Cove** is a pretty anchorage, protected from westerlies but exposed to the east. Several years ago we anchored near the head of Tsakonu Cove for a quiet lunch, while outside a 20-knot inflow wind blew Knight Inlet into an uncomfortable chop. Driftwood logs on the shore suggest that outflow winds in Knight Inlet probably roar into Tsakonu Cove, accompanied by substantial seas.

Hoeya Sound. Hoeya Sound is pretty, but deep and completely exposed to the westerly winds that are prevalent in the summer.

Glendale Cove. Glendale Cove offers minimal protection from strong northeast winds that often blow down the inlet. "We anchored on a sloping bottom off the east side, just north of some old pilings. The second night four other pleasure boats were there. Every place else seemed to be less than 6 feet, or more than 150 feet." [Evertz]

Glendale Cove has one of the highest concentrations of Grizzly Bears, also referred to as Brown Bears, on the west coast of British Columbia. In spring, bears are feeding on tidal area sedge; and by mid-August, they are feeding continuously on salmon. Pleasure boaters anchored in the cove are often approached by the First Nations, who hand out bear viewing guidelines established by the Commercial Bear Viewing Association. These helpful guidelines are intended to protect the bears from feeling crowded and becoming displaced, as well as common sense safety tips for those viewing the bears. Dogs should never be brought ashore. Boaters should be respectful of boat speed, noise, distance, and viewing time. Being good stewards and respectful boaters is always important for future preservation of these special places. Knight Inlet Lodge, located on the east side of Glendale Cove, is a private resort providing Grizzly Bear tours to their fly-in guests. Reservations are booked well in advance for this distinctive lodge. The Lodge does not provide transient moorage and doesn't have any services for boaters visiting the area.

Wahshihlas Bay. Located at the mouth of the Sim River, Wahshihlas Bay is a possible anchorage. Although we've never tried it, Correspondents Bruce and Margaret Evertz have. "It was settled weather and we anchored in the northwest corner, just off the shoal. There were some snags to avoid. If we expected any winds we could have moved away from the shoal a little and anchored with a stern tie to shore or to some old pilings. The bay is far from 'bomb proof,' but we felt secure with the weather we had." *[Evertz]*

Port Elizabeth. Port Elizabeth is a great big bay bounded on the west by low hills that let westerlies in. A substantial log booming operation is in the cove in the northwest corner. You can find good anchorage near the booming site and along the western shore, west of the largest of the three islands. The two smaller islands are joined on the west by drying flats.

Correspondents John and Lorraine Littlewood provided us with the following extra information:

"The unexpected difficulty with the anchorage in Duck Cove at the west end of Port Elizabeth is that in any winds from 0 to 180 degrees you will feel the full force. We were getting gusts to 30 knots in a southeaster, supposedly sheltered. The only real shelter is in the extreme southeastern end of Port Elizabeth, except in a northwest blow." *[Littlewood]*

Sargeaunt Passage. Sargeaunt Passage connects Knight Inlet and Tribune Channel, and has anchorage at either end of the narrows, although one cruiser warned us about old logging cables fouling their anchor on the southeast side. The passage runs between steep-sided mountains, and is beautiful. The shoal in the middle extends from the east shore across much of the passage. Favor the west shore. We found the depth at the narrow part was less than shown on the chart.

Tribune Channel. Tribune Channel borders the east and north sides of Gilford Island. The only marina on Tribune Channel is at Kwatsi Bay. Lacy Falls can be stunning.

Kumlah Island Anchorage. Kumlah Island is in Tribune Channel, roughly across from the mouth of Thompson Sound. Waggoner reader Joel Erickson found suitable anchorage in 16 to 24 feet behind Kumlah Island, between it and Gilford Island. We haven't spent the night, but would consider anchoring there in settled weather. The view is beautiful.

Thompson Sound. Thompson Sound is surrounded by forested mountains so steep that the hillsides are scarred by many landslides. Earlier editions of the Waggoner said Thompson Sound has no good anchorages, but Correspondents John and Lorraine Littlewood set us straight with this email: "There is excellent anchorage at the head of Thompson Sound, on the shelf between the mudflats at the mouth of the Kakweiken River. You can explore the river for a couple miles at high tide; there is lots of bear sign, and we don't mean black bears, either!"

A reader reported that when they tried to anchor, they found the shelf dotted with crab trap buoys, leaving no room. They anchored briefly in the lee of Sackville Island, with a stern-tie to shore.

Bond Sound. In the past, we reported that Bond Sound had no good anchorages. But inspired by Bill Proctor's wonderful book, *Full Moon, Flood Tide*, readers Jim and Marsha Peters anchored their Grand Banks

The happy hour potlucks are legendary at Kwatsi Bay Marina.

At Kwatsi Bay, take the dinghy over to the beach and hike to the waterfalls.

42 Dev's Courage at the head of the sound in settled weather and took the dinghy some distance up the Ahta River. They said it was beautiful. Correspondents Steve and Elsie Hulsizer say to go up about two hours before high water. Another reader, Bill Cooke, told us that cutthroat trout fishing is good at the head of the sound. Correspondents John and Lorraine Littlewood add this note from an early September cruise:

"Bill Proctor's book, *Full Moon, Flood Tide,* led us to the Ahta River at the head of Bond Sound, an absolutely pristine salmon spawning river teeming with every sort of wildlife, from very large, dead salmon that have just completed their life cycle, to much larger hairy brown mammals that feed on them (and just about anything else they want to). The place is like something from a fairy tale. It is not all that easy to find and explore, but very much worth it. Anchorage is tricky just off the drying bar at the mouth of the rivers (there are two: Ahta Creek on the left as you face the estuary and the Ahta River on the right). The Ahta River, with a smaller opening, is deep, fast and clear. Don't tell a soul."

Note: Strong winds can funnel through Bond Sound, making it mostly unsuitable for overnight anchorage.

③ **Kwatsi Bay.** The inner cove of Tribune Channel's Kwatsi Bay is a stunning anchorage, one of the most impressive on the coast,

surrounded by a high, sheer bowl of rock. Sunrises and sunsets are magnificent. Our log says, "Wow!" The bay is deep, though, over 100 feet deep in much of the inner cove. We had a peaceful night in 60 feet with good holding off the two streams that empty into the western bight of the inner cove. The next morning, we found several other possible places to anchor in 48 to 72 feet. We have been told that the spot we anchored in is rocky and we should have anchored on the south side of the back bay, east of the entrance. [Hale]

③ **Kwatsi Bay Marina.** Simoom Sound P.O., Simoom Sound, V0P 1S0; (250) 949-1384; kwatsibay@kwatsibay.com; www.kwatsibay. com. Monitors VHF 66A. Moorage, water, small gift store, Wi-Fi during set hours. No shore power. Visa and Mastercard accepted.

Max Knierim and his wife Anca Fraser opened Kwatsi Bay Marina in 1998. Together with their daughter Marieke and son Russell, they carved out a place to live in the bush. Marieke and Russell have grown up and are pursuing their own careers. Max and Anca are empty nesters, except for the many friends and guests who visit Kwatsi Bay during the summer.

The store is small but classy, with a selection of local arts and crafts ranging from pottery and jewelry to woodwork. It also carries souvenir T-shirts, caps and sweatshirts. Reservations are recommended for July and August, email is best. Short hiking trails are nearby, reached by dinghy. One leads to a beautiful waterfall. Max or Anca can provide directions. Kwatsi Bay often hosts a potluck happy hour on the dock in the evening.

This is not a luxury resort; this is the wilderness, at its gentle but hardworking best.

Watson Cove. Watch for a rock in the entrance, and favor the north shore when entering. Watson Cove is surrounded by beautiful rock, stunning waterfalls, and dense forest. A fish farm and floathouse have been moved from inside the cove to just outside. This makes the cove accessible for anchoring (60 feet, about halfway in), although we've heard the bottom is foul with logging debris. Don't tie to the aquaculture float; a barge is moored there overnight.

At the head of Watson Cove a dinghy can be tied to a length of large logging chain and you can scramble up the rock to a trail leading to the 1000-year-old cedar tree mentioned in Billy Proctor's *Full Moon, Flood Tide.* On an otherwise quiet afternoon at Kwatsi Bay, Anca took a bunch of us over in the speedboat to see the tree. The forest was beautiful and the tree was a memorable sight.

Lacy Falls. Just west of Watson Cove, Lacy Falls washes down an expanse of smooth black rock and tumbles into the sea. The boat can be brought up close, but not too close. The bottom at the base of the falls is rocky. Note: During dry periods, water does not fan across the rocks.

Wahkana Bay. The inner cove of Wahkana Bay is attractive, but 120 feet deep except near shore. The south shore has spots where you can anchor in 48 to 72 feet with swinging room, however. Parts of the east shore are reported to be foul with logging debris and old pilings beneath the surface. The head of the inner

It's worth the trek through the forest to see the 1000-year-old cedar tree at Watson Cove.

Reserve your space at Echo Bay's popular marina docks or try their Cliffside option on the other side of the bay.

cove shoals rapidly so watch out. Wind can blow through the saddle that reaches to Viner Sound.

Viner Sound. Viner Sound is pretty, but narrow and shallow. An indent on the north side, a short distance down the narrow channel, will hold one boat near the opening. Just inside that indent the water shoals immediately. Two public mooring buoys are in the little cove on the north side. The long shoaling area shown on the chart at the head of Viner Sound is real. Watch your depths as you explore.

Scott Cove. Scott Cove once was a busy logging camp, but the camp is now closed. This was the location of Pierre's Bay Marina, which moved to Echo Bay in 2008. We're told a surprising number of people still show up every summer mistakenly looking for Pierre's Bay Marina in Scott Cove.

LOCAL KNOWLEDGE

POWELL ROCK WARNING: A nasty drying rock lies off Powell Point, the southwest corner of Scott Cove. A boat running between Tribune Channel and Echo Bay or Cramer Passage could easily run up on this rock. Give Powell Point (and the rock) a big, wide offing.

④ **Echo Bay.** Echo Bay has been a gathering place for thousands of years, and for more than 100 years it has been a center for loggers, fishermen, and now summertime boaters. In 2008 Pierre and Tove (pronounced "Tova") Landry bought the Echo Bay Resort and moved Pierre's Bay Marina from nearby Scott Cove to Echo Bay. The Echo Bay Resort docks were scrapped and new docks, with upgraded power, were built and installed. The store was refurbished and restocked. A new fuel dock was built. In a span of about three months the resort was transformed—a remarkable achievement in a remote location where help is scarce and everything must be barged in.

Since then Pierre has continued expanding and improving the facilities. The blue roofed

event building, on the concrete breakwater, is the first sight upon entering. What used to be called Windsong Sea Village, under the cliff opposite Pierre's, is now part of Pierre's, known as The Cliffside. In 2017 the event building was expanded out towards the water and is now connected to the building where the store is housed.

Echo Bay has much to offer. Visit Billy Proctor's museum of local artifacts. A short but steep trail leads from Pierre's to the museum. An easier trail begins at the Cliffside docks. Or take the dinghy over to Shoal Harbour and see local author and artist Yvonne Maximchuk's SeaRose Studio *www. yvonnemaximchuk.com.*

A deep midden at the head of Echo Bay is easily investigated from the beach. A schoolhouse once stood on shore, but the school-age population of the area has fallen below the threshold needed to keep the school open. The school closed in 2008, and was removed in fall 2014. A good hike begins behind where the former schoolhouse stood, and leads back into the hills past two dams, across a couple of bridges, and onto a logging road. The logging road is heavily overgrown with

alder; however, and you probably won't go much farther. Be bear aware and make noise when hiking the area.

Slow down: The wakes from passing vessels and the following wake from approaching vessels can get inside the bay and set things a-rocking. Please slow down well outside the marina when approaching.

Caution: See Pym Rocks warning.

④ **Pierre's Echo Bay Lodge & Marina.** c/o General Delivery, Simoom Sound PO, BC V0P 1S0; (250) 713-6415; info@pierresbay. com; www.pierresbay.com. Monitors VHF 66A. Phone coverage is spotty in the area. Best to contact the marina by email. Open all year, gasoline, diesel, propane, 15, 30 & 50 amp power, rental cabins, store, ice, water, washrooms, showers, laundry, limited Wi-Fi; a cell phone booster is located in the dining hall. Ample guest moorage, reservations recommended mid-July through mid-August. Floatplane service by Kenmore Air and NW Seaplanes.

This is a busy destination in the Broughtons, with wide, sturdy docks, ample electric power, fuel dock and a well-stocked store for marina guests. The protected bay, with dramatic sheer rock faces, is beautiful. Pierre and Tove Landry have made Echo Bay a popular destination.

Pierre's is a social place. Happy hour gatherings are common and sometimes lead to potluck dinners. Visitors enjoy sitting around a cozy fire pit located onshore above the docks. During summer, Pierre and Tove host several weekly food events, such as fish n' chips night and prime rib night. Saturday night pig roasts, their signature event, run from the last weekend in June to the first weekend in September. Many visitors arrive on Fridays to get a good spot on the dock. Reservations are just about essential. Check their website for schedules and themes, some of which merit a costume or funny hat.

After many years of providing great service and events for boaters, Pierre and Tove

Guests relax around a cozy fire at Pierre's.

Billy Proctor's museum is filled with artifacts from a lifetime in the Islands. The Gift Shop has an impressive selection of local and nautical books.

have made the decision to retire and have put the marina on the market. They will continue to be involved with the marina, and boaters can expect the same special events.

④ **Pierre's Echo Bay - The Cliffside.** Formerly Windsong Sea Village, acquired by Pierre's at Echo Bay in 2013. The Cliffside offers overflow moorage for Pierre's at Echo Bay. Water, no power. For cruisers who prefer less hustle-and-bustle, The Cliffside is a good alternative to the main docks at Pierre's. A ramp to shore leads to a trail through the woods to Billy Proctor's Museum.

④ **Echo Bay Marine Park.** The dock has been condemned and is now closed. The holding bottom can be poor; anchor with care. The park has walk-in campsites and picnicking. A nice beach is often used as a landing for kayakers.

Shoal Harbour. Shoal Harbour has good, protected anchorage, mud bottom. We would anchor just to the right, inside the entrance. Study the charts and use caution when transiting the narrow entrance. Watch the depths; the main head and northern arm shoal quickly.

Billy Proctor's Museum. Open 9:00 a.m. to 5:00 p.m. A trail, rough in places, leads from Pierre's at Echo Bay. An easier trail begins at The Cliffside. By boat, if you leave Echo Bay and turn left toward Shoal Harbour, you can follow the shoreline around the peninsula and into a cozy bay with a home, small dock and marine railway haulout. This is where legendary Billy Proctor, who has logged, trapped and fished on the coast all of his many years, lives and has his museum.

Over a lifetime, Billy Proctor has collected a treasure of Chinese opium bottles, Chinese and Japanese beer bottles, engine plates, tools, arrowheads, bone fish hooks, a 1910 mimeograph machine from Minstrel Island, a crank telephone, a scale from the old Simoom Sound post office, and thousands of other artifacts of the coast's past.

Finally, in a structure he built from lumber he milled himself, the remarkable collection

is displayed. Out the back door is a fish pond. Out the front door is another building he put up himself, housing a small book and gift shop, and more treasures. Everything has a story, even the windows and doors.

A few years ago, Billy built a replica of a hand logger's cabin, circa 1900. All the wood came from a single cedar log he found floating. Recently, he built a small schoolhouse and filled it with items from the old Echo Bay schoolhouse. Visitors can write on the old blackboards and look through old pictures. The kids love it.

No admission charge for the museum or schoolhouse, but a box marked "donations," which go to salmon enhancement, is next to the door. Billy also has an excellent selection of books on the area, including his own.

If you want to call ahead, try *Ocean Dawn* on VHF 16 or 06. Hike the occasionally challenging trail from Pierre's. Meet Billy and go have a look. We think you'll be glad you did.

Pym Rocks. *Caution*: When crossing from the vicinity of Echo Bay bound for Simoom Sound, Shawl Bay, Greenway Sound and so forth, Pym Rocks, off the northeast tip of Baker Island, lie very close to your probable course. We know of one experienced skipper whose attention wandered briefly and he went

right up on the rocks. We had a close call with the rocks ourselves, but steered clear in time. The rocks are farther out than they ought to be, and unless you're on autopilot they keep drawing the boat toward them. *[Hale]*

Burdwood Group. The Burdwood Group is a beautiful little clutch of islands, a gunkholer's dream. The group is dotted with rocks and reefs, and Chart 3515 (1:80,000) doesn't show a lot of detail. With a sharp lookout, however, small boats can slowly maneuver among the islands. Anchorages are scarce, deep and rocky, and recommended in settled weather only. Given the opportunity, the cruising boat should at least patrol through these islands.

Simoom Sound. Simoom Sound is a dogleg inlet, very scenic, but most of it is too deep for convenient anchoring. The best anchorages are in **O'Brien Bay** at the head of Simoom Sound, and in **McIntosh Bay** and the bays adjacent, along the north shore. You'll be in 48 to 60+ feet in O'Brien Bay, and 18 to 36 feet in the McIntosh Bay area. We spent a quiet night in McIntosh Bay behind the small island. The views took our breath away. In an emergency you could find anchorage off the northeast corner of Louisa Islet, and near the mouth of a creek on the Wishart Peninsula side.

⑤ **Laura Bay.** Laura Bay is a pretty and popular anchorage. Anchorage is in two sections: one, with a challenging entry, is in the long neck that extends westward behind the outer anchorage; the other is the outer anchorage in the cove between Trivett Island and Broughton Island. The cove behind Trivett Island is lovely. A little islet is in the cove, but the chart incorrectly shows good water all around. A rock is in the narrow passage to the east of the islet. Entering the cove, leave the islet to starboard.

Caution: A major drying reef lies a short distance inside the entry to the neck of the bay that extends westward from the outer anchorage. This reef is shown on small scale Chart 3515, but without enough detail to indicate how to get around it. Our

Laura Bay has room for several boats to anchor.

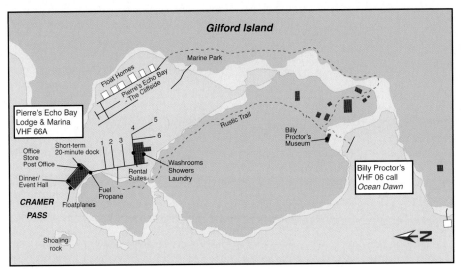

Echo Bay

FLAG ETIQUETTE

The National Flag

Vessels should fly the National Flag in which they are registered. As a general rule, the ship's National Flag should be 1 inch for each foot of the vessel's overall length; be sure this flag is not too small in proportion to your vessel. The National Flag is properly flown from a staff pole at the stern of a power boat, and from the leech of the most aftersail of a sailboat. Older tradition called for the flag to be removed from the gaff or leech when not under sail, and the flag placed on a staff pole at the stern. Most sailboats today fly the National Flag from the stern when under sail and under power. The Flag should be flown from 0800 to sunset, and at half-staff on Memorial Day until 12:00.

Courtesy Flag

As a courtesy, vessels should fly the National Flag of a foreign nation when cruising in their waters. Proper placement is on the mast of a power boat, or on the end of the starboard spreader for sailboats. For sailboats with more than one mast, the Courtesy Flag is flown from the starboard spreader of the forward mast. A power vessel without a mast, may fly the Courtesy Flag from the bow in lieu of a burgee; or preferably, on the starboard antenna strong enough to support it. Be sure your Courtesy Flag is not torn or in disrepair, and not too small. For sizing purposes, use one-half inch for each foot of the vessel's overall length. Most importantly, never fly a Courtesy Flag from the bow of your vessel unless you are a power boat without a mast. The Courtesy Flag is raised only after clearing customs, and usually takes the place of the yellow quarantine flag. Don't forget to remove the Courtesy Flag once you leave the waters of your host country.

Burgee

A burgee is a small flag with a symbol indicating membership in a yacht club or boat club. The burgee is flown from the bow on power boats and usually at the end of the lowest starboard spreader on sailboats. Only one burgee should be flown at a time, indicating the group or activity in which you are participating. Burgees can be sized to one-half inch for each foot of the vessel's overall length.

Quarantine Flag

In early times, a yellow flag indicated that there was a disease or illness aboard the ship, which was then isolated for 40 days. In modern times, it's the opposite, the yellow flag signals that the ship is free of disease and requests boarding and inspection. Boaters should fly the yellow Quarantine Flag from the mast just prior to reaching a customs dock or assigned slip, and the flag should be removed once you have cleared customs. There's a side benefit to the bright yellow flag, it's often easier for a customs agent to locate your vessel in a large marina, resulting in a quicker response to your request for clearance.

observations indicate that the reef extends from the south shore until somewhat past the middle of the channel. Approaching the reef, favor the north side at dead slow with an alert bow watch.

Field Correspondent Deane Hislop reports that Laura Bay and Laura Cove are favorite locations for commercial crabbers. Recreation boaters have been known to snag pot lines that stretch under water over a hundred feet.

Sir Edmund Bay. Sir Edmund Bay should be entered east of Nicholls Island to avoid a rock west of the island. This rock is farther offshore than you might expect. Fish farms take up considerable space, but anchorage is possible in a cove at the northwest corner of the bay, and in another cove at the south corner.

The northwest cove is 48 to 60 feet deep until well in. Then it shoals to 30 feet before the shelf is reached. An all-chain anchor rode would yield a small enough swinging circle; boats with combination chain and rope may need to stern-tie to a tree. The cove is not very pretty and wouldn't be our first choice.

The southern cove has anchorage behind a charted drying rock. Some years ago, we visited near the bottom of a 7-foot low tide and failed to locate the rock. Others who have anchored there say the cove is a good spot, however. Until we know more we neither recommend nor discourage anchoring.

⑥ **Shawl Bay & Moore Bay.** Shawl Bay and Moore Bay are a short distance inside the entrance to Kingcome Inlet on the east side. The bays are connected by a narrow channel that reportedly is navigable at half tide or better. Moore Bay has no marinas. Anchorage is behind Thief Island in the south part of Moore Bay, or in 36 feet close behind the 55-meter island near the north shore. Two other nooks along the east shore might also be workable anchorages, depending on the weather. Along the north shore, near where a stream from Mt. Plumridge enters the bay, the Ministry of Forests installed a dinghy dock and four campsites with picnic tables and an outhouse.

Shawl Bay Marina. c/o General Delivery, Simoom Sound, BC V0P 1S0; (250) 483-4022; shawlbaymarina@gmail.com; www.shawlbaymarina.com. New owners purchased Shawl Bay Marina in 2016 and closed the marina for renovations, which began in 2017. Construction continued through 2018, and we were told that the marina most likely will not be open until 2020. See WaggonerGuide.com for updates.

Reid Bay. Reid Bay, on the western shore just inside the entrance to Kingcome Inlet, is open, deep, and uninteresting. It is no place to anchor. Just south of Reid Bay, however, an unnamed cove has possibilities. It is rather pretty and has good protection from westerlies. The chart indicates depths of approximately 6 fathoms throughout the bay, but our depth sounder showed 60 to 80

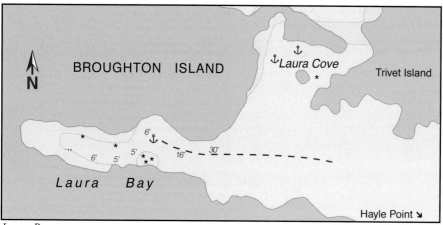

Laura Bay

feet, except about 36 feet close to the head. If you go into this cove, give a wide berth to the point at the south entrance. We saw one uncharted rock just off the point; Chappell's guidebook says there are two.

KINGCOME INLET

Kingcome Inlet extends 17 miles inland between high and beautiful mountains, terminating at the delta of the Kingcome River. The water is milky from glacier runoff and the surface band of water can be surprisingly fresh. Just beyond Petley Point at the head of the inlet, a magnificent new pictograph, a real work of art, is painted high on a rock cliff on the north shore. It is the work of Native artist Marianne Nicolson. The pictograph is brilliant red in color, and measures 28 feet wide and 38 feet high. A half mile south of the new pictograph, there is a much older Native pictograph. The book, *Two Wolves at the Dawn of Time*, by Judith Williams, describes the project. The book's prose is a bit rich, but the story is interesting.

Kingcome Inlet's great depths and sheer rock walls allow virtually no suitable anchorages in the upper portions, except in settled weather.

Wakeman Sound. Wakeman Sound branches off Kingcome Inlet and extends about 7 miles north into the mountains. Although it has no good anchorages, on a clear day the scenery is beautiful. Wakeman Sound is a center for logging activity. Watch for drift in the water.

Belleisle Sound. Belleisle Sound branches off Kingcome Inlet to the south. Entry is between two high green mountains—the kind that make you feel small. Belleisle Sound is beautiful and remote-feeling, but generally too deep for easy anchoring. Only a small area just inside the entrance is usable. Chappell and Sailing Directions warn that strong westerlies can blow through. On the day of our visit the surface was mirror-calm. The water was warm and people on another boat took a swim, right out in the middle. We spent the night in Belleisle Sound without difficulty, anchored and stern-tied to the little islet across from the entrance. [Hale]

SUTLEJ CHANNEL

Cypress Harbour. Cypress Harbour is a pretty spot, but a large fish farm occupies part of Miller Bay, and two log booms are present in Berry Cove farther in. Good anchorage, removed from the fish farm and log boom, is in lovely Stopford Bay in the southeast corner of Cypress Harbour. Be sure to avoid the charted rock. We've had a report of a stretch of logging cable lying on the bottom a short distance before the rock is reached. Watch the depths in Stopford Bay; the bottom grows increasingly shoal until it becomes drying flats. Recommended if you want a quiet, tucked-away anchorage.

Field Correspondent Deane Hislop reports that the Forest Service Recreation site on Clawston Point offers 5 camp sites with picnic tables, fire pits, and a pit toilet.

Broughton Lagoon. "The entrance to Broughton Lagoon is a reversing tidal rapids. At Alert Bay high slack, water pours in through the narrow passage, trying to fill the lagoon. At Alert Bay low slack, water pours out at a ferocious rate. The calmest time to enter Broughton Lagoon is about 1 hour 15 minutes after Alert Bay high slack. For about 30 minutes around that time the rapids are at their least flow. Use the north entry channel only. The other channel often dries. This is a beautiful lagoon. It has plenty of width and depth for powerful dinghies. Not recommended for larger craft without local knowledge." *[Tom Taylor]*

Greenway Sound. Greenway Sound has several good anchorages. The bay behind Broughton Point, at the east end of Carter Passage, is nice.

Depending on conditions, anchorage is in a number of little nooks on both sides of Greenway Sound and behind Simpson Island, near the head of the sound. Leave Simpson Island to starboard when approaching the head of Greenway Sound. For exercise, Broughton Lakes Park, with access from a dinghy dock on the west shore of the bay due east of Greenway Point, received much work in recent years and has excellent hiking. The bay itself is a little deep for anchoring, so anchor elsewhere and take the dinghy over. Good trout fishing at the lakes (fresh water license required), beautiful views.

Cartwright Bay. This bay is open to the wakes from passing traffic in Sutlej Channel, but offers easy anchorage at its inner end.

⑦ **Sullivan Bay Marina Resort.** Box 6000, Port McNeill, BC V0N 2R0; (604) 484-9193; sullivanbaymarina@gmail.com; www.sullivanbay.com. Monitors VHF 66A. Fuel open year-round, store and moorage seasonal. Recycling and burn barrel. Services include gasoline, diesel, propane, 15, 30 & 50 amp power, water, washroom, showers, laundry, exercise room, and limited Wi-Fi at the happy hour tent for moored guests.

Everything except the fuel storage tanks is on

At the head of Kingcome Inlet you can see this native pictograph.

floats, in cozy float houses that date from the mid-20th century. Guests often gather around 5:00 p.m. for drinks and appys at the "Sullivan Square" area. Golfers can try their hands on the 1-hole golf course. Depending on tide and wind, the floating target is 100 to 140 yards out. Last year, there were two holes in one.

Sullivan Bay is legendary among cruising boaters. It has ample moorage (3000 feet), a well-stocked grocery store with liquor agency, bait and tackle, and is pet friendly. They also offer fresh-baked pastries, pies, and cinnamon buns. The restaurant is open Monday, Wednesday, and Friday with a fixed price, buffet-style dinner; we have received rave reviews, especially over the prime rib dinner, call for reservations.

This is a popular turnaround point for Broughtons cruisers. Daily floatplane service to Seattle and elsewhere. Boat sitting available. The resort offers fishing charters.

The annual July 4th celebration and parade on the docks is hugely popular. Reservations recommended.

A community of handsome vacation float homes occupies a portion of the Sullivan Bay moorage. Improvements continue every year. Debbie Holt is the attentive manager. Tucker, the four-legged assistant manager, is an enthusiastic member of the community. He is happy to show other dogs the 'poop deck' located behind the fuel dock.

Atkinson Island. Find anchorage in either end of the passage south of Atkinson Island.

GRAPPLER SOUND

Grappler Sound, north of Sutlej Channel and Wells Passage, has several good anchorages.

Kinnaird Island. The bay in the northeast corner of the island is reported to be good in settled weather.

Hoy Bay. Some anchorage is possible in Hoy Bay, behind Hopetown Point, west of Hopetown Passage.

LOCAL KNOWLEDGE

DANGEROUS CURRENTS: If Hopetown Passage is attempted at all, it should be done cautiously, at high water slack in a shallow draft boat.

Hopetown Passage. The eastern entrance to Hopetown Passage is blocked by a drying reef. Strong currents, tidal overfalls and shallow depths make this a challenge. Explore by dinghy first.

⑧ **Carriden Bay.** Carriden Bay is located just inside Pandora Head, at the entrance to Grappler Sound. The holding is reportedly good, if a little deep when away from the shoreline. One reader calls Carriden Bay "a special spot." As you look in, the spectacular knob of Pandora Head rises on the left, and when you're in, you see a beautiful vista of mountains out the mouth of the bay. This vista makes Carriden Bay exposed to east winds, however. It could be an uncomfortable anchorage in such winds.

⑨ **Claydon Bay.** This is a popular anchorage. Entering or leaving, favor the Morton Point side. Foul ground, shown on the chart, extends from the opposite side of the entry. In Claydon Bay you can pick the north arm or south arm, depending on which way the wind is blowing. An islet is in the entry to the north arm. Leave this islet to starboard when entering. Note also that the drying reef surrounding the islet extends a considerable distance southeast of the islet. The northern arm has room for about a dozen boats; holding is good with a thick mud bottom. Crabbing is reportedly good.

Woods Bay. Woods Bay is deep until close to shore, and exposed to westerly winds. This bay has been reported to be a good spot in settled weather, but we think other anchorages in the area are more appealing.

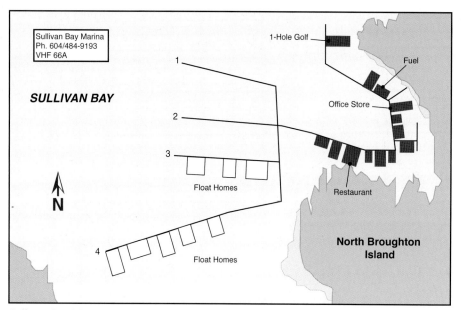

Sullivan Bay Marina Resort

Embley Lagoon. Too shallow for anything but dinghies, but an interesting exploration.

⑩ **Turnbull Cove.** Turnbull Cove is a large, popular, and beautiful bay, with lots of room and good anchoring in 30 to 50 feet. Avoid the areas in front of recent slides. The bottom there probably is foul with debris. Chappell warns that an easterly gale can turn the entire bay into a lee shore, so be aware if such winds are forecast.

The Ministry of Forests built a trail from Turnbull Cove over the mountain to Huaskin Lake. Field Correspondents Brett and Sue Oemichen report that an old steam donkey, somewhat hidden by trees, is to the right of the dinghy landing near the trailhead to the lake. A large float for swimming, a picnic table, a tent platform, and a fire pit are at the lake. It's really nice. The trail goes straight up and straight back down, and it's muddy in places. Steps and even a handrail are on the lake side. They make a big difference. The lake is scenic and looks as if it goes forever.

Approach: Currents of 2+ knots flow through the channel leading to the entry. The currents are not hazardous, but they can come as a surprise. The west side of the entry to Turnbull Cove is charted as clear, but lots of kelp is growing there. A mid-channel course is recommended.

Nepah Lagoon. The adventuresome might want to try Roaringhole Rapids into Nepah Lagoon. Transit, by dinghy with an outboard motor, should be attempted only at high water slack, which lasts 5 minutes and occurs 2 hours after the corresponding high water at Alert Bay. The channel is only 3 feet deep at low water. Nepah Lagoon doesn't appear to have any useable anchorages, except possibly a little notch about a mile from the rapids.

MACKENZIE SOUND

Kenneth Passage. Kenneth Passage has sufficient depths at all stages of tide, being careful of a covered rock off Jessie Point. Currents can be quite strong and whirlpools sometimes appear. Slack water entry is advised, especially on spring tides. The best advice is to take a look and decide if conditions suit you and your boat.

Steamboat Bay. Steamboat Bay is a good anchorage, with room for a few boats. The bay shoals to drying flats all around. Watch for the drying rocks along the east shore at the entrance.

Burly Bay. Burly Bay is a good anchorage, mud bottom, but the muddy shoreline makes going ashore difficult. The little notch just to the west of Blair Islet is better. Blair Islet has ample room for two boats to swing at anchor in 20-30 feet, mud bottom. At low tide, a drying, rocky bar separates Blair Islet from Burly Bay. At high tide, you can take the dinghy across the rapids just around the corner to explore the east end of Hopetown Passage. From the open water on the north side, the views of Mt. Stephens are stunning.

Little Nimmo Bay and Nimmo Bay. Little Nimmo Bay is a pretty anchorage, and the rock-strewn entrance is not as difficult as it appears on the chart—except on a low tide. The Nimmo Bay Wilderness Resort is located there. Anchor in 24 feet, mud bottom. Several small waterfalls tumble through the forest. With care it is possible to go through to Nimmo Bay, which has roomy anchorage offering 15-40 foot depths, with a sticky, mud bottom. At low tide, an extensive, drying flat forms from the head of the bay. In late summer, the bear watching here is excellent with numerous bears roaming the beaches at low tide.

⑪ **Nimmo Bay Wilderness Resort.** Box 696, Port McNeill, BC V0N 2R0; (800) 837-4354; heli@nimmobay.com; www.nimmobay.com. Nimmo Bay Wilderness Resort is a luxury destination resort. Dock space is limited to 60 feet on a first-come, first-served basis and available only to guests with dinner or spa reservations. With advanced reservations, visiting boaters may enjoy a gourmet dining experience at the lodge and "fire dock." Massage services with the use of the waterfall-side hot tubs are also available with advanced reservations. Larger vessels can anchor in Mackenzie Sound or Nimmo Bay and take the tender to the resort's dock for dinner or spa treatments. Floatplane service available from Kenmore Air and NW Seaplanes.

DRURY INLET

Drury Inlet is much less visited than other waters in the area. The entrance, off Wells Passage, is clearly marked on the charts, as is Stuart Narrows, 1.5 miles inside the entrance. Good anchorage is in two arms of Richmond Bay (choose the one that protects from the prevailing wind); near Stuart Narrows; in Jennis Bay; and in Sutherland Bay, at the head of Drury Inlet. Approach Sutherland Bay around the north side of the Muirhead Islands, after which the bay is open and protected.

Our sister publication, *Cruising the Secret Coast*, available at WaggonerGuide.com, by Jennifer and James Hamilton, devotes an entire chapter to exploring Drury Inlet and Actaeon Sound, with details about interesting hikes.

Helen Bay. Helen Bay is just east of Stuart Narrows. It is reportedly a good anchorage. Halibut are said to be caught in the area.

Stuart Narrows. Currents in Stuart Narrows run to a maximum of 7 knots, although on small tides they are much less. Times of slack are listed under Alert Bay, Secondary Current Stations, in the Tide & Current Tables Vol. 6, and Ports and Passes. The skipper of a tug towing a log boom through Stuart Narrows advised us that he times slack for 10 minutes

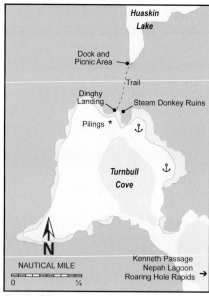

Turnbull Cove

after both high and low tides at Alert Bay, which is in line with the tide and current tables information. The only hazard is Welde Rock. You will most likely see the kelp. Get way over to the south side of the channel. The current flows faster south of Welde rock, although passage can be made north of the rock as well. Leche Islet should be passed to the north. A study of the chart shows a rock patch to the south.

Note that Stuart Narrows is well inside the mouth of Drury Inlet.

Richmond Bay. Located just south of the west entrance to Stuart Narrows, Richmond Bay contains three coves. The southwest inner cove is filled with a float house and a large work float. The best anchorage is in 50 feet just off the work float.

⑫ **Jennis Bay.** Jennis Bay is the site of a logging camp and booming ground, with good anchorage in the cove northwest of Jennis Bay Marina.

⑫ **Jennis Bay Marina.** P.O. Box 456, Port McNeill, BC V0N 2R0; (778) 762-3037, jennismarina@gmail.com; www.jennisbay. com. VHF 66A. Jennis Bay Marina is a historic logging camp with a quaint, rustic

feel. Moorage available year-round, 300 feet of transient moorage space for up to 11 boats depending upon size and rafting options. Free Wi-Fi; reader Joanne Wilshin reports good, reliable internet. No power at the docks. Burn barrel for trash. TV room, washroom and shower. Four cabin rentals. Kayaking, mountain biking, hiking, and miles of logging roads and trails for exploring. The marina offers a truck for rent to tour the local area; email ahead to check availability. Happy Hour potlucks are ad-hoc, organized by visiting pleasure boaters at the covered barbecue area.

From Drury Inlet, enter Jennis Bay around either end of Hooper Island. If entering during limited visibility, the west end may be safest. Keep to a mid-channel course to avoid rocks along the shores. Leave the floating log breakwater and yellow buoys to starboard entering the marina.

Caution: Obstructions in the water lie about 500 feet southeast of the marina's log boom breakwater, consisting of a float plus a separate 'standing boom,' neither of which are lit.

Davis Bay. Davis Bay looks inviting on the chart, but is not very pretty and is open to westerlies. Enter on the south side of Davis Islet, strongly favoring the Davis Islet shore. Anchoring depths of 24-30 feet.

Muirhead Islands. The Muirhead Islands, near the head of Drury Inlet, are rock-strewn but beautiful. They invite exploring in a small boat or kayak. The cove on the northeast side, behind the dot island, is a suitable anchorage, as is the cove on the south side, immediately west of the 59-meter island.

Actress Passage and Actaeon Sound. Actress Passage, connecting Drury Inlet with Actaeon Sound, is rock- and reef-strewn, narrow and twisting. Careful navigation is required. There are two theories: some feel high water slack is best to have more water; others feel low water slack is best to allow a better chance of seeing the rocks and hazards in the water. One approach is to enter Actress Passage between Dove Island and the mainland to the north, avoiding the charted rock. Tugs and tows and other commercial traffic, however, use the shorter channel east of Dove Island, splitting rocks marked with sticks at the entrance to Drury Inlet.

Once into Actress Passage, the overriding navigation problem is the area between Skene Point and Bond Peninsula, where a careful S-shaped course around the rocks is required, hence the local name Snake Passage. Another choice is to follow Chappell's suggestion of crossing from Skene Point to Bond Peninsula,

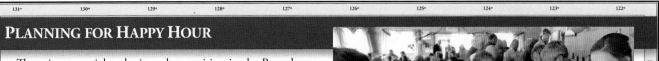

PLANNING FOR HAPPY HOUR

The primary social gathering when cruising in the Broughtons is Happy Hour. This ritual typically begins around 4:00 to 5:00 p.m. and can extend well past dinnertime. I am told a movement is underway at some marinas to move the start of happy hour to 3:00 p.m., or maybe sometime after lunch. If a Happy Hour is not scheduled it could happen spontaneously when a group is hanging around the dock with nothing to do. All of a sudden someone gasps, "Hey, we ought to have a Happy Hour!" The drinks start flowing and food emerges.

During our early years of cruising the Inside Passage, we never seemed to have the right provisions for a proper Happy Hour contribution. We once showed up at an impromptu Happy Hour with a plate of store bought Oreo cookies (oh, the horror!), though the Oreos always disappeared. No one had briefed us on Happy Hour etiquette, and our cruising guides lacked this critical information.

With a few seasons under my belt I now begin preparing for Happy Hour at the beginning of the cruising season. In addition to making sure we have an adequate supply of oil, filters, and belts, I make sure we have plenty of items for whipping up a jaw-droppingly impressive Happy Hour hors d'oeuvre, preferably something that will stack or mound to 8-12 inches high or more.

What is my secret? A good supply of cream cheese and crackers!

At the beginning of the season I make a special trip to my local warehouse store for bricks of cream cheese. In order to carry sufficient quantities, I purchased and installed a dedicated refrigerator. I also buy a variety of crackers, boxes of them. I stock onion soup mix, different spice combinations, canned smoked salmon, canned crab, and even canned shrimp. Just in case I end up cruising to multiple locations with the same people, I also have a number of sweet mixes for cream cheese to change things up. Dried cherries, cran-raisins, dried apricots, and a few syrups to add color and flavor.

Now, cream cheese adaptations go over well, but I have noticed some captain and first mate teams look for extra points in the unspoken Happy Hour competition. They bring a dip with fresh caught crab (sometimes even artfully arranged in the shell) with chunks of crabmeat. Or, they show up with a bowl of fresh prawns caught that morning, still warm from a spiced boil. I really hate the guy who shows up with his salmon caught that morning and smoked on the dock next to his boat. How does he do this? He is one competitive Happy Hour cruiser!

Other Happy Hour recipes show up too. I long for the pea salad like my mother used to make, or the spicy coleslaw someone brings in an antique bowl. Sometimes someone will bring a simple green salad with fresh tomatoes and basil brought over from Vancouver Island that morning, garnished with pine nuts. Fresh brownies are a wonderful contribution, and yes, I might even sneak an Oreo cookie or two when one of the first-timers joins the party on the dock.

Our best galley advice for cruising in the Broughtons? Be ready and go bold for Happy Hour. Mix it up, mound it high, and watch it fly. Fellow cruisers will love the end result!
– Anonymous

and working past the charted hazards around the corner.

In our sister publication, *Cruising the Secret Coast*, the Hamiltons have extensively explored this area and present specific directions for this passage and the area.

WELLS PASSAGE

Tracey Harbour. Tracey Harbour indents North Broughton Island from Wells Passage. It is pretty and protected. No anchorage is viable, however, until near the head of the bay. There, you can find anchorage on mud bottom in Napier Bay, or on rocky bottom in the bay behind Carter Point. You're apt to find log booms in Napier Bay, and leftover buildings from an old logging operation. Anchor near the head of the cove behind Carter Point. The cove is beautiful and cozy-feeling, but the bottom feels like a thin layer of mud on top of rock and it wouldn't take much to drag the anchor.

Carter Passage. Since Carter Passage is blocked in the middle by a boulder-strewn drying shoal, it is actually two harbors, one off Wells Passage and one off Greenway Sound, with good anchorages in each end. The west entrance has tidal currents to 7 knots, and should be taken at or near high water slack. A reef extends from the south shore, so keep north of mid-channel. Two pleasant anchorages are in this west end.

The east entrance, off Greenway Sound, is somewhat easier, in terms of both tidal currents and obstructions. John Chappell's *Cruising Beyond Desolation Sound* describes how to safely transit the drying shoal between the two ends of Carter Passage.

Dickson Island. Dickson Island is near the mouth of Wells Passage. The small anchorage on the east end of the island provides good protection from seas, but the low land allows westerly winds to blow across the bay. Two other bays along the west side of Broughton Island are too exposed to westerly weather to be good anchorages.

Polkinghorne Islands. The Polkinghorne Islands are outside the mouth of Wells Passage. A channel among the islands is fun, particularly on the nice day. The anchoring bottom we've found is not too secure, so an overnight stay is not recommended. [*Kincaid*]

FIFE SOUND

Cullen Harbour. Cullen Harbour is on the south side of Broughton Island, at the entrance to Booker Lagoon. It is an excellent anchorage, with plenty of room for everyone. You might rock a little if the wind is blowing from northwest. The bottom is mud, and depths range from 24 to 50 feet.

LOCAL KNOWLEDGE

UNCHARTED ROCK: Correspondents John and Lorraine Littlewood did some independent chart work surveying Booker Lagoon, and found a ledge of rock not shown on the charts (see Booker Lagoon map). Its presence was confirmed by two bent props, one bent skeg and one bent rudder — "a real boat-eater," according to John.

Booker Lagoon. The entrance to Booker Lagoon is from Cullen Harbour through Booker Passage, a narrow channel bounded by reefs on both sides. The channel is about 50 feet wide and has ample depths. Best to transit at slack water. Use the Sunday Harbour secondary station in Canadian Tide and Current Tables Vol. 6, or Ports and Passes. On big tides the duration of slack water is about 10 minutes, and the stream can build to 7 knots or more. The aquaculture pens that once occupied the four arms of Booker Lagoon have been removed, so it's a good anchorage again on a sticky mud bottom. Don't enter Booker Lagoon through the passage on the west side of Long Island. The passage is shoal and choked with kelp.

Once in Booker Lagoon you'll be in a secluded coastal paradise. The lagoon is quite large, and deep in the middle. Watch

for a couple of hazards near the entrance to the west arm, they appear to be low floating buoys, which are difficult to see. Explore around, then anchor in one of the arms, perhaps away from other anchored boats; it's that kind of place.

Deep Harbour. In the past the inner part of Deep Harbour was blocked by boomed logs and the center of the bay taken over by aquaculture pens. It is now clear and there are little nooks around the edges with room for one boat.

BROUGHTON ARCHIPELAGO

Much of the Broughton Archipelago is now a marine park. Some of the islands are private, however, so use discretion when going ashore.

Our journal, written while at anchor after a day of exploring, reads, "A marvelous group of islands and passages, but few good anchorages. We navigated around Insect Island and through Indian Passage. Very pretty—many white shell beaches. Rocks marked by kelp. A different appearance from Kingcome Inlet or Simoom Sound. The trees are shorter and more windblown. The west wind is noticeably colder than farther east. Fog lay at the mouth of Fife Sound; a few wisps blew up toward us. Great kayaking, gunkholing country." [*Hale*]

This large group of islands west of Gilford Island does have anchorages, including Sunday Harbour, Monday Anchorage, and Joe Cove. The area is dotted with rocks, reefs, and little islands, which in total provide good protection, but also call for careful navigation.

M. Wylie Blanchet (*The Curve of Time*) was blown out of Sunday Harbour, and we've heard mixed reports about Monday Anchorage. Chappell wasn't impressed with either one. Joe Cove is considered to be a good anchorage. Chart 3546 (1:40:000) should be studied carefully before going into these waters, and kept close at hand while there. Currents run strongly at times through the various passages.

⑬ **Sunday Harbour.** Sunday Harbour is formed by Crib Island and Angular Island, north of the mouth of Arrow Passage. The bay is very pretty, although exposed to westerly winds. We would anchor in the middle for a relaxing lunch on a quiet day. The little cove in the northeast corner looks attractive but is full of rocks.

⑭ **Monday Anchorage.** Monday is a large and fairly open anchorage between Tracey Island and Mars Island. There are a number of bays, bights and coves with varying depths. Field Correspondent Deane Hislop set the hook between the most eastern islet and Tracey Island in 30 feet of water and spent time exploring tide pools and a large midden on Tracey Island. When entering the anchorage from the south, beware of the foul ground shown on the chart, extending from Tracey Island to starboard.

Wells Passage connects western Broughtons with Queen Charlotte Strait.

⑮ **Joe Cove.** Joe Cove, perfectly protected and private feeling, indents the south side of Eden Island. The best anchorage is near the head. A little thumb of water extends southeast near the head of the cove, but access is partially blocked by several rocks. It is possible, however, to feel your way in by hugging the shore to starboard as you enter. The passage is narrow but clear. The float in the cove has deteriorated to the point where it is no longer safe to use; a sign warning not to use the float has been posted.

East of Eden (Lady Boot Cove). Lady Boot Cove is what Don and Reanne Douglass call this nice little anchorage in *Exploring the South Coast of British Columbia*. Locals tell us the correct name is East of Eden. The cove indents the northeast corner of Eden Island, with Fly Island directly off the mouth. As the chart shows, the southern indent is shoal and foul with a drying reef. The northern indent is beautifully protected with room for 3-4 boats; room to swing is limited so a stern-tie is best.

RETREAT PASSAGE

Seabreeze Cove. This otherwise unnamed lovely little anchorage in Gilford Island was suggested by Correspondents James and Jennifer Hamilton. It lies behind the 70-meter island due east of Seabreeze Island, at the western entrance to Retreat Passage. Their report: "We anchored in 18 feet south of the 70-meter island and held very well in sticky mud. Some southwest winds did blow through, but nothing major. The water was

barely rippled. Caught three big Dungeness crabs overnight."

Be aware that the bottom shoals rapidly once past the 70-meter island.

Bootleg Bay. South of False Cove, a thumb-like island protrudes northwest from Gilford Island. The cove south of that island has about 30 feet at the entrance, shoaling gently toward the head. No name appears on the charts. According to Chappell it is known locally as Bootleg Bay. A wrecked fish boat has been reported at the head of the bay. Anchoring depths 20-40 feet.

⑯ **Waddington Bay.** Waddington Bay indents the northeast corner of Bonwick Island. The bay is popular, with room for several boats. It has good holding in 18 to 30 feet. The approach is off the little pass that connects Retreat Passage and Arrow Passage. Turn to leave the 46-meter island to starboard, and go on in. Be sure you have the right island; they all look alike. The approach is wide enough, but rocks are all around and careful piloting is called for. Know your position at all times. Waddington Bay shoals at the head. The wind direction and your depth sounder will tell you where to put the hook down. Wind will get in when the westerly is blowing, but there's no fetch for seas to build. This is a tranquil anchorage—a good place to hide out for a few days.

Grebe Cove. Grebe Cove indents the east side of Bonwick Island off Retreat Passage. The cove shallows to 40 to 50 feet about 200 yards from the head, and 30 to 40 feet near the head, mud bottom, with good depths side

to side. A saddle in the hills at the head might let westerlies in, but the seas would have no fetch. On one visit, a couple in a 20-foot pocket cruiser called out, "Great anchorage! The otters will entertain you!"

Carrie Bay. Carrie Bay indents Bonwick Island across Retreat Passage from Health Bay. The head of the bay is pretty and protected from westerly winds. The bottom shoals rapidly from 40 to 50 feet in much of the bay to around 20 feet at the head. Good holding in sand and shell bottom.

Health Bay. The Health Bay Indian Reserve, with a small dock offering overnight moorage with power, fronts on Retreat Passage, ask for Charlie. Health Bay itself is strewn with rocks. Anchorage is best fairly close to the head of the bay, short of the first of the rocks. Field Correspondents Brett and Sue Oemichen report reliable cell signal in Retreat Passage in front of the Health Bay community.

BLACKFISH ARCHIPELAGO

The name Blackfish Archipelago does not appear on the charts or in Sailing Directions, but generally refers to the myriad islands and their waterways adjacent to Blackfish Sound.

Goat Island Anchorage. You'll find a good anchorage in the cove that lies off the southeast corner of Crease Island.

Enter Goat Island Anchorage between Crease Island and Goat Island, leaving Goat Island to port and Crease Island to starboard. The chart makes the preferred entry clear. Caution for the charted shoals northeast of Goat Island as you approach the preferred entrance. Chart 3546 in raster mode appears to mislabel a smaller island to the south of Goat Island, along Village Channel, as Goat Island. Vector mode charts correctly show Goat Island as the small island immediately southeast of a short peninsula on Crease Island.

Anchor in 12 to 18 feet on a sometimes rocky bottom, wherever it looks good. The cove is excellent for crabbing. Weed on the bottom might foul some anchors. A reader reported that their anchor found a large diameter line on the bottom, probably left over from earlier logging. Where there's one cable there might be more. It would be a good idea to rig a trip line to the crown of the anchor. The view to the southeast is very pretty.

Leone Island. A bay lies between Leone Island and Madrona Island. Tom Kincaid has anchored there and recommends it. "'Friends, with extensive experience, also recommend it. We, however, tried to set our anchor four times over a 2-day period, and failed each time. Twice the anchor did not penetrate large, leafy kelp. Once it refused to set in thin sand and reedy weed. On the last try the anchor seemed to set, but it dragged with only moderate power in reverse." [*Hale*]

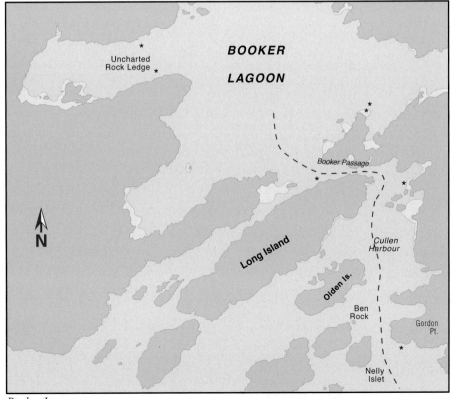

Booker Lagoon

Mound Island. The cove behind Mound Island is a good anchorage, paying mind to the rocks (shown on the chart) that line the shores. Tom Sewid at Village Island told us that 14 depressions in the earth were once the sites of big houses. Correspondent Pat Shera reports that the depressions are obvious, just inland from the beach at the western end of the island.

⑰ **New Vancouver.** (250) 974-2703. Monitors VHF 78. Moorage, with 30 amp power. Cash only payment. Washrooms, showers and laundry are located in a trailer unit. Trails to camp sites are in the area. The small store has gifts and convenience snacks, cash only. Open June 1 through September 15. New Vancouver, traditionally known as Tsatsisnukwomi Village, is on the north side of Harbledown Island, a short distance west of Dead Point, the entrance to Beware Passage. The location is marked IR on the chart, for Indian Reserve. It is the ancestral home of the Da'naxda'xw Native Band, who moved from Knight Inlet in the 1960s. Efforts are underway to protect eelgrass in the area, anchor in deeper water. The band is welcoming and offers cultural tours of the village and bighouse for a fee; we have heard that the tour is very interesting.

Farewell Harbour. You'll find good anchorage in Farewell Harbour close to the Berry Island side. The Farewell Harbour Marine Resort, shown on the chart, is actually a luxury fishing resort and doesn't cater to visiting yachties.

Chiefs Bathtub. The Chiefs Bathtub is located on Village Channel on the north side of Berry Island, at approximately 50°36.45'N /126°39.56'W (NAD 83). It's a sculpted-out depression in a rock cliff, a little below the high water line. According to Tom Sewid, up-and-coming chiefs had to sit in this bathtub four times a day for four days as the cold waters of the tide washed in. If you take the dinghy to see the tub more closely, don't touch the pictographs on the rock. Skin oils attack the paint.

⑱ **Village Island.** (250) 287-2955; A site on the western shore of Village Island is often known incorrectly as Mamalilaculla. It is the uninhabited village of Mimkwamlis and the ancestral home of the Mamalilikulla First Nation (MFN). Uplands are protected Indian Reserve property and access is by permission of the Mamalilikulla First Nation Band office. The Band charges $20 per person ($10 for children) to tour the village site, with its empty school building, collapsing houses, fallen totem poles and big house remains. All fees go to the clean up of the village site and support the Band's guardian watchmen program.

Anchor in the bay north of the village site; be sure of your set. In 2018, a new 160-foot private dock was installed in the bay north of the village to provide improved access for band members and visitors with permission to go ashore. This is a private dock and tie-up is allowed only by permission from the Mamalilikulla First Nation; maximum stay of 2 hours. Mimkwamlis is protected under the Heritage Conservation Act; respect the village property; leave all artifacts and remains as they lie; and do not enter any of the buildings. No camping or fires ashore; leave only footprints.

For permission to go ashore and to pay visitor fees, contact the MFN Band office at (250) 287-2955 or visit their website at Mamalilikulla.ca, or by mail at Mamalilikulla First Nation, 1441B 16th Ave Campbell River, BC V9W 2E4.

Native Anchorage. Native Anchorage is located at the southwest corner of Village Island. It's no place to be in a southerly storm, but in all other winds it's a fine anchorage. Put the hook down in 18 to 24 feet. Excellent mud bottom.

Canoe Passage. Canoe Passage runs east-west between Turnour Island and Village Island. The waterway dries at low tide, but can be transited at higher tides, depending on a vessel's draft.

CLIO CHANNEL

Cracroft Inlet. Cracroft Inlet is on the south side of Dorman and Farquharson Islands. While we have not anchored there (yet), it is reportedly well protected, with good holding bottom on either side of the large charted rock. Lagoon Cove, on the other side of Farquharson Island, can be reached by taking the dinghy around the east end of the island. The passage is shallow, so check the tides and be sure of your depths.

Bones Bay. The entire bay is fairly open, although you may find temporary anchorage behind the islets along the south shore. Watch for rocks around the islets. A floating fishing lodge is moored behind these islets.

Bend Island. Bend Island is connected to West Cracroft Island by a drying ledge, but good anchorage is in either end. Friends have anchored in the tiny nook just east of Bend Island, with a stern-tie to shore.

Docks at the Native Village of New Vancouver

⑲ **Potts Lagoon.** The outer bay behind Klaoitsis Island and the 119-meter headland is open for anchorage; the previous log booming operation has been removed, only the landing site remains. Two inner bays provide good protection from all winds. The inner bay to the southeast of the 41-meter island is the more popular and spacious with anchoring depths of 18 to 24 feet. Ruins from an old pier along with a few float homes add to the character of this hidden scenic anchorage. A smaller but more private cove is found to the northeast of the outer cove.

Klaoitsis Island. Anchorage might be found in the bay northwest of Klaoitsis Island, and in a notch on the south shore of Jamieson Island. Currents can run through these anchorages. For most boats, Potts Lagoon is a better choice.

Beware Passage. Place names from Chart 3545 for Beware Passage might scare you away; Beware Passage, Caution Rock, Caution Cove, Beware Rock, Beware Cove, and Dead Point. Beware Passage is aptly named, but you can get through safely. Sailing Directions recommends transiting at low water when rocks are visible. There are two routes through Beware Passage; Care Island route and Harbledown Island route. Both routes are shown on the Beware Passage map. Locals prefer the Harbledown Island route and suggest only using the Care Island route at low water slack, when rocks can be seen and current isn't making course changes difficult. We recommend proceeding dead slow with a careful watch on depth sounder and a bow watch for both routes. Assuming a passage from east to west, both routes start by entering just off Nicholas Point on Turnour (pronounced "Turner") Island. There are several Native pictographs on a rock face 300 yards west of Nicholas Point. After Nicholas Point and the pictographs, both routes follow mid-channel between Kamano Island and the unnamed islet north of Kamano Island. At the west end of Kamano Island, the two routes separate. For Harbledown Island route, turn to heading 275° magnetic when the west end of Kamano Island is abeam your port side. Proceed to the Harbledown Island side of Beware Passage and a narrow channel between Harbledown Island and a pair of small islands that lie just offshore from Harbledown Island. This narrow channel has kelp, and a charted shoal on the Harbledown Island side. Exit this narrow channel on a heading of 305° magnetic. Turn to port and continue northwest on Beware Passage when Dead Point is on a course of 273° magnetic. For Care Island route, when the west end of Kamano Island is abeam your port side, turn to a heading of approximately 346° magnetic. Turn to a heading of approximately 266° magnetic when you see a forested rock outcropping on Turnour Island shore to your starboard. Check your GPS chartplotter to confirm this critical turn to the west making sure you avoid the rock awash to port and the charted rock that dries at 1.2 meters. Proceed, favoring the Care Island side until past Care Island. Then turn to heading 271° magnetic. For both routes, pass between Beware Rock and the charted rock that dries at 0.9 meters and proceed to Dead Point.

Caution Cove. Caution Cove is open to prevailing winds, but the bottom is good. Caution Rock, drying at 4 feet, is in the center of the entrance. The rock is clearly shown on Chart 3545, as are the rocks just off the drying flats at the head of the cove. An extensive logging operation may be operating in the cove. Beware Cove might be a better option.

Beware Cove. Beware Cove is a good anchorage, very pretty, with protection from westerlies but not southeasterlies. Easiest entry is to the west of Cook Island, leaving Cook Island to starboard.

⑳ **Monks' Wall.** The ruins of a massive and mysterious rock wall lies hidden just inside the treeline on Harbledown Island, at the north end of Beware Passage. Chinese Buddhist monks are reported to have been on the island more than a century ago, and some have speculated that they are the ones who built the wall. It makes an intriguing story: far from their homeland, devout Buddhists in their robes carrying and positioning huge stones for what?—a temple, perhaps.

The real story is not as intriguing, but it is at least as inspiring. The wall was not built by monks. It was built by white settlers, William Herbert Galley and his wife Mary Anne Galley. In the late 1800s, Galley acquired 160 acres on Harbledown Island and built a trading post there. According to Galley's great-granddaughter, great-grandfather Galley married Mary Anne Wharton in 1889. Together they cleared the land, planted 125 fruit trees, and kept cows, pigs, chickens, ducks and sheep. The homestead was defined by carefully-built rock walls, straight and solid. An archway marked the entrance to the trading post. It is said that Mary Anne Galley carried rocks in her apron. Those rocks are big. Some apron. Some great-grandmother.

The Monks' Wall is located on the west side of Beware Passage, a short distance south of Dead Point. It is on the point of land separating two large, shallow bays, at lat. 50°35.40'N. (This latitude was measured on the chart, and is approximate.) Anchor in the bay north of that point of land and row the dinghy in. The

353

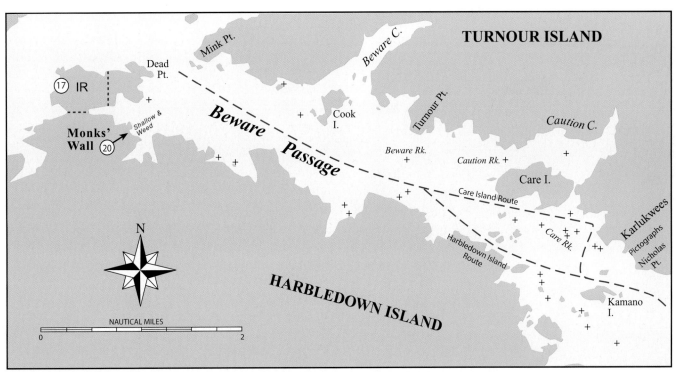

Beware Passage

bottom shoals when approaching the cove, and is dense with weeds that could foul a propeller. Working from north to south, identify the third little nook on the point of land. It's a definite indent. The ruins of the magnificent walls are just inside.

If you hike through the woods around the area you'll find more walls; taken together they're impressive. All built by hand. Straight and true. Enveloped now by the relentless forest. The archway has since collapsed.

Although Monks' Wall is a misnomer, it looks like the name will stick. Our thanks to Galley great-granddaughter Kathy Young for her historical background, and to Billy Proctor for his quickly-drawn map that showed us where to find the site.

Request: The wall and the lesser walls in the surrounding forest are a treasure. Please, no souvenirs, no destruction, no litter.

Dead Point. The unnamed cove just inside Dead Point offers protection from westerlies.

LOCAL KNOWLEDGE

CURRENT DIRECTIONS: Current in Baronet Passage floods west and ebbs east, the opposite of the flows in Johnstone Strait a mile south, and in Knight Inlet 4 miles north.

Baronet Passage. Baronet Passage is very pretty. It's partially obstructed by Walden Island, with the preferred passage in the deeper channel to the north of Walden Island. This is a well-used passage for boats heading to and from Blackfish Sound.

㉑ Growler Cove. Growler Cove, on the west end of West Cracroft Island, is an excellent anchorage, with ample room and good protection from westerlies and easterlies. It is popular with commercial fishermen who work Johnstone Strait and Queen Charlotte Strait. During prime commercial fishing months of July and August, Growler Cove is apt to be full of commercial boats, with little room for pleasure craft.

If you're approaching from the east, enter along West Cracroft Island, favoring the island as you work your way in. We saw an extensive kelp bed, not shown on the chart, off the point that leads to the entrance. We would keep clear of that kelp. If you're approaching from the west, enter between Sophia Islands and Baron Reef, both shown on the chart. Inside, keep a mid-channel course, favoring the north side to avoid a charted rock about halfway in. Good anchoring near the head in 18 to 24 feet.

Hanson Island. The rugged and beautiful north shore of Hanson Island is indented by a number of bays and coves that are a gunkholer's paradise. The most popular anchorage is in Double Bay, also the location of the Pacific Outback Resort, a private fishing lodge. Enter only along the west side of the bay. The bay behind Spout Islet, to the east of Double Bay, is also a good anchorage. Field Correspondent Deane Hislop writes: "We spent a night in the beautiful bay to the east of Spout Islet. The holding was good and provided protection from the summer afternoon westerlies. The view of the whales in Blackfish Sound, the Miriam Range, and 1238-meter Mt. Mathison were spectacular."

FIRST-AID SUPPLIES & PREPAREDNESS

A good first-aid kit is critical when cruising in some of the more remote places. Medical help could be a day or more away. Consider adding a few additions not always included in First Aid kits that fit your lifestyle. We try to cover a reasonable range of potential medical emergencies or discomfort.

Dressings:
Hydrogen Peroxide
Adhesive Bandages
Band-Aids (various sizes)
Gauze Pads, Rolls & Tape
Blister Pads such as Moleskin

Equipment:
Surgical Gloves
Tweezers and Scissors
Splinting Material
Thermometer
Gel Packs (heat/cold)

Ointments:
Antibacterial ointment
Aquaphor for cracks and dry skin
Insect sting relief (medicated pads)

Medications:
Pain Relivers
Anti-acids
Allergy medication such as Benadryl
Sea Sickness medication - Dramamine
Cold & Flu medications

Native village ruins and midden beach at Village Island

FULL MOON FLOOD TIDE, BILL PROCTOR'S RAINCOAST
By Bill Proctor and Yvonne Maximchuk

Publisher: Harbour Publishing; ISBN: 9781550172911

Bill Proctor has spent over 80 years fishing, trapping, and hand-logging among the **Broughton Islands**, as did his predecessors who shaped his life and taught him the skills of survival, an art that is now found only on the written pages of history. Most boaters who have cruised the Broughton Islands have met Bill while visiting his museum, a collection of artifacts and pieces of history that he discovered, or that were donated by friends and Natives he knew from childhood. Bill's book, illustrated by Yvonne, is a delightful read – full of stories about people, places, historical tidbits, and life among the islands. Like a guidebook for the past, Bill points the way to lost villages, logging camps, and early homesteads. Bill also includes a short history about Echo Bay, a popular stop in the Broughtons even to this day. It's a book that can be read at leisure, starting with any chapter.

People: Bill Proctor tells of the many friends he met over the years, with insights into their character and the remote life-style they chose, including Blondy Carlson, a hand-logger and trapper who lived in a float house in Shawl Bay; Tom Hyde, a beloved blacksmith; trapper Matt Rose, who came from the Yukon and whose trapping books are on display at Bill's museum; and many other notable characters. You won't want to miss the incredible story of Bill Baker, who moved from the prairies of Saskatoon to Axe Point on Knight Inlet and learned to hand-log, fish and hunt; or the intriguing story of 'Rough House Pete,' a big Swede who trolled for salmon in the summers and had a trapline at Vernon Lake in the winters. Bill Proctor includes some of his own personal stories,

FULL MOON FLOOD TIDE

First Nations people smoked chum salmon in this building, which once stood by the mouth of the Viner River. There's not much left of it now.

A lot of A-frame logging took place here starting in 1918, and from 1924 to 1932 George O'Brien owned a railroad logging camp at the head of the sound. The railroad brought the timber down the valley to the head of the sound, and the camp sat on floats that rested on the mud at low tide. The row of pilings on the left (north) side near the head are all that remains of the track and the log dump, and here and there bits of machinery lie rusting. The entire railroad was moved around from place to place by piling the tracks on the log-hauling cars, starting with the back end. After George left Viner, he moved the railroad to Trestle Bay.

The Viner River is a historically rich river with coho, pink, chum and sockeye salmon and steelhead, Dolly Varden and cutthroat trout. Before 1991 chum were abundant—runs of thirty to sixty

including when he almost froze to death when out trapping one day.

Places: Bill Proctor's book includes reference maps showing the many Native villages that once were, old homestead cabin sites, and logging camps. Some remnants can still be found today, like the steam donkeys on Baker Island and at Scott Cove on **Gilford Island**; or the interesting rock carvings at the head of **MacKenzie Sound**; remains of a sawmill at Watson Point; and rail tracks at Trestle Bay, Carriden Bay, and Claydon Bay, all used for logging purposes. Bill also points out old logging roads and trails to lakes and along rivers. Bill remembers visiting the Native village of Wahkash Creek in **Knight Inlet** as a kid, where he saw totem poles and cannonballs on the beach; apparently the cannonballs were traded for furs. Bill explains how Minstrel Island was once the hub of the Broughtons. Many people made their home there and raised their children. **Minstrel Island** had a boat repair shop, boat ways, school, hotel, dance hall, several cafes, and a lot of bootleggers.

Historical Tidbits: Each chapter in the book is interspersed with interesting stories and tidbits, like the Legend of the Lost Gold Mine in **Hoeya Sound**; Hand-Logging Techniques; and A Trapper's Life, including trapping methods and preparing pelts. Other articles include The Life of a River; Fishing Techniques; and The Rowboat Fishermen. Having lived the remote island life, Bill has seen the big picture and interdependence between animals, birds, and marine life and now spends his time participating in government chum egg enhancement projects.

Echo Bay: Early on in the book, Bill shares the previous history of **Echo Bay**, now referred to as Pierre's Echo Bay. One of the first settlers to arrive here was Louie McCay in 1910; he purchased land all around the bay, built a home, and raised his two daughters with his wife Hazel. The first school house was built in 1923, serving a growing community of loggers; at one time there were fifteen float houses tied against the cliffs. With the new influx of people, Louie McCay built a store, gas float, and fish-buying camp. In 1930, McCay and Vic Botta started a mink and fox farm on the south side of the head of the bay, currently Bill Proctor's property; but the venture didn't do well as it was too wet for the fox. Around the same time Joe Vasseur came to Echo Bay and operated a shingle mill, under the name of Gilford Island Mills; seventy-five men worked at the mill, mostly Chinese. Louie & Hazel McCay ran a store there from 1920 to 1950, when he sold to Jim Wardrop, who ran it until 1959. Jim Wardrop sold to Bob Martineau, who sold to Norpack Fish in 1970. The fish company stayed for only two years and then closed down the business.

The next time you visit Echo Bay, be sure to walk the trail to Bill Proctor's museum and book store to purchase your copy of *Full Moon Flood Tide*. As Bill and Yvonne explain, the book title is fitting since tides affect the movements of both humans and animals. More fish are around during high tides; clamming is best at low tides; towboat captains like to motor with a flood tide; hand-loggers prefer flood tides to get their logs off the 'foreshore;' and a flood tide is the time to put a boat on the ways for repairs, so goes the life of those who live by the sea.

~ 62 ~

355

North Vancouver Island

CHAPTER 13

WEYNTON PASSAGE
Bauza Cove • Telegraph Cove
Beaver Cove • Pearse Islands

BROUGHTON STRAIT
Port McNeill • Alert Bay • Sointula

QUEEN CHARLOTTE STRAIT
Beaver Harbour • Port Hardy • Bear Cove

North Island refers to the eastern side of Vancouver Island from Sayward (Kelsey Bay) to the top of the island. North Island is served by Highway 19 and is the center of commerce for both sides of the Inside Passage in this area. Port McNeill and Port Hardy are the principal towns. Alert Bay on Cormorant Island and Sointula on Malcolm Island also have facilities.

Boats cruising the Broughtons or continuing farther up the coast usually stop at one or more of the North Island towns for supplies, repairs, fuel, and water. For this reason, the North Island chapter opens with comments about crossing Queen Charlotte Strait.

Kelsey Bay and Robson Bight are covered in the Johnstone Strait section.

Hospitals: Port McNeill and Port Hardy have fully-staffed hospitals. The Cormorant Island Community Health Centre in Alert Bay is in a new building, behind the U'mista Cultural Centre. It has a doctor on duty every day.

Queen Charlotte Strait. Queen Charlotte Strait is about 15 miles wide. The prevailing winds are from the northwest in the summer and the southeast in the winter. In the summer, winds are often lighter in the morning.

Typically, by late morning or early afternoon a sea breeze will begin, and by mid-afternoon it can increase to 30 knots with very rough seas. The sea breeze usually quiets at sundown.

Tom Taylor, owner of the now-closed Greenway Sound Marina Resort, has crossed the strait between Wells Passage and Port McNeill hundreds of times, and tells us that in good weather he could go (in a fast boat) as late as 2:00 p.m. Any given day can go against the norm, however. Skippers should treat Queen Charlotte Strait with great respect.

Weather information: The wind report from Herbert Island, in the Buckle Group, can be a good reference for approaching northwesterly winds. If it's not blowing at Herbert Island, there's a good chance Queen Charlotte Strait will be okay. If Herbert Island is windy, however, Queen Charlotte Strait probably will be next.

Bauza Cove. Bauza Cove is an attractive but deep bay with good protection from westerly swells. It is open to the wakes of passing traffic in Johnstone Strait.

① **Telegraph Cove.** Telegraph Cove is postcard picturesque. The boardwalk is lined with old, brightly painted buildings on pilings, including a good restaurant and pub. The old homes are now cottages for resort guests. The place is the embodiment of the word "charming." A whale museum is located at the end of the docks and a whale watch excursion boat leaves several times each day. Tide Rip Grizzly Tours takes groups up Knight Inlet by fast boat to see grizzly bears. Charter fishing boats head out to fish for salmon, and a kayak operator takes groups out to the islands and Johnstone Strait.

Locals relax on the beach in front of U'mista Cultural Centre.

The Telegraph Cove Resort moorage is to starboard as you enter. Moorage is primarily for small boats, but some room is available for larger boats at the dock near the entrance. To port as you enter, Telegraph Cove Marina has some side-tie guest moorage for larger boats, and a considerable number of guest slips for boats to 30 feet.

Be advised, though, that Telegraph Cove isn't very big. There's room to maneuver, but "spacious" is not the word that comes to mind, especially when the wind picks up.

① **Telegraph Cove Marina.** Box 1-8, 1642B, Telegraph Cove, BC V0N 3J0; (250) 928-3163; (877) 835-2683; reservations@ telegraphcove.ca; www.telegraphcove.ca. Monitors VHF 66A. Open all year, 130 slips to 30 feet, limited side-tie moorage to 65 feet. Mostly permanent moorage, limited transient space. Potable water, some slips have 15, 30 & 50 amp power. Concrete launch ramp. Showers, laundry, and washrooms. Wi-Fi available for a fee. Reservations requested.

It's an easy walk around the cove to

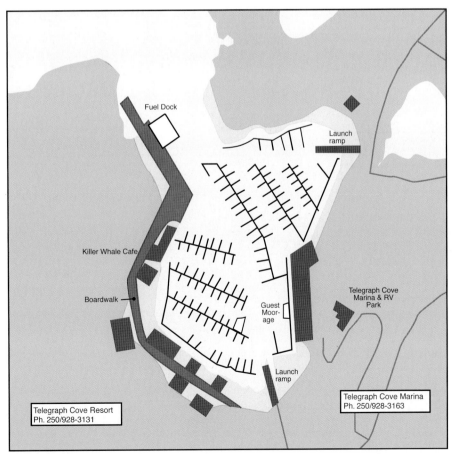
Telegraph Cove

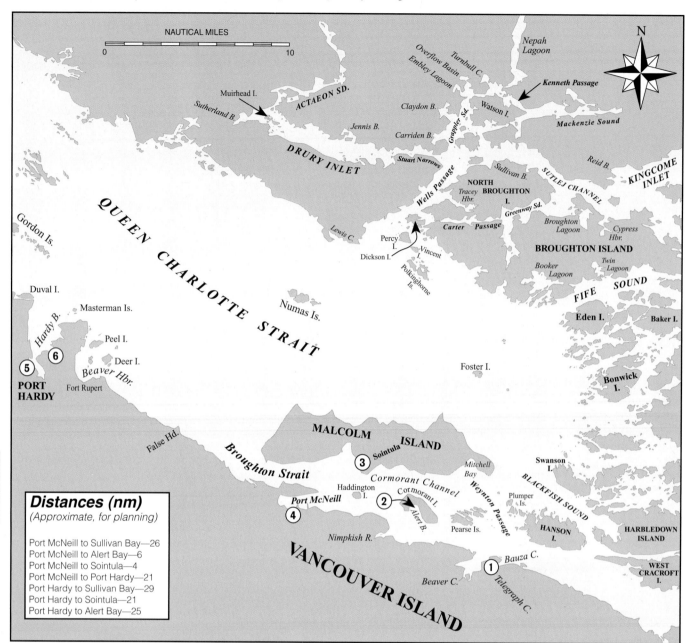

North Vancouver Island

Distances (nm)
(Approximate, for planning)

Port McNeill to Sullivan Bay—26
Port McNeill to Alert Bay—6
Port McNeill to Sointula—4
Port McNeill to Port Hardy—21
Port Hardy to Sullivan Bay—29
Port Hardy to Sointula—21
Port Hardy to Alert Bay—25

amenities and tour operators, such as whale watching, grizzly bear viewing, and kayak tours. The Seahorse Cafe has good food and a great view over the marina.

① **Telegraph Cove Resort.** Box 1, Telegraph Cove, BC V0N 3J0; (250) 928-3131; (800) 200-4665; info@TelegraphCoveResort. com; www.telegraphcoveresort.com. Open seasonally with gasoline (no diesel), launch ramp, restaurant, pub, two coffee shops, general store with gifts and fishing tackle. Slips for boats to 25 feet. Larger boats may be able to overnight on the fuel dock, check with management. No power or water. Cabins and campsites available for rent. The resort maintains the historic boardwalk, with cottages and buildings from when this was a telegraph station during the early 1900s. Attractions include fishing charters, whale and bear watching tours, and the Whale

Interpretive Centre. The restaurant and pub are good.

Beaver Cove. Fairly deep anchorage can be found along the shores of Beaver Cove, the site of an old sawmill. Logs may be boomed in the bay, and the bottom is almost certainly foul with sunken logs and debris.

Pearse Islands (Cormorant Channel Marine Park). Careful piloting is called for when exploring this area because of rocks, reefs, and strong currents in the narrow channels between the islands. Correspondents James and Jennifer Hamilton report:

"We anchored in 30 feet (zero tide) just north of the 72-meter islet, about where the 9.8-meter sounding is on Chart 3546. A little wind blew through from the northwest, but we saw very little boat traffic. It was a lovely spot with an excellent view down Broughton

Strait. Good holding—the anchor set instantly with 150 feet of rode out. It looks like excellent dinghy-exploring country, but it had been a long day and we didn't have the strength.

The next morning the current was really whipping through the passage, but we held just fine. When we left, we found the current very strong off the tip of the 88-meter island, with whirlpools and upwellings." [Hamilton]

Correspondent Pat Shera reports that when the current is flooding east in Broughton Strait, a strong westward countercurrent is present when approaching the Pearse Islands from the south.

② **Alert Bay.** One can learn more about native culture here, in less time, than anywhere on this part of the coast.

Chart 3546 shows Alert Bay in good detail and shows where current runs up to 4 knots.

Alert Bay
Discover our World

Arts | Culture | Heritage

U'mista Cultural Centre
Alert Bay Visitor Centre
and Art Gallery
Alert Bay Museum
Big House & World's
Tallest Totem Pole
'Namgis Burial Ground with
stand of totems
Traditional dance performances
in Big House

Activities

Whale watching
Fishing
Nature Trails
Traditional Canoes
Skate Park
Cultural Playground

Health

Hospital and Health Centre
Personal Care Services

Business

Full service Marina
Accommodations -
Hotels, B&B's Cabins
Campground
Grocery Store | Pharmacy
Restaurants | Pubs
Liquor Store | Post Office
Churches | Banking | Hair Salon

For general inquiries and cultural planning:

Alert Bay Visitor Centre

Phone: (250) 974-5024
Fax: (250) 974-5026
E-mail: info@alertbay.ca
www.alertbay.ca

U'mista Cultural Centre
For events and cultural activities check here
www.facebook.com/Umista.Cultural.Society
(250) 974-5403 or 1-800-690-8222 | **www.umista.ca**

Living Tradition
online museum:
umistapotlatch.ca

ALERT BAY — THE SPIRIT OF U'MISTA

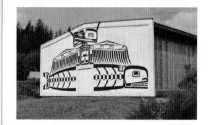

The heritage of the Inside Passage is a rich tapestry of man's life on the land and his utilization of its waters for both transportation and sustenance. Today we enjoy the beauty of the islands and animals, the fjords and waterfalls. And, occasionally, nature's bounty, hauled to the surface in a crab pot or caught on the end of a fishing line. But for thousands of years, since long before Europeans arrived, the area was carefully occupied by First Nations people.

The First Nations people depended on the environment around them in ways often lost in modern life. Their beliefs and customs are inextricably linked to the Inside Passage. A glimpse into their culture reveals a belief in family and clan and an interest in preserving life and land. They believe in sustaining their people by maintaining nature's balance.

They are also a giving people, always ready to share. Perhaps there is no better example of their culture of sharing than their potlatch ceremonies.

Potlatches bring together neighboring families and nearby tribes. Cultural traditions, like songs and dances, are performed and ceremonial regalia, like coppers, masks and robes, are shown off. Feasts are prepared. Gifts, ranging from blankets to berries, are given. Successful potlatches can be reminisced about for years. Potlatches may celebrate marriage, birth, death or other rites of passage. Regardless of the reason for celebration, potlatches are a vehicle for giving. The more a family shares, the better the event is remembered.

In 1885, the government of Canada banned potlatches. Unwilling to give up centuries old traditions, the celebrations secretly continued. But in the early 1920s, a new Director of Indian Affairs gave orders to enforce the potlatch laws. First Nations members were arrested and some were jailed for up to two months. Regalia was confiscated, packed and shipped to Ottawa for storage. Some masks were kept for the personal collection of the Superintendent General of Indian Affairs.

Beginning in the 1960s, the Canadian government slowly repatriated the items they had taken. They reached an agreement where the regalia would be returned and placed on display in two museums, the Nuyumbalees Cultural Centre near Cape Mudge, and the U'mista Cultural Centre in Alert Bay. When a person returns from a restricted life, they are said to have "u'mista," and the same can be said for the potlatch regalia that has now been returned to the First Nations people.

Today, the spirit of u'mista is alive in the coppers, robes and masks on display in the U'mista Cultural Centre.

Welcoming office and docks at Sointula on Malcolm Island

Baked goods and coffee are featured at the cafe on First Street.

Protected moorage is available in the Boat Harbour basin at the head of the bay.

A small public float is in front of the main part of town. The float is exposed to all winds, and currents can run swiftly, but it is convenient when provisioning at the nearby grocery. Deeper in the bay, the breakwater-protected Boat Harbour basin, northwest of the ferry landing, has moorage. Anchorage is available in the bay; be sure to anchor clear of the ferry dock and its approach.

The Alert Bay village is about a half-mile walk from the Boat Harbour. At the top of the dock, take a right and walk along the waterfront. The village has a grocery store, pharmacy, pub, liquor store, restaurants, salon and spa, ATM, post office, and walk-in emergency clinic. An excellent Visitor Centre is on the water side of the road, about midway into the commercial area. It's open 7 days a week during the season. You will get good information about the attractions in Alert Bay: the world's tallest totem pole

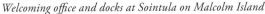

Alert Bay Boat Harbour
Tel. 250/974-5727
VHF 66A

Alert Bay Boat Harbour

(whose top blew off in a 2007 winter storm); the U'mista Cultural Centre and gift shop; the Ecological Park, where you can see culturally modified cedar trees (trees partly stripped of bark to make baskets, regalia, and clothing); the burial grounds; and the Anglican church that dates back to 1879. Brochures give information and map routes for self-guided tours. Interpretive displays have been installed. U'mista Cultural Centre is about a one-mile walk to the left from the Boat Harbour docks. Five awakwas (places to meet) along the way represent the five clans of the 'Namgis First Nation.

Cruisers moored at Port McNeill can walk-on the BC ferry to Alert Bay. Catch the 8:40 a.m. ferry from Port McNeill and return on the 5:55 p.m. or 8:25 p.m. ferry from Alert Bay. Bring your camera. The entire town of Alert Bay is walkable and photogenic.

Hiking trails: Cormorant Island has an extensive system of predator-free hiking trails. Ask for a map in the Visitor Centre or harbor office.

Seafest: Fourth weekend in July along the boardwalk. Table vendors, music, fun contests, and Artfest.

Alert Bay 360: B.C. Day is the first Monday of August. Observe or take part in the paddling race around Cormorant Island.

② **Alert Bay Boat Harbour.** 20 Fir Street, Bag 2800, Alert Bay, BC V0N 1A0; (250) 974-5727; boatharbour@alertbay.ca; www.alertbay.ca. Monitors VHF 66A. Excellent docks, 30 amp power, water, pumpout. This is the breakwater-protected public wharf and floats in Alert Bay, located next to the ferry landing. The harbor manager's office features showers and flat-rate laundry with nice machines. Removal of derelict boats and general sprucing up of the harbour area has recently taken place.

② **U'mista Cultural Centre.** P.O. Box 253, Alert Bay, BC V0N 1A0; (250) 974-5403; (800) 690-8222; info@umista.ca; www.umista.ca; www.facebook.com/umista.cultural.society. We doubt that anyone could see this collection of historical coppers, masks and other ceremonial regalia without

being affected. Open daily 9:00 a.m. to 5:00 p.m. from Canada Day to Labor Day, and Tuesday through Saturday, 9:00 a.m. to 5:00 p.m. in winter.

The displays portray the history of the area and the significance of the potlatch. In 1885 the government attempted to outlaw potlatch ceremonies, but the law was generally ignored and unenforced. In 1921, however, 45 people in the village were charged with violating a revised version of the law. Twenty-two people received suspended sentences, in an agreement where potlatch paraphernalia and ceremonial regalia, including masks and coppers, were turned over to the Indian Agent at Alert Bay. The items were sent to museums; some ended up in the personal collection of a government official. The people of Alert Bay successfully negotiated the return of their property in the 1960s, with the stipulation that museums be constructed for their display in Alert Bay and in Yaculta, near Cape Mudge. The result in Alert Bay is the U'mista Cultural Centre.

If you can, schedule your visit to see the T'sasala Cultural Group dance performance, Thursdays through Saturdays at 1:15 p.m. in the 'Namgis Bighouse: $20 adults, $10 for 4-12 year olds; no charge for children under 4. They explain and perform traditional dances, complete with regalia and masks. The audience joins in a dance at the end. Afterward, a visit to the U'mista Cultural Centre takes on greater importance. The artifacts on display are extraordinary. You can participate in a variety of free drop-in programs such as cedar bark weaving, traditional medicine, and story telling, to name a few. Check their Facebook page for free events and classes during the summer. The children's play area is a natural playground of trees and rocks that kids can climb. Future plans include an open-air longhouse.

③ **Sointula.** Sointula is a pleasant stop with amenities including an Info Centre, Co-op grocery store and bakeries. The Malcolm Island Lions Harbour Authority marina has space in the summer for visiting boats in both the north and south sections. The Sointula Co-op, across the road from the south docks, carries charts and a good selection of marine hardware.

See Area Map Page 358 - Maps Not for Navigation

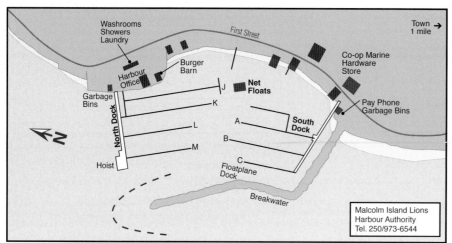

Malcolm Island (Sointula)

A Co-op grocery store in the village, closed on Sundays and Mondays, has a small liquor agency. The Co-op does not use plastic bags. Bring your own bags for purchases. A farmer's stand, actually a box on the side of the Info Centre, carries local items including eggs and breads and uses an honor box for payment. An ATM is in the co-op store in the village and at the hotel, which also has a restaurant and gift shop featuring local artisans.

Sointula means "place of harmony" in Finnish, and was settled by Finnish immigrants as a utopian cooperative shortly after the turn of the 20th century. Utopia didn't last, but the Co-op store is a reminder of earlier days. There's no doubting the Finnish influence as you walk around—the town is clean, well-maintained and orderly. You'll find well-tended lawns and gardens, with unique wood fencing.

Schedule time to see the museum. It's nicely done, and volunteers on duty love to share the town's history.

Sointula is a place where drivers wave as they go by, and are apt to stop and ask if you'd like a ride. It's a place where people put down what they are doing to chat briefly and exchange a small joke or two.

You can also visit Sointula by walking on the BC ferries from Port McNeill.

Note: the concrete float that used to be next to the BC Ferries dock in front of the town center has been removed.

③ **Malcolm Island Lions Harbour Authority**. P.O. Box 202, Sointula, BC V0N 3E0; (250) 973-6544; milha@cablerocket. com; www.sointulaharbour.com. Monitors VHF 66A. Excellent docks with 20 & 30 amp power, some 50 amp; water, laundry, showers, garbage drop, Wi-Fi. Office hours are 8:30 a.m. to 4:30 p.m. in summer, 8:30 a.m. to 12:30 p.m. in winter. Downtown Sointula is an easy bike ride away, loaner bicycles are available at the Harbour Office.

Sointula's extensive public docks are behind a rock breakwater at the head of Rough Bay, 1 mile north of the ferry landing. The docks are divided into north and south sections. Both sections are available to visiting boats and it's an easy walk on the road between the two. Each set of docks has a garbage drop and pay phone. The north docks also have washrooms, showers, and laundry, built and maintained by the Malcolm Island Lions Club. Solar panels on the roof provide the hot water. Both sections have potable water on the docks. All moorage is first-come, first-served, side-tie only, no reservations, rafting allowed. Moor where it makes sense. Pay at the office in the north section. Lorraine Williams is the manager. The office staff is happy to provide you with more information on the town.

The Burger Barn, a local favorite, with good hamburgers, wraps, and fish & chips, is in the bright red building in the parking lot.

Tarkanen Marine Ways (250) 973-6710, capable of major and emergency work, is located near the boat basin. Tarkanen has three marine ways with varying size cradles that can accommodate vessels up to 60 feet. With the closing of the Quarterdeck Boatyard in Port Hardy, this is the only marine ways between Campbell River or Lund and Shearwater. It is often busy serving commercial fishing boats. Tarkanen Marine Ways was completely rebuilt after a fire in 2016 and re-opened for business in 2017.

Mitchell Bay. Mitchell Bay, near the east end of Malcolm Island, is a good summertime anchorage, protected from easterlies and northwest winds. Not suitable in south or southwest winds. A public dock managed by the Malcolm Island Lions Harbour Authority is located on the east side of the bay; first-come, first-served. The L-shaped public dock has approximately 150 feet of moorage on the outside. Inside portion of the docks are usually occupied by smaller, local boats. Self-registration and payment box located at the head of the ramp. Don't miss visiting the bright 'Red Net Shed' at the head of the pier, where you can purchase antiques and other collectibles. A log boom area is north of the public dock.

④ **Port McNeill.** Port McNeill is a modern small city on Highway 19, which runs the length of Vancouver Island. It has banks,

NORTH ● ISLAND MARINA
PORT McNEILL
BRITISH COLUMBIA

Gateway to the Broughtons and Northern BC

Friendly Service

- *Transient and Guest Moorage for yachts up to 285'*
- *In berth fueling for Marine Diesel, Marine Gas, Avgas and Jet Fuel*
- *Propane*
- *Laundromat, Chandlery and Parts Store*
- *BBQ and Patio Area*
- *Free WiFi*

Reservations: 855-767-8622 • Marina: 250-956-4044 • Winter: 250-956-3336
VHF 66a • info@northislandmarina.com • www.northislandmarina.com

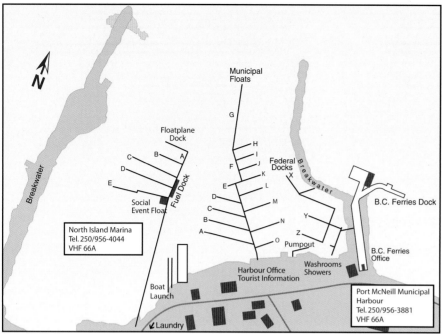

Port NcNeill

stores, hotels, restaurants, and transportation to the rest of Vancouver Island. With nearly all services located within easy walking distance of the boat harbor, Port McNeill is an excellent resupply point for boats headed north, south, or into the Broughton Islands. A Saturday Market is held from 9:00 a.m. to 1:00 p.m. on the lawn in front of the Port Authority and Visitor Center building.

Port McNeill has two marinas: the North Island Marina, and the Town of Port McNeill Harbour. Both are protected by an extensive breakwater. The Port Harbour docks are the first, to port as you round the end of the breakwater. North Island Marina and fuel dock is to starboard. Both facilities are close to shopping, restaurants and a modern laundromat with free Wi-Fi. The well-stocked IGA is in a shopping center a few blocks from the docks. The IGA has a van and will make deliveries. Fishing tackle, post office, large liquor store, drug store and more are within a few minutes' walk.

An auto parts store is just beyond the head of the North Island Marina docks and carries marine parts, batteries and lubricants. If parts are not available locally, they can be ordered and often flown in the next day. While there is no boat yard in Port McNeill, there are a number of resources for marine services and repairs. Both marinas can provide a list of boat service providers. The Shop-Rite marine and logging store handles outboard repairs.

Regular floatplane service connects down-island. Kenmore Air and NW Seaplanes fly to Seattle from North Island Marina. The Port Hardy International Airport, with air service north and south, is a 30-minute taxi ride from Port McNeill.

If the Port Harbour docks and the North Island Marina are full, anchorage is possible across the bay from the marinas. Good holding in thick, sticky mud.

Be sure to see the Port McNeill & District Museum, which showcases the history of logging in the area. It is a short walk from the docks. Nearby, the world's largest burl is on display.

BC Ferries operates a ferry from Port McNeill with service to Sointula and Alert Bay. Many dock their boat in Port McNeill and walk-on the ferry to Sointula and Alert Bay.

④ **Port McNeill Harbour.** 1594 Beach Drive, P.O. Box 1389, Port McNeill, BC V0N 2R0; (250) 956-3881; info@portmcneillharbour.ca; town.portmcneill.bc.ca/harbour. Monitors VHF 66A. When approaching, call on the VHF for a slip assignment. Open all year, guest moorage, 20, 30, 50 & 100 amp power, water, washrooms, showers, pumpout, waste oil disposal, garbage drop. This is a comfortable marina, with friendly management and room for all sizes of boats. No reservations; first-come, first-served. The marina office is in the Visitor Centre building, above the marina. The BC Ferries landing, with service to Alert Bay and Sointula, is east of the marina.

The Harbour showers are located above the BC Ferries landing and are $5 per day, payable at the Harbour Office. A passcode for the combination lock to the showers is provided with payment.

Federal Docks. Located behind the breakwater within Port McNeill Harbour. These are working docks, mostly taken by government and commercial vessels. Guest moorage is first-come, first-served, subject to rafting.

④ **North Island Marina.** P.O. Box 488, Port McNeill, BC V0N 2R0; (250) 956-4044; info@portmcneill.com; www.portmcneill.com. Monitors VHF 66A. Formerly Port McNeill Fuel Dock and Marina. Open all year with 2100 feet of guest moorage for vessels to 285 feet. 30, 50 (120/208 volt) and 100 amp (single and three phase) power, water, Wi-Fi. Garbage and recycling at the head of the dock. The main dock has a security gate; get the passcode from the marina office. Reservations highly recommended.

The fuel dock has gasoline, diesel, 100 LL and Jet A aviation fuel, propane. A long fuel hose and reel allows for in-berth fueling. The dock store has ice, lubricants and some marine parts. This is a friendly and well-staffed marina located adjacent to the municipal floats.

You can't miss the large "Happy Hour" float with wind-break and awning cover, which has become the gathering place for special events. The 10-foot long custom made charcoal grill is started each evening during the summer season for your steak, burgers, or just-caught salmon. The custom-made tables have built-in stainless tubs for ice to keep beverages chilled.

North Island Marina offers many services, including a courtesy car, and pick-up and drop-off at the Port Hardy airport, about 24 miles away. The marina staff can arrange for heli-tours, golf or other services, including boat watch. For those who need to return home, North Island Marina is a good spot to leave your boat. Their customer service is outstanding with concierge type services. Kenmore Air and Northwest Seaplanes leave directly from the North Island Marina floatplane dock with flights to Seattle.

Historic Fort Rupert overlooking Beaver Harbour and Deer Island

Bruce and Nancy Jackman have owned and operated the marina for many years. Their son Alan and other family members continue to be involved with the managment and care of the marina.

Beaver Harbour. The islands in Beaver Harbour are picturesque. The west side of the Cattle Islands is protected; anchor on a mud bottom in 30 to 45 feet. Patrician Cove has been recommended to us. Several white shell midden beaches are located throughout the islands. Reader Jack Tallman reports fresh northwesterly winds get in and can make for a "troublesome night."

Our sister publication, *Cruising the Secret Coast*, by Jennifer and James Hamilton, devotes a chapter to Beaver Harbour and the Native village of Fort Rupert.

Fort Rupert. Located in Beaver Harbour past Thomas Point. Exposed to north and east winds, but with several areas that serve well for day anchorage or overnight in settled weather. The town of Fort Rupert consists of two distinct areas, the newer town on the southwest shore of Beaver Harbour and the Native Reserve on the southernmost shore. Both areas are accessible by dinghy or kayak. Storey's Beach Park on the southwest offers a sandy beach and picnic tables. The south shore is the site of the Kwakiutl Band Longhouse and cemetery with exceptional carvings and paintings by Calvin Hunt, a well-known Master Carver and local resident. Visitors are welcome at the community carving shed located near the Longhouse and at Calvin Hunt's art gallery located on Copper Way.

Anchor off the south beach in 16 to 30 feet of water and dinghy to shore, look for the public gazebo for a landing spot. Position the dinghy appropriately for the charted extensive drying beach. A short trail leads to the cemetery and longhouse; the small Fort Rupert General Store is nearby.

This area was once the site of a Hudson's Bay Company fort, built in 1849, first commanded by William Henry McNeill. The fort burned down in 1889. One of the remaining eight-pound cannons is displayed in front of the Longhouse.

⑤ **Port Hardy.** Port Hardy is the northernmost community on Vancouver Island. Moorage is at the seasonal Seagate T-Floats, formerly called the City Dock (summer only), Quarterdeck Marina, and Port Hardy Harbour Authority.

The seasonal Seagate T-Floats are adjacent to the Coast Guard wharf, and have the closest access to town and shopping. If the floats are full, you can anchor out and take the dinghy in.

The Quarterdeck Marina and the Harbour Authority floats are a mile or so farther into Hardy Bay, past a narrow entry channel. It's a one-mile walk from this inner bay to downtown. Stryker Electronics Ltd. (250) 949-8022, with marine electronics, repairs and a chandlery is across the street.

A large Save-on Foods supermarket is at Thunderbird Mall. For items with "Regular price/Member price" shelf tags, we found that non-members can get the Member price by asking the checker for a tourist card. The store will pay the cab fare to deliver large orders to the Seagate Summer Floats, Harbour Authority floats, and Quarterdeck Marina. They didn't give us an exact amount, but something around $100 probably would qualify.

Port Hardy is clean and friendly. A park is along the shore with a seaside promenade past tidy waterfront homes. The Visitor Centre is next to the park. Be sure to read the sign commemorating completion of the Carrot Highway. A nearby library houses a small but excellent museum.

Port Hardy has city amenities, including a hospital and airport with scheduled flights to and from Vancouver. Nearby Bear Cove is the terminus for the BC Ferry that runs to Prince Rupert during the summer. Coastal Mountain Fuels is in Bear Cove. There is a recreational boat marina in Bear Cove with portapotties and two lane boat ramp.

Dining: Port Hardy has several restaurants. We've had a good lunch and dinner at the Quarterdeck Pub at the

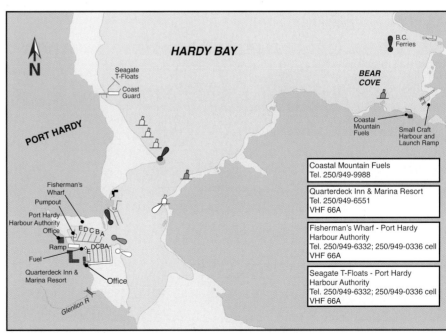

Port Hardy

Quarterdeck Marina. In town, breakfast at Captain Hardy's is a local favorite, complete with oversized portions. Cafe Guido has excellent coffee, sandwiches and baked goods. The Book Nook, the West Coast Community Craft Shop and The Drift are co-located with Cafe Guido. A local favorite, The Sporty Bar & Grille is down the street. A recent addition to Port Hardy is the beautiful Kwa'LiLas Hotel, formerly the Port Hardy Inn. Three Native tribes; Nakwaxda'xw People, Gwa'sala People, and Kwakiutle People came together to completely rebuild the structure, making extensive use of local cedar as an expression of native culture. The Kwa'LiLas Hotel houses the fine dining Ha'me' Restaurant with an excellent menu. Ha'me' is open for lunch and dinner; (250) 949-8884 for reservations. Taxi transportation is available in the area; Town Taxi (250) 949-7877; Waivin Flags Taxi (250) 230-7655.

Museum: The museum on the main street in town is small but superb. It also houses the finest collection of local history and local interest books we've seen. We recommend it.

Fuel: Fuel is available on the east side of Hardy Bay at Coastal Mountain Fuels in Bear Cove, and at Quarterdeck Marina farther in the bay.

Walkway & Nature Trail: A walking trail with picnic tables and viewpoints starts near the Quarterdeck Marina, leads past the Glen Lyon Inn, and continues along the edge of Hardy Bay. At the head, you can turn north and walk to the Quatse River estuary, or take the Quatse River loop through the woods to the Quatse River Salmon Hatchery (www.quatsehatchery.ca or call (250) 949-9022 to arrange a tour). The trail is very easy, and much of it is wheelchair-accessible. It's a great side-trip that offers a different perspective of Port Hardy. [*Hamilton*]

Port Hardy's Quarterdeck Marina has transient moorage.

LOCAL KNOWLEDGE

FLOATPLANE OPERATIONS FLASHING LIGHTS: Two floatplane pilot-activated white flashing lights in Port Hardy's inner harbour, when flashing, indicate floatplane aircraft take-off and landing activity. Both lights are charted, one is located on the east shore 300 yards south of red and green inner harbour entrance markers, and the other is located on the tip of the south shore breakwater.

DANGEROUS REEF: South of the Port Hardy Seagate T-Floats in the outer bay, yellow buoys mark a large drying reef. If proceeding to the inner bay, pass well east of the reef.

⑤ **Fisherman's Wharf -** Port Hardy Harbour Authority. 6600 Hardy Bay Rd., Port Hardy, BC V0N 2P0; (250) 949-6332; (250) 949-0336 cell; porthardyharbour@gmail.com; www.porthardy.ca. Monitors VHF 66A. The

finger floats have mostly 20 amp power, some 30 amp. The main float has increased the number of 30 and 50 amp outlets. Although this basin is primarily for commercial fishing vessels, there is limited room for pleasure craft in the summer when the fleet is out. The facility has washrooms, pumpout, and launch ramp; no showers or laundry.

⑤ **Quarterdeck Inn & Marina Resort.** 6555 Hardy Bay Rd., P.O. Box 910, Port Hardy, BC V0N 2P0; (250) 949-6551; (250) 902-0455; marina@quarterdeckresort.net; www.quarterdeckresort.net. Monitors VHF 66A. Open all year, gasoline, diesel, propane, guest moorage, 15, 30 & 50 amp power, washrooms, showers, laundry, Wi-Fi access, liquor store. During winter the fuel dock and marina office are closed on Sundays. The Quarterdeck Pub & Restaurant is on the same property.

Quarterdeck's 40-room hotel is attractive and well-appointed. It has full wheelchair access, ocean views, and a covered walkway to the pub, with a nice area for families.

The boatyard and Travelift are no longer operating.

⑤ **Seagate T-Floats -**Port Hardy Harbour Authority. (250) 949-6332; (250) 949-0336 cell; porthardyharbour@gmail.com; www.porthardy.ca. Monitors 66A. Seasonal floats with 30 amp power, water, and garbage drop. Close to town and shopping. Side-tie for boats up to 60 feet. Docks are best used in settled weather as the area is exposed to the north. Docks are managed by Port Hardy Harbour Authority; moorage payment can be made with credit card by telephone or to Harbour Authority staff who come to the floats twice daily. This is a convenient place to stop and fill water tanks before heading around Cape Caution or into the Broughtons.

⑥ **Coastal Mountain Fuels** (Bear Cove). 6720 Bear Cove, Port Hardy, BC V0N 2P0; (250) 949-9988. Monitors VHF 16. Open all year, gasoline, diesel, kerosene, propane. Despite commercial appearance, they welcome pleasure boats. Washrooms, bait, ice, waste oil pump and disposal. Located near the BC Ferries terminal. Launch ramp and convenience store.

Port Hardy basin, home to Fisherman's Wharf and Quarterdeck Marina

SOINTULA ISLAND UTOPIA - By Paula Wild

Publisher: Harbour Publishing; ISBN: 978-1-55017-456-4

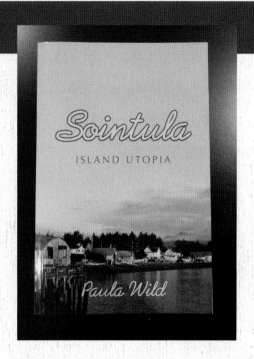

You can follow the quest of early Finnish settlers who sought a new social life on **Malcom Island** in British Columbia, free from Russian opposition and church dogma in Paula Wild's book, *Sointula Island Utopia*. Paula Wild tells the story of two Socialist leaders, Matti Kurikka and Austin Makela, who were instrumental in establishing the village of **Sointula** (place of harmony). The early settlers faced many hardships and challenges. The author takes us from the 1920's through the 1970's, describing the Island community as it moved through socialism and cooperative business ventures. The book provides insights to the times and political background which lead individuals to seek other options for purposeful living.

Finland was under the control of Russia; and when Russian Czar Nicholas II came to power in 1896, Finnish language and culture were censored and working conditions were deplorable. An exodus from Finland took Finn workers to Sweden, Australia, and North America. Finns found work in the mines, logging camps, and in the fishing industry of British Columbia. Wishing to improve working conditions, twenty Finn immigrants met in 1891 to lay plans to form a utopian, socialist community; Matti Kurikka was called upon to be their leader. Matti Kurikka, owner and editor of a popular Finnish Newspaper, was well known among the greater Finnish community. His parents were originally wealthy landowners in Finland, but were forced to become peasants under Russian rule.

Matti Kurikka arrived in **Nanaimo** in the fall of 1900 and spent several weeks in Canada spreading the dream of a utopian society, "a new Finland," where work, education, and entertainment would be experienced communally. Men and women would receive equal pay for equal work plus meals and clothing. Members of the newly organized Kalevan Kansa Society, were asked to purchase stock in the company created to benefit the Society. Unfortunately, expenses mounted and the list of creditors grew; newcomers weren't always able to purchase shares but were still welcomed. Matti Kurikka was a charismatic dreamer who wasn't always able to think through the practical matters. Ideas were plentiful but so were the expenses of establishing a local Finnish Newspaper (the Aika), logging timber, working a quarry to make brick, clearing land for farming, purchasing a boat for shipments, and building a make-shift mill to cut lumber. Members of the Kalevan Kansa became disillusioned.

Differences in opinion began to build between Matti Kurikka and Austin Makela, creating two factions in the community. The status of free property and the question of free love widened the gap. Kurikka left the island with 24 men in 1905 to start a new commune, while Austin Makela took on the role of leader for those who stayed at **Sointula**.

While Makela was level-headed, he lacked Kurikka's charisma and imagination. Makela wasn't able to convince the outside world that Sointula was viable. Makela preferred to be a political commentator rather than an activist and was content with the quiet island life. In 1907, Makela took the position of lighthouse keeper at Pulteney Point on the east end of the island, but retained an active presence in Sointula, guiding the commune until his death.

Paula Wild's book, *Sointula Island Utopia*, is filled with stories of perseverance, hard work, and inventiveness, including a local fisherman's invention of a mounted drum to haul in fishing nets. Numerous historic photos are found throughout the book; many of the buildings in the photos are still recognizable today. Visitors to **Sointula** will find that this community retains its quiet island lifestyle and the co-op grocery store remains a social center for the community.

West Coast of Vancouver Island

CHAPTER 14

HARDY BAY TO QUATSINO SOUND
God's Pocket • Goletas Channel • Nahwitti Bar
Cape Scott • Sea Otter Cove

QUATSINO SOUND TO KYOQUOT
Winter Harbour • Quatsino Narrows • Coal Harbour
Brooks Peninsula • Bunsby Islands

KYOQUOT SOUND TO ESPERANZA INLET
Clear Passage • Zeballos • Esperanza • Tahsis Narrows

NOOTKA SOUND TO HOT SPRINGS COVE
Tahsis • Critter Cove • Friendly Cove • Estevan Point

CLAYOQUOT SOUND
Bacchante Bay • Ahousat • Lemmens Inlet • Tofino

BARKLEY SOUND
Ucluelet • Broken Group • Port Alberni • Bamfield

Cuising West Coast Vancouver Island. For many, the area from Port Hardy, at the top of the east coast of Vancouver Island, down the west coast of Vancouver Island to the mouth of the Strait of Juan de Fuca, is the finest cruising ground in the Northwest—except, perhaps, Alaska. Little can compare with the variety, beauty, ruggedness, remoteness, and sheer satisfaction of this voyage. Please allow enough time when you make the trip. Plan for three weeks, two weeks at a minimum. This is a large cruising area to cover and you may have to allow for being weathered in.

The West Coast is broken into five inlets and sounds that snake their way into the heart of Vancouver Island. Mountains rise all around. Rocks lurk in the waters. Fish and wildlife abound. Only the hardy (and occasionally the foolhardy) are out there with you. This is Northwest cruising writ large.

Except for the rounding of Cape Scott and the long run down the Strait of Juan de Fuca, the distance between inlets and sounds is in the 20- to 30-mile range. Wait for good weather and dash around. Once inside, let the wind outside blow. You're safe.

Clockwise or counter-clockwise? Most boats travel the west coast of Vancouver Island traveling counter-clockwise. For sailboats, the prevailing summertime westerly winds combine with the westerly swells of the Pacific Ocean, and create some splendid downwind offshore sailing. Most powerboats have an easier time running with the seas than into them, so they prefer the prevailing conditions. "Prevailing," though, does not mean guaranteed, and the wind can blow from the south.

The difficulty with a counter-clockwise trip is the time it takes. To go down-island on the outside, you first must go up-island on the inside, and the weeks go by. Those who do not have the luxury of time to circumnavigate Vancouver Island can cruise the West Coast by running out the Strait of Juan de Fuca to Barkley Sound. They begin their explorations from Barkley Sound, traveling clockwise up the coast, perhaps only as far as Nootka Sound and then back down the coast. They must pick their weather for outside passages up-island into the prevailing swells, but that can be done. And if weather delays a passage

for a day or even a few days, at least the time is spent on the West Coast, not in traveling up the Inside Passage.

Strait of Juan de Fuca. For boats coming from Puget Sound or Vancouver/Victoria, the Strait of Juan de Fuca can be a difficult body of water. The typical summer weather pattern calls for calm conditions in the early morning, with a sea breeze building by afternoon, often to 30+ knots. When wind and tidal current oppose, large, steep seas result.

On the American side, boats can leave Port Townsend at first light and get to Sequim Bay, Port Angeles, Pillar Point or even Neah Bay before the wind builds. From there they can cross to the Canadian side for the run to Ucluelet Customs the next day. Weather permitting, a fast boat can make it in one day.

On the Canadian side, boats can depart Victoria or Sooke at first light, and reach Port San Juan or even Barkley Sound, conditions and boat speed permitting. The distance from Victoria to Bamfield is approximately 92 nautical miles.

These thoughts are for typical conditions.

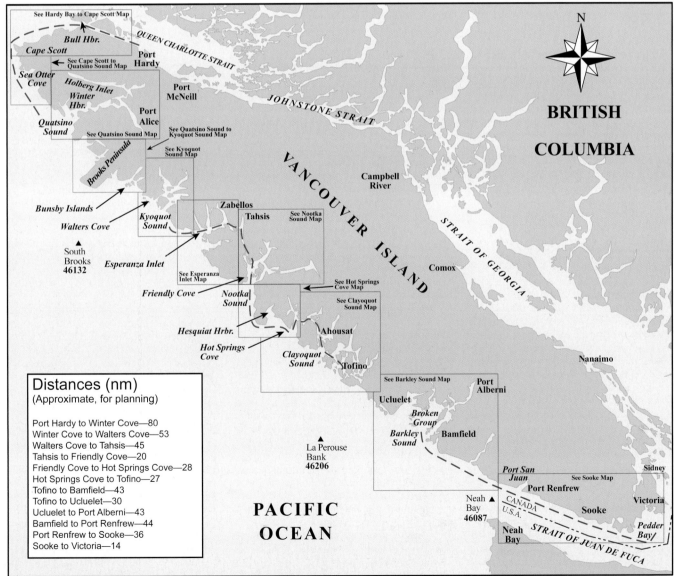

Distances (nm)
(Approximate, for planning)

Port Hardy to Winter Cove—80
Winter Cove to Walters Cove—53
Walters Cove to Tahsis—45
Tahsis to Friendly Cove—20
Friendly Cove to Hot Springs Cove—28
Hot Springs Cove to Tofino—27
Tofino to Bamfield—43
Tofino to Ucluelet—30
Ucluelet to Port Alberni—43
Bamfield to Port Renfrew—44
Port Renfrew to Sooke—36
Sooke to Victoria—14

West Coast Vancouver Island

Variations often change typical conditions. We have seen the strait windy all day and calm all day. Listen to the weather broadcasts, watch the barometer and sky, and be cautious.

The boat. Large or small, a boat for the West Coast should be seaworthy, strong, and well-equipped. The seas encountered on the offshore passages will be a test, especially at Cape Scott, Brooks Peninsula, Tatchu Point, Estevan Point, the entrance to Ucluelet, Cape Beale, and in the Strait of Juan de Fuca.

The wind accelerates as it is diverted at the capes and points, and the ocean's currents grow confused. Between wind and current, the seas grow noticeably higher and steeper. Even on moderate days, a boat can be suddenly surrounded by whitecaps. At Cape Scott and off Brooks Peninsula, pyramid-shaped waves can appear, break (or crumble into foam), and sweep past.

These 'rogue' waves can come from directions different from the prevailing seas. Assuming a summertime westerly wind and a course in following seas, they can grab the broad sterns of many powerboats and make broaching a hazard. A double-ender, especially a double-ended sailboat with a large rudder, will not be affected as much. In fact, sailing in these seas with a 25-knot breeze from astern could be high points of the trip. But a planing-hull powerboat skipper will pay close attention to the waves and their effect.

It is at times such as these that the skipper and crew know they are in serious water, and that their boat and equipment must be dependable. It is no place for old rigging, uncertain engines, sticky steering, intermittent electrical power, broken antennas, small anchors, unswung compasses, or clogged pumps. For a lifelong city-dweller, the West Coast is a wild coast with open seas and rocks a mile offshore. It pays to be prepared.

There are essentially no repair services between Port McNeill/Port Hardy and Ucluelet. Where service is available, it is oriented towards sport fishing vessels, with limited capabilities and parts to service inboard engines, onboard auxiliary systems and electronics. Even if you have the parts, the shop will very likely not have the time to help you since their bread and butter is the sport and commercial fishery.

You, the owner and operator of the boat, must decide which systems are critical to continuing the voyage and carry your own spares and learn how to install them. Parts not common to sport fishing vessels may be available from Campbell River, the nearest large town with an industrial base. Make sure that you have the maintenance and parts books available and the tools needed. With the right parts and tools, another cruiser may be able to help.

Most consider radar all but essential. The local boats, even the little ones, have radar. A GPS chartplotter will add to your navigational peace of mind. Even on clear days in mild conditions, GPS can identify turning points and confirm visual navigation. A chartplotter

can take the anxiety out of navigating among ugly black rocks. In thick weather or fog, radar and electronic navigation will raise the comfort level aboard dramatically.

Weather. Winter on the West Coast is stormy, and not a place for pleasure craft. In early spring, conditions begin to improve, and by June or July the pattern of calm early mornings followed by rising westerly winds establishes itself. In the evening, the winds subside. That said, even in summer, serious storms can hit the West Coast.

Northwest winds coming down the coast tend to turn inland at the entrances to sounds and inlets. Sailors making a downwind run along the coast will often be able to carry that wind into the sounds, ending their day with a glorious sail on smooth water.

Fog can be a problem, particularly in August and September. We've heard the month of August referred to as "Foggust." The typical fog forms in early morning and burns off in late morning or early afternoon—just as the westerly fills in. If an outside passage is planned but the morning is blanketed in fog, the skipper will appreciate having radar and a chartplotter. It is also important to have your day's route layed out and saved on your chartplotter, complete with waypoints.

Plan for rain and cool temperatures as well as sunshine during a visit of two to four weeks or more.

The Coast Guard broadcasts continuous weather information from several locations along the way. The reports are limited in scope to weather that affects the West Coast, and include wind and sea state reports from lighthouses and weather-monitoring stations. In surprisingly short time, a visitor who's paying attention learns how to interpret the weather broadcasts and decide whether the time is right for an outside passage.

Lighthouse weather reports are particularly valuable. These reports include visibility, wind speed and direction, human-observed sea state, and swell height and direction. Reports are issued every three hours, but light keepers can often be reached on VHF 82 for up-to-the-minute weather information.

Fuel. Although the West Coast is a wilderness, it is a wilderness with fuel. Gasoline and diesel are available all along the way, within workable ranges for virtually any boat capable of safely being out there. The fuel stations exist to serve the fishing fleet, logging camps, and the pockets of permanent residents, especially Native communities. Fuel can be found at Winter Harbour, Coal Harbour, Fair Harbour, Zeballos, Esperanza, Tahsis, Critter Cove (gasoline only), Newston Cove, Moutcha Bay, Ahousat, Tofino (gasoline and biodiesel only), Ucluelet, Bamfield, Poett Nook (gasoline only), Port Alberni, Port San Juan (gasoline only), Sooke, and Victoria.

Note: The above list of fuel stops is subject to change. Check for the latest updates at www.WaggonerGuide.com.

Ice. Although finding block ice can be a

challenge, it is becoming more common on the west coast. Where commercial fishing is allowed, the fish processing plants may have flaked ice for the fish boats, which take it on by the ton. A polite inquiry usually will yield enough ice for the icebox or cooler—sometimes for a charge, often not. Fish ice is "salt ice," and not recommended for the cocktail hour.

Water. Ask locals before filling the tank.

Fresh vegetables. Uneven quality. Best to plan ahead and stock accordingly. Port Alice, Tofino and Ucluelet are the only towns with real supermarkets.

Public docks. Every community has a public dock with moorage fees collected by a local resident. At some of the docks the local resident isn't around, or doesn't bother to come collecting. Accept the no-charge tie-ups where you find them, pay gladly where the charge is collected.

Reference books and guidebooks. The Canadian Tide and Current Tables, Vol. 6 (blue cover) gives tides and currents south to Port San Juan. Vol. 5 (green cover) covers the Strait of Juan de Fuca and inland waters of Strait of Georgia and Puget Sound. Ports and Passes Tides and Currents covers the entire west coast. Sailing Directions, B.C. Coast, South Portion, is the official government publication, and should be considered essential. Note that Sailing Directions is intended for large vessels. A cove listed as good for anchoring may be too deep or exposed for small craft, but a passage listed as tortuous may be easily run by small craft.

Useful book: *Voyages to Windward* by Elsie Hulsizer, paperback edition, 2015. Well-told stories of West Coast adventures packed with information about the coast's history, people, and natural history. Excellent photos. Provides a good sense of what it's like to cruise this challenging and interesting coast.

For those with limited space, we recommend carrying the the most current edition of the *Waggoner Cruising Guide* for updated information on facilities (only the Waggoner is truly up-to-date) and a second guidebook of your choice. Three other good guidebooks exist, and we carry all three in the Waggoner Store. The three are very different. Look for the one that most matches your cruising style.

The first is Don and Reanne Douglass' *Exploring Vancouver Island's West Coast*, 2nd ed., published in 1999. The book is clear, easy to understand, and describes a large percentage of bays and coves along the West Coast. Not every bay described is a desirable anchorage, but the Douglasses tell the reader what to expect if forced to enter.

The second is Anne and Laurence Yeadon-Jones' *Dreamspeaker Cruising Guide, Vol. 6: The West Coast of Vancouver Island*, published in 2009 by Fine Edge in the U.S. and Harbour Publishing in Canada. They

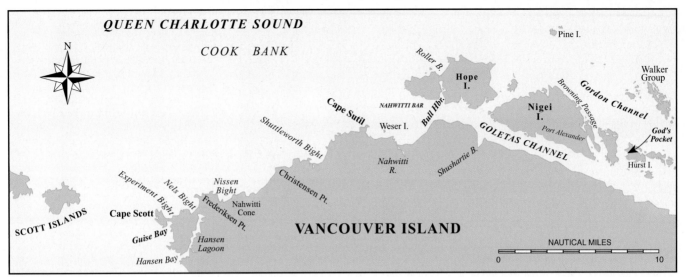

Hardy Bay to Cape Scott

favor stern-tieing and tight anchorages which some boaters may not care for, particularly since stern-tieing is rarely necessary on the west coast.

The third is Don Watmough's *Cruising Guide to the West Coast of Vancouver Island*, published in 1984 as part of the Pacific Yachting series on British Columbia cruising, and republished (unrevised) in 1993 by Evergreen Pacific Publishing Co. The rocks have not moved since 1984, and the excellent aerial photos by George McNutt will help with navigation. The book was written before boats had GPS and radar. The author's dependence on traditional coastal navigation skills is instructive. Watmough gives a good picture of what the coast was like in the 1980s. Keep in mind that the coastal towns have gone through dramatic economic changes with declines in both fishing and logging and the closing of pulp and sawmills.

Charts. The Canadian Hydrographic Service has more than 30 charts that cover the coast between Port Hardy and Trial Island. Buy them all. Let the few that you don't use be insurance that you will have the chart you need, regardless of where you are. The charts are of excellent quality and easy to read. The West Coast is no place for approximate navigation. If a $20 chart can take even a moment's anxiety out of a passage, the $20 is well spent. Canadian Hydrographic Service electronic charts are available for all of West Coast Vancouver Island and Haida Gwaii as a package, PAC-01, for $175.

Coast Guard. The Canadian Coast Guard stationed along the West Coast is simply incredible. They watch like mother hens over the fleets of fish boats, pleasure boats and work boats, ready to deploy helicopters and rescue craft instantly. They know what the weather is doing and where the traffic is. They know where to find help. A call to the Coast Guard brings action.

Local communities can often respond even faster than the Coast Guard. In the area off Kyuquot Sound, for example, we were told

that a call to Walters Cove on VHF 06 or 14 would bring help a-running. Be sure to call the Coast Guard on channel 16, too.

Insurance. Insurance policies for most inshore boats do not cover the west coast of Vancouver Island. Read your policy and check with your agent about extending the coverage for the period of your trip.

Communications. Cell phone service is found in Ucluelet, Bamfield, Tofino, Hot Springs Cove and in many locations in Quatsino Sound. Wi-Fi, found at marinas, coffee shops, restaurants and as commercial services is usually satellite based, which is slower than you may be used to.

Oregon's Secret. Many of the boats cruising the West Coast come from Oregon. For years it's been their playground, their little secret. The reason is obvious. After the trip along the Washington coast, their first stop is the west coast of Vancouver Island. In good weather it's a long but easy run. Boats from the population centers of Puget Sound or Vancouver/Victoria must fight the Strait of Juan de Fuca or go around the top of Vancouver Island. Often, it is easier for them to enjoy cruising in the protected waters inside Vancouver Island.

Trailer Boats. Launch ramps are available on each of Vancouver Island's sounds and inlets. Many kayakers choose whatever part of the West Coast they wish without making a summer of it. The West Coast truly is kayak country, with kayak delivery services from small speedboats with kayak racks, to the coastal freighters the Frances Barkley and Uchuck III.

HARDY BAY TO CAPE SCOTT

We will start from the north as though leaving from Port McNeill or Port Hardy, both excellent ports with provisioning and other services. Most importantly, you can watch the internet for the right weather window. Many cruisers like to watch for a 1-3 day settled weather window for the trip leg from the top of Vancouver Island south past Brooks Peninsula.

Goletas Channel stretches west-northwest 23 miles between Duval Point (entrance to Hardy Bay) and the western tip of Hope Island. At the west entrance of Goletas Channel the notorious Nahwitti Bar blocks westerly swells from entering. Goletas Channel's shorelines are steep-to. Winds can funnel between them and grow stronger, but

Rounding remote Cape Scott is a part of the West Coast Vancouver Island experience.

When the wind and current are calm, Nahwitti Bar can be easily negotiated.

in usual summer conditions the channel, while it can get pretty choppy, is not known for dangerous seas. Be alert, however, for turbulence and debris in the water where Christie Passage, Browning Passage and Bate Passage join Goletas Channel. The mouth of Hardy Bay can be slow going as you pick your way through drift. Bull Harbour indents Hope Island at the west entrance to Goletas Channel. It is the usual waiting point for slack water on Nahwitti Bar.

God's Pocket is a favorite layover in Christie Passage on the west side of Hurst Island, just off Goletas Channel. Boats bound around Vancouver Island probably will not see God's Pocket unless to escape a chop in Goletas Channel. But boats planning a direct crossing of Queen Charlotte Sound to Haida Gwaii (Queen Charlotte Islands), or boats bound past Cape Caution, find God's Pocket to be a good departure spot. God's Pocket is a local name, not shown on the chart.

God's Pocket Resort. P.O. Box 130, Port Hardy, BC V0N 2P0; (250) 949-1755; info@godspocket.com; www.godspocket.com. This is primarily a diving resort with friendly people. Room for three to four boats at the dock, or anchor out. No power or water on the docks. No washrooms and no showers. Breakfast, lunch and dinner are available for the resort's diving guests; others can be accommodated on an as-available basis, with reservations.

Port Alexander. Port Alexander, indenting Nigei Island west of Browning Passage, is a good anchorage for boats bound for Cape Scott or around Cape Caution. Anchor near the head in 50 to 60 feet. The beach is good for dog walking. The westerly wind blows in across the island, but has no fetch for seas to build. The west side of the bay seems more protected than the east. The accumulation of large logs on the beach indicates that this is no place to be in a southerly storm.

Clam Cove. Clam Cove is a local name, not shown on the chart, for an anchorage on the Gordon Channel side of Nigei Island, where Browning Passage meets Gordon Channel. The entrance is approximately 0.7 miles southeast of Hougestal Point. The entrance is guarded by rocks, but Correspondent Bruce Evertz reports that with attention, entry isn't a problem. Correspondents Carol-Ann Giroday and Rick LeBlanc tell us the entry is wider than it appears on the chart and kelp marks the shallow spots. The basin has room for several boats, with protection from all winds. An easily-walked trail leads from the south end of Clam Cove to Port Alexander. A cluster of float homes is located at the north end of the inner-most part of the cove.

Shushartie Bay. "We stopped for breakfast in Shushartie Bay after rounding the top end of Vancouver Island (clockwise circumnavigation). A 30-knot southeasterly wind was blowing against a strong flood current, making Goletas Channel very rough. We went deep into the bay and dropped the hook in 50 feet just inside the 30-meter line, west of some dolphins marked 'Dns' on the chart. Holding was good in thick mud. This is no Prideaux Haven, but considering the conditions outside, the swell that came in wasn't too bad. The Douglasses description of Shushartie Bay is fairly negative, and we don't know how it would be in a westerly. But it worked for us that day." [*Hamilton*]

Bull Harbour. Bull Harbour is a lovely bay almost landlocked in Hope Island. It is the place to wait for weather and for slack water on Nahwitti Bar.

Enter Bull Harbour around the east side of Norman Island, which blocks the southern entrance. A light marks the entrance. 3-knot speed limit inside the harbour. Parts of Bull Harbour grow quite shoal on a low tide. Check the depths and tide tables before anchoring for the night. The bottom is mud and holding is excellent. Sailing Directions says the southern portion of the harbor is reported to be foul with old chain and cable. During the fishing season, commercial fish

boats often crowd the harbor. The entrance should be kept clear for floatplane landings and departures. The Coast Guard station, once active here, has been decommissioned.

All of Hope Island, including Bull Harbour, at the west end of Goletas Channel, is the property of the Tlatlasikwala Native Band. Boaters may tie-up at the Band's dock in mid-harbour but may not go ashore on Hope Island, all of which is private Indian Reserve land. Moorage is first-come, first-served. The northern most section of the dock is reserved for floatplanes. A detached float just past Norman Island near the harbour entrance is also available for moorage. Payment for moorage can be mailed to the Band at Tlatlasikwala First Nation, PO Box 339, Port Hardy, BC V0N 2P0. See their website at www.tlatlasikwala.com.

Westerly winds can enter Bull Harbour, as can southeast gales. If you are anchored, be sure the anchor is well set with adequate scope.

Nahwitti Bar. Nahwitti Bar should be attempted only at or near slack. Slack water and current predictions are shown in Tide and Current Tables, Vol. 6. Maximum tidal currents over the bar reach 5.5 knots. From seaward, the bar shoals gradually to a least depth of approximately 35 feet. When ocean swells from deep water hit the bar, friction from the shallowing bottom slows the water there, while the top of the swell continues its pace. As a result the waves grow high and steep. If a strong ebb current opposes westerly winds, dangerous and heavy breaking seas will develop.

It is often said that the ideal time to cross Nahwitti bar is at high slack water, when the typical westerly wind blows with the flood current. This tends to keep seas down and permits crossing a few minutes before the slack. The subsequent ebb current flows to 3 knots along the coast all the way to Cape Scott.

A crossing at high slack is not without its disadvantages, though. First, the ebb that follows will oppose the prevailing westerly wind, and could build a steep chop along the run to Cape Scott. Second, if you cross Nahwitti Bar at slack, you are almost guaranteed to arrive at Cape Scott around mid-tide, when currents could be kicking up the seas. One alternative is to take the inner route around Nahwitti Bar prior to high or low slack at the bar, timing your arrival at Cape Scott for high or low water.

Thus the wise skipper considers all factors before crossing Nahwitti Bar: current direction and speed, weather, time of day, and vessel speed. At least 30 minutes should be allowed to get through the swells on the bar. Even fast boats usually must proceed slowly. At slack water in windless conditions, we found impressive swells extending 2.5 miles out to Whistle Buoy *MA* before they died down.

Nahwitti Bar Inner Route. A September 1992 *Pacific Yachting* article by June Cameron describes a quieter inner route that avoids Nahwitti Bar altogether. While in Bull Harbour, an old and grizzled commercial fisherman told us he hadn't gone across the bar in years, and we were nuts if we didn't take the inner route. Cross to the bay on the south shore of Goletas Channel and work in behind Tatnall Reefs. Follow the Vancouver Island shoreline around the bay, passing on either side of Weser Island. If the westerly is blowing, you can hide in the little nook behind Cape Sutil. We did it and it works. We don't plan to cross Nahwitti Bar again. [*Hale*]

Cape Sutil to Cape Scott. Sailing Directions says the distance from Cape Sutil to Cape Scott is 15 miles, but this understates the actual running distance after crossing Nahwitti Bar. A more realistic distance would be measured from Whistle Buoy *MA*, and would be approximately 16.5 miles. Although the run across the bottom of Queen Charlotte Sound is exposed to westerlies, except for the relentless Pacific swell the early morning conditions are often quiet. Rocks extend as much as a mile offshore all along the way. Stay well off.

According to Sailing Directions, temporary anchorage can be found in Shuttleworth Bight, Nissen Bight, Fisherman Bay (southwest corner of Nissen Bight), Nels Bight, and Experiment Bight. Study the chart before entering, and watch the weather.

Cape Scott is the westernmost point of Vancouver Island. Dangerous rocks extend 0.5 mile offshore, northward and westward. The cape itself is a low piece of land connected by a narrow neck with the main body of Vancouver Island. The Cape Scott Light, on a square tower 13 feet high, is on higher ground about a quarter-mile inland from Cape Scott.

Currents flowing on both sides of the cape meet at Cape Scott. Especially when opposed by wind, the currents can produce heavy seas and overfalls, dangerous to small craft. Even in calm conditions, seas can emerge seemingly from nowhere, the result of colliding currents. With its seas, rocks, and shortage of convenient hidey-holes, Cape Scott is not a place to treat lightly. A vessel in trouble at Cape Scott could be in serious trouble, and quickly.

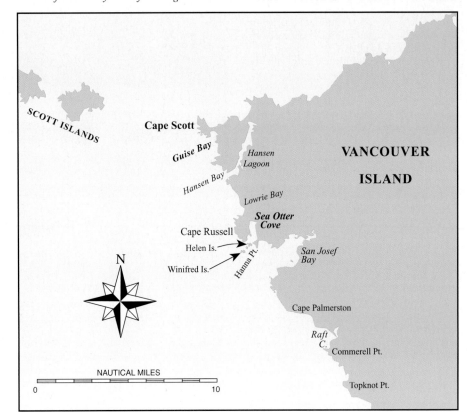

Cape Scott to Quatsino Sound

It is with good reason that guidebooks (including this one) and magazine articles emphasize the dangers and cautions at Cape Scott. The waters can be treacherous. Yet in settled summer conditions, a well-managed seaworthy vessel, with a good weather eye, can make a safe and satisfying rounding. The standard advice is to round Cape Scott at slack. Other factors may persuade a skipper to round at times other than slack. Each situation, each boat, is different. What worked yesterday may not work today. A careful skipper, fully aware that safety of the vessel and crew truly are at risk at Cape Scott, must judge conditions and make the right choices.

Weather information: The Cape Scott lighthouse weather report is regularly updated with wind speed and direction, sea conditions, and visibility information. The automated weather station on Sartine Island provides wind speed and direction. Listen to the continuous marine broadcast for the latest weather information.

CAPE SCOTT TO QUATSINO SOUND

Depending on the courses chosen, the run from Cape Scott to the entrance of Quatsino Sound is approximately 28.5 miles. To stay clear of off-lying rocks and reefs, the general advice is to follow the 20-fathom curve all the way down the coast. Douglass says he prefers the 30-fathom curve for an extra margin of safety. We are inclined toward Douglass' 30-fathom standard. In moderate conditions with excellent visibility, we felt comfortable in 25 to 30 fathoms. Had conditions worsened, we would have moved out.

With the summer westerly in place, the run between Cape Scott and Quatsino Sound is a downhill sleigh ride. Powerboaters, especially those with planing hulls, will have to saw away at the helm and play with the throttle to stay in harmony with the relentless procession of rollers. They will arrive tired. The sailboaters will have all the fun, especially if the boat and crew can handle a spinnaker. They too will arrive tired, but exhilarated.

Given the conditions, many boats make a direct passage between Cape Scott and Quatsino Sound, and leave the bays between for another day. Sailboats, after a long passage at 6 knots, will be apt to put into one of those bays, particularly Sea Otter Cove. Boats heading clockwise, toward Cape Scott, might also be more apt to investigate the shoreline, choosing to spend the night in Sea Otter

God's Pocket Resort has space for a few boats and is a good jumping-off point when rounding Cape Scott.

Cove. They could make an early departure the next morning and round Cape Scott before the westerly fills in.

Weather information: At the north end, the Cape Scott lighthouse weather report informs mariners of wind and sea conditions. At the south end, the Quatsino lighthouse report does the same. Listen to the continuous marine broadcast for the latest weather information.

Guise Bay. Guise Bay is just south of Cape Scott. Sailing Directions says the entrance to Guise Bay is encumbered with rocks, and local knowledge is called for. The chart suggests that entrance is possible, but Douglass says that the rocks are often covered with foam and a strong heart is needed. Correspondents Gil and Karen Flanagan, however, put in to Guise Bay, and here is their report:

"Guise Bay is a great anchorage. The shore is so interesting we would consider overnighting there. The walk to the lighthouse is well used, and pretty easy. The anchorage area is about 600 yards long by 600 yards wide. The swell that day was only

A community boardwalk skirts the shoreline at Winter Harbour.

a few inches. Behind the island, the main south entrance channel is 1000 feet wide and 42 feet deep. If it is a reasonably nice day, don't pass it by." [Flanagan]

Hansen Bay. Hansen Bay was the location of a Danish settlement around 1900. Supply vessels could anchor in good weather only. The settlement failed. Sailing Directions says Hansen Bay "affords no shelter," although commercial fish boats do hole up there.

Sea Otter Cove. Sea Otter Cove, south of Cape Scott, is described in Sailing Directions as "indifferent shelter." Nevertheless, Sea Otter Cove is a favorite of fish boats, and well-known to yachtsmen. The rocks and islets outside the entrance are awesome in their ruggedness. Inside, you feel safe but surrounded by hostile ground. Sea Otter Cove is an exciting place to be. We recommend it.

Enter from the south, between Hanna Point and the Helen Islands. Watmough's book shows swells breaking almost across the entrance, but careful attention to the chart will bring you through. The channel is narrow, and grows shallower as you go in. Deep draft vessels should be careful if they anchor there due to the shallow depths. Four storm mooring buoys were in place in 2015; least depth was about 8 feet at zero tide.

San Josef Bay. San Josef Bay is protected from northerly winds, but open to westerly and southerly winds. Anchor in settled weather.

QUATSINO SOUND

Quatsino Sound is the northernmost of the five sounds that indent the west coast of Vancouver Island. Despite fish farms and logging operations, Quatsino Sound still provides scenic coves and interesting anchorages. With the exception of North Harbour and Winter Harbour on the north side near the entrance, Quatsino Sound is probably the sound least explored by cruising yachts.

Quatsino Sound is the first quiet anchorage after the 50-mile run from Bull Harbour, and a welcome sight it is after anxiety at Cape

Scott and hours of rolling seas. The entrance is straightforward. Using large-scale Chart 3686, identify South Danger Rock and Robson Rock (both of them well away from land), stay close to Kains Island, and proceed into Forward Inlet. North Harbour and Browning Inlet are good anchorages, or you can continue to Winter Harbour.

For those coming from Haida Gwaii or the Central Coast, Quatsino Sound offers the opportunity to do major provisioning, either at Port Alice or by taking a bus to Port Hardy from Coal Harbour.

VHF: We are told the fishermen work on channels 73, 84, and 86.

Cell phones: There is Telus service throughout most of Quatsino Sound except Forward Inlet north of Montgomery Point.

① **Winter Harbour.** Winter Harbour once was a commercial fishing outpost, and B.C. Packers owned the first major set of docks as you enter, including the fuel dock. With the closing of fishing, their docks and fuel facility have been taken over by the company that owns and runs the Outpost store. Today Winter Harbour has 12 full time residents and about 70 summer residents.

Beyond the Outpost and its facilities is the campground of the Winter Harbour Lodge, followed by the Qualicum Rivers Fishing Resort (the large white building), and finally, the Winter Harbour Authority public dock.

The library, located above the public dock, has irregular hours. Pay phones are on the far side of this building. A post office and book exchange is located in a small building to the right of the public wharf. For-fee Wi-Fi is available in Winter Harbour.

Van Isle 360: The Van Isle 360 sailboat race, held in odd-numbered years, visits Winter Harbour. They fill the docks when they arrive.

① **Outpost at Winter Harbour, Grant Sales Ltd.** 108 Winter Harbour Rd., Winter Harbour, BC V0N 3L0; (250) 969-4333; winterharbour@telus.net; www.winterharbour.ca. Monitors VHF 19. Open all year, moorage for boats to 75 feet, gasoline, diesel, oil, laundry, washrooms & showers,

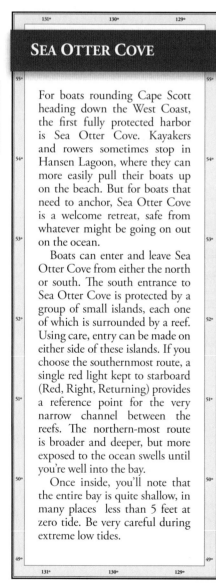

SEA OTTER COVE

For boats rounding Cape Scott heading down the West Coast, the first fully protected harbor is Sea Otter Cove. Kayakers and rowers sometimes stop in Hansen Lagoon, where they can more easily pull their boats up on the beach. But for boats that need to anchor, Sea Otter Cove is a welcome retreat, safe from whatever might be going on out on the ocean.

Boats can enter and leave Sea Otter Cove from either the north or south. The south entrance to Sea Otter Cove is protected by a group of small islands, each one of which is surrounded by a reef. Using care, entry can be made on either side of these islands. If you choose the southernmost route, a single red light kept to starboard (Red, Right, Returning) provides a reference point for the very narrow channel between the reefs. The northern-most route is broader and deeper, but more exposed to the ocean swells until you're well into the bay.

Once inside, you'll note that the entire bay is quite shallow, in many places less than 5 feet at zero tide. Be very careful during extreme low tides.

general store, water at fuel dock, campsites. The showers are in a small building on a dock near the Outpost. The general store has frozen foods including some frozen meat, canned goods, packaged foods and ice. Produce is limited. Grocery availability may depend on delivery schedules. The Outpost also carries liquor, clothing, charts, fishing equipment, and miscellaneous tools. The liquor agency has a decent wine selection. Wi-Fi can be purchased and used at an attractive patio area overlooking the harbor. Greg Vance is the owner.

① Winter Harbour Authority. (800) 960-2646 rob@qualicumrivers.com; Moorage on 450 feet of dock, water, waste oil disposal, garbage drop, recycling, 15, 20, & 30 amp power. Power is run to the dock by extension cord; quality varies. A pay phone is at the top of the dock. Cruisers may need to go to the Outpost to use the for-fee WiFi. A tidal grid is available. Qualicum Rivers, the fishing lodge next door, operates June through September and sells flaked ice to cruisers and has a restaurant. Reservations required at the seasonal restaurant.

A sign on the dock asks shallow draft boats to allow deeper draft boats priority on the outer side. Larger boats also anchor to the north of the public dock and at the head of Winter Harbour.

North Harbour. North Harbour, north of Matthews Island in Forward Inlet, is an excellent anchorage, popular with boats planning a morning departure from Quatsino Sound. A small float house is moored close to shore and does not significantly interfere with anchorage. North Harbour is sheltered and quiet, yet close to the mouth of Quatsino Sound.

Browning Inlet. Browning Inlet is narrow and sheltered from seas and swells, with good holding in 18 to 30 feet. Crabbing is reportedly good. In strong northwesterlies, winds blow from the valley to the north. In those conditions North Harbour or Winter Harbour are preferable.

Koskimo Bay. Koskimo Bay has a couple of anchorages, one behind Mabbott Island and one at Mahatta Creek. The Koskimo Islands are at the east end of Koskimo Bay.

Mabbott Island. The little area behind Mabbott Island would be a cozy spot to drop the hook if the large fish farm and float house didn't take much of the anchorage.

Mahatta Creek. In Koskimo Bay. Work your way east of the mouth of the creek, anchor in 30 to 45 feet. At high tide you can explore the creek. Waves can build across the sound in strong northwesterlies. On those days it's best to move north to East Cove.

Koskimo Islands. Explore by dinghy. The narrow passage between the largest of the islands and Vancouver Island can be run (carefully), but with safe water just outside the islands we see no need to.

Koprino Harbour. Most of Koprino Harbour is too deep for pleasure craft to anchor, but the area of East Cove, near the northeast corner of Koprino Harbour, is excellent.

East Cove. East Cove is tranquil, snug and tree-lined, with good dinghy access to shore—cruising as it should be. If East Cove were in Desolation Sound instead of Koprino Harbour, it would be filled with 25 boats every night, all stern-tied to shore. But because East Cove is on the west coast of Vancouver Island, you will probably be the only boat at anchor and won't need a stern-tie. Another cove, almost as delightful, is just to the north, behind a group of little islets. The largest of these islets is identified on the chart as Linthlop Islet.

Pamphlet Cove. Pamphlet Cove, part of a provincial recreation reserve, is located on the north side of Drake Island, about 3.5 miles west of Quatsino Narrows. Pamphlet Cove is scenic and protected, an ideal anchorage. You can go ashore and enjoy the reserve. At high tide several small lagoons make for good exploring by dinghy or kayak.

Julian Cove. Southeast of Drake Island and east of Kultus Cove. Protection is excellent and holding is good. Probably the most pristine cove in Quatsino Sound, Julian Cove has room for four or five boats. Beautiful forested hills surround it without a clearcut in sight. At the head of the bay

a stream crosses a marsh and salmonberries grow along the shore. Watch for bears. Entry is direct and easy.

Smith Cove. It's been reported that a large float and separate float house, with cables running to shore, occupies much of Smith Cove. Nearby Julian Cove is a better choice.

Atkins Cove. Atkins Cove is well protected except south. Good holding over a mud bottom.

"Early Bird Cove," Douglass' name for the almost-landlocked cove accessed through the narrows on the north side of Atkins Cove, is also a good anchorage. We went through the narrow, shallow entrance strongly favoring the west shore. On an 8.5-foot high tide we saw depths of 6.5 feet.

Neroutsos Inlet. "The wind blows hard every afternoon in Neroutsos Inlet," one knowledgeable local told us. Neroutsos Inlet is long and straight-sided, with little diversion along the way. A former pulp mill is at Port Alice near the south end.

② Port Alice. Port Alice, properly Rumble Beach, but locally called Port Alice, is a friendly, former cellulose-mill town struggling to adjust to the recent sale and subsequent closure of the mill. Amenities include a liquor store, and a grocery market that almost qualifies as a supermarket (and the best grocery shopping between Port Hardy and Tofino). Restaurants are scarce. Fuel is available from a service station near the public dock at the north end of town for a $20 fee. A tricky 9-hole golf course is located at the site of the former mill, the real Port Alice, about a mile south of the town. Showers and laundry are available at the campground half a mile south of the yacht club and Rumble Beach Marina.

Visitors are warmly welcomed in Port Alice. It is a delightful stop and a good alternative to a bus ride into Port Hardy from Coal Harbour for provisioning.

② Rumble Beach Marina. (250) 209-2665; (250) 284-3391. Open all year with moorage to 100 feet. This marina, just south of the Port Alice Yacht Club, is the best moorage prospect

375

Harbour Authority float at Winter Harbour

Julian Cove is an outstanding anchorage.

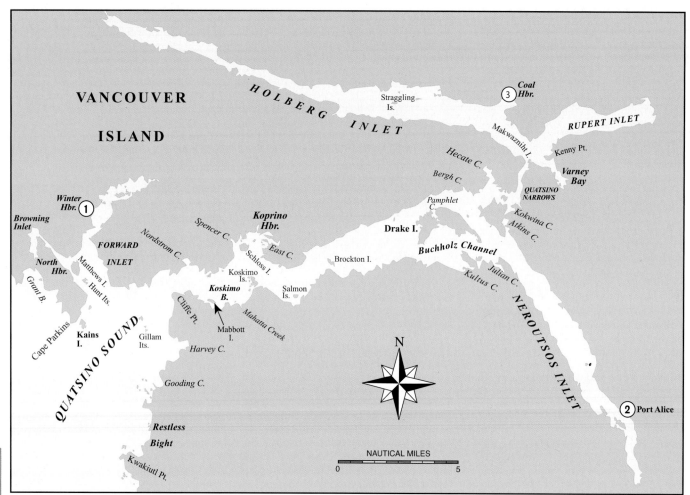

Quatsino Sound

in Port Alice. Potable water and garbage drop. No power, laundry or showers.

The marina is operated by the city and is within walking distance of all Port Alice amenities.

② **Port Alice Yacht Club.** You must belong to a yacht club with reciprocal privileges to tie up here. A log breakwater protects the yacht club and the public dock/launch ramp to the south. Moorage is available in members' vacant slips. Slips are generally not available in July and August. Boats that have been trailered to Port Alice cannot stay at the yacht club.

Although the yacht club is designed primarily for smaller boats, it may have room for larger boats if two adjacent moorage spaces are open. A volunteer worker may point you to your slip, help you tie up, then show you around town. Good water and 20 amp power on the docks. If you come in after hours, the gate is locked but the phone numbers of volunteers are posted. A public park with picnic tables and playground equipment is immediately to the north. We were told that boats can anchor south of the Frigon Islets.

Quatsino Narrows. Quatsino Narrows connects with Rupert Inlet and Holberg Inlet, and the village of Coal Harbour. With tidal streams near Makwazniht Island running to 9

knots on the flood and 8 knots on the ebb, it is best to take the narrows near slack. Predictions for Quatsino Narrows are shown as a secondary station based on Tofino in Canadian Tide & Current Tables Vol. 6, and Ports and Passes. You'll find considerable turbulence near Makwazniht Island. The range on the eastern shore of the narrows is for large ships with 30-foot drafts; small boats need not stay on the range. Turbulence, though less than that found near Makwazniht Island, is present near the south entrance to Quatsino Narrows. At slack water, watch for tugs with log boom tows.

Varney Bay. Varney Bay, at the mouth of the Marble River and east of the north entrance to Quatsino Narrows, is scenic, tranquil and protected. A dinghy ride up the Marble River is worth a trip through Quatsino Narrows. Anchor inside Kenny Point behind the 3-meter island, and watch for rocks and deadheads as you enter. Varney Bay is a fish preserve. No fishing. Correspondents Gil and Karen Flanagan add this report: "After you cross the rather large delta, the Marble River flows through a canyon. The river has undercut some of the canyon walls, forming fantastic caverns. We went up the river about 2.7 miles to a rapids, where we found a huge cavern, measuring at least 30 feet by 30 feet. A must-see." To ensure enough water to safely cross the delta and reach the cavern,

plan to be at the rapids as close to high tide as possible.

Rupert Inlet. Rupert Inlet is the site of the giant Utah Mines open pit copper mine, now closed and flooded.

③ **Coal Harbour.** Coal Harbour has a small village with launch ramp, marina, and museum. It is 8 miles by road from Port Hardy.

Thrice-daily bus service to Port Hardy, with connections to Port McNeill, leaves from the village.

During World War II, Coal Harbour was a Royal Canadian Air Force seaplane base. The large building on the waterfront was the hangar. The Coal Harbour Whaling Station, the last whale-processing site on the West Coast, later operated out of these same facilities. Whaling operations ceased in 1967. The hangar and adjacent land now serve as seaplane storage, launching facilities, and water taxi service.

Three rooms in the hangar make up a museum, with artifacts, newspaper clippings and photographs from Coal Harbour's years as an RCAF base and a whaling station. Ask at the desk to see it. If you're lucky you'll get a guided tour. No charge. The large whale jawbone shown in photos of Coal Harbour has been repaired and is on display in the hanger. Recommended.

③ **Quatsino First Nations Dock**. 322 Quattishe Road, Coal Harbour, BC V0N 1K0; (250) 949-6870; Moorage, gas, diesel, water, some 20 amp power. Showers and laundry facilities available beyond the wharfinger office. The floats can be busy with commercial boats. Floats can accommodate vessels up to 60 feet.

Holberg Inlet is 18 miles long, narrow and deep, a classic fjord. It has few places to anchor, and not much for the cruising yachtsman. With its 36-mile round trip and no facilities or attractions, it is seldom traveled by cruising yachts.

Quatsino Village. The public dock at Quatsino Village is mostly for smaller boats and loading/unloading. We tucked into the only larger space available only to be shouted at by a taxi boat operator who appeared to have plenty of space to maneuver. We walked into the village and to the 1898 Anglican church, open for visitors. A small museum and snack shop are open one hour per day, several days a week. Chart 3681 shows the details for entry. Room to anchor off the dock if necessary.

BROOKS BAY

Brooks Bay is between Quatsino Sound and Brooks Peninsula. It's about 19 miles from a departure point south of Kains Island (at the entrance to Quatsino Sound) to a point about 2 miles west of Solander Island. Depending on the course chosen, it's another 22 to 25 miles from Solander Island to Walters Cove—a total of at least 40 miles in the open sea. If wind and seas are favorable, those heading south will want to seize the opportunity to round Brooks Peninsula. They can be excused for not exploring Brooks Bay. If the weather is unfavorable, Brooks Bay is a good place to explore while waiting for a weather window. If you have the time, it is recommended.

The entrance to Klaskish Basin is narrow.

Two inlets, Klaskino Inlet and Klaskish Inlet, are beautiful and have good anchorage, although portions of Klaskino Inlet have been logged. Brooks Bay is dotted with unmarked (but charted) rocks and reefs that make navigation exciting. Plot courses carefully.

④ **Klaskino Inlet.** Assuming an approach from the north, leave Lawn Point approximately 2 miles to port. (Lawn Point's grassy-looking slopes are in fact covered with low bushes). Continue, leaving Scarf Reef to port. Then turn to leave Rugged Islets to starboard. Turn to pass midway between Buoys *M17* and *M18*, then turn to enter Klaskino Inlet.

For a quick anchorage, skirt around Anchorage Island into Klaskino Anchorage or into the small bight north of Klaskino Anchorage.

If you'd like to explore further, go through Scouler Pass. Use the more open northern channel, leaving Buoy *M23* to port. The kelp will be close enough to hold your attention. Anchor in the bight between the 67- and 53-meter islands, in the area shown as 7 meters at zero tide. The drying flats of the river mouth come up sharply. Be sure you don't swing onto them.

Correspondent Gil Flanagan went all the way to the head of Klaskino Inlet (about 4 miles from Scouler Pass), and recommends the anchorage behind the little island near the head. He says shore access is excellent, with logging roads for walking. Make noise; bears frequent the woods.

Leaving Klaskino Inlet, the safest route is back between Buoys *M17* and *M18*. Although it's possible to take a route westward through Steele Reefs, we're not sure we'd do it again. Our course took us directly over the word "Steele" on the chart. We had good depths, but even on a quiet day the surf crashing on the rocks seemed closer than we expected. [*Hale*]

⑤ **Klaskish Inlet**. If you run from Quatsino Sound directly to Klaskish Inlet, your probable course will take you very near to Hughes Rock, which dries 5 feet. Hughes Rock is clearly shown on the chart. Don't run over it.

Consider anchoring in magnificent Klaskish Basin, reached through a knockout, must-see narrow gorge with vertical rock sides overhung with dense forest. Once through, you are separated from the rest of the world. All the mooring buoys shown on the chart have been removed.

Brooks Peninsula. Brooks Peninsula and the waters off Cape Cook are, together with Cape Scott, the most hostile on the west coast of Vancouver Island. Like rounding Cape Scott, rounding the Brooks is a milestone in a circumnavigation. The peninsula itself is a mountainous, rectangular promontory that extends 6 miles out from Vancouver Island, like a growth on the side of an otherwise handsome face. Rocks and reefs guard much of the shoreline. Tangles of driftwood make beaches impassable. Cliffs rise from the

Docks at Rumble Beach Marina are within walking distance to Port Alice.

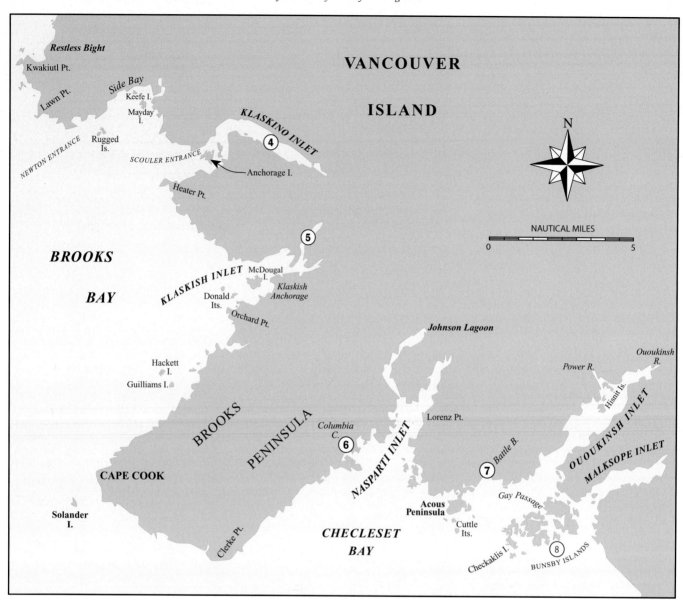

Brooks Peninsula

beaches. At the tops of the cliffs, wilderness. Much of the peninsula is a provincial park, preserved for its wildness. Twenty thousand years ago, when glaciers covered most of Vancouver Island, the Brooks Peninsula remained ice-free. Plant species wiped out in glaciated areas are still found here. Park status helps preserve those species.

Cap on the Cape: When a cloud forms on top of Brooks Peninsula over Cape Cook, it often means that strong northwesterly winds will follow.

Cape Cook & Solander Island. Cape Cook is the northwestern tip of Brooks Peninsula. Rocks and shoals extend offshore from Cape Cook nearly to Solander Island.

The Cape Cook/Solander Island area can be a dangerous patch of water. When conflicting currents meet accelerating winds, conditions can sink a boat. Cape Cook has driven back large ships. The marine weather broadcasts often talk of "local winds off the headlands" of 35 knots. The headland they have in mind is Cape Cook. While no headland on the West

Coast should be taken lightly, Cape Cook (and Cape Scott) should be given the greatest respect. Listen to the weather broadcasts. If conditions sound questionable, wait. When your opportunity comes, seize it.

On all but the quietest days, the safe route past Cape Cook is well offshore from Solander Island. If you are one of the rare lucky ones to round the Brooks on a quiet day and can approach Solander Island more closely, you'll see Steller sea lions hauled out on the base of the island and puffins swimming near your boat.

Weather information: An automated weather station on Solander Island provides wind speed and direction, updated hourly. Listen to the continuous marine broadcast for the latest weather information.

Clerke Point. Clerke Point marks the southeast corner of Brooks Peninsula. Shoals extend at least 0.5 mile offshore. Following the 20-fathom curve will leave ample room for safety. The pyramid-shaped seas we had battled at Solander Island disappeared completely by Clerke Point.

Once past Brooks Peninsula, the winds slacken, the weather warms and conditions improve.

CHECLESET BAY

Checleset Bay has a number of anchorages, including the Shelter Sheds, Columbia Cove, and the Bunsby Islands. If you have just rounded Brooks Peninsula, Shelter Sheds or Columbia Cove are good stops. Columbia Cove is exceptional.

Shelter Sheds. The Shelter Sheds are lines of reef extending from Brooks Peninsula into Checleset Bay. Fishermen have found shelter in their lee, hence the name. Correspondent Gil Flanagan reports that Shed 4 has by far the finest beach his family has found—better even than West Beach at Hakai. The water was near 70° F. A trail leads to Columbia Cove, but Correspondents Steve and Elsie Hulsizer report that windfall has made the trail difficult, especially the first 200 yards.

⑥ **Columbia Cove.** Beautiful Columbia Cove is known locally as Peddlers Cove. Neither name is on the chart. The cove is immediately north of Jackobson Point, snugged up against the base of Brooks Peninsula. Depths in Columbia Cove are shallower than charted.

Be sure to enter between Jackobson Point and the 215-foot island. Columbia Cove has experienced some silting over the years and anchoring room has become limited. The mouth of the cove, between Jackobson Point and the 215-foot island, is safe in a northwesterly. In southerlies, winds and waves make this area uncomfortable, leaving room for only about three boats in the cove itself. Columbia Cove is a voluntary no-discharge zone. Please volunteer.

The name Columbia Cove comes from Captain Robert Gray's ship Columbia, which overnighted here twice. If you think Columbia Cove is crowded with three boats, now imagine it with the Columbia, the schooner Adventure, and the ship Margaret, of Boston, all at the same time. A sometimes muddy trail across the small peninsula formed by Jackobson Point leads to a beautiful sandy ocean beach. Great beachcombing. Take the dinghy up the stream to the trailhead, but watch the tide. You can be stranded, with a long walk across tideflats dragging your dinghy or kayak.

Weather Note: When strong winds from the northwest are forecast south of Brooks Peninsula, the Brooks provides a lee for Columbia Cove and adjacent waters. Winds may be strong but seas will be quiet. It's a good place to wait out a northwest gale. It's not a good place to wait out a southeast gale.

⑦ **Battle Bay.** Battle Bay, north of the Bunsby Islands, has acceptable anchorages roughly off the Indian reserve, and in the nook that makes up the northeast shore. Approach the Longback Islands before making your turn into Battle Bay. One interesting anchorage is immediately west of Battle Bay, against the east shore of Acous Peninsula. To reach that anchorage, leave the Skirmish Islands to

Brooks Peninsula is famous for high winds and rough water. It demands respect.

starboard as you approach. From there you'll look across a sea of islands and rocks to the Bunsbys.

The Indian Reserve on the Acous Peninsula is the former home of the Checleset Band, now located in Walters Cove. You can find fallen totem poles serving as nurse logs, and the depressions of old longhouses.

⑧ **Bunsby Islands.** "Did you get to the Bunsbys?" That's what people ask when they learn you've been down the west coast of Vancouver Island. Don't disappoint them by saying no. The Bunsby Islands are rocky, rugged, and beautiful. They were named for a character in the Charles Dickens novel *Dombey and Son*. A number of other features in the area also carry names from that novel.

Study the chart and know your location at all times. Enter the Bunsby Islands only through Gay Passage. Two anchorages are off this passage: either the cove in the southern island or the slightly larger bay in the northern island. Enter the northern island's bay favoring the north shore to avoid a shoal extending from the south side. In this larger bay, note the rock directly beneath the 6-fathom sounding. The lagoon adjacent to this bay may be fine for an adventuresome trailerable boat.

The cove on the west side of Gay Passage is guarded by two rocks that dry 4 feet. The rocks are easy to identify and avoid if you're paying attention. The cove has room for several boats.

Checleset Bay has a large population of sea otters, the successful result of a 1969 effort to re-establish these delightful creatures. From the Bunsbys, where they were first re-introduced, the sea otters have spread up and down the coast, as far south as Barkley Sound and as far north as the Cape Caution area on the mainland. You'll sometimes see them in "rafts," groups of otters hanging together, in kelp beds.

If weather allows, take the dinghy or kayak around the islands. The rugged, windswept rocks and islets are too stunning to try to describe. It's easy to get disoriented. Carry a chart, compass, handheld GPS and handheld VHF radio.

KYUQUOT SOUND

With the exception of the outer islands and Rugged Point, Kyuquot (pronounced "Ki-YU-kit") Sound is protected and pretty, surrounded by high mountains, with easy waters. On the inside, Dixie Cove and Don Douglass' "Petroglyph Cove" (known locally as Blue Lips Cove) are excellent anchorages, and several others are attractive. The settlement of Walters Cove is a favorite.

From the south, enter Kyuquot Sound past Whistle Buoy *M38*. Leave the buoy to starboard, and proceed through Kyuquot Channel. Most visiting pleasure craft, however, will approach from the north and stop at Walters Cove before entering Kyuquot Sound proper.

⑨ **Walters Cove.** For communication, call on VHF channels 06 or 14. The little settlement of Walters Cove has almost everything you might need after a week or two of working your way along the coast: outpost hospital, ice, charts, a small general store, pay phone, a restaurant and coffee shop, relaxed and friendly people, happy kids and lazy dogs. The store at the public dock, on

Solander Island off Cape Cook, the Cape of Storms, on a rare calm summer afternoon.

The Bunsby Islands are not to be missed. The rugged scenery and sandy beaches are a highlight of the west coast of Vancouver Island.

the south side, is open Monday, Wednesday and Friday; and the store above the dock, on the Kyuquot side, is open evenings only. The Kyuquot Inn Restaurant, also known as Java The Hut, is open daily with free Wi-Fi for customers; cash only.

One thing Walters Cove does not have is liquor. Walters Cove is dry, by vote of the Kyuquot Native community, and there's not a drop to be bought. Nor is liquor in evidence, even on the dock.

Another thing you won't find is fuel. Be sure you have enough fuel in your tanks. The nearest fuel is in Fair Harbour.

From seaward, the safest approach to Walters Cove in all weather is from Whistle Buoy *MC*, at the entrance to Brown Channel. Use Chart 3683. Go through Brown Channel and turn to starboard on a course to leave Gayward Rock to starboard. At Gayward Rock go to large scale Chart 3651 to work your way past the east side of Walters Island and into Walters Cove.

Boats coming down from the Bunsby Islands probably will follow Chart 3683's rather obvious passage along the Vancouver Island shoreline, leaving Cole Rock to starboard, and McLean Island and Chief Rock Buoy *M29* to port. At Gayward Rock they would move to large-scale Chart 3651.

On Charts 3623 and 3683, take note of the charted rock awash at 10 ft (50°03'06"N/127°27'07"W). This rock is along your probable shoreline passage course. At a depth of 10 feet at zero tide the rock is not a concern for most boats, but you should know it's there.

Without Chart 3651, entry to Walters Cove would be a tricky matter. Although it is marked by buoys and a daybeacon, the channel past the east side of Walters Island is easy to misread, and the unwary skipper could be on a rock. With Chart 3651 the channel is apparent, and following the rule of Red, Right, Returning, entry is safe. The one daybeacon along the way marks the narrow passage that leads directly into Walters Cove. Don't cut it close. Remember that beacons are attached to the earth; rock extends well into the passage from the beacon. Use a mid-channel course favoring the north side between the beacon and the 51-meter island opposite. The chart makes the route clear.

Several locals insist, "Don't anchor in Walters Cove!" The bottom, they say, is foul with debris. Furthermore, the floor of the bay is crisscrossed by high voltage submarine electrical cables, a Telus phone line, and the water lines serving the community.

Instead of anchoring, tie up at the public wharf to port as you enter. Long mooring floats are on each side of the public wharf. The general store and post office is at the head of the wharf. Open Monday, Wednesday, and Friday 1:00 p.m. to 5:00 p.m. Stock arrives once per week. Walters Cove Resort also offers moorage, reservations recommended.

Java the Hutt Coffee Shop, which began its life as a "boat-through" rather than "drive-through" coffee shop on the Kyuquot Inn dock, is now located in the renovated school house at the inn with an expanded menu. They serve coffee, pastries and a variety of burgers and salads. Free Wi-Fi is provided. Showers are available at the inn. Owner Eric Gorbman is among one of the friendliest people on the coast.

The best time to arrive at Walters Cove is Thursday afternoon. The *Uchuck III* arrives that day, sometime around 5:00 p.m., depending on the other stops they have scheduled. Walters Cove becomes a bustle of activity when the ship lands, with skiffs arriving from all over the cove and outlying areas. Watching the *Uchuck III* unload its cargo is a slice of West Coast life you won't

want to miss. Everyone pitches in. Fuel barrels, boxes, even washers and dryers are loaded off the boat's starboard side into waiting skiffs. Pallets of groceries are loaded off the port side onto carts on the dock.

Because the ship overnights at Walters Cove, passengers spend the night at lodges and B&Bs. For dinner, passengers eat at the Java The Hutt Coffee Shop. When there is space, the Java The Hut also feeds boaters, guests at the lodges, and anyone else who asks by mid-afternoon. Dinner is delicious. Guests eat family-style at a long table.

For medical matters, contact the VIHA (Vancouver Island Health Authority) outpost hospital at Walters Cove, (250) 332-5289.

Good water is available at the store for a small fee.

The Kyuquot Band Native community of approximately 200 is across the bay, served by its own public dock. We met a resident of the Native community who told us that she operates a small store near the head of the dock selling snacks, soft drinks, some groceries and native crafts.

All transport is by boat in Walters Cove, and from an early age the Kyuquot children (and Native children all along the coast) are accomplished boat handlers. Their outboard-powered craft seem to have but two directions: forward and reverse; and two throttle settings: full-power and off.

Walters Cove has been a popular gathering place for decades. Years ago it was home to five fish camps in the summer. When people were stuck in port waiting for the weather to break, the talk flowed. Long ago Walters Cove got its local name of Bull--t Bay, BS Bay in polite company. A cafe in Walters Cove was called the BS Cafe. (The BS Cafe, with its memorabilia-laden walls, burned in 1998.)

⑨ **Walters Cove Resort.** (250) 332-5274; (250) 287-2223; gofishing@walterscoveresort. com; www.walterscoveresort.com. Monitors VHF 78A. Open in summer with moorage, water, ice, Wi-Fi. No power. Reservations required. This is a first class fishing lodge that

The public dock at Walters Cove. The building at the head of the dock is a post office and well-stocked store.

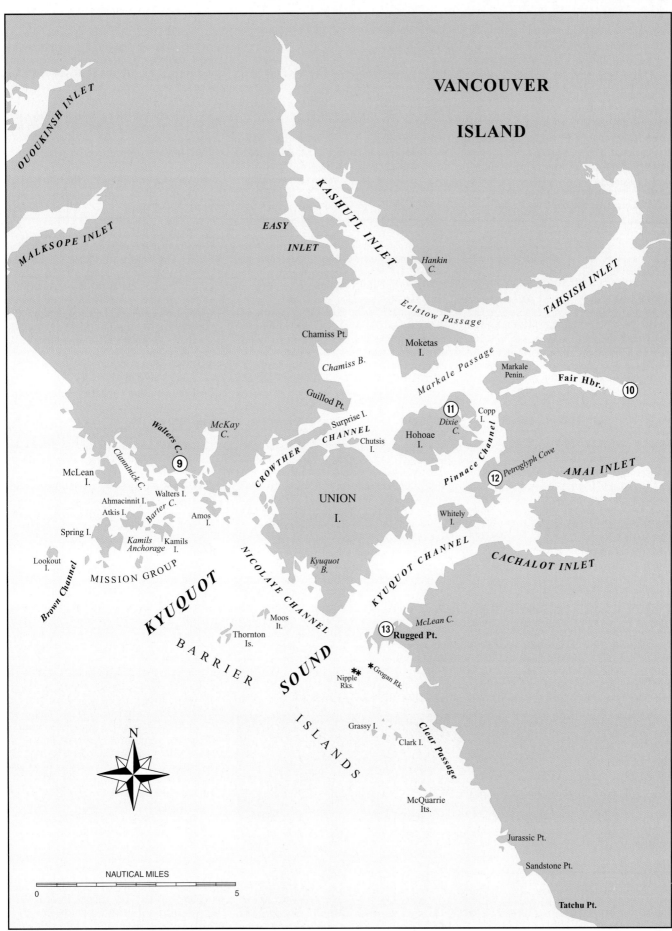

VANCOUVER

ISLAND

OUOUKINSH INLET

MALKSOPE INLET

KASHUTL INLET

EASY INLET

Hankin C.

Eelstow Passage

TAHSISH INLET

Chamiss Pt.

Chamiss B.

Moketas I.

Markale Passage

Markale Penin.

Fair Hbr.

⑩

Guillod Pt.

Walters C.

McKay C.

Surprise I.

CROWTHER CHANNEL

Chutsis I.

⑪ Dixie C.

Copp I.

Hohoae I.

Pinnace Channel

⑫ Petroglyph Cove

AMAI INLET

⑨

McLean I.

Clanninick C.

Ahmacinnit I.

Walters I.

Barter C.

Atkis I.

Amos I.

Spring I.

Kamils Anchorage

Kamils I.

UNION I.

Whitely I.

Lookout I.

Brown Channel

MISSION GROUP

KYUQUOT

NICOLAYE CHANNEL

Kyuquot B.

KYUQUOT CHANNEL

CACHALOT INLET

McLean C.

⑬ **Rugged Pt.**

BARRIER

SOUND

Moos It.

Thornton Is.

ISLANDS

Nipple Rks. ✱✱ ✱ Grogan Rk.

Grassy I.

Clark I.

Clear Passage

McQuarrie Its.

Jurassic Pt.

Sandstone Pt.

Tatchu Pt.

N

NAUTICAL MILES

0   5

Kyoquot Sound

381

provides transient moorage when space is available. Showers available with room rental. A take-out menu from Walters Cove Bistro is available with dine-in options as space allows. Moorage guests have full access to resort amenities, including hot tub, lounge, kayaks, and SUPs. Fishing charters and fish packing available.

Barter Cove. Barter Cove, in the Mission Group islands outside Walters Cove, is open, unprotected and not as interesting as anchorages inside Kyuquot Sound. Leave Ahmacinnit Island and the tiny islet east of Ahmacinnit Island to starboard, and feel your way in.

Kamils Anchorage. Kamils Anchorage in the Mission Group islands is more exposed than Barter Cove. Enter, very carefully, through Favourite Entrance.

Amos Island. From Walters Cove, the easiest entrance to Kyuquot Sound is around the east side of Amos Island into Crowther Channel. Use Chart 3651 to identify the channel between Walters Cove and Nicolaye Channel, then Chart 3682 to find the route past Amos Island. The passage east of Amos Island is deep but narrow, and bounded by rocks. The first time through can be unsettling, but after you've done it once, it's easy.

Surprise Island. Surprise Island, steep, round, and logged off to stumps, is located in Crowther Channel. On the south side of Surprise Island, Crowther Channel is deep and open, but on the north side a narrow passage is interesting. At zero tide least depths in this passage are approximately 18 feet. A ledge of rock, shown on the chart, extends from the north shore. Favor the Surprise Island side all the way through.

Hankin Cove. Hankin Cove is located near the mouth of Kashutl Inlet, on the east side. It is a beautiful little cove with good holding and completely protected. Stands of small trees covering the hillsides show evidence of past logging. Correspondents Gil and Karen Flanagan anchored in the southeast cove, and add, "Chart 3682 is way off on the shoal in this cove. The shoal extends only halfway

across from the east shore. Depths are 12 to 18 feet along the west shore, almost to the south end of the cove."

⑩ **Fair Harbour.** Enter Fair Harbour south of Karouk Island, leaving the two lighted beacons to port. The passage north of the island has two reported rocks, not shown on the chart.

Fair Harbour has a wide dirt launch ramp at the head, with a small campground and ample parking. A dirt road leads from Zeballos to Fair Harbour, the only road access to Kyuquot Sound. This is a popular trailer boat launch point. A good-sized public wharf, with a long float, is at the head. If the float is full, anchor in approximately 60 feet.

⑩ **Fair Harbour Marina & Campground.** (250) 483-3382; fairharbourmarina@gmail.com; www.gatewaytokyuquot.com. Open all year. Limited moorage, gas, diesel, propane, water, garbage drop, boat launch. No power on the docks. This is the only fuel in Kyuquot Sound. A small store carries fishing tackle, ice, convenience food.

⑪ **Dixie Cove.** Dixie Cove indents the east side of Hohoae Island, and is a wonderful anchorage. Enter south of Copp Island, through a narrow but deep passage to the first of two anchorages. The outer anchorage is approximately 30 feet deep, with good holding. Another narrow passage leads to the inner cove, completely secluded, with rock cliffs on one side. Depths here are approximately 18 feet, mud bottom with excellent holding. Landing on shore is a problem, so you're restricted to the boat. As a place to put the hook down, though, Dixie Cove is highly recommended.

⑫ **Petroglyph Cove** (Blue Lips Cove). In his excellent book, *Exploring Vancouver Island's West Coast*, Don Douglass describes this previously-unnamed anchorage and calls it "Petroglyph Cove." In the second edition of his book, Douglass acknowledged that others had not been able to find the petroglyphs. Hulsizer reported finding what looked like a faded pictograph (red ochre painting) and noted that the local name for the cove is Blue

Lips Cove—because when residents went swimming the water was so cold their lips turned blue. Petroglyph, Pictograph or Blue Lips, the cove is located near the mouth of Amai Inlet, roughly due west of Amai Point. The narrow entry is hidden until you're right on it. The channel shallows to a least depth of 12 to 18 feet, but has no hazards. Once inside you are protected. While in our opinion Petroglyph Cove is not as pretty as Dixie Cove, it is an excellent spot.

Volcanic Cove. Exposed to the north, small, no room to swing. Temporary only for small boats, in our view.

⑬ **Rugged Point Marine Park**. Rugged Point marks the southern entrance to Kyuquot Sound. Our notes read, "Wow!" The beaches on the ocean side are spectacular, and deserve a visit. Anchor along the inside beaches in 18 feet on a kelp-covered hard sand bottom, and dinghy ashore. The Pacific swell, though diminished, can get into the anchorage. The anchorage is protected from southeasterlies and westerlies but is subject to occasional nighttime outflow winds. Be sure you anchor far enough offshore to avoid swinging onto shallows if outflow winds develop.

A trail, now upgraded with a boardwalk, leads through the park to the ocean beaches. Bear and cougar prints have been sighted, so be noisy. Once on the ocean beach, you will find a series of paths leading around headlands all the way to the Kapoose Creek. Some of the paths are steep and involve climbing ladders or using ropes for assistance.

Cachalot. Cachalot, the site of a former industrial whaling center, makes an interesting lunch stop or afternoon exploration. Locate it by finding the abandoned pilings between Cachalot Inlet to the east and Cachalot Creek to the west. Although pronounced locally as "catch a lot," the name means sperm whale in French (and in French would be pronounced "caa-shaa-low"). The whaling center operated between 1907 and 1926, then served as a pilchard reduction plant until the 1940s.

Anchor off the old pilings in 30 to 60 feet of water and take the dinghy ashore. You'll find old whale bones, crockery, and miscellaneous hardware on the beach, and rusty equipment in the forest. Next to the creek, a ferrocement statue of a sperm whale serves as a memorial to the whales that were processed at this site. The statue was placed there by Vancouver Island artist Wayne Adams in the 1970s. Hulsizer gives the history of the site in her book *Voyages to Windward*.

When anchoring, avoid the drying shoal on the north end of the site near the river and be sure to anchor in at least 30 feet of water to avoid your anchor being entangled in kelp.

Kyuquot Sound to Esperanza Inlet. Depending on the course chosen, it is approximately 13.5 miles between Rugged Point and the entrance to Gillam Channel, which leads into Esperanza Inlet. In good

Walters Cove Resort caters to fishing guests but accommodates cruising boats by reservation. Meals are excellent.

visibility the route through Clear Passage is smooth and interesting. In poor visibility, we would head seaward from Rugged Point to entrance Buoy *M38*, then turn southeastward toward Gillam Channel.

Clear Passage to Tatchu Point. Clear Passage takes you about 4 miles along the coast in waters protected by the Barrier Islands, past a steady display of rugged rocks and rock islets. The channel is free of hazards. To enter Clear Passage, leave Grogan Rock to starboard, watching carefully for the rock to port, marked by kelp, that dries at 4 feet. Heading down-island, we got a little close to Grogan Rock, and the depths came up sharply. We moved off to port and they went back down. You will have no trouble identifying Grogan Rock. It is an awful 23-foot-high black pinnacle and it commands attention. Lay a course to take you north of McQuarrie Islets, and exit Clear Passage leaving McQuarrie Islets to starboard. The rocks and islets along Clear Passage all look alike. It helps to plot a waypoint at the spot where you intend to turn to exit past McQuarrie Islets. Clear Passage is also a good route when heading north. Leave McQuarrie Islets and Grogan Rock to port.

The island just south of Grassy Isle is a good place to hunt fossils. "We anchored south of Clark Island and took the dinghy ashore to a shell beach on the southeast corner of the island. The fossils were just lying on the beach. We recommend doing this on a calm day only. With a more detailed metric chart, it might be possible to find anchorage between Grassy Isle and Clark." [*Hulsizer*]

Local fishermen say the waters from Jurassic Point past Tatchu Point can be an "ugly patch of water." Use caution and careful judgment.

⑭ **Rolling Roadstead** (Catala Island Provincial Park). Rolling Roadstead offers acceptable anchorage in fair weather. From the west the approach can be tricky. Douglass and Watmough describe the approach in their books. Careful navigation is called for, including the finding and identifying of the various rocks and reefs in the entrance. The hazards are easily identified, either by the breaking surf or kelp growing in the shallows. With the hazards accounted for, the entry is reported to be safe. All agree that it should be run in fair weather only, with good visibility.

If you're coming down from Tatchu Point, especially in a fresh westerly, it's easier to enter via Gillam Channel, leaving Black Rock and Entrance Reef to port and approach Rolling Roadstead from the southwest. Anchor in the lee of the point of land that juts abruptly from Catala Island.

Catala Island, which protects Rolling Roadstead, is a provincial marine park. The beach on Catala Island is beautiful. Several sea caves are accessible.

Gillam Channel. Gillam Channel, more than one-half mile wide and well-buoyed, is the safe entrance to Esperanza Inlet. Approaching, leave the entrance buoy *M40*

At anchor in lovely Hankin Cove

and buoy *M42*, which marks the west end of Blind Reef, to starboard. Leave buoy *M41* to port, and continue into Esperanza Inlet.

ESPERANZA INLET

Esperanza Inlet is on the west side of Nootka Island, and ultimately connects with Nootka Sound. The inlet is part of the "inside route" through this portion of the coast. This route is served by three communities—Zeballos, Tahsis, and Gold River—and by the Esperanza Mission, with its fuel dock and excellent water. The waterways are beautiful, and contain several good stopping places. Tahsis Narrows connects Esperanza Inlet with Tahsis Inlet on the Nootka Sound side, and is not difficult to run.

Nuchatlitz Inlet. Reader Don Thain reports that Mary Basin is a delightful and protected anchorage with good holding in mud. A pretty waterfall on Laurie Creek is reachable by dinghy on a 7-foot tide. The inner basin is a tidal lagoon.

⑮ **Nuchatlitz Provincial Park.** Nuchatlitz Provincial Park is a beautiful and interesting stop with a well-protected anchorage. It's a favorite among kayakers and campers. The area contains a number of archeological treasures, including burial canoes on land and burial caves on the outer islands.

The entry to Nuchatlitz is very complex with numerous rocks and reefs; a careful study of the charts is warranted. Inside, a large bay has a uniform bottom with approximately 30- to 40-foot anchoring depths. In good weather, if you choose an anchoring spot where you can see over the islands towards the northwest, you may be rewarded with a magnificent sunset. The anchorage can be absolutely calm when the wind dies in the evening, but you can hear the surf breaking on the outer islands.

The abandoned Indian village of Nuchatlitz is on the shore of a 44-meter island marked Indian Reserve, above a marvelous beach. At low tide you can walk the drying sand bar from the reserve island to a second 44-meter island to the west. Although the village was

moved from this site to Espinosa in the 1980s, the site is still visited by the band. Local kayak tours use it as a landing site.

A number of private homes dot the shores of a privately-owned unmarked island on the south side of the anchorage. Private buoys mark the route past submerged rocks to homes on the island's back side and to a shallow lagoon. Use Chart 3676, which reflects hydrographic survey work performed between 1992 and 1996 at the cost of many survey launch propellers.

The easy but long entry to Nuchatlitz is from the northeast, passing east of Rosa Island. From there the chart makes the course clear: Follow the winding channel east of the 37-meter and 34-meter islands, and east of the two red spar buoys *M46* and *M48* (Red, Right, Returning). At Buoy *M48* the bay opens up. Both Douglass and Yeadon-Jones describe a second, more direct entrance, leaving the light on the 37-meter island (known locally as Entrance Island) to starboard as you enter.

⑯ **Queen Cove.** Queen Cove is a short distance inside the entrance to Port Eliza, the first inlet to port as you enter Esperanza Inlet. It is a safe and satisfying spot to put the hook down and go exploring, although not as beautiful as Nuchatlitz on the east side of Gillam Channel. Queen Cove is a popular anchorage among island circumnavigators. Anchor here and you'll soon have company. The cove is well protected, and has excellent holding in 20 to 40 feet. It is large enough for several boats to swing. We have received reports that the Queen Cove Band collects a fee for anchorage. A cabin with a dock is at the north end of Queen Cove. The Park River enters at the north end, and makes for good dinghy exploration.

The most protected anchorage is the nook at the south end of Queen Cove, between the little island and the rock that dries at 3.4 meters (11 feet). Swinging room is a little restricted, but the anchorage is workable. We overnighted in Queen Cove, anchored in the wider and much more exposed northern area. At 5:00 p.m. the wind came in, and built to about 25 knots before dying at sundown. We sailed back and forth on

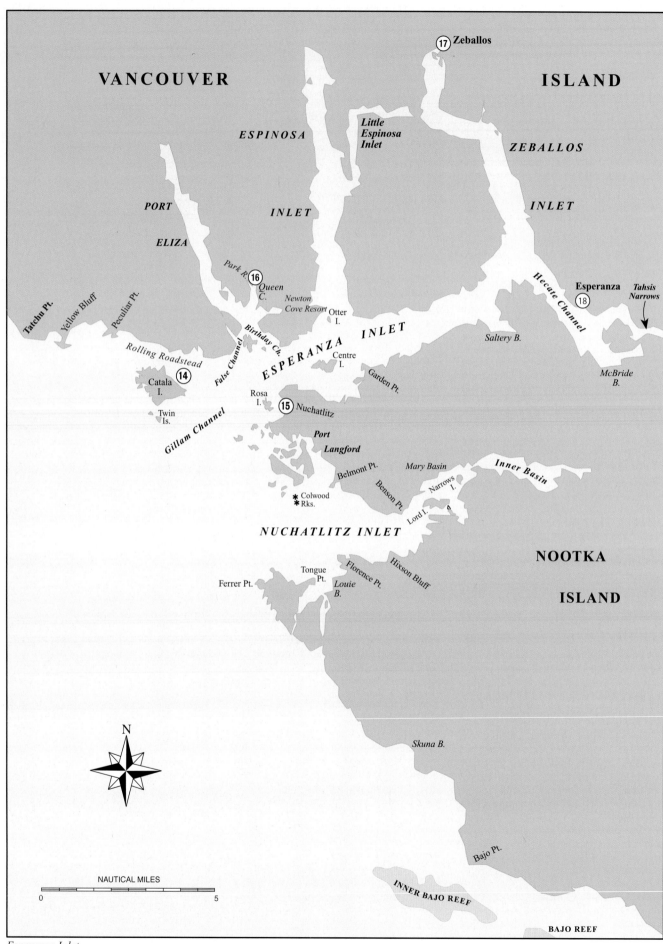

VANCOUVER

ISLAND

⑰ **Zeballos**

ESPINOSA

Little Espinosa Inlet

ZEBALLOS

PORT

ELIZA

INLET

INLET

Park R.

⑯ Queen C.

Newton Cove Resort

Otter I.

Hecate Channel

Esperanza

⑱

Tahsis Narrows

Tatchu Pt.

Yellow Bluff

Peculiar Pt.

Birthday Ch.

ESPERANZA INLET

Saltery B.

Rolling Roadstead

False Channel

Centre I.

McBride B.

Catala I.

⑭

Rosa I.

⑮ Nuchatlitz

Garden Pt.

Twin Is.

Gillam Channel

Port Langford

Belmont Pt.

Mary Basin

Inner Basin

✳ Colwood
✳ Rks.

Benson Pt.

Narrows I.

NUCHATLITZ INLET

Lord I.

NOOTKA

Tongue Pt.

Florence Pt.

Hixson Bluff

ISLAND

Ferrer Pt.

Louie B.

N

Skuna B.

NAUTICAL MILES

0   5

INNER BAJO REEF

Bajo Pt.

BAJO REEF

Esperanza Inlet

384

Zeballos is bounded by impressive mountains.

our anchor, but we didn't budge. [*Hale*].

Espinosa Inlet. Espinosa Inlet is deep and high-walled. No place to anchor. The Native village of Ocluje is located at its head.

Newton Cove Resort. (877) 337-5464; info@nootkamarineadventures.com; www. nootkamarineadventures.com. Monitors VHF 06. Call ahead for availability. Moorage, 30 & 50 amp power, restaurant, lodging, fishing charters, fish packing. Fuel dock has gas and diesel, ice, and bait. Located near the mouth of Espinosa Inlet.

⑰ **Zeballos.** www.zeballos.com. Zeballos (pronounced "Ze-BAH-los") is the most unexpected town on the west coast of Vancouver Island. While other settlements range from fishing camp (Winter Harbour) to bustling town (Tofino), Zeballos stands alone.

The trip up Zeballos Inlet is an especially scenic one, with bulbous-topped odd-shaped mountains, and sheer rock faces rising above the shores. Zeballos is a mining town that looks like Cicily, Alaska, the fictional town made famous by the television show *Northern Exposure*, with wandering streets, false-fronted buildings, and a museum. The town is built at the mouth of the Zeballos River, next to mountains that go *straight up.*

The museum, located on the main road heading out of town, is one of the town's main attractions. It's small but fascinating, with mining paraphernalia, photographs, and a full-scale model of a mine entrance. In 2016 it was staffed by a full-time curator, but in previous years has not always been open regularly. If you arrive at the museum during the workweek and no one is there, inquire at the municipal hall and someone will give you a tour.

The town recently constructed a boardwalk trail through the Zeballos River estuary. It's a beautiful walk along the river.

Much gold has been taken out of the highly mineralized mountains around Zeballos. Over dinner at the hotel on our first visit, we talked with a wildcat prospector whose eyes burned bright as he told of pockets of gold still waiting to be taken. He insisted that he didn't have gold fever, *but he knew where the gold was.* [*Hale*]

Tie up at the public dock, to the right of the fuel dock as you approach. Pay telephones are at the head of the dock and on the seaplane dock. The village has a wharf to the left of the fuel dock, but it is for large vessels, loading and unloading only. The small float next to the wharf is for short-term (a few hours) tie-up. A bird-viewing platform overlooks the estuary.

A fish-processing plant is shoreward of the fuel dock and is one of the town's economic mainstays. It's a good place to purchase chipped ice.

Provisioning: Cruising boaters often ask whether they should stop at Zeballos or Tahsis for provisioning. The answer is you may need to stop at both for everything you need. At present, no good store exists in Zeballos. The store near the fuel dock carries ice cream and convenience foods, as well as frozen meat and bread, and liquor. The Rosa Island General Store also offers limited items including staples, snacks, and cigarettes. Fruits and vegetables were in short supply at both stores. Zeballos is a good place to spend the night. The inlet leading to the town is long and beautiful. There's no point going both ways in one day.

⑰ **Zeballos Fuel Dock Inc.** P.O. Box 100, Zeballos, BC V0P 2A0; (250) 761-4201. Open all year. Gasoline, diesel, propane, kerosene, petroleum products, some marine supplies. Candace Saulkner is the owner.

⑰ **Village of Zeballos Municipal Wharf.** (250) 761-4229. Open all year. For large vessels, loading and unloading only. The small float next to the wharf is for short-term (a few hours) tie-up. Some overnight moorage with permission. Access to power and water if absolutely necessary.

⑰ **Zeballos Small Craft Harbour.** P.O. Box 99, Zeballos, BC V0P 2A0; (250) 761-4991. Monitors VHF 06. Open all year with 400 feet of moorage, 30 amp power, year-round washrooms & showers, water, waste oil collection, all tide launch ramp, long term parking (launch ramp is run by the village). A sign on the east side of the easternmost dock warns of shallow water, but the Hulsizers report finding 2.7 meters when sounding the depth with a lead line at low tide.

Map:

Vancouver Island

N

Washrooms
Showers

Parking

All Tide
Launch Ramp

Zeballos
Store

Zeballos Small
Craft Harbour
Tel. 250/761-4333
VHF 06

Zeballos Municipal Wharf
Tel. 250/761-4229

Load & Unload
Only

Mid-Island
Ice

200 ft.

200 ft.

Zeballos Fuel Dock
Tel. 250/761-4201
VHF 68

Zeballos
Inlet

Zeballos

The floats at Zeballos are well maintained, with power and water.

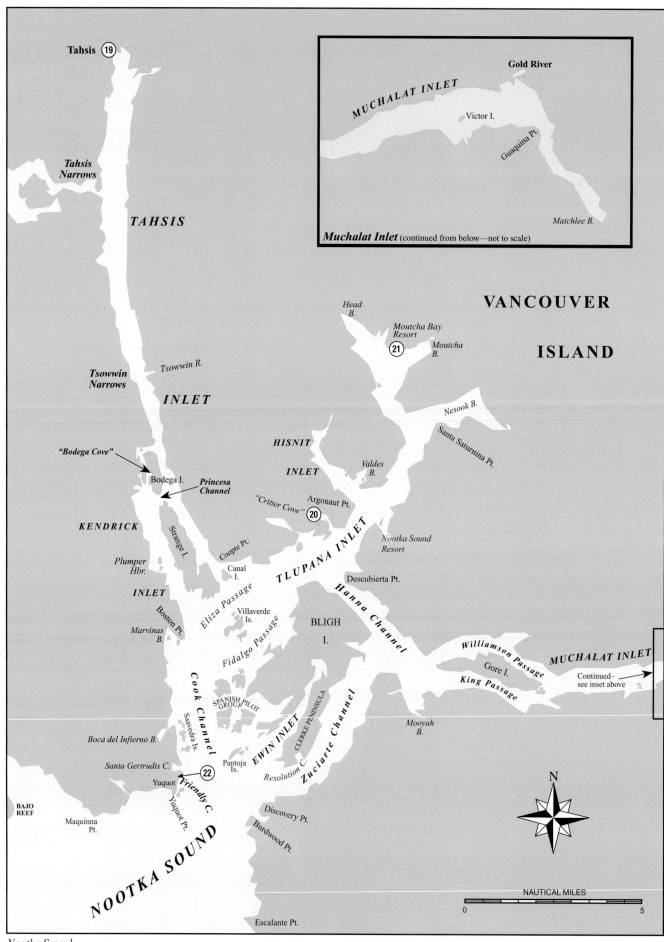

Tahsis ⑲

Tahsis Narrows

TAHSIS

Tsowwin R.

Tsowwin Narrows

INLET

VANCOUVER

ISLAND

Head B.

Moutcha Bay Resort ㉑

Moutcha B.

Nesook B.

Santa Saturnina Pt.

HISNIT

INLET

Valdes B.

"Bodega Cove"

Bodega I.

Princesa Channel

"Critter Cove" ⑳

Argonaut Pt.

Nootka Sound Resort

KENDRICK

Strange I.

Coopte Pt.

TLUPANA INLET

Descubierta Pt.

Plumper Hbr.

Canal I.

Hanna Channel

INLET

Eliza Passage

Villaverde Is.

BLIGH

I.

Williamson Passage

MUCHALAT INLET

Boston Pt.

Gore I.

Marvinas B.

Fidalgo Passage

King Passage

Continued— see inset above

SPANISH PILOT GROUP

Cook Channel

Saavedra Is.

EWIN INLET

CLERKE PENINSULA

Mooyah B.

Boca del Infierno B.

Pantoja Is.

Zuciarte Channel

Santa Gertrudis C.

㉒

Resolution C.

Yuquot

Friendly C.

Discovery Pt.

BAJO REEF

Yuquot Pt.

Maquinna Pt.

Burdwood Pt.

NOOTKA SOUND

N

Escalante Pt.

NAUTICAL MILES

0   5

Inset (top right):

Gold River

MUCHALAT INLET

Victor I.

Guaquina Pt.

Matchlee B.

Muchalat Inlet (continued from below—not to scale)

Nootka Sound

386

⑱ **Esperanza (Nootka Mission).** P.O. Box 368, Tahsis, BC V0P 1X0; (250) 483-4162; www.esperanza.ca. info@esperanza.ca Monitors VHF 06. Fuel dock open all year from 7:00 a.m. to 9:00 p.m. with gasoline, diesel, lube oil. Excellent water, phone service and free Wi-Fi for one hour for customers. A small store, with fishing gear and limited groceries, is on the fuel dock; no alcohol or tobacco. Moorage is available at the dock for boats up to 120 feet in front of the old boathouse, except during the month of July; call ahead. The mission runs camps for local children. When a camp is in session, facilities may not be available.

Esperanza is the home of the Nootka Mission. Its story goes back to 1937, when the Shantyman Mission began a hospital at Esperanza. This was in the tradition of the Mission, founded in northern Ontario in 1907 to serve shanty dwellers in outlying areas. The Esperanza hospital no longer operates and the property is now owned by the Esperanza Ministries Association, serving people of the west coast of Vancouver Island. The property is immaculately kept. The fuel dock is an important source of revenue.

Inquire about availability for visiting boaters. Showers, washrooms, some 15 amp power, water, ice, and laundry are available. Sometimes, fresh Esperanza-grown produce and canned cheesecake are available for purchase.

Tahsis Narrows. Tahsis Narrows connects the Esperanza Inlet side of Nootka Island with the Nootka Sound side. From the chart, one would think reversing tidal currents rage through the narrows four times a day, but they do not. The narrows are deep and free of hazards, with little tidal current activity. Passage can be made at any time.

TAHSIS INLET

Tahsis Inlet (Tahsis is pronounced with a short-a, as in cat) is long and narrow, and bounded by mountains. The wind funnels and blows up-inlet or down, depending on conditions. The normal situation in prevailing westerly winds is for light or outflow winds in the morning and strong inflow winds in the afternoon, building stronger as you approach the town. But during extended periods of warm weather, strong outflow winds can also develop, especially at night and early morning. Gale-force easterlies rarely reach upper Tahsis Inlet, making it a good place to wait out a storm.

⑲ **Tahsis.** At the head of the inlet the sawmill town of Tahsis once had full facilities, but the mills closed and have been dismantled. The loss of the mills just about killed the town. Now, Tahsis is struggling but surviving. Outsiders bought the houses at bargain prices, which, at least initially, gave the economy a small boost. Through it all, the Westview Marina has remained an outstanding operation.

In town, the Tahsis Supermarket has consolidated many of the operations previously run by others. The Supermarket sells groceries, liquor and fuel. It also has a small cafe. This is a small town, and grocery selection is limited. Tahsis Building Centre, a hardware store, is just north of the Supermarket. A post office is located at the other end of town, near the seaplane dock.

The Tahsis library, in the municipal building, has free Wi-Fi and an excellent view. It's a wonderful place to while away a stormy afternoon.

⑲ **Westview Marina & Lodge.** P.O. Box 248, Tahsis, BC V0P 1X0; (250) 934-7672; (800) 992-3252; info@westviewmarina.com; www.westviewmarina.com. Monitors VHF 06. The fuel dock has gasoline, diesel, lubricants, and marine parts. Mechanic available 24/7. Washrooms, showers, laundry, free Wi-Fi, small store with ice and good gift selection, licensed restaurant with patio, and the Island Attitude Coffee Café. The Café opens at 5:00 a.m. during the summer. Moorage with 15, 30 & 50 amp power and potable water. Kayak rentals and eco tours. Courtesy car available. Email your provisioning list a week ahead and they'll have it ready for you.

This marina, at the head of Tahsis Inlet, is set up to serve the summer flotilla of small sportfishing boats. Cruisers are welcome, too, and the marina has just about anything a cruising boater might need. Reservations recommended May to September, but the marina will always try to fit you in. The restaurant has live music and steak dinners on Friday nights, June through September. Each year, we hear good things from readers, praising the facilities and the treatment they receive. The marina is neat and attractive, the people helpful, and the fuel dock easy to approach.

Tsowwin Narrows. The major navigation danger in Tahsis Inlet is Tsowwin Narrows, created by the outfall from the Tsowwin River. A beacon marks the edge of the shoal. Pass between that beacon and another beacon on the west shore of the inlet. Remember that beacons are attached to the earth, and shoal water can extend into a channel from a beacon. Give each beacon a good offing.

While we did not see much debris, Tahsis Inlet is reported to have considerable drift and deadheads, depending on logging activity. Keep a close watch on the water ahead.

Princesa Channel. Princesa Channel runs between Bodega Island and Strange Island, and connects Tahsis and Kendrick inlets. A route through Princesa Channel gets a boat out of the Tahsis Inlet chop and cuts some distance off a passage for southbound boats heading to Friendly Cove, but the Tahsis Inlet entrance to Princesa Channel is narrow and partly guarded by underwater rocks.

From Tahsis Inlet to Kendrick Inlet (east to west) the problem is the flood tide. The flood current flows northward into Tahsis Inlet, and a boat entering Princesa Channel will find a definite northward set to its course. This northward set will tend to put the boat onto a submerged rock charted about 200 feet north of the Princesa Channel light, at the east entrance to Princesa Channel. Don Douglass, in his book *Exploring Vancouver Island's West Coast*, believes the rock is closer to 100 feet from the light. Whether 100 feet or 200 feet, the rock is not far away. The goal is to wrap around the Princesa Channel light but avoid yet another charted rock south of the light, while not being set onto the rock 100 to 200 feet north of the light. Chart 3675 shows the rocks clearly. Study the chart and you will understand not only the challenge but the decisions required to meet the challenge.

We ran Princesa Channel in a stout flood current and had no problems. In our case, we ran south in Tahsis Inlet until the Princesa Channel light bore 235° magnetic, then turned toward the light. We kept the light on our nose (we had to crab to make good our course) until the light was close aboard, then laid off to starboard to give the light 50 feet of clearance, and entered the channel. The key was to be aware of the rock 100 to 200 feet north of the light and keep our course south of that rock. Once past the light we held a mid-channel course and waltzed on through. [*Hale*]

Bodega Cove. Douglass calls this previously unnamed anchorage "Bodega Cove" and

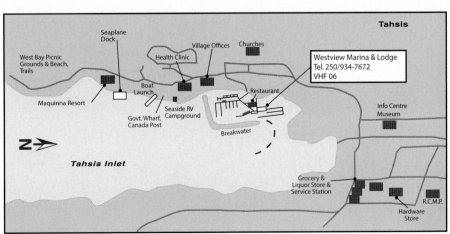

Tahsis Inlet

we see no reason to argue. Bodega Cove lies at the head of Kendrick Inlet, between Nootka Island and Bodega Island. The area has been logged, so the scenery is not that of primeval forest. Protection is excellent, however, and the shores are accessible. A reef extends from the Nootka Island side of the entrance. Favor the eastern, Bodega Island, side. The recommended approach is to divide the entry channel in half, then split the eastern, Bodega Island, portion in half again (in other words, three-quarters of the way toward the eastern shore), and run down that line.

A large log dump and booming ground is on Nootka Island near the head of Kendrick Inlet. When it's in operation, you can watch huge machines dumping piles of logs into the water.

NOOTKA SOUND

Nootka Sound is where European influence in the Northwest began. Although Captain Cook first landed at Resolution Cove in 1778, it was at Friendly Cove that Captain Meares built the *Northwest America*, 48 feet on deck, the first ship ever built on the west coast, and launched it in 1788.

The long arms (Muchalat Inlet and Tlupana Inlet) that reach out from Nootka Sound have few anchorages, and they tend to be deep. The Port of Gold River is at the head of Muchalat Inlet. The town of Gold River is 9 miles from the dock. Trailerable boats, most of them here for salmon fishing in Nootka Sound, are launched at Gold River.

㉔ Critter Cove. Critter Cove is the name given by Cameron Forbes to this previously unnamed spot about 1 mile south of Argonaut Point on Tlupana Inlet. Cameron has established a sportfishing resort in the cove and named it after his nickname of "Critter," when he played hockey. The inner cove is no longer suitable for anchoring.

The Island Attitude Coffee Café at Westview Marina.

㉔ Critter Cove Marina. P.O. Box 1118, Gold River, BC V0P 1G0; (250) 412-6029; info@crittercove.com; www.crittercove.com. Fuel dock carries mid-grade gasoline, oil, ice, bait, coffee, convenience food, fishing tackle, and ocean-themed pottery. Fuel dock hours are 10:00 a.m. to 6:00 p.m. in June, and 8:00 a.m. to 9:00 p.m. in July and August. Moorage, cabins, lodge rooms, suites, restaurant, showers, washrooms. No power or water on the docks. Showers are for overnight guests only.

Cameron Forbes, one of the nicest guys you'll meet, has quite a sportfishing camp here. Most of Critter Cove is on floats, including the licensed restaurant and some of the accommodations. The Critter Cove Cafe is open for breakfast, lunch and dinner. Boaters who are not overnight guests are welcome at the cafe. There are also self-contained beach cottages on the land adjacent to and behind the floating portion of the resort. Most of the boats at Critter Cove are trailered into Gold River, where they are launched. They do have room for a few visiting cruisers.

Nootka Sound Resort. (877) 337-5464; VHF 06 info@nootkamarineadventures.com; www.nootkamarineadventures.com. Call ahead to check moorage availability. Moorage, power, water, restaurant, lodging, fishing charters. Located in Galiano Bay.

Hisnit Inlet. Hisnit Inlet extends north from Tlupana Inlet. Hisnit is one of the few anchorages in Nootka Sound that is well-protected, shallow enough for convenient anchoring, and large enough for a number of boats. Two submerged rocks lie almost mid-channel a short distance into Hisnit Inlet. Do not be deceived by the open and safe appearance of the inlet as you arrive or depart. Favor the south shore.

The view of mountains up the stream at the head of the inlet is stunning. A marble quarry once operated on the east shore. Piles of white marble are visible on the beach and in the nearby forest. The quarry itself is buried under fallen trees and is difficult (and dangerous) to locate. Near the head of

It is a short walk from Friendly Cove to this beautiful beach overlooking Nootka Sound.

the inlet on the same east shore is a large rock shaped like a human head.

Anchorage at the head of the inlet is in 40 to 60 feet. It is open but protected. The shoreline is accessible.

㉑ **Moutcha Bay Resort.** (877) 337-5464; info@nootkamarineadventures.com; www. moutchabay.com. Moutcha Bay Resort is a full service marina, with moorage to 150 feet, fuel dock with gasoline, diesel and propane, water, 15 & 30 amp power, pumpout, Wi-Fi, and a concrete launch ramp. Washrooms and showers are at the top of the docks. The docks are beautifully built, wide and stable. A small store carries limited groceries, gift items, and ice.

The restaurant is good and features local seafood, meat, and produce. Fishing charters, guided and unguided, are available on a fleet of rental boats. Fish processing and packing is offered. Yurts, chalets, and campsites can be rented. The staff is helpful and courteous. This is a luxury resort with facilities to match.

Ewin Inlet. Ewin Inlet indents the south side of Bligh Island some 3 miles, with no anchorages until the head is reached. The cove to the west at the head of the inlet is quite protected and has depths of 30 to 40 feet. "We rounded the little islet in the cove at low tide, about 100 feet off, and the depth sounder abruptly but briefly showed a depth of 15 feet. We suspect it found an uncharted rock." [*Hale*]

Resolution Cove. Historic Resolution Cove is on Bligh Island, near the south end of Clerke Peninsula. In March, 1778, Captain Cook anchored his two ships there and found and fitted a new foremast for the *Resolution*. A flagpole and plaques commemorating Cook's visit have been placed on a knoll above the cove. Anchor in 40 to 50 feet, either with a stern-tie to shore or enough room to swing. You'll probably make your visit a short one. Swells from the ocean wrap around the Clerke Peninsula into the cove.

Santa Gertrudis Cove. The western cove in Santa Gertrudis Cove is an excellent

anchorage: cozy, good holding, protected. As you enter you will see an island in the northern cove. A submerged rock extends from that island a considerable distance toward the south shore, farther than we expected. Be sure to identify this rock and give it room as you favor the south shore. There is sufficient room to pass between this rock and the drying rock shown off the south shore on the chart. The north cove of Santa Gertrudis Cove, around the island, is foul and tight.

㉒ **Friendly Cove.** Friendly Cove is where Captains Vancouver and Quadra met in 1792 and attempted to negotiate the final details of the Nootka Convention of 1790, in which Spain relinquished to England all its claims to Northwest lands. Hulsizer, in her book *Voyages to Windward*, gives an interesting and succinct explanation of the complicated events in Friendly Cove that brought Spain and Great Britain to the brink of war before they worked out their differences in the Nootka Convention.

Friendly Cove is shallow and fairly protected from typical summertime winds, with good anchoring for four or five boats on a sand bottom. Outflow winds can make Friendly Cove bumpy. Nearly all the land ashore belongs to the Mowachaht Band, and a fee ($12 per person, no credit cards) must be paid for landing. The band has summertime staff on hand who monitor VHF 66A and collect the fee. The landing fee is the same, whether you dinghy in from an anchored boat or tie up at the wharf and floats on the west side of the bay.

When you anchor, be aware that the Uchuck III delivers tourists and freight to the dock regularly. To watch the Uchuck wind its way through anchored boats is awe-inspiring—and terrifying if you're on one of the boats.

A trail runs through campgrounds and above the ocean beach. It passes the Native graveyard and leads to a lake that's good for swimming. Six rental cabins, small and rustic, are just beyond the lake. The spired Catholic church is filled with Native carvings, and has two marvelous stained glass windows. They depict the transfer of authority over the area

from Spain to England in 1792, and were a gift from the government of Spain. A carved welcome figure stands on the far shore of the cove, facing the open sea.

㉒ **Nootka Light Station.** You can walk from the Friendly Cove beach to the Nootka Light Station on San Rafael Island. A well-maintained series of stairs leads up from the beach to the light station. Once at the station, be sure to sign the guest book.

Nootka is a repeater station for Prince Rupert Coast Guard radio, and has considerable radio equipment. Every three hours from early morning until nightfall, the Nootka station reports weather conditions for the marine weather broadcast, including estimated wind strength and sea conditions offshore.

Thanks to the miracle of the Fresnel lens, the light uses only a 35-watt LED bulb to cast a beam that can be seen for 15 miles.

The Nootka Light Station and its light keepers are powerful arguments for retaining manned light stations along the coast. They are invaluable for timely and accurate weather information, and for communication in areas that may not have good cell phone coverage. The lightkeepers monitor VHF channel 82. We are told that many of the lightkeepers maintain an open Wi-Fi signal for visiting boaters.

Estevan Point. Estevan Point is the southwest corner of Hesquiat Peninsula, another of the headlands where winds and seas build and become confused. Estevan Point can be ugly in a storm, but in more settled conditions does not present the challenge found at Cape Cook or Cape Scott. In fog, the problem with Estevan Point is its low, flat terrain, which makes its shoreline a poor target for radar. The rocks more than a mile offshore make Estevan Point unforgiving for the navigator who is off-course.

From Nootka Sound, a rounding of Estevan Point first must clear Escalante Rocks and Perez Rocks, both of them on the west side of Hesquiat Peninsula. Unfortunately for the navigator, no single chart shows all of Estevan Point from Nootka Sound to

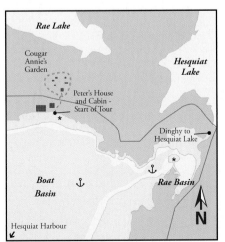

Boat Basin & Rae Basin

Moutcha Bay Resort's lodge is first class.

BOARDWALK PLANKS BEING REPLACED AT HOT SPRINGS COVE BC

Boardwalk at Hot Springs Cove is being rebuilt.
In the fall of 2018, BC Provincial Parks began a project to replace and widen the failing boardwalk at Hot Springs Cove. Located on the West side of Vancouver Island, this remote park site was originally accessible only by boat. Today, a number of Tofino based tour operators bring large numbers of visitors to this park by seaplane and high-speed tour boat. The 2 km (1 ¼ mile) boardwalk, from Maquinna Marine Park dock to the hot springs, has hundreds of individually carved planks commemorating boaters' visits to the park and hot springs. The long history of carved boardwalk planks holds an often surprisingly artistic dated chronology of boat names, dates, and trivia.

History of Carved Planks at Hot Springs Cove
A long time ago, when boats were wood or steel, boaters came to enjoy the hot springs at Hot Springs Cove. The 2 km trail from the anchorage area to the hot springs was a rustic muddy trek. Locals and visiting boaters over time constructed the first boardwalk path by voluntarily bringing individual planks to add to the growing boardwalk. Reportedly, the very first planks were hand-split from sections of logs on-site. Boat names, dates, and messages were inscribed on the planks; and thusly, the record of this unique boardwalk was created.

After a number of years — probably about the time the first fiberglass boats appeared — the original boardwalk and planks needed to be replaced. The boardwalk was rebuilt with all new 2x6 planks and the history of the first planks went with it. However, the tradition of carved planks with boat names didn't die; and very soon after the construction of the new boardwalk, carved boat names and dates began to appear once again.

It's okay to Carve the Planks – But Don't Pick the Flowers
In the more recent past, BC Parks facilitated carved boardwalk planks. BC parks had been providing plank dimensions for those who wanted to pre-carve a plank and leave with park rangers for later installation. To make it even easier, BC Parks sold bare planks which you could carve and leave with them for installation. This is one of those rare instances where it was okay to leave your mark at a park.

As access by seaplanes and tour boats brought increasing numbers of vistors, carved planks appeared from other than boaters. In 2012, a romantic suitor had a carved plank placed on the boardwalk that read "Clara, Will you marry me?" For those who immediately ask the question; it is reported that Clara said "yes."

Where are the artfully carved planks going?
We at Waggoner Guide learned of the boardwalk replacement project during the summer of 2017 and at that time, the future plans for individually carved planks was undetermined. Following the suggestion of the Waggoner Guide team, BC Parks intends to consolidate the best planks and re-purpose them in a special feature within the park. Plans include interpretive signage capturing the history of the carved planks.

Will the Carved Plank Tradition Live-On?
The answer is, NO. Today's safety and construction standards preclude future carvings along the boardwalk. BC Parks expresses their appreciation and thanks the public for participating in the past boardwalk program. The Waggoner Guide team is appreciative that BC Parks is preserving this piece of northwest boating history.

Visitors will continue to have access to the park and hot springs during cruising season.

- Leonard and Lorena Landon, Managing Editors

Hot Springs Cove

Hesquiat Bay in large scale. You will be forced to plot your course on small scale Chart 3603, which doesn't give much close-in detail. Once at Estevan Point, you can use Chart 3674 to continue to Hot Springs Cove.

Especially with the lack of a single good large scale chart for the west side of Hesquiat Peninsula, the general advice is to give Estevan Point "lots of room." Give Escalante Rocks and Perez Rocks lots of room, too. This applies when heading north as well.

Weather Information: The Estevan Point lighthouse provides updated wind, sea, and atmospheric conditions every three hours. Listen to the continuous marine broadcast for the latest weather information.

Hesquiat Harbour. Hesquiat Harbour is protected from westerly winds, and Hesquiat Bar (24 feet deep) knocks down the Pacific swell. Crossing the bar may be unsafe in a southeasterly; storm seas can break over it. Anchorage depths can be found in **Boat Basin** located at the northeast end of Hesquiat Harbour; but Rae Basin provides better protection since Boat Basin is open to the south. Most of the upland areas around Hesquiat Harbour and Boat Basin are included within the Hesquiat Peninsula Provincial Park. **Rae Basin** is a well-protected anchorage in the northeast corner of Boat Basin and offers bear viewing opportunities at low tide. Rae Basin consists of an outer basin anchorage and an inner basin anchorage. Most boats will prefer anchoring in the outer area of Rae Basin. Anchorage is possible for shallow draft vessels in Rae Basin's inner area. At a tide of 11 feet or higher, you can dinghy into Hesquiat Lake from Rae Basin.

From Boat Basin or Rae Basin, you can take the dinghy to **Cougar Annie's Garden** for an interesting educational tour. Pioneers Ada Anne (Cougar Annie), and husband William Rae-Arthur, cleared land for a homestead in 1915 at Boat Basin where they raised their three children and established a large garden. Today, the garden is maintained as a heritage site with research studies in temperate rainforest ecology. Tours are arranged through the Boat Basin Foundation (www.boatbasin.org); email boatbasinfoundation@gmail.com or call (250) 726-5096 a couple of days before your arrival. Admission is charged to help pay for the restoration and ongoing research there; credit card payment preferred. Field Correspondent Mary Campbell reports that the visit is well worth the $30 donation fee. Land or anchor your dinghy off the beach in front of Peter's house and cabin located along the north shore of Boat Basin. Peter,

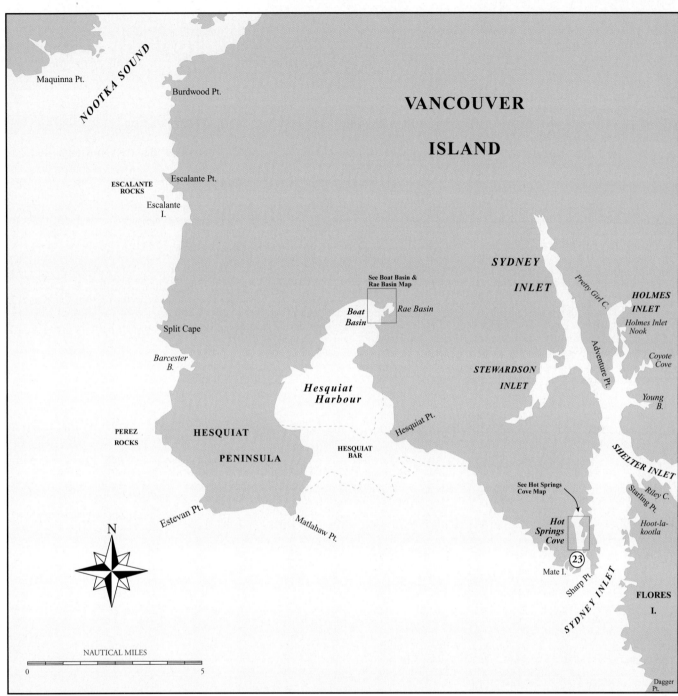

Hot Springs Cove

who acts as guide, will accompany you along the trail to Cougar Annie's Garden.

Hot Springs Cove Area. Hot Springs Cove is adjacent to Sydney Inlet, the northern entrance to Clayoquot Sound. Depending on the points of departure and arrival and the exact course chosen, the distance from Nootka Sound around Estevan Point, past Hesquiat Peninsula, and east to Hot Springs Cove, is approximately 30 to 31 miles. When traveling south, once you are past Chief Matlahaw Point, you can duck into the lee of Hesquiat Peninsula to avoid the worst of the ocean swells.

㉓ **Hot Springs Cove.** www.env.gov.bc.ca/bcparks/. Hot Springs Cove is home to

Maquinna Marine Provincial Park and Protected Area, and **Ramsay Hot Springs**. The park and hot springs are reasons why cruising boats do the West Coast. The challenge of getting to Hot Springs Cove is sufficient to make the reward—a soothing bath in comforting water (no soap, please)—worth the entire trip. In earlier times, most visitors came the hard way, up from Barkley Sound or down from Cape Scott. Now tour boats, floatplanes, and even helicopters carrying visitors who have arrived without effort at Tofino, visit Hot Springs Cove many times a day. An hour by high-speed boat, and they are there.

The cove is easy to enter. Chart 3674 shows that the mouth is open and the channel free of dangers. The marine park public dock

is approximately 1.7 miles farther into the cove from the hot springs themselves. You can anchor in 24 feet, or boats less than 12 meters (40 feet) can tie to the Park dock; self-registration and fee payment box on shore at the Park Information Shelter. Hot Springs Cove is within the Ahousat First Nation territory; the Ahousaht Stewardship Program may collect donation fees for anchorage, look for the yellow *Ahous Hakoon* vessel; they can answer questions and will provide you with a receipt.

A 1.2-mile walk along a well-maintained boardwalk leads to the hot springs. A $3 per person park fee is payable at a drop box near the head of the dock. In the past, visiting craft had a tradition of bringing a plank to add to the boardwalk. On the plank would be carved the name of the boat and the year of the visit. Many of the planks showed remarkable artistic talent. This practice has been discontinued by the parks department. A multi-year project to replace and widen the boardwalk from the dock to the hot springs was started in 2018. Access to the hot springs is open during construction. The hike through the rainforest to the hot springs is easy and beautiful. Toilets are available at the end. The modest will find a pleasant changing room in which clothes may be doffed and a bathing suit put on. Traditionalists will lament that the hot springs no longer can be enjoyed in the old way, sans bathing suit. The place is popular. Although a constant stream of bathers hike the trail and soak in the springs during the day, savvy boaters know that if they come before 9:00 a.m. or after 6:00 p.m., they will share the springs only with other boaters. Note: pets not permitted beyond the start of the boardwalk; alcoholic beverages not permitted within the park.

The B&B boat *InnChanter*, with attached dinghy floats, is normally anchored nearby and may have space for visiting boaters for dinner or breakfast. Call Shaun on the *InnChanter* at (250) 670-1149. Hot Springs has campsites, often used by kayakers. A cell phone tower in the Native village across from the Park now provides four to five bars of cell phone service (Bell).

CLAYOQUOT SOUND

Clayoquot Sound is a series of inlets and passages with entrances at both its north and south ends. By traveling inside Clayoquot Sound you can explore many coves and anchorages, and avoid 20 miles of ocean swells. Tofino is the only major town, although fuel and some groceries are available at Ahousat. There is cell coverage around Tofino and Hot Springs Cove, but coverage is spotty in outlying areas and inlets.

Much of Clayoquot Sound is within the traditional territory of the Ahousaht First Nation, who have established a Stewardship Guardian Program. First Nation representatives of the **Ahousaht Stewardship Program** collect donation fees at various anchorages within the Clayoquot Sound in support of their programs which include care for beaches and trails, search and rescue support, management and cultural interpretation for visitor access, and training in first aid. Receipts for payment are provided via a representatative aboard the *Ahous Hakoon* vessel. Guardians monitor VHF channel 65A and may be contacted if you are in need of support. For more information call Ahousaht Stewardship Operations at (250) 731-6957.

Sydney Inlet. Sydney Inlet is the northern entrance to Clayoquot Sound. It is adjacent to Hot Springs Cove and leads approximately 11 miles into the mountains of Vancouver Island, with several good anchorages. Rounding Sharp Point after leaving Hot Springs Cove, be aware of two charted but unmarked off-lying rocks. The first is fairly close to Sharp Point and easy to avoid. The second is about 0.2 mile off. Most boats will choose to pass between the two rocks. Be sure you know where you are. Once in Sydney Inlet, the fairway is open and unencumbered. Reader Don Thain reports that sea otters are now well established in Sydney Inlet and that crabbing is poorer where the sea otters have colonized.

Sydney Inlet Unnamed Cove. This is the cove that lies behind the 65-meter island about 0.5 mile south of Hootla-Kootla Bay, at latitude 49°21.85'N on the east shore of Sydney Inlet. (Douglass, in both editions of *Exploring Vancouver Island's West Coast,* mistakenly calls this cove Hootla-Kootla, but the chart leaves it unnamed and calls the next cove to the north Hootla-Kootla.) Enter from the south. You'll see a beautiful white beach. Although the water is a little shallow near the beach, it's the prettiest spot in the cove. You could also anchor at the north end of the cove, behind the 65-meter-high island. Do not attempt to enter the cove at the north end. It is foul.

Young Bay. Young Bay, on the east side of Sydney Inlet, is a lovely place to anchor, although a little deep until you get close to shore. The middle is 50 to 60 feet deep, but along the shore it's easy to find 35- to 40-foot depths. On the south shore a stream connects with Cecilia Lake, one-half mile away. A rough trail leads up the stream to the lake. Trout fishing at the lake is reported to be good. A copper mine and a pilchard reduction plant both operated here in the past. Only a few concrete platforms and pieces of machinery remain.

Enter Young Bay right down the middle, to avoid shoals that extend from either side. Once inside you will see a small islet with trees on it. Pass to the south of that islet.

Bottleneck Bay (Coyote Cove). This is an otherwise unnamed bay that cruising guide author Don Watmough fell in love with. Bottleneck Bay is located just north of Young Bay, east of Adventure Point. The entrance is narrow but deep. Inside, the high, treed hills make the feeling of seclusion complete. Easy anchoring in 30 feet.

Holmes Inlet Nook. An intimate back cove in Holmes Inlet, with room for 2 to 3 boats over a mud bottom; anchoring depths of 20 feet. Swinging room is tight so you may want to stern-tie.

Hootla-Kootla Bay. Hootla-Kootla Bay is located about 0.25 mile north of the 65-meter-high island on the east shore of Sydney Inlet, approximately 1.6 miles from the mouth of the inlet. This cove is known locally as Baseball Bay, but the chart shows it as Hootla-Kootla Bay. The entrance is shallow, and is partly blocked by a charted rock just south of mid-channel. Divide the channel north of the rock in half, and enter the northern half "mid-channel." "Least depth on the depth sounder was 12.5 feet near the bottom of a 3.6-foot low tide at Tofino. Anchorage is good once inside." [Hale]

Riley Cove. Riley Cove is just east of Starling Point, on the northwest tip of Flores Island. It may not be the best choice for an anchorage. The cove is open and uninteresting, and a little deep for anchoring until close to the head. At the head, Riley Cove is divided into two smaller coves; the cove to the west has a sandy beach. A rock, not shown on the chart, is just off the point that separates the two coves. A shoal extends from the east shore near the entrance of Riley Cove. Favor the west shore.

Steamer Cove. Steamer Cove is on the north side of Flores Island, behind George Island. The small cove at the southwest corner of Steamer Cove is well protected and has easy anchoring depths.

㉔ **Bacchante Bay.** Bacchante Bay, at the east end of Shelter Inlet, is a dramatic anchorage, with steep cliffs on both sides, an inviting grassy meadow at the head and a snow-capped mountain beyond. The narrow, shallow entrance is hidden until you are close. Bacchante Bay is part of Strathcona Provincial Park. Minimum depth at entry is 18 feet; a shallowing bar, just outside the entrance, has a minimum depth of 16 feet.

Bacchante Bay has ample room to anchor in 40 to 50 feet. Holding is excellent. If you

Lennard Island Lighthouse along the west coast of Vancouver Island. Photo by John Forde, The Whale Centre.

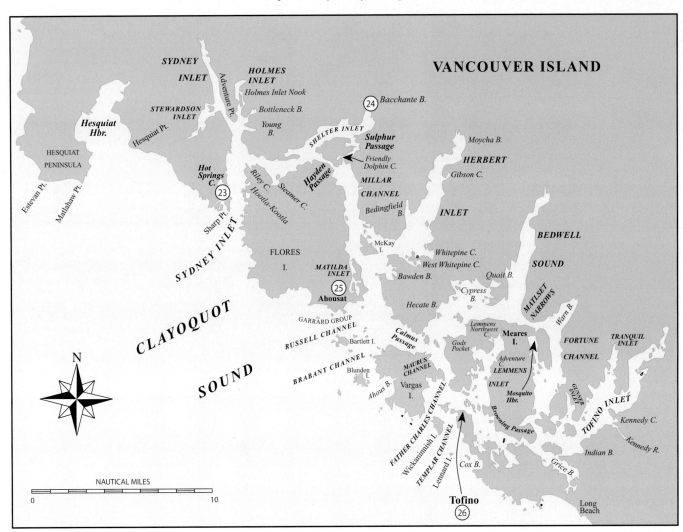

Clayoquot Sound

run to the head of the bay, watch for abrupt shoaling off the meadow. At high tide explore Watta Creek by dinghy.

Readers Mike and Sandy Cecka report fouling their anchor in Bacchante Bay. They anchored on the west side of the bay, below steep cliffs. We've had no problem anchoring in the middle of the bay.

Hayden Passage. Hayden Passage is on the west side of Obstruction Island, and connects Shelter Inlet with Millar Channel. Tidal current predictions are shown with Hayden Passage as a secondary station based on Tofino in the Tide and Current Tables, Vol. 6 and Ports and Passes. The flood sets southeast; the ebb, northwest. Be sure to pass west of the red daymarker beacons (Red, Right, Returning).

Because the flood currents meet at Hayden Passage, you may find that the currents don't behave as predicted. The cautious passage would be at slack water. If transiting sometime other than slack water, maintain a constant watch for current set, and crab as needed to stay in the channel.

Sulphur Passage. Sulphur Passage connects Shelter Inlet and Millar Channel on the east side of Obstruction Island and is far more tortuous

than Hayden Passage. The northern portion of Sulphur Passage is the tricky part. There, the channels twist and turn and are bounded by submerged rocks. Don Douglass ran Sulphur Passage along the east side of the 38-meter island in the northern portion, and reported it to be a period of "high anxiety." Locals favor passing on the west side of 38-meter island, where the Landons found a minimum depth of 35 feet on the south end of the narrow channel, between 38-meter island and Obstruction Island. Tidal current predictions are in Tides & Currents Vol 6 and Ports & Passes as a secondary station based upon Tofino.

Friendly Dolphin Cove. Friendly Dolphin is Douglass' name for the cove that indents Obstruction Island, just inside the south entrance to Sulphur Passage. The cove is pretty, private and appealing. Well protected from wind and current. Anchor near the head in 40 to 50 feet, probably with a stern-tie ashore to control swinging, or in 50 to 60 feet with room to swing. Space for 3 or 4 boats. The Landons reported a pleasant stay early in the season.

Shark Creek. 49°23.95'N/126°04.00'W. "This is a kayakers' secret: a beautiful 70-foot-high waterfall in a chimney, accessible at high

tide by dinghy only. It is located in Millar Channel, just north of Atleo River. Anchor north of the small island and dinghy in. Best in late afternoon when sunlight makes a rainbow on the rocks behind the falls." [*Hulsizer*]

Matilda Inlet indents the southeast corner of Flores Island and is bordered on the east by McNeil Peninsula. Anchorage is possible near the head of Matilda Inlet. From the anchorage, a warm springs in Gibson Marine Park can be visited (best at high tide; at low tide it's a muddy hike) or a trek made to the beach. Don Watmough describes the area in fond detail. The Native community of Marktosis is on McNeil Peninsula. Across the inlet and a short distance north are the store and fuel dock of Ahousat.

㉕ **Ahousat.** General Delivery, Ahousat, BC V0R 1A0; (250) 670-9575. Ahousat, with its general store, fuel dock and marine ways, is on the west shore of Matilda Inlet, at the southeast corner of Flores Island. Ample moorage for transient boaters; high dock with metal facia, may need to adjust fenders. Gasoline and diesel at the fuel dock, washrooms, 15 amp power, showers and laundry, haulout to 30

Ahousat, with a general store, fuel and haulout, has ample side-tie moorage.

feet. Potable water, pay phone, post office, and motel rooms are available. The store is a rough-and-ready place, with a cougar head on the wall, but with luck, it may have what you need: groceries, miscellaneous hardware and marine supplies. No charts or liquor.

Marktosis. Marktosis is the Native village across Matilda Inlet from Ahousat. Carved Native canoes can be seen on the beach and at the shed by the Government Wharf. Docks at the wharf are filled with commercial fish boats and sport fish boats; transient moorage is limited. Permits for the Wild Side Trail can be purchased at the fuel dock; the trail is mostly boardwalk to White Sand Cove (www.wildsidetrail.com). You can anchor south of Ahousat in the bay near the "slightly warm" springs, and take the dinghy back to the village. Leave the dinghy at the Government Wharf and touch base with the band office before exploring further. The fuel dock (250-670-6803) was completed in 2017; rocks make the approach hazardous; larger boats should enter only at high tide.

Gibson Marine Park. Gibson Marine Park is at the head of Matilda Inlet, past Ahousat. At one time, Hugh Clarke, at the Ahousat General Store, hacked out a trail from the head of the inlet to the hot springs. Boots are necessary on the trail, which transits some boggy areas. Clarke recommends going in at half tide on a rising tide, to avoid tramping across the mud flats. Correspondent Gil Flanagan tells us that you can hike for many miles on the ocean beach to the west. The only problem, Flanagan says, are bands of gravel that make barefoot walking uncomfortable. He adds that the beach is popular with kayakers and tourists from Tofino. The park requests that dogs are kept out of the park as there have been incidents of wolves killing the dogs.

Herbert Inlet. The run up Herbert Inlet is even more spectacular than many other inlets along the coast. High mountains and rock walls line the shores. Deep alpine river valleys

lead away into the mountains. Snowcapped peaks can be seen in the distance.

West Whitepine Cove. Although unnamed, both Watmough and Douglass call this delightful anchorage West Whitepine Cove, and we shall do the same. West Whitepine Cove lies to the west of Whitepine Cove, near the mouth of Herbert Inlet. Entry to the inner bay is along the south side of the 67-meter island. We entered slowly, strongly favoring this island. Rocks were visible underwater and easily skirted. Once inside, the cove is lovely and protected. Bears are reported to frequent the south shore.

A charted rock is in the cove, off the tip of the little peninsula that extends southeast from the 94-meter island. When anchoring, stay away from it.

Gibson Cove. Gibson Cove indents the west side of Herbert Inlet, about 5 miles north of Whitepine Cove. Since Gibson Cove is not on the way to anyplace else, we suspect it sees few visitors. Those who do visit are in for a treat. Gibson Cove is beautiful, but a little deep for anchoring. Although it appears protected, strong afternoon westerlies can bring wind and waves.

Quait Bay. The entrance to nearly landlocked Quait Bay is located on the northeast side of Cypress Bay. Watch for the numerous crab pot buoys in Cypress Bay. From Cypress Bay, enter Quait Bay passing 45-meter island off your starboard side, favoring the port-side of the channel. The chart makes the course clear. A large floating lodge, with no services for boaters, is just inside the entrance on the left. Quait Bay has room for many boats. Anchor nearly anywhere in 20-40 feet of water. Southwesterly winds do find their way into the bay.

The most popular spot is in the little cove in the east corner in about 10 feet. A submerged concrete structure (49° 16.603N 125° 50.843W) lies in the mouth of the two nooks at the back of this cove. The structure dries at 2 feet. A private 40-foot float is located on the north shore.

For a peek at what life is like for Clayoquot Sound's year-round floating home residents, take your dinghy out the entrance of Quait Bay, enter the unnamed cove south of Quait Bay (49° 15.86N 125° 51.57W) and continue all the way to the head of the cove to visit Wayne Adams and Catherine King in their floating garden on their magenta and turquoise floating home. Wayne and Catherine must hold the record for interviews and feature articles about Clayoquot Sound residents.

Matlset Narrows. Matlset Narrows runs to a maximum of 4 knots on spring tides. The flood sets east. Sailing Directions warns of strong tide-rips in the vicinity of the Maltby Islets at the east end of the narrows. We ran the narrows against a west-flowing ebb. We saw definite current activity, but had no problem. We suspect any tide-rips would be on a flood.

Calmus Passage to Heynen Channel. The route from Millar Channel to Heynen Channel via Calmus Passage and Maurus Channel is the beginning of shallower water. The channels are well marked by buoys and beacons but the navigator must stay alert, keep an eye on the depth sounder, and know the vessel's position at all times. Large-scale Chart 3685 is extremely helpful.

Lemmens Inlet. Lemmens Inlet indents Meares Island, just a few miles from the town of Tofino. Be sure to use large scale Chart 3685 while navigating around Tofino and into Lemmens Inlet. The entry channel to the inlet is amply deep, but bordered by drying flats. Once inside, you have your choice of three possible anchorages—although float homes now are moored in all of Lemmens Inlet's coves, so anchoring may be a challenge. Watch for numerous crab pot buoys throughout the Inlet.

Adventure Cove. Adventure Cove, where Capt. Robert Gray built the small schooner *Adventure* in 1792, is filled with history. The beach is easy to land on. While walking in the woods we could almost feel the presence of Gray's Fort Defiance and the shipbuilding activity. Though the area is now overgrown with large trees, some say you can feel as though *something went on here.* Watmough and Douglass describe the history well. Hulsizer discusses it more thoroughly in *Voyages to Windward.* Unfortunately, a floathouse and a fish farm take up most of the cove, leaving little room for anchoring. Discarded fish farming equipment on the beach makes beach access challenging. A reader tells us an uncharted rock lies SSW of the island in the mouth of Adventure Cove.

Lemmens Northwest Cove. Lemmens Northwest Cove is Douglass' name for this anchorage in the northwest corner of Lemmens Inlet. It is identified on the chart by the 39-meter island. Two charted drying rocks east of 39-meter island and a large oyster farm obstruct entrance to the cove. Rows of oyster aquaculture farming fill the area on both sides of these two drying rocks to the shoreline to the northwest. Enter the cove with 39-meter island on your port side and the oyster farm very close on your starboard side. Caution for the charted shoals on the northeast side and north tip of 39-meter island. Bow watch is recommended. Once inside, you'll find good anchoring depths and adequate protection; caution for the charted shallow spot. Several float homes are tucked into various areas of the cove.

Gods Pocket. Gods Pocket is the cove northwest of Lagoon Island, on the west side of Lemmens Inlet. Protection is good, with anchorage in 25 to 30 feet. Aquaculture is in the cove with buoys set in half of Gods Pocket. Three or four float homes are tucked into bights along the northern shore.

Fortune Channel. Fortune Channel connects Tofino Channel with Matlset Narrows, which in turn connects with the waters of upper and western Clayoquot Sound. In Fortune Channel you can choose from three good anchorages: Windy Bay, Heelboom Bay and Mosquito Harbour. Chances are, you won't see much boat traffic in this area.

Mosquito Harbour. Although not as scenic and cozy as Heelboom Bay, Mosquito Harbour is big and open and easily entered. Anchor in 20 feet behind the Blackberry Islets. Approach on either side of the Wood Islets, but from Fortune Channel you'll probably approach by way of Plover Point or Dark Island. Kelp marks the rocks off the north end of Dark Island. Note the location of Hankin Rock. We would trend toward Plover Point before turning to enter Mosquito Harbour.

Heelboom Bay. Heelboom Bay, located near the south end of Fortune Channel, is a good anchorage, surrounded by lush evergreen forests. Room for 3-4 boats. We found outstanding holding in 35 feet. This Bay was the site of a major protest against logging in Clayoquot Sound and is considered almost sacred by some residents. Approaching, favor the east shore and stay well clear of rocks off the western shore. One of these rocks is considerably detached from the shoreline. Chart 3685 helps understanding.

Windy Bay. Windy Bay is beautiful. The south shore is heavily forested, and the north shore is sheer rock wall. Westerly winds accelerate over the saddle at the head of the bay, but they have no fetch to build up seas. With 15 knots of wind outside Windy Bay, we had gusts to 30 knots inside. Anchor in 30 to 35 feet with excellent holding.

Browning Passage and Tsapee Narrows. Rocks abound and shoals threaten. The larger scale Chart 3685 will show you the way. If you are coming from Heynen Channel or Lemmens Inlet, the course will be clear: Pass west of Morpheus Island and east of Buoy Y35, and continue down Browning Passage and through Tsapee Narrows. Note that currents on springs can run to 5 knots near Morpheus Island and 4 knots at the narrows. Go slowly. Look ahead and identify all buoys, islands and visible rocks well in advance. Keep a close reference between your charts and your navigation electronics. Done this way, the passage should not be difficult.

If you are departing Tofino, leave Buoy Y29, opposite the 4th Street dock, to starboard, and run toward Arnet Island until you can safely turn to run south, along the west side of Riley Island. Favor Riley Island to pass clear of the rocks shown on the chart. Once south of Riley Island you are in Browning Passage.

TOFINO INLET

Island Cove. Island Cove is easy to enter around either side of Ocayu Island. Study the chart to avoid the rocks that lie off the southwest shore of the approach. Unfortunately, the hillsides surrounding Island Cove have been logged down to the water's edge and the cove isn't very pretty. Anchor in 40 to 50 feet, close to the west shore.

Gunner Inlet. It's tricky to get into the inlet and not very scenic when you make it. Approach favoring the east shore and use a small low islet with a distinctive white top as your leading mark. Make an S-turn around the islet and follow the chart in. Anchoring depths vary, 20-60 feet.

Tranquilito Cove. Tranquilito Cove is the name Douglass gave this unnamed cove on the east side of Tranquil Inlet, near the head. This cove is secluded and beautiful. The rock wall on the north side has been strikingly sculpted by glaciers. Favor the northern side of the entry to avoid a shoal that extends from the point of land on the south side. Anchor in 20 feet.

Cannery Bay. Cannery Bay, at the mouth of the Kennedy River, provides good protection and is easy to get in. Despite its flat terrain, it's rather pretty. Consider the nook just to port as you enter. Anchor in 15 to 20 feet over mixed mud and sand with excellent holding.

Kennedy Cove. Kennedy Cove is easy to enter by favoring the 68-meter island. Anchor wherever you like in 15 to 30 feet. It's a pretty spot. A private dock and water slide is on the north shore, labeled "ruin" on some charts. Farther in the bay is a private gazebo overlooking the cove from IR Land.

㉖ **Tofino.** If you come from up-island, Tofino will be your first major town since Port McNeill or Port Hardy, and it's more vibrant than either of them. During the summer season, Tofino's bustle and busyness may surprise you. After growing accustomed to the slower life up-island, Tofino, with its commerce, tourists, fast traffic and loud engines, can cause culture shock. Welcome to the city.

As long as you're in the city you might as well spend some money. You can choose from several good restaurants, the kind that serve meals without french fries. Gift shops and galleries—at last!—are available for mementos and presents. The Co-op store, close to the waterfront, is a complete supermarket and will deliver if asked. The Co-op also carries clothes. Showers are available at the 4th Street Dock and at the laundromat at 4th & Campbell. The laundromat has enough machines to do all the crew's laundry in one cycle. Common Loaf is all-organic and features a local favorite: peasant bread. SoBo, open for lunch and dinner, uses locally grown ingredients in their dishes; reservations recommended (250) 725-2341. The "1909 Restaurant" at Tofino Resort & Marina is also excellent. For a guided food tour, contact Tofino Food Tours at 800-656-0713.

Be sure to allow enough time to see all the sights that Tofino has to offer. The Tofino Botanical Gardens (250) 725-1220 located 1.5

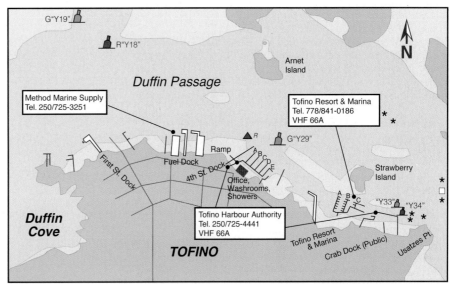

Tofino

miles out of town, is worth a visit and is open daily. A network of paths and boardwalks are contained within the 12 acres of gardens, forest, and shoreline. Tofino is known for its beautiful beaches and has several surf shops in town. You often see surfboards strapped to bicycles, as surfers make their way to the beaches. Surf reports are given for North & South Chesterman Beach and Cox Beach. Other beaches include Mackenzie, Middle, and Tonquin Beaches, with Tonquin being the closest to Tofino.

The Tofino Transit Shuttle (250-725-2871) on Campbell Street can take you out to the beaches, or call the Tofino Water Taxi (250-725-8844). Bike rentals are available next to the Tofino Bus station. A dedicated bike path follows the highway south of town; plans include extending the bike path to Ucluelet junction. Bus service was recently extended to Ucluelet.

The Big Trees Trail on nearby Mears Island is another worthwhile excursion. A dinghy dock on the west side of the island is available while hiking the 3 km loop trail, which takes about 2 hours. A small fee to hike the trail is collected by a guard on duty, or you can use the on-site payment box. Some of the largest trees in B.C. are found here, ranging in age from 1,000 years to 1,500 years old. The largest tree is known as "the hanging garden." The Tofino Water Taxi makes stops at the Big Trees Trail.

Opitsaht First Nations Village, located on the southwest end of Mears Island, is the oldest, continuously run Native settlement. A campground/hostel above the beach is a starting point for the popular Lone Cone Trail to the summit of Lone Mountain, contact (250) 725-2169 or go to www.LoneConeTrail.ca for more information. The Water Taxi from Tofino can take you to the Opitsaht Dock.

Hot Springs Cove, located 28 nautical miles northwest of Tofino, is a popular destination. The high-speed Tofino Water Taxi makes runs to Hot Springs Cove and is a nice option for visitors arriving in Tofino by private boat or by car.

From seaward, enter Tofino via Templar Channel. While Chart 3673 gives a good overall view for the close navigation needed, we strongly recommend large scale Chart 3685. Note how the buoyed fairway twists and turns to avoid shallows. Identify each buoy as you proceed, and leave the buoys off the proper hand.

From the north, enter Tofino via Deadman Pass, narrow and bordered on both sides by drying flats. Be sure to use large scale Chart 3685. Note that while you may be returning to Tofino, the buoyage system in Deadman Pass is not. As you head south in Deadman Pass you will leave the red buoys to port.

The approach to Tofino, whether through Templar Channel or Deadman Pass, is one of the few places on this coast where you need to carefully watch the currents. Time your arrival for slack water to avoid the strong currents that swirl around the docks.

Stay close to the docks once at Tofino. A serious drying reef lies a short distance off.

Anchoring can be a challenge because of strong currents that sweep through the harbor. Although Tofino has several public docks, moorage for visiting boats is limited. The District of Tofino Dock (called the Whiskey Dock) near Grice Point is closest to the Co-op and the liquor store, but is busy day and night with water taxis and locals. Moorage may be available at the Method Marine Supply fuel dock. It tends to be full during the busy season, but you can check.

The most popular moorage is the Tofino Harbour Authority 4th Street Public Dock. Farther east, the Tofino Resort & Marina may have space, but without advance reservations the docks often are taken by their sport fishing guests. The easternmost public dock is called the Crab Dock. The Crab Dock is a longer walk from the commercial district, however. Currents can make landing on a flood tide tricky. Do not proceed eastward past the Crab Dock. A major rock blocks the channel.

㉖ **Tofino Harbour Authority 4th Street Public Dock.** P.O. Box 826, Tofino, BC V0R 2Z0; (250) 725-4441; tofharbour@gmail.com; www.tofinoharbour.ca; Monitors VHF 66A. Maddy Prince is the harbormaster. Open all year, 20 & 30 amp power, water, pumpout, washrooms, showers, laundry, for fee Wi-Fi. This is the closest moorage to Tofino, convenient to the commercial district. Watch the current. Office open daily 11:00 a.m. to 1:00 p.m. in summers; open Tuesday, Wednesday and Thursday during the off season.

A shoal extends into the channel from a piling east of the easternmost dock, and leads across the ends of B, C and D docks. Dredging was completed in 2017. Minimum depth is 8 feet at 0 tide.

This is a commercial fishing harbour with some recreational moorage available on E-dock, first-come, first-served. Rafting encouraged up to two deep. Permanent spaces used for guest moorage when available. The Harbour Authority tries to fit everyone in. A short-term two-hour dock in front of the ramp is available while shopping, suitable for dinghies and small craft.

The dock water system operates by a 'loonie' timer, similar to pay showers. Make sure all the other faucets are closed, then feed a loonie to the timer, which pressurizes the dock system for about 15 minutes. Water pressure is good and one dollar should get you about 100 U.S. gallons of water. Be all set up before you start the system. Car day parking available for puchase.

㉖ **Method Marine Supply.** Box 219, 380 Main Street, Tofino, BC V0R 2Z0; (250) 725-3251; sbernard@methodmarine.ca; www.methodmarine.ca. Open all year. Gasoline, bio-diesel, lube oils, propane, water, ice, divers' air, vacuum waste oil disposal.

Method Marine Supply is Tofino's fuel dock and marine supply source.

Moorage has electrical hookup, but moorage often is fully reserved in the busy season. This is a modern, well-run facility, with a good chandlery that carries a wide range of equipment and supplies, including sport fishing gear, fishing licenses, bait, snacks, foul weather wear, and charts. Storm Light Outfitters, a well-stocked outdoor gear store, is right behind, up on the street.

㉖ **Tofino Resort & Marina.** 634 Campbell St, Tofino, BC V0R 2Z0; (844) 680-4184 ext. 002; (778) 841-0186; marina@tofinoresortandmarina.com; www.tofinoresortandmarina.com. Monitors VHF

66A. This is a high-end resort with secure gated docks, open all year. 15 & 30 amp power, water, showers, laundry, Wi-Fi and fitness room. Most of the slips and side-tie are for smaller boats with limited side-tie moorage for medium sized boats on the 'T' ends of several docks. There is a side-tie area for yachts up to 130 feet with 100 amp power. Reservations requested. The fuel dock has marine gasoline, no diesel. Harbour Air Service available from the dock. The upland '1909 Restaurant' offers fine dining, with casual eats available at the adjacent 'Hatch Pub'. Adventure tours to Hot Springs Cove, hiking excursions through National Parks, and

whale/bear watching are offered through the upland resort/marina office.

㉖ **Tofino Harbour Authority Crab Dock.** P.O. Box 826, Tofino, BC V0R 2Z0; (250) 725-4441; tofharbour@gmail.com Monitors VHF 66A. Maddy Prince is the harbormaster. This is the easternmost dock on the Tofino waterfront. Some transient recreational moorage for vessels up to 40 feet, 20 & 30 amp power, water, Wi-Fi. First-come, first-served. Use caution upon approach as there are rocks off the northeast end of the docks and a shoal located just north of the dock; check your charts. Bull rails were replaced in 2018. Docks move considerably so fender well. New chains to secure the docks are planned to be installed during 2019.

CLAYOQUOT SOUND TO UCLUELET

It is approximately 19 miles from Lennard Island, at the southern entrance to Clayoquot Sound, to Whistle Buoy *Y42* offshore from Ucluelet Inlet. These 19 miles cross the ocean face of the Pacific Rim National Park; but since you'll probably be about 3 miles out, you won't see much of the park. Sailing Directions says to stay 2 miles off the coast; Watmough likes 3 miles. So do we. Plot a waypoint for Whistle Buoy *Y42*, go 3 miles offshore from Lennard Island, turn left, and make for the buoy. In fog, radar is a big help in avoiding

the many fish boats that work these waters. Sport fishing boats that travel full speed even in thick fog are especially worrisome. Absent a GPS and radar, in fog we would go out to at least 30 fathoms deep and follow the 30 to 40 fathom curve to Buoy *Y42*.

Weather Information: The Lennard Island lighthouse, just outside of Clayoquot Sound, and the Amphitrite Point lighthouse, just outside of Barkley Sound, provide a picture of outside weather conditions. Listen to the continuous marine broadcast for the latest weather information or you can attempt to call the lighthouse keepers on VHF 82.

Amphitrite Point. Amphitrite Point, at the end of the Ucluth Peninsula, can present a challenge. The essential navigation problem is to get around Amphitrite Point while staying well clear of Jenny Reef, shown on the chart, yet staying off the Amphitrite Point shoreline. The problem is made more difficult in fog, when the radar may lose Buoy *Y43* against the shoreline.

Carolina Channel is the entry suggested by Sailing Directions, except in thick weather, when Carolina Channel can be too rough for safe navigation. The outer entrance to Carolina Channel is marked by Whistle Buoy *Y42*, about 0.5 mile offshore. The channel leads past Bell Buoy *Y43*, which lies but 300 meters off the rocky shore. In reduced visibility, life can get interesting when you're trying to raise Buoy *Y43*. If you have trouble seeing the buoy against the rocky shoreline, the light structure on the east side of Francis Island could serve as a leading mark.

As you approach Carolina Channel, leave Whistle Buoy *Y42* close to starboard, and turn to a course of 037° magnetic to raise Buoy *Y43*. After passing close south of Buoy *Y43*, Sailing Directions suggests using the summit of South Beg Island as a leading mark. It should bear approximately 075° magnetic. Run approximately 0.2 mile until the eastern extremity of Francis Island is abeam, then round Francis Island and enter Ucluelet Inlet.

BARKLEY SOUND

Depending on your direction, Barkley Sound is the first sound on the way north or the last sound on the way south. Barkley Sound is named after English Capt. Charles William Barkley, who in 1787 sailed into the sound on his ship *Loudoun*, which he had illegally renamed *Imperial Eagle* (Austrian registry) to avoid paying a license fee to the East India Company. With Capt. Barkley was his 17-year-old bride, Frances Trevor Barkley. Capt. Barkley came to trade with the Indians for furs. You'll find reminders of the Barkleys in many names around Barkley Sound, including Imperial Eagle, Loudon and Trevor Channels.

Barkley Sound is roughly square in shape, measuring 15 miles across its mouth and approximately 12 miles deep, not counting the 20-mile-long canal to Port Alberni. The sound is dotted with rocks and islands, and the

waters are famous for their excellent fishing. A cruising boat could spend weeks in Barkley Sound, fishing, exploring, and moving from one nook to another. In fact, many boats do just that, coming directly from Puget Sound, Oregon, or the Strait of Georgia region.

During the summer months, fog often forms just offshore. In minutes, it can sweep in, even with no wind. It is essential, therefore, that the navigator know the vessel's position at all times. GPS and electronic navigation will prove useful in foggy conditions. Radar is a big help. Most boats cruising Barkley Sound, large and small, have radar. Even with electronic help, the navigator must remain alert and aware.

If approaching from up-island, you will probably enter Barkley Sound from Ucluelet. Note that a course across Sargison Bank from Ucluelet to the Broken Group takes you very close to a rock that lies approximately 0.7 miles east of Chrow Island. The rock is shown on the chart not with a rock symbol, but by a depth of 0.5 meters. It is easy to overlook while scanning the chart for hazards.

If approaching from the Strait of Juan de Fuca or Oregon, leave Cape Beale at least one-half mile to starboard, which will leave the offshore rocks a safe distance off. If the boat is coming from the United States, it must go directly to Ucluelet for Canadian Customs, although it may duck into Barkely Sound to get out of the ocean swells. A good option is to enter Imperial Eagle Channel, leave Effingham Island to port, and proceed west between Clarke and Benson Islands to Loudoun Channel and Ucluelet.

In Barkley Sound you will find superb exploring everywhere: Pipestem Inlet, the Pinkerton Islands, Julia Passage, the Chain Group, the Deer Group and the famous Broken Group. Settled summer weather makes it possible to anchor in any of hundreds of coves or nooks and explore by dinghy.

We do not cover all the areas mentioned above, an unfortunate consequence of limited exploration time. Other references—especially Douglass' *Exploring Vancouver Island's West Coast* are excellent resources. In the end, your own inquisitiveness and derring-do will determine the range of your exploring.

Ucluelet. Ucluelet is pronounced "You-CLOO-let." With moorage, fuel, provisions, repairs and good dining, the village of Ucluelet (pop. approx. 1800) is the commercial center of Barkley Sound. The channel leading into Ucluelet is well buoyed. Following the rule of Red, Right, Returning, you will have no problems. Spring Cove, to port a short distance inside the channel, is where fish boats used to discharge their catches. The plant deep in the cove is closed and the docks are posted with No Trespassing signs. Spring Cove is a good anchorage.

Ucluelet has one fuel dock, located on the town side. Several fish processing plants and public docks used by large commercial boats are also on the town side of the inlet. Small public docks used by the Ucluelet Native

Band are on the east side of the inlet, across from town.

West of the north tip of Lyche Island, the Ucluelet Small Craft Harbour is the principal marina, and the one we recommend. Another marina to consider is Island West Resort, on the west side of the inlet just before the turn to the small craft harbor. The docks are built almost entirely for trailerable boats. They have no designated guest dock, so call ahead by phone.

In town, halfway up Ucluelet Inlet, Pioneer Boat Works (250-726-4382) has a marine railway for haulout and repairs. Their chandlery, next to the ways, has a good stock of marine supplies, commercial and sportfishing tackle, and charts. Cruisers will find what they need there. For engine repairs and electrical services, contact Erik Larsen, LLC (250-726-7011). They are the only shop on the Vancouver West Coast that deals with diesel engines.

Around the winding streets of Ucluelet you will find gift shops, art galleries, including an excellent Native Gallery, the Ucluelet Aquarium, dining from casual to quite nice, a large co-op grocery, an excellent bakery, general merchandise store and other essential services.

It's a pleasant hike or bike ride out the road to the Coast Guard Station at Amphitrite Point Lighthouse. The Wild Pacific Trail begins just beyond He-Tin-Kis Park, near the Coast Guard Station.

In Ucluelet Inlet, Lyche Island can be passed on either side. If passing on the west side (the town side), check Chart 3646 and leave the buoys and beacons off the proper hands.

Customs: Ucluelet is the only customs reporting station on the west coast of Vancouver Island. Open all year. The 52 Steps Dock in Ucluelet Inlet, a short distance beyond buoy *Y44*, is the official Customs dock. Call (888) 226-7277 by cell or at the on-dock payphone.

㉗ **Eagle Marine, Ltd./Columbia Fuels.** 1231 Eber Road, Ucluelet, BC V0R 3A0; (250) 726-4262; www.columbiafuels.com. Open 7 days a week all year, summer 7:30 a.m. to 6:00 p.m., winter 8:00 a.m. to 5:00 p.m. Gasoline, diesel, lubricants, water, ice, bait, tackle, convenience items, garbage drop.

Whiskey Landing. 1645 Cedar Rd, Ucluelet, BC V0R 3A0, Canada; (250) 726-2270; www.whiskeylanding.com; info@whiskeylanding.com. Guest moorage for hotel guests.

㉘ **Ucluelet Small Craft Harbour.** 200 Hemlock St., Ucluelet, BC V0R 3A0; (250) 726-4241; (250) 725-8190; kcortes@ucluelet.ca. The marina has 30 amp and some 50 amp power, water, washrooms, tidy showers and laundry, pumpout, garbage drop, recycle, waste oil disposal, and for-fee Wi-Fi. The outside basin, before entering the large main basin, has three floats that are usually for commercial boats, with a pumpout at the

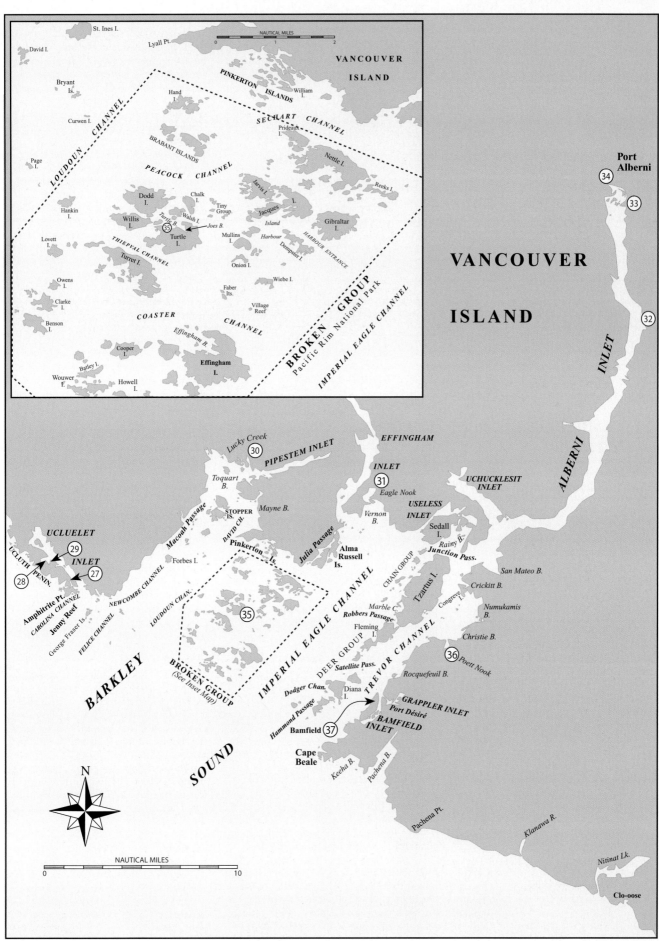

Barkley Sound

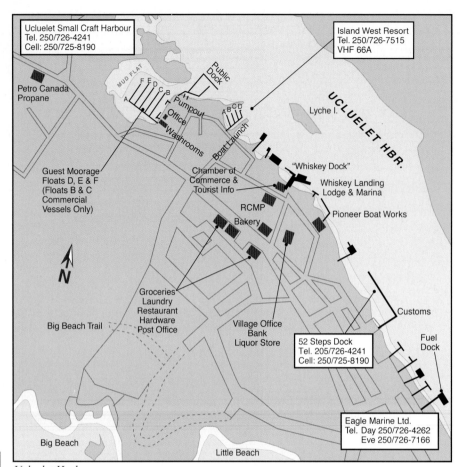

Ucluelet Harbour

bottom of the ramp. Docks B & C in the main basin are marked for commercial boats only; docks D, E & F are for recreational and commercial boats. The facility is completely protected, well maintained, and quiet. It's where most cruising boats tie up. The staff is attentive and helpful. Kevin Cortes is the wharfinger.

㉘ **Island West Resort.** Box 879, 1990 Bay St., Ucluelet, BC V0R 3A0; (250) 726-7515; fish@islandwestresort.com; www.islandwestresort.com. Open all year, reservations accepted. Limited moorage for larger boats up to 40 feet, call ahead. A busy sportfishing resort, often fully reserved a year ahead for July and August. Limited 15 amp power, washrooms, seasonal showers and laundry, free Wi-Fi, portapotty dump, launch ramp, marine supplies, ice, convenience groceries, excellent pub. Fishing charters.

㉙ **52 Steps Dock.** (250) 726-4241; (250) 725-8190; kcortes@ucluelet.ca. Located on the west side, north of the fuel dock and south of town, open all year with moorage on both sides of a 450 foot float. Water, no power, no restrooms or showers. This facility is managed by the Small Craft Harbour wharfinger. Pay by phone or when the wharfinger makes his rounds at the dock, twice daily. 52 Steps dock is a designated customs dock.

WESTERN BARKLEY SOUND

The western part of Barkley Sound, from Ucluelet to Pipestem Inlet and over to the Pinkerton Islands, is relatively open and easily run. As long as you stay in the middle, Newcombe Channel and Macoah Passage present no problems. They lead to the Stopper Islands and, beyond them, to Pipestem Inlet. Pipestem Inlet is where the magical falls at Lucky Creek await.

Stopper Islands. The Stopper Islands are quite pretty and beg exploration by dinghy or kayak. Anchor between Larkins Island and the large island.

Toquaht Bay Marina.   www. secretbeachcampground.com. On the west side of Toquaht Bay behind a breakwater constructed of orange railroad tankers. Boat launch and moorage for trailerable boats.

Pipestem Inlet. Pipestem Inlet is long, beautiful and bordered by high mountains. Most of the inlet is too deep for anchoring, but there are several good anchorages near the mouth and at the head of the inlet. Anchorages near the mouth are behind **Bazett Island** in the southwest cove and southeast cove. The southwest cove has a fish farm work float and a number of large yellow buoys. The southeast cove is in the little thumb-shaped inlet; an adjacent shore

provides stern-tie opportunities. A third anchorage option at the mouth of the inlet is on the north side of **Refuge Island**, a bit east of the 16-meter island. These anchorages are within easy dinghy commute to Lucky Creek. At the head of the inlet, you can tuck behind 32-meter island, or continue to the very end to anchor in a basin formed by a shoaling area.

㉚ **Lucky Creek.** The late John Schlagel, fearless longtime explorer, did not suggest that we see Lucky Creek, he instructed us to see Lucky Creek, and he was right. This is a window-of-opportunity trip and the window corresponds with high tide.

We suggest taking the outboard-powered dinghy up to the falls an hour before high water and coming out an hour after. Former Managing Editor Sam Landsman took a shallow-draft, outboard powered 22' C-Dory in, and wouldn't want to go in anything much bigger.

The entrance is directly across Pipestem Inlet from Bazett Island. After crossing the shallow entry (bordered by meadow grass and wildflowers), the channel winds through marvelous mature forest, with overhanging cedars. The deeper part of the channel tends to follow the outside of the bends, river-style. The water is clear. We kept our eye on the bottom. Close to the falls the bottom shoals and we sought out the narrow, U-shaped channel to follow.

Suddenly, before our eyes was a storybook waterfall directly out of Walt Disney's imagination. Seeing that waterfall, we knew Tinker Bell was around; she was just too quick for us to see. When you go, tie the dinghy off to the side and climb up to a series of bathing pools. Be careful, the rocks can be slippery. And remember, just as Cinderella had to run when the clock tolled twelve, you cannot stay. If you tarry too long the falling tide will close you in.

You probably won't be alone at Lucky Creek. The lodges and resorts in the area are fully familiar with Lucky Creek and the boat drivers know the channel well. We got to Lucky Creek a half-hour after high tide, and the guests were all leaving—at top speed in the narrow waterway that was unfamiliar to us. They came right at us and swooped past, all smiles and happiness as we splashed through their wakes. No matter, the trip was worth it. [*Hale*]

Entrance Inlet. Entrance Inlet indents Vancouver Island at the northeast corner of Mayne Bay. Anchor in the outer basin in 40 feet. During the day you will have boat traffic from the fishing resort in Cigarette Cove.

Cigarette Cove. You can anchor in Cigarette Cove, but the resort takes up much of the space. The entry is narrow and bounded by rocks. If you pay attention, you will have no problems.

Southeast Cove. This cove is open to the west, but is good in settled weather. Anchor in 35 to 40 feet.

Take the train to visit Historic McLean Mill, a working steam-powered mill.

Pinkerton Islands. Far from the wildness of the outer islands, the Pinkerton Islands are north of the Broken Group, next to Vancouver Island. The Pinkertons are small and protected, with narrow channels, and are ideal for gunkholing. Watch for rocks. The easiest anchorage is in the cove northwest of Williams Island. Unless several boats want to share the cove, no stern-tie is required. A study of the chart will suggest a number of other possibilities, most of which will require a stern-tie to shore.

UPPER BARKLEY SOUND

Effingham Inlet. Sailing Directions says Effingham Inlet is high, steep and deep, with few if any anchoring possibilities. Correspondents Bruce and Margaret Evertz explored Effingham Inlet and here is their report:

"We found anchorage in the bay on the west side of Effingham Inlet about one-quarter of the way in. The center of the bay is fairly flat and approximately 75 feet deep. Our anchor set well at 49°00.959'N/125°10.659'W. Another secure spot would be at the south corner of the bay in 30 to 40 feet with a stern-tie. We were told that boats often anchor on the north side of the small peninsula near John Islet, at the entrance.

"While several oyster farms are in the lower part of Effingham Inlet, we saw few signs of man farther in. It isn't Princess Louisa, but like Pipestem Inlet it's still pretty. The sides are high, steep and forested, with many interesting cliffs. We saw only two waterfalls. We didn't see many anchoring opportunities unless you want to stern-tie, and there were many small bights for that. We were told that afternoons can be windy, but the trees grow right to the high water line so we don't think the winds amount to much." [*Evertz*]

(31) **Jane Bay/Franks Bay.** This bay, known locally both as Jane Bay and Franks Bay, is not named on the chart. It is located at the back of Barkley Sound, connected by a narrow but safe passage with Vernon Bay at 48°59.80'N/125°08.80'W. Anchor, carefully, near the head before the flats

shoal too much. A water line is clearly marked with yellow buoys. Or tie up at Eagle Nook Lodge.

(31) **Eagle Nook Resort and Spa (Vernon Bay).** P.O. Box 289, Ucluelet, BC V0R 3A0; (800) 760-2777; (604) 357-3361; info@ eaglenook.com; www.eaglenook.com. Monitors VHF 73. Marina is immediately to starboard as you enter the bay. Moorage to 100 feet, 30 & 50 amp power, water, Wi-Fi, washrooms and showers. Reservations recommended, especially for larger boats. The lodge's exterior is Pacific Northwest style, interior is traditional lodge. Open May to mid-September. An elite high-end restaurant, spa, and guided fishing are available to visiting boaters. Well-maintained walking trails lead through the forest.

Useless Inlet. Useless Inlet contains a number of aquaculture leases and recreational float homes. Entry to the inlet is made interesting by a series of large rocks that are covered except at lower stages of the tide. The rocks were covered when we were there and the wind rippled the water, making them hard to see. The obvious safe entry is along the north shore, to avoid the rocks in the middle. We attempted that route twice but didn't feel comfortable. We did see several trailerable sport fishing boats roar in and out of Useless Inlet, running between the rocks in the middle. They knew where the channel was; we didn't.

Correspondents Bruce and Margaret Evertz went into Useless Inlet. They report that "Useless Nook," described in the Douglass book, has an oyster farm in it, and a sign on shore that says, "No anchorage or trespassing in bay—oyster farm."

Rainy Bay Cove. Located on the north side of Junction Passage on Seddall Island. Tucked behind the smaller Boyson Islands, a narrow passage leads into Rainy Bay Cove, home to a quiet community of float cabins along the western shore. Good anchorage at the north end of the cove to the west of the shoaling nook; anchoring depths of 30 feet over a mud bottom.

ALBERNI INLET

Alberni Inlet begins between Chup Point and Mutine Point, where it meets with Trevor Channel and Junction Passage. The inlet continues some 21 miles into the heart of Vancouver Island to the town of Port Alberni. Alberni Inlet is narrow and high-sided. A well-protected detached public float is in San Mateo Bay, near the mouth of the inlet, and in Hook Bay about half way up the inlet. China Creek Marina, about 6 miles down-inlet from Port Alberni, has limited guest moorage for larger vessels. Tidal current flows are less than 1 knot both directions, but the surface current can flow as fast as 3 knots when wind and current direction are the same.

In the summer, an up-inlet thermal wind develops at 1:00 p.m. ("You can set your clock by it," says a friend in Port Alberni), and will increase to 25 to 30 knots by mid-afternoon. The wind produces a short, uncomfortable chop. We would run Alberni Inlet in the morning.

Port Alberni. In our opinion, the McLean Mill National Historic Site, accessed via a 1954 diesel locomotive train, is the highlight and reason to visit Port Alberni. Port Alberni offers several moorage options for pleasure boaters. Port Alberni is also very popular as a saltwater trailer boat destination, giving. trailer boaters safe and easy access to Barkley Sound, one of the most diverse and interesting cruising grounds in the Northwest. It's a 21-mile run down the Alberni Inlet to Barkley Sound.

To get to Port Alberni from the mainland, trailer the boat to the BC Ferries terminal at Tsawwassen, near the U.S. border, or to the Horseshoe Bay terminal, north of Vancouver. Large, comfortable ferries will take you to Nanaimo's Duke Point or Departure Bay terminals. (Or, if you are coming from the

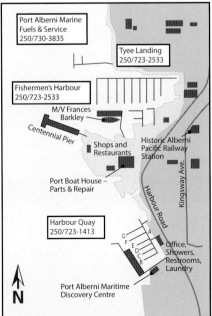

Port Alberni

south, take the private ferry Coho from Port Angeles, Wash. to Victoria.) Our trailer boat friends tell us the fares for trailered boats are not inexpensive, so be prepared. From the Duke Point ferry terminal at Nanaimo, an easy and often beautiful 1½- to 2-hour drive on paved highway will take you to Port Alberni.

Along the way, be sure to stop at Cathedral Grove for a walk through a towering forest of 1000-year-old cedar, hemlock and Douglas fir. The trail is easy and well-maintained. If you hurry along, you can walk it in 20 minutes. If you linger to absorb more of the majesty, it could take about an hour. Interpretive signs explain everything.

To reach Port Alberni you do have to go over a 1230-foot-high mountain pass, with an 8 percent grade on the east side and a 6 percent grade on the west. Be sure your rig has enough power and brakes.

Once at Port Alberni, you'll find good launch ramps at Clutesi Haven Marina at the mouth of the Somass River, and at China Creek, located 6 miles down the Alberni Inlet. Long-term parking is available at both locations. All the marinas are operated by the Port Alberni Port Authority; www. portalberniportauthority.ca.

In Port Alberni you'll find complete services including hospital, shopping, marine supplies and a boatyard. The "Port Boat House" (250-724-5754) provides service for trailerable boats.

A 1954 diesel locomotive pulls a train that runs from downtown Port Alberni to the McLean Mill National Historic Site, the only working steam-operated sawmill in Canada. It takes about 35 minutes each way. The McLean Mill is a fascinating tour, with interpretive signs to explain what you are looking at. The cookhouse, blacksmith shop, workers' housing and other buildings have been restored. Mill demonstrations and a guided theatrical experience are offered as scheduled. Logs are in the mill pond. A trip to the McLean Mill is a step back in time. The entire family will enjoy it. Call (250) 723-1376. Better yet, for latest information and schedules see www.alberniheritage.com.

For information on other attractions and events, contact the Alberni Valley Chamber of Commerce, (250) 724-6535.

Salmon Festival: Port Alberni's Salmon Festival & Derby (www.salmonfestival.ca) is held Labour Day weekend each year at Clutesi Haven Marina. We are told that the Somass River is the third largest salmon stream in B.C. Only the Fraser River and the Skeena River have larger returns.

Haulout: Alberni Engineering and Shipyard has haulout and complete repairs for boats to 100 feet. Call (250) 723-0111.

Fuel: Marine gasoline and diesel are available at Tyee Landing in Port Alberni and in China Creek.

San Mateo Bay. Located at the junction of Trevor Passage and Junction Passage on the east side. A 70-foot public float, managed by Port of Alberni Port Authority, offers overnight side-tie moorage at no charge. Moorage available on both sides of the float, which is detached from shore. The float, tucked behind Bernard Point, provides shelter from most winds. Depths in the bay are too deep for anchoring.

Uchucklesit Inlet. A branch near the entrance of Port Alberni Inlet, Uchucklesit leads northwest to Snug Basin. The east shore of this deep inlet is lined with float homes, summer cabins and year-round residences; watch your speed and wake. The variety of homes makes for an interesting cruise. About half way up the inlet on the east shore near Case Creek is the small community post office on floats; this is also the landing for the M/V Barkley Sound passenger vessel. No services for pleasure boaters. Anchorage can be found in **Snug Basin**, with good protection in depths of 50-60 feet over a flat mud bottom.

Green Cove. Located east of Cheeyah Island at the entrance to Uchucklesit Inlet, Green Cove offers protected anchorage from all except northwesterly winds which have fetch. Anchorage depths are as charted, with a flat mud and sand bottom. Upland homes and cabins dot the shoreline, some with fanciful names. In 2018 the Landons noted a non-operational fuel dock just inside the cove entrance on the north shore of Strawberry Point peninsula. No log booms were observed in the cove in 2018.

Limestone Bay. Located on the west side of Alberni Inlet, just north of the entrance to Uchucklesit Inlet. Use only the southwest entrance into the bay. The small bay has space for one or two boats to anchor at the northwest head of the bay. Two float cabins, both with log breakwaters, are not a factor for anchoring. Anchoring depths of 12 feet over mixed mud and sand, protection from northerlies but open to south westerlies.

㉜ **China Creek Marina & Campground.** (250) 723-9812; www.campchinacreek. com; chinacreek@alberniport.ca. Open April through September, 88 slips and 2300 feet of side-tie moorage, 4-lane launch ramp. Gasoline, diesel, propane, 15, 20 & 30 amp power, washrooms, showers, laundry, ice, garbage drop, fish cleaning stations, playground. Campsites and RV sites are adjacent. Shallow depths with shifting sandbars make the marina entrance challenging.

Hook Bay. Located about half way up Port Alberni Inlet on the west shore, Hook Bay provides protection from up-inlet winds. Anchor in 30-40 feet over a flat bottom. A 50-foot public float, managed by the Port Alberni Port Authority, is available for overnight moorage at no charge; side-tie on both sides of the float, which is not connected to shore.

㉝ **Harbour Quay.** 2900 Harbour Rd., Port Alberni, BC V9Y 7X2; (250) 723-1413; www. portalberniportauthority.ca; harbourquay@ alberniport.ca. Harbour Quay has 15 slips and 2000 lineal feet of side-tie moorage, 20 & 30 amp power, washrooms, showers, laundry, potable water on the floats, garbage drop and secured gate access. This is a breakwater-protected marina close to downtown. The docks have been reconfigured to create more side-tie moorage, making it attractive for larger boats. Check ahead for availability. Adjacent to the Maritime Heritage Discovery Centre, located in a genuine west coast lighthouse.

㉝ **Fishermen's Harbour.** 3140 Harbour Rd., Port Alberni, BC V9Y 7X2; (250) 723-2533; www.portalberniportauthority.ca; fishermensharbour@alberniport.ca. Open all year, 7600 feet of moorage, 20, 30 and some 50 amp power, water, washrooms & showers, garbage drop and pumpout. Shipyard, marine ways and a two-ton electric winch on site. Fishermen's Harbur is adjacent to downtown Port Alberni, with all the services of downtown close by. They never turn anyone away, but be prepared to raft. June is the busiest month.

㉝ **Tyee Landing.** 3140 Harbour Rd., Port Alberni, BC V9Y 7X2; (250) 723-2533; www.portalberniportauthority.ca; fishermensharbour@ alberniport.ca. 160 feet of side-tie moorage is located north of Fishermen's Harbour and to the shore side of the fuel dock. Contact the Port Authority for availability.

Harbour Quay provides moorage for pleasure boaters visiting Port Alberni.

㉝ **Port Alberni Marine Fuels & Services.**
990-3300 Harbour Rd., Port Alberni, BC
V9Y 7X2; (250) 730- 3835; At the end of
the Tyee Landing dock, located just north of
Fishermen's Harbour, this fuel facility opened
in 2016. Marine gasoline and diesel including
high-speed diesel. Convenience store. Open
Monday through Friday 9:00 a.m. to 5:00
p.m.; Saturday, Sunday, and holidays 9:00
a.m. to 3:00 p.m.

㉞ **Clutesi Haven.** (250) 724-6837; www.
portalberniportauthority.ca; clutesihaven@
alberniport.ca. Open all year. Moorage
sometimes available, call ahead. Water, 15,
20 & 30 amp power, washrooms, garbage
drop, 4-lane launch ramp. Clutesi Haven is
located behind a breakwater near the mouth
of the Somass River. Best suited to boats 40
feet or less. This is a popular launching spot
for trailerable boats. Hotels, pubs, and liquor
store are nearby. Groceries are 5 blocks away.

BROKEN GROUP

The Broken Group extends from the wind-
and-wave-lashed outer islands to peaceful
islands deep inside Barkley Sound. The
Broken Group is part of the Pacific Rim
National Park, to be preserved in its natural
state in perpetuity. For many Northwest
boaters, a holiday spent in the Broken Group
is the fulfillment of a lifelong dream.

Boats visiting the Broken Group will find
dozens of little nooks and bights to put the
hook down, depending on weather and the
mood on board. Don Watmough, Don
Douglass, and the Yeadon-Joneses all describe
a number of them in their guides. The major
anchorages are Effingham Bay, Turtle Bay
and Nettle Island.

Pets: The Broken Group is part of Pacific
Rim National Park. In order to protect native
flora and fauna, pets are not permitted on
shore anywhere in the Broken Group.

Effingham Bay. Effingham Bay is large,
pretty, and protected. On the nights of our
visits we have shared the bay with 10 to 20
other boats, yet everyone had room to swing
and we didn't feel crowded. The chart shows
the entrance. Anchor in 30 to 50 feet, good
holding. Sunsets, seen out the mouth of the
bay, can be dramatic. Because Effingham Bay
is open to the west, westerly winds can make
the anchorage a bit bumpy.

Take the time to dinghy ashore and hike to
the ancient Native village site on the east side
of Effingham (Village) Island. The trail begins
on the right side (as you face the land from the
water) of the little thumb of water at the head
of Effingham Bay and leads through lush and
mature forest. Take care to turn right, the left
side leads in the wrong direction. Don't be
fooled; the wrong trail leads to mud, fallen trees
and other obstacles. The sign warns of wolves
on the island. Do pay attention to what it says:

"When in a group, act in unison to
send a clear message to the wolves they
are not welcome.

Turtle Bay is a large, scenic anchorage.

Back away slowly, do not turn your back
on the wolf.

Make noise, throw sticks, rocks and sand
at the wolf."

The trail across the island is generally
easy, but a little primitive and challenging
in places. The village site, on the eastern
shore, is mystical. Widely-spaced trees
suggest the location of the main village.
The large midden, with shells poking
out of it, indicates a long and populous
habitation. Near the beach you can find
an old longhouse beam that now serves as
a nurse log. A sea cave is located there, but
is inaccessible at high tide. Late in the day
the view eastward from the beach—the sea,
with the mountains of Vancouver Island
painted in low reddish light—is inspiring.

Benson Island. In settled weather you can
take anchorage off the east shore of Benson
Island, in the cove opposite the water faucet
icon on the chart. A trail leads across the
island to a scenic rocky beach with a blowhole
that sounds just like a whale blowing.

Clarke Island. Temporary or settled weather
anchorage can be found on the east side of
Clarke Island.

Turret Island. The cove formed by the
36-meter island on the southwest side of
Turret Island is okay for anchoring, though
the bottom is thick with kelp. The surrounding
area has interesting rock formations and is
good for exploring by dinghy or kayak.

㉟ **Turtle Bay.** Turtle Bay is a local name for
the bay formed by Turtle Island, Willis Island,
and Dodd Island. Joes Bay, an appendage of
Turtle Bay, indents Turtle Island. It is the little
nook where Salal Joe, the Hermit of Barkley
Sound, made his home.

The best entrance to Turtle Bay is from the
north, off Peacock Channel, between Dodd
Island and Chalk Island. A study of the
chart shows the entrance channel bounded
by rocks and drying rock outcroppings
along the way. A careful entry, proceeding
slowly and identifying the hazards, will
bring you in safely. Those who have been in

a few times know where the rocks are and
roar right in.

Anchor in 25 to 30 feet on a mud bottom,
good holding.

Nettle Island. Nettle Island has three good
anchorages—one in the large bay that indents
the southern shore, and the other two in the
channel between Nettle Island and Reeks
Island to the east. In Nettle Island's large bay
we prefer the eastern portion, off the park
ranger's float cabin. The center of the bay is a
little deep (50 to 60 feet, depending on state
of tide), but you can find depths of 20 to 30
feet near the shore north of the ranger's cabin.
Reader Dick Drinkow reports that the park
ranger warns that boats have grounded on
the shelf, and recommends anchoring in the
center of the bay.

Watmough describes two other anchorages
along the east side of Nettle Island, opposite
Reeks Island. These nooks will hold a couple
of boats each, and Watmough says they are
delightful. The charted rocks are easy to
identify and avoid.

Outer Islands. The outer islands of the
Broken Group are marked by twisted
trees, the result of relentless onshore winds,
especially in the winter. If your needs include
the desire to navigate "at the edge," the outer
islands can satisfy that need. Here, you'll
have your opportunity to run in wind and
fog, with the Pacific Ocean swells beating
against the rocks. Navigate carefully. The
low islands are easy to get mixed up. Rocks
and reefs are charted, but they're everywhere.
This is beautiful, raw country. The kayakers
have it best. The favored anchorage is at
Wouwer Island.

Wouwer Island. Wouwer Island is
breathtaking, both in its scenery and
gunkholing. At half tide or higher, most boats
can make it through the slit between Batley
Island and Wouwer Island. A bow watch will
only scare you.

We anchored temporarily in a nook south of
two islets, west of the slit between Batley and
Wouwer Islands. A trail leads across the island
to a lovely beach with great beachcombing.

EASTERN BARKLEY SOUND

㊱ **Poett Nook**. Poett Nook is on the eastern shore, at lat 48°53'N. It doesn't look like a nook when you see it. It is a spacious, rather pretty bay, with good anchoring in 25 to 35 feet. The entry is narrow but deep. The Poett Nook Marina, a large sport fishing resort, is on the eastern side of the bay.

㊱ **Poett Nook Marina & Campground.** Mailing: P.O. Box 1083, Port Alberni, BC V9Y 7L9; (250) 758-4440; (250) 720-9572; poettnookmarina@gmail.com; www.poettnook.com. Gasoline at the fuel dock, washrooms, showers. No power, non-potable water. A small store carries convenience food, ice, and tackle. Fee-based garbage drop. This is a busy small-boat sportfishing resort, with 123 RV/camping sites and berths for 174 boats. Maximum length 36 feet. Most boats launch at Port Alberni or China Creek.

Robbers Passage. Robbers Passage leads between Fleming Island and Tzartus Island in the Deer Group, and is a likely route for boats bound between points near the head of Barkely Sound and Bamfield. A rock that dries 1 meter is in the western approach to Robbers Passage. Although the rock is clearly charted, people at the Port Alberni Yacht Club swear this is one rock that moves. Give the rock a wide berth. The S-shaped channel leading into Robbers Passage requires close attention, but with attention it is safe. A study of large-scale chart 3668 will make the route clear. Inside the passage, the Port Alberni Yacht Club has its floating clubhouse and docks. Several large buoys might be mistaken for mooring buoys. These buoys are not designed for mooring and have dragged when boats tied to them.

Port Alberni Yacht Club. Consider spending at least one night at the Port Alberni Yacht Club. The facility is clean and well-maintained, and the folks are friendly and helpful. They have a wealth of local knowledge to share. Be sure to walk the beautiful trails around the peninsula behind the yacht club. The moorage charge is modest and goes back into the facility. All are welcome; no yacht club membership needed. Washrooms, showers, and non-potable water available. Note that upland trails and facilities are private property and are for yacht club members and paying overnight guests. If you anchor out, do not come ashore.

Fleming Island. The day was sunny with only a gentle breeze, so we left the boat at the yacht club and motored the dinghy around Fleming Island. The impossibly rugged shoreline is dotted with sea caves. We were told that some of the caves extend far into the rock. For thousands of years the First Nations people in Barkley Sound put some of their dead in bentwood boxes and hid them in sea caves. We were fascinated by the stories.

We did, however, ease the dinghy through a narrow cleft in the rock and up to the mouth of one cave. The opening loomed above us, and we could see the floor of small boulders rise and disappear in darkness. The rock walls of the cleft were covered with orange and purple sea stars. Other neon-hued sea life waved in the surge. The word impressed does not begin to describe the effect on us. [Hale]

Tzartus Cove. Tzartus Cove (our preferred anchorage on Tzartus Island) is the name Douglass gives to this excellent anchorage about 0.5 mile north of Marble Cove. Rocks extend from both shores, so go right down the middle when you enter. Anchor near the head in 25 to 30 feet. Sea caves are nearby. Reader Dick Drinkow reports that a bit of northwest swell can get into the cove and that kelp fouled their anchor.

Marble Cove. Marble Cove is on the west side of Tzartus Island, and often is mentioned as a good anchorage (we would choose instead the cove one-half mile north). A rock stack between two islands and reddish rocks on the shore add to the scenic nature of the cove. A float house is on the north side of Marble Cove. Anchor in 25 to 30 feet off the gravel beach on the island opposite the float house. This is a good place to explore tidepools at low tide.

Grappler Inlet. Grappler Inlet joins near the mouth of Bamfield Inlet and leads to Port Désiré, a protected anchorage with a launch ramp and a public dock. Although Grappler Inlet is beautiful, it is surrounded by homes.

㊲ **Bamfield Inlet.** Bamfield Inlet is open and easy to enter. The village of Bamfield is along the shores of the inlet. Several docks open to the public are located on each side. Moorage is limited, but space usually can be found for pleasure craft. West Bamfield public dock has the most moorage space. East Bamfield public dock has limited space available. At the head of the inlet, past Rance Island, is a quiet basin where boats can anchor, although an overhead power cable limits mast height to 17 meters (55 feet). Larger boats anchor off the East Bamfield public dock. There are no mooring buoys open to the public.

㊲ **Bamfield.** They call the inlet "Main Street." The village of Bamfield covers both sides of the inlet, and the west side is not connected by road with the east side. You cross by dinghy or water taxi (250-728-1212). The Bamfield General Store, with liquor agency, is on the west side of the inlet. A boardwalk runs along the homes and businesses on the west side, and folks get around by walking. The seasonal Boardwalk Bistro located near the West Bamfield public dock serves espresso drinks and delicious salmon burgers.

The east side has roads that tie its businesses and homes together. They connect with the 60-mile-long dirt logging road that leads to Port Alberni. The east side has a hardware store and a marine store, motel with a pub, and a convenience grocery store with a cafe. The trail to Cape Beale begins on the east side of the inlet. Anchorage and a launch ramp are at nearby Port Désiré.

A small Outpost Hospital is located on the east side. It is set up to treat illness or injury, deliver babies, and dispense medication. The hospital is operated by registered nurses, and a visiting physician calls on a regular schedule. They work closely with the Coast Guard for emergency helicopter transport when needed. A fee schedule accommodates non-Canadians who need medical attention.

Fiber optic cables were installed at Bamfield in 2018. Some docks and lodges may now offer Wi-Fi.

The large building on the east side of the inlet near the entrance houses the Bamfield Marine Research Station. The station is owned by five universities in British Columbia and Alberta, and began operation in 1971. Visitors are welcome and tours are offered during the summer, 1:00 p.m. to 2:30 p.m. Wednesdays, Fridays and Sundays, no charge, donations appreciated. This facility once was the eastern terminus of the transpacific cable that connected North America with Australia. Its first message was sent on November 1, 1902; its last message was sent in 1959. See their website at www.bms.bc.ca.

Bamfield offers several events during

The Port Alberni Yacht Club docks are in Robbers Passage.

the year, including the Music by the Sea Festival (250-728-3887), with classical and jazz musicians from all over. Lodging is at a premium, but boaters can stay on board. See www.bamfieldchamber.com/events.html for events and dates or call (250) 728-3006. The festival welcomes boaters. The first time you attend, they will award you a festival burgee to fly from your boat. Come a subsequent year, and they'll give you a second burgee with two stars on it. Repeat as many times as you want and get as many burgees as your number of visits, each with more stars. The experience of sitting in the Bamfield Marine Research Station's modern auditorium and watching the sun set over Barkley Sound through floor to ceiling glass windows while listening to wonderful music is well worth repeating.

While in Bamfield, don't miss the Kiixin Tour (pronounced Keein). The Native village of Kiixin, located in Pachena Bay, is a National Historic Site with significant remains of a traditional First Nations village and is the most complete known on the southern B.C. coast. Call or book online with the Huu-ay-aht First Nation to reserve a tour of the village. A tour bus leaves from the East Bamfield Public Dock to the trail head, scheduled during the summer months. Contact Kiixintours@huuayaht.org or call (250) 735-3432.

For a fine dining experience, book reservations at Pacific Wilderness Gateway Lodge (888-493-8933) located at the north tip of West Bamfield. Dinner guests can tie their dinghy at the dock belonging to the lodge. Dinners are available seasonally, beginning June 1st.

㊲ **East Bamfield Public Dock**. (250) 728-3231; hfnmarket@gmail.com hfndevelopmentlp.org; Located on the east side at the south end, 100 feet of guest moorage on the outside of the western-most float for vessels up to 15 meters (50 feet); water, for-fee garbage drop, 20 & 30 amp power at one stanchion located under the ramp. No washrooms. Dinghy landing space can usually be found. Preferred method to register and pay is at nearby upland "The Motel - Bamfield" (250-728-3231) or self-registration and pay with cash at the box located at the top of the ramp. Managed by the Huu-ay-aht Development Limited Partnership which also manages the nearby convenience store and "The Motel - Bamfield."

㊲ **Kingfisher Marina.** 211 Nuthatch Rd., Bamfield, BC V0R 1B0; (250) 728-3231; frontdesk@hunayaht.com. Located on the east side of the inlet opposite the "Y54" red spar buoy. Open all year, limited side-tie guest moorage behind the fuel dock. Gas and diesel at the fuel dock. Laundry service, Wi-Fi, and ice. No power, no water. Waterfront suites are available upland.

㊲ **West Bamfield Public Dock.** (250) 720-7548; bhadockmanager@gmail.com. Side-tie

West Bamfield Public dock, your best option for moorage

moorage on both sides of 500 feet of floats, 20 & 30 amp power, water. No washrooms, no garbage drop. Reservations recommended during July and August. Self-registration and payment box located at the head of the ramp. If the public docks are full, contact Bamfield Lodge (250-728-3419) located directly behind the public docks. **Bamfield Lodge** accepts overflow moorage at their dock as space allows.

㊲ **Harbourside Lodge.** (250) 728-3330; (604) 328-1656; requests@harboursidelodge.com; www.harboursidelodge.com. VHF 06 & 72. Open June to mid-September with guest moorage, 30 & 50 amp power, water, washroom, and showers. Gasoline and diesel. Located on the west side of the inlet, just past the public dock. Convenience store has ice, bait, tackle.

㊲ **McKay Bay Lodge.** (250) 728-3323; mckaybay@island.net; www.mckaybaylodge.com. Located on the west side of the inlet at the south end. Transient moorage as space available; lodging guests have priority; call ahead. They usually have space early and late in the season but often full in July and August. Gasoline, limited quantity of diesel, tackle, ice. Reservations are taken for dinner at the lodge. Washroom, guest rooms.

Dodger Channel. A small basin on the south portion of the channel, just east of Haines Island off the southwest corner of Diana Island, provides anchorage in settled weather; anchorage is open to the northwest and southwest. A drying rock lies on the west side of the north entrance to Dodger Channel. The south entrance from Trevor Channel is shallow, with rocks on both sides. Field Correspondent Mary Campbell reports that the south basin anchorage serves well as an early morning departure point from Barkley Sound. "It's the perfect anchorage for a good night's sleep before the run down the Strait of Juan de Fuca and has shallow depths, good crabbing and good views of the open sea. Diana Island is reminiscent of beaches in the South Pacific."

BARKLEY SOUND TO BECHER BAY

The final leg of a counter-clockwise circumnavigation of Vancouver Island is from Barkley Sound into the Strait of Juan de Fuca. On the Canadian side, Port Renfrew is the only protection between Barkley Sound and Sooke.

The typical summer weather pattern calls for calm conditions in the early morning, with a westerly sea breeze building by afternoon, often to 30+ knots.

Currents in the Strait of Juan de Fuca can be strong. This can speed up the passage, especially for sailboats. Or, they can substantially slow the trip. When the wind blows against the current, steep, sometimes-dangerous seas result. Pay attention to the current when planning to transit the Strait of Juan de Fuca.

Several weather resources make the trip less nerve-racking. Lighthouses at Cape Beale, Pachena Point and Carmanah Point provide regular weather updates. Automated stations at Shearingham Point and Race Rocks report hourly wind speed and direction. The Neah Bay weather buoy (46087) provides regular wind speed updates, and the New Dungeness buoy (46088) provides wind speed, direction, and sea state. Put together, you can get a picture of conditions on the Strait before venturing out.

Cape Beale. Cape Beale, surrounded by off-lying rocks, marks the eastern entrance to Barkley Sound. Trevor Channel exits at Cape Beale, and is the safest entry to, or exit from, Barkley Sound in thick weather or poor visibility. Seas can be difficult off Cape Beale when an outflowing current from Barkley Sound meets the longshore current outside. The collision of currents, combined with wind and shallow depths around the cape, can make for heavy going.

The usual advice is to round Cape Beale in early morning, before the summertime westerly wind gets up.

The local lightkeepers have provided this bit of local knowledge: A nasty reef is one-quarter of a mile in front of the lightstation. Beware of coming in close to take photos. Lightkeepers have had to summon the Bamfield Lifeboat crew a good many times to rescue overturned sports-fishing and pleasure craft occupants.

Pacific Gateway Marina, the only protected marina between Sooke and Bamfield

Nitinat Narrows. Nitinat Narrows connects Nitinat Lake with the Pacific Ocean. Entrance to the narrows is obstructed by rocks and a shallow bar. An onshore wind can cause breaking seas. A crossing of this bar and negotiation of the narrows to Nitinat Lake is considered a supreme Northwest navigation challenge by a small number of adventurers. Each year a few boats do make it through.

Many years ago Don Douglass took his 32 Nordic Tug across the bar, through the narrows, and into Nitinat Lake. His guidebook, *Exploring Vancouver Island's West Coast, 2nd Ed.* describes the experience, including the comment that his crew refused to ever try it again.

㊳ **Port San Juan.** For shelter off the Strait on the Canadian side consider Port San Juan, about halfway between Victoria and Barkley Sound. Port San Juan is a rectangular notch in Vancouver Island, with Port Renfrew on the eastern shore near the head of the bay. The breakwater protected marina at Port Renfrew offers year-round moorage and services. A public dock at Port Renfrew has limited moorage for smaller boats. The village and surrounding area has a grocery, pub, and several cafes.

The historic hotel and pub, at the head of the public dock, is a great place to relax over drinks. Port Renfrew is at the end of the road; hundreds of hikers, kayakers and sight-seers pour through town during the summer months.

Thrashers Cove. About one-third of a mile north of Quartertide Rocks, just off Hobbs Creek along the west shore of Port San Juan is a small bight with good anchoring depths and fair protection from northwesterly winds. Upland areas are part of the Pacific Rim National Park Reserve and the West Coast Trail. On shore you will see trail hikers camped for the night. A permit is required to visit the Park Reserve and hike the trail.

Woods Nose. Anchorage can be found close to shore behind Woods Nose on the south shore of Port San Juan. Woods Nose head breaks up the swell. Trees ashore block southerly winds, but the anchorage is open to northerly and westerly winds. In 2018, Landons reported that a private float and crab trap buoys occupied much of the desirable anchoring area.

㊳ **Port Renfrew Community Dock.** 17280 Parkinson Rd., Port Renfrew, BC V0S 1K0; (250) 647-5431. VHF 06 & 68 "Medd-O Base." Floats with room for 20 boats are installed from mid-May through mid-September. All are taken by charter boats. No electrical power; water is on the wharf but not on the floats. Best to call ahead for availability and reservations. Stan Medd is the harbormaster.

㊳ **Pacific Gateway Marina.** (250) 412-5509; contact@pacificgatewaymarina.ca; www.pacificgatewaymarina.ca. VHF 66A. Open year round. 60 slips designed for small sport fishing boats and 80 feet of side-tie for larger vessels. Larger vessels should call ahead for availability. Reservations highly recommended. Water and 30 amp power are available on A and B docks. Free Wi-Fi. Gasoline and diesel. Launch ramp. This marina is owned and managed by the Mill Bay Group. Washrooms, showers and 50 amp power are planned for the 2019 season. Repairs to the breakwater and docks have been completed following storm damage from January 2018. Bridgemans West Coast Eatery is open seasonally overlooking the marina with views of Port San Juan. SUP and sea kayak tours and rentals available nearby. A general store with groceries is within walking distance of the marina. The Botanical Beach Provincial Park is 3 km away; the marina may be able to help with transportation.

Renfrew Marina and RV Park. 7505 Gordon River Rd., Port Renfrew, BC V0S 1K0; (250) 483-1878; info@portrenfrewmarina.com; www.portrenfrewmarina.com. Open seasonally May through September. Monthly and daily moorage for small craft when available. First-come, first-served. Marine gasoline and launch ramp. Renfrew Marina is located at the head of Port San Juan, 1-mile up the Gordon River. River bar access is only navigable by shallow draft smaller vessels at mid to high tide (3 foot plus) with local knowledge; check tides.

SOOKE AND BECHER BAY

㊴ **Sooke Harbour.** Enter between Company Point and Parsons Point. The harbor is protected by Whiffen Spit, which nearly blocks the passage. Enter by keeping Whiffen Spit close to port. Two intersecting ranges mark the entrance channel. Follow the marked channel to town on the west bank. An area just inside Whiffen Spit, with charted depths of 7 meters (3 ¾ fathoms), has good anchorage, although wakes from passing boats make it rolly. Sooke Harbour Marina is the first set of docks. Just north of that is Jock's Docks, then Prestige Resort and a little farther up is Sooke Harbour Authority wharf with guest moorage. Sooke Harbour Marina and Jock's Docks have moorage for smaller vessels. Two day-use floats are located at the north end of the city boardwalk north of the of Harbour Authority city floats. Currents run quite strongly along the city waterfront, take care when landing.

Sooke Basin, the innermost harbor, is seldom visited by pleasure craft. The shallow channel follows the curve of the shoreline east of Middle Ground, between Eliza Point and Trollope Point. Notices to Mariners advises that entry to Sooke Basin be made after low water during daylight hours, when the drying banks are visible. Sooke is 15 miles closer to Barkley Sound than downtown Victoria, and often used as a departure point for boats heading up the west coast of Vancouver Island.

Sooke has a wide variety of services close to the Harbour Authority city floats, including a marine railway and machine shop, groceries, fuel, and restaurants. Just south of the Harbour Authority docks is the beautiful Prestige Oceanfront Resort, which houses the West Coast Grill. Shops, grocery, and restaurants are in town about half a mile north from the Harbour Authority docks. Follow the road the full half-mile distance or take the trail to the boardwalk for the last quarter-mile. The trail to the boardwalk starts in McGregor Park and follows the shoreline before climbing a hill into town.

No customs clearance is available in Sooke. The nearest Canadian Port of Entry is Victoria.

㊴ **Sooke Harbour Resort & Marina.** 6971 West Coast Road, Sooke, BC V9Z 0V1; (250) 642-3236; reservations@sookeharbourmarina.

WHITE SLAVES OF MAQUINNA JOHN R. JEWITT'S NARRATIVE OF CAPTURE AND CONFINEMENT AT NOOTKA

Publisher: Heritage House; ISBN: 978-1-894384-02-5

John Jewitt and John Thompson were the only survivors of an attack by the Mowachaht tribe of **Nootka Sound** who boarded the sailing ship *Boston*, along with their King, or Head Chief, Maquinna. After Jewitt was rescued, he wrote a book of his experiences, which appeared in 1815, and became known as *Jewitt's Narrative*. It proved to be so popular that it was reprinted for the next 185 years. In 1987, Heritage House published a version of the Jewitt Narrative called *White Slaves of the Nootka*, and the book title was subsequently renamed in 2000 to *White Slaves of Maquinna* as the term Nootka is no longer the preferred name for the Nuu-chah-nulth people of Vancouver Island's west coast.

Born 1783, in Great Britain, John Jewitt received schooling to become a surgeon and was given an apprenticeship with a doctor; but Jewitt was more interested in his father's shop which forged metal, particularly for vessels. This opportunity gave Jewitt his introduction to sailors and their accompanying stories of adventure. In 1802, the ship Boston, of Boston, Massachusetts commanded by Captain Salter, arrived in England to take on cargo for trade with the natives on the Northwest Coast of America in exchange for furs, which then were to be brought to China. Wishing to visit foreign countries, John Jewitt begged his father to let him go along. As an armorer, he would be paid 30 dollars per month plus furs set aside in his name. After an emotional goodbye to his parents, he was at sea and employed in forging muskets, daggers, knives, and small hatchets for trade.

In March 1803, after rounding Cape Horn, they arrived in **Nootka Sound**, where Captain Salter anchored to supply the ship with wood and water before continuing north. The following morning, several natives came by canoe from their village in **Friendly Cove**, along with their king called Maquinna. Having encountered other English and American ships, Maquinna had learned a number of English words and could make himself understood. Maquinna and his tribe seemed pleased to trade with the *Boston*, enjoying tea, coffee, and molasses, and were especially interested in iron weapons and tools. Maquinna dined with the captain on several occasions and natives came onboard daily, bringing an abundance of fresh salmon. On one occasion, Maquinna informed Captain Salter that there were plenty of wild ducks and geese near Friendly Cove. As a token of thanks, the captain presented him with a double-barreled fowling gun.

On the 21st, Maquinna returned with nine pair of wild ducks as a present and had also brought with him the gun; Maquinna had broken one of the locks, saying that the gun was peshak (bad). Captain Salter was offended and called the king a liar along with other offensive terms and asked John Jewitt if he could fix the gun. The following morning the natives came with the usual gift of salmon and remained onboard. About noon, Maquinna came alongside with a considerable number of his chiefs and men in their canoes. After the customary examination, they were admitted onto the ship. Working on his vice-bench in the steerage, Jewitt heard a commotion; putting his head above deck, he was caught by the hair and hit in the head with an axe, falling back into the hold unconscious. The natives had gotten possession of the ship and had slaughtered all aboard. When Jewitt regained consciousness, Maquinna ordered that Jewitt not be killed, for he was the armorer and would be of use to them.

Jewitt was taken ashore to Maquinna's house and was told his life had been spared in order to serve as a slave for Maquinna and his tribe. Jewitt was careful to show affection for the king's eleven-year

old son, which immediately pleased Maquinna. During one sleepless night, Jewitt heard natives arriving around midnight to inform the king that there was one of the white men alive who had come aboard the ship at night; this was John Thompson, the sail maker. To spare his life, Jewitt claimed that 40-year old Thompson was his father; and that if his father was killed, that his wish was to be killed as well. Maquinna believed the story, and Thompson's life was spared. The Chief ordered his natives to begin stripping the Boston of her sails, rigging, spars, masts, and gather supplies off the ship. Jewitt and Thompson were obliged to help. In the cabin, Jewitt found a prayer book which he collected for himself along with some tools and a journal kept by the second mate. As word spread among other tribes regarding Maquinna's captured property, tribes from north and south arrived by canoe at Nootka; Maquinna proudly held a feast and ordered Thompson to fire the cannon as part of the ceremony.

All hope for an immediate escape for the white slaves vanished when it was reported early one morning that the ship was on fire. One of the natives had gone aboard with a firebrand at night for the purpose of plunder; sparks fell into the hold igniting combustibles, creating a fire that engulfed the ship. Jewitt soon began writing a journal. He used Raven feathers for writing quills; and after a number of trials, created black ink by boiling the juice of the blackberry mixed with a finely powdered charcoal, then filtering it through a cloth. Jewitt's narrative includes fascinating accounts of the natives' dress, face-painting, building techniques, fishing, whaling, and cooking, along with religious beliefs and ceremonies. As a slave, Jewitt produced spears, harpoons, daggers, jewelry and other ornaments in addition to cutting and hauling wood to the village from several miles distance, a back-breaking job; and Thompson had made a fine sail for the king's canoe, which earned his favor. On Sundays, Thompson and Jewitt retreated in private for a Christian service, praying that a ship would one day arrive and provide release from "a savage world."

As summer grew to a close, Maquinna and his tribe moved their camp to **Tahsis**, bringing with them planks and frames to cover their houses. The move was made again in order to spend the winter months at Coopte, located farther up the Sound. Jewitt and Thompson had now lived among the natives for two years, and each time they left the coast, their hope of ever being rescued faded. Having learned enough of the native language, Jewitt came to learn why Maquinna had attacked their ship. According to Maquinna, other European ships had done him ill and killed many of his people. As noted by Jewitt, "these injuries had excited in the breast of Maquinna an ardent desire of revenge, the strongest passion of the savage heart." Indeed, Maquinna had asked Jewitt to participate in a war against the A-y-chart tribe, located 50 miles to the south, due to some controversy that had arisen. Many of the A-y-chart people were killed; John Jewitt took four captives of which Maquinna said they could belong to John. Jewitt was also told he must take a wife among one of the area tribes, the details of which are included in his narrative.

Jewitt and Thompson were eventually rescued. Under great risk to himself and Thompson, Jewitt devised a plan of escape and rescue. To learn how he arrived safely home to his parents, don't miss reading John Jewitt's narrative of capture and confinement at Nootka; Heritage House published version.

Sooke

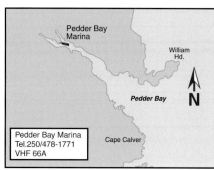

Pedder Bay Marina

ca; www.sookeharbourmarina.ca. Open all year with side-tie guest moorage to 50 feet along outside breakwater. Inside docks are for boats up to 25 feet. First-come, first-served. Services include washrooms, showers, 30 & 50 amp power, Wi-Fi on shore, and 2-lane concrete launch ramp. This is the first marina as you come into the harbor.

㊴ **Jock's Dock.** 6947 West Coast Rd., Sooke, BC V9Z 0V1 (778) 425-2703. Open all year; 60 slips for small sport fishing boats and runabouts; occasional guest moorage when available; first-come, first-served, call ahead. Water at the docks; two launch ramps, fishing charters. The upland Crab Shack (250-642-4410), open May to October, sells smoked fish, prawns and live crab.

㊴ **Sooke Harbour Authority.** 1800 Maple, Sooke, BC V9Z 1H5; (250) 642-4431; (250) 893-6578 cell; sookeharbour@ telus.net. Open all year, first-come, first-served guest moorage along both sides of 400 foot A-dock, 20 & 30 amp power, water, garbage drop, used oil disposal; no washrooms or showers. Rafting required. Gate secured floats are well maintained.

Watch for current. Walking distance to town and park entrance to the boardwalk.

Sunny Shores Resort & Marina. 5621 Sooke Rd., RR 1, Sooke, BC V9Z 0C6; (250) 642-5731; www.sunnyshoresresort. com. Gasoline and diesel at fuel dock. Guest moorage for 6 to 10 smaller boats, call ahead for availability. Docks are in an advanced stage of deterioration. Washrooms, showers, laundry, 15 amp power, haulout. Motel accommodations and campground. Store carries ice, fishing tackle, limited groceries. Taxi to town 3 miles away.

Becher Bay. Becher Bay is a good alternative to Sooke for boaters wishing to avoid a difficult entry in fog. Although Becher Bay is farther east than Sooke, the time not spent winding your way past Whiffen Spit makes up for it. Campbell Cove on the west side of Becher Bay is a pleasant anchorage, but be careful of a drying rock near the south end. It's a good departure point for the run to Barkley Sound. Kelp is on the bottom; be sure of your set. Murder Bay, at the north end, is another recommended anchorage, also with kelp, though. Another pleasant anchorage lies to the east of Wolf Island. For a bit of

gunkholing, enter between Wolf and Lamb Islands. Be sure to avoid the submerged power cable when anchoring.

㊵ **Becher Bay Marina & Campground**. 241 Becher Bay Rd., Sooke, BC V9Z 1B7; (250) 642-3816. Open May 1 to September 30. Limited guest moorage by reservation only, maximum boat length 30 feet. Services include washrooms, no showers, 2-lane concrete launch ramp, no power. Smokin' Tuna Cafe on site. RV parking.

Pedder Bay. Pedder Bay is a mile-long inlet, shallow and narrow, just south of William Head. No anchoring in bay due to submerged utility pipes. A launch ramp with floats is at the head.

㊶ **Pedder Bay Marina.** 925 Pedder Bay Drive, Victoria, BC V9C 4H1; (250) 478-1771; pbm@obmg.com; www.pedderbay. com. Monitors VHF 66A. Open all year, gasoline only at fuel dock. Permanent and visitor moorage available for vessels up to 50', call ahead for larger boats. Washrooms, showers, laundry, 30 amp power, free Wi-Fi, 3-lane concrete launch ramp, year-round RV resort, camping, coffee shop, chandlery with bait, tackle, and ice. Approaching, use Chart 3410; watch the wind. Located between Pearson College and Dept. of National Defence (don't stop there; it's a prison). The marina is part of Oak Bay Marina Group.

Harbour-side boardwalk leads to the town of Sooke.

Rounding Cape Caution

CHAPTER 15

PINE ISLAND ROUTE
Pine Island • Egg Island

WALKER ISLAND GROUP ANCHORAGE
Kent Island • Staples Island

PULTENEY POINT–JEANETTE ISLAND ROUTE
Malcolm Island • Jeanette Islands • Harris Island
Hot Spring Island • Richards Channel • Allison Harbour

MAINLAND ROUTE
Blunden Harbour • Allison Harbour • Miles Inlet
Nakwakto Rapids • Southgate Group

Cape Caution, for some, is a fearsome barrier to exploring the remote and beautiful northern areas of British Columbia and on to Southeast Alaska. Like many of the challenging cruising areas of the Inside Passage, careful planning, attention to the weather reports, patience and time can lead to a smooth and uneventful crossing. We have met cruisers who may wait for days for the right settled conditions. Good weather for a crossing happens more often than you might think.

To get to the central and northern B.C. Coast you first must round Cape Caution. Although the distance in open water is only about 40 miles, the seas can be high and steep. The bottom shoals from 100+ fathoms off the continental shelf to 20-70 fathoms in Queen Charlotte Sound itself, causing seas to heap up. The problem is made worse when these seas are met by the outflowing ebb currents from Queen Charlotte Strait, Smith Sound, Rivers Inlet and Fitz Hugh Sound.

After more than 30 crossings, we've refined our "go, no-go" decisions to six factors: weather forecast; time of day; lighthouse wind and sea reports; flood or ebb tide; size of tidal exchange (spring tide or neap tide); and the automated combined wave (wave and swell) height reports from the West Sea Otter Buoy.

Weather Forecast. Regardless of other factors, we want a favorable forecast or we're not going. Fog, while limiting visibility, often indicates little to no wind, favorable for a crossing if you are skilled operating your radar. Radar is very helpful as it is not unusual to have opposing traffic in this area during periods of settled conditions, when others want to round Cape Caution.

Time Of Day. The typical summertime weather pattern calls for calm early mornings, followed in late morning or early afternoon by a rising westerly sea breeze, sometimes to gale force. "Typical," however, does not mean every day. We've seen windy mornings and flat-calm late afternoons.

Lighthouse Wind And Sea Reports. From south to north, lighthouses, and automated stations, at Scarlett Point, Herbert Island, Pine Island, Egg Island, and Addenbroke Island report conditions approximately every four hours, posted on the Continuous Marine Broadcast. Pine Island and Egg Island are the most relevant. Addenbroke Island, inside the mouth of Fitz Hugh Sound, often reports quiet conditions when Pine Island and Egg Island are much rougher. Scarlett Point, just off the north part of Vancouver Island, usually is quieter than Pine Island and Egg Island.

Flood Or Ebb Tide. Flood tide is preferred. On a flood, the incoming swells and prevailing westerly wind are aligned and the seas are flattened. The ebb is the reverse: outflowing ebb currents meet the westerly swells, making them higher and steeper. One year we made the mistake of crossing the mouth of Rivers Inlet in a mounting sea breeze that was blowing against a strong outflowing ebb, and we took a beating. We *will not* do that again.

Size Of Tidal Exchange. If possible, cross during a time of neap tides (half moon). If that can't be done, try to cross on a flood. If that can't be done, try to cross at the end of one tide, when currents are growing less, and the beginning of the next tide, while currents are still low. Avoid crossing the mouth of Rivers Inlet on an ebb.

West Sea Otter Buoy. When West Sea Otter Buoy reports seas 1.3 meters or less, with a dominant wave period greater than 8 seconds, crossing is likely to be pleasant. Combine this information with the weather forecast, lighthouse reports, and flood and ebb tides.

VTS Radio Note. South of Cape Caution, Victoria VTS, channel 71, controls large vessel traffic. North of Cape Caution, traffic is controlled by Prince Rupert VTS, channel 11. Especially in reduced visibility, one radio should be monitoring VHF 16 and a second radio should be scanning channels 11 and 71.

Pine Island Route. This is the most popular route from Vancouver Island. It begins at Scarlett Point at the mouth of Christie Passage on Gordon Channel, and ends at Fury Cove, at the north end of Rivers Inlet. The distance is approximately 40 miles. Boats often provision and refuel in Port McNeill or Port Hardy, and move to a departure point near Christie Passage for a crossing the next morning. God's Pocket in Christie Passage, Port Alexander in Browning Passage, or Clam Cove in Gordon Channel just west of Browning Passage, are often used. Another good spot is the cove between Staples Island and Kent Island in the **Walker Group**.

The Pine Island route leads westward in Gordon Channel to Pine Island, then northward past the tip of the Storm Islands, past Egg Island, and on to Smith Sound, Rivers Inlet or Cape Calvert. This route will give Cape Caution an offing of 1.5 to 2.5 miles.

Gordon Channel is a principal passage for commercial vessels. Display a radar reflector. In thick weather or fog, having radar, GPS and AIS is extremely helpful. Especially in low visibility or fog, most commercial traffic can be avoided by crossing Gordon Channel to the Redfern Island/Buckle Group side, and favoring that side to Pine Island.

Pulteney Point to Jeanette Islands Route. If Queen Charlotte Strait is behaving, this can be a good route from Port McNeill, on Vancouver Island, to the mainland side. From Pulteney Point at the west tip of Malcolm Island, turn to a course of 309° magnetic. This will leave the charted kelp patch to port. Twenty miles later you will arrive at the Jeanette Islands on the mainland side of Queen Charlotte Strait. Turn to approximately 290° magnetic and proceed through Richards Channel until flashing green Whistle Buoy *N31* is abeam to port. Alter course slightly to leave Harris Island to starboard and Allen Rocks Lighted Whistle Buoy *N33* to port. From there a course of approximately 293° magnetic will take you to a common intersection point west of Cape Caution.

Caution in Richards Channel. On an ebb, especially a big ebb, Richards Channel can be difficult. One year, although the wind was

---

ROUNDING CAPE CAUTION GO-NOGO CHECKLIST

Tides & Currents - See Ports & Passes; Canadian Tides & Current Tables Vol. 7
- ☐ Phase of the moon – Spring or Neap Tide: Neap Tides are preferred
- ☐ Check for Slack Water time at Slingsby Channel
- ☐ Flood or Ebb; Flood is preferred

Weather System Predictions – via Internet or satellite
- ☐ Check NOAA Ocean Prediction Center forecasts for any approaching significant weather systems
- ☐ Check Windy.com, Predictwind.com, SiriusXM Marine, or Sailflow.com
- ☐ See Environment Canada forecast for the Synopsis report for Central Coast From McInnes Island To Pine Island

Weather & Seas Forecasts – via Internet, phone, or VHF
- ☐ See Environment Canada Forecast for Central Coast; Check for warnings, note wind speed and direction, wave height and interval, and trends of forecast conditions
- ☐ Check Environment Canada Forecasts for Queen Charlotte Sound, and West Coast Vancouver Island North; forecast conditions that are much different than the forecast for Central Coast may signal changing conditions

Observations & Present Conditions – via Internet, phone, or VHF
- ☐ Check Buoy Report for West Sea Otter (46204); note wind and sea conditions
- ☐ Check Lighthouse Reports from Scarlett Point, Herbert Island, Pine Island, Egg Island, and Addenbroke Island; note wind speed, wind direction, and sea conditions

Go-NoGo Decision
- √ Check wind and wave direction in relation to direction of travel.
- √ Is there a northwest wind against an ebb current situation?
- √ Do the wind and wave conditions exceed your limits?

Fail-Safe Contingency Plans
- √ Duck-in locations along the route: Allison Harbour, and Millbrook Cove

See *Chapter 1 Interpreting Northwest Weather* section for telephone numbers, website addresses, VHF channels, and buoy numbers.

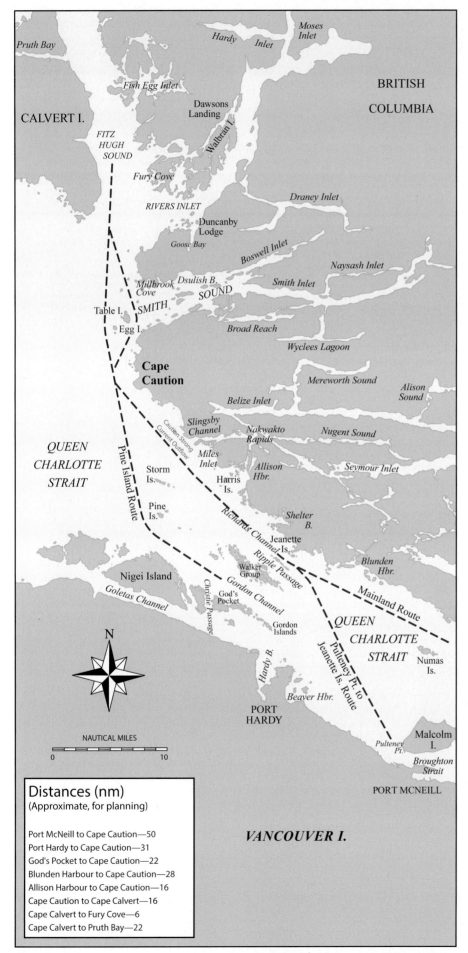

Distances (nm)

Distances (nm)
(Approximate, for planning)

Port McNeill to Cape Caution—50

Port Hardy to Cape Caution—31

God's Pocket to Cape Caution—22

Blunden Harbour to Cape Caution—28

Allison Harbour to Cape Caution—16

Cape Caution to Cape Calvert—16

Cape Calvert to Fury Cove—6

Cape Calvert to Pruth Bay—22

---

calm, a big ebb set up a 2.5-knot outflowing current that opposed the incoming swells, creating larger and more threatening seas. We aborted our crossing and anchored instead in Allison Harbour. High winds kept us in Allison Harbour the following day and night.

Mainland Route. The mainland route offers more shelter in case of a blow and lets you visit Blunden Harbour, Allison Harbour, Miles Inlet, and Milbrook Cove in Smith Sound. You could even take a major side trip through famed Nakwakto Rapids (at slack) and spend time in Seymour Inlet and Belize Inlet. Many boats prefer the mainland route for its greater interest and possibility of shelter. The major cautions are Richards Channel on an ebb (above) and the waters off Slingsby Channel on an ebb.

Slingsby Channel Caution. Slingsby Channel is the primary drain for the hundreds of miles of inlets behind Nakwakto Rapids. What Slingsby Channel does to Queen Charlotte Strait on a big ebb can be terrifying. Outer Narrows at the mouth of Slingsby Channel runs to 9 knots on an ebb. The water fire-hoses into Queen Charlotte Strait, where it collides with the Pacific Ocean's incoming swells. If a westerly is blowing against this vast outpouring, conditions can be as bad as the worst at Cape Mudge.

Outer Narrows currents turn 10 minutes before Nakwakto Rapids, both flood and ebb. We departed our anchorage in Allison Harbour at 8:00 a.m., not realizing that two hours earlier the maximum ebb at Nakwakto Rapids was 11.4 knots. Shortly after 8:00 a.m. Slingsby Channel was still roaring. Although not a breath of wind was stirring, we found ourselves in large, steep seas that lifted the bow high, then crashed us down into the troughs. We pressed on, hoping not to meet a log in the bottom of a trough, and got through without injury or damage. The turbulence diminished but persisted all the way to Cape Caution, which we rounded at 10:10 a.m., a half-hour after the turn to flood in Slingsby Channel.

Summing up. Rounding Cape Caution is more than simply rounding the Cape itself. From the departure points to arriving in Fitz Hugh Sound, you will transit different areas with varying weather and sea conditions. The total experience involves planning for and choosing a route through the various sections. These sections include: staging and anchoring the night before; transiting of Queen Charlotte Strait; avoiding conditions off Slingsby Channel; rounding the Cape itself; and passing outside or inside Egg Island. You might include in your plan a stop in Smith Sound. You will need to choose the day's stopping point: Millbrook Cove, Fury Cove, Goose Bay, or go all the way to Pruth Bay. Patience and diligence in planning is the key. Start the planning process well ahead of time; start watching the forecast weather and the subsequent buoy and lighthouse observations a week ahead to familiarize yourself with conditions and place names.

WHERE FATE BECKONS, THE LIFE OF JEAN-FRANCOIS DE LÁ PEROUSE - By John Dunmore

Publisher: University of Alaska Press; ISBN: 978-1-60223-003-3

Where Fate Beckons, by John Dunmore, is the fascinating story of French explorer and naval officer Jean-Francois de la Perouse – his adventures, discoveries, and the fateful end to a scientific exploration around the world.

La Perouse began his naval career in the mid 1700's at the age of 15, participating in supply expeditions to New France, present day northeastern Canada. British ships were attempting to block the supply route to the cities of Quebec and Montreal, which later led to La Perouse serving as an officer on several frigates. La Perouse also served in the French West Indies, protecting merchant ships. In 1773, La Perouse was given command of his own ship, along with the task of bringing order to France's island territories. During his career with the French Navy, La Perouse recognized that the strong class system, not only within his country, but within the Navy itself, caused jealousies and in-fighting for social standing. He warned that if the French Navy was to become a stable and efficient force, changes must be made. He did not hesitate to face the class structure that caused problems of recruitment and retention in the Navy.

He carried these beliefs into his personal life as well. During a visit to Isle de France, he met Eleonore, a woman of his intellect; but she was considered not of equal social standing, and La Perouse's father forbade their marriage. Their love story reads like an opera filled with joy, sorrow, and ultimate tragedy. La Perouse was absent from Eleonore during his military campaigns, protecting French interests and supporting the efforts of the Americans' War of Independence. Over time, his father and family slowly relented, and Jean-Francois La Perouse married Eleonore Broudon on July 8, 1783.

La Perouse greatly admired James Cook, and had long dreamed of sailing the Pacific. His dream came true when he was appointed by Louis XVI and by the Secretary of the Navy to lead a scientific expedition around the world. The mission was to establish trade contacts, complete missing pieces on navigation maps, and enrich French scientific collections. On July 12, 1785, La Perouse with his ship Boussole, and De Langle with his ship the Astrolabe, departed for their trip to the Pacific.

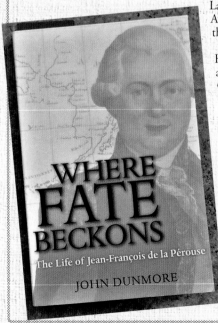

After rounding Cape Horn, they dropped anchor in the Bay of Conception, where the Spanish supplied the expedition with fruit, vegetables, and meat. La Perouse then sailed directly to Easter Island and on to the Sandwich Islands (Hawaiian Islands), arriving at the end of May, 1786. From Oahu, La Perouse set a course due north towards the Alaskan coast.

They identified Mount St Elias and reached the point where Vitus Bering had sailed in 1741.

Author John Dumore goes on to describe in his book the discovery of Lituya Bay. West of Mount Fairweather, an opening appeared, a bay that was not shown on any of their maps; La Perouse had discovered Lituya Bay. The bay provided protected anchorage, but the bar entrance is narrow and treacherous. His scientists brought their instruments ashore and spent a number of weeks studying the T-shaped bay. When La Perouse began to ready his ships for departure, he sent out two longboats to take soundings in the bay for charting purposes. He warned his men not to venture too close to the rocks near the entrance, but the tide had turned and the small boats were helplessly carried away. As they reached the bar and the open sea, the boats capsized – six officers and fifteen men drowned.

Heading south, La Perouse's ships reached Cross Sound and the Alexander Archipelago in early August; then came Sitka Sound, Baranof Islands, Christian Sound and Prince of Wales Island. Through a thick fog, he was able to find Cook's Nootka Sound on August 25th. La Perouse had been given less than three months to survey the Alaskan and northern Canadian coast, an impossible task. By September 15, he reached Monterey, being the first non-Spanish foreign vessel to visit the harbor. They next set sail for China, the Philippines, and then north to Kamchatka via Taiwan and Japan. No other expedition had ventured into Korea Strait or the Sea of Japan.

After landing at Petropovlovsk, the only village on Russia's Kamchatka Peninsula, La Perouse was met there by Barthelemy de Lesseps (uncle of Ferdinand de Lesseps of Suez Canal fame, and Panama Canal infamy), who took La Perouse's journals overland to Moscow and on to France. The account of Barthelemy de Lesseps' journey overland is a fascinating story unto itself, which Dunmore summarizes in his book. From Kamchatka, La Perouse sailed to Australia, crossing the equator for the third time. Unfortunately, another tragedy befell them. When De Langle, captain of the Astrolabe, went ashore to fill water barrels, De Langle was attacked and killed by the Samoans, along with eleven of his men. La Perouse named the site on Tutuila Island, Massacre Bay. Departing with a heavy heart, La Perouse reached Botany Bay, Australia on January 2, 1788. The unexpected arrival of two French frigates caused a stir; but knowing that La Perouse was on a scientific voyage, the English provided the crucial service of bringing La Perouse's letters and journals back to Europe. Among the letters were those written to Eleonore.

These letters would be his last words to Eleonore. On March 10, 1788, the *Boussole* and *Astrolabe* set sail for home, and were never heard from again. Eleonore went to Paris to await news of her beloved. Forty years later, remnants of the *Boussole* and *Astrolabe* were found on Vanikoro Island, southeast of the Solomon Islands – a ship's bell and guns with identification markings.

Northern B.C. Coast

CHAPTER 16

See Area Map Page 415 - Maps Not for Navigation

Planning a Trip to the Northern B.C. Coast. Most cruisers limit their voyages to the waters south of a line that runs between Wells Passage on the mainland to Port Hardy on Vancouver Island. North of this line the northern part of Queen Charlotte Strait is a natural barrier. It takes time, a strong boat, and good navigation skills to proceed farther up the coast. To be fair, a lifetime of cruising could be spent south of that line with complete satisfaction.

But—to those with the time and inclination—the coast north of Wells Passage is a special experience. The scenery is magnificent, the population is small and self-sufficient, the fishing can be exceptional and you can even take a warm soak at one of several hot springs. You can anchor in bays with no other boats and take in the scenery all by yourself.

This is the part of the coast where you'll find the famous names: Nakwakto Rapids, Rivers Inlet, Fish Egg Inlet, Hakai, Bella Bella, Ocean Falls, Ivory Island, Fiordland, Butedale, Grenville Channel, Prince Rupert. It's a coast filled with history and possibilities. If it's wilderness you seek, you can find it here.

Be self-reliant. Between Port Hardy and Prince Rupert, there are few marinas with services for pleasure boats. Be glad the facilities are there, and don't complain if they're a little rough and maybe a bit more expensive. Don't expect marina help to come down to take your lines as you land.

Most facilities and businesses are set up to take credit cards. ATMs are limited except for a machine at Shearwater and sometimes in Klemtu, and you have full banking in Prince Rupert. Cell phone coverage is spotty. To determine whether you have cell phone coverage or roaming in this area, check with your provider. There are several areas with cell phone coverage between Port Hardy and Prince Rupert. Generally speaking you will find coverage at Shearwater/New Bella Bella, Klemtu, Hartley Bay, Kitimat, and Bella Coola. Some boats rent or purchase satellite phones when cruising this area. Satellite based messaging devices, such as the Garmin InReach system, with weather forecast delivery options, are useful in isolated areas with no VHF radio reception. Land line pay phones are in Bella Coola, Shearwater, New Bella Bella, Ocean Falls, and Klemtu.

Insurance. Some vessel insurance policies don't cover these waters without a special rider. Check with your marine insurance broker before you leave.

The boat. Not many small boats cruise the northern coast. You'll sometimes see jerry cans filled with extra fuel or water lashed to the rails or in the cockpits. Radar and GPS should be considered standard equipment. This is remote country. The boat should be in top mechanical condition. Complete spares should be carried.

Many anchorages along this coast are 60 to 90 feet deep, with shallower water too close to

Dall's Porpoise love to accompany boats.

shore to swing in comfort. You'll need ample anchor rode—300 feet should be considered the minimum.

Bottoms often are rocky. Because of its resistance to bending and its ability to set and hold in nearly any bottom, including rock, Bruce is a popular anchor. Manson Supreme, Rocna, CQR, Ultra and Delta anchors also are popular. You don't see as many Danforth style anchors. Danforth style anchors are good in sand and mud, but they have trouble setting in rock, and once wedged they are easily bent.

Be sure to carry at least two anchors. Whatever the style of anchors chosen, they should be big, strong, and ready to deploy.

Fuel and water. Fuel is plentiful, both gasoline and diesel, all the way up the coast. Rivers Inlet has gasoline and diesel at Dawsons Landing. You can get gasoline and diesel at Bella Coola, Shearwater, New Bella Bella, Klemtu, Kitimat, Hartley Bay, and Prince Rupert. The longest distance between fuel stops is roughly 70 miles.

Water is available all along the way. Some of it may be tinged brown from cedar bark tannin, but people have been drinking cedar water for decades with no ill effects. The dock at Ocean Falls has sparkling clear, purified water. New Bella Bella, Klemtu and Hartley Bay have multi-million-dollar water treatment plants that deliver clear, pure water.

Weather. Bring clothes for all conditions, from cold and rainy to hot and sunny. Expect wet weather at least part of the time. The residents of Ocean Falls call themselves "The Rainpeople" for good reason. Some years have been so wet that a few boats quit their cruise.

Plan for clouds down on the deck, for fog, for rain (both vertical and horizontal), and for storms. Leave enough flexibility in the schedule to anchor through serious foul weather. Be sure the boat is well-provisioned and equipped with generator or battery power to spend several days at anchor in one location.

Plan on sunshine, too, maybe a lot of

sunshine. It can get *hot*. Bring bug spray, and equip the boat with screens on doors, hatches, opening ports, and windows.

You should have a heat source while underway and a heat source to be used at anchor. A hydronic system, with heat exchanger and furnace, can be used for both. There are various combinations of different heaters that can provide warmth.

Sailboaters will want some sort of cockpit protection, from a companionway dodger to full cockpit enclosure. Keep the cabin warm and dry, or you'll be miserable.

Marinas. There aren't many marinas on this coast. In Rivers Inlet, Dawsons Landing has moorage, fuel and supplies. The Native band stores at New Bella Bella and Klemtu have a good grocery selection. Shearwater, near New Bella Bella, has moorage, a restaurant and pub, groceries, chandlery, fuel, water, haulout and repairs. Ocean Falls has moorage, power, water, Wi-Fi and a pub in nearby Martin Valley. Farther north, Hartley Bay has fuel, water, and limited moorage. Prince Rupert has just about everything.

If you're in a jam, you could seek help at one of the sportfishing lodges along the coast, but remember that their business is serving their fly-in fishing guests, not recreational boats.

Dogs and hiking. Shorelines often are steep and rocky along this part of the coast, with few good places to walk the dog or take a walk yourself. Although we have seen many pets on board, we've met a number of cruisers who feel it's just too difficult to get a dog ashore. People who enjoy regular walks and hikes will find their options limited. All agree that the coast is beautiful, but some would welcome more opportunity for exercise.

Repairs. While it's best to carry complete spares and know how to fix whatever goes wrong, nobody can be ready for everything. Parts and mechanics can be flown in anyplace along the coast between Port Hardy and Prince Rupert. The only full-service shipyard

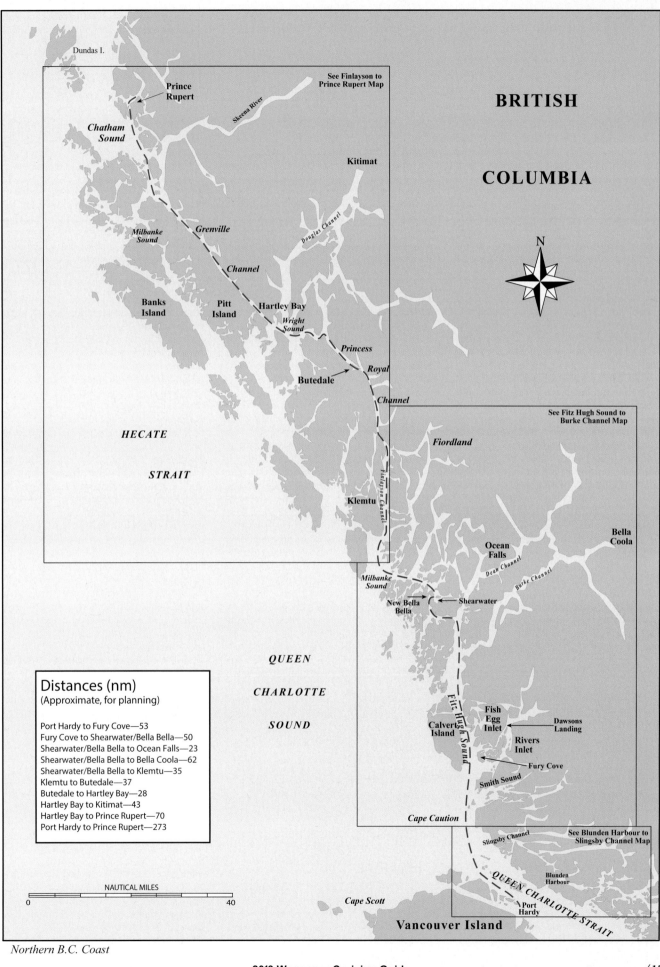

Dundas I.

Prince
Rupert

See Finlayson to
Prince Rupert Map

*Chatham
Sound*

Skeena River

BRITISH

Kitimat

COLUMBIA

Grenville

Douglas Channel

*Milbanke
Sound*

N

Channel

**Banks
Island**

**Pitt
Island**

Hartley Bay

*Wright
Sound*

Princess

Royal

Butedale

HECATE

Channel

See Fitz Hugh Sound to
Burke Channel Map

Fiordland

STRAIT

Finlayson Channel

Klemtu

*Ocean
Falls*

Dean Channel

**Bella
Coola**

Burke Channel

*Milbanke
Sound*

New Bella
Bella

Shearwater

QUEEN

CHARLOTTE

SOUND

Fitz Hugh Sound

**Calvert
Island**

Fish
Egg
Inlet

Dawsons
Landing

**Rivers
Inlet**

Fury Cove

Smith Sound

Cape Caution

See Blunden Harbour to
Slingsby Channel Map

Slingsby Channel

*Blunden
Harbour*

Distances (nm)
(Approximate, for planning)

Port Hardy to Fury Cove—53
Fury Cove to Shearwater/Bella Bella—50
Shearwater/Bella Bella to Ocean Falls—23
Shearwater/Bella Bella to Bella Coola—62
Shearwater/Bella Bella to Klemtu—35
Klemtu to Butedale—37
Butedale to Hartley Bay—28
Hartley Bay to Kitimat—43
Hartley Bay to Prince Rupert—70
Port Hardy to Prince Rupert—273

QUEEN CHARLOTTE STRAIT

Port
Hardy

NAUTICAL MILES

0   40

Cape Scott

Vancouver Island

Northern B.C. Coast

415

is at Shearwater. Parts can be easily flown in to New Bella Bella. Kitimat has facilities and a yard for repairs. Prince Rupert has full services, though they primarily serve the fishing fleet.

Charts and reference books. The Canadian Hydrographic Service has more than 65 charts that cover the coast from Wells Passage to Prince Rupert. Boaters that like to use paper charts will make the passage with fewer than 65 charts, but the number of charts on board likely will be closer to 65 than 35. Consider buying every chart, both small scale and large scale, in the area you plan to cruise. Include a few extra charts for unplanned side trips, unless your schedule calls for a straight passage up the main route (Interstate 5, as it is sometimes called). It takes a capital investment to cruise this coast safely and enjoyably.

Many boats carry a copy of Marine Atlas, Vol. 2, especially for those who rely on their chartplotter or laptop navigation system. The charts in the atlas are long out of date and many of the place names have changed, but the course lines are helpful. The book is a good quick reference and backup.

Tides and currents are shown in Ports and Passes and Canadian Tide and Current Tables, Vol. 7, (the purple book). North of Cape Caution you may want to consider getting the 3-volume set of Sailing Directions for the North Coast, PAC 200, 205, and 206.

The most complete guidebook is *Exploring the North Coast of British Columbia, 3rd Ed.*, by Don Douglass and Réanne Hemingway-Douglass, published and updated in 2017. Check www.WaggonerGuide.com/store for information on the updated edition. *Cruising the Secret Coast*, by Jennifer and James Hamilton, opens up anchorages in some of the most scenic, out-of-the-way locations for this area and others.

For the latest updates, sign up for WaggonerGuide.com email alerts. We also recommend a subscription to *Pacific Yachting* magazine, published in Canada. This is a well-done monthly magazine with cruising articles and updates on boating along the B.C. coast.

BLUNDEN HARBOUR TO SLINGSBY CHANNEL

The entrance to Blunden Harbour is approximately 11 miles northwest from the mouth of Wells Passage.

Blunden Harbour. Blunden Harbour is a lovely, well-protected bay, with excellent holding ground. As you approach the entrance it is important to identify Siwiti Rock and leave it to starboard. Study the 1:15,000 Blunden Harbour inset on Chart 3548 or your chartplotter. Note the several rocks along both sides of the passage into Blunden Harbour. These rocks make a somewhat serpentine route necessary as you go in.

Anchor anywhere in the large basin, or between Moore Rock and Byrnes Island. We feel that Moore Rock is closer to Byrnes Island than the chart suggests. An abandoned Indian village is on the north shore, and the beach is littered with relics. A large "no trespassing" sign warns against exploring the uplands, however.

You can explore Bradley Lagoon in the northeast corner of Blunden Harbour. Those who have say it's interesting. Take the dinghy through the rapids at high water slack.

Southgate Group. The Southgate Group is a cluster of islands at the corner of the route between Blunden Harbour and Allison Harbour. A passage between Southgate Island and Knight Island makes for a scenic, sheltered shortcut. Basins on either side of the narrows appear just right for anchoring. Chart 3921 shows the passage in large detail.

Allison Harbour. Allison Harbour is large, long and nicely protected, with room for many boats. Log booms may be tied to shore. Crabbing is said to be good. The best holding ground is toward the head, in 20 to 25 feet. *Favor the western shore as you enter and leave,* *to avoid a rock that lies almost mid-channel, about halfway in.*

Murray Labyrinth. This one is for the brave, who will be rewarded. *Exploring the North Coast of British Columbia* has a good description of Murray Labyrinth, and *Best Anchorages...* authors Kelly and Vipond describe Murray Labyrinth in glowing terms. Waggoner Correspondents Lorraine and John Littlewood report:

"The inner cove is a special place to us and nearly a perfect anchorage. It's guarded by what looks to be an impossibly tortuous, kelp-choked entrance, so most boats pass on by (in 10 years, we've not seen another boat there). It's not that hard, though, and the reward is that extreme rarity on the coast: a landlocked, completely protected anchorage with access at any tide and endless exploration potential by kayak or dinghy.

We took our 43-foot Ocean Alexander in twice, and other boats before. It was a piece of cake each time—just keep a bow watch and go dead slow, in and out of gear as necessary to give yourself plenty of time to react. All obstacles are plainly visible or charted. Use the south entry only. Do not attempt to enter or leave through the northern passage in anything other than a kayak or dinghy. It's foul, and what appear to be two rocks are really one rock with the middle part awash at low tide." [*Littlewood*]

Skull Cove. Skull Cove is on Bramham Island, roughly opposite Murray Labyrinth. It is one of the prettier anchorages you will find. If approaching from the south, we would pass behind Southgate Island and follow the eastern mainland shore almost to City Point. Then we would turn northwest, leaving Town Rock to port, and go through the passage between the Deloraine Islands and Murray Labyrinth, thus avoiding all the rocks and reefs that lie offshore. If approaching from the north, follow the Bramham Island shore.

Enter Skull Cove on the east side of the unnamed island and take anchorage in the cove immediately to port, in 20 to 25 feet. The view on the west side of the island is superb.

Miles Inlet. Miles Inlet indents the west shore of Bramham Island and is beautiful. The narrow passage is lined with silver snags. The trees are not tall, suggesting wind from winter storms blows strongly in the inlet. The entrance is narrow, but using McEwan Rock as a reference, the entrance is easy to locate. Offlying rocks are on each side of the entrance. Go directly down the middle. Once inside, anchor in a little nook on the north side of the entrance channel or at the T intersection. The two arms of the T shoal rapidly, but the north arm has more room.

Schooner Channel. Schooner Channel, along the east side of Bramham Island, is narrow and requires constant attention to avoid rocks and reefs. With attention, however, the channel is not difficult to run. Watch tidal currents closely. The flood runs

Blunden Harbour is a beautiful anchorage, with room for many boats. It's a good starting point for an early morning rounding of Cape Caution.

Boat name signs attached to trees on Turret Rock in Nakwakto Rapids

Treadwell Bay. Treadwell Bay is a good, protected anchorage at the east end of Slingsby Channel. It is often used by boats awaiting slack water at Nakwakto Rapids. Favor the east shore as you enter to avoid rocks off the Anchor Islands. The rocks are shown clearly on the charts. Inside, beware of rocks shown on the chart off the south shore of the bay.

Nakwakto Rapids. Nakwakto Rapids is among the world's fastest. Especially on spring tides, they must be transited at slack water only. At neap tides the window of safety opens a little wider. We have been told that high water slack is much preferred over low water slack. On big tides in particular, take this advice very, very seriously.

During the full rush of a maximum tidal current, the sound and action of the rushing water give the impression that Turret Rock actually trembles. Brave mariners have nailed boards with their boat names to trees on Turret Rock. Favored passage is on the west side.

Behind Nakwakto Rapids lie the extensive waterways of Seymour Inlet, Belize Inlet, Nugent Sound, and Alison Sound.

Note: Our sister publication *Cruising the Secret Coast*, by Jennifer and James Hamilton, devotes three chapters to the approaches to Nakwakto Rapids and the extensive waters of Seymour Inlet and Belize Inlet. Highly recommended.

to 5 knots and the ebb to 6 knots. Schooner Channel currents are shown in Ports and Passes and Canadian Tide and Current Tables, Vol. 6, as a secondary station based on Nakwakto Rapids.

An unnamed bay opposite Goose Point at the north end of Schooner Channel is mentioned in Sailing Directions as a good anchorage for small craft.

LOCAL KNOWLEDGE

Tide-Rip: Mike Guns, a commercial fisherman with much experience in these waters, reports that when an ebb current opposes a westerly wind, the entrance to Outer Narrows and Slingsby Channel is on par with the worst conditions that Nahwitti Bar or Cape Mudge can produce. He has seen "noticeable turbulence" as long as 3 hours after maximum ebb at Nakwakto Rapids. Take this patch of water seriously.

Slingsby Channel. Slingsby Channel runs between the mainland and the north side of Bramham Island. Currents in Outer Narrows, between the Fox Islands and Vigilance Point, run to 7 knots on the flood and 9 knots on the ebb. Outer Narrows is shown as a secondary station based on Nakwakto Rapids in Canadian Tide and Current Tables, Vol. 6 or Ports and Passes.

You can enter Slingsby Channel via a narrow, scenic channel that runs between the Fox Islands and Bramham Island, thus avoiding Outer Narrows entirely. Sailing Directions mentions the channel but does not encourage it. We found the channel easy to run, and deeper than the chart shows. [Hale]

SMITH SOUND

Smith Sound doesn't see many pleasure boats, but it's reputed to be full of fish. We visited during an opening for gillnet commercial salmon fishing, and the boats turned out in force. Picking our way among the nets required close attention, but all went well.

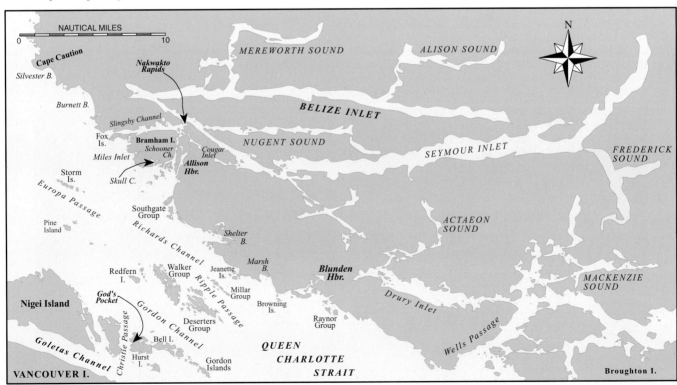

Blunden Harbour to Slingsby Channel

NAKWAKTO RAPIDS AND BELIZE INLET

If you are looking for a much less-traveled area with remote anchorages and intriguing, majestic scenery, the labyrinth of waterways lying southeast of Cape Caution is the place to be. How often do boaters on their way to or from Southeast Alaska focus on getting around Cape Caution instead of stopping for the cruising opportunities awaiting in the variety of inlets behind Cape Caution?

Allison Harbour, located south of Bramham Island, serves as a starting point for timing a passage through Nakwakto Rapids, the gate to this labyrinth of remote inlets.

On a recent trip, we anchored for the night in Allison Harbour and departed the following day, allowing 40 minutes to reach Nakwakto Rapids before slack. One of the world's fastest rapids, Nakwakto can attain speeds of 14.5 knots on large ebb tides and holds a record second only to Sechelt Rapids. Like other boaters, we had heard about these rapids and had seen photographs which tend to deter boaters from taking this passage. As we discovered, however, transiting the rapids at slack is a non-event; admittedly, timing the rapids is crucial. Not only is it the speed that makes Nakwakto treacherous, but also the whirlpools and eddies. Nakwakto Rapids is not one to challenge in anything but slack; within 15 minutes of slack, you can see turbulence and eddies. While transiting the rapids at slack is easily done, it's not uncommon to meet a tug pulling a raft of logs. As we neared the entrance to Nakwakto Rapids, we saw a tug approaching from the opposite direction and circled around a small islet to wait for the tug to be well clear before continuing into the passageway. Normally, seeing tugs at rapids is often a concern; but in this case, they serve as a confirmation that it's time to go through. Turret Rock, known locally as 'Tremble Island,' lies in the middle of the narrow Nakwakto Rapids. Boaters can pass around either side of Turret Rock; the west side is considered the preferred side. On our return trip, however, we passed on the east side with equal ease. Transiting each side allowed us to see all of the boat names attached to trees on this tiny rock island, a long-standing tradition.

Once through Nakwakto Rapids, boaters have three main headings to explore: east into Nugent Sound; southeast into Seymour Inlet which includes Frederick Sound; or northeast into Belize Inlet which includes Mereworth Sound and Alison Sound. Seldom visited by pleasure boaters, we found ourselves completely alone among these isolated scenic inlets, hidden from the outside world. With limited time, we chose the beautiful Belize Inlet route, a fjord-like channel with steep mountains and numerous waterfalls. Putting the nose of Got d' Fever up close to one of the falls, we took in the quiet, undisturbed majesty of this remote backcountry.

While traversing through the bends and turns admiring the variety of geological formations and vegetation, we couldn't help but marvel that this area was once home to the Nakwaktok people. Pictographs in the area give evidence of their previous life here. A pictograph on the northern shore of Belize Inlet (near the entrance to Alison Sound) depicts a sailing ship and some canoes, men in the canoes appear to be holding what looks like rifles. As we turned up Alison Sound following the narrow, twisting channel lined with more mountain peaks and cascading waterfalls, we found a second pictograph on the north shore showing a row of canoes with one lone canoe approaching. It is reported that a Native Nakwaktok camp in Village Cove of Mereworth Sound was fired upon in 1868 in retaliation for an assault on a trading vessel named Thorton; perhaps these pictographs record this incident. History indicates that a main village, as well as summer camps, were established throughout these inlets.

For us, our journey took us to the head of Belize Inlet ending at a delta. Backtracking a short distance, we found anchorage at Summers Bay over an irregular bottom in about 60 feet of water. The still quiet evening was interrupted only by the sound of a nearby waterfall and the chirping of birds as the sun went behind the peaks above Chief Nollis Bay at the western end of Alison Sound.

– Lorena Landon

One of many scenic stops on Belize Inlet on the way to Alison Sound

Dramatic scenery on Belize Inlet where very few boaters venture

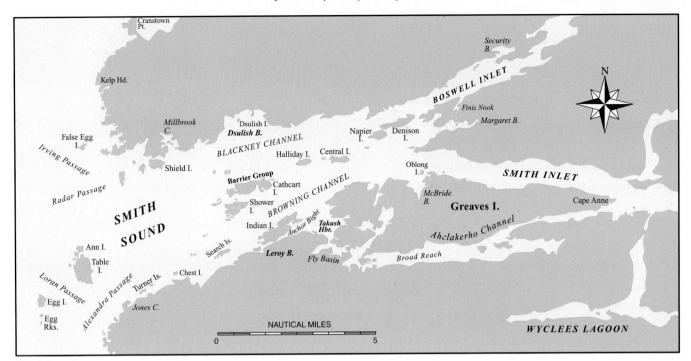

Smith Sound

You're on your own in Smith Sound itself. There are no resorts or settlements. Several bays are good for anchoring, although only one, Millbrook Cove, really appeals to us.

From the south, enter Smith Sound through Alexandra Passage, between North Iron Rock and Egg Rocks. From the west, enter through Radar Passage. From the north, enter through Irving Passage. We suggest that you plot waypoints to keep clear of rocks. This is especially true in reduced visibility.

Table Island. Table Island is in the mouth of Smith Sound, and the casual visitor would not think of it as an anchorage. But fish boats anchor there and have no problems. A boat waiting to make a southerly dash around Cape Caution could find this anchorage useful, as could a boat seeking shelter from a westerly in Queen Charlotte Sound. The Hulsizers report spending a rolly night at this anchorage.

Crossing Smith Sound at Blackney Channel for a night's anchorage in Millbrook Cove.

Jones Cove. Jones Cove is on the south shore of Smith Sound, near the mouth. The cove is cozy and well protected and often used by commercial fish boats. Anchor in 20 feet with limited swinging room. Depending on the rise and fall of the tide and the presence of other boats, you may choose to run a stern-tie to shore.

Fly Basin. Fly Basin is on the south side of Smith Sound at 51°16.35'N/127°36.20'W. "It is very private and protected, but entry requires care. Study of the chart will show that you should favor the western shore until opposite the point of land extending from the eastern shore. Then swing to the east side of the channel. The charted rocks can be difficult to see except at low water. Once in, anchor in 15 to 25 feet (zero tide) in the eastern section of the bay, excellent holding in mud." [*Hamilton*]

Correspondents John and Lorraine Littlewood report the western basin is also good. Work your way in past the rocks, and anchor in pristine surroundings on a good mud bottom. They begged us to not tell a soul about this anchorage, but since we are friends we feel safe letting you in on it.

McBride Bay. This bay is on the north side of Greaves Island, at the east end of Browning Channel. It is deep until near the head, which has 30 to 40 foot anchoring depths. Protection is excellent, but swinging room is a little limited.

Ahclakerho Channel. Ahclakerho Channel leads along the south side of Greaves Island. The current runs hard in the channel. Transit at slack water, especially on big tides. Slack appears to be around the time of high and low water at Bella Bella. Correspondent Gil Flanagan reports: "This is an overlooked gem. The narrow part of the channel is probably 200 feet wide. The anchorage on the east side of the 78-meter east Ahclakerho Island gives good protection from west winds in Smith Sound. We stern-tied among numerous rocks and small islands. It was beautiful."

Margaret Bay. Margaret Bay is at the head of Smith Sound, on the point of land that separates Boswell Inlet and Smith Inlet. Chambers Island, rather small, is in the middle of the bay, about halfway in. West of Chambers Island depths are too great for anchoring. East of the island they shallow to 50 to 55 feet. The head shoals sharply, and old pilings take up much of the room at the head. Protection is excellent.

Ethel Cove. Ethel Cove is just outside the mouth of Margaret Bay. It looks right out to sea, however, and we found a very low surge coming in. Get close to shore or anchor in 50 to 60 feet farther out.

Millbrook Cove is a quiet, protected anchorage at the entrance of Smith Sound.

Finis Nook. Finis Nook is located near the mouth of Boswell Inlet, on the south shore, sort of "around the corner" from Margaret Bay. It is nearly landlocked and completely protected; it seems a perfect anchorage. A log boom blocks the back bay, however, and a float house is on the east side, with the wreck of a fish boat. Anchoring depths in the area not already taken are approximately 35 feet. We were disappointed, and went back to Millbrook Cove to overnight. (In *Cruising the Secret Coast,* the Hamiltons like Finis Nook).

Dsulish Bay. Dsulish Bay, with beautiful white sand beaches, is on the north shore of Smith Sound. A trail reportedly leads to Goose Bay to the north. The best anchorage is behind the 46-meter island, deep inside the bay. It is a little open but workable. We have seen fish boats anchored along the west side of Dsulish Bay. In the right conditions it would be a good lunch stop, though we're not so sure about overnight.

Millbrook Cove. This is the outermost anchorage on the north side of Smith Sound. To us it is the favored anchorage. The cove is completely landlocked, with 25 to 35 foot depths, good holding ground, and ample room.

Getting in will hold your attention, at least the first time. Find the red spar buoy *E6* marking Millbrook Rocks. The buoy has a small radar reflector on top. Leave this buoy to starboard (Red, Right, Returning), and aim the boat toward the 30-meter island. Keep a sharp lookout for rocks on both sides, especially the west side, as shown on the chart. The 30-meter island can be passed on either side, although the east side is a little deeper.

Once in, watch for a drying rock a short distance off the northeast corner of the 30-meter island. Minding your depths, anchor anywhere.

RIVERS INLET

Note: Cruising the Secret Coast, by Jennifer and James Hamilton, contains an entire chapter devoted to cruising the parts of Rivers Inlet not covered here, with a little overlap.

Rivers Inlet is a famed salmon fishing area and, at one time, had 18 salmon canneries. All the canneries are closed now and most are sinking into ruin. Absent its commerce of former years, Rivers Inlet is prime cruising ground. The scenery is beautiful and the

anchorages excellent. The area is served by Dawsons Landing and private fishing lodges. In Goose Bay, a substantial concrete dock provides access to the Goose Bay Cannery, but no amenities.

Open Bight. Open Bight, well named, is just inside Cranstown Point at the entrance to Rivers Inlet. Anchorage, with protection from westerlies but not easterlies or northerlies, is along the south and west shores. The west shore is preferred. We would put the hook down outside the kelp line in 25 to 30 feet, within view of a stunning white shell midden beach. Gentle swells will rock the boat.

Home Bay. Home Bay, on the south shore a short distance inside the mouth of Rivers Inlet, is a pretty spot.

Just west of Home Bay is another nook, which Douglass calls West Home Bay in *Exploring the North Coast of British Columbia*. The bay has anchorage behind the first of two islets inside. Contrary to Douglass' illustration, however, low tide reveals rocks that foul the western side of that first islet. We would pass the islet only to the east.

Other anchoring possibilities lie in the unnamed group of islands just west of Duncanby Lodge. Larger boats will find good anchoring in deep water in the unnamed cove marked with 29-meter and 35-meter soundings. The large island with the

105-meter hill is at the north end of this cove. Smaller boats can creep into the unnamed cove east of the deep water cove. This cove is marked with a 9-meter sounding in the mouth and a 16-meter sounding inside. A fishing resort outpost is moored on the eastern shore. The little nook at the northeast end of the cove offers quiet anchorage in 60 to 120 feet, but be careful when you enter this nook. A reef extends northward nearly halfway across the entrance, much farther than the chart suggests. Favor the north side.

Duncanby Lodge. (604) 628-9822; (877) 846-6548; www.duncanby.com. Duncanby is a high-quality fly-in fishing resort. Meals, lodging and charter boats are all inclusive as a guest package. The restaurant and docks are no longer open to the general boating public. No fuel service.

Goose Bay. Anchorage is good in 20 to 50 feet on a sticky bottom across the bay from the cannery buildings. Crabbing is reported to be good.

Goose Bay Cannery Dock. (778) 373-6346; Monitors VHF 06. Open during peak summer season. This is a private facility which is at the discretion of the owners to permit visitors to come ashore. The historic cannery in Goose Bay, built in 1926, processed and canned salmon from 1927-1957; 350 people once worked and lived at the cannery. A clean, sturdy 175-foot concrete dock is available for short-term and overnight stays on a first-come, first-serve basis; no power; no water. Leave space on the dock for floatplanes. A self-registration payment box is located at the end of the dock ramp, expect a donation fee of $1 per foot. Fees collected go towards making improvements on the cannery buildings. Projects are ongoing and shared among the multiple owners of the property. A two-bedroom cabin is available for rent. Depending on which owner you meet and the work scheduled for that day,

Visitor moorage at Goose Bay Cannery. Sign in at the head of the dock.

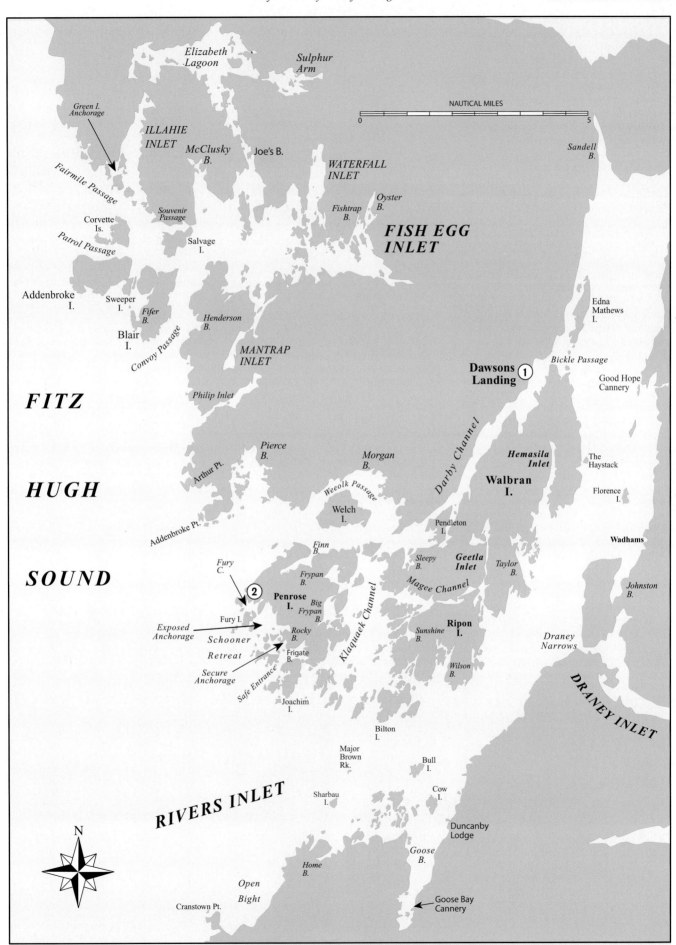

NAUTICAL MILES

0   5

Elizabeth Lagoon

Sulphur Arm

Green I. Anchorage

ILLAHIE INLET

McClusky B.

Joe's B.

WATERFALL INLET

Sandell B.

Fishtrap B.

Oyster B.

FISH EGG INLET

Fairmile Passage

Souvenir Passage

Salvage I.

Corvette Is.

Patrol Passage

Addenbroke I.

Sweeper I.

Fifer B.

Henderson B.

Edna Mathews I.

Blair I.

Convoy Passage

MANTRAP INLET

Dawsons Landing ①

Bickle Passage

Good Hope Cannery

FITZ

Philip Inlet

HUGH

Pierce B.

Morgan B.

Weeolk Passage

Darby Channel

Hemasila Inlet

Walbran I.

The Haystack

Florence I.

Arthur Pt.

Welch I.

Wadhams

SOUND

Addenbroke Pt.

Finn B.

Fury C.

Frypan B.

②

Penrose I.

Big Frypan B.

Fury I.

Exposed Anchorage

Rocky B.

Schooner

Retreat

Frigate B.

Secure Anchorage

Safe Entrance

Klaquaek Channel

Pendleton I.

Sleepy B.

Geetla Inlet

Taylor B.

Magee Channel

Ripon I.

Sunshine B.

Johnston B.

Draney Narrows

Wilson B.

Joachim I.

Bilton I.

DRANEY INLET

RIVERS INLET

Major Brown Rk.

Bull I.

Cow I.

Sharbau I.

Duncanby Lodge

Goose B.

N

Home B.

Open Bight

Cranstown Pt.

Goose Bay Cannery

Rivers Inlet & Fish Egg Inlet

421

you might be able to finesse an invitation for a brief tour of the grounds and cannery. With permission, hiking the 1 mile trail to a dam located above the cannery may be of interest, but be "bear aware" and take appropriate precautions. A waterfall, and a suspension bridge built in the 1940's can be seen near the dam. Correspondents Knut and Christine Hildebrand report that the trail is challenging. Use at your own risk.

Hemasila Inlet. "Entry to the inner basin looks impossible on the chart, but isn't. The charted rock is central in a 200-foot-wide channel and is visible except at very high tides. Favor the east side—it has slightly more room and the shore is steep. We anchored in 35 feet just north of the 9.1-meter sounding with plenty of room to swing. Holding was excellent in thick mud. It was sheltered and pretty, with a small creek at one side and a small waterfall at the other side. Watch for a rock 2.5 meters deep at zero tide in the mouth of the inlet where the R symbol and 24 meter sounding are located." [*Hamilton*]

Taylor Bay. Taylor Bay indents the east shore of Walbran Island and has tranquil, lovely anchorage in 35 to 50 feet, although swinging room is limited. Anchor all the way in or try the nook behind the north end of the inner island, between the inner island and Walbran Island. Protected from most winds except east and southeast.

Draney Narrows & Draney Inlet. The current runs hard in Draney Narrows. We looked in 1½ hours before the predicted turn and decided against it. Fifteen minutes before the turn the narrows were flat. Predictions are shown in Canadian Tide & Current Tables, Vol. 7 and Ports and Passes as a secondary station based on Prince Rupert Tides.

Draney Inlet, approximately 24 miles long, is surrounded by high, steep mountains. It's beautiful. Because it is not on the way to anyplace else, it sees little pleasure craft traffic. Good anchorage in 30 to 35 feet is available in Fish Hook Bay, a short distance inside the narrows. When we visited, a float home with

Frypan Bay, a sizzling place to anchor with plenty of room.

two floating outbuildings was on the south shore of Fish Hook Bay, near the entrance. A large sign read, "Warning, Private Property, No Trespassing." A convincing watchdog greeted our boat with don't-mess-with-me barks and growls. We didn't argue.

Note: Our sister publication, *Cruising the Secret Coast*, by Jennifer and James Hamilton, devotes a chapter to Draney Inlet, with much information about anchorages and what to see.

Johnston Bay. Johnston Bay, on the east shore of Rivers Inlet just south of Wadhams, is a former cannery site. The bay is quiet and beautiful, but deep until very near the head. As the chart shows, a reef lies in the center of the outer part of Johnston Bay, and a rock is close to the eastern shore at the entrance. Favor the western shore all the way in and you'll have ample depths of 30-50 feet.

Sandell Bay. "North shore of Rivers Inlet, where the inlet takes that east bend. Anchor well into the bay in 25 feet, zero tide. Excellent holding in mud/sand/rock/shell. Kind of like

a cement mix, and held like it, too. Sandell Bay looks exposed on the chart, but is actually protected. It was blowing 30 knots in Rivers Inlet when we came in, and from the anchorage we could see a line of whitecaps out there. But hardly any wind or fetch reached us." [*Hamilton*]

Good Hope Cannery. Good Hope Cannery is the large, white building visible when cruising past Draney Inlet. The facility is a high-end fly-in sport fishing resort. No services for cruising boats.

① **Dawsons Landing** (Dawsons Landing General Store). (604) 629-9897; dawsonslanding@gmail.com; www.dawsonslanding.ca. Monitors VHF 06. Phone service is spotty; it's often best to communicate by email. Open all year, gasoline and diesel fuel. Guest moorage, hardware, groceries, charts, ice, fishing licenses, fishing and hunting gear, liquor, washroom, showers, laundry, post office, two rental cabins with kitchenettes. Satellite based Wi-Fi available for a fee, pay at the general store. Locally

Informal owner-conducted tours of the Goose Bay Cannery might be available as owner's time permits.

The short, narrow entrance to Big Frypan Bay is straight-forward and easy to transit.

Relax and enjoy the view of Rivers Inlet at Dawsons Landing.

Dawsons Landing has plenty of dock space.

produced water available on the dock. A heli-pad takes up part of the south end dock. They have scheduled air service from Wilderness Seaplanes and NW Seaplanes.

Dawsons Landing is owned by Rob and Nola Bachen, and has been in the family since 1954. This is a real general store, with an excellent stock of standard grocery items and an astonishing accumulation of tools and hardware. One year, for example, we needed an in-line fuse holder to replace a spare we had used. Dawsons had it.

Note that instead of cleats, you'll tie to loops of rope set into the planks. Absent bull rails, it's easier and safer to clear the docks of snow in the winter. The one dock with bull rails is used by float planes.

Smoked salmon: It's almost worth a trip to Dawsons Landing simply to stock up on the Bella Coola Valley Seafoods smoked wild Pacific salmon that Nola carries in the store. Several smoke flavors to choose from; time of year varies depending on the commercial fishing season.

Darby Channel (Schooner Pass). Darby Channel, locally called Schooner Pass, borders the west side of Walbran Island, and is easily run. Southbound boats should favor the west shore of the channel to avoid being lured into foul ground behind Pendleton Island. The rock off the southwest corner of Pendleton Island is clearly marked by a beacon and easily avoided.

Pierce Bay. Exercise caution, because Pierce Bay contains dangerous rocks not necessarily shown on the chart. One of the rocks is east of the south tip of the largest island, at 51°31.665'N/127°45.667'W. This rock is in relatively open water, and could surprise a person. Another is off the northwest point of the large island, where the anchorage opens up.

Frypan Bay. Frypan Bay, spacious, scenic and well protected, is at the northeast corner of Penrose Island. Anchoring depths, along the south shore, are 25 to 40 feet and, in the

middle, 50 to 85 feet with good holding. This anchorage is a favorite of many cruisers. The narrow entrance has an uncharted shoal on the port side shore as you enter.

Big Frypan Bay. Located on the east side of Penrose Island, this large bay has ample room for numerous boats; anchoring depths of 68 feet on a sand-mud bottom. Shallower depths can be found in a couple of coves within the bay. The short, narrow entrance to Big Frypan is straight-forward and easy to transit.

Finn Bay. Finn Bay, on the north side of Penrose Island, is well protected. An abandoned sport fishing camp is in the bay. Anchoring depths of 36-66 feet can be found in the bay.

Sunshine Bay. Tucked in the middle of Ripon Island, the bay is entered through a narrow channel off of Klaquaek Channel. The charted shoal on the south shore at the neck of the entrance is not as extensive as depicted on the charts. Anchoring depths are 25 to 30 feet over a flat mud bottom. This intriguing bay is

See Area Map Page 421 - Maps Not for Navigation

home to a hidden community of float-homes. During the off-season, this bay is the parking location for several fishing lodge buildings.

② **Fury Cove.** The cove behind Fury Island is a beautiful and a popular anchorage, with a perfect white shell beach. Fury Cove, as it is commonly called, is entered by leaving Cleve Island to port, then turning to port towards the narrow entrance.

Fury Cove is a good place to spend the night before a southbound rounding of Cape Caution, or when headed north after crossing Cape Caution. It is popular and occasionally fills up; consider Big Frypan Bay as an alternative. While at anchor, you can look across the beach and see the conditions on Fitz Hugh Sound. Inside, avoid the charted rock that dries at 10 feet close to Fury Island. Consider taking the dinghy to shore to explore the beach and tide pools. A cabin used by kayakers is nestled in the woods on the north shore of Fury Island.

Cleve Island is mentioned in Sailing Directions, but shown on the chart only as a 61-meter island—no name. **Breaker Pass** separates Fury Island from Cleve Island. We have run through the pass in calm weather, but we could tell it wouldn't take much of a southwesterly for Breaker Pass to live up to its name.

No Discharge Zone: No black water overboard discharge, please. Fury Cove does not flush well.

Philip Inlet. Philip Inlet indents the mainland side of Fitz Hugh Sound approximately 3 miles south of Addenbroke Island. The entrance can be hard to identify. Use caution when entering: ledges of rock extend from each side of the inlet near the mouth. About halfway in, a small island creates a rock-strewn, tight and tricky narrows. A bow watch is recommended. Field Correspondents Jim Norris and Anita Fraser report: "We came here to hide from an approaching southeast gale. We entered midway on the flood and found the entrance narrow in one spot, but well charted on Chart 3934. Least depth was 18 feet at half tide with very slight current. We anchored in 55 feet in the middle of the bay with good holding. The next morning Addenbrook Island lighthouse reported southeast 15 knot winds; we had northwest 3 knots."

Fifer Bay. Fifer Bay indents the western side of Blair Island, with lovely 6- to 12-foot anchorage for small craft at the head of the southernmost cove. There's room for one boat if it swings, more if all stern-tie to shore. When entering, favor Sweeper Island to avoid the rocks lying off the southern side of the entrance. When clear of the rocks, turn south and work your way into the anchorage.

FISH EGG INLET

Fish Egg Inlet indents the east side of Fitz Hugh Sound, behind Addenbroke Island. This is beautiful cruising country, and is

Fury Cove is well-protected with sandy beaches and windows to Fitz Hugh Sound.

becoming one of the popular spots on the coast. Those who say you'll be all alone are wrong. The gunkholing possibilities are many, but here are notes on some of the better-known anchorages.

Mantrap Inlet. Once you're inside, Mantrap Inlet offers good anchorage. The entrance, however, is narrow, made narrower by an uncharted ledge of rock that extends from the west shore. Consider going through at half tide or higher, dead slow, with a lookout.

Oyster Bay. Oyster Bay, next to Fish Trap Bay at the head of Fish Egg Inlet, is a nice anchorage with a remote feel to it. We had a late and relaxed lunch there, anchored in 20 feet near the head of the bay. Recommended. [*Hale*]

Fish Trap Bay. Awfully tight, but room for one boat, stern-tied. At lower water levels the Native fish trap is clearly visible.

Waterfall Inlet. Pretty spot, but we couldn't find any comfortable anchorages. We felt that the west entry, leaving the 99-meter island to starboard, was safest. Go slowly and watch for rock ledges that extend from each side of the narrow pass.

Joe's Bay. Joe's Bay has become quite popular. When we visited in early July one year, five

other boats were already anchored. Joe's Bay is worth the crowds, though. It's tranquil, tree-lined and snug. Anchoring is straightforward in the southern basin; rocks and reefs make the northern portion somewhat trickier. A stern-tie to shore might be called for to keep the boat from swinging onto a rock. Once anchored, the tidal rapids leading to Elizabeth Lagoon and Sulphur Arm are worth exploring with the dinghy.

Souvenir Passage. Sailing Directions says that Souvenir Passage is very narrow at its eastern end and the chart shows a rock on the north shore. We have found good water all the way by favoring the south side of the passage.

Illahie Inlet. The head of Illahie Inlet would be a delightful anchorage in 30 to 40 feet, mud bottom, with good protection. Favor one shore or the other as you enter Illahie Inlet. Rocks lie in the middle of the channel, partway in.

Green Island Anchorage. Green Island Anchorage, just off Fitz Hugh Sound at the mouth of Illahie Inlet, is about as cozy as an anchorage needs to be. Excellent holding in 35 to 40 feet. From seaward, wrap around the 70-meter island and follow the shoreline in. This is a good spot to rest after crossing Queen Charlotte Sound.

Entrance to the very well-protected Sunshine Bay on Ripon Island

RAIN PEOPLE, THE STORY OF OCEAN FALLS   *- By Bruce Ramsey*

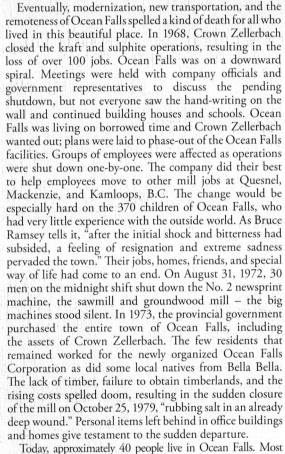

Publisher: Ocean Falls Library Association; ISBN: 0-968192-0-X

Boaters never seem to tire of visiting the modern-day ghost town of Ocean Falls, scattered with ghostly reminders, including dishes still in the cupboards and children's books lying on the floor of abandoned houses. There's something fascinating and endearing about this special place, which continues to capture the hearts and minds of all who visit. The sad, yet inspiring story of this once active mill town of 5,000 people is told by Bruce Ramsey in his book, *Rain People, The Story of Ocean Falls.*

The story begins in 1902 when Robert Thompson and Charles Baker, from Washington State, formed the Bella Coola Pulp & Paper Company. After locating timberlands and a waterfall in Cousins Inlet, they began their enterprise. Land was cleared in 1906 for the townsite, which included a store, school, and hospital to meet the needs of workers coming to the area. By 1912, a hotel had been built to accommodate 250 guests, and 33 houses had been completed. When a recession hit in 1913, Archie B. Martin, of Bellingham, Washington was appointed general manager.

Things started looking up in 1915 when a Canadian corporation, Pacific Mills Limited, took over at Ocean Falls; Martin agreed to stay on as general manager. (Pacific Mills would later become a division of the Crown Zellerbach Corporation.) A new concrete gravity dam, 677 feet long and 60 feet high, was constructed over the falls. By May 1917, Ocean Falls was turning out newsprint paper at a rate of 600 feet a minute. The hotel was enlarged, a new fire hall was built along with apartments, churches, a customs building, and warehouse. As WWI set in, area mills turned their attention to Sitka spruce for the building of aircraft as did Ocean Falls. Bruce Ramsey goes on to describe in his book the various logging practices that developed over the years. Like other towns, Ocean Falls experienced its share of the roaring 20's with band concerts, theatre performances, community celebrations, and many sporting activities and clubs.

Ocean Falls was not without its house of ill repute, which operated in the 1930's; author Ramsey puts it this way, "the palace of 'Venus' was located around the bend from Ocean Falls, out of sight of the town, and it was known for what it was for miles around. All the ships coming in to pick up paper, as well as the regular coastal steamers, would give a shrill blast of their whistles as they passed by." The 1930's saw the dark days of the Great Depression, and Archie Martin was forced to cut wages by ten percent in order to keep the mills afloat.

In September of 1939, Canada was plunged into war with Germany for a second time. Mills once again focused their attention on the Sitka spruce of the northwest coast for fighter and bomber aircraft frames. Labor shortage for the mills was an acute problem; the men that remained were put on extra shifts, and women were employed where possible, which required the construction of separate apartment buildings. At the end of WWII, men began to return to their jobs at

Ocean Falls; 1945 also saw the passing of Archie Martin. In July 1947, the new Martin Inn opened with 265 rooms, and another 105 rooms were added in 1952, making the Inn the third largest hotel in British Columbia. It was a happening town, and the local newspaper was filled with community events. It was during the 1940's, 50's, and 60's that the Swim Team earned world recognition, turning out Pan-American and Olympic champions. This was also the period that homes were being constructed in Martin Valley, the small community located down the road from Ocean Falls.

Eventually, modernization, new transportation, and the remoteness of Ocean Falls spelled a kind of death for all who lived in this beautiful place. In 1968, Crown Zellerbach closed the kraft and sulphite operations, resulting in the loss of over 100 jobs. Ocean Falls was on a downward spiral. Meetings were held with company officials and government representatives to discuss the pending shutdown, but not everyone saw the hand-writing on the wall and continued building houses and schools. Ocean Falls was living on borrowed time and Crown Zellerbach wanted out; plans were laid to phase-out of the Ocean Falls facilities. Groups of employees were affected as operations were shut down one-by-one. The company did their best to help employees move to other mill jobs at Quesnel, Mackenzie, and Kamloops, B.C. The change would be especially hard on the 370 children of Ocean Falls, who had very little experience with the outside world. As Bruce Ramsey tells it, "after the initial shock and bitterness had subsided, a feeling of resignation and extreme sadness pervaded the town." Their jobs, homes, friends, and special way of life had come to an end. On August 31, 1972, 30 men on the midnight shift shut down the No. 2 newsprint machine, the sawmill and groundwood mill – the big machines stood silent. In 1973, the provincial government purchased the entire town of Ocean Falls, including the assets of Crown Zellerbach. The few residents that remained worked for the newly organized Ocean Falls Corporation as did some local natives from Bella Bella. The lack of timber, failure to obtain timberlands, and the rising costs spelled doom, resulting in the sudden closure of the mill on October 25, 1979, "rubbing salt in an already deep wound." Personal items left behind in office buildings and homes give testament to the sudden departure.

Today, approximately 40 people live in Ocean Falls. Most of the buildings have collapsed or were bulldozed earlier; but several homes still stand along paved streets leaving us clues of this once vibrant, attractive community. The hotel and other office buildings, as well as the homes, continue to be taken over by vines that crawl up their sides and into open windows as if possessed. Thanks to the many photographs of the town's prosperous past, the images of happier times remain safe in the hearts of all who visit this unique place.

The Crown Zellerbach company boat "Leeward" was used to en... paper buyers. This was a crabbing trip in June 1953.

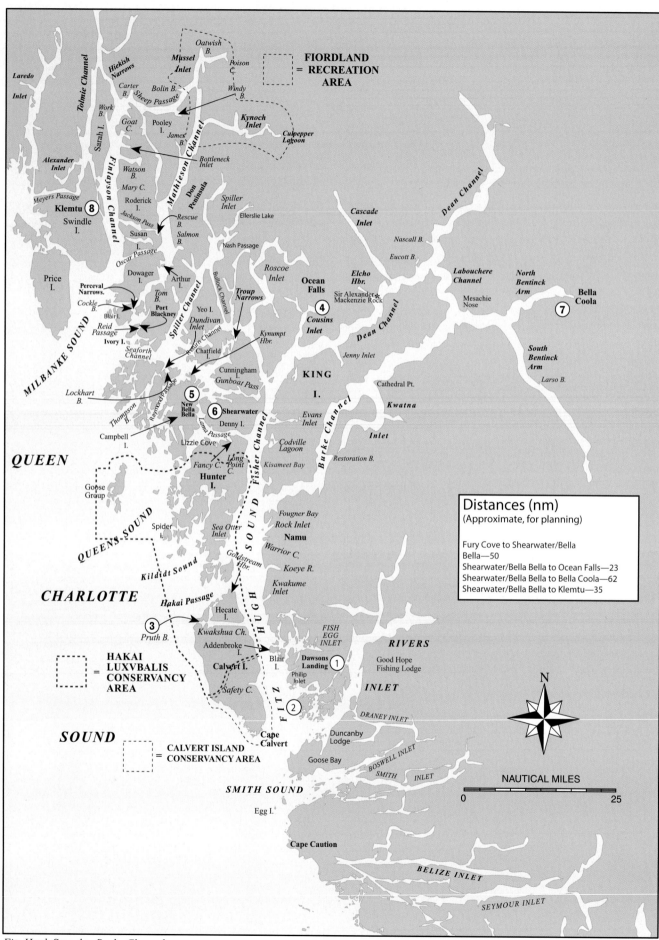

FIORDLAND = RECREATION AREA

Distances (nm)
(Approximate, for planning)

Fury Cove to Shearwater/Bella
Bella—50
Shearwater/Bella Bella to Ocean Falls—23
Shearwater/Bella Bella to Bella Coola—62
Shearwater/Bella Bella to Klemtu—35

□ = **HAKAI LUXVBALIS CONSERVANCY AREA**

□ = **CALVERT ISLAND CONSERVANCY AREA**

NAUTICAL MILES
0   25

N

Fitz Hugh Sound to Burke Channel

FITZ HUGH SOUND

Fitz Hugh Sound begins at Cape Calvert and continues north to Fisher Channel. Boats crossing Queen Charlotte Sound from the south will find the ocean swells quickly vanish once Cape Calvert is behind them. A southwesterly can still make things nasty, especially in a south flowing ebb current. Even in settled conditions, expect to find rougher water where Hakai Passage joins Fitz Hugh Sound.

Northbound boats that don't stop at Rivers Inlet probably will stop in Fifer Bay, Safety Cove, or Pruth Bay. Green Island Anchorage is another good choice for passing traffic.

Safety Cove. Safety Cove is a steep-walled, uninteresting bay that indents Calvert Island approximately 7 miles north of Cape Calvert. The bottom shoals sharply a fair distance from the head of the bay. Sailing Directions recommends anchoring immediately when the depth reaches 100 feet. If you press in to find shallower water, watch your swing or you could find yourself aground on the shelf at low tide. Despite its name and regular use, Safety Cove is not our first choice of anchorages in the area.

③ **Pruth Bay.** Pruth Bay is at the head of **Kwakshua Channel,** some 7 miles north of Safety Cove. Pruth Bay has long been a favorite stopover point. It offers ample room, 40- to 50-foot anchoring depths, and a flat bottom with good holding. Storms coming off the ocean can make the bay quite windy.

This entire area is part of the **Hakai Luxvbalis Conservancy Area**, a huge provincial park that includes the northern half of Calvert Island, the southern two-thirds of Hunter Island, and Goose Island.

Correspondents James and Jennifer Hamilton have anchored in about 50 feet

West Beach near Pruth Bay is arguably the best beach anywhere on the west coast.

with good holding in the unnamed cove west of Keith Anchorage, on the south shore of Kwakshua Channel, a short distance east of Pruth Bay. Anchor in this cove or one of the others that indent that shore, in Pruth Bay itself, or in the bay north of the thumb of land marked by Whittaker Point.

Southbound, we often overnight at Pruth Bay before rounding Cape Caution. Hakai Beach Institute provides free Wi-Fi in the bay, handy for downloading weather information.

Note: Our sister publication, *Cruising the Secret Coast*, by Jennifer and James Hamilton, devotes a chapter to this area. It describes anchorages not included in the Waggoner, and includes coverage of anchorages at the mouth of Hakai Passage.

③ **Hakai Beach Institute.** In 2010 the luxury fly-in fishing resort at the head of Pruth Bay was purchased by the Tula Foundation and became the Hakai Beach Institute.

The facility is now used for research and as a conference center. Visitors are welcome to moor their dinghies and use the marked walk-way and trail to the Pacific side of the Institute's grounds.

No fuel or commercial services are available at Hakai Beach Institute. When arriving by dinghy, moor only at the clearly marked "dinghy dock" section of the float. The Institute requests that visitors sign the guest log at the Welcome Centre, at the head of the dock. A public washroom is adjacent.

The grounds are immaculate. Follow the signs for the trail to West Beach, one of the finest beaches on the coast. The trail is substantially covered with a boardwalk, but unfinished and muddy in some places. Carry bug spray. After a pleasant and flat hike of almost a half-mile, you hear the ocean and break out of the forest to a beautiful beach, with white sand extending in both directions. On a sunny day it seems almost tropical.

Easy trail from Pruth Bay brings you to West Beach.

HAKAI BEACH INSTITUTE – PRUTH BAY

Pruth Bay has always been a good overnight stop along the Inside Passage. The bay, at the head of Kwakshua Channel, is well protected and scenic. But the real attractions are West Beach and North Beach, two of the most beautiful sand beaches in the Northwest.

Access to the beach areas, however, has not always been easy. As the owners of the property have changed, the state of the trail leading across Calvert Island has ranged from poor to acceptable.

A few years back the property, formerly a fishing lodge, was acquired by the Tula Foundation and rechristened as the Hakai Beach Institute. Eric Peterson and Christina Munck, the principals of the Tula Foundation, have since transformed the property into a world-class conference and research center.

The improvements are apparent as soon as you arrive. Beautiful new docks have been installed, welcoming signage posted, and top-notch facilities constructed. Signs direct visitors

to the West Beach trail, a well-maintained boardwalk and gravel pathway.

Researchers and educators use the facilities to investigate and collaborate. Areas of research include local archaeology, ecology, and First Nations culture. The institute has a fleet of boats available to transport personnel and equipment throughout the area and scientific labs to support research activities.

Due to its location, the Hakai Beach Institute is totally off the grid. Electricity is generated by a 50 kw solar farm feeding into a nearly 10,000 amp hour battery bank. Water is collected on site. Sewage is heavily treated before being released. And perhaps most welcome for visiting boaters, internet is piped in through nine satellite links and distributed wirelessly throughout the property and anchorage (please, no streaming video or other bandwidth intensive tasks).

We are fortunate to have people like Eric and Christina, focused on understanding our environment and sharing the beauty of this area with visiting boaters.

You can learn more about the Hakai Beach Institute and the work of the Tula Foundation on their blog and website, www.hakai.org.

– Mark Bunzel

On an overcast day, with crashing waves, it carries the beauty and furor of the wild Pacific Ocean. A less-developed trail leads north to North Beach, a sandy beach facing Hakai Pass; and a longer more challenging trail leads south to nine scenic west facing beaches.

Visiting boats are welcome to anchor in Pruth Bay, as long as they stay 100 meters from the dock so seaplanes have room to maneuver. Free Wi-Fi covers the entire bay. Wi-Fi internet use is limited to 300mb of data per device per day. The best reception is close to the head of the bay.

Meay Inlet. Meay Inlet leads north from Kwakshua Channel to Hakai Pass. Immediately after the turn past Whittaker Point is a small scenic cove with room for 4 or 5 boats. The Hamiltons, in *Cruising the Secret Coast*, named this cove Whitaker Point Cove and report anchorage in 40 to 60 feet, with good holding in mud mixed with shell.

The Hakai Lodge (hakai-lodge.com) fly-in fishing resort, owned by the principals of NW Seaplanes, is in a nearby cove from late June until September. The resort has almost daily floatplane service to the Renton/Seattle area, making this a good place to drop off or

pick up crew or parts. The lodge serves meals to visiting boaters, reservations required 24-hours in advance for breakfast, lunch, and dinner. Reservations also accepted for guided fishing tours. Email ccarlson@hakailodge.com or hail on VHF 16 for meal reservations. This is a seasonal resort, floats are removed in the off-season.

Hakai Passage. Hakai Passage is one of the great fishing spots, yielding 50- to 60-pound salmon and large bottom fish. Since Hakai Passage opens to the Pacific Ocean, it can get rough. Treat it with respect. On an otherwise pleasant afternoon we overheard two well-managed boats discussing on the radio whether the swells they were facing in Hakai Passage began in Japan or just Hawaii.

Goldstream Harbour. Goldstream Harbour is a lovely little anchorage at the north end of Hecate Island. Enter from the east favoring Hat Island, which extends from the south shore about 0.2 mile inside. Don't favor Hat Island too closely, though; rocks extend out from it. Hat Island is not named on the chart, but its height (39 meters) is shown. Once past Hat Island, pass Evening Rock, which dries

at 1.2 meters, leaving it to starboard. Evening Rock lies about 300 feet off the northwest corner of Hat Island (it helps to refer to the chart as you read these instructions). Inside, the middle of Goldstream Harbour is about 30 feet deep. Rocks extend out from the shore, so pick your anchoring spot carefully to swing safely. This is a nice protected spot with an opening in rocks to look out at the conditions in Hakai Pass.

Ward Channel. Ward Channel connects Hakai Passage with Nalau Passage. Running it is straightforward as long as you follow the chart to keep track of the rocks.

Edward Channel. Edward Channel, west of Ward Channel, also connects Hakai Passage with Nalau Passage, but the southern entry is much tighter than Ward Channel. Pass between the 27-meter and 31-meter islets, staying well clear of the detached rock that dries at 1.6 meters off the south tip of the 27-meter islet. Chart 3935 (1:40,000) is quite clear. Don't try the south entry with the older Chart 3727 (1:73,584). It doesn't show enough detail where you need it. The primary reason to be in Edward Channel is the lovely anchorage of Lewall Inlet.

Lewall Inlet. Lewall Inlet indents the east shore of Stirling Island and is a delightful anchorage. Run all the way to the bend and anchor in 10 to 20 feet, north of the north shore of the entry channel. Stay well off the little treed islet near the south shore. A ledge of drying rock reaches out from that islet.

Uncharted rock: An uncharted rock lies mid-channel just north of the anchorage bend at approximately 51°46.150'N/128°06.266'W. The rock dries on a +2 foot tide. Use extreme caution if going north of the bend at the anchorage.

Nalau Passage. Nalau Passage, scenic and open, separates Hunter Island and Stirling Island, and connects Fitz Hugh Sound with Kildidt Sound. A conservative, mid-channel course has no hazards. The western entrance, however, is made interesting by drying rocks offshore from the north side of the passage. Eastbound boats crossing Kildidt Sound may have anxious moments finding the exact entrance. We used the following waypoint for the western entrance successfully: 51°47.10'N/128°07.20'W.

SPIDER ISLAND AREA

Note: Our sister publication, *Cruising the Secret Coast*, by Jennifer and James Hamilton, contains extensive coverage of these cruising grounds, including Kildidt Sound, Kildidt Inlet, the Goose Group, the McNaughton Group, and other wild areas between Hakai Passage and Seaforth Channel.

Kildidt Sound. Kildidt Sound is remote and beautiful with many anchorage possibilities. Consult *Cruising the Secret Coast* for more information on the numerous islets and anchorages in this area.

Serpent Group. Correspondents James and Jennifer Hamilton have anchored successfully in the cove on the easternmost side of the 57-meter island, southwest of the 31-meter island. Their anchorage was tranquil, but when they dinghied ashore and climbed to the seaward side they found windblown trees barely holding to the shore.

Kildidt Narrows. Kildidt Narrows is the reversing tidal rapids at the entrance to Kildidt Inlet, which the Waggoner does not yet cover. We include it here only because observations by Waggoner Correspondents James and Jennifer Hamilton, and confirmed by Canadian Hydrographic Service, indicate that the Sailing Directions times are incorrect. High water slack occurs approximately 1.5 hours after high water at *Bella Bella*. The time difference for low water slack varies with the height of the tide. For a low water of 0.4 meter, slack occurs approximately 2 hours after low water at *Bella Bella*; for a low water of 2.5 meters, slack occurs approximately 1 hour after low water at *Bella Bella*. Bella Bella is italicized because Sailing Directions calls

James & Jennifer Hamilton found this perfect anchorage in Kildidt Sound's Serpent Group. Photo by James Hamilton.

for Prince Rupert tides.

For complete coverage of Kildidt Narrows and Kildidt Inlet, see *Cruising the Secret Coast*.

Brydon Channel. Brydon Channel connects Kildidt Sound and Spider Anchorage. Westbound across Kildidt Sound, lay a course well south of Lancaster Reef, then turn north toward the Brydon Channel entrance. When studying the chart, you will see the

easternmost dogleg in Brydon Channel is foul with rocks. Mike Guns, a commercial fisherman with much experience in these waters, told us the safe route through is to hug the northwest end of the 72-meter island at the eastern end of the channel. This keeps you clear of the rocks farther out. See the reference map.

Brydon Anchorage. Brydon Anchorage extends northward into Hurricane Island

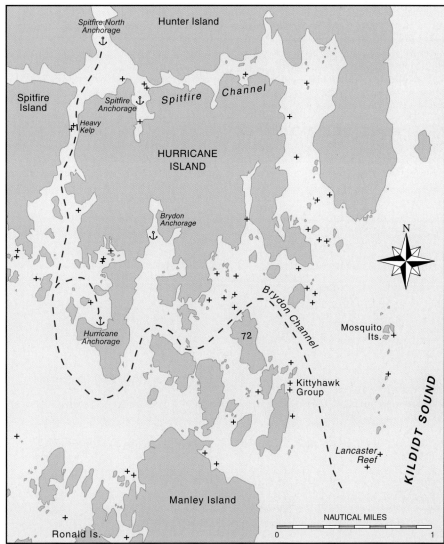

Kildidt Sound and Brydon Channel

at the west end of Brydon Channel at 51°50.25'N/128°12.25'W (NAD 83). Correspondents James and Jennifer Hamilton anchored in 30 feet near the very head. They report, "An amazing view to the south, not a soul around. It was an astonishingly quiet and beautiful anchorage—like no other. Most places remind us of somewhere else. This one stands alone." [*Hamilton*]

Spider Island area. This area is beautiful, raw, remote feeling, and little visited. The waters are also full of rocks. This is perfect gunkholing country, a paradise for kayakers.

You have a choice of two ways to get there, outside or inside. The outside route goes out the mouth of Hakai Passage into Queens Sound, then bends northwest toward the west side of Spider Island. Breadner Point, on the west side of Spider Island, is a famous hot spot for spring salmon. South of Spider Island, enter through Fulton Passage, or north of Spider Island through Spider Channel.

The inside route goes through Nalau Passage, across Kildidt Sound, and through rock-choked Brydon Channel into Spider Anchorage. An alternate to the Brydon Channel portion is Spitfire Channel, along the north side of Hurricane Island. Spitfire Channel has one spot so tight, however, we recommend you explore by dinghy before committing the mother ship. Near high tide, and with a lookout on the bow, we squeezed through in a 52-foot Grand Banks.

The following information is an overview of the main places. It would take several days to poke around all the delights of this area.

Passage between Spider Anchorage and Spitfire Channel. This passage separates Spitfire Island and Hurricane Island. The route shown was recommended to us by Mike Guns. The passage is clear until the north end, where rocks extend from Spitfire

Spitfire Passage is narrow, challenging and beautiful. Here three Grand Banks yachts from NW Explorations pass through carefully with a bow watch ready to call out the clearance to the rocks.

Island. This area is fairly well covered with bull kelp floating on the surface and thick leaf kelp below. We went in near the top of a high tide without difficulty. Next morning we departed 1½ hours after a 3.3-foot low tide and gathered a heavy glop of leaf kelp on our props and rudders. A low-powered fin keel sailboat could have been stopped dead. This passage is best run near high water.

Hurricane Anchorage. "Hurricane Anchorage" is Douglass' name for the otherwise unnamed cove in the hook formed by the south end of Hurricane Island. As shown on the reference map, enter north of the group of islets that make up the hook. Well protected and scenic.

Spitfire West Anchorage. This is Douglass' name for the otherwise unnamed cove that indents Hurricane Island, immediately west of the Spitfire Channel narrows. Several people have recommended it to us. Douglass says the bottom offers only fair to poor holding, however.

Spitfire North Anchorage. This is our name for the otherwise unnamed cove that indents Hunter Island, west of the Spitfire Channel narrows. Mike Guns recommended it to us. We would anchor in the outer part only. At low water the mouth leading to the inner lagoon appeared to be impassable or nearly so. The east side of the outer cove had a bottom that felt like a thin layer of mud on top of rock, and we dragged easily. The west side of the cove yielded good holding in 50 to 55 feet.

Spitfire Channel. Spitfire Channel separates Hurricane Island and Hunter Island, and except for the narrows at the west end, is easily run. The narrows are another matter. A medium-size cruiser can go through these narrows without difficulty, but with great caution and a sharp lookout. Underwater rocks extend into the channel, especially from the north side. Plan your transit at high water slack—high water, to get the greatest width possible; slack because we wouldn't want current pushing us where we didn't want to go. Least depth is 1.9 meters (approximately 6 feet) at zero tide.

FITZ HUGH SOUND, CONTINUED

Kwakume Inlet. Kwakume Inlet is a beautiful and roomy anchorage, but study your chart closely before entering. A rock awash at zero tide is shown outside the

Bonsai tree on wind-swept island near Spider Anchorage and Spitfire Channel

entrance, and you'll want to steer a course to avoid it. Mike Guns, a commercial fisherman with 35 years' experience in these waters, says the preferred approach is from the north. He recommends favoring the mainland shore, to pass between the rock and the shore.

Once past the rock, pass between the larger islet in the entrance and the little dot islet south of the larger islet. Inside, two rocks are shown a short distance along the north shore, one of them dries at 1.5 meters. Near the head of the main basin and south of its islet, another rock is shown, this one dries at 1.8 meters.

The south cove immediately inside the entrance has been recommended as an anchorage, but might be filled with aquaculture. Other aquaculture is located along the north side of Kwakume Inlet. Fortunately, it doesn't occupy any favored anchorages.

With the south cove taken, the best anchorage is in 25 to 30 feet (zero tide) at the head of the inlet, between the shore and a rock shown as drying at 1.8 meters. Anchor either there or in the inner basin.

If you can get into it, the inner basin is unusually secluded and snug feeling. Be aware, however, that the short fairway leading to the inner basin is narrow, and that a substantial drying rock lies in the middle, with more rocks on each side. *High water only, this little pass, dead slow bell, with alert lookouts.* We favored the north side.

Having a high tide when we arrived in early evening, we felt our way into the inner basin for the night. We were treated to glass-smooth water and the most plaintive loon's call we've ever heard. As we slipped out at high water early the next morning we were stopped cold by a wolf's cry—a long lonesome troubled howl, repeated just once. [Hale]

Koeye River. A charted rock lies north of Koeye Point. Enter north of that rock and wrap around into the cove behind the point. A lodge is near the point.

A few years ago we talked with the lodge caretaker, who told us that an onshore wind blowing out of Hakai Passage creates large seas that roll into the bay. He also said this is grizzly bear country. Later, we talked with a boat that experienced the seas mentioned above. The skipper said the seas were awful. They had come back from the mine and had much trouble getting from the dinghy to the boat. Stay away in a westerly.

Although in our opinion Koeye (pronounced "Kway") River is not a good spot for overnight anchoring, several people have told us a dinghy trip up the river to the mine ruins is beautiful. At the mine you'll find two open pits connected by a tunnel. The remains of a shop are there, and a huge old 1-cylinder steam engine. The buildings on the point at the mouth of the river are a Bella Bella Native band summer camp. [Hale]

Sea Otter Inlet & Crab Cove. Sea Otter Inlet, on Hunter Island, has two arms that form a "T" at the entrance. Crab Cove, the northern arm, was recommended by a park ranger at Pruth Bay. Anchor near the head in 30 to 35 feet. The south arm is prettier than Crab Cove and more private feeling. Anchor near the head of the south cove in 35 to 40 feet.

Kiltik Cove. Mouth of cove at 51°53.80'N /128°00.05'W. Kiltik Cove indents the east side of Hunter Island, approximately across from Namu. It is extremely well protected. The bottom shoals abruptly just past the tiny rock islet on the east shore of the arm. We would anchor in 35 to 40 feet a short distance north of that rock.

Warrior Cove. Warrior Cove is on the mainland (east) side of Fitz Hugh Sound, approximately 1.5 miles south of Namu. With a typical westerly wind, a following sea will chase you into the cove, but the seas subside when you pass the 82-meter island (in a southeast gale a lump may get in). The inner cove is pretty and protected. Scout around for just the right spot, and put the hook down in 20 to 25 feet, good holding.

Namu. The falling-down cannery at Namu went through a transition. For many years caretakers Pete and Rene (pronounced "Reenie") Darwin, and Rene's longtime friend Theresa, managed the facility. They created a unique destination on a collection of floats, complete with a covered common area, gift store, workshop, greenhouse, and docks. They transformed the uplands of the old cannery with art and and creative landscaping. Pete and Rene have moved on, physically moving their floats to Lizzie Cove on Lama Passage. See Lizzie Cove entry for more information.

Anchorage is still available at Namu or in nearby Rock Inlet.

Navigation note: The beacon is gone from Loo Rock, between the Namu floats and the entrance to Rock Inlet, but Loo Rock still exists. The Namu Harbour inset on Chart 3936 shows the rock's location. Watch for another rock located in front of the abandoned cafe building and for other possible obstacles in the area.

Rock Inlet. Rock Inlet extends northeast from Whirlwind Bay (Namu), and it's a good, protected spot. Entering or departing, be sure to identify Verdant Island, near the mouth, and pass east of it. Keep a mid-channel course and watch for rocks. The chart shows the way. Inside, anchor in 25 to 40 feet. The bottom is rocky, and our anchor skipped across for some distance before setting.

FISHER CHANNEL

The north end of Fitz Hugh Sound divides into Burke Channel and Fisher Channel. Burke Channel leads eastward to Bella Coola, which is connected by road to Williams Lake and the highways inland. Bella Coola has facilities and is mentioned often by the few residents on this part of the coast, but is little visited by pleasure craft.

Fisher Channel is a continuation of the Inside Passage route, although the Inside Passage soon leads west and north, via Lama Passage or Gunboat Passage, to Bella Bella and Shearwater. If you remain in Fisher Channel you will reach Cousins Inlet. Ocean Falls, at the head of Cousins Inlet, is the most complete and interesting ghost town on the coast.

Humchitt Island. Humchitt Island is immediately off the south tip of King Island, at the intersection of Fitz Hugh Sound, Burke Channel and Fisher Channel. "With 15-knot southeasterlies blowing up Fitz Hugh Sound, we overnighted in the cove on the northeast shore of Humchitt Island. The seas were 2 to 3 feet outside, but our anchorage was tranquil and calm, with an amazing view up Fisher Channel. Anchor in 10 to 20 feet, moderate to good holding over rock, with a 150-foot swing radius." [Hamilton]

Kisameet Bay. Kisameet Bay is on King Island, about 3.5 miles north of the mouth of Burke Channel, roughly east of Fog Rocks. Correspondents John and Lorraine Littlewood report: "A splendid anchorage. The northernmost part of the bay, behind the island, is the place to be. It's quiet and fully protected from wind and sea, with a 'window' out into Fisher Channel to

The Kisameet Bay anchorage is somewhat smaller than this photo suggests. Work your way in around rocks, all of them charted.

This sandy beach at Sagar Lake is reached by trail from Codville Lagoon.

observe conditions." This is a very pleasant place to hide out. Anchor in 30 to 40 feet. We overnighted in this anchorage three seasons ago before heading south to cross Cape Caution. We found it to be just as the Littlewoods described and recommend it.

Codville Lagoon. Codville Lagoon is a provincial park on the east side of Fisher Channel. It is a popular anchorage, protected and pretty. Readers John and Deb Marshall reported that strong winds will work their way to the back cove. The narrow entrance is hard to locate, but Codville Hill, its moonscape of three peaks and barren rock slopes, is a good landmark. Favor the south side of the entrance to avoid a rock off the north shore. Anchor in 40 to 50 feet at the eastern head of the inlet. A trail runs from the northeastern shore of the anchorage to sandy beaches at beautiful Sagar Lake. Field Correspondent Jim Norris warns of vicious sand fleas. This is bear country. Make noise as you walk.

The Trap. The Trap is located behind Clayton Island on the west side of Fisher Channel, about 2 miles south of Lama Passage. North entrance at 52°02.35'N/127°56.80'W. South entrance at 52°01.05'N/127°56.80'W. We read about this spot in Iain Lawrence's *Far Away Places* (now out of print). Southbound on a windy, rainy afternoon we decided

to tuck in for a look. The passage behind Clayton Island is as Lawrence describes it: deep, but protected from the wind. Lawrence says the bottom is rocky and requires a stern-tie to shore to prevent swinging. The Trap itself is the bay at the very south end of the passage. Lawrence says this bay empties at low tide, revealing a labyrinth of ancient fish traps.

Long Point Cove. Long Point Cove is located on the west side of Fisher Channel, approximately 1 mile south of Lama Passage. Although Sailing Directions mentions Long Point Cove as a good anchorage for small craft, it isn't as scenic or interesting as other anchorages in the area. On entering, favor the west shore to avoid a rock that dries some 250 to 300 yards north of Long Point. The rock is shown on the chart.

④ **Ocean Falls (Cousins Inlet).** Ocean Falls is a favorite destination. Although a ghost town, Ocean Falls is a busy ghost town. The winter population of 25 swells to 100 in the summer, but services are limited. Two bed and board inns offer services to their guests. Saggo's Saloon in nearby Martin Valley is usually open Mondays, Wednesdays, and Fridays from 4:00 p.m. to 7:00 p.m.; check the bulletin board at the top of the dock.

A right turn at the top of the ramp from the Small Craft Harbour leads to Ocean

Falls proper. Other than the small gift store in the corner of the marine ways building, Ocean Falls Lodge (formerly Darke Waters), and the Old Bank Inn (formerly the Ocean Falls Fishing Lodge) are the only operating businesses.

The dam dominates the head of the inlet and supplies electrical power for Ocean Falls, Shearwater, and New Bella Bella. The dam also provides water and power for the town's multi-million dollar hatchery and rearing pen facility for Atlantic salmon smolt for fish farms. Some 30 large green fiberglass rearing pens have been installed beside the former Crown Zellerbach mill site. Mixing ponds, where freshwater and saltwater are blended in exact proportions for the developing smolt, have been blasted out of the rocky mountainside leading to the dam. High tech has arrived in Ocean Falls. In early 2018, a computer-based cryptocurrency "mining" entity leased a building with a computer processing facility, which requires large amounts of electrical power.

A trip to Ocean Falls is not complete without a hike to the dam with vistas of Link Lake and views of the once busy mill town below. A walk through this "ghost town" can't help but stir the imagination. Make noise—you might meet a bear. Trout fishing in Link Lake is said to be excellent.

A left turn at the top of the dock leads visitors on a 1.5-mile road to Martin Valley. It's an easy, scenic stroll. The first house you come to is Saggo's Saloon. A little farther along, a concrete launch ramp serves amphibious planes.

The houses in Martin Valley were taken over by the province when Ocean Falls was abandoned. They have since been sold to people who enjoy the beauty and solitude of the area. Visitors as well as locals arrive at Ocean Falls by ferry service from Bella Bella, Shearwater, and Bella Coola (check BC Ferries for the scheduled service).

Crabbing is excellent off the old mill site. Halibut and salmon can be caught in Cousins Inlet. Consider dropping a prawn trap in Wallace Bay on your way up the inlet. We think Ocean Falls is a "don't miss" stop for its unique charm and beauty.

The view of Ocean Falls from the Small Craft Harbour.

Ample side-tie at Ocean Falls Small Craft Harbour

Lodging can be found in Ocean Falls at Old Bank Inn and Ocean Falls Lodge. Martin River Lodge, in nearby Martin Valley, offers fishing charteres and B&B guest rooms. Air service to and from Ocean Falls is available through Wilderness Seaplanes.

④ **Ocean Falls Small Craft Harbour.** General Delivery, Ocean Falls, BC V0T 1P0; (250) 289-3859; www.oceanfalls.ca/blog/ofha. Open all year, public dock with ice, potable water, free Wi-Fi, 20 & 30 amp power, no fuel.

Ample dock space with reasonable rates and all the Link Lake water you need. The water is sweet and pure and has gone through a further purification process.

"The Shack," a yellow float house next to the ramp, has a book exchange, computer with internet, and tables and chairs. Pay moorage in The Shack, or wait for the wharfinger to come down the docks in the morning or late afternoon. Visa and MasterCard accepted.

Harbor owner Herb Carpenter runs the marine ways. Herb built Melissa, the gold-colored mermaid who welcomes boats to the docks. In the downstairs corner of the marine ways building, Herb's wife Lena has set up a little gift shop called C' shores Gift Shop.

Upstairs is Nearly Normal Norman's Ocean Falls Museum, filled with items left behind by former residents of Ocean Falls. Those of us over 50 will recognize many of the objects. If the door is not open, ask around. Norman will open up for visitors. Donations accepted. Children will love visiting the "Fairy Rock" located a short distance from the docks on the road to Martin. Children take great delight in finding coins hidden in the Rock. Be sure to let the wharfinger know if you plan to visit Fairy Rock so the fairies can be alerted; you can contribute coins at The Shack in support of this long-standing tradition at Ocean Falls. Another fun tradition is the Annual Salmon Derby Barbecue weekend held in late August, a popular event drawing participants from other nearby communities. Tickets for the barbeque can be purchased at The Shack.

No garbage drop: Recycling bins for plastic, glass, tin, aluminum and burnables are located at The Shack. Take everything else with you.

Weather radio channel WX 1: The signal is spotty. If necessary, walk along the dock with a handheld VHF until you find reception, or use the computer in The Shack to check the forecast online.

④ **Ocean Falls Lodge.** (250) 289-3585; greenway.galloway@gmail.com; www.darkewaters.com. New owners purchased the former Darke Waters Inn, the historic hospital bulding across from the marine ways building. Ocean Falls Lodge offers rooms, hot showers, and coin laundry. The new owners have plans to renovate the building in the near future.

④ **Old Bank Inn.** (250) 289-9624; info@lemarston.com. Les and Toni LeMarston purchased the former fishing lodge near the historic Ocean Falls Hotel and converted the lodge into a cozy bed and board guesthouse offering comfortable, nicely-appointed rooms with breakfast, lunch and dinner included in the daily rate. You guessed it, the building was originally the bank in Ocean Falls.

Lama Passage. Lama Passage leads westward and northward from Fisher Channel to New Bella Bella and Shearwater. Cruise ships and BC Ferries use this passage regularly. Keep a sharp lookout ahead and astern.

Fancy Cove. Fancy Cove is on the south shore of Lama Passage and is a delightful little anchorage. Don and Reanne Douglass write about the cove in their book *Exploring the North Coast of British Columbia*. This nearly landlocked cove is well protected. Anchor in 10 to 25 feet.

Fannie Cove. Fannie Cove is in Cooper Inlet on the south shore of Lama Passage. It's a beautiful little spot, with an obvious anchoring nook on its eastern shore just inside the entrance. Unfortunately, the holding ground is only fair. We tried twice to get a good set in the little nook and once farther out, but each time we dragged without much effort. We would overnight in settled weather only. Study the chart before entering. Leave Gus Island and the little dot islet west of Gus Island to port as you approach.

The once charming homes of Ocean Falls are now in disrepair.

Children love visiting the Fairy Rock for hidden coins at Ocean Falls, a long-standing tradition from years past.

Visit Lizzie Cove for a genuine taste of island living.

Lizzie Cove. Monitors VHF 10. Their hospitality has been a favorite of cruisers for many years. Pete and Rene Darwin moved their floats, BBQ shelter, and gift shop from Namu to Lizzie Cove. Tucked inside the southeast end of Lizzie Cove, there is 100 feet of side-tie moorage for visitors and overnight guests. Cash only. No power or water. Don't miss the gift shop filled with custom-made wood working items and other crafts. Their self-sufficient gardens are impressive and include a hothouse with fruit trees.

Two routes, Hogan Rock Route and Gus Island Route bring you into Lizzie Cove from Lama Passage. Two privately maintained buoys mark the channel for red right returning to Lizzie Cove from Lama Passage. Buoys are privately maintained and may not be in place; red and green markings may be faded or obscured by marine growth. Bow watch is recommended.

Hogan Rock Route - leave Hogan Rock and the awash rock northwest of Hogan Rock to port; then proceed south-southwest passing the reef that dries at 3-meters to port and the private red buoy marker to starboard; then turn west-northwest passing the private green marker buoy, which marks the 41-meter island shoal, to port; and wrap around the 41-meter island. Give the northwest end of 41-meter

island shoal a wide berth. Gus Island Route – leave Gus Island to port; proceed south-southwest; then turn northwest, passing 41-meter island to port and the reef that dries at 2.1-meters to starboard; and wrap around the 41-meter island, passing the private green marker buoy to port and the private red buoy marker to starboard. Give the northwest end of 41-meter island shoal a wide berth.

Jane Cove. Jane Cove, on the south shore of Lama Passage in Cooper Inlet, offers shelter but lacks scenic quality. Study the chart carefully before entering to avoid shoals and rocks. Fannie Cove, despite its marginal holding, or Fancy Cove, which is spectacular by comparison, are preferred.

⑤ **New Bella Bella.** New Bella Bella (Waglisla) is a major Native village, with fuel, potable water, garbage drop, and a grocery store and nice cafe; cell phone service is

good. The village has a hospital. The closest laundromat is at Shearwater. The BC Ferries terminal is located south of town.

The main pier and floats are busy with water taxis and local boat traffic. Moorage is filled with commercial and local boats; there is no transient moorage but always room for a dinghy. The fuel dock (250-957-2440) has gas and diesel, call ahead for service. The attendants are courteous, but religious about their lunch hour. You may have to be patient. New Bella Bella's water treatment plant provides a steady stream of clear, potable water at the fuel dock.

A new, large grocery store opened in 2018 and includes a bakery and meat department. This is a fun place to shop for gifts and food items to re-stock your galley. The supply barge arrives weekly on Sundays. Just north of this store is the Waglisla Senior Centre, with native artwork. The locals are friendly and eager to share their stories. Visitors are also welcome to tour the K-12 Bella Bella Community School.

Guests at Shearwater can take the water taxi to New Bella Bella to shop at the band store or to drop off or pick up passengers or parts from the airport. Scheduled airline service runs throughout the day.

The New Bella Bella airport is about 2 miles from the village. You can walk along the road or take a taxi. The taxi is often standing by before or after a flight or call (250) 957-2582 or on VHF channel 14. They know the schedules. Wilderness Seaplanes serves New Bella Bella with multiple flights per day.

Bella Bella. Bella Bella (Old Bella Bella) is on Denny Island on the northeastern shore of Lama Passage. The excellent docks and lovely buildings ("Whistler North") house the Coast Guard Search and Rescue vessel *Cape Farewell*, its crew and support staff, and Fisheries and Oceans personnel. No transient moorage.

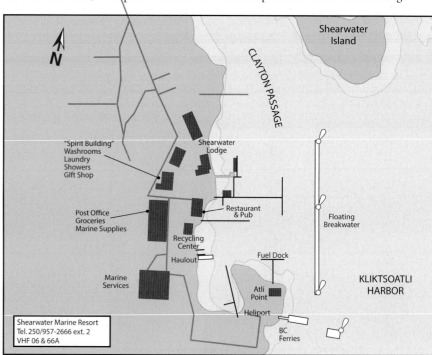

Lizzie Cove

Shearwater Marine Resort

The sculptures commemorate the area's war veterans.

The coffee bar is a nice addition at Shearwater.

Kliktsoatli Harbour. Shearwater Resort & Marina is located in Kliktsoatli Harbour, 2 miles east of New Bella Bella on the north side of Denny Island. Good anchorage can be found on the eastern shore.

⑥ **Shearwater Resort & Marina.** (250) 957-2666; moorage@shearwater.ca; hotel@shearwater.ca; www.shearwater.ca. Monitors VHF 06 & 66A, the fuel dock monitors VHF 08. Open all year, 1500 feet of guest moorage, 15, 30 & 50 amp power all the way out the main float, free Wi-Fi and for-fee premium Wi-Fi. Potable water is available on the guest dock. Seasonally, there are two waterlines for different uses; one carries potable water, and the other is for washdown. White hoses carry potable water, and the green hoses are for washdown. Please be sparing and sharing with the potable water. During prime season, register and pay for moorage at the dockside harbourmaster's office, or at the hotel during shoulder season. Moorage reservations are highly recommended during the busy summer months. If the main docks are full, you can moor on the inside of the breakwater docks, no power or water. Cellular service is good. 200 additional feet of guest moorage was planned for 2018; at press time the project was not completed.

The fuel dock has diesel, gasoline, lubricants, propane, Avgas and Jet A. On shore you'll find an ATM, washrooms, showers, laundry, ice, restaurant, pub, haulout, launch ramp, facilities for waste oil dump, garbage drop and recycling center. There is a small fee for recycling to cover the costs of barging the material to Richmond B.C. A well-stocked grocery store, liquor store, and marine supply store are on site along with a post office, coffee pastry bar, and gift shop. The showers and laundry room, in the building across from the store, are excellent.

The popular pub, with live entertainment, has a nice deck for outdoor dining. It's a great place to meet other boaters and locals, who often share a table.

Shearwater is the most complete marine facility between Campbell River and Prince Rupert. The shipyard can haul boats to 70 tons and handle almost anything, from

See Area Map Page 426 - Maps Not for Navigation

toilet repairs to electronics to repowers. They can order parts for you and coordinate their arrival by air if needed. Shearwater has its own 3,000-foot airstrip for private aircraft. Scheduled airline service to Port Hardy and Vancouver is available at New Bella Bella. Shearwater is also a stop for the BC Ferries system. Shearwater Helicopter Tours (778-899-0513) can provide airport transfers and sightseeing excursions. The Sea-Bus water taxi connects Shearwater and New Bella Bella (Waglisla) with a 10-minute, 2.5-mile ride. In calm weather you can scoot over in a dinghy. Shearwater is the crossroads of the northern coast and gets a full range of visitors.

The marina was the site of a WWII Royal Canadian Air Force seaplane base. The large historic hangar now serves as the shop. In 2013, Craig Widsten, the principal owner of this family-owned resort, created two special tributes to the heritage of Shearwater and the surrounding area. When a wall of the shop needed replacement, Craig had it rebuilt and commissioned muralist Paul Gartua to paint the images of seventeen people who had an impact on the growth and development of Shearwater. They include tribal leaders, medical professionals, the original manager of the Hudson's Bay Co. outpost, and even Craig's father, Andrew, the founder of Shearwater. Measuring 120 feet wide and 22 feet tall, the mural is quite striking.

Craig also installed a cenotaph to commemorate Shearwater and New Bella Bella residents' war service. He commissioned the casting of a 17-foot scale replica of the Stranraer flying boat that was based at Bella Bella during WWII. Nearby, a carved Eagle pole commemorates First Nations veterans, and an obelisk commemorates other veterans from the area.

Kakushdish Harbour. Kakushdish Harbour, long and narrow, extends into Denny Island immediately east of Kliktsoatli Harbour (Shearwater). An overhead power cable with 23 meters (75 feet) vertical clearance crosses the entrance. "We favored the north shore through the entrance bar and saw a minimum depth of 11 feet, zero tide. Anchor in 20 to 25 feet, good holding in mud. The anchorage was surprisingly deserted and tranquil." [*Hamilton*]

LOCAL KNOWLEDGE

NAVIGATION NOTES: The trickiest spot in Gunboat Passage is the narrow fairway between Denny Point and Maria Island. Use caution to navigate away from the rocks. A second tricky spot is the reef that extends from the southern shore toward Dingle Island. Watch the currents in this area. A red nun buoy marks the outer end of this reef. Red, Right, Returning assumes you are returning eastbound, from the sea. The third tricky spot is the range at the west end of Gunboat Passage. Entering or departing, stay on the range.

Gunboat Passage. Gunboat Passage connects Seaforth Channel with Fisher Channel and is a scenic route between Ocean Falls and New Bella Bella/Shearwater. The passage is littered with reefs and rocks, but well marked with aids to navigation.

Beales Bay. The entrance looks tricky on the chart, but if you leave the small islet to port as you enter, you'll have good water. Anchor inside in 30 to 40 feet. Stay well clear of the mouth of Beales Lagoon. At least two detached drying rocks lie in the cove off the lagoon's mouth. Excellent protection.

Gosse Bay. Gosse Bay is west of Maria Island, a good anchorage on the west side of the westernmost cove.

Forit Bay. Forit Bay, on the eastern approach to Gunboat Passage, is an excellent, protected anchorage in 15 to 25 feet. The entrance, however, is encumbered by a large rock between Flirt Island and the point of land that marks the inner part of the bay. The rock is not visible at high tide, but is visible through the water at a little less than half tide.

Enter Forit Bay by wrapping around the north tip of Flirt Island, leaving the island to port.

BURKE CHANNEL, DEAN CHANNEL, BELLA COOLA

Important chart note: In October, 2011, Canadian Hydrographic Service (CHS) released new Chart 3974 and cancelled Charts 3729 and 3730. All coverage of this area is now shown on 3900-series charts—Chart 3936 for the mouth and western portion of Burke Channel, and Chart 3939 for the mouth and western portion of Dean Channel.

Burke Channel and Dean Channel border the south and north sides of King Island and plunge deep into the Coast Range mountains. We had been told that this is some of the most beautiful and awe-inspiring country imaginable, but after seeing so much beautiful country all along the B.C. coast, we expected it to be just more of the same. We were wrong. A circumnavigation of King Island will astonish you. Gone is the raw coast with its low, wave-pounded islands. A short distance up either channel puts you inland, bounded on each side by high mountains. If you're going to spend some time on this coast, see these waters.

LOCAL KNOWLEDGE

EBB CURRENT: On warm summer days, heating of inland air produces an up-channel sea breeze in Burke Channel that can begin as early as 10:00 a.m. and blow strongly until sundown. Make your runs early and find shelter before the wind starts blowing.

TIDE-RIPS: The surface water in Burke Channel is often in an almost constant ebb, the result of fresh water flowing toward the sea. When this surface ebb meets a spring flood, tide-rips, whirlpools, and general confusion results.

Burke Channel. Burke Channel leads 38 miles inland, beginning at Edmund Point, just north of Namu. From Edmund Point to Restoration Bay, the lower reaches of Burke Channel are subject to strong tidal currents and heavy tide-rips, but in the upper reaches the tidal streams are weak.

The north end of Burke Channel divides into South Bentinck Arm and North Bentinck Arm (Bella Coola is at the head of North Bentinck Arm), and Labouchere Passage, which leads to Dean Channel. When the ebb current is flowing and the up-channel sea breeze is blowing, expect rough seas at the confluence of these channels. Early morning, before the B.C. interior heats up, is often the calmest time of day.

All these cautions make Burke Channel sound impenetrable, which isn't the case. The prudent skipper simply will avoid being out there in the wrong conditions.

The best anchorage along Burke Channel is at the head of Kwatna Inlet, with a second-best choice being the small cove just north of Cathedral Point.

Fougner Bay. Fougner Bay is near the mouth of Burke Channel on the south side, just east of Edmund Point. The outer part of the bay is somewhat protected, with anchorage in 40 to 60 feet. To us it feels uninviting. An inner cove, however, is a perfect spot.

Find the 4.1-meter sounding back in the bay. That's the cove. To get in, the chart shows good water by leaving the + symbol (indicating a dangerous underwater rock 2 meters or less at zero tide) to starboard. Once clear of the rock, loop into the back cove. Very cozy and protected. Study the chart carefully before entering Fougner Bay. The rocks off the entry are easy to avoid, but you want to know where they are and where you are.

Kwatna Inlet. Kwatna Inlet extends some 12 miles into the mainland and is too deep for anchoring until near the head. Watch carefully for the drying flats at the head. We are told by several people that it is an excellent place to put the hook down.

Cathedral Point. Cathedral Point, a weather reporting station, marks the north entrance to Kwatna Inlet, and is easily identified by its white building and tower. Just north of the point, a tiny cove with dramatic granite walls makes a good anchorage in 25 feet. The cove has excellent protection from up-channel winds, but the mass of large logs on the south beach suggests that down-channel winds and seas blow right in. We patrolled the cove but did not stay. Early Correspondent Bill Hales, from Victoria, anchored for the night and reported a pleasant experience.

South Bentinck Arm. South Bentinck Arm, 25 miles long, lies between high mountains.

436

The Bella Coola docks look more spacious in this photo than when we were trying to raft off in 20-knot winds.

The relatively few cruisers who have gone all the way up the arm say it is beautiful. We have gone as far as Larso Bay, which has good anchorage in 35 to 70 feet. The mountains across from Larso Bay are beautiful. Correspondent Gil Flanagan found one of the largest red cedars in B.C. by walking about 1 km up a logging road that begins in the north part of the bay. The tree is on the right side of the road, marked with a plaque.

Tallheo Hot Springs. Tallheo Hot Springs is about one-quarter mile north of the mouth of Hotsprings Creek on the west shore of South Bentinck Arm, a short distance south of Bensins Island. Anchorage is exposed.

North Bentinck Arm. The water in North Bentinck Arm is green and milky, the result of the Bella Coola River emptying into the head of the arm. We found no good anchorages, so you have to hope for room at the Bella Coola docks. Watch for drift. Windy Bay is on the south side of North Bentinck Arm, near the junction with Burke Channel. When we crossed the mouth of

Windy Bay in early afternoon we learned how it got its name. Whew!

LOCAL KNOWLEDGE

WEATHER TIP: The wind can blow almost constantly at Bella Coola, making for rough seas going in or out. There aren't many places to hide from the weather, either. Be aware of the tendency for strong inflow and outflow winds before deciding to go to Bella Coola.

⑦ **Bella Coola.** Bella Coola is seldom visited by yachts but interesting nonetheless. The government floats are run by the Bella Coola Harbour Authority, and they are making improvements. Water is available all the way out the docks, with 20 & 30 amp power. Showers and washrooms are at the head of the ramp.

The Columbia Fuels fuel dock is adjacent to the public floats.

Correspondent Gil Flanagan says the best way to visit is to overnight in Larso Bay in

South Bentinck Arm or Eucott Bay on Dean Channel, and come over in the morning. A visitor at the Seattle Boat Show recommended anchoring in Bryneldsen Bay, near the north end of Labouchere Channel, and going to Bella Coola early the next morning. Use Chart 3974. Bryneldsen Bay is behind the thumb of land that extends southeast, approximately 0.8 miles from Ram Bluff. The bay is not labeled, but Chart 3974 does show an anchor symbol beside it.

The town of Bella Coola is 3 kilometers (about 2 miles) from the dock. Taxis may be available. The Bella Coola Estuary makes for a beautiful stroll. Stay on the water side of the road, since it's wider and safer for walking.

We urge you to see the Bella Coola Museum, housed in buildings dating from 1892 and 1898. It is on the edge of town along the road from the marina. Bella Coola is where, in 1793, Alexander Mackenzie touched saltwater on his transcontinental crossing of Canada. Much of the museum's display is about Mackenzie. We bought a booklet of Mackenzie's journal entries (including comment about the unrelenting wind) in the Bella Coola and Dean Channel area.

The town has provincial and federal government offices, a post office, hospital, motel, liquor store, laundromat, showers, and a well-stocked co-op grocery store and Moore's Organic Market. Take a tour of the area on the Bella Coola Valley Bus for $2.50; call (250) 799-0079 before 8:00 p.m. the day before you want to ride the bus.

Correspondents Bruce and Margaret Evertz add the following: "A worthwhile attraction in this area are the petroglyphs. The Native band wants them preserved, so they are not marked on any maps. Guides may be available. You can get information about them at the museum."

Correspondents Gil and Karen Flanagan report that rental cars are available (Bella Coola Vehicle Rentals 250-957-7072). "We put about 150 miles on a Dodge Caravan, all on good paved roads. The spectacular drive to Tweedsmuir Park inland is rated as one of the 10 most scenic drives in Canada."

Bella Coola is the B.C. Interior's window on the coast. Each year, a remarkable number of boats are trailered from the Interior to Bella Coola, where they stay the summer, either tied to the dock or on trailers.

⑦ **Bella Coola Harbour Authority.** P.O. Box 751, Bella Coola, BC V0T 1C0; (250) 799-5633; bellacoolaharbour@gmail.com. They try to monitor VHF channels 06 & 16. Open all year with guest moorage. Facilities include 20 & 30 amp power (20 amp shore power breakers have 20 amp receptacles—bring adaptor), water, washrooms, laundry and showers (showers closed November through March), tidal grid, garbage drop, waste oil drop, pumpout, launch ramp, pay phones, Wi-Fi. Fuel dock adjacent. The harbor office is at the head of the pier. Office hours June through September 8:00 a.m. to 6:00 p.m. and off season Monday through

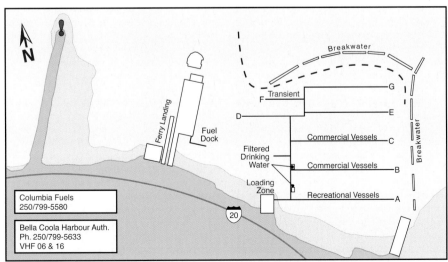

Bella Coola

See Area Map Page 426 - Maps Not for Navigation

Saturday 8:00 a.m. to 12:00 p.m.

Float "A" is dedicated for visiting pleasure craft 14 meters and longer. The float is exposed to westerly winds. Smaller boats can tie up there, but if a boat 14 meters or longer arrives, the smaller boats will have to move.

Bella Coola is a popular launch point for trailerable boats. The Harbour Authority has added additional boat launch floats to make launching and retrieving easier.

The marina is tight and the wind can blow almost constantly. Rafting is required. If necessary, take temporary moorage at the loading zone. Put out lots of fenders, both sides. Of all the places we have landed, Bella Coola is one of the most challenging.

The floats are located south of a rock breakwater, behind a floating log breakwater. They are home port to a large number of commercial fish boats. All of A dock and the south side of B dock are reserved for pleasure craft, however. You may have to raft to a permanent boat. The channel on the land side of A dock is narrow, especially at low tide. Feel your way in and find a spot.

Now that the local Harbour Authority is running the facility, more interest is devoted to visiting boaters. Even so, Bella Coola is not a "resort marina." Self-reliance is the key.

Columbia Fuels Fuel Dock. (250) 799-5580. Open Monday through Friday 9:00 a.m. to 4:00 p.m. all year. Call (250) 305-8333 for off-hours service. Gasoline, diesel, lubricants. Dwayne Saugstad is the manager. Dwayne's great-great-grandfather led the original band of Norwegian settlers to Bella Coola. Dwayne's great-grandfather remained, as did Dwayne's grandfather, Dwayne's father, and now Dwayne and his two children. All have called or presently call Bella Coola their home. Six generations.

Labouchere Channel. Labouchere Channel connects the north end of Burke Channel with Dean Channel. **Mesachie Nose**, at the confluence of the two channels, is a magnificent glacier-smoothed rock prominence on the north shore. Tidal currents combined with winds and surface water runoff can create very difficult seas in this area. If the water is flat, see Mesachie Nose, up close.

The waters of Labouchere Channel itself are generally smooth and wind-free. The scenery, with waterfalls spilling from high mountains, is fabulous. Our notes say, "So many waterfalls!"

LOCAL KNOWLEDGE

WEATHER TIP: Strong up-channel sea breezes can develop when warm temperatures in the Interior heat the air and suck cold ocean air up the various inlets. This sea breeze can begin as early as 10:00 a.m. and last until sundown. Because summertime freshets often create a nearly permanent ebb surface current, an ugly chop can develop when the wind blows against the current.

This monument marks Sir Alexander Mackenzie Rock, where Mackenzie ended his overland westward explorations in 1793.

Dean Channel. Dean Channel connects with Fisher Channel at the mouth of Cousins Inlet (Ocean Falls) and continues 53 miles northward. It is bordered on both sides by high mountains; Burke Channel offers some of the finest scenery along the coast. In Dean Channel we felt as if we were high up in the mountains on a huge lake, like we should be chewing gum to clear our ears. The concept of being at sea level in these surroundings was hard to grasp.

The principal points of interest on Dean Channel are Elcho Harbour, Sir Alexander Mackenzie Rock, and Eucott Bay and hot springs. Cascade Inlet is stunning, but not a good place to anchor.

Jenny Inlet. If Jenny Inlet were someplace else it might be interesting. But we found it ordinary, too deep for anchoring, with a logging camp near the head. Elcho Harbour, 8 miles farther up Dean Channel, or Cousins Inlet (Ocean Falls), 5 miles down-channel, are better choices.

Elcho Harbour. If you are looking for a scenic spot, Elcho Harbour qualifies. It's stunning. The inlet reaches a little more than 2 miles back between steep high mountains, and appears perfectly protected from all winds. Waterfalls plummet from the sides. A lovely bowl is at the head of the inlet, with the obligatory stream that creates an estuary and mudflat. Anchor in 90 to 110 feet off a delightful waterfall on the west side, about one-third of the way in. Or anchor at the head in 90 feet before it shelves up to mudflat. Take the dinghy back out to Sir Alexander Mackenzie Rock for a little history.

Sir Alexander Mackenzie Rock. Sir Alexander Mackenzie Rock is marked by a cairn at the mouth to Elcho Harbour. On 22 July 1793 Mackenzie completed his overland journey across Canada to the Pacific Ocean, and marked his accomplishment with ochre paint on the rock. Later, the inscription was

carved into the stone. You can bring the boat right up to the monument, watching for underwater rocks close to shore, and take your own picture of it. Or you can anchor out and dinghy ashore, leaving somebody aboard in case the wind kicks up.

Apparently, Mackenzie ended his westward trek here because the waters beyond were Bella Bella Indian country, and his Bella Coola Indian guides could not guarantee safety. A few miles west on the north side of Dean Channel, ochre pictographs on white cliffs are thought to be boundary markers. They are a short distance east of Frenchman Creek. We found the pictographs about 0.6 nautical miles south of the daymark near Hokonson Point.

Eucott Bay. Eucott Bay is a gorgeous spot, about as pretty as any we have anchored in. The mountains along the eastern and northeastern sides remind us of Yosemite. Photographers, bring your camera—Half Dome exists in Eucott Bay. Eucott Hot Springs is near the head of the bay, inshore of a line of pilings. The hot springs have been improved with concrete to make an excellent soaking basin. The water used to be too hot for soaking, but now the temperature can be adjusted.

Craig Widsten, principal owner of Shearwater Marine Resort, told us that in 1948 his father and he journeyed to Eucott Bay to pack mud and hot spring water for sale to health and beauty fanatics in Europe. We're sure it was elegant—hot spring water and mud from the remote Canadian coast, to smooth away the wrinkles and cure what ails you.

Enter Eucott Bay along the east (starboard) side. We are told the entrance has silted up, and is much shallower than charted. Once inside, a large basin unfolds. Find a good spot in the middle and put the hook down. Take the dinghy up to the hot springs. Insect repellant might be needed to protect against deer flies ("those man-eating winged demons," one reader wrote). At low tide wear boots. The beach is muddy.

Nascall Bay. Nascall Hot Springs is near the mouth of Nascall Bay. You'll recognize the buildings by their blue roofs. Previous owners had ambitious development plans, but they didn't work out. The facility is private with posted No Trespassing signs.

SEAFORTH CHANNEL, MILBANKE SOUND, FINLAYSON CHANNEL

LOCAL KNOWLEDGE

Navigation Note: Although Seaforth Channel is connected with the sea, west of Lama Passage the buoyage system defines "returning from the sea" as returning from south to north, not west to east. If you are outbound in Seaforth Channel, west of Lama Passage you will leave red aids to navigation (buoys, beacons, lights) to starboard (Red, Right, Returning from the south). If you are inbound in Seaforth Channel, west of Lama Passage, leave red aids to navigation to port.

"Returning from the sea" changes at Lama Passage. East of Lama Passage, inbound vessels will leave red buoys, beacons and lights to starboard.

Seaforth Channel. Seaforth Channel connects the New Bella Bella/Shearwater area with Milbanke Sound to the west and is part of the Inside Passage route. Ivory Island is at the western entrance.

Troup Passage. Troup Passage runs between Chatfield Island and Cunningham Island, and leads to Roscoe Inlet. Troup Narrows is at the northern end. Near the southern end of Troup Passage an unnamed bay sometimes called Discovery Cove is an excellent anchorage.

Discovery Cove. Discovery Cove at lat 52°13.50'N, unnamed on the charts, is the only major indent of Cunningham Island from Troup Passage. It was first recommended to us by John and Evonne MacPherson, who spent many summers cruising the coast in their perfectly-maintained 45-foot Grenfell, Malacandra. The chart shows rocks on the southwest shore of the entry, but if you go in along the northeast shore you'll have no problems. This is one of the most beautiful coves on the coast. It is surrounded by mountains and seemingly immune to any storm winds that might be about. Anchor in either of the two nooks along the north shore or the area to the east.

Troup Narrows. Troup Narrows, with maximum tidal currents of only about 2 knots, is easily run. Assuming a passage from south to north, identify the reef that dries 15 feet near the south entrance to the narrows. Leave the reef to port, and slide west to the beautiful rock cliffs of Chatfield Island. Stay

Roscoe Inlet has some of the most awe-inspiring scenery on the coast.

on the Chatfield Island side until the point of land on Cunningham Island is abeam, then trend east to the far shore of Cunningham Island to avoid the reef that extends from the 65-meter island. Study the chart to find the rocks you must avoid.

Roscoe Inlet. Roscoe Inlet is drop-dead beautiful. Beginning where Johnson Channel meets Return Channel, Roscoe Inlet winds some 21 miles back through high mountains that plunge straight down into the sea. Exquisite bowls and valleys lead into the mountains. Sheer cliffs tower overhead. In some places you can bring the boat alongside a vertical granite wall that rises to a mountain peak 3600 feet above and still have more than 450 feet of water below. Dramatic.

Good anchorages are scarce. For a day trip, we suggest motoring up in the morning, dropping the hook for lunch at the head of the inlet, and motoring back in the afternoon. You can overnight, of course.

Other than the head of the inlet, in our opinion **Boukind Bay** is the easiest anchorage along the way. A large, 25- to 30-foot-deep area allows plenty of room to swing. If an inflow wind is blowing, however, it might be a little bouncy. **Quartcha Bay** is a visually stunning anchorage, although deep until close to the sides or the mud flats at the head. Waterfalls tumble down the mountain sides. From near the head you can look back into two glacier-polished bowls of rock (called cirques) and extensive meadows. Correspondent Gil Flanagan reports that evidence of ancient fish traps can be found on the large tide flats. **Shack Bay** and **Ripley Bay** are exposed to inflow winds, and deep until very close to shore. We didn't like them. **Clatse Bay**, at the south end of Roscoe Inlet,

is a good anchorage. Go all the way to the head and anchor in 40 to 50 feet.

Bugs: Several readers have warned about ravenous deer flies. Bring insect repellant.

Morehouse Bay. Morehouse Bay, indenting Chatfield Island off Return Channel, has a lovely one-boat anchorage (more, if all are stern-tied to shore) in a cove at the very back, or room for more boats in 60-foot depths outside the back cove. To enter the outer anchorage, leave the 53-meter island to port and the 44- and 59-meter islands to starboard. The more secluded back cove is in the south part of the bay, behind the 59-meter island. Leave a large rock, shown as a 1.2-meter depth, to starboard as you enter. The entry is easy—just be sure you know where that rock is. Anchor in 25 to 35 feet.

Wigham Cove. Wigham Cove, on the south shore of Yeo Island, is a popular anchorage and an excellent place to overnight before transiting Seaforth Channel. Favor the west shore as you enter, until abeam the islets in the middle of the bay. Then turn to pass north of the islets to the favored anchorage in the northeast nook of the cove. This nook has room for several boats. We have shared this anchorage with a 60-footer and a 43-footer with no crowding at all. An 80-footer was anchored in the southeast cove.

Dangerous rock: Be careful if you enter the southernmost nook of Wigham Cove. A dangerous underwater rock with a depth of 0.5 meters at zero tide is reported lying close to and just east of the northernmost of the three drying rocks that extend from the eastern shore of the entrance to Wigham Cove. When entering this nook, favor the islets to the east.

Ivory Island Lighthouse marks the decision point, a northeast turn to protected Reid Passage, or continue west up Milbanke Sound.

Spiller Channel. Spiller Channel and Bullock Channel run north from Seaforth Channel on either side of Yeo Island and lead to famed Ellerslie Lagoon, whose entrance rocks have bumped many a boat. Neither run is particularly scenic. Compared with other areas, the hillsides are low.

Neekas Cove, across the channel from the north tip of Yeo Island, is the only easy anchorage in the southern part of Spiller Channel. Yeo Cove, near the south entrance to Spiller Channel, has a rock-studded entry and only limited anchorage deep in the southeast corner. Tate Lagoon, which leads into Don Peninsula, has a treacherous entrance. This lagoon is shown as unnamed on Chart 3940. Douglass describes both places.

The top of Spiller Channel is a little better. The hidden anchorage Douglass calls "Nash Narrows Cove" is lovely. Decent anchorage can be found in the bay immediately south of Ellerslie Lagoon.

Neekas Cove. Neekas Cove is opposite the north tip of Yeo Island in Spiller Channel. The cove is narrow and pretty, but deep until close to the head, where the bottom shelves rapidly. Anchor in 50 feet (zero tide) if cautious; 35 feet if braver; less, at your peril. Watch for bears on the shore here.

Nash Passage. Nash Passage (Douglass' name for this otherwise unnamed winding channel), separates Coldwell Peninsula from a good-sized unnamed island on the approach to Ellerslie Bay, just before Spiller Inlet. The chart shows rocks, but the ones to watch out for dry at 4.3 meters, so they should be visible much of the time.

Nash Narrows Cove (Douglass' name again), is the little cove at the turn of Nash Passage. It is beautiful, and would be a good spot to put the hook down.

A peninsula separates Ellerslie Lagoon from a substantial bay immediately to the south. Anchorage is in the inner bay, east of an islet in the middle of the fairway. Pass either side of the islet. Our preferred spot is in 60 feet (zero tide) on the south side, under a towering cliff. The north side of the bay might get down to 40-foot depths, but isn't as protected or cozy feeling.

Ellerslie Lagoon. Because of dangerous rocks, a spring tide high water entry is called for. Two sets of narrows lead in. Ellerslie Lake pours a lot of water into the lagoon; expect the outflowing current through the narrows to last longer than usual.

Spiller Inlet. Spiller Inlet extends northward from the top of Spiller Channel. The sides are steep and the water is deep until near the head, where the depths shoal rapidly to a shelf. Near the head of the inlet, the granite cliff on the east side has fractured and fallen away to create Weeping Woman, a Picasso-like natural sculpture on the mountainside. It's quite dramatic.

Bullock Channel. Bullock Channel is a straight run between Return Channel and the top of Yeo Island. Study the chart and favor the Coldwell Peninsula side of the channel. The shoal areas on the Yeo Island side have a tendency to be right where you think you should be going.

The only good Bullock Channel anchorages are on the Coldwell Peninsula side—one at the south end, the other at the north end (where we overnighted). We checked the purported anchorages on the Yeo Island side, but they weren't satisfactory. We found poor holding in the northernmost anchorage, and rock, rock, rock in the bight a little south of the north anchorage.

The water is warm near the top of both channels. In colder waters we like our cabin heat in the morning, but we had no need for it there. [Hale]

Bullock Channel North Cove. This is Douglass' name for the otherwise unnamed anchorage behind the 39-meter island at the north end of Bullock Channel, on the Coldwell Peninsula side. We found excellent overnight holding in 50 feet (zero tide) opposite the west opening to the cove. The chart shows a rock awash at zero tide in this west opening. Enter and depart this cove from the north.

Bullock Spit Cove. Again, Douglass' name for this unnamed anchorage located inside the 70-meter island on the Coldwell Peninsula side, near the south entrance to Bullock Channel. As the chart shows, you don't want to go very far in or you'll run aground. We found good holding in 35 feet just south of the tip of the island.

Kynumpt Harbour. Kynumpt Harbour indents the north tip of Campbell Island, east of Raymond Passage. Sailing Directions says the local name is Strom Bay. The entrance is open and easy, but study the chart carefully to identify and avoid rocks on the western and southern shores. The northernmost indent on the eastern shore is reported to be a good anchorage, as is Strom Cove, the arm that extends to the southeast. We poked around Strom Cove to find a good lunch stop, but saw mostly 55 to 75 feet on the sounder. At those depths, even a 3:1 scope would swing us too close to rocks near shore, so we anchored in the outer bay, 40 feet, west of Spratt Point.

Dundivan Inlet. Dundivan Inlet indents Dufferin Island west of Raymond Passage. It's a pretty spot with several islets to break up the scenery, but the water is deep except near hazards. Two arms make up Lockhart Bay, near the head. The western arm is the more attractive anchorage. For overnight we would run a stern-tie to a tree. The eastern arm is deep (60 feet) until very near the head and requires a stern-tie. Dundivan Inlet would not be our first choice unless weather was ugly and we were looking for a place to hole up.

Raymond Passage. Raymond Passage connects Seaforth Channel with Queens Sound and sees few pleasure craft. The passage is open, free of hazards, and connects with Codfish Passage at the south end. If you're looking for a raw and exposed wilderness experience and have the boat and navigation skills to manage it, Raymond Passage is a good choice.

Thompson Bay. Thompson Bay is on the west side of Potts Island. Examine the area on your chartplotter or study Chart 3938. This entire area is beautiful and seldom visited. At the northeast corner of Thompson Bay an excellent, protected cove indents Potts Island. Enter the cove from the north, at 52°09.75'N/128°20.75'W.

To get from Raymond Passage to Thompson Bay, run a course of approximately 239° magnetic from the southern tip of

This photo at low tide shows you should pass to the east of Carne Rock in Reid Passage.

Alleyne Island to the 45-meter island, then turn to a course of approximately 292° magnetic to Agnew Islet. You will leave Seen Island approximately one-quarter mile to the south. Rocks will be all around you, but stay in the pass and you will have water.

St. John Harbour. Enter from the north, leaving red buoy *E46*, marking Rage Reefs, to starboard. Several floating fishing resorts are around Dyer Cove. We prefer the back cove; be sure to avoid the drying shoal. The shallowest point of the channel is at least 7 feet deep. Holding is good.

Milbanke Sound. Milbanke Sound is the shortest route north or south for boats trying to make time along the Inside Passage. In quiet conditions Milbanke Sound is easy. But if the wind is blowing the crossing can be brutal.

From Seaforth Channel to Finlayson Channel, leave Ivory Island to starboard and lay a course that passes north of Susan Rock and west of Vancouver Rock Buoy *E54*. From there, lay a course to the mouth of Finlayson Channel. Our course took us fairly close to Jorkins Point and the east side of Swindle Island. Total distance was about 12 miles. We've seen boats pass east of Vancouver Rock and take Merilia Passage. This saves about a mile.

Tuno Creek Anchorage. "At the south end of Reid Passage, Blair Inlet extends nearly 2 miles eastward into the Don Peninsula. Tuno Creek empties into the head of Blair Inlet. Anchor south of the creek in 25 to 30 feet, good holding over mud. Strong westerly winds probably will reach the anchorage, but wind protection is good from other directions." [*Hamilton*]

Reid Passage & Port Blackney. If there's much wind at all, most pleasure craft headed north or south will avoid Milbanke Sound and use the Reid Passage route east of Ivory Island. Chart 3710 makes navigation straightforward. At the south end, be sure to identify all the rocks and islets, and Buoy *E50*. In the middle of Reid Passage, pass to the east of Carne Rock. Port Blackney, at the north end of Reid Passage, has two

anchorages, Boat Inlet and Oliver Cove, that can be used before crossing to Perceval Narrows.

Boat Inlet. Boat Inlet, at the southwest corner of Port Blackney, has a delightful basin for anchorage, with an untouched feeling. The passage that leads to the basin is shallow, however, and rocks encumber the south shore and middle of the channel. Favor the north shore all the way in, with an alert lookout for underwater rocks. The little bay on the north shore at the east end of the passage is shallow and rocky. Stay out. Depending on your vessel's draft, wait for half tide or higher before running Boat Inlet.

Oliver Cove. Oliver Cove Marine Provincial Park, on the east side of Port Blackney, is a safe and pretty anchorage. Enter carefully, avoiding a charted rock in the middle of the fairway and another on the south side. Put the hook down in 35 feet. A few years ago we saw a bear and her cubs on the rocky shore.

Perceval Narrows. The Inside Passage route leads across Mathieson Channel between Port Blackney and Perceval Narrows. Tidal current predictions are found as a secondary station under Prince Rupert in Tide and Current Tables, Vol. 7 and Ports and Passes. From south to north, lay a course that gives Cod Reefs a good offing to port as you leave Port Blackney. Then turn to approximately 270° magnetic and cross Mathieson Channel toward Martha Island, leaving Lizzie Rocks to starboard. We found turbulence in Mathieson Channel off Lizzie Rocks on an ebb tide.

Cockle Bay/Lady Douglas Island. Cockle Bay, a short distance north of Perceval Narrows, has a beautiful beach and good protection from westerlies. You can find 30- to 35-foot depths along the south shore and 60 to 90 feet in the middle, as shown on the chart.

Tom Bay. Tom Bay is on the east side of Mathieson Channel at lat 52°24.20'N. It's a good anchorage, though scarred by recent logging. As with most bays on this coast,

441

See Area Map Page 426 - Maps Not for Navigation

Tom Bay shoals at the head. Anchor in 60 to 70 feet.

Dowager Island & Arthur Island. The coves north of Arthur Island, approximately 1.5 miles south of Oscar Passage on the west side of Mathieson Channel, are mentioned in Sailing Directions as a small boat anchorage. Neither cove is very scenic and driftwood clogs the eastern cove. We would choose Rescue Bay on Susan Island, Salmon Bay to the north, or Tom Bay to the south.

Salmon Bay. Salmon Bay is on the east side of Mathieson Channel, opposite the mouth of Oscar Passage. It is deep until the very head, where the bottom comes up to 50 to 60 feet. The bay is cozy and we heard a loon—always a soothing sound.

Oscar Passage. Oscar Passage is the wide-open Inside Passage route between Mathieson Channel and Finlayson Channel. On an ebb, however, the seas can heap up where Oscar Passage joins Finlayson Channel, the result of swells from Milbanke Sound meeting outflowing current. Larger vessels often use Oscar Passage rather than Jackson Passage.

Rescue Bay. Rescue Bay is the most popular anchorage in this area. It is well protected with good holding, and has room for many boats. Study the chart carefully before entering, and steer a determined mid-channel course between the two islands and their reefs that mark the entrance. Once inside Rescue Bay, scout around with the depth sounder and pick your spot carefully. We saw one boat on the western side find the bottom at low tide, after being too eager to get the anchor down.

Note the drying rock in the southeast corner of the bay. Note also the drying reef that extends from the east side of the bay, south of the round islet. The reef covers at high water, and we anchored a little close to it. After checking things out by dinghy and seeing how near the reef was, we re-anchored farther out. At low water the reef showed itself. We were glad we had moved.

Jackson Passage. Jackson Passage is the scenic route between Mathieson Channel and Finlayson Channel. The passage is easily navigated, except for a tight spot at Jackson Narrows at the eastern end, where the depth shows as low as 12 feet on the charts. The fairway through the eastern end of Jackson Narrows is quite narrow and shallow; kelp marks the rocks. Larger vessels may prefer Oscar Passage to the south. While neither the chart nor Sailing Directions shows the current directions, our observations from several transits indicate the flood current sets east and the ebb current sets west.

Jackson Narrows is blind. Before entering, either direction, it's a good idea to call ahead on VHF channel 16, low power, to announce your intentions *(Securité, securité, this is the 34-foot motor vessel* Happy Days, *about to enter Jackson Narrows westbound. Any*

At anchor in Rescue Bay on the east end of Jackson Passage

eastbound traffic please advise, channel one-six). One year, to our astonishment, a boat approaching from the other end called back on channel 16. Since we were about to enter, the other boat waited until we got through. Strongly favor the south shore all the way through the narrows, and keep a sharp lookout. A transit near high water slack would be the least anxious, although we have gone through at low water slack with no difficulty.

James Bay. James Bay, on the west side of Mathieson Channel, is open to southerly winds, but gets you out of the chop in the channel. It is a pretty spot, but the bottom shoals abruptly in the northwest corner. Anchor in 75 feet, where the little anchor symbol is on the chart.

FIORDLAND RECREATION AREA

The Fiordland Recreation Area was established in 1987, and is some of the most striking country on the coast. The mountains are sheer and beautiful and the wildlife abundant, but anchorages are just about nonexistent. Fortunately, good anchorage can be found in Windy Bay, only a short distance away.

Fiordland begins just east of Bolin Bay at the north end of Sheep Passage, and includes Mussel Inlet and Kynoch Inlet. We include Bolin Bay in this section because it is so pretty, and Windy Bay because it is the best anchorage near Fiordland.

Windy Bay. Windy Bay is on the south shore of Sheep Passage, near the eastern end. The chart shows anchorage in the middle, but more protected anchorage is in 60 feet in what we call Cookie Cove, just east of the little island at the northeast corner of the bay. Excellent holding.

Bolin Bay. Bolin Bay is set in a bowl of sheer rock mountains with a beautiful drying flat at

the head. We didn't anchor, but we did find a few spots with depths of 35 to 60 feet near the head of the bay. With care you might get a safe amount of scope out and stay off the flats. Windy Bay is a better choice.

Oatwish Bay. Oatwish Bay is at the north end of Mussel Inlet. Amazing Lizette Falls will have you reaching for the camera. The bay is too deep for anchoring. We enjoyed lunch there, drifting, engines off.

Poison Cove. At the northeast end of Mussel Inlet lies Poison Cove and Mussel Cove/Mussel River. This is a protected wildlife area for bears and mountain goats which is jointly monitored by BC Parks and the Mussel River Watchmen program. When arriving at the area, boaters should contact the Watchmen on VHF Channel 06. A maximum number of people/boats are allowed in the area at one time. For more information go to www.env.gov.bc.ca/bcparks/explore/parkpgs/fiordland/. The run to the east of Mussel Inlet to Poison Cove left us awestruck. Our notes say, "Poison Cove dwarfed us. I ran out of superlatives."

Kynoch Inlet. Located off Mathieson Channel, Kynoch Inlet is a spectacular deep water fiord with unsurpassed beauty. Words such as amazing, awesome, incomparable and magnificent suggest but do not capture the grandeur of this inlet. Black rock mountains rise straight up and waterfalls spill down the mountain faces. The inlet is so narrow and the sides are so steep that our GPS lost its satellites. The only anchoring in the Inlet is in deeper water off the drying flats of Kainet Creek. Correspondents Elsie and Steve Hulsizer reported in 2018 that waters off Kainet Creek have silted, and they touched bottom with a 6 foot keel where the chart showed 10 meters. They also reported strong inflow afternoon winds blow up Kynoch Inlet; and suggested

The size, scale and grandeur of Fiordland are awe inspiring.

Waterfalls abound in Kynoch Inlet.

planning a visit to Culpepper Lagoon during neap tides to provide longer slack water intervals for entering and exiting.

Culpepper Lagoon. Enter or depart Culpepper Lagoon around high water slack. Correspondent Bill Hales reports that current in the entrance turns 15 to 30 minutes before high or low water at Bella Bella, and a least depth of 10 to 15 feet. Correspondent Gil Flanagan adds that he entered Culpepper Lagoon around high slack without difficulty. Coming out the next morning, they departed an hour or two before low water slack. He reports: "We heard the roar of the rapids well before seeing the narrows in fog. It was quite a ride. We estimated the current at 7.5 knots, and sure we dropped more than a foot. The depth sounder was unusable because of the turbulence. We didn't have time to look anyway. There was no turning back. Just steer the sled to the bottom of the hill and hope we miss the Kainet Creek mudflats. Yahoo!" After comparing Bella Bella tides with Hiekish Narrows current predictions, Flanagan thinks Hiekish Narrows might be a better predictor of slack water. Waggoner draws no conclusions, except to arrive early

and—unlike our correspondent— wait for slack water before going through. On our visit to Culpepper Lagoon we went through the narrows an hour after low water at Bella Bella with no difficulty. We tried to anchor off Riot Creek but couldn't find a place we liked to put the hook down. Flanagan anchored south of the Lard Creek mudflats at the head of Culpepper Lagoon, inshore from the 60-foot sounding.

FINLAYSON CHANNEL TO PRINCE RUPERT

Nowish Cove. Nowish Cove is on the east side of Finlayson Channel, south of Jackson Passage, at the entrance to Nowish Inlet. Despite being shown as an anchorage, we weren't impressed. The bottom is 85 feet deep and currents from Nowish Narrows swirl through the bay. If protection is needed from a southerly storm, we would consider this cove. Otherwise, if we were looking for a place to hide and had the time, Bottleneck Inlet, 11 miles farther north, is a better choice.

⑧ **Klemtu**. The fuel dock (250-839-1233) and Kitasoo band store are at the north end

of town. Both are open Monday through Saturday, closed for lunch 12:00 p.m. to 1:00 p.m., limited hours Sundays. Boaters may tie-up at the fuel dock when shopping for groceries at the band store as space permits. The band store has an ATM. You'll find gasoline, diesel, propane, stove oil, and ample clear water from the village's water treatment system. The fuel dock faces the channel and wakes from passing boat traffic are apt to bounce you against the dock. Be sure you are well-tied and well-fendered. If the attendant is not in the office shack on the pier, try calling First Nations Fuel on VHF 06 or ask someone in town what the fuel situation is. The fuel dock is closed Sundays, but someone might be available to turn on the pumps.

Klemtu is the last fuel stop until Hartley Bay, approximately 65 miles north. In several recent instances, Hartley Bay has temporarily run out of fuel. Choose fuel stops accordingly.

BC Ferries and Wilderness Seaplanes have scheduled service into Klemtu.

An 11-foot-wide, 210-foot-long concrete dock has been installed in the bay near the village. The dock has no power. The docks can get crowded with local fishing boats and nets are often stacked on the floats. Be prepared to anchor, being mindful of large drying shoals on the south and west sides of the bay.

The village has a K-12 school, good cell phone coverage, two nurses, a post office and three stores. We have shopped in two of the stores: the band store at the fuel dock, and Robinson-Mason General Store in the village.

The band store at the head of the fuel dock pier carries a good selection of groceries and other essentials (no liquor), but the stock can thin a few days after scheduled ferry deliveries. On our last visit, we watched the last gallon of milk get snatched up. The store receives supplies only once every two weeks. A small restaurant with breakfast, burgers, and Chinese food is in the entry to the store. You can dine in or order takeout. A pay telephone is just outside the store.

If you'd like to see the extraordinary Big House overlooking the harbor, contact the band. Tours are $10 per person. A boardwalk runs around the harbor from the fuel dock to the long house. In 2017 we were surprised

Deep water anchorage at the head of Kynoch Inlet near the entrance to Culpepper Lagoon

Reference Only – Not for Navigation

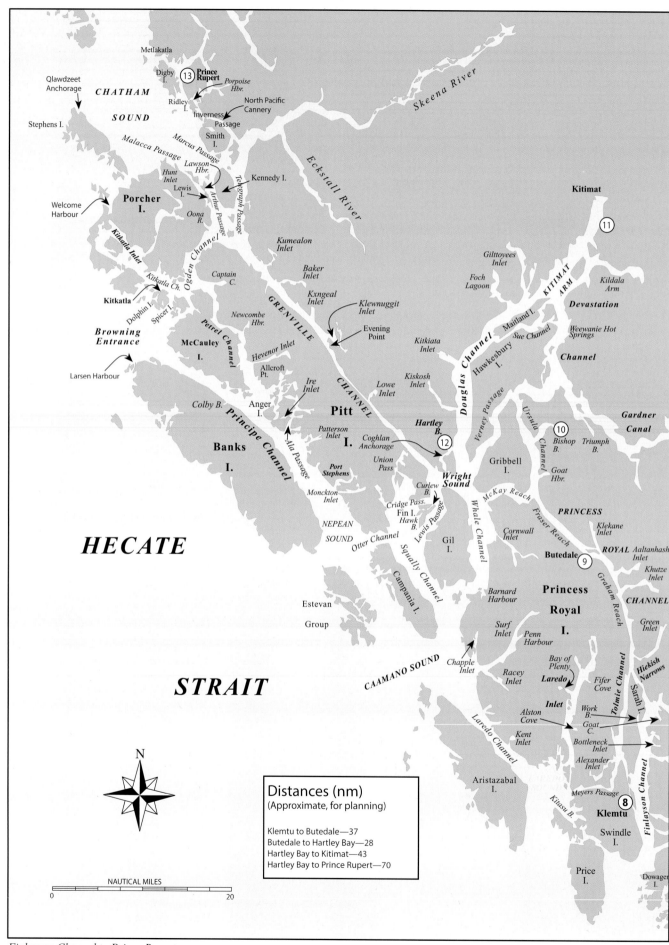

Metlakatla
Qlawdzeet Anchorage
CHATHAM
Digby I.
(13) **Prince Rupert**
Porpoise Hbr.
SOUND
Ridley I.
North Pacific Cannery
Inverness Passage
Stephens I.
Smith I.
Skeena River
Marcus Passage
Malacca Passage
Lawson Hbr.
Hunt Inlet
Lewis I.
Kennedy I.
Eckstall River
Telegraph Passage
Welcome Harbour
Porcher I.
Oona R.
Arthur Passage
Kitimat
Kitkatla Inlet
Kitkatla Ch.
Ogden Channel
Kumealon Inlet
(11)
Gilttoyees Inlet
Foch Lagoon
KITIMAT ARM
Kildala Arm
Kitkatla
Dolphin I.
Spicer I.
Captain C.
Baker Inlet
Kxngeal Inlet
Klewnuggit Inlet
Devastation
Browning Entrance
Newcombe Hbr.
GRENVILLE
Hevenor Inlet
Evening Point
Kitkiata Inlet
Maitland I.
Sue Channel
Weewanie Hot Springs
Channel
Larsen Harbour
McCauley I.
Petrel Channel
Allcroft Pt.
CHANNEL
Kiskosh Inlet
Douglas Channel
Hawkesbury I.
Verney Passage
Ire Inlet
Lowe Inlet
Colby B.
Anger I.
Pitt I.
Hartley B.
(10)
Ursula Channel
Bishop B.
Triumph B.
Gardner Canal
Principe Channel
Ala Passage
Patterson Inlet
Coghlan Anchorage
(12)
Gribbell I.
Goat Hbr.
Banks I.
Port Stephens
Union Pass
Wright Sound
Curlew B.
Monckton Inlet
Cridge Pass.
Fin I.
Hawk B.
Lewis Passage
McKay Reach
PRINCESS
Klekane Inlet
NEPEAN SOUND
Otter Channel
Gil I.
Whale Channel
Cornwall Inlet
Fraser Reach
HECATE
Squally Channel
Campania I.
Barnard Harbour
Butedale
(9)
ROYAL
Aaltanhash Inlet
Khutze Inlet
Estevan Group
Surf Inlet
Penn Harbour
Princess Royal I.
Graham Reach
CHANNEL
Green Inlet
STRAIT
CAAMANO SOUND
Chapple Inlet
Racey Inlet
Bay of Plenty
Laredo
Fifer Cove
Tolmie Channel
Hickish Narrows
Inlet
Alston Cove
Work B.
Goat C.
Sarah I.
Laredo Channel
Kent Inlet
Bottleneck Inlet
Alexander Inlet
Aristazabal I.
Meyers Passage
(8)
Kitasu B.
Klemtu
Price I.
Swindle I.
Finlayson Channel
Dowager I.

N

Distances (nm)
(Approximate, for planning)

Klemtu to Butedale—37
Butedale to Hartley Bay—28
Hartley Bay to Kitimat—43
Hartley Bay to Prince Rupert—70

NAUTICAL MILES
0   20

Finlayson Channel to Prince Rupert

The Native village of Klemtu has a Band Grocery and fuel dock.

to see a medium sized cruise ship stopped at Klemtu. It waited near the ferry landing while its tender shuttled passengers to the Big House and Cultural Center.

Clothes Bay. Clothes Bay is south of Klemtu on the west side of the channel between Swindle Island and Cone Island. The bay is well protected except from southeasterly winds. We anchored for the night behind the north tip of Star Island at the mouth of the bay. At low tide, we discovered that the charted "something," extending from Base Point north of us, was a substantial drying reef. The bay has good holding but limited room for only a couple of boats. Being near Klemtu, there is cell phone service in the bay.

Alexander Inlet. Alexander Inlet extends 5 miles into Princess Royal Island, beginning where Meyers Passage and Tolmie Channel meet. If you're fed up with the throngs of boaters and crowded anchorages on this part of the coast (we're joking), here is where you can escape. The early sections of Alexander Inlet are bordered by steep mountains, and are beautiful. The head, however, is surrounded by low hills and is rather ordinary. But, being 5 miles off the beaten path, chances are you'll be the only boat.

The chart shows the inlet well. The only tricky part is near Bingham Narrows. After clearing the drying reef before you reach Bingham Narrows, sag to the west shore to avoid the drying rocks, marked by kelp, just before the narrows themselves.

The head of the inlet is wide open, with ample room to avoid the rock that dries at 2.4 meters lying off the west shore. Anchor in 30 to 35 feet with outstanding holding.

One of the hilltops looks like the profile of a woman lying on her side, and we called it Sleeping Woman. See if you agree. We saw a pair of birds that our field guide identified as red-throated loons, not seen as often as common loons. A lagoon pours into the very head of the inlet, making fluffs of white foam on the water's surface. We rowed over

and took pictures, but didn't take the time to explore further. It's very pretty.

The next morning our final note, written after the previous day's notes called the head of Alexander Inlet rather ordinary, reads, "This is a neat spot." [Hale]

OUTSIDE ROUTE – PRINCESS ROYAL ISLAND & PITT ISLAND

At this point we step away from the main Inside Passage route to describe the routes west of Princess Royal and Pitt Islands. Those continuing through Finlayson or Tolmie Channels, past Butedale, and through Grenville Channel will find that information resuming on page 449.

Without question, the preferred Inside Passage route to Prince Rupert and beyond is through Finlayson or Tolmie Channels (past Klemtu), past Butedale, and up through Grenville Channel. The waters are protected, the scenery is outstanding, and there's enough boat traffic that if you have a problem, somebody will be along to help out.

An alternate route is on the outside of Princess Royal and Pitt Islands. This route is popular with sailors and adventuresome power boaters. It's as beautiful as the traditional route, but wilder and much less traveled, with more islands and anchorages but fewer waterfalls. Sailors will find more consistent and stronger winds due to the wider channels and lower hills. There's even room for tacking. Because of their remoteness, we recommend these passages for more experienced cruisers only.

From south to north, the outside route first leads up the west side of Princess Royal Island. It begins by running west through Meyers Passage (near Klemtu), then through Laredo Channel and Whale Channel, and rejoins the Inside Passage at Wright Sound. To cruise the outside of Pitt Island, the route runs west from Wright Sound (south end of Grenville Channel), and north through Principe Channel and Petrel Channel, then east through Ogden Channel to rejoin the Inside Passage.

On the outside of either island you could travel all day and only see one or two other pleasure boats, although you're sure to see a few fish boats, perhaps a tug and barge or even a cruise ship. You'll find good anchorages on the outside. In many cases you'll be the only boat.

Weather permitting, you could travel the traditional Inside Passage going one way and all or part of the outside route going the other. The inside and outside routes are roughly the same distance. However, if you take only part of the outside route, going back and forth between the inside and the outside, your total trip will be longer. If you are considering the outside route, carry Sailing Directions PAC 206, and *Exploring the North Coast of B.C.*, by Don Douglass and Réanne Hemmingway-Douglass. The Waggoner Guide describes only the most direct outside routes and focuses on good anchorages. The other books cover a wider area and describe places that require caution and may be more challenging than some skippers would like. If you have the desire for a coastal cruising challenge, with the boat and skills to meet that challenge, the west coast of Princess Royal Island and Pitt Island are excellent cruising areas.

If winds are favorable, sailboats (or slower powerboats) can cut almost a day off their time on the outside route with an open water passage that avoids Klemtu and Meyers Passage. Northbound exit Seaforth Channel, cross Milbanke Sound, and transit Catala Passage. Or, go around McInnes Island, then north up Laredo Sound to Laredo Inlet. This open water route has no stops until you reach Higgins Passage, so pick your weather window carefully. Pay careful attention to your navigation in Catala Passage. The islands and rocks are easily confused, especially in fog. Watch for cruise ships and freighters that occasionally use Laredo Sound.

WEST SIDE OF SWINDLE ISLAND

Higgins Passage. Higgins Passage connects the north end of Milbanke Sound to Laredo Sound, between Swindle and Price Islands.

The middle section of the passage, however, has strong currents, many turns, and dries on a six foot tide.

Anchorage can be found in the western end of Higgins Passage. From Laredo Sound, enter Higgins Passage south of Kipp Islet. **Grant Anchorage** is deep and not well protected from southeast winds. Proceed through the anchorage and anchor in 30 to 40 feet on the west side of **Lohbrunner Island.** This anchorage is well protected from all winds, mud bottom.

Kitasu Bay. Kitasu Bay is between Wilby Point and Meyers Passage. Several anchorages are available, ranging from good to excellent. The bay itself is exposed to northwesterly winds, which blow straight down Laredo Channel into **Parson's Anchorage.** In southeasterly or southwesterly weather, however, Parson's Anchorage provides good holding.

The **Marvin Islands** provide shelter from northwest winds. Anchor on the southeast side of the islands in about 50 feet. Several boats can anchor in this location and protected from moderate winds. Gale force northwesterly winds can make this anchorage uncomfortable.

Jamieson Point Anchorage (also known as Coward's Cove) is just east of Jamieson Point and provides total protection from all winds. Stay mid-channel when entering to avoid a rock on the west side of the entrance. This rock is usually marked by kelp. Once inside, anchor in 30 to 40 feet over a sticky mud bottom.

The eastern basin of **Osment Inlet** provides good anchorage in most weather but the bottom is rocky and irregular.

WEST SIDE OF PRINCESS ROYAL ISLAND

LOCAL KNOWLEDGE

NAVIGATION NOTE: Red spar Buoy *E70* is in the middle of the tight spot in Meyers Passage. Pass north of the buoy, midway between the buoy and the north shore. Currents to 3 knots flood east and ebb west. Sailing Directions says least depth at zero tide is 4 feet. Kelp shows the places to avoid.

Meyers Passage. Meyers Passage separates Swindle Island and Princess Royal Island and is the low-anxiety way to travel between Finlayson Channel and Laredo Sound. The only tricky spot is kelp-choked Meyers Narrows. Although the narrows are not difficult to run, kelp may be present. Current can run to 3 knots in the narrows.

We went through slowly, avoiding the kelp as best we could. When we got through we said, "Piece of cake."

Field Correspondents Jim Norris and Anita Fraser confirmed that there's good anchorage in 45 feet in the bay on the south shore of the passage.

Laredo Channel. Laredo Channel separates Princess Royal Island and Aristazabal Island, and connects Laredo Sound at the south end with Caamaño Sound and Campania Sound at the north end. Aristazabal Island, on the west side of Laredo Channel, is incompletely charted and considered extremely challenging.

While several inlets lead off Laredo Channel into Princess Royal Island, Laredo Inlet at the south end and Surf Inlet at the north end are the major indents.

LOCAL KNOWLEDGE

INACCURATE CHART: We've heard reports that Chart 3737 is based on an unknown datum, resulting in significant inaccuracies. Electronic charts based on Chart 3737 have similar inaccuracies.

Laredo Inlet. Laredo Inlet is about 10 miles long, and is well protected from westerly storms. If you're approaching from the south, such as from Meyers Passage, the closest entry is through Thistle Passage. Rocks extend first from the east side of the narrows, then from the west side. They aren't shown well on the chart. We went through at the top of a 12.8-foot tide. We didn't see any sign of the rocks and they were not marked by kelp. Caution advised. The chart shows 4½ fathoms least depth at the north end of the narrows.

Palmer Anchorage. Fisherman Mike Guns suggests Palmer Anchorage at the south end of Thistle Passage as a good wait-and-see temporary anchorage in a northwest gale, but it's deep, and not what we'd select as the best overnight cruising anchorage.

While several overnight anchorages are available in Laredo Inlet, we think you'll be choosing between Quickly Creek Cove, Alston Cove, Bay of Plenty, and perhaps Fifer Cove. We spent the night in Alston Cove and explored Fifer Cove and Bay of Plenty.

Quigley Creek Cove. From the top of Thistle Passage, turn east just beyond the first small island, leaving the remaining islands to port, then follow the shore into a landlocked basin at the mouth of Quigley Creek. The basin has a depth of about 60 feet at zero tide. A beautiful spot, protected by surrounding islands from wind and waves. This is one of the few outer channel anchorages that you might share with another boat.

Alston Cove. Mouth 52°45.10'N/128°45 .75'W. Lovely Alston Cove is easy to enter and is surrounded by mountain peaks. We put the hook down in sticky brown mud just onto the 6½-fathom area on the north side of the cove, near the flats. When we departed the next morning we were glad to have the anchor washdown system. It took a long time to hose the chain and anchor clean.

Fifer Cove. Mouth 52°52.15'N/128°45 .15'W. Fifer Cove is surrounded by mountain peaks and is very scenic, but most of the cove is too deep for easy anchoring. To enter, wrap around Tuite Point, leaving it to starboard. We found 40- to 50-foot depths near the head of the cove, off the stream mouth. Correspondents James and Jennifer Hamilton report the creek shoals out much farther than the chart indicates or they expected, and holding was poor.

Kohl Island Anchorage. "Kohl Island is in Weld Cove, directly south of Bay of Plenty. The bight at the northwest tip of Kohl Island is a sheltered anchorage with mountain views. Approach between Kohl and Pocock Islands and turn west when clear of the rocks off the north tip of Kohl Island. The anchorage is at 52°49.00'N/128°46.09'W between two uncharted rocks. One rock rarely covers and the other is awash at 12 feet. We dropped the anchor between the rocks and pulled back 150 feet to stern-tie onto Kohl Island. Holding was good in 10 to 20 feet over mud and shell." [*Hamilton*]

Bay of Plenty. Bay of Plenty was recommended to us by Correspondents Mike Guns and Laurie and Anita Dowsett. On our chart, Guns drew the entrance channel south of the 120-foot island, and north of the little islet in the middle of the Bay. Anchor in 30 feet, short of the flats. Those flats, by the way, come out a long way. The bay is open to southwest storms.

Field Correspondent Jim Norris reports good anchorage, but his empty crab pot had him renaming this spot "Bay of Not so Much."

Buie Creek. "A spectacular two-level waterfall is a short distance up Buie Creek at the head of Laredo Inlet. To visit, anchor temporarily off the head of Laredo Inlet at 52°58.128'N/128°39.763'W in 90 feet with a 250-foot swing radius, moderate holding." [*Hamilton*]

Kent Inlet. Kent Inlet is on the east side of Laredo Channel. Once inside, Kent Inlet is scenic and appears to be well protected. To get inside, however, you must go through Philip Narrows, which is guarded by rocks. Sailing Directions says currents through Philip Narrows run to 8 knots at spring tides, and recommends a transit at slack water only.

We arrived at Kent Inlet near high water slack, so we went in. Kelp marked the rocks at the entrance, off Laredo Channel, and they were not a problem. Kelp did *not* mark the rocks a short distance east of Loap Point. Rocks are out in the middle, exactly where you think you want to be. Stay south of those rocks. Give them room.

At slack water Philip Narrows was easy. Correspondents Laurie and Anita Dowsett recommended anchoring either near the west shore immediately inside Phllip Narrows, or in the back basin off the tidal waterfall. Favor

These extraordinary falls are at the head of Surf Inlet.

the north shore to get to the back basin. Note the rocks on the south side when entering the back basin. The water in Kent Inlet was dark with rain runoff when we visited; we couldn't see more than a foot or two into it. We had good depths all around the point that defines the back basin. This anchorage is beautiful, marred only by many diseased trees.

 LOCAL KNOWLEDGE

CHARTPLOTTER ERRORS: In Surf Inlet, one of our chartplotters placed our boat several hundred feet from where it actually was. Navigate cautiously in this area.

Surf Inlet. Beautiful Surf Inlet stretches 13 miles into Princess Royal Island at the north end of Laredo Channel, ending at a stunning waterfall over a dam that separates Bear Lake from the inlet.

An abandoned concrete power house is on a point below the dam at the head of Surf Inlet. A road leads to a point below the falls. We've been told that if you can get a dinghy or kayak up to the dam (the road looks like the way to go), you can go up Bear Lake to an old mining camp that is surprisingly intact.

Chapple Inlet, at the mouth of Surf Inlet, has a few anchorage possibilities, but Surf Inlet itself has only one, Penn Harbour.

Penn Harbour. Penn Harbour is beautiful and spacious, with a straightforward entry and ample anchoring room in 40 to 50 feet near the head. A stream cascades into the east end and makes little white icebergs of foam on the surface—except that on the night of our visit the icebergs weren't white, they were tan. The water was brown and the anchor turned brown as it penetrated the surface. It disappeared altogether within a foot or two.

Chapple Inlet. Chapple Inlet leads north from the mouth of Surf Inlet, and has anchorage possibilities. These include a little

nook on the west shore at Doig Anchorage, another nook behind Chettleburgh Point, and in Kiln Bay. Entry to Chapple Inlet is easy at Mallandaine Point. Follow a midchannel course along the east shore.

At **Doig Anchorage**, try the area just north of the point at 52°55.10'N/ 129°07.80'W. We didn't verify the depths, but we saw three rafted powerboats anchored and stern-tied to shore.

Behind **Chettleburgh Point**, we would anchor in 60 feet, with ample swinging room. This is where you will appreciate an all-chain anchor rode so you can swing in a smaller circle on shorter scope. If you move closer in for shallower water, you'll probably want to run a stern-tie to shore.

In **Kiln Bay**, anchor in 60 feet, north of the little island.

 LOCAL KNOWLEDGE

CHARTPLOTTER ERRORS: In Emily Carr Inlet, one of our chartplotters placed our boat several hundred feet from where it actually was. Navigate cautiously in this area.

Emily Carr Inlet. Emily Carr Inlet is on the north side of Surf Inlet, right at the mouth. The inlet is beautiful, and the main body of the inlet is open. With close attention it should present no problems. A reef, however, extends from Webber Island nearly across Holgate Passage, making the entry from Chapple Inlet a little tricky.

We went through Emily Carr Inlet from north to south, then turned northeast to complete our circumnavigation of Princess Royal Island. Although the winds were light, we got into a nasty tide-rip off the 207-foot island south of Duckers Island and wet the boat down pretty thoroughly. It wasn't fun. We crowded over close to Duckers Island and found calmer water. [*Hale*]

Barnard Harbour. Mouth, west side of Borde Island, 53°04.90'N/129°07.75'W; east side

of Borde Island, 53°05.20'N/129°06.65'W. Barnard Harbour is shown on planning Charts 3737 and 3742, see Chart 3911 for detail.

Barnard Harbour is big, open, and beautiful. It was a center for fly-in sport fishing lodges, but these lodges have since moved. Anchor in Cameron Cove along the west shore in 30 to 35 feet or in 40 to 60 feet off the mouth of Barnard Creek.

Campania Island. Campania Island, with its bald, knobby mountaintops, is recognizable from miles away. Several inlets on Campania Island's west shore provide sheltered anchorages, interesting views, and opportunities for exploration by kayaks and dinghies. All are well charted; use Charts 3724 and 3912.

McMicking Inlet. McMicking Inlet, in Estevan Sound on the west side of Campania Island, is one of the few places in the outer channels where, at least in July and August, you might have competition for the best anchoring spots. The looming granite mass of Pender Mountain makes for a dramatic anchorage, and twisted cedars growing among the rocks add to the scenic character. Use Charts 3724 and 3912. Although the entrance to McMicking Inlet is open to the south, islets, rocks and reefs diminish any swells. Enter south and east of a chain of islets and drying reefs extending from the south end of Jewsbury Peninsula. Anchor north of the narrows.

Weinburg Inlet. Located off Estevan Sound on the west side of Campania Island, Weinburg Inlet is the maze of islets and lagoons that include Anderson Passage and Dunn Passage, and related bays, coves, and basins. Approximately 3 miles of passage ways lead from Estevan Sound to the head of Weinburg Inlet.

At the head of **Anderson Passage** is a large basin where there is good anchorage with swinging room for several boats. This is the easiest way to enter Weinburg Inlet in limited visibility. Larger boats can anchor in the center of the basin in about 13 fathoms. Small boats can anchor in the more scenic and intimate southeast nook.

The head of **Dunn Passage** provides good anchorage among a labyrinth of rocks and islets. There is room for one or two boats, but swinging room is limited. Field Correspondent Jim Norris reports spending three nights anchored here in 2016, waiting out a southeast gale, with good holding but limited swinging room on a 5 to 1 scope.

WEST SIDE OF PITT ISLAND

This route leads from the south end of Grenville Channel.

Otter Channel. Two possible anchorages appear to be available on the south tip of Pitt Island (the north side of Otter Channel). The first is Dillon Bay, where we saw a sailboat anchored. The second is Saycuritay Cove.

Knobby Campania Island

Patterson Inlet, Princess Diana Cove

Saycuritay Cove. The small cove east of Fleishman Point on the southwest corner of Pitt Island. Approach from 53°12.67'N/129°33.54'W, heading north. Favor the Pitt Island shore beyond the islet at the entrance, and wrap around the north side of the first of the three small islets inside. Minimum depth on entry is 10 feet. Anchor in 25 feet with room to swing between the first and second of the three small islets. Holding is good over a soft bottom, with reasonable wind protection and views out between the islets. Good anchoring depths also are at the 6-fathom sounding on the chart. The ruins of an old settlement, now a kayaker camp, are on the east shore of the bight in the north side of the large islet that makes up the south shore of the cove." [*Hamilton*]

Monckton Inlet. Monckton Inlet indents Pitt Island at lat 53°18.65'N. The inlet is well protected, with three anchorage possibilities. The first is in 60 feet on the back side of Monckton Point, a short distance inside the inlet on the north side. If you can get in and out near high water, this would be a marvelous, snug anchorage. With propellers and rudders hanging down, however, low water access is scary.

The second anchorage is about three-quarters of the way into the inlet in the bay that extends north almost a mile behind Roy Island. Go up near the head, past the two rocks marked with a + on the chart. Anchor with lots of room in 40 to 50 feet, mud bottom. We tried to find the two rocks mentioned above, but didn't see them. They were not marked by kelp. Be aware.

The third anchorage is at the very head of Monckton Inlet in 50 to 60 feet, mud bottom. It's not very interesting.[*Hale*]

Kooryet Bay. Kooryet Bay, on Banks Island, roughly across Principe Channel from Monkton Inlet, can provide a convenient escape when fog sets in or winds kick up in Principe Channel. Inside the bay you'll have a good vantage point for watching changing conditions in the channel. In southerly winds, anchor in the south cove. In northerly winds, anchor off the creek bed or northwest of Kooryet Island.

Patterson Inlet/Princess Diana Cove. Patterson Inlet is narrow, beautiful, and appears well protected. The head of the inlet divides into a north arm and a south arm. The south arm is very pretty, with a stunning rock wall on the north side near the entry. The bottom is 90 feet deep, though, and a grown-over log booming ground is near the head. We see no need to anchor in the south arm.

The north arm is known as Princess Diana Cove. We overnighted there. It was a perfect anchorage, 25 to 30 feet deep, thick mud bottom. Anchor in the middle. Rocks and reefs sneak up along the shores.

Note: A reader tells us this bay was not good in a southeast gale.

Ire Inlet. Ire Inlet is entered from Ala Passage at latitude 53°30'N. The entry is narrow and quite dramatic, but the fairway is clear. The hillsides are covered with remarkable trees, tall and straight with very short limbs. They look like green pipe cleaners. The trees on top of the rock mountain on the north side of Ire Inlet are twisted and have few limbs. From our distance they looked like bonsai trees.

The little cove on the south shore has rocks as shown on Chart 3984 but not on 3741. Not a good spot. A much better anchorage is between the little islet and the head of the inlet in 20 to 25 feet. Pass north of the little islet. Rocks lie off the south side, and a large drying shoal extends from the south shore of the inlet.

If you visit Ire Inlet (recommended), study the chart carefully before entering Ala Passage. A number of islets and drying rocks must be identified and located. Know where you are at all times and check for fallen trees before entering.

Azimuth Island. Mike Guns put us onto this one. A small unnamed island lies southwest of Azimuth Island, and a convenient anchorage is behind that island at 53°31.45'N/129°59.50'W on the chart. Anchor in 60 to 65 feet. Be sure to enter this anchorage from the north. The southern entry is foul with rocks.

Tangent Island. Tangent Island lies in a cluster of islands located north of Anger Island, near the intersection of Petrel and Principe Channels. The cove on the east side of Tangent Island provides good protection, with a view to the mountains of Pitt Island to the east. Although the anchorage is 100 feet deep, it has good holding and is well protected. Tangent Island also provides an opportunity to refresh your geometry. Enter via Markle Passage, passing between Sine Point to the west, Tangent Point to the east and Logarithm Point to the south.

Colby Bay. Colby Bay is on Banks Island, the west side of Principe Channel, at latitude 53°32.10'N. Go down the middle and anchor in 30 feet where the bay opens up. You'll be surrounded by mountains and protected from northwest or southeast gale winds in Principe Channel. Mike Guns, who first recommended Colby Bay to us, called this spot "a joy."

Petrel Channel. Petrel Channel begins at the south tip of McCauley Island and winds along the west side of Pitt Island to Captain Cove. It has four anchorages, all on the Pitt Island side.

Allcroft Point. Just south of Allcroft Point, at lat 53°35.65'N, is an unnamed bay that gets you off Petrel Channel. Anchor in 75 to 90 feet when you get to the wide spot. The chart shows a rock awash at zero tide obstructing access to the back cove. You may prefer Hevenor Inlet.

Hevenor Inlet. Hevenor Inlet stretches 5 miles into Pitt Island's mountains and you have to go all the way to the head of the inlet for suitable anchorage. The hills on both sides have been clearcut, but already are green again. Anchor in 35 to 60 feet off the falls (you'll see them) or off the mouth of the lagoon.

Newcombe Harbour. Newcombe Harbour is a fine, well-protected anchorage. Motor straight in and anchor off the drying flats in 40 to 50 feet. We wouldn't bother with the little nook on the east shore, a short distance inside the entrance. It is rather tight and not that exciting. With such good, easy anchorage only a little farther in, it's not worth the effort. The log booms reported in the Douglass *Exploring the North Coast of British Columbia* were not there when we visited.

Signs like this one at Newcombe Harbour mark several anchorages.   *The public dock in Kitkatla. When maneuvering, stay close to the dock.*

Captain Cove. Captain Cove is a cozy, protected anchorage at the northwest corner of Pitt Island, near the south entrance to Ogden Channel. Anchor in 60 to 80 feet in the large basin behind the 84-foot island, or in the 5-fathom basin along the south shore, behind the little dot islet. We have anchored twice in the 5-fathom basin and once behind the 84-foot island. If you don't mind 70 to 80 feet, the anchorage behind the island is excellent.

Kitkatla. (250) 848-2214. Kitkatla is a Native village on the north end of Dolphin Island, west of Ogden Channel. The dock has 20 & 30 amp power but no other amenities. Most of the dock is taken by local boats. Fuel is available by jerry jug; pay in advance at the band office.

Kitkatla is a pleasant community. Ann's B&B has a nice display of small baskets and conical hats, which Ann wove in years past. Several small convenience stores operate out of homes.

Don't plan to stop at Kitkatla on weekends. Most of the village goes shopping in Prince Rupert.

We left Bully Island to port and went up Kitkatla Channel, leaving the Kitkatla Islands to starboard. Sailing Directions says a church spire is a significant Kitkatla landmark from the water, but new construction makes the spire less significant. Green Buoy *E95* marks the end of a rocky shoal when you get close to the moorage area, and a little island lies beyond. Leave Buoy *E95* to port and turn toward shore. Head for the large loading dock, leaving the little island to starboard. Go slowly. Kelp marks the shallow spots. Once past the island, run right along the public dock or as close as the rafted boats allow. Rocks lie along the island.

Deep draft boats beware: Depth alongside the dock is approximately 6.5 feet at zero tide.

Spicer Islands. Located off Beaver Passage, between Spicer Island and South Spicer Island. Follow the channel to the well-protected, roomy basin. Anchor in 25 feet, good holding.

Larsen Harbour. Larsen Harbour, at the northwest corner of Banks Island, is a scenic anchorage. Low-lying rocks surround the anchorage and storm-battered trees line the shore. Field Correspondent Jim Norris reports that there is no significant kelp blocking the entrance and that the anchorage is well-protected from swells originating in Hecate Strait but not from northwest winds which can build steep waves at the entrance. Jim also reports that there are no buoys in the harbour, contrary to some other guidebooks.

Conditions on Hecate Strait are visible from within the anchorage, making it a good place to stage a trip across the strait to Haida Gwaii. Anchor in 15-25 feet, with fair holding on a rocky bottom with patchy kelp.

Welcome Harbour. Welcome Harbour is on the east side of Henry Island. A maze of rocks and islets guard the entrance; navigate carefully. The channel on the west side of Dancey Island leads to Secret Cove. Welcome Harbour is a favorite of many Prince Rupert boaters.

INSIDE PASSAGE ROUTE, CONTINUED

Mary Cove. Mary Cove is on the east side of Finlayson Channel across from Klemtu. It is a pleasant little cove, but it appears open to southwest winds. Anchor in 50 to 55 feet inside. A salmon stream empties into Mary Cove.

Bottleneck Inlet. Bottleneck Inlet, at latitude 52°42.8'N on the east side of Finlayson Channel, is an outstanding anchorage. It is protected and beautiful, and large enough for a number of boats. The north side of the inlet has superb rock walls. The chart shows a least depth of just over a fathom in the narrow entry, and a rock shelf extends from the south shore at the narrow part. Favor the north shore. Deeper draft vessels should enter cautiously at low tide. The chart fails to show a 13-15 fathom hole a short distance inside the entry sill. The bottom then comes up to 25-30 feet.

Although we have anchored in Bottleneck Inlet several times now, one night in particular was memorable. That was the night a forewarned on-shore gale struck the coast. Four people died in that storm. At 1:30 a.m. the winds hit. We could see clouds racing overhead and hear the wind roaring in the trees above us, but except for four tongues of strong wind that slammed into our boat between 1:30 a.m. and 4:00 a.m., the air around us was almost calm. [*Hale*]

Goat Cove. Goat Cove indents the eastern shore near the north end of Finlayson Channel. An inner basin is reached by running through a narrow neck. Inside, Sailing Directions says good anchorage can be had in 17 fathoms, which is pretty deep. Don Douglass likes this inner basin, too, and would anchor near the head in 36 feet. We don't like it at all. We

The view out the mouth of Bottleneck Inlet the morning after a storm. At high tide the entry looks wide, but a rock ledge extends from the south shore.

went in during a gathering storm, and wind gusts found their way to us with nothing to stop them. The bottom shoaled too quickly for us to anchor in 36 feet and pay out scope to stand up to the wind. "Oversold!" we decided, and left. We must add that since then, we have met other cruisers who like Goat Cove, so perhaps it comes down to what the weather is doing. [*Hale*]

Work Bay. Work Bay is on the west side of Finlayson Channel near the north end. The bay appears open to southerly winds, but we anchored there in the southerly storm that chased us out of Goat Cove, and found no wind and only remnants of a few rollers from Finlayson Channel. In our opinion Work Bay has room for just one boat at anchor unless all boats stern-tie. The bay is 40 to 50 feet deep. With only a 3:1 scope (150 feet) of anchor rode out, you must be in the center or you will swing onto shore or onto the drying shelf at the head of the bay.

Lime Point Cove. Lime Point Cove, on Griffin Passage, is an indentation just south of the north end of Pooley Island. For years it has been passed by after the area above the cove was logged. New growth has filled in and once again it is a quiet, scenic anchorage, although exposed to southerlies passing up through Griffin Passage. Anchor in the shallow areas of the cove in 36 to 70 feet.

Carter Bay. Carter Bay is on the north side of Sheep Passage at the east entry to Hiekish Narrows. The bones of the steamship Ohio, which ran up on Ohio Rock in 1909, are there. Knowing he was sinking, the captain of the Ohio made it across the mouth of the narrows and into Carter Bay, where he grounded the ship. Of the 135 passengers and crew, only four were lost. Anchoring depths of 54 feet near the head of the bay. The anchorage is exposed to southwest winds.

Hiekish Narrows. Hiekish Narrows connects with Sheep Passage and Finlayson Channel at the south end, and Graham Reach, the continuation of the Inside Passage, at the north end. Current predictions are given under Hiekish Narrows in Ports and Passes and Canadian Tide and Current Tables, Vol. 7. Currents run to 4.5 knots on the flood, 4 knots on the ebb. The flood sets north. The water behind Hewitt Island appears to be a possible anchorage, but the current runs strongly through it.

Graham Reach & Fraser Reach. Graham Reach and Fraser Reach are wide, straight and deep, and lined with beautiful waterfalls. Cruise ships make this their highway. The principal stopping point for pleasure craft is Butedale.

Horsefly Cove. Horsefly Cove is a short distance inside the mouth of Green Inlet on the east side of Graham Reach. The cove is cozy and protected, but 80 to 90 feet deep. You may have to stern-tie to shore to restrict your swing.

This humpback was spotted in Fraser Reach just a few miles from Butedale.

Swanson Bay. Swanson Bay is on the east side of Graham Reach. This bay is exposed, but interesting. Ruins of an old sawmill and pulp mill are on the beach and back in the trees. A 3-story concrete building is just inside the treeline. Farther back, a tall red brick chimney is hidden in the trees. Although the chart shows the chimney as a landmark, summer foliage has almost obscured it from view.

We had trouble finding a comfortable place to anchor at Swanson Bay, settling finally for the shallower water off the creek mouth. Current from the creek kept the boat from swinging. Ashore are the ruins of what once was a formidable shipping center. We have seen a photo of a long wharf at Swanson Bay, with a large square-rigger tied alongside. The wharf is gone, and only a few pilings remain. Unfortunately, the dense forest inhibited our exploration on land.

Our notes say that Swanson Bay shipped its first load of pulp in 1909, and in the 1920s had a population of 500. Its last shipment was in 1934. For some reason the notes don't show the source of this information, so no guarantees as to accuracy.

A few years ago we saw a black-colored wolf on the south shore of Swanson Bay. It watched as our boat slowly approached. Then, with a dismissive, air it ambled back into the forest. [*Hale*]

Khutze Inlet. Khutze Inlet stretches eastward from Graham Reach nearly 5 miles and rewards visitors with a stunning anchorage near the head. From there you can look across the drying flats of the Khutze River into a broad valley with mountains on both sides. Don't get too close to the flats. The water can be murky and the bottom comes up sharply. A long and beautiful waterfall tumbles down the mountain to your right. The outfall stream forms an alluvial fan off its mouth. We've seen boats anchored there, and earlier editions suggested that you could find a good spot on that fan to put the hook down. A few years ago, however, a 42-foot boat anchored in that location, but swung too close to shore and went aground.

We have anchored toward the river mouth in 90 to 100 feet, and between the river mouth and the waterfall in 60 feet. Approach the drying flats slowly until you reach your depth, and put the anchor down. Note that

a drying spit extends from the south shore of the Khutze River into the bay. You want to anchor on the south side of that spit.

You can also anchor behind Green Spit near the mouth of the inlet. One good spot is along the south shore, just west of the stream mouth. The chart shows the right spot.

⑨ **Butedale.** Located on Princess Royal Island, at the south end of Fraser Reach, Butedale is the site of an historic cannery. Only a few original buildings remain after clearing the area for new development.

The Butedale property was puchased in 2013 and plans to re-develop the property have been ongoing. Clearing of the uplands was underway in 2018 and access to the uplands was closed. Signs on the dock warn visitors that using the dock is at their own risk and access to uplands is closed until further notice. Please respect all signage. Boaters seeking shelter won't be turned away. The docks are still primitive, but they're the only docks between Klemtu and Hartley Bay. Untreated water is available on the dock. No other services; upland access not permitted.

Anchorage is possible, though the bottom near the dock may be foul with cable. The nearby waterfall is lovely. It's not known at this time what type of new development will take place; additional investors are currently being sought. See www.WaggonerGuide.com for updates.

⑩ **Bishop Bay Hot Springs.** Bishop Bay Hot Springs is located at the head of Bishop Bay, on the east side of Ursula Channel. This is one of the don't-miss stops along the northern B.C. coast. Local residents have done an outstanding job building and maintaining the bathhouse and boardwalk. A voluntary use fee was initiated in 2017 with an honor box upland on the way to the hot springs. At the bathhouse, the hot spring water is an agreeable temperature and odor-free. The boardwalk parallels the shoreline through fabulous, moss-covered and moss-hung forest.

The dock is small, maximum boat size is 36 feet, plan on rafting. Fish boats sometimes raft-up at this dock. Anchoring is only fair to poor, because the bottom slopes quickly to deep water. A stern-tie would make anchoring more comfortable. A short distance south of the dock a shoal, not shown on the charts, extends into the bay from the shoreline. Be aware of that shoal and plan your swing to stay well off it. The three mooring buoys marked "Private" actually are for public use, use at your own risk. We have seen some boats drag on the mooring balls.

Verney Passage. Verney Passage, along the west side of Gribbell Island, must be one of the more beautiful places on earth. It is lined, both sides, with raw, polished rock mountains, 3500 feet high. Great glacier-carved bowls, called cirques, are hollowed into the mountains. From the water you can see their forested floors and sheer rock walls. Especially on a sunny day, a visit to Bishop Bay Hot Springs should include a circumnavigation of Gribbell Island, to see Verney Passage.

Weewanie Hot Springs. Midway up Devastation Channel, Weewanie Hot Springs is a beautiful small bay, surrounded by sheer rock walls and forest. One mooring buoy was available in 2015.

Though the anchorage is beautiful, the hot springs on shore are the primary attraction. The Kitimat Aquanauts Scuba Club built a rustic bathhouse and soaking tubs. Land a dinghy on the rocky beach and follow the trail past a campsite to the bathhouse. Or, land the dinghy on the rocks just below the bathhouse, tie to a log ashore, and climb up to the bathhouse. We've found Weewanie Hot Springs quiet and tranquil, less crowded than popular Bishop Bay.

Proper hot spring etiquette is to pull the plug on the lower tub, drain, then replug. The tub will fill again from the hose connected to the underground hot springs.

⑪ **Kitimat.** Kitimat, pop. 10,000, is a small city located at the head of Douglas Channel. While it has shopping for nearly everything one might need, the town itself is located about 5 miles from the nearest marina, MK

Bay Marina. Taxi service (Coastal Taxis, 250-632-7250), if available, is about $25 each way. We suspect a person needing to get to town for shopping could find a ride.

Kitimat is a classic company town, built by Alcan in the 1950s to make aluminum. In the middle of the shopping area, the small Kitimat Museum and Archives has several exhibits that show how the town was built, including the massive tunnels and hydroelectric power dam for the smelting plant. The Alcan plant was one of the largest non-defense construction projects of the 1950s. Today, new owners continue updating and operating the plant.

Just a few miles west on Douglas Channel you can see the clearing and construction for a Liquid Natural Gas plant planned for sometime in the future. When completed, this will be the terminus for an LNG pipeline beginning in the Interior. The gas will be processed, chilled into liquid form, and loaded on ships for distribution.

⑪ **MK Bay Marina.** 4935 Kitimat Village Rd, Kitimat, BC V8C 2G7; (250) 632-6401; contact@mkbay.ca; www.mkbaymarina.ca. Monitors VHF 68. Open all year, 420 feet of guest side-tie moorage on D-dock and occasional slip moorage. 20, 30 & 50 amp power, water, washrooms, showers, laundry, and free Wi-Fi. Convenience store with fishing supplies, ice, and a deli. Gas and diesel fuel, haulout to 20 tons, and launch ramp. The marina is on the east side of Kitimat Arm.

Boats on the seaward side of the dock should consider extra fenders. Inflow winds, common in the afternoon, produce significant chop. The marina is co-owned by The Mill Bay Group and Haisla Nation. Walkways were upgraded and new washing machines installed in 2018. A full-service campground opened in August 2018. Future plans include additional moorage slips and 3-phase power. An overnight guest house is available at the marina. The marina recommends calling ahead, especially larger vessels.

WEATHER TIP: When crossing Wright Sound in an outflow wind in Douglas Channel, it is better to lay a course to Juan Point, at the north end of Gil Island. We tried this route in an outflow wind, and found it much smoother than our previous crossing, in which we tried a direct (and wet) route between Point Cumming and Cape Farewell.

Wright Sound. Wright Sound is at the junction of Grenville Channel, Douglas Channel, Verney Passage and McKay Reach. All these passages pour their currents into Wright Sound, where the waters collide and mix. Especially on an ebb, not much wind is needed to make conditions ugly.

Coghlan Anchorage. Coghlan Anchorage is behind Promise Island, and is connected by Stewart Narrows with Hartley Bay. The anchorage is open to the south, but still decently protected. There are no mooring buoys in the anchorage. One year we anchored briefly in 35 to 40 feet just north of Brodie Point. The protection and holding ground were excellent, if not scenic. Anchorage is also possible on the shore opposite Brodie Point, off Otter Shoal. [*Hale*]

⑫ **Hartley Bay.** Band Office, 320 Hayimiisaxaa Way, Hartley Bay, BC V0V 1A0; (250) 841-2500; hbvc@gitgaat.ca. Open all year. Gasoline and diesel, pure water (from the water treatment plant) at the fuel dock, 30 amp power on the floats. Garbage drop, but only separated recycling accepted. Major credit cards accepted.

Hartley Bay, near the south end of Douglas Channel, is a friendly and modern-looking Native village, population 160-200, with a no-charge government dock behind a rock breakwater. The Cultural Centre is upland near the fuel dock. No liquor. No pay phone, but cell phones work. A medical clinic has two nurses and a visiting doctor.

Fuel dock hours are Monday through Thursday 8:00 a.m. to 12:00 p.m., and 1:00 p.m. to 5:00 p.m.; Friday through Sunday on call, VHF 06, Hartley Bay Fuel. Hartley Bay has run out of fuel several times in recent years. Boats that must take on fuel at Hartley Bay should call ahead to ensure availability. It is a pleasure to walk the Native village of Hartley Bay where homes and public buildings are all connected by a series of wide, substantial boardwalks. There are no roads in town except for the wide boardwalks used occasionally by ATV's and Smart Cars; residents generally get around by bicycle or on foot. For supplies and groceries locals must ride the foot ferry to Prince Rupert, an 80-mile journey one way. This interesting community has a small fishing fleet and a fish hatchery. A trail along Kukayu River leads to the fish hatchery, where visitors are welcome. Continuing farther along the trail

Floats are available at Butedale, but uplands are closed until further notice.

Hartley Bay is a pleasant boardwalk community.

Beautiful Devastation Channel connects Verney Passage to Kitimat Arm. Weewanie Hot Springs is on the east side.

we discovered the "local swimming hole" where you can hike down the stairs to enjoy a natural pool. Rumor has it that locals know where you might see a "Spirit Bear," stop by the Band Office for more information.

Fin Island. Fin Island lies between Lewis Passage and Cridge Passage, immediately west of Gil Island. Fin Island is fairly low and not particularly interesting, but it has two workable anchorages, Curlew Bay and Hawk Bay. Hawk Bay is the better of the two.

Curlew Bay. Curlew Bay indents the northeast corner of Fin Island. It isn't a destination anchorage by any means, but it will do in settled weather or a southerly. The bay appears open to a northerly and to outflow winds from Douglas Channel. The chart shows shoaling a short distance west of the narrows. We anchored in 20 feet at the east end of the narrows. The anchor bumped twice on what felt like rock, then set solidly. [Hale]

Hawk Bay. Hawk Bay, on the west side of Fin Island, is more scenic and has more room than Curlew Bay. The anchorage is somewhat open to westerly winds and you'll swing around if it's blowing. Anchor in the middle in 60 feet.

Grenville Channel. Sometimes called "The Ditch," Grenville Channel is a straight and unobstructed 45-mile-long channel running between Wright Sound in the south and Arthur Passage in the north. The Sailing Directions indicate that currents in Grenville Channel reach a maximum of 2 knots, but between Lowe Inlet and Evening Point, in the narrowest portion of the channel, we've seen as much as 3 to 4 knots on the flood and up to 6 knots on the ebb, especially near Lowe Inlet. Canadian Hydrographic Service does not provide current predictions for Grenville Channel but does provide corrections for high and low water at Lowe Inlet, based on Bella Bella. These corrections can be found in Ports and Passes and the Canadian Tide and Current Tables, Vol. 7. NOAA provides secondary corrections for Grenville Channel, but they are based on Wrangell Narrows and

are suspect. Virtually all software predictions for currents in Grenville Channel are based on the NOAA data, and are equally suspect.

Tidal currents flow in and out of each end of Grenville Channel. According to Sailing Directions, flood currents meet near Evening Point, about 25 miles from the south entrance, and ebb currents separate about one mile further to the northwest. This advice is misleading because it is true only in certain circumstances.

Height of the tide at each end of the channel is what drives the flood current to the central parts of the channel. The timing and strength of these currents would be reasonably predictable if that was all there was to it. But many other factors combine to make the currents in Grenville Channel very difficult to

predict. High water occurs at different times and reaches different heights in Wright Sound and Chatham Sound. Depending on which end has the higher tide, the strength of the current, and even its direction, may change significantly.

The meeting and separating points of flood and ebb are also variable. The wind regime in Chatham Sound and Wright Sound may be considerably different and may have a strong influence on tidal heights. When onshore winds pile up water in Chatham Sound, Wright Sound may be under the influence of outflow winds from Douglas Channel, diminishing the height of the tide. This scenario forces the meeting point of the currents to the southeast.

When the Skeena River is in flood, vast

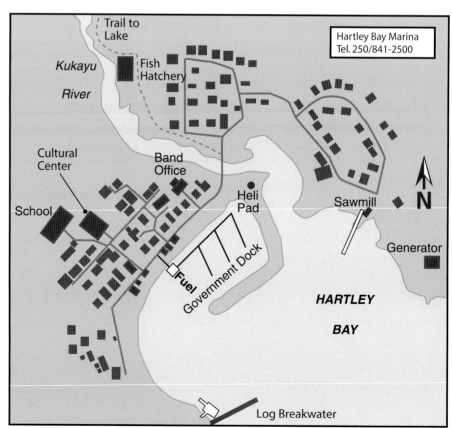

Hartley Bay

Hartley Bay's government dock is behind the breakwater to the right.

amounts of fresh water are deposited into the northern end of Grenville Channel. This forces the meeting point of the currents far to the southeast, and when combined with certain wind conditions, pushes it nearly all the way to Wright Sound.

Finally, though Grenville Channel appears to be well protected, when strong currents in the northern, more open part of Grenville Channel oppose strong winds from the NW or SE, a heavy chop develops, making travel very uncomfortable. At those times, conditions in the northern end of Grenville Channel may actually be worse than in the open waters of Chatham Sound.

Be sure to give Morning Reef, north of Evening Point, a wide berth.

Grenville Channel is a major waterway on the Inside Passage. You may see tugs with tows, all types of fish boats and large commercial vessels, the BC Ferries, and cruise ships. In limited visibility, radar is essential and AIS is helpful. We monitor Prince Rupert Vessel Traffic Service on VHF 11. Large vessels have Call-in Points shown on the charts. Their check-ins with VTS will help you develop a mental picture of the large vessels that may be a factor on your passage, especially those approaching from ahead or overtaking from astern.

Union Passage. Union Passage, on the west side of Grenville Channel, is served by Hawkins Narrows from Grenville Channel, and Peters Narrows from the south. It is one of those places people talk about but not many visit. The problem is the two sets of narrows. The chart shows 8-knot currents in Hawkins Narrows and 7-knot currents in Peters Narrows. Hawkins Narrows slack is shown as 5 minutes in duration. Neither the chart nor Sailing Directions say much about Peters Narrows. Once inside, the scenery is not remarkable.

The currents often are much less than shown, and the window of least current much wider than 5 minutes. We entered Union Passage through Hawkins Narrows at low water slack, poked around for a few minutes, then departed the way we came. The day was windy, rainy and cold. Our spirit was with the

great explorers, but our resolve that day was weak. [Hale].

The entrance to Hawkins Narrows is at latitude 53°22'N. The channel is open until the inner end is approached. There, a rock awash at zero tide lies off the eastern shore. Favor the western shore to avoid it.

Lowe Inlet (Verney Falls). Lowe Inlet, a provincial park 14.5 miles from the southern entrance to Grenville Channel, is an excellent spot to overnight. You can anchor either in the outer basin or in Nettle Basin, the cozier inner cove. Walt Woodward, in his book *How to Cruise to Alaska Without Rocking the Boat Too Much*, recommends anchoring directly in front of Verney Falls where they pour into Nettle Basin. Current holds the boat in place, and you are treated to a wonderful view of the falls. Depending on the time of year, you may see bears fishing in the falls. Holding ground is only fair, so be sure the anchor is well set and you have ample scope for high tide. An alternative is to anchor far enough from the falls that the current, while still enough to hold the boat steady, is not very strong.

Douglass, in *Exploring the North Coast of British Columbia*, likes the Verney Falls anchorage, but also suggests an anchorage along the south shore of Nettle Basin, off the shelf formed by a creek that empties into that area. We tried to put the hook down in 60 feet off that shore, but found that we would swing too close to the shelf. After two tries in wind squalls and heavy rain showers, we moved out to the middle and anchored in 100 feet with 300 feet of rode out. Shortly after we were settled another boat came in, tried to anchor as we earlier tried, then moved out to the middle as we had. Our holding ground was excellent. We had trouble tripping the anchor the next morning.

Lowe Inlet is beautiful. Our notes read, "If you're looking for a scenic spot, this is it." [Hale]

Klewnuggit Inlet. At approximately 120 feet, Klewnuggit Inlet is too deep for most boats to anchor. We talked with some folks, however, who found excellent crabbing near the head of the inlet.

East Inlet. East Inlet is adjacent to Klewnuggit Inlet. The inner cove of East Inlet is a superb anchorage, surrounded by high mountains and protected from seas. In a storm, however, winds might swirl through. Anchor near the head of the inner basin in 50 to 55 feet. You can also find anchorage in the little cove on the south shore, just inside the entrance to the inner basin.

We anchored at the head of East Inlet, a perfect night in a perfect place. Mountains reflected in the calm water. A small stream drained from a lake into the head of the inlet, and waterfalls poured down from the sides. We found an inukshuk, a small, stonehenge-like marker, next to the stream mouth. [*Hale*]

Kxngeal Inlet. Kxngeal Inlet, on the north side of Grenville Channel approximately 4 miles northwest of Klewnuggit Inlet, is a beautiful bowl in the mountains. Favor either shore as you enter to avoid a nasty rock that dries 16 feet in the entrance. The inlet is at least 130 feet deep until it shelves at the head, and when it shelves, it shelves right now. Trees are at the head of the inlet, with logged areas on each side. The shelf is on a line with the points where the trees begin. Anchor in 90 feet.

Watts Narrows. Watts Narrows is a short passage that connects Baker Inlet with Grenville Channel. A dogleg turn near the inner entrance makes the passage blind. Before entering, either direction, announce your intentions on VHF 16, low power. Sound the ship's horn as you approach the turn. The current runs swiftly through the narrows, but people tell us they have gone through in the presence of current without trouble. We have waited for slack water, which occurs about the times of high and low water at Prince Rupert. As the chart shows, the narrows are narrow, but they are deep. A mid-channel course will get you through safely.

Baker Inlet. Baker Inlet, entered through Watts Narrows, is wonderful. The best overnights are at the head of the inlet, 60 feet, good bottom, mountains all around. Beautiful.

Kumealon Island/Kumealon Inlet. The little cove behind Kumealon Island is a good anchorage for a small number of boats. The much larger Kumealon Inlet, immediately south, also is good. Behind Kumealon Island, anchor in 15 to 25 feet north of the island, near the head.

Kumealon Inlet is well protected and has beautiful scenery. Anchor in the inner basin, behind the little island. Find a good spot and put the hook down in 50 to 70 feet. A reader reported that two uncharted rocks lie close to shore near the southeast corner.

Oona River. The village of Oona River, a tiny Swedish fishing and boatbuilding community, indents Porcher Island at the east end of Ogden Channel. A public dock is behind a stone breakwater, and is served by a narrow channel through drying mudflats. From the white buoy, line up on the private range markers on the rock jetty and proceed along the markers set in the entrance. Use caution, but depths should be adequate for most pleasure vessels. Call "Oona River" on VHF channel 06 for additional information, though you may not always get an answer.

Cell phones work near Oona River.

Arthur Passage to Chatham Sound. Assuming a northbound route, begin your run west of Watson Rock (west of Gibson Island) at the northern entrance to Grenville Channel. Continue north to a waypoint off the flashing light on the southwest shore of Kennedy Island. Then turn westward slightly to run past the southwest corner of Hanmer Island and leave Bell Buoy *D9*, marking Cecil Patch, to port. Continue to a waypoint in the passage west of Genn Island, then to a waypoint east of Holland Rock.

From Holland Rock, run to a waypoint west of Barrett Rock at the entrance to Prince Rupert Harbour. The entire area is well-buoyed, but it is easy to get the buoys confused.

LOCAL KNOWLEDGE

WEATHER TIP: Chatham Sound can be downright ugly when the wind blows. Especially on an ebb, when the onshore wind meets the combined ebb current and Skeena River runoff, seas can get high, steep and close together. On the VHF weather channel, listen to the hourly updates for Holland Rock. If it's blowing at Holland Rock, conditions can be rough when you try to cross.

Lawson Harbour/Kelp Passage. Kelp Passage is on the west side of Lewis Island, across Arthur Passage from Kennedy Island.

Lawson Harbour indents the top of Lewis Island. Neither would be our first choice for scenery, but each serves as an anchorage if needed. A reef extends from the western shore inside Lawson Harbour. Anchor near the south end of the reef in 35 to 40 feet.

In Kelp Passage, anchor in the area marked 8.8 meters on Chart 3947, mud bottom. The small basin at the south end of Kelp Passage provides good protection in a northerly wind.

Qlawdzeet Anchorage. A large bay on the north end of Stephens Island, well protected from all but northerly winds. This anchorage is often used by fishing vessels and has plenty of room for a number of boats. Anchorage can be found in the main bay or tucked into small bights. Use Chart 3909.

Porpoise Harbour. (250) 628-9220; info@peharbour.ca. Located at Port Edward, Porpoise Harbour gives priority to long-term year-round customers. Transient moorage available on first-come, first-served basis, best to call ahead, 15 & 30 amp power, water,

Bears search for food along the shore.

garbage drop, washrooms, showers, laundry. Approach using the range south of Ridley Island marked with a buoy for Porpoise Channel.

The harbor is close to the North Pacific Cannery, a museum showing what cannery life was all about. Bus service to Prince Rupert is available.

North Pacific Cannery Dock. (250) 628-3538; www.northpacificcannery.ca info@northpacificcannery.ca. Hours: 10:00 a.m. to 5:00 p.m., May-September, max. 4-hour stay. Located on the north shore of Inverness Passage, the North Pacific Cannery National Historic Site/Museum has a concrete 45-foot day-use dock available for boaters visiting this interesting, picturesque historic cannery. Available on a first-come, first-serve basis, no charge for use of the dock. Located about 5 miles up the Inverness Passage from Chatham Sound, a short side-trip on your way to or

from Prince Rupert. Inverness Passage is well charted but open to river flow from the Skeena River which can carry wood debris. To minimize river flow influence, time your visit around high tide. Follow the west side of Smith Island to enter Inverness Passage, use Charts 3947 and 3958. Fender and secure well as current runs past the dock. A boomstick was recently attached to the up-river corner of the dock to deflect some of the windfall debris coming down the Skeena River.

The North Pacific Cannery is the oldest standing cannery on the West Coast and is a National Historic Site. The cannery operated from 1889 to 1968. Visitors can tour the cannery buildings including the processing plant, check in at the museum entrance. Guided tours are available three times daily, July through September; and Tuesday through Sunday during May and June. Tour boats occasionally reserve the dock, call ahead for availability.

Small boats can anchor just beneath Verney Falls where the current prevents you from swinging into the rocks. If the salmon are running, the bear viewing is fantastic.

LOCAL KNOWLEDGE

SPEED LIMIT: A 5-knot speed zone in Prince Rupert Harbour is enforced within 600 yards of the Prince Rupert shore. It is up to you to gauge the distance as there are no speed limit buoys.

⑬ **Prince Rupert.** As you approach Prince Rupert, it's a good idea to monitor Prince Rupert Traffic (VTS) on VHF 71 in case a large ship decides to depart while you're coming in. The fairway gets narrow in places. This is especially important in poor visibility.

As you approach, the large coal and grain loading areas are part of the Port of Prince Rupert's Ridley Terminals. From Barrett Rock at the entrance to Prince Rupert Harbour, it is another 5.5 miles of slow speed travel to town. Four marinas serve Prince Rupert: Fairview at the south end, the new Cow Bay Marina in front of Atlin Terminal, Prince Rupert Rowing and Yacht Club in the middle, and Rushbrooke at the north end.

Rushbrooke Floats, Fairview Small Craft Docks, and Porpoise Harbour are all managed by the Port Edward Harbour Authority, (250) 628-9220.

Fairview is primarily a commercial boat moorage, although some pleasure boats do tie up there. It is fairly far from downtown, with limited bus service. Rushbrooke, at the north end, has better facilities for pleasure boats, but during the commercial fishing months many fish boats occupy the slips. The walk from Rushbrooke to town is long but manageable. Most pleasure boats go directly to the Cow Bay Marina and the Prince Rupert Rowing and Yacht Club, located at Cow Bay. In the past, the Prince Rupert Rowing and Yacht Club would quickly fill during the summer months. The recently constructed Cow Bay Marina is a welcome addition to the Cow Bay area, offering ample moorage. This is a secure marina with key cards issued to overnight guests. Good anchorage is in Pillsbury Cove, across the harbor. Northwest Fuels operates a large fuel dock in Cow Bay, just past the Prince Rupert Rowing & Yacht Club.

Prince Rupert ("Rainy Rupert"), population 12,500, is a complete city. With a large fishing fleet to support, you can find anything you need for your boat. What isn't there can be flown in. Fuel and waste oil disposal are available at Northwest Fuels in Cow Bay.

A shopping mall is a pleasant walk uptown, or you can take a cab. A Wal-Mart is now located in the mall. A large Safeway is located between Cow Bay and the mall. The Save-On-Foods market (formerly Overwaitea market), farther uptown, is another option for provisions, and will deliver to the docks for a fee. The provincial liquor store is close to the Safeway parking lot and the yacht club. A smaller, private liquor store is at Cow Bay.

The Museum of Northern British Columbia is excellent, and sponsors a variety of informative day and evening programs during the summer. Highly recommended. Several restaurants are in town and in the Cow Bay area, some of them quite good. The Port Interpretive Centre, located on street level in Atlin Terminal, gives free tours about the past, present and future of the Port of Prince Rupert. Recommended.

Located above Cow Bay, Sea Sport Outboard Marina and Clothing has an excellent selection of clothing, fishing equipment, safety gear, and marine parts. They also have a machine shop on site.

The King Coin laundromat in the center of town will do your laundry for a reasonable

NORTH PACIFIC CANNERY
A CENTURY OF SALMON

Imagine a century ago, when hundreds of fishing boats would be out on the Skeena and Nass Rivers for 4-5 days per week, 24 hours per day during the salmon runs, in all kinds of weather and sea conditions. Tender boats would shuttle the salmon catch back to the docks of the North Pacific Cannery. Imagine a dock with thousands of silvery salmon being cued up for processing. It was tough work done by specialists of different ethnic backgrounds. In the beginning the work was all manual, even the cans were made by hand. As time went on, new machines and processes improved the efficiency and ability to can more salmon.

The North Pacific Cannery was more than just a cannery. It was a small town, processing salmon for over 90 continuous years from 1889 to 1968, and remains the oldest standing cannery on the West Coast. A tour of the North Pacific Cannery is a glimpse back in time, where you get a sense of how these hardy people

fished, processed the salmon, and lived in different housing areas onsite. As you tour the buildings and grounds, you can almost hear and feel what it must have been like.

The North Pacific Cannery museum captures what cannery life was like for the Japanese, Chinese, First Nations, and Europeans working in this plant. You can walk from building to building and see how a cannery worked, see the company store, office building, and rows of houses. You can tour the cannery on your own, or take one of the group tours to learn more about the canning process and the social aspects of life here.

The North Pacific Cannery is located 22 km south of Prince Rupert. You can rent a car in town or take the local bus which stops right in front of the cannery. Allow about 3 hours for a docent's tour of the facility. The Crew Kitchen, a small café at the cannery, sells baked goods and is open for lunch. Don't forget to stop by the gift shop.

The North Pacific Cannery is accessible by boat, 5 miles up Inverness Passage from Chatham Sound. The cannery has a 45-foot guest dock for stays up to 4 hours on a first-come, first serve basis. It's best to time your visit around high tide to minimize the effects of river flow from the Skeena River.

PRINCE RUPERT MARKETPLACE

RESTAURANTS & SHOPS

MUSEUM OF NORTHERN BC
Explore the Museum of Northern BC's collection of art and artifacts and discover the wealth of history and culture on BC's Northwest Coast. Witness the legacy of oral history, archaeological discoveries and unique artifacts that depict ten thousand years of ancient history.
250.624.3207 • 100 First Avenue West
www.museumofnorthernbc.com

NORTH PACIFIC CANNERY
Experience the history of BC's oldest surviving salmon cannery. Built in 1889, North Pacific Cannery is now a designated national historic site and museum.
Exhibits, guided tours, original architecture, historically-inspired cuisine and the pristine wilderness surroundings tell the story of an industry that played an integral role in BC's economic, cultural and natural development over the last century.
250-628-3538 • 1889 Skeena Drive • Port Edward
www.northpacificcannery.ca

ICE HOUSE GALLERY
The Ice House Gallery is the the Northwest Coast Artists' Cooperative, where you'll find a wide range of high quality, original artwork created by Northwest Coast artists.
The artists share their art, skills, information, vision and culture, providing a high quality display of regionally produced art including cards, carvings, knitting, paintings, glass and jewelry.
250-624-4546 • Suite 190-215 Cow Bay Road
www.icehousegallery.ca

THE PORT INTERPRETIVE CENTRE
The Port Interpretive Centre is where Prince Rupert goes to find out what's happening at the Port. Our ambassadors answer your questions with the assistance of interactive exhibits, video experiences and children's activities to explore the port's world. Learn about the products, vessels and vehicles moving through the Port of Prince Rupert, the communities and countries that we connect to, and the types of people and partners who make it all possible.
250-624-4559 • 215 Cow Bay Road • www.rupertport.com

Visit Here To Learn About Annual Events
www.visitprincerupert.com/see-and-do/annual-events

COWBAY CAFÉ
We offer big and bold rustic Italian flavours with our fresh house pastas, bright salads and traditional stone oven pizzas. Perfect alone or for sharing di famiglia. These classics are paired with our own take on modern westcoast cuisine through our chef-inspired menu board, featuring seasonally harvested ingredients and locally sourced seafood. An integral part to dining with us is wine and we take it just as seriously. We have chosen select award-winning British Columbian, Italian and International wines to enhance our cuisine.
250-627-1212 • 205 Cow Bay Road
www.cowbaycafe.com

WHEELHOUSE BREWING COMPANY
Wheelhouse Brewing Company is the vision of three friends who fell in love with a remote North Coast town. Established in 2013, the Wheelhouse Brewing Company was created to satisfy the demand for great quality, great tasting beer on British Columbia's North Coast. But more than that, the partners simply love making and sampling varieties of beer and want to share that love with the people they live with.
A typical visit to Wheelhouse is a lively affair and a great opportunity to mix with the locals! Also look for wheelhouse on tap and in bottles while visiting the restaurants around Prince Rupert
250-624-2739 • 217 1st Ave East
www.wheelhousebrewing.com

The green "Lightering Dock" is for Customs check-in and clearance.

Cow Bay Marina opened in 2016 and offers 51 slips and side-tie moorage.

charge. It's a treat for us to leave all the ship's sheets, towels and dirty clothes at the laundromat and go for dinner at one of the local restaurants. A few hours later we pick up the laundry, clean, dry, and neatly folded.

Up at 617 2nd Avenue, just beyond the mall, we found Gary's Lock and Security Shop Ltd., a lock shop with a twist. Gary Weick, the longtime owner, collects things. His shop is a museum. In the window were wonderful toys from the 1930s and 40s, Canadian Pacific Railroad conductors' caps, old photos–and a stuffed and mounted fur-bearing trout, very rare. It was caught in Lake Superior, from depths so great trout grow fur to keep warm. This trout's fur is white. Everything is explained on the sign next to the specimen. You have to see it.

If you have time, take the bus to Port Edward for a tour of the North Pacific Cannery, now a museum. You'll see how the workers lived and worked.

Prince Rupert was hurt by the decline of the commercial fishing and forest industries, and then the pulp mill closed. The town lost about one-third of its population. In the last ten years it has become a major deepwater seaport, in heavy competition with Vancouver, Puget Sound and California. Prince Rupert is closer to Asia than any other west coast port, and CN Rail owns tracks from Prince Rupert to Memphis, Tennessee. Transit time from Asia to the heartland of the U.S. is cut by at least two days. Not only can

Prince Rupert handle the largest container ships now afloat, it will be able to handle the largest on the drawing board.

Prince Rupert is the last major city in British Columbia before transiting Dixon Entrance on the way to Ketchikan and Southeast Alaska. While there is good shopping and a liquor store in Prince Rupert, vessels bound for Alaska may want to wait to provision until Ketchikan to avoid customs issues with liquor, produce, and meat. On the way south from Alaska, Prince Rupert is the best place to stock up on produce, meat and liquor.

Customs clearance: Tie up at the 100-foot-long green-painted "Lightering Dock," where a dedicated toll-free phone for customs clearance is installed. The dock is located beneath the large shopping mall building at the top of the hill. The railroad museum building is near the shore, and a whale sculpture. Lat/Lon 54°18.827'N/130°19.930'W. Touch-and-go for customs clearance only. A locked gate prevents shore access.

You can also clear customs by telephone at Rushbrooke, the Prince Rupert Rowing and Yacht Club, Cow Bay Marina and Fairview Government Dock by calling 888-226-7277, or on a dedicated phone at each of the four marinas. Calls now go to a call center in Hamilton, Ontario. Agents have the option of calling out a local customs agent for an inspection.

Trailer and Vehicle Storage: For those

trailering boats to Prince Rupert and looking for places to store their tow vehicle and boat trailer, contact: Coastal Propane (250) 624-5011; Bandstra Transport (250) 624-6826; Bridgeview Marine (250) 624-5809.

Car Rentals: National, (250) 624-5318. Located on the west end of town in the Highline Hotel.

Cruise Ships: A cruise ship will call once or twice a week during the summer. When a

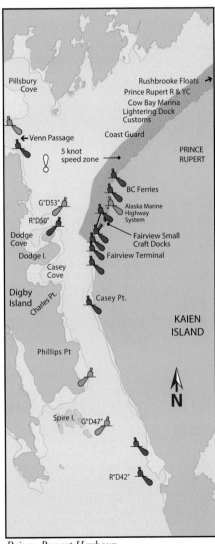

Prince Rupert Harbour

Cow Bay shops and restaurants near Cow Bay Marina and Rowing Club

ship is in town, the streets and stores are apt to be crowded.

Fairview Small Craft Harbour. (250) 624-3127; info@peharbour.ca. Open 7 days a week 5:00 a.m. to 8:00 p.m. during the summer; 8:30 a.m. to 5:00 p.m. Monday through Friday the rest of the year. This is the first set of docks as you approach Prince Rupert. Commercial vessels primarily, but sometimes room for a few pleasure boats. Water, 15 & 30 amp power, garbage drop, washrooms. First-come, first-served.

⑬ **Cow Bay Marina.** (250) 622-2628; www.cowbaymarina.ca. Monitors VHF 66A. Open all year with moorage for boats up to 80 feet and can accommodate larger yachts up to 120 feet on the breakwater docks, 30, 50 & 100 amp power, washrooms, showers, laundry, water, garbage drop, recycling, and Wi-Fi. Reservations recommended. This is a new 51-slip marina located in Cow Bay in front of the Atlin Terminal building. Be sure to fender well as wakes from passing boats find their way into the marina despite the posted "no wake" sign. A pub and microbrewery is nearby and the marina is close to the center of town.

Cow Bay Marina is a welcome addition to the previously tight moorage options at Prince Rupert and offers clean, modern shower and laundry facilities for visiting boats.

⑬ **Prince Rupert Rowing and Yacht Club.** P.O. Box 981, 121 George Hills Way, Prince Rupert, BC V8J 1A3; (250) 624-4317; info@prryc.com. Monitors VHF 73. Open all year, 30 & 50 amp power, new washroom and shower, recycling, water, pay phone, garbage drop, Wi-Fi, fish-cleaning station. Waste oil dump at the Northwest Fuels facility next door.

This is more of a marina than a traditional yacht club. There is no reciprocal moorage. Although reservations are not accepted, visitors are encouraged to call at least 24 hours ahead to get on a wait list for moorage. Cell phones work for calling the Yacht Club from Hartley Bay and Oona River. As you approach, call on VHF 73. The dock staff can be busy.

The yacht club docks are strong and safe, but well used. The main dock has been replaced, and more replacements are planned. New docks or old, be aware that you will be squeezed in more tightly than at most marinas. If the commercial salmon fishing

fleet is in the midst of an opening, the boats will come and go all night, and moorage at the outermost docks can be pretty bouncy. Put out lots of fenders.

A new club house, with a bright red roof, was completed in 2018. The yacht club is close to good dining in Cow Bay or you can walk or take a cab uptown.

⑬ **Northwest Fuels Ltd.** (250) 624-4106. Located in Cow Bay next to the Yacht Club. Monitors VHF 71. Open every day, extended hours in summer. Petro Canada gasoline, diesel, lubricants, washrooms and showers. Block, cube and salt ice. Small convenience store on the pier with a surprising number of marine and fishing tackle items. Garbage drop, waste oil disposal. Propane is available a few blocks away. This fuel dock is often busy; be prepared to wait for a space to clear.

⑬ **Rushbrooke Floats Small Craft Harbour.** (250) 624-9400; info@peharbour.ca. Open all year, water, 15 amp power, washrooms, showers. Commercial vessels have priority in the summer, but there can be room for pleasure craft too. Rafting required. Located about a mile north of town. Rushbrooke has the only launch ramp in Prince Rupert. First-come, first-served.

Pillsbury Cove. Pillsbury Cove, on the west side of Prince Rupert Harbour, is an excellent anchorage: level bottom, great holding, beaches and tide pools, and lots of crab. If the marinas in Prince Rupert are all full or you prefer anchoring, this is a good choice. Prince Rupert is a 3-mile dinghy ride away. Field Correspondent Jim Norris notes that entering Pillsbury Cove can be intimidating due to the extensive aquaculture floats crowding the east side of the entrance channel; hug close to these floats on your starboard side as you enter.

THINGS TO DO

1. Cow Bay. Several good restaurants and shops. One casual favorite is Cowpuccino's for coffee, fresh baked goods and excellent Wi-Fi.
2. Khutzeymateen Sanctuary. Also called "Valley of the Grizzly," this is the only park of its kind in Canada. It contains one of the largest populations of grizzly bears–about 50 –in British Columbia. Located 45 km NE of Prince Rupert.

3. North Pacific Cannery. The oldest, most completely preserved cannery remaining of 200-or-so that once dotted B.C.'s northwest coast. Now a bus or car ride away from town.

4. Museum of Northern British Columbia. An impressive collection about the northwest coast. A First Nations longhouse describes the history of the people and area going back to the last ice age. It contains well-preserved,

Cow Bay Marina is just one block from shops and restaurants and three blocks up to town.

historical Tsimshian and other First Nations works of art, clothing, baskets and more. A short walk from the marinas.

5. Firehall Museum. Focused on the history of the local fire department since 1908. A rebuilt red fire truck from 1925 sits in the middle of the museum.

6. Kwinitsa Railway Museum. Authentic railway station with artifacts from the early 1900s, the heyday of the Grand Trunk Pacific Railway. On the waterfront, near the Lightering Dock.

7. Farmer's Market. In town on Sunday afternoons during the summer season.

8. Earl Mah Aquatic Center. A short walk from Cow Bay.

9. Seafest. The town's biggest annual festival, held each June.

10. Port Interpretive Centre. Free guided tours about the Port of Prince Rupert. Hands-on activities let visitors explore the growth of Prince Rupert's commerce including, containers, coal and grain.

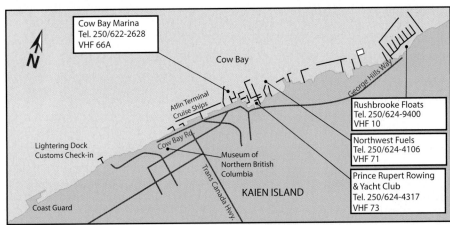

Prince Rupert Waterfront

Haida Gwaii

CHAPTER 17

Located 130 miles north of Vancouver Island and 65 miles west of the B.C. coast's mainland islands, Haida Gwaii offers some of the Northwest's most spectacular cruising. Haida Gwaii, formerly called the Queen Charlotte Islands, is an archipelago of over 150 islands, best explored by boat. It is remote and pristine with a unique geological history. Glaciers once covered this area and receded 2,000 years before the rest of British Columbia, resulting in an ecosystem with some species of plants and animals not seen anywhere else. It has been referred to as the "Galapagos of the Northwest" with hundreds of species of birds, unique species of bears and many trees and plants growing in areas from the rain forests of the western coast to the dry forests on the eastern coast.

Haida Gwaii means "Islands of the People" in the language of the first people to settle here. The Haida were revered and respected along the coast as ambassadors and warriors, with a unique culture. The islands had a population of more than 10,000 until the 1800s when many succumbed to smallpox and other diseases from Europe. By 1900, only 350 remained. A visit to Haida Gwaii and the Gwaii Haanas National Park will take you to a place where you can see what remains of this once great culture. As you walk the trails through the rain forest and moss-covered rock canyons around the old villages you may even feel the presence of the people who inhabited this rugged and beautiful area.

Haida Gwaii experienced the impact of an imbalance caused by western man. In the 1800s sea otters were hunted almost to extinction. Their pelts were highly valued around the world and greed took over. In time the sea urchin population grew out of control without the sea otters to keep them in check. Later, the health of the kelp beds was affected by the overabundance of sea urchins. Nature's balance was thrown off. Today the symbol of Haida Gwaii is the sea otter and the sea urchin, a reminder to keep the ecosystem in balance.

Fishing and crabbing are allowed within the Gwaii Haanas Reserve except in

Buddy-boating helps with difficult anchorages at Gwaii Haanas Watchmen Sites.

designated closed areas, which are described at orientation. Appropriate fishing licenses required.

Permits. The Gwaii Haanas National Park Reserve, a Protected Area, was created in 1987 and encompasses the southern third of the Haida Gwaii archipelago. The Reserve is jointly managed by the Haida and the government of Canada. It is unique in Canada, covering both land and sea. A visit to Gwaii Haanas requires a permit for the time you will be in the Reserve. The daily fee is $49.00 for families (up to 7 people, max of 2 people over 18), $19.60 for adults, $16.60 for seniors (65 and over), and $9.80 for youths (6 to 16 years). No limit on the number of days you may stay within the Reserve; however, after six days, it is more cost effective to purchase a Season Pass.

Only 100 people are permitted in Gwaii Haanas National Park Reserve at once. Advance reservations are recommended to ensure you'll get a permit. An orientation is required for all visitors, either in advance by DVD or at the **Haida Heritage Centre** in Skidegate. The Heritage Centre has a gift shop. Orientation sessions are typically at 9:00 a.m. Monday-Friday in June and after mid-August, and Monday-Saturday

July to mid-August. Orientation sessions can be scheduled by appointment if staff is available. Reserving space for scheduled orientations is not required. A permit tag is issued at the time of orientation and must be carried ashore within the Park Reserve. The excellent orientation covers the history of Gwaii Haanas as well as the procedures to visit the different sites within the park. All protected sites are managed by Haida Watchmen. They can be reached on VHF 06 prior to going ashore at each site. They manage the number of people on shore at a time. They also provide interpretive talks about the site and are very welcoming.

A fee is not required between October 1st and April 30th, but visitors must register and attend an orientation session. Check the Parks Canada Gwaii Haanas website for more information. Call (877) 559-8818 (8:30 a.m. to 4:30 p.m. Monday through Friday after April 2nd) for more information or to arrange for a permit (www.pc.gc.ca/gwaiihaanas). As a convenience, orientation sessions are generally offered in early March in Vancouver BC, Victoria, or Sidney; check their website for the year's schedule. If planning to enter Gwaii Haanas from the south, it may be possible to get an orientation package by mail for a fee; contact the Haida Heritage Centre.

Getting to and from Haida Gwaii. Separated from mainland British Columbia by Hecate Strait; from Vancouver Island by Queen Charlotte Sound; and from Alaska by Dixon Entrance, getting to Haida Gwaii by boat requires crossing some of the Northwest's most feared bodies of water. Hecate Strait is notorious for rough water. With shallow depths in the northern portion, ranging from 50 to 115 feet, winds can quickly whip up big, uncomfortable seas. Tides move large volumes of water through Hecate Strait and Dixon Entrance. When wind blows against current, dangerous conditions can result. Particularly during spring tides, be mindful of possible wind-against-current situations. Nevertheless, we have had several smooth passages by timing the transit to the correct conditions and forecast.

Orientations for Gwaii Haanas National Park are held at the Haida Heritage Center in Skidegate.

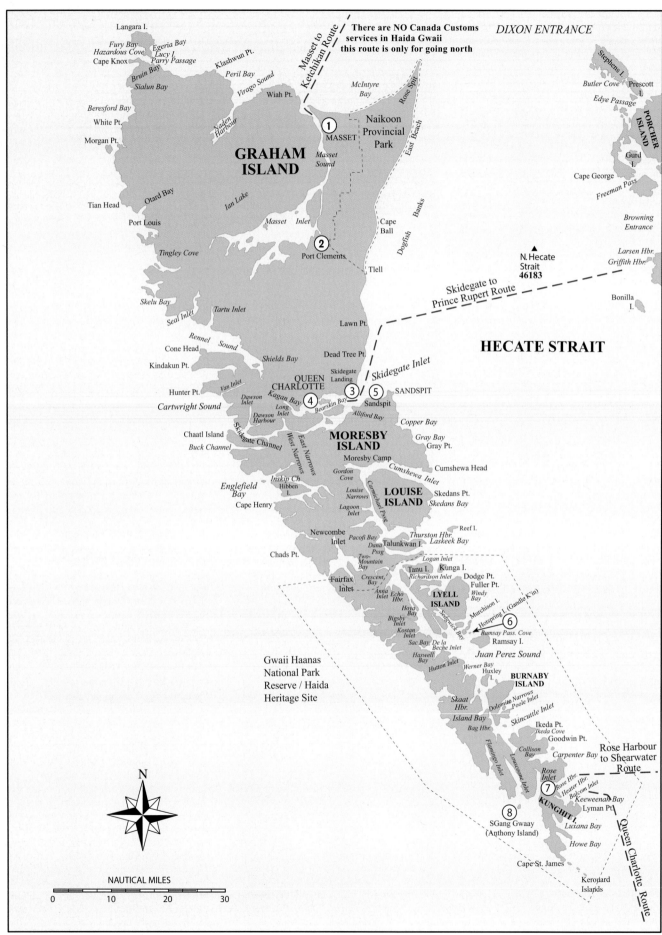

DIXON ENTRANCE

There are NO Canada Customs services in Haida Gwaii this route is only for going north

Langara I.
Fury Bay
Hazardous Cove
Cape Knox
Egeria Bay
Lucy I.
Parry Passage
Bruin Bay
Sialun Bay
Klashwun Pt.
Peril Bay
Virago Sound
Wiah Pt.
Beresford Bay
White Pt.
Morgan Pt.
Naden Harbour
Masset to Ketchikan Route
McIntyre Bay
Rose Spit
① MASSET
Naikoon Provincial Park
East Beach
GRAHAM ISLAND
Masset Sound
Masset Inlet
② Port Clements
Cape Ball
Dogfish Banks
Tlell
Tian Head
Otard Bay
Ian Lake
Port Louis
Tingley Cove
Skelu Bay
Tartu Inlet
Seal Inlet
Lawn Pt.
Dead Tree Pt.

N. Hecate Strait 46183
Larsen Hbr.
Griffith Hbr.
Bonilla I.

Skidegate to Prince Rupert Route

HECATE STRAIT

Rennel Sound
Cone Head
Kindakun Pt.
Shields Bay
Skidegate Landing
Skidegate Inlet
Hunter Pt.
Van Inlet
Cartwright Sound
Dawson Inlet
Kagan Bay
Long Inlet
Dawson Harbour
QUEEN CHARLOTTE
④ ③ ⑤ SANDSPIT
Bearskin Bay
Sandspit
Alliford Bay
Copper Bay
Gray Bay
Gray Pt.
Chaatl Island
Buck Channel
Skidegate Channel
West Narrows
East Narrows
MORESBY ISLAND
Moresby Camp
Cumshewa Inlet
Cumshewa Head
Englefield Bay
Inskip Ch
Hibben I.
Gordon Cove
Louise Narrows
Lagoon Inlet
Carmichael Psg
LOUISE ISLAND
Skedans Pt.
Skedans Bay
Cape Henry
Newcombe Inlet
Pacofi Bay
Dana Pssg
Talunkwan I.
Thurston Hbr.
Laskeek Bay
Reef I.
Chads Pt.
Two-Mountain Bay
Logan Inlet
Tanu I.
Kunga I.
Richardson Inlet
Dodge Pt.
Fuller Pt.
Fairfax Inlet
Crescent Bay
Anna Inlet
Echo Hbr.
Hoya Bay
Bigsby Inlet
Kostan Inlet
Windy Bay
LYELL ISLAND
Sedgwick Bay
Murchison I.
Hotspring I. (Gandle K'in)
⑥ Ramsay Pass. Cove
Ramsay I.
Sac Bay
De la Beche Inlet
Haswell Bay
Hutton Inlet
Werner Bay
Huxley I.
Juan Perez Sound
BURNABY ISLAND
Gwaii Haanas National Park Reserve / Haida Heritage Site
Skaat Hbr.
Dolomite Narrows
Poole Inlet
Island Bay
Bag Hbr.
Skincuttle Inlet
Ikeda Pt.
Ikeda Cove
Goodwin Pt.
Flamingo Inlet
Collison Bay
Carpenter Bay
Rose Harbour to Shearwater Route
Louscoone Inlet
Rose Inlet
Rose Hbr.
Heater Hbr.
Balcom Inlet
Keeweenah Bay
Lyman Pt.
⑦ **KUNGHIT I.**
⑧ SGang Gwaay (Anthony Island)
Luxana Bay
Howe Bay
Queen Charlotte Route
Cape St. James
Kerouard Islands

Stephens I.
Butler Cove
Prescott I.
Edye Passage
PORCHER ISLAND
Gurd I.
Cape George
Freeman Pass
Browning Entrance

N

NAUTICAL MILES
0   10   20   30

Haida Gwaii

462

There are basically three options for getting to and from Haida Gwaii; Crossing Hecate Strait from mainland BC Coast is the shortest open water route and the most common; Crossing Queen Charlotte Sound from Vancouver Island is the most direct but the longest open water route; Crossing Central Dixon Entrance to the north is only possible when departing Haida Gwaii as there are no Canada customs clearance locations in Haida Gwaii.

Crossing Hecate Strait. Shearwater, Bella Bella, and Klemtu in the south, and Prince Rupert in the north, are the popular starting points. There are a number of anchorages on the islands between Hecate Strait and BC mainland's Inside Passage. Routes from these anchorages offer the shortest open water crossings, ranging from 85 miles for southerly departure points and 65 miles from the northerly departure points. Many boats depart for Haida Gwaii from Prince Rupert. This route offers the shortest crossing (roughly 60 to 65 miles of open water), allowing boaters to minimize their exposure to potentially hazardous weather. Prince Rupert is a major city, and has anything a cruising boater might need before heading out to explore Haida Gwaii. With fuel, provisions, and internet access for weather information, Prince Rupert makes a logical starting point. After leaving Prince Rupert, several anchorages provide a place to spend the night and wait for better weather before crossing Hecate Strait. Larsen Harbour, anchorages in the Spicer Islands, and Welcome Harbour are good choices. In the past we have been warned of extreme kelp in Larsen Harbour. More recently we have been told that Larsen Harbour is easily navigable. It is the shortest point of crossing to Lawn Point on Graham Island. During our recent trip, we anchored in the Spicer Islands. For our early morning departure we listened for the wind and wave report from the North Hecate Strait weather buoy Station 46183 and navigated directly across Hecate Strait, passing the buoy on the way to Lawn Point. Note the shoal area leading north from the entrance to Skidegate Inlet. If headed to Sandspit Harbour or Queen Charlotte, follow the deeper channel to Skidegate Inlet or Shingle Bay. In settled conditions and higher tides, we have crossed just north or south of Bar Rocks near the green can buoy.

Shearwater, Bella Bella, and Klemtu have provisions, fuel, water, and internet access and are good southern starting locations. Departing from Shearwater, Bella Bella, or Klemtu, boaters can take one of several routes from the Inside Passage to what Douglass terms the Outer Passage, where you will find several anchorages on Aristazabal Island before crossing Hecate Strait to Rose Harbour on Moresby Island. Because Rose Harbour is within the Gwaii Haanas National Park Reserve, you will be required to have a permit and have already completed the required Park orientation. This 85 mile crossing can be done in one long summer daylight

Protected moorage at Sandspit Harbour, northeast end of Moresby Island

day. This route crosses the southern area of Hecate Strait, which is not as shallow as the northern portion. There are no services at Rose Harbour, so boaters landing in Rose Harbour need to have fuel, provisions, and water until arriving in Queen Charlotte or Sandspit. Field Correspondent Mary Campbell has had four smooth crossings along this route. She suggests Borrowman Bay or Weeteeam Harbour for overnight anchorages. This route is also a good option when returning from Haida Gwaii after your stay in Gwaii Haanas Park.

Crossing Queen Charlotte Sound. Haida Gwaii can also be accessed from Vancouver Island to the south. The trip is long— about 160 nautical miles—and exposed to the full brunt of the open Pacific Ocean. Sailboats and slow powerboats will have to make an overnight passage. For faster boats in settled weather, the trip can be completed in a very long day. Keep in mind, however, that sea conditions may not be conducive to high-speed operation. Also remember that fuel is not available anywhere south of Sandspit. You will need a Gwaii Haanas National Park Reserve permit and have completed the required orientation. From the south, plot a route from the area north of Vancouver Island to Houston Stewart Channel and Rose Harbour. Use West Sea Otter weather buoy, Station 46204, and the South Hecate Strait weather buoy Station 46185 for wind and wave reports for the area. This might also be your return route when leaving Haida Gwaii for points south.

Crossing Central Dixon Entrance. Boats returning to British Columbia from Alaska may be tempted to cross Dixon Entrance to Masset instead of Prince Rupert. Unfortunately, there are no Canadian Government customs offices anywhere in Haida Gwaii. Boats southbound from Alaska must first clear customs in Prince Rupert. Boaters going north from Haida Gwaii and into Alaska may cross Dixon Entrance and proceed to Ketchikan for required U.S. Customs clearance. Keep in mind that you

may not anchor or make landfall anywhere in U.S. waters before clearing customs in Ketchikan. From Masset to Ketchikan is approximately 85 miles, which can be done in one long day. Check weather, current, and conditions in Dixon Entrance carefully. Use Central Dixon Entrance weather buoy, Station 46145 for wind and wave reports.

Fuel. Fuel is available at Masset on the north end of Graham Island, at Sandspit, and in the town of Queen Charlotte in Skidegate inlet. Cruising in Haida Gwaii is wilderness cruising with no major repair services or boatyards.

Water. Masset, Port Clements, Sandspit, and Queen Charlotte have potable water. Parks Canada maintains fresh water hoses at Hoya Bay and at Louscoone Inlet; water at both locations is untreated.

Garbage Drops. In the remote and protected areas all trash must be carried out with you.

Insurance. Not all vessel insurance policies cover Haida Gwaii, check with your insurance agent to ensure that you have coverage for this area.

Provisioning. Groceries are available in Masset, Skidegate, Queen Charlotte, and Sandspit. Deliveries are usually once a week. Selection may be limited.

Trailering. BC Ferries serve Masset, Skidegate, Sandspit, and Alliford Bay. Check www.bcferries.com for schedules and rates. Boat launches are located at Alliford Bay, Sandspit, Masset, and Copper Bay. Trailering small boats to Haida Gwaii may save time and money and can minimize weather delays.

Resources. Don and Reanne Douglass *Exploring the North Coast of British Columbia* is the most complete cruising guide for Haida Gwaii. It has been updated in 2017.

Queen Charlotte Harbour Authority floats, with Bearskin Bay anchorage in the background

GRAHAM ISLAND

① **Masset.** During the summer months, Masset, the northernmost community on Haida Gwaii, is a hub of sport fishing operations. The local airport offers regular flights to Vancouver, and floatplanes run regularly from Prince Rupert. You'll find restaurants, a liquor store, three grocery stores, a hardware store, pubs, car rentals and an internet cafe.

Local businesses cater to tourists, with sightseeing trips and fishing charters. Hikes give boaters the opportunity to stretch their legs and see a different side of Haida Gwaii. The 9-hole Dixon Entrance Golf Club is 5 kilometers outside of town. The Dixon Entrance Maritime Museum showcases the maritime history of the area.

① **North Arm Transportation.** (250) 626-3328; nat@northarm.bc.ca; www.northarm.

bc.ca. Open all year. Located at the government dock. Gas, diesel, and lubricants available.

① **Delkatla Slough Harbour Authority.** (250) 626-5487. Open all year, first-come, first-served, primarily a commercial boat facility. Power and water on the docks, garbage drop, tidal grid. Rafting required.

Refuge Cove. Known locally as 7-mile Cove, Refuge Cove provides good protection from weather and has 600 feet of dock space. This is a good place to wait out a storm, or to wait for favorable currents to enter Masset. Use caution entering Refuge Cove. The fairway is narrow, about 100 feet wide, with 6-foot depths at zero tide. In stormy conditions, swells can break across the entrance channel, making it impassable. Fishing outside Refuge Cove is reportedly excellent.

Langara Island. Langara Island, the northernmost island in the archipelago, is known for its exceptional salmon fishing. Sport fishing lodges on the island cater to fly-in guests. Several anchorages are available, although they are typically busy with sport fishing boats.

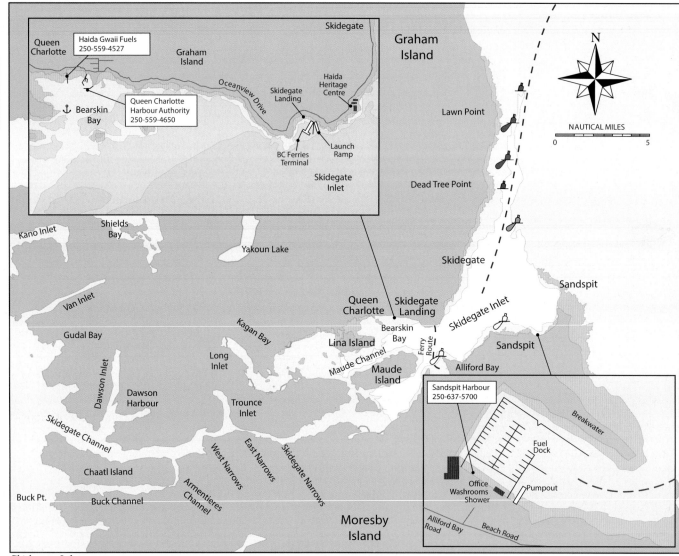

Skidegate Inlet